THE ROUTLEDGE COMPANION TO MANAGEMENT INFORMATION SYSTEMS

The field of Information Systems has been evolving since the first application of computers in organizations in the early 1950s. Focusing on information systems analysis and design up to and including the 1980s, the field has expanded enormously, with our assumptions about information and knowledge being challenged, along with both intended and unintended consequences of information technology.

This prestige reference work offers students and researchers a critical reflection on major topics and current scholarship in the evolving field of Information Systems. This single-volume survey of the field is organized into four parts. The first section deals with Disciplinary and Methodological Foundations. The second section deals with Development, Adoption and Use of MIS – topics that formed the centrepiece of the field of IS in the last century. The third section deals with Managing Organizational IS, Knowledge and Innovation, while the final section considers emerging and continuing issues and controversies in the field – IS in Society and a Global Context. Each chapter provides a balanced overview of current knowledge, identifying issues and discussing relevant debates.

This prestigious book is required reading for any student or researcher in Management Information Systems, academics and students covering the breadth of the field, and established researchers seeking a single-volume repository on the current state of knowledge, current debates and relevant literature.

Robert D. Galliers is the University Distinguished Professor at Bentley University, USA. He also holds a fractional appointment as Professor of IS at Loughborough University, UK. His work has been published in many of the leading IS journals and has been cited over 10,000 times. He is editor-in-chief of the *Journal of Strategic Information Systems*. He received the AIS LEO Award for exceptional lifetime achievement in 2012, and is a Fellow of the AIS, the British Computer Society and the Royal Society of Arts.

Mari-Klara Stein is an Associate Professor at the department of Digitalization, Copenhagen Business School, Denmark. She has published her work in leading IS journals (e.g., *MIS Quarterly, Journal of Information Technology, Information & Organization, European Journal of IS*). Mari is also the recipient of the 2016 European Research Paper of the Year award from CIONET – a leading community of IT executives in Europe.

ROUTLEDGE COMPANIONS IN BUSINESS, MANAGEMENT AND ACCOUNTING

Routledge Companions in Business, Management and Accounting are prestige reference works providing an overview of a whole subject area or sub-discipline. These books survey the state of the discipline including emerging and cutting-edge areas. Providing a comprehensive, up-to-date, definitive work of reference, Routledge Companions can be cited as an authoritative source on the subject.

A key aspect of these Routledge Companions is their international scope and relevance. Edited by an array of highly regarded scholars, these volumes also benefit from teams of contributors that reflect an international range of perspectives.

Individually, Routledge Companions in Business, Management and Accounting provide an impactful one-stop-shop resource for each theme covered. Collectively, they represent a comprehensive learning and research resource for researchers, postgraduate students and practitioners.

Titles in this series include:

The Routledge Companion to Accounting and Risk
Edited by Margaret Woods and Philip Linsley

The Routledge Companion to Wellbeing at Work
Edited by Sir Cary L. Cooper and Michael P. Leiter

The Routledge Companion to Performance Management and Control
Edited by Elaine Harris

The Routledge Companion to Management Information Systems
Edited by Robert D. Galliers and Mari-Klara Stein

The Routledge Companion to Critical Accounting
Edited by Robin Roslender

The Routledge Companion to Trust
Edited by Rosalind Searle, Ann-Marie Nienaber and Sim Sitkin

THE ROUTLEDGE COMPANION TO MANAGEMENT INFORMATION SYSTEMS

Edited by Robert D. Galliers and Mari-Klara Stein

LONDON AND NEW YORK

First published 2018
by Routledge
2 Park Square, Milton Park, Abingdon, Oxon OX14 4RN

and by Routledge
711 Third Avenue, New York, NY 10017

Routledge is an imprint of the Taylor & Francis Group, an informa business

© 2018 selection and editorial matter, Robert D. Galliers and Mari-Klara Stein; individual chapters, the contributors.

The right of Robert D. Galliers and Mari-Klara Stein to be identified as the authors of the editorial material, and of the authors for their individual chapters, has been asserted in accordance with sections 77 and 78 of the Copyright, Designs and Patents Act 1988.

All rights reserved. No part of this book may be reprinted or reproduced or utilised in any form or by any electronic, mechanical, or other means, now known or hereafter invented, including photocopying and recording, or in any information storage or retrieval system, without permission in writing from the publishers.

Trademark notice: Product or corporate names may be trademarks or registered trademarks, and are used only for identification and explanation without intent to infringe.

British Library Cataloguing-in-Publication Data
A catalogue record for this book is available from the British Library

Library of Congress Cataloging-in-Publication Data
Names: Galliers, Robert, 1947– editor. | Stein, Mari-Klara, editor.
Title: The Routledge companion to management information systems / [edited by] Robert D. Galliers and Mari-Klara Stein.
Description: Abingdon, Oxon ; New York, NY : Routledge, 2017. | Includes bibliographical references and index.
Identifiers: LCCN 2017008362 (print) | LCCN 2017025828 (ebook) | ISBN 9781315619361 (eBook) | ISBN 9781138666450 (hardback : alk. paper)
Subjects: LCSH: Management information systems. | Information technology—Management.
Classification: LCC HD30.213 (ebook) | LCC HD30.213 .R6795 2017 (print) | DDC 658.4/038—dc23
LC record available at https://lccn.loc.gov/2017008362

ISBN: 978-1-138-66645-0 (hbk)
ISBN: 978-1-315-61936-1 (ebk)

Typeset in Times New Roman
by Apex CoVantage, LLC

 Printed in the United Kingdom
by Henry Ling Limited

CONTENTS

List of figures	*ix*
List of tables	*xii*
Notes on contributors	*xiii*
Acknowledgements	*xvii*
Foreword	*xviii*

PART 1
Disciplinary and methodological foundations   1
Robert D. Galliers and Mari-Klara Stein

1 Taking IS history seriously   5
 Nik Rushdi Hassan

2 Philosophy and method: making interpretive research interpretive   30
 Allen S. Lee

3 Information systems as a reference discipline: current debate and future directions   47
 Richard L. Baskerville and Michael D. Myers

4 On theory   57
 Shirley Gregor

5 What literature review type should I conduct?   73
 Ana Ortiz de Guinea and Guy Paré

6 Coming of age: interpretive research in information systems   83
   Michael D. Myers

7 NeuroIS   94
   René Riedl

8 Ethnography in information systems research: Quo vadis?   108
   Ulrike Schultze

PART 2
Development, adoption and use of MIS   121
Mari-Klara Stein and Robert D. Galliers

9 The future of software development methods   125
   Brian Fitzgerald and Klaas-Jan Stol

10 Agility in information systems development   138
   Kieran Conboy, Denis Dennehy, Lorraine Morgan, and Roger Sweetman

11 IT use: notes from a journey from use to effective use   152
   Andrew Burton-Jones, Mark Bremhorst, Fang Liu and Van-Hau Trieu

12 Affect in the ICT context   166
   Jasy Liew Suet Yan and Ping Zhang

13 Research on user resistance to information technology   183
   Liette Lapointe and Suzanne Rivard

14 Information systems strategising: the role of ambidextrous
   capabilities in shaping power relations   202
   Marco Marabelli and Robert D. Galliers

15 Digitalization as a strategy practice: what is there to learn
   from strategy as practice research?   218
   Viktor Arvidsson and Jonny Holmström

16 Affordance theory and how to use it in IS research   232
   Olga Volkoff and Diane M. Strong

PART 3
Managing organisational IS, knowledge and innovation   247
Robert D. Galliers and Mari-Klara Stein

17   Generativity in digital infrastructures: a research note   253
      Kalle Lyytinen, Carsten Sørensen, and David Tilson

18   The role of enterprise systems in innovation in the contemporary organization   276
      Darshana Sedera and Sachithra Lokuge

19   Digital capability: scaffolding for rewiring a company for digital   290
      Joe Peppard

20   Sourcing information technology services: past research and future research directions   307
      Mary Lacity, Aihua Yan, and Shaji Khan

21   Innovation in healthcare settings: the power of everyday practices   328
      Marco Marabelli and Sue Newell

22   Aligning in practice   341
      Anna Karpovsky and Robert D. Galliers

23   Digital innovation – a definition and integrated perspective   360
      Philipp Hukal and Ola Henfridsson

24   Knowledge collaboration in organizations: from information processing to social knowing   370
      Samer Faraj, Karla Sayegh and Linda Rouleau

PART 4
IS in society and a global context: emerging – and continuing – issues and controversies   387
Mari-Klara Stein and Robert D. Galliers

25   Organizational intelligence in the digital age: analytics and the cycle of choice   391
      Stella Pachidi and Marleen Huysman

26	Datification in action: diffusion and consequences of algorithmic decision-making *Sue Newell and Marco Marabelli*	403
27	Digital divides: past, present, and future *Maria Skaletsky, James B. Pick, Avijit Sarkar, and David J. Yates*	416
28	The developmental effects of the digital revolution *Chrisanthi Avgerou and Atta Addo*	444
29	Beyond mobile IT: ubiquitous digitality and work *Carsten Sørensen*	466
30	Technology-driven changes in the economy *Roman Beck*	481
31	Staying alive: the IS field at the half century mark *Ning Su, John Leslie King, and Jonathan Grudin*	490

Index   *505*

FIGURES

4.1	Unfinished workshop demonstration of use of the canvas	66
4.2	Diagrammatic representation of theoretical background	68
4.3	Completed example of research contribution canvas	68
5.1	Decision tree	78
7.1	The human nervous system and brain lobes	96
9.1	Software Crisis 2.0	126
9.2	Height of software printout stack in Mercedes S-Class	127
9.3	Software scaling as a multi-dimensional phenomenon	128
10.1	The evolution of agile from small co-located teams to portfolios of projects spanning multiple organizations	139
10.2	Value-based measurement of agility	140
10.3	The simplistic view of project portfolio management	143
10.4	The reality of project portfolio management	144
11.1	A map to guide a research program on effective use	154
12.1	The circumplex model	168
12.2	A model of individual interaction with IT (IIIT)	169
12.3	Causal relationships among affective responses during an ICT interaction episode	171
12.4	Sample AUs from FACS	173
14.1	Galliers's 2011 ISS framework	206
14.2	A rejuvenated framework of ISS	208
14.3	Generative dance of knowing and power in strategising processes	210
17.1	Conceptual model of the socio-technical structure of digital infrastructures	257
18.1	Comparison of enterprise systems and digital technologies	277
18.2	Maturity and innovation	282
18.3	Software focus and innovation	283
18.4	Vendor agnosticism and innovation	284
18.5	Software management approach and innovation	285
19.1	Schematic of hierarchy for digital capability	294

19.2	Basic scaffolding for a digital capability	295
19.3	The pillars and core domains for digital	296
19.4	Leadership and governance: framing the digital capability	299
19.5	Social capital providing the environment for organizational knowing	301
19.6	Mobilizing resources to create digital competences	302
20.1	Independent variables that determine ITO decisions	311
20.2	Independent variables that determine ITO outcomes	311
20.3	Categories of independent variables that determine ITO decisions and ITO outcomes	321
21.1	Time line of events and data collection at Dooly	331
22.1	Aligning: an analytical framework	346
25.1	The cycle of choice with organizational learning dysfunctions	394
26.1	Privacy and discrimination in the big and little data era	412
27.1	Four successive types of access in the appropriation of an ICT	419
27.2	Global changes in ICT adoption, 2000–2015	420
27.3	Internet users in 2014 (% of population)	421
27.4	Mobile-cellular subscriptions per 100 inhabitants in 2014	422
27.5	Mobile-broadband subscriptions per 100 inhabitants in 2015	422
27.6	Digital divides in developed vs. developing countries, 2015	424
27.7	ICTs in ITU world regions in 2015	425
27.8	Household adoption of computer, internet, and broadband (% of households), 1997–2012	427
27.9	Internet use in the United States by gender	429
27.10	Internet use in the United States by age	429
27.11	Internet use in the United States by education level	429
27.12	Households with a computer (% of households) in US states in 2003	430
27.13	Households with Internet access (% of households) in US states in 2003	431
27.14	Households with computers in US states in 2013	431
27.15	Households with high-speed Internet access in 2013	432
27.16	Broadband adoption in US states in 2013: percent of households using broadband in areas where broadband is available	432
27.17	Wireless-only households in US states in 2012	433
27.18	Household access to PCs and Internet in Russia, 2010–2014	434
27.19	Internet use by age in 2014	435
27.20	Internet use by urban and rural population in 2014	435
27.21	Number of mobile subscriptions per 100 people in 2000	436
27.22	Number of mobile subscriptions per 100 people in 2014 (excluding St. Petersburg)	436
27.23	Number of active mobile subscriptions using the Internet per 100 people in 2014	437
28.1	Illustration of Aadhaar's architecture	455
29.1	Illustration of the common architecture of edge-devices off-loading computational complex tasks through high-speed networking to cloud services	468
29.2	Illustration of six categories of affordances related to mobile and ubiquitous computing technologies	470

29.3 Mobile performances occur when individuals apply mobile IT affordances as a means of optimising decisions and actions within a context of contradictory work requirements and situations 471
29.4 The breadth and interconnectedness of organisational technologies span digital dust and global infrastructures – far beyond the traditional IS perspective centered around an organisational locus of information processing 476

TABLES

1.1	Narratives in historical paradigms	14
1.2	Historical IS studies categorized by paradigms	15
4.1	Definition of different theory types	61
6.1	Klein and Myers's (1999) principles for interpretive research	89
7.1	Important reference disciplines of NeuroIS	97
7.2	Results of NeuroIS paper classification ($N = 76$)	103
7.3	Overview of NeuroIS tools	104
9.1	Exemplar scaling scenarios in each dimension and their implications	134
10.1	Metrics used to manage flow	141
10.2	Challenges in combining agile and open approaches	146
11.1	Recent studies on effective use	155
11.2	Summary of current research in progress	156
12.1	Affective responses	170
13.1	Explaining resistance independently from acceptance	185
13.2	Studying resistance and acceptance jointly	186
13.3	Definitions of resistance	192
13.4	Conceptualizations of resistance to IT	194
14.1	ISS and organisational tensions	204
15.1	Five movements in IS strategy and strategizing	220
15.2	Definitions of key conceptual elements of the Huang et al. (2014) framework	223
19.1	Macro- and micro-competences definitions	297
20.1	Empirical articles used in review	309
21.1	The power of ongoing practices	336
22.1	Aligning activities: coding and categorization	344
24.1	Synthesis of approaches to knowledge collaboration	374
25.1	The effect of analytics on organizational learning dysfunctions	399
27.1	Measures of digital divides tracked by the United Nations (UN) sources	418
28.1	What the Aadhaar is	453

CONTRIBUTORS

Atta Addo is a PhD candidate in the Information Systems Group of the Department of Management at the London School of Economics and Political Science, UK.

Viktor Arvidsson is a postdoctoral fellow at the Research Group for Information Systems, Department of Informatics, University of Oslo, and affiliated with the Swedish Center for Digital Innovation, Sweden.

Chrisanthi Avgerou is Professor of Information Systems in the Department of Management at the London School of Economics, UK.

Richard Baskerville is Regents' Professor and Board of Advisors Professor at Georgia State University, USA, and Professor of Information Systems at Curtin University, Australia.

Roman Beck is Professor for Information Systems at IT University of Copenhagen, Denmark.

Mark Bremhorst is a PhD candidate in Business Information Systems at the University of Queensland Business School, Australia.

Andrew Burton-Jones is a Professor of Business Information Systems at the University of Queensland Business School, Australia.

Kieran Conboy is a Professor in Information Systems and co-Principal Investigator of the Lero Irish Software Research Centre at NUI Galway, Ireland.

Denis Dennehy is a postdoctoral researcher at Lero – the Irish Software Research Centre, NUI Galway, Ireland.

Samer Faraj is Professor and Canada Research Chair at McGill University, Canada.

Brian Fitzgerald is Director of Lero – the Irish Software Research Centre and holds the Frederick A Krehbiel II Chair at the University of Limerick, Ireland.

Contributors

Robert D. Galliers is the University Distinguished Professor at Bentley University, USA, and holds a fractional appointment as Professor of IS at Loughborough University, UK; he is founding editor-in-chief of the *Journal of Strategic Information Systems*.

Shirley Gregor is Professor of Information Systems and Associate Dean Research in the College of Business and Economics, Australian National University, Australia.

Jonathan Grudin is a researcher at Microsoft and Affiliate Professor at the University of Washington, USA.

Nik Rushdi Hassan is Associate Professor of MIS at the University of Minnesota Duluth, USA, and is the Department Editor of the History and Philosophy of Information Systems section of the *Communications of the Association for Information Systems*.

Ola Henfridsson is Professor and Head of the Information Systems and Management group at Warwick Business School, University of Warwick, UK.

Jonny Holmström is Professor of Informatics at Umeå University and Director and co-founder of the Swedish Center for Digital Innovation, Sweden.

Philipp Hukal is a PhD student of Information Systems and Management at Warwick Business School, University of Warwick, UK.

Marleen Huysman is Professor and Head of the KIN Research Group, VU Amsterdam, the Netherlands.

Anna Karpovsky is a Visiting Assistant Professor at Bentley University, USA.

Shaji Khan is Assistant Professor of Information Systems at the University of Missouri–St. Louis, USA.

John Leslie King is W. W. Bishop Professor of Information in the School of Information at the University of Michigan, USA.

Mary Lacity is Curators' Distinguished Professor of Information Systems and an International Business Fellow at the University of Missouri-St. Louis, USA.

Liette Lapointe is Associate Professor and Associate Dean, Undergraduate Programs at the Desautels Faculty of Management of McGill University, Canada.

Allen S. Lee is Professor of Information Systems at Virginia Commonwealth University, USA.

Fang Liu is a PhD candidate in Business Information Systems at the University of Queensland Business School, Australia.

Sachithra Lokuge is an early career academic at the University of Queensland, Australia.

Contributors

Kalle Lyytinen is the Iris S. Wolstein Professor of Management Design; Department Chair and Professor, Design and Innovation; and Faculty Director, Doctor of Management program, Weatherhead School of Management, Case Western Reserve University, USA.

Marco Marabelli is an Assistant Professor at Bentley University, USA, and holds a joint appointment at the University of Warwick in the Information Systems Management group, UK.

Lorraine Morgan is a lecturer in the J.E. Cairnes School of Business and Economics, NUI Galway, Ireland.

Michael Myers is Professor of Information Systems at the University of Auckland Business School in Auckland, New Zealand.

Sue Newell is a Professor of Information Systems and Management, and Head of Business & Management, School of Business, Management & Economics, Sussex University, UK.

Ana Ortiz de Guinea is an Associate Professor and holder of the Professorship in Strategy and Management Information Systems at HEC Montréal, Canada.

Stella Pachidi is Lecturer in IS at Judge Business School, University of Cambridge, UK.

Guy Paré is Professor of IT and holder of the Research Chair in Digital Health at HEC Montréal, Canada, and is a member of the Royal Society of Canada.

Joe Peppard is a Professor at ESMT Berlin, Germany.

James B. Pick is Professor of Business at University of Redlands, USA.

René Riedl is Professor in the Digital Business Management programme, a joint initiative of the University of Applied Sciences Upper Austria and Johannes Kepler University Linz, Austria.

Suzanne Rivard holds the HEC Montréal Endowed Chair in Strategic Management of Information Technology, Canada, and is a member of the Royal Society of Canada.

Linda Rouleau is Professor of Strategy and Organization Theories in the Management Department of HEC Montréal, Canada.

Avijit Sarkar is Professor of Operations Research at University of Redlands School of Business, USA.

Karla Sayegh is a doctoral candidate at the Desautels Faculty of Management, McGill University, Canada.

Ulrike Schultze is Associate Professor in Information Systems and Information Technology at Southern Methodist University, USA.

Contributors

Darshana Sedera is an Associate Professor at the Queensland University of Technology, Australia.

Maria Skaletsky is Senior Research Consultant at Bentley University, USA, and researches living standards and the digital divide.

Carsten Sørensen is Associate Professor (Reader) in Digital Innovation at the London School of Economics and Political Science, UK.

Mari-Klara Stein is Associate Professor at Copenhagen Business School, Department of IT Digitalization, Denmark.

Klaas-Jan Stol is a Principal Investigator and Research Fellow with Lero – the Irish Software Research Centre, Ireland.

Diane M. Strong is Professor of IT and Director of IT programs in the Foisie Business School at Worcester Polytechnic Institute, USA.

Ning Su is Associate Professor and J. J. Wettlaufer Faculty Fellow at the Ivey Business School of Western University, Canada.

Roger Sweetman lectures in Information Technology at Maynooth University, Ireland.

David Tilson is a Clinical Associate Professor of Computer and Information Systems and the Associate Dean of the Full-Time MBA Program at the Simon Business School, University of Rochester, USA.

Van-Hau Trieu is an Associate Lecturer at the University of Melbourne, School of Computing and Information Systems, Australia.

Olga Volkoff researches the challenges of implementing and effectively using large package software. She recently retired from the Beedie School of Business at Simon Fraser University, Canada.

Aihua Yan studies IT-enabled outsourcing strategy and governance at the University of Missouri–St. Louis, USA.

Jasy Liew Suet Yan is a Senior Lecturer at the School of Computer Sciences, Universiti Sains Malaysia.

David J. Yates is Associate Professor of Computer Information Systems at Bentley University, USA.

Ping Zhang is Professor in the School of Information Studies at Syracuse University, USA.

ACKNOWLEDGEMENTS

First and foremost, we wish to thank all our contributors for so willingly responding to our call for the chapters that make up this Companion volume. Their insightful reflections on key topics in the field of Management Information Systems add much to our understanding of this complex and ever-changing field of study, and help us as an academy to set new directions for exciting, relevant and impactful research in the future.

We also wish to thank John Wiley & Sons Ltd. for permission to use and further develop material first published in the *Information Systems Journal* in Chapter 14: "Information systems strategising: The role of ambidextrous capabilities in shaping power relations" by Marco Marabelli and Bob Galliers. Similarly, we acknowledge Palgrave Macmillan to use and further develop material first published in the *Journal of Information Technology* in Chapter 20: "Sourcing Information Technology Services: Past Research and Future Research Directions" by Mary Lacity, Aihua Yan and Shaji Khan, and in Chapter 22: "Aligning in Practice" by Anna Karpovsky and Bob Galliers. We also acknowledge Oxford University Press for Sue Newell and Marco Marabelli's chapter, "Innovation in healthcare settings: The power of everyday practices" (Chapter 21), which extracts and develops material from a previously published chapter of theirs.

The references to the original works are

Karpovsky, A. and Galliers, R.D. (2015). Aligning in Practice: From Current Cases to a New Agenda, *Journal of Information Technology*, 30(2): 136–160.
Lacity, M., Khan, S. and Yan, A. (2016). Review of the Empirical Business Services Sourcing Literature: An Update and Future Directions, *Journal of Information Technology*, 31(2), 1–60.
Marabelli, M. and Galliers, R.D. (2016). A Reflection on Information Systems Strategizing: The Role of Power and Everyday Practices, *Information Systems Journal*. doi:10.1111/isj.12110.
Newell, S. and Marabelli, M. (2016). Knowledge Mobilization in Healthcare Networks: The Power of Everyday Practices. In Mobilizing Knowledge. In *Healthcare: Challenges for Management and Organization*, J. Swan, D. Nicolini and S. Newell (Eds.), Oxford: Oxford University Press.

Our thanks too go to Amy Laurens (Commissioning Editor, Business and Management), Nicola Cupit (formerly Senior Editorial Assistant, Business & Management), and Laura Hussey (Editorial Assistant, Business & Management) at Routledge for their help in bringing this work to fruition during its various stages of development.

Bob Galliers and Mari-Klara Stein

FOREWORD

Since the very first business application of computing – the LEO computer that began operations in London in November 1951[1] (Williams, 2011), and the first university programme in business computing – developed by Börje Langefors at the Royal Institute of Technology and the University of Stockholm in Sweden in 1965 (Hirschheim and Klein, 2011), both the practice and the academic field of Information Systems (IS) has grown enormously over the past 60 years and more. For example, global spending on Information and Communication Technology (ICT) is forecast to reach $3.5 trillion in 2017 (Gartner, 2016), and the membership of the international IS academy – in the form of the Association for Information Systems (AIS)[2] – now approaches 5,000, located in approximately 100 countries worldwide.

The diversity of the IS field has grown over the years in addition, due in part from the expanding range of technologies available but also due to its ubiquity and widespread impacts, as noted by us in the foreword to the *Routledge Handbook on Management Information Systems* that we edited previously (Galliers and Stein, 2015). In that Handbook, we attempted to represent the development and diversity of the IS field by reprinting seminal works and more recent publications that might guide the future agenda in four volumes:

- Volume I: Disciplinary and Methodological Foundations of the Information Systems Field
- Volume II: Development, Adoption and Use of MIS
- Volume III: Managing Organizational IS, Knowledge and Innovation
- Volume IV: IS in a Global Context, Emerging Issues and Controversies.

In this Companion volume, we have complemented this material by seeking novel contributions from established and emerging IS academics from around the world. No single volume can of course do justice to such a wide-ranging and diverse field as IS, but we have attempted to follow the general course of the Handbook by, for example, laying a foundation for a comprehensive consideration of the field in terms of its history, philosophy and methods; considering the application, impacts and management of ICT in organizations and society; and further reflecting on ethical and sustainability concerns. We end with a critical reflection on the field's potential future.

We have taken the opportunity to invite contributions that are deliberately thought-provoking, critical and forward-looking. This has enabled the Companion contributors to freely reflect on their topics and the IS field outside the usual constraints of journal articles. The result, we feel, is a collection of imaginative and discerning chapters that tackle head-on many of the digital transformations and upheavals characterizing phenomena of interest for the IS field – from new digital methods to digital innovation and transformation capabilities to new digital inequalities.

As with the Handbook, we trust that this Companion volume will be a useful source of ideas not just for students and those entering the IS field but also for established academics who wish to reflect further on key topics and controversies with a view to finding inspiration for new agendas as the field continues to develop and grow.

Notes

1 The first Lyons Electronic Office computer (LEO I) is officially recognized as the First Business Computer by Guinness World Records (www.guinnessworldrecords.com/world-records/first-business-computer).
2 https://aisnet.org/page/AboutAIS

References

Galliers, R.D. and Stein, M.K. (eds.) (2015). *Management Information Systems: Critical Perspectives on Business and Management*, Vols I–IV, London and New York: Routledge.
Gartner (2016). Gartner Says Global IT Spending to Reach $3.5 Trillion in 2017, October 19, www.gartner.com/newsroom/id/3482917, last accessed January 18, 2017.
Hirschheim, R. and Klein, H.K. (2011). Tracing the History of the Information Systems Field. In R.D. Galliers and W.L. Currie (eds.) *The Oxford Handbook of Management Information Systems: Critical Perspectives and New Directions*, Oxford: Oxford University Press, 16–61.
Williams, C. (2011). How a Chain of Tea Shops Kickstarted the Computer Age, November 10, www.telegraph.co.uk/technology/news/8879727/How-a-chain-of-tea-shops-kickstarted-the-computer-age.html, last accessed January 18, 2017.

PART 1

Disciplinary and methodological foundations

Introduction

Part 1 of this Companion volume focuses on the disciplinary and methodological foundations of Information Systems (IS) as a field of study. This foundation is extremely important in the context of this Companion given the diversity and changing nature of IS, and the various schools of thought and debates that have characterised the field over the years.[1] Hirschheim and Klein note in Chapter 1 of the *Routledge Handbook on MIS* (Galliers & Stein, 2015) that the IS literature can be characterised as 'diverse and pluralistic' (see Hirschheim & Klein, 2012[2] for the original article), while King et al. (2010) view the field in terms of 'harmonious pluralism.' Were the latter to be entirely the case! The field's very diversity is seen as a strength by some (e.g., Galliers, 2003, 2006; Robey, 1996), but as a weakness by others (e.g., Benbasat & Weber, 1996; Benbasat & Zmud, 2003).

The history of the IS field provides some clues as to why it is that esteemed colleagues take such contrasting views as these, and this is why we commence, in Chapter 1, with a further reflection, by Nik Hassan, on historical developments.

While limited progress has been made in providing histories of the IS field in recent years,[3] this chapter builds on such earlier studies as these and introduces the major paradigms of historiography to highlight various features of such histories and their potential to encourage new, insightful research that can help in establishing the identity and relevance of IS not just for the field itself but also on behalf of cognate fields. By doing so, this chapter highlights existing gaps and future opportunities for further IS research and can be seen as something of a precursor to our consideration of IS as a reference discipline in and of itself, in Chapter 3.

As is pointed out by Hassan,

> Writing history is very different from writing traditional IS research. Taking IS history seriously first starts when the differences between the behavioral research that IS researchers are accustomed to and historical studies are clear in the mind of the researcher. It demands a major shift in outlook about research and about why IS history is being written.

Given its inherently reflexive nature, such research tells us what has been achieved in the past, and exposes the field's intellectual structures. Further, such studies can identify *what* and *how* we have studied chosen phenomena. Thus, in reviewing historical studies, Chapter 1 helps, potentially at least, in resolving long-standing issues of identity and relevancy within the IS field. If we can agree on past accomplishments, then the 'communication deficit' that remains between different research communities within the IS academy – and externally with practitioner colleagues – may be reduced, resulting in a greater likelihood of agreement concerning appropriate future research agendas.

The diversity, changing nature and alternative perspectives that characterise the IS field require us to delve more deeply into philosophical and methodological issues, and this is a topic that is considered by Allen Lee in Chapter 2. Titled "Philosophy and Method: Making Interpretive Research Interpretive," this chapter raises three key questions: (1) What makes interpretive research interpretive? (2) How is interpretive research valid? (3) Why are these two questions important for the conduct of research in Information Systems? In answering these questions, Chapter 2 calls upon such topics as phenomenology, hermeneutics, ethnography and hypothetico-deductive logic to problematise and interpret meaning, and to assess the validity of interpreted meaning. Key ideas are applied and illustrated with a reconstructed example (Sarker & Lee, 2006) of a walk-through of the interpretation of the meaning of technological tools used for business process change in two organisations.

Following on from these considerations, the field of IS has for long been seen to be reliant on such 'reference disciplines' as Computer Science, Management Science, Systems Theory, and various subfields of Management (Keen, 1980). More recently, this thinking has been turned on its head given the trans-disciplinary nature of the subject matter, with the IS field itself being viewed as a reference discipline in its own right, able to inform other fields of study. Thus, for example, we see recent calls from management strategists for insights from the IS field given the impact of IS/IT on opening up organisational strategising (e.g., Whittington, 2014).[4] As a result of this rethinking, Richard Baskerville and Michael Myers discuss IS as a reference discipline in Chapter 3, based in part on their earlier article on the topic (Baskerville & Myers 2002) – an article that for the first time questioned conventional wisdom and asked whether it was time for IS to be considered as a reference discipline in and of itself. The chapter, thus, reflects on the authors' original article, reviews the various contributions that have been made to the debate in subsequent contributions and proposes a future research agenda. Baskerville and Myers conclude that the IS field "is simply one academic discipline among others exchanging knowledge in a free flow of ideas. Information Systems is simply one of many 'contributing disciplines' to an ever-changing discourse related to information technology."

Having provided this foundation, we turn in Chapter 4 to the question of the theory – theories rather – upon which our research is based and to which it might contribute. Written by Shirley Gregor, this chapter aims to illustrate how different perspectives on theory and theorizing have accompanied historical movements in the philosophy of science. Recognising that theory can take on different forms depending on its purpose and how it is to be used, and building on her taxonomy of theory (Gregor, 2006), the process of theory development is discussed in terms of the context of discovery (*theory building*) and the context of justification (*theory testing*). Arising from this, a 'Theory Contribution Canvas' is presented to assist IS researchers in demonstrating their contribution to ongoing theory development.

These first four chapters provide us with a firm basis to next consider *how* we might go about undertaking research in the IS field given its expanding universe. Whatever method we choose,[5] IS researchers have to locate their work in the context of extant theory, and thus, literature reviews that do not simply replicate what has already been said are crucial. What added value does the review provide? What gaps and controversies does it uncover? And what questions arise from a critical and reflexive treatment of what has been studied previously?

These are the kind of questions a thorough literature review will answer, and very helpful guidance on undertaking literature reviews is the topic covered by Ana Ortiz de Guinea and Guy Paré in Chapter 5. The authors note the "recent explosion of interest . . . investigating literature reviews as a research method." They discern two main topics in this literature: (1) advice on how to conduct and assess the quality of literature reviews and (2) the development of a typology of literature reviews that are considered relevant to the IS field.

We go on to consider alternative research approaches and considerations in the next three chapters. Interpretive research is covered by Michael Myers in Chapter 6. NeuroIS is considered by René Riedl in Chapter 7, while Chapter 8, written by Ulrike Schultze, focuses on ethnography. Thus, in Chapter 6, Myers talks of interpretive research in IS "coming of age" in that, over the past decade and more, this form of research has established itself as a key research philosophy – among others, of course. He makes the point that "approximately one-quarter of all IS research articles" in the field's major journals take an interpretive perspective. The chapter considers the reasons for the rise of interpretive research in our field, together with the contributions it is making, concluding with a vision of how interpretive research might evolve in the future.

From interpretive research that has 'come of age,' we then move to a research perspective that is only beginning to find its footing in the IS field, but has tremendous potential – 'NeuroIS.' A chapter by René Riedl explains that "NeuroIS is a field . . . which makes use of neurophysiological tools and knowledge to better understand the development, adoption, and impact of information and communication technologies." Riedl poses and addresses four questions: (1) What is NeuroIS? (2) Why is NeuroIS important? (3) What are possible NeuroIS topics? (4) How to conduct NeuroIS research? The chapter provides a consolidation of the concepts and methods that have been used in NeuroIS in order to contribute to further development of the topic.

We conclude Part 1 of the Companion with an overview of ethnography and its use in IS research, with a view to identifying future research directions. The chapter is written by Ulrike Schultze, who notes that, while ethnographic research is a method originally developed by anthropologists to study foreign cultures, it has more recently been adopted by IS researchers. Following a partial review of a number of ethnographic IS studies, Schultze identifies three types of ethnographies that are particularly evident in IS: (1) *organisational,* (2) *digital* and (3) *design* ethnographies. Building on this, she notes that a key challenge for IS research is that the phenomena of interest are changing as a result of technological innovation . . . at once becoming more individual/personal (e.g., wearables) and more digital, distributed and global (e.g., grid computing, digital traces), while simultaneously becoming more fleeting. Schultze points to the implication that such methods require adaption to better capture contemporary phenomena. The chapter draws to a close by highlighting three types of ethnographic research: (1) *mobile,* (2) *sensory* and (3) *visual* ethnography that hold considerable promise for future IS research.

Having considered these important disciplinary, philosophical and methodological aspects of the IS field, all of which underpin our research agenda, we turn to questions of the development, adoption and use of IS in Part 2.

Notes

1 See, for example, King and Lyytinen (2006).
2 See also Hirschheim and Klein (2011).
3 See, for example, Galliers and Whitley (2007) and Stein et al. (2016) for historical reflections on the European Conference on IS since its inception.

4 See also Huang et al. (2013) and Baptista et al. (2017) for examples of the use of social media in 'open' strategy.
5 See, for example, Galliers et al. (2007) for a consideration of alternative approaches to IS research.

References

Baptista, J., Wilson, A., Galliers, R.D. & Bynghall, S. (2017). Social media and the emergence of reflexiveness as a new capability for open strategy, *Long Range Planning*, 50(3), 322–336.

Baskerville, R.L. & Myers, M.D. (2002). Information systems as a reference discipline, *MIS Quarterly*, 26(1), 1–14.

Benbasat, I. & Weber, R. (1996). Rethinking diversity in information systems research, *Information Systems Research*, 7(4), 389–399.

Benbasat, I. & Zmud, R. (2003). The identity crisis within the IS discipline: defining and communicating the discipline's core properties, *MIS Quarterly*, 27(2), 183–194.

Galliers, R.D. (2003). Change as crisis or growth? Toward a trans-disciplinary view of information systems as a field of study – A response to Benbasat and Zmud's call for returning to the IT artifact, *Journal of the Association for Information Systems*, 4(6): 337–351.

Galliers, R.D. (2006). 'Don't worry, be happy'... A post-modernist perspective on the information systems domain, in J.L. King & K. Lyytinen (eds.), *Information Systems: The State of the Field*. Chichester: Wiley, 324–331.

Galliers, R.D. & Stein, M.K. (eds.) (2015). *Management Information Systems: Critical Perspectives on Business and Management*, Vols. I-IV, London: Routledge.

Galliers, R.D. & Whitley, E.A. (2007). *Vive les differences*? Developing a profile of European information systems research as a basis for international comparisons, *European Journal of Information Systems*, 16(1), 20–35.

Galliers, R.D., Markus, M.L. & Newell, S. (eds.) (2007). *Exploring Information Systems Research Approaches: Readings and Reflections*, London: Routledge.

Gregor, S. (2006). The nature of theory in information systems, *MIS Quarterly*, 30(3), 611–642.

Hirschheim, R. & Klein, H.K. (2011). Tracing the history of the information systems field. In R.D. Galliers & W.L. Currie (eds.) (2011). *The Oxford Handbook of Information Systems: Critical Perspectives and New Directions*, Oxford: Oxford University Press, 16–61.

Hirschheim, R. & Klein, H.K. (2012). A glorious and not-so-short history of the information systems field, *Journal of the Association for Information Systems*, 13(4), 188–235.

Huang, J. Baptista, J. & Galliers, R.D. (2013). Reconceptualizing rhetorical practices in organizations: The impact of social media on internal communications, *Information & Management*, 50(2–3), 112–124.

Keen, P.G.W. (1980). MIS research: Reference disciplines and a cumulative tradition. *ICIS 1980 Proceedings*, Paper 9. http://aisel.aisnet.org/icis1980/9.

King, J.L. & Lyytinen, K. (eds.) (2006). *Information Systems: The State of the Field*, Chichester: Wiley.

King, J.L., Myers, M.D., Rivard, S., Saunders, C., and Weber, R. (2010). What do we like about the IS field? *Communications of the Association for Information Systems*, 26(20). http://aisel.aisnet.org/cais/vol26/iss1/20.

Robey, D. (1996). Diversity in information systems research: Threat, promise, and responsibility, *Information Systems Research*, 7(4), 400–408.

Sarker, S. & Lee, A.S. (2006). Does the use of computer-based BPC tools contribute to redesign effectiveness? Insights from a hermeneutic study, *IEEE Transactions on Engineering Management*, 53(1), 130–145.

Stein, M.K., Galliers, R.D. & Whitley, E.A. (2016). Twenty years of the European information systems academy at ECIS: Emergent trends and research topics, *European Journal of Information Systems*, 25(1), 1–15.

Whittington (2014). Information systems and strategy-as-practice: A joint agenda, *Journal of Strategic Information Systems*, 23(1): 87–91.

1
TAKING IS HISTORY SERIOUSLY

Nik Rushdi Hassan

Introduction

Historical research in information systems (IS) represents an enigma. Recognizing the potential for historical research in IS, Harvard University initiated the MIS History Project in 1988 to develop a historical tradition in management information systems (MIS) research (Mason et al. 1997a). The first article published under that program began with a quote from Francis Bacon:

> Histories make men wise; poets, witty; the mathematics, subtle; natural philosophy, deep; moral, grave; logic and rhetoric, able to contend.

The project produced several exemplary studies demonstrating the effectiveness of IT and systems on companies and industries, including the case of American Airlines' Sabre electronic reservation system (Copeland and McKenney 1988) and Bank of America's electronic banking system (McKenney et al. 1997). Except for several notable studies of Texaco's information technology (IT) function (Hirschheim et al. 2003; Porra et al. 2005. 2006), it would take another quarter of a century before Frank Land (2010) reminded the IS field that they had not yet established that historical tradition and may be missing such an opportunity. Realizing this state of affairs, an effort to rejuvenate historical research began taking shape in 2012 concluding in the Association of Information Systems (AIS) council setting up the AIS History Task Force in 2013, and the appointment of the AIS first historian, Ping Zhang (2015) from Syracuse University. Consequently, the IS field saw more historical studies published, including a book chapter (Hirschheim and Klein 2011) and two special issues on history in the *Journal of the AIS* and the *Journal of Information Technology*, with several of those studies receiving best paper awards (Hirschheim and Klein 2012; Porra et al. 2014). This development indicates how much the field values and supports the effort to produce more historical studies, with the *Communications of the AIS* leading the way by establishing a permanent History section to continue these efforts at a broader level of participation. Despite such encouraging developments, the IS field faces considerable challenges in its endeavors to establish a historical tradition. Writing history is not like your everyday IS research study. History is both science and art, and as we shall see, a good dose of philosophy in applying a method – the historical method – that is unlike any method the IS researcher is familiar with. It is not surprising that these efforts to encourage more historical IS studies are facing challenges.

The historical method and historiography of information systems

Francis Bacon's expectations in the merits of history and its potential already made it challenging enough for any discipline to embark on the project of writing its history. It is more so with the IS field, which has seen in its own history its fair share of debates surrounding its identity (Ackoff 1967; Benbasat and Zmud 2003; Dearden 1966; Dearden 1972; Hirschheim and Klein 2003; Keen 1980; Thurston 1962), its subject matter (Banville and Landry 1989; Benbasat and Weber 1996; Hassan and Will 2006; Mingers and Stowell 1997; Robey 1996; Taylor et al. 2010) and its relevance (Applegate 1999; Benbasat and Zmud 1999; Desouza et al. 2006; Grover et al. 2008; Keen 1991; Rosemann and Vessey 2008; Straub and Ang 2011). It is easy enough to write about the history of computers with its conveniently available treasure trove of artifacts, documents and living legends associated with that subject matter. But we can all agree that the history of computers is not the history of IS, even taking in consideration the obvious overlaps. If we are not writing about computers per se, the question then is, what history is there to write about? Therein lies the value of researching and writing history for the IS field. As Bryant and colleagues (2013) eloquently deliberated, the process of researching and writing the history of IS addresses most, if not all of the aforementioned concerns the field is struggling with. What identity would nations have if not for the history about them? The subject matter of the arts would not be defined if not for art history, and the same can be said for any other discipline. And as far as relevancy goes, anything of significance is recognized and becomes relevant when we say that it "will go down in history." In other words, if we can document such momentous IS-related events and describe them, the relevancy of the field becomes less of an issue.

The historian's task in the making of history is not a matter of documenting a parade of personalities, events and dates, a nostalgic trip down memory lane, or even as Humboldt puts it, "to present what actually happened" (Ranke 1973, p. 5). Even before such "facts" can be collected, the historian is burdened with choosing which is to be considered significant enough to be historical, and to discard the rest as unhistorical. Not all historical events in computer science are relevant to IS, and what is *historic* in IS need not be the same as what is historic in computer science. This argument applies to historical figures. Many historic figures in computer science, such as Codd (1970) and Chen (1976) for databases, Brook's (1975) work on software engineering and the numerous scientists responsible for the Internet such as Vint Cerf and Tim Berners-Lee (Leiner et al. 2016), can hardly be claimed as historic IS figures. A historical fact or historical figure only becomes historical for a field of study when a historian in that field decides so. As Carr (1965) notes, "the facts speak only when the historian calls on them" (p. 9). Thus, a relatively unknown but large UK company, J. Lyons & Co., that owns teashops and hotels, and supplies bread, cakes and pastries, becomes the AIS's symbol of such a "momentous" event taking the shape of the first implementation in 1953 of a computer-based IS in the world (Caminer 1997; Ferry 2003). Whether or not this event is worthy of such accolades is up to debate. But the fact that the AIS chose this event has significant implications on the subject matter of the field that appropriates it as being historical. The IS field could have easily chosen the implementation of the EDSAC computer, also in the UK, when it first calculated a table of squares four years earlier in 1949 (Anonymous 2011). Or, the AIS could have chosen UNIVAC's accomplishment to predict the outcome of the US presidential elections (Brinkley 2006) in 1952 as that major IS historical event, or any other significant computer-related history. In this sense, General Electric's (GE) implementation of UNIVAC to automate its clerical tasks and payroll that took place at about the same time, or Metropolitan Life Insurance Company's plans to use computers for insurance equally qualify as historical IS events. But what made J. Lyons & Co. most significant as far as the IS field is concerned was because they not only sponsored the EDSAC project, but because they also designed, built and implemented an EDSAC-derivative system, the LEO (Lyons Electronic Office) that automated the company's office tasks and developed what would be called a decision-support system (DSS) for management decision making (Land 2010; Land 2015). The architect of that system, John Simmons, would later describe how he accomplished that historical achievement in one of the earliest texts on IS (Simmons 1962). Such a network of related events makes the LEO an historic event to the IS field.

The nature of the event, its technical (constructing the computer) as well as its social, business and political connotations in the form of developing the requirements for the LEO that fit the needs of the company, the leadership in Simmons as the prototypical chief information officer (CIO), the successful adoption and implementation of the new system within uncharted waters, and the spin-off of the LEO into a range of similar models that would service a number of industries, all characterize something other than computer science, management or any other discipline and would be distinguished as the subject matter of IS. When analyzed historically, these events and significant developments simultaneously resolve the issues of identity, subject matter and relevancy.

The historical method and the historiography that systematically and artfully organize such developments can be found in standard historical methods and historiographical texts and in IS studies (Bryant et al. 2013; Farhoomand and Drury 1999; Hirschheim and Klein 2012; Land 2010; Land 2015; Mason et al. 1997a; Porra et al. 2005, 2006, 2014; Straub 2015; Zhang 2015). Because the historical method does not follow the hypothetico-deductive research method that the IS community is familiar with, it is summarized in the following sections, in its briefest of form and with apologies to historians, as a guide to the IS researchers interested in undertaking this under-researched area of study. This chapter focuses more on materials that are not already described in other publications (Bryant et al. 2013; Hirschheim et al. 2003; Mason et al. 1997a; Mason et al. 1997b; Porra et al. 2005, 2006, 2014), and the reader is encouraged to refer to those publications for details. Historical studies inevitably lead to epistemological (what distinguishes historical knowledge from other knowledge), methodological (how is historical knowledge constructed), ontological (what is the nature of history), and ethical (how ought history be applied) controversies (Keulen and Kroeze 2012), and it is important for the IS researcher interested in writing history to be familiar with these issues. One of the goals of this chapter is to introduce the IS researcher to the original sources of the historical method, their distinct epistemology, methodology, ontology and ethics dating back to antiquity so that the IS researcher can nurture a deeper appreciation of the historical account.

History of the historical method

The foundational Greco-Roman historical method

Herodotus's (c. 484–425 BCE) legacy laid the foundations for history as a science (Breisach 1983; Collingwood 1946). For Herodotus, history is considered a science because it is (1) scientific – the word "history" is Greek for inquiry and investigation and it begins by asking questions, (2) humanistic – concerned with actions of man at determinate times, (3) rational – appeals to evidence, and (4) self-revelatory – tells man what he has done. Even though the

Greeks gave value to permanence and the absolute (through Plato), they appreciated the dynamic nature of the changing world, and still saw value in history because the rhythm of its changes is likely to repeat itself with similar antecedents leading to similar consequences (as per Aristotle's four causes), thereby providing a basis for prognostic judgments, even if it's not demonstrable. For Herodotus, the historian sets out to find the truth, and the historical method consists of gathering and reporting of facts given by reliable eyewitnesses. This requirement became a limitation to the Greek historical method, tying them to the length of living memory. The Greek historical method also depended on significant events that happened to be maintained in living memory to decide on the subject of historical study, not the historian's choice of what to study. Third, the histories themselves remain as particularistic fragments, not whole, aggregated universal histories. The Roman historical method was able to extend the Greek particularistic view to a more universal view of the history of the world, albeit viewing themselves as *the* world. The Roman historical method was focused on substantialism, treating what is significant in history (i.e., the Roman empire) as being changeless and eternal. As a result, their method prevents historians from studying how the characteristics of Roman institutions molded the Roman character or how Rome came to be what it was.

The cyclical theocentric Christian historical method

The Christians jettisoned both the optimistic humanist ideas of the Greco-Roman historical method and the substantialist idea of eternal entities (Breisach 1983; Collingwood 1946). They introduced the doctrine of the spirit of man as immaterial creations of God, replacing history as the study of human actions and deeds with the study of God's actions through human agents and His Providence. Rome therefore was not seen as an eternal entity but a transient thing that came into existence at the appropriate time in history to fulfill God's purpose. History no longer stood as a continuity, but a series of cyclical creations and destructions, where all men stood equal in front of God and involved in the workings of God's purpose, a universal history of mankind (e.g., Eusebius of Caesarea as cited by Collingwood). With history as a series of epochs, the task that lay before the medieval historians was to discover and expound on this divine plan, through its stages. In a way, the Christian historical method brought the pendulum that began from the theocentric pre-Herodotus period to the abstract and humanistic Herodotus, back to the theocentric view into the medieval period, but with an epochal perspective with its cycles of ups and downs. And because history is God's divine plan, the cyclical theocentric Christian method lacked a critical component necessary for the scientific study of the actual facts of history.

The verisimilitude of the Muslim historians

The Muslim historians and philosophers (al-Khawarizmi 780–850 CE, al-Tabari 839–923 CE, Avicenna 987–1037 CE, Averroes 1126–1198 CE and Ibn Khaldun 1332–1406 CE, among others) preserved and expanded the philosophy and scientific method of the Greco-Roman historians and philosophers, while retaining the theocentric outlook of the Christian method, to produce one of the world's most advanced practices of historiography (Robinson 2003; Rosenthal 1952). Although Islamic historiography prioritized oral tradition and eyewitnesses, they extended reliable sources to authenticated documents and systematically transmitted the Greco-Roman sciences to the scholars of the Renaissance. History to the Muslims is synonymous with practical philosophy taking various forms of wisdom and knowledge such as *akhbaar* (reports), *seera* and *hadith* (biography), *tabaqat* (annals or chronological history) and *tareekh* (modern sociological historiography). Verisimilitude, or the spirit of approaching the truth, characterized these historical forms. In the *Muqaddimah* (Prolegomena) to his 13-volume treatise on *Tareekh* (History), Ibn Khaldun (1377/1967) elaborates that the science of history

> requires proper interpretation and thoroughness that lead the historian to the truth and keeps him from slips and errors. If he trusts historical information in its plain transmitted form and has no clear knowledge of the principles resulting from custom, the fundamental facts of politics, the nature of civilization, or the conditions governing human social organization . . . he often cannot avoid stumbling and slipping and deviating from the highroad of truth.
>
> (p. 1)

The critical Renaissance historical method

It was not until the 16th and 17th centuries that the critical spirit embodied in Ibn Khaldun's work and the Muslim historians would be picked up by the early historians of the Renaissance period. Tillemont's *History of the Roman Empire* demonstrated that by reconciling statements of various authorities, Descartes's skepticism of history in his *Discourse on Method* could be overcome (Collingwood 1946). It would take a revolution in the form of Vico (1668–1744 CE) to resurrect the philosophy of history established by the earlier historians, which made possible a reconstruction of earlier methods into a systematic set of principles (*verum et factum*) separating ideas from facts, and perception from the interpretation of history. With this stroke of insight, Vico rebuilt the modern idea of the subject matter of history in which its form and matter is created by mankind – essentially the science of human nature – and can therefore be critically studied without Cartesian skepticism. Using this modern method, sources of errors in history from exaggerations of wealth and power, conceit of nations or the learned could be identified, and the historian did not have to depend on an unbroken tradition but could reconstruct by scientific methods, a picture of the past. This critical method culminated in the form of historical works of Locke, Berkeley and Hume, putting history at least in the same footing as other sciences.

All of these principles of historiography are applied in different forms or paradigms depending on the goals, rules and background of the historian. It is important that IS researchers distinguish between historical studies and other kinds of studies that include some kind of historical analysis (see Porra et al. 2014 for a comparison of historical studies with case studies, longitudinal studies, ethnography and field studies). Without a clear distinction of these different kinds of studies, historical research may fall into the same quagmire that the management and organizational sciences experienced in their efforts to write about their history. Even with dedicated journals for historical studies (e.g., *Management & Organizational History, Business History, Business History Review, Journal of Management History*), the organizational science struggled with differences between, say, historical studies and studies in the social sciences, and the relationship between history and theory. In a response to Kieser's (1994) plea for organizational sciences to embrace historical analysis, Goldman (1994) replied, "without agreed-upon theory that transcends time and place, history becomes data, not explanation" (p. 622) and "insofar as theory refers to principles of organization that transcend time and space, historical . . . data can test the generalizability and utility of a theory" (p. 623). This reply reflects the epistemological hold that has taken over the organizational sciences and blinds some of their researchers to the richness and potential of historical studies. Perhaps the organization sciences may not be the best tutor for the IS field when it comes to historical studies. A rich tradition has developed within historiography that deserves a careful study by IS researchers interested in this genre. The following section briefly introduces several of the major paradigms of historiography.

Historiographical paradigms

Rationalistic enlightenment paradigm

Primarily French, the Enlightenment paradigm gave weight to the present as the moment of exceptional importance in the history of the world. To the historians of the Enlightenment like Montesquieu (1689–1755), Voltaire (1694–1778) and Hume (1711–1776), history was viewed as a chain of developments founded on freeing human life and thought from superstition, the Christian church and other irrational authorities, toward the optimistic present that, with the help of science and rationality, promises a bright future. Human nature was thought to be an unchanging constant, in the nature of the Western Europeans of the 18th century, making it difficult for these historians to accept the idea of a history of, and variation in, human nature. The notion of the spirit of humanity was to be abolished, to be replaced by the concept of mental processes that are ready-made and unchanging, that need only to be sharpened by mathematics, physics and metaphysics. Montesquieu, for example, saw the history of other nations to be the necessary effects of natural causes, of climate or geography, not the development of human reason. To these historians, any history before that period paled in significance to the rational and philosophical forms of knowledge of the 18th century. Gibbon's (1737–1752) *History of the Decline and Fall of the Roman Empire* (1788) reflected the barbarism of the past and accentuated the primacy of the present, as did Condorcet (1743–1794) when he wrote in *Outlines of an Historical View of the Progress of the Human Mind* (1795, p. 327):

> The time will therefore come when the sun will shine only on free man who know no other master but their reason; when tyrants and slaves, priests and their stupid or hypocritical instruments will exist only in works of history and on the stage . . . to maintain ourselves in a state of vigilance . . . and to learn how to recognize and so to destroy, by force of reason, the first seeds of tyranny and superstition, should they ever dare to reappear among us.

As a result, less focus is placed on analyzing genuine historical causes because they were not sufficiently interested enough in history for its own, in the development of who they thought to be barbaric peoples, or had any insights into what from their point of view were non-rational periods of history.

This paradigm views history in their own modern scientific spirit as being practical and forward-looking, not theoretical or backward-looking. In Britain, a similar strand of this historical thought was taken up by "Whig historians," predominantly Christian, Anglican thinkers, who used the historical origins of the great British Empire from the Reformation as a means of uniting the empire. Butterfield (1931), in *The Whig Interpretation of History*, highlighted the hubristic dangers of writing history that aggrandized the present (Bentley 1999; Berger et al. 2003). This paradigm is not limited to that period in history. It can be found lurking in oft-mentioned phrases like "How can this be happening? This is the 21st century . . ." or "How did we ever survive without the [computer, cellphone, other technologies . . .]?" Despite these proclivities, this paradigm has its strengths, especially in drawing attention to otherwise unknown aspects of the object of study.

The literary Romantic paradigm

The reaction to the Enlightenment movement came in the form of Romanticism, which accepted a more sympathetic investigation of past history and its significance, and saw positive values in civilizations different from its own (Bentley 1999; Collingwood 1946). The Romantic historian believed that the masses of humanity could be changed and improved through literature, the arts and education. This principle could be applied not only to the contemporary civilized world of the 18th century, but also to the history of all races and all times. Herder (1744–1803), in *Ideas upon Philosophy and the History of Mankind* (Herder 1784/1803), insisted that the unit of analysis of history was the *Volk*, the people, their rational and moral life, having their own physical and mental peculiarities, each differentiated with its own ideal of life. It was this kind of thinking of history that helped him give birth to the new field of anthropology. His own teacher Emmanuel Kant, the product of the Enlightenment, did not agree with some of Herder's ideas, but he did produce some insights concerning the teleological view of history such that it is possible for the historian to envisage historical events as part of some kind of orderly phenomenon that follows some laws unlike those of the natural sciences. With this understanding, history can then be studied just like any other science, with its truth-claims that needed to be tested and validated. Thus in Kant, although the real history or *thing-in-itself*, cannot be known, the knowing subject gains her knowledge of history by processing various kinds of sense-data available.

Both these ideas from Herder and Kant are found in what became known as *Historicism*, which rejects the universalist empiricism and rationalism of the Enlightenment, and places importance on cautious, rigorous and contextualized interpretation of history. For historicists, the diverse nature of human life cannot possibly be universally generalized or contained; instead each aspect of life demonstrates its own sublime beauty, order and distinction. The vehicle to perform this task of enriching history, describing all manner of experiences, the uncovering of the human values and spirit, intelligence and moral freedom was the narration. The narrative of *The French Revolution: A History* by Carlyle (1837/1934) became more than just a dry procession of events; its readers felt the terror in the streets, tasted the decadence of the monarchy and saw the blood spilling from the guillotine, while at the same time understood the context and philosophy surrounding it (Hindley 2009). Great personalities played major roles in this historical narrative. For historicism, every society must be viewed as a complex of values to be understood in its own terms instead of by reference to standards external to the society.

Rankean paradigm of scientific history

The need to find order in history materialized in Humboldt's lecture *On the Tasks of the Historian* as he elaborated on finding form within chaos, locating historical events as part of organic wholes that combined a trustworthy reconstruction of the past with literary excellence. This movement began in Germany in the early 18th century with the establishment of the University of Berlin, where Leopold Ranke established seminars for historians in the critical examination of medieval documents and the scientific method. This method is not limited to critically examining historical documents; it also involves penetrating the external events to understand (*verstehen*) the causal nexus within history and God's plans. Thus, the professionalized historical scholarship involved both a demand for strict objectivity on the one hand and the particularistic political and cultural analysis on the other. This German model of historicism became the standard model for Europe and the new United States as historians on both continents refer to Ranke as the "father of historical science."

An example of this empirical approach to history can be seen in Garfield and colleagues' historiographic approach to scientometrics (Garfield 1963; Garfield et al. 1964). Citation indexing epitomizes Ranke's scientific approach to historical documents. Scientometrics can pinpoint how a particular scientific discovery emerged and identify the bibliographic antecedents and descendants of that area. For example, by tracing the methods and solutions used in historiographical material before the discovery of the double helix structure of DNA, Garfield (2004) found several original works that were critical to the discovery but were never acknowledged.

The social science paradigm of history

The classical historicism of Ranke's scientific method and its political narrative did not give a large enough role to society, economy and culture. Although the Rankean paradigm emphasized the establishment of facts by means of rigorous research, it rested on the metaphysical assumption that certain historical forces or ideas were at work, and did not consciously ask theoretical questions or apply methodological approaches for explaining those forces (Iggers 2005). This crisis that historicism faced coincided with the development in the social and cultural sciences as philosophers like Dilthey (1833–1911), Windelband (1848–1915) and Rickert (1863–1936) began working out a clearer methodology for their incipient science separate from that of the natural sciences. Windelband's (1980) notion of the idiographic (or individualizing) nature of the social sciences sought to understand the meaning of human actions in its concrete, social and historical setting, whereas the nomothetic (or generalizing nature of the natural sciences) sought to derive laws that explain types or categories of objective phenomena. Combining the two in Max Weber's (1864–1920) terms, for example, meant that the intuitive approach of the historicists needed to be replaced by abstract analytical concepts (or ideal types) in order for understanding (*verstehen*) to take place (Weber 1919/1968). The social science paradigm of history sought out the attitudes and values that were unique to the character of the society and culture.

Among the many different social sciences traditions, the French *Annales* exerted an influence in historiography as the one that challenged the dominant linear view of historical progress. Its prognosticators included Febvre (1878–1956) and Bloch (1886–1944), who together established the journal *Annales d'historie economique et sociale*, from which the movement got its name. Le Goff (1924–2014) and Nora (1934–) continued this tradition in the form of France's *New History* movement. While traditional historicism elevated the role of the state as both goal and means with other disciplines subordinated to that role, the *Annales* historians broke down the boundaries between the traditional disciplines to open historiography to other directions and new approaches. This interdisciplinary approach to historiography that became a "science of man" included economics, sociology, anthropology, linguistics, semiotics, literature and the arts placed emphasis on the complex structures in history rather than on personalities or politics. As a result, it became possible for historiography to accept and quantify multiple coexisting time lines that proceeded differently (Iggers 2005).

One application of coexisting timelines can be found in the social construction of technology (SCOT) studies. Bijker and colleagues (Bijker et al. 1987; Pinch and Bijker 1984) developed a new way of thinking that integrated abstract models, historical narratives and political analysis "to understand the relations between technology and society and to act on issues of sociotechnical change" (Bijker 1995, p. 6). This approach involves focusing on the problem–solution underlying technological change, uncovering the strategies taken by relevant social groups to resolve those problems through time, and the artifacts that emerge as a result of the inter- and intra-group relations. The form of historicism in SCOT plays a major role in demonstrating how particularistic changes in social behavior and society throughout history impacts technology.

Critical and Marxist paradigm

At the same time the social science paradigm was exerting an influence on historians, Marx (1818–1883), partly inspired by Hegel's (1770–1831) *Philosophy of History*, was formulating his own version of human history. Marx's inspiration, Hegel, viewed the development of human freedom as the development of human consciousness. Thus in order to understand history, it became necessary to understand what people thought of their political or social conditions, and the resultant action from their thoughts. These actions that take the form of the historical process were therefore logical processes that could be predicted. Thus, Hegel argues, every historical process is a dialectical process in which one form of life (thesis) generates its own opposite (antithesis), and out of this opposition, there arises a better form (synthesis).

Marx took these principles and applied them to economic and social history. Whereas Hegel's dialectic began with thought forming nature, Marx began with nature forming thought, asserting therefore that historical events had natural causes (dialectical materialism) (Collingwood 1946). Many interpret this historical materialism as taking the form of economic forces and means of production as primary causal structures, while others view Marx focusing instead on human needs and the irrationality of the capitalistic social formation. Nevertheless, the conception of class struggle, and the displacement of one social formation over another, dominate the popular view of Marxian history, and there is no shortage of diverging interpretations. For example, Thompson (1963) rejects the three Marxist concepts of the primacy of economic forces, the objectivity of the scientific method and the idea of progress. Instead, Thompson prefers a more open investigative approach and critique of the culture as embodied in traditions, value systems, ideas and institutions, and not necessarily understood dogmatically according "to a text written one hundred and twenty years ago" (p. 383). This critical tradition was not Marx's or Hegel's invention. It can be traced back to Socrates's methods and Kant's three critiques (Kant 1790/1964; Kant 1781/1978; Kant 1788/1956), and was carried in the traditions of Nietzsche, Weber, Lukacs and others after that. Critical historiography becomes an essential part of writing history, especially with the tendency of certain historians toward misinterpretation and revisionism (Bloch 1992).

Postmodern paradigm

The work of historians like Thompson (1963) anticipated the changes that overtook the world as it faced the deleterious effects of modernization, expanding industrialization as well as social upheavals triggered by among others, the civil rights movement and the Vietnam War, for which none of the earlier paradigms offered any satisfactory historical explanations (Iggers 2005). Historians began questioning these structuralist paradigms that essentially attempt to provide a cohesive scientific explanation of historical change, often supported by quantification, and economic and demographic determinism (Stone 1979). They turned away from these macrohistorical methods and returned back to the microhistorical narratives of the human and cultural sciences that repudiated the positivism inherent in some of the earlier paradigms. For this kind of historical research, the post-structuralist approaches of Jacques Derrida (1930–2004), Michel Foucault (1926–1984) and cultural anthropologists represented by writers like Clifford Geertz (1926–2006) served as models. In the case of Derrida (1976), his historical analysis of text highlights the futility of arriving at positivistic absolute concepts, and that each concept has to be carefully differentiated from other similar concepts contingent on the historical context. Geertz (1973), for example, introduces the method of "thick description" that allows each culture to be analyzed according to that culture's symbolic values, free of any theory-guided questions that deprive that culture of their vitality.

By and large, historical methods lean toward idealistic methods that are inherently subjective. Even the Rankean (1973, p. xliv) paradigm extols the "doctrine of ideas," which in a historical event "is only partially visible to the world of the senses: the rest has to be added by intuition, inference, and guesswork." Postmodernism rejects studying history like the natural sciences, and eschews efforts to discover "laws" of historical phenomena. However, this idealistic foundation of history when taken to the extreme in postmodernism, and its "linguistic turn," puts no limit on the number of permitted readings of historical documents and essentially divorces the historical text from past events. So historians have essentially occupied the middle ground that neither relies on positivist realist evidence nor falls victim to relativism; instead, the scholarly procedures in historiography maintain an avenue of inquiry that is closest to the "real" and as far removed as possible from the absurdities of relativism (Tosh 2000).

Brief analysis of IS historical studies

Based on these paradigms of history, a brief analysis of historical studies in IS highlights the opportunities as well as limitations of historical studies in IS (Table 1.1). Each of the studies were categorized based on the concept of the Kuhnian paradigm as exemplary work (Kuhn 1970; Kuhn 1977) in historical studies or standard illustrations of analyzing history. Studies that analyze IS historical studies are excluded from the brief analysis. Specific summarized narratives were used to categorize each study (Table 1.1).

Table 1.1 Narratives in historical paradigms

Historical paradigm	Narrative
Enlightenment paradigm	Exceptionalism in present history, rationalistic, practical spirit freeing mankind from superstition
Romantic paradigm	Literary, heroic leadership, spiritual values, teleological, optimism in people's potential, appreciation for particularism and contextualized study (historicism)
Rankean paradigm	Scientific method, order, objectivity, organic whole, rigorous reconstruction, content and scientometric historiography
Social science paradigm	Philosophy and methodology of social science, focus on society, politics, economy and culture, social structures (structuralism), theoretical abstractions, interpretivism, generalizing categories
Critical paradigm	Human consciousness, class struggle, social action, dialectical process, domination, emancipation
Postmodern paradigm	Post-structuralism, idiographic, genealogy, textual analysis and hermeneutics, deconstruction, cultural anthropology and ethnography

Table 1.2 Historical IS studies categorized by paradigms

	Enlightenment paradigm	Romantic paradigm	Rankean paradigm	Social science paradigm	Critical paradigm	Postmodern paradigm
Chen and Hirschheim (2004)			X	X		
Clarke (2013)			X			
Copeland and McKenney (1988)			X	X		
Culnan (1986)			X			
Culnan (1987)			X			
Epstein (2013)				X		
Farhoomand and Drury (1999)			X			
Galliers and Whitley (2007)			X			
Grover et al. (2006)			X			
Hassan (2014)					X	X
Hassan (2016)						X
Hirschheim and Klein (2003)	X			X		
Hirschheim and Klein (2011)				X		
Hirschheim and Klein (2012)				X		
Jakobs (2013)			X	X		
Mason et al. (1997a)	X	X	X			
Mason et al. (1997b)	X	X	X			
McKenney et al. (1997)	X	X	X			
Mitev (2006)				X		
Orlikowski and Baroudi (1991)			X	X		
Pollock and Williams (2008)			X	X		
Porra et al. (2005)				X		
Porra et al. (2006)	X			X		
Stein et al. (2016)			X			
Wade et al. (2006)			X			
Whitley and Galliers (2007)			X			

As the analysis summarized in Table 1.2 shows, the vast majority of IS historical studies follow the Rankean or social science paradigm, which is not surprising, given the background and training of IS researchers. Exceptions include early studies from the IS History Project (Mason et al. 1997a) that combined several paradigms to address questions surrounding the organic changes and technological transformations in business, and studies of the Texaco IT function (Hirschheim et al. 2003; Porra et al. 2006) that analyzed the role of CEOs and CIOs in the history of the company. Why did the change come when it did? Why did it take the form it did? What was the result, and what role did IT have in the process? The view of IS in the studies of American Airlines and Bank of America as part of an organic whole impacting business, and the use of the central notion of "dominant design" in a coherent explanation for changes in the banking and airline industries, reflect the Rankean scientific paradigm. The depiction of the champions at a very personal level leading those transformations in these studies and in the Texaco IT function follows the Romantic paradigm that injects a sense of purpose and richness of experience into those responsible for the transformation. At the same time, the ideal types abstracted from the analysis (leaders, maestro and supertech personalities) demonstrate how that IS history makes use of the Weberian social science paradigm. Altogether, these descriptions fulfill what Bryant et al. (2013) consider to be the major goals of writing IS history. First, it is not just about computing or technology, nor it is just about how the managers overcame their challenges – it is directly relevant to field of IS and thus establishes its identity, an issue that continues to concern the IS field (Hirschheim and Klein 2011; Hirschheim and Klein 2012). This method of writing IS history provides a process of how IS history unfolds without succumbing to the extremes of technological determinism or organizational imperatives. Third, it allows us to see the discontinuities taking place as a means of discovering "other" perspectives of that history, and therefore be better able to confront the difficulties of the present.

Within the Rankean paradigm are studies that compare IS with the perspectives of "others" using "objective methods" such as content analysis, co-citation and other scientometric-related methods. Content analysis methods in IS history (Farhoomand and Drury 1999) examine journals and conferences representing secondary sources of historical data to infer about methodological or thematic trends in IS research. Co-citation studies map the development of the IS fields and its interaction with its reference disciplines over several decades (Culnan 1986; Culnan 1987). By applying both content analysis and scientometric methods, Galliers and Whitley (2007) and Whitley and Galliers (2007) find that historically, European IS research demonstrates a different profile compared to other conferences (ICIS, AMCIS or PACIS) especially that of the American tradition. A follow-up study (Stein et al. 2016) not only finds similar trends continuing into the last decade, it finds evidence of convergence toward conservatism between the European and the American research traditions. The debate between Grover et al. (2006) and Wade et al. (2006) concerning IS as a reference discipline demonstrates the power of citation networks in drawing up different interpretations and perspectives surrounding the historical development of the field. Like seeing oneself in the mirror, the power of seeing others allows the field to face itself, and grow with the help of insights from the other. The successful conclusion of this exercise only takes place when the IS field goes beyond mirroring what they see in others. However, the IS field has consistently mirrored, borrowed and replicated what it sees in its reference disciplines (Hassan 2011). And not surprisingly, the same can be seen in the IS field's historical studies. Because the IS historical tradition itself is still being developed, IS authors tend to fashion their history following either the history of computing (Bannister 2002) or the history of management (Kieser 1994). The former follows a well-established tradition in computer science (Eames and Eames 1990; Goldstine 1972; Zientara 1981) that focuses on the technology and its development. The latter focuses on how organizations apply strategies involving technologies to accomplish goals (Chandler 1962; Porter 1980), the history of diffusion of technology (Rosenberg 1972), or history of innovation in technologies and their business implications (Teece 1986), primarily through case studies of companies. As Mason et al. (1997a) note, this computer science model may not reveal "forces [that] changed businesses, organizations, and industries" (p. 261). On the other extreme, the organizational focus may omit important considerations relating to the technology that only an expert in the technology appreciates. For example, the Bank of America study (Mason et al. 1997a) was undertaken in the context of technologies of the 1950s. Experts that understand the capabilities and limits of 1950s technologies can provide more insights into the series of events that took place.

Finding the right balance between purely managerial concerns and purely technologies concerns can be challenging. One study on the governance of the Internet (Epstein 2013) sought to describe a different kind of governance system that prevailed over the Internet as compared to the traditional state-centric mechanisms of the telecommunications system. The study followed the creation of the Internet Governance Forum to demonstrate how these two different governance systems affected notions of legitimacy and authority. The result of the analysis delved into institutional history, but focused primarily on the political interests and values with only tangential conclusions on how the technology played a role, reflecting its social science paradigm. On the other end, a description of the beginnings of the Web in Australia (Clarke 2013) described in detail the technological development of the Internet in data networks, file transfers and browser navigation, and how early individual and organizational adopters applied them, but remained very much a technological study. IS historical studies require a balance that combines social organizational concerns with technological concerns, and ideally addresses questions about some major historical event. In a study that answers the question as to why the X.400 email standard failed, Jakobs (2013) not only combined both technical and societal concerns, but the study also explains why despite being associated with the very influential OSI standards, and using technology more sophisticated than SMTP, the X.400 standard failed anyway. The answer lies in the socio-technical. In describing the technology, Jakobs (2013) compared the implications stemming from the close integration of the X.400 system with the OSI stack against the simplicity of the Internet's SMTP. This technical analysis demonstrates the objective Rankean paradigm. The study also described the contextual business variables that contributed to its demise, providing a detailed historical narrative of what happened to the X.400 while at the same time offering valuable lessons for future designers. This interpretation of the business environment applied the social science paradigm.

Some may claim that historical patterns do generalize over time and those lessons can be taken as "laws of society." Even though historical studies involve a search for patterns (e.g., the cyclical nature of history), each pattern is unique and contextually dependent on that particular age. Innovation may go through cycles; however, the nature of innovation in the case of the TV or the phone is not the same as the innovation of the Internet. TV and phone technologies took a much longer time to be adopted compared to the Internet, and they impacted people and organizations in different ways. Even though such cycles may appear in the guise of old technology that takes new forms (Porra et al. 2014), the different context and particular processes of innovation require a much more nuanced study that the historical method is well adapted to provide. Pollock and Williams's (2008) study of the explosive success of the enterprise resource planning (ERP) system led by SAP is an example of this kind of nuanced approach. By combining technological and organizational concerns under the guidance of the social science paradigm (especially social construction of technology), they proposed the notion of the "biography of the artifact" to make salient what would otherwise be silent about the development of the technology in the organization. Using this concept, it became possible for the researchers to address multiple historical time frames around the object, and events or activities that needed to be analyzed.

A historical study need not be in search of theories (Marwick 1989), as the Rankean and social science paradigms stipulate. Several IS studies successfully mirrored such goals. A study of the failure of the computerized reservation system at French Railways (Mitev 2006) focused on the interaction of macro-social and historical factors and showed how price changes instituted by the system challenged existing regional and national development plans. The design of the system and its fare structure disrupted the already established subsidies that were region-specific based on their stage of economic development. In trying to emulate the success of the airline reservation systems, French Railways incorporated interface design that did not fit rail travel needs. The study concluded with the theory that the numerous micro-social level conflicts and problems that the system introduced had major macro-social organizational, economic and political implications.

Other studies in the Rankean and social science paradigms challenge existing assumptions and theories by uncovering the historical background that enacted or reified those assumptions. In IS, Orlikowski and Baroudi (1991) and Chen and Hirschheim (2004) uncovered the philosophical traditions that have dominated IS research in the past 20 years. They both found that while the positivist tradition has maintained its dominance, the critical tradition has yet to show progress. Despite the publications of special issues (Cecez-Kecmanovic et al. 2008), handbooks (Howcroft and Trauth 2005) and a major article on the principles of critical research (Myers and Klein 2011), this paradigm of research continues to struggle in IS (Richardson and Robinson 2007). It is not surprising that very little is accomplished in the field with the critical historical paradigm. Of the few that could be mentioned, Hassan (2014) analyzes the historical impact of one of the field's most influential article, "Can the Field of MIS Be Disciplined?" on how the Kuhnian paradigm is applied in the IS field and its impact on the IS field's progress. By going behind the historical events leading to the publication of that article and its subsequent acceptance into the collective memory of the IS community, Hassan applies Gadamer's hermeneutics, one of the techniques available for historical analysis in the postmodern paradigm, to understand how the IS field's antipathy toward the Kuhnian paradigm affected the field's disciplinary structures.

In another article inspired by the postmodern paradigm, Hassan (2016) distills the nearly 60-year history of the IS field into two major intellectual and discursive activities of *informatizing* and *systematizing*. Using Foucault's archeological analysis and Bourdieu's (1977) and Pickering's (1995) practice theories, Hassan (2016) deconstructs these two essential activities of the IS field into six dimensions of automating, informating, complexing, analyzing/synthesizing, sensemaking and enacting. This diverse image of the IS field enables IS researchers to find their place and to connect the dots related to their work, despite the field's apparent theoretical diversity and incongruity. Focusing on what the IS field does throughout its history helps build a distinctive identity for the field, opens up possibilities for theorizing the IT artifact and enables IS researchers to theorize not only traditional IS topics, but especially novel, unpredictable and emergent socio-technical phenomena.

Following Üsdiken and Kieser (2004), Mitev and de Vaujany (2012) categorized 64 papers published between 1972 and 2009 that they considered to be historical in their content and related to IS. Given the novel nature of historical studies in IS, and the large number of papers their research method selected, it is likely that they might have included case studies, field studies, ethnographic and longitudinal studies into their pool of historical studies. They found that most of these papers were supplementarist with limited uses of the historical method. Supplementarist application of historical methods makes history as just another contextual variable alongside other social variables, and merely complements the dominant positivist approach albeit with a longer time span. If they did include other kinds of studies with historical studies, then, this result is not surprising because the vast majority of IS research are case studies, field studies or longitudinal studies, which are not strictly historical studies per Porra et al.'s (2014) categorization.

What is common with the positivist tradition is the nomothetic nature of their analysis. For example, two studies that are referred to as historical studies of the failure of the baggage handling system at the launch of the Denver Airport follow this nomothetic approach. The emphasis of the first study (Montealegre and Keil 2000) was on how to de-escalate a project that was doomed to fail. As the authors correctly noted, the use of history as an antecedent to explain the de-escalation process, and collection of data from the field and interviews, makes this kind of research a case study rather than a historical study (Porra et al. 2014). The second study (Neufville 1994) focused on the complexity of the design of the baggage system and sought to arrive at lessons that could be generalized to other cases of complex design. This too qualifies as case study research that abstracts laws to explain the phenomenon of interest. This nomothetic approach sidelines rich descriptions that add valuable insights to the historical event. The deep description in the Romantic paradigm provides this insightful understanding of the times, and even creates an image of a theory, although not in the positivistic sense that can be tested. Thus a historical analysis of the Denver Airport could be enriched with a detailed description of how the people on the front lines suffered as a result of the breakdown – with the goal of enriching the knowledge of any future designers or builders of systems – to understand the dire implications, not so much that they arrive at certain list of things to do or not to do, but to provide a vivid description of the experiences of those involved to serve as valuable input for future plans.

What is even more significant is how Üsdiken and Kieser (2004) characterize what they consider to be closer to historical studies, which they describe as either integrationist, or better yet, reorientationalist. Integrationist studies use history to extend existing theoretical frameworks by integrating historical techniques and theories into organizational research. Examples include studies of new institutionalism and organizational ecology that have become "more historical" with an increase in longitudinal studies, or with an increase in use of historical databases. Reorientationalist studies, akin to critical research, make extensive use of historical data, deconstruct existing theoretical frameworks and propose new frameworks. Their exemplars for this kind of studies include history as science studies and actor-network theory-based critical organizational analyses. A comparison of the richness and diversity of the historiographical paradigms described earlier with these two categories demonstrates the rather narrow depiction of historical studies in organizational science, and their reluctance to view the historical tradition as a different form of scholarship. Mitev and de Vaujany's (2012) attempt to link the characterization of IS research into positivist, interpretive and critical studies with Üsdiken and Kieser's (2004) categories of historical research in organizational science only reaffirms, just like its reference discipline, how deep-seated and invested IS research has become in the social science or behavioral paradigm.

Thus, while Mitev and de Vaujany's (2012) found that 60% of historical studies in IS journals are supplementarist and nearly 40% are integrationist, the foregoing brief analysis suggests that given the smaller pool of historical studies in IS (as opposed to case studies, field studies, ethnographic or longitudinal studies), not only does the IS field have a larger proportion of reorientationalist studies as shown in Table 1.1, but the future is also bright for a vibrant historical tradition in IS and the field may yet capture that missed opportunity (Land 2010). However, IS researchers need to seriously engage with the historical method and embrace its many diverse paradigms instead of relying on just the two paradigms, the Rankean and social science paradigms, that they are familiar with. To assist researchers in this direction, a brief guide based on Garraghan's (1946) classic historiography, adapted to the IS field following Mason et al.'s (1997b) seven steps, is provided next.

Historiography's seven steps

These seven steps are not meant to be a cookie-cutter approach for writing historical studies. According to Garraghan (1946), historical methods can be categorized into three major operations: (1) historical heuristics – search for material and sources of information, (2) criticism – appraisement of the materials or sources from the viewpoint of evidential value, and (3) synthesis and exposition – assembling the body of historical data and presentation of their significance. All three are not necessarily taken in strict succession, and they often overlap.

The danger of following these steps unreflectively can be clearly seen in the case of design science research in IS, when researchers latch on to Hevner et al.'s (2004) prescription on how to perform design science research, much to the dismay of design science's own champions (Gregor and Hevner 2013). Historical writing is by definition original, fresh, insightful and ideally, exciting. Major differences between historical research and the traditional research models in IS are highlighted within these steps, and the description of the same steps adds important considerations that were absent in previous studies (Mason et al. 1997b; Porra et al. 2006; Porra et al. 2014).

Formulating historical questions

Both Mason et al. (1997b) and Porra et al. (2014) suggest beginning by asking the right questions that will help the researcher focus on the goals and directions to the writing process. The deceptive simplicity of this important step hides its distinguishing elements that are necessary for the study to be historical. For example, about the Bank of America, Mason et al. (1997b) formulated questions concerning any perceived competitive crises that threatened the organization, why IT was proposed as a solution and how the technology was selected and incorporated into the organization – all contributing to the goal of describing how the bank achieved competitive advantage and later lost it (McKenney et al. 1997). Porra et al. (2006) formulated questions concerning the significant changes the Texaco IT function faced, related changes in the oil industry and in the IT industry all contributing to the goal of describing the perceptions management had about the IT function. It is not enough to ask the five W's (what, who, when, where and why) and the "how" questions that are also asked in any research study. It is not enough to study a phenomenon just because it is interesting. Although, it need not always be the case, the questions in an historical study *should ask what was it that was truly historic.*

The selection by the researcher as to *what makes history* founds the motivation behind the study. In the case of the former study of Bank of America, what was historic was how the bank successfully created, with the help of technology, the concept of branch banking in the US, to become for a period in history, the largest bank in the world, surpassing even J.P. Morgan. The latter history of the Texaco IT function was concerned more about management perceptions of success and failure, an important question to consider, but perhaps not necessarily as historic as the former.

Once the significance of the question is clear, a decision needs to be made as to which paradigm and which philosophy of history best fits the goals of the historical study. Is the study aiming to describe the experiences of IT professionals as they faced difficult decisions during the dotcom crash? If so, the Romantic paradigm may guide the researcher toward this end. Is the study asking why, despite all signs pointing to the growing tech bubble, did IT investors and industry pundits not predict the dotcom crash? If that is the goal, then, the social science paradigm or the postmodern paradigm may be well suited for the task. Even the Enlightenment paradigm, despite its apparent bias and Whiggish tradition, provides a useful heuristic for writing history. For a field like IS that is asking questions surrounding its identity, relevancy and legitimacy, the Enlightenment paradigm of history that views the rest of history from its own present exceptional circumstances, provides IS history the necessary heuristic to free itself from its reliance on its reference disciplines and narrow antiquarian viewpoints, much like the role the British historians played in building the British Empire. Historians like Goldwin Smith (and his anti-imperial writings in *The Empire*) and John Seeley (and his pro-imperial writings in *The Expansion of England*) contributed to the discussion and the establishment of an imperial power both military and economic that was unmatched in the late 1800s. These historical writings became like the "bible" for politicians and patriots alike (Gooch 1959). Analogically, such institution building can also take place in fields of studies and disciplines. Even though the IS field as an academic institution did not take shape until the late 1960s, the subject matter had existed as soon as programmable computers were invented in the 1940s (Hassan and Will 2006). Thus, highlighting those development enacts the history of IS beyond strict academic boundaries and allows the IS historian to construct an identity comparable with the other sciences.

Specifying the IS domain

This step is an important step that distinguishes IS history, and therefore, the IS field, by defining the kind of perspective the historical study takes. This step doesn't just specify the unit of analysis – which in the case of a historical study could be anything from a person to the whole world – it defines the subject matter. Is this study about the history of the IS field or about the history of IS? What aspect in the history of IS is being investigated? A few of the studies analyzed in this paper focused on either the history of the computer, networks, the Internet or the history of management, both of which are related to IS, but are not strictly the history of IS. The ontology and nature of the study determines the methods most suited for it. The scope of the study should not be too wide or too narrow; it should be just right to provide a potential wealth of sources, but does not necessarily put limits on the historian.

If the domain is about the history of IS, then as Mason et al. (1997b) suggest, it could be about the implementation, use and management of information and communications technology (ICT). But the history of IS can be much more than that. McKenney et al.'s (1997) Bank of America history was not just about computing. It does relate very detailed technical aspects of the NCR, IBM and Burrough's check-processing machines, but it also described how the requirements for branch banking led to innovations in banking procedures and check format. Similarly, Porra et al.'s (2006) history of the IT function at Texaco wasn't just about the technology, it was about how benefits from automation and technology were obscured. The heuristic provided by the various paradigms also help define the domain of study. For example, following the SCOT paradigm, it could be about the history of the changing impacts of ICT on society, and the impact of society on ICT. Guided by the critical paradigm, it could be about how ICT differs from other technologies of the industrial revolution, and how these differences factor into the shaping of the post-industrial information revolution (Bell 1973). If the domain is about the field of IS, the extensive background from Hirschheim and Klein's (2012) *A Glorious and Not-So-Short History of the Information Systems Field* and Zhang's (2015) *The IS History Initiative: Looking Forward by Looking Back* provide a treasure of historical events that could be investigated in order to arrive at why the IS field has become what it is. What happened to all the pioneering works of Churchman, Langefors, Blumenthal and Mumford that built the foundations of the IS field? Where have all those key concepts and practical lessons that endeared themselves to the practitioners of that age gone? What historical lessons can be distilled from the early experiences of the information revolution, and how were they applied during the dotcom era?

Gathering evidence – a focus on primary sources

Although establishing what constitutes the historical facts can be challenging, historians have always preferred primary sources, whether they be in the form of eyewitnesses, original documents, reports, artifacts, autobiographies, letters, or business or government records

(Marwick 1989). Because the majority of studies in IS find data in surveys, field studies, interviews and often secondary sources (journal articles that cite other journal articles or primary sources), these primary sources of evidence are not what IS researchers are used to. An example of such primary sources are the interviews that Zhang and Land collected of key researchers who lived through the establishment of the IS field in the UK (Land 2015). Researchers that lean toward positivist approaches are less sensitive to the subjective, irrational and volatile nature of human behavior and the crucial role of perception, often found in these primary sources. History for them is data that needs to be tested, while human agency and man's often irrational and creative choices receive less attention (Keulen and Kroeze 2012). These choices and their evidence in the form of relics and traces that come into existence during the actual period of the past that the historian is investigating require a set of unique skills in searching as well as in interpreting.

For example, in historical studies, surviving objects are treated as documents. A coin with the mark "In God We Trust" implies that the people of that period have belief in liberty and God. To historians, an article reviewing the belief of that period carries less credibility than the coin. For some historians (Marwick 1989, p. 199), "without the study of primary sources there is no history." But primary sources are not the only acceptable evidence. Sources that are not completely composed or created during the time period being studied (e.g., autobiographies) are also acceptable, as are secondary sources, but should be noted as such. Such hybrid or secondary sources cannot be taken entirely at face value and must be critically assessed.

Caminer's (1997) collection of chapters from the "insiders" closely associated with the history of the LEO forms an exemplary case of such a hybrid study of primary sources and autobiographies. It vividly describes how the idea for the first business computer was hatched by a caterer and teashop company no less, how this idea was realized with the assistance of numerous experts in both technical and business domains, and the impact it made on industry as a whole. Writing from the outside as a science writer, Ferry's (2003) historical analysis surrounded the conflict that the Lyon's company faced in developing its own technology, and the challenges it faced in attempting to market that technology unsuccessfully to others.

Critiquing the historical evidence

Porra et al. (2014) present a long list of criteria to evaluate the accumulated evidence to ensure their credibility. Much of these criteria are derived from the principle of verisimilitude established by the Muslim historians. Embedded in verisimilitude are the related principles of authenticity, veracity, corroboration and consistency, all of which are organized by historians into the two methods of external criticism and internal criticism (Garraghan 1946). External criticism concerns the authenticity of historical evidence. Fabrication is rampant, so tests are necessary not only to prevent blatant fraud but also to moderate the abuse of evidence that takes place in historical studies. Preventing fraud was the original goal of Garfield's citation index (Garfield 1955). In the IS field, there may be a tendency to appropriate works from other disciplines and claim it as belonging to IS (e.g., Codd's and Chen's database studies, or the development of the Internet), whereas those scholars have little association with the IS research community per se.

Once the sources of evidence or the evidence itself passes external criticism, the evidence needs to undergo internal criticism to establish its credibility. While external criticism establishes that the historical fact actually happened, by examining the contents, form, style and other related criteria of the evidence, internal criticism establishes that it is close to what actually happened. It is possible that the source originated at the period being studied, but it may have been falsified or edited in transmission. Both external and internal criticism take place with the help of sophisticated and critical processes that order the mass of historical evidence into a coherent and intelligible narrative.

Determining patterns

At this stage, the assemblage of admissible and ordered facts must now be interpreted and its meaning comprehended. The value added by historians is to interpret the facts and explain them, perhaps with the help of other disciplines: philosophy, scientometrics, statistics, anthropology, epigraphy, linguistics, geography, political science, numismatics and archeology. Various methods are available to synthesize the mass of historical facts into patterns. Analogical reasoning argues that resemblance of two events in one or more respects suggest a necessary resemblance also in other respects. This process helps reveal new aspects and relations of historical facts, uncover points of agreements and disagreements and suggest new data. At the same time, the historian has to look out for faulty analogies (Garraghan 1946).

Generalization is another powerful process of historical analysis. Although history is concerned with the idiographic, single individual facts, generalizing these facts enables the historian to grasp the sheer volume of what appear to be disparate events into manageable units. IS researchers are used to applying statistics to reach conclusions. These statistical methods can also be useful in generalizing historical facts. In seeking to reason things out, historians also formulate conjectures and hypotheses that bring together possible causes and effects. The historian distinguishes between conjectures and hypotheses: the former deals more with individual and particular facts, whereas the latter deals with bodies of facts with wider range and significance. Neither can be undertaken gratuitously and must be based on sound evidence. Even the lack of evidence provides an argument for interpreting history – argument from silence. Historians argue against an alleged historical fact because contemporary sources fail to say anything about it and use this silence to challenge the credibility of the evidence. Evidence that exists prior to the occurrence of the historical event (e.g., known characters, antecedents, habits) may be legitimately applied to argue for the existence of certain processes operating after the event. All forms of interpretation – factual, linguistic, technical, logical, psychological – should be marshalled to find those patterns.

Telling the story – the power of the narrative

As Mason et al. (1997b, p. 317) emphasize, "the penultimate step in an historical study is to tell the story." The success of popular guru books in management speaks of the power of the narrative (e.g., *In Search of Excellence*, *Iacocca: An Autobiography*, and *Good to Great*). The advantage of the narrative over the hypothetico-deductive method lies in the ability of the narrative to (1) highlight the differences between periods, places and people, each with its own logics; (2) embed rich contextual and structural elements that are often ignored in rationalistic descriptions; (3) avoid deterministic descriptions of traditions or the appearance of linear progress; and (4) include both micro- and macro-level forces operating during the period (Keulen and Kroeze 2012). The synthesis of all the historical work thus far culminates in what Paul Ricoeur (2012, p. ix) calls the plot: "by means of the plot, goals, causes, and chances are brought together within the temporal unity of a whole and complete action," as in a story that has a beginning, a middle and an end. The narrative is just like a building that is made up of a combination of bricks represented by the historical facts, and everything else (structure, fittings, design) that together represent the interpretation of those facts (Keulen and Kroeze 2012). That doesn't mean that the narrative is fictional or any less scientific than historicism.

Writing the history

No history is written until the historian sits down and starts writing. This step, often assumed to be the last step, rarely concludes the process because as the writing begins, the historian reflects over the chosen strategy. For example, the historian may have decided to write a critical assessment of how Google captured the imagination of both investors and the public in the search space, but realizes as soon as the manuscript is written, it lacks the necessary elements to be convincing. Guided by the Romantic paradigm, the IS historian may decide to inject into the writing personal stories of entrepreneurs that had worked in the same industry before Google came onto the scene, or following the SCOT paradigm, relate how developments in information retrieval during that period in society shaped the direction that Google took in designing its technology. These changes require the historian to go back to previous steps in searching for other evidence, critiquing the evidence and constructing new plots in the story.

This reflective process takes place continuously as writing proceeds, and it is enhanced by what Garraghan (1946, p. 362) calls "putting oneself in the past." Doing so requires the historian to share thoughts, emotions and viewpoints of the people during that period and to judge them by the standards of their day rather than of the present. The historian needs to be imbued "with the life and spirit of the time," which invariably demands an examination of prior assumptions held when writing started. Additionally, a consideration of the audience is paramount, and the historian needs to formulate a convincing thesis that will help hold the attention of the audience as the plot of the writing moves from one event to another, and from one concept to the next.

Conclusion

Writing history is very different from writing traditional IS research. Taking IS history seriously first starts when the differences between the behavioral research that IS researchers are accustomed to and historical studies are clear in the mind of the researcher. It demands a major shift in outlook about research and about why IS history is being written. This shift can be bewildering, but the potential is enormous for a field like IS. Because historical research is inherently reflexive and literally tells the field what the field has done, it shines light on the intellectual structures of the field and how the IS field studies its chosen phenomena. Additionally, in historical studies, the identity of the subject matter is core to the research and because the choice of what is being researched is supposed to be historic, the study itself addresses the question of its relevance. These two characteristics of historical studies potentially resolve long-standing issues of identity and relevancy within the IS field.

By helping the IS community agree on past accomplishments, historical studies address the communication deficit that exists internally between different research communities and externally with practitioners (Klein and Hirschheim 2008). A better grasp of the history of IS helps improve mutual understanding among differing research communities in the field, and with that mutual understanding, the IS field will be able to build a more coherent inter-community programs of research (Hirschheim and Klein 2012). Our field's relatively younger age means that we have not yet missed the opportunity to build our historical tradition, but that opportunity needs to be grasped with an understanding and approach that take full advantage of insights from one of humanity's oldest disciplines – history.

References

Ackoff, R. L. 1967. "Management Misinformation Systems," *Management Science* (14:4) pp. 147–156.
Anonymous. 2011. "Pioneer Computer to Be Rebuilt," *Cambridge Alumni Magazine* (62) p. 65.
Applegate, L. M. 1999. "Rigor and Relevance in MIS Research-Careers on the Line," *MIS Quarterly* (23:1) pp. 17–18.
Bannister, F. 2002. "The Dimension of Time: Historiography in Information Systems Research," *Electronic Journal of Business Research Methods* (1:1) pp. 1–10.
Banville, C., and Landry, M. 1989. "Can the Field of MIS Be Disciplined?," *Communications of the ACM* (32:1) pp. 48–60.
Bell, D. 1973. *The Coming of the Post-Industrial Society: A Venture in Social Forecasting*, New York: Basic Books.
Benbasat, I., and Weber, R. 1996. "Rethinking Diversity in Information Systems Research," *Information Systems Research* (7:4) pp. 389–399.
Benbasat, I., and Zmud, R. W. 1999. "Empirical Research in Information Systems: The Practice of Relevance," *MIS Quarterly* (23:1) pp. 3–16.
Benbasat, I., and Zmud, R. W. 2003. "The Identity Crisis Within the IS Discipline: Defining and Communicating the Discipline's Core Properties," *MIS Quarterly* (27:2) pp. 183–194.
Bentley, M. 1999. *Modern Historiography: An Introduction*, New York: Routledge.
Berger, S., Feldner, H., and Passmore, K. (eds.). 2003. *Writing History: Theory & Practice*, London: Oxford University Press.
Bijker, W. E. 1995. *Of Bicycles, Bakelites, and Bulbs: Toward a Theory of Sociotechnical Change*, Cambridge, MA: MIT Press.
Bijker, W. E., Hughes, T. P., and Pinch, T. J. 1987. *The Social Construction of Technological Systems*, Cambridge, MA: MIT Press.
Bloch, M. 1992. *The Historian's Craft*, Translated by P. Putnam, Manchester, UK: Manchester University Press.
Bourdieu, P. 1977. *Outline of a Theory of Practice*, Cambridge, UK: Cambridge University Press.
Breisach, E. 1983. *Historiography: Ancient, Medieval, and Modern*, Chicago: University of Chicago Press.
Brinkley, A. 2006. *American History: A Survey*, 12th ed., New York: Glencoe/McGraw-Hill.
Brooks Jr., F. P. 1975. *The Mythical Man-Month: Essays on Software Engineering*, Reading, MA: Addison-Wesley.
Bryant, A., Black, A., Land, F., and Porra, J. 2013. "Information Systems History: What Is History? What Is IS History? What IS History? . . . And Why Even Bother With History?" *Journal of Information Technology* (28:1) pp. 1–17.
Butterfield, H. 1931. *The Whig Interpretation of History*, London: G. Bell and Sons.
Caminer, D. T. (ed.). 1997. *LEO: The Incredible Story of the World's First Business Computer*, New York: McGraw-Hill.
Carlyle, T. 1837/1934. *The French Revolution: A History*, New York: Modern Library.
Carr, E. H. 1965. *What Is History?* New York: Alfred A. Knopf.
Cecez-Kecmanovic, D., Klein, H. K., and Brooke, C. 2008. "Editorial: Exploring the Critical Agenda in Information Systems Research," *Information Systems Journal* (18:2) pp. 123–135.
Chandler, A. D. 1962. *Strategy and Structure: Chapters in the History of the Industrial Enterprise*, Cambridge, MA: MIT Press.
Chen, P. P.-S. 1976. "The Entity-Relationship Model – Toward a Unified View of Data," *ACM Transaction on Database Systems* (1:1) pp. Sep-36.
Chen, W., and Hirschheim, R. 2004. "A Paradigmatic and Methodological Examination of Information Systems Research From 1991 to 2001," *Information Systems Journal* (14:3) pp. 197–235.
Clarke, R. 2013. "Morning Dew on the Web in Australia," *Journal of Information Technology* (28:2) pp. 93–110.
Codd, E. F. 1970. "A Relational Model of Data for Large Shared Data Banks," *Communications of the ACM* (13:6) pp. 377–387.
Collingwood, R. G. 1946. *The Idea of History*, Oxford, UK: Clarendon Press.
Condorcet, M. D. 1795. *Outlines of an Historical View of the Progress of the Human Mind*, London: J. Johnson.
Copeland, D. G., and McKenney, J. L. 1988. "Airline Reservation Systems: Lessons From History," *MIS Quarterly* (12:3) pp. 353–370.

Culnan, M. J. 1986. "The Intellectual Development of Management Information Systems, 1972–1982: A Co-Citation Analysis," *Management Science* (32:2) pp. 156–172.

Culnan, M. J. 1987. "Mapping the Intellectual Structure of MIS, 1980–85: A Co-Citation Analysis," *MIS Quarterly* (11:3) pp. 340–353.

Dearden, J. 1966. "Myth of Real-Time Management Information," *Harvard Business Review* (44:3) pp. 123–132.

Dearden, J. 1972. "MIS Is a Mirage," *Harvard Business Review* (50:1) pp. 90–99.

Derrida, J. 1976. *Of Grammatology*, Baltimore, MD: Johns Hopkins University Press.

Desouza, K. C., El Sawy, O. A., Galliers, R. D., Loebbecke, C., and Watson, R. T. 2006. "Beyond Rigor and Relevance Towards Responsibility and Reverberation: Information Systems Research That Really Matters," *Communications of the AIS* (17:16) pp. 341–353.

Eames, C., and Eames, R. 1990. *A Computer Perspective: Background to the Computer Age*, Cambridge, MA: Harvard University Press.

Epstein, D. 2013. "The Making of Institutions of Information Governance: The Case of the Internet Governance Forum," *Journal of Information Technology* (28:2) pp. 137–149.

Farhoomand, A. F., and Drury, D. H. 1999. "A Historiographical Examination of Information Systems," *Journal of the AIS* (1:19).

Ferry, G. 2003. *A Computer Called LEO: Lyons Teashops and the World's First Office Computer*, London, UK: Fourth Estate.

Galliers, R. D., and Whitley, E. A. 2007. "Vive Les Differences? Developing a Profile of European Information Systems Research as a Basis for International Comparisons," *European Journal of Information Systems* (16) pp. 20–35.

Garfield, E. 1955. "Citation Indexes for Science: A New Dimension in Documentation Through Association of Ideas," *Science* (122:3159) pp. 108–111.

Garfield, E. 1963. "Citation Indexes in Sociological and Historical Research," *American Documentation* (14:4) pp. 289–291.

Garfield, E. 2004. "Historiographic Mapping of Knowledge Domains Literature," *Journal of Information Science* (30:2) pp. 119–145.

Garfield, E., Sher, I. H., and Torpie, R. J. 1964. *The Use of Citation Data in Writing the History of Science*, Philadelphia, PA: Institute for Scientific Information (ISI).

Garraghan, G. J. 1946. *A Guide to Historical Method*, New York: Fordham University Press.

Geertz, C. 1973. *The Interpretation of Cultures*, New York: Basic Books.

Gibbon, E. 1788. *The History of the Decline and Fall of the Roman Empire*, Dublin: Luke White.

Goldman, P. 1994. "Searching for History in Organizational Theory: Comment on Kieser," *Organization Science* (5:4) pp. 621–623.

Goldstine, H. H. 1972. *The Computer From Pascal to Von Neumann*, Princeton, NJ: Princeton University Press.

Gooch, G. P. 1959. *History and Historians in the Nineteenth Century*, Boston: Beacon Press.

Gregor, S., and Hevner, A. R. 2013. "Positioning and Presenting Design Science Research for Maximum Impact," *MIS Quarterly* (37:2) pp. 337–355.

Grover, V., Ayyagari, R., Gokhale, R., Lim, J., and Coffey, J. 2006. "A Citation Analysis of the Evolution and State of Information Systems Within a Constellation of Reference Disciplines," *Journal of the Association for Information Systems* (7:5) pp. 270–325.

Grover, V., Lyytinen, K., Srinivasan, A., and Tan, B.C.Y. 2008. "Contributing to Rigorous and Forward Thinking Explanatory Theory," *Journal of the AIS* (9:2) pp. 40–47.

Hassan, N. R. 2011. "Is Information Systems a Discipline? Foucauldian and Toulminian Insights," *European Journal of Information Systems* (20:4) pp. 456–476.

Hassan, N. R. 2014. "Paradigm Lost . . . Paradigm Gained: A Hermeneutical Rejoinder to Banville and Landry's 'Can the Field of MIS Be Disciplined?,'" *European Journal of Information Systems* (23:6) pp. 600–615.

Hassan, N. R. 2016. "Doing Information Systems: Informatizing and Systematizing From a Practice Lens," *European Conference on Information Systems, June 12–15*, Istanbul, Turkey: Association for Information Systems.

Hassan, N. R., and Will, H. J. 2006. "Synthesizing Diversity and Pluralism in Information Systems: Forging a Unique Disciplinary Subject Matter for the Information Systems Field," *Communications of the AIS* (17:7) pp. 152–180.

Herder, J.G.V. 1784/1803. *Outlines of the Philosophy of the History of Mankind*, London: J. Johnson.
Hevner, A.R., March, S.T., Park, J., and Ram, S. 2004. "Design Science in Information Systems Research," *MIS Quarterly* (28:1) pp. 75–105.
Hindley, M. 2009. "The Voracious Pen of Thomas Carlyle," *Humanities* (30:2) pp. 22–26.
Hirschheim, R.A., and Klein, H.K. 2003. "Crisis in the IS Field? A Critical Reflection on the State of the Discipline," *Journal of the Association for Information Systems* (4:5) pp. 237–293.
Hirschheim, R., and Klein, H.K. 2011. "Tracing the History of the Information Systems Field," in *The Oxford Handbook of Management Information Systems*, R.D. Galliers and W.L. Currie (eds.), Oxford, UK: Oxford University Press, pp. 16–62.
Hirschheim, R., and Klein, H.K. 2012. "A Glorious and Not-So-Short History of the Information Systems Field," *Journal of the Association for Information Systems* (13:4) pp. 188–235.
Hirschheim, R., Porra, J., and Parks, M.S. 2003. "The Evolution of the Corporate IT Function and the Role of the CIO at Texaco – How Do Perceptions of IT's Performance Get Formed?," *Data Base for Advances in Information Systems* (34:4) pp. 8–27.
Howcroft, D., and Trauth, E.M. (eds.). 2005. *Handbook of Critical Information Systems Research: Theory and Application*, Cheltenham, UK: Edward Elgar.
Iggers, G.G. 2005. *Historiography in the Twentieth Century*, Middletown, CT: Wesleyan University Press.
Jakobs, K. 2013. "Why Then Did the X.400 E-Mail Standard Fail? Reasons and Lessons to Be Learned," *Journal of Information Technology* (28:1) pp. 63–73.
Kant, I. 1790/1964. *The Critique of Judgement*, Translated by J.C. Meredith, Oxford, UK: Clarendon Press.
Kant, I. 1781/1978. *The Critique of Pure Reason*, New York: E.P. Dutton.
Kant, I. 1788/1956. *The Critique of Practical Reason*, New York: Liberal Arts Press.
Keen, P.G.W. 1980. "MIS Research: Reference Disciplines and a Cumulative Tradition," in *International Conference on Information Systems (ICIS)*, E. McLean (ed.), Philadelphia, PA: ACM Press pp. 9–18.
Keen, P.G.W. 1991. "Relevance and Rigor in Information Systems Research: Improving Quality, Confidence, Cohesion and Impact," in *Information Systems Research: Contemporary Approaches and Emergent Traditions*, H.-E. Nissen, H.K. Klein and R. Hirschheim (eds.), North-Holland: Elsevier Science Publishers B.V., pp. 27–49.
Keulen, S., and Kroeze, R. 2012. "Understanding Management Gurus and Historical Narratives: The Benefits of a Historic Turn in Management and Organization Studies," *Management & Organizational History* (7:2) pp. 171–189.
Khaldun, I. 1377/1967. *The Muqaddimah: An Introduction to History I*, Translated by F. Rosenthal, Princeton, NJ: Princeton University Press.
Kieser, A. 1994. "Why Organization Theory Needs Historical Analyses – and How This Should Be Performed," *Organization Science* (5:4) pp. 608–620.
Klein, H.K., and Hirschheim, R. 2008. "The Structure of the IS Discipline Reconsidered: Implications and Reflections from a Community of Practice Perspective," *Information and Organization* (18:4) pp. 280–302.
Kuhn, T.S. 1970. *The Structure of Scientific Revolutions*, 2nd ed., Chicago: University of Chicago Press.
Kuhn, T.S. 1977. *The Essential Tension: Selected Studies in Scientific Tradition and Change*, Chicago: University of Chicago Press.
Land, F. 2010. "The Use of History in IS Research: An Opportunity Missed?" *Journal of Information Technology* (25:4) pp. 385–394.
Land, F. 2015. "Early History of the Information Systems Discipline in the UK: An Account Based on Living Through the Period," *Communications of the Association for Information Systems* (36:1) pp. 563–575.
Leiner, B.M., Cerf, V.G., Clark, D.D., Kahn, R.E., Kleinrock, L., Lynch, D.C., Postel, J., Roberts, L.G., and Wolff, S. 2016. *A Brief History of the Internet*, Reston, VA: Internet Society, Retrieved Oct 27, 2016, from www.internetsociety.org/internet/what-internet/history-internet/brief-history-internet
Marwick, A. 1989. *The Nature of History*, Chicago: Lyceum Books.
Mason, R.O., McKenney, J.L., and Copeland, D.G. 1997a. "Developing an Historical Tradition in MIS Research," *MIS Quarterly* (21:3) pp. 257–278.
Mason, R.O., McKenney, J.L., and Copeland, D.G. 1997b. "An Historical Method for MIS Research: Steps and Assumptions," *MIS Quarterly* (21:3) pp. 307–320.

McKenney, J. L., Mason, R. O., and Copeland, D. G. 1997. "Bank of America: The Crest and Trough of Technological Leadership," *MIS Quarterly* (21:3) pp. 321–353.
Mingers, J., and Stowell, F. (eds.). 1997. *Information Systems: An Emerging Discipline?* London: McGraw-Hill.
Mitev, N. N. 2006. "More Than a Failure? The Computerized Reservation Systems at French Railways," *Information Technology & People* (9:4) pp. 8–19.
Mitev, N. N., and Vaujany, F.-X.D. 2012. "Seizing the Opportunity: Towards a Historiography of Information Systems," *Journal of Information Technology* (27:2) pp. 110–124.
Montealegre, R., and Keil, M. 2000. "De-Escalating Information Technology Projects: Lessons from the Denver International Airport," *MIS Quarterly* (24:3) pp. 417–447.
Myers, M. D., and Klein, H. K. 2011. "A Set of Principles for Conducting Critical Research in Information Systems," *MIS Quarterly* (35:1) pp. 17–36.
Neufville, R.D. 1994. "The Baggage System at Denver: Prospects and Lessons," *Journal of Air Transport Management* (1:4) pp. 229–234.
Orlikowski, W. J., and Baroudi, J. J. 1991. "Studying Information Technology in Organizations: Research Approaches and Assumptions," *Information Systems Research* (2:1) pp. 1–28.
Pickering, A. 1995. *The Mangle of Practice: Time, Agency, and Science*, Chicago: University of Chicago Press.
Pinch, T. J., and Bijker, W. E. 1984. "The Social Construction of Facts and Artefacts: Or How the Sociology of Science and the Sociology of Technology Might Benefit Each Other," *Social Studies of Science* (14:3) pp. 399–441.
Pollock, N., and Williams, R. 2008. *Software and Organizations: The Biography of the Enterprise-Wide System or How SAP Conquered the World*, New York: Routledge.
Porra, J., Hirschheim, R., and Parks, M. S. 2005. "The History of Texaco's Corporate Information Technology Function: A General Systems Theoretical Interpretation," *MIS Quarterly* (29:4) pp. 721–746.
Porra, J., Hirschheim, R., and Parks, M. S. 2006. "Forty Years of the Corporate Information Technology Function at Texaco Inc. – a History," *Information and Organization* (16:1) pp. 82–107.
Porra, J., Hirschheim, R., and Parks, M. S. 2014. "The Historical Research Method and Information Systems Research," *Journal of the Association for Information Systems* (15:9) pp. 536–576.
Porter, M. E. 1980. *Competitive Strategy: Techniques for Analyzing Industries and Competitors*, New York: Free Press.
Ranke, L.V. 1973. *The Theory and Practice of History*, Indianapolis, IN: Bobbs-Merrill.
Richardson, H., and Robinson, B. 2007. "The Mysterious Case of the Missing Paradigm: A Review of Critical Information Systems Research 1991–2001," *Information Systems Journal* (17:3) pp. 251–270.
Ricoeur, P. 2012. *Time and Narrative, Volume 1*, Translated by K. McLaughlin and D. Pellauer, Chicago: University of Chicago Press.
Robey, D. 1996. "Diversity in Information Systems Research: Threat, Promise, and Responsibility," *Information Systems Research* (7:4) pp. 400–408.
Robinson, C. F. 2003. *Islamic Historiography*, Cambridge, UK: Cambridge University Press.
Rosemann, M., and Vessey, I. 2008. "Toward Improving the Relevance of Information Systems Research to Practice: The Role of Applicability Checks," *MIS Quarterly* (32:1) pp. 1–22.
Rosenberg, N. 1972. "Factors Affecting the Diffusion of Technology," *Explorations in Economic History* (3:1) pp. 3–33.
Rosenthal, F. 1952. *A History of Muslim Historiography*, Leiden, Holland: E. J. Brill.
Simmons, J.R.M. 1962. *Leo and the Managers*, London, UK: Macdonald.
Stein, M.-K., Galliers, R. D., and Whitley, E. A. 2016. "Twenty Years of the European Information Systems Academy at ECIS: Emergent Trends and Research Topics," *European Journal of Information Systems* (25:1) pp. 1–15.
Stone, L. 1979. "The Revival of Narrative: Reflections on a New Old History," *Past & Present* (85) pp. 3–24.
Straub, D. W. 2015. "The Critical Role of Historiography in Writing IS History," *Communications of the Association for Information Systems* (36:1) pp. 593–598.
Straub, D. W., and Ang, S. 2011. "Editor's Comments-Rigor and Relevance in IS Research: Redefining the Debate and a Call for Future Research," *MIS Quarterly* (35:1) pp. iii–xii.
Taylor, H., Dillon, S., and Van Wingen, M. 2010. "Focus and Diversity in Information Systems Research: Meeting the Dual Demands of a Healthy Applied Discipline," *MIS Quarterly* (34:4) pp. 647–667.

Teece, D. J. 1986. "Profiting From Technological Innovation: Implications for Integration, Collaboration, Licensing and Public Policy," *Research Policy* (15:6) pp. 285–305.

Thompson, E. P. 1963. *The Making of the English Working Class*, London: V. Gollancz.

Thurston, P. H. 1962. "Who Should Control Information Systems?" *Harvard Business Review* (40:6) pp. 135–138.

Tosh, J. 2000. *The Pursuit of History*, 3rd ed., New York: Pearson.

Üsdiken, B., and Kieser, A. 2004. "Introduction: History in Organization Studies," *Business History* (46:3) pp. 321–330.

Wade, M., Biehl, M., and Kim, H. 2006. "Information Systems Is Not a Reference Discipline (And What We Can Do About It)," *Journal of the Association for Information Systems* (7:5) pp. 247–269.

Weber, M. 1919/1968. "Basic Sociological Terms," in *Economy and Society: An Outline of Interpretive Sociology*, G. Roth and C. Wittich (eds.), New York: Bedminster Press, pp. 4–15, 17–23, 24–26.

Whitley, E. A., and Galliers, R. D. 2007. "An Alternative Perspective on Citation Classics: Evidence From the First 10 Years of the European Conference on Information Systems," *Information & Management* (44:5) pp. 441–455.

Windelband, W. 1980. "Rectorial Address, Strasbourg, 1894," *History and Theory* (19:2) pp. 169–185.

Zhang, P. 2015. "The IS History Initiative: Looking Forward by Looking Back," *Communications of the Association for Information Systems* (36:1) pp. 477–514.

Zientara, M. 1981. *The History of Computing: A Biographical Portrait of the Visionaries Who Shaped the Destiny of the Computer Industry*, Framingham, MA: CW Communications.

2
PHILOSOPHY AND METHOD
Making interpretive research interpretive

Allen S. Lee

Introduction

What makes interpretive research interpretive? How is interpretive research valid? Why are these two questions important for the conduct of research in the information systems discipline?

Interpretive research is not only qualitative research. It is qualitative research in which a researcher does not take for granted but interprets the meanings expressed by the people whom the researcher is observing, much as one person would interpret the words expressed by others speaking a foreign language with which the former is not very familiar. Rather than risk imposing his or her own meaning for, and misunderstanding of, what the people themselves mean, the researcher engages in a deliberate effort of interpretation. One of the objectives of this chapter is to examine what constitutes this research effort of interpretation – in other words, what makes interpretive research interpretive. And when interpretation has taken place, how may the researcher know that it is valid? Providing a basis for the examination will be phenomenology, a field of study that has made the investigation of meaning its *raison d'être*.

The approach taken in this chapter is from the perspective of philosophy and method. By one definition, "philosophy is thinking about thinking" (Quinton 2005). Method, in the sense of research method, refers to

> the specific techniques, instruments, and procedures used to obtain information for the purposes of research and for the analysis of the information gathered or generated [and] [i]ncludes observations (measurements), interviews, questionnaires, archival and literature searches, and the gamut of quantitative and qualitative techniques.
>
> (Duignan 2016)

In other words, rather than simply advance research methods in the spirit of how to use them, this chapter will regard research methods themselves as objects of research upon which we further think and reflect. As such, this chapter is intended to add to the body of philosophical and methodological research on interpretivism in information systems, of which just a few prominent examples are Walsham (1993, 1995a, 1995b, and 2006), Klein and Myers (1999), and Myers (1999, 2013).

The first section of this chapter, following this introduction, will offer examples problematizing meaning. The second section will offer suggestions for how to interpret meaning. The third section will offer discussion about assessing the validity of interpreted meaning.

Problematizing meaning

Meaning is not to be taken for granted. I offer three examples to make this point – two originating in the work of Martin Heidegger and one in the work of Alfred Schutz.

For the first example, I turn to Harman (2013), who relates this story from his own reading of Heidegger (pp. 22–23):

> As he stands in a lecture hall in Freiburg, addressing his students from the podium, Heidegger notes that professor and students all use the various objects in the room, taking them for granted. The podium is simply used, not consciously seen. The desks of the students, their pens and notebooks, are also taken for granted as useful items before they are ever clearly and consciously noticed. Heidegger now asks us to imagine what would happen if a [person from a tribe that has had no contact with the rest of the world] suddenly entered the room. This . . . foreigner might have no concept at all of a lecture hall and its usual equipment. He might be utterly confused by the podium and have no idea of how to use it. Even so, he would not see the podium and the desks as meaningless colors and shapes. Instead, he might think of the podium as an item for [his religion], or as a barrier for hiding from [offensive weapons]. [This person's] failure [from the perspective of the professor and students] to understand the room does not mean that the room is a sheer perception without any practical use. Instead, he would encounter the room as a form of "equipmental strangeness."
>
> This is what the world means for the young Heidegger: it is not a spectacle of colors and shapes, but rather an environment in which all things have a special significance for us and are linked with one another in a specific way. What we learn from the [foreigner] is that objects always have a highly specific meaning even when they are not lucidly present in consciousness.

The lessons are about meaning – not only what meaning the "podium" might have for the foreigner, but also the taken-for-granted meaning of the "podium" for the professor and students. And just as we might be intrigued by how the foreigner comes to form whatever meaning he does for the "podium," we should be equally intrigued by how the professor and students themselves understand the "podium" in the way that they do. There is, moreover, another lesson, about equipment; we will examine this lesson in detail shortly.

Consider now an information system in place of the podium. Consider the engineers (who created the information system) in place of the professor and students. And consider the middle-level managers and clerks (who see this information system for the first time) in place of the foreigner. Suppose the information system ends up being a failure. What role in the failure could have been played by the differing meanings that the information system had for the engineers on the one hand, and for the managers and clerks on the other? How did the respective meanings originate in the first place? By what method may a researcher, conducting a study of the information systems failure, come to interpret the meanings that the information system has for the different people rather than simply impose his or her own taken-for-granted meaning (or misunderstanding) of it?

For our second example, we again go to Heidegger and a description by Harman (pp. 1–2):

> Consider Heidegger's famous example of a hammer . . . In one sense, a hammer remains invisible to us: we tend to use our tools without noticing them, and focus instead on the house or ship we are building. The hammer usually withdraws from view. But even when we notice it, such as when it breaks, the hammer will always be more than whatever we see or say about it. This means that the being of the hammer is always absent; it labors silently in invisible depths, and is not "present-at-hand," to use Heidegger's term. But absence is only one side of the story. Hammers, candles, and trees cannot be only absent, because then we would never see anything or have any relations with anything at all. Yet quite obviously, the hammer is also present: I see its wooden handle and metallic head, feel its weight, and interpret it either as a tool for building, an item of hardware priced for sale, or a weapon for hand-to-hand combat. For a dog, a baby, an ant, or a parrot, most of the hammer's usual properties are not there at all, which shows that the presence of a thing is also determined by those who encounter it.

The lesson here is about equipment. The meaning of something, such as a hammer, is not fixed by whatever its dictionary definition might be. Its meaning to a person depends on what purpose or use, if any, it might serve at the moment to the person, as if it were one or another piece of equipment.

Consider now an information system in place of the hammer. The information system would include the complex of hardware, software, data structures, networks, procedures, and operations comprising an enterprise resource planning system. Applying Harman's discussion of Heidegger, we can say the following. Whatever the information system, we tend to use it without noticing it, focusing instead on the task that we are using it for, so that the information system withdraws from view. But even when the information system fails to work and we then notice it, it is more than what we happen to notice at the moment. And for people not directly using the information system – that is, for whom it is not equipment – most of the information system's usual properties are not there at all, which shows that the meaning that an information system has is relational, determined by those who encounter it at the moment. By what method may a researcher, conducting a study of an information system, come to interpret the meaning(s) that the information system has?

For the third and final example problematizing meaning, we turn to Alfred Schutz (1962a, p. 54):

> The same overt behavior (say a tribal pageant as it can be captured by the movie camera) may have an entirely different meaning to the performers. What interests the social scientist is merely whether it is a war dance, a barter trade, the reception of a friendly ambassador, or something else of this sort.

The lesson here is about the meaning that a researcher imputes to overt behavior manifested by the people who he or she is observing. Consider overt behavior in the form of a person's deliberate non-use of an information technology. Does the person's non-use of the technology indicate that the technology carries the meaning of little or no "usefulness" or "ease of use" to this person? Does the person's non-use of the technology indicate the meaning of "resistance to technology" from this person? Or does the person's non-use of the technology indicate that the person regards the effects of the technology as potentially harmful to others and is therefore acting protectively and benevolently (Mohajeri 2014)? By what method may a researcher, conducting a study of some people's overt behaviors relating to a technology, come to interpret the meaning(s) underlying the overt behaviors?

The three preceding examples make the point that the meanings held by the people in a study are pivotal to the outcome of the study. Interpreting the meanings differently would result in a different study. And for a researcher not to interpret the meanings at all, but to somehow proceed with implicit assumptions about what they are, would likely result in an incomplete or outright invalid study. By what method or methods may a researcher deliberately interpret the meanings that are present in a research setting? We address this question next.

Interpreting meaning

I offer two complementary approaches to the task of how to interpret meaning. The first approach is primarily philosophical, drawing on phenomenology. (Heidegger and Schutz, just mentioned, are phenomenologists.) The full range of phenomenological philosophy can hardly be captured in any single essay, so just some leading concepts of it (relying on the work of Schutz (1962b) as a guide) will be touched upon.

Definitions of phenomenology are deceptively straightforward. The *Oxford English Dictionary* (2005a) offers this definition:

> A method or procedure, originally developed by the German philosopher Edmund Husserl (1859–1938), which involves the setting aside of presuppositions about a phenomenon as an empirical object and about the mental acts concerned with experiencing it, in order to achieve an intuition of its pure essence; the characteristic theories underlying or resulting from the use of such a method. In more recent use: any of various philosophical methods or theories (often influenced by the work of Husserl and his followers) which emphasize the importance of analysing the structure of conscious subjective experience.

The Encyclopaedia Britannica (Biemel 2016) states:

> **phenomenology**, a philosophical movement originating in the 20th century, the primary objective of which is the direct investigation and description of phenomena as consciously experienced, without theories about their causal explanation and as free as possible from unexamined preconceptions and presuppositions.

In both definitions, any straightforwardness is deceptive owing to the challenge involved in freeing oneself from "unexamined preconceptions and presuppositions" in achieving the "pure essence" of a phenomenon. As for the subtleties and complexity involved in phenomenology, consider the following hypothetical situation that Schutz provides (1962b, p. 106):

> I perceive the blossoming tree in the garden. This, my perceiving of the tree as it appears to me, is an indubitable element of the stream of my thought. And the same is valid for the phenomenon "blossoming-tree-as-it-appears-to-me," which is the intentional object of my perceiving. This phenomenon is independent of the fate of the real tree in the outer world. The tree in the garden may change its colors and shades by the interplay of sun and cloud, it may lose its blossoms, it may be destroyed

by fire. The once perceived phenomenon "blossoming-tree-as-it-appears-to-me" remains untouched by all these events . . .

In any case, each act of perceiving and its intentional object are indubitable elements of my stream of thought; and equally certain is the doubt I may have about whether the "tree as it appears to me" has a correlate in the outer world. The foregoing example has illustrated the fact that my cogitations and their intentional objects are elements of my stream of thought which are not influenced by the changes that may happen to their correlates in the outer world. But this does not mean that the cogitations are not subject to modification by events happening within my stream of consciousness. In order to make this clear let us first distinguish between the act of perceiving and the perceived, between the *cogitare* and the *cogitatum* or, to use Husserl's technical term, between the Noesis and the Noema.

A key takeaway from this example is the distinction between the correlate in the outer world (the blossoming tree in the garden) and the intentional object of my perceiving (the blossoming-tree-as-it-appears-to-me, in my thinking). What the former "means" to me is the latter.

An additional, rich complication arises regarding the meaning held by a researcher, as distinct from the meaning held by a research subject, namely, a person whom the researcher is observing or who is a part of the social scene that the researcher is studying. For the researcher, there is the distinction between the correlate in the outer world (here, it is [the blossoming-tree-as-it-appears-to-the-research-subject, in the research subject's thinking]) and the intentional object of the researcher's own perceiving ([[the blossoming-tree-as-it-appears-to-the-research-subject, in the research subject's thinking] as this appears to the researcher, in the researcher's thinking]). (NB: The reason for the use of brackets will be made clear.) Strictly speaking, the meaning held by the researcher is a second-order meaning; it is the researcher's meaning of the meaning held by the research subject. The seriousness of the challenge in forming a second-order meaning becomes apparent when we return to the example of the foreigner in Heidegger's classroom – the person from a tribe that has had no contact with the rest of the world. How do I, as a researcher, learn the meaning that the podium has, or comes to have, for this person?

There is the associated task of my "setting aside of presuppositions about a phenomenon as an empirical object and about the mental acts concerned with experiencing it." How do I, as a researcher, set aside my own presuppositions about the podium when my presuppositions are invisible to me, in much the same way as, according to Harman's example involving Heidegger, "a hammer remains invisible to us"? According to this line of thinking, I would need to identify and set aside my presuppositions so that I, as a researcher, may come to know what an object (such as a podium or a hammer) or an overt action means to a person in a social setting that I am researching.

For an information-systems example, consider overt behavior in the form of a research subject's deliberate non-use of a new information system. Consider also that the focus of the research, at the moment, is not on the new information system itself, but on [the overt behavior in the form of the research subject's deliberate non-use of the new information system]. In other words, the correlate in the outer world is [the overt behavior in the form of the research subject's deliberate non-use of the new information system]. Suppose, on the one hand, the intentional object of the information-systems researcher's perceiving ([the overt behavior in the form of the research subject's deliberate non-use of the new information system] as this appears to the information-systems researcher) is "resistance to technology," but on the other hand, the intentional object of the research subject's own perceiving ([the overt behavior in the form of the research subject's deliberate non-use of the new information system] as this appears to the research subject) is instead "protection of the well-being of my co-workers and clients." In this situation, what is or what should be the relationship between the second-order meaning ("resistance to technology") and the first-order meaning ("protection of the well-being of my co-workers and clients")? Under what conditions is the second-order meaning better or worse, or even justifiable in the first place? In past interpretive research in information systems, have researchers related the two meanings or even recognized the distinction between them in the first place?

Helping to bring some clarity to this methodological situation is what phenomenology calls *bracketing*. As the previous usage of brackets suggests, it involves setting aside a group of elements (much as bracketing is performed in mathematics, from which this term is borrowed), which are then treated not only as a group, but are also subjected to the question, "what is this?" In this sense, the same function could be served by scare quotes, which are "quotation marks used to foreground a particular word or phrase, esp. with the intention of disassociating the user from the expression or from some implied connotation it carries" (*Oxford English Dictionary* 2005b). One's belief of what is bracketed, or is placed in scare quotes, is placed in temporary suspension as one no longer takes its meaning for granted but instead wonders anew about what it is.

According to Schutz (p. 104), "Husserl called this procedure 'putting the world in brackets' or 'performing the phenomenological reduction.'" He continues (pp. 104–105):

> Although "phenomenological reduction" does not require any magic or mysterious faculty of mind, the technique of bracketing which it suggests is by no means a simple one if applied with the necessary radicalism. What we have to put in brackets is not only the existence of the outer world, along with all the things in it, inanimate and animate, including fellow-men, cultural objects, society and its institutions. Also our belief in the validity of our statements about this world and its content, as conceived within the mundane sphere, has to be suspended. Consequently, not only our practical knowledge of the world but also the propositions of all the sciences dealing with the existence of the world, all natural and social sciences, psychology, logic, and even geometry – all have to be brought within the brackets.

The foregoing approach to the task of how to interpret meaning, drawing on Schutz, is philosophical, where the task of interpreting meaning can be as challenging as it is abstract.

We now consider a complementary approach, from the perspective of research methods. It remains challenging but is less abstract and more practical. In other words, step by step, how may an information systems researcher interpret the meanings that are present in, say, the organizational setting where she is studying an information systems failure? Casebier, Kuhn, and Kanter each provide some pointers.

Casebier (2014) provides an illustration of bracketing that can be particularly practical for social scientists:

> It is important to realize that utilizing the reduction or bracketing is not some special kind of introspection. It is rather a process much like what often occurs in philosophy and other inquiries in whatever tradition, including Anglo-American analytic philosophy. The method is best described as cognitive transformation. In legal settings, the experience of novels, and many other contexts, we are familiar with cognitive transformation. For example, in a legal setting, it may be significant that for purposes

of a trial in progress someone testifies to the court that Maggie was upstairs in the mansion when the owner was killed. Normally, in our lived experience, such information directs our attention to the state of affairs represented, involving Maggie and upstairs in the mansion and at a certain time. In cases of testimony in court, however, a retreat may be made. We suspend our judgment on the truth of the claim – Maggie was upstairs then – we consider only the fact that, according to the witness, Maggie was upstairs at the time that the owner was killed. We have thus made a cognitive transformation. We have been taken from the original use of a basic sentence (Maggie was upstairs then) to a transformed sentence expressly about what has been asserted, questioned, commanded, and so forth. We have thus bracketed whether Maggie was upstairs then to focus only on the representational content and mode of the original sentence. We may be noncommittal about whether what the witness testified to was true.

Especially in a social-science context, not only a legal context, we can be noncommittal about whether what organizational members (or others whom we, as researchers, interview or otherwise observe) tell us is true. And even in the event that what they say turns out not to be true, we would remain no less interested in what they meant; indeed, this is a point of a 1979 article by Van Maanen, the telling title of which begins, "The Fact of Fiction. . . ." In other words, in continuing to reason along the path of what the preceding discussion has alternatively called a cognitive transformation, the phenomenological reduction, and bracketing, we focus on what Casebier calls the "transformed sentence" (literally, regarding the comments we hear and, figuratively, regarding the overt actions we see), whereupon the meaning behind the words and actions may emerge.

Kuhn, as a scholar in the history and sociology of science, also offers some concrete advice in this regard. He states, in the preface to an anthology of his essays, *The Essential Tension* (Kuhn 1977, p. xii, also cited in Lee 1991, p. 348; emphasis added):

> When reading the works of an important thinker, look first for the **apparent absurdities** in the text and ask yourself how a sensible person could have written them. When you find an answer . . . when those passages make sense, then you may find that more central passages, ones you previously thought you understood, have changed their meaning.

In other words, when reading a passage, one may actually ascribe to the passage a meaning that simply and naturally occurs to oneself – indeed, even a meaning rich in one's own (as yet unidentified) preconceptions and presuppositions. Of course, such a meaning could very well turn out to be incorrect (the passage that is read with such a meaning might not then make sense in relation to other passages), whereupon one would then need to depart from the presumed meaning and try out re-reading the text with a different meaning – namely, one that "a sensible person" might have meant. And in the event that the re-reading contains any remaining apparent absurdities, or new ones appear, the process is repeated.

The beauty of this approach is that it does not require a researcher to explicitly perform the phenomenological reduction, where the researcher would explicitly identify and set aside her "unexamined preconceptions and presuppositions" in pursuit of the "pure essence" of a phenomenon. In contrast, this approach would actually allow the researcher to wholeheartedly embrace the presence of his preconceptions and presuppositions, all in the spirit of accepting that they provide a mere starting point in the researcher's quest for the text's meaning. Indeed, the greater any apparent absurdity that subsequently arises, the richer the material for identifying previously unexamined preconceptions and presuppositions.

Of course, for Kuhn and for others following an interpretive tradition, this manner of interpreting text is not only for interpreting text, but for all else that can be "read" as "text analogues," such as spoken words that a researcher might hear in an interview or overt actions a researcher might observe in people working in an organization. Where a research subject's spoken words and overt behaviors are text analogues, the interpretation of meaning proceeds in the same way as in the reading of text.

In other words, when a researcher observes behavior that he or she considers to be puzzling or nonsensical (i.e., an "apparent absurdity"), the researcher then re-"reads" the problematic "passage" with a changed meaning – one that a sensible person, engaging in this behavior, might have meant. The researcher keeps on trying out different meanings in a trial-and-error manner, until the passage makes sense. As Kuhn points out, the change in meaning ascribed to the passage could call for the meanings of related "passages" also to be changed, thereby altering the meaning of the overall "text" or the overall organization if the object of research is an organization.

Kanter, in her book *Men and Women of the Corporation*, offers a similar tack (1977, p. 291):

> With Michel Crozier, I wanted to demonstrate that everyone is rational, that everyone within an organization, no matter how absurd or irrational their behavior seemed, was reacting to what their situation made available, in such a way as to preserve dignity, control, and recognition from others.

The practical rule of thumb here is: for the scientific observer, do not presume irrationality, but entertain meanings that presume the observed behavior or spoken words are rational, or have a rationale behind them. This is akin to Kuhn's advice of considering "how a sensible person" could have written text that initially appears puzzling to the reader.

In other words, for Kanter, if a person makes comments or engages in overt behaviors that appear to the scientific observer (such as an information systems researcher) to be irrational, then either the person is acting in a way that he himself would consider to be irrational (which is not likely) or the interpretation of irrationality is not correct; the rule of thumb for the scientific researcher is to make the second choice.

The scientific researcher's posture is to depart from ascribing any meaning that harbors even a hint of irrationality and to try out different meanings in a trial-and-error manner until the person's comments and overt behaviors would make sense *to the person herself*. What might the comments and overt behaviors mean if the person is attempting to preserve her dignity in her work environment? . . . if the person is acting to maintain some sort of control over the resources she needs to get her job done? . . . if the person is moving ahead with her goal to gain recognition as an outside-of-the-box thinker in the eyes of her supervisors? In other words, a necessary condition for a scientific observer's ascribing of a plausible meaning to the observed people's comments and overt behaviors is that the meaning not be seen as irrational, self-defeating, counterproductive, uncomplimentary, unethical, or otherwise negative in the eyes of the observed people themselves. The interpreted meaning should be, in Schutz's term, "subjectively meaningful," namely, it would need to be regarded as meaningful in the eyes of the research subjects themselves.

To recapitulate up to this point, the researcher's task of interpreting meaning can take an approach based on phenomenological philosophy (involving the phenomenological reduction and bracketing), as well as an approach based on practical methods (such as those inspired by

Casebier, Kuhn, and Kanter). However, once a researcher has conducted interpretive research, which involves the interpretation of the meanings present in a setting that he or she is studying, how may he or she know that the interpreted meanings are valid?

Assessing the validity of interpreted meaning

Applying a philosophy or research method for interpreting meaning is one thing; assessing the goodness of the resulting interpretation is quite another thing. This is a case of the difference between formative validity and summative validity. As Lee and Hubona explain (2009, p. 246): "A theory achieves formative validity by following one or another accepted procedure in the process of its being formed. A theory, once formed, achieves summative validity by surviving an empirical test that uses the logic of modus tollens." Whereas Lee and Hubona are addressing theory, the same lesson applies to meaning. I will demonstrate this with ideas from Føllesdal (1979), Hirsch (1967), and Agar (1986). Føllesdal and Hirsch offer their ideas in the context of hermeneutics; Agar, in ethnography. All are compatible, indeed inseparable, from the phenomenological thinking informing the preceding portion of this chapter.

Another common theme across the works of Føllesdal, Hirsch, and Agar is hypothetico-deductive logic. Føllesdal and Hirsch recognize this explicitly; Agar recognizes this implicitly and, as I will show, necessarily. First, I will provide a general explanation of hypothetico-deductive logic as an application of modus tollens, which I will illustrate with ideas from Føllesdal, Hirsch, and Agar. Second, I will provide an illustration of the iterative process of applying hypothetico-deductive logic in assessing the validity of an interpretation, drawing on the work of Sarker and Lee (2006).

Modus tollens is a form of the syllogism. The major premise is "if p is true, then q is true." The minor premise is "q is not true." The conclusion is "therefore p is not true."

Hypothetico-deductive logic is an application of modus tollens used in empirical inquiry where p stands for a universal or general statement and q stands for a statement of particular, such as a fact resulting from an observation. Furthermore, hypothetico-deductive logic considers p to stand for a hypothesis and q to be a fact that would be observed to be true if the hypothesis is true. If it is observed not to be true, then the hypothesis is considered incorrect.

Suppose instead that q is observed to be true, so that the minor premise, instead of being "q is not true," is "q is true." At first blush, one might think, given the major premise, "if p is true, then q is true," that this allows the conclusion to be "therefore p is true," but this would be incorrect. Consider the major premise, "if *it is raining outside* is true, then *the street is wet* is true." We observe that *the street is wet*. We may not conclude that the hypothesis *it is raining outside* is true because the street could be wet for any number of other reasons. Indeed, to conclude incorrectly that the hypothesis p is true based on q's being true has the general name, "the fallacy of affirming the consequent." For this reason, the term "consistent with" rather than "prove" is often used in scientific discussions; for example, one may assert that the facts are consistent with the hypothesis, but not that the facts prove the hypothesis. This also means that, because evidence may never prove a hypothesis true, empirical testing (involving the collection of facts through, for instance, experiments or surveys) continues *ad infinitum*, at least in principle, until contradictory facts appear, whereupon the hypothesis would have to be revised.

A presumption about hypothetico-deductive logic is that the hypothesis p is (what information systems researchers and others would consider to be) a positivist theory, such as a theory of physics; however, there is nothing in the logic itself that precludes the hypothesis p from standing for something interpretive, such as "the new information system's meaning to the managers and clerks is a loss of jobs and job advancement opportunities." Indeed, Føllesdal and Hirsch each claim explicitly that hermeneutic interpretation employs hypothetico-deductive logic.

Føllesdal describes hypothetico-deductive logic as follows (1979, p. 321): "As the name indicates, it is an application of two operations: the formation of hypotheses," referred to earlier as p, "and the deduction of consequences from them," referred to earlier as q, "in order to arrive at beliefs which – although they are hypothetical – are well supported, through the way their deductive consequences fit in with" or are, as referred to earlier, *consistent with* "our experiences and with our other well-supported beliefs." Føllesdal continues: "The beliefs that make up such a hypothetico-deductive system are not justified 'from above,' as they are in an axiomatic system, where the axioms are supposed to be justified by some special kind of insight or necessity. Instead, they are justified from below, through their consequences," referred to earlier as consistent observations in the form of q. "In a hypothetico-deductive system, the hypotheses are never known with certainty. From a system of hypotheses an infinite number of consequences follow and there is always a risk that some of these consequences may turn out not to fit in with our experience," referred to earlier as the need to continue empirical testing *ad infinitum*, at least in principle, until contradictory facts appear, whereupon the hypothesis would need to be revised.

Then, in contradistinction to those who might insist that hypothetico-deductive logic may pertain only to positivist science, Føllesdal offers a refutation in the form of hermeneutic interpretation using hypothetico-deductive logic in an example of literary criticism of Henrik Ibsen's *Peer Gynt* (p. 324):

> The pattern of this interpretation is clearly hypothetico-deductive. One sets forth an hypothesis [p], that the strange passenger is Ibsen the author himself, and then deduces a number of consequences [q] from it, that are shown to fit in with [i.e., are consistent with] the text.

Føllesdal adds (p. 331):

> As we saw in the example from Peer Gynt, one proceeds, however, hypothetically-deductively when one uses the hermeneutic method, and instead of contrasting the two methods ["explaining" as in the natural sciences and "hermeneutic" as in the social sciences], we have found it natural to say that the hermeneutic method is the hypothetico-deductive method applied to meaningful material.

Hirsch is no less a proponent of the use of hypothetico-deductive logic in hermeneutics than is Føllesdal. He states in his book, *Validity in Interpretation*, "the hypothetico-deductive process is fundamental in both of them [the sciences and the humanities], as it is in all thinking that aspires to knowledge" (1967, p. 264, cited in Packer and Addison 1989, p. 276). Hirsch also states (1967, pp. 203–204, cited in Packer and Addison 1989, p. 276): "The act of understanding is at first a genial (or a mistaken) guess," which corresponds to the previous exhortation for a researcher to wholeheartedly embrace the presence of his or her preconceptions and presuppositions, all in the spirit of accepting that they provide a mere starting point in the researcher's quest for the text's meaning, "and there are no methods for making guesses, no rules for generating insights." Hirsch continues:

> The methodological activity of interpretation commences when we begin to test and criticize our guesses. These two sides of the interpretive process, the hypothetical

and the critical, are not of course neatly separated when we are pondering a text . . . But the fact that these two activities require and accompany one another in the process of understanding should not lead us to confuse the whimsical lawlessness of guessing with the ultimately methodical character of testing.

"The hypothetical" refers to the formulation of the hypothesis p in modus tollen's major premise, "if p is true, then q is true." "The critical" refers to the search for instances fitting the minor premise "q is not true," the absence of which may never prove p to be true, but only at best to provisionally qualify p as valid; elsewhere Hirsch notes: "Since we can never prove a theory to be true simply by accumulating favorable evidence," which would be committing the fallacy of affirming the consequent, "the only certain method of choosing between two hypotheses is to prove that one of them is false" (1967, p. 180). Hirsch emphasizes, "there is no way of compelling a right guess by means of rules and principles. Every interpretation begins and ends as a guess, and no one has ever devised a method for making intelligent guesses" (p. 170). Where every theory, hypothesis, and interpretation is a guess, the guess must therefore, after formulation, be subjected to testing, the manner of which is described by Hirsch, as well as Føllesdal, as hypothetico-deductive.

Agar, like Føllesdal and Hirsch, adopts a logic that is hypothetico-deductive, but unlike them, does not label it explicitly as such. In his description of how ethnographic understanding proceeds, he refers to "coherence," "breakdown," and "resolution," which he ties together with what he calls "strips."

Agar bases his notion of coherence on the work of Schutz, whose work we earlier referred to. Agar states (1986, p. 25):

> From Schutz we get an elaborate description of coherence. It requires the reflective examination of an action as an act,[1] whether distantly observed or shared as lived experience with informants. The act is coherent if it fits into a plan that we imagine it might have been a part of, where plan is a cover term for an organization of goals and frames.

A breakdown, in turn, is described by Agar as follows (1986, p. 20, emphasis in the original): "When the different traditions are in contact," which refers to the traditions of the people being observed and the traditions of the observing ethnographer, "an ethnographer focuses on the *differences* that appear. Expectations are not met; something does not make sense; one's assumption of perfect coherence is violated. For convenience, the differences noticed by an ethnographer are called *breakdowns*." In other words, a breakdown occurs in my empirical investigation whenever I, in my role as a researcher, observe organizational members or other research subjects acting in a way that would be incoherent from the perspective of the traditions that I, as a researcher, hold. For example, as an information systems scholar who propounds the rationality of the procedures of systems analysis and design, I would regard the refusal of managers to use an information system – one that they previously agreed satisfies all the formally documented information requirements – to be incoherent from my perspective, leading to a breakdown in my understanding. This would qualify as an apparent absurdity (for Kuhn), as an apparently irrational behavior (for Kanter), and as a breakdown – "something [that] does not make sense" where the researcher's "assumption of perfect coherence is violated" (for Agar).

A resolution involves the restoration of coherence, which occurs as follows. "Ethnographic coherence, in brief, is achieved when an initial breakdown is resolved by changing the knowledge in the ethnographer's tradition so that the breakdown is now reinterpreted as an expression of some part of a plan" (Agar 1986, p. 25). The ethnographer, or the interpretive researcher in general, performs this by no longer being beholden to her own preconceptions and presuppositions about how people behave, and by instead building up her knowledge of the schema with which the observed people themselves understand their own world and with which they plan and engage in actions to achieve their own goals. Just as Kuhn asked how a sensible person could have written a passage initially appearing nonsensical to a reader (what would the passage mean to the author?), an interpretive researcher asks what schema would lead a sensible person to engage in the action initially difficult for the interpretive researcher to understand (what would the action mean to an observed person?).

With a new schema, the interpretive researcher continues making observations as well as reviewing old ones. For Agar, the unit of investigation for the purpose of checking for any additional breakdowns is called a "strip," which could be "an observed social act," "an informal interview," "a more structured interview or experiment," "a document of some sort," or "any bounded phenomenon against which an ethnographer tests his or her understanding" (1986, pp. 27–28). A new schema stands until it meets a strip rendering it invalid, whereupon it is revised and stands until it meets a strip rendering it invalid, and so forth. Even in the event that a schema meets no strip rendering it invalid, the interpretive researcher may never claim that she has discovered the actual schema that the observed people follow; she may, at best, only claim that the schema she has constructed is consistent with the one followed by the observed people.

The logic that Agar uses is therefore hypothetico-deductive, where p refers to the latest schema and q refers to "any bounded phenomenon" that would be observable and that would follow from the schema p. A schema's never being proved true, but at best only being consistent with all the strips it has encountered so far, is an instance of the hypothetico-deductive stance that p may never be proved true, but may at best only be considered to be consistent with all of the q's it has encountered so far.

Sarker and Lee (2006), in their hermeneutic study of business process change (BPC) tools in two organizations, provide material with which to illustrate how to assess the validity of interpretation using hypothetico-deductive logic. In these organizations, MANCO (a manufacturing firm) and TELECO (a telecommunications firm), what is the meaning of the BPC tools that were present? This question is not unlike, "what is the meaning of a hammer?," posed in our earlier discussion on Heidegger, where we quoted Harman as stating: "For a dog, a baby, an ant, or a parrot, most of the hammer's usual properties are not there at all, which shows that the presence of a thing is also determined by those who encounter it." Likewise, Sarker and Lee interpret the meaning of the BPC tools in relation to the people (the business process redesigners) who encounter it in MANCO and TELECO. I will reconstruct, as hypothetico-deductive, Sarker and Lee's hermeneutic reasoning for assessing the validity of their interpretations of the meaning that the BPC tools had for the people using them.

First, Sarker and Lee adopted, as a starting point, the preconceptions and presuppositions of the BPC academic and trade literature itself for the meaning of BPC tools (2006, p. 137, references suppressed):

> Our preunderstanding, based on the BPC literature [both the academic and trade literature], was that computerized BPC tools (especially those for flowcharting/process-mapping and project management) enhance redesign effectiveness by providing: 1) a necessary structure to the complex redesign process involving multiple redesigners over an extended period of time; 2) cognitive support to the redesigners who are

overwhelmed by the amount of information and the linkages between them; and 3) a standardized/shared notation for representing business processes and other related information.

Where this preunderstanding of the meaning of the BPC tools can be designated as the antecedent p_1 in hypothetico-deductive logic, Sarker and Lee observed consistent observations at TELECO but inconsistent observations (i.e., *not q_1*) at MANCO, where a key player discontinued her use of a "user-friendly and easy-to-learn" BPC tool and "team-members stated that the tools would not have made the redesign more effective" (2006, p. 138). The consistent observations at TELECO do not prove the interpretation *p* to be true (lest the fallacy of affirming the consequent be committed) and the inconsistent observations at MANCO lead to the conclusion *not p_1*, thereby requiring a revision in p_1, the interpreted meaning of the BPC tools.

Second, Sarker and Lee embarked with a new guess as to an improved interpretation, based on an "outburst" from a TELECO redesigner whom they quoted (2006, p. 138): "The problem is, if you have a tool, you become a slave to that tool . . . The business of producing and documenting was very cumbersome . . . we refined the hell out of this thing and toolsmithed it so many times, it was ridiculous!" Thus, Sarker and Lee moved away from p_1, the initial meaning of the BPC tools (based on the academic and trade literature), to p_2, a new interpretation of the meaning (based on practice) that "BPC tools have a negative effect on redesign effectiveness" (p. 138), which they noted was also possibly the case at MANCO. Still, given the weight of the academic and trade literature, Sarker and Lee felt that "the new interpretation that computer-based BPC tools have a negative effect on redesign seemed unsatisfactory," where this observation is the minor premise *not q_2* "and constituted an anomaly for us to explore further" (p. 138).

Third, again motivated by a remark from an organizational member, Sarker and Lee were inspired to make a new guess, this time that BPC tools need not necessarily have just either positive effects or negative effects, but could have positive as well as negative effects depending on contextual factors with "the 'net' direction of effects being dependent on the circumstances surrounding use" (2006, p. 139). In other words, Sarker and Lee were no longer interpreting the BPC tools as having an inherent meaning of good or bad, or useful or not, for the redesigners at MANCO and TELECO, but instead offering p_3, the interpretation that the meaning of these tools for the organizational members depended on the members themselves and the situations they found themselves in.

Fourth, Sarker and Lee returned to "two apparent absurdities that had emerged earlier" (2006, p. 139). The first one pertained to this: where p_4 is "the BPC tools do have (in certain circumstances) a positive influence on redesign effectiveness by providing structure, cognitive support, and standardized notation" and "Because structure, cognitive support, and notation become more relevant with increasing size [of the firm], it seemed sensible for us to assume that a larger BPC team (or a BPC team in a larger organization) would experience the benefits from using the tools" (p. 139). However, TELECO was, by far, larger than MANCO, where the BPC tools were largely not used after their introduction (hence, *not q_4*). The second absurdity pertained to this: if "a respected member of the BPC team [at MANCO] had expressed, through the text 'It would have provided us with some guidance,' the need for a computer-based tool to provide support to the redesign process" (i.e., p_5), then why was it that "MANCO had discontinued the use of the BPC tools that it had acquired" (i.e., *not q_5*)?

To resolve the former absurdity, Sarker and Lee

> reached the interpretation [i.e., p_6] that, even in large organizations that would seemingly require the use of computerized BPC tools, the distantiation and the resulting

designs [in a politicized redesign process] can outweigh the tools' intended benefit, and even lead to harmful effects (which can include . . . depersonalization of the redesigns, "meaningless" changes being made, and frustration experienced by the redesigners).

(2006, p. 140)

To resolve the latter absurdity, Sarker and Lee posited the following interpretation (p_7) that the BPC tools had for the people using them: "in a smaller company such as MANCO whose employees enjoyed a cooperative working environment, there was no need to win justification for a redesign through formalizing or otherwise embellishing its appearance" (2006, p. 140).

Both p_6 and p_7 can be regarded as specifications of p_3, the interpretation that the meaning of the BPC tools for the organizational members can be "can be positive or negative, depending on the circumstances" (2006, p. 140) that the members themselves found themselves in.

Fifth, Sarker and Lee considered an additional interpretation (i.e., p_8) "that BPC tools should be used only in the early stages of the redesign or to satisfy bureaucratic requirements," which would fit the situations at both MANCO and TELECO. However, Sarker and Lee quickly noted, "yet, many organizations (including ones that cannot be characterized as 'bureaucratic' have been reported to use the tools effectively throughout the redesign phase of their BPC initiatives" (i.e., *not* q_8). Sarker and Lee, after revisiting and analyzing remarks made by people in the two organizations, then revised their interpretation (i.e., p_9) as follows: "The interpretation that now emerged was that decisions to use BPC tools, and their beneficial or harmful effects, are dependent on *the political and organizational-culture context of their use*" (2006, p. 140, emphasis in the original). The last interpretation that Sarker and Lee offered was consistent with all of the earlier observations they considered (i.e., "strips," in Agar's terminology), including the comments of the organizational members.

In essence, Sarker and Lee treated the people at MANCO and TELECO much as if, regarding the earlier Heidegger example, they were persons who are from a tribe that has had no contact with the rest of the world and who come into contact with the podium, or BPC tools, for the first time. Sarker and Lee investigated the meaning of the podium/BPC tools for these people. Always accepting that the people were acting in ways that they themselves would consider sensible, Sarker and Lee formulated guesses to interpret the meanings the BPC tools had for the people at MANCO and TELECO and used hypothetico-deductive logic to test the goodness of their interpretations.

Discussion

Some points require elaboration. Is the phenomenological reduction, as earlier described, necessary? What is the relation between meaning and theory in interpretive research? And is hypothetico-deductive logic compatible with interpretive research?

First, Sarker and Lee demonstrate how to interpret meaning, just as do Kuhn, Kanter, and Agar, all without mentioning the phenomenological reduction. This, however, does not mean that the phenomenological reduction is unnecessary; instead, it means that an interpretive researcher, following Sarker and Lee, Kuhn, Kanter, and Agar, nonetheless strives for the "pure essence" of what the observed people mean through the interpretive researcher's successively testing – and therefore successively examining and eliminating – his or her previously "unexamined preconceptions and presuppositions," where this successively applied method aims for each iteration of testing to achieve an interpretation closer to what the observed people mean. The phenomenological reduction can thus be achieved even if it is not explicitly named.

Second, an interpreted meaning alone is not a theory, but it may be a part of a theory. One plausible conception of interpretive theory is that it is theory which delineates the social structure and the culture for the people being studied; Lee and Hovorka offer this description of social structure and culture (2015, p. 4922):

> A particularly clear form of social structure is kinship structure [which consists of] a durable collection of roles, of the relationships between them, and of "the rules of social life" (Giddens 1984, p. 21) pertaining to roles and relationships throughout the structure. Different rules are associated with different roles, where knowledge of the rules are shared by all members of the kinship structure, and where the shared knowledge forms the core of the group's culture. Such rules can pertain to, among other things, what a role allows or enables its occupant to do, as well as what two different roles allow or enable their respective occupants . . . to do with respect to each other.

Culture, as such, also refers to the body of shared meanings within the social structure, such as the meanings of routine social actions engaged in by members of different roles as well as the meanings that can be ascribed to certain artifacts (such as a podium or a hammer). A theory about how a technology diffuses throughout a group of people, for instance, would consist of not only a collection of interpreted meanings that the people have for their social actions and technological artifacts, but also propositions built upon these meanings, such as "a necessary condition for the use of a technology to diffuse among the people in this organization is that the people experience no irremediable conflict in the political and organizational-culture context of the technology's use." In other words, there is a long distance to be traveled from the point of merely interpreting meaning, which has been the focus of this chapter, to the point of having built and tested a theory.

Third, the hermeneutic interpretations performed by Sarker and Lee, Føllesdal, and Hirsch all constitute proofs by demonstration that hypothetico-deductive logic is compatible with interpretive research. There exists the perception among some that positivist research has a monopoly on logic; however, logic was already in existence long before positivism was even conceived. Furthermore, symbolic logic, which is the home of modus tollens and hypothetico-deductive logic, is a part of the discipline of philosophy, which is one of the humanities. In this sense, interpretive research is not so much appropriating as it is rightfully re-appropriating hypothetico-deductive logic.

Conclusion

The question – what makes interpretive research interpretive? – is important because meaning is problematic. It is not easily observed. Its interpretation is a calculated effort. Just as the observation of numerical data can benefit from the support of instrument development and other methods, the observation of meaning can benefit from the support of interpretive methods, which may include those shared by Casebier, Kuhn, Kanter, and Agar, as well as the support of underlying philosophies, such as those of Husserl, Heidegger, and Schutz.

The question – how is interpretive research valid? – is important because the interpretation of meaning is not arbitrary. Not all interpreted meanings are necessarily good, much less valid. Science, which includes interpretive research, requires the criterion of validity. Hypothetico-deductive logic, through which validity can be demonstrated, is no less applicable in the human sciences than in the natural sciences, as clarified by Hirsch and Føllesdal and as illustrated with the work of Sarker and Lee.

Both questions are especially important for the conduct of research in the information systems discipline because, ultimately, all information systems are systems of meanings. And to proceed, research on systems of meanings requires the meanings to be interpreted and the interpretations to be valid – where these include not only the meanings of technological artifacts, but also the meanings that the technological artifacts can be used to create and convey.

Finally, one may define interpretive research in any way that one wishes, but to live up to its name, interpretive research needs to be interpreting *something*. In this chapter, I have defined it as research that involves the interpretation of meaning. I look forward to insightful examinations of what else interpretive research may be framed as interpreting, such as action, culture, artifacts, rules, and beliefs.

Note

1 Agar defines action as "the lived experience of the actor at the time of its doing" and act as "a reflectively contemplated action" (1986, pp. 24–25). Using Schutz's terminology from earlier in this chapter, we may describe an action as the correlate in the outer world and the act as the intentional object.

References

Agar, M.H. 1986. *Speaking of Ethnography*. Thousand Oaks, CA: Sage.
Biemel, W. 2016. "Phenomenology," in: *Encyclopaedia Britannica*, Britannica Academic.
Casebier, A. 2014. "Phenomenology," in: *Encyclopedia of Aesthetics*, M. Kelly (ed.). Oxford: Oxford University Press.
Duignan, J. 2016. "Research Method," in: *A Dictionary of Business Research Methods*. Oxford: Oxford University Press.
Føllesdal, D. 1979. "Hermeneutics and the Hypothetico-Deductive Method," *Dialectica* (33:3/4), pp. 319–336.
Giddens, A. 1984. *The Constitution of Society: Outline of the Theory of Structuration*. Berkeley: University of California Press.
Harman, G. 2013. *Heidegger Explained: From Phenomenon to Thing*. Chicago: Open Court.
Hirsch, E.D. 1967. *Validity in Interpretation*. New Haven, CT: Yale University Press.
Kanter, R.M. 1977. *Men and Women of the Corporation*. New York: Basic Books.
Klein, H.K. and Myers, M.D. 1999. "A Set of Principles for Conducting and Evaluating Interpretive Field Studies in Information Systems," *MIS Quarterly* (23:1), pp. 67–93.
Kuhn, T.S. 1977. "Preface," in *The Essential Tension: Selected Studies in Scientific Tradition and Change*. Chicago: University of Chicago Press, pp. ix–xxiii.
Lee, A.S. 1991. "Integrating Positivist and Interpretive Approaches to Organizational Research," *Organization Science* (2:4), pp. 342–365.
Lee, A.S. and Hovorka, D. 2015. "Crafting Theory to Satisfy the Requirements of Interpretation," *48th Hawaii International Conference on System Sciences*: IEEE, pp. 4918–4927.
Lee, A.S. and Hubona, G.S. 2009. "A Scientific Basis for Rigor in Information Systems Research," *MIS Quarterly* (33:2), pp. 237–262.
Mohajeri, K. 2014. *Theorizing When User Reaction to IT Implementation Is Neither Resistance nor Acceptance, but Constructive Behavior: A Case Study of Healthcare IT Implementation*. Doctoral Dissertation, Department of Information Systems, Virginia Commonwealth University.
Myers, M.D. 1999. "Investigating Information Systems With Ethnographic Research," *Communications of the Association for Information Systems* (2:23), pp. 1–20.
Myers, M.D. 2013. *Qualitative Research in Business and Management*. Thousand Oaks, CA: Sage.
Oxford English Dictionary. 2005a. "Phenomenology." Oxford: Oxford University Press.
Oxford English Dictionary. 2005b. "Scare Quotes." Oxford: Oxford University Press.
Packer, M.J. and Addison, R.B. 1989. "Evaluating an Interpretive Account," in: *Entering the Circle: Hermeneutic Investigation in Psychology*, M.J. Packer and R.B. Addison (eds.). Albany: State University of New York Press, pp. 275–292.

Quinton, The Rt. Hon. Lord. 2005. "Philosophy," in: *The Oxford Companion to Philosophy*, T. Honderich (ed.). Oxford: Oxford University Press.

Sarker, S. and Lee, A. S. 2006. "Does the Use of Computer-Based BPC Tools Contribute to Redesign Effectiveness? Insights From a Hermeneutic Study," *IEEE Transactions on Engineering Management* (53:1), pp. 130–145.

Schutz, A. 1962a. "Concept and Theory Formation in the Social Sciences," in: *Alfred Schutz Collected Papers 1*, M. Natanson (ed.). Dordrecht, the Netherlands: Kluwer Academic, pp. 48–66.

Schutz, A. 1962b. "Some Leading Concepts of Phenomenology," in: *Alfred Schutz Collected Papers 1*, M. Natanson (ed.). Dordrecht, the Netherlands: Kluwer Academic, pp. 99–117.

Van Maanen, J. 1979. "The Fact of Fiction in Organizational Ethnography," *Administrative Science Quarterly* (24:4), pp. 539–550.

Walsham, G. 1993. *Interpreting Information Systems in Organizations*. New York: John Wiley & Sons.

Walsham, G. 1995a. "The Emergence of Interpretivism in IS Research," *Information Systems Research* (6:4), pp. 376–394.

Walsham, G. 1995b. "Interpretive Case Studies in IS Research: Nature and Method," *European Journal of Information Systems* (4:2), pp. 74–81.

Walsham, G. 2006. "Doing Interpretive Research," *European Journal of Information Systems* (15:3), pp. 320–330.

3
INFORMATION SYSTEMS AS A REFERENCE DISCIPLINE
Current debate and future directions

Richard L. Baskerville and Michael D. Myers

Introduction

In our 2002 article we suggested that it might be time for the field of information systems to be considered as a reference discipline for others (Baskerville and Myers 2002). For the previous two decades the conventional wisdom among information systems (IS) researchers had been that IS is an applied discipline drawing upon other, more fundamental, reference disciplines. These reference disciplines were seen as having foundational value for IS. Before our 2002 article the only arguments concerning this topic had been about which disciplines should be regarded as reference disciplines. No one had actually questioned this conventional wisdom, that perhaps it was time for IS itself to be considered as a reference discipline for others. In our 2002 article we did not claim that IS had in fact achieved the status of a reference discipline; rather, we suggested that it was time to at least consider this question. We said that our paper was designed to be provocative and rhetorical in order to stimulate discussion about the nature and status of our field.

Our aim in writing the article was certainly achieved. The 2002 article sparked much discussion and debate in the IS research literature, with one special issue of the *Journal of the Association for Information Systems* devoted to this issue. Our article has now received more than 500 citations, with scholars coming down on both sides of the argument.

The purpose of this chapter, therefore, is to discuss our original argument for IS to be considered as a reference discipline, review the various contributions that have been made to the debate since then and suggest a way forward for future research.

The outline of this chapter is as follows. The next section briefly summarizes our original argument as to why IS should be considered as a reference discipline, as per our 2002 article. The following section reviews the various contributions that have been made to the debate by IS scholars since then. The final section suggests some possible future directions for further work on this important topic.

IS as a reference discipline?

In this first section we briefly summarize our original argument as to why IS should be considered as a reference discipline.

The idea that the field of information systems is an applied discipline drawing upon other, more fundamental, reference disciplines, was first suggested by Peter Keen at the first International Conference on Information Systems (ICIS) in 1980. Because these reference disciplines were more mature, Keen argued that IS researchers could borrow and learn from the theories, methods and exemplars of good research in these reference disciplines (Keen 1980). Following on from Keen's original ICIS paper, IS scholars spent much time and effort debating which disciplines should be counted as reference disciplines. For example, as well as the usual suspects of engineering, computer science, mathematics, management science and behavioral decision theory, IS scholars suggested that many other related disciplines should be added to the list. These additional disciplines included accounting, management, architecture and anthropology. But until our 2002 article no one had really considered the idea that other fields might borrow and learn from the theories, methods and exemplars of good research in IS. The flow of knowledge and information was assumed to be entirely one way.

The conventional wisdom regarded IS as having many reference disciplines but not its own research tradition, and that it had few, if any, referring disciplines. We suggested that this view of the nature of our field might be outdated for four reasons (Baskerville and Myers 2002).

First, the field of information systems has developed its own research tradition. By 2002 the field had at least one major journal (*MIS Quarterly*) that was established more than 25 years ago, the field's major international conference (ICIS) was more than 20 years old and most major universities had IS departments. As well as having its own international society (the Association for Information Systems), the field has a distinct subject matter, a distinct research perspective and a well-developed communication system that includes respected journals (Baskerville and Myers 2002).

Second, we argued that IS has much to offer researchers in many other disciplines. This contribution is especially important because information technology and systems had already become ubiquitous in the developed world by 2002. We provided two examples of IS research articles that had been well cited by researchers from other disciplines, one by Markus, the other by Davenport and Short. Markus's classic article on resistance to IS implementation (Markus 1983) had been cited over 200 times over the previous decade (Lee et al. 2000) in such diverse disciplines as Communication (Lewis 2000), Education (Telem 1997), Human Resources (Fincham 1994), Manufacturing (Guimaraes et al. 1995), Medical Informatics (Kaplan 1997), Organizational Behavior (Singh and Ginzberg 1996), Organizational Change Management (Kaarst-Brown 1999), Sociology (Rachel and Woolgar 1995) and Urban Planning (Budic and Godschalk 1994). Davenport and Short's (1990) original article on business process reengineering had been cited more than 250 times by 2002 in fields such as Behavioral Science (Paul et al. 1999), Systems Science (Gross and Traunmuller 1996), Government (Caudle 1996), Manufacturing and Engineering (Harris 1996; Li 1996) and Medical Informatics (Buetow and Roland 1999). As an aside, Markus's 1983 article has been cited more than 2,600 times, and Davenport and Short's 1990 article more than 4,300 times.

Third, given the rapid and unrelenting digitization of business and society as a whole, we suggested that researchers from many other fields would soon start to recognize the importance of IS research.

Hence we suggested that IS has an opportunity to become established as a reference discipline for other research fields because almost every other human discipline was now a potential consumer of IS research discoveries.

Fourth, we suggested that IS could be seen as one part among many knowledge creation networks throughout the world. Seen in this way, IS would cease to be regarded as a referring discipline with many reference disciplines, but one of many reference disciplines exchanging ideas in an intellectual discourse with other disciplines. IS would be seen as one "reference discipline" or "contributing discipline" among others (Baskerville and Myers 2002).

In order for the field to take its place as one reference discipline among others, we suggested that there were at least two arenas for concentrated improvement. The first arena was a change in our own mind-set as to the audience for IS research. As well as our existing constituency, we suggested that we needed to address a much broader audience in our work – this audience to include scholars in any field that would be affected by the use and application of information technology and systems. The second arena involved making sure that our research is easily accessible to researchers in other fields. We suggested that our research articles needed to be visible, readily available, and understandable to others.

We concluded our 2002 piece by suggesting that there was an opportunity for IS scholars to take a more visible and active leadership role within a larger community of scholars. Taking a position of leadership would mean transforming our research agendas and clearly explaining the broad value of our research discoveries. It would also mean working toward the situation where scholars from many other fields look to our top journals for leadership and guidance. Our research articles would need to be of sufficient quality, substance and depth that scholars in other fields would find IS research increasingly useful (Baskerville and Myers 2002).

To summarize, the main purpose of our 2002 paper was to stimulate discussion about the nature and status of our field. Our 2002 article suggested that it was time to question the conventional wisdom that IS was simply a consumer of knowledge from other fields, and consider instead whether it was also a contributor. We argued that the IS field had come of age, although whether IS had in fact become a reference discipline at that time was still an open question. We thought that 2002 was certainly an appropriate time to consider the question of whether IS had emerged as a reference discipline in its own right, although we acknowledged that there was still much work to be done.

The subsequent reference discipline discourse

It might be said that our 2002 paper represented a milestone in the disciplinary debate. It offered one path away from the inwardly focused information systems "identity crisis" (Benbasat and Zmud 2003), instead focusing outwardly on the intellectual utility of information systems research. If not a milestone, it certainly became something of a lightning rod. It precipitated a discourse about the usefulness of the scholarly knowledge proceeding from the field. This discourse includes work of an empirical nature, with conclusions based on citation analyses of the research literature, to work of a more theoretical nature.

We suggest that the subsequent discourse can be grouped into three types of argument: (1) information systems is an intellectual black hole; (2) information systems is a rising star; and (3) information systems scholars should move on to consider a different set of questions.

Information systems is an intellectual black hole

The first type of argument in the subsequent discourse is that the discipline of information systems only absorbs knowledge from other fields. We can characterize this first type of argument as *the black hole proposition*. IS scholars taking this line of argument say that knowledge flows into the discipline, but relatively little, if any, flows out of the discipline. This view reiterates the idea that the field of information systems is not a reference discipline, or at least not yet.

A leading work taking this perspective is Wade, Biehl and Kim's article titled "Information Systems Is Not a Reference Discipline (And What We Can Do About It)" (2006b). Using a citation analysis of 22 journals (1990–2001) anchored to the *Financial Times* list of research journals, they found it "difficult to conclude that the IS field is a reference discipline" (p. 256). Further, based on a social network analysis, they offer evidence that IS is not even a contributing discipline. A time series analysis that the authors conducted produced no indications that any spread of IS knowledge is developing. They say that their findings

> cast doubt on Baskerville and Myers' conclusion that IS is ready to attain the status of a reference discipline. [The findings] also draw into question the extent to which the IS field has become a contributing discipline for other management fields.
>
> (p. 260)

In "Relationships Among the Academic Business Disciplines: A Multi-Method Citation Analysis," Biehl et al. (2006) delivered a more general analysis of the *Financial Times* list of management journals (1985–2001) using social network analysis. In their study of the relationships among the research publications in the management disciplines, they found indications that information systems was highly interdisciplinary in that it seemed to draw its reference base from broadly across other management disciplines. However, the other disciplines, even those that were most cited within information systems, were not citing IS research from information systems journals.

Polites and Watson (2009), in "Using Social Network Analysis to Analyze Relationships Among IS Journals," used social network analysis of the core journals in information systems in relation to journals in allied disciplines (2003–2005). They say that their

> findings support the conclusions of Wade et al. (2006) based on 1990–2001 data from 31 top business journals and others that IS has not yet achieved status as a full-fledged reference discipline, in that it is not being extensively cited by other disciplines.
>
> (pp. 608–609)

Larsen and Levine, in "Searching for Management Information Systems: Coherence and Change in the Discipline" (2005) use a co-word analysis of the literature to identify 62 different centers of coherence in the information systems discipline. They find only weak evidence of theory building. With so much diversity, they believe that any kind of cumulative tradition continues to elude the field of information systems. They conclude:

> No end appears to be in sight for the now familiar and longstanding discussions on the status of MIS. This debate touches upon the identity and value of MIS as a field within the university and in relation to industry practice.
>
> (p. 377)

We can see, therefore, that the first discourse disagrees with any proposition that IS has achieved the status of a reference discipline; rather, the evidence for the building of a coherent, cumulative tradition of IS research is weak, and any knowledge that flows into IS tends to disappear into a black hole, that is, once it enters our field it stays there, never to see the light of day anywhere else.

Information systems is a rising star

The second argument in this discourse takes an opposing line of argument to the first. This discourse takes the view that the discipline of information systems is indeed diffusing knowledge into other fields. We call this line of argument *the rising star proposition*. It takes the general view that knowledge is not only being drawn into the discipline, but is increasingly flowing out of the discipline. IS scholars taking this view argue that the field of information systems is well on the way to becoming a reference discipline, if it is not one already.

A leading work taking this perspective is Grover et al.'s (2006b) "A Citation Analysis of the Evolution and State of Information Systems Within a Constellation of Reference Disciplines." In their citation analysis of 16 management journals during the period 1990–2003, they find:

> In general, these results support the contention that IS is becoming an exporter of ideas. . . . Our analysis suggests that our traditional reference disciplines are increasingly drawing . . . from IS; in a sense the tables have turned. It is also evident that fields like engineering . . . and ergonomics . . . are also benefactors of our knowledge base. Therefore, despite the diversity of the field, there seems to be an intellectual engine emerging that can contribute to more "mature" disciplines.
>
> (pp. 292–294)

Katerattanakul, Han and Rea, in "Is Information Systems a Reference Discipline?" (2006), conducted a citation analysis of the 4,668 journals indexed in the Social Science Citation Index and the Science Citation Index. They analyzed the citations to the 1,120 articles in the top six information systems journals.

> Results from this study provide strong evidence that the information systems discipline has become a reference discipline for others. That is, IS research published in IS journals is frequently cited by other disciplines, even those fields that previously served as reference disciplines for IS (such as computer science, management, and organization science).
>
> (p. 117)

In "Defining the Intellectual Structure of Information Systems and Related College of Business Disciplines: A Bibliometric Analysis," Pratt et al. (2012) seek to identify the reciprocal impact of scholarly contributions between information systems and five other business disciplines. Basing their co-citation analysis on a selection of 115 journals (25 in each discipline, including overlaps), and using the Thomson Reuters Web of Knowledge, they analyzed 148,009 papers. They conclude that

> there is an increased export of IS literature to other COB disciplines with the sharpest increases to Marketing and Entrepreneurship. The increased export of IS knowledge to other COB disciplines demonstrates the growing influence of IS on other disciplines and further supports the argument that IS is becoming a reference discipline.
>
> (p. 301)

We can see, therefore, that the second argument in this discourse agrees with the proposition that IS has achieved the status of a reference discipline, or at least is well on the way to becoming one. Knowledge is increasingly flowing out of IS into other fields.

Why the contradictions in the citation evidence?

The somewhat equally weighted yet diametrically opposing citation evidence for each argument is intriguing. Surprisingly, two of these contradictory articles, namely, Wade et al. (2006b) and Grover et al. (2006b), appeared in the very same issue of the *Journal of the Association for Information Systems* dedicated to the subject. Scientometric studies such as those described earlier are sometimes superficial, but not in this case. Both these papers are extremely rigorous and thorough, characterized by one of the special issue editors as raising "the level of the discourse to the highest level" (Straub 2006, p. 243). In fact, all six of the studies mentioned are very well executed.

One possible explanation for the apparently contradictory results lies in the selection of journals included in the studies. For example, is *Decision Sciences* an information systems journal or a management science journal (cf. the arguments of Wade et al. (2006a) on this point)? Over time, journals change editorial policies, for example, *Communications of the ACM* changed in its scope (cf. the arguments of Grover et al. (2006a) on this point). Another possible explanation is the varying assumptions about whether all papers published in information systems journals ought to be considered information systems papers (Wade et al. 2006a). Yet another is whether citations can provide an appropriate measure to indicate a reference discipline anyway. These are a matter of degree and the degree is a matter of opinion (Grover et al. 2006a). Finally, the analytical tools used in each paper might affect the results. Social network analysis seems to support the black hole proposition, and other forms of co-citation analysis seem to support the rising star proposition (Polites and Watson 2009).

The subsequent discourse to our 2002 article thus includes well-designed and well-executed citation-based scientometric studies that support *both* the black hole proposition *and* the rising star proposition. This outcome leads us to concur with Grover et al. (2006b) that it may well be a faulty conceptualization of the two propositions that supposes them as being in opposition to each other. Perhaps a reframing of the two propositions might yield some useful insights.

Reframing the two propositions

The two opposing arguments discussed earlier have attracted alternative ways of reframing the two propositions. As for the black hole proposition, Gill and Bhattacherjee (2009) reframed this proposition in their article titled "Whom Are We Informing? Issues and Recommendations for MIS Research From an Informing Sciences Perspective." They argued that the various clients of the information systems academic discipline include students, practitioners and other academics (outside of information systems). They positioned their work as focusing on the degree to which information systems is informing practice; or more particularly, informing important problems facing practice. They argue that all business disciplines in general (and not just IS) do a poor job of informing practice. In Europe, they note how the information systems discipline is better aligned with practice than in North America.

As for the rising star proposition, our subsequent paper titled "Fashion Waves in Information Systems Research and Practice" (Baskerville and Myers 2009) reframed this proposition as related to the use of IS research by IS practice, not the use of IS research by other academic disciplines. We considered whether the fashion-following tendencies known to inhabit management practice (Abrahamson 1991; Abrahamson 1996) were also a feature of the IS field; namely, whether information systems practice mirrored those fashions found in information systems research. Using bibliographic analysis, we found indications that both IS research and practice are closely aligned. We showed how the discipline's research tracked, and occasionally led, practice. Our findings suggested that there were opportunities for information systems not only to contribute knowledge to other academic disciplines, but to contribute in the formulation of new trends and fashions in practice.

We can see, therefore, that the subsequent reframing of the discourse has only continued the apparent disagreement over the state of the IS field (Myers et al. 2011). Some authors have continued to argue in favor of the black hole proposition, saying that IS research is irrelevant to practice, whereas others such as ourselves have continued to argue in favor of a slightly modified version of the rising star proposition, saying that IS research is not only relevant but closely aligned to IS practice.

IS scholars should move on to consider a different set of questions

While reframing the two original arguments has helped to broaden the discourse to include the degree to which information systems research has contributed to practice, a third type of argument in the subsequent discourse to our 2002 article is that IS scholars should move on to consider a different set of questions. That is, grounding their work in the foregoing reference discipline debate, these researchers have sought to frame the discourse in a different way.

Kjaergaard and Vendelø (2015) suggest that any proposition that information systems is a reference discipline will more likely depend on the nature of the theory adaptation taking place in particular research projects. In "The Role of Theory Adaptation in the Making of a Reference Discipline," they examine the particular case of sense-making theory, its adaptation in information systems research and the subsequent impact of such research. Using a set of 323 articles from nine leading information systems journals ranging from 1997 until 2006, they identified 19 articles that adapt and use sense-making theory as a central construct in a theoretical framework. They conducted a citation analysis of these articles using the Web of Knowledge and Web of Science and compared the referencing of these articles to the results of the Wade et al. (2006b) study mentioned earlier. They conclude that this set of sense-making articles "are remarkably more successful in attracting citations from outside the IS discipline, and therefore conclude that theory adaptation matters for external referencing" (p. 144). Hence these scholars have moved the discourse forward from simply discussing whether knowledge flows in or out of the field of information systems. Instead, they consider how it flows, looking at the bi-directional flow of knowledge both into IS and subsequently out of IS.

Bernroider et al. (2013) used citation and co-citation analysis across the AIS basket or eight journals together with 825 journals in 22 business and management fields (1995–2011). They identified general management as the original main reference discipline for information systems, but say its influence has declined over time, giving way to a more diverse set of reference disciplines (notably marketing, business strategy and social science). Their analysis focused on the information systems discipline's increased advocacy for its jurisdiction over certain problem areas (Abbott 2001). They found evidence that this advocacy initially rose, then fell, then rose again over the history of the field. They regard the multi-disciplinarity of information systems and its fluid boundaries as essential for the field's continued formation, saying "the multi-disciplinary and hybrid nature of the developing IS discipline remains visible over time as it equally shares its discourses with inputs from non-IS disciplines, and as a discipline has established different levels of jurisdiction over time" (p. 85). Hence this article also moves the debate forward by establishing which areas of knowledge are in effect "owned" by IS.

Córdoba et al. (2012) examine the field of information systems from the perspective of the sociology of science. Using Abbott's (2001) theories of disciplinary emergence, they propose three concepts as being relevant: differentiation (jurisdiction over problem areas), competition (externally with other disciplines and internally, e.g., over research methods) and absorption (winning rights to a jurisdiction). Using evidence from citation analysis (see Bernroider et al. 2013), their insights "indicate that IS has gone through stages of differentiation, competition and is currently in a stage of absorption, in what appears to be a consolidation of positivist and behaviourally oriented research oriented to study and manage IS acceptance and use" (p. 492). Like the previous article, this work focuses on what areas of knowledge are unique to IS.

We can see, then, that the third discourse moves on from the original debate about whether information systems is a reference discipline or not. Instead, these scholars adopt a more dynamic perspective and consider which areas of knowledge are continuously *owned* by IS and which areas exhibit ownership that *flows dynamically* between disciplines over time.

Summarizing the discourse

Has the field of information systems now achieved the status of a reference discipline? Was our original argument right or wrong? We have seen that the evidence, whether it is citation, co-citation or social network analyses, is mixed and somewhat equivocal. The answer depends on the assumptions that are made about which journals to include in the studies and the analytical methods that are employed. More recent work has suggested alternative ways to reframe the argument. These more nuanced ways of analyzing the flow of knowledge within and between disciplines now lead us to suggest a way forward for future research.

Future directions

As we have just mentioned, the most recent work related to the IS as a reference discipline debate actually moves on from considering whether knowledge flows in one direction or the other. Rather, recent work builds on the idea that knowledge flows in many directions, whether from one academic discipline to another, or from academia to practice (and vice versa). Seen in this way, the field of IS can be seen as one part among many intertwining knowledge creation networks throughout the world. The field of information systems is simply one academic discipline among others exchanging knowledge in a free flow of ideas. Information Systems is simply one of many "contributing disciplines" to an ever-changing discourse related to information technology (Baskerville and Myers 2002). Hence, we suggest that one future direction of IS research could be to document and analyse this multi-directional flow of knowledge over time. We regard Kjaergaard and Vendelø's (2015) article as an exemplar of this kind of future work.

Another future direction for further work builds on a suggestion that we made in our 2002 article. We suggested that there was an opportunity for IS scholars to take a more visible and active leadership role within a larger community of scholars. We said that we as IS scholars should work toward the situation where scholars from many other fields would look to our top journals for leadership and guidance (Baskerville and Myers 2002). So an appropriate question to ask, approximately 15 years since our original article, is this: has IS taken up a position of leadership not only within academia, but also with IS practitioners and society as a whole with respect to the discourse related to development, use, application and impact of IT? While we would argue that our research is being cited and used in these various arenas, we think that there is still a long way to go before we are seen as thought leaders. The idea of having grand challenges for the IS discipline is one step in the right direction (Baskerville et al. 2006; Limayem et al. 2011), but much more work remains to be done. Hence this remains a work in progress.

References

Abbott, A. 2001. *Chaos of Disciplines*. Chicago: University of Chicago Press.

Abrahamson, E. 1991. "Managerial Fads and Fashions: The Diffusion and Rejection of Innovations," *Academy of Management Review* (16:3), pp. 586–612.

Abrahamson, E. 1996. "Management Fashion," *Academy of Management Review* (21:1), pp. 254–285.

Baskerville, R. L., and Myers, M. D. 2002. "Information Systems as a Reference Discipline," *MIS Quarterly* (26:1), pp. 1–14.

Baskerville, R. L., and Myers, M. D. 2009. "Fashion Waves in Information Systems Research and Practice," *MIS Quarterly* (33:4), pp. 647–662.

Baskerville, R. L., Scubert, P., Watters, C., Winter, R., and Wulf, V. 2006. "Panel: Grand Challenges for Information Systems Research," in: *European Conference on Information Systems*. pp. 1–2.

Benbasat, I., and Zmud, R. W. 2003. "The Identity Crisis Within the IS Discipline: Defining and Communicating the Discipline's Core Properties," *MIS Quarterly* (27:2), pp. 183–194.

Bernroider, E. W., Pilkington, A., and Córdoba, J.-R. 2013. "Research in Information Systems: A Study of Diversity and Inter-Disciplinary Discourse in the AIS Basket Journals Between 1995 and 2011," *Journal of Information Technology* (28:1), pp. 74–89.

Biehl, M., Kim, H., and Wade, M. 2006. "Relationships Among the Academic Business Disciplines: A Multi-Method Citation Analysis," *Omega* (34:4), pp. 359–371.

Budic, Z. D., and Godschalk, D. R. 1994. "Implementation and Management Effectiveness in Adoption of GIS Technology in Local Governments," *Computers Environment and Urban Systems* (18:5), pp. 285–304.

Buetow, S. A., and Roland, M. 1999. "Clinical Governance: Bridging the Gap Between Managerial and Clinical Approaches to Quality of Care," *Quality in Health Care* (8:3), pp. 184–190.

Caudle, S. L. 1996. "Strategic Information Resources Management: Fundamental Practices," *Government Information Quarterly* (13:1), pp. 83–97.

Córdoba, J.-R., Pilkington, A., and Bernroider, E.W.N. 2012. "Information Systems as a Discipline in the Making: Comparing EJIS and MISQ between 1995 and 2008," *European Journal of Information Systems* (21:5), pp. 479–495.

Davenport, T., and Short, J. 1990. "The New Industrial Engineering: Information Technology and Business Process Redesign," *Sloan Management Review* (31:4), pp. 11–27.

Fincham, R. 1994. "Computing Occupations – Organizational Power, Work Transition and Collective Mobility," *New Technology Work and Employment* (9:1), pp. 43–53.

Gill, G., and Bhattacherjee, A. 2009. "Whom Are We Informing? Issues and Recommendations for MIS Research From an Informing Sciences Perspective," *MIS Quarterly* (33:2), pp. 217–235.

Gross, T., and Traunmuller, R. 1996. "Methodological Considerations on the Design of Computer-Supported Cooperative Work," *Cybernetics and Systems* (27:3), pp. 279–302.

Grover, V., Ayyagari, R., Gokhale, R., and Lim, J. 2006a. "About Reference Disciplines and Reference Differences: A Critique of Wade et al.," *Journal of the Association for Information Systems* (7:5), p. 336.

Grover, V., Ayyagari, R., Gokhale, R., Lim, J., and Coffey, J. 2006b. "A Citation Analysis of the Evolution and State of Information Systems Within a Constellation of Reference Disciplines," *Journal of the Association for Information Systems* (7:5), pp. 270–325.

Guimaraes, T., Yoon, Y., and Oneal, Q. 1995. "Success Factors for Manufacturing Expert-System Development," *Computers & Industrial Engineering* (28:3), pp. 545–559.

Harris, S. B. 1996. "Business Strategy and the Role of Engineering Product Data Management: A Literature Review and Summary of the Emerging Research Questions," *Proceedings of the Institution of Mechanical Engineers Part B – Journal of Engineering Manufacture* (210:3), pp. 207–220.

Kaarst-Brown, M. L. 1999. "Five Symbolic Roles of the External Consultant – Integrating Change, Power and Symbolism," *Journal of Organizational Change Management* (12:6), pp. 540–561.

Kaplan, B. 1997. "Addressing Organizational Issues Into the Evaluation of Medical Systems," *Journal of the American Medical Informatics Association* (4:2), pp. 94–101.

Katerattanakul, P., Han, B., and Rea, A. 2006. "Is Information Systems a Reference Discipline?," *Communications of the ACM* (49:5), pp. 114–118.

Keen, P.G.W. 1980. "MIS Research: Reference Disciplines and a Cumulative Tradition," *Proceedings of the First International Conference on Information Systems*, Philadelphia, PA, pp. 9–18.

Kjaergaard, A., and Vendelø, M. T. 2015. "The Role of Theory Adaptation in the Making of a Reference Discipline," *Information and Organization* (25:3), pp. 137–149.

Larsen, T. J., and Levine, L. 2005. "Searching for Management Information Systems: Coherence and Change in the Discipline," *Information Systems Journal* (15:4), pp. 357–381.

Lee, A. S., Myers, M. D., Paré, G., and Urquhart, C. 2000. "Three Perspectives: If Markus' 1983 Classic Study, 'Power, Politics, and MIS Implementation,' Were Being Reviewed Today," *Twenty First International Conference on Information Systems*, Brisbane, pp. 724–726.

Lewis, L. K. 2000. "'Blindsided by That One' and 'I Saw That One Coming': The Relative Anticipation and Occurrence of Communication Problems and Other Problems in Implementers' Hindsight," *Journal of Applied Communication Research* (28:1), pp. 44–67.

Li, H. 1996. "The Role of IT Manager in Construction Process Re-engineering," *Building Research and Information* (24:2), pp. 124–127.

Limayem, M., Niederman, F., and Slaughter, S. A. 2011. "What Are the Grand Challenges in Information Systems Research? A Debate and Discussion," in: *International Conference for Information Systems*. pp. 1–5.

Markus, M. L. 1983. "Power, Politics, and MIS Implementation," *Communications of the ACM* (26:6), pp. 430–444.

Myers, M. D., Baskerville, R. L., Gill, G., and Ramiller, N. 2011. "Setting Our Research Agendas: Institutional Ecology, Informing Sciences, or Management Fashion Theory?," *Communications of the AIS* (28:1), pp. 357–372.

Paul, R. J., Giaglis, G. M., and Hlupic, V. 1999. "Simulation of Business Processes," *American Behavioral Scientist* (42:10), pp. 1551–1576.

Polites, G. L., and Watson, R. T. 2009. "Using Social Network Analysis to Analyze Relationships Among IS Journals," *Journal of the Association for Information Systems* (10:8), pp. 595–636.

Pratt, J. A., Hauser, K., and Sugimoto, C. R. 2012. "Defining the Intellectual Structure of Information Systems and Related College of Business Disciplines: A Bibliometric Analysis," *Scientometrics* (93:2), pp. 279–304.

Rachel, J., and Woolgar, S. 1995. "The Discursive Structure of the Social-Technical Divide – the Example of Information-Systems Development," *Sociological Review* (43:2), pp. 251–273.

Singh, D. T., and Ginzberg, M. J. 1996. "An Empirical Investigation of the Impact of Process Monitoring on Computer-Mediated Decision-Making Performance," *Organizational Behavior and Human Decision Processes* (67:2), pp. 156–169.

Straub, D. 2006. "The Value of Scientometric Studies: An Introduction to a Debate on IS as a Reference Discipline," *Journal of the Association for Information Systems* (7:5), pp. 241–246.

Telem, M. 1997. "The School Computer Administrator's (New) Role Impact on Instruction Administration in a High-School – a Case Study," *Computers & Education* (28:4), pp. 213–221.

Wade, M., Biehl, M., and Kim, H. 2006a. "If the Tree of IS Knowledge Falls in a Forest, Will Anyone Hear?: A Commentary on Grover Et Al.," *Journal of the Association for Information Systems* (7:1), pp. 326–335.

Wade, M., Biehl, M., and Kim, H. 2006b. "Information Systems Is Not a Reference Discipline (And What We Can Do About It)," *Journal of the Association for Information Systems* (7:5), pp. 247–266.

4
ON THEORY

Shirley Gregor

There is nothing as practical as a good theory.

(Lewin 1945, p. 129)

Introduction

Contributing to theoretical knowledge is a primary goal in all scientific endeavours, including information systems (IS). Publishing in journals requires a contribution to knowledge of some form. Yet there is a range of views on what is meant by the term "theory" and what is involved in "theorizing." In management, Feldman (2004, p. 565) notes:

> We tell authors that their papers do not make theoretical contributions, but often do not give authors much insight into what counts as a theoretical contribution or how to build stronger theories.

The situation in IS is similar and is perhaps compounded because IS is at the intersection of the natural, human and technological sciences and our researchers draw on traditions from a number of fields. A further complication is that the phenomena of interest in IS are moving targets, changing rapidly with advances in information technology.

As the opening quote from Lewin indicates, good theory in disciplines such as IS can inform practice and provide benefits to individuals, organizations and societies. Being able to say what counts as a theory is important to academics because when we make a claim at the end of a journal article that we have made a contribution to theory we should be able *to point to the theory or body of systematized knowledge to which we are contributing*. This insight is a simple one but it is one that escapes many writers – the author included, at times. It was recognition of this insight that led to the development of the "Theory Contribution Canvas" that is presented in the latter part of this chapter. The canvas also highlights the need for contributions to theory and knowledge to be interesting, to answer the "so what" question. Theories are often more interesting when they address important practical problems.

The goals of the chapter are twofold. The first aim is to examine views of what constitutes theory and how theorizing occurs. The second aim is to describe how one can demonstrate in a journal article that one has made a contribution to theory using the Theory Contribution

Canvas as a tool. A practical takeaway from the chapter is the demonstration of how, at the conclusion of a research article, you can state clearly what theory you have contributed to and how you have done this (for example, building, testing, qualifying or expanding theory).

The chapter takes a pragmatic view of theory, recognizing that different forms of theory suit different purposes, and follows Gregor (2006) in recognizing five separate types of theory, being those for (1) analysis, (2) explanation, (3) predicting, (4) explaining and predicting and (5) design and action. Further, the word "theory" is used, as in Gregor (2006), in a broad sense to encompass what might be termed elsewhere models, frameworks or a systematized body of knowledge.

The structure of the chapter is as follows. The second section gives an overview of how theory is conceptualized, showing how different philosophical perspectives influence the view of theory and presenting the theory taxonomy of Gregor (2006). The third section covers the theorizing process. The fourth section aims to give some practical advice on how authors can demonstrate a contribution to theory in a single piece of work such as a journal article, using the Theory Contribution Canvas. The fifth section provides some concluding remarks.

What is theory?

The issue of what constitutes theory is a difficult one and many researchers tend to shy away from the use of the word, preferring to say, for example, that they are contributing to theoretical models or nascent theories. Weick (1995, p. 386) says:

> We would like writers to feel free to use theory whenever they are theorizing. Modesty is all very well, but leaning over too far backward removes a good word from currency.

Using the word "theory" means that we need to engage more carefully in thinking about what we are doing and how our work relates to traditions in other fields – a good thing. However, there can be issues when an overly restrictive view of theory is taken, for instance when the term is reserved for what might be called theory with a capital "T," as in a named high-level formal theory with general law-like statements: for instance, the Theory of Reasoned Action. Avison and Malaurent (2014) decry a "theory fetish" in IS, seemingly in response to a focus in scholarly practice on a formal traditional view of theory. An absence of a formal or named theory, however, need not mean that work is atheoretical or "theory light," but depends on what perspective on theory is adopted, as will be seen in the following discussion.

The term theory has different meanings and varying definitions, for example:

> A scientific theory is an attempt to build together in a systematic fashion the knowledge that one has of some particular aspect of experience.
> (Ruse 1995, p. 870)

> Scientific theories are universal statements. Like all linguistic representations they are systems of signs or symbols. Theories are nets cast to catch what we call "the world"; to rationalize, to explain and to master it. We endeavour to make the mesh even finer and finer.
> (Popper 1980, p. 59)

> By theory, I mean a particular kind of model that is intended to account for some subset of phenomena in the real world. (p. 4). Theories provide a representation of

how a subset of real-world phenomena should be described. In this light, they can be conceived as specialized ontologies.

(Weber 2012, p. 3)

Others stress that "scientific" theory should be well supported by empirical evidence. Hempel (1966) argues that support for hypothesis depends not only on the amount of confirmatory evidence, but also on its variety: "the greater the variety, the stronger the resulting support" (p. 34). Also in this light is the definition:

Theory: In science, a well-substantiated explanation of some aspect of the natural world that can incorporate facts, laws, inferences and tested hypotheses.

(National Academy of Sciences 1999, p. 2)

Although not always explicitly stated, most views of theory recognize that theory is knowledge that is abstract and general, not knowledge of specific facts alone.

Why do the different definitions of theory exist? Some differences reflect the different positions that writers have taken in terms of the philosophy of science, where issues of epistemology (how knowledge is developed) and ontology (what things exist, including theory) are debated. An important point is that the philosophy of science itself has a history and that this history reflects both developments in science and the interplay between science and the external environment (see Godfrey-Smith 2003; Scharff and Dusek 2003). It is impossible to give an adequate representation of changes in the philosophy of science even in the recent past in a single chapter, and all that can be done here is point to some of the more notable movements. It should be recognized that the representations of "isms" here are simplifications and that there were differences in thought within as well as between movements. Moreover, some philosophers changed their own positions over time.

Relatively recent movements that have influenced how theory is regarded include *logical positivism*, a strong form of empiricism developed in the Vienna Circle in Europe in the 1920s. Subsequently, in the 1920s to 1950s *logical empiricism* flourished as a successor to logical positivism and, although encompassing a diversity of ideas, there were concerns for scientific methodology, the use of logic and mathematics and the role that science could take in shaping society. From about 1940, work on computers, cybernetics (Wiener 1948) and general systems theory (von Bertalanffy 1950) changed thinking across a broad range of disciplines. In 1962 Kuhn challenged prevailing views with "The Structure of Scientific Revolutions," which suggested that the evolution of science was in part sociologically determined. In 1969, Herbert Simon, a Nobel prize winner in economics, produced the first edition of "Sciences of the Artificial," the foundational work that aimed to give (traditional) scientific status to fields dealing with the construction of artifacts (technology), such as management, economics and computer science. This work was the seminal work for what in IS is termed the design science approach and arguments for the need for design theory (e.g., see Gregor and Jones 2007). In 1975 Feyerabend presented "an anarchist theory of knowledge" that questioned the supremacy of *a* single scientific method. The so-called Science Wars in the 1990s saw postmodernists, with those from other fields such as cultural studies and science and technology studies, pitted against those proposing more traditional views of science. Recent work gives more sophisticated treatment of the philosophy of science that transcends some of the arguments between opposing camps (for example, see Papineau 2002). These brief historical reflections indicate how ideas in the philosophy of science and ideas of theory have changed over time. Recent considerations of what is meant by theory acknowledge that there may be a range of views.

It is important to be aware of differences, as some researchers may hold fixed views, without considering the value of a more encompassing position, or that their own views are not universally shared.

Winther (2016) identifies three perspectives on theory,[1] which although they may have commonalities, have dominant features that distinguish them:

- The *Syntactic View* focuses on the way theory is formally expressed and emerged out of the work of the Vienna Circle and logical positivism. Theories are sets of sentences in a specific logical domain language. There are two languages in each domain: the theoretical language (often mathematical) and the observational language, with correspondence rules linking the two. The link to common understandings in research in IS and neighbouring disciplines are clear, with the familiar discussion of theoretical constructs and associated empirical indicators. This position is also referred to as the "received view" (Suppe 2000). Winther notes that this perspective has active and able defenders today.
- The *Semantic View* investigates meaning and representation and argues that analyzing theory structure requires tools other than symbolic logic.[2] Proponents of this perspective include Suppes (1957) and Van Frassen (1989). According to Suppe (2000 S105), "the basic idea is that theory structures are connected with suitably connected families of models." Suppe claims that the Semantic View avoids problems with correspondence rules in the Syntactic View and shows how the relationship between theory and experiments is mediated by a non-deductive hierarchy of models for the experiment, for data, experimental design and ceteris paribus conditions (citing Suppes 1962). Frigg and Hartmann (2017) suggest examples of theoretical models are the Bohr model of the atom, evolutionary models in the social sciences and general equilibrium models of markets. In addition to countering difficulties perceived in the syntactic view, the semantic view also has a strong flavour of system theory concepts, including system boundaries, open and closed systems (models) and so on (e.g., see Dubin 1978). Winther concludes that the Semantic View is also "alive and well as a family of analyses of theory structure, and continues to be developed in interesting ways" (p. 30).
- The *Pragmatic View* explores theory use and studies how theorizing is actually done. Scientific theory is seen as internally and externally complex and includes a rich variety of both formal and non-formal components such as analogies, metaphors, values, ontological assumptions, natural kinds and classifications, stylized facts, mathematical concepts and techniques and computer modelling. Examples of analogies include the atom as a planetary system and the benzene ring as a snake biting its own tail (Kekulé). Proponents include Cartwright (1983) and Hacking (1983). Winther cites influences on this view as including Kuhn (1962). Supporters of this view do not necessarily reject the Syntactic and Semantic Views, but argue for the inclusion of informal in addition to formal components. Winther concludes that the Pragmatic View remains "under construction." "It acknowledges that scientists use and need different kinds of theories for a variety of purposes" (p. 45).

The Gregor (2006) essay on the nature of theory can be seen as congruent with the Pragmatic View because it categorizes theories in terms of their purpose and can be applied in fields such as IS where the purposes of theory include specifying design knowledge. The purposes of theory in the Gregor categorization are to analyze and describe, explain, predict and prescribe. As these aims are addressed to a greater or less extent in different types of theory, there is not one but five definitions of theory depending on its place in the theory taxonomy. Table 4.1 shows

Table 4.1 Definition of different theory types

Theory Type	Definition and Information Systems Examples
I. Analysis	This type of theory says what is. It does not extend beyond analysis and description, no causal relationships are specified and no predictions are made. Variants of this type are classifications, schema, frameworks or taxonomies. An example is Iivari, Hirschheim and Klein's (1988) dynamic framework for classifying IS development approaches and methodologies.
II. Explanation	This type of theory says what is, how, why, when and where. It provides causal explanations but does not aim to predict with any precision and has no testable propositions. These theories could be labelled as theories for understanding, or sense-making, as they lead to others viewing the world in a certain way. An example is Orlikowski's (1992) structurational model of technology.
III. Predicting	This type says what is and what will be. It has testable propositions but does not give explanations for the propositions. This type of theory is not common in information systems. Example may be found in economics and finance, where accurate predictions can be very valuable, even if the underlying causal mechanisms for assumptions are unknown. An example is the work by Moore (1965), who proposed Moore's law, relating improved technology circuits and cost.
IV. Explaining and Predicting	This type says what is, how, why, when, where and what will be. It predicts and has testable propositions and causal explanations. This is the most common and well-recognized type in information systems and may be equated with traditional scientific-type theory. An example is Bhattacherjee and Premkumar's (2004) work on temporal changes in user beliefs and attitudes toward IT usage.
V. Design and Action	This type gives guidance on how to do something. It is different in nature from the other types as it will contain imperative, prescriptive, statements: e.g., Do X1, X2, X3, . . . or Provide the system with the following functions and components . . . to achieve an outcome O. An example is Markus, Majchrzak and Gasser's (2002) theory for systems that support emergent knowledge processes.

Source: Adapted from Gregor (2006).

the definition for each type. The Gregor taxonomy still also has in part a semantic flavour, as it drew on Dubin (1978) for identifying the structural components of theory: means of representation, constructs, statements of relationship, scope and possibly also causal explanations, testable propositions and prescriptive statements.

Encouragingly, recent work in IS indicates that the discipline may be progressing to integrated bodies of knowledge with theory of different types, a focus on IS phenomena and what can be termed "native" IS theory. An example is the review and synthesis paper of Wiener et al. (2016, p. 471) that develops "an expanded theoretical framework for IS project control with supporting conjectures." Alter's Work System Theory is another example (Alter 2013). The *MIS Quarterly Research Curations* initiative can also be regarded in this light. The curation on research on trust and information and communication technology by Söllner et al. (2016) brings together articles with a range of theory types. In their overview of the progression of trust research, the curation team are able to identify what they term "thematic advances in knowledge," but could also be called theory. The team point to both "insights into how systems should be designed so that their users perceive them as being more trustworthy" (Type V design theory) and also testable propositions, such as "with regard to trust in virtual teams, multiple studies have shown the importance of trust among team members as an antecedent of team success" (Type IV theory). Further work that is relevant to IS and fits with the Pragmatic View is Brian Arthur's (2009) theory of the origins and evolution of technology. Arthur advances the proposition that rather than arising from insight moments of individual genius, new technology evolves by creating itself out of itself. Arthur uses many examples in his theorizing and also analogies, such as the relation of the forces of good and evil in Star Wars to humans' relationships with technology.

Having now made an argument for recognition of different types of theory in IS, we can turn to the question of how theories are developed.

The theorizing process

The process by which theories are developed is as important as the form in which a theory is expressed. Further, there are divergent views on how theorizing should occur, paralleling the different perspectives on what theory is. Again, these divergent views in part reflect historical developments in the philosophy of science and should be understood in terms of the context in which they were advanced.

A distinction that persists across viewpoints is that between theory building and theory testing, both of which can be considered as part of an overall theory development process. This distinction is also characterized as being between the "context of discovery" and the "context of justification" (Reichenbach 1938). The context of discovery refers to the generation of a new idea, hypothesis or theory and the context of justification to the test or verification of it. Perhaps unfortunately, some disciplines that influence research and journal practice in IS, such as management, emphasized for many years the importance of the context of justification (theory testing) at the expense of the context of discovery (theory building). In this they followed the falsificationist thinking of Popper (1980, p. 31), who stated:

> The question of how it happens that a new idea occurs to a man – whether it is musical theme, a dramatic conflict, or a scientific theory – may be of great interest to empirical psychology; but is it irrelevant to the logical analysis of scientific knowledge. This latter is concerned . . . only with questions of justification or validity.

Schickore (2011) concludes that the impact of this view on the philosophy of science for most of the 20th century can hardly be overestimated. Congruent with an emphasis on theory testing is the hypothetico-deductive method (H-D method), in which a hypothesis is put forward, perhaps derived from existing theory and then tested with observational data. The H-D method emphasizes deductive reasoning and avoids reliance on inductive reasoning, which Popper and others found problematic. Space precludes a detailed examination of the problem of induction, but Papineau (2002) provides good coverage of recent thinking. Further, the distinction between the two contexts is somewhat artificial. Hempel (1966) describes how in the early stages of reasoning about phenomena, attempts at theoretical explanations will be influenced by preliminary hypotheses about how phenomena are connected, which will guide analysis and classification of data. Theory building (the context of discovery) can involve an iterative process of imagination, initial hypothesizing, testing and data gathering until a researcher believes that a new theory provides a reasonable account for what is observed.

The ongoing concern for IS is that there has not been a great deal written for the context of discovery that supplements the H-D method and gives guidance on how theories are constructed. Grounded theory methods are an exception, but are certainly not the only method, as can be seen in the many forms of reasoning and experimentation employed in theory development (see Hempel 1966; Baggini 2016). For design science, Fischer and Gregor (2011) present an idealized model for theory development that shows that induction, abduction and deduction can all play a role in the context of discovery.

One reference is Jaccard and Jacoby (2010) who produced the monograph "Theory Construction and Model-Building Skills." This work has a focus on building theoretical models that link "variables" and lead to hypotheses that can be tested with statistical methods. It deals primarily with Type IV theory for explanation and prediction in the Gregor taxonomy. The authors do recognize, however, that qualitative methods such as grounded theory approaches exist and that these can lead to process-oriented theory.

A valuable and interesting work is "Great Minds in Management" (Smith and Hitt 2005), which brings together influential theorists in management and gives their reflections on their processes of theory development and their personal accounts of the gestation of these theories. Contributors include Argryis on double-loop learning, Barney on resource-based theory, Scott on institutional theory, Weick on sense-making and Mintzberg on theorizing itself. In their epilogue, Smith and Hitt reflect on the common themes in these firsthand accounts of the development of management theory. They conclude:

> We believe that the best way to learn how to develop theory is by studying the masters, who have developed important management theories. For the most part, the process of theory development is causally ambiguous, involving tacit and difficult-to-observe processes. Although well intentioned, prior literature on theory development has often been produced by scholars with limited experience in developing prominent theory.
>
> (pp. 572–573)

Smith and Hitt note that the various processes the master theorists used to develop their theories were complex and unique. Nevertheless, they distinguish four separate stages characterizing these processes.

1 *Tension/Phenomena*. For many of the theorists the starting point was a conflict or dissonance between the scholar's view of the world and observations of the world that represented contradictory findings, puzzles and so on. For example, Barney was motivated to develop the resource-based view to resolve conflict around different views on the nature of equality. Others found tensions arising from data that violated an accepted viewpoint. For example, Scott concluded from work on authority systems that work structures were determined by social and political processes rather than economic laws.

2 *Search*. In this phase there is exploration and discovery. There is discourse and interaction with other scholars, and career paths, location and serendipity may all play a role. The process is seen as a creative one where new theory results from exposure to and combinations of "new and seemingly unrelated matrices of thought and ideas" (p. 577).

3 *Elaboration/Research*. The process of elaboration is described variously as induction, detective work, sensemaking and research. It is noted that elaboration appears to occur in different ways based on the level of theoretical abstraction. When the theoretical concepts are closer to measurement, then elaboration is more like the scientific model of

quantitative research. In this case, other scholars may join in the process of testing and refining the theory. In other cases, where the concepts in the theory are further removed from measurement, elaboration is closer to a path that involves diagrams, description, and more qualitative research. Interestingly, Barney says that his framework for the resource-based view was never intended for empirical testing, but was meant to lead scholars to think about the attributes of resource-based logic.

4 *Proclamation/Presentation.* In this final phase the theory is presented to appropriate constituencies. A number of the eminent theorists struggled to get their ideas accepted, especially in top academic journals. Some had to write a series of conceptual and empirical articles that had to pass a threshold before acceptance. For example, Locke and Latham relied on 25 years of research in their book on goal setting in 1990. Other theorists have written books to propound their ideas without a series of journal articles beforehand. For example, Vroom published his monograph on *Work and Motivation* when only 28 years old and reflects later that he was "presumptuous." A number of the scholars express concerns about the academic publishing processes that made it hard for them to get their work accepted initially, possibly because they questioned norms at the time.

Interestingly, Smith and Hitt (2005, p. 581) conclude that "the purpose underlying the theory is important to the way it evolves. . . . The idea that theory can serve **multiple purposes**, from sensemaking to empirical testing, has not been well acknowledged in the literature" (emphasis added). This conclusion, based on the personal accounts of how eminent theorists developed important theories in management, is compatible with the description given earlier of the pragmatic perspective where different types of theories serve different ends. It is also compatible with the recognition of different types of theory in Gregor's 2006 taxonomy.

Given the overall theorizing process as represented by eminent theorists, we might reflect on how each of us can contribute to this process, without necessarily being bold enough to attempt an entirely new theory, but being more likely to attempt discrete contributions to theory in individual journal articles. Some insights into how this effect can be achieved are provided by Colquitt and Zapata-Phelan (2007), who reviewed the theoretical contributions made in articles in the 50 years from 1958 to 2007 in the *Academy of Management Journal*. These authors developed a taxonomy that reflects the theoretical contribution of empirical articles along two dimensions: *theory building* and *theory testing*. In their account, theory building is described as an inductive approach that can involve building on cases, using the grounded theory approach or ethnography. Inductive empirical articles typically conclude with a set of propositions that summarize the resulting theory, perhaps with a new framework or diagram. On the other hand, theory testing typically adopts the H-D approach, where hypotheses are proposed from theory then tested. From their taxonomy, Colquitt and Zapata-Phelan identify five types of contributions: (1) reporters – low on both testing and building (for example, replications); (2) testers – high on testing, low on building; (3) qualifiers – moderate levels of both (for example, adding a new moderating variable); (4) builders – high on building, low on testing; and (5) expanders – high on both building and testing (for example, focussing on constructs, relationships or processes that are linked to an existing theory but have not been studied. Colquitt and Zapata-Phelan find that articles that are rated moderate to high in terms of both theory building and theory testing enjoyed the highest rates of citations (that is, qualifiers and expanders).

The Colquitt and Zapata-Phelan taxonomy dimensions bear some resemblance to the Smith and Hitt (2005) theory building process in that theory building is akin to stages one and two of tension/phenomena and search, and theory testing is akin to some types of theory elaboration/

research. However, Colquitt and Zapata-Phelan's descriptions of theory building and testing are narrower, in that they do not capture the richness and variety of the processes, including creativity, described by the eminent theorists in Smith and Hitt. They do not include the role of review articles that synthesize a stream of research in their description of theory building. Nevertheless, Colquitt and Zapata-Phelan's taxonomy may be of use to researchers who want to identify the type of theoretical contribution their article makes in language that is acceptable to journals that follow a pattern similar to management journals, as many IS journals do.

The journal *MIS Quarterly* now has a section for theory and review articles and Suzanne Rivard (2014), a senior editor in this section, gives insights into what is expected for review articles that develop theory. She notes the needs for the motivation for a new theory, for definitional clarity, specification of the boundaries of the theory, for erudition and scholarship, for imagination, for explanation of relationships, for clear presentation, for cohesion and for a demonstrated contribution to knowledge.

For researchers wanting to contribute to design science, rather than more traditional forms of theory, Gregor and Hevner (2013) propose a framework that shows how different types of contributions can be made. Their taxonomy shows contributions in terms of two dimensions based on the existing state of knowledge in both the solution and problem domains for the research domain in question.

The theory contribution canvas

To summarize, thus far this chapter has shown different types of theory, described different views of the theorizing process and shown different ways of making contributions to knowledge in journal articles. This section takes up the topic of journal article contributions again and introduces a tool developed by the author that researchers can use when preparing an article for publication – *The Theory Contribution Canvas*.[3] These individual journal article contributions can be seen as individual steps in a larger encompassing theory development process.

The canvas allows researchers to depict an outline of their work in graphical form. It was developed in a series of workshops for PhD students and researchers. A number of the people who have been shown the canvas continue to use it, including the author. It can be used at any stage in planning and documenting research and can be revised as ideas mature and change. Using the canvas in groups and workshops is a good idea, as it allows one to explain the main argument in a piece of work to others and see how the argument can be clarified. Figure 4.1 shows an example of a canvas that was prepared in an initial workshop in Nuremberg, documenting the underlying structure of the knowledge claims in Komiak and Benbasat (2006) for demonstration purposes. The messy nature of this first effort is typical – a tidied-up version is shown later in the chapter.

The point of preparing the canvas is to expose the underlying argument in an article at a high-level, so one can separate "the wood from the trees." An important point, not yet added to Figure 4.1, is that one should be able to draw an arrow from the final section 5 back to the "theoretical background" section 2, to indicate exactly what theory has been contributed to and how. The motivation from the canvas came from the author having recently experienced the rejection of a journal article, which, in hindsight was warranted because of a failure to make this link explicit.

Note there are other devices and aids that can be used to help structure journal article submissions: the canvas is different because of its graphical form. It is meant as an aid and should not be used too prescriptively. The process of completing the canvas has some similarities with the model of engaged scholarship in Van de Ven (2007), whose work is strongly recommended

Shirley Gregor

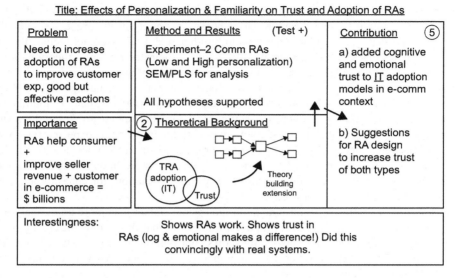

Figure 4.1 Unfinished workshop demonstration of use of the canvas

as further reading. Van de Ven also stresses the importance of the formulation of the research problem as a first step, and quotes Medawar (1979, p. 20):

> Any scientist of any age who wants to make important discoveries must study important problems. Dull or piffling problems yield dull or piffling answers.

There are four steps in using the canvas:

1 Start with an important problem;
2 Identify relevant existing theory, if any;
3 Plan the type of contribution (building/testing) and carry out the study with an acceptable method;
4 Tell the story – show the contribution to knowledge/theory and its "interestingness."

Each step is now described in more detail.

Step 1: describe the problem and its importance (motivation)

The process described here suggests starting with an important problem, one where others will be interested in the answer. Saying that one is addressing a gap in the literature is not usually sufficient in itself. Although there may be a theoretical gap, the gap might exist because that particular aspect of a problem area is not really of much interest. Rivard (2014) expresses similar views. Important problems will often be based in the real world, but some may address problems that are important for research itself, as in Gregor's (2006) work on theory. Alvesson and Sandberg (2011) also question the practice of spotting "gaps" in the literature as a basis for research questions and propose that research questions be generated through "problematization," where assumptions underlying existing theories are challenged, leading to more influential theories.

Some examples of real-world problems follow:

- Indigenous adoption of ICT in Australia is low. This problem is important because adoption can enhance employment opportunities for indigenous communities.
- Influences on the flow experience of web users are not well understood. This problem is important because flow is a desirable state to prolong web visits and increase revenue.
- There is a need to develop a new enterprise architecture for governments to handle complexity. The problem is important because current enterprise architecture methods do not allow trace-back to legislation.

The problem identified should relate to IS, otherwise there are likely to be difficulties publishing in IS journals. Identification of the problem and its importance then leads to the research goal, which is to solve the problem.

Step 2: identify relevant theory and prior knowledge

The next step is to identify the existing theory that relates to the problem being addressed. This step is incredibly important but difficult, in part because the complex problems in IS mean that many prior theories can relate to them. A suggestion is to ask, what is the classic concern that is being addressed? To what class of problems does my problem belong? It appears that the more the author can express this concern at a higher level of abstraction, the better. For example, many problems are associated at a high level of abstraction with decision making assisted by information technology, a long-standing classic concern in IS. In some areas there are now some classic concerns that are reasonably well recognized and review articles exist that draw prior work together and indicate important theory that others have used. Examples are Alavi and Leidner (2001) for knowledge management systems and Li and Karahanna (2015) for online recommendation systems. The MISQ curated sections now provide another useful resource.

A further suggestion at this point is to draw a diagram that can be added to the contribution canvas. This diagram may not appear in a published article but it can help make sense of different streams of research. For example, Venn diagrams as in Figure 4.2 can help represent theories and knowledge that relate to the problem and their inter-relationships. Tables can be used to summarize the results of prior empirical studies directly addressing the problem at hand, as in Kim et al. (2011) and also in the MISQ curated section on trust.

Step 3: choice of genre and method

The next step is the choice of genre, or the type of research that will be undertaken, and the research method. The problem and the existing state of knowledge should help in identifying the type of contribution. When thinking in terms of the Colquitt and Zapata-Phelan (2007) taxonomy, the author can identify whether the genre is reporter, tester, qualifier, builder or expander, or more simply theory building versus theory testing.

The choice of the method is usually the most straightforward step, in that there are well-documented methods to suit whatever genre has been chosen. If theory building, then one can choose methods such as theory building from cases, grounded theory methods or theoretical reviews including prior empirical work. If theory testing, then there are many choices also: for example, experiments, surveys and so on. Researchers engaged in design science can consult work such as Peffers et al. (2007–2008) or Kuechler and Vaishnavi (2012). Work such as Galliers (1991) can help guide the choice of method.

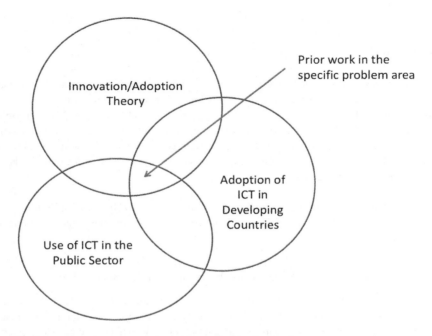

Figure 4.2 Diagrammatic representation of theoretical background
Source: Adapted from Imran (2010).

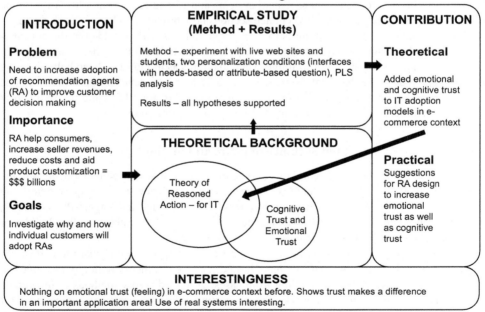

Figure 4.3 Completed example of research contribution canvas
Source: Based on Komiak and Benbasat (2006).

Step 4: tell the story

The final step is to complete the story by explicitly showing in the final sections of an article what the contribution to knowledge is, as well as any other aspects of the study that demonstrate its interestingness. It should be possible to make an explicit link between the statement of the contribution made and a body of knowledge/theory that was presented in Step 2, as shown by the arrow in Figure 4.3. This step completes the canvas.

Searching the article by Komiak and Benbasat (2006) shows wording that explicitly makes this linkage:

> In terms of contributions to theory, these findings, if supported by additional research, would indicate that adding emotional trust and cognitive trust to IT adoption models in e-commerce contexts is appropriate.
>
> (p. 957)

Discussion

This chapter has discussed the conceptualization of theory in IS, showing that different views on theory can be linked to underlying perspectives in the philosophy of science. Three overarching perspectives are identified, namely, the Syntactic, Semantic and Pragmatic Views. Current thinking suggests that a pragmatic perspective on theory is appropriate, where different kinds of theories are recognized as being used depending on the purposes of researchers. Gregor's (2006) taxonomy of theory is presented. The taxonomy has a pragmatic flavour as it recognizes different types of theory in terms of the different aims that theory serves, namely, description, explanation, prediction and prescription (design and action).

The work of Smith and Hitt (2005) is used as a basis for depicting theorizing processes as complex, but with recognizable stages of tension/phenomena, search, elaboration/research and proclamation/presentation. This depiction of theorizing has the merits of being based on the reflections of scholars who themselves developed prominent management theories. A comparison is made between this grounded view and the stylized depiction of theory building (Context of Discovery) and theory testing (Context of Justification) phases used in analyzing management journal practices. These grounded reflections also lead to the conclusion that theory can serve multiple purposes, from sense-making to predicting, compatible with the Gregor taxonomy.

The final section of the chapter introduces the Theory Contribution Canvas, a graphical tool that is designed to assist individual researchers in their goal to demonstrate how their own efforts are part of the grand journey of theory development and knowledge building.

Acknowledgements

Thank you to participants in workshops at universities in Nuremberg, Canberra, Singapore and Brisbane who helped refine the ideas in this chapter. Further thanks are due to Izak Benbasat, Ulrich Frank, Alexander Maedche, Guido Schryen, Mikko Siponen, Gerit Wagner and Ron Weber, who commented on earlier versions of the chapter. Support from Albrecht Fritzsche and the Schoeller Research Center at the Friedrich Alexander University Erlangen-Nuremberg is gratefully acknowledged.

Notes

1 The labels for the three perspectives correspond to terminology introduced in semiotics by Morris (1938).

2 Lorenzano (2013) argues that the "structuralist" view should also be included in the semantic perspective.
3 A debt for the idea of using a "canvas" is acknowledged to Osterwalder, Pigneur et al. and their book on *Business Model Generation* (2010).

References

Alavi, M. and Leidner, D. (2001). Review: Knowledge Management and Knowledge Management Systems: Conceptual Foundations and Research Issues. *MIS Quarterly*, 25, 1.
Alter, S. (2013). Work System Theory: Overview of Core Concepts, Extensions, and Challenges for the Future. *Journal of the Association for Information Systems*, 14, 2, 72–121.
Alvesson, M. and Sandberg, J. (2011). Generating Research Questions Through Problematization. *Academy of Management Review*, 36, 2, 247–271.
Arthur, B. (2009). *The Nature of Technology: What It Is and How It Evolves*. London: Allen Lane.
Avison, D. and Malaurent, J. (2014). Is Theory King? Questioning the Theory Fetish in Information Systems. *Journal of Information Technology*, 29, 4, 327–336.
Baggini, J. (2016). *The Edge of Reason*. New Haven: Yale University Press.
Bhattacherjee, A., and Premkumar, G. (2004). Understanding Changes in Belief and Attitude Towards Information Technology Usage: A Theoretical Model and Longitudinal Test. *MIS Quarterly*, 28, 2, 229–254.
Cartwright, N. (1983). *How the Laws of Physics Lie*. New York: Oxford University Press. St Lucia, Qld: University of Queensland Press.
Colquitt, J. and Zapata-Phelan, C. (2007). Trends in Theory Building and Theory Testing: A Five-Decade Study of the Academy of Management Journal. *Academy of Management Journal*, 50, 6, 1281–1303.
Dubin, R. (1978). *Theory Building*. New York: Free Press.
Feldman, D. (2004). What Are We Talking About When We Talk About Theory? *Journal of Management*, 30, 5, 565–567.
Feyerabend, P. (1975). *Against Method: Outline of an Anarchist Theory of Knowledge*. Atlantic Highlands, NJ: New Left Books.
Fischer, C. and Gregor, S. (2011). Forms of Reasoning in the Design Science Research Process. In Jain, H., Sinha, A. and Vitharana, P. (Eds.). *Service-Oriented Perspectives in Design Science Research (6th DESRIST), Lecture Notes in Computer Science*, Heidelberg: Springer, pp. 17–31.
Frigg, R, and Hartmann, S. (2017). Models in Science. *Stanford Encyclopedia of Philosophy* (Spring 2017 Edition), Edward N. Zalta (ed.), URL: https://plato.stanford.edu/archives/spr2017/entries/models-science/.
Galliers, R. (1991). Choosing Appropriate Information Systems Approaches: A Revised Taxonomy. In Nissen, H-E., Klein, H. K. and Hirschheim, R. (Eds.). *Information Systems Research: Contemporary Approaches and Emergent Traditions*, Amsterdam: North Holland, pp. 327–345.
Godfrey-Smith, P. (2003). *Theory and Reality: An Introduction to the Philosophy of Science*. Chicago: University of Chicago Press.
Gregor, S. (2006). The Nature of Theory in Information Systems. *MIS Quarterly*, 30, 3, 611–642.
Gregor, S. and Hevner, A. (2013). Positioning and Presenting Design Science Research for Maximum Impact. *MIS Quarterly*, 37, 2, 337–355.
Gregor, S. and Jones, D. (2007). The Anatomy of a Design Theory. *Journal of the Association of Information Systems*, 8, 5, 312–335.
Hacking, I. (1983). *Representing and Intervening: Introductory Topics in the Philosophy of Natural Science*. Cambridge: Cambridge University Press.
Hempel, C. (1966). *Philosophy of Natural Science*. Englewood Cliffs, NJ: Prentice-Hall.
Imran, A. (2010). *Information Communication Technology Adoption in Governments of the Least Developed Countries: A Case Study of Bangladesh*. Unpublished PhD Thesis, Australian National University.
Iivari, J., Hirschheim, R., and Klein, H. K. (1998). A Paradigmatic Analysis Contrasting Information Systems Development Approaches and Methodologies. *Information Systems Research*, 9, 2, 164–193.
Jaccard, J. and Jacoby, J. (2010). *Theory Construction and Model-Building Skills*. New York: Guilford Press.
Kim, G., Shin, B., Kim, K. K., and Lee, H. G. (2011). IT Capabilities, Process-Oriented Dynamic Capabilities, and Firm Financial Performance. *Journal of the Association for Information Systems*, 12, 7, 1.

Komiak, S. and Benbasat, I. (2006). The Effects of Personalization and Familiarity on Trust and Adoption of Recommendation Agents. *MIS Quarterly*, 30, 4, 941–960.

Kuechler, W. and Vaishnavi, V. (2012). A Framework for Theory Development in Design Science Research: Multiple Perspectives. *Journal of the Association for Information Systems*, 13, 6.

Kuhn, T. (1962). *Structure of Scientific Revolutions*. Chicago: University of Chicago Press.

Lewin, K. (1945). The Research Centre for Group Dynamics at Massachusetts Institute of Technology. *Sociometry*, 8, 126–135.

Li, S. and Karahanna, E. (2015). Online Recommendation Systems in a B2C E-Commerce Context: A Review and Future Directions. *Journal of the Association for Information Systems*, 16, 2, 2.

Lorenzano, P. (2013). The Semantic Conception and the Structuralist View of Theories: A Critique of Suppe's Criticisms. *Studies in History and Philosophy of Science*, 44, 4, 600–607.

Markus, M., Majchrzak, L.A., and Gasser, L. (2002). A Design Theory for Systems That Support Emergent Knowledge Processes. *MIS Quarterly*, 26, 3, 179–212.

Medawar, P.B. (1979). *Advice to a Young Scientist*. New York: Harper & Row.

Moore, G.E. (1965). Cramming More Components Onto Integrated Circuits. *Electronics*, 38, 8, 114–117.

Morris, C. (1938). Foundations of a Theory of Signs. In Neurath, O., Carnap, R. and Morris, C. (Eds.). *International Encyclopedia of Unified Science*, Chicago: University of Chicago Press, pp. 77–138.

National Academy of Sciences (1999). *Science and Creationism: A View From the National Academy of Sciences* (2nd ed.). National Academic Press.

Orlikowski, W.J. (1992). The Duality of Technology: Rethinking the Concept of Technology in Organizations, *Organization Science*, 3, 3, 398–427.

Osterwalder, A., Pigneur, Y. and Smith, A. and 470 Practitioners From 45 Countries (2010). *Business Model Generation*, self-published.

Papineau, D. (2002). Philosophy of Science. In Bunnin, N. and Tsui-James, E.P. (Eds.). *The Blackwell Companion to Philosophy*, Hoboken, NJ: John Wiley & Sons, pp. 286–316.

Peffers, K., Tuunanen, T., Rothenberger, M. and Chatterjee, S. (2007–8). A Design Science Research Methodology for Information Systems Research. *Journal of Management Information Systems*, 24, 3, 45–77.

Popper, K. (1980). *The Logic of Scientific Discovery*. London: Unwin Hyman.

Reichenbach, H. (1938). *Experience and Prediction: An Analysis of the Foundations and the Structure of Knowledge*. Chicago: University of Chicago Press.

Rivard, S. (2014). Editor's Comments: The Ions of Theory Construction. *MIS Quarterly*, 38, 2, ii–xii.

Ruse, M. (1995). Theory. In Honderich, T. (Ed.). *The Oxford Companion to Philosophy*, Oxford, UK: Oxford University Press, pp. 870–871.

Scharff, R. and Dusek, V. (2003). *Philosophy of Technology: The Technological Condition: An Anthology*. Malden, MA: Blackwell.

Schickore, J. (2011). Scientific Discovery. In Zalta, E., Nodelman, U., Allen, C. and Perry, J. (Eds.). *Stanford Encyclopaedia of Philosophy*. URL: https://plato.stanford.edu/entries/scientific-method/ (Accessed Dec. 2016).

Simon, H. (1969). *The Sciences of the Artificial*. Cambridge, MA: MIT Press.

Smith, K. and Hitt, M. (Eds.). (2005). *Great Minds in Management: The Process of Theory Development*. Oxford: Oxford University Press.

Söllner, M., Benbasat, I., Gefen, D., Leimeister, J.M. and Pavlou, P.A. Trust. In *MIS Quarterly Research Curations*, Ashley Bush and Arun Rai, (Eds.). http://misq.org/research-curations, October 31, 2016.

Suppe, F. (2000). Understanding Scientific Theories: An Assessment of Developments, 1969–1998. *Philosophy of Science*, 67 (Proceedings), pp. S102–S115.

Suppes, P. (1957). *Introduction to Logic*. Princeton: D. Van Nostrand.

Suppes, P. (1962). Models of Data. In Nagel, E., Suppes, P. and Tarski, A. (Eds.). *Logic, Methodology and Philosophy of Science: Proceedings of the 1960 International Congress*, Stanford: Stanford University Press, 252–261.

Van de Ven, A. (2007). *Engaged Scholarship: A Guide for Organizational and Social Research*. Oxford: Oxford University Press.

van Frassen, B. (1989). *Laws and Symmetry*. New York: Oxford University Press.

von Bertalanffy, L. (1950). An Outline of General Systems Theory. *British Journal of Philosophy of Science*, 1, 139–164.

Weber, R. (2012). Evaluating and Developing Theories in the Information Systems Discipline. *Journal of the Association for Information Systems*, 13, 1, 1–30.

Weick, K. (1995). What Theory Is Not, Theorizing Is. *Administrative Science Quarterly*, 40, 3, 385–390.

Wiener, N. (1948). *Cybernetics: Control and Communication in the Animal and the Machine*. New York: Wiley.

Wiener, M., Mähring, M., Remus, U. and Carol Saunders, C. (2016). Control Configuration and Control Enactment in Information Systems Projects: Review and Expanded Theoretical Framework, *MIS Quarterly*, 40, 3, 741–774.

Winther, R. (2016). The Structure of Scientific Theories. In Zalta, E., Nodelman, U., Allen, C. and Perry, J. (Eds.). *Stanford Encyclopaedia of Philosophy*. URL: https://stanford.library.sydney.edu.au/archives/fall2016/entries/structure-scientific-theories/ (Accessed Dec. 2016)

5
WHAT LITERATURE REVIEW TYPE SHOULD I CONDUCT?[1]

Ana Ortiz de Guinea[2] and Guy Paré

> Good research builds on that which was done before, and uses previous research to ground current research in theory and as a lens for interpreting results.
> (Jennex 2015, p. 140)

Introduction

The growth of the information systems (IS) field has created new knowledge at a rate outpacing our individual capacity for recall, sense-making, and use (Paré et al. 2016). The number of peer-reviewed journals currently publishing IS research and the number of IS-related academic conferences has been steadily on the rise. Most likely, the IS knowledge base will continue to expand in the coming years. While this must be interpreted as a clear sign of relevance and vitality, our domain's expansion also translates into a body of knowledge that is increasingly fragmented (Paré et al. 2016).

Our current situation arises partly from historic trends in IS scholarship – as a relatively new discipline, we have tended to privilege development of new frameworks and models over confirmatory studies. A diversity of business and technology contexts results in a tendency to freely modify existing constructs and models (Tate et al. 2015), with the result that the extent to which even studies that purportedly use the same theory are actually commensurable is often unclear. However, we cannot continue to plead the newness of our discipline and the novelty of our phenomena indefinitely. After four decades of research, and thousands, even tens of thousands of research articles in some key areas of the discipline, it is reasonable to expect that by now we would be able to synthesize and accumulate that knowledge in a rigorous way (Templier and Paré 2015). Failure to do this has many risks, which have the potential to undermine our reputation and status as an academic discipline. Some of these risks include underuse of research evidence by IS researchers and practitioners, overuse of limited or inconclusive findings, and misuse and "cherry picking" of existing research by basing conclusions on a few studies at the expense of the larger body of research evidence. Put simply, much of the effort and expense that goes into the creation of individual knowledge artifacts is wasted if that knowledge cannot become part of a greater whole.

Fortunately, there has been a recent explosion of interest in editorials and regular articles investigating literature reviews as a research method in our field, IS. As we see it, the recent literature on literature reviews can be divided into two main topics. First, efforts have been made at providing authors with advice on how to conduct literature reviews as well as how to assess or evaluate their quality. For example, Templier and Paré (2015) proposed a set of guidelines for evaluating the level of rigor of families of reviews. Others have proposed a standardized methodology for conducting literature reviews (Okoli 2015), developed a typology of review types to be considered relevant to the IS field (Paré et al. 2015), and contributed to a debate about the importance of systematicity in conducting reviews (Boell and Cecez-Kecmanovic 2015; Schultze 2015). Second, efforts have also aimed at developing a set of specific tools and methods for conducting high-quality literature reviews. For instance, Bandara et al. (2015) provided insights on how to use qualitative data analysis and tools for conducting literature reviews, Houy et al. (2015) adapted the stylized facts method from economics as a tool for summarizing when conducting reviews, and Wall et al. (2015) proposed critical discourse analysis as a literature review methodology.

Despite these recent, yet important contributions, we posit that one particular issue remains underlooked. Given the diversity of literature review genres and types, to our knowledge there exists no tool that helps IS scholars and graduate students decide which particular type of literature review to conduct in a given situation. Hence, the present chapter primarily aims to fill this important gap. Before moving to the next section, we would like to provide a definition of what we understand by literature review in this chapter. Our aim goal is to present a general definition that encompasses all types of reviews and that is aligned with existing definitions (e.g., Okoli 2015; Paré et al. 2015; Rowe 2014; Schryen 2015; Webster and Watson 2002). So, *a stand-alone literature review is a document which provides a synthesis of the body of knowledge on one or several specified domains, topics, theories or research methods.*

The remaining of this chapter is structured as follows. We first identify and illustrate various types of reviews that are considered to be most relevant to IS. Second, we propose and explain a decision tree (along with its dimensions) that aims to help prospective authors of reviews decide how to best position their contribution. Finally, we end this chapter with a brief discussion of the main contributions and limitations of our work.

Main types of reviews relevant to the information systems field

With the growing interest in literature reviews, there have been several papers that have developed typologies or taxonomies of the existing types of literature reviews (e.g., Paré and Kitsiou 2016; Paré et al. 2015; Schryen 2015). Building upon the work of these authors, we present 10 types of literature reviews that are considered to be most relevant to the IS community.

First, *narrative reviews* describe what has been written on a given domain or topic (Hart 2003). These reviews are usually unsystematic in the sense that they do not follow a set of well-specified criteria or they do not report it, and as a result they suffer from subjectivity (Paré and Kitsiou 2016; Paré et al. 2015). Narrative reviews usually do not claim generalization of cumulative knowledge (Paré et al. 2015), and their general purpose is to provide a comprehensive background on a topic as well as some directions for future research (Paré and Kitsiou 2016). As an example of a narrative review, Vaast and Walsham (2013) reviewed a selected set of articles dealing with grounded theory and electronically mediated social contexts and they drew some recommendations for future research.

Second, *descriptive reviews*, also called quantitative systematic reviews (Pickering and Byrne 2014), aim to evaluate the extent to which prior research shows any trends or interpretable patterns about research outcomes, methods, or theories (Paré and Kitsiou 2016; Paré et al. 2015). In comparison to narrative reviews, the search and screening processes as well as the data extraction and analysis methods of descriptive reviews are more structured and transparent (Paré and Kitsiou 2016). In a descriptive review each article included in the sample represents a unit of analysis (Paré et al. 2015). As an example, Paré et al. (2008) reiterated the observations and suggestions made by Markus and Robey (1988) on the causal structure of IT impact theories and carry out an analysis of empirical research published in four major IS journals between 1991 and 2005.

Third, *scoping reviews* aim to provide an initial indication of the potential size and nature of the available literature on a emergent topic (Paré et al. 2015, p. 187). In line with their main objective, scoping reviews usually conclude with the presentation of a detailed research agenda for future works along with potential implications for practice and research (Paré and Kitsiou 2016). Unlike narrative and descriptive reviews, the whole point of scoping an emergent topic is to be as comprehensive as possible, including gray literature (Arksey and O'Malley 2005). The review process is systematic and transparent and the coding of articles is usually performed by multiple raters (Paré et al. 2015). As an example of a scoping review in our field, Smith et al. (2011) surveyed prior information privacy research, mapped the extant literature in different ways, and drew several conclusions. In an appendix, they provided a description of the approach they followed to identify a relevant set of articles.

Fourth, *critical reviews* usually look for inconsistencies, contradictions, and weaknesses in prior research (Paré and Kitsiou 2016; Paré et al. 2015) through an approach called problematization (Alvesson and Sandberg 2011). Problematization goes beyond gap spotting by "challenging assumptions of underlying existing literature" (Alvesson and Sandberg 2011, pp. 251–252). Unlike other review types, critical reviews attempt to take a reflective account of the research that has been done in a particular area of interest, and assess its credibility by using appraisal instruments or other methods. An exemplar of this review type is the article by Schryen (2013) on IS business value. In this review, the author provides a synthesis of the extant literature and pinpoints a few critical problems including the heterogeneity in the relation between IS investments and productivity across companies and the mismeasurement of key constructs.

Fifth, a *conceptual review* usually focuses on a single concept along with its basic elements (Walker and Avant 2010). The main idea is to examine the structure and function of a given concept in order to help in distinguishing it from other related concepts (Walker and Avant 2010). Conceptual reviews involve the identification of the ways in which a given concept has been defined and the identification of its core attributes as well as its antecedents and consequences (Walker and Avant 2010). For example, Alavi and Leidner (2001) reviewed the related concepts of knowledge, knowledge management, and knowledge management systems in order to shed light onto organizational knowledge management processes such as knowledge transfer across individuals and groups.

Sixth, the main purpose of *theory development reviews* (Webster and Watson 2002) is to provide plausible explanations of a phenomenon (Paré et al. 2015) and build solid theories (Schryen 2015). These reviews not only synthesize literature often bringing different streams of research together but they go a step further in developing a theoretical framework or model often in the form of research hypotheses or propositions (Paré et al. 2015). A good example in our field is a review of the banner processing literature by Sun et al. (2013). The authors review the literature on how people process advertising banners online and they develop both a process model that explains the different transitions between banner processing modes and a variance model that helps explain individuals' attention to banners.

The next three types of review all aim at theory testing. First, a *meta-analysis* uses statistical techniques to summarize and synthesize prior empirical results on a given topic (King and

He 2005). Meta-analyses provide precise estimates of relations between variables because they adjust for sample size and reliability of measures (Lipsey and Wilson 2001). It is important, however, to note that meta-analyses are not recommended if there is too much heterogeneity in prior studies (Paré and Kitsiou 2016). In fact, some argue that the topics composing the IS field do not meet the methodological requirements of meta-analyses, nor can they provide adequate data due to heterogeneity reasons (Houy et al. 2015). Despite these claims, several meta-analyses have been published in IS research. For example, Ortiz de Guinea et al. (2012) conducted a meta-analysis of virtualness on team processes and outcomes. They found that moderators like analysis at the group or individual level, and the short or long time orientation of a team played a central role in some of the relations between virtualness and processes and outcomes.

But there are situations in which it is not appropriate to pool studies together using meta-analytic (statistical) methods simply because there is too much heterogeneity between the included studies or variation in measurement tools, comparisons, or outcomes of interest. In these situations, systematic reviews can use qualitative synthesis approaches or methods such as vote counting, content analysis, and thematic analysis, as an alternative approach to narratively synthesize the results of the studies included in the sample (Paré and Kitsiou 2016). This form of aggregative review is known as *qualitative systematic review*. An example of this type of review in our field is the article by Petter et al. (2008) which reviews 180 papers found in the academic literature for the period 1992–2007 dealing with some aspect of IS success. Using the six dimensions of the DeLone and McLean (1992) model – system quality, information quality, service quality, use, user satisfaction, and net benefits – 90 empirical studies were analyzed and the results summarized. A total of 15 pairwise associations between the success constructs were investigated. The final type of theory-testing review is called *umbrella review* (Thomson et al. 2010). In comparison with meta-analyses and qualitative systematic reviews who analyze research findings from primary studies, umbrella reviews aim at synthesizing the findings of prior systematic reviews (Thomson et al. 2010). This is why they are often referred to as tertiary types of evidence synthesis (Paré and Kitsiou 2016). As an example, Kitsiou et al. (2015) conducted a review of systematic reviews in order to test the magnitude of the effects of home telemonitoring interventions on patients with chronic heart failure.

As explained earlier, theory-testing reviews are concerned with relationships or causal associations. Such logic is most appropriate for fields like medicine and education, where findings of randomized controlled trials can be aggregated to see whether a new treatment or intervention does improve outcomes (Paré and Kitsiou 2016). However, many argue that it is not possible to establish such direct causal links between interventions and outcomes in fields such as management and IS, where for any intervention there is unlikely to be a consistent outcome (Oates 2011; Rousseau et al. 2008). In such fields, *realist reviews* can be of great value. Their main goal is to understand the mechanisms by which a particular outcome occurs (or not) in a particular context. So, instead of asking the question – what works? – which is usually associated with meta-analyses and qualitative systematic reviews, a realist review asks: what is it about this intervention that works, for whom, in what circumstances, in what respects, and why? An example of a realist review is the article by Otte-Trojel et al. (2014) that synthesized prior findings on patient web portals and their outcomes. In this review, the authors observed among others that when patient portals are part of integrated health networks they lead to more positive outcomes (Otte-Trojel et al. 2014).

Before we move to the next section, it is interesting to note that not all review types are prevalent in our domain. Indeed, a recent survey by Paré et al. (2015) showed that theoretical and narrative reviews are the most frequently published forms of reviews while realist and umbrella reviews are yet to be found in our top-tier outlets.

Choosing the most appropriate review type

Choosing the most appropriate review type in a given situation is a strategic decision that depends on several factors. The decision tree we propose in Figure 5.1 builds upon a set of dimensions or characteristics that we borrowed from existing taxonomies (e.g., Cooper 1988; Rowe 2014). As mentioned earlier, to our knowledge this is the first attempt to develop such a decision tool.

The first dimension of our decision tree corresponds to the overarching goal of the review with respect to theory. According to Rowe (2014), there are four possibilities: describing (atheoretically), understanding, explaining, and theory testing. First, describing means to summarize prior research in categories or to classify what is known about a particular topic (Rowe 2014). As shown in Figure 5.1, three types of review fall under this category, namely, narrative, descriptive, and scoping reviews. The second possibility refers to providing an understanding of a "new phenomenon or problem through related concept(s) that have been proposed in former research" (Rowe 2014, p. 244). The idea is to synthesize prior research and develop an overall understanding of a given topic or phenomenon. A related goal of understanding is to identify key results, issues, and ways to solve such issues (Rowe 2014). There are two particular types of review that belong to this category, namely, critical and conceptual reviews. The third goal with respect to theory is called explaining. Reviews whose main objective is to provide a novel explanation often produce new theories, models, or frameworks. Hence, theoretical and realist reviews belong to this category. The fourth goal with respect to theory is theory testing. Aggregative reviews, which can take the form of meta-analyses, qualitative systematic reviews, or umbrella reviews, focus on synthesizing quantitatively or qualitatively prior empirical findings pertaining to a given theory, model, or hypothesis.

The second dimension refers to the twin concepts of systematicity and transparency. On the one hand, systematicity is an important part of trustworthiness of a review that strongly relates to its internal validity or credibility (Paré et al. 2016). With the exception of narrative reviews, the other review types described earlier show a high level of systematicity, in that they employ structured methods to search, screen, and evaluate relevant literature. It is important to note, however, that although reviews may be conducted in a systematic manner, many do not report on such methods. In other words, they do not show a high level of transparency (Paré et al. 2016). Transparency is paramount for the reliability (in the positivist tradition) or consistency (in the interpretivist tradition) of stand-alone reviews (Paré et al. 2016). It is recognized that umbrella reviews, meta-analyses, and qualitative systematic reviews are the most systematic and transparent forms of reviews (King and He 2005; Okoli 2015; Paré and Kitsiou 2016).

The third dimension is called focus. It refers to the main or primary lens of the literature review (e.g., Cooper 1988). Narrative and scoping reviews usually focus on a particular topic, whereas descriptive reviews focus on a topic, a research method, or even a given field. As an example, Dubé and Paré (2003) provided a descriptive review of the extent to which positivist IS case studies published between 1990 and 1999 were rigorously conducted. Critical reviews, for their part, focus on the underlying assumptions of a given literature whereas conceptual reviews are concept centric and thus, they focus on the synthesis and development of concepts. Theoretical reviews center on elements of theories such as hypotheses or propositions whereas

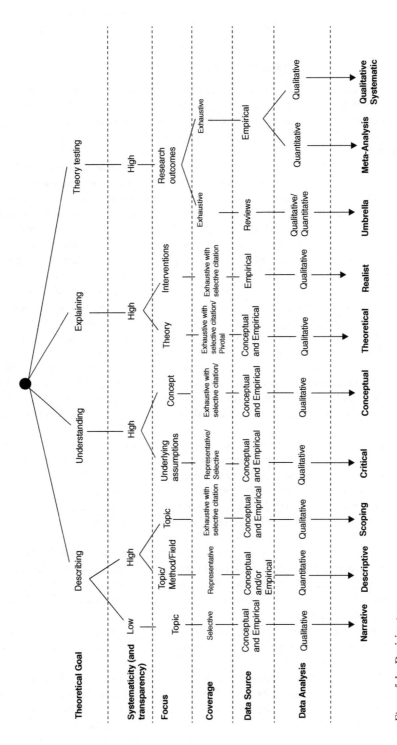

Figure 5.1 Decision tree

the focal point of realist reviews are complex interventions such as the deployment of enterprise systems like enterprise resource planning (ERP) and customer relationship management (CRM) systems in organizations. Finally, umbrella, meta-analytic, and qualitative systematic reviews focus on research outcomes.

The fourth dimension is called coverage, that is, how review authors "search the literature and how they make decisions about" the suitability of the material (Cooper 1988). While systematicity has to do with the existence of appropriate and well-defined methods to search the literature, evaluate, and extract data from the input materials, coverage deals with the exhaustivity of the literature search and the presentation of materials. According to Cooper (1988) and Paré et al. (2015), there are five coverage strategies. First, exhaustive coverage involves the inclusion of all relevant literature (or most of it). This type of coverage is a fundamental characteristic of all forms of aggregative reviews, that is, meta-analyses, qualitative systematic reviews, and umbrella reviews. The second type of coverage "bases conclusions on entire literatures, but only a selected sample of works is actually described" in the review (Cooper 1988, p. 111). Cooper (1988) calls this strategy exhaustive coverage with selective citation. Reviews that aim at explaining (i.e., theoretical and realist reviews), as well as conceptual and scoping reviews, often use this particular form of coverage. Third, representative coverage refers to the presentation of "works that are representative of many other works in a field" (Cooper 1988, p. 111). Several descriptive reviews in our field have surveyed the materials published in a sample of journals, often associated with the "basket of eight" (e.g., Paré et al. 2008). Fourth, central or pivotal coverage is when a review concentrates on works that have had a pivotal role in a given topic or domain (Cooper 1988). Theoretical reviews occasionally use this form of coverage (e.g., Briggs et al. 2008; Greenaway and Chan 2005). Last, selective coverage is when the authors of a review survey only the evidence that is readily available to them (Paré et al. 2015). Narrative reviews are often criticized because the authors selectively ignore or limit the attention paid to certain studies in order to make a point. In this rather unsystematic approach, the selection of information from primary articles is highly subjective, lacks explicit criteria for inclusion, and can lead to biased interpretations or inferences (Paré and Kitsiou 2016).

The fifth dimension refers to the data source or the types of papers (input) that feed the literature review. Conceptual papers refer to theoretical works whereas empirical works refer to papers that have some primary/secondary and qualitative/quantitative data. Most literature reviews, such as narrative, scoping, critical, conceptual, and theoretical reviews are very inclusive and will consider both conceptual and empirical papers. Descriptive reviews can include both or either conceptual and/or empirical papers. Umbrella reviews include only review articles as they are overviews of reviews. Lastly, meta-analyses and qualitative systematic reviews are restricted to empirical works because their primary goal is to test theory.

The sixth and final dimension refers to data analysis, that is, how the extant literature is being reviewed and analyzed. In descriptive and meta-analysis reviews, for instance, quantitative techniques are employed such as frequency analysis and meta-analytic statistical analyses. Many types of reviews, such as narrative, scoping, critical, conceptual, theoretical, realist, and qualitative systematic use qualitative data analysis techniques such as narrative summary, content or thematic analysis, or other interpretive methods such as grounded theory. Finally, umbrella reviews can employ either qualitative methods or quantitative ones.

To summarize, the purpose of the decision tree presented in Figure 5.1 is to help prospective authors of review articles make the appropriate decision with regard to the type of review to conduct. According to Gregor (2006), classifications attempt to analyze the "what" instead of forecasting predictions or explaining causality. To some, this type of classification is the most basic type of theory (Fawcett and Downs 1986), which is a prerequisite to good scientific method by providing the uniformities and differences of the different review types covered in this chapter (Gregor 2006). It is thus important to note that the decision tree proposed here shows the similarities and differences across review types and as such, each path of the decision tree is characterized by a high level of internal coherence.

Concluding remarks

In our viewpoint, literature reviews are critical for the development and evolution of any discipline, and the IS field is no exception. With this in mind, our main objectives in this chapter are threefold. First, our intention is to help prospective authors of review articles to better understand the main similarities and differences among the most relevant review types to the IS community. Second, the decision tree proposed here can contribute further in helping IS scholars and graduate students choose the type of review that best suits their goals. Third, our decision tree can also help reviewers and editors in the assessment of submitted review articles. According to Jennex (2015) there are several factors that lower the quality of a review article: (a) when the review contains materials from some relevant journals but not others, (b) when the search criteria is weak, (c) when the search criteria is artificial, (d) when the author does not go to the original source, and (e) when the author does not understand the source. Such factors point to two important dimensions covered in our decision tree, namely, systematicity and coverage. Several authors have highlighted the importance of these two criteria when evaluating the quality of a review article (Paré et al. 2016). These dimensions shall guide reviewers and editors in terms of what to expect and what to look for when they are faced with a particular review article. On the one hand, our decision tree indicates that not all reviews must conduct an exhaustive coverage strategy to be considered of high quality. On the other hand, consistent with Paré et al. (2016), our decision tree shows that systematicity (and transparency) shall be considered an important trait of virtually all review types.

Although our decision tree covers a wide variety of review types, we do not pretend that it is exhaustive. Indeed, we recognize that there are other types of reviews such as meta-synthesis (Hoon 2013) and meta-ethnography (Lee et al. 2015) that could contribute to building a cumulative tradition in our field. Future extensions of our work shall consider these review types. Importantly, although we believe most literature reviews would fit well in one of the 10 paths included in our decision tree, we must acknowledge that some reviews share characteristics of two or more review types. These are called hybrid reviews (Paré et al. 2015) or mixed-methods reviews (Schryen 2013). For instance, Joseph et al. (2007) performed three distinct yet complementary types of reviews in order to investigate the factors influencing turnover of IS professionals. As another example, Chiasson et al. (2008) conducted a narrative review followed by a descriptive review in order to evaluate action research in the IS discipline.

To conclude, we hope our classification of review types along with the decision tree will help members of the IS community better understand and appreciate the wide diversity of review types available to them and, most importantly, select the one that best corresponds to their particular situation.

Notes

1 Both authors contributed equally to this book chapter.
2 Corresponding author: ana.ortiz-de-guinea@hec.ca.

References

Alavi, M., and Leidner, D. E. 2001. "Knowledge Management and Knowledge Management Systems: Conceptual Foundations and Research Issues," *MIS Quarterly* (25:1), pp. 107–136.

Alvesson, M., and Sandberg, J. 2011. "Generating Research Questions Through Problematization," *Academy of Management Review* (36:2), pp. 247–271.

Arksey, H., and O'Malley, L. 2005. "Scoping Studies: Towards a Methodological Framework," *International Journal of Social Research Methodology* (8:1), pp. 19–32.

Bandara, W., Furtmueller, E., Gorbacheva, E., Mikson, S., and Beekhuyzen, J. 2015. "Using Insights From Qualitative Data Analysis and Tool Support for Rigorously Reviewing the Literature," *Communication of the Association for Information Systems* (37:8), pp. 154–204.

Boell, S., and Cecez-Kecmanovic, D. 2015. "On Being 'Systematic' in Literature Review in IS," *Journal of Information Technology* (20), pp. 161–173.

Briggs, R. O., Reinig, B. A., and de Vreede, G. J. 2008. "The Yield Shift Theory of Satisfaction and Its Application to the IS/IT Domain," *Journal of the Association for Information Systems* (9:5), pp. 267–293.

Chiasson, M., Germonprez, M., and Mathiassen, L. 2008. "Pluralist Action Research: A Review of the Information Systems Literature," *Information Systems Journal* (19), pp. 31–54.

Cooper, H. M. 1988. "Organizing Knowledge Syntheses: A Taxonomy of Literature Reviews," *Knowledge, Technology & Policy* (1:1), pp. 104–126.

DeLone, W. H., and McLean, E. R. 1992. "Information Systems Success: The Quest for the Dependent Variable," *Information Systems Research* (3:1), pp. 60–95.

Dubé, L., and Paré, G. 2003. "Rigor in Information Systems Positivist Case Research: Current Practices, Trends, and Recommendations," *MIS Quarterly* (27:4), pp. 597–635.

Fawcett, J., and Downs, F. S. 1986. *The Relationship of Theory and Research*. Norwalk, CT: Appleton-Century-Croft.

Greenaway, K. E., and Chan, Y. E. 2005. "Theoretical Explanations for Firms' Information Privacy Behaviors," *Journal of the Association for Information Systems* (6:6), pp. 171–198.

Gregor, S. 2006. "The Nature of Theory in Information Systems," *MIS Quarterly* (30:3), pp. 611–642.

Hart, C. 2003. *Doing a Literature Review: Releasing the Social Science Research Imagination*. London, UK: SAGE.

Hoon, C. 2013. "Meta-Synthesis of Qualitative Case Studies: An Approach to Theory Building," *Organizational Research Methods* (16:4), pp. 522–556.

Houy, C., Fettke, P., and Loos, P. 2015. "Stylized Facts as an Instrument for Literature Reviews and Cumulative Information Systems," *Communication of the Association for Information Systems* (37:10), pp. 225–256.

Jennex, M. E. 2015. "Literature Reviews and the Review Process: An Editor-in-Chief's Perspective," *Communication of the Association for Information Systems* (36:1), pp. 139–146.

Josepth, D., Ng, K. Y., Koh, C., and Ang, S. 2007. "Turnover of Information Technology Professionals: A Narrative Review, Meta-Analytical Structural Equation Modeling, and Model Development," *MIS Quarterly* (31:3), pp. 547–577.

King, W. R., and He, J. 2005. "Understanding the Role and Methods of Meta-Analysis in IS Research," *Communications of the Association for Information Systems* (16:1), pp. 665–686.

Kitsiou, S., Paré, G., and Jaana, M. 2015. "The Effects of Home Telemonitoring Interventions on Patients With Chronic Heart Failure: An Overview of Systematic Reviews," *Journal of Medical Internet Research* (17:3), p. e63.

Lee, R. P., Hart, R. I., Watson, R. M., and Rapley, T. 2015. "Qualitative Synthesis in Practice: Some Pragmatics of Meta-Ethnography," *Qualitative Research* (15:3), pp. 334–350.

Lipsey, M. W., and Wilson, D. B. 2001. *Practical Meta-Analysis*. Thousand Oaks, CA: Sage.

Markus, M. L., and Robey, D. 1988. "Information Technology and Organizational Change: Causal Structure in Theory and Research," *Management Science* (34:5), pp. 583–598.

Oates, B. 2011. Evidence-Based Information Systems: A Decade Later, *European Conference on Information Systems*: paper 222.

Okoli, C. 2015. "A Guide to Conducting a Standalone Systematic Literature Review," *Communication of the Association for Information Systems* (37:1), pp. 879–910.

Ortiz de Guinea, A., Webster, J., and Staples, D. S. 2012. "A Meta-Analysis of the Consequences of Virtualness on Team Functioning," *Information & Management* (49:6), pp. 301–308.

Otte-Trojel, T., de Bont, A., Rundall, T., and van de Klundert, J. 2014. "How Outcomes Are Achieved Through Patient Portals: A Realist Review," *Journal of the American Medical Informatics Association* (21), pp. 751–757.

Paré, G., Bourdeau, S., Marsans, J., Nach, H., and Shuraida, S. 2008. "Re-Examining the Causal Structure of Information Technology Impact Research," *European Journal of Information Systems* (17), pp. 403–416.

Paré, G., and Kitsiou, S. 2016. "Methods for Literature Review," in *Handbook of Ehealth Evaluation: An Evidence-Based Approach*, F. Lau and C. Kuziemsky (eds.), Vol. 3: University of Victoria Library Press, pp. 281–299.

Paré, G., Tate, M., Johnstone, D., and Kitsiou, S. 2016. "Contextualizing the Twin Concepts of Systematicity and Transparency in Information Systems Literature Reviews," *European Journal of Information Systems* (25), pp. 493–508.

Paré, G., Trudel, M. C., Jaana, M., and Kitsiou, S. 2015. "Synthesizing Information Systems Knowledge: A Typology of Literature Reviews," *Information and Management* (52), pp. 183–199.

Petter, S., DeLone, W., and McLean, E. 2008. "Measuring Information Systems Success: Models, Dimensions, Measures, and Interrelationships," *European Journal of Information Systems* (17), pp. 236–263.

Pickering, C. M., and Byrne, J. 2014. "The Benefits of Publishing Systematic Quantitative Literature Reviews for PhD Candidates and Other Early Career Researchers," *Higher Education Research and Development* (33), pp. 534–548.

Rousseau, D. M., Manning, J., and Denyer, D. 2008. "Evidence in Management and Organizational Science: Assembling the Field's Full Weight of Scientific Knowledge Through Syntheses," *Academy of Management Annals* (2:1), pp. 475–515.

Rowe, F. 2014. "What Literature Review Is Not: Diversity, Boundaries and Recommendations," *European Journal of Information Systems* (23:3), pp. 241–255.

Schryen, G. 2013. "Revisiting Is Business Value Research: What We Already Know, What We Still Need to Know, and How We Can Get There," *European Journal of Information Systems* (22), pp. 139–169.

Schryen, G. 2015. "Writing Qualitative IS Literature Reviews – Guidelines for Synthesis, Interpretation and Guidance of Research," *Communication of the Association for Information Systems* (37:12), pp. 286–325.

Schultze, U. 2015. "Skirting SLR's Language Trap: Reframing the 'Systematic' vs 'Traditional' Literature Review Opposition as a Continuum," *Journal of Information Technology* (30), pp. 180–184.

Smith, H., Dinev, T., and Xu, H. 2011. "Information Privacy Research: An Interdisciplinary Review," *MIS Quarterly* (35:4), pp. 989–1016.

Sun, Y., Lim, K. H., and Peng, J. Z. 2013. "Solving the Distinctiveness-Blindness Debate: Unified Model for Understanding Banner Processing," *Journal of the Association for Information Systems* (14:2), pp. 49–71.

Tate, M., Evermann, J., and Gable, G. 2015. "An Integrated Framework for Theories of Individual Attitudes Towards Technology," *Information and Management* (52:6), pp. 710–727.

Templier, M., and Paré, G. 2015. "A Framework for Evaluating Literature Reviews," *Communication of the Association for Information Systems* (37:6), pp. 112–137.

Thomson, D., Russell, K., Becker, L., Klassen, T., and Harling, L. 2010. "The Evolution of a New Publication Type: Steps and Challenges of Producing Overviews of Reviews," *Research Synthesis Methods* (1:3/4), pp. 198–211.

Vaast, E., and Walsham, G. 2013. "Grounded Theorizing for Electronically Mediated Social Contexts," *European Journal of Information Systems* (22:1), pp. 9–25.

Walker, L., and Avant, K. 2010. *Strategies for Theory Construction in Nursing*. San Francisco, CA: Prentice Hall.

Wall, J., Stahl, B., and Salam, A. 2015. "Critical Discourse Analysis as a Review Methodology: An Empirical Example," *Communication of the Association for Information Systems* (37:11), pp. 257–285.

Webster, J., and Watson, R. T. 2002. "Analyzing the Past to Prepare for the Future: Writing a Literature Review," *MIS Quarterly* (26:2), pp. xiii–xxiii.

6
COMING OF AGE
Interpretive research in information systems

Michael D. Myers

Introduction

Over the past 10 to 15 years interpretive research has come of age. In fact, one might say that it has almost become normal science, or an accepted way of doing research in Information Systems (IS). Various surveys of the IS research literature paint a reasonably consistent picture, showing that approximately 25% of all articles published in our top journals are interpretive (Liu and Myers, 2011). This proportion of interpretive to positivist research has not changed much for over a decade (Chen and Hirschheim, 2004). Although some argue that there is a lack of diversity in IS research (Mingers, 2003) and criticize the 'methodological monism' and narrowness of IS research (Davison and Martinsons, 2011), at least a reasonable amount of interpretive research is being conducted and published on a regular basis.

This was not always the case. Back in the late 1980s and early 1990s many IS scholars complained about the fact that almost all IS research was of a similar nature, that is, it was almost all quantitative and positivist. For example, Galliers and Land (1987) lamented the lack of diversity in IS research and called for a wider interpretation of what should be considered acceptable IS research. Orlikowski and Baroudi (1991) said that any one perspective is always only a partial view, and unnecessarily restrictive. They argued that there was much that could be gained if a plurality of research perspectives was effectively employed to investigate information systems phenomena. Landry and Banville (1992), likewise, suggested that no single method could ever capture all the richness and complexity of organizational reality, and that a diversity of methods, theories, and philosophies was required (Landry and Banville, 1992, p. 78). There were many other similar calls at around the same time for IS researchers to value a diversity of methods and paradigms (Lee, 1991).

By the early 2000s, however, interpretive research had taken its place as one valuable paradigm or research philosophy alongside positivist research. From the early 2000s onwards a steady stream of interpretive research articles began to be published in all of our best journals. One obvious question to ask is this: What happened in the mid- to late 1990s that paved the way for more diversity in the IS field? What changed the minds of the senior scholars (the gatekeepers) within the discipline to allow a reasonable number of interpretive articles to be published? Although a small number of journals had welcomed interpretive research before 2000 (mostly the European-based journals such as *European Journal of Information*

Systems, *Information Systems Journal*, and *Journal of Strategic Information Systems*), from approximately 2000 onwards almost all IS major journals began to welcome such work. The senior scholars of these journals started to appoint a few interpretive researchers as associate and senior editors, and they in turn appointed 'qualified reviewers,' that is, those with some expertise in interpretive research – to evaluate interpretive manuscripts. These appointments to virtually all of our best journals enabled and facilitated the publishing of a greater number of interpretive research articles.

I suggest the main thing that happened was the publication of a few articles that defined and explained the interpretive research paradigm, along with articles that proposed or established principles or criteria for the evaluation of interpretive research manuscripts. Of course, all the various calls for diversity helped to set the scene, so to speak, but I believe it was the publication of various evaluative criteria that made all the difference. These articles helped to legitimize interpretive research as valid way of conducting research on IS phenomena, and they provided a justification as to why interpretive research was valuable and needed. Of course, the ones that needed convincing were not interpretive researchers themselves, but rather the gatekeepers, that is, the majority of senior IS scholars and editors of journals, who even today adopt mostly positivist approaches to research.

Two early articles that helped to pave the way were published by Geoff Walsham. In the first article he discussed the emergence of interpretive and suggested that his paper could be used as "a reference point" for further work (Walsham, 1995a). In the second article he explicitly provided some guidance for those wanting to conduct interpretive case studies (Walsham, 1995b). He suggested how interpretive researchers could contribute to theory and make generalizations from interpretive case studies. Subsequently, Markus and Lee edited a special issue of *MIS Quarterly* that had as its explicit purpose the establishment of appropriate criteria for evaluating various qualitative and interpretive methods. They said they were concerned that some IS scholars were inappropriately using "positivist criteria to judge interpretivist intensive research" (Markus and Lee, 1999, p. 36). Hence the special issue was explicitly designed to provide some exemplars of how such research could be evaluated. I believe the goals of the special issue were certainly achieved: the first two articles that were published as part of the special issue have since been widely cited, with the first one (Walsham and Sahay, 1999) being cited more than 650 times and the second (Klein and Myers, 1999) more than 4,500 times. The latter suggested a set of principles for the evaluation of interpretive field studies, drawing on hermeneutics and phenomenology as its philosophical base.

Having said this, however, I think many interpretive IS scholars seem to have misinterpreted the main purpose of these articles. I have received a few comments from IS colleagues saying that their paper was rejected because it did not meet all of the principles outlined in our 1999 paper (Klein and Myers, 1999). In other words, the Klein and Myers (1999) paper was being used as some kind of stick with which to discipline their work. The Klein and Myers (1999) principles were being seen as some kind of orthodoxy which all interpretive papers must follow.

But this use (or rather, misuse) of our article suggests to me that some scholars have been using our paper inappropriately. A careful reading of our paper will show that we explicitly stated that our proposed principles should not be used like a checklist and that their use was not mandatory. In fact, to guard against our paper being used in this way, we made this same point twice, in both the introduction and conclusion. We said, and I quote, "We caution, however, that our proposed set of principles cannot be applied mechanistically. It is incumbent upon interpretive scholars to appropriate them and use their own judgement as to their specific application" (Klein and Myers, 1999, p. 88). We also said that our proposed set of principles was just **one set**, and additional sets of principles would be welcome. The idea that our principles are the one and only way to evaluate interpretive research is a complete misinterpretation of our paper.

Given this misinterpretation, which unfortunately seems to be rather common (Jones, 2004), I think I need to restate what was the main purpose of our 1999 paper: the main purpose of our Klein and Myers (1999) paper was to help establish interpretive research as a legitimate paradigm for IS research. The main audience was positivist IS researchers: we wanted to convince them that interpretive research was a valid paradigm for IS and such research should be welcomed in our journals. Heinz and I had no intention of forcing interpretive IS researchers to slavishly follow the principles, even though that may have been the unintended result in a few instances.

Overall, however, I think it is fair to say that the main purpose of our paper was achieved. It is now relatively easy to justify the use of interpretive research in IS research and even positivist IS researchers, while they may not conduct interpretive research themselves, at least recognize its value. They realize that the interpretive research should not be judged by inappropriate positivist criteria, although I would add that not all interpretive research should be judged by the Klein and Myers (1999) criteria, either. Interpretive research has taken its place as one valuable research paradigm among others. Most interpretive IS scholars seem to use our principles appropriately.

I will now discuss the nature of interpretive research and how it differs from positivist research. Both positivist and interpretivist research aim at improving the understanding of phenomena, but differ in how this can be achieved.

The nature of interpretive research

All research is based on some underlying philosophical assumptions. These philosophical assumptions are concerned with our beliefs about reality, how knowledge can be obtained about this reality, and how this knowledge can be justified (Myers, 1997). I will discuss just two paradigms or research philosophies in this chapter: positivism and interpretivism. Although there are other paradigms, such as the critical research paradigm (Brooke, 2002; Kvasny and Richardson, 2006; Myers and Klein, 2011; Richardson and Robinson, 2007; Stahl and Brooke, 2008), the positivist and interpretivist paradigms are the most common in IS research.

Positivism is the most commonly used paradigm in information systems, as it is in most other social science and business disciplines, although most positivist IS researchers would probably classify themselves as post-positivist researchers today (Burton-Jones, 2005; Straub et al., 2004). One of the most basic assumptions of positivism (or post-positivism) is that reality is objectively given and can be described by measurable properties which are independent of the observer (researcher) and his or her instruments (Bernstein, 1983). In practice this means that a positivist IS researcher will seek to test one of more hypotheses against a particular data set. The data set is assumed to be a reasonably accurate representation of the real world "out there." While post-positivist researchers accept the idea that their models and theories are social constructions, they still believe that the reality they are studying exists independently of the observer. Hence it is important for positivist researchers to be objective and not let their own biases or values affect (or 'taint') the results. One of the worst accusations that can be made against a positivist researcher is that they were biased either in their analysis of the data or in the writing up of their results.

The interpretivist paradigm is not as commonly used in information systems as the positivist paradigm, but is used in approximately one-quarter of all articles published in top

IS journals (Liu and Myers, 2011). Unlike positivist researchers, who assume that a theory or hypothesis can be tested against a data set, interpretive researchers assume that data are not detachable from theory, because what counts as data is determined in the light of some theoretical interpretation (Bernstein, 1983). Interpretive researchers assume that access to reality (given or socially constructed) is only through social constructions such as language, consciousness, shared meanings, and instruments (Klein and Myers, 1999). Interpretive researchers also assume, given the hermeneutic concept of prejudice or prejudgement, that the researcher's background, methods, and the interactions with the phenomena under study influence the findings. Hence it is impossible for an interpretive researcher to claim to be completely unbiased. However, this does mean that an interpretive researcher should only find what they are looking for – they should be open to new discoveries. It also does not mean that the findings from interpretive research are less valuable than those from positivist research. Rather, the validity of the generalizations derived from interpretive research depends more upon "the plausibility and cogency of the logical reasoning used in describing the results from the cases, and in drawing conclusions from them" (Walsham, 1993, p. 15). Interpretive studies generally attempt to understand phenomena through the meanings that people assign to them and interpretive methods of research in IS are "aimed at producing an understanding of the *context* of the information system, and the *process* whereby the information system influences and is influenced by the context" (Walsham, 1993, pp. 4–5). Interpretive research does not predefine dependent and independent variables, but focuses on the full complexity of human sense-making as the situation emerges (Kaplan and Maxwell, 1994). Hence interpretive researchers in IS tend not to test any hypotheses or suggest propositions.

The applicability of interpretive research

Information systems are used by people in a variety of social and organizational situations. By definition, IS scholars conducting research on IS phenomena look at both the technology and people and how the two interact. One challenge for IS researchers is that the technology is always changing, as are the people, and yet another challenge is that the social contexts within which people live, work, and play are changing as well. In other words, everything is changing at once. For example, new mobile technology models are introduced every year; and as for the people, the younger generation of digital natives interact with technology in a different way than digital immigrants (Vodanovich et al., 2010; Wang et al., 2013); and as for the social and organizational context within which people and technology interact, this is constantly changing as well – for example, the laws concerning e-business, data sharing, and/or privacy seem to be updated every few years. This means that an IS researcher needs to try to understand not just the technology and the people and how these two interact, but also the social and organizational context within which they interact. This real-life context is forever changing, with people having different ideas about what is happening and why. And this is where interpretive research comes into its own – interpretive research provides a paradigm and a way of exploring this context. Hence the goal of interpretive field research is to improve our understanding of human thought and action through the interpretation of human actions in their real-life context.

In short, interpretive research is applicable especially in real-life situations where that situation is messy and rather complicated. I have found that interpretive research is especially valuable when we are trying to understand a new phenomenon or re-think an old problem in a new way.

The two most common research methods that interpretivist researchers tend to use are case study research (Walsham, 1993, 1995b) and ethnographic research (Harvey and Myers, 1995;

Myers, 1999). Case study research and ethnographic research are similar in the sense that both involve talking to people in their real-life context, except that the latter relies more on fieldwork and participant observation. The ethnographer "immerses himself in the life of people he studies" (Lewis, 1985, p. 380) and seeks to place the phenomena studied in its social and cultural context.

As Yin explains,

> Ethnographies usually require long periods of time in the "field" and emphasise detailed, observational evidence . . . In contrast, case studies are a form of enquiry that does not depend solely on ethnographic or participant observation data. One could even do a valid and high-quality case study without leaving the library and the telephone.
>
> (Yin, 1994, pp. 21–22)

As well as case study research and ethnographic research, the interpretive paradigm can inform action research studies. Action research is an interventionist research method where the researcher seeks to solve a practical problem as well as a research problem (Baskerville, 1999). Normally action research is carried out in collaboration with practitioners. The idea is that the researcher contributes to practice as well as to the scholarly community (Baskerville and Myers, 2004). Action research is usually seen as a cyclical process that involves diagnosing a problem situation, planning action steps, and implementing and evaluating outcomes. The evaluation may lead to starting another action research cycle based on the insights previously gained. The main idea is that action research uses a scientific approach to study important organizational or social problems together with the people who experience them (Elden and Chisholm, 1993). An example of an interpretive approach to action research is Peter Checkland's work in developing soft systems methodology (SSM). SSM is a methodology for enquiry into 'soft' or ill-structured situations. SSM has been used in information systems to understand problem situations, and then to recommend taking action to improve them (Checkland and Holwell, 1993, 1998; Checkland and Scholes, 1990).

The interpretive paradigm can also be used in conjunction with grounded theory studies. The basic idea of grounded theory is that the concepts and theory should emerge from the data. Rather than using preconceived ideas, the researcher uses a coding scheme and has to constantly compare and contrast qualitative data in the search for similarities and differences (Urquhart et al., 2010). An example of an interpretive approach to grounded theory is Cathy Urquhart's work on analyst–client communications (Urquhart, 1997).

Examples of interpretive research

I will now discuss a few empirical examples of interpretive IS research.

Boland was one of the first IS researchers to adopt an interpretive paradigm in his research work (Boland, 1979, 1985, 1987, 1991; Boland and Day, 1989). He suggested hermeneutics and phenomenology as a means of looking at the sense-making process in information systems development. Klein and Hirschheim (1983) provided a brief introduction to the hermeneutic approach to IS research.

Almost a decade later, Walsham became one of the leading advocates of interpretive research (Walsham, 1993, 1995a, b; Walsham and Sahay, 1999). In one of his articles with Waema, the IS strategy formation and implementation process in a medium-sized UK building society was analyzed. One of their conclusions was that the IS strategy formation and implementation process is a dynamic one, involving time-varying relationships, multilevel contexts, and cultural and political aspects (Walsham and Waema, 1994).

Also in the 1990s, both Lee (1991, 1994) and Myers (1994, 1995) used hermeneutics in their studies of information systems. Lee (1994) looked at richness in email communications by exploring the wider social and political context within which the email communications took place, while Myers (1994, 1995) examined the implementation of an information system from a critical hermeneutic perspective.

Using ethnographic research, Orlikowski (1991) studied a large, multinational software consulting firm. She found that, contrary to the theoretical position of much of the IS research literature at that time, which assumed that information technology will transform existing bureaucratic organizational forms and social relations, the use of new information technology led to the existing forms of control being intensified and fused. Her research was informed by Giddens's theory of structuration (Giddens, 1984). In a similar way, Hirschheim and Newman (1991) critiqued current IS development approaches by looking at the role of myth, metaphor, and magic.

Toward the end of the decade a few interpretive research articles discussed various aspects of using interpretive research as a research method (e.g., Butler, 1998; Nandhakumar and Jones, 1997). The *Journal of Information Technology* published a special issue on interpretive research in 1998 (Myers and Walsham, 1998).

In 2000 Trauth and Jessup (2000) analyzed the same IS phenomena (group support system use) from both positivist and interpretivist perspectives. They found that, while the positivist analysis provided useful information, the interpretive analysis provided a richer understanding of the same evidence. Their paper thus contributed to a better understanding of the added value of interpretive research in information systems.

From about 2000 onwards many interpretive research articles began to be published in almost all IS journals. In this chapter it is simply not possible to mention them all, so I will just mention a few excellent examples.

Iversen et al. (2004) used interpretive research to study the management of risk in software process improvement initiatives. As well as proposing an approach to understand and manage risks in SPI teams, the authors proposed how it might be possible to tailor risk management to specific contexts.

Madon (2005) adopted a "practical reflexive-interpretive" methodological approach to encourage the development and reshaping of theoretical ideas about governance. Madon studied the sustainability of a telecentre project in India.

Levina (2005) used an interpretive approach in her study of a Web-based application development project. She proposed that multiparty collaborative practice can be understood as constituting a "collective reflection-in-action" cycle through which an information systems design emerges as a result of agents producing, sharing, and reflecting on explicit objects.

Sarker et al. (2012) used interpretive case study research to explore value creation in relationships between an ERP vendor and its partners. Their research uncovered different mechanisms underlying value co-creation within B2B alliances, and also pointed to several categories of contingency factors that influence these mechanisms.

Echoing the earlier study by Trauth and Jessup (2000), Lee and Dennis (2012), in their study of a controlled laboratory experiment, showed how interpretive research, and specifically hermeneutics, can complement and reinforce positivist research.

Quite a few studies have used interpretive research to provide new insights into IT outsourcing (Levina and Ross, 2003) and IT offshoring. For example, Gregory et al. (2013) looked at the control dynamics associated with IS development (ISD) offshoring projects, whereas Ravishankar et al. (2013) focused on IT offshoring within the context of postcolonialism.

Although most interpretive research articles in IS have tended to use case study research or ethnographic research, a good example of an interpretive action research study is provided by Braa et al. (2007). The authors helped to provide a strategy to standardize health information systems and information infrastructures that are appropriate for the context of developing countries. Another example of an interpretive action research study is Smith et al.'s (2010) analysis of power relationships during an information systems security standards adoption and accreditation process. The authors found that a strategy based on organization subunit size could be helpful in motivating and assisting organizations to attain government mandated accreditation of their security processes and procedures (Smith et al., 2010).

As can be seen, IS researchers have used interpretive research to provide insights into a variety of IS topics. Although interpretive research is often said to be most useful for "exploring" a new phenomenon, there are good examples of interpretive research being use to provide fresh insights into long-established areas such as IT outsourcing and offshoring.

Evaluating interpretive research manuscripts

The Klein and Myers (1999) principles for interpretive research are summarized in Table 6.1. The seven principles they suggest were derived from hermeneutic philosophy and phenomenology and applied to an IS context.

Table 6.1 Klein and Myers's (1999) principles for interpretive research

1. **The Fundamental Principle of the Hermeneutic Circle**
   This principle suggests that all human understanding is achieved by iterating between considering the interdependent meaning of parts and the whole that they form. This principle of human understanding is fundamental to all the other principles.
2. **The Principle of Contextualization**
   Requires critical reflection of the social and historical background of the research setting, so that the intended audience can see how the current situation under investigation emerged.
3. **The Principle of Interaction between the Researchers and the Subjects**
   Requires critical reflection on how the research materials (or "data") were socially constructed through the interaction between the researchers and participants.
4. **The Principle of Abstraction and Generalization**
   Requires relating the idiographic details revealed by the data interpretation through the application of Principles 1 and 2 to theoretical, general concepts that describe the nature of human understanding and social action.
5. **The Principle of Dialogical Reasoning**
   Requires sensitivity to possible contradictions between the theoretical preconceptions guiding the research design and actual findings ("the story which the data tell") with subsequent cycles of revision.
6. **The Principle of Multiple Interpretations**
   Requires sensitivity to possible differences in interpretations among the participants as are typically expressed in multiple narratives or stories of the same sequence of events under study. Similar to multiple witness accounts even if all tell it as they saw it.
7. **The Principle of Suspicion**
   Requires sensitivity to possible 'biases' and systematic "distortions" in the narratives collected from the participants.

Although the Klein and Myers (1999) principles are the most widely recognized criteria of judging interpretive research manuscripts (Jones, 2004), they are not the only ones that have been suggested. For example, Walsham suggested four criteria for the evaluation of interpretive case studies: interpretive case studies should develop new concepts, contribute to theory, draw specific implications, and contribute rich insight into IS phenomena (Walsham, 1995b). Schultze, drawing on Golden-Biddle and Locke (1993)'s work, suggested three criteria for ethnographic research in general, namely, authenticity, plausibility, and criticality (Schultze, 2000), with two additional criteria for ethnographic work of a confessional nature.

Jones (2004) says there is a danger of researchers unreflexively adopting criteria such as those mentioned as measures of quality. The fulfilment of these criteria could become the objective in itself, without reference to the wider aims of the research. While I agree with him that this is a danger, in actual fact I believe that most IS researchers have used these criteria appropriately. I have not read many papers that use these criteria unthinkingly – in fact, most IS scholars only to refer to the principles in passing without getting bogged down in the detail. Hence I believe the publication of these criteria was good for the IS field as a whole in that they helped to legitimize interpretive research among the wider community of IS scholars, especially among those IS researchers who adopt positivist research methods.

Conclusion

Interpretive research has come a long way over the past one or two decades, with approximately one-quarter of all IS research articles now adopting an interpretive perspective. Interpretive research is well suited to providing information systems researchers with rich insights into the human, social, and organizational aspects of information systems development and application. It is especially valuable in exploring the messy, confused, and often complicated social contexts within which IT phenomena are developed and used. However, with interpretive research in effect becoming normal science, there is a danger that only a certain way of doing interpretive research might become the norm. Hence my plea is that IS scholars continue to show some flexibility to ensure that interpretive researchers continue to come up with interesting and creative insights. Perhaps some IS scholars will also take up the challenge of suggesting different sets of principles for the evaluation of interpretive research? However, given that most IS scholars do not seem to be slavishly following the existing published criteria for conducting and evaluating interpretive research, that task might not be as urgent as it once was.

References

Baskerville, R. (1999) Investigating Information Systems With Action Research, *Communications of the AIS* 2(19): online.

Baskerville, R. and Myers, M. D. (2004) Special Issue on Action Research in Information Systems: Making IS Research Relevant to Practice-Foreword, *MIS Quarterly* 28(3): 329–335.

Bernstein, R. J. (1983) *Beyond Objectivism and Relativism*, Philadelphia: University of Pennsylvania Press.

Boland, R. (1979) Control, Causality and Information System Requirements, *Accounting, Organizations and Society* 4(4): 259–272.

Boland, R. (1985) Phenomenology: A Preferred Approach to Research in Information Systems, in: Mumford, E., Hirschheim, R. A., Fitzgerald, G., Wood-Harper, A. T. (Eds.), *Research Methods in Information Systems*, Amsterdam: North Holland, pp. 193–201.

Boland, R. (1987) The In-Formation of Information Systems, in: Boland, R. J., Hirschheim, R. A. (Eds.), *Critical Issues in Information Systems Research*, New York: John Wiley and Sons, pp. 363–394.

Boland, R. (1991) Information System Use as a Hermeneutic Process, in: Nissen, H.-E., Klein, H.K., Hirschheim, R.A. (Eds.), *Information Systems Research: Contemporary Approaches and Emergent Traditions*, Amsterdam: North-Holland, pp. 439–464.

Boland, R.J. and Day, W.F. (1989) The Experience of System Design: A Hermeneutic of Organizational Action, *Scandinavian Journal of Management* 5(2): 87–104.

Braa, J., Hanseth, O., Heywood, A., Mohammed, W., Shaw, V. and Town, C. (2007) Developing Health Information Systems in Developing Countries: The Flexible Standards Strategy, *MIS Quarterly* 31: 381–402.

Brooke, C. (2002) What Does It Mean to Be 'Critical' in IS Research? *Journal of Information Technology* 17: 49–57.

Burton-Jones, A. (2005) *New Perspectives on the System Usage Construct*, Computer Information Systems, Atlanta: Georgia State University, p. 242.

Butler, T. (1998) Towards a Hermeneutic Method for Interpretive Research in Information Systems, *Journal of Information Technology* 13(4): 285–300.

Checkland, P. and Holwell, S. (1993) Information Management and Organizational Processes: An Approach Through Soft Systems Methodology, *Journal of Information Systems* 3(1): 3–16.

Checkland, P. and Holwell, S. (1998) *Information, Systems and Information Systems: Making Sense of the Field*, Chichester: Wiley.

Checkland, P. and Scholes, J. (1990) *Soft Systems Methodology in Action*, Chichester: Wiley.

Chen, W.S. and Hirschheim, R. (2004) A Paradigmatic and Methodological Examination of Information Systems Research From 1991 to 2001, *Information Systems Journal* 14(3): 197–235.

Davison, R.M. and Martinsons, M.G. (2011) Methodological Practice and Policy for Organisationally and Socially Relevant IS Research: An Inclusive-Exclusive Perspective, *Journal of Information Technology* 26(4): 288–293.

Elden, M. and Chisholm, R.F. (1993) Emerging Varieties of Action Research: Introduction to the Special Issue, *Human Relations* 46(2): 121–142.

Galliers, R.D. and Land, F.F. (1987) Choosing Appropriate Information Systems Research Methodologies, *Communications of the ACM* 30(11) (November): 900–902.

Giddens, A. (1984) *The Constitution of Society: Outline of a Theory of Structure*, Berkeley: University of California Press.

Golden-Biddle, K. and Locke, K. (1993) Appealing Work: An Investigation of How Ethnographic Texts Convince, *Organization Science* 4(4): 595–616.

Gregory, R.W., Beck, R. and Keil, M. (2013) Control Balancing in Information Systems Development Offshoring Projects, *MIS Quarterly* 37: 1211–1232.

Harvey, L. and Myers, M.D. (1995) Scholarship and Practice: The Contribution of Ethnographic Research Methods to Bridging the Gap, *Information Technology and People* 8(3): 13–27.

Hirschheim, R. and Newman, M. (1991) Symbolism and Information Systems Development: Myth, Metaphor and Magic, *Information Systems Research* 2(1): 29–62.

Iversen, J.H., Mathiassen, L. and Nielsen, P.A. (2004) Managing Risk in Software Process Improvement: An Action Research Approach, *MIS Quarterly* 28: 395–433.

Jones, M. (2004) Debatable Advice and Inconsistent Evidence: Methodology in Information Systems Research, in: Kaplan, B., Truex, D.P., Wastell, D., Wood-Harper, A.T. and DeGross, J.I. (Eds.), *Information Systems Research: Relevant Theory and Informed Practice*, Dordrecht: Kluwer Academic, pp. 121–142.

Kaplan, B. and Maxwell, J.A. (1994) Qualitative Research Methods for Evaluating Computer Information Systems, in: Anderson, J.G., Aydin, C.E. and Jay, S.J. (Eds.), *Evaluating Health Care Information Systems: Methods and Applications*, Thousand Oaks, CA: Sage, pp. 45–68.

Klein, H.K. and Hirschheim, R. (1983) Issues and Approaches to Appraising Technological Change in the Office: A Consequentialist Perspective, *Office: Technology and People* 2: 15–24.

Klein, H.K. and Myers, M.D. (1999) A Set of Principles for Conducting and Evaluating Interpretive Field Studies in Information Systems, *MIS Quarterly* 23(1): 67–93.

Kvasny, L. and Richardson, H. (2006) Critical Research in Information Systems: Looking Forward, Looking Back, *Information Technology and People* 19(3): 196–202.

Landry, M. and Banville, C. (1992) A Disciplined Methodological Pluralism for MIS Research, *Accounting, Management and Information Technologies* 2(2): 77–97.

Lee, A.S. (1991) Integrating Positivist and Interpretive Approaches to Organizational Research, *Organization Science* 2(4): 342–365.

Lee, A. S. (1994) Electronic Mail as a Medium for Rich Communication: An Empirical Investigation Using Hermeneutic Interpretation, *MIS Quarterly* 18(2): 143–157.

Lee, A. S. and Dennis, A. R. (2012) A Hermeneutic Interpretation of a Controlled Laboratory Experiment: A Case Study of Decision-Making With a Group Support System, *Information Systems Journal* 22: 3–27.

Levina, N. (2005) Collaborating on Multiparty Information Systems Development Projects: A Collective Reflection-in-Action View, *Information Systems Research* 16(2): 109–130.

Levina, N. and Ross, J. W. (2003) From the Vendor's Perspective: Exploring the Value Proposition in Information Technology Outsourcing, *MIS Quarterly* 27: 331–364.

Lewis, I. M. (1985) *Social Anthropology in Perspective*, Cambridge: Cambridge University Press.

Liu, F. and Myers, M. D. (2011) An Analysis of the AIS Basket of Top Journals, *Journal of Systems and Information Technology* 13(1): 5–24.

Madon, S. (2005) Governance Lessons From the Experience of Telecentres in Kerala, *European Journal of Information Systems* 14: 401–416.

Markus, M. L. and Lee, A. S. (1999) Special Issue on Intensive Research in Information Systems: Using Qualitative, Interpretive, and Case Methods to Study Information Technology – Foreword, *MIS Quarterly* 23(1): 35–38.

Mingers, J. (2003) The Paucity of Multimethod Research: A Review of the Information Systems Literature, *Information Systems Journal* 13(3): 233–249.

Myers, M. D. (1994) A Disaster for Everyone to See: An Interpretive Analysis of a Failed IS Project, *Accounting, Management and Information Technologies* 4(4): 185–201.

Myers, M. D. (1995) Dialectical Hermeneutics: A Theoretical Framework for the Implementation of Information Systems, *Information Systems Journal* 5(1): 51–70.

Myers, M. D. (1997) Interpretive Research in Information Systems, in: Mingers, J. and Stowell, F. (Eds.), *Information Systems: An Emerging Discipline*, London: McGraw-Hill, pp. 239–266.

Myers, M. D. (1999) Investigating Information Systems With Ethnographic Research, *Communications of the AIS* 2(23): 1–20.

Myers, M. D. and Klein, H. K. (2011) A Set of Principles for Conducting Critical Research in Information Systems, *MIS Quarterly* 35(1): 17–36.

Myers, M. D. and Walsham, G. (1998) Guest Editorial: Exemplifying Interpretive Research in Information Systems: An Overview, *Journal of Information Technology* 13(4): 233–234.

Nandhakumar, J. and Jones, M. (1997) Too Close for Comfort? Distance and Engagement in Interpretive Information Systems Research, *Information Systems Journal* 7: 109–131.

Orlikowski, W. J. (1991) Integrated Information Environment or Matrix of Control? The Contradictory Implications of Information Technology, *Accounting, Management and Information Technologies* 1(1): 9–42.

Orlikowski, W. J. and Baroudi, J. J. (1991) Studying Information Technology in Organizations: Research Approaches and Assumptions, *Information Systems Research* 2(1): 1–28.

Ravishankar, M. N., Pan, S. L. and Myers, M. D. (2013) Information Technology Offshoring in India: A Postcolonial Perspective, *European Journal of Information Systems* 22(4): 387–402.

Richardson, H. and Robinson, B. (2007) The Mysterious Case of the Missing Paradigm: A Review of Critical Information Systems Research 1991–2001, *Information Systems Journal* 17(3): 251–270.

Sarker, S., Sarker, S., Sahaym, A. and Bjørn-Andersen, N. (2012) Exploring Value Co-creation in Relationships Between an ERP Vendor and Its Partners: A Revelatory Case Study, *MIS Quarterly* 36: 317–338.

Schultze, U. (2000) A Confessional Account of an Ethnography About Knowledge Work, *MIS Quarterly* 24(1): 3–41.

Smith, B. S., Bunker, D. and Jamieson, R. (2010) Circuits of Power: A Study of Mandated Compliance to an Information Systems Security De Jure Standard in a Government Organization, *MIS Quarterly* 34: 463–486.

Stahl, B. C. and Brooke, C. (2008) The Contribution of Critical IS Research, *Communications of the ACM* 51(3): 51–55.

Straub, D., Boudreau, M.-C. and Gefen, D. (2004) Validation Guidelines for IS Positivist Research, *The Communications of the Association for Information Systems* 13(1): 380–427.

Trauth, E. M. and Jessup, L. M. (2000) Understanding Computer-Mediated Discussions: Positivist and Interpretive Analyses of Group Support System Use, *MIS Quarterly* 24(1): 43–79.

Urquhart, C. (1997) Exploring Analyst-Client Communication: Using Grounded Theory Techniques to Investigate Interaction in Informal Requirements Gathering, in: Lee, A. S., Liebenau, J. and DeGross, J. I. (Eds.), *Information Systems and Qualitative Research*, London: Chapman and Hall, pp. 149–181.

Urquhart, C., Lehmann, H. and Myers, M. D. (2010) Putting the Theory Back Into Grounded Theory: Guidelines for Grounded Theory Studies in Information Systems, *Information Systems Journal* 20(4): 357–381.

Vodanovich, S., Sundaram, D. and Myers, M. D. (2010) Digital Natives and Ubiquitous Information Systems, *Information Systems Research* 21(4): 711–723.

Walsham, G. (1993) *Interpreting Information Systems in Organizations*, Chichester: John Wiley and Sons.

Walsham, G. (1995a) The Emergence of Interpretivism in IS Research, *Information Systems Research* 6(4): 376–394.

Walsham, G. (1995b) Interpretive Case Studies in IS Research: Nature and Method, *European Journal of Information Systems* 4(2): 74–81.

Walsham, G. and Sahay, S. (1999) GIS for District-Level Administration in India: Problems and Opportunities, *MIS Quarterly* 23(1): 39–65.

Walsham, G. and Waema, T. (1994) Information Systems Strategy and Implementation: A Case Study of a Building Society, *ACM Transactions on Information Systems* 12(2): 150–173.

Wang, Q., Myers, M. D. and Sundaram, D. (2013) Digital Natives and Digital Immigrants, *Business and Information Systems Engineering* 5(6): 409–419.

Yin, R. K. (1994) *Case Study Research, Design and Methods*, 2nd ed., Newbury Park: Sage.

7
NEUROIS

René Riedl

Introduction

NeuroIS is a field in Information Systems (IS) which makes use of neurophysiological tools and knowledge to better understand the development, adoption, and impact of information and communication technologies. The idea of applying physiological measurement in IS research is not a recent one. Galletta and colleagues, for example, already wrote more than 20 years ago that a "lack of actual measures" (p. 78) exists, and they suggested heart rate and hormone measurement, among others, as complements to the more traditional measurement techniques (Huston et al., 1993). However, despite the fact that a very limited number of publications on IS phenomena and neurophysiological measurement have been available for more than ten years, the idea of applying cognitive neuroscience approaches in IS research appeared at the 2007 International Conference on Information Systems (ICIS) and at pre-ICIS workshops (for details, see Riedl and Léger, 2016). Since that time, NeuroIS has been developing at a stunning pace.

A number of NeuroIS papers, both conceptual and empirical in nature, have been published in mainstream IS journals, including papers in premium outlets such as *MIS Quarterly, Information Systems Research, Journal of Management Information Systems*, and *Journal of the Association for Information Systems*. Analysis of the extant NeuroIS literature reveals that the papers vary in terms of the IS phenomena studied and the research tools employed. In a recent NeuroIS book, Riedl and Léger (2016) indicate that NeuroIS contributions address the following phenomena (topics), among others: attention and memory, avatars, business process modelling, e-commerce, emotions in human-computer interaction, enterprise systems, information behavior, IS design science, IT security, knowledge processes, mental workload, multitasking, music and user interfaces, neuro-adaptive systems, risk, social networks, software development, technology adoption and acceptance, technostress, trust, usability, virtual worlds, and website design. Moreover, based on an analysis of the extant literature, Riedl and Léger (2016) indicate that IS scholars have used a vast range of neurophysiological tools, such as functional magnetic resonance imaging (fMRI), electroencephalography (EEG), functional near-infrared spectroscopy (fNIRS), transcranial direct-current stimulation (TDCS), electrocardiogram (EKG), galvanometer (i.e., measurement of the conductance of the skin), oculometry and pupillometry (i.e., eye movement and pupil dilation measurement), and hormone measurement.

Against the background of the fact that NeuroIS has been established as a research field in the IS discipline in the past decade, it is useful to provide a reflection on the foundations and the status of the field. The present chapter has the goal to provide such a brief reflection. However, NeuroIS is a relatively young field, and hence we observe an ongoing development of concepts and methods. It follows that it is possible that concepts and methods that are considered essential today will become less important in the future. Likewise, new concepts and methods that have not yet received attention in the NeuroIS literature will eventually become crucial in the future. In other words, the author of this chapter believes that a final consolidation of the concepts and methods in the NeuroIS field has not yet taken place. This fact makes it even more interesting to observe, or to directly contribute to, the future development of the field. Thus, it is also hoped that the present chapter creates interest in NeuroIS.

What is NeuroIS?

This section gives an overview of the NeuroIS field, including its genesis in 2007. Other themes in this section are notes on foundations of human neurobiology and a brief description of reference disciplines of NeuroIS.

The idea of applying cognitive neuroscience approaches in IS research appeared at ICIS in December 2007. In his keynote presentation for the Sixth Annual Workshop on Human-Computer Interaction Research in Management Information Systems, a pre-ICIS event, Fred D. Davis, among other themes, outlined the potential of cognitive neuroscience for technology acceptance research. Two other presentations in this workshop also dealt with topics at the nexus of neuroscience and human-computer interaction (Adriane B. Randolph: paper 12, René Riedl: paper 15; see http://sighci.org/). Moreover, Angelika Dimoka presented an ICIS paper entitled "Neuro-IS: The Potential of Cognitive Neuroscience for Information Systems Research" in the track "Breakthrough Ideas in Information Technology" (Dimoka et al., 2007). Today, it is an established fact that these presentations in the context of ICIS 2007 constitute the genesis of the NeuroIS field.

Dimoka et al. (2007) defined the term NeuroIS as "the idea of applying cognitive neuroscience theories, methods, and tools in Information Systems (IS) research." Later, based on a discussion of 15 IS and neuroscience scholars at the inaugural Gmunden Retreat on NeuroIS, an annual academic conference on research at the nexus of information systems and neuroscience (see www.neurois.org/), Riedl et al. (2010, p. 245) put forward the following definition:

> NeuroIS is an interdisciplinary field of research that relies on knowledge from disciplines related to neurobiology and behavior, as well as knowledge from engineering disciplines. NeuroIS pursues two complementary goals. First, it contributes to an advanced theoretical understanding of the design, development, use, and impact of information and communication technologies (IT). Second, it contributes to the design and development of IT systems that positively affect practically relevant outcome variables such as health, well-being, satisfaction, adoption, and productivity.

Sound application of neuroscience approaches in IS contexts implies a reasonable degree of knowledge on human neurobiology. As outlined in more detail in Riedl and Léger (2016, Chapter 2), the ancient areas of history reveal evidence of human awareness of the brain. It follows that basic investigations into the anatomy and functions of the brain date back thousands of years, with significant scientific contributions starting after the Middle Ages. Hence, a vast amount of knowledge on human neurobiology exists today, documented in tens of thousands of journal articles and in a wealth of textbooks.

The human nervous system is necessary for perceptions, thoughts, feelings, and behavior and it consists of two parts: the central nervous system (CNS; brain and spinal cord) and the peripheral nervous system (PNS; neural tissue except for the CNS). Despite the fact that these two systems are anatomically separate units, their functions are interrelated. The PNS can be subdivided into the somatic nervous system (SNS) and the autonomic nervous system (ANS), and the latter consists of the sympathetic division (activates the body) and parasympathetic division (relaxes the body). Riedl et al. (2014) indicate that the brain (i.e., the information processing unit) and the ANS (i.e., the unit that keeps the body in balance; referred to as homeostasis) are the major units of analysis in NeuroIS research, while the spinal cord and the SNS are less important. A primer on neurobiology and the brain for information systems scholars is available in Riedl and Léger (2016, see chap. 2).

Figure 7.1 shows a conceptual illustration of the human nervous system; moreover, it shows that the human brain consists of four lobes (frontal, temporal, parietal, occipital), each of which is related to specific functions (example functions are indicated in Figure 7.1). However, it is important to note that a one-to-one mapping between a cognitive function and an anatomical region in the brain does not exist. Thus, the brain does not operate in a simple one-to-one fashion (Price and Friston, 2005). Today it is an established fact that a network of regions and the interaction between them are critical for the emergence of cognitive functions (Riedl et al., 2017a; see Appendix C in their paper, Sporns, 2011).

In addition to general knowledge of human neurobiology, research in several other scientific disciplines has revealed insights into biological foundations and applications relevant to IS research. Riedl and Léger (2016) analyzed various scientific disciplines and developed a

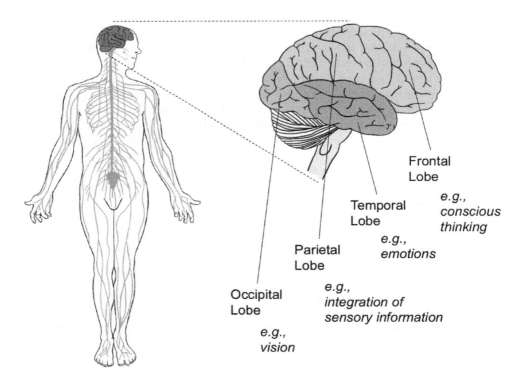

Figure 7.1 The human nervous system and brain lobes

Table 7.1 Important reference disciplines of NeuroIS

Reference Disciplines	Description
Cognitive neuroscience	A discipline geared toward understanding how the brain works, how its structure and function affect behavior, and ultimately how the brain enables the mind.
Neuropsychology	A discipline that holds the notion that the mind acts through the brain to produce higher functions, whereas the brain alone is responsible for lower functions that we have in common with other animals.
Neuroeconomics	A discipline with the objective to provide a single, general theory of human behavior for understanding the processes that connect sensation and action by revealing the neurobiological mechanisms by which decisions are made.
Neuromarketing	A discipline focused on the application of neuroimaging methods to product marketing.
Neuroergonomics	A discipline defined as the study of brain and behavior at work.
Affective computing	A discipline with the objective to positively influence effectiveness in human-computer interaction, based on the assignment of the human capabilities of observation, interpretation, and generation of emotional features to computers.
Brain-computer interaction	A discipline with the objective to provide a non-muscular channel for sending messages to the external world in order to provide a communication possibility for "locked in" patients (i.e., people who are completely paralyzed and unable to speak, but who are cognitively intact).

Note: Sources of definitions can be found in Riedl and Léger, 2016, section 1.3.

list of reference disciplines of NeuroIS. Among others, cognitive neuroscience, neuropsychology, neuroeconomics, decision neuroscience, social neuroscience, consumer neuroscience, neuroergonomics, affective computing, and brain-computer interaction have been identified as important reference disciplines. Table 7.1 summarizes the disciplines.

Why is NeuroIS important?

Based on Riedl and Léger (2016), this section outlines ten contributions available from the application of neurobiological approaches to IS research and practice. Each contribution is explained based on a concrete example. Examples include both published research and research ideas.

1 The neuroscience literature can inform the design of IT artifacts, as well as IS investigations in general (e.g., by motivating behavioral experiments), and can do so without application of neuroscience methods and tools.

   Example: Brain research indicates that humans have a preference toward curved objects, if compared to sharp-angled objects, because perception of the latter may result in activation of the amygdala (Bar and Neta, 2007). This brain area is related to arousal, threat, and fear. Based on this brain research knowledge, a recommendation for software engineers could be to avoid using sharp-angled objects on a graphical user interface (e.g., button design). This, in turn, is expected to prevent negative user feelings, and fewer negative responses are likely to positively affect important outcome variables, such as user satisfaction.

2. Brain activity, or any other neurophysiological activation (e.g., hormones, heart rate, skin conductance, pupil dilation, or muscle tension), can be used as a mediator between the IT artifact and IT behavior or antecedents of IT behavior (e.g., beliefs or behavioral intentions), thereby introducing a biological level of analysis and explaining why and how an IT artifact influences the IT behavior or its antecedents.

    Example: Technostress has become an important research topic in IS research (e.g., Riedl et al., 2012, Tams et al., 2014). Computer hassles, such as system breakdowns or long and variable response times, are an important stress factor in human-computer interaction. Researchers have studied the effects of computer hassles on physiological activation of the user and subsequent IT behavior, as well as antecedents of IT behavior (for a review, see Riedl, 2013).

3. Application of neuroscience and psychophysiological methods and tools can shed light on theoretical mechanisms underlying the influence of the IT artifact on IT behavior or antecedents of IT behavior.

    Example: Consider that experimental research reveals that the integration of a trust seal into an e-commerce environment positively influences purchase intention. While it is not difficult to establish such a research finding, determination of the reason of this effect is a more sophisticated task because alternative explanations may result in this finding. On the one hand, it is possible that the trust seal reduces a user's uncertainty perceptions. On the other hand, it is also possible that the seal increases the trustworthiness of the online shop. Because it is, at least in some cases, difficult to investigate specific phenomena (including uncertainty and trust) based on self-report questionnaires, application of neuroscience tools may lead to novel theoretical insights. Because neural correlates of uncertainty and trustworthiness have already been identified in neuroscience research, these findings could shed light on the question of whether reduced uncertainty or increased trustworthiness has led to the influence of the trust seal on purchase intention. A NeuroIS study could reveal activation of the neural correlates of trustworthiness. All other things being equal, this would suggest that elevated purchase intention is a result of increased trustworthiness perceptions.

4. Brain activity, or any other biological activation, can be used to inform IT artifact evaluation.

    Example: Brain research has found that trust is associated with activity in the caudate nucleus (for a review, see Riedl and Javor, 2012). Software developers could implement two prototypes of a user interface and evaluate the trust-inducing potential of each version, based on fMRI. Moreover, EEG research identified neural correlates of cognitive workload (for a review, see Müller-Putz et al., 2015). Developers could evaluate the cognitive workload effects of different prototypes.

5. Neuroscience and psychophysiological methods and tools make possible the measurement of constructs that cannot be reliably measured on the basis of self-report techniques such as interviews or questionnaires.

    Example: Flow is a mental state in which an individual performing an activity is immersed in a feeling of focus, complete involvement, and enjoyment in the process of the activity.

It follows that the measurement of flow based on questionnaire is difficult because, at least in case of concurrent measurement, the flow necessarily becomes interrupted. Mauri et al. (2011) have used a combination of neurophysiological measures to evaluate the flow state of Facebook users, and their results show that physiological activation patterns can be used to explain Facebook's success.

6. Biological states and processes can be better predictors of behaviorally relevant outcome variables (e.g., user health) than self-report measures.

    Example: Medical evidence indicates that repeated and chronic elevations of stress hormones may have detrimental health effects (see, for example, the review by Riedl, 2013, which shows reports on the stress hormones adrenaline and cortisol). Also, it is an established fact that conscious perception of stress, measured by means of questionnaires, frequently does not significantly correlate with the unconscious elevations of stress hormones (e.g., Tams et al., 2014). This finding suggests that hormone measurements are better predictors of future health states than self-reports. Yet, it is important to note that the best way to predict dependent variables is often to use complementary forms of measurement.

7. Neuroscience and psychophysiological methods and tools make possible an understanding of whether the use of IT artifacts alters the brain, and if so, how this occurs.

    Example: It is reported that IT use may lead to addiction, and that this behavioral addiction is based on structural and/or functional changes in the brain (He et al., 2017, Montag and Reuter, 2015).

8. Biological states and processes can be used in real time to design adaptive systems that may positively affect practically relevant outcome variables such as health, well-being, satisfaction, and productivity.

    Example: It has been demonstrated that bio-signals indicating the cognitive and affective states of users (e.g., facial expressions, pupil dilation, skin conductance, or brain waves) may be automatically monitored so that a neuro-adaptive system can dynamically adapt the interface to a user's states. Adam et al. (2016), for example, present a design blueprint for stress-sensitive adaptive enterprise systems; one of the major characteristics of this blueprint is the use of neurophysiological measures (e.g., skin conductance) as real-time stress indicators.

9. Provision of real-time information on a user's own biological state, based on a specific physiological indicator, constitutes an important foundation for a user to consciously control the physiological indicator. Such biofeedback systems may have positive effects on outcome variables such as health or performance.

    Example: If a person observes his or her own level of arousal (e.g., in the form of a graph on a computer screen) based on real-time measurement of the arousal state with non-obtrusive measures (e.g., skin conductance), this greater awareness improves conscious control of the arousal level. Arousal has a significant influence on human performance (Yerkes and Dodson, 1908); thus, users may benefit from biofeedback systems.

10. Electrophysiological measures of brain function can be used to replace input devices (e.g., mouse or keyboard) in human-computer interaction, which may positively affect outcome variables such as enjoyment or productivity.

Example: Navigation in virtual worlds is possible through BCI technologies (e.g., Scherer et al., 2008). A long-term goal of brain-computer interaction (BCI) research in the business domain has been proposed (Byrne and Parasuraman, 1996; Lee and Tan, 2006; Loos et al., 2010; Riedl, 2009), namely that such systems may contribute to the automatization of process steps in workflows (e.g., a system recognizes a user's intentions and information processing begins automatically).

What are possible NeuroIS topics?

In the previous section, several NeuroIS topics have already been outlined. This section provides a brief publications retrospective of NeuroIS papers. The identification of the research topics, and the neuroscience tools that have been applied to examine the topics, is based on analysis of papers published between 2010 and 2016. The following discussion is illustrative. It follows that this brief review of papers is not exhaustive.

Based on fMRI, Dimoka (2010) found that trust in online environments is related to the brain's reward (caudate nucleus, putamen), prediction (anterior paracingulate cortex), and uncertainty areas (orbitofrontal cortex), while distrust is related to the brain's emotion (amygdala) and fear of loss areas (insular cortex). Moreover, this study found that the identified brain areas may predict price premiums in simulated online shopping and the levels of brain activation have a stronger predictive power than the corresponding self-report measures. Using the same brain imaging technique, Riedl et al. (2010) examined gender differences in online trust and found some similarities (e.g., insular cortex related to disgust, uncertainty, or anticipation of pain) and substantial differences (e.g., caudate nucleus, putamen, and thalamus related to reward, or prefrontal structures related to anticipation of future decision consequences, or hippocampus related to memory) between neural processing in women and men. In a further fMRI study, Riedl et al. (2014) studied trust in avatars and humans. Findings indicate that people are better able to predict the trustworthiness of humans than the trustworthiness of avatars. Moreover, it was found that decision making about whether or not to trust another actor activates the medial frontal cortex significantly more during interaction with humans, if compared to interaction with avatars (note that this brain region is of high importance for the prediction of other individuals' thoughts and intentions, referred to as mentalizing, a crucial ability in trust situations). Finally, results indicate that the trustworthiness learning rate is similar, whether interacting with humans or avatars.

In addition to trust studies, several NeuroIS papers examined stress and arousal. Nunamaker et al. (2011) developed and evaluated an automated kiosk that uses embodied intelligent agents to interview individuals and detect changes in arousal, behavior, and cognitive effort by using psychophysiological information systems. In essence, the authors describe the contribution of their study as follows:

> [T]his research demonstrates how even a single sensor [measuring vocal pitch, people speak with a higher pitch and with more variation in pitch or fundamental frequency when under increased stress or arousal], properly modeled, can provide . . . awareness of human emotion or behavior.
>
> (p. 42)

Riedl et al. (2012) examined user stress resulting from system breakdown. Using salivary measurement of the stress hormone cortisol, it was found that system breakdown in the form of an error message is an acute stressor that may elicit cortisol elevations as high as in non-HCI (human-computer interaction) stress situations such as public speaking. In a similar experiment, Riedl et al. (2013) studied the role of gender in computer users' physiological reactions to malfunctioning technology. Based on theories explaining that men, in contrast to women, are more sensitive to "achievement stress," they hypothesized that, in cases of system breakdown during execution of a human-computer interaction task under time pressure (as compared to a breakdown situation without time pressure), male users would exhibit higher levels of stress than women. Using electrodermal activity as a stress indicator, the hypothesis was confirmed.

Astor et al. (2013) developed and evaluated a neuro-adaptive system in a financial decision-making context, based on unobtrusive and real-time heart rate measurement. Their study demonstrated the efficacy of a biofeedback-based NeuroIS tool aimed at supporting decision makers with improving emotion regulation capabilities. In another study on technostress, Tams et al. (2014) examined effects of stress on performance on a computer-based task. This study showed that physiological and self-report measures can diverge. Importantly, this divergence precludes them from constituting alternative forms of measurement; rather, both forms of measurement seem to be complementary. This complementarity was demonstrated by using the physiological measure (salivary alpha-amylase, a precursor substance of a major stress hormone in the human body) to explain additional variance in performance on a computer-based task, variance to which the self-reported stress measure was blind. Thus, the authors concluded that "the value of NeuroIS research lies in its capacity to complement traditional IS methods so that a more complete understanding of IS phenomena can be obtained and more powerful predictive relationships achieved" (p. 744).

Léger et al. (2014a) report on an experiment that used an enterprise resource planning (ERP) system in a decision-making context to investigate differences between the emotional responses of expert and novice users. Specifically, it was examined how such a difference affects information sourcing behavior. In a simulated ERP business environment (i.e., SAP), subjects' emotional responses during business decisions were measured based on electrodermal activity recording. Results show that both expert and novice SAP users exhibit significant electrodermal activity during their interaction with SAP, showing that ERP use can be an emotional process for both groups. Moreover, results show that experts' emotional responses lead to their sourcing information from SAP, while novices' emotional responses lead to their sourcing information from other people. Altogether, Léger et al. (2014b) concluded that emotions can lead to different behavioral reactions, depending on whether the user is an expert or novice.

In another stream of research based on EEG, Gregor et al. (2014) examined user emotions during interaction with websites. They found that positive and negative emotion-inducing stimuli were associated with positive and negative emotions when viewing the websites; note that emotions were measured based on self-reports and EEG data. Findings also indicate that the EEG measure had some predictive power for the outcome variable e-loyalty. Li et al. (2014) examined user game engagement through software gaming elements. Findings demonstrated that cognitive-related gaming elements (classified as game complexity and game familiarity) influence the density of theta oscillations from the left side of the dorsolateral prefrontal cortex and game engagement.

Hu et al. (2015) studied information security and self-control. Using event-related potentials, an EEG-based technique, findings indicate that subjects with low self-control had lower levels of neural recruitment in both hemispheres relative to those with high self-control, in particular with respect to areas in or near the dorsal lateral prefrontal cortex and inferior frontal cortex. The authors argue that their study

> extend[s] the findings in neuroscience literature related to the role of self-control in decision making in general, and validate a new paradigm for use with the electroencephalography/event-related potentials (EEG/ERP) technique to examine theoretical questions in information security and criminology research.
>
> (p. 7)

Another study also examined information security. Specifically, Vance et al. (2014) studied users' perception of and response to information security risks. Findings indicate that participants' P300 amplitude, a specific EEG measure, in response to losses in a risk-taking experimental task strongly predicted security warning disregard in a subsequent and unrelated computing task. Importantly, self-reported measures of information security risk did not predict security warning disregard. The study also found that after simulating a malware incident on the participants' computing devices, post-test measures of information security risk perception did predict security warning disregard. Thus, the results of this experiment suggest that self-reported measures of information security risk can significantly predict security behavior, but only when security risks are salient. In contrast, the P300, an EEG-based risk measure in this study, was a significant predictor of security behavior both before and after the security incident. The authors concluded that their results "highlight the robustness of NeuroIS methods in measuring risk perceptions and their value in predicting security behavior" (p. 704). A recent fMRI study by Warkentin et al. (2016) on the neural correlates of protection motivation for secure IT behaviors confirms the assessment of Vance and colleagues that NeuroIS methods may provide significant value to IT security researchers.

In addition to trust, technostress and arousal, and security, IS researchers have examined several other topics based on neurophysiological measurement. Léger et al. (2014a) used frequency analysis to examine the neural correlates of cognitive absorption in the context of IS training. Results indicate that subjects with high EEG Alpha and low EEG Beta (indicating calmness, relaxation, and low vigilance) reported being more cognitively absorbed than subjects who did not display these patters.

So far, I discussed different NeuroIS topics based on example studies. A more systematic review of NeuroIS research is provided in Riedl and Léger (2016, section 4.2). This review classified 76 papers published in the 2011–2014 proceedings of the Gmunden Retreat on NeuroIS (for details, see www.neurois.org/). Classification is based on four categories described in Dimoka et al. (2012, p. 691): cognitive processes, emotional processes, social processes, and decision-making processes. Table 7.2 summarizes the main results of this analysis.

Cognition and emotion, importantly, are involved in both social and decision-making processes. It follows that the results indicate that NeuroIS research has thus far explored only the two fundamental processes, namely cognition and emotion, and has not yet comprehensively investigated their application with regard to social and decision-making processes. Because both social neuroscience and decision neuroscience are two fields which have been developing at a stunning pace, it is likely that future NeuroIS research will also study social and decision-making processes more intensively (because a wealth of relevant research findings are available in social neuroscience and decision neuroscience).

With respect to the adoption rate of neuroscience tools, Riedl and Léger (2016), based on their analysis of papers published in the proceedings of the Gmunden Retreat on NeuroIS, found the following result: (1) EEG, (2) eye-tracking (including pupillometry),

Table 7.2 Results of NeuroIS paper classification ($N = 76$)

Category	# Papers	Percent	Example Topics
Cognitive	33	43%	Information search, mental workload in HCI
Emotional	30	39%	Technostress, website impression formation
Social	11	14%	Trust, coordination in IS initiatives
Decision-making	2	3%	Online payment method choice, risk processing
Sum	76	100%	

Note: Original data of this analysis can be found in Riedl and Léger, 2016, section 4.2. Sum of percents of rows is not 100% due to rounding differences. HCI: Human-Computer Interaction.

(3) electrodermal activity, (4) fMRI, (5) metrics related to heart rate, and (6) hormone assessment. Other tools (e.g., fNIRS) have been applied less frequently. It follows that NeuroIS researchers have applied tools related to both measurement of CNS activity (e.g., EEG, fMRI, or fNIRS) and measurement of ANS activity (e.g., pupillometry, electrodermal activity, metrics related to heart rate, or hormone measurement). I consider this variety as a major strength of the NeuroIS field.

How to conduct NeuroIS research?

This section gives an overview of important concepts of a NeuroIS research methodology. I start this section with a brief summary of major neurophysiological tools (see Table 7.3). More comprehensive tool descriptions are provided in Riedl et al. (2010), Dimoka et al. (2012), and particularly in Riedl and Léger (2016, see chap. 3).

Table 7.3 shows that each NeuroIS tool is either related to measurement of CNS or ANS activity. Moreover, it is also shown what specific parameter a tool actually measures. As an example, fMRI and fNIRS do not directly measure neuronal activity. Rather, neuronal activity is inferred based on other physiological indicators. Also, Table 7.3 shows an assessment of a tool's intrusiveness and the costs of application. Note that the main goal of this classification is to give the reader an impression of the relative intrusiveness and costs. As explained in detail in Riedl et al. (2014, section 5.6), intrusiveness can be conceptualized with three dimensions: degree of movement freedom during task execution, degree of natural position during task execution (which is usually a sitting or standing position in human-computer interaction), and degree of invasiveness (defined as the extent to which the recording device of a measurement instrument has to be inserted into or attached to the body).

Based on the notion that NeuroIS researchers deliberately select a tool in a specific research situation, a number of papers have been published that deal with specific guidelines. Dimoka (2012) published guidelines for conducting fMRI studies in social science research. These guidelines were later complemented by Hubert et al. (2012, 2017) who introduced connectivity analysis of brain imaging data to NeuroIS research. Gefen et al. (2014) discuss the potential role of fNIRS in IS research. In another paper, Léger et al. (2014c) introduced the Eye-Fixation Related Potential (EFRP) method to IS research. The EFRP method allows synchronization of eye-tracking data with EEG recordings to precisely capture users' neural activity at the exact time when processing of a stimulus begins (e.g., processing an event on the screen.). In essence, EFRP complements and overcomes shortcomings of the traditional ERP method, which can only stamp the time at which a stimulus is presented to a user. It follows that the

Table 7.3 Overview of NeuroIS tools

	Tool measures...	Intrusiveness	Costs of application
Tools related to CNS activity measurement			
fMRI	Neural activity is inferred based on magnetic properties of oxygenated and deoxygenated blood in the brain	high	high
fNIRS	Neural activity is inferred based on oxy-hemoglobin and deoxy-hemoglobin concentration changes in the cortical tissue of the brain	medium	medium
PET	Neural activity is inferred based on metabolic activity (visualized by injection of radioactive isotopes)	high	high
EEG	Measurement of electrical activity on the scalp, which constitutes the manifestation of the activity of populations of neurons in the brain	medium	medium
MEG	Measurement of magnetic fields induced by activity in the brain	high	high
Tools related to ANS activity measurement			
EDA	Measurement of the conductance of the skin in a specific context, or in response to a particular stimulus (often measured in the palm of the hand)	low	low
EKG	Measurement of electrical activity of the heart on the skin	low	low
Pupillometry	Measurement of pupil dilation	low	medium
fEMG	Measurement of electrical activity resulting from contraction and relaxation of facial muscles	medium	low
Hormone assessment	Measurement of hormones in blood, saliva, or urine	low (except drawing of blood samples)	low

EFRP method increases preciseness of measurement in NeuroIS research. Müller-Putz et al. (2015) discuss EEG as a research tool in the IS discipline, and specifically deal with the tool's foundations, measurement principles, and applications in the IS field.

Moreover, vom Brocke and Liang (2014) have published general guidelines for neuroscience studies in IS research. In essence, this paper takes an IS perspective in deriving six phases for conducting NeuroIS research and describes five guidelines for planning and evaluating NeuroIS studies: to advance IS research, to apply the standards of neuroscience, to justify the choice of a neuroscience strategy of inquiry, to map IS concepts to bio-data, and to relate the experimental setting to IS-authentic situations.

Riedl et al. (2014), in a paper titled "Towards a NeuroIS Research Methodology: Intensifying the Discussion on Methods, Tools, and Measurement," argue that six factors with respect to a measurement instrument, among others that will become evident in future discussions, are critical for a rigorous NeuroIS research methodology. The six factors are (definitions taken from Riedl et al., 2014, p. xxix):

1. *Reliability*: The extent to which a measurement instrument is free of measurement error, and therefore yields the same results on repeated measurement of the same construct.
2. *Validity*: The extent to which a measurement instrument measures the construct that it purports to measure.
3. *Sensitivity*: A property of a measure that describes how well it differentiates values along the continuum inherent in a construct.
4. *Diagnosticity*: A property of a measure that describes how precisely it captures a target construct as opposed to other constructs.
5. *Objectivity*: The extent to which research results are independent from the investigator and reported in a way so that replication is possible.
6. *Intrusiveness*: The extent to which a measurement instrument interferes with an ongoing task, thereby distorting the investigated construct.

Riedl et al. (2014) argue that NeuroIS researchers – independent from whether their role is editor, reviewer, or author – should carefully give thought to these factors.

Concluding comments

The genesis of NeuroIS took place in 2007. Since then, a number of IS scholars have started to use concepts and tools from neuroscience to better understand human cognition, emotion, and behavior in IS contexts. In my opinion, the NeuroIS field has developed at a stunning pace in the past decade. As outlined in this paper, a number of IS topics have been studied based on a variety of neuroscience tools. Moreover, several conceptual papers and a recent textbook (Riedl and Léger, 2016) have discussed the great potential of neuroscience for IS research. Also, papers contributing to the methodological development of the field were published. However, despite these positive developments in the past, recent evidence (Riedl et al., 2017b) indicates that the NeuroIS field is still in a relatively nascent stage. Therefore, it is critical that more IS scholars get engaged in NeuroIS, thereby increasing the number of community members who are potential editors, reviewers, and authors. Importantly, newcomers must become familiar with the basic theories, concepts, methods, tools, and measurements that are used in cognitive neuroscience, neurobiology, and psychophysiology. Based on a higher degree of familiarity, IS scholars can better evaluate whether or not a specific theory, concept, method, tool, or measurement is suitable to study a specific IS research question, or may form the basis for the development of a neuro-adaptive information system. It is hoped that increasingly more IS scholars will recognize the indisputable potential of neuroscience for IS research and will be able to develop the knowledge and infrastructure basis to conduct high-quality NeuroIS research. It will be rewarding to see what insights future research will reveal.

References

Adam, M.T.P., Gimpel, H., Maedche, A., and Riedl, R. (2016). Design blueprint for stress-sensitive adaptive enterprise systems. *Business and Information Systems Engineering*. First Online: 05 September 2016.

Astor, P.J., Adam, M.T.P., Jerčić, P., Schaaff, K., and Weinhardt, C. (2013). Integrating biosignals into information systems: A NeuroIS tool for improving emotion regulation. *Journal of Management Information Systems*, 30, 247–277.

Bar, M., and Neta, M. (2007). Visual elements of subjective preference modulate amygdala activation. *Neuropsychologia*, 45, 2191–2200.

Byrne, E. A., and Parasuraman, R. (1996). Psychophysiology and adaptive automation. *Biological Psychology*, 42, 249–268.

Dimoka, A. (2010). What does the brain tell us about trust and distrust? Evidence from a functional neuroimaging study. *MIS Quarterly*, 34, 373–396.

Dimoka, A. (2012). How to conduct a functional magnetic resonance (fMRI) study in social science research. *MIS Quarterly*, 36, 811–840.

Dimoka, A., Banker, R. D., Benbasat, I., Davis, F. D., Dennis, A. R., Gefen, D., Gupta, A., Ischebeck, A., Kenning, P., Müller-Putz, G., Pavlou, P. A., Riedl, R., vom Brocke, J., and Weber, B. (2012). On the use of neurophysiological tools in IS research: Developing a research agenda for NeuroIS. *MIS Quarterly*, 36, 679–702.

Dimoka, A., Pavlou, P. A., and Davis, F. D. (2007). NEURO-IS: The potential of cognitive neuroscience for information systems research. *Proceedings of the 28th International Conference on Information Systems*.

Gefen, D., Ayaz, H., and Onaral, B. (2014). Applying functional near infrared (fNIR) spectroscopy to enhance MIS research. *AIS Transactions on Human-Computer Interaction*, 6, 55–73.

Gregor, S., Lin, A.C.H., Gedeon, T., Riaz, A., and Zhu, D. (2014). Neuroscience and a nomological network for the understanding and assessment of emotions in information systems research. *Journal of Management Information Systems*, 30, 13–48.

He, Q., Turel, O., and Bechara, A. (2017). Brain anatomy alterations associated with social networking site (SNS) addiction. *Scientific Reports*, 7(paper 45064), 1–8.

Hu, Q., West, R., and Smarandescu, L. (2015). The role of self-control in information security violations: Insights from a cognitive neuroscience perspective. *Journal of Management Information Systems*, 31, 6–48.

Hubert, M., Linzmajer, M., Riedl, R., Hubert, M., Kenning, P., and Weber, B. (2017). Using Psychophysiological Interaction Analysis with fMRI data in IS research: A guideline. *Communications of the Association for Information Systems*, 40, Article 9.

Hubert, M., Linzmajer, M., Riedl, R., Kenning, P., and Hubert, M. (2012). Introducing connectivity analysis to NeuroIS research. *Proceedings of the 33rd International Conference on Information Systems*.

Huston, J., Galletta, D. F., and Huston, T. (1993). The effects of computer monitoring on the medical transcriptionist's performance and stress. *Journal of the American Health Information Management Association*, 64, 77–81.

Lee, J. C., and Tan, D. S. (2006). Using a low-cost electroencephalograph for task classification. *ACM Symposium on User Interface Software and Technology*, 19, 81–90.

Léger, P.-M., Davis, F. D., Cronan, T. P., and Perret, J. (2014a). Neurophysiological correlates of cognitive absorption in an enactive training context. *Computers in Human Behavior*, 34, 273–283.

Léger, P.-M., Riedl, R., and vom Brocke, J. (2014b). Emotions and ERP information sourcing: The moderating role of expertise. *Industrial Management and Data Systems*, 114, 456–471.

Léger, P.-M., Sénecal, S., Courtemanche, F., Ortiz de Guinea, A., Titah, R., Fredette, M., et al. (2014c). Precision is in the eye of the beholder: Application of eye fixation-related potentials to information systems research. *Journal of the Association for Information Systems*, 15, Article 3.

Li, M., Jiang, Q., Tan, C.-H., and Wei, K.-K. (2014). Enhancing user-game engagement through software gaming elements. *Journal of Management Information Systems*, 30, 115–150.

Loos, P., Riedl, R., Müller-Putz, G., vom Brocke, J., Davis, F. D., Banker, R. D., and Léger, P.-M. (2010). NeuroIS: Neuroscientific approaches in the investigation and development of information systems. *Business and Information Systems Engineering*, 395–401.

Mauri, M., Cipresso, P., Balgera, A. et al. (2011). Why is Facebook so successful? Psychophysiological measures describe a core flow state while using Facebook. *Cyberpsychology Behavior and Social Networking*, 14, 723–731.

Montag, C., and Reuter, M. (Eds.). (2015). *Internet addiction: Neuroscientific approaches and therapeutical interventions*. Series in Neuroscience, Psychology & Behavioral Economics. Heidelberg: Springer.

Müller-Putz, G., Riedl, R., and Wriessnegger, S. (2015). Electroencephalography (EEG) as a research tool in the information systems discipline: Foundations, measurement, and applications. *Communications of the Association for Information Systems*, 37, 911–948.

Nunamaker, J. F., Derrick, D. C., Elkins, A. C., Burgoon, J. K., and Patton, M. W. (2011). Embodied conversational agent-based Kiosk for automated interviewing. *Journal of Management Information Systems*, 17–48.

Price, C. J., and Friston, K. J. (2005). Functional ontologies for cognition: The systematic definition of structure and function. *Cognitive Psychology*, 22, 262–275.

Riedl, R. (2009). Zum Erkenntnispotenzial der kognitiven Neurowissenschaften für die Wirtschaftsinformatik: Überlegungen anhand exemplarischer Anwendungen. *NeuroPsychoEconomics*, 4, 32–44.

Riedl, R. (2013). On the biology of technostress: Literature review and research agenda. *DATA BASE for Advances in Information Systems*, 44, 18–55.

Riedl, R., Banker, R. D., Benbasat, I., Davis, F. D., Dennis, A. R., Dimoka, A., Gefen, D., Gupta, A., Ischebeck, A., Kenning, P., Müller-Putz, G., Pavlou, P. A., Straub, D. W., vom Brocke, J., and Weber, B. (2010). On the foundations of NeuroIS: Reflections on the Gmunden Retreat 2009. *Communications of the AIS*, 27, 243–264.

Riedl, R., Davis, F. D., and Hevner, A. R. (2014). Towards a NeuroIS research methodology: Intensifying the discussion on methods, tools, and measurement. *Journal of the Association for Information Systems*, 15(10), Article 4.

Riedl, R., Davis, F. D., Banker, R. D., and Kenning, P. (2017a). *Neuroscience in information systems research: Applying knowledge of brain functionality without neuroscience tools*. Berlin, Heidelberg: Springer.

Riedl, R., Fischer, T., Léger, P.-M. (2017b). *A decade of NeuroIS research: Status quo, challenges, and future directions*. Working paper (currently under review).

Riedl, R., Hubert, M., and Kenning, P. (2010). Are there neural gender differences in online trust? An fMRI study on the perceived trustworthiness of eBay offers. *MIS Quarterly*, 34, 397–428.

Riedl, R., and Javor, A. (2012). The biology of trust: Integrating evidence from genetics, endocrinology and functional brain imaging. *Journal of Neuroscience, Psychology, and Economics*, 5, 63–91.

Riedl, R., Kindermann, H., Auinger, A., and Javor, A. (2012). Technostress from a neurobiological perspective: System breakdown increases the stress hormone cortisol in computer users. *Business & Information Systems Engineering*, 4, 61–69.

Riedl, R., Kindermann, H., Auinger, A., and Javor, A. (2013). Computer breakdown as a stress factor during task completion under time pressure: Identifying gender differences based on skin conductance. *Advances in Human-Computer Interaction*, Article ID 420169.

Riedl, R., and Léger, P.-M. (2016). *Fundamentals of NeuroIS – Information systems and the brain*. Berlin/Heidelberg: Springer.

Riedl, R., Mohr, P., Kenning, P., Davis, F., and Heekeren, H. (2014). Trusting humans and avatars: A brain imaging study based on evolution theory. *Journal of Management Information Systems*, 30, 83–113.

Scherer, R., Schlögl, A., Leeb, R., Bischof, H., and Pfurtscheller, G. (2008). Toward self-paced brain-computer communication: Navigation through virtual worlds. *IEEE Transactions on Biomedical Engineering*, 55, 675–682.

Sporns, O. 2011. *Networks of the brain*. Cambridge, MA: MIT Press.

Tams, S., Hill, K., Ortiz de Guinea, A., Thatcher, J., and Grover, V. (2014). NeuroIS – Alternative or complement to existing methods? Illustrating the holistic effects of neuroscience and self-reported data in the context of technostress research. *Journal of the Association for Information Systems*, 15, Article 1.

Vance, A., Anderson, B. B., Kirwan, C. B., and Eargle, D. (2014). Using measures of risk perception to predict information security behavior: Insights from electroencephalography (EEG). *Journal of the Association for Information Systems*, 15, Article 2.

vom Brocke, J., and Liang, T.-P. (2014). Guidelines for neuroscience studies in information systems research. *Journal of Management Information Systems*, 30, 211–234.

Warkentin, M., Walden, E., Johnston, A. C., and Straub, D. W. (2016). Neural correlates of protection motivation for secure IT behaviors: An fMRI examination. *Journal of the Association for Information Systems*, 17, Article 1.

Yerkes, R. M., and Dodson, J. D. (1908). The relation of strength of stimulus to rapidity of habit-formation. *Journal of Comparative Neurology and Psychology*, 18, 459–482.

8
ETHNOGRAPHY IN INFORMATION SYSTEMS RESEARCH

Quo vadis?

Ulrike Schultze

What is ethnography?

Ethnography is a research approach originally developed in anthropology, where its primary objective was to gain a holistic and multi-faceted understanding of the role of culture, that is, the socially acquired and shared knowledge held by the members in a social setting, in human activity. Providing a "thick description" (Geertz, 1973) of the social setting under study was the primary product of ethnographic research. Today, ethnographic methods are applied in many academic disciplines, including sociology, organization studies and information systems, as well as in commercial settings (e.g., new product development might rely on insights into consumer lifestyles and preferences developed by ethnographers). Understanding how people make sense of things, events and phenomena in their everyday lives is a key goal of the ethnographic endeavor, thereby making meaning and knowing its central focus.

Practically speaking, doing ethnographic research has traditionally implied

> a long period of intimate study and residence in a well-defined community employing a wide range of observational techniques including prolonged face-to-face contact with members of local groups, direct participation in some of the group's activities, and a greater emphasis on intensive work with informants than on the use of documentary or survey data.
>
> (Conklin, 1968: 172)

A defining feature of the ethnographic approach is thus the researcher's immersion in a social setting referred to as the field, as well as his engagement with its participants. There is an expectation of remaining co-present in the field for an extended amount of time (e.g., one year) and relying on firsthand, in-situ participant observation for data collection. This implies that the researcher is visible (and accountable) to the people whose everyday lives he is studying.

Additionally, ethnographic research is marked by writing: not only does the ethnographer record in as much detail as possible what she observed in the field (i.e., field notes), but also what she experienced while in the social situation, for example, how it feels to be in a place and to do certain activities; things that are puzzling and frustrating (i.e., diary).

Even though ethnographic research is flexible in terms of data collection strategies and typically includes interviews with participants and review of texts (e.g., documents, emails, social media posts), observing people doing things in their minute detail from a vantage point of immersive co-presence, quintessentially defines the ethnographic endeavor. Wherever possible, the ethnographer should also try her hand at the activities enacted by the people being studied, so as to gain an embodied, affective understanding of what life is like in the social setting. With such an immersive approach, the researchers do not only gain access to what is going on in the field, but also to how people make sense of it (i.e., what they say about it). This promises to generate in-depth insights, which is one of ethnography's key value propositions (Myers, 1999).

Analytically, ethnography entails distinguishing facts from fiction, and deriving second-order concepts from first-order facts (van Maanen, 1979). Determining the facts of the situation requires the ethnographer to separate events from participants' descriptions thereof, as the latter are likely to be influenced by the appearances that informants want to maintain vis-à-vis the researcher. Facts should be limited to observed activities (e.g., behavior) and be separated from the self-presentations put forth by participants as they talk about these activities. Generating second-order concepts (i.e., generalizable statements that explain the patterning of specific activities/events) from observed first-order data (i.e., facts) requires the ethnographer to derive the invisible structures and taken-for-granted assumptions that underlie people's actions and interpretations. These second-order concepts become the building blocks of the researcher's theory development, which ultimately elevates the rich description of the field into a scientific contribution.

Importantly, this analytical work is only feasible when bits of information can be assessed by comparisons across time, informants and situations. The extended time period in the field is thus a crucial element in ethnography, not only because it allows the researcher to build rapport with informants and observe similar events on multiple occasions under different circumstances, but also because it gives the researcher time to reflect on events and theories, test and discuss them with participants, and revise categories while co-present in the field.

Ethnography in IS research

One indicator of whether ethnographic methods are valued in IS research is their rate of publication in IS journals. Paré et al. (2008) found that ethnographies represented a mere 2.6% of the 189 publications they identified in their review of all empirical papers on the impact of IT published between 1991 and 2005 in *Management Information Systems Quarterly, Information Systems Research, Information & Organization,* and *European Journal of Information Systems*. More recently, Rowe (2012) argued that ethnographic research is rare in IS and, in order to encourage ethnographic studies, he announced a new category of IS research genres, namely, Ethnographies and Narratives, for the *EJIS*. Some papers in this category have already been published (e.g., Utesheva, Simpson, & Cecez-Kecmanovic, 2016).

Another indicator of ethnography's perceived value in the field of IS, is the number of calls for ethnographic research that are made. While calls for ethnographic studies are frequently made in order to answer research questions or resolve inconsistent findings in a specific domain (e.g., Overby, Slaughter, & Konsynski, 2010), Ramiller et al. (2008) make a particularly strong case for the role of ethnographic research in addressing the discipline's struggles with producing insights relevant to industry. They propose a type of study that they label "boundary ethnography" to investigate research projects that involve both academics and practitioners. They anticipate that such studies might develop a set of best practices for research collaboration across the industry–academia divide.

While the review of the ethnographic studies in IS that is presented in this section is admittedly partial, it nevertheless highlights that ethnographies are published fairly regularly in our leading journals. It also points to the diversity of topics and approaches that fall under the umbrella of ethnography in IS.

Organizational ethnographies

Ethnographic research methods have been embraced in IS research particularly as a way of studying the organizational implications of information technology in use. Studies of work practice frequently rely on organizational ethnographies, whose purpose is to "uncover and explicate the ways in which people in particular work settings come to understand, account for, take action and otherwise manage their day-to-day situation" (van Maanen, 1979: 540). Importantly, the study of practice is not just focused on what people do (i.e., the actions they take), but also on the social structures that enable and constrain their agency. From a structurational perspective (Giddens, 1984), practice thus encompasses both structure, agency and the recursive, constitutive relationship between them (also Bourdieu, 1977).

The work practices that have been studied as organizational ethnographies in IS are varied but nevertheless tend to focus on knowledge creation and coordination. For example, in their study of task-based offshoring afforded by transformational technologies that enable the creation of digital artifacts, Leonardi and Bailey (2008) relied on a multi-sited ethnography of engineers in India, Mexico and the United States, to identify five new knowledge transfer practices. Levina (2005) followed the development of a Web application in a media company in order to gain insight into systems development practices that required collaboration among different professional groups (e.g., marketing, sales, IT). Knowledge practices found to be conducive to successful collaborative system design included reflection in action and boundary spanning.

In their nine-month ethnography of knowledge integration practices in a manufacturer of semiconductors, Howard-Grenville and Carlile (2008) identified how knowledge regimes – some of which were more powerful than others – were sources of incompatibilities that challenged the design of knowledge integration systems. Ravishankar, Pan, and Myers (2013) were similarly concerned with issues of asymmetries of power, albeit in a more global setting. The purpose of their eight-month ethnography of an Indian IT outsourcer was to understand the role of historical power asymmetries between the West and former colonies in the contemporary off-shoring relationships.

A key feature of organizational ethnographies is that the field site is an institutionally defined place of work (e.g., an office building, a hospital, a lab) and as such a geographic space that the researcher can physically enter in order to study the phenomenon of interest. The ethnographer is co-present and able to both observe events and ask people about their understanding of them. Even though the boundaries of the field emerge as the researchers decide who or what to follow in their data generation efforts, the definition of the field is nevertheless based largely on established organizational parameters (e.g., work groups, projects, artifacts).

Nevertheless, the organizational ethnographies in IS vary on a number of dimension. For example, when it comes to length of stay in the field, Garud and Kumaraswamy (2005) relied on 45 days of firsthand, ethnographic observation of knowledge processes to enrich their study of vicious and virtuous circles in the management of knowledge. In contrast, Vieira da Cunha (2013) stayed in the field over a 15-month period and completed 307 days of observation of a new sales unit in a telecommunication's firm. Generally, the length of stay in organizational ethnographies in IS lies between six and 12 months.

The location of the research site also varies tremendously. While Wales et al. (2007) and Mazmanian et al. (2014) studied NASA engineers, whose technology-intensive work revolved around the use of software, data and screens, Miscione (2007) did participant observations of healthcare and healing practices in rural areas of the Upper Amazon, Peru, where a telemedicine system was being implemented. While some of the studies are single-sited (e.g., Leonardi, 2013; Oborn, Barrett, & Davidson, 2011; Schultze & Orlikowski, 2004), others rely on multiple sites (e.g., Leonardi & Bailey, 2008).

Another distinction between the studies is their data collection strategy, specifically with respect to what and or who is followed. While some researchers make either a project (e.g., Levina, 2005) or a class of artifact (e.g., Mazmanian et al., 2014) their key focus, others focus on an organizational unit (Mattarelli, Bertolotti, & Macrı, 2013).

We have also seen some diversity in terms of the style with which ethnographic material is presented. For example, Schultze (2000) and Mathiassen and Sandberg (2013) relied on confessional styles of writing that make the researcher's role as research instrument, generating both data and theoretical insights, evident. While these two studies are examples of reflexive ethnography, Lin et al.'s (2015) work is a critical ethnography, which "is concerned with social issues such as freedom, power, social control and values with respect to the development, use, and impact of information technology" (Myers & Klein, 2011: 17). In their presentation of their ethnographic material, Lin et al.'s (2015) highlight the macro-sociological power relationships at play in the implementation of an educational technology in rural Taiwan.

Digital ethnographies

There are also some examples of digital ethnographies in IS research. Digital ethnography is the study of phenomena that are created through computer-mediated social interaction by relying on the researcher's firsthand observations of human behavior in online spaces. Phenomena that require digital adaptations of classic ethnographic approaches include virtual teams, online communities, virtual (game) worlds and digital social networks. While these distributed and technology-mediated social settings challenge the assumptions of physical co-presence and independent observation of embodied practices (i.e., such that a wink is a powerful marker of meaning) that have traditionally been a requirement of ethnographic research, digital ethnography recognizes that people are operating in virtual spaces that are characterized by a degree of uncertainty associated with users' lack of access to the physically embodied person taking action online (Hine, 2015). Understanding how people live and work in these mediated settings and how they make sense of virtuality is thus of keen interest to digital ethnographers.

There is some disagreement among practitioners of digital ethnography about whether data about the participants' online actions should be enhanced by engaging with them in their physically embodied selves in off-line settings as well. Because one of the ethnographer's key challenges is separating fact from fiction, there is some concern about taking participant's online actions and presentations of self at face value. Hine (2015), for example, argues that collecting data about online phenomena by interacting with the actual user enhances the validity of data and should therefore be pursued in digital ethnographies. In contrast, Boellstorff (2008) maintains that digital environments, like virtual worlds, are social spaces in their own right. Even though events and cultures in digital settings are intertwined with those of the actual world, they are real and legitimate to users. Boellstorff (2008: 61) writes:

> If during my research, I was talking to a woman, I was not concerned to determine if she was "really" a man in the actual world, or even if two different people were taking

turns controlling "her." Most Second Life residents meeting this woman would not know the answer to such questions, so for my ethnographic purposes it was important that I not know either.

Despite the divergence over how best to address the distinctions between virtual phenomena enacted by digitally embodied users who are nevertheless physically embodied and located in a geographical place, there is little controversy over the need for digital ethnographers to make themselves visible (and accountable) in the virtual space (Hudson & Bruckman, 2004) and to remain active in it for an extended period of time. The digital ethnographies published in IS provide us examples of how ethnographers can engage in the virtual setting for firsthand data collection.

In their study of virtual teams, Sarker and Sahay (2004) relied on their active role as instructors throughout a 14-week course that brought together students from an American and a Norwegian university for a systems development project. Because the project teams were composed of students from each geographic location, the authors were able to physically observe and interact with half the students, while relying on the digital project spaces to symbolically observe and interact with the other half. Sarker and Sahay (2004) thus drew on three sources of data for their digital ethnography: digital communications among team members (i.e., messages posted, files shared and chat interactions on the learning management platform the students were using), reflections of team members at the end of the course and their own impressions of the virtual teams' collaborative practices throughout the course.

In order to study collaboration in virtual, open source communities, Howison and Crowston (2014) conducted a digital ethnography. Aware of the need to derive insights from reflection on his lived experience in the virtual community, Howison chose an open source project with relevance to his work life as a student. He then proceeded to engage with a bibliographic management software project daily for four years. He not only used the product, but followed the mailing list and bug tracker. While it is unclear whether Howison made himself visible in the community through active participation (e.g., by reporting bugs or contributing to their resolution), his long-time observations of the open source community were nevertheless contemporaneous and provided the authors with the kind of historical/cultural insight they needed to narratively reconstruct the software developers' coordination practices from the trace data that the project archives represented.

The process of making digital trace records (e.g., transaction logs, version histories, source code, email messages) meaningful by attaching them to lived experience, which the authors refer to as "trace ethnography" (Geiger & Ribes, 2011), played a central analytical role in this Howison and Crowston's (2014) study. Rather than using the voluminous amounts of digital traces that the developers' work generated for quantitative analysis, the authors instead relied on their understanding of the activities, people and technologies that produced these digital records to invert the traces and generate qualitatively rich descriptions of different actors' practices.

Chua and Yeow (2010) also studied open source development projects. They were particularly interested in the practices of cross-project coordination, which arose when multiple projects were working on a single piece of software in the open source environment. They observed this phenomenon in an open source game, Jagged Alliance 2 (JA2), whose ongoing development relied on modding different components, for example, developing new weapons or characters. Instead of just relying on the archival data of the 40 modding projects, the authors also used secondary data from wikis and online forums associated with some of these projects. What gave the project its ethnographic quality, however, was the fact that one of the co-authors was not only a player of JA2, but had also been observing the JA2 mod discussion board for three years. Even though it is not clear that the co-author made himself visible as a participant observer within the modding community during this time, his years of observation suggest that he had gained the kind of insider perspective that comes from being immersed in a community.

Greenhill and Fletcher's (2014) study of labor practices in virtual game worlds similarly relied on the researchers' active engagement in two games – Puzzle Pirates and Farmville – over an extended period of time. The researchers played Puzzle Pirates for three years and Farmville for 12 months. While they relied on blog posts and other third-party publications of people's experience with Puzzle Pirates for additional insight on this game, they also conducted interviews and analyzed visual representations for insights that extended beyond their own experience of Farmville.

Design ethnographies

While ethnography draws on a variety of largely qualitative data collection and analysis methods, it can also become part of other research traditions. In IS, in particular, ethnography frequently forms part of design research (Crabtree, 2004; Sharrock & Randall, 2004). For example, in their action research project, Bjørn et al. (2009) relied on the insights they had gained from ethnographic observation to point out inconsistencies between the proposed designs and existing work practices during design workshops. Carugati (2008) relied on his position as a member of a systems development team to collect in-depth data on the development process.

The distinction between organizational ethnography and action research might not always be clear. Even though Crabtree (2004) advocates for the hybridization of ethnography and design research, the distinction he makes between using ethnography for *design critique* versus *design practice* is helpful in characterizing a study that encompasses both observational ethnography and interventionist design. To the extent that the ethnographic data is used to support an intervention (e.g., the design of a new technology or the implementation of a system in an organizational setting), the study is more design ethnography or action research. However, if the ethnographic material is used to evaluate a design approach without the lessons being implemented in the empirical context (i.e., design critique), the study can more readily be characterized as an organizational ethnography (e.g., Gasson, 2006).

Ethnography in IS research: Quo vadis?

Research methods should ideally be chosen to illuminate phenomena of interest. This suggests that changes in the phenomena a discipline wants to study need to be met with new methods or adaptations to existing methods. In IS, technological advancement is continuously changing the issues and questions researchers want to explore. For example, technological developments are fundamentally changing the nature of work and institutions as the workforce is becoming more mobile, virtual and global. This implies that work life is more fleeting, distributed and multiple than in the past. The distinctions between organizations and their customers are being challenged in an era of open innovation (Thorén, Ågerfalk, & Edenius, 2014). As more and more human activity is mediated and recorded by technology, digital traces are a key resource that can be mined through (big data) analytics. And increasingly complex IT infrastructures, including grid computing (Venters, Oborn, & Barrett, 2014), are being deployed.

Furthermore, technology is becoming so entangled in individuals' everyday lives, that traditional boundaries of work versus play, actual versus virtual, and human versus machine can no longer be taken for granted. Additionally, this increasing intertwining of the human and the non-human renders the user's experiences with technology increasingly sensory, emotional and kinesthetic.

This list of trends highlights that IS research needs to grapple increasingly with the highly personal uses of technology (e.g., wearable technology and ubiquitous computing), where issues of multiple embodiments and the integration of technology with the user as an embodied, sensory being need to be explored. At the same time, the increasingly distributed, global and digital nature of large-scale infrastructures (e.g., digital traces, analytics) represent the other area of research that challenges our extant tools.

The increasingly fleeting nature of technology-mediated settings highlights the inadequacies of traditional social science methods (Law & Urry, 2004). Increasingly IS researchers are therefore seeking to not only study technological phenomena that occur outside of organizational settings (Yoo, 2010), but also understand the constitutive entanglement between the social and the technological in new ways. Socio-material theorizing represents a recent movement that challenges how IS phenomena are theorized, studied and represented (Orlikowski & Scott, 2008).

We also hear calls in IS for methodological approaches capable of analyzing visual data (Diaz Andrade, Urquhart, & Arthanari, 2015), as well as digital traces (Howison, Wiggins, & Crowston, 2011). Multi-sited, biographical approaches to the study of enterprise software are being advocated as an alternative to single-sited, organizational ethnographies (Williams & Pollock, 2012).

Ethnography, both as a method and as a genre of representation, has much to offer with regard to contributing key insights into these emerging phenomena of interest. However, ethnographic methods need to be adapted to deal more effectively with the ephemeral, distributed, sensory and embodied nature of contemporary phenomena. Law and Urry (2004: 403–404) maintain that our social science methods deal poorly

> with the fleeting – that which is here today and gone tomorrow, only to re-appear again the day after tomorrow. They deal poorly with the distributed – that is to be found here and there but not in between – or that which slips and slides between one place and another. They deal poorly with the multiple – that which takes different shapes in different places. They deal poorly with the non-causal, the chaotic, the complex. And such methods have difficulty dealing with the sensory – that which is subject to vision, sound, taste, smell; with the emotional – time – space compressed outbursts of anger, pain, rage, pleasure, desire, or the spiritual; and the kinaesthetic – the pleasures and pains which follow the movement and displacement of people, objects, information and ideas.

There are some forms of ethnography emerging in other fields that hold much promise for ethnographic inquiry of contemporary phenomena in IS. While these modes of ethnographic inquiry may challenge some of the tenets of ethnography as traditionally conceived, they nevertheless tend to preserve the core research practice of the researcher becoming immersed in the phenomenon/social setting for an extended period of time.

Mobile ethnography

Developed in the discipline of human geography over the last ten years (Novoa, 2015), mobile ethnography is part of a mobility paradigm that emphasizes movement – including networks, relations, flows and circulation – over fixed places (Sheller & Urry, 2016). Nevertheless, it considers movement and moorings and seeks to examine different forms of mobility – for example, corporeal travel of people, physical movement of goods, virtual person-to-person communication – and their complex combinations. Instead of focusing on phenomena and people within a situation, mobile approaches to research seek to understand patterns of connection and circulation of ideas and people.

In operational terms, mobile ethnographies imply traveling with participants in order to gain insight into the embodied, sensory experience and constitutive aspects of movement. As a method, mobile ethnographies entail

> inquiries on the move – such as the shadowing, stalking, walk-alongs, ride-alongs, participatory interventions and biographies we describe – enable questions about sensory experience, embodiment, emplacement, about what changes and what stays the same, and about the configuration and reconfiguration of assemblies of objects, spaces, people, ideas and information.
> (Büscher, Urry, & Witchger, 2011: 13)

Experiencing and participating in the everyday movement of people in a co-present manner, is of utmost importance to this method. As such,

> mobile ethnography is a translation of traditional participant observation onto contexts of mobility. It means that the ethnographer is not only expected to observe what is happening, but also to experience, feel and grasp the textures, smells, comforts and discomforts, pleasures and displeasures of a moving life. It means following people around and engaging with their worldviews. It means focusing on mobility.
> (Novoa, 2015: 99)

Applied to IS research, the sensibilities of mobile ethnographies seem particularly valuable in studies of ubiquitous, mobile technologies and experiential computing (Yoo, 2010). Shadowing users of smartphones or mobile games (e.g., Pokemon Go) using these methods promises to provide us with rich insight into the role of sensations, embodiment and movement in the experience (or performance) of geographic space, thus rendering geographies more fleeting and ephemeral. In studies of less mobile technologies such as virtual worlds (Tom Boellstorff et al., 2012), online services such as Freecycle (Hine, 2015), or sharing economy applications (e.g., Uber), mobile ethnography might enable the exploration of the meaning and patterns with which online and off-line venues are traversed.

Sensory ethnography

Sensory ethnography takes as "its starting point the multisensoriality of experience, perception, knowing and practice" (Pink, 2015: xi). It invites the researcher to do ethnography through the senses – vision, touch, taste, smell and hearing – and to account for perception that draws on the culturally shaped and intertwined nature of the senses in the research process. Sensory ethnography thus challenges the notion that ethnography relies primarily on observation, insisting instead that it is a highly reflexive and experiential process. Participant *sensing* (or sensory participation) – rather than participant *observation* – forms the cornerstone of this methodological adaptation.

An example of sensory ethnography is presented by Edvardsson and Street (2007), who were studying how different health care environments affected the understanding and provisioning of care. They noted that nurse-ethnographer David Edvardsson's senses were gradually changing during the fieldwork and that the insights he gained and the questions he asked shifted accordingly. Edvardsson and Street (2007: 26) explain:

> While being at the ward as a participating observer, DE found that he instinctively joined the brisk pace habitually used by the nurses as they moved around at the unit . . . he found that the brisk movement and sound of the hurried steps of staff prompted the sensation of wanting to move with the pace of the unit . . . [this] led him to understand the way that corridors were used in these units as spaces of passage and not for lingering or chance encounters . . . This epiphany stimulated his curiosity to explore further how people moved around the unit and what this movement might mean.

Pink (2015) highlights that walking with others, that is, sharing their pace and rhythm, is a powerful practice of sensory ethnography, as it provides the researcher insight into others' experiential world. It however also creates affinity, empathy and a sense of belonging with the participants in the field of study. By using walking as a form of research, sensory ethnography thus overlaps with mobile ethnography; however, it might enhance mobile ethnographies by making more explicit the palette of sensations that informs the experience of movement.

As the ethnographer relies on her own sensate experience as a guide to the experiential world of others, autoethnography features prominently in sensory ethnography (Pink, 2015). Autoethnography relies on the researcher's narration of the self in order to engage in cultural analysis and interpretation (Chang, 2008). It is particularly effective in the investigation of phenomena that are not only highly distributed but also sensory in nature, because the researcher can rely on her own experience as the primary source of data (Hine, 2015).

While there appear to be few published examples of autoethnographies in IS to date, those that are available rely on researchers' self-narratives of being in virtual worlds. For example, Silva and Mousavidin (2015) drew on diaries of their own gameplay in World of Warcraft (WoW) over a three-month period in order to gain insights into how players develop strategic thinking; and O'Riordan (2014) relied on her experience of being in Second Life to explore what it means to be digital. Arguing that the hybridic state of existing simultaneously in actual and virtual spaces challenges basic assumptions about existence and experience, O'Riordan (2014) suggests that the narration of one's own experience gives researchers the freedom to express their struggle to make sense of their experience in their unique, emotionally expressive voice. It is thus the complexly entangled nature of a self that is enacted in multiple venues through a variety of (digital) bodies that motivates O'Riordan (2014) to rely on self-observation as her primary data source.

Sensory ethnography can be fruitfully used in IS research. For example, Pantzar & Ruckenstein (2014) propose studying the emotional implications of data analytics, specifically in the context of the Quantified Self movement, where individuals rely on biometric trackers to monitor their bodies. What emotions do these analytics produce and how do people deal with them? Similar questions might be asked of social media, which rely on quantifications and rankings, for example, the number of likes on Facebook or number of followers on Twitter. What do such popularity and social influence analytics do – in terms of sensations – to users' identities and sense of self? By asking these kinds of questions, sensory ethnography might significantly enrich our understanding of social media and other experiential technologies.

Visual ethnography

As Diaz Andrade et al. (2015: 646) assert, "the information systems field is overwhelmingly visual in nature." Websites and social media (especially Facebook and Instagram) are rich in images and video, and individuals are increasingly relying on their smartphone cameras to capture textual information as images (e.g., photographs of a document or whiteboard). Researchers too increasingly rely not only on audio recording in their fieldwork, but also on photography and video recording (Pink, 2007). Visual ethnography offers one way of generating insights from these still and moving images. To date, however, IS research has failed to leverage such images (Diaz Andrade et al., 2015).

Visual ethnography can take one of three forms (Pink, 2007): studying society by producing images (e.g., the researcher producing photographs and/or video); examining visual representations that have already been produced, thus providing information about the social setting; or collaborating with research participants in the production of still and/or moving images that represent society. Ethnographers who take images of the social setting as part of their data generation effort find that the sharing of these images with their informants offers an occasion for sense-making and storytelling (Pink, 2007). As such, it is the conversation about visual representations during the course of ethnographic research that generates valuable insights. This approach is potentially viable in organizational and design ethnographies in IS.

Studying the visual representation of companies (e.g., websites) or individuals (e.g., social media profiles, avatars) is particularly promising in digital ethnographies in IS. How identities are produced through such digital images and what they come to mean in different settings are potential research topics.

Another approach to visual ethnography is the use of photo-diaries that are produced by research participants (Pink, 2007). Particularly effective in situations where the phenomenon of interest is difficult to observe – for example, because they occur in highly distributed, private spaces such as people's homes – participants are asked to create visual representations of events and document them by describing the image in some way (e.g., when it was taken and why). They are later interviewed about their photo-diaries in order to elicit the meaning of the images further (Latham, 2003). This data generation method effectively turns research participants into apprentice ethnographers as they reflect on events and the material surroundings of their everyday lives. These photo-diaries may even approximate autoethnographies (Pink, 2007).

While Schultze (2014) relied on the photo-diary interview method in her work on the avatar–self relationship in Second Life, this work cannot be classified as a visual ethnography because the researcher was not immersed in the social situation under study (i.e., the virtual world) for an extended period of time. Even though she had an avatar and was periodically active in-world, Schultze (2014) did not spend the kind of time in-world as her research participants did. This highlights that reliance on photo-diaries as a data collection method alone does not make a study a visual ethnography; the researcher's prolonged immersion in the social setting under study remains a core requirement of ethnographic research.

Conclusion

Ethnography as a method for generating and representing knowledge about culturally shaped phenomena (e.g., work practices) is well established in the field of IS. Even though the publication of ethnographic studies in IS journals is relatively rare (Rowe, 2012), ethnographic research is being conducted and shared publicly on what appears to be a fairly regular and ongoing basis. Currently, the types of ethnographic research that are predominant in IS are organizational, digital and design ethnographies.

Because information technology is changing the nature of the phenomena of interest by rendering them more fleeting, distributed and global, social science research methods – including ethnography – need to be adapted in order to provide insight into these phenomena. While styles of ethnography – especially trace ethnography (Geiger & Ribes, 2011) – hold much promise for future IS research that involves digital trace data, this chapter highlights three types of ethnography – mobile, sensory and visual – that focus on the human experience of technology, especially as it pertains to mobility, sensation and embodiment. The hope is that this introduction to new modalities of ethnographic research stimulates experimentation with this research approach, which has much to offer as the field of IS grapples with the changing nature of phenomena.

References

Bjørn, P., Burgoyne, S., Crompton, V., MacDonald, T., Pickering, B., & Munr, S. (2009). Boundary factors and contextual contingencies: configuring electronic templates for healthcare professionals. *European Journal of Information Systems*, *18*, 428–441.

Boellstorff, T. (2008). *Coming of Age in Second Life: An Anthropologist Explores the Virtually Human*. Princeton, NJ: Princeton University Press.

Boellstorff, T., Nardi, B., Pearce, C., & Taylor, T.L. (2012). *Ethnography and Virtual Worlds*. Princeton, NJ: Princeton University Press.

Bourdieu, P. (1977). *Outline of a Theory of Practice*. Cambridge and New York: Cambridge University Press

Büscher, M., Urry, J., & Witchger, K. (Eds.). (2011). *Mobile Methods*. Abington: Routledge.

Carugati, A. (2008). Information system development activities and inquiring systems: An integrating framework. *European Journal of Information Systems*, *17*, 143–155.

Chang, H. (2008). *Autoethnography as Method*. Walnut Creek, CA: Left Coast Press.

Chua, C.E.H., & Yeow, A.Y.K. (2010). Artifacts, actors, and interactions in the cross-project coordination practices of open source communities. *JAIS*, *11*(12), 838–867.

Conklin, H. (1968). Ethnography. In D.L. Sills (Ed.), *International Encyclopedia of the Social Sciences* (pp. 115–208). New York: Free Press.

Crabtree, A. (2004). Taking technomethodology seriously: Hybrid change in the ethnomethodology – design relationship. *European Journal of Information Systems*, *13*, 195–209.

Diaz Andrade, A., Urquhart, C., & Arthanari, T.S. (2015). Seeing for understanding: Unlocking the potential of visual research in information systems. *JAIS*, *16*(8), 646–673.

Edvardsson, D., & Street, A. (2007). Sense or no-sense: The nurse as embodied ethnographer. *International Journal of Nursing Practice*, *13*(1), 24–32.

Garud, R., & Kumaraswamy, A. (2005). Vicious and virtuous circles in the management of knowledge: The case of Infosys Technologies. *MIS Quarterly*, *29*(1), 9–33.

Gasson, S. (2006). A genealogical study of boundary-spanning IS design. *European Journal of Information Systems*, *15*, 26–41.

Geertz, C. (1973). *The Interpretation of Cultures*. New York: Basic Books.

Geiger, R.S., & Ribes, D. (2011). Trace ethnography: Following coordination through documentary practices. Paper presented at the 44th HICSS, Hawaii.

Giddens, A. (1984). *The Constitution of Society: Outline of the Theory of Structuration*. Cambridge: Polity Press.

Greenhill, A., & Fletcher, G. (2014). Laboring online: Are there "new" labor processes in virtual game worlds? *JAIS*, *14*(11), 672–693.

Hine, C. (2015). *Ethnography for the Internet: Embedded, Embodied and Everyday*. London: Bloomsbury Academic.

Howard-Grenville, J.A., & Carlile, P.R. (2008). The incompatibility of knowledge regimes: Consequences of the material world for cross-domain work. *European Journal of Information Systems*, *15*, 473–485.

Howison, J., & Crowston, K. (2014). Collaboration through open superposition: A theory of the open source way. *MIS Quarterly*, *38*(1), 29–50.

Howison, J., Wiggins, A., & Crowston, K. (2011). Validity issues in the use of social network analysis with digital trace data. *JAIS, 12*(12), 767–797.

Hudson, J.M., & Bruckman, A. (2004). "Go Away" participant observations to being studied and the ethics of chatroom research. *Information Society, 20*, 127–139.

Latham, A. (2003). Research, performance and doing human geography: Some reflections on the diary-photograph, diary-interview method. *Environment and Planning A, 35*(11), 1993–2017.

Law, J., & Urry, J. (2004). Enacting the social. *Economy and Society, 33*(3), 390–410.

Leonardi, P.M. (2013). When does technology use enable network change in organizations? A comparative study of feature use and shared affordances. *MIS Quarterly, 37*(3), 749–775.

Leonardi, P.M., & Bailey, D.E. (2008). Transformational technologies and the creation of new work practices: Making implicit knowledge explicit in task-based offshoring. *MIS Quarterly, 32*(2), 411–436.

Levina, N. (2005). Collaborating on multiparty information systems development projects: A collective reflection-in-action view. *Information Systems Research, 16*(2), 109–130.

Lin, C.I.C., Kuo, F.-Y., & Myers, M. (2015). Extending ICT4D studies: The value of critical research. *MIS Quarterly, 39*(3), 697–712.

Mathiassen, L., & Sandberg, A. (2013). How a professionally qualified doctoral student bridged the practice-research gap: A confessional account of collaborative practice research. *European Journal of Information Systems, 22*, 475–492.

Mattarelli, E., Bertolotti, F., & Macrì, D.M. (2013). The use of ethnography and grounded theory in the development of a management information system. *European Journal of Information Systems, 22*, 26–44.

Mazmanian, M., Cohn, M., & Dourish, P. (2014). Dynamic reconfiguration in planetary exploration: A sociomaterial ethnography. *MIS Quarterly, 38*(3), 831–848.

Miscione, G. (2007). Telemedicine in the upper amazon: Interplay with local health care practices. *MIS Quarterly, 31*(2), 403–425.

Myers, M.D. (1999). Investigating information systems with ethnographic research. *CAIS, 2*(23).

Myers, M.D., & Klein, H. (2011). A set of principles for conducting critical research in information systems. *MIS Quarterly, 35*(1), 17–36.

Novoa, A. (2015). Mobile ethnography: Emergence, techniques and its importance to geography. *Human Geographies, 9*(1), 97–107.

Oborn, E., Barrett, M., & Davidson, E. (2011). Unity in diversity: Electronic patient record use in multi-disciplinary practice. *Information Systems Research, 22*(3), 547–564.

O'Riordan, N. (2014). *Autoethnography: Proposing a new research method for information systems research*. Paper presented at the European Conference on Information Systems, Tel Aviv.

Orlikowski, W.J., & Scott, S.V. (2008). Sociomateriality: Challenging the separation of technology, work and organization. *Annals of the Academy of Management, 2*(1), 433–474.

Overby, E., Slaughter, S.A., & Konsynski, B. (2010). The design, use, and consequences of virtual processes. *Information Systems Research, 21*(4), 700–710.

Pantzar, M., & Ruckenstein, M. (2014). The heart of everyday analytics: Emotional, material and practical extensions in self-tracking market. *Consumption Markets and Culture, 18*(1).

Paré, G., Bourdeau, S., Marsan, J., Nach, H., & Shuraida, S. (2008). Re-examining the causal structure of information technology impact research. *European Journal of Information Systems, 17*, 403–416.

Pink, S. (2007). *Doing Visual Ethnography*. London: Sage.

Pink, S. (2015). *Doing Sensory Ethnography* (2nd ed.). London: Sage.

Ramiller, N.C., Swanson, E.B., & Wang, P. (2008). Research directions in information systems: Toward an institutional ecology. *JAIS, 9*(1), 1–22.

Ravishankar, M.N., Pan, S.L., & Myers, M.D. (2013). Information technology offshoring in India: A postcolonial perspective. *European Journal of Information Systems, 22*, 387–402.

Rowe, F. (2012). Toward a richer diversity of genres in information systems research: New categorization and guidelines. *European Journal of Information Systems, 21*, 469–478.

Sarker, S., & Sahay, S. (2004). Implications of space and time for distributed work: An interpretive study of US-Norwegian systems development teams. *European Journal of Information Systems, 13*, 3–20.

Schultze, U. (2000). A confessional account of an ethnography about knowledge work. *MIS Quarterly, 24*(1), 3–41.

Schultze, U. (2014). Understanding cyborgism: Using photo-diary interviews to study performative identity in second life. In U. Plesner & L. Phillips (Eds.), *Researching Virtual Worlds: Methodologies for Studying Emergent Practices* (pp. 53–75). London: Routledge.

Schultze, U., & Orlikowski, W. J. (2004). A practice perspective on technology-mediated network relations: The use of internet-based self-serve technologies. *Information Systems Research, 15*(1), 87–106.

Sharrock, W., & Randall, D. (2004). Ethnography, ethnomethodology and the problem of generalisation in design. *European Journal of Information Systems, 13*, 186–194.

Sheller, M., & Urry, J. (2016). Mobilizing the new mobilities paradigm. *Applied Mobilities, 1*(1), 10–25.

Silva, L., & Mousavidin, E. (2015). Strategic thinking in virtual worlds: Studying World of Warcraft. *Computers in Human Behavior, 46*, 168–180.

Thorén, C., Ågerfalk, P. J., & Edenius, M. (2014). Through the printing press: An account of open practices in the Swedish newspaper industry. *JAIS, 15*, 779–804.

Utesheva, A., Simpson, J. R., & Cecez-Kecmanovic, D. (2016). Identity metamorphoses in digital disruption: A relational theory of identity. *European Journal of Information Systems, 25*, 344–363.

van Maanen, J. (1979). The fact of fiction in organizational ethnography. *Administrative Science Quarterly, 24*, 539–550.

Venters, W., Oborn, E., & Barrett, M. (2014). A trichordal temporal approach to digital coordination: The sociomaterial mangling of the cern grid. *MIS Quarterly, 38*(3), 927–949.

Vieira da Cunha, J. (2013). A dramaturgical model of the production of performance data. *MIS Quarterly, 37*(3), 723–748.

Wales, R. C., Shalin, V. L., & Bass, D. S. (2007). Requesting distant robotic action: An ontology for naming and action identification for planning on the Mars exploration Rover mission. *JAIS, 8*(2), 75–104.

Williams, R., & Pollock, N. (2012). Moving beyond the single site implementation study: How (and why) we should study the biography of packaged enterprise solutions. *Information Systems Research, 23*(1), 1–22.

Yoo, Y. (2010). Computing in everyday life: A call for research on experiential computing. *MIS Quarterly, 34*(2), 213–231.

PART 2

Development, adoption and use of MIS

Introduction

The development, adoption and use of information systems (IS) in and across organisations has arguably been a major focus of research in MIS (Córdoba, et al., 2012). This part, thus, offers an insightful collection of chapters reflecting on these key topics with an eye toward incorporating important insights from the past while developing their treatment in novel and forward-looking ways. We begin with a chapter by Brian Fitzgerald and Klaas-Jan Stol, who leverage their extensive knowledge gathered over decades of research into software development (e.g., Fitzgerald, 2006; Fitzgerald and Stol, 2015) to highlight how the current software landscape is being disrupted by elements such as software ecosystems, servitisation, the Internet of Things, parallel processing, cognitive computing and quantum computing. These disruptions mean that organisations are increasingly developing software in environments where they may need to rapidly scale their products, services or systems (to reach new markets and create new offerings), their organisation or business domain (to collaborate with new partners, suppliers or workforce) and their processes and methods (to expand their repertoire of techniques). Software development methods, therefore, need to be adjusted accordingly. This chapter is complemented by the chapter on agility in information systems development by Kieran Conboy, Denis Dennehy, Lorraine Morgan and Roger Sweetman. The chapter provides an excellent overview of the evolution of agile methods (see also Conboy, 2009), followed by the consideration of the next 'wave' of agile methods that could also help address many of the present and coming challenges identified in the previous chapter. The readers can find illuminating reflections on questions such as whether agile methods scale to open innovation environments (scaling outside the organisation and in terms of processes) and to whole project portfolios (scaling across a range of products).

From the topic of IS development we then move to IS adoption and use – while development and use are often studied separately to reduce analytical complexity, this boundary has been recognised as artificial (Leonardi, 2009). We thus hope that considerations of effective use, affect and resistance will not only be useful for researchers of adoption and use, but also to researchers of development. We begin with a chapter by Andrew Burton-Jones, Mark Bremhorst, Fang Liu and Van-Hau Trieu that summarises the current state of the art in IT use studies (the largest single body of research in the IS field). The chapter proposes that IS researchers shift their attention from use to effective use – from just using IT to using it in ways that help attain relevant goals (see also Burton-Jones and Grange, 2012). Lessons learned from multiple research studies show the authors' evolving thinking around the topic of effective use. For example, the chapter highlights that effective use also involves conveying messages that contain emotion and human elements, not just 'the facts.' Emotions have in recent years become an increasingly focal topic in IS as researchers are looking to go beyond goal-oriented and rational explanations of IT in organisations (McGrath, 2006). From here, we thus move to Chapter 12 on affect in the ICT context by Jasy Liew Suet Yan and Ping Zhang. While the cognitive and attitudinal antecedents and outcomes of technology use have been studied extensively (Hsieh, et al., 2008; Venkatesh and Brown, 2001), emotions and affect are only recently entering the field of research. In line with the general forward-looking principle of this book, as well as with trends elsewhere (e.g., affective economics, see Andrejevic, 2011), we chose to focus on the topic of emotions because we believe it will grow in importance and emphasis in the coming years. Jasy and Ping begin by briefly reviewing the state of research on affect in the information and communication technologies (ICT) context in the IS field. Building on Ping's influential Affective Response Model (ARM) (Zhang, 2013), various affective concepts that represent interactions between users and ICT are then discussed, providing a useful overview of how various affective evaluations (including emotions) may arise from as well as influence technology use. Jasy and Ping then take the discussion further, by considering how ICTs can be used to detect affective responses from users. Interest in using computers for automated and accurate emotion detection from various signals (text, neuro, speech, facial) has been growing steadily (Dimoka, et al., 2011; Stieglitz and Dang-Xuan, 2013). Not only can this help understand technology users better, but it can also be used to personalise and adapt technology (e.g., user interfaces) to user reactions in real time (Hibbeln et al., 2017). As with many other shifts toward increased automation and data-driven or algorithmic decision making, many ethical and privacy concerns arise, posing a major upcoming challenge for the IS field (Newell and Marabelli, 2015). We then move to Chapter 13 by Liette Lapointe and Suzanne Rivard, who offer an updated look on the topic of user resistance to information technology (building on their earlier groundbreaking research, e.g., Lapointe and Rivard, 2005; Rivard and Lapointe, 2012). The chapter considers various conceptualisations of resistance – for example, resistance as behavior, as intention, as a negative perception, as a cognition, as an attitude and as a mindset. The chapter also problematises two often taken-for-granted assumptions in resistance research – first, that implementers are always supportive of new technologies, and second, that new technologies are in fact always considered normatively good and as something that should be implemented. Relaxing both assumptions can lead to interesting new research on resistance that does not just focus on users, but all manner of stakeholders (including developers and implementers). This shift in emphasis is in line with the general trend of user and consumer empowerment observed with the digital transformation of business and society. Users and consumers of IT are increasingly also seen as potential developers and producers (Yoo, et al., 2010). In this changing landscape, resistance is thus less and less about user resistance in response to management mandates of new technologies, and rather more about multi-directional negotiations.

The next two chapters in Part 2 elaborate on this line of thinking by developing our understanding of the process of IT and IS strategising in organisations. Traditionally seen as top-down activity lead by management, strategising is increasingly being re-conceptualised as also involving emergent, bottom-up processes (Besson and Rowe, 2012). Marco Marabelli and Bob Galliers describe these two processes of strategising and the corresponding models of power (diffusion and translation). They highlight how both an understanding of the actions of powerful actors in an organisational hierarchy pushing for a certain change as well as the 'tinkering' done on the change effort by heterogeneous actors across the organisation are important strategy research. Viktor Arvidsson and Jonny Holmström then consider how organisations escape political and economic inertia and pick strategic options intended for the digital era through various digitalisation practices. Notably, when almost anyone can become a digital entrepreneur (McQuivey, 2013), the locus of innovation shifts from central, resource-rich actors to the edges. Strategic change can thus increasingly happen without managerial oversight and involvement, as also described in one of the cases studied by Jonny and Viktor. However, as also noted by the chapter, many systemic inequalities (such as class- and gender-related) persist, posing often unrecognised obstacles to innovation. Many IS topics that have relied on neat distinctions between management and users (such as resistance and acceptance) may thus need revisiting in the coming years.

We end Part 2 with a chapter that informs a large stream of research that has been gathering momentum in studies of development, adoption and use of MIS: affordances (Majchrzak and Markus, 2012). Olga Volkoff and Diane Strong, in their chapter on affordance theory and its use IS research, offer an invaluable set of principles and guidelines for anyone undertaking a study utilising affordance theory. They also sort out much of the existing confusion around what affordances are and are not. A few unresolved issues in affordance research are also pointed out. We chose affordance theory to conclude this part, as in our view it represents one of the few perspectives that has the potential of explaining and understanding the many varied outcomes of IT, regardless whether the focus is on development, implementation and/or use, accommodating both managerial and user perspectives, and regardless of the technology under investigation (as the literature cited in Olga and Diane's chapter readily demonstrates). Looking to the future, we see a great need for the conceptual integration of goal-oriented perspectives (e.g., affordances and effective use) and emotion-oriented perspectives (e.g., ARM).

References

Andrejevic, M. (2011). The work that affective economics does. *Cultural Studies*, 25(4–5), 604–620.
Besson, P., & Rowe, F. (2012). Strategizing information systems-enabled organizational transformation: A transdisciplinary review and new directions. *Journal of Strategic Information Systems*, 21(2), 103–124.
Burton-Jones, A., & Grange, C. (2012). From use to effective use: A representation theory perspective. *Information Systems Research*, 24(3), 632–658.
Conboy, K. (2009). Agility from first principles: Reconstructing the concept of agility in information systems development. *Information Systems Research*, 20(3), 329–354.
Córdoba, J.R., Pilkington, A., & Bernroider, E.W. (2012). Information systems as a discipline in the making: Comparing EJIS and MISQ between 1995 and 2008. *European Journal of Information Systems*, 21(5), 479–495.
Dimoka, A., Pavlou, P.A., & Davis, F.D. (2011). Research commentary-NeuroIS: The potential of cognitive neuroscience for information systems research. *Information Systems Research*, 22(4), 687–702.
Fitzgerald, B. (2006). The transformation of open source software. *MIS Quarterly*, 30(3), 587–598.
Fitzgerald, B., & Stol, K.J. (2015). Continuous software engineering: A roadmap and agenda. *Journal of Systems and Software*, 123, 176–189.
Hibbeln, M., Jenkins, J.L., Schneider, C., Valacich, J.S., and Weinmann, M. (2017). How is your user feeling? Inferring emotion through human-computer interaction devices, *MIS Quarterly*, 41(1), pp. 1–21.
Hsieh, J.P.A., Rai, A., & Keil, M. (2008). Understanding digital inequality: Comparing continued use behavioral models of the socio-economically advantaged and disadvantaged. *MIS Quarterly*, 32(1), 97–126.
Lapointe, L., & Rivard, S. (2005). A multilevel model of resistance to information technology implementation. *MIS Quarterly*, 29(3), 461–491.

Leonardi, P. M. (2009). Crossing the implementation line: The mutual constitution of technology and organizing across development and use activities. *Communication Theory, 19*(3), 278–310.

Majchrzak, A., & Markus, M. L. (2012). Technology affordances and constraints in management information systems (MIS). In E. Kessler (Eds.), *Encyclopedia of management theory*. Thousand Oaks, CA: Sage.

McGrath, K. (2006). Affection not affliction: The role of emotions in information systems and organizational change. *Information and Organization, 16*(4), 277–303.

McQuivey, J. (2013). *Digital disruption: Unleashing the next wave of innovation*. Forrester Research. Las Vegas: Amazon.

Newell, S., & Marabelli, M. (2015). Strategic opportunities (and challenges) of algorithmic decision-making: A call for action on the long-term societal effects of 'datification.' *Journal of Strategic Information Systems, 24*(1), 3–14.

Rivard, S., & Lapointe, L. (2012). Information technology implementers' responses to user resistance: Nature and effects. *MIS Quarterly, 36*(3), 897–920.

Stieglitz, S., and Dang-Xuan, L. (2013). Emotions and information diffusion in social media – sentiment of microblogs and sharing behavior. *Journal of Management Information Systems, 29*(4), 217–248.

Venkatesh, V., & Brown, S. A. (2001). A longitudinal investigation of personal computers in homes: Adoption determinants and emerging challenges. *MIS Quarterly, 25*(1), 71–102.

Yoo, Y., Lyytinen, K. J., Boland, R. J., & Berente, N. (2010). The next wave of digital innovation: Opportunities and challenges: A report on the research workshop 'Digital Challenges in Innovation Research.' Available at SSRN 1622170.

Zhang, P. (2013). The affective response model: A theoretical framework of affective concepts and their relationships in the ICT context. *MIS Quarterly, 37*(1), 247–274.

9

THE FUTURE OF SOFTWARE DEVELOPMENT METHODS

Brian Fitzgerald and Klaas-Jan Stol

Introduction

There is a distinct half-life obsolescence with respect to software development methods, in that the principles and tenets that become enshrined in methods can become obsolete due to the emergence of new challenges and issues as the technological environment evolves. This has been labeled the 'problem of tenses' (cf. Fitzgerald 2000; Friedman 1989). The software development methods and processes that are popular today have been derived from principles that were first identified many decades ago – the systems development life cycle, object orientation, agile and lean methods, open source software, software product lines, and software patterns, for example. However, there are a number of fundamentally disruptive technological trends that suggest that we need an 'update of tenses' in relation to the software development methods that can cater to this brave new world of software development. Fitzgerald (2012) has coined the term Software Crisis 2.0 to refer to this new disruptive age. The original software crisis (Software Crisis 1.0, as we might refer to it), identified in the 1960s, referred to the fact that that software took longer to develop and cost more than estimated, and did not work very well when eventually delivered. The diligent efforts of many researchers and practitioners has had a positive outcome in that this initial software crisis has been resolved to the extent that software is one of the success stories of modern life.

Software Crisis 2.0

Notwithstanding the achievements made that have helped to address Software Crisis 1.0, this success has also helped to fuel Software Crisis 2.0. Fitzgerald (2012) identifies a number of 'push factors' and 'pull factors' that combine to cause Software Crisis 2.0. Push factors include advances in hardware such as that perennially afforded by Moore's law, multiprocessor and parallel computing, big memory servers, IBM's Watson platform for cognitive computing, and quantum computing. Also, developments such as the Internet of Things (IoT) and Systems of Systems (SoS) have led to unimaginable amounts of raw data which fuel the field of data analytics – a field that is commonly referred to as "big data." Pull factors include the insatiable appetite of 'digital native' consumers – those who have never known life without computer technology – for new applications to deliver initiatives such as the quantified self, life-logging, and wearable computing. Also, the increasing role of software is evident in the concept of software defined * (where * can refer to networking, infrastructure, data center, or enterprise). The Software Crisis 2.0 bottleneck arises from the inability to produce the volume of software necessary to leverage the absolutely staggering increase in the volume of data being generated, in turn allied to the enormous amount of computational power offered by the many hardware devices also available, and both complemented by the demands of the newly emerged digital native consumer in a world where increasingly software is the key enabler. Figure 9.1 summarizes these 'push' and 'pull' factors.

"Software is eating the world!"

This quote from Netscape founder Marc Andreessen colorfully captures the extent to which software is becoming predominant, to the extent that we claim that *all* companies are becoming software companies.

> Our organization has become a software company. The problem is that our engineers haven't realized that yet!

This is how the vice president for research of a major semiconductor manufacturing company, traditionally seen as the classic hardware company, characterized the context in which software solutions were replacing hardware in delivering his company's products. This organization knew precisely the threshold of reuse level for its hardware components before designing for reuse became cost-effective. However, this level of sophistication was not yet present in its software development processes. There was a tendency to approach each software project in a once-off fashion, and a repeatable and formalized software development process had not been fully enacted.

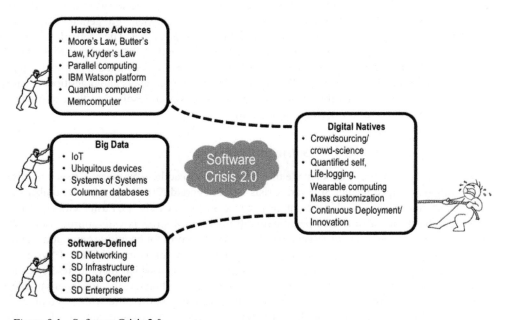

Figure 9.1   Software Crisis 2.0

The future of software development methods

We have seen this situation replicated across several business domains as the transformation to software has been taking place for quite some time. The telecommunications industry began the move to *softwareization* in the 1970s with the introduction of computerized switches, and currently, the mobile telephony market is heavily software focused. The automotive industry has very noticeably been moving toward softwareization since the 1960s – today, 80%–90% of innovations in the automotive industry are enabled by software (Mössinger 2010; Swedsoft 2010). This is evidenced in the dramatic increase in the numbers of software engineers being employed in proportion to the numbers employed in traditional engineering roles. A striking example of the growing importance of software in the automotive industry is conveyed in the following: In 1978, a printout of the lines of code would have made a stack about twelve centimeters high; by 1995, this was already a stack three meters high; and by 2015, it is a staggering 830 meters, higher than the Burj Khalifa – the tallest man-made structure in the world (see Figure 9.2).

Another example of a domain in which software has increased dramatically in importance is the medical device sector. Traditionally, medical devices were primarily hardware with perhaps some embedded software. However, a 2010 EU Medical Device Directive classifies stand-alone software applications as active medical devices (McHugh et al. 2011). This has major implications for the software development process in many organizations, as they now find themselves subject to regulatory bodies such as the US Food and Drug Administration (FDA).

Thus, we have a context where software, traditionally seen as secondary and a means to an end in many sectors, moves center stage. The implications of this global shift are frequently underestimated. It requires the software development function to transform itself in order to provide the necessary foundation to fulfill this central role, which in turn requires an expansion of the set of concerns that need to be integrated into any software solution. The increasing

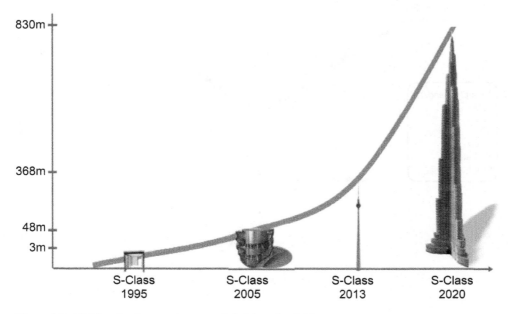

Figure 9.2 Height of software printout stack in Mercedes S-Class
Source: Schneider (2015).

importance of software is not only a matter of 'scale' in the traditional sense, measured in lines of code, transactions per second, or capacity, but the scaling of software causes the need for changes in other dimensions, too. This has implications for the methods that we use to guide software development practice.

The future of software development methods: an expanded view

This expanded role for the software development function requires a multi-dimensional perspective. Figure 9.3 illustrates three inter-related dimensions that have been drivers for software scaling over the past 20 years. The inner, dark-shaded circle represents the traditional view that was concerned with individual products developed within traditional organizational boundaries using conventional software development processes – or as is the case in many organizations, no formal development process at all. However, the move to services, the emergence of topics such as open innovation, organizational ecosystems, various forms of sourcing (outsourcing, open-sourcing, innersourcing, crowdsourcing; we use the term '*-sourcing') (Ågerfalk et al. 2015a; 2015b), and IoT have caused an expanded focus in each of these dimensions. We characterize each of these dimensions in more detail later in this chapter.

Scaling products, systems and services

Companies are also seeking to extend beyond the current state-of-the-art in service-oriented architectures (SOA) to build products. Many companies are actively using open source components

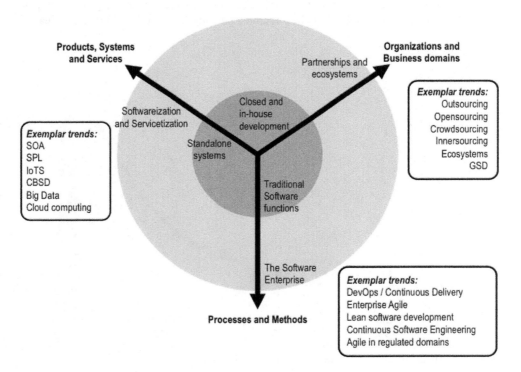

Figure 9.3 Software scaling as a multi-dimensional phenomenon

and are also providing middleware functionality to provide the glue layer which allows them to incorporate various popular social media applications into their product and service offerings. Software reuse, component-based software development and software product line (SPL) approaches are established means that facilitate the scaling of software systems in the traditional sense.

It is estimated that 35 billion devices are currently connected in the IoT scenario, a figure that is expected to rise to 100 billion by 2020 (Feki et al. 2013). The exponential increase in the volume of available data – Big Data – allied to the ubiquitous devices that are available to process the data also leads to a demand for additional software systems to process into market relevant knowledge. So, not only do software systems become bigger, the number of systems (however small these may be) is growing exponentially.

Another trend is that of *servitization*. Rather than selling products to customers, organizations sell services that could not exist without software. Airbnb is the world's largest supplier of accommodation, but the company owns no real estate. Likewise, Uber is the world's largest taxi company, but owns no taxis of its own. This shift from products to services is continuing and has significant implications for how companies conduct business.

Scaling processes and methods

Software processes and methods are subject to scaling, as building larger systems requires adjusting those processes. New software development paradigms, such as Open Source (Feller et al. 2005), Inner Source (Stol and Fitzgerald 2014), lean software development (Fitzgerald et al. 2014; Poppendieck and Cusumano 2012), and DevOps (Fitzgerald and Stol, 2017), are emerging, and are at varying levels of maturity. Global software development with distributed teams, for example, requires that methods that were not intended for such settings (e.g., agile methods) be tailored. Furthermore, the increasing reliance and prevalence of software solutions in regulated domains (e.g., automotive, medical, and financial sectors, as mentioned earlier) also requires tailoring of both new and traditional development approaches.

While the move from traditional to agile methods is well under way, it is worth noting that agile methods were originally proposed as only suited to small projects with co-located teams developing software in non-critical domains (Boehm 2002). While agile has moved well beyond this space, with frequent use of agile methods on projects with globally distributed teams, many challenges remain in relation to social issues such as cultural differences, communication breakdowns, and optimum practices for distributing development work across sites. Furthermore, the need for Enterprise Agile, or Agile 2.0, whereby agile principles need to permeate beyond the software development function to other organizational functions such as finance, marketing, and human resources, is very apparent. Individual successes such as mentioned earlier rely heavily on their particular organizational context, which is increasingly recognized as an important factor (Dybå et al. 2012).

Agile methods and regulated environments are often seen as incommensurable (Turk et al. 2005). The reason for this is probably evident in the Agile Manifesto, which identifies a number of fundamental value propositions for agile – for example, that working software and developer interaction should be viewed as more important than documentation or processes and plans. In regulated environments where traceability is paramount, documentation, processes, and plans are critical. Likewise, in regulated domains, the agile goal of improving time-to-market is secondary to the need to ensure safety is never compromised to satisfy market demands, as the consequences of system failure can lead to loss of life as well as multi-million-dollar compensation claims. Nevertheless, there are encouraging signs to suggest that agile methods can be successfully scaled to regulated environments (Fitzgerald et al. 2013), although this will require organizational changes as well.

Software systems are becoming larger. The obvious expansion is first in terms of lines of code, as demonstrated in Figure 9.2. For example, an average Fortune 100 company maintains 35 million lines of code, adding about 10% each year in enhancements alone – as a result, the amount of code maintained was previously estimated to double every seven years (Müller et al. 1994), but with the ever-increasing ubiquity of computing devices, this is likely to be a conservative estimate. Furthermore, many organizations are faced with mission-critical legacy software systems that are written in older technologies such as COBOL or even assembly language. This represents major risks for many organizations that wish to modernize their systems. Again, there is a tension in relation to the use of agile methods for such modernization projects. Certainly, the use of agile methods in large development projects remains a significant challenge (Booch 2015), with little empirical evidence of the successful deployment of agile in large projects (e.g., Cao et al. 2004; Kähkönen 2004). The extant literature tends to assume that scaling agile methods can be done in a linear fashion; Rolland et al. (2016) have argued that this approach has limitations and that such assumptions must be re-evaluated.

Scaling organizations and business domains

As software assumes greater importance in companies, traditional concepts such as software architecture, software product lines, software reuse, and formalized software development processes become more important. These in turn require significant organizational change in order to be successfully implemented. A major task here is the education of management and the broader engineering workforce to the complexities and challenges of software development and the benefits of a systematic approach in the areas just mentioned.

Software organizations are now adopting global software development (GSD) strategies such as opensourcing, outsourcing and offshoring, and even crowdsourcing to accommodate the increasing need to deliver larger software systems more quickly in order to stay competitive (Stol and Fitzgerald 2014). Acquisition of companies that possess critical technology or software resources is another common trend. Ensuring a proper governance model and selecting the right partnerships are key challenges. Another trend is that organizations are entering new domains as they increasingly rely on software. Domains that were traditionally dominated by hardware-based solutions are now moving to software solutions. Consequently, companies find themselves in new business markets with new competitors.

Another phenomenon which is relevant in this context is the erosion of strict organizational boundaries as organizations seek to leverage open innovation. One concrete form of open innovation is the building of organizational partnerships or ecosystems with suppliers (e.g., commercial off-the-shelf (COTS) vendors and open source software (OSS) communities) (Bosch and Bosch-Sijtsema 2010). A topic that has started to draw more attention is the creation of open source–style communities within one or a consortium of commercial organizations: (proprietary) software is developed in-house using OSS development practices (Stol and Fitzgerald 2014). This is called Inner Source, and has been adopted in several large organizations such as Allstate, Bloomberg, Bosch, Ericsson, Paypal, Philips, and Sony Mobile. There is growing evidence that an organization's people and culture play a pivotal role in adopting new methods (Conboy et al. 2011). However, there is little insight into how "Communities of Practice" (CoP) can be built within commercial organizations, which must take business considerations and sustainability into account (Tamburri et al. 2013).

Industry vignettes

We believe the three dimensions in Figure 9.3 are inter-related and suggest that to scale successfully in any one dimension requires that related challenges in the other dimensions be resolved simultaneously. This can be difficult as the software development function in many organizations today is not in a position to mandate organizational change in other organizational functions, yet the latter is critical for success. A case in point is the current focus on DevOps and continuous deployment, which requires buy-in from an operations team to be able to deliver new versions at a fast pace (Stol and Fitzgerald 2014).

We illustrate these challenges with a number of industry vignettes describing real-world scenarios where organizations are faced with these challenges. These vignettes represent real organizational contexts in which we have been involved through funded research projects (Fitzgerald et al. 2013). Each vignette is primarily driven from one dimension but challenges in terms of the other dimensions are clearly evident. The first vignette presents the case of QUMAS and relates to the Scaling Processes and Methods dimension.

Scaling processes and methods: the case of QUMAS

QUMAS is an example of a company developing software for a regulated market. The software development process in QUMAS must adhere to a number of standards. QUMAS previously employed a waterfall-based approach. However, this approach resulted in a long time-to-market and a large release overhead, which were seen as drawbacks in the quickly changing market that QUMAS is operating in. As a consequence, they have adopted and augmented the Scrum methodology.

Agile methods were initially assumed to be limited to small development projects with co-located teams working on non-safety critical development projects. In order to introduce a new agile process, QUMAS have to interact with external organizations in the regulatory bodies that monitor compliance with the relevant standards. Also, the agile process that QUMAS have adopted requires the Quality Assurance (QA) function to assess compliance of the software produced at the end of each three-week sprint. This was a fundamental change in work practice for QA as they currently assess regulatory compliance more or less annually to coincide with new releases of the product. Because QA are required to be independent of the software development function in a regulated environment, senior management need to support such a large organizational change initiative.

QUMAS see this approach as also altering the product and services they offer. New functionality in interim software products at the end of sprints can be demonstrated to customers and their feedback sought more frequently than in the typically annual big-bang release of a new product as per the traditional waterfall-based process.

QUMAS's transformation started on the *processes and methods* dimension, but resulted in significant changes in the product and organizational dimensions. The need to involve other parts of the organization to make a process transformation is clearly relevant to the *organizational* dimension. In regulated domains, the QA function is required to be an independent department from the software development function, and thus the agile transformation also required other parts of the organization to transform. The change to an incremental process facilitated the concept of *continuous compliance*. Whereas the waterfall approach validated the product under development only at the very end, in the new process the compliance auditing took place incrementally as well. The incremental development and frequent delivery also facilitated presales of the product before the software was finished – something unheard of in a waterfall approach. Finally, given the new incremental development approach also affected the implementation of the product, as its design now had to facilitate incremental addition of features.

The second vignette presents the case of Husqvarna, a leading manufacturer of gardening machinery, and represents a company transforming primarily in relation to the Products, Systems and Services dimension, but with major implications for the Organization and Business Domains and the Processes and Methods dimensions.

Scaling products, systems, and services: the case of Husqvarna

Husqvarna is an example of a company on the journey of transformation to becoming a software company. Ten years ago, Husqvarna was primarily a retailer of gas-powered machinery. Now, an increasing number of machines are battery powered. This changes dramatically the competitive business domain in which Husqvarna operates, as they are now faced with new competitors.

Software is now becoming a key factor. In the past, software development was often done by the robotics staff at Husqvarna, who would have taken programming courses at college. Software development was perceived in Husqvarna as largely equivalent to coding. However, it is estimated that coding only represents about 7% of the effort in software development, and the majority of the work has to do with requirements, architecture and system design, documentation, testing, and other higher-level activities. Husqvarna has moved to the adoption of more formalized software development processes, and a software product line approach is being introduced to rationalize software development across the Husqvarna product range.

A range of new services will be enabled through software in the future. For example, Husqvarna currently incurs a high cost through products being returned as faulty under warranty, which in many cases is due to customer misuse. Adopting an IoT approach, Husqvarna will interrogate built-in sensors in their products deployed in the field worldwide to recover diagnostic and statistical information on the functioning of their equipment. This will enable Husqvarna to proactively advise customers as to whether the equipment needs servicing, and whether it is being used properly and efficiently. If not, a message will be sent to the customer advising them that the product is likely to malfunction, which will require it to be returned to Husqvarna and thus not be available to the customer for some period of time.

Also, Husqvarna robotic lawn mowers will be able to monitor weather forecasts to ensure grass is cut before imminent rainfall, and also will remember previous grass-cutting routes to ensure that new routes will be chosen each time. All these innovations are enabled by software.

There are several key lessons in the vignette. First, as Husqvarna was moving from gas-driven to electrically powered machinery, they found themselves in a new business domain that was already inhabited by other companies producing similar devices, and hence were faced with new competitors. In order to introduce new products and services, new approaches such as software product lines and a formalized development process were necessary. Furthermore, the need to deliver more software required an organizational expansion as a result of the hiring of trained software developers.

The final vignette relates to the Scaling Organizations dimension, and we draw on the experiences of Sony Mobile.

Scaling organizations: the case of Sony Mobile

Sony Mobile is an example of a large company in the mobile phone domain, a highly dynamic and competitive market with a number of significant competitors looming. Staying innovative is key and delivering new features is of the utmost importance. This in turn results in a higher demand for a large pool of developers that can deliver those features quickly. To overcome this organizational barrier to scale their software development capacity, Sony Mobile is expanding the development organization in two ways. First Sony Mobile is actively participating and contributing in open source communities. Sony Mobile's phones are based on the Android platform and more than 85% of their software is based on open source. Second, Sony Mobile is adopting Inner Source (adopting open source practices within organizational boundaries). Inner Source facilitates developers across the organization to collaborate on common projects without formal team membership. Engagement with OSS projects and adopting Inner Source has implications for the product and process dimensions as well. Teams interacting with communities of 'unknown' developers must comply with community norms and common practices so as to ensure that their contributions can be integrated.

Similar to the companies in the other vignettes, Sony Mobile has also been facing the challenge to deliver more software and more quickly. In their domain, they chose to adopt the Android platform for their mobile phones, and consequently were facing the need to collaborate with other stakeholders outside their organization – in this case, open source communities. At the same time, the company is also adopting innersource managing projects that involve such external and internal communities requires considering new and unknown forces (Höst et al. 2014). Many other large organizations are actively involved in open source communities, including Hewlett-Packard and Wipro. These organizations must learn how to interact with these external communities of developers that may have a different agenda and motivations. To that end, many of these companies are now employing dedicated Open Source Community Experts.

In each of the three vignettes described earlier, the primary focus was on scaling in one dimension, but the companies involved ultimately had to deal with changes in all three dimensions. For example, QUMAS started their scaling transformation in the *process* dimension, but consequentially had to make changes to their *organization* and *product* dimensions. Likewise, Husqvarna is scaling primarily in the *product* dimension, leading to subsequent changes to their *processes* and *organization*. Sony Mobile focused primarily on expanding their *organization* by leveraging open source and innersource communities, which in turn led to changes in the *product* architecture (e.g., dependency on the open source Android platform) and *process* changes.

Implications for research

The three industry vignettes demonstrate how different organizations are scaling in different ways. What they have in common, however, is that no matter which direction they scale in initially, they will eventually have to scale along all three dimensions. This interdependency

Table 9.1 Exemplar scaling scenarios in each dimension and their implications

Scaling Dimension	Exemplar Scaling Scenario	Implications for Other Dimensions	Implications for Practice, Research, and Education
Products, Systems and Services	Organizations are changing their product offerings and moving to 'softwareization' and 'servitization.'	Companies need to scale on organizational aspects, e.g., hire trained software engineers instead of relying on hardware engineers, and adopt an appropriate software development process that suits the product development context.	The range of software development contexts will become much more varied, which increases the importance of context in research and education of software engineers.
Organizations and Business Domains	Organizations are becoming increasingly dependent on external suppliers and workforces, and offer participation to third-party suppliers in ecosystems.	Trends such as open sourcing, outsourcing, and crowdsourcing require changes to an organization's internal development processes. Outsourcing organizations should also consider the product architecture in coordinating external workforces and integrating externally developed software. Keystone players in ecosystems offering platforms to third parties to develop plug-ins or apps must consider constraints of the product architecture.	Organizations must carefully consider the implications of their sourcing and partnership strategies. Software may take an organization to new business domains that are already inhabited by others, thus facing new competition.
Processes and Methods	Organizations are adopting contemporary and emerging software development practices and techniques, including agile methods, DevOps, continuous deployment, and continuous software engineering.	Organizations need to consider other stakeholders in the organization affected by a changing process, e.g., to adopt DevOps and continuous delivery, teams responsible for operations must be involved. Top-level management support is required to get different departments involved. If applicable, constraints due to regulatory compliance must be considered. Product architectures must be amenable to a continuous delivery approach.	Software transcends the software development function, which must be linked to the whole organization – the software enterprise. Software engineering education must address the interactions with other functions, including marketing and sales.

across these three dimensions has thus far received limited attention; studies tend to focus on one dimension exclusively. For example, cloud computing, software product lines (SPL), and service-oriented architectures (SOA) are all means to scale software products. While the SPL community has also recognized the impact on process and organization, for example through the BAPO framework (van der Linden et al. 2007), there has not been a systematic approach to considering all three interlinked dimensions for all the contemporary developments that we can identify in the modern software research or industry landscapes.

We believe future research on software development should include considerations across all three key dimensions discussed earlier. In Table 9.1, we summarize exemplar scaling scenarios for each dimension, together with the implications for other dimensions, and also some relevant implications for practice, research, and education.

Conclusion

The domain of software development is expanding and reaching far beyond mere technical solutions that involve algorithms, software architectures, and ultra-large systems. The ability to deliver this increasing amount of software is an immediate and pressing concern for many organizations – this has been termed Software Crisis 2.0 (Fitzgerald 2012). Software development must take a holistic view and consider the various interdependencies between trends such as softwareization and servitization, the organizational aspects that are affected by an increasing 'pull' for software-based solutions, and the processes and methods that are used to deliver this software.

These trends will have far-reaching consequences. First, the tension that arises due to the push and pull factors discussed earlier may increase the pressure to deliver software more quickly, which inevitably will lead to compromises in the quality of the software produced. Software that is constructed quickly, without proper design, review, and quality assurance is far more likely to exhibit defects down the road, thus increasing the cost of maintenance, which in turn exacerbates Software Crisis 2.0.

Second, the pull factors also imply an increasing need for talented software developers. As software systems are becoming increasingly complex, the reliance on self-educated and software hobbyists is no longer sufficient; instead, companies need well-trained staff. The lack of well-trained staff is an oft-cited reason for companies to outsource their software development.

Another challenge that is perhaps not receiving enough attention is our society's ever-increasing reliance on software systems. Software systems are truly ubiquitous, but many of these systems are very dated legacy systems. Many critical systems (e.g., operating at banks, insurance companies, and government institutions) were developed in the '60s and '70s on technology platforms that are now considered dated, such as COBOL. While developers who are able to maintain these systems are currently still available, this may no longer be the case 20 or 30 years from now. An incredible amount of software is being written today on a variety of technologies that rapidly become obsolete and will inevitably have to be replaced at some point. As systems are becoming ever more intertwined and interdependent, this will become increasingly problematic.

With the realization that software development transcends algorithms and techniques, we believe research should include considerations across all three key dimensions: products, services, and systems; processes and methods; and organizations and business domains. An increased understanding of the different types of scaling challenges that organizations face will help the software industry to overcome them, and will help in deriving new software development methods better suited to the needs of the prevailing software development environment.

Acknowledgments

This work was supported, in part, by Enterprise Ireland, grant IR/2013/0021 to ITEA-SCA-LARE, Science Foundation Ireland grant 15/SIRG/3293 and 13/RC/2094 and co-funded under the European Regional Development Fund through the Southern & Eastern Regional Operational Programme to Lero – the Irish Software Research Centre (www.lero.ie).

References

Ågerfalk, P.J., B. Fitzgerald and K. Stol (2015a) *Software Sourcing in the Age of Open: Leveraging the Unknown Workforce*, New York: Springer.

Ågerfalk, P.J., B. Fitzgerald and K. Stol (2015b) "Not so shore anymore: The new imperatives when sourcing in the age of open," *Proceedings of the European Conference on Information Systems (ECIS)* Münster, Germany.

Boehm, B. (2002) "Get ready for agile methods, with care," *IEEE Computer*, vol. 35, pp. 64–69; doi:10.1109/2.976920.

Booch, G. (2015) Keynote at the International Conference on Software Engineering, SEIP Track, Florence, Italy.

Bosch, J. and P. Bosch-Sijtsema (2010) "From integration to composition: On the impact of software product lines, global development and ecosystems," *Journal of Systems and Software*, vol. 83, no. 1, pp. 67–76; doi:10.1016/j.jss.2009.06.051.

Cao, K., P. Mohan, P. Xu and B. Ramesh (2004) "How extreme does extreme programming have to be? Adapting XP practices to large-scale projects," in *37th Hawaii International Conference on System Science*.

Conboy, K., S. Coyle, X. Wang and M. Pikkarainen (2011) "People over process: Key challenges in agile development," *IEEE Software*, vol. 28, no. 4, pp. 48–57.

Dybå, T., D.I.K. Sjøberg and D.S. Cruzes (2012) "What works for whom, where, when, and why? On the role of context in empirical software engineering," *Proceedings of Empirical Software Engineering and Measurement*, pp. 19–28.

Feki, M.A., F. Kawsar, M. Boussard and L. Trappeniers (2013) "The internet of things: The next technological revolution," *IEEE Computer*, vol. 46, no. 2, pp. 24–25.

Feller, J., B. Fitzgerald, S. Hissam, and K. Lakhani (2005) *Perspectives on Free and Open Source Software*, Cambridge, MA: MIT Press.

Fitzgerald, B. (2000) "Systems development methodologies: the problem of tenses," *Information Technology & People*, vol. 13, no. 3, pp. 174–185.

Fitzgerald, B. (2012) "Software Crisis 2.0," *IEEE Computer*, vol. 45, no. 4, pp. 89–91.

Fitzgerald, B., M. Musial and K. Stol (2014) "Evidence-based decision making in lean software project management," *Proceedings of International Conference on Software Engineering*, vol. 2, Hyderabad, India.

Fitzgerald, B. and K. Stol (2017) "Continuous software engineering and beyond: A roadmap and agenda," *Journal of Systems and Software*, vol. 123, pp. 176–189.

Fitzgerald, B., K. Stol, R. O'Sullivan and D. O'Brien (2013) "Scaling agile methods to regulated environments: An industry case study," *Proceedings of International Conference on Software Engineering*, vol. 2, pp. 863–872.

Friedman, A. (1989) *Computer Systems Development: History, Organisation and Implementation*, Chichester: Wiley & Sons.

Höst, M., K. Stol and A. Orucevic-Alagic (2014) "Inner source project management," in: G. Ruhe and C. Wohlin (Eds.) *Software Project Management in a Changing World*, Berlin: Springer, pp. 343–367.

Kahkonen, T. (2004) "Agile methods for large organisations – building communities of practice," in *Agile Development Conference*.

McHugh, M., F. McCaffery and V. Casey (2011) "Standalone software as an active medical device," *Proceedings of 11th International SPICE Conference*, pp. 97–107.

Mössinger, J. (2010) "Software in automotive systems," *IEEE Software*, vol. 27, no. 2, pp. 92–94.

Müller, H., K. Wong, and S. Tilley (1994) "Understanding software systems using reverse engineering technology," *Proceedings of the 62nd Congress of L'Association Canadienne Française pour l'Avancement des Sciences (ACFAS)*, vol. 26, no. 4, pp. 41–48.

Poppendieck, M. and M. Cusumano (2012) "Lean software development: A tutorial," *IEEE Software*, vol. 29, no. 5, pp. 26–32.

Rolland, K., B. Fitzgerald, T. Dingsøyr and K. Stol (2016) "Problematizing agile in the large: Alternative assumptions for large-scale agile development," *Proceedings 37th International Conference on Information Systems*, Dublin, Ireland.

Schneider, J. (2015) "Software-innovations as key driver for a green, connected and autonomous mobility," *ARTEMIS-IA/ITEA-Co-Summit*.

Stol, K. and B. Fitzgerald (2014) "Two's company, three's a crowd: A case study of crowdsourcing software development," *Proceedings of the 36th International Conference on Software Engineering* (Technical Track), Hyderabad, India.

Stol, K. and B. Fitzgerald (2015) "Inner source – adopting open source development practices in organizations: A tutorial," *IEEE Software*, vol. 32, no. 4.

Swedsoft, A Strategic Research Agenda for the Swedish Software Intensive Industry, 2010.

Tamburri, D., P. Lago and H. van Vliet (2013) "Uncovering latent social communities in software development," *IEEE Software*, vol. 30, no. 1, pp. 29–36.

Turk, D., R. France and B. Rumpe (2005) "Assumptions underlying agile software-development processes," *Journal of Database Management*, vol. 16, no. 4, pp. 62–87.

van der Linden, F., K. Schmid and E. Rommes (2007) *Software Product Lines in Action*, Berlin: Springer.

10
AGILITY IN INFORMATION SYSTEMS DEVELOPMENT

Kieran Conboy, Denis Dennehy, Lorraine Morgan, and Roger Sweetman

The chapter is divided into three parts.

- The first part provides a brief overview of the evolution of agile methods, how the application of agile methods from small to large co-located teams, to a variety of other contexts has emerged over time, and the predominant schools of thought on how agility is and should be evaluated.
- The second part provides a description of the next 'wave' of agile and how concepts such as flow are changing how we think about and apply agile in information systems development (ISD).
- The third part describes areas of ISD where agile methods have not been effectively applied, despite an ever-increasing need to do so (see Figure 10.1). These are project portfolio management and open innovation environments. It also considers how the next 'wave' of agile could help address existing issues.

Evolution of agility and agile evaluation in ISD

The concept of *agility* was formally introduced to ISD through the publication of a manifesto (Fowler and Highsmith, 2001) and embodied through approaches such as XP and Scrum (cf. Boehm, 2002; Highsmith and Cockburn, 2001; Highsmith, 2002). These approaches rejected the plan-driven bureaucratic thinking of the time in favour of faster, user-centric, and more dynamic methodologies that enabled continuous delivery, requirements change and reflection. These were employed with success across diverse contexts and domains (Boehm, 2002; Lindvall et al., 2002; Turk et al., 2002) and even extending to heavily regulated environments such as biomedical (e.g., Kane et al., 2006) and healthcare (e.g., Aronsson et al., 2011). There are two dominant perspectives in the agility literature, in terms of the enablement and evaluation of agility.

First, and more prevalent, is an adherence-based perspective, whereby agility is measured by implementation of commercially labelled 'agile' practices. In particular, examples can be found of measuring adherence or the application of metrics to XP (Layman, 2004; Williams et al., 2004; Mangalaraj et al., 2009) and Scrum (Scharff et al., 2012; Scharff, 2011). However, an extensive review and synthesis of discussion around the concept of agility identified

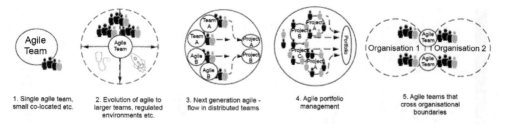

Figure 10.1 The evolution of agile from small co-located teams to portfolios of projects spanning multiple organizations

a number of significant failings of this adherence-based view (Conboy, 2009). For instance, the methodologies that form the basis of adherence suffer from shortcomings such as a lack of clarity, a lack of theoretical glue, a lack of parsimony, limited applicability, and naivety regarding the evolution of the concept of agility in other fields such as manufacturing. As a result, adherence-based assessments of agility make it difficult to compare methodologies, assess in-house methodologies, apply staged adoption of agility, and consider context. In addition, valuing adherence also contradicts the agile principle of using working software as the primary measure of success.

A second approach to agility assessment is a value-based enquiry. Failings of the adherence-based view are bridged with a focus upon goals and values (Agerfalk and Fitzgerald, 2005; Lindstrom and Jeffries, 2004). Rather than assessing the number of practices implemented from a predefined menu of commercial methodologies, one would assess the level of agility (the value) afforded by a practice or set of practices. Conboy (2009) developed a definition and formative taxonomy of agility for this exact purpose (depicted in Figure 10.2). This taxonomy was based on a structured literature review of agility across a number of disciplines, such as manufacturing and management where the concept originated, matured, and has been applied and tested thoroughly over time. The taxonomy addresses some of the shortcomings of an adherence-based view of agility in that it (1) considers the inherent agility-adding value of a set of practices rather than simply measuring whether or not commercially labelled agile practices are used; (2) allows agility to be assessed 'in context,' thus acknowledging the differences between design environments; and (3) allows a staged adoption of agility for those environments where more extreme levels of agility are not feasible or indeed necessary.

Agility and flow

Organisations are progressively seeking new approaches to improve their ISD process in order to increase agility and scale in software project management. Flow is part of the next generation of agile methods and is proving to be a catalyst for increasing agility and scale, especially in knowledge-intensive work activities such as software project management (Anderson, 2010; Petersen and Wohlin, 2011; Reinertsen, 2009; Power and Conboy, 2015). Although utilisation of the flow method is gaining momentum in the IS community, it is important to establish how flow brings agile methods to the next level.

Flow is about managing a continuous and smooth flow of value-creating activities throughout the entire software development process (Anderson, 2010; Reinertsen, 2009; Petersen and Wohlin, 2011; Poppendieck and Poppendieck, 2003). Flow emphasises the continuous movement of valuable work, rather than a sequence of discrete activities, performed by distinct

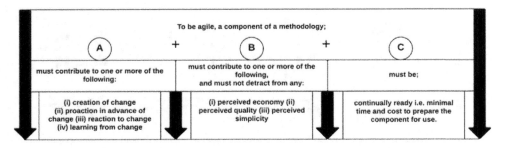

Figure 10.2 Value-based measurement of agility

Source: Adapted from Conboy (2009).

teams or departments (Fitzgerald and Stol, 2014). Flow focuses on managing queues, rather than managing time lines and project phases or simple waste elimination, which makes it distinct from traditional project management (Power and Conboy, 2015; Anderson, 2013; Anderson et al., 2011).

Flow in product development is defined as "the progressive achievement of tasks along the value stream so that a product proceeds from design to launch, order to delivery, and raw materials into the hands of the customer with no stoppages, scrap, or backflows" (Womack and Jones, 2010, p. 306). In the context of XP, Beck (2000, p. 30) defines flow as "delivering a steady flow of valuable software by engaging in all activities of development simultaneously."

One technique used to manage the continuous and smooth flow of work is the Kanban scheduling system, which uses a pull system rather than a push system. Kanban encourages the visualisation of workflow states as work passes through different states (e.g., Planned, In Progress, Done) in the ISD process (Anderson, 2010; Power and Conboy, 2015). Work-in-progress (WIP) limits are used to manage the quantity of WIP at any given stage in the workflow, as well as explicit policies frequently called entry and exit criteria that determine when a work item can be pulled from one state to another (Power, 2014). A system of coloured cards is used for signalling between upstream and downstream processes, as well as to enable team members to observe WIP.

Kanban has significant differences when compared to other agile methods in software development practices: (1) WIP limits are explicit rather than implicit; (2) it does not artificially time box sprints; (3) work items can vary in size, as there is no explicit rule that it must fit a specific time box; (4) release methodology is continuous delivery as opposed to the end of a sprint, and (5) change can occur at any time (Sjøberg et al., 2012; Cawley et al., 2013; Kniberg and Skarin, 2010). Research has also indicated that using Kanban leads to a higher level of productivity, as it is more responsive to change when compared to other agile methods (Sjøberg et al., 2012).

Cumulative Flow Diagrams (CFDs) are another tool that is used to visualise and manage workflow states in ISD. With origins in queuing theory, CFDs show the amount of work in each of the defined work states and are useful for understanding the behaviour of queues, and for diagnosing problems that are interrupting the fluent flow of work (Power, 2014; Reinertsen, 2009).

Complementary to the Kanban technique and CFDs is a number of key metrics used for understanding and managing the flow of work in software development practices (see Table 10.1).

Table 10.1 Metrics used to manage flow

Metric	Description
Throughput rate	Reveals the rate of work through the system over time, and when combined with demand analysis shows how much work is value demand (e.g., customer requesting something new such as a new product feature) versus failure demand (e.g., when a product or product feature does not meet the customer's needs and generates additional work).
Cycle time	Shows how long individual work items spend in specific workflow states and are used to understand how work flows through individual or combinations of work states.
Lead time	Shows how long it takes for individual work items to move through a system – from initial request to delivery to end user.
Queue size	Queues are the underlying cause of various forms of economic waste: longer cycle time, increased risk, increased overhead, and lower quality.

Source: Power and Conboy (2015); Reinertsen (2009).

Metrics in flow-based product development are used to understand the inputs, processes, outputs, and outcomes related to the flow of work and impediments (Power and Conboy, 2015). Impediments in software development are defined as "anything that obstructs the smooth flow of work through the system and/or interferes with the system achieving its goals" (Power and Conboy, 2014, p. 2). Impediments to the flow of work are broadly categorised: extra features, delays, handovers, failure demand, (too much) work-in-progress, context switching, and unmet human potential (Power and Conboy, 2014, p. 2).

While there is strong anecdotal evidence to suggest that awareness and indeed use of flow techniques is gaining popularity across the software development community (cf. Anderson, 2013; Nord et al., 2012; Petersen and Wohlin, 2011; Poppendieck and Cusumano, 2012; Power and Conboy, 2015; Reinertsen, 2009), the current body of knowledge on flow in ISD is nascent. Moreover, there are challenges that inhibit both its utility and theoretical development. These challenges are highlighted in the next section.

Challenges of reapplying flow in agile

Despite its growth in popularity, the utility of flow is driven by practice-led research, which is not unusual for novel and emergent ISD methods (Conboy, 2009; Dybå and Dingsøyr, 2008). It does, however, present a corresponding set of challenges due to the complexities, scales, and contexts associated with contemporary ISD. First, the effectiveness of flow has largely been supported by anecdotal evidence (Sjøberg et al., 2012; Ebert et al., 2012). Second, the assumption that flow is suited to complex ISD environments has been subject to harsh criticism (Ebert et al., 2012). Third, as flow is a metric-driven process, it is critical that such metrics are interpreted in context because failure to understand the context will limit the understanding and the usefulness of the results (Kitchenham, 2010). Fourth, the absence of value-based research on flow-method use will result in a repeat of the mistakes witnessed with the adherence-based approach.

These challenges highlight a need for rigorous research on the assimilation of flow techniques in the real-world context for which its uses were intended and to understand the challenges of assimilating flow techniques in software development practices. The need for a deeper understanding of adaptability and extension of software development methods in practice and in a rigorous research approach were identified as significant shortcomings in the current body of knowledge (Conboy, 2009; Dybå and Dingsøyr, 2008).

These challenges provide opportunities for the future development of agile and flow, which are presented in the following section.

Future development of agile and flow

The future development of agile and flow is contingent on the following four interrelated research activities. First, there is an opportunity to evaluate the adoption and use of flow techniques in practice. This would ensure that the effectiveness of the flow method is based on data that has been accumulated objectively rather than relying on anecdotal evidence. Second, given the complexity and socially embedded nature of the flow method, there is an opportunity to develop a flow maturity model. This would provide a roadmap for managers who are responsible for the implementation of flow techniques across distributed ISD teams, while also creating awareness that adoption of ISD methods is not a binary activity. Third, applying a suit of appropriate metrics to establish a baseline of the current state of flow and to monitor the improvements and transitions across the various adoption stages would demonstrate the value-add of flow in the context of ISD. Finally, having a deep understanding of agility and flow at a project level will provide the ideal platform for researchers and practitioners to effectively scale flow techniques to a portfolio level.

Agility and project portfolio management

Having considered the evolution of agile at the project level, it is now appropriate to consider its deployment in a multi-project environment and more specifically, its implications for a portfolio approach to information systems development. Traditionally, agile methods had been considered as constrained to small co-located projects carried out by individual teams (Hoda et al., 2010; Abrahamsson et al., 2009; Dybå and Dingsøyr, 2008). However, portfolio management has been identified as one of the most important topics for research in agile software development (Dingsøyr and Moe, 2013). This section introduces information systems project portfolio management (IS PPM), discusses the problems associated with it in agile portfolios, and describes how research can help address the shortcomings in both agile and IS PPM.

IS PPM is the ongoing identification, selection, prioritisation, and management of the complete set of an organisation's information systems projects that share common resources in order to communicate portfolio success, maximise returns to the organisation, and achieve strategic business objectives (Meskendahl, 2010; Cooper et al., 1999; Blichfeldt and Eskerod, 2008; PMI, 2013). A review of the literature reveals that IS PPM consists of four components: (1) the identification, selection, and prioritisation of projects; (2) resource management; (3) strategic alignment; and (4) portfolio performance management.

A portfolio approach considers the total return on a complete set of components as opposed to the return on each of the individual components. This approach has been applied successfully in a number of disciplines such as research and development (Stummer and Heidenberger, 2003; Mikkola, 2001) and new product portfolio development (Cooper et al., 2001). However, despite being first applied over 30 years ago (McFarlan, 1981), the application of portfolio management in IS has had limited success. Studies have shown that up to 75% of IS portfolios fail to meet budget, time, and performance expectations (Whittaker, 1999; Keil et al., 2000; Bartis and Mitev, 2008; Gartner, 2014; Singh et al., 2009; Pervan, 1998). Moreover, IS portfolio failure is not restricted to certain industry sectors or project types; rather it occurs with some regularity in organisations of all types and sizes such as health (Greenhalgh and Keen, 2012; Mark, 2007), finance (Drummond, 1999; Charette, 2005), telecommunications (Boonstra and van Offenbeek, 2010) and consulting (Conboy, 2010). Overall, there is little evidence to suggest the trend of portfolio failure is improving.

The continued high rates of IS portfolio failure highlight the problems with scaling agile. While agile methods have been shown to reduce the incidence of project failure (Conboy 2010), paradoxically, the difficulties with PPM are greater in organisations practicing agile (Stettina and Hörz, 2015). PPM has traditionally assumed that success is achieved by selecting the 'right' projects and executing each one effectively. Indeed, most PPM research focuses solely on the initial prioritisation and selection of the project mix (Cooper and Edgett, 1997; Meskendahl, 2010, de Reyck et al., 2005) and there is little research looking at the day-to-day management of portfolios (Frey and Buxmann, 2012). The idealistic perspective where all projects proceed in a linear fashion, with no need to consider change or interdependencies, is illustrated in Figure 10.3 (Stettina and Hörz, 2015).

While this approach may work in traditional industries (e.g., construction) or even in IS where a waterfall approach is appropriate and there is little change to projects, it is totally at odds with an agile approach that embraces change, even late in projects. The combination of constant change, interdependencies, and social and technical issues results in a complex dynamic portfolio that can prove difficult to manage (Orlikowski and Scott, 2008; Daniel et al., 2014) (see Figure 10.4).

While one may argue that the management of a portfolio is no different from the management of a single project, the scaling of management to the portfolio level is difficult for a number of reasons. First, individual project success does not ensure portfolio success (Billows,

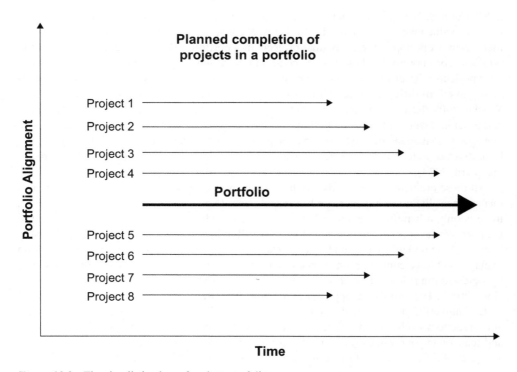

Figure 10.3 The simplistic view of project portfolio management

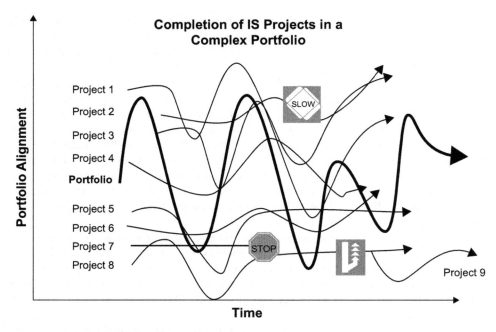

Figure 10.4 The reality of project portfolio management

2001; Conboy, 2010), and sometimes the entire portfolio is technically sound but offers little business value (Weill and Vitale, 1999). Consequently, the view that a good project management framework applied to individual projects in a portfolio inevitably leads to a successful portfolio does not always hold true. Second, in a portfolio there is a mix of short- and long-term projects with disparate and dyssynchronous time horizons. This makes the simultaneous management of different project time lines within the overall portfolio difficult (Collyer and Warren, 2009, Jeffery and Leliveld, 2004). Third, a portfolio requires management of projects and programs with multiple, conflicting goals and the management of multiple managers by a manager or management group. This can be problematic when project and portfolio managers have diverse preferences or nuances toward certain management types (Hansen and Kraemmergaard, 2013).

All these problems are exacerbated in an agile environment. However, while agile project management literature has increased in recent years (e.g., Fernandez and Fernandez, 2008), there is only a handful of empirical studies that has addressed the issues of scaling agile to the portfolio level (e.g., Stettina and Hörz, 2015; Rautiainen et al., 2011) and the relationship between them remains poorly understood. That said, a number of approaches to agile portfolio management have come to prominence in recent years. These approaches generally originate in the consulting literature and have been subject to little empirical validation (Stettina and Hörz, 2015). Two prominent approaches are now discussed.

Leffingwell (2007, 2010) developed the Scaled Agile Framework (SAFe) to implement agile practices at the enterprise level. The framework has three levels (portfolio, program, and team) and four values (alignment, code quality, transparency, and program execution). The portfolio management team prioritises the portfolio backlog and allocates resources. At the program level, product managers participate in program prioritisation, and at the team level, five to ten agile teams deliver projects. However, the Scaled Agile Framework has been criticised by agile pioneers as being overly complicated and rigid (Schwaber, 2013) as well as being "relentlessly top down," with no requirement for organisational agility (Jeffries, 2014). Furthermore, when compared with the definition of agile as illustrated in Figure 10.2, a number of issues arise. First, the focus on execution of programs as prioritised at the portfolio level can impair the enterprise's capacity to either react to change or learn from it. Second, agile must not detract from perceived simplicity, whereas the SAFe adds to organisational complexity.

Krebs (2008) proposes "Agile Portfolio Management" to deliver a dynamically managed portfolio based on agile principles. Portfolio management is divided between projects, resources, and assets with a dashboard recommended to monitor the whole portfolio. Progress, quality, and team morale are proposed as project metrics. Resource transparency and the establishment of a Project Management Office (PMO) are considered key to agile portfolio management (Stettina and Hörz, 2015). Again there is little experimental validation of this framework. Like SAFe, it can be criticised as overly prescriptive. It assumes that what works in one organisation will work in all organisations, and there is little scope for "method tailoring" (Conboy and Fitzgerald, 2010) that has helped to make agile successful at the project level.

Future development of agile PPM

While agile promotes a bottom-up approach, its original development was aimed at single teams of around eight people. It is therefore unsurprising that agile has proven difficult to scale, and it should be noted that many of the criticisms aimed at agile approaches to portfolio management are merely extensions of criticisms that have been directed at agile software development (e.g., practitioner led, hard to scale). However, while it is not unusual for research in ISD to be practice led, it is necessary for academic research to address the shortcomings arising from this approach, develop effective theory to underpin practice, provide empirical data to support (or refute) claims of effectiveness, and illuminate limitations of such methods.

Indeed, academic research is seeking to both validate IS PPM and to provide a theoretical underpinning to existing frameworks as well as develop new frameworks (Stettina and Hörz, 2015; Vähäniitty, 2012). For example, principles for scaling agile have been developed that seek to address the additional challenges associated between managing multiple teams across organisational levels (Dingsøyr and Moe, 2014). Furthermore, by articulating the challenges associated with agile at the portfolio level, academics may influence the next wave of agile methodologies in order to make them more scalable. Concepts such as flow (discussed earlier), which are currently being incorporated into agile, have the potential to help manage a dynamic portfolio of interdependent IS projects. For example, the focus on value in flow (Wang et al., 2012) can help with performance management at the portfolio level. Furthermore, flow's use of visualisation techniques (Petersen et al., 2014) provides the necessary transparency to ensure resources can be moved rapidly around the portfolio as priorities change.

Agility and openness

While the previous sections focused on the evolution of agile at the project and portfolio level, this section reflects on how open collaborative practices can augment agile software development. A particular strength of agile approaches is that they move away from reclusive development, where the team building the system is disconnected from the customer. Instead,

Table 10.2 Challenges in combining agile and open approaches

Challenges	Explanation
Agile methods open development to the customer only.	The customer plays an essential and integrated role in agile development. However, this practice does not extend to include other stakeholders in an open ecosystem.
Open development practices require significant time and resource investment from multiple stakeholders, as well as from the development team.	Often there are conflicts of interest that need to be addressed on a continuous basis. Thus, there has to be a high level of commitment from various participants. Furthermore, due to the commitment required, staff may miss or not prioritise their commitment due to time constraints or required work on multiple initiatives.
Open innovation can be difficult to implement when there is a level of competition or diverse interests between teams and business units.	Some developers are happy to discuss the ideas of others while being protective of their own.
Agile can damage visibility in open environments	Agile methods attempt to optimise the use of documentation and eliminate waste paperwork. This may be a significant concern if trying to create an open network of development teams.

Source: Conboy and Morgan (2014).

agile approaches continually involve the customer in the development process, often resulting in the development of a more innovative and valuable software product (Conboy and Morgan, 2014, 2011). Nonetheless, it is useful to contemplate how agile software development could benefit from more openness and transparency between agile teams and other stakeholders across an organisation. A previous study by Conboy and Morgan (2014) highlighted a number of challenges (see Table 10.2) that organisations need to consider when combining agile and open innovation.

Despite these challenges, however, there is great potential for agile and open development practices to be combined to enhance the effectiveness of software development inside organisations. While companies might think they have to make a clear choice between the two, this choice has more to do with the range of participants and the openness of the process to other stakeholders than it does with the philosophy of design and development (Goldman and Gabriel, 2005). Open collaborative development via communities, for example, open source software, is widely understood and accepted, and organisations are now realising that these characteristics can be applied to improve their own internal software development process as well, with many looking to apply them to enhance their own internal software development methods, typically in conjunction with agile or lean methodologies (Yeaton, 2012).

Future development of agile and open

Given the notable success of open source communities and projects (Linux, Apache, etc.), many organisations are now applying open source development practices within their own internal software development environments, a phenomenon that is termed innersource (Stol et al., 2011). Comparable to open source development, innersource applies an open, concurrent model of collaboration and has been referred to as a good example of intra-organisational open innovation (Morgan et al., 2011). Innersource development implies benefits analogous to distributed ownership and control of code, early and frequent releasing, developer rotation, many continuous feedback channels, and improved innovation. Indeed, innersource can be a great tool to help break down silos, encourage internal collaboration, accelerate new engineer on-boarding, and improve overall productivity (Oram, 2015).

On the surface, agile methods and innersource might appear to be drastically different. However, the two share many of the same principles and values. For example, agile methods such as Scrum are highly prevalent in software development practices and often praised for being flexible and lightweight, thus enabling creativity and innovation given their emphasis on communication and collaboration and valuing people over process (Conboy and Morgan, 2014; Beck, 2000). Moreover, innersource is considered a development philosophy that focuses more on principles of egalitarianism, self-organisation, developer rotation, transparency, and meritocracy (Riehle et al., 2009; Agerfalk et al., 2015). Indeed, there is significant overlap between agile and innersource methods, as both approaches foster teamwork and collaboration, certainly essentials that assist in addressing some of the challenges outlined in Table 10.2. Nonetheless, to effectively take advantage of implementing innersource, there are a number of prerequisites that need to be put in place.

First, top management support is vital, particularly when developers may be contributing to another team's project. Second, open development practices like innersource require a mindset of collaboration and cooperation. Thus, there need to be incentives that recognise contributions and provide the motivation for collaboration and willingness to share with other stakeholders.

Third, developing an innersource reference model that can feed into an organisation-wide common development process, namely establishing a rich taxonomy, or pattern language, consisting of patterns (each defining a context, recurring problem, and common solution) is important. The reference model can help with the dissemination of expertise, coaching, and training activities of agile teams.

Fourth, project managers need to plan appropriately for cross-team collaboration. Standards need to be clearly defined and followed, therefore, organisations should develop an effective governance framework and communications plan with supporting strategies and tactics for successful and sustainable agile development and innersourcing. This aspect should focus on the integration between organisational structures necessary to serve the business needs of the organisation (e.g., timely delivery of product release deadlines) as well as internal processes and relational mechanisms that serve to engage all stakeholders. Finally, developing metrics will help in quantifying and monitoring agile and open initiatives. Metrics may include the number of active projects and contributors, the distributions of contributions across projects, and so on.

Conclusions

Agile methods were designed with contemporary ISD environments in mind. However, the emergent and complex nature of ISD has increased, even since the original agile manifesto was conceived.

This chapter provided a brief overview of the evolution of agile methods since the early 2000s, and compared the ways agility is and should be evaluated today. The chapter also introduced the emerging concept of flow and discussed the ways it is changing how we think about and apply agile in ISD. The chapter then described project portfolio management and open innovation environments – areas of ISD where agile methods have not been effectively applied despite an ever-increasing need to do so.

When first drafting the sections on flow, project portfolio management, and open innovation, we considered each individually. However, it is interesting to note that across each of these areas we see similar issues – a lack of knowledge regarding how these concepts are applied in practice, a lack of research as to how they link and accommodate agility, and concern regarding the clarity and applicability of the concepts in practice. This chapter therefore raises some interesting issues regarding these concepts going forward.

References

Abrahamsson, P., Conboy, K. & Wang, X. 2009. 'Lots Done, More To Do': The Current State of Agile Systems Development Research. *European Journal of Information Systems*, 18, 281–284.

Agerfalk, P.J., Fitzgerald, B., Stol, K. 2015. *Software Outsourcing in the Age of Open: Leveraging the Unknown Workforce*. Springer, Heidelberg.

Anderson, D. 2013. *Lean Software Development*. Lean Kanban University (LKU), Seattle.

Anderson, D., Concas, G., Lunesu, M.I. & Marchesi, M. 2011. *Studying Lean-Kanban Approach Using Software Process Simulation. Agile Processes in Software Engineering and Extreme Programming*, pp. 12–26. Springer, Heidelberg.

Anderson, D.J. 2010. *The Kanban Principles*. Blue Hole Press, Sequin, WA.

Aronsson, H., Abrahamsson, M., and Spens, K. 2011. Developing Lean and Agile Health Care Supply Chains. *Supply Chain Management*, 16(3), 176–183.

Bartis, E. & Mitev, N. 2008. A Multiple Narrative Approach to Information Systems Failure: A Successful System That Failed. *European Journal of Information Systems*, 17, 112–124.

Beck, K. 2000. *Extreme Programming Explained: Embrace Change*. Addison-Wesley, Reading, MA.

Billows, D. 2001. *Managing Complex Projects*, Hampton Group, Denver, CO.

Blichfeldt, B.S. & Eskerod, P. 2008. Project Portfolio Management – There's More to It Than What Management Enacts. *International Journal of Project Management*, 26, 357–365.

Boehm, B. 2002. Get Ready for Agile Methods, With Care. *Computer*, 35, 64–69.

Boonstra, A. & Van Offenbeek, M. 2010. Towards Consistent Modes of E-Health Implementation: Structurational Analysis of a Telecare Programme's Limited Success. *Information Systems Journal*, 20, 537–561.

Cawley, O., Wang, X. & Richardson, I. 2013. *Lean Software Development – What Exactly Are We Talking About? Lean Enterprise Software and Systems*, pp. 16–31. Springer, Heidelberg.

Charette, R.N. 2005. Why Software Fails [Software Failure]. *Spectrum, IEEE*, 42, 42–49.

Collyer, S. & Warren, C.M.J. 2009. Project Management Approaches for Dynamic Environments. *International Journal of Project Management*, 27, 355–364.

Conboy, K. 2009. Agility From First Principles: Reconstructing the Concept of Agility in Information Systems Development. *Information Systems Research*, 20, 329–354.

Conboy, K. 2010. Project Failure En Masse: A Study of Loose Budgetary Control in ISD Projects. *European Journal Of Information Systems*, 19, 273–287.

Conboy, K. & Fitzgerald, B. 2010. Method and Developer Characteristics for Effective Agile Method Tailoring: A Study of XP Expert Opinion. *ACM Transactions on Software Engineering and Methodology (Tosem)*, 20, 2.

Conboy, K. & Morgan, L. 2011. Beyond the Customer: Opening the Agile Systems Development Process. *Journal of Information and Software Technology*, 53, 535–542.

Conboy, K. & Morgan, L. 2014. Embracing Open Innovation in Agile Software Development. *Engineers Journal* [online], available at: www.engineersjournal.ie/2014/02/13/embracing-open-innovation-in-agile-software-development/.

Cooper, R.G. & Edgett, S.J. 1997. Portfolio Management in New Product Development: Lessons From the Leaders – I. *Research Technology Management*, 40, 16.

Cooper, R.G., Edgett, S.J. & Kleinschmidt, E. 1999. New Product Portfolio Management: Practices and Performances. *Journal of Product Innovation Management*, 16, 333–351.

Cooper, R.G., Edgett, S.J & Kleinschmidt, E. 2001. *Portfolio Management for New Products*. Perseus Books, Cambridge, MA.

Daniel, E.M., Ward, J.M. & Franken, A. 2014. A Dynamic Capabilities Perspective of IS Project Portfolio Management. *Journal of Strategic Information Systems*, 23, 95–111.

De Reyck, B., Grushka-Cockayne, Y., Lockett, M., Calderini, S. R., Moura, M. & Sloper, A. 2005. The Impact of Project Portfolio Management on Information Technology Projects. *International Journal of Project Management*, 23, 524–537.

Dingsøyr, T. & Moe, N. B. 2013. Research Challenges in Large-Scale Agile Software Development. *ACM Sigsoft Software Engineering Notes*, 38, 38–39.

Dingsøyr, T. & Moe, N. B. 2014. Towards Principles of Large-Scale Agile Development. *Agile Methods: Large-Scale Development, Refactoring, Testing, and Estimation*, pp. 1–8. Springer, Heidelberg.

Drummond, H. 1999. Are We Any Closer to the End? Escalation and the Case of Taurus. *International Journal of Project Management*, 17, 11–16.

Dybå, T. & Dingsøyr, T. 2008. Empirical Studies of Agile Software Development: A Systematic Review. *Information and Software Technology*, 50, 833–859.

Ebert, C., Abrahamsson, P. & Oza, N. 2012. Lean Software Development. *IEEE Software*, 22–25.

Fernandez, D. J. & Fernandez, J. D. 2008. Agile Project Management – Agilism Versus Traditional Approaches. *Journal of Computer Information Systems*, 49, 10–17.

Fitzgerald, B. & Stol, K.-J. Continuous Software Engineering and Beyond: Trends and Challenges. Proceedings of the 1st International Workshop on Rapid Continuous Software Engineering, 2014. Acm, 1–9.

Fowler, M. & Highsmith, J. 2001. The Agile Manifesto. *Software Development*, August, 28–32.

Frey, T. & Buxmann, P. 2012. IT Project Portfolio Management – A Structured Literature Review. *ECIS 2012*.

Gartner. 2014. *Gartner PPM & IT Governance Summit* [Online]. Available: www.Gartner.Com/Technology/Summits/Na/Program-Management/Agenda.Jsp [Accessed 10/04/2014 2014].

Goldman, R. & Gabriel, R. P. 2005. *Innovation Happens Elsewhere: Open Source As a Business Strategy*. Morgan Kaufmann, Amsterdam.

Greenhalgh, T. & Keen, J. 2012. England's National Programme for IT. *Lancet*, 379, 29–30.

Hansen, L. K. & Kraemmergaard, P. 2013. Transforming Local Government by Project Portfolio Management: Identifying and Overcoming Control Problems. *Transforming Government: People, Process and Policy*, 7, 50–75.

Highsmith, J. 2002. What Is Agile Development? *Journal of Defense Software Development*, 15.

Highsmith, J. & Cockburn, A. 2001. Agile Software Development: The Business of Innovation. *Computer*, 34, 120–127.

Hoda, R., Kruchten, P., Noble, J. & Marshall, S. 2010. Agility in Context. ACM SIGPLAN Notices, ACM, 74–88.

Jeffery, M. & Leliveld, I. 2004. Best Practices in IT Portfolio Management. *MIT Sloan Management Review*, 45, 41–49.

Jeffries, R. E. 2014. Safe – Good But Not Good Enough. [Online]. Available: Http://Ronjeffries.Com/Xprog/Articles/Safe-Good-But-Not-Good-Enough/ [Accessed 11/05/2016 2016].

Keil, M., Mann, J. & Rai, A. 2000. Why Software Projects Escalate: An Empirical Analysis and Test of Four Theoretical Models 1, 2. *MIS Quarterly*, 24, 631–664.

Kitchenham, B. 2010. What's Up With Software Metrics? – A Preliminary Mapping Study. *Journal of Systems and Software*, 83, 37–51.

Kniberg, H. & Skarin, M. 2010. Kanban and Scrum – Making the Most of Both, Lulu.com.

Krebs, J. 2008. *Agile Portfolio Management*, Microsoft Press, Redmond, WA.

Layman, L., Williams, L. and Cunningham, L., 2004, June. Exploring Extreme Programming in Context: An Industrial Case Study. In Agile Development Conference, 2004 (pp. 32–41). IEEE.

Leffingwell, D. 2007. *Scaling Software Agility: Best Practices for Large Enterprises*, Addison-Wesley, Reading, MA.

Leffingwell, D. 2010. *Agile Software Requirements: Lean Requirements Practices for Teams, Programs, and the Enterprise*, Addison-Wesley Professional, Reading, MA.

Lindstrom, L. & Jeffries, R., 2004. Extreme Programming and Agile Software Development Methodologies. *Information Systems Management*, 21(3), 41–52.

Lindvall, M., Basili, V., Boehm, B., Costa, P., Dangle, K., Shull, F., . . . Zelkowitz, M., 2002, August. Empirical findings in agile methods. In *Conference on Extreme Programming and Agile Methods*, pp. 197–207. Springer, Heidelberg.

Mangalaraj, G., Mahapatra, R. & Nerur, S., 2009. Acceptance of software process innovations: The case of extreme programming. *European Journal of Information Systems*, 18(4), 344–354.

Mark, A. L. 2007. Modernising Healthcare – Is the NPfIT for Purpose? *Journal of Information Technology*, 22, 248–256.

Mcfarlan, F. W. 1981. Portfolio Approach to Information Systems. *Harvard Business Review*, 59, 142–150.

Meskendahl, S. 2010. The Influence of Business Strategy on Project Portfolio Management and Its Success – A Conceptual Framework. *International Journal of Project Management*, 28, 807–817.

Mikkola, J. H. 2001. Portfolio Management of R&D Projects: Implications for Innovation Management. *Technovation*, 21, 423–435.

Morgan, L., Feller, J. and Finnegan, P. 2011. Exploring Inner Source as a Form of Intra-Organisational Open Innovation. *Proceedings of the 19th European Conference on Information Systems (Ecis)*, Helsinki, Finland, June 6th–9th.

Nord, R. L., Ozkaya, I. & Sangwan, R. S. 2012. Making Architecture Visible to Improve Flow Management in Lean Software Development. *Software, IEEE*, 29, 33–39.

Oram, A. 2015. *Getting Started With Innersource*. San Francisco, O'Reilly Media.

Orlikowski, W. J. & Scott, S. V. 2008. Sociomateriality: Challenging the Separation of Technology, Work and Organization. *Academy of Management Annals*, 2, 433–474.

Pervan, G. 1998. How Chief Executive Officers in Large Organizations View the Management of Their Information Systems. *Journal of Information Technology*, 13, 95–109.

Petersen, K., Roos, P., Nyström, S. & Runeson, P. 2014. Early Identification of Bottlenecks in Very Large Scale System of Systems Software Development. *Journal of Software: Evolution and Process*, 26, 1150–1171.

Petersen, K. & Wohlin, C. 2011. Measuring the Flow in Lean Software Development. *Software: Practice and Experience*, 41, 975–996.

PMI 2013. *The Standard for Portfolio Management*, 3rd Ed., Project Management Institute, Newtown Square, Pennsylvania.

Poppendieck, M. & Cusumano, M. A. 2012. Lean Software Development: A Tutorial. *IEEE Software*, 29, 26–32.

Poppendieck, M. & Poppendieck, T. 2003. Lean Software Development: An Agile Toolkit. Addison-Wesley, Reading, MA.

Power, K. 2014. Definition of Ready: An Experience Report From Teams at Cisco. *Agile Processes in Software Engineering and Extreme Programming*, pp. 312–319. Springer, Heidelberg.

Power, K. & Conboy, K. 2014. Impediments to Flow: Rethinking the Lean Concept of 'Waste' in Modern Software Development. *Agile Processes in Software Engineering and Extreme Programming*, pp. 203–217. Springer, Heidelberg.

Power, K. & Conboy, K. 2015. A Metric-Based Approach to Managing Architecture-Related Impediments in Product Development Flow: An Industry Case Study From Cisco. *Software Architecture and Metrics (Sam), 2015 IEEE/ACM 2nd International Workshop On*, IEEE, 15–21.

Rautiainen, K., Von Schantz, J. & Vähäniitty, J. 2011. Supporting Scaling Agile With Portfolio Management: Case. *Paf.Com*.

Reinertsen, D. G. 2009. *The Principles of Product Development Flow: Second Generation Lean Product Development*. Celeritas Redondo Beach.

Riehle, D., Ellenberger, J., Menahem, T., Mikhailovski, B., Natchetoi, Y., Naveh, B., and Odenwald, T. 2009. Open Collaboration Within Corporations Using Software Forges. *IEEE Software*, 26, 2, 52–58.

Scharff, C., 2011, May. Guiding global software development projects using Scrum and Agile with quality assurance. In Software Engineering Education and Training (CSEE&T), 2011 24th IEEE-CS Conference on (pp. 274–283). IEEE.

Schwaber, K. UnSAFe at any speed. Ken Schwaber's Blog: Telling it like it is, 2013. https://kenschwaber.wordpress.com/2013/08/06/unsafe-at-any-speed/.

Singh, R., Keil, M. & Kasi, V. 2009. Identifying and Overcoming the Challenges of Implementing a Project Management Office. *European Journal of Information Systems*, 18, 409–427.

Sjøberg, D. I., Johnsen, A. & Solberg, J. 2012. Quantifying the Effect of Using Kanban Versus Scrum: A Case Study. *Software, IEEE*, 29, 47–53.

Stettina, C. J. & Hörz, J. 2015. Agile Portfolio Management: An Empirical Perspective on the Practice in Use. *International Journal of Project Management*, 33, 140–152.

Stol, K., Babar, M. A., Avgeriou, P. & Fitzgerald, B. 2011. A Comparative Study of Challenges in Integrating Open Source Software and Inner Source Software. *Information and Software Technology (IST)*, 53(12), 1319–1336.

Stummer, C. & Heidenberger, K. 2003. Interactive R&D Portfolio Analysis With Project Interdependencies and Time Profiles of Multiple Objectives. *Engineering Management, IEEE Transactions On*, 50, 175–183.

Sutherland, J., Downey, S. & Granvik, B., 2009, August. Shock therapy: A bootstrap for hyperproductive scrum. In Agile Conference, 2009. AGILE '09. (pp. 69–73). IEEE.

Vähäniitty, J. 2012. *Towards Agile Product and Portfolio Management*. Unigrafia Oy, Helsinki.

Wang, X., Conboy, K. & Cawley, O. 2012. "Leagile" Software Development: An Experience Report Analysis of the Application of Lean Approaches in Agile Software Development. *Journal of Systems and Software*, 85, 1287–1299.

Weill, P. & Vitale, M. 1999. Assessing the Health of An Information Systems Applications Portfolio: An Example From Process Manufacturing. *MIS Quarterly*, 23, 601–624.

Whittaker, B. 1999. What Went Wrong? Unsuccessful Information Technology Projects. *Information Management and Computer Security*, 7, 23–29.

Williams, L., Krebs, W., Layman, L., Antón, A. & Abrahamsson, P., 2004. Toward a framework for evaluating extreme programming. *Empirical Assessment in Software Engineering (EASE)*, 11–20.

Womack, J. P. & Jones, D. T. 2010. *Lean Thinking: Banish Waste and Create Wealth in Your Corporation*. Simon and Schuster, New York.

Yeaton, T. 2012. Inner Sourcing: Adopting Open Source Development Processes in Corporate IT. *Business* [Online], Available at: http://Osdelivers.Blackducksoftware.Com/2012/08/29/Inner-Sourcing-Adopting-Open-Source-Development-Processes-In-Corporate-It/

11
IT USE

Notes from a journey from use to effective use

Andrew Burton-Jones, Mark Bremhorst, Fang Liu and Van-Hau Trieu[1]

Introduction

For some years, my colleagues and I have been on a journey to move from studying the use of information systems to their effective use. This chapter has given us a chance to look upon the research more reflectively. While we believe we are on the right path, we are in the early stages of our journey and our steps have been slow and sometimes tentative. In this chapter, we describe the background to our journey and the steps we have been taking. We hope this chapter can interest other researchers in this program of work and hopefully even entice some to join the journey with us.

From use to effective use

Our research on effective use stemmed from the prior work of one of us on system use (Burton-Jones 2005). That work was motivated by the fact that system use was the most researched concept in the IS field, but it needed to be studied in new ways. Specifically, when I (Burton-Jones) spent much of 2001–2003 reviewing that literature, I found vast differences in how researchers defined, viewed and measured system use. Also, I found that researchers typically conceptualized and measured it in what I called a 'lean' way, for example, just measuring use versus non-use, or extent of use (Burton-Jones and Straub 2006). In my view, such research was explaining a phenomenon of questionable relevance. After all, many systems should not be used, should be used less, or should be worked around (Gasser 1986; Lucas and Spitler 1999). I felt that the key issue in practice was how actors achieve their goals, and the key issue for researchers was to understand *how* systems should be used (or not) to achieve them. This would mean, for researchers studying system use, that they should focus on the aspects of use that are relevant in a context and only then turn to building theories to explain that type of use.[2]

The prior work on system usage informed our work on effective use in three main ways. First, the prior work suggested that because systems can be used in so many ways, and researchers can study use in so many ways, researchers should try to identify *subtypes* that matter in specific contexts (Burton-Jones and Straub 2006). From this perspective, effective use is just one subtype of use. In our view, it is simply the most *important* subtype. After all, if we agree that information systems are designed and implemented to facilitate desired goals, and if we agree that the impacts of systems depend on how they are used (DeSanctis and Poole 1994; Zuboff 1988), then the key question is how the systems should be used to achieve the desired goals. In this light, effective use is the lynchpin through which an information system achieves its potential. It is surprising, therefore, that Burton-Jones and Grange (2013) found that only a handful of studies had examined effective use in detail.

Second, the prior work suggested that all types of system use involve three elements: users, systems, and tasks. Accordingly, Burton-Jones and Grange (2013, p. 633) wrote:

> We define effective use as using a system in a way that helps attain the goals for using the system. Our definition is adapted from Burton-Jones and Straub (2006), who defined system use in terms of a user, system, and task, and defined a task as a "goal-directed activity" (p. 231). To move from use to effective use, we simply shifted the emphasis from using the system to perform a goal-directed activity to using it in a way that helps attain the relevant goal.

We adopt the same definition. In terms of a scale, we see effective use lying on a scale from completely ineffective to completely effective. Ineffective just means 'not' effective. It reflects a negative outcome in that it reflects an opportunity cost of time/effort, but it does not capture degrees of negativity. A different construct, such as destructive use, negligent use, or maladaptive use would be needed to capture such notions (Caplan 2006; Skibell 2003). Meanwhile, complete effectiveness is likely to be unknowable and dynamic because any system (information system or work system) has emergent properties (Truex et al. 1999). Achieving maximum effectiveness presumably requires leveraging or even creating such properties.

Third, the prior work suggested the need to tailor conceptualizations of effective use to the context studied. In particular, we can distinguish between the ontological context (the real-world context the researcher wishes to study, such as a specific organization with its specific users, systems, and tasks), and the epistemological context (the knowledge about the world that a researcher wishes to gain, such as the relationship between effective use and performance, or instead its relationship with some other factor). An assumption of our research program is that depending on the ontological and epistemological context, effective use may be quite different and may be studied quite differently.

A program of research: a map and first steps

Using the ideas in the prior section, my colleagues and I began a program of research on effective use about a decade ago. Figure 11.1 shows a diagram that one of us used to structure our thinking in the area (Burton-Jones 2012). The figure shows three domains:

- *Philosophical domain*: Our work is informed by and hopes to inform views on the nature of information systems. That is, we are not interested in the effective use of just *any* artifact; we want to contribute IS-specific insights and contribute back to our understanding of information systems. We have been testing this approach using 'Representation Theory' (RT) as a guiding lens (Weber 1997; Weber 2003), and we will try other lenses over time.
- *Specific research domain*: We wish to learn how theories or views on information systems (such as RT) might help us think about effective use (Burton-Jones and Grange 2013).

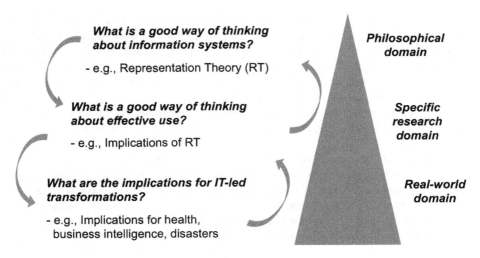

Figure 11.1 A map to guide a research program on effective use

Likewise, we believe an ideal way to reach a deeper understanding of information systems is to understand what it takes to use them effectively (Winograd and Flores 1986, p. 137).

- *Real-world domain*: We are interested in IT-led transformations. This is because we wish to inform ongoing real-world concerns (Agarwal and Lucas 2005). We also expect we will learn unexpected insights from these domains that we can use to update our thinking.

The triangle on the right of Figure 11.1 shows the amount of time we aspire to spend on each domain, that is, more time in the field, a middling amount of time reading and writing studies on our topic of interest, and less time on philosophical concerns. Meanwhile, the arrows show how the work in each domain interrelates. For instance, we have been studying what RT implies for effective use (Burton-Jones and Grange 2013) and meanwhile conducting a grounded theory study of effective use in community care to learn what insights we can gain from the field (Burton-Jones and Volkoff 2016).

To illustrate the approach we are following, we briefly describe the first published study in our program: Burton-Jones and Grange (2013). They explained (p. 650) how they derived a theory of effective use by drawing on several premises of RT:

- The premise that an information system serves to provide users with representations of a real-world domain through a surface structure (interface) and physical structure (machine). They drew on this idea to propose that one dimension of effective use is 'transparent interaction,' defined as "the extent to which a user is accessing the system's representations unimpeded by the system's surface and physical structures" (p. 654).
- The premise that users desire faithful representations of the domain represented by an information system. They drew on this idea to propose that a second dimension of effective use is 'representational fidelity,' defined as "the extent to which a user is obtaining representations that faithfully reflect the domain that the system represents" (p. 654).
- The premise that faithful representations of a domain are desired because they enable users to take actions, and more faithful representations provide a better basis for action than unfaithful ones do. They drew on this idea to propose that a third dimension of

Table 11.1 Recent studies on effective use

Aspect of Effective Use	Relevant References
Nature of effective use (routinization, infusion, extended use, intensity and extent of use, interaction transparency, representational fidelity, informed decision)	(Grublješič and Jaklič 2014; Grublješič and Jaklič 2015; Haake et al. 2015; Huber and Dibbern 2014; Kretzer et al. 2015; Liang et al. 2015; Sarkar 2014; Serrano and Karahanna 2016; Sorgenfrei et al. 2014; Stein et al. 2014a; Trieu 2013; Zou et al. 2014)
Causes or enablers of effective use (e.g., user adaptation, management support, training, usability, organizational capabilities or culture, tensions/frictions)	(Anand et al. 2014; Esposito 2015; Grublješič and Jaklič 2014; Grublješič and Jaklič 2015; Haake et al. 2015; Huber and Dibbern 2014; Kettinger et al. 2013; Kretzer et al. 2015; Lauterbach et al. 2014; Liang et al. 2015; Odusanya et al. 2015; Park et al. 2015; Pearce 2014; Stein et al. 2014a; Trieu 2013; Venkatachalam 2015; Weber et al. 2015; Weeger et al. 2014; Zou et al. 2014)
Consequences of effective use (e.g., firm performance, decision-making performance, work effectiveness/ efficiency/ engagement)	(Anand et al. 2014; Huber and Dibbern 2014; Pearce 2014; Sarkar 2014; Serrano and Karahanna 2016; Trieu 2013; Venkatachalam 2015; Zou et al. 2014)
Moderators of effective use (innovation climate, recommendation faithfulness, routine reconfiguration, learning styles)	(Anand et al. 2014; Haake et al. 2015; Kretzer et al. 2015; Liang et al. 2015; Park et al. 2015)

effective use is 'informed action,' defined as "the extent to which a user acts on faithful representations that he or she obtains from the system to improve his or her state in the domain" (p. 654).

Although we focus this chapter on our ongoing work, and how it builds on or extends Burton-Jones and Grange (2013), many other researchers are taking steps on this journey too. To get a sense for this work, we used Google Scholar to search for studies that cited Burton-Jones and Grange (2013) until June 2016. We found 89. We then reviewed each paper to find the subset that we felt contributed to research on effective use; we found 25. We then categorized them into those that contributed insights regarding the *nature* of effective use, *causes* or *enablers*, *consequences*, or *moderators*. Table 11.1 shows our categorization. Even though many of these studies are preliminary (e.g., theses and conference papers), a vibrant body of work is emerging. We do not have the space here to give justice to these papers, but we hope Table 11.1 can provide readers with a launching point from which to learn more about how researchers are taking steps toward understanding effective use.

Our research in progress

In this section, we briefly discuss our current research projects and how they have enacted the research approach in Figure 11.1. Table 11.2 provides a summary. As the table shows, we have either been working down from RT, working up from the field, or both. When we have worked up from the field, we have been able to generate new inductive insights not covered by RT. In

Table 11.2 Summary of current research in progress

	Effective use of electronic health records in community care	*Effective use of business intelligence systems in universities*	*Effective use of broadcast social media tools in disasters*	*Effective use of reporting systems in clinical networks*
Deduction from RT	N/A (grounded theory study)	Representational fidelity is a key dimension of effective use	Transparent interaction and representational fidelity are key dimensions of effective use	Representational fidelity and informed action are key dimensions of effective use
Inductive insight from fieldwork	Effective use involves reflection-in-action. Reflection-in-action acts like a valve, setting appropriate levels of accuracy and consistency	Effective use involves not just representing reality but presenting a desirable but still justifiable image	Effective use involves conveying messages that contain emotion and human elements, not just 'the facts'	Effective use involves not just representational fidelity but also requires 'truce frames' to guide informed action
Alternative theory that help with understanding field-based insight	Reflection-in-action and practice perspectives (Schon 1983; Yanow and Tsoukas 2009)	Presentation theory (Goffman 1959)	Theories of emotion and communication (Berger and Milkman 2012; Heilman 1997; Reisenzein 1994)	Frames and framing theory (Burke 1937; Davidson 2006)

these instances, we have also been turning to other alternative theories to help shed more light on our inductive findings.

Case study 1: effective use of electronic health records in community care

One of our projects (Burton-Jones and Volkoff 2016) involves studying the effective use of electronic health records (EHRs) in community care. This is a very relevant context in practice in which to study effective use, because the US government offers funds to healthcare providers who can show they use their EHR systems meaningfully, where 'meaningful' and 'effective' are defined similarly (Blumenthal 2011). Thus, healthcare providers are interested in what effective use involves.

Rather than starting from RT's premises, Burton-Jones and Volkoff used grounded theory methods (GTM) (Glaser and Strauss 1967). To learn what dimensions of effective use were relevant, Burton-Jones and Volkoff took an affordance lens (Gibson 1979), asking groups of users in a Canadian health authority how they used their EHR system to accomplish their tasks and what distinguished between more and less effective use. Across different users and different affordances, users described effective use in similar ways. From users' descriptions, Burton-Jones and Volkoff induced three dimensions of effective use: *accuracy* (i.e., how well information in or derived from the EHR reflects the reality it was designed to reflect) (CIHI 2009, p. 6), *consistency* (i.e., variation among instances of use of a given type) (CIHI 2009, p. 41), and *reflection-in-action* (i.e., a practice-based rationale driving the user's actions). Of these dimensions, only the first was discussed (in terms of representational fidelity) by Burton-Jones and Grange (2013).

Burton-Jones and Volkoff found that reflection-in-action was perhaps the most important dimension of effective use, in that it acted like a valve determining the appropriate levels of accuracy and consistency in users' work settings. RT is not well-suited to providing insights on reflection-in-action because it does not consider users or their work settings (Wand and Weber 1990, p. 1282; 1995, p. 205). Thus, Burton-Jones and Volkoff turned to other theories for insights, particularly the literature on reflection-in-action (Boud 2010; Schon 1983; Yanow and Tsoukas 2009). As in Figure 11.1, we can then ask if these practice-based insights may allow us to reach a deeper understanding of the nature of information systems. For instance, it may be that RT is unable to provide a sufficient perspective on information systems and that other theories are required, for example, combining representation- and practice-based insights. Some studies have taken this approach in the past (e.g., Zuboff 1988), offering an opportunity to extend such ideas further in the future (Burton-Jones 2014).

Case study 2: effective use of business intelligence systems in universities

In a second case study, we have been examining transformations occurring close to home. Specifically, many university executives have been turning to business intelligence (BI) systems to help them understand, improve and report on their performance (Goldstein 2005), a trend that is accelerating with the rise of influential and controversial assessment regimes (Hicks 2012; Nica 2014). This is an interesting context in which to study effective use and reach a deeper understanding of information systems, because a core assumption of BI systems is that they offer a 'single-source of truth' (Watson and Wixom 2007). Such an assumption may not be tenable in an academic setting because much academic research is a social construction (Pinch and Bijker 1984) (adding complexity to the notion of 'truth'), and academics and administrators can shape how they present their research to others (Bonnell 2016; Stein et al. 2013) (adding complexity to the notion of a 'single source' of truth).

Motivated by the practical importance of effective use in this context, we conducted a case study of the effective use of a BI system in an Australian university (Trieu and Burton-Jones 2016). The Australian government requires Australian universities to report their research performance to the federal government. Given the political context in which these assessments are produced and used, each university clearly wishes to present its performance in the best light possible. Working down the triangle in Figure 11.1, we began with Burton-Jones and Grange's (2013) deduction from RT that a key dimension of effective use is representational fidelity. Meanwhile, working up the triangle, we asked if representational fidelity would still be relevant, and if so, how, in the university assessment context.

The university we studied had developed a BI system for identifying, categorizing, and reporting on research outputs. Through interviews with users of the BI system, and subsequent qualitative coding of the data, we obtained mixed views on the importance of representational fidelity. On the one hand, we learned that representing performance faithfully was important, consistent with the academics' traditional moral of respect for truth. On the other hand, we also learned how the representation fidelity of a system can depend heavily on the perceptions and practices of those using the system, and it can be perceived differently by people, for example, due to interpreting research and/or research categories differently (Boyd and Crawford 2012; Snowden and Boone 2007). Because RT does not consider the user context, it is unable to provide insights into the latter findings. We therefore turned to another theory – presentation theory (or 'self-presentation' theory) (Goffman 1959) – for insights.

Through analysis of our data, we ultimately concluded that stakeholders' main goal was not to faithfully represent their performance, as RT would predict, nor was it to misrepresent it. Rather, effective use involved faithfully representing a *story about their performance* that would both remain faithful to their actual performance *and* impress key stakeholders. This conclusion offers a way to contribute back to our understanding of information systems. Rather than seeing an information system as an artifact for representing reality, as RT suggests, or simply as a method for impression management, as a presentation perspective might suggest, our study sees the information system as a fused product of the two – the information system provides a faithful representation of a presentation (a story) and equally provides a presentation of a faithful representation (a story about their true performance). To our knowledge, the literatures on RT (e.g., Wand and Weber 1995; Weber 1997; Burton-Jones and Grange 2013) and presentation theory (e.g., da Cunha 2013; Hee-Woong et al. 2012; Leonardi and Treem 2012; Meng and Agarwal 2007) have not been combined to date, offering an opportunity for future research.

Case study 3: effective use of broadcast social media tools in disasters

A very different context in which the effective use of information systems is increasingly important is the use of social media in disasters, such as the use of Twitter to communicate during and about floods, wildfires and terrorism. In such contexts, social media can cause negative impacts if used ineffectively (e.g., arousing panic) (Abdullah et al. 2015), but it can equally bring about positive impacts if used effectively (e.g., minimizing impacts and supporting recovery) (Chan 2014). To understand effective use in this context, we followed a dual strategy of making deductions from RT while also analyzing social media (in particular,

Twitter) data from three disasters (Oklahoma tornado, 2013; Boston Marathon bombing, 2013; and New South Wales bushfires, 2013).

Given citizens' need for an accurate understanding of the current state of a disaster, we initially took the importance of representational fidelity as a given and focused on how to increase it. In particular, we focused on the deduction from RT that transparent interaction facilitates representational fidelity (Burton-Jones and Grange 2013). This led us to ask what might, in turn, facilitate transparent interaction. One feature of social media tools that could help we call *convenience for evidencing*, that is, a tool's ability to allow a message sender to easily find and include evidence in a message. We predicted that messages sent from tools with greater convenience for evidencing would show higher levels of representational fidelity. To test this prediction, we compared messages sent during the three disasters from desktops with those sent from mobile devices, and found that compared to messages sent from mobile devices, messages sent from desktops are more likely to include evidence (e.g., pictures, videos or external URLs), which can help faithfully reflect the state of a disaster (Liu et al. 2016). In line with our prediction, we concluded that this was because it is easier for message senders to search for and attach evidence about real-world situations in a message on desktops. When people use social media apps on mobile devices (Perreault and Ruths 2011), they have to switch to other apps (i.e., browser or search engine) to search for evidence, and due to the smaller font and keyboard size, they must exert more effort to adjust the selection to copy and paste the evidence (Chen et al. 2014).[3]

While this finding supported our prediction, our exploration of the data led us to additional insights. Specifically, when we viewed messages on Twitter in the three disasters, we noticed that many messages (tweets) were retransmitted messages (retweets). Therefore, one way for disaster managers to think about effective use is the extent to which they can tailor their messages to enhance the likelihood that their messages will be *retransmitted*, because this will get the information out faster to a larger audience (Liu et al. 2016). What might RT imply for how messages should be tailored? The concept of representational fidelity would suggest that the most desirable messages would be those that provide a window on reality. In the communications field, the window metaphor is associated with newswriting that focuses on 'the facts' (Bird and Dardenne 1990, p. 33). However, communication researchers have long debated whether agencies should focus their messages on the facts alone (e.g., communicating dry, official messages) or instead imbue their messages with emotions and human elements (Bird and Dardenne 1990; Cross and Ma 2015; Pewitt-Jones 2014). Based on our analysis of our data and theories of emotion (Berger and Milkman 2012; Heilman 1997; Reisenzein 1994), we would argue that if disaster managers want their messages to be retweeted, they should take the latter approach and convey emotion and human elements (e.g., stories and pictures of individuals) in their messages rather than just simply the facts. Given that RT does not offer any insights into human emotions, a lesson from this research has been that we may need to infuse our understanding of effective use, and information systems in general, with an understanding of emotion, just as we need to do in our understanding of information systems more broadly (Stein et al. 2014b).

Case study 4: effective use of reporting systems in clinical networks

In our final case study, we have been studying ways to manage the rising tide of chronic disease. One approach used in several nations to tackle chronic disease is to establish *clinical networks*, which are networks of clinicians employed across diverse organizations who can benefit from information sharing and goal setting (Cunningham et al. 2012; Greene et al.

2009). One of our projects involves studying the effective use of reporting systems in such networks. In the network we are studying, a major function of the network is to agree on performance indicators and to use a clinical reporting system to report on them across the network and make decisions accordingly.

In this study, we focused on two dimensions of effective use that Burton-Jones and Grange (2013) deduced from RT: the notion that effective use involves taking informed action on the basis of information from the system, and the notion that representational fidelity enables informed action. In addition to these deductions, we also carried out fieldwork in a particular clinical network. During the fieldwork, it became clear to us that clinical administrators and practitioners did not view the reports in a denotational fashion (simply interpreting the numbers 'as is'). Rather, as in other prior studies (e.g., Boland 1991), they applied social and cognitive processes to inform their interpretation and use of the information. We concluded, therefore, that an adequate theory of effective use in this context must account for such social and cognitive processes. Given that RT explicitly excludes such social and cognitive processes (Wand and Weber 1990, p. 1282; Wand and Weber 1995, p. 205), we looked elsewhere for insights.

We found theories of frames/framing (Davidson, 2006) to be helpful. The concept of a technological frame of reference (TFR) refers to

> a subset of members' organizational frames that concern the assumptions, expectations, and knowledge they use to understand technology in organizations. This includes not only the nature and role of the technology itself, but the specific conditions, applications, and consequences of that technology in particular contexts.
> (Orlikowski and Gash 1994, p. 178)

The concept of a TFR implies that the users of a system develop a frame of reference that shapes their "perceptions of and actions towards" it (Gal and Berente 2008, p. 135).

Can theories of frames be reconciled with RT? Partially, we believe it is possible to incorporate the concept of frames into RT through Strong and Volkoff's (2010) notion of 'latent structures' (which complement Wand and Weber's (1995) original conceptualization of surface, deep, and physical structures). Specifically, one could argue that users' frames are embedded into both the deep and latent structure of a system. However, to account for frames fully, we believe there is a need to go further and account for users' frames as users use the information in their work. For instance, in our fieldwork, we have found that different clinicians have conflicting frames, and effective use therefore appears to involve the emergence of a new, negotiated frame that resolves the conflict – a 'truce frame' (Azad and Faraj 2008; 2011) – that allows clinicians to make decisions in the network that are acceptable to its members. Given that there has been little relationship between RT and the literature on frames/framing (Davidson 2002; Davidson 2006; Lin and Cornford 2000; Lin and Silva 2005), we believe this insight offers a good opportunity to improve perspectives on effective use, as well as the nature of information systems in general.

Two lessons from our case studies

We are still in the early stages of our journey toward understanding effective use. As a result, our insights remain limited and tentative. However, we feel confident in two insights.

First, our data has supported the deductions from RT in Burton-Jones and Grange (2013), such as the importance of transparent interaction (in our studies of Twitter use), representational fidelity (in all four studies) and informed action (in our study of clinical networks). Thus, we feel increasingly confident in the relevance of these dimensions, and the relevance of RT, for understanding effective use, and understanding information systems in general.

Second, all four studies have shown that RT is insufficient, on its own, to explain effective use. In particular, all four studies have shown that we either need a richer perspective on representational fidelity, or we need to supplement representational fidelity with other constructs. Effective users *reflect* on how faithful the representation should be (case study 1); choose how to present representations to impresses external stakeholders (case study 2); imbue their representations with human emotion (case study 3); and negotiate frames of reference that allow them to produce, understand and act on the representations (case study 4). The challenge and opportunity for us is to determine how best to reconcile these findings with RT, or instead how to move away from RT to other perspectives that will allow a better understanding of effective use or of information systems. Only time will tell which of these solutions will prove more satisfactory. However, it is unlikely that any one theory or perspective will work for all contexts. Therefore, in our own work, we plan to continue cycling between the domains of Figure 11.1, conceiving of research as an ongoing and collective process of discovery, treading a line between the idealism of building general theory and the pragmatism of solving real-world problems. We might be wrong, but we suspect the success of our journey will depend on how well we tread this line over time.

Conclusion

This chapter has reviewed our progress on a journey from studying use to effective use. We described the basis for our journey, the steps we have been taking and the insights we have learned to date. We searched the literature to identify others who are contributing to this journey, too. Overall, the research is driven by the simple view that information systems need to be used effectively to achieve their potential. The simplicity of this notion is important, as we believe it is an idea that almost all researchers and practitioners interested in information systems can understand and agree to. The destination is clear. At the same time, learning what effective use actually involves is a complex challenge. The route is long and difficult. We hope this short chapter can allow researchers to assess the journey we have been taking and potentially even entice some to join the journey with us.

Acknowledgements

We thank Mari-Klara Stein for her helpful comments on an earlier version of this paper.

Notes

1. When writing this chapter, Mark, Fang and Hau were Andrew Burton-Jones' doctoral students at the University of Queensland. They are listed alphabetically.
2. I did not realize then that I was making my own questionable assumptions. I later realized there *are* contexts in which use versus non-use (and greater/lesser use) matter. For instance, online vendors are interested in getting users to use their websites, and use them for longer, because it means more advertising exposure.
3. To clarify this point, we note that it is easier to obtain *direct* evidence about a situation (e.g., take photos) using mobile devices. However, in an online environment, one's own evidence is typically just a very small subset of all the information already online, and it is easier to select from and include such evidence in a message using the surface structure (interface) and physical structure (mouse and keyboard) of a desktop application.

References

Abdullah, N. A., Nishioka, D., Tanaka, Y., and Murayama, Y. "User's Action and Decision Making of Retweet Messages Towards Reducing Misinformation Spread During Disaster," *Journal of Information Processing* (23:1) 2015, pp. 31–40.

Agarwal, R., and Lucas, H. C. "The Information Systems Identity Crisis: Focusing on High-Visibility and High-Impact Research," *MIS Quarterly* (29:3) 2005, pp. 381–398.

Anand, A., Sharmar, R., and Kohli, R. "Routines, Reconfiguration, and the Contribution of Business Analytics to Organizational Performance," in: *Proceedings of the 24th Australasian Conference on Information Systems*, RMIT University, Melbourne, Australia, 2014, pp. 1–10.

Azad, B., and Faraj, S. "Making E-Government Systems Workable: Exploring the Evolution of Frames," *Journal of Strategic Information Systems* (17) 2008, pp. 75–98.

Azad, B., and Faraj, S. "Social Power and Information Technology Implementation: A Contentious Framing Lens," *Information Systems Journal* (21) 2011, pp. 33–61.

Berger, J., and Milkman, K. L. "What Makes Online Content Viral?" *Journal of Marketing Research* (49:2) 2012, pp. 192–205.

Bird, S. E., and Dardenne, R. W. "News and Storytelling in American Culture: Reevaluating the Sensational Dimension," *Journal of American Culture* (13:2) Summer 1990, pp. 33–37.

Blumenthal, D. "Wiring the Health System – Origins and Provisions of a New Federal Program," *New England Journal of Medicine* (365:24) 2011, pp. 2323–2329.

Boland, R. J. "Information System Use as a Hermeneutic Process," in: *Information Systems Research: Contemporary Approaches and Emergent Traditions*, H. Nissen, H. K. Klein and R. Hirschheim (eds.), Elsevier Science, North-Holland, 1991, pp. 439–458.

Bonnell, A. G. "Tide or Tsunami? The Impact of Metrics on Scholarly Research," *Australian Universities' Review* (58:1) 2016, pp. 54–61.

Boud, D. "Relocating Reflection in the Context of Practice," in: *Beyond Reflective Practice: New Approaches to Professional Lifelong Learning*, H. Bradbury, N. Frost, S. Kilminster and M. Zukas (eds.), Routledge, Abingdon, UK, 2010, pp. 25–36.

Boyd, D., and Crawford, K. "Critical Questions for Big Data: Provocations for a Cultural, Technological, and Scholarly Phenomenon," *Information Communication and Society* (15:5) 2012, pp. 662–679.

Burke, K. *Attitudes Towards History*, New Republic, New York, 1937.

Burton-Jones, A. *New Perspectives on the System Usage Construct*, Unpublished Doctoral Dissertation Department of Computer Information Systems, Georgia State University, 2005.

Burton-Jones, A. "Extending the Theoretical Program of Representation Theory," in: *Proceedings of the Information Systems Foundations Workshop*, S. Gregor (ed.), Australian National University, 2012.

Burton-Jones, A. "What Have We Learned From the Smart Machine?" *Information and Organization* (24:2) 2014, pp. 71–105.

Burton-Jones, A., and Grange, C. "From Use to Effective Use: A Representation Theory Perspective," *Information Systems Research* (24:3) 2013, pp. 632–658.

Burton-Jones, A., and Straub, D. "Reconceptualizing System Usage," *Information Systems Research* (17:3) 2006, pp. 228–246.

Burton-Jones, A., and Volkoff, O. "What Does It Mean to Use an Organizational Information System Effectively? Insights From Users of a Community Care Electronic Health Record System," *Working paper, University of Queensland*, 2016.

Caplan, S. E. "Relations Among Loneliness, Social Anxiety, and Problematic Internet Use," *CyberPsychology & Behavior* (10:2) 2006, pp. 234–242.

Chan, J. C. "The Role of Social Media in Crisis Preparedness, Response and Recovery," *RAHS Programme Office (RPO)* (Retrieved 5 May 2016, from www.oecd.org/governance/risk/The%20role%20of%20Social%20media%20in%20crisis%20preparedness,%20response%20and%20recovery.pdf) 2014.

Chen, C., Perrault, S. T., Zhao, S., and Ooi, W. T. "Bezelcopy: An Efficient Cross-Application Copy-Paste Technique for Touchscreen Smartphones," in: *Proceedings of the 2014 International Working Conference on Advanced Visual Interfaces*, ACM, Como, Italy, 2014, pp. 185–192.

CIHI. *The CIHI Data Quality Framework*. Canadian Institute for Health Information, Ottawa, Canada, 2009.

Cross, M. K. D., and Ma, X. "EU Crises and Integrational Panic: The Role of the Media," *Journal of European Public Policy* (22:8) 2015, pp. 1053–1070.

Cunningham, F.C., Ranmuthugala, G., Westbook, J.I., and Braithwaite, J. "Net Benefits: Assessing the Effectiveness of Clinical Networks in Australia Through Qualitative Methods," *Implementation Science* (7:108) 2012, pp. 1–13.

da Cunha, J.V. "A Dramaturgical Model of the Production of Performance Data," *MIS Quarterly* (37:3), September 2013, pp. 723–748.

Davidson, E. "Technology Frames and Framing: A Socio-Cognitive Investigation of Requirements Determination," *MIS Quarterly* (26) 2002, pp. 329–358.

Davidson, E. "A Technological Frames Perspective on Information Technology and Organizational Change," *Journal of Applied Behavioral Science* (42:1) 2006, pp. 23–39.

DeSanctis, G., and Poole, M.S. "Capturing the Complexity in Advanced Technology Use: Adaptive Structuration Theory," *Organization Science* (5:2) 1994, pp. 121–147.

Esposito, M. "End User Participation in Information Systems Development: Why Does Collaboration Remain Elusive?," in: *Proceedings of the Southern Association for Information Systems*, Hilton Head Island, SC, 2015, pp. 1–6.

Gal, U., and Berente, N. "A Social Representations Perspective on Information Systems Implementation: Rethinking the Concept of 'Frames,'" *Information Technology and People* (21) 2008, pp. 133–145.

Gasser, L. "The Integration of Computing and Routine Work," *ACM Transactions on Office Information Systems* (4:3) 1986, pp. 205–225.

Gibson, J.J. *The Ecological Approach to Visual Perception*. Taylor & Francis, New York, 1979.

Glaser, B.G., and Strauss, A.L. *The Discovery of Grounded Theory*, Aldine, Chicago, 1967.

Goffman, E. *The Presentation of Self in Everyday Life*, Doubleday, Garden City, New York, 1959.

Goldstein, P.J. "Academic Analytics: The Uses of Management Information and Technology in Higher Education," Published online (https://net.educause.edu/ir/library/pdf/ecar_so/ers/ers0508/EKF0508.pdf) December 2005, pp. 1–12.

Greene, A., Pagliari, C., Cunningham, S., Donnan, P., Evans, J., Emslie-Smith, A., Morris, A., and Guthrie, B. "Do Managed Clinical Networks Improve Quality of Diabetes Care? Evidence From a Retrospective Mixed Methods Evaluation," *BMJ Quality and Safety* (18:6) 2009, pp. 456–461.

Grubljesic, T., and Jaklic, J. "Customer Oriented Management Practices Leading to BIS Embeddedness," *Online Journal of Applied Knowledge Management* (2:1) 2014, pp. 11–27.

Grubljesic, T., and Jaklic, J. "Conceptualization of the Business Intelligence Extended Use Model," *Journal of Computer Information Systems* (55:3) 2015, pp. 72–82.

Haake, P., Mädche, A., Mueller, B., and Lauterbach, J. "The Effect of User Adaptation on the Effective Use of Enterprise Systems," in: *Proceedings of the 36th International Conference on Information Systems*, Fort Worth, TX, 2015, pp. 1–12.

Hee-Woong, K., Chan, H.C., and Kankanhalli, A. "What Motivates People to Purchase Digital Items on Virtual Community Websites? The Desire for Online Self-Presentation," *Information Systems Research* (23:4) 2012, pp. 1232–1245.

Heilman, K. "The Neurobiology of Emotional Experience," *Journal of Neuropsychiatry* (9:3) 1997, pp. 439–448.

Hicks, D. "Performance-Based University Research Funding Systems," *Research Policy* (41:2) 2012, pp. 251–261.

Huber, T., and Dibbern, J. "How Collaboration Software Enables Globally Distributed Software Development Teams to Become Agile-an Effective Use Perspective," in: *International Workshop on Global Sourcing of Information Technology and Business Processes*, Springer International, Switzerland, 2014, pp. 49–63.

Kettinger, W.J., Zhang, C., and Chang, K.-C. "Research Note – A View From the Top: Integrated Information Delivery and Effective Information Use From the Senior Executive's Perspective," *Information Systems Research* (24:3) 2013, pp. 842–860.

Kretzer, M., Nadj, M., and Mädche, A. "The Effect of Recommender Systems on Users' Situation Awareness and Actions," in: *Proceedings of the 36th International Conference on Information Systems*, Fort Worth, TX, 2015, pp. 1–12.

Lauterbach, J., Kahrau, F., Mueller, B., and Maedche, A. "What Makes 'the System' Tick? Explaining Individuals' Adaptation Behavior Towards Effective Use in Enterprise System Implementations," in: *Proceedings of the 35th International Conference on Information Systems*, Auckland, NZ, 2014, pp. 1–21.

Leonardi, P.M., and Treem, J.W. "Knowledge Management Technology as a Stage for Strategic Self-Presentation: Implications for Knowledge Sharing in Organizations," *Information and Organization* (22:1) 2012, pp. 37–59.

Liang, H., Peng, Z., Xue, Y., Guo, X., and Wang, N. "Employees' Exploration of Complex Systems: An Integrative View," *Journal of Management Information Systems* (32:1) 2015, pp. 322–357.

Lin, A., and Cornford, T. "Framing Implementation Management," in: *Proceedings of the 21st International Conference on Information Systems*, W.J. Orlikowski, S. Ang, P. Weill, H.G. Hrcmar and J. DeGross (eds.), Brisbane, Australia, 2000, pp. 197–205.

Lin, A., and Silva, L. "The Social and Political Construction of Technological Frames," *European Journal of Information Systems* (14) 2005, pp. 49–59.

Liu, F., Burton-Jones, A., and Xu, D. *Facilitating the Spread of Information Rather Than Rumor in a Disaster: Insights From Twitter*, Working paper, University of Queensland, 2016.

Lucas, H.C., and Spitler, V.K. "Technology Use and Performance: A Field Study of Broker Workstations," *Decision Sciences* (30:2) 1999, pp. 1–21.

Meng, M., and Agarwal, R. "Through a Glass Darkly: Information Technology Design, Identity Verification, and Knowledge Contribution in Online Communities," *Information Systems Research* (18:1) 2007, pp. 42–67.

Nica, E. "The Corporate Restructuring of the University System," *Economics, Management, and Financial Markets* (9:1) 2014, pp. 142–147.

Odusanya, K., Coombs, C., and Doherty, N.F. "Assessing Individual Benefits Realization Capability: An IT Culture Perspective," in: *Proceedings of the 36th International Conference on Information Systems*, Fort Worth, TX, 2015, pp. 1–11.

Orlikowski, W.J., and Gash, D.C. "Technological Frames: Making Sense of Information Technology in Organizations," *ACM Transactions on Information Systems* (12) 1994, pp. 174–207.

Park, I., Al-Ramahi, M., and Cho, J. "The Effect of Perceived IS Support for Creativity on Job Satisfaction: The Role of Effective IS Use in Virtual Workplaces," in: *Proceedings of the 36th International Conference on Information Systems*, Fort Worth, TX, 2015, pp. 1–11.

Pearce, D.E. *Developing a Method for Measuring "Working Out Loud,"* Unpublished Doctoral Dissertation, University of Kentucky, 2014.

Perreault, M., and Ruths, D. "The Effect of Mobile Platforms on Twitter Content Generation," in: *Proceedings of the 5th International AAAI Conference on Weblogs and Social Media*, Barcelona, Spain, 2011, pp. 289–296.

Pewitt-Jones, *Narrative Literary Journalists, Ethical Dilemmas, and Ethics Codes*, Unpublished Doctoral Dissertation, Texas Tech University, 2014.

Pinch, T.J., and Bijker, W.E. "The Social Construction of Facts and Artefacts: Or How the Sociology of Science and the Sociology of Technology Might Benefit Each Other," *Social Studies of Science* (14:3) 1984, pp. 399–411.

Reisenzein, R. "Pleasure-Arousal Theory and the Intensity of Emotions," *Journal of Personality and Social Psychology* (67:3) 1994, pp. 525–539.

Sarkar, S. *New Perspectives on Implementing Health Information Technology*, Unpublished Doctoral Dissertation, Georgia State University, Atlanta, 2014.

Schon, D.A. *The Reflective Practitioner: How Professionals Think in Action*. Basic Books, New York, 1983.

Serrano, C., and Karahanna, E. "The Compensatory Interaction Between User Capabilities and Technology Capabilities in Influencing Task Performance: An Empirical Assessment in Telemedicine Consultations," *MIS Quarterly* (40:3) 2016.

Skibell, R. "Cybercrimes and Misdemeanors: A Reevaluation of the Computer Fraud and Abuse Act," *Berkeley Technology Law Journal* (18:3) 2003, pp. 909–944.

Snowden, D.J., and Boone, M.E. "A Leader's Framework for Decision Making," *Harvard Business Review* (85:11) 2007, pp. 1–11.

Sorgenfrei, C., Ebner, K., Smolnik, S., and Jennex, M.E. "From Acceptance to Outcome: Towards an Integrative Framework for Information Technology Adoption," in: *Proceedings of the 22nd European Conference on Information Systems*, Tel Aviv, Israel, 2014.

Stein, M.-K., Lim, E.T., and Tan, C.-W. "Tensions to Frictions? Exploring Sources of Ineffectiveness in Multi-Level IT Use," in: *Proceedings of the 35th International Conference on Information Systems*, Auckland, 2014a, pp. 1–10.

Stein, M.-K., Newell, S., Galliers, R.D., and Wagner, E.L. "Classification Systems, Their Digitization and Consequences for Data-Driven Decision Making: Understanding Representational Quality," in: *Proceedings of the International Conference on Information Systems* Milan, Italy, 2013.

Stein, M.-K., Newell, S., Wagner, E. L., and Galliers, R. "Felt Quality of Sociomaterial Relations: Introducing Emotions Into Sociomaterial Theorizing," *Information & Organization* (24:3) 2014b, pp. 156–175.

Strong, D. M., and Volkoff, O. "Understanding Organization-Enterprise System Fit: A Path to Theorizing the Information Technology Artifact," *MIS Quarterly* (34:4) 2010, pp. 731–756.

Trieu, T. V.-H. "Extending the Theory of Effective Use: The Impact of Enterprise Architecture Maturity Stages on the Effective Use of Business Intelligence Systems," in: *Proceedings of the 34th International Conference on Information Systems*, Milan, Italy, 2013, pp. 1–11.

Trieu, T. V.-H., and Burton-Jones, A. Producing Representational Fidelity: An Investigation in the Business Intelligence Systems Context, Working paper, University of Queensland, 2016.

Truex, D., Baskerville, R., and Klein, H. "Growing Systems in Emergent Organizations," *Communications of the ACM* (42:8) 1999, pp. 117–123.

Venkatachalam, Leveraging of Software as a Service by Small and Medium Enterprises: Information Systems Capabilities and Organisational Complementarities, Unpublished Doctoral Dissertation, QUT, 2015.

Wand, Y., and Weber, R. "An Ontological Model of an Information System," *IEEE Transactions on Software Engineering* (16) 1990, pp. 1282–1292.

Wand, Y., and Weber, R. "On the Deep Structure of Information Systems," *Information Systems Journal* (5) 1995, pp. 203–223.

Watson, H. J., and Wixom, B. H. "The Current State of Business Intelligence," *IEEE Computer* (40:9) 2007, pp. 96–99.

Weber, M., Gewald, H., and Weeger, A. "Disruptions of the Tripartite Structure of System Usage: Exploring Factors Influencing the Effective Usage of Information Systems in German Hospitals," in: *Proceedings of the 23rd European Conference on Information Systems*, Munster, Germany, 2015, pp. 1–15.

Weber, R. *Ontological Foundations of Information Systems*, Coopers & Lybrand and Accounting Association of Australia and New Zealand, Melbourne, 1997.

Weber, R. "Editor's Comments: Still Desperately Seeking the IT Artifact," *MIS Quarterly* (27:3) 2003, pp. iii–xi.

Weeger, A., Neff, A., Gewald, H., and Haase, U. "Exploring Determinants of Effective Use: The Role of Misfits Between a Hospital and Its Information Systems," *Multikonferenz Wirtschaftsinformatik*, 2014, pp. 1–13.

Winograd, T., and Flores, F. *Understanding Computer and Cognition: A New Foundation for Design.* Ablex, New Jersey, 1986.

Yanow, D., and Tsoukas, H. "What Is Reflection-in-Action? A Phenomenological Account," *Journal of Management Studies* (46:8) 2009, pp. 1339–1364.

Zou, P. X., Keating, B., Yang, R. J., Campbell, J., and Zhao, L. "Achieving Building Sustainability Through Application of Information System and Stakeholder Alignment," in: *Smart Construction and Management in the Content of New Technology (ICCREM)*, American Society of Civil Engineers (ACSE), 2014, pp. 113–125.

Zuboff, S. *In the Age of the Smart Machine: The Future of Work and Power.* Basic Books, New York, 1988.

12
AFFECT IN THE ICT CONTEXT

Jasy Liew Suet Yan and Ping Zhang

Introduction

It is a bright and sunny day. You walk into office in a good mood. Powering up your computer, you are notified that the company has just started a new information system and the self-training module has to be done. Your attitude toward new technology has always been apprehensive. With a slight frown on your face, you log in to the system and are greeted by a playful game-like user interface that leads you to a series of effortless steps that touch upon your job closely. Your frown gradually disappears as you explore the new system. Without knowing it, you become absorbed in the training module and complete the module without realizing how much time has passed. By the end of it, you are thinking: this new system seems to be a useful and fun system to use.

This scenario illustrates that humans do not judge and behave in an emotional vacuum in their everyday interaction with information and communication technologies (ICTs). It has been well established that affect is a fundamental aspect of human beings, one that influences reflex, perception, cognition, and behavior within many social contexts including where humans interact with ICTs (Norman, 2002; Slovic, Finucane, Peters, & MacGregor, 2002; Zhang, 2013; Zhang & Li, 2005).

Existing research in information systems (IS) and other social science studies have shown that affect influences job satisfaction (Weiss, Nicholas, & Daus, 1999), consumer shopping behaviors (Childers, Carr, Peck, & Carson, 2001), creative problem solving (Isen, Daubman, & Nowicki, 1987), group work (Chin & Gopal, 1995; Kelly & Barsade, 2001), risk taking and decision making (Mittal & Ross, 1998) and organizational behavior (Brief, 2001; Loiacono & Djamasbi, 2010). Failure to take into account of the affective aspect in human behaviors can lead to frustration and disadvantage.

ICT use has grown into nearly every facet of our lives. Users' choices of ICTs have grown tremendously too, with many competing ICT products and services available for similar purposes. Such technological changes have prompted the interest in understanding affect and are particularly timely and relevant as we seek to understand individuals' use and exploration behaviors, as well as the potential implications of such understanding on ICT design, deployment and management (Zhang, 2013).

Over the past two decades, affect has received much attention among IS researchers. The conceptualizations and findings, however, show high inconsistencies and discrepancies. The inconclusive results can be caused by a number of factors, such as (1) the lack of agreement on names, labels and definitions, (2) operationalizing the loaded concept of affect without first delineating more specific affective phenomena of interest, and (3) inconsistencies in the measurement of affect. It is understandable that the study of affect in the ICT context is analogous to the story of the blind men appraising an elephant. Each provides a partial viewpoint and has some validity in its own right, yet few studies, with some exceptions, have considered many viewpoints to provide an overview of the phenomenon. There are great opportunities and need for further research in these areas.

This chapter is an effort to continue the dialogue and discovery of various issues on affect in the ICT context. In the next section, we introduce two conceptualizations of affective concepts from outside the IS field. We then provide a brief review of the state of research on affect in the IS field. Besides showcasing some of the long-time efforts and findings on various affective concepts, we utilize a theoretical framework (Zhang, 2013) that attempts to unify many related affective concepts and their relationships. In the third section, we focus on various affective concepts that represent interactions between users and ICT. This type of affective concept is mostly studied in the IS field but with inconsistent findings. The section again utilizes Zhang's framework and shows propositions that outline the causal relationships among affective concepts. In the fourth section, we introduce research efforts and findings on using ICT to detect affective signals from users during their interaction with ICT. This addresses limitations of using largely self-report surveys and provides alternative ways of understanding users' affective responses. With the measurement tools and methods becoming more mature and affordable, our research efforts and findings can be greatly enhanced and validated. At the end of the chapter, we point out several possible future research directions and call for more research efforts in this area.

Affective concepts

"Affect" is an umbrella term for a number of concepts that are considered "hot," including attitude, mood, emotion, feelings, and temperament, among others (Bagozzi, Gopinath, & Nyer, 1999; Russell, 2003). There are several ways of conceptualizing affective concepts systematically.

The first, known as the *categorical view*, conceptualizes affect as a set of mutually exclusive, discrete categories (Cowie, 2009; Zachar & Ellis, 2012). Each category represents a distinct affect defined by prototypical members or a set of features (e.g., joy, sadness, or anger). Classification can be based on facial expressions (Ekman, 1984), action tendencies or behavioral responses (Frijda, 1986; Plutchik, 1980), patterns of autonomic nervous system activity (Ekman, Levenson, & Friesen, 1983), brain structures or neurotransmitters (Panksepp, 1982), cognitive appraisals or structures (Ortony, Clore, & Collins, 1988; Scherer, 1984), and emotive language (Kövecses, 2007). For example, Ekman's basic emotion framework (anger, fear, sadness, disgust, surprise, and joy) follows the categorical view (Ekman, 1999).

The second view, *dimensional view*, conceptualizes affect in terms of dimensions. Affect is structured as a "coincidence of values on a number of strategic dimensions" (Bradley & Lang, 1999, p. 1). The dimensional model aims to represent affect in simpler and more general dimensions as opposed to discrete categories. It holds that all affective phenomena share the same fundamental structure, and can be identified from the composition of two or more independent dimensions (Zachar & Ellis, 2012). Russell and Mehrabian (1977) postulated three bipolar dimensions that are necessary and sufficient to adequately detect all affective concepts: valence, arousal, and dominance/submissiveness. Valence refers to the pleasantness or unpleasantness of the affective concept. Arousal refers to the degree of activation, which can range from calm to excited. Dominance/submissiveness refers the extent of control one has on events or surroundings, and can range from feeling a total lack of control to feeling in total control. Russell (1980) subsequently proposed the circumplex model of affect mapping affective terms based on two independent dimensions (valence and arousal). The circumplex model of affect can be used as the base to measure all affective concepts. Every affective concept can be represented by a particular value on both valence and arousal dimensions, as illustrated by Figure 12.1.

In the IS field, there has been an increasing interest in researching affective concepts and their effects pertinent to interacting with ICT. For example, the following is a list of just some of the terms that gained long-term attention from scholars in the ICT disciplines:

- Satisfaction (Au, Ngai, & Cheng, 2008; Briggs, Reinig, & Vreede, 2008; Chin & Newsted, 1995; Doll, Xia, & Torkzadeh, 1994; Hiltz & Johnson, 1990; Ives, Olson, & Baroudi, 1983; Karimi, Somers, & Gupta, 2004; Liang, Lai, & Ku, 2006; McKeen, Guimaraes, & Wetherbe, 1994; Mejias, Shepherd, Vogel, & Lazaneo, 1996; Sethi & King, 1999; Te'eni & Feldman, 2001; Woodroof & Burg, 2003).
- Computer playfulness (Atkinson & Kydd, 1997; Hackbarth, Grover, & Yi, 2003; Martocchio & Webster, 1992; Webster & Martocchio, 1995; Woszczynski, Roth, & Segars, 2002; Yager, Kappelman, Maples, & Prybutok, 1997).

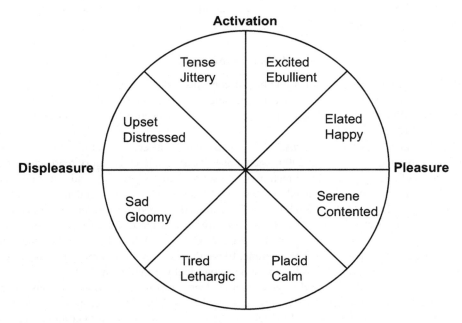

Figure 12.1 The circumplex model
Source: Russell (2003).

- Computer anxiety (Desai, 1995; Hackbarth et al., 2003; Igbaria & Parasuraman, 1989; Karahanna, Ahuja, Srite, & Galvin, 2002; Meier, 1985; Thatcher & Perrewé, 2002; Webster, Heian, & Michelman, 1990).
- Emotion (Beaudry & Pinsonneault, 2010; Brave & Nass, 2009; de Guinea & Markus, 2009; Éthier, Hadaya, Talbot, & Cadieux, 2004; Furneaux & Nevo, 2008; Kim, Lee, & Choi, 2003; Kim & Moon, 1998; Lam & Lim, 2004; Oatley, 2004; Sturdy, 2003; Venkatesh, 2000).
- Affect (Deng & Poole, 2010; George, Lankford, & Wilson, 1992; Hassenzahl, Diefenbach, & Göritz, 2010; Hudlicka, 2003; Sun & Zhang, 2006; Zhang, 2009; Zhang & Li, 2007).
- Flow (Chen, Wigand, & Nilan, 2000; Finneran & Zhang, 2003, 2005; Ghani, 1995; Ghani & Deshpande, 1994; Ghani, Supnick, & Rooney, 1991; Guo & Poole, 2009; Hedman & Sharafi, 2004; Hsu & Lu, 2004; Jiang & Benbasat, 2004; Koufaris, 2002; Nah, Eschenbrenner, & DeWester, 2011; Pace, 2004; Pilke, 2004; Trevino & Webster, 1992; Webster, Trevino, & Ryan, 1993).

A significant portion of IS research focuses on people's reactions toward ICT. Such reactions can be cognitive, affective, and behavioral. Sun and Zhang surveyed the IS literature and identified a number of affective concepts, as well as their relationships with some cognitive concepts (Sun & Zhang, 2006). In their Individual Interaction with Information Technology model (IIIT), as shown in Figure 12.2, they posited that IT-related traits, such as computer playfulness and personal innovativeness of IT, influence both affective reaction toward using IT and cognitive reaction toward using IT, and both types of reactions would influence IS use.

Realizing the confusions on conceptualizations and measurements, as well as inconsistent findings with regard to affective concepts, Zhang (2013) provides a comprehensive framework, the Affective Response Model, to classify various affective concepts and the relationships among them in the ICT context. In this chapter, we describe some of these concepts and related research findings, with the emphasis on providing a background to introducing some common affective responses users experience when they interact with ICT.

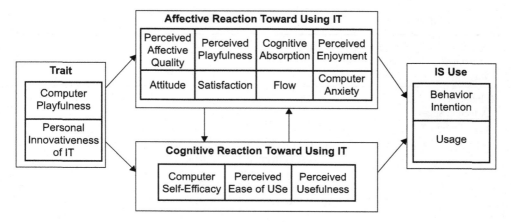

Figure 12.2 A model of individual interaction with IT (IIIT)
Source: Sun & Zhang (2006).

Affective responses toward ICT

Affective responses are of great interest to IS researchers because users' affective responses toward the ICT stimuli can significantly influence their cognitive and behavioral reactions toward ICT. Such broad understanding can offer implications for ICT design, adoption, management, and deployment.

Affective response is a broader term encompassing "both a person's emotion induced by a stimulus and affective evaluations of the stimulus" (Zhang, 2013, p. 254). It is important to note that affective responses reside within the interaction between the human and the ICT stimuli.

For the same ICT-related stimuli, different people may respond differently, and the same person may respond differently to different ICT stimuli. Thus, affective responses are the interplay between people as users and the ICT.

According to the Affective Response Model (Zhang, 2013), several dimensions can be used to further classify affective responses. Table 12.1 depicts the classification. The specific affective response categories are described in general terms. The numbers inside the brackets are the IDs Zhang uses for the concepts. To ensure consistency and convenience for later discussion, we keep these IDs in Table 12.1.

In the IS literature, Zhang found that the same terms or labels, such as attitude or affect, can belong to more than one category, and each category can have several affective concepts being studied. Thus the terms themselves are not sufficient to indicate their meanings and one needs to focus on their semantics in the context of the original study. Keeping this in mind will help interpret the findings and continue building our collective understanding.

Besides clarifying the concepts, Zhang also conceptualized the nomological network on the relationships among affective responses. Figure 12.3 depicts the causal relationships during an ICT interaction episode.

Apart from the discrepancies on conceptualization of the affective terms, the operationalization and measurement have also caused inconsistent findings. In the IS literature, most measures for affective responses use self-reported surveys, which occur after the interaction episode. Either two-dimensional (valence and arousal) or categorical (anger, anxiety, happiness) may be used in surveys where subjects are asked to rate in Likert scales. Besides

Table 12.1 Affective responses

Temporally Constrained (State)	Temporally Unconstrained (Disposition)			
(4) Induced Affective States (e.g., Emotion)		*Particular Stimulus*		*General Stimulus*
		Process-Based	*Outcome-Based*	
	Object Stimulus	(5.1) Process-based affective evaluation toward a particular object	(5.2) Outcome-based affective evaluation toward a particular object	(7) Learned affective evaluation toward a type of objects
	Behavior Stimulus	(6.1) Process-based affective evaluation toward behaviors on a particular object	(6.2) Outcome-based affective evaluation toward behaviors on a particular object	(8) Learned affective evaluation toward behaviors on a type of objects

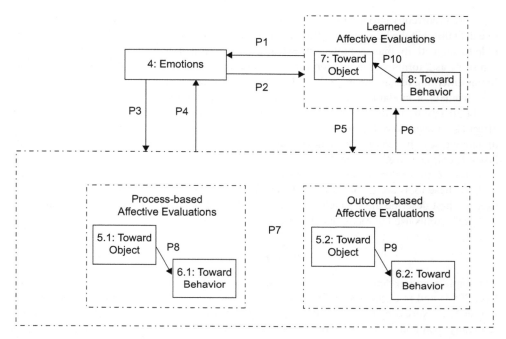

Figure 12.3 Causal relationships among affective responses during an ICT interaction episode

this quantitative approach, affective responses can also be acquired using a more descriptive (qualitative) approach, wherein users are instructed to describe how they feel about the ICT stimuli using affect-related adjectives (Weiss et al., 1999). These recall-based methods can be suitable for certain affective concepts, such as Categories 5 and 6, which are post-episode evaluations, or Categories 7 and 8, which are learned and stored in one's memory. They are not suitable for other affective concepts that are time sensitive, such as affective states (i.e., emotions) – the values of such concepts are gone once the inducing condition is gone. In addition, sometimes, a subject's reported affective response may not be what she or he feels at the moment. This leads to the next section, where ICT can be used to detect human's affective responses in a more objective way.

Affect detection by ICT

An emotion can be communicated in a variety of ways directly through bodily reactions or through linguistic means. For example, the emotion *fear* can be expressed through physiological signals such as increased heart rate and the skin breaking into a sweat. Fear can also be observed through the facial expression that is characterized by widened eyes, eyebrows slanted upwards, and the mouth, which is usually opened. One can also use linguistic expressions such as "scared," "frightened," or "having butterflies in my stomach" to describe the experience of fear.

The advancement of affective computing (Picard, 1998) has breathed new life in the study of affect in the context of ICT through the use of innovative covert channels to capture human emotion. Affect detection or recognition by computers is framed as a pattern classification problem in which computers are trained to recognize patterns that underlie the experience of an emotion from the affective signals.

There is currently strong interest in IS research to capture presumably more objective affective data through the human body and linguistic cues. Such measures of affect are less susceptible to subjectivity bias, complement existing sources of data collected from self-report, and can serve as a form of triangulation across different measures of affect (Dimoka et al., 2010). In this emerging research area in IS, ICT is used as tools to capture affective signals from various channels or modalities, such as written text, spoken words, facial images, body surface, and brain activity (Calvo & D'Mello, 2010). Interests to adopt more reliable tools to measure affect as a means to overcome the weaknesses of self-report measures has led to the genesis of a new research area in 2007, coined Neuro-Information Systems (NeuroIS) (Dimoka et al., 2010; Riedl, Davis, & Hevner, 2014).

In this section, we provide a broad overview of the research in each modality with the focus on how these tools are employed to detect affect toward ICT-related stimuli. In each subsection, we first describe the characteristics of the affective signals from each modality and then review the tools used to recognize the affective signals.

Textual signals

Automatic emotion detection in text falls in the general area of sentiment analysis (Pang & Lee, 2008) and is concerned with the use of computational models to identify segments of written text expressing emotions. Interest in automatic emotion detection in text is fueled by the ready availability of subjective user-generated content on the Web, as well as the need to scale emotion detection in text in a cost-effective manner, because manual annotation is expensive. Such tools are particularly useful in detecting or mining emotions from massive amounts of social media texts (Stieglitz & Dang-Xuan, 2013), blogs (Chau & Xu, 2012), and online reviews (Goes, Lin, & Au Yeung, 2014; Hong, Huang, Burtch, & Li, 2016; Yin, Bond, & Zhang, 2014).

Processing textual signals requires understanding of the language used to express emotions in written text. Emotion expressions in text can occur in two forms: explicit emotion cues and implicit emotion cues (Kövecses, 2007). Explicit emotion cues consist of words (e.g., happy, sad, surprise, hope, pride, love, yuck, wow, haha) or typographical symbols (emoticons such as :-), :), :-(, :(, :O) that denote emotions. Implicit emotion cues are figurative descriptions of emotion, which are expressed implicitly through the use of a broad range of linguistic devices such as metaphors, metonymies, similes, and idioms. In addition, implicit emotion cues can also be embedded within the linguistic structure. For example, emotions may be expressed in the form of actions associated with an actor toward an object (e.g., "I cried because I failed my exam" is an expression of sadness) (Balahur, Hermida, & Montoyo, 2012) or the relationships between different entities (e.g., "the mother scolded her daughter" is an expression of anger) (Kövecses, 1990).

Some IS studies perform lexical analysis based on an emotion lexicon to automatically detect emotions in text. Given a lexicon of emotion terms, lexicon-based emotion detectors use a simple matching algorithm to extract emotion keywords from text based on the list of terms found in the lexicon. One such approach used the Linguistic Inquiry and Word Count (LIWC) (Pennebaker, Francis, & Booth, 2001) to analyze text for positive, negative, or specific emotion categories (Goes et al., 2014; Hong et al., 2016; Yin et al., 2014). Another approach employed SentiStrength (Thelwall, Buckley, & Paltoglou, 2011; Thelwall, Buckley, Paltoglou, Cai, & Kappas, 2010), a slightly more advanced text analysis tool combining an emotion lexicon with additional linguistic rules for negations, intensifiers, and emoticons to generate the sentiment polarity score for each tweet used in political analysis (Stieglitz & Dang-Xuan, 2013).

Many of the tools currently used to detect textual signals assume that emotions are expressed explicitly using a handful of emotion words. Thus, the tools may perform favorably in the detection of explicit emotion cues but may result in poor performance when the meaning of the word is changed by the context in which it is used. Also, the lexicon-based approach only relies on obvious surface cues, and cannot deal with text segments that convey emotions through the use of non-emotional words (i.e., implicit emotion cues). Non-lexicon approaches are just starting to be explored as evidenced by recent studies on the use of machine learning classifiers trained on thousands of user-tagged data to detect, analyze, and visualize emotions on social media text (Zimmerman, Stein, Hardt, Danielsen, & Vatrapu, 2016; Zimmerman, Stein, Hardt, & Vatrapu, 2015).

More sophisticated computational linguistic techniques used to detect emotions in text are reviewed in Liew (2016). On top of identifying the meaning of words, emerging applications such as IBM Watson's Tone Analyzer[1] also detect emotional tones expressed in text. Further exploration is required to examine how these advanced techniques can be adapted into IS research. At the same time, as automatic emotion detection in text is quickly gaining traction in human subject research, the balance of privacy versus data access is going to receive greater scrutiny. Researchers engaging in such research investigations should be aware of ethical issues, such as obtaining participant consent to mine publicly available text for emotion signals or acquiring data from the public domain beyond the terms of use allowed by target websites.

Facial signals

The face acts as an indicator of a person's emotions, which can be measured through the muscle movement of the face. The smallest observable component of facial movement or change in facial appearance (e.g., eyebrow lift or nose wrinkle) is called an Action Unit or AU (Ekman & Friesen, 1978). The Facial Action Coding System (FACS) developed by (Ekman & Friesen, 1975) decoded the human face into a set of identifiable AUs associated with each basic emotion (i.e., anger, sadness, fear, disgust, surprise, and happiness). Examples of a few AUs are shown in Figure 12.4. Note that the AUs concentrate on a few features of the face, such as the eyes and lips, which are usually more expressive than others.

AU	Description	Facial muscle	Example image
1	Inner Brow Raiser	*Frontalis, pars medialis*	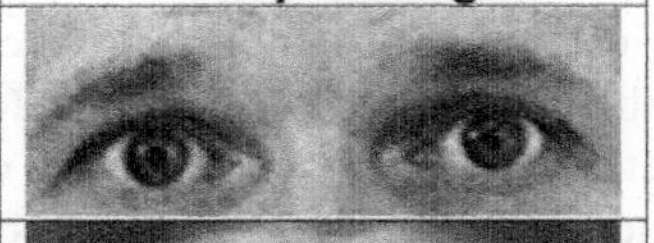
2	Outer Brow Raiser	*Frontalis, pars lateralis*	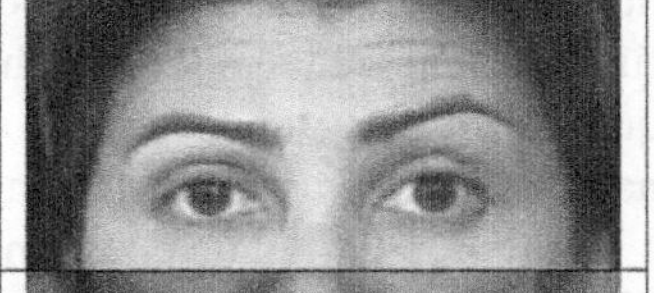
15	Lip Corner Depressor	*Depressor anguli oris*	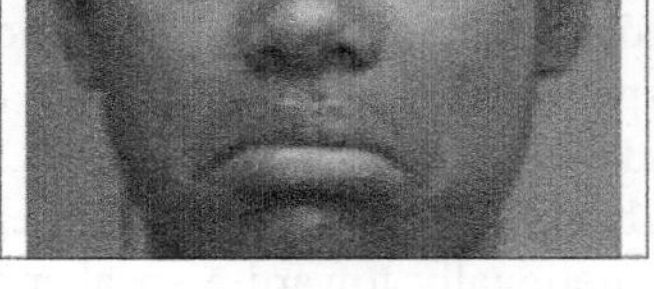

Figure 12.4 Sample AUs from FACS
Source: Ekman & Friesen (1978).

Three methods are commonly used to detect the expression of emotions through facial actions: (1) manual coding, (2) facial electromyography (EMG), and (3) automatic analysis of facial actions through image processing of a single image or a sequence of images of the human face (Cohn & Kanade, 2007). Manual coding is rarely used because the method is time-consuming and resource intensive. Similarly, EMG is less popular due to its intrusiveness, as surface electrodes have to be attached to the skin in order to measure muscle movement on the face. Automatic analysis, which is made possible by the advancement in computer vision, involves a two-step process. First, the facial features on different points on the face are extracted from digitized images. The facial features are then be classified into AUs (Bartlett et al., 1996) or basic emotion categories (Padgett & Cottrell, 1997; Pantic & Rothkrantz, 2000).

Automatic analysis using the FACS framework has been applied successfully in detecting students' affective states in an electronic learning (e-learning) environment (Ray & Chakrabarti, 2012) and identifying drowsy drivers (Vural et al., 2007). Recent advances in affective computing have produced more accurate facial detection applications such as Emotient and Affectiva. These facial detection applications for emotion recognition are also equipped with advanced functionalities that can delineate the contours in the eyes, lips, and nose, as well as detect facial expressions even in poor lighting conditions. These emerging applications are becoming impressively accurate and reliable. For instance, scientists were able to predict which advertisements shown during Super Bowl 2015 were more likely to go viral by tracking viewers' facial expressions of emotions using Emotient (Mone, 2015).

With the prevalence of online communication tools such as video conferencing and online learning, facial emotion analysis can potentially help researchers to capture an individual's emotion expressions on the face in real time and over a longer period of time. These tools not only help reliably measure affective states that are time sensitive but also avoid the need to prompt the user for affective data.

Speech signals

Speech emotion analysis focuses on the analysis of acoustic properties or vocal behaviors as markers of affect (e.g., the sound of sobbing and sniffing is a marker for sadness) (Scherer, 2003). It is assumed that our voice carries emotional information and a set of voice parameters or features can be used to objectively measure the affective state a person is currently experiencing. For example, our voice is intensified when expressing anger and our voice tends to shake when feeling anxiety. Each emotion can be identified by a distinct set of voice parameters. Only non-verbal aspects of the speech are taken into account (how something is said), not the semantic information contained within words. Voice cues revealing emotions include fundamental frequency or pitch, vocal perturbation or variability in sound production, voice quality, intensity, and temporal aspects of speech (e.g., speech rate), as well as various combinations of these aspects (Anagnostopoulos & Skourlas, 2014; Scherer, 2003).

Tools for automatic emotion detection from speech signals commonly employ algorithms for phonetic (articulation sound) and acoustic (speech wave) analysis. EmoVoice, an online speech recognition tool, is an example that utilizes both phonetic and acoustic analysis to identify emotions from voice (Vogt, André, & Bee, 2008). EmoVoice, which is freely available, serves as the intelligent emotion detection engine for Greta, a virtual agent that reacts emotionally toward a speaker based on the voice (Rosis, Pelachaud, Poggi, Carofiglio, & Carolis, 2003), and Barthoc, a humanoid robot that expresses joyful and fearful expressions when listening to fairy tales. Another example, Cogito, uses voice analysis algorithms to assist customer service agents to monitor changes in the customer voice (e.g., pitch variations) as a means to gain better awareness of the customer's emotions. Speech emotion recognition has also found its way into health (e.g., depression diagnosis) and security applications (Allen, 2016).

Speech emotion analysis becomes extremely useful in situations where face-to-face interaction is not possible or where real-time detection is required, such as in the case of an online call center. In such cases, voice becomes the only channel that can be used to infer what a customer or caller is feeling. On a similar note, speech emotion analysis opens up the possibility for IS researchers to objectively measure affective states purely from voice data.

Neurosignals and biosignals

Of the different modalities described, detecting neurophysiological signals is one area that has received heated attention among IS scholars, so much so that IS research applying neuroscience theories, methodologies, and tools is called Neuro-Information Systems or NeuroIS (Riedl et al., 2014). Much of the research pertaining to emotions is based on the idea that it is possible to identify the neural and physiological correlates of many emotional processes (Gregor, Lin, Gedeon, Riaz, & Zhu, 2014). According to neuroscience research, emotion is linked to the limbic system, and specific regions of the human brain have specialized functions for emotional processes. For example, fear is found to activate the amygdala while sadness engages the subcallosal cingulate, according to neuroimaging studies with positron emission tomography (PET) and functional magnetic resonance imaging (fMRI) (Phan, Wager, Taylor, & Liberzon, 2002). Also, the growing body of evidence reporting physiological patterns (e.g., heart rate) associated with emotions makes automatic emotion detection from one's physiological state viable.

A wide range of neurophysiological tools are available to detect neural signals from the brain and physiological signals from the body. Generally, neurophysiological tools can be divided into two types:

1 Psychophysiological tools: pupillometry, electrocardiogram (EKG), skin conductance response or electrodermal activity, and eye tracking;
2 Neuro imaging tools: functional magnetic resonance imaging (fMRI), electroencephalography (EEG), and position emission topography (PET).

In IS research, the neurophysiological tools are not adopted as replacement to the traditional self-report measures of emotion. Rather, these tools are often used to complement or supplement existing sources of data. Neurophysiological tools are promising as they can be used to reveal latent or unconscious affect-related processes that cannot be obtained with the more traditional tools. Such tools are particularly valuable to measure affective concepts that are difficult or impossible for people to share willingly or honestly (Dimoka et al., 2010).

Although NeuroIS is still in its infancy, the use of neurophysiological tools in the evaluation of IT artifacts is starting to reveal interesting findings about the neurobiological processes associated with affect in response to the ICT stimuli. Using fMRI, Riedl, Hubert, and Kenning (2010) revealed that activity changes in certain regions of the brain differ between women and men when evaluating the trustworthiness of eBay offers. The EEG data provided by Gregor et al. (2014) affirmed that positive and negative emotions were related to positive and negative emotion-inducing stimuli on websites. In another study, Leger, Riedl, and Brocke (2014) measured emotional responses based on electrodermal activity, and found that both experts and novices display substantial electrodermal activities during their interaction with an enterprise resource planning (ERP) system for decision making. Thus, it can be inferred that ERP use is an emotionally charged activity for both groups. Based on heart rate and skin conductivity measurements, Adam, Krämer, and Weinhardt (2012) showed that emotions elicited during online auction participation influences the final price.

Attempts to integrate the neurophysiological tools as built-in functions of an IT artifact is also starting to emerge. For instance, Astor, Adam, Jerčić, Schaaff, and Weinhardt (2013) incorporated a neurophysiological tool in a serious game, which will continuously detect and display the individual's emotional states via biofeedback. On top of that, the game would automatically adapt and adjust the difficulty of the game based on emotional states. The advent of neurophysiological technologies in IS promises new and exciting means for understanding affective constructs associated with the development, adoption, and use of ICT.

Conclusions and future directions

Understanding people's affective reactions toward ICT has great implications to ICT design, use, management, and impact. On the conceptual level, there are still open questions regarding what affective concepts are relevant in IS research, what conceptualization is well suited for IS studies, as well as how these affective concepts related to one another and to other cognitive and behavioral concepts. One important step to maintain consistency and reliability in research findings is to continue our efforts to works toward achieving common definitions and obtaining greater clarity for the different affective concepts relevant to IS. In this chapter, we attempted to dissect the "elephant" that is affect and to clarify the different affective concepts common in IS research. It is important to ensure that ongoing and future research on affect will not be stymied by disagreements in the definitions, names, labels, and measures.

Given how quickly technologies evolve over time, there are also interesting questions regarding if our affective responses have changed dramatically in the presence of faster and more interactive ICTs. In the past when ICTs were considered to be a scarce resource, our emotions were less likely to be negatively affected by ICT features or behaviors. How have our affective systems evolve over time due to increased exposure and interaction with ICTs? Are we more likely to be flustered and annoyed over a one-minute wait for a response from a computer system now that processing power has increased tremendously? Can ICT technologies instill fear in our hearts (e.g., fear of system crashing or fear of data loss)? These questions that require longitudinal observation remain promising territories to explore. Our research on affect in the ICT context can make a significant contribution to strengthening the scientific study of affect.

One natural next step of research and practice is to effectively use ICT to address people's emotion-related issues. For example, a group of scholars investigated the effect of expressive writing intervention on Facebook in helping alleviate depressive symptoms and improving their emotional states (Lee et al., 2016). Another natural step is to integrate ICT detection of emotions into IS research. IS scholars are less interested in developing such technologies or algorithms but more interested in using such technologies as measuring tools to detect emotions in social contexts. The current IS literature shows a relatively spotty application of such ICT tools to measure emotions in the ICT context. This may change dramatically with the tools becoming more affordable and easy to use.

Although ICT detection of emotions in IS research is still in a nascent stage, the need for more objective measures of affect is encouraging researchers and practitioners to venture into using multimodal measurement of affect instead of using only one modality (e.g., only facial signals). Some emotions (e.g., happiness and surprise) can be more accurately recognized through facial signals, while other emotions (e.g., sadness and disgust) are more clearly recognized through speech signals (Virvou, Tsihrintzis, Alepis, Stathopoulou, & Kabassi, 2007). The tools that are currently available afford us the opportunity to obtain a more holistic view of affect in the context of ICT, which is analogous to piecing together the different accounts from the blind men in order to see the elephant as a whole.

Note

1 IBM Watson's Tone Analyzer: https://tone-analyzer-demo.mybluemix.net/

References

Adam, M.T.P., Krämer, J., & Weinhardt, C. (2012). Excitement up! Price down! Measuring emotions in Dutch auctions. *International Journal of Electronic Commerce, 17*(2), 7–40.

Allen, S. (2016). Giving voice to emotion: Voice analysis technology uncovering mental states is playing a growing role in medicine, business, and law enforcement. *IEEE Pulse, 7*(3), 42–46.

Anagnostopoulos, T., & Skourlas, C. (2014). Ensemble majority voting classifier for speech emotion recognition and prediction. *Journal of Systems and Information Technology, 16*(3), 222–232.

Astor, P.J., Adam, M.T., Jerčić, P., Schaaff, K., & Weinhardt, C. (2013). Integrating biosignals into information systems: A NeuroIS tool for improving emotion regulation. *Journal of Management Information Systems, 30*(3), 247–278.

Atkinson, M., & Kydd, C. (1997). Individual characteristics associated with World Wide Web use: An empirical study of playfulness and motivation. *SIGMIS Database, 28*(2), 53–62.

Au, N., Ngai, E.W.T., & Cheng, T.C.E. (2008). Extending the understanding of end user information systems satisfaction formation: An equitable needs fulfillment model approach. *Management Information Systems Quarterly (MISQ), 32*(1), 43–66.

Bagozzi, R.P., Gopinath, M., & Nyer, P.U. (1999). The role of emotions in marketing. *Journal of the Academy of Marketing Science, 27*(2), 184–206.

Balahur, A., Hermida, J.M., & Montoyo, A. (2012). Detecting implicit expressions of emotion in text: A comparative analysis. *Decision Support Systems, 53*(4), 742–753.

Bartlett, M.S., Viola, P.A., Sejnowski, T.J., Golomb, B.A., Larsen, J., Hager, J.C., & Ekman, P. (1996). Classifying facial action. In *Advances in neural information processing systems* (pp. 823–829). Cambridge, MA: MIT Press.

Beaudry, A., & Pinsonneault, A. (2010). The other side of acceptance: Studying the direct and indirect effects of emotions on information technology use. *Management Information Systems Quarterly (MISQ), 34*(4), 689–710.

Bradley, M.M., & Lang, P.J. (1999). *Affective norms for English words (ANEW): Instruction manual and affective ratings*. University of Florida: Center for Research in Psychophysiology.

Brave, S., & Nass, C. (2009). Emotion in human-computer interaction. In *The human-computer interaction handbook: Fundamentals, evolving technologies and emerging applications* (pp. 53–68). Boca Raton, FL: CRC Press.

Brief, A.P. (2001). Organizational behavior and the study of affect: Keep your eyes on the organization. *Organizational Behavior and Human Decision Processes, 86*(1), 131–139.

Briggs, R.O., Reinig, B.A., & Vreede, G.-J. de. (2008). The yield shift theory of satisfaction and its application to the IS/IT domain. *Journal of the Association for Information Systems, 9*(5), 267–293.

Calvo, R.A., & D'Mello, S. (2010). Affect detection: An interdisciplinary review of models, methods, and their applications. *IEEE Transactions on Affective Computing, 1*(1), 18–37.

Chau, M., & Xu, J. (2012). Business intelligence in blogs: Understanding consumer interactions and communities. *Management Information Systems Quarterly (MISQ), 36*(4), 1189–1216.

Chen, H., Wigand, R.T., & Nilan, M. (2000). Exploring Web users' optimal flow experiences. *Information Technology & People, 13*(4), 263–281.

Childers, T.L., Carr, C.L., Peck, J., & Carson, S. (2001). Hedonic and utilitarian motivations for online retail shopping behavior. *Journal of Retailing, 77*(4), 511–535.

Chin, W. W., & Gopal, A. (1995). Adoption intention in GSS: Relative importance of beliefs. *SIGMIS Database*, *26*(2–3), 42–64.

Chin, W. W., & Newsted, P. R. (1995). Research report – The importance of specification in causal modeling: The case of end-user computing satisfaction. *Information Systems Research*, *6*(1), 73–81.

Cohn, J. F., & Kanade, T. (2007). Use of automated facial image analysis for measurement of emotion expression. In *The handbook of emotion elicitation and assessment* (pp. 222–238). New York: Oxford University Press.

Cowie, R. (2009). Perceiving emotion: Towards a realistic understanding of the task. *Philosophical Transactions of the Royal Society of London B: Biological Sciences*, *364*(1535), 3515–3525.

de Guinea, A. O., & Markus, M. L. (2009). Why break the habit of a lifetime? Rethinking the roles of intention, habit, and emotion in continuing information technology use. *Management Information Systems Quarterly (MISQ)*, *33*(3), 433–444.

Deng, L., & Poole, M. S. (2010). Affect in Web interfaces: A study of the impacts of Web page visual complexity and order. *Management Information Systems Quarterly (MISQ)*, *34*(4), 711–730.

Desai, M. S. (1995). Computer anxiety and performance: A model and a recommendation. In *Proceedings of the annual meeting – decision sciences institute* (pp. 777–779). Boston, MA.

Dimoka, A., Banker, R. D., Benbasat, I., Davis, F. D., Dennis, A. R., Gefen, D., Gupta, A., Ischebeck, A., Kenning, P., Pavlou, P. A., Müller-Putz, G., Riedl, R., Brocke, J. V., & Weber, B. (2010). On the use of neurophysiological tools in IS research: Developing a research agenda for NeuroIS. *Management Information Systems Quarterly (MISQ)*, *36*(3), 679–702.

Doll, W. J., Xia, W., & Torkzadeh, G. (1994). A confirmatory factor analysis of the end-user computing satisfaction instrument. *Management Information Systems Quarterly (MISQ)*, *18*(4), 453–461.

Ekman, P. (1984). Expression and the nature of emotion. In *Approaches to emotion* (Vol. 3, pp. 319–343). New York: Psychology Press.

Ekman, P. (1999). Basic emotions. In *Handbook of cognition and emotion* (pp. 45–60). West Sussex: John Wiley & Sons.

Ekman, P., & Friesen, W. V. (1975). *Unmasking the face: A guide to recognizing emotions from facial clues*. Los Altos, CA: Malor Books.

Ekman, P., & Friesen, W. V. (1978). *Manual for the facial action coding system*. Palo Alto, CA: Consulting Psychologists Press.

Ekman, P., Levenson, R. W., & Friesen, W. V. (1983). Autonomic nervous system activity distinguishes among emotions. *Science*, *221*(4616), 1208–1210.

Éthier, J., Hadaya, P., Talbot, J., & Cadieux, J. (2004). Business-to-consumer web site quality and web shoppers' emotions: Exploring a research model. In *Proceedings of the International Conference on Information Systems (ICIS)* (pp. 889–900).

Finneran, C. M., & Zhang, P. (2003). A person-artefact-task (PAT) model of flow antecedents in computer-mediated environments. *International Journal of Human-Computer Studies*, *59*(4), 475–496.

Finneran, C. M., & Zhang, P. (2005). Flow in computer-mediated environments: Promises and challenges. *Communications of the Association for Information Systems*, *15*(1), 4.

Frijda, N. H. (1986). *The emotions*. Cambridge: Cambridge University Press.

Furneaux, B., & Nevo, D. (2008). Beyond cognitions: A call for greater consideration of emotion in information systems decision theories. In *Proceedings of the 41st annual Hawaii International Conference on System Sciences* (pp. 451–451).

George, C. E., Lankford, J. S., & Wilson, S. E. (1992). The effects of computerized versus paper-and-pencil administration on measures of negative affect. *Computers in Human Behavior*, *8*(2–3), 203–209.

Ghani, J. A. (1995). Flow in human computer interactions: Test of a model. In *Human factors in information systems: Emerging theoretical bases* (pp. 291–311). Norwood, NJ: Ablex.

Ghani, J. A., & Deshpande, S. P. (1994). Task characteristics and the experience of optimal flow in human–computer interaction. *Journal of Psychology*, *128*(4), 381–391.

Ghani, J. A., Supnick, R., & Rooney, P. (1991). The experience of flow in computer-mediated and in face-to-face groups. In *Proceedings of the Twelfth International Conference on Information Systems (ICIS)* (Vol. 91, pp. 229–237). New York, NY.

Goes, P. B., Lin, M., & Au Yeung, C.-M. (2014). "Popularity effect" in user-generated content: Evidence from online product reviews. *Information Systems Research*, *25*(2), 222–238.

Gregor, S., Lin, A.C.H., Gedeon, T., Riaz, A., & Zhu, D. (2014). Neuroscience and a nomological network for the understanding and assessment of emotions in information systems research. *Journal of Management Information Systems*, *30*(4), 13–48.

Guo, Y. M., & Poole, M. S. (2009). Antecedents of flow in online shopping: a test of alternative models. *Information Systems Journal, 19*(4), 369–390.

Hackbarth, G., Grover, V., & Yi, M. Y. (2003). Computer playfulness and anxiety: Positive and negative mediators of the system experience effect on perceived ease of use. *Information & Management, 40*(3), 221–232.

Hassenzahl, M., Diefenbach, S., & Göritz, A. (2010). Needs, affect, and interactive products – Facets of user experience. *Interacting with Computers, 22*(5), 353–362.

Hedman, L., & Sharafi, P. (2004). Early use of Internet-based educational resources: Effects on students' engagement modes and flow experience. *Behaviour & Information Technology, 23*(2), 137–146.

Hiltz, S. R., & Johnson, K. (1990). User satisfaction with computer-mediated communication systems. *Management Science, 36*(6), 739–764.

Hong, Y., Huang, N., Burtch, G., & Li, C. (2016). Culture, conformity and emotional suppression in online reviews. *Journal of the Association for Information Systems*.

Hsu, C.-L., & Lu, H.-P. (2004). Why do people play on-line games? An extended TAM with social influences and flow experience. *Information & Management, 41*(7), 853–868.

Hudlicka, E. (2003). To feel or not to feel: The role of affect in human-computer interaction. *International Journal of Human-Computer Studies, 59*(1–2), 1–32.

Igbaria, M., & Parasuraman, S. (1989). A path analytic study of individual characteristics, computer anxiety and attitudes toward microcomputers. *Journal of Management, 15*(3), 373–388.

Isen, A. M., Daubman, K. A., & Nowicki, G. P. (1987). Positive affect facilitates creative problem solving. *Journal of Personality and Social Psychology, 52*(6), 1122–1131.

Ives, B., Olson, M. H., & Baroudi, J. J. (1983). The measurement of user information satisfaction. *Communications of the ACM, 26*(10), 785–793.

Jiang, Z., & Benbasat, I. (2004). Virtual product experience: Effects of visual and functional control of products on perceived diagnosticity and flow in electronic shopping. *Journal of Management Information Systems, 21*(3), 111–147.

Karahanna, E., Ahuja, M., Srite, M., & Galvin, J. (2002). Individual differences and relative advantage: The case of GSS. *Decision Support Systems, 32*(4), 327–341.

Karimi, J., Somers, T. M., & Gupta, Y. P. (2004). Impact of environmental uncertainty and task characteristics on user satisfaction with data. *Information Systems Research, 15*(2), 175–193.

Kelly, J. R., & Barsade, S. G. (2001). Mood and emotions in small groups and work teams. *Organizational Behavior and Human Decision Processes, 86*(1), 99–130.

Kim, J., Lee, J., & Choi, D. (2003). Designing emotionally evocative homepages: An empirical study of the quantitative relations between design factors and emotional dimensions. *International Journal of Human-Computer Studies, 59*(6), 899–940.

Kim, J., & Moon, J. Y. (1998). Designing towards emotional usability in customer interfaces – trustworthiness of cyber-banking system interfaces. *Interacting With Computers, 10*(1), 1–29.

Koufaris, M. (2002). Applying the technology acceptance model and flow theory to online consumer behavior. *Information Systems Research, 13*(2), 205–223.

Kövecses, Z. (1990). *Emotion concepts*. New York: Springer-Verlag.

Kövecses, Z. (2007). *Metaphor and emotion: Language, culture, and body in human feeling*. New York: Cambridge University Press.

Lam, R., & Lim, K. (2004). Emotions in online shopping: Fulfilling customer's needs through providing emotional features and customizing website features. In *Proceedings of the International Conference on Information Systems (ICIS)*, p. 71.

Lee, S. W., Kim, I., Yoo, J., Park, S., Jeong, B., & Cha, M. (2016). Insights from an expressive writing intervention on Facebook to help alleviate depressive symptoms. *Computers in Human Behavior, 62*, 613–619.

Leger, P.-M., Riedl, R., & Brocke, J. vom. (2014). Emotions and ERP information sourcing: The moderating role of expertise. *Industrial Management & Data Systems, 114*(3), 456–471.

Liang, T.-P., Lai, H.-J., & Ku, Y.-C. (2006). Personalized content recommendation and user satisfaction: Theoretical synthesis and empirical findings. *Journal of Management Information Systems, 23*(3), 45–70.

Liew, J.S.Y. (2016). *Fine-grained emotion detection in microblog text*. Syracuse, NY: Syracuse University Press.

Loiacono, E., & Djamasbi, S. (2010). Moods and their relevance to systems usage models within organizations: An extended framework. *AIS Transactions on Human-Computer Interaction, 2*(2), 55–72.

Martocchio, J. J., & Webster, J. (1992). Effects of feedback and cognitive playfulness on performance in microcomputer software training. *Personnel Psychology, 45*(3), 553–578.

McKeen, J. D., Guimaraes, T., & Wetherbe, J. C. (1994). The relationship between user participation and user satisfaction: An investigation of four contingency factors. *Management Information Systems Quarterly (MISQ), 18*(4), 427–451.

Meier, S. T. (1985). Computer aversion. *Computers in Human Behavior, 1*(2), 171–179.

Mejias, R. J., Shepherd, M. M., Vogel, D. R., & Lazaneo, L. (1996). Consensus and perceived satisfaction levels: A cross-cultural comparison of GSS and non-GSS outcomes within and between the United States and Mexico. *Journal of Management Information Systems, 13*(3), 137–161.

Mittal, V., & Ross, W. T. (1998). The impact of positive and negative affect and issue framing on issue interpretation and risk taking. *Organizational Behavior and Human Decision Processes, 76*(3), 298–324.

Mone, G. (2015). Sensing emotions. *Communications of the ACM, 58*(9), 15–16.

Nah, F. F.-H., Eschenbrenner, B., & DeWester, D. (2011). Enhancing brand equity through flow and telepresence: A comparison of 2D and 3D Virtual Worlds. *Management Information Systems Quarterly (MISQ), 35*(3), 731-747.

Norman, D. A. (2002). Emotion and design: Attractive things work better. *Interactions Magazine, 9*(4), 36–42.

Oatley, K. (2004). The bug in the salad: The uses of emotions in computer interfaces. *Interacting With Computers, 16*(4), 693–696.

Ortony, A., Clore, G. L., & Collins, A. (1988). *The cognitive structure of emotions.* Cambridge: Cambridge University Press.

Pace, S. (2004). A grounded theory of the flow experiences of Web users. *International Journal of Human-Computer Studies, 60*(3), 327–363.

Padgett, C., & Cottrell, G. W. (1997). Representing face images for emotion classification. In M. I. Jordan & T. Petsche (Eds.), *Advances in neural information processing systems 9* (pp. 894–900). Cambridge, MA: MIT Press.

Pang, B., & Lee, L. (2008). Opinion mining and sentiment analysis. *Foundations and Trends in Information Retrieval, 2*(1–2), 1–135.

Panksepp, J. (1982). Toward a general psychobiological theory of emotions. *Behavioral and Brain Sciences, 5*(3), 407–422.

Pantic, M., & Rothkrantz, L.J.M. (2000). Automatic analysis of facial expressions: The state of the art. *IEEE Transactions on Pattern Analysis and Machine Intelligence, 22*(12), 1424–1445.

Pennebaker, J. W., Francis, M. E., & Booth, R. J. (2001). *Linguistic inquiry and word count: LIWC 2001.* Mahwah, NJ: Lawrence Erlbaum Associates.

Phan, K. L., Wager, T., Taylor, S. F., & Liberzon, I. (2002). Functional neuroanatomy of emotion: A meta-analysis of emotion activation studies in PET and fMRI. *NeuroImage, 16*(2), 331–348.

Picard, R. W. (1998). *Affective computing.* Cambridge, MA: MIT Press.

Pilke, E. M. (2004). Flow experiences in information technology use. *International Journal of Human-Computer Studies, 61*(3), 347–357.

Plutchik, R. (1980). A general psychoevolutionary theory of emotion. *Emotion: Theory, Research, and Experience, 1*(3), 3–33.

Ray, A., & Chakrabarti, A. (2012). Design and implementation of affective e-learning strategy based on facial emotion recognition. In S. C. Satapathy, P. S. Avadhani, & A. Abraham (Eds.), *Proceedings of the International Conference on Information Systems Design and Intelligent Applications 2012 (INDIA 2012)* (pp. 613–622). Visakhapatnam, India.

Riedl, R., Davis, F. D., & Hevner, A. R. (2014). Towards a NeuroIS research methodology: Intensifying the discussion on methods, tools, and measurement. *Journal of the Association for Information Systems, 15*(10), i–xxxv.

Riedl, R., Hubert, M., & Kenning, P. (2010). Are there neural gender differences in online trust? An fMRI study on the perceived trustworthiness of eBay offers. *Management Information Systems Quarterly (MISQ), 34*(2), 397–428.

Rosis, F. de, Pelachaud, C., Poggi, I., Carofiglio, V., & Carolis, B. D. (2003). From Greta's mind to her face: Modelling the dynamics of affective states in a conversational embodied agent. *International Journal of Human-Computer Studies, 59*(1–2), 81–118.

Russell, J. A. (1980). A circumplex model of affect. *Journal of Personality and Social Psychology, 39*(6), 1161–1178.

Russell, J. A. (2003). Core affect and the psychological construction of emotion. *Psychological Review, 110*(1), 145–172.

Russell, J. A., & Mehrabian, A. (1977). Evidence for a three-factor theory of emotions. *Journal of Research in Personality, 11*(3), 273–294.

Scherer, K. R. (1984). On the nature and function of emotion: A component process approach. In *Approaches to emotion* (pp. 293–317). New York: Psychology Press.

Scherer, K. R. (2003). Vocal communication of emotion: A review of research paradigms. *Journal of Speech Communication – Special Issue on Speech and Emotion, 40*(1–2), 227–256.

Sethi, V., & King, R. C. (1999). Nonlinear and noncompensatory models in user information satisfaction measurement. *Information Systems Research, 10*(1), 87–96.

Slovic, P., Finucane, M., Peters, E., & MacGregor, D. G. (2002). Rational actors or rational fools: Implications of the affect heuristic for behavioral economics. *Journal of Socio-Economics, 31*(4), 329–342.

Stieglitz, S., & Dang-Xuan, L. (2013). Emotions and information diffusion in social media – Sentiment of microblogs and sharing behavior. *Journal of Management Information Systems, 29*(4), 217–248.

Sturdy, A. (2003). Knowing the unknowable? A discussion of methodological and theoretical issues in emotion research and organizational studies. *Organization, 10*(1), 81–105.

Sun, H., & Zhang, P. (2006). The role of affect in IS research: A critical survey and a research model. In *Human-computer interaction and management information systems: Foundations* (Vol. 5, pp. 295–329). Armonk, NY: M. E. Sharpe.

Te'eni, D., & Feldman, R. (2001). Performance and satisfaction in adaptive websites: An experiment on searches within a task-adapted website. *Journal of the Association for Information Systems, 2*(1), 1–30.

Thatcher, J. B., & Perrewé, P. L. (2002). An empirical examination of individual traits as antecedents to computer anxiety and computer self-efficacy. *Management Information Systems Quarterly (MISQ), 26*(4), 381–396.

Thelwall, M., Buckley, K., & Paltoglou, G. (2011). Sentiment in Twitter events. *Journal of the American Society for Information Science and Technology, 62*(2), 406–418.

Thelwall, M., Buckley, K., Paltoglou, G., Cai, D., & Kappas, A. (2010). Sentiment strength detection in short informal text. *Journal of the American Society for Information Science and Technology, 61*(12), 2544–2558.

Trevino, L. K., & Webster, J. (1992). Flow in computer-mediated communication electronic mail and voice mail evaluation and impacts. *Communication Research, 19*(5), 539–573.

Venkatesh, V. (2000). Determinants of perceived ease of use: Integrating control, intrinsic motivation, and emotion into the technology acceptance model. *Information Systems Research, 11*(4), 342–365.

Virvou, M., Tsihrintzis, G. A., Alepis, E., Stathopoulou, I.-O., & Kabassi, K. (2007). Combining empirical studies of audio-lingual and visual-facial modalities for emotion recognition. In B. Apolloni, R. J. Howlett, & L. Jain (Eds.), *Knowledge-based intelligent information and engineering systems* (pp. 1130–1137). Berlin: Springer.

Vogt, T., André, E., & Bee, N. (2008). EmoVoice – A framework for online recognition of emotions from voice. In E. André, L. Dybkjaer, W. Minker, H. Neumann, R. Pieraccini, & M. Weber (Eds.), *Perception in multimodal dialogue systems* (pp. 188–199). Berlin: Springer.

Vural, E., Cetin, M., Ercil, A., Littlewort, G., Bartlett, M., & Movellan, J. (2007). Drowsy driver detection through facial movement analysis. In M. Lew, N. Sebe, T. S. Huang, & E. M. Bakker (Eds.), *Human-computer interaction* (pp. 6–18). Berlin: Springer.

Webster, J., Heian, J. B., & Michelman, J. E. (1990). Computer training and computer anxiety in the educational process: An experimental analysis. In *Proceedings of the International Conference on Information Systems (ICIS)* (pp. 171–182).

Webster, J., & Martocchio, J. J. (1995). The differential effects of software training previews on training outcomes. *Journal of Management, 21*(4), 757–787.

Webster, J., Trevino, L. K., & Ryan, L. (1993). The dimensionality and correlates of flow in human-computer interactions. *Computers in Human Behavior, 9*(4), 411–426.

Weiss, H. M., Nicholas, J. P., & Daus, C. S. (1999). An examination of the joint effects of affective experiences and job beliefs on job satisfaction and variations in affective experiences over time. *Organizational Behavior and Human Decision Processes, 78*(1), 1–24.

Woodroof, J., & Burg, W. (2003). Satisfaction/dissatisfaction: Are users predisposed? *Information & Management, 40*(4), 317–324.

Woszczynski, A. B., Roth, P. L., & Segars, A. H. (2002). Exploring the theoretical foundations of playfulness in computer interactions. *Computers in Human Behavior, 18*(4), 369–388.

Yager, S. E., Kappelman, L. A., Maples, G. A., & Prybutok, V. R. (1997). Microcomputer playfulness: Stable or dynamic trait? *SIGMIS Database, 28*(2), 43–52.

Yin, D., Bond, S., & Zhang, H. (2014). Anxious or angry? Effects of discrete emotions on the perceived helpfulness of online reviews. *Management Information Systems Quarterly (MISQ), 38*(2), 539–560.

Zachar, P., & Ellis, R. D. (2012). *Categorical versus dimensional models of affect: A seminar on the theories of Panksepp and Russell* (Vol. 7). Amsterdam: John Benjamins.

Zhang, P. (2009). Theorizing the relationship between affect and aesthetics in the ICT design and use context. In *Proceedings of the International Conference on Information Resources Management*. Dubai, United Arab Emirates.

Zhang, P. (2013). The affective response model: A theoretical framework of affective concepts and their relationships in the ICT context. *Management Information Systems Quarterly (MISQ), 37*(1), 247–274.

Zhang, P., & Li, N. (2005). The importance of affective quality. *Communications of the ACM, 48*(9), 105–108.

Zhang, P., & Li, N. (2007). Positive affect and negative affect in IT adoption: A longitudinal study. In *Proceedings of Pre-ICIS HCI workshop*. Montreal, Canada.

Zimmerman, C., Stein, M.-K., Hardt, D., Danielsen, C., & Vatrapu, R. (2016). emotionVis: Designing an emotion text inference tool for visual analytics. In *Tackling society's grand challenges with design science* (pp. 238–244). Switzerland: Springer International.

Zimmerman, C., Stein, M.-K., Hardt, D., & Vatrapu, R. (2015). Emergence of things felt: Harnessing the semantic space of Facebook feeling tags. In *Proceedings of the 36th International Conference on Information Systems (ICIS)* (pp. 1–20).

13
RESEARCH ON USER RESISTANCE TO INFORMATION TECHNOLOGY

Liette Lapointe and Suzanne Rivard

Introduction

Information technology (IT) innovations have challenged how people thought about behavior at work since the second half of the 20th century. Indeed, through time, efforts to introduce new IT in organizations, from early "electronic data-processing equipment" (Mann and Williams 1960) to recent Enterprise Social Networks (Choudrie and Zamani 2016), have encountered users' resistance.

Early on, researchers have acknowledged resistance toward IT as a critical obstacle that often prevents organizations from reaping the potential benefits of its implementation (Ginzberg et al. 1984). While some have identified resistance as an important barrier to IT implementation, often leading to project failure (Kendall 1997; Ang and Pavri 1994), others have seen it as a means for the users to communicate their discomfort with a system that might be flawed (Keen 1981; Marakas and Hornik 1996).

Along with other researchers, our perspective is that resistance to IT is neither good nor bad (Ferneley and Sobreperez 2006; Markus 1983). Indeed, a recent study suggests that implementers' responses to user resistance play a role in explaining whether resistance is functional or dysfunctional (Rivard and Lapointe 2012). First, resistance that is left unattended – either because implementers are not aware of users resisting, choose not to respond, or feel that they do not have the means to respond – or that is merely acknowledged can spiral into organizational disruption. Similarly, implementers' responses to resistance that aim at rectifying the situation are likely to lead to increased resistance if the rectification is not congruent with the object of resistance – either the system or its significance. Likewise, dissuasive efforts from implementers will have a similar effect if these efforts are not credible. This implies that only when implementers' efforts to rectify the situation are congruent with the object of resistance or when their dissuasive messages are credible in the eyes of the users that resistance will decrease. These results stress the importance of implementers understanding the phenomenon of resistance, in particular of why users resist a new IT. They also stress the importance of researchers' contributions to that understanding by developing explanatory models of resistance.

Therefore, our first objective was to uncover and synthesize the explanations of user resistance to IT offered in the literature. During our literature review we observed that not all extant models of resistance share the same conceptualization of resistance. Some authors theorize on resistance as behaviors (Lapointe and Rivard 2005), others on resistance as intention (Kim and Kankanhalli 2009) or as a negative perception of a new technology (Bhattacherjee and Hikmet 2007). Our second objective was thus to unpack the concept of resistance to IT implementation. To do this, we broadened our literature search and identified several definitions and conceptualizations of resistance. These two different readings of the literature on IT resistance lead us to identify some gaps that also constitute interesting research opportunities.

We then adopted a different perspective to analyze the literature, that of problematization, which implies relaxing one or several well-received assumptions about a phenomenon (Whetten 2002) and even challenging them (Alvesson and Sandberg 2011). We identified two such assumptions – *managers fully embrace the new IT* and *technology is good* – and we suggest that relaxing either assumption might lead to new and insightful explanations of the phenomenon of resistance to IT.

Explaining resistance

Although user resistance has often been portrayed as the culprit of failed implementations, there exist relatively few efforts to explain how and why resistance emerges. Several years ago, we reviewed 25 years of literature, and we identified and presented four such models (Lapointe and Rivard 2005). Extending this review to the contributions published in the AIS Senior Scholars' Basket of Journals[1] from 2005 to 2016, we now add eight new articles that purport to explain resistance.

The models of resistance we reviewed are based on two different assumptions about resistance and acceptance. One set of works assumes that resistance and acceptance are explained by different antecedents (cf. Table 13.1). The second assumes that acceptance and resistance are part of the same decision process regarding an IT being implemented, and thus often incorporate both in their explanation (cf. Table 13.2).

Explaining resistance independently from acceptance

Markus (1983) studies resistance to IT implementation through power relations within groups. She uses a political variant of interaction theory to explain empirical findings drawn from a case study. She suggests that resistance can be explained by an interaction between the information system being implemented and the context of use, which will translate into conflicts. If a group of actors considers that the use of the system is likely to support their position of power, they will be inclined to use it. If they expect that it will reduce their power, they will resist.

Joshi's (1991) explanation of user resistance is based on equity theory. The underlying assumption held here is that there is no fundamental resistance to change, only concern with the fairness of an exchange when users compare their inputs into the exchange to the outcomes they obtain from it. Joshi suggests an equity-implementation model to understand resistance better when a system is implemented. The model supposes that users will assess their equity status on from three strata of analysis. The first stratum is the self, where users focus on themselves and where the net change in equity status can be defined as the resulting change – due to a new system – in their outcomes and inputs. When the net gain is negative, users will be unfavorably inclined toward the system, will resent it and be inclined to resist. The second stratum of analysis is considering the fair sharing of profits between self and the employer. If users feel that their employer has obtained greater relative gains, they will consider the system-induced

Table 13.1 Explaining resistance independently from acceptance

Article	Object	Initial conditions	Perceived threat	Explanation	Conceptualization of resistance	Subject
Markus 1983	Patterns of interaction prescribed by the system	Patterns existing in the political setting where the IS is introduced	Power loss for a group, power gain for another	Mismatches [may] create resistance-generating conditions	Behavior	Group
Joshi 1991	Inputs and outcomes prescribed by the IS (self, group of reference, employer)	Existing inputs and outcomes (self, group of reference, employer)	Distress of inequity or loss of equity	Mismatches [may] create a perceived threat	Behavior	Individual
Marakas and Hornik 1996	New routines and modes of work brought about by a new IT	Established routines and modes of work Individual's rigidity and resentment	Stress and fear	Interaction between difference in demands of the IT and established modes of work, with rigidity and resentment	Passive behavior	Individual
Lapointe and Rivard 2005	• System features • System significance • System's advocates	Work conditions, status, power structure	Modifications of conditions that threaten well-being	Expected impact of the object on initial conditions	Behavior	Individual and group
Klaus and Blanton 2010	System	Promises regarding individual, system, organization, process	Breach of contract	Equity comparison and breach of contract interpretation	Behavior	Individual
Selander and Henfridsson 2012	• System features • System's advocates	Control panacea, implementation incompetency, work premises, defeatism	None for cynicism Modifications of conditions that threaten well-being	Seeing through implementers' espoused claims	Cynicism as a form of passive resistance Behavior – active forms of resistance	Individual

Source: Adapted from Lapointe and Rivard (2005).

Table 13.2 Studying resistance and acceptance jointly

Article	Object	Antecedents	Construct(s) being explained	Subject
Martinko et al. 1996	Characteristics of the IT	Individual differences Efficacy expectations Outcome expectations	User reactions to IT implementation (acceptance, reactance, and resistance)	Individual
Bhattacherjee and Hikmet 2007	Change in work practices introduced by a new information system	Perceived threat: fear of losing control over work practices	Resistance to change as an antecedent of perceived usefulness, perceived ease of use and intention to use	Individual
Kim and Kankanhalli 2009	Change associated with a new IS implementation	Increase: Switching costs Decrease: Perceived value Organizational support for change	User resistance	Individual
Stein et al. 2015	IT stimulus event Affective characteristics (cues) of the IT stimulus event	Emotions (induced affective states) Affective evaluations	User affective responses (including acceptance, resistance and ambivalence)	Invididual
Laumer et al. 2016a	Characteristics of the IS	User perceptual resistance to change Perceived usefulness Perceived ease of use Dispositional resistance to change	User behavioral resistance to change	Individual
Laumer et al. 2016b	Characteristics of the new work routines associated with a new IS	Technology perception (perceived ease of use; perceived usefulness) Work routine perception (perceived ease of use; perceived usefulness)	User behavioral resistance to change	Individual

change unfavorable and will be more likely to resist. Finally, the third stratum pertains to the asymmetry in results between a user and his/her reference group. When users feel that they have benefited less than others from the new system, they will experience inequity, will assess the change as unfavorable, and will tend to resist.

Addressing resistance from a psychoanalytic and psychological perspective, Marakas and Hornik (1996) challenge the view that resistance is dysfunctional. They consider that resistance may be the result of sincere doubts about the relevance of a particular IT introduction. In adapting a model of passive resistance misuse to IT implementation, the authors explain behavior as the consequences of passive-aggressive responses to the threats or stresses that a given individual will, rightly or wrongly, associate with a new information system. The model suggests that, within an IS implementation, passive resistance misuse will manifest itself through resistance behavior that will translate in different actions and reactions.

Lapointe and Rivard (2005) propose a process model of user resistance to IT implementation. Their model consists of five key constructs: the object of resistance, the subject of resistance, initial conditions, perceived threats, and resistance behaviors. The model, developed from the analysis of three cases of clinical information systems implementation, suggests that resistance behaviors occur when users perceive threats due to the interaction between an object of resistance – a system, system significance, or system's advocates – and a set of initial conditions. When a system is first implemented, it is likely to modify the initial conditions of the user environment. The interaction between the system and those conditions may create a situation wherein a user feels threatened. In such a case, resistance behaviors, which may vary from apathy to refusal to use the system, strikes, and even sabotage, will ensue. Over the course of an implementation, the subject of resistance may vary, from the system to its significance, to the system's advocates themselves. The model further suggests that group-level resistance emerges from the individual level, over the course of an IT implementation project. At the beginning of a project, individual-level resistance behaviors are rather independent. During the project, however, if group-level initial conditions are affected, individual level behaviors will converge and become increasingly similar.

Klaus and Blanton (2010) anchor their explanation of the development of user resistance in the psychological contract literature, which they enrich with a focus group and interviews conducted with informants from three organizations that implemented an enterprise system. Although the authors recognize that an attitude that opposes implementation plans may develop before, during, and after system implementation, their explanation focuses on behavioral resistance as it occurs during implementation. They define behavioral resistance as "the behavioral expression of a user's opposition to a system implementation during the implementation" (p. 627). The authors adopt the view of a psychological contract as "beliefs that individuals hold regarding promises made, accepted, and relied on between themselves and another" (Rousseau 1995, p. 9, as cited by Klaus and Blanton 2010, p. 626). The authors' thesis is that user resistance occurs when users develop a perception of a violation of the psychological contract that links them to their organization. They borrow from Morrison and Robinson's (1997) concept and explanation of violation – a major psychological contract breach – that occurs when employees perceive that the promises that have been made to them are unmet. Klaus and Blanton suggest that an enterprise system user experiencing a violation "would likely have strong negative perceptions towards the ES [enterprise system] and the change" (p. 627). The authors refined their explanation with a qualitative study. The resulting model suggests that in the context of an enterprise system there are four domains of perceived unmet promise: individual issues, system issues, organizational issues, process issues. According to the model, users will conduct equity comparisons on the unmet promises. This equity comparison will play the role of a moderator of the relationship between unmet promises and perceived breach of contract. Users then interpret the breach of contract to determine whether it is significant enough to be considered a violation. The result of the interpretation may be that the severity of the breach justifies resistant behaviors; it may also be that it does not justify such behaviors. Klaus and Benton thus conceptualize breach of contract interpretation as moderating the relationship between perceived breach of contract and resistant behavior.

Focusing on cynicism, which they conceptualize as a passive form of resistance, and building on Lapointe and Rivard's (2005) process model of resistance, Selander and Henfridsson (2012) address the question of "what is the process by which cynicism emerges and is constituted as part of resistance in IT implementation?" (p. 290). The authors refer to cynicism as "cognitively distanced resistance that constitutes negative affect towards the IT implementation and manifests a perception of seeing through espoused goals of the implementers" (p. 293). The authors analyze data from a case study of a customer relationship management (CRM) system implementation and confirm the explanation offered by Lapointe and Rivard's model. Also, their theoretical explanation suggests that the notion of cynicism adds to this earlier model in that it allows for capturing antecedents of resistance other than perceived threats. Indeed, they posit that that cynicism does not result from perceived threats as do active forms of resistance, but that instead, it emerges from seeing through espoused claims of the implementers and experiencing negative affect toward these claims. They also suggest that cynicism and active forms of resistance may co-occur and that the degree of cynicism is not constant but may vary during an implementation.

Studying resistance and acceptance jointly

The second stream of explanations considers resistance as one aspect of users' decisions regarding an information technology (Laumer and Eckhardt 2012). As such, they propose models that integrate explanations of IT resistance with antecedents of IT acceptance – mostly perceived ease of use and perceived usefulness (Davis et al. 1989). We identified five such models in the literature we surveyed.

Martinko et al. (1996) offer a theoretical explanation of resistance to IT implementation at the individual level as part of an attributional model of reactions to IT. The authors' thesis is that the intensity and the nature of user reactions depend on the interaction of some factors: external and internal influences as well as the individual's prior experience with the technology. The model posits that a new technology, along with external influences (e.g., co-worker behavior and management support) and internal influences (e.g., prior experience and attributional style), combined with an individual's prior success and failure at tasks involving similar technologies evokes causal attributions. In turn, these attributions influence the individual's expectations regarding the outcomes in terms of efficacy and outcomes of future performance, which then drive his/her reactions toward the system, be they behavioral (i.e., acceptance, resistance, and reactance) or affective (e.g., satisfaction, hostility, fear, or self-esteem). The reactions result in actual outcomes, the nature of which will in turn influence the nature of future attributions.

Bhattacherjee and Hikmet's (2007) model is one of IT acceptance, more precisely of intention to use IT. Because the model incorporates user resistance to change as a hinderer to IT acceptance and that it proposes one hypothesis regarding an antecedent of user resistance, we included it in our survey. The authors explain their choice of combining resistance and acceptance within the same model with the assumption that "user resistance is clearly a barrier to IT usage in organizations" (p. 726). Based on this assumption they propose a model aimed at explaining intention to use with three antecedents. The first two antecedents are the well-accepted perceived usefulness and perceived ease of use from the Technology Acceptance Model (TAM) (Davis et al. 1989), which are hypothesized to influence intention to use an IT positively. The authors operationalized resistance to change as the extent to which users did not want the system being implemented to change how they worked. In the context of the study – health information systems to be used by physicians – this referred to the extent to which physicians did not want the system to change the way they ordered clinical tests, made clinical decisions, interacted with others on their job, and the overall nature of their job (p. 731). Along with the user resistance to IT implementation literature, the model posits that resistance is influenced by users perceiving threats from the system being implemented, more precisely a fear of losing control over their work practices. The model was tested with a survey of 131 practicing physicians. The empirical study provided support for the resistance-related hypotheses, that is, perceived threats are positively related to resistance to change, which in turn negatively influences intention to use the system.

Kim and Kankanhalli (2009) propose an explanation of user resistance that aims at filling the gaps in "understanding of the psychological and decision-making mechanisms underlying resistance to [a] new IS" (p. 567). To fill this gap, the authors introduce the concept of status quo bias, which refers to user preference for the current situation as compared to a situation that would involve a new system. The model they propose integrates user acceptance and user resistance literature with status quo bias. Adopting a conceptualization that is similar to that of Bhattacherjee and Hikmet (2007), the authors define user resistance as the "opposition of a user to change associated with a new IS implementation" (p. 568). The authors build their model from the theory of planned behavior (Ajzen 1991), the equity-implementation model (Joshi 1991), and status quo bias theory. The model hypothesizes some antecedents that will have the effect of reducing user resistance. These resistance-reducing antecedents are: perceived value of the new system, switching benefits – the benefits one would get by switching from an existing to a new system – self-efficacy, organizational support for change, and favorable opinion of a colleague. In turn, as per status quo bias theory (Samuelson and Zeckhauser 1988), the model hypothesizes that switching costs – related to "the perceived disutility a user would incur in switching from the status quo to the new IS and consist of three components, transition costs, uncertainty costs, and sunk costs" (p. 572) – will increase user resistance. The model was tested in a survey of 202 employees who were facing the implementation of a new enterprise system. The results support the hypothesis that switching costs increase user resistance and that perceived value and organizational benefits contribute to decreasing it.

Stein et al. (2015) propose a model that explains specific IT use patterns, including ambivalence, acceptance, and resistance. Their analysis of two case studies of two North American universities that implemented a software package to improve administrative functions efficiency and productivity showed the role of emotions in how such IT use patterns emerge. More precisely, the authors analyzed the relationships between affective cues, affective responses, and IT use patterns. They suggest that three of the five cues identified in their study (IT instrumentality, IT symbolism, identity work) tend to play a key role in IT implementations and will affect users' responses, which sheds light on user acceptance and resistance. Their theoretical development extends Beaudry and Pinsonneault (2010) and builds upon Bagayogo et al. (2013). It shows, on the one hand, that users react to uniform emotions with clear adaptation strategies. On the other hand, their study reveals that users appear to react to ambivalent emotions with a mixture of different adaptation behaviors. Faced with ambivalent emotions, users go back and forth between focusing on positive and negative aspects of the situation. Such reactions appear, however, to ultimately lead to active and positive user engagement and positive organizational impacts.

Laumer et al. (2016a) formulate the general explanation that user resistance behavior results from a person's assessment of a new information system and their predisposition to resisting change. The authors introduce the construct of dispositional resistance to change – a personality trait – as the main cause of employees' resistance to IT-induced change. They borrow from the psychology literature and define dispositional resistance to change "an individual's dispositional inclination to resist change" (Oreg 2003, p. 680, as cited in Laumer et al. 2016a, p. 69). The construct is conceptualized as including four dimensions: routine seeking, emotional reaction, short-term focus, and cognitive rigidity. Laumer et al. posit that dispositional resistance to change will not only influence one's resistance behavior but also their appreciation of a system. More precisely, they hypothesize that dispositional resistance to change will have a negative effect on perceived ease of use and perceived usefulness and a positive impact on perceptual resistance to change. Adopting Bhattacherjee and Hikmet's (2007) construct of behavioral resistance to change, the authors further hypothesize that perceived ease of use and perceived usefulness will negatively influence behavioral resistance to change and that perceived resistance to change will have a positive effect on behavioral resistance. The empirical test, conducted with a sample of 106 human resource employees, provides support for the influence of dispositional resistance to change.

Laumer et al. (2016b) propose a model that posits that behavioral resistance to change (adopted from Bhattacherjee and Hikmet 2007) is not only induced by the change required by new technology being implemented but also by the new work processes this new technology is likely to imply. More precisely, the model hypothesizes that perceived ease of use and perceived usefulness of the new information system being implemented and of the new work processes the system entails will negatively influence behavioral resistance to change. The model further suggests that perceptions regarding technology are determinants of work routine perceptions. More precisely, the model hypothesizes that the perceived ease of use of the technology and its perceived usefulness will influence those perceptions regarding the work processes that go along with the technology. The empirical test provides support for the model.

Identifying gaps

The models presented here enrich our understanding of how, when, and why users resist IT implementation. Anchored in different theoretical foundations, such as organizational behavior (e.g., psychological contract; Klaus and Blanton 2010) and psychology (e.g., dispositional resistance to change; Laumer et al. 2016a) or indigenous to the IT domain (e.g., Lapointe and Rivard 2005), the models we reviewed illuminate different antecedents and manifestations of user resistance. Notwithstanding the richness of these contributions, we identified gaps that we consider as opportunities for future research.

In addition to focusing their explanations on resistance itself, independently from acceptance, the models from the first stream of research share the characteristic of being process explanations, that is, explaining the overall pattern that generates a series of events or explaining "how one event leads to and influences subsequent events" (Van de Ven and Poole 2005, p. 1384). Those models are either conceptual elaborations (Joshi 1991; Marakas and Hornik 1996) or based on a small number of case studies (Klaus and Blanton 2010; Lapointe and Rivard 2005; Markus 1983; Selander and Henfridsson 2012). Indeed, there does not exist any large-scale validation of these models. Although process explanations do not readily lend themselves to validation through large-scale surveys, other methods such as simulation can be used for testing this type of model (Van de Ven and Poole 2005).

In contrast, five of the six models that provided explanations of resistance along with acceptance were variance models, four of them including an empirical test. Although they show that there exist relationships between acceptance and resistance, being variance models, they are silent on the dynamics of these interactions. Only Stein et al. pave the way to such an explanation. Future research could explore further these dynamics, for example, through a longitudinal model of users' acceptance and resistance behaviors, their antecedents, and their associated impacts. Indeed, by identifying the dynamics underlying acceptance and resistance to IT, it would be possible to understand how antecedents, manifestations, and outcomes come together over time and to provide a better understanding of the evolving reactions to IT that sometimes evolve from acceptance to resistance or vice versa.

The third gap we observed constitutes an important hindrance to the advancement of knowledge on user resistance, as it pertains to the definition of resistance itself. Indeed, as synthesized in Tables 13.1 and 13.2, although all 12 studies we analyzed use the term user resistance, it often appears to refer to different concepts. A number of models are based on a conceptualization of resistance as behavior (e.g., Markus 1983, Lapointe and Rivard 2005, Laumer et al. 2016a), others conceptualize it more as an intention (Kim and Kankanhalli 2009) or as a negative perception that is an antecedent of acceptance (Bhattacherjee and Hikmet 2007). Such a difference implies that although the models pertain to a common phenomenon, they do not constitute a solid base on which to develop an integrated explanation. Having a clear conceptualization of the construct of interest being a critical issue of research on user resistance, we devote the next section to a new analysis of the literature with the objective of better illuminating it.

Defining and conceptualizing resistance

The previous section clearly highlighted inconsistencies in how resistance is defined and conceptualized in the models that explain the resistance phenomenon in IS research. To further explore this gap, we expanded our literature search to include top conferences papers and a broader set and range of academic journals. From this literature review, we identified several definitions of resistance that were proposed, over time. Then, we focused on the different conceptualizations of resistance that exist in the extant literature on resistance.

Defining resistance

As illustrated in Table 13.3, there is no consensus on how resistance to IT ought to be defined. A first, maybe disturbing, observation is that many authors do not even offer a clear definition of how they apprehend resistance in their research. A second observation is that the few authors who do offer a definition of resistance tend to emphasize different particularities of the phenomenon. A key differentiator in the way resistance is defined appears to relate to its valence. Indeed, many authors portray resistance neutrally, as a *reaction* or a *response* from users while several take a more negative stance, claiming that resistance is a *problem*, an *opposition*, or an *obstruction*. Finally, it must be noted that a few authors refer to 'positive resistance,' referring to a *manifestation of user unease that is functionally useful* or to a *clue to what went wrong*.

Conceptualizing resistance

With regard to conceptualizations of resistance in IS research, our analysis of the literature confirms an observation made by Kim (2010), and reveals that there exist two main

Table 13.3 Definitions of resistance

"Resistance is defined as behavioural reactions expressing reservation in the face of pressure exerted by change supporters seeking to alter the status quo (Waddell and Sohal 1998; Coetsee 1999; Lapointe and Rivard 2005; Meissonier and Houzé 2010)." (p. 436)	Van Offenbeek et al. (2013)
"We define cynicism as cognitively distanced resistance that constitutes negative affect towards the IT implementation and manifests a perception of seeing through the espoused goals of the implementers (cf. Kunda 1992; Dean et al. 1998; Fleming 2005)." (p. 290)	Selander and Henfridsson (2012)
Resistance, defined as "Opposition, challenge or disruption to processes or initiatives," occurs in response to a perceived threat. The list of behaviours included under the heading of user resistance range from passive to active and through to aggressive. (p. 2)	Carroll and Fidock (2011)
"It was behaviourally defined as an adverse reaction (Hirschheim and Newman 1988) or the opposed intention of users to proposed changes resulting from IS implementation or use of system (Kim and Kankanhalli 2009; Markus 1983)." (p. 3)	Kim (2010)
User's resistance is defined as a subjective process psychologically based at the individual level. (p. 541)	Meissonier and Houzé (2010)
The literature has been dominated by negative connotations associated with resistance, often concluding that it is undesirable and detrimental to an implementation's success (Schein 1988; Kossek et al. 1994); that it is a product of employees' opposition to control and domination (Cook et al. 1999) and that it inhibits strategic change (Ansof 1988). However, resistance is emerging as a more complex phenomenon than previously thought and need not always be viewed negatively (Hirschheim and Newman 1988; Lapointe and Rivard 2005). Indeed, resistance may be a manifestation of user unease with a flawed system (Mumford et al. 1978; Keen 1981; Hirschheim and Klein 1994; Marakas and Hornik 1996) or may even be regarded as functionally useful (Markus 1983). (p. 345)	Ferneley and Sobreperez (2006)
Resistance to system use has long been recognized as a problem to successful implementation of information systems (IS). However, most studies have focused on studying system acceptance and construed resistance as being the flip side of it. (p. 1297)	Lauer and Rajagopalan (2002)
Routine workplace resistance refers to less visible [than formal resistance] and more indirect form of opposition that take place within the everyday world of organizations. (p. 388)	Prasad and Prasad (2000)
Resistance is often portrayed by the sponsors of change as a pejorative term conjuring images of unlawful or unwarranted acts. (p. 130)	Newman (1989)
Resistance is not a problem to be solved so that a system can be installed as intended: it is a useful clue to what went wrong and how the situation can be righted. (p. 441)	Markus (1983)
"Sees resistance as a signal from a system in equilibrium that the costs of change are perceived as greater than the likely benefits." (p. 27)	Keen (1981)

conceptualizations of resistance: attitudinal or behavioral. We here distinguish between the conceptualization of resistance as a behavior or as a psychological state. In her seminal piece on resistance, Markus (1983) has depicted resistance as being a *behavior*, which will be enacted to prevent implementation or use. Several authors (e.g., Marakas and Hornik 1996; Lapointe and Rivard 2005; Kim and Kankanhalli 2009; Campbell and Grimshaw 2015; Klaus and Blanton 2010) have adopted a similar conceptualization of resistance in their work. Other authors have proposed an alternative conceptualization of resistance, claiming that rather than being a behavior, resistance is akin to a *psychological state*. In that perspective, some portray resistance as *cognition* claiming that it is "a cognitive force precluding potential behavior" (Bhattacherjee and Hikmet (2007, pp. 727–728). Others conceptualize it as a *psychological reaction* that typically occurs when one assesses negatively IT implementation impacts (e.g., Ang and Pavri 1994; DeSanctis and Courteney 1983; Lorenzi and Riley 2000; Zuboff 1988). Some authors have adopted a conceptualization of resistance as an *attitude* (e.g., Robey 1979, Kim 2010) or as an *affect* (e.g., Stein et al. 2015). In the case where it is conceptualized as an affect, it has for example been construed as a "negative affect towards the IT implementation and manifests a perception of seeing through the espoused goals of the implementers" (Selander and Henfridsson 2011, p. 293).

A finer-grained analysis of conceptualizations of resistance is offered in Lapointe and Beaudry (2014). Table 13.4 synthesizes and enriches their analysis. In addition to the conceptualizations mentioned earlier, they identify a wider array of conceptualizations of resistance and propose a new, all-encompassing conceptualization of resistance, that is, as a *user mindset*, which ultimately translates into behaviors.

As pointed out by Lapointe and Beaudry, resistance has been conceptualized at times in a narrow fashion under the labels *avoidance* implying for "the individual has the opportunity and even the need, but consciously circumvents using the system" (Kane and Labianca 2011, p. 505) or *opposition*, that is, as "opposition of a user to change associated with a new implementation" (Kim and Kankanhalli 2009, p. 688), "an adverse reaction to a proposed change" (Hirschheim and Newman 1988, p. 398), or *organizational disruption* (Keen 1981, p. 27).

In a few instances, such as in Ferneley and Sobreperez (2006), resistance has been conceptualized as a *process*. The authors suggested that resistance is a two-phase process: an initial phase that is cognitive or emotional and a second one consisting of the decision to resist. They argue that resistance typically manifests in user workarounds, which are deviations from set procedures. Last, Lapointe and Rivard (2005) and Rivard and Lapointe (2012) conceptualize resistance as a *multidimensional construct* where resistance to IT implementation can be construed

> as behaviors that occur following perceptions of threats associated with the interaction between an object and initial conditions. During implementation, some triggers can either modify or activate initial conditions; a modification of the object of resistance may ensue. From the interaction of this new object and new set of initial conditions, different resistance behaviors may follow.
> (Lapointe and Beaudry 2014, p. 4621)

Lapointe and Beaudry argue that resistance, akin to acceptance, is a mindset, which they define as

> a complex multidimensional mental state that is based on cognitions, emotions, and attitudes that predispose an individual to perform IT-related behaviors of a certain type. More specifically, we argue that acceptance and resistance to IT comprise an emotional dimension (e.g., fear, anxiety, excitement), a cognitive dimension (e.g., performance expectancy, self-efficacy, perceived ease of use), and an attitudinal dimension (e.g., like/dislike, good/bad). Taken together, these three dimensions will, in turn, be associated to behavioral manifestations, which can be many and

Table 13.4 Conceptualizations of resistance to IT

Conceptualization	Evidence	Representative References
A process	"The concept of resistance is seen as a two-phase process, the first phase being the internal individual/group cognitive or emotional process that results in the decision to resist, the second phase being the resultant workaround behavior." (p. 355)	Ferneley and Sobreperez (2006)
An attitude	"In the present study, user resistance is conceptualized as the individual's attitude towards the change." (p. 3)	Kim (2010)
A cognition	"Resistance is not a behavior but a cognitive force precluding potential behavior." (pp. 727–728)	Bhattacherjee and Hikmet (2007)
A behavior	"Behaviors intended to prevent the implementation or use of a system or to prevent system designers from achieving their objectives." (p. 443)	Markus (1983)
A psychological reaction	"A normal psychological reaction when the perceived consequences (e.g., loss of power) are negative." (p. 130)	Ang and Pavri (1994)
An affect	"Negative affect towards the IT implementation." (p. 293)	Selander and Henfridsson (2012)
A disruption	"A signal from a system in equilibrium that the costs of change are perceived as greater than the likely benefits." (p. 27)	Keen (1981)
An avoidance	"IS avoidance, however, occurs when the individual consciously chooses to avoid IS despite having time, need, and ability." (p. 505)	Kane and Labianca (2011)
An opposition	"As opposition of a user to change associated with a new implementation." (p. 688)	Kim and Kankanhalli (2009)
A multidimensional construct	"The multilevel and dynamic nature of resistance." (p. 467)	Lapointe and Rivard (2005)
A mindset	"In our proposed conceptualization of acceptance and resistance, we define a user's mindset as a complex multidimensional mental state that is based on cognitions, emotions, and attitudes that predisposes an individual to perform IT-related behaviors of a certain type." (p. 4622)	Lapointe and Beaudry (2014)

varied (e.g., user or task adaptation, venting, usage, and even sabotage). This definition implies the existence of frames that shape one's actions through a repertoire of potential reactions and responses. Though a mindset may be shared across a group, there will nevertheless be variation, and these differences will translate into a wide array of possible behavioral reactions within a given group.

(2014, p. 4622)

While Lapointe and Beaudry (2014) propose an umbrella conceptualization of acceptance and resistance, in extant research most authors have conceptualized resistance and acceptance as independent constructs, most construing resistance as being the flip side of acceptance. As explained in the previous section, apart from the few authors (including, for example, Bhattacherjee and Hikmet 2007; Bhattacherjee et al. 2013; Kim 2010; Smith et al. 2014; Laumer et al. 2014) who have conceptualized acceptance and resistance together in combination with perceived ease of use (PEOU) and perceived usefulness (PU), only a handful of authors have studied or conceptualized resistance and acceptance within a unified model or framework.

The first paper to present a unified model is that of Martinko et al. (1996), who proposed an attributional model of reactions to IT. According to this model, when faced with the introduction of a new technology, users develop positive and/or negative expectations regarding the impacts of IT use, which will drive their psychological and behavioral reactions. Lauer and Rajagopalan (2002) have looked at the relationship between acceptance and resistance, taking into account the time dimension. They argue that a system may appear to be accepted early on but may come to be resisted, eventually resulting in failure and, vice versa, that a system may be initially resisted, but that as a result of effective management may become accepted. More recently, Van Offenbeek et al. (2013) proposed a model that integrates acceptance and resistance. The framework they propose conceptualizes acceptance and resistance from a behavioral standpoint and identifies four categories of user reaction. The framework distinguishes between two dimensions; one ranging from high use to non-use, and the other from enthusiastic support to aggressive resistance. Bagayogo et al. (2013) view acceptance and resistance as a psychological reaction that is associated with a complex mix of behaviors. They argue that acceptance does not always imply effective use and resistance does not necessarily imply non-use. Finally, as mentioned earlier, Lapointe and Beaudry (2014) construe acceptance and resistance as mindsets.

In conclusion, our analysis of the literature confirms that there is overall no consensus on the definition or conceptualization of resistance. While this is not a fatal flaw of the current research on resistance per se, as it allows to explore different aspects and dimensions of the phenomenon, it nonetheless raises a red flag to which researchers should be sensitive. Indeed, to ensure the proper advancement of knowledge and the conceptual and methodological relevance of the research that focuses on resistance, it is critical to ensure conceptual clarity of the construct (Barki 2008). In the words of the author, "there are many opportunities for contributing to information systems (IS) research and practice through careful conceptualization and measurement of constructs, thereby providing a better understanding and explanation of interesting and important information technology (IT) phenomena" (Barki 2008, p. 9). We argue that this logic applies to the resistance to IT phenomenon and that the usefulness of well conceptualizing the resistance construct is becoming paramount.

Problematizing the literature

Our review of the literature presented earlier led us to identify gaps that we deem merit researchers' attention. We now take another perspective to reflect upon extant literature, that of problematization, which implies identifying well-accepted explanations of phenomena and relaxing the assumptions on which they are based (Whetten 2002) and even challenging them (Alvesson and Sandberg 2011). To do this, we re-analyzed the literature on resistance to IT implementation to unearth some of its most basic assumptions. Two of these assumptions – *managers fully embrace the new IT* and *technology is good* – are common to most of the works we reviewed. We suggest, however, that they are at times erroneous and that relaxing them could allow for new and interesting explanations of the phenomenon.

Assumption 1 – managers fully embrace the new IT

The literature on user resistance rests on the assumption that managers, when they are responsible for a unit where an IT is implemented, embrace the new system and feel accountable for its successful implementation. This assumption does not exclude the possibility that managers, when they are themselves the target users of a new system, may resist. In such a circumstance they would be studied as "users." However, when they are invested with the responsibility of having users in their unit adopt a system, managers are not expected to manifest resistance. A similar assumption underlies research in the domain of change management in general, where managerial resistance is rarely investigated (Page 2011).

A careful examination of accounts of IT implementation experiences suggests that managerial resistance may indeed be an important obstacle to successful IT implementation. For instance, the project director of a large ERP implementation commented as follows:

> The unit directors may feel threatened by the project [. . .] A common defense mechanism is a resistance, which can manifest in different ways. One of them is lukewarm support. A director may agree in principle with the new system. Yet, their actions may create difficulties for the project. Someone will claim their support and at the same time wish that the project will fail [. . .] Another manifestation of resistance is the reluctance of a director to allocate his/her best resources to the project. Or to make critical decisions so slowly that the delay is interminable from a project point of view. [. . .] Another protection mechanism from unit directors is to attack the project director's credibility.
>
> (Landry and Rivard 2001, p. 57)

A recent study of the development of an information system aimed to support the merger of three previously independent hospitals into a single organization documents resistance manifestations on the part of one of the unit managers who was actually in charge of playing the role of boundary-shaker during the project (Vieru et al. forthcoming). Indeed, the role of boundary shakers is to act as change agents and to contribute to the elimination of boundaries between groups given collaboration (Balogun et al. 2005). Rather than fully embracing this role, one manager – from a pediatric hospital that was part of the merger – used her influence on the other parties involved in the project to resist the integration and reinforce the boundaries between the merging units, thus becoming a boundary consolidator. The actions of this manager are described as follows:

> instead of focusing on commonalities and dependencies between the three sites, the Pediatric manager's efforts and energy were invested in highlighting the differences (e.g. children vs. adult patients, no information exchange between the Pediatric and the Adult sites) as well as the uniqueness of the Pediatric site (e.g. in terms of procedures, clerical tasks, etc.). The Pediatric manager's forerunner attitude as well as her legitimacy, based on her charisma, her experience and her reputation, enabled her to mobilize support around the idea that the Pediatric site on one side and the Adult sites on the other, had different ways of working and required different [information systems].
>
> (Vieru et al. forthcoming, p. 12)

These examples open an avenue for adding to the explanation of IT implementation failures. Indeed, if the very people who are in charge of ensuring user acceptance of a new information system do themselves resist, the contextual boundaries of studies of resistance will have to be expanded. This would imply including managers' attitudes and actions in addition to those of users in studies of user resistance. It would also be important to develop explanations of managers' resistance to IT implementation. Because the existing models of user resistance would not readily provide such explanations, new models might need to be developed, building on what we have learned from user resistance. A promising starting point might be the generic model components identified by Lapointe and Rivard (2005), which were common to several of the user resistance explanations we reviewed. Indeed, using the concepts of the object of resistance, subject of resistance, initial conditions, perceived threats, and resistance manifestations might allow for the development of explanations that would add to our current understanding of the phenomenon.

Assumption 2 – technology is good

The common view on IT is that it brings many benefits to individuals, organizations, and even society. Early on, IT has been depicted as having the potential for improving workers' performance and bringing in organizational benefits (Davis et al. 1989; Zuboff 1988). In extant research, IT usage has long been considered a key indicator of IS success (Delone and McLean 2003), contributing to individual productivity and resulting in significant economic benefits for organizations. With the pervasiveness of IT in all aspects of organizational and even social life, IT is typically seen as a positive innovation, for example, by enabling effective and efficient information sharing and collaboration.

From a research perspective, the IS literature mostly provides a monolithic view of the IT use phenomenon, treating all usage behaviors equally (Bagayogo et al. 2013) where use is considered a desirable behavior. However, as reported in recent studies (Tarafdar et al. 2013), the use of IT – in its various forms – can have a downside and may lead to unexpected or undesired outcomes, especially when it is excessive, compulsive, and uncontrolled. A growing body of research has started to explore some negative aspects and outcomes of IT usage, for example, IT addiction (Turel et al. 2011), misuse (Bulgurcu et al. 2010), work overload (D'Arcy et al. 2009), and interruptions (Gupta et al. 2013). In the words of Tarafdar et al. 2013:

> considering that the ubiquitous and functionally pervasive nature of IT use is expected to expose users to ever greater levels of conditions that are potent for experiencing negative outcomes. Networked enterprises further aggravate the situation [Barjis et al. 2011]. Research occurring in these areas is embryonic and offers significant opportunity for conducting high-impact theoretical and applied studies.
> (p. 270)

Research in different domains, including psychology, psychiatry, and information systems, already indicates that excessive and compulsive IT use may cause serious individual, organizational, and societal problems (LaRose et al. 2003; Block 2008; Vaghefi et al. 2017). In particular, IT addiction is increasing viewed as a serious and alarming matter in most professional settings. In recent years, calls have been made for further research on this phenomenon and for designing strategies to control and regulate excessive IT use, which can help remedy the potential consequences of addiction on the performance and well-being of such users.

While technology addiction might be an obvious drawback of IT use, there are more insidious negative consequences that can be associated with it. Due in large part to the advent of more ubiquitous and more sophisticated technologies that enable near constant contact with the workplace, the issue of work–life balance brings in new, disturbing questions about the role of IT in organizations and society. Recent research shows that in response to changes brought about in large part because of technology usage, individuals tend to feel that they have to be constantly available for their organizations, "fixated on 24/7 connectivity, productivity, and multitasking" (Cook 2015, p. 17). Workplace technostress is increasing among employees and impacts both physical and mental health, costing employers lost productivity, higher absenteeism, higher turnover, lower engagement levels, missed deadlines, and low morale (Ayyagari et al. 2011; Tarafdar et al. 2011). All in all, evidence suggests that IT use may be blurring work–family boundaries with negative consequences for individuals and even organizations (Chesley 2005). Organizations now appear to feel pressured to implement work practices intended to facilitate employees' efforts to fulfill both their organizational and their personal responsibilities (Wang et al. 2008; Ayyagari et al. 2011).

Conclusion

In this chapter, our first objective was to identify and synthesize models of resistance to IT implementation that are proposed in the literature. We found that these models were anchored in different theoretical foundations, thus illuminating different antecedents and manifestations of user resistance and enriching current knowledge of how, when, and why users resist IT implementation. Notwithstanding the richness of these contributions, we identified gaps that we consider as opportunities for future research.

The first gap pertains to the subset of models that offer a process explanation of resistance to IT. Being either conceptual or based on a small number of cases, those models have not been empirically tested. We suggest that although process explanations do not lend themselves to validation through large-scale surveys, other methods, such as simulation, can be used for testing this type of model.

The second gap pertains to the variance models that provided explanations of resistance along with acceptance. Although these models show relationships between acceptance and resistance, they do not explain the dynamics of these relationships. Future research could explore these dynamics, for example, using longitudinal models, thus providing a better understanding of the evolving reactions to IT that sometimes evolve from acceptance to resistance or vice versa.

The third gap is an important limitation to the advancement of knowledge on user resistance, as it pertains to the definition of resistance itself. Although the models pertain to a common phenomenon, they do not constitute a solid conceptual base for the development of an integrated explanation.

Following this observation, our second objective was to analyze the literature, focusing on definitions and conceptualizations of resistance to IT implementation. Our analysis confirms the lack of consensus on the definition or conceptualization of resistance. While this is not a fatal flaw of the current research on resistance per se, it unearths an important research issue. Indeed, to ensure the proper advancement of knowledge and the conceptual and methodological relevance of the research that focuses on resistance, we invite researchers to work toward achieving conceptual clarity of the construct.

Our third objective was to problematize the literature so as to pave the way to the exploration of unchartered territories. To do so, we would suggest two well-received assumptions that researchers may want to relax. The first is that of *managers fully embracing the new IT*. Relaxing this assumption would imply including managers' attitudes and actions in addition to those of users in studies of user resistance. The second assumption is that of *technology is good*, that is, IT brings many benefits to individuals, organizations, and even society. However, research has revealed that IT has a dark side and may lead to unexpected or undesired outcomes, especially when its use is excessive, compulsive, and uncontrolled. More research in this direction is thus warranted.

In brief, although resistance to IT has been investigated for many decades, it remains a contemporary research and management issue. Furthermore, it offers opportunities for researchers to make new insightful and meaningful contributions.

Note

1 https://aisnet.org/?SeniorScholarBasket: European Journal of Information Systems; Information Systems Journal; Information Systems Research; Journal of AIS; Journal of Information Technology; Journal of MIS; Journal of Strategic Information Systems; MIS Quarterly.

References

Ajzen, I., "The Theory of Planned Behavior," *Organizational Behavior and Human Decision Processes*, Vol. 50, 1991, pp. 179–211.
Alvesson, S., Sandberg, J., "Generating Research Questions Through Problematization," *Academy of Management Review*, Vol. 36, No. 2, 2011, pp. 247–271.
Ang, J., and Pavri, F., "A Survey and Critique of the Impacts of Information Technology," *International Journal of Information Management*, Vol. 14, 1994, pp. 122–133.
Ayyagari, R., Grover, V., Purvis, R., "Technostress: Technological Antecedents and Implications," *MIS Quarterly*, Vol. 35, No. 4, 2011, pp. 831–858.
Bagayogo, F., Beaudry, A., Lapointe, L., "Impacts of IT Acceptance and Resistance Behaviors: A Novel Framework," *Proceedings ICIS 2013*, 2013, pp. 1–19.
Balogun, J., Gleadle, P., Hailey, V. H., and Willmott, H., "Managing Change Across Boundaries: Boundary-Shaking Practices," *British Journal of Management*, Vol. 16, No. 4, 2005, pp. 261–278.
Barjis, J., Gupta, A., Sharda, R., "Knowledge Work Challenges in Networked Enterprises," *Information Systems Frontiers*, Vol. 13, No. 5, 2011, pp. 615–619.
Barki, H., "Thar's Gold in Them Thar Constructs," *ACM SIGMIS Database*, Vol. 39, No. 3, 2008, pp. 9–20.
Beaudry, A., Pinsonneault, A., "The Other Side of Acceptance: Studying the Direct and Indirect Effects of Emotions on Information Technology Use," *MIS Quarterly*, Vol. 34, No. 4, 2010, pp. 689–710.
Bhattacherjee, A., Davis, C., Hikmet, N., "Physician Reactions to Healthcare IT: An Activity-Theoretic Analysis," *Proceedings 46th Hawaii International on System Sciences Conference*, 2013, pp. 2545–2554.
Bhattacherjee, A., Hikmet, N., "Physicians' Resistance Toward Healthcare Information Technology: A Theoretical Model and Empirical Test," *European Journal of Information Systems*, Vol. 16, 2007, pp. 725–737.
Block J. J., "Issues for DSM-V: Internet Addiction," *American Journal of Psychiatry*, Vol. 165, No. 3, 2008, pp. 306–307.
Bulgurcu, B., Cavusoglu, H., Benbasat, I., "Information Security Policy Compliance: An Empirical Study of Rationality-Based Beliefs and Information Security Awareness," *MIS Quarterly*, Vol. 34, 2010, pp. 523–548.
Campbell, R. H., Grimshaw, M., "Enochs of the Modern Workplace," *Journal of Systems and Information Technology*, Vol. 17, No. 1, 2015, pp. 35–53.
Carroll, J., Fidock, J., "Beyond Resistance to Technology Appropriation," *Proceedings 44th Hawaii International Conference on System Sciences*, 2011, pp. 1–9.
Chesley, N., "Blurring Boundaries? Linking Technology Use, Spillover, Individual Distress, and Family Satisfaction," *Journal of Marriage and Family*, Vol. 67, No. 5, 2005, pp. 1237–1248.
Choudrie, J., Zamani, E. D., "Understanding Individual User Resistance and Workarounds of Enterprise Social Networks: The Case of Service Ltd," *Journal of Information Technology*, Vol. 30, 2016, pp. 130–151.
Cook, L. N., "Restoring a Rhythm of Sacred Rest in a 24/7 World: An Exploration of Technology Sabbath and Connection to the Earth Community," *International Journal of Religion and Spirituality in Society*, Vol. 5, No. 4, 2015, pp. 17–27.
D'Arcy, J., Hovav, A., Galletta, D., "User Awareness of Security Countermeasures and Its Impact on Information Systems Misuse: A Deterrence Approach," *Information Systems Research*, Vol. 20, No. 1, 2009, pp. 79–98.

Davis, F. D., Bagozzi, R. P., Warshaw, P. R., "User Acceptance of Computer Technology: A Comparison of Two Theoretical Models," *Management Science*, Vol. 35, No. 6, 1989, pp. 982–1003.

Delone, W. H., McLean, E. R., "The DeLone and McLean Model of Information Systems Success: A Ten-Year Update," *Journal of Management Information Systems*, Vol. 19, No. 4, 2003, pp. 9–30.

DeSanctis, G., Courteney, J. F., "Toward Friendly User MIS Implementation," *Communications of the ACM*, Vol. 26, No. 10, 1983, pp. 732–738.

Ferneley, E. H., Sobreperez, P., "Resist, Comply or Workaround? An Examination of Different Facets of User Engagement With Information Systems," *European Journal of Information Systems*, Vol. 14, No. 4, 2006, pp. 345–356.

Ginzberg, M. J., Schultz, R., Lucas, H. C., "A Structural Model of IT Implementation," *Applications in Management Science: Management Science Implementation*, Schultz, R. (Ed.), JAI Press, Greenwich, CT, 1984.

Gupta, A., Li, H., Sharda, R., "Should I Send This Message? Understanding the Impact of Interruptions, Social Hierarchy and Perceived Task Complexity on User Performance and Perceived Workload," *Decision Support System*, Vol. 55, No. 1, 2013, pp. 135–145.

Hirschheim, R., Newman, M., "Information Systems and User Resistance: Theory and Practice," *Computer Journal*, Vol. 31, No. 5, 1988, pp. 398–408.

Joshi, K., "A Model of Users' Perspective on Change: The Case of Information Systems Technology Implementation," *MIS Quarterly*, Vol. 15, No. 2, 1991, pp. 229–240.

Kane, G. C., G. Labianca, "IS Avoidance in Health-Care Groups: A Multilevel Investigation," *Information Systems Research*, Vol. 22, No. 3, 2011, pp. 504–522.

Keen, P. G. W., "Information Systems and Organizational Change," *Communications of the ACM*, Vol. 24, No. 1, 1981, pp. 24–33.

Kendall, K. E., "The Significance of Information Systems Research on Emerging Technologies: Seven Information Technologies That Promise to Improve Managerial Effectiveness," *Decision Sciences*, Vol. 28, No. 4, 1997, pp. 775–792.

Kim, H. W., Kankanhalli, A., "Investigating User Resistance to Information Systems Implementation: A Status Quo Bias Perspective," *MIS Quarterly*, Vol. 33, No. 3, 2009, pp. 567–582.

Kim, H.-Y., "Managing User Resistance to Open Source Migration," *Proceedings ICIS 2010*, St. Louis, 2010.

Klaus, T., Blanton, J. E., "User Resistance Determinants and the Psychological Contract in Enterprise System Implementations," *European Journal of Information Systems*, Vol. 19, 2010, pp. 625–636.

Landry, R., Rivard, S., "Le projet Harmonie," *Gestion*, 2001, pp. 56–64.

Lapointe, L., Beaudry, A., "Identifying IT User Mindsets: Acceptance, Resistance and Ambivalence," *Proceedings of the 47th Hawaii International Conference on System Sciences*, 2014, pp. 4619–4628.

Lapointe, L., Rivard, S., "A Multilevel Model of Resistance to Information Technology Implementation," *MIS Quarterly*, Vol. 29, No. 3, 2005, pp. 461–491.

LaRose, R., Lin, C. A., Eastin, M. S., "Unregulated Internet Usage: Addiction, Habit, or Deficient Self-regulation?" *Media Psychology*, Vol. 5, No. 3, 2003, pp. 225–253.

Lauer, T., Rajagopalan, B., "Examining the Relationship Between Acceptance and Resistance in System Implementation," *Proceedings AMCIS*, 2002, pp. 1297–1303.

Laumer, S., Eckhardt, A., "Why Do People Reject Technologies: A Review of User Resistance Theories," Y. K. Dwivedi et al. (Eds.), *Information Systems Theory: Explaining and Predicting Our Digital Society*, Springer, 2012, pp. 63–86.

Laumer, S., Maier, C., Eckhardt, A., Weitzel, T., "Why Are They Grumbling About My New System? Theoretical Foundation and Empirical Evidence of Employee Grumbling as a User Resistance Behavior," *Proceedings ICIS 2014*.

Laumer, S., Maier, C., Eckhardt, A., Weitzel, T., "User Personality and Resistance to Mandatory Information Systems in Organizations: A Theoretical Model and Empirical Test of Dispositional Resistance to Change," *Journal of Information Technology*, Vol. 31, 2016a, pp. 67–82.

Laumer, S., Maier, C., Eckhardt, A., Weitzel, T., "Work Routines as an Object of Resistance During Information Systems Implementations: Theoretical Foundation and Empirical Evidence," *European Journal of Information Systems*, Vol. 25, 2016b, pp. 317–343.

Lorenzi, N. M., Riley, R. T., "Managing Change," *Journal of the American Medical Informatics Association*, Vol. 7, No. 2, 2000, pp. 116–124.

Mann, F. C., and Williams, L. K., "Observations on the Dynamics of a Change to Electronic Data-Processing Equipment," *Administrative Science Quarterly*, Vol. 5, No. 2, 1960, pp. 27–38.

Marakas, G. M., and Hornik, S., "Passive Resistance Misuse: Overt Support and Covert Recalcitrance in IS Implementation," *European Journal of Information Systems*, Vol. 5, No. 3, 1996, pp. 208–220.

Markus, M. L., "Power, Politics, and MIS Implementation," *Communications of the ACM*, Vol. 26, No. 6, 1983, pp. 430–444.

Martinko, M. J., Henry, J. W., and Zmud, R. W., "An Attributional Explanation of Individual Resistance to the Introduction of Information Technologies in the Workplace," *Behaviour and Information Technology*, Vol. 15, No. 5, 1996, pp. 313–330.

Meissonier, R., Houzé, E., "Toward an 'IT Conflict-Resistance Theory': Action Research During IT Pre-Implementation. *European Journal of Information Systems*," Vol. 19, No. 5, 2010, pp. 540–561.

Morrison, E. W., Robinson, S. L., "When Employees Feel Betrayed: A Model of How Psychological Contract Violation Develops," *Academy of Management Review*, Vol. 22, No. 1, 1997, pp. 226–256.

Newman, M. "Some Fallacies About Information Systems Development," *International Journal of Information Management*, Vol. 9, 1989, pp. 127–143.

Oreg, S., "Resistance to Change: Developing an Individual Differences Measure," *Journal of Applied Psychology*, Vol. 88, No. 4, 2003, pp. 680–693.

Page, D., "From Principled Dissent to Cognitive Escape: Managerial Resistance in the English Further Education Sector," *Journal of Vocational Education and Training*, Vol. 63, No. 1, 2011, pp. 1–13.

Prasad, P., Prasad, A., "Stretching the Iron Cage: The Constitution and Implications of Routine Workplace Resistance," *Organization Science*, Vol. 11, No. 4, 2000, pp. 387–403.

Rivard, S., Lapointe, L., "Information Technology Implementers' Responses to User Resistance: Nature and Effects," *MIS Quarterly*, Vol. 36, No. 3, 2012, pp. 897–920.

Robey, D. "User Attitudes and Management Information System Use," *Academy of Management Journal*, Vol. 22, No. 3, 1979, pp. 527–538.

Rousseau, D. M., *Psychological Contracts in Organizations: Understanding Written and Unwritten Agreements*, Sage, Thousand Oaks, CA, 1995.

Samuelson, W., Zeckhauser, R., "Status Quo Bias in Decision Making," *Journal of Risk and Uncertainty*, Vol. 1, 1988, pp. 7–59.

Selander, L., Henfridsson, O., "Cynicism as User Resistance in IT Implementation," *Information Systems Journal*, Vol. 22, 2012, pp. 289–312.

Smith, T., Grant, G., Ramirez, A., "Investigating the Influence of Psychological Ownership and Resistance on Usage Intention Among Physicians," *Proceedings of the 47th Hawaii International Conference on System Sciences*, 2014, pp. 2808–2817.

Stein, M. K., Newell, S., Wagner, E. L., Galliers, R. D., "Coping With Information Technology: Mixed Emotions, Vacillation, and Nonconforming Use Patterns," *MIS Quarterly*, Vol. 39, No. 2, 2015, pp. 367–392.

Tarafdar, M., Gupta, A., Turel, O., "The Dark Side of Information Technology Use," *Information Systems Journal*, Vol. 23, No. 3, 2013, 269–275.

Tarafdar, M., Ragu-Nathan, T. S., Ragu-Nathan, B. Tu, Q., "The Impact of Technostress on Role Stress and Productivity," *Journal of Management Information Systems*, Vol. 24, 2007, pp. 307–334.

Tarafdar, M., Tu, Q., Ragu-Nathan, T. S., Ragu-Nathan, B. S. "Crossing to the Dark Side: Examining Creators, Outcomes, and Inhibitors of Technostress," *Communications of the ACM*, Vol. 54, No. 9, 2011, pp. 113–120.

Turel, O., Serenko, A., Giles, P., "Integrating Technology Addiction and Use: An Empirical Investigation of Online Auction Users. *MIS Quarterly*, Vol. 35, No. 4, 2011, pp. 1043–1062.

Vaghefi, I., Lapointe, L., Boudreau-Pinsonneault, C., "A Typology of User Liability to IT Addiction," *Information Systems Journal*, Vol. 27, No. 2, March 2017.

Van de Ven, A. H., Poole, M. S., "Alternative Approaches for Studying Organizational Change," *Organization Studies*, Vol. 26, No. 9, 2005, pp. 1377–1404.

Van Offenbeek, M., Boonstra, A., Seo, D., "Towards Integrating Acceptance and Resistance Research: Evidence From a Telecare Case Study," *European Journal of Information Systems*, Vol. 22, No. 4, 2013, pp. 434–454.

Vieru, D., Rivard, S., Boudreau, S., "From Boundary Shaker to Boundary Consolidator by Ways of Symbolic Discourses in a Post-Merger Integration Context," *Proceedings ICIS 2016*, forthcoming.

Wang, K., Shu, Q., Tu, Q., "Technostress Under Different Organizational Environments: An Empirical Investigation," *Computers in Human Behavior*, Vol. 24, No. 6, 2008, pp. 3002–3013.

Whetten, D. A., "Modelling-as-Theorizing: A Systematic Methodology for Theory Development," *Essential Skills for Management Research*, D. Partington (Ed.), Sage, Thousand Oaks, CA, 2002, pp. 45–71.

Zuboff, S., *In the Age of the Smart Machine: The Future of Work and Power*. Basic Books, New York, 1988.

14
INFORMATION SYSTEMS STRATEGISING

The role of ambidextrous capabilities in shaping power relations

Marco Marabelli and Robert D. Galliers

Introduction[1]

The concept of IS strategising has developed since the 1970s in what is now an established theorising of how organisations engage in the on-going processes and practices of strategy making involving Information Systems (IS) and Information Technology (IT) (e.g., Chen et al. 2010; Teubner 2013). Strategising principles include a high-level, holistic view of how IS strategy develops as a dynamic, iterative and knowing/learning set of practices, both formal and informal (e.g., Galliers 2004). Conceptualisations of IS strategising have taken an explicit socio-technical approach (e.g., Ciborra 2000; Hanseth 2004; Mumford 2006). Early literature (Green 1970; Land 1976; Land 1982) noted that the focus of IS strategising should not be solely on the IT artefact but also on how organisational actors are able to explore and exploit opportunities and challenges associated with IT (Chen et al. 2010; Henfridsson and Lind 2014). To this end, IS strategising involves a number of tensions (Galliers 2004; 2011); examples include those between formal and informal approaches, between human and IT aspects, and between standardised procedures such as business process 'engineering' hand in hand with enterprise systems (Howcroft et al. 2004; Wagner et al. 2005), and flexible knowledge management systems (KMS) aimed at organisational 'knowing' (Newell et al. 2003). In addition, IS strategising highlights dynamic processes that are conducted jointly by IT and business personnel (Ciborra 2000; Hanseth 2004; Mumford 2006), thereby strengthening ongoing alignment (Karpovsky and Galliers 2015; Wilson et al. 2013).

In this chapter, we first position the ISS framework within the broader IS literature; second, we examine our most recent elaboration of Galliers's framework (Marabelli and Galliers 2017) and, adopting a practice-based perspective (Bourdieu 1990; Schatzki 2001; Schatzki 2010), we discuss power as enacted through ongoing practices as well as 'exercises' through formal relationships, such as in organisational charts with formal roles that necessarily follow a vertical hierarchy (Latour 1986; Marshall and Rollinson 2004). We conclude the chapter by laying out some relevant theoretical implications.

IS strategy and strategising: an overview

Strategising and the IS literature

Strategy is a cross-disciplinary topic in business-related disciplines such as Management, Marketing, Economics and IS, and includes contributions from such eminent scholars as Alfred Chandler (1962), Henry Mintzberg (1979) and Michael Porter (1991), as well as practitioners such as Bruce Henderson, founder of the Boston Consulting Group and initiator of the 'strategic consultants' idea. Additionally, authors of highly cited academic papers and books on strategy include Gary Hamel and C. K. Prahalad (e.g., Hamel and Prahalad 1992; Prahalad and Hamel 1994). Those strategy researchers who emphasise the practices of strategy making include Paula Jarzabkowski, Andreas Spee and Richard Whittington (e.g., Jarzabkowski and Spee 2009; Whittington 1996, 2006a).

Strategising through IT has long been a 'hot' topic (Barney 1991; Bhatt et al. 2005; McFarlan 1984; Porter and Millar 1985) and has been a major concern confronting CIOs over four decades (Brancheau and Wetherbe 1987; Luftman 2011; Luftman and Derksen 2012; Luftman et al. 2013; Niederman et al. 1991; Watson et al. 1997). IS strategising "provides a shared understanding across the organization to guide subsequent IT investment and deployment decisions" (Chen et al. 2010, p. 239). Recalling Earl's (1993) "organizational view" of IS strategy and reflecting the ongoing assessment of organisational needs to promote the ability (or capability) to innovate (Chan and Reich 2007; Shollo and Galliers 2016), gaining the sought-after benefits is not without its tensions. Scholars have highlighted the relevance of exploring and exploiting IS/IT in organisational contexts by conceptualising it as an "IS capability" (Bharadwaj 2000) that "is embedded within the fabric of the organization" (Peppard and Ward 2004, p. 170).

IS strategising and organisational tensions

The dynamic process of strategising contrasts planned strategy with its execution, acknowledging that aspects of the actual strategy are emergent (Mintzberg 1979). This implies that tensions exist between exploiting existing plans, ideas and resources and exploring new and emerging means to achieve organisational objectives (March 1991). In Table 14.1, we identify a number of strategic elements that have, over the years, appeared in the (IS) strategising literature, and that are associated with exploitative and exploratory activities. While, for analytical purposes, we retain the distinction between exploration and exploitation, we should remember that these tensions are not to be seen as separate but instead are mutually constituted and reinforcing, occurring at the same time (March 1991; Utterback 1994). As an example, Galliers (1993, p. 201) points to the conflictual nature of strategising processes by arguing that "the one [is] creative and synthetical; the other mechanistic and analytical" – here referring to aligning issues between business and IT. The need to combine different approaches and philosophies thus becomes necessary to form(ulate) and execute a coherent strategy within organisations. This involves being 'ambidextrous' (Adler et al. 1999; Gibson and Birkinshaw 2004; O'Reilly and Tushman 2008).

As can be noted from Table 14.1, planned strategies involve exploitation in line with existing cognitive beliefs, such as those related to managerial experience, market data and forecasts arising, for example, from business intelligence (Shollo and Galliers 2016) or 'big

Table 14.1 ISS and organisational tensions

Tensions/focus	Exploitation	Exploration
Over-arching view	*Planned strategy*	*Emerging strategy*
IT artefact	ERP systems (repository view)	Social media (network view)
Hierarchical aspects	Standardised procedures and roles	Communities of practice, virtual teams, task forces
Human resources	Individuals (attempt to) execute the planned strategy	Knowledge brokers, boundary spanners provide a link between the planned strategy and emerging circumstances that might deviate from the planned strategy
Organisational environment (organisational climate and culture)	Formal relationships, little or no strategy negotiations, top-down approach	Informal relationships, bottom-up or interactive processes of negotiation; clan control
Regulatory and competitive environment (e.g., institutional forces)	Maintaining supply-chain relationships; consolidating alliances; taking advantage of experience and know-how in a static market	Responding quickly to unpredictable changes (e.g., the need to be compliant with a new law/regulation); disruptive innovations can suddenly change an industry's equilibrium (see Kodak and its incapacity to adapt)

data analytics' (Chen et al. 2010; Galliers et al. 2015; George et al. 2014). In comparison, emerging strategies focus on the protagonists of strategising – the *practitioners* (Whittington 2006b). Here, the focus is on *how* strategy is enacted in practice (Hackney and Little 1999; Johnson et al. 2003; Nolan 2012), making it relevant to reflect on the concept of alignment (in a dynamic and ongoing sense) between IT and business, as a key aspect of strategising (Chan et al. 1997; Chan and Reich 2007; Hirschheim and Sabherwal 2001; Karpovsky and Galliers 2015). Moreover, planned and emerging strategy, as with exploitation and exploration, are not viewed as sequential but overlapping (Henfridsson and Bygstad 2013; Merali et al. 2012). Emerging practices are the outcome of the everyday *doings* of strategy and can change the initial assumptions (inherent in planned strategy), in that they are constantly refined and adapted to new contexts, needs and circumstances (Jarzabkowski et al. 2013; Mintzberg and Waters 1990; Whittington 2014).

In considering the IT artefact, it is not uncommon that the implementation of enterprise systems (ES), for example, create efficiencies as they are intended to 'speed up business processes,' as argued, *inter alia*, by Cooper and Zmud (1990) and Davenport (2000). However, conversely and paradoxically, they can create invisible barriers to informal knowledge sharing (Newell et al. 2001), as 'everything' becomes codified, with little room being left for improvisation, flexibility and individuals' ability to deal with emerging contingencies (Ciborra 2000). To this end, informal knowledge sharing systems can be implemented together with ES (Newell et al. 2003) to mitigate the rigidity that is idiosyncratically embedded in such technologies (Elbanna 2006). The tension between the repository view (static information, such as in a file server) and the network view (dynamic information such as a forum or a social media platform) has been recently illustrated by Newell and Marabelli (2014), while Huang and colleagues (2013) show how a network strategy can facilitate 'bottom-up' and 'sideways' strategy formation via the use of social media within organisations.

Thus, strategising acknowledges the limits of considering it as an exclusively 'top-down' exercise, where execution follows planning in a relatively straightforward fashion (see e.g., Lederer and Gardiner 1992; Premkumar and King 1994; Segars and Grover 1999; Segars et al. 1998). Strategy is a much more messy and emergent phenomenon than this (Mintzberg and Waters 1990). For instance, Newkirk et al. (2003) note that too much planning can constrain flexible execution, thus inhibiting innovation, while too little planning appears nebulous and ambiguous to those who attempt its execution. This suggests that a balance should be achieved between formal planning and emerging strategies, tactics and practices.

The focus on human resources is also relevant from the point of view that strategists are constantly challenged by the conflicting demands of exploiting existing organisational knowledge to create efficiencies and, at the same time, exploring new knowledge in being innovative (Newell 2015). Thus, while strategists are required to implement "codified solutions" (Galliers 2011, p. 331) – for instance, those prescribed by Kaplan and Norton's Balanced Scorecard (BS) framework (1996; Kaplan and Norton 2001) as applied in Martinsons et al. (1999) – they often face the need to improvise (Ciborra 2000) when the planned strategy cannot be accomplished in its entirety. To this end, for instance, the stages of growth framework (Galliers and Sutherland 1991) provides means of asking pertinent questions as regards the likely feasibility of strategies *as they are being formulated* on the basis of the various elements contained therein,[2] while feedback facilitates strategising processes involving review, ongoing learning and revisions of current strategy *in light of actual experience*.

Additionally, strategising is a social process, often undertaken in project teams. Teams, either physical or virtual (Ardichvili et al. 2003), often face emerging, unpredictable issues associated with collaboration and trust (Jarvenpaa and Leidner 1998; Ridings et al. 2002) requiring things to be worked out 'on the hoof.' This might require revising project deadlines or intermediate objectives, and even major changes in thinking. Additionally, Newell and Edelman (2008) consider issues associated with cross-project learning.

Either explicitly (Galliers 2004; 2011) or implicitly (Henfridsson and Bygstad 2013; Nolan 2012), the IS strategising literature recognises that a balance between exploitation and exploration is required (Durcikova et al. 2011), viewing it as an *ambidextrous set of activities*. Drawing on March (1991), the ambidexterity literature proposes that organisations are more successful if they can pursue both exploratory and exploitative activities at the same time (Durcikova et al. 2011; He and Wong 2004; Katila and Ahuja 2002). To this end, using ambidexterity to explain tensions arising from ongoing strategising helps to reconcile the need for flexibility *and* efficiency when planning and executing strategy. How the balance between exploiting (cf. planned strategy) and exploring (cf. emerging strategy) occurs in practice requires an examination of practices themselves. In this chapter, we aim to do so by taking a practice-based view (Bourdieu 1990; Schatzki 2001; Schatzki 2010). This, we believe, is an appropriate choice because it reflects the very nature of the ISS framework (see Figure 14.1), which focuses on the actions taken by strategists through their everyday practices and the consequences that these practices have for those involved (Feldman and Orlikowski 2011; Marabelli et al. 2016) – the practitioners. A focus on practices necessarily brings to the surface power considerations (Barad 2003; Hardy and Thomas 2014; Marshall and Rollinson 2004; Nicolini 2012). Moreover, as we argue, the balance between planned and emergent strategy has political implications – namely, power plays an important role in enabling an organisation to shift from planning to improvising and vice versa (Ciborra 2000). In the next two sections we illustrate the link between ISS and power, based on this practice perspective, and then we expand on how power can be used as

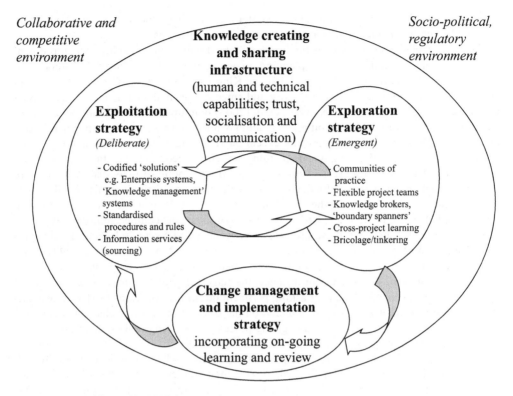

Figure 14.1 Galliers's 2011 ISS framework

an explanatory construct that enables ambidextrous capabilities – the capabilities that promote smooth and speedy shifts between exploitative and exploratory strategies, involving all those who enact strategy, practitioners as well as top management.

IS strategising and power

Power and the practice-based view

In the last two decades, a focus on practices – the "practice turn" (Schatzki 2001) – and on how knowledge is produced through these practices has become a relevant topic initially in the Sociology and Management fields (Cook and Brown 1999; Gherardi 2000; Swan et al. 2002) and subsequently in the IS field, where scholars, drawing on the contributions of Wanda Orlikowski (2007; 2008) began adopting the so-called practice-based view (Feldman and Orlikowski 2011). According to this practice-based view, knowledge is emergent, unpredictable and always *becoming* (Marabelli and Newell 2012) in contrast to more 'traditional' views of knowledge (Nonaka 1994; Nonaka and Konno 1998) that conceive it as a (solely) cognitive effort, a product of our minds (Trkman and Desouza 2012) and something that is, to some extent, "tangible" (Newell et al. 2009). The traditional view – also known as "possession perspective" of knowledge (Cook and Brown 1999; Newell 2015; Newell et al. 2009) assumes that knowledge originates at the individual level (Simon 1991) and subsequently is elaborated at the team (Tsai 2001) and organisational levels (Cohen and Levinthal 1990), albeit with difficulty, because knowledge is sticky by definition (Szulanski 1996). Thus, knowledge sharing or transfer processes are challenging (Spender 1996). The practice-based view – also known as the "practice perspective" (Cook and Brown 1999; Newell 2015; Newell et al. 2009), in contrast, suggests that knowledge (or better 'knowing') originates at the collective level and knowledge 'transfer' is far from automatic, as knowledge is not simply sticky but is, instead, a social and material accomplishment that occurs through practices – or *doings* (Marabelli and Newell 2014).

Following the seminal work of Michael Foucault (1977; 1980a; 1980b), scholars associated with the practice-based view suggest that knowledge (creation, sharing, exploitation and exploration) should be studied along with the underpinning power dynamics (Barad 2003; Latour 1986) as power is a product of knowledge and vice versa (Townley 1993). For instance, Nicolini (2012, p. 6) notes that a practice-based view foregrounds "the centrality of interest in all human matters and therefore put[s] emphasis on the importance of power, conflict, and politics as constitutive elements of the social reality we experience."

To this end, in our most recent revision of the ISS framework we noted that, while the IS literature has considered power extensively (and examples include Backhouse et al. 2006; Hart and Saunders 1997; Levina 2005; Markus and Silver 2008; Pozzebon and Pinsonneault 2012; Silva and Backhouse 2003; Silva and Fulk 2012) and political processes are extremely relevant for strategising (Mintzberg 1994), IS scholars have only seldom discussed power and IS strategy (and strategising) jointly (Marabelli and Galliers 2017). Thus, next we aim to unpack the construct of power in light of the strategy literature and briefly summarise the main insights that we outlined in our 2016 article on IS strategising that appeared in the *Information Systems Journal* (and upon which this chapter draws).

Power and strategising

Drawing on Marxian and Weberian philosophy, power has been traditionally seen as a resource that can be used by 'the powerful' to achieve the strategic objectives that *they* set (Dahl 1957; Emerson 1962; Pfeffer and Salancik 1974). More recent literature suggests that this (resource) view of power is quite limiting in that it requires the constant *exploitation* of organisational assets such as status, influence and the associated power to reward and/or coerce. Others (Clegg 1989; Hardy 1996; Hardy et al. 2005; Lukes 1974), however, argue that viewing power simply as a resource does not reflect the complexity of the construct (Dhillon 2004). Along these lines, we can pose that power is situated (Contu and Willmott 2003), translated (Latour 1986), and immanent[3] in practice (Nicolini 2012).

Foucault (1977; 1980a) departs from the idea that power is owned by individuals or groups who use it as an instrument of coercion, and moves toward a view where power is seen as translated rather than diffused: "embodied and enacted rather than possessed, discursive rather than purely coercive, and constitutes agents rather than being deployed by them" (Gaventa 2003, p. 1). Additionally, Foucault (1980a, p. 93) argues that "power is everywhere: not because it embraces everything, but because it comes from everywhere . . . Power is not an institution, nor a structure, nor a possession. It is the name we give to a complex strategic situation in a particular society."

Latour (1986) embraces Foucault's view of power as being translated, and provides a useful example that contrasts this view with one that views power as a resource. For Latour, an order, a claim or an artefact (described as a token) can be proposed by a powerful individual (or group), and the token, according to the principle of inertia, will move in the direction given by the powerful actor (the actor with resource power) as long as there are no obstacles (e.g., frictions or resistances). In this 'diffusion' exercise of power, the order (the token) does not need to be explained, and the greater the strength with which the token is delivered, the more the token will travel and overcome resistances. In other words, powerful individuals exploit their hierarchical position or influence to give orders. However, ultimately, the token will encounter resistance and this will slow down the order's pace of impact so that the original force (power) is reduced.

In contrast, power can be seen as performative, and this relates to the idea that the spread of the token "is in the hands of people" (Latour 1986, p. 267). Its displacement is not caused by the initial impetus (i.e., being dependent on the resources of the person attempting to make the change), because the token here has no impetus; instead, it is the energy given to the token by people, who keep it going. In this context, the token is not a 'mandatory' order, but is something that people reshape, by "modifying it, or deflecting it, or betraying it, or adding to it, or appropriating it" (Latour 1986, p. 267). Latour calls this a 'translation' model (in contrast to the 'diffusion' model), because power relates to social processes where the order is negotiated, rather than 'executed' (or spread). Latour's translation model is illustrative of this idea of power that resides in everyday practices that are imbued with particular values, cultures, symbols and meanings in particular organisational settings (Foucault 1980b; Vaara and Whittington 2012). In line with the translation model, therefore, power is seen as a relational construct where people constantly negotiate emerging practices that are associated with the accomplishment of a strategy (Hardy and Maguire 2016).

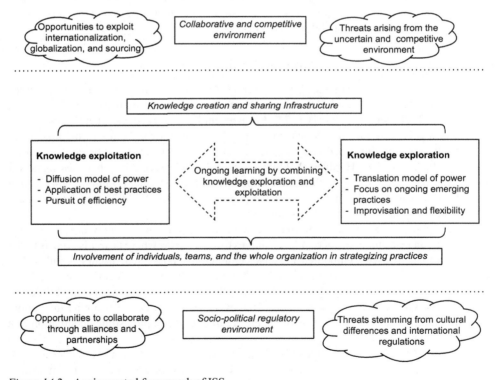

Figure 14.2 A rejuvenated framework of ISS

From Marabelli and Galliers (2017, p. 355).

In our recent reconceptualisation of the ISS framework (see Figure 14.2), we noted that highlighting tensions between power diffused and translated (Latour 1986), and between strategy formulated and emerging (Mintzberg and Waters 1990), will promote the ability to both explore and exploit organisational resources and capabilities (here, with a particular focus on knowledge, through practices, social interactions and ongoing learning).

This way of seeing the tension between knowledge exploration and exploitation as concurring conceptualises power as a command-based as well as a more relational and enacted construct and is helpful in capturing the twofold nature of strategising, and finds support in the literature (e.g., Marshall and Rollinson 2004).

Discussion

In this chapter, we have argued that IS strategising is a dynamic and complex accomplishment of everyday practices. We revisited the IS strategising literature and identified core contributions, particularly in regard to strategising activities that account for the tensions at play in exploiting existing assets and resources (planned strategy) while exploring new ways to gain and maintain a differential advantage, through improvisation, flexibility, informality, and communication/collaboration practices (emerging strategy). Thus, organisations are necessarily developing capabilities that involve both the achievement of efficiencies while retaining a degree of flexibility – a point that echoes Thompson's (1967) conceptualisation of basic organisational tradeoffs, which is both challenging (Burns and Stalker 1961; Lawrence and Lorsch 1967) and topical (Benner and Tushman 2015).

We also noted that the construct of power has not been discussed by prior IS strategising literature (at least, not explicitly) – an exception being the strategy-as-practice literature (Jarzabkowski and Paul Spee 2009; Jarzabkowski and Whittington 2008; Spee and Jarzabkowski 2009; Whittington 1996; 2006a), which highlights how strategising is an ongoing unfolding of practices, and points to the relevance of power discourses. These discourses reflect negotiations and dialogue that occur in everyday social interactions between strategists, when planned strategic initiatives require refinement because of contingencies (Whittington 2006b; Whittington 2014). We drew on Latour's (1986) models to illustrate the difference between hierarchical power (which we argue can help in launching strategic initiatives), and performative power (that generally leads to more durable strategic changes). We link the diffusion model to 'exploitation' – as exercising hierarchical power necessarily involves exploiting a dominant position (Pfeffer 1981). Likewise, we link the translation model to 'exploration,' because the token (in Latour's terms) is constantly shaped, reshaped and appropriated by users through back-and-forth practices that are illustrative of the co-development of an IS (Boudreau and Robey 2005) leading to innovation (Scarbrough et al. 2015; Swan et al. 2007). This view of knowledge/power describes the constructs as having a twofold nature: an exploitative nature if we refer to knowledge as 'possessed' by individuals/strategists and straightforwardly executed throughout the power of the chain of command; and an exploratory nature, if we think of the emerging (and often bottom-up) strategy that needs to be collectively negotiated between top executives and those who are supposed to execute it.

This view of knowledge/power that we adopt in the context of IS strategising echoes Cook and Brown's (1999) 'mutual constitution view' of knowledge and knowing (Marabelli and Newell 2012; Nicolini 2011). Cook and Brown (1999) discuss the relationship between knowledge and knowing as a "generative dance." Although there is a practical component to all knowledge and power and, therefore, the practice-based view provides the theoretical touchstone through which both knowing/relational power and knowledge (individual, possessed) can be interpreted – knowledge and knowing are complementary, and develop jointly. Putting it differently and linking it to the ISS framework, an individual's possessed knowledge and power exists only insofar as it was created using social categories derived from practice that gave sense to these constructs (Marabelli and Newell 2014). This view (the generative dance), which nevertheless supports the central role of knowing, is helpful to further understand the overarching tension of the ISS model that refers to planned versus emerging strategies: it is through enacted power that knowing is translated (Latour 1986) throughout an organisation, and this legitimises power that is merely 'executed,' and where knowledge (of, for example, a specific strategy) is simply 'diffused' (Latour 1986). As we pointed out earlier, these two activities are not sequential but rather continuously overlapping – or interlocked in this generative dance. Figure 14.3 illustrates the generative dance in light of the ISS framework.

From Figure 14.3 it is clear that practices play a key role in enabling the development of both knowledge exploitation (and planned strategy) and knowledge exploration (and emergent strategy). This interplay between knowledge and knowing has been recently noted during fieldwork that we conducted at a software development company (that we call Alpha) headquartered in Massachusetts. The software developed team was initially engaged in a project (creation of a CRM or customer relationship management system) that at the onset was conducted with a pure 'waterfall' methodology – a traditional approach to develop software involving several (and planned) sequential phases (design, coding, testing, rollout, and maintenance). This approach failed (the rollout was unsuccessful) because the rigidity of the methodology did not allow changing any system features while undertaking the various phases, and the programmers, testers and trainers were never on the same page. Management suggested to start over from scratch; the development team would have to go back to the design phase and adopt a more flexible, 'agile' approach, which involves 'back and forth' interactions between the various development phases.

This new approach, albeit challenging in that relies on decentralisation of power (for instance, programmers are free to customise software discretionally and test new code right away. However, as the rollout is limited to very small parts of the system at any time, and

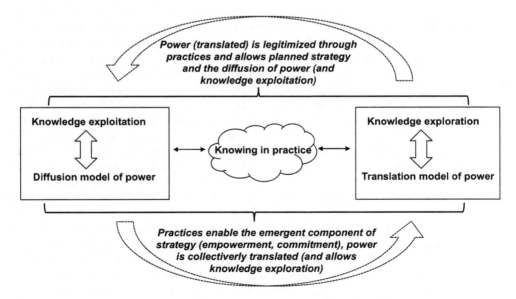

Figure 14.3 Generative dance of knowing and power in strategising processes

involves mainly power users, it benefits from the continuous review of "what works and what does not work." The 'relaunch' (as the second development was called) was successful mainly because the team benefitted from the informal environment where various parts of the project development were assigned to programmers and testers on the basis of trust (i.e., they did not have to report each and every activity related to the development of the CRM). Trainers were free to recruit 'super-users' (IT-savvy users, purposely selected for testing the systems' functionality in a beta environment) at any time and to provide training to users on even very small parts of the new software. Moreover, trainers started to take on a 'help desk' role, spontaneously making themselves available to users to solve problems via email or in person (even though the need for this type of support was not foreseen at the onset of the relaunch).

Almost paradoxically, the very few planned objectives – involving milestones, particular system requirements and deadlines – were achieved with little problem. The project manager almost never had to check whether planned objectives were being achieved. The various project actors (the team) spontaneously (and often) contacted the project manager with updates but also in a more proactive way, by suggesting the creation of unplanned (yet in their opinion very useful and innovative) functionalities, stemming from ideas that emerged through the development of the 'core' features of the CRM.

This example illustrates that the sole application of the diffusion model of power does not work, because planned strategy often needs to be tweaked (or even drastically disrupted). Emerging and unpredictable hurdles challenge strategists, and the possibility to change plans 'in the making' makes the difference in relation to the achievement of holistic (organisational) objectives. For instance, at Alpha, the initial software development project focused exclusively on knowledge exploitation (various 'by the book' phases, characteristic of the waterfall methodology). The development of informality and trust between team members during the relaunch allowed informal knowledge sharing (working together on the daily challenges associated with failures and successes typical of IS developments). Knowledge was exploited when deadlines had to be met, but was also explored by 'peers' (e.g., trainers independently recruited super-users and helped them out with troubleshooting – even if they did not have to), and in a bottom-up fashion (e.g., programmers often contacted the project manager to suggest new functionalities). In sum, planned strategy (and knowledge exploitation) was successfully pursued because emergent strategy (and knowledge exploration) was enabled (and supported by management). Thus, the diffusion model of power (here referred to as the 'mandatory' orders related to specific system requirements and deadlines) could work because the translation model of power (based on trust and informality) enabled it to do so. This supports our point about the coexistence of the diffusion and translation models of power (Figure 14.3). We next provide some concluding remarks related to our contribution.

Implications

Our theorising (Marabelli and Galliers 2017) provides relevant insights and implications for IS strategising scholars. First, with respect to the tensions involving knowledge/power in practical settings, tensions emerge, and these require that organisational actors to engage in exploratory and exploitative activities. Were we to assume that knowledge can be treated (exclusively) as a tangible asset, the likely outcome is that learning processes (exploration) do not occur (cf. Newell et al. 2009). In this regard, Levinthal and March's (1993, p. 95) paper on the "Myopia of Learning" highlights how organisations need to balance "the competing goals of developing new knowledge (i.e., exploring) while exploiting current competencies in the face of dynamic tendencies to emphasize one or the other."

Second, power might spread (or attempts to spread) from powerful individuals to the whole organisation. However, when an attempt to exercise power is made without empowering those who will put strategies into practice (the practitioner strategists), limited effects are achieved. In other words, this type of hierarchical power – here conceptualised using Latour's (1986) diffusion model – is less effective. Instead, engagement and empowerment of practitioners (cf. the translation model) result in more durable effects, as back-and-forth interactions between executives (those who 'give the orders') and practitioners (those who execute them) allow the latter to negotiate and revise strategies during execution. This translation perspective is illustrative of why planned strategy cannot always be executed *in toto*, given emerging, often unpredictable issues. However, while other literatures conceptualise power in a way that is similar to Latour's translation model (cf. the previously mentioned strategy as practice literature), here we argue that both the diffusion and the translation models are helpful to understand strategising processes (see Figure 14.2): while the diffusion model reflects exploitation (of power and knowledge), the translation model is more related to exploration (again, of power and knowledge). A tension between the diffusion and the translation models exists because, in practical settings, it is not always possible to exercise power in a way that gives voice to those who 'practice' the strategy. Our interpretation of this tension is that they are illustrative of a never-ending process of *becoming* where strategy is pursued by the constant effort to reach a balance between exploratory and exploitative practices – always in need to refinement, because of the unpredictable and emerging issues being confronted.

In conclusion, while our revised IS strategising framework can provide guidance to strategists, at any organisational level, it does not aim to provide specific recommendations on how to plan and manage strategy in organisations. While it does provide a set of non-prescriptive principles that are helpful in better understanding the messy unfolding of practices involving strategic initiatives, it is better for strategists to be aware that strategising is an emergent and emerging process, and that it needs to be treated as such.

Notes

1 This chapter is based in large part on and extends Marabelli and Galliers (2017).
2 In this case, based on the so-called 7 S's of Pascale and Athos (1981).
3 Power is immanent in practice in that it cannot be separated from people's *doings* as it is the emergent product of collective practices.

References

Adler, P. S., Goldoftas, B., and Levine, D. I. 1999. "Flexibility Versus Efficiency? A Case Study of Model Changeovers in the Toyota Production System," *Organization Science* (10:1), pp. 43–68.

Ardichvili, A., Page, V., and Wentling, T. 2003. "Motivation and Barriers to Participation in Virtual Knowledge-Sharing Communities of Practice," *Journal of Knowledge Management* (7:1), pp. 64–77.

Backhouse, J., Hsu, C. W., and Silva, L. 2006. "Circuits of Power in Creating De Jure Standards: Shaping an International Information Systems Security Standard," *MIS Quarterly* (30), pp. 413–438.

Barad, K. 2003. "Posthumanist Performativity: Toward an Understanding of How Matter Comes to Matter," *Signs* (28:3), pp. 801–831.

Barney, J. 1991. "Firm Resources and Sustained Competitive Advantage," *Journal of Management* (17:1), pp. 99–120.

Benner, M. J., and Tushman, M. L. 2015. "Reflections on the 2013 Decade Award – Exploitation, Exploration, and Process Management: The Productivity Dilemma Revisited Ten Years Later," *Academy of Management Review* (40:4), pp. 497–514.

Bharadwaj, A. S. 2000. "A Resource-Based Perspective on Information Technology Capability and Firm Performance: An Empirical Investigation," *MIS Quarterly* (24:1), pp. 169–196.

Bhatt, G. D., Grover, V., and Grover, V. 2005. "Types of Information Technology Capabilities and Their Role in Competitive Advantage: An Empirical Study," *Journal of Management Information Systems* (22:2), pp. 253–277.
Boudreau, M.-C., and Robey, D. 2005. "Enacting Integrated Information Technology: A Human Agency Perspective," *Organization Science* (16:1), pp. 3–18.
Bourdieu, P. 1990. *The Logic of Practice*. Stanford, CA: Stanford University Press.
Brancheau, J. C., and Wetherbe, J. C. 1987. "Key Issues in Information Systems Management," *MIS Quarterly* (11:1), pp. 23–45.
Burns, T. E., and Stalker, G. M. 1961. *The Management of Innovation*. London: Tavistock.
Chan, Y. E., Huff, S. L., Barclay, D. W., and Copeland, D. G. 1997. "Business Strategic Orientation, Information Systems Strategic Orientation, and Strategic Alignment," *Information Systems Research* (8:2), pp. 125–150.
Chan, Y. E., and Reich, B. H. 2007. "IT Alignment: What Have We Learned?," *Journal of Information Technology* (22:4), pp. 297–315.
Chandler, A. D. 1962. *Strategy and Structure: Chapters in the History of the American Enterprise*. Cambridge, MA: MIT Press.
Chen, D. Q., Mocker, M., Preston, D. S., and Teubner, A. 2010. "Information Systems Strategy: Reconceptualization, Measurement, and Implications," *MIS Quarterly* (34:2), pp. 233–259.
Ciborra, C. 2000. *From Control to Drift: The Dynamics of Corporate Information Infrastructures*. Oxford: Oxford University Press.
Clegg, S. R. 1989. "Radical Revisions: Power, Discipline and Organizations," *Organization Studies* (10:1), pp. 97–115.
Cohen, W. M., and Levinthal, D. A. 1990. "Absorptive Capacity: A New Perspective on Learning and Innovation," *Administrative Science Quarterly* (35:1), pp. 128–152.
Contu, A., and Willmott, H. 2003. "Re-Embedding Situatedness: The Importance of Power Relations in Learning Theory," *Organization Science* (14:3), pp. 283–296.
Cook, S. D., and Brown, J. S. 1999. "Bridging Epistemologies: The Generative Dance Between Organizational Knowledge and Organizational Knowing," *Organization Science* (10:4), pp. 381–400.
Cooper, R. B., and Zmud, R. W. 1990. "Information Technology Implementation Research: A Technological Diffusion Approach," *Management Science* (36:2), pp. 123–139.
Dahl, R. A. 1957. "The Concept of Power," *Behavioral Science* (2:3), pp. 201–215.
Davenport, T. H. 2000. *Mission Critical: Realizing the Promise of Enterprise Systems*. Boston: Harvard Business School Press.
Dhillon, G. 2004. "Dimensions of Power and IS Implementation," *Information & Management* (41:5), pp. 635–644.
Durcikova, A., Fadel, K. J., Butler, B. S., and Galletta, D. F. 2011. "Research Note – Knowledge Exploration and Exploitation: The Impacts of Psychological Climate and Knowledge Management System Access," *Information Systems Research* (22:4), pp. 855–866.
Earl, M. J. 1993. "Experiences in Strategic Information Systems Planning," *MIS Quarterly* (17), pp. 1–24.
Elbanna, A. R. 2006. "The Validity of the Improvisation Argument in the Implementation of Rigid Technology: The Case of ERP Systems," *Journal of Information Technology* (21:3), pp. 165–175.
Emerson, R. M. 1962. "Power-Dependence Relations," *American Sociological Review*, pp. 31–41.
Feldman, M. S., and Orlikowski, W. J. 2011. "Theorizing Practice and Practicing Theory," *Organization Science* (22:5), pp. 1240–1253.
Foucault, M. 1977. *Discipline and Punish: The Birth of the Prison*. New York: Vintage.
Foucault, M. 1980a. *The History of Sexuality. Volume One: An Introduction*. New York: Random House.
Foucault, M. 1980b. *Power/Knowledge: Selected Interviews and Other Writings, 1972–1977*. New York: Pantheon.
Galliers, R. D. 1993. "Towards a Flexible Information Architecture: Integrating Business Strategies, Information Systems Strategies and Business Process Redesign," *Information Systems Journal* (3:3), pp. 199–213.
Galliers, R. D. 2004. "Reflections on Information Systems Strategizing." In C. Avgerou, C. Ciborra & F. Land (eds.). *The Social Study of Information and Communication Technology: Innovation, Actors, and Contexts*. Oxford: Oxford University Press, pp. 231–262.
Galliers, R. D. 2011. "Further Developments in Information Systems Strategizing: Unpacking the Concept." In R. D. Galliers & W. L. Currie (eds.). *The Oxford Handbook of Management Information Systems: Critical Perspectives and New Directions*. Oxford: Oxford University Press, pp. 329–345.

Galliers, R. D. and Sutherland, A. R. 1991. "Information Systems Management and Strategy Formulation: The 'Stages of Growth' Model Revisited," *Information Systems Journal* (1:2), pp. 89–114.

Galliers, R. D., Newell, S., Shanks, G., and Topi, H. 2015. "The Challenges and Opportunities of 'Datification' Strategic Impacts of 'Big' (and 'Small') and Real Time Data – for Society and for Organizational Decision Makers. Special Issue Call for Papers." *Journal of Strategic Information Systems* (24:1), pp. II–III.

Gaventa, J. 2003. *Power after Lukes: An Overview of Theories of Power since Lukes and Their Application to Development*. Brighton: Participation Group, Institute of Development Studies.

George, G., Haas, M. R., and Pentland, A. 2014. "Big Data and Management," *Academy of Management Journal* (57:2), pp. 321–326.

Gherardi, S. 2000. "Practice-Based Theorizing on Learning and Knowing in Organizations," *Organization* (7:2), pp. 211–224.

Gibson, C. B., and Birkinshaw, J. 2004. "The Antecedents, Consequences, and Mediating Role of Organizational Ambidexterity," *Academy of Management Journal* (47:2), pp. 209–226.

Green, J. F. 1970. "Management Information Systems and Corporate Planning," *Long Range Planning* (2:4), pp. 74–78.

Hackney, R., and Little, S. 1999. "Opportunistic Strategy Formulation for IS/IT Planning," *European Journal of Information Systems* (8:2), pp. 119–126.

Hamel, G., and Prahalad, C. K. 1992. "Strategy as Stretch and Leverage," *Harvard Business Review* (71:2), pp. 75–84.

Hanseth, O. 2004. *Knowledge as Infrastructure*. Oxford: Oxford University Press.

Hardy, C. 1996. "Understanding Power: Bringing About Strategic Change," *British Journal of Management* (7:S1), pp. S3–S16.

Hardy, C., Lawrence, T. B., and Grant, D. 2005. "Discourse and Collaboration: The Role of Conversations and Collective Identity," *Academy of Management Review* (30:1), pp. 58–77.

Hardy, C., and Maguire, S. 2016. "Organizing Risk: Discourse, Power, and 'Riskification,'" *Academy of Management Review* (41:1), pp. 80–108.

Hardy, C., and Thomas, R. 2014. "Strategy, Discourse and Practice: The Intensification of Power," *Journal of Management Studies* (51:2), pp. 320–348.

Hart, P., and Saunders, C. 1997. "Power and Trust: Critical Factors in the Adoption and Use of Electronic Data Interchange," *Organization Science* (8:1), pp. 23–42.

He, Z.-L., and Wong, P.-K. 2004. "Exploration vs. Exploitation: An Empirical Test of the Ambidexterity Hypothesis," *Organization Science* (15:4), pp. 481–494.

Henfridsson, O., and Bygstad, B. 2013. "The Generative Mechanisms of Digital Infrastructure Evolution," *MIS Quarterly* (37:3), pp. 907–931.

Henfridsson, O., and Lind, M. 2014. "Information Systems Strategizing, Organizational Sub-Communities, and the Emergence of a Sustainability Strategy," *Journal of Strategic Information Systems* (23:1), pp. 11–28.

Hirschheim, R., and Sabherwal, R. 2001. "Detours in the Path Toward Strategic Information Systems Alignment," *California Management Review* (44:1), pp. 87–108.

Howcroft, D., Newell, S., and Wagner, E. 2004. "Understanding the Contextual Influences on Enterprise System Design, Implementation, Use and Evaluation," *Journal of Strategic Information Systems* (13:4), pp. 271–277.

Huang, J., Baptista, J., and Galliers, R. D. 2013. "Reconceptualizing Rhetorical Practices in Organizations: The Impact of Social Media on Internal Communications," *Information & Management* (50:2), pp. 112–124.

Jarvenpaa, S. L., and Leidner, D. E. 1998. "Communication and Trust in Global Virtual Teams," *Journal of Computer-Mediated Communication* (3:4), doi:10.1111/j.1083–6101.1998.tb00080.x.

Jarzabkowski, P., and Paul Spee, A. 2009. "Strategy-as-Practice: A Review and Future Directions for the Field," *International Journal of Management Reviews* (11:1), pp. 69–95.

Jarzabkowski, P., Spee, A. P., and Smets, M. 2013. "Material Artifacts: Practices for Doing Strategy With 'Stuff,'" *European Management Journal* (31:1), pp. 41–54.

Jarzabkowski, P., and Whittington, R. 2008. "A Strategy-as-Practice Approach to Strategy Research and Education," *Journal of Management Inquiry* (17:4), pp. 282–286.

Johnson, G., Melin, L., and Whittington, R. 2003. "Micro Strategy and Strategizing: Towards an Activity-Based View," *Journal of Management Studies* (40:1), pp. 3–22.

Kaplan, R. S., and Norton, D. P. 1996. *The Balanced Scorecard: Translating Strategy Into Action.* Boston: Harvard Business School Press.

Kaplan, R. S., and Norton, D. P. 2001. "Transforming the Balanced Scorecard From Performance Measurement to Strategic Management: Part I," *Accounting Horizons* (15:1), pp. 87–104.

Karpovsky, A., and Galliers, R. D. 2015. "Aligning in Practice: From Current Cases to a New Agenda," *Journal of Information Technology* (30:2), pp. 136–160.

Katila, R., and Ahuja, G. 2002. "Something Old, Something New: A Longitudinal Study of Search Behavior and New Product Introduction," *Academy of Management Journal* (45:6), pp. 1183–1194.

Land, F. 1976. "Evaluation of Systems Goals in Determining a Design Strategy for a Computer-Based Information System," *Computer Journal* (19:4), pp. 290–294.

Land, F. 1982. "Adapting to Changing User Requirements," *Information & Management* (5:2), pp. 59–75.

Latour, B. 1986. "The Powers of Association." In J. Law (ed.). *Power, Action and Belief: A New Sociology of Knowledge.* London: Routledge, pp. 264–280.

Lawrence, P. R., and Lorsch, J. W. 1967. "Differentiation and Integration in Complex Organizations," *Administrative Science Quarterly* (12:1), pp. 1–47.

Lederer, A. L., and Gardiner, V. 1992. "The Process of Strategic Information Planning," *Journal of Strategic Information Systems* (1:2), pp. 76–83.

Levina, N. 2005. "Collaborating on Multiparty Information Systems Development Projects: A Collective Reflection-in-Action View," *Information Systems Research* (16:2), pp. 109–130.

Levinthal, D. A., and March, J. G. 1993. "The Myopia of Learning," *Strategic Management Journal* (14:S2), pp. 95–112.

Luftman, J. 2011. "Key Issues for IT Executives," *MIS Quarterly Executive* (4), pp. 269–286.

Luftman, J., and Derksen, B. 2012. "Key Issues for IT Executives 2012: Doing More With Less," *MIS Quarterly Executive* (11), pp. 207–218.

Luftman, J., Zadeh, H. S., Derksen, B., Santana, M., Rigoni, E. H., and Huang, Z. D. 2013. "Key Information Technology and Management Issues 2012–2013: An International Study," *Journal of Information Technology* (28:4), pp. 354–366.

Lukes, S. 1974. *Power: A Radical View* (Vol. 1). London: Palgrave Macmillan.

Marabelli, M., and Galliers, R. D. 2017. "A Reflection on Information Systems Strategizing: The Role of Power and Everyday Practices," *Information Systems Journal* (27:3), pp. 347–366.

Marabelli, M., and Newell, S. 2012. "Knowledge Risks in Organizational Networks: The Practice Perspective," *Journal of Strategic Information Systems* (21:1), pp. 18–30.

Marabelli, M., and Newell, S. 2014. "Knowing, Power and Materiality: A Critical Review and Reconceptualization of Absorptive Capacity," *International Journal of Management Reviews* (16:4), pp. 479–499.

Marabelli, M., Newell, S., and Galliers, R. D. 2016. "The Materiality of Impression Management in Social Media Use: A Focus on Time, Space and Algorithms," *36th International Conference of Information Systems*, Dublin, Ireland: AIS.

March, J. G. 1991. "Exploration and Exploitation in Organizational Learning," *Organization Science* (2:1), pp. 71–87.

Markus, M. L., and Silver, M. S. 2008. "A Foundation for the Study of IT Effects: A New Look at DeSanctis and Poole's Concepts of Structural Features and Spirit," *Journal of the Association for Information Systems* (9:10/11), pp. 609–632.

Marshall, N., and Rollinson, J. 2004. "Maybe Bacon Had a Point: The Politics of Interpretation in Collective Sensemaking," *British Journal of Management* (15:S1), pp. S71–S86.

Martinsons, M., Davison, R., and Tse, D. 1999. "The Balanced Scorecard: A Foundation for the Strategic Management of Information Systems," *Decision Support Systems* (25:1), pp. 71–88.

McFarlan, F. W. 1984. "Information Technology Changes the Way You Compete," *Harvard Business Review*, May.

Merali, Y., Papadopoulos, T., and Nadkarni, T. 2012. "Information Systems Strategy: Past, Present, Future?," *Journal of Strategic Information Systems* (21:2), pp. 125–153.

Mintzberg, H. 1979. "An Emerging Strategy of 'Direct' Research," *Administrative Science Quarterly* (24:4), pp. 582–589.

Mintzberg, H. 1994. "The Fall and Rise of Strategic Planning," *Harvard Business Review* (72:1), pp. 107–114.

Mintzberg, H., and Waters, J. 1990. "Studying Deciding: An Exchange of Views Between Mintzberg and Waters, Pettigrew, and Butler," *Organization Studies* (11:1), pp. 1–6.

Mumford, E. 2006. "The Story of Socio-Technical Design: Reflections on Its Successes, Failures and Potential," *Information Systems Journal* (16:4), pp. 317–342.

Newell, S. 2015. "Managing Knowledge and Managing Knowledge Work: What We Know and What the Future Holds," *Journal of Information Technology* (30:1), pp. 1–17.

Newell, S., and Edelman, L. F. 2008. "Developing a Dynamic Project Learning and Cross-Project Learning Capability: Synthesizing Two Perspectives," *Information Systems Journal* (18:6), pp. 567–591.

Newell, S., Huang, J. C., Galliers, R. D., and Pan, S. L. 2003. "Implementing Enterprise Resource Planning and Knowledge Management Systems in Tandem: Fostering Efficiency and Innovation Complementarity," *Information and Organization* (13:1), pp. 25–52.

Newell, S., and Marabelli, M. 2014. Knowledge Management. In A. B. Tucker (ed.). *Information Systems and Information Technology, Computer Science Handbook*. Chapman and Hall, pp. 17.11–17.21.

Newell, S., Pan, S. L., Galliers, R. D., and Huang, J. C. 2001. "The Myth of the Boundaryless Organization," *Communications of the ACM* (44:12), pp. 74–76.

Newell, S., Robertson, M., Scarbrough, H., and Swan, J. 2009. *Managing Knowledge Work and Innovation*. London: Palgrave Macmillan.

Newkirk, H. E., Lederer, A. L., and Srinivasan, C. 2003. "Strategic Information Systems Planning: Too Little or Too Much?" *Journal of Strategic Information Systems* (12:3), pp. 201–228.

Nicolini, D. 2011. "Practice as the Site of Knowing: Insights From the Field of Telemedicine," *Organization Science* (22:3), pp. 602–620.

Nicolini, D. 2012. *Practice Theory, Work, and Organization: An Introduction*. Oxford: Oxford University Press.

Niederman, F., Brancheau, J. C., and Wetherbe, J. C. 1991. "Information Systems Management Issues for the 1990s," *MIS Quarterly* (15:4), pp. 475–500.

Nolan, R. L. 2012. "Ubiquitous IT: The Case of the Boeing 787 and Implications for Strategic IT Research," *Journal of Strategic Information Systems* (21:2), pp. 91–102.

Nonaka, I. 1994. "A Dynamic Theory of Organizational Knowledge Creation," *Organization Science* (5:1), pp. 14–37.

Nonaka, I., and Konno, N. 1998. "The Concept of BA: Building a Foundation for Knowledge Creation," *California Management Review* (40:3), pp. 40–54.

O'Reilly, C. A., and Tushman, M. L. 2008. "Ambidexterity as a Dynamic Capability: Resolving the Innovator's Dilemma," *Research in Organizational Behavior* (28), pp. 185–206.

Orlikowski, W. J. 2007. "Sociomaterial Practices: Exploring Technology at Work," *Organization Studies* (28:9), pp. 1435–1448.

Orlikowski, W. J. 2008. "Using Technology and Constituting Structures: A Practice Lens for Studying Technology in Organizations." In *Resources, Co-Evolution and Artifacts*. New York: Springer, pp. 255–305.

Pascale, R. T., and Athos, A. G. 1981. "The Art of Japanese Management," *Business Horizons* (24:6), pp. 83–85.

Peppard, J., and Ward, J. 2004. "Beyond Strategic Information Systems: Towards an IS Capability," *Journal of Strategic Information Systems* (13:2), pp. 167–194.

Pfeffer, J. 1981. *Power in Organizations*. Cambridge, MA: Ballinger.

Pfeffer, J., and Salancik, G. R. 1974. "Organizational Decision Making as a Political Process: The Case of a University Budget," *Administrative Science Quarterly*, pp. 135–151.

Porter, M. E. 1991. "Towards a Dynamic Theory of Strategy," *Strategic Management Journal* (12:S2), pp. 95–117.

Porter, M. E., and Millar, V. E. 1985. "How Information Gives You Competitive Advantage," *Harvard Business Review*, July–August, pp. 149–152.

Pozzebon, M., and Pinsonneault, A. 2012. "The Dynamics of Client-Consultant Relationships: Exploring the Interplay of Power and Knowledge," *Journal of Information Technology* (27:1), pp. 35–56.

Prahalad, C. K., and Hamel, G. 1994. "Strategy as a Field of Study: Why Search for a New Paradigm?," *Strategic Management Journal* (15:S2), pp. 5–16.

Premkumar, G., and King, W. R. 1994. "The Evaluation of Strategic Information System Planning," *Information & Management* (26:6), pp. 327–340.

Ridings, C. M., Gefen, D., and Arinze, B. 2002. "Some Antecedents and Effects of Trust in Virtual Communities," *Journal of Strategic Information Systems* (11:3), pp. 271–295.

Scarbrough, H., Robertson, M., and Swan, J. 2015. "Diffusion in the Face of Failure: The Evolution of a Management Innovation," *British Journal of Management* (26:3), pp. 365–387.

Schatzki, T. R. 2001. *The Practice Theory*. London: Routledge.
Schatzki, T. R. 2010. *Site of the Social: A Philosophical Account of the Constitution of Social Life and Change*. University Park, PA: Pennsylvania State University Press.
Segars, A. H., and Grover, V. 1999. "Profiles of Strategic Information Systems Planning," *Information Systems Research* (10:3), pp. 199–232.
Segars, A. H., Grover, V., and Teng, J. T. 1998. "Strategic Information Systems Planning: Planning System Dimensions, Internal Coalignment, and Implications for Planning Effectiveness," *Decision Sciences* (29:2), pp. 303–341.
Shollo, A., and Galliers, R. D. 2016. "Towards an Understanding of the Role of Business Intelligence Systems in Organisational Knowing," *Information Systems Journal* (26:4), pp. 339–367.
Silva, L., and Backhouse, J. 2003. "The Circuits-of-Power Framework for Studying Power in Institutionalization of Information Systems," *Journal of the Association for Information Systems* (4:1), p. 14.
Silva, L., and Fulk, H. K. 2012. "From Disruptions to Struggles: Theorizing Power in ERP Implementation Projects," *Information and Organization* (22:4), pp. 227–251.
Simon, H. A. 1991. "Bounded Rationality and Organizational Learning," *Organization Science* (2:1), pp. 125–134.
Spee, A. P., and Jarzabkowski, P. 2009. "Strategy Tools as Boundary Objects," *Strategic Organization* (7:2), pp. 223–232.
Spender, J.-C. 1996. "Organizational Knowledge, Learning, and Memory: Three Concepts in Search of a Theory," *Journal of Organizational Change and Management* (9:1), pp. 63–78.
Swan, J., Bresnen, M., Newell, S., and Robertson, M. 2007. "The Object of Knowledge: The Role of Objects in Biomedical Innovation," *Human Relations* (60:12), pp. 1809–1837.
Swan, J., Scarbrough, H., and Robertson, M. 2002. "The Construction of Communities of Practice in the Management of Innovation," *Management Learning* (33:4), pp. 477–496.
Szulanski, G. 1996. "Exploring Internal Stickiness: Impediments to the Transfer of Best Practice Within the Firm," *Strategic Management Journal* (17:S2), pp. 27–43.
Teubner, R. A. 2013. "Information Systems Strategy," *Business & Information Systems Engineering* (5:4), pp. 243–257.
Thompson, J. D. 1967. *Organizations in Action: Social Science Bases of Administrative Theory*. New York: McGraw-Hill Book Company.
Townley, B. 1993. "Foucault, Power/Knowledge, and Its Relevance for Human Resource Management," *Academy of Management Review* (18:3), pp. 518–545.
Trkman, P., and Desouza, K. C. 2012. "Knowledge Risks in Organizational Networks: An Exploratory Framework," *Journal of Strategic Information Systems* (21:1), pp. 1–17.
Tsai, W. 2001. "Knowledge Transfer in Intraorganizational Networks: Effects of Network Position and Absorptive Capacity on Business Unit Innovation and Performance," *Academy of Management Journal* (44:5), pp. 996–1004.
Utterback, J. M. 1994. *Mastering the Dynamics of Innovation. How Companies Can Seize Opportunities in the Face of Technological Change*. Cambridge, MA: MIT Press.
Vaara, E., and Whittington, R. 2012. "Strategy-as-Practice: Taking Social Practices Seriously," *Academy of Management Annals* (6:1), pp. 285–336.
Wagner, E., Howcroft, D., and Newell, S. 2005. "Special Issue Part II: Understanding the Contextual Influences on Enterprise System Design, Implementation, Use and Evaluation," *Journal of Strategic Information Systems* (14:2), pp. 91–95.
Watson, R. T., Kelly, G. G., Galliers, R. D., and Brancheau, J. C. 1997. "Key Issues in Information Systems Management: An International Perspective," *Journal of Management Information Systems* (13:4), pp. 91–115.
Whittington, R. 1996. "Strategy as Practice," *Long Range Planning* (29:5), pp. 731–735.
Whittington, R. 2006a. "Completing the Practice Turn in Strategy Research," *Organization Studies* (27:5), pp. 613–634.
Whittington, R. 2006b. "Learning More From Failure: Practice and Process," *Organization Studies* (27:12), pp. 1903–1906.
Whittington, R. 2014. "Information Systems Strategy and Strategy-as-Practice: A Joint Agenda," *Journal of Strategic Information Systems* (23:1), pp. 87–91.
Wilson, A., Baptista, J. J., and Galliers, R. 2013. "Performing Strategy: Aligning Processes in Strategic IT," *31st International Conference of Information Systems*. Milan, Italy.

15
DIGITALIZATION AS A STRATEGY PRACTICE
What is there to learn from strategy as practice research?

Viktor Arvidsson and Jonny Holmström

Introduction

Information technology (IT) has caught strategy scholars' attention for over 50 years (Peppard et al. 2014). Because IT resources were initially costly to develop and implement, strategic uses of IT have historically been subordinated to the predominant business strategy (Galliers 1993). Information systems (IS) strategy scholars have therefore drawn extensively on strategic management theories. The influence of classic perspectives of strategy on IS strategy research is not the least palpable in notions of strategic alignment and positioning whereby organizational transformation is about control and planned implementations of simple sets of IT resources, carefully selected to grant the organization a competitive position within a stable environment. Around 25 years ago, the strategic promises of creating digital infrastructures within and across organizations started to render IT uses more socio-technically complex (Ciborra 1997). Because only senior managers have sufficient economic and political resources to undertake such a task, IT resources mostly remained subordinate to the business strategy; however, new IT use soon generated innovation and organizational change far beyond senior management's reach and control (Jarvenpaa and Ives 1996), making environments more uncertain. Today, IT enjoys a ubiquitous presence in organizations (Holmström and Robey 2005), but even as most contemporary IT resources are malleable enough to extend upon for actors on all organizational levels (Bygstad 2015), many organizations still visibly struggle to put new IT resources into good use (Tilson et al. 2010). Some organizations even seem blind to the strategic opportunities that already implemented IT resources afford (Arvidsson et al. 2014). Hence, it is high time for IS strategy scholars to step out of the boardroom and reveal how local organizational actors mobilize IT resources as entrepreneurial means for promoting digital business strategies (Jarvenpaa and Ives 1996).

In recent years, strategy-as-practice has emerged as an approach focused on strategizing and the doing of strategy. While the notion of strategizing entered the strategy discourse early on to make sense of why strategies rarely unfold as planned, strategy-as-practice focuses on the day-to-day actions that lead to strategic outcomes as they occur in context (Mintzberg 1973). This shift from a process-based to a practice-based view of strategy making grew out of frustration with classic assumptions regarding the nature and cause of change. For example, Vaara and

Whittington (2012) argued that as organizations' environments undergo socio-technical and economic transformations as a result of digitalization, we must rethink the notion of strategy. Strategy-as-practice can afford IS strategy scholars new insight into how IT promotes digital strategies, because to keep up with digitalization organizations must often build a new IT capability base from the ground up (Bharadwaj et al. 2013). This typically requires collective action by actors with distinct resource commitments, interests, and horizons (Henfridsson and Yoo 2014). To direct attention to how IT resources promote such digitalization processes by distributing innovation and localizing organizational change, this chapter charts out possible applications of strategy-as-practice in IS strategy research. In so doing, we extend on calls to examine how structures emerge, and how actors configure IT resources to undo information silos that block digital business strategies (Besson and Rowe 2012, Bharadwaj et al. 2013).

The chapter is organized as follows. First we argue that digitalization has expanded the scope of IS strategy research to the point where classic perspectives are stretched to their limits. We then propose strategy-as-practice as an alternative approach, and demonstrate its uses through three empirical vignettes that each reveals a facet of the challenges organizations face in using IT resources strategically. Finally, we discuss some ways in which strategy-as-practice offers IS strategy scholars insight into the digitalization practices of current strategic organizations.

From IT strategy to digital strategizing

IS strategy research has assumed many forms over the years. Peppard et al. (2014: 2) outlines five movements, each of which is influenced by strategic management theories albeit lagging some years behind (Table 15.1). These theories influence on IS strategy research is visible in the conventional assumption that IT resources come aligned with predominant business strategies and are implemented in organizations to achieve an *a priori* known goal that senior managers support. Because IT implementations associated with strategy change have carried a high cost and risk, this assumption is historically valid. However, it has also limited our understanding of the challenges organizations face in using IT resources strategically to mainly psychological and cognitive aspects of organizational inertia (Besson and Rowe 2012). Even as most IT resources are now malleable enough to extend upon for organizational actors on every level (Bygstad 2015), little is accordingly known of how local organizational actors can mobilize IT as an entrepreneurial means for overcoming economic and political inertia that block the materialization of digital business strategies (Besson and Rowe 2012, Bharadwaj et al. 2013).

Peppard et al. (2014) nicely summarizes how digitalization has caused organizations to embed IT resources and associated capabilities at an increasing depth, in effect blurring the boundary between IT and business strategies. For example, using IT resources to spot and locally act on new strategic opportunities is now vital for most organizations (Whittington 2014). Due to the low cost and high scalability of IT resources today (Bygstad 2015), we could therefore say that every employee is a potential champion of a digital business strategy. If digital infrastructures lower the bar for participation in strategizing, however, IS strategy scholars must re-examine the mechanisms and conditions that influence bottom-up organizational change – for example, how changes must be sequenced and staged for local innovations to scale (Jarvenpaa and Ives 1996), and how IT governance frameworks and architectures affect the coevolution of IT and business strategies by generating socio-technical, economic, and political inertia (Besson and Rowe 2012). In this chapter, we argue that completing this movement entails abandoning the assumption that IT resources carry a certain use, which

Table 15.1 Five movements in IS strategy and strategizing

IS strategy movements	Praxis	Practitioners	Practices	Description
Ad hoc bottom-up approach to determining IS	Ad hoc approach to determining EDP and computing requirements	IT staffs	Emphasis on building systems rather than determining strategy	Ad hoc, bottom-up, primarily driven by technology requirements. IS plan operational in focus, for the most part identifying individual applications (cf. Galliers and Sutherland 1991)
IS planning	Top-down approach to determining IS needs to meet business goals	IT staffs	Planning based on an informal network of a few key individuals	Formal top-down planning for IS. IS plans reactive to business plans.
Strategic planning for information systems (SPIS)	Team approach involving multiple stakeholders	Senior management and IT staffs	IS plans periodically reviewed to adapt to changing circumstances	Proactively seeking opportunities for competitive advantage from IT
Building an IS capability	IS capability embedded in fabric of the organization	All employees have a role to play	Influenced by organizational culture; and information orientation of organization	Acknowledging that having a strategy is only part of what is required. Ability to continually identify opportunities, deploy technology, implement change and use information and IT.
IS strategizing	Cognitive and intellectual dimensions	All employees	Co-evolution of business and IT strategies	IS strategy is something that organizations do rather than have

Source: Adapted from Peppard et al. (2014).

senior management will support once it is rendered obvious. Although IS strategy scholars increasingly note that IT implementation is merely the beginning (Arvidsson et al. 2014), and that strategic responses to digitalization require organizational actors to develop, combine, and reposition IT resources in unexpected ways (Henfridsson and Yoo 2014), we believe that IS strategy research has only scratched the surface concerning the entrepreneurial means IT resources afford processes of innovation and organizational change, as well as their material nature. To investigate this nature is important because IT resources help to counter the fact that even good ideas that originate in the bottom tend to "die early and quiet deaths," having failed to capture the senior managers' imagination and attention (Jarvenpaa and Ives 1996: 119). But it is also required to account for the myriad of ways that digital infrastructures have rendered organizations socio-technically complex ever since IT resources were first introduced in organizations (Tilson et al. 2010, Zuboff 1988).

Today, CEOs have learned that having an IS plan is only part of the strategizing process. The long-term success of most organizations is dependent on its capability to develop and promote increasingly innovative uses of IT resources over time, and to navigate associated uncertainty. These dependences stem from the need to strike a balance between the pace by which new IT resources can be developed and the rate by which IT uses can be reasonably replaced, and the unexpected opportunities digital infrastructures' inter-generational (generative) effects create. If classic assumptions no longer hold, navigating digitalization will be hard; once a matter of control and planned implementations of simple sets of IT resources, carefully selected by IT staff and executives to grant organizations competitive positions, digitalization then requires distributed forms of innovation. Hence, organizations must create conditions for IT resources to be enacted as a part of multiple organizational practices, in pursuit of contradictory goals (Berente and Yoo 2012). Although IS strategy research makes evident that environments grow uncertain as organizations imbue their products and services with IT capabilities (Nolan 2012, Ward 2012), it is unclear how organizations transform as a result of rapid, openly distributed innovation processes, subject to many more or less digital organizing logics (Yoo et al. 2012).

For IS strategy research to explain how organizational actors use IT to overcome inertia built into prevailing information silos, and pave the way for digital business strategies (Besson and Rowe 2012, Bharadwaj et al. 2013), practice perspectives are needed. Examining IT resources as entrepreneurial means indeed entails recognizing the fact that if all operations have an IT component, IT resources are no longer subordinated to business strategies. Rather, they make up the generative substances and forms with which new digital business strategies are developed. Many scholars have argued for fusing IT and business strategy more comprehensively under the notion of digital business strategy (Bharadwaj et al. 2013, Grover and Kohli 2013), but we thus emphasize the need to take the digital for real. In the next section, we discuss how strategy-as-practice can offer IS strategy scholars such insight. While strategy-as-practice can grant insight into how IT resources constitute a nexus for collective action in numerous ways (Orlikowski 2013), we center our upcoming discussion on two key aspects of the relationship between IT and business strategy, which digitalization has transformed (Peppard et al. 2014).

1 Digital business strategy success is in everyone's hands. IT resources are increasingly modular and layered, and therefore no longer possible to control by the IT unit or align simply with the will of the senior management. Thanks to standardized interfaces, it is always possible to combine and repurpose local IT resources in innovative ways. Yet, champions of novel IT uses are likely to run into heavy economic and political inertia. IS

strategy research must thus admit the distributed nature of innovation, and theorize the scaling processes by which local organizational actors use IT resources as a means for mobilizing external allies to support the materialization of new strategic outcomes.
2   Digital business strategizing is emergent rather than planned. Strategic uses of IT now unfold in open and expanding environments, and tend to diverge from predominant IT resource commitments by cutting across information silos and functional units. Because IT resources can be easily modified, highly embedded work systems live long lives for economic and political reasons, but also come to create contradictory realities and user experiences. An important part of digital strategizing is therefore to admit that IT uses are ephemeral, and create IT governance systems that balance the needs to implement, maintain, and roll back IT resources to constantly pave way for new organizing logics.

Digitalization as a strategy practice

Strategy-as-practice examines the processes and contents of strategy making (Jarzabkowski et al. 2007). To bring organizational actors back onto the stage, strategy-as-practice scholars use verbs rather than nouns, but also recognize that different actors make different sense of shared situations, because they belong to different communities of practice (Chia and Mackay 2007, Jarzabkowski 2004). Because each community's resource uses are subject to its institutionalized logics, exploring strategy practices such as digitalization requires a framework of strategizing much different from classic approaches to strategic management (Jarzabkowski et al. 2007).

Because of the strong emphasis on strategy as a process that occurs in a context (Mintzberg 1973), strategy-as-practice shifts attention from rational accounts of IT use to rich accounts of how organizational actors rearrange messy organizational realities, in studies of digitalization (Ciborra 1996). Strategy-as-practice scholars work around three parameters: *practitioners* (the focal strategizing actors), *practices* (the historical, symbolic, and material processes that guide their activities), and *praxis* (the sequence by which activities unfold *in situ*). However, what truly unites the literature is a commitment to explain what actors do and why (Jarzabkowski et al. 2007, Jarzabkowski 2004), which in our context then entails attending to IT resources both as material means and utilities. Huang et al. (2014) accordingly adapted this framework for IS strategy research by expanding on the idea of praxis to direct specific attention to the *strategy site*. In light of IT resources' unique materiality (Kallinikos et al. 2013) and the unbounded nature of IT innovations (Yoo et al. 2012), a digital strategy site is here conceptualized as the environment where organizational practices and IT resources are bundled together as part of a *strategy praxis* (thus carrying the material means and resources for its own transformation). In this way, strategy-as-practice can help IS scholars capture digitalization as a material practice.

By isolating the strategy site (Table 15.2), Huang et al. (2014) showed that IS strategy research is conceptually ready to develop a material understanding of what it means for all employees to take part in digital strategizing. Specifically, they revealed how the employees "who perform and engage in strategy practices" promoted a digitalization outcome at a Chinese strategy site by using IT resources as means for ambidexterity (Huang et al. 2014: 30) – that is to say, to simultaneously exploit and explore the strategic opportunities that digital infrastructures create over time. As such, the authors showed that a strategy site can be conceptualized as different bundles of IT resources, organizational structures, and practitioner roles that constitute different alignments, and undergo change, as a new praxis for digital strategizing is established. This view renders evident how strategizing occurs both in and as a material arrangement of actors and resources.

Table 15.2 Definitions of key conceptual elements of the Huang et al. (2014) framework

Key concept	Definition
IS strategy practices	Institutionalized routines that guide IS strategic activity, based on traditions, norms and procedures that exist both within the organization and beyond its boundaries
Strategy practitioners	Those individual actors who shape and actualize IS strategy, including actors within a focal firm but also, for example, external policy makers, regulatory bodies, competitor organizations
IS strategy praxis	The actual activity of creating and enacting an IS strategy that may be more or less similar to the institutionalized routines because of the sensemaking/interpretation of the particular practitioners involved and because of unanticipated events that can disrupt routine practices
Strategy site	The social and relational space where IT-enabled practices are bundled together in particular ways by the practitioners involved and that can change over time as an outcome of praxis

We have argued that classic assumptions of strategic management have prevented IS strategy research from understanding digitalization as an (IS) strategy practice. In particular, we argue that the literature as a result has failed to account for the ways in which digital infrastructures change the conditions and mechanisms for innovation and organizational change (Besson and Rowe 2012, Tilson et al. 2010). As Huang et al. (2014) noted, this gap also presents itself in a lack of case studies that reveal how organizational practices and strategy sites are transformed over time as result of digitalization, rather than as the expected result of a one-shot, top-down IT implementation. In the remainder of the chapter, we expand on this claim to demonstrate that IS strategy scholars can build on the notion of strategy site to reveal what it means for all workers to participate in digital strategizing. In particular, we show that strategy-as-practice can open up three avenues for IS strategy scholars to investigate digitalization as a strategy practice: (1) how technologies-in-use at a strategy site act as material carriers of institutions that enable and constrain strategic outcomes when new IT resources are introduced; (2) how IT resources thanks to their material nature can be used as entrepreneurial means for digital business strategizing; and (3) how digital infrastructures and platforms moderate conditions and mechanisms for innovation and organizational change. To chart out these avenues, we next present three empirical vignettes. Because these vignettes only offer snapshots, they do not provide a complete description of all the actors and dependencies associated with digital strategizing processes. They do, however, provide solid illustrations of how digital business strategies differ due to the material role of IT resources, and consequently the need for digital strategizing practices to recognize the ways digitalization challenges existing boundaries.

Digital strategizing in practice

For IT implementations to prove strategic, IT resources must form a material nexus for novel assemblies of organizational practices, and generate associated resource commitments in use (Boudreau and Robey 2005). Counter to classic assumptions of strategic management, digital strategizing therefore requires more than senior management decree and strategically aligned IT resources; many successful IT implementations initially buttress existing information silos that must be undone for organizations to harness generative infrastructures. Indeed, rational and common-sense uses of IT resources often reinforce predominant structures and norms by *digitizing* cow-paths (Tilson et al. 2010). By contrast, *digitalization* requires organizations to improvise in their use of IT (Orlikowski 1996) and enable power users and thought leaders to champion IT innovation (Boudreau and Robey 2005, Jarvenpaa and Ives 1996). Digitalization processes are thus visible in how organizations continually work to cultivate and reveal digital options in the existing base of social and technical capabilities with varied IS strategy success.

Papermill was among the last pulp and paper mills, owned and operated by an international conglomerate, to implement a new enterprise IT architecture. By standardizing three core IT systems at each mill, the conglomerate's global paper division intended to move upmarket and create new revenue. For example, the enterprise architecture was aligned to pave the way for a more agile paper production process, and to facilitate deeper product-service integration. In a recent paper (Arvidsson et al. 2014), we demonstrated how as the final system – the mill execution system, responsible for translating the sales division's replenishment requirements into reels of paper ready for shipment – was being implemented, Papermill persisted in using its paper-born production routines. Such persistence can initially be viewed as the result of a cognitive form of entrenchment that occurs as organizing logics sediment in routines and IT use norms, which the material arrangement of the strategy site then serves to maintain. For example, the enormous paper machine had over the decades anchored the idea that 'paper production has a certain way to it' – an organizing logic to which all other practices at the pulp and paper mill had to bend. Since then, we have analyzed this case in further depth to reveal how the paper machine not only was loud and trembling but in praxis also constituted fixed subject positions, IT use commitments, and organizational identities (Arvidsson 2016). Indeed, by creatively implementing the mill execution system around existing work systems, Papermill digitized a historical divide between workers and planners, inhibiting new IT use.

To illustrate, production planners worked in a pink building adjacent to the mill. They saw as their main challenge 'to minimize the trim' – that is to say, minimize the waste that occurs as combinations of paper reels of marketable quality, length, and breadth are cut from huge rolls of paper, several meters in width. For the white-collar planners, who worked in nice climate-controlled offices, the new mill execution system was welcome, but no occasion for change. Graphical user interfaces and drag-and-drop operations made it simple to tune and compare different paper production scenarios, but they saw no little need to transform how paper was produced. It was only a replacement (e.g., the old system had once been repaired using parts from a technology museum, and although highly efficient carried many known risks). In fact, even as the mill management was otherwise aware of the urgent need for new work routines, 'it was not part of the plan.' The production planners' stubbornness was a cause for cynicism at the production floor, where blue-collar shift workers operated around the clock to produce paper, in a massive hall packed with buzzing machinery. Because of paper-born routines, the workers could not adjust production plans despite local capabilities and skills. Many thus felt that the planners busted their balls – a sentiment many truck operators shared as reels arrived in a disorderly way from their point of view. Large-scale production processes frustrate downstream workers by default, but digitized cow-paths was also a source of frustration upstream. The regional sales office had to market many products of different kinds at short notice; one sales person with experience of working at the mill could not fathom 'why the production is still so rigid.' Because the mill had taken measures to ensure that all workers were represented in the system implementation, it is puzzling that the mill still saw the outcome as a success.

Examining why actors who could make a novel strategic choice often fail to recognize that a choice is present is a timeless avenue for IS strategy research. The Papermill vignette shows how strategy-as-practice can unpack such organizational dynamics. For example, it portrays how the site's paper-bound and mechanic materiality constituted two types of masculinity – one rough, the other respectable (Horowitz, 2013) – which served to maintain the historical divide between blue- and white-collar workers by corrupting and constraining the use of IT. Strategy-as-practice research has observed masculinity to shape the discursive formation of organizational strategies and criticized its influence on strategic management, but can thus be extended to explain IT resources' role as material carriers of organizing logics (Gosain 2004, Vaara and Whittington 2012). Indeed, a practice view on digitalization *per se* directs attention to the alterity of those who must be managed (Zuboff 1988). Consider the production worker: if the production planners' response can be seen as corrupt (Stensaker and Falkenberg 2007), why did they also fail to 'pick up' the IT resources at hand? One reason is found in the way rough masculinities are steeped in resistance and so foster behaviors sustaining the idea that some men must be managed for their own good. Mastery is a cultured form of resistance.[1] It allows workers to one-up the management because skilled work entails resource delegation and knowledge dependencies that workers can exploit to enforce idiosyncratic routines beyond managerial control. For example, Papermill's executives were concerned that paper machine operators insisted on running the production process based on their gut (and embodied experience from working at the mill), as their idiosyncratic behaviors created 'visible' losses during work shifts; but the managers also knew that 'you cannot change their work routines using an IT system.' Because a masculine self-preservation underscored Papermill's blindness, it is likely that IT resources were left unused in part because they threatened existing forms of mastery.[2]

If IS strategy research is cast in classic, rational assumptions, strategy-as-practice can enable IS scholars to advance a more material and emotional (situated) understanding of the organizational dynamics of digitalization. As the first vignette shows, such understanding is crucial as strategy blindness is rooted in paper-born routines and information infrastructures, which material carriers must be transformed alongside their use logics for digitalization to succeed. As portrayed in our second vignette, strategy-as-practice enables IS scholars to examine how weak but resourceful actors can use IT to navigate this challenge (Besson and Rowe 2012).

Goldcity is the local administration of a Swedish city that in 2000 embarked on a decade-long digitalization effort. By launching a digital service center, the city hoped to catalyze IT-based service innovation and back-end process redesign. Like Papermill, however, the organization initially refused to put otherwise successfully implemented IT resources into good use. In an upcoming paper, we explain how strategy blindness occurs when organization's incumbents use IT as a façade to protect their resource privileges. For example, Goldcity's service units made only minimal changes to its service routines and used the document and workflow system implemented alongside the new service to digitize existing organizational structures. In fact, the new service center was eventually sidestepped completely when the service units struck deals with the IT vendors to deliver simple forms of IT-based services (limited to each IT vendor's proprietary information siloes and service processes that the units controlled). As organizations can so easily decouple legitimizing talk from their actual use of IT resources, it is likely that successful digitalization will often rest on champions to hide behind such facades until they can produce convincing economic justifications and gain support for additional IT investments needed to showcase innovative IT use logics in practice (Aanestad and Hanseth 2002, Jarvenpaa and Ives 1996). However, combatting strategy blindness may also require IT use manipulation. One reason for this is that IT resources can solve many different problems simultaneously and so foster multiple resource use commitments, which generates drift and surfaces contradictions that are not easily resolved (Berente and Yoo 2012, Ciborra 1997).

To illustrate, a skunk works team in Goldcity's periphery learned the hard way that strategic IT uses are not at all obvious in the near term. The centralized service strategy they pursued was blocked for nearly a decade by incumbents, who refused to yield control over crucial IT and service resources because they saw the change as a threat to their privileged position in the city. To digitalize both the city's citizen-facing service routines and its back-end service processes based on a centralized organizing logic, the team thus had to learn how to exploit the organization's blindness. Unable to capture their unit managers' attention or imagination, they ultimately decided to deploy a new IT platform as a 'Trojan horse' that could push for digitalization from within by overloading the service routines that the units hoped to protect. The platform made this outcome possible because it on the one hand made it easy to develop rather sophisticated apps using mature web technologies, which reduced development costs and enabling component reuse. By leveraging digital infrastructures to reduce the economic inertia associated with digitalizing services, the skunk works team in this way paved the way for a distributed and periphery-driven strategic change of the city's service delivery processes. As such, strategy-as-practice can help IS scholars explore how IT resources can be configured and used to produce strategic change rather than blindness by scrutinizing why digitalization processes so often generate contradictions and unexpected events, which organizational actors must navigate to promote innovation and organizational change. For example, in Goldcity contradiction was a potent source of conflict, but thus also enabled the skunk works team to exploit the city's strategy blindness and digitalize its service delivery. While it is common that organizations lack capacity for digital strategy little is still known about how associated multiplicity can be harnessed in the configuration and use of IT (Robey and Boudreau 1999).

If the strategy practices that lead to successful digitalization comprise collective actions and entrepreneurial activities that are distinct but related as they must resonate for the implementation and use of IT resources to have a strategic effect (Besson and Rowe 2012, Lyytinen et al. 2009), it is time for IS scholars to forget about the boardroom and view digitalization as a strategy practice. For example, to explain how organizational actors can create conditions for bottom-up innovation and organizational change, and learn to exploit the mechanisms that digitalization affords. On the one hand, this process is well understood: successful bottom-up change typically relies on a local champion that enjoys the backing of the management team, who can provide necessary economic and political resources to push change through once a novel IT resource use logic has emerged (cf. Jarvenpaa and Ives 1996). On the other hand, however, little attention has been paid to how digital infrastructures and platforms influence such processes by rendering IT innovations open and distributed (Nambisan 2016), and why some organizations successfully reconcile contradictory organizing logics in novel forms of IT, materializing new strategies where others fail (Berente and Yoo 2012, Tilson et al. 2010).

To explore these issues, we are currently conducting a longitudinal case study of the design and implementation of a digital planning system at a Norwegian rehab hospital. The *Clinic*, our final strategy site, is located a short boat ride away from Oslo, and has entrepreneurship and innovation built into its walls. Digital planning systems and similar types of innovations were considered a strategic necessity at the hospital, as it helped the hospital board maintain autonomy despite its small size, and ward off increasing pressures for a centralized IT and health system governance (all hospitals in the region are decoupled around administrative and health-professional work roles, and almost all IT-related activities are furthermore the responsibility of a software company owned by the regional health authority). The new time planning system was enabled by a stand-alone application, originally developed by a Swedish company, that as a result of the trial underwent further development to become an integrated part of the regional health authority's IT platform, brimming with its own mechanisms and IT use conditions, which the local IT unit and a clinical team-coordinator (and champion) had to learn how to navigate *in situ* (e.g., the platform would grant security certificates needed to put patient data into the application, but demanded compliance with regional architectures and standards). The decision to go ahead with the implementation was significant: the Clinic had sought to digitalize planning ever since the introduction of the PC, and yet had not succeeded to get rid of the paper-born routines that the chief of clinic herself devised in an early attempt to showcase the many clinical opportunities of IT use; moreover, even though the budgeted cost was less than 1 million NOK, the cost was still too big for the local IT budget (by comparison, IT systems designed to digitalize patient journals can have costs exceeding 1 billion NOK for a large hospital in the region). What impact then did the regional IT platform have?

To illustrate, the digital time planning project was instigated by the local IT unit and took off once an innovation officer found a clinical team coordinator willing to champion the system. During a routine follow-up interview, we found the project champion in distress. Although the trial of the new planning system proved positive – the coordinator's department at the Clinic had many short-term patients with highly condensed trajectories meaning that planning was key but also that change of plans was normal and medically justifiable – and the application seemed capable to make planning more reliable – patient treatment plans were presently made using a Word template, printed, and then carried to a number of places in the hospital; based on the patient's specific condition, this triggered another set of paper-born routines e.g., in the gym or the pool – and also accountable for – through complex cost per patient measures the system would ultimately grant the controllers with hard facts e.g., in case of patient complaints concerning the hours and types of treatments received, but the data would also allow Clinic to measure the effect and optimal intensity of their specialized rehab treatments, and cut back on their resource use – she expressed frustration. The outcome was highly uncertain, and she had little insight into or ability to influence the decision. Because local resources were scarce, the project was indeed fraught by the risk of the project getting stuck in the ever-growing backlog IT portfolio at the clinic. The platform in this way did not only enable an investment in the present, based on a future promise, but also imposed limits on the development, two of which were striking: whenever information was to be encoded into the system, it became accountable to a range of laws, norms, and regulations (e.g., the application could not integrate patient data during the trial, limiting feedback to user experience issues rather than local workflow issues); being on the regional platform solved this problem but required first passing a costly, lengthy, and uncertain review process that all applications go through to review their security classing. This meant funds had to be released before they could innovate around IT resources in use.

Digital infrastructures put IT resources in reach for actors on all organizational levels, but as the Clinic's experience shows they also introduce new forms of inertia because of the growing complexity that digitalization brings to organizations. The implementation, planned for the beginning of 2017, will, indeed, not be straightforward at all. Once resources were freed the IT vendor finally secured the buy-in to make their application compliant with the IT platform: should Clinic succeed, the application can easily be sold and distributed to other hospitals in the region and allowed for local configurability by design. But the application is at the same time implemented in the dark, because the new system could not be tested without it first being redeveloped for the healthcare context. For example, nurses – who had a front-row seat to the patients' frustration with uncertain information and knew the value of the time they spent with the physicians were all but excluded from the trial. The routine exclusion of nurses constitutes a great risk in IT development projects because they are coupled with patients *in situ*, and is not only indicative of a sexist development practice that fosters development conditions in which medically indefensible IT use decisions too often becomes the after-thought of white men in suits (e.g., during an innovation cluster meeting at the Clinic a member of the audience noted that the just presented strategic group for lightweight innovation only comprised men), but also telling of the ways in which the local decoupling of administration and clinical work at all Norwegian hospitals has caused a situation where innovation is all but impossible, because the shared administration renders power to be both distant and concealed from local activities.

Boudreau and Robey (2005) showed that delayed strategic responses to new IT resources can be explained by the time it takes local power users to turn failed IT implementations around – mastery of new IT resources and manipulation of related IT use dependencies, for example, enforcing a specific workflow to help co-workers, can grant them the ability to make others comply with their IT resource logics. It remains to be seen whether such a process can accumulate at the Clinic and digitalize the existing workarounds and shadow systems that stops planning from being both reliable and accountable. IS scholars should in light of such uncertainties continue to theorize failures (e.g., uncover why users make limited uses of IT even when they are given considerable opportunities to learn; Cooper 2000), but we argue that also in studies of success it will be of particular importance to consider not only the ways in which platforms and digital infrastructures make new information visible, but also how they distance and conceal certain information (Leonardi 2014), and classify who/what matters (Cecez-Kecmanovic et al. 2014).

Concluding remarks

For over 25 years, IS scholars have known that IT resources often fail to create more strategic work due to "the rather disappointing outcomes in which automation, driven by the dominant elites and their will to control, erodes and undoes the promise of a transparent and multivalent workplace in which information could have played an enlightening role" (Kallinikos 2010: 2). The three vignettes offer some ways to appreciate the material role IT resources play in both day-to-day and entrepreneurial activities as they occur *in situ*. While *Papermill* exhibited the opportunities for materially grounded theorizing of complex digitalization outcomes (such as when organizations view smooth transitions into new IT use as successful because they are blind to digital options; Arvidsson et al. 2014, Cecez-Kecmanovic et al. 2014), *Goldcity* indicates that digital entrepreneurs can configure IT resources to leverage such blindness against those privileged by it. *Clinic*, in turn, revealed how digital infrastructures will render such activities increasingly distributed, emotionally complex, and politically challenging (Besson and Rowe 2012, Stein et al. 2015). The point of this chapter was accordingly not to make a clever point about how organizations should strategize, but instead to reveal the degree of complexity that a strategy-as-practice perspective can handle. However, we do suggest that those interested in exploring these issues think of ways to develop the idea of a strategy site (Huang et al. 2014); for example, by examining the physicality of paper-based routines and other material carriers, recognizing that even as IT resources promote certain interests, their impact on organizations ultimately depends on how they are fitted into the existing material arrangement (Arvidsson et al. 2014), which other self-interested actors will seek to maintain (Markus 1983, Sayer 1998).

Research into how local organizational actors pool scarce resources to undo inertia built into information siloes, and how to managers can better govern and support associated innovation and organizational change processes, could facilitate an encompassing agenda for strategy-as-practice and IS research (with ample theoretical and methodological support in Zuboff 1988). In recent decades, the proliferation of strategic IT uses in relations within and across multiple organizations (Tilson et al. 2010, Nolan 2012) have made organizations reliant on their ability to spot and act on digital options, and yet relatively little is known about how existing IT uses (and other technologies-in-use) restrict organizations to exploit such options beyond the scope of the institutionalized work system (and related praxis). Such knowledge is vital if we are to teach students responsible and sustainable governance of digital innovation and organizational change; and to managers in organizations that struggle to turn information silos into powerful digital platforms (cf. Bharadwaj et al. 2013, Hanseth et al. 2006). It is known that digitizing of cow-paths often coincides with the use of IT as a means to streamline, procedurally optimize, and speed up organizational processes in search for efficiency (Zuboff 1988). Beyond the scope of this chapter, it is therefore the need to recognize that what is viewed as efficient is "the outcome of a particular social order and the interests it accommodates and renders legitimate," an agenda which practice theories support (Cecez-Kecmanovic et al. 2014). Insofar as the three lessons strategy-as-practice teaches IS research all entail examining the impact IT has on life beyond the strategy site, scholars adopting such view would do well to also anchor their reference theory and concepts into the IS context (e.g., using ideas of digital materiality, or extending on the idea of IT as a material carriers of institutional logics (Gosain et al. 2004).

Notes

1 Mastery also influenced trim planners' behaviors. Thanks to algorithms, mill execution systems can recommend advanced production strategies, but trim planners were always looking to beat the system.
2 While trim planners were blinded by control, no production worker wanted to be accused of 'playing for the pink team' (an allusion meant to render the trim planners' unmanly, based on the color of their building), in large part because harsh working conditions required their compliance with rough virtues.

References

Aanestad, M., & Hanseth, O. (2002). Growing networks: Detours, stunts and spillovers. In *COOP* (pp. 38–49).
Arvidsson, V. (2016). Strategy blindness as disciplined IT-use practice: Looking past the 'unintended and unexpected' through the practice lens. In *2016 49th Hawaii International Conference on System Sciences (HICSS)* (pp. 4644–4653). IEEE.
Arvidsson, V., Holmström, J., & Lyytinen, K. (2014). Information systems use as strategy practice: A multi-dimensional view of strategic information system implementation and use. *Journal of Strategic Information Systems*, 23(1), 45–61.
Berente, N., & Yoo, Y. (2012). Institutional contradictions and loose coupling: Postimplementation of NASA's enterprise information system. *Information Systems Research*, 23(2), 376–396.
Besson, P., & Rowe, F. (2012). Strategizing information systems-enabled organizational transformation: A transdisciplinary review and new directions. *Journal of Strategic Information Systems*, 21(2), 103–124.
Bharadwaj, A., El Sawy, O.A., Pavlou, P.A., & Venkatraman, N.V. (2013). Digital business strategy: Toward a next generation of insights. *MIS Quarterly*, 37(2), 471–482.
Boudreau, M.C., & Robey, D. (2005). Enacting integrated information technology: A human agency perspective. *Organization Science*, 16(1), 3–18.
Bygstad, B. (2015). The coming of lightweight IT. In *Proceedings of the ECIS Conference*, Munster, May.
Cecez-Kecmanovic, D., Kautz, K., & Abrahall, R. (2014). Reframing success and failure of information systems: A performative perspective. *MIS Quarterly*, 38(2), 561–588.
Chia, R., & MacKay, B. (2007). Post-processual challenges for the emerging strategy-as-practice perspective: Discovering strategy in the logic of practice. *Human Relations*, 60(1), 217–242.
Ciborra, C.U. (1997). De profundis? Deconstructing the concept of strategic alignment. *Scandinavian Journal of Information Systems*, 9(1), 2.

Ciborra, C. U. (1996). The platform organization: Recombining strategies, structures, and surprises. *Organization Science*, 7(2), 103–118.
Cooper, R. B. (2000). Information technology development creativity: A case study of attempted radical change. *MIS Quarterly*, 24(2), 245–276.
Galliers, R. D. (1993). IT strategies: Beyond competitive advantage. *Journal of Strategic Information Systems*, 2(4), 283–291.
Gosain, S. (2004). Enterprise information systems as objects and carriers of institutional forces: The new iron cage? *Journal of the Association for Information Systems*, 5(4), 6.
Grover, V., & Kohli, R. (2013). Revealing your hand: Caveats in implementing digital business strategy. *MIS Quarterly*, 37(2), 655–662.
Hanseth, O., Jacucci, E., Grisot, M., & Aanestad, M. (2006). Reflexive standardization: Side effects and complexity in standard making. *MIS Quarterly*, 30 (August), 563–581.
Henfridsson, O., & Yoo, Y. (2014). The liminality of trajectory shifts in institutional entrepreneurship. *Organization Science*, 25(3), 932–950.
Holmström, J., & Robey, D. (2005). Understanding IT's organizational consequences: An actor network theory approach. In Czarniawska, B. and Hernes, T. (eds.), *Actor-network theory and organizing* (pp. 165–187). Stockholm: Liber.
Horowitz, R. (2013). *Boys and their toys: Masculinity, class and technology in America*. London: Routledge.
Huang, J., Newell, S., Huang, J., & Pan, S. L. (2014). Site-shifting as the source of ambidexterity: Empirical insights from the field of ticketing. *Journal of Strategic Information Systems*, 23(1), 29–44.
Jarvenpaa, S. L., & Ives, B. (1996). Introducing transformational information technologies: The case of the World Wide Web technology. *International Journal of Electronic Commerce*, 1(1), 95–126.
Jarzabkowski, P. (2004). Strategy as practice: Recursiveness, adaptation and practices-in-use. *Organization Studies*, 25, 529–60.
Jarzabkowski, P., Balogun, J., & Seidl, D. (2007). Strategizing: The challenges of a practice perspective. *Human Relations*, 60(1), 5–27.
Kallinikos, J. (2010). The "age of smart machine": A 21st century view. *Encyclopedia of Software Engineering*, 1(1): 1097–1103.
Kallinikos, J., Aaltonen, A., & Marton, A. (2013). The ambivalent ontology of digital artifacts. *MIS Quarterly*, 37(2), 357–370.
Leonardi, P. M. (2014). Social media, knowledge sharing, and innovation: Toward a theory of communication visibility. *Information Systems Research*, 25(4), 796–816.
Lyytinen, K., Newman, M., & Al-Muharfi, A.R.A. (2009). Institutionalizing enterprise resource planning in the Saudi steel industry: a punctuated socio-technical analysis. *Journal of Information Technology*, 24(4), 286–304.
Markus, M. L. (1983). Power, politics, and MIS implementation. *Communications of the ACM*, 26(6), 430–444.
Mintzberg, H. (1973). Strategy-making in three modes. *California Management Review*, 16(2), 44–53.
Nambisan, S. (2016). Digital entrepreneurship: Toward a digital technology perspective of entrepreneurship. *Entrepreneurship Theory and Practice*.
Nolan, R. L. (2012). Ubiquitous IT: The case of the Boeing 787 and implications for strategic IT research. *Journal of Strategic Information Systems*, 21(2), 91–102.
Orlikowski, W. J. (1996). Improvising organizational transformation over time: A situated change perspective. *Information Systems Research*, 7(1), 63–92.
Orlikowski, W. J. (2013). Practice in research: Phenomenon, perspective and philosophy. In D. Golsorkhi, L. Rouleau, D. Seidl and E. Vaara (Eds.), *Cambridge handbook of strategy as practice* (pp. 23–33). Cambridge: Cambridge University Press.
Peppard, J., Galliers, R. D., & Thorogood, A. (2014). Information systems strategy as practice: Micro strategy and strategizing for IS. *Journal of Strategic Information Systems*, 23(1), 1–10.
Polites, G. L., & Karahanna, E. (2012). Shackled to the status quo: The inhibiting effects of incumbent system habit, switching costs, and inertia on new system acceptance. *MIS Quarterly*, 36(1), 21–42.
Sayer, K. (1998). Denying the technology: Middle management resistance in business process re-engineering. *Journal of Information Technology*, 13(4), 247–257.
Stein, M. K., Newell, S., Wagner, E. L., & Galliers, R. D. (2015). Coping with information technology: Mixed emotions, vacillation, and nonconforming use patterns. *MIS Quarterly*, 39(2), 367–392.
Stensaker, I., & Falkenberg, J. (2007). Making sense of different responses to corporate change. *Human Relations*, 60(1), 137–177.

Tilson, D., Lyytinen, K., & Sørensen, C. (2010). Research commentary – digital infrastructures: The missing IS research agenda. *Information Systems Research, 21*(4), 748–759.

Vaara, E., & Whittington, R. (2012). Strategy as practice: Taking social practices seriously. *Academy of Management Annals, 6*(1), 285–336.

Ward, J. M. (2012). Information systems strategy: Quo vadis? *Journal of Strategic Information Systems, 21*(2), 165–171.

Whittington, R. (2014). Information systems strategy and strategy-as-practice: A joint agenda. *Journal of Strategic Information Systems, 23*(1), 87–91.

Yoo, Y., Boland, R. J., Lyytinen, K., & Majchrzak, A. (2012). Organizing for innovation in the digitized world. *Organization Science, 23*(5), 1398–1408.

Zuboff, S. (1988). *In the age of the smart machine: The future of work and power*. New York: Basic Books.

16
AFFORDANCE THEORY AND HOW TO USE IT IN IS RESEARCH

Olga Volkoff and Diane M. Strong

Nothing is so practical as a good theory.

—Kurt Lewin

When Andrew van de Ven (1989) used Lewin's quote as the title for his editorial comments regarding theory in organizational research, he was probably not thinking about Affordance Theory. It would, however, have been a very apt example. As various articles in that special issue of *Academy of Management Review* (AMR) argue, the key to good theory requires not just that we identify key constructs and describe how they are related, but that those constructs and the relationships among them help us explain real-world issues. Good theory should help us explicate the generative mechanisms that underlie the phenomena we observe and want to understand (Tsoukas, 1989). Affordance Theory provides building blocks for such explanations that both explicitly incorporate the IT artifact into the analysis and are well aligned with the way practitioners who are deploying and using IT think about the challenges they face.

Not surprisingly, interest in Affordance Theory has surged among IS researchers. While there have been some growing pains during the developmental process of translating this theory from its original domain of ecological psychology to IS, including inconsistent definitions of constructs and sloppy use of terms, the enthusiasm has been rewarded with interesting and useful findings. In this chapter we aim to bring clarity to the discussion by providing clear definitions and guidelines for researchers. We also examine some of the interesting directions that have been explored to date and several thorny issues that have arisen, and highlight several questions that remain open as we move forward.

Origins of affordance theory

The IS literature already has many excellent overviews of the history of Affordance Theory (e.g., see Fayard and Weeks, 2014; Majchrzak and Markus, 2012; Markus and Silver, 2008; Robey et al., 2013; Zammuto et al., 2007, among others). Rather than repeat that material here, we provide a short overview, drawing out some specific elements that relate to the guidelines we propose for using Affordance Theory in information systems (IS) research.

Gibson (1977, 1979) articulated the original tenets of Affordance Theory to express his view that a goal-directed actor perceives an object in the environment in terms of how it can be used (what it "affords" the actor in terms of action possibilities for meeting that goal), and not as a set of characteristics or features that is inherent to the object and independent of the actor. Furthermore, these affordances are perceived directly (if they are perceived), not requiring cognitive analysis of object characteristics and features. They also exist independently of whether the actor perceives them or not. Thus a chair affords an adult human the possibility of sitting (if he or she wants to) and does not depend on that person consciously analyzing the chair's height, stability or solidity. Similarly, an email system affords a user who has appropriate capabilities the possibility of communicating.

Subsequent to Gibson's original work, a debate ensued among ecological psychologists to clarify various ontological issues. While Turvey (1992) considered affordances to be a property of the environment, paired with and relative to actors who have the capability to actualize those affordances, Stoffregen (2003, p. 123) argued that affordances do not exist in the objects or the environment alone, but "are relational (i.e., emergent) properties of the animal-environment system." Chemero (2003) disagreed that affordances are properties of the relationship, and defined them as the relations themselves between particular aspects of animals and particular aspects of situations. Within a few years, these different authors converged on a shared understanding. In a joint article, Chemero and Turvey (2007) wrote that "both Turvey and Chemero understand their views of affordances as claiming that affordances are emergent, relational properties of animal-environment systems" and presented a united front to oppose those who defined affordances as mental representations, arguing that such views directly contradicted Gibson's intention.

Before this debate was resolved, researchers in other fields started to adopt the notion of affordances with the inevitable result that the term has been used in contradictory ways. Fortunately, some dominant themes are appearing. A main theme in technology-related fields mirrors the Chemero and Turvey perspective previously noted, that affordances arise from the relation between users and technology (and are not of the technology itself). Another theme is that affordances relate to action possibilities for goal-directed actors, not to actual actions, and also not to objects or states. This latter distinction, however, has often been blurred in the IS literature, as will be discussed later.

Before turning to our discussion of the issues involved with using Affordance Theory in IS research, we briefly explore one of the main alternative uses of Affordance Theory in technology-related literature, namely its application to the design of everyday objects and its resultant use in human-computer interaction studies, as inspired by Norman (1988). As opposed to the view that affordances are "real," existing apart from the actor's perception, but arising from the relation between the object and the actor (i.e., the view of Chemero, 2003; Robey et al., 2012; and the view subscribed to in this chapter), Norman (1988) used the term to refer to both perceived and actual properties of an object, without reference to an associated actor. While even in this original use Norman acknowledged his deviation from Gibson, some years later he publicly regretted his use of the term, as it had taken on several new and sometimes inappropriate meanings. Specifically, Norman (1999) points out the differences across three related but separate elements, namely (a) an affordance, (b) an actor's perception of that affordance (where the two may or may not coincide), and (c) the visual feedback or information the object supplies to suggest an affordance. Interface designers are interested in ensuring that the visual feedback available, (c), helps ensure that the other two, (a and b), are in sync. Human-computer interaction (HCI) research is about how to make that happen. One helpful distinction is to recognize that the HCI/Norman view of affordances relates to the usability of an object, whereas the original Gibsonian view relates to its usefulness (McGrenere and Ho, 2000). This latter, functional perspective focuses on what the potential actions afforded by the technology-user relationship are intended to accomplish, rather than the details of those actions in any particular situation. We now turn to this functional perspective, that is, to Gibson's original view, and its application to IS research.

Adapting affordance theory for IS research

Among the perennial topics in IS research is the exploration of how technology is selected and used, either by individuals or groups of organizational actors, and the resulting changes in organizational processes and structures. An ongoing challenge in this work has been to adequately acknowledge the materiality of technology while avoiding the two extremes of technological determinism and social constructivism (Leonardi and Barley, 2010; Robey et al., 2012). Affordance Theory takes a socio-technical perspective that lets us be specific about the technology while simultaneously incorporating social and contextual elements. Over the past decade, these possibilities offered by traditional Gibsonian Affordance Theory have been recognized and calls made to employ it in our work (Markus and Silver, 2008; Zammuto et al., 2007). Those calls have been answered by many researchers who have made interesting and useful discoveries.

As mentioned earlier, early writers in this area focused on introducing and examining Affordance Theory itself by looking at its origins and what it promises the IS field. Subsequently there were a variety of second-order reflections on the use of Affordance Theory in IS research. For example, the transition from individual to organizational use of artifacts required not only a new definition of affordances with implications for theory building (Strong et al., 2014) and a discussion of underlying ontology (Volkoff and Strong, 2013), but also an introduction of new constructs, such as consideration of shared and collective affordances (Leonardi, 2013), and new methodologies, such as using an affordance approach to support computational analysis of routines (Gaskin et al., 2014).

Where Affordance Theory really becomes useful, however, is when we start utilizing it as a lens for changing how we look at a variety of IS topics rather than simply examining the theory itself. One theme that has emerged is a fresh look at the familiar topic of IS adoption, adaptation and organizational change. For example, Leonardi (2011) uses an affordance lens to build his theory of imbrication to explain adaptations users make either to routines or to the technology they use. In contrast to examining emergent change as per Leonardi, Seidel et al. (2013) used an affordance lens to understand how technology might proactively support a desired change, in their case to change business practices to be more environmentally sustainable. More recently, Glowalla et al. (2014) used an affordance lens to examine differences in how organizations appropriate business intelligence software.

Within this general theme of organizational change viewed through an affordance lens, the study of organizational routines has emerged as an interesting subtheme (Robey et al., 2012). Examples include looking at a health information system implementation in a hospital (Goh et al., 2011), at the relationship between mobile apps and routines (Boillat et al., 2015) and a process of looking at networks of actualized affordances to analyze routines (Pentland et al., 2015).

One specific domain where the affordance lens has been used productively is the adoption and use of social media. For example, Treem and Leonardi (2013) examined how social media use within organizations can affect such processes as socialization, knowledge sharing, and the exercise of power. Majchrzak et al. (2013) show how four different affordances associated with the use of social media to support knowledge sharing induce a shift from a process that is centralized, intermittent and repository based to a set of continuous online communal knowledge conversations that are decentralized, continuous and emergent. Jung and Lyytinen (2014) provide an "ecological account" of media choices made by users, that is, one that is grounded simultaneously in the materiality of each medium and social interaction factors.

Another specific domain has been the use of an affordance lens to look at software development. For example, van Osch and Mendelson (2011) looked at users and developers as they used various tools, from which they developed a typology of affordances as designed, improvised or emergent. More recently Krancher and Luther (2015) employed an affordance lens to explain how the use of platform-as-a-service changes the work of software development teams.

Unfortunately, while there have been many valuable contributions based on Affordance Theory, it has also been used in ways that are inconsistent with each other, and that contradict Gibson's original intention. These concerns apply even to some of the otherwise notable examples given earlier. Furthermore, the theory has, to some extent, become the "flavour of the month." As a result, Affordance Theory is included in many papers (whether of value or not) and anything and everything related to IT artifacts is being labelled an affordance.

One reason for the confusion about how to use Affordance Theory in IS research has been the challenge of translating Affordance Theory from its origins as an examination of individual actors engaging with individual objects to a study of groups of organizational actors engaging with complex, somewhat opaque objects, namely information systems. This has required a number of extensions to the original theory. For example, Strong et al. (2014), wanting to study the implementation of an electronic health record system in a multi-site medical group, found they had to address three key issues in using Affordance Theory.

First, while they determined that Affordance Theory provided a useful lens, its originators had focused on a different type of question, namely, how an actor sees an object in the environment, but not what happens when, after seeing it, that actor engages with it to do something. While the possibilities for action are important in IS research, so are the actual actions taken and the outcomes of those actions. Thus Strong et al. found they had to distinguish clearly between the affordance itself (the possibilities for goal-directed action), its actualization (the actions actually taken), and the outcomes of those actions.

Second, while at any given moment it is an individual that engages with the technology, that individual is part of various organizational structures, from local work groups engaged in collective tasks to the far-flung multi-level hierarchy that is the modern organization. This introduces a problem, namely that while an affordance relates to a goal-directed actor, we still need to know, "which or whose goal"? Not only does each actor have many goals, from personal goals to task-related goals, but he or she is also subject to group and organizational goals. Strong et al.'s approach was to focus, not on overarching goals, but rather on immediate concrete outcomes of the task being executed during the affordance actualization process.

Third, not only are there multiple actors using a complex object, but there are multiple affordances, what we call bundles of affordances (Strong et al., 2014), arising from any object-actor relation. Thus actualizing an affordance does not happen in a vacuum, and we need to consider the bundles of affordances and the ways these affordances interact.

With all these issues in mind, Strong et al. (2014) proposed a definition for the word "affordance" to accommodate the nature of affordances in organizations:

> *An affordance is* the potential for behaviors associated with achieving an immediate concrete outcome and arising from the relation between an artifact and a goal-oriented actor or actors.
>
> (p. 69)

Six principles for using affordance theory in IS research

Several key points flow from the preceding definition of an affordance and the analysis that led up to it. We articulate these points as six principles for using Affordance Theory in IS research (Strong and Volkoff, 2016).

Principle 1: remember that an affordance arises from the user/artifact relation, not just from the artifact

While already discussed several times, it is important to remember that affordances arise from the relation between the technology and the actor. It is very easy for authors writing about affordances to slip into language and arguments that treat affordances as though they are the same as features of the technology. A technical artifact does not have any affordances except in relation to a goal-directed actor. That said, it does not have to be a specific actor (until we move to actualization), but can be thought of as an archetypal actor with a set of defined tasks related to a specific goal.

Principle 2: maintain the distinction between an affordance and its actualization

The preceding definition highlights the critical distinction between an affordance and its actualization. The affordance, as the potential for action with respect to an actor's goals, refers to function (what the affordance is useful for or the purpose of the action), that is, an affordance is the potential for achieving a goal. As such its definition will be somewhat abstract and applies across potential actors with that goal and associated capabilities. The actualization, as the action itself, is specific and relates to structure, not function, where structure focuses not on the purpose of the action, but the actual configuration of behaviours that make up the action (Burton-Jones and Gallivan, 2007; Morgeson and Hofmann, 1999). Thus, while affordances relate to potential actions and the purpose they are intended to achieve, actualization relates to a particular individual actor and details regarding the specific actions that actor will take or has taken.

Principle 3: focus on the action, not the state or condition reached after taking the action

An affordance is about potential action, not about the state or condition that is reached after an action is taken. The immediate concrete outcome is the state reached after an affordance has been actualized. The problem is that when we focus on the state or condition reached, the research differs little from IS impacts research, and in particular, can lose sight of the need to understand the role of technology and user actions, that is, the mechanisms involved that provide the explanatory power that is a core contribution of using Affordance Theory. To accomplish this focus, it helps to be careful in our naming conventions for affordances by using a verb participle, such as "sitting" or "communicating," reserving noun forms for the immediate concrete outcome that results.

Principle 4: select an appropriate level(s) of granularity for the affordances

The definition of an affordance says nothing about the level of granularity that is appropriate, other than that it relates to an actor or actors who are capable of action and an artifact with various features. In fact, Gibson makes it clear that in his view affordances are nested. He uses the example that at one level an apple affords a human the possibility of eating, but that this is composed of lower-level affordances such as biting, chewing and swallowing. Similarly, an individual using an email system is afforded not only the possibility of communicating, but also the possibility of first composing and then sending a message.

The appropriate level of analysis is dictated by the question at hand. Of course just as an affordance can be decomposed into lower-level affordances, affordances can also be aggregated into higher level, and generally more abstract, affordances.

It is often at this more abstract level where the distinction between action potential and state or outcome (Principle 3) becomes somewhat blurred. Thus, for example, our literature contains many references to a "visibility" affordance. This is, however, a state, and masks the associated actions – and even the actor. Visibility is associated with two types of actors, the provider of the information and the receiver. The former, by "inputting data," might, in the course of "making information visible" be engaging in various activities, from "revealing information" (sometimes inadvertently), "telling" (deliberately), or "promoting" (actively). Similarly, the receiver, by "accessing data," may be "observing," "monitoring" or "investigating." The outcome "visibility" might be the subject of many interesting research questions. The power of the Affordance lens is that it helps to pinpoint the actors involved and the variety of potential actions they might engage in as they use the technology. Actualizing those affordances results in a particular outcome, namely visibility.

Principle 5: identify all salient affordances and how they interact

In addition to the affordances that are nested within any affordance, there are many other affordances available arising from the relation between the technical artifact and the actors. These are not independent, but rather interact. Unlike Gibson, we are generally not interested in a single affordance, but in the bundles of affordances that arise from the many potential uses of an IT artifact. Often, more sophisticated affordances (such as monitoring) depend on successful actualization of more basic affordances (such as inputting data), generating a dependence network of affordances (Strong et al., 2014). Affordances may support other affordances or may interfere with them, generating a number of interesting research questions. Again, the identification of which affordances to focus on depends on the research question being asked.

Principle 6: recognize social forces that affect affordance actualization

Affordances are not actualized in a vacuum, but rather in a social context. Thus, social forces, arising from the groups within which the actors operate, also affect how, how well, or even whether any affordance will be actualized. In addition to analyzing traditional social mechanisms such as group or cultural norms that can enhance or constrain the actualization of an affordance (Bloomfield et al., 2010), we need to consider how the presence of other people using the same artifact for similar or related purposes will affect an actor's behaviour.

One way to do this is to use Leonardi's (2013) differentiation among individual, shared, and collective affordances. An individual affordance is actualized by one actor acting independently of others; a shared affordance is the same affordance being actualized by many people in similar ways; while a collective affordance involves many people doing different things to accomplish a joint goal. For IT artifacts used in an organizational context, the concepts of shared and collective affordances are important. As computing becomes more ubiquitous, IS researchers are also interested in individual affordances, for example, for individual healthcare support apps. In all three cases, IS researchers are likely to be more interested in the bundles of affordances available to users, often across more than one IT artifact, than in investigating a single affordance.

Unresolved issues

These six principles are fairly straightforward, and if followed consistently with rare violations, they can go a long way toward removing the confusion and inconsistencies that can occur when IS researchers apply Affordance Theory without due consideration. There remain, however, some unresolved, vexing questions for researchers applying an Affordance lens to IS research.

Issue 1: do affordances have to be perceived to be actualized?

The first of these issues is the various views that have been expressed regarding what it means to "perceive" an affordance, and whether affordances must be perceived to be actualized. Part of the issue is how the word "perceived" is defined in the first place. When Gibson introduced Affordance Theory, his whole purpose was to understand how actors perceive objects in the environment; that is, Affordance Theory is a theory about and redefinition of perception. His insight was that actors, in general, do not process what they see through cognitive filters, but rather that they process the information in a more intuitive manner, focusing on affordances. What he also said, however, is that affordances do not need to be perceived to be actualized.

This leads to two points. The first is that the construct "perception" needs to be carefully defined before being used. At present it is used to cover everything from mindful, cognitive awareness through practical or physical awareness, to subliminal or intuitive awareness. While all of these are legitimate possibilities, Gibson's whole argument is that the first form is not the way we generally operate. Thus an actor wanting a drink of water will automatically, and with little or no thought, reach for a cup, not a fork.

The second point is that an actor may actualize an affordance without being aware of its existence at all, not even at an intuitive level. This is particularly true when the artifact in question is complex and somewhat opaque, such as an information system. For example, a person using a technology such as Facebook, who is deliberately actualizing a "communicating" affordance by posting something for his or her friends to see is often simultaneously actualizing a "broadcasting" affordance whereby unknown others also have access to the information (for example if it gets commented on or tagged by someone and so ends up appearing in other places). A similar situation arises when the user of an enterprise system enters data – actualizes a "data inputting" affordance. That actor may not be as aware of actualizing the associated "broadcasting" affordance, which in turn triggers or enables additional affordances, such as a "monitoring" affordance, for other actors such as managers.

Of course, while an actor does not "need" to perceive an affordance to actualize it, it may well be that mindful actualization makes the user of an artifact more effective. This leads to a variety of interesting research questions regarding threshold levels of awareness needed for effective use, or the types of affordances for which unintentional actualization is more likely to occur. Similarly, such an analysis may help to explain or prevent unexpected outcomes.

Given these concerns, the term "perceived affordances" should be avoided. It introduces confusion because Gibson's theory is already a theory of perception and because the concept of "perceived" means many things. As such, the term "level of awareness" of an affordance may provide better terminology than referring to "perceived affordances."

Issue 2: are affordances both enabling and constraining or only enabling?

A different question relates to whether affordances can be both enabling and constraining, or whether affordances are only enabling, and constraints are different. Certainly our literature has examples of both perspectives. In support of the "just enablement" view, it could be argued that the plain language meaning of the word "affording" refers to enablement. In addition, it seems unlikely that an actor would deliberately actualize an affordance that constrained his or her actions.

Hutchby (2001), one of the earlier researchers to apply Affordance Theory to technology, used it to argue that technical objects cannot be viewed simply as "texts" that are read and interpreted by users with complete flexibility. Although an individual's interpretations and social processes do influence how such objects are used, technical objects also have material properties that both enable and constrain users while not determining what those users will do, nor what the outcomes of use of such an object will be. What is not clear from his work is whether the associated affordances embody both enablement and constraint, or only the former. The case for both enablement and constraint is made clearer by Zammuto et al. (2007, p. 752), when they state that "An affordance perspective recognizes how the materiality of an object favors, shapes, or invites, and at the same time constrains, a set of specific uses."

Like Zammuto et al., we argue that affordances embody both enablement and constraint; that is, like most things, affordances are often two-edged swords. When one thing is enabled, something else is simultaneously constrained, simply because the two are incompatible, and the enabling and constraining aspects are not separable. Thus a locking mechanism on a door affords an actor a barricading affordance, which might be seen as enabling if the actor's goal is privacy or protection, but would also be seen as constraining by preventing that individual from escaping if threatened. Similarly, using an enterprise system to actualize a data inputting affordance enables an actor to record the day's activities (which may be required for payment of wages) but simultaneously constrains the same actor from hiding the long lunch hour taken. It is because of this two-sided nature that we subscribe to the "affordances as both enabling and constraining" point of view. This also aligns with Gibson's original views on this topic.

Issue 3: how "capable" does an actor have to be for an affordance to apply?

Finally, Affordance Theory implies that the actor involved is "capable" of actualizing the associated affordance. The question that arises is whether this means "physically capable" (i.e., has the manual dexterity and strength required) or whether it also demands knowledge of how to execute the action. Gibson mostly considered simple everyday objects such as rocks or stairs where physical ability mattered, but skill *per se* did not.

When we are confronted with a new system on which we have not yet been trained, are there any affordances? One answer might be "no" because we may have insufficient knowledge to have any sense of potential actions we might take or of the likely outcomes of such actions. In our view the answer is "yes," in large part because knowledge is not a binary characteristic, but rather an emerging and ever-changing one. An actor might actualize an affordance ineffectively to start with, but over time and with training their skill level will increase. In the same way that affordances exist whether or not an actor is aware of them, we contend that the affordance as a theoretical "potential for action" exists whether or not the knowledge for how to actualize it has been acquired yet, as long as the physical capacity is there. Among other benefits, this perspective makes it easier to ask questions related to training and its outcomes.

Consistency of affordance theory with underlying philosophical perspectives

In our discussion to this point, we have not explicitly addressed the question of which underlying philosophical perspectives fit best with Affordance Theory. Specifically, Affordance Theory, like any theory, has underlying ontological assumptions about the nature of reality and underlying epistemological assumptions about what we can know. These assumptions can be more or less consistent with various philosophical perspectives and research methods typically used by IS researchers. Thus, we examine how Affordance Theory fits with the philosophical perspectives used by IS researchers.

Although Gibson does not state his philosophical orientation, others have described the critical realist nature of ecological psychology in general, and Gibson in particular (Markus and Silver, 2008; Michaels, 2003; Volkoff and Strong, 2013). Ontologically, critical realists assert the existence of an objective reality separate from us (and that includes both the physical world, and the non-physical, such as social structures). Epistemologically, they assert this reality is unknowable because researchers view it through their existing knowledge and biases. Furthermore, researchers can only view empirically observable events, a subset of all actual events. They cannot directly view the generative mechanisms that cause actual events, nor the elements within the objective reality, and the relations between them, from which the generative mechanisms arise (O'Mahoney and Vincent, 2014; Mingers, 2004). From their observations of events, researchers can, however, retroduce what those mechanisms must be. Stating that affordances exist whether or not an actor is aware of them or not indicates an underlying realist perspective – affordances are real and while they exist in relation to the actor, they do not exist only in the mind of the actor. The extent to which the actor is aware of them (if at all) will affect the actualization, but not the existence of the affordance.

Assuming the IS researcher wanting to utilize Affordance Theory is a critical realist, what does it mean for the research itself and the way it is conducted? For those of us who are critical realists, the objective of doing research is to identify the underlying mechanisms that generate the phenomena we want to understand. Those mechanisms are not deterministic, so the goal is not to predict outcomes, but to explain them. The better we understand the bundle of affordances at play in a situation – both what they are and how they interact – the better we are able to understand events as they unfold and likely directions going forward. That said, Affordance Theory is not the explanation itself, but rather provides a new way of seeing things that makes identifying the mechanisms easier.

For the many IS researchers who are not critical realists or who focus on research questions that are not seeking to find explanatory mechanisms, Affordance Theory can also be useful, as long as we appreciate the underlying philosophical assumptions. For example, those of us taking a positivist perspective and aiming to build causal models hold ontological views similar to critical realists, namely that an objective reality exists, separate from us. Where these two camps diverge is over epistemology, as positivists believe reality is knowable, and hence our research should focus on that which we can see and measure in order to test theoretical propositions. Positivists will find that Affordance Theory does not directly generate predictions that can be tested. First, because they are potentials for action that users may not even be aware of, and in any case may never actualize, affordances cannot be treated as measurable constructs. Second, affordance actualization captures a non-deterministic process guided by various users' goals, thus lacking the causality needed for predicting actualization outcomes.

That said, the real nature of affordances is aligned with a positivist perspective. By using Affordance Theory as a lens for thinking about the interactions between a technical artifact and users, we can ask questions that would be amenable to developing and testing causal models. For example, as mentioned earlier, we might explore the extent to which mindful actualization mattered more for some affordances than others, a question that can be examined empirically. The key would be first to understand the bundle of affordances and how they interact well enough to see where actualization without mindfulness inhibits effective use of a system. Similarly, issues of training – what to train on and how to design training – can be explored once the bundle of affordances is identified. Identifying the bundle of affordances, however, is easier after actualization, but even then, some affordances may still not be recognized or may only be recognized and actualized by a few of the many users.

While not often articulated (for exceptions see Carlsson, 2010; Gregg et al., 2001; Purao, 2013), the ontology of design science focuses on a reality that has not yet been created, although, like positivism and critical realism, it accepts that this reality exists separate from us once created. The difference between design science and positivism is that while the latter focuses on understanding relationships as they are, design science focuses on what reality might look like in the future – and recognizes that the outcome is not preordained. Indeed, both the products of design and the design process itself evolve. As with critical realism, then, design science has a focus on the mechanisms underlying the process. For that reason, Affordance Theory should serve an IS researcher taking a design science approach extremely well. By identifying potential affordances, both those that are explicitly designed and those that emerge, arising because of interactions or even unintended uses, our designs can be improved. In fact, affordances are similar in many ways to use case scenarios.

While Affordance Theory is, in general, a useful lens, it seems less appropriate for use by those of us who are pure interpretivists, as we would be less comfortable with the notion of affordances being real and existing whether or not they are recognized. What Affordance Theory does offer is an inexorable connection between the social and the technical. Affordances do not exist in either the artifact or the user – they are of the relation between the two. The difference between this view and pure socio-materiality is that even in the relation the social and the material are held apart – they are not so intermingled as to be indistinguishable, just as the two strands that make up the double helix of a DNA molecule are both integral to that molecule yet remain separate. In this sense, Affordance Theory provides a lens consistent with the perspective of those of us who prefer a socio-technical perspective.

Conducting IS research using an affordance theory lens

Affordance Theory, used correctly (i.e., following the six principles discussed earlier), provides a variety of research opportunities for IS researchers to be specific about the technology while also incorporating the social context. In this section, we highlight a few of those opportunities.

Before doing so, we note two caveats. First, when thinking about using Affordance Theory, IS researchers should consider the underlying philosophical perspective they are using to be sure Affordance Theory provides an appropriate and consistent lens for their research. Second, IS researchers should consider whether and how Affordance Theory adds value to a study. Affordance Theory provides IS researchers with many new opportunities, but it is not a good fit for every study, nor is it a replacement for the many different approaches we already have for conducting excellent IS research.

For IS researchers, Affordance Theory, although a theory itself, provides a lens for developing a variety of mid-level socio-technical theories. That is, using Affordance Theory in IS research is not simply an application of an existing theory, but rather is a new way of thinking about the artifact/user relationship that can be useful for generating new socio-technical theories. Those new theories are necessarily mid-level rather than grand theories because they are grounded in specific technologies and users.

One area of IS research opportunity is identifying affordances. When we study affordances, we can connect them to artifacts at various levels – from the broad system level such as "an enterprise system" to a feature level such as different types of input media. Generalizability is not to all technology (which makes the artifact vanish), but rather to common functional aspects of a type of technology. Enterprise systems are different from each other, but they are even more different from gaming platforms. There will be generalizations we can make about the former once we understand how the features that are common to enterprise systems are implicated in affordances with typical enterprise system users. Similarly, we can explore various affordances arising from actors engaging with different social media. We can also compare affordances across technology and user types, as Volkoff and Strong (2013) did in their re-analysis of their enterprise systems study and Leonardi's engineering support systems study. We can generate useful knowledge by developing theory around affordances and their connections to technology features and to user characteristics, goals and capabilities. For example, connecting affordances to associated technology features can help us better understand and conceptualize the IT artifact, which in turn can help us create better IT artifact designs. Similarly, by connecting affordances to associated user characteristics, goals and capabilities, we can design artifacts that are easier to use, and also can better understand training needs and create better training materials.

When identifying affordances, we must remember that an IT artifact provides multiple affordances, that is, bundles of affordances, to users, and these affordances are interconnected and interdependent in various ways. These connections and interdependencies can be studied. For example, Strong et al. (2014) proposed studying temporal networks of affordance dependencies, focusing on the sequence in which affordances could be actualized because the actualization of some affordances depend on previous actualization of other affordances. Lindberg et al. (2014) proposes studying the ecology or configuration of affordances across multiple IT artifacts because in practice users are choosing to actualize multiple affordances available from multiple IT artifacts simultaneously.

Another area of IS research opportunity focuses more on affordance actualization and seeks to identify mechanisms for organizational change. Focusing on actualization provides the foundation for our ultimate goal of increasing our understanding of the resulting changes in organizations as affordances are actualized. In doing so, we can provide practical insights to managers attempting to effect change through effective use of technologies. Using the Affordance Theory lens, we explicitly acknowledge that technology does not determine effects, but also that there is the possibility of guiding the actualization process so that desired effects are more likely and unintended consequences are recognized and managed. With a focus on actualization, we can build mid-range theories of IT implementation and IT-enabled organizational change that focus on specific technologies and specific organizational goals.

An emerging opportunity is to use more quantitative techniques to study affordances and their actualization. For example, as we think of bundles of affordances and their actualizations in terms of networks, sequences or configurations of these affordances, we could employ various network analysis tools to analyze and understand those configurations. Furthermore, because actualizing many of the affordances of interest to IS researchers typically involves using an IT artifact, that usage can be tracked, enabling associated "market basket" analysis of which artifact features are used together (Lindberg et al., 2014). While feature use is not the same as an affordance actualization, one can track who the user was and perhaps develop an understanding of the user goals.

Finally, although early IS researchers using Affordance Theory have done much to adapt Affordance Theory to the IS research context, there are still unresolved issues as noted earlier. We expect that, as IS researchers continue to use Affordance Theory, adaptations will continue to evolve to capture how Affordance Theory can be best used across the many research perspectives that underlie IS research.

Conclusion

Affordance Theory's focus on the relation between the IT artifact and users, while also maintaining the distinction between them, is what allows us to bring the IT artifact back into our research. Through Affordance Theory we finally have a way to be specific about the technology while incorporating the social context in mid-range socio-technical theories. To do so, we must focus on mid-range theories to avoid generalizing so much that we lose the artifact again.

As noted in the opening quote by Lewin, good theory can provide practical guidance to managers as they try to address real-world issues. Managers need actionable suggestions, and can become frustrated when presented with abstract notions that are often largely self-evident. Research employing Affordance Theory can provide useful guidance in many ways, enabling IS researchers to provide research results of relevance to managers. For example, simply identifying individual affordances enables managers to ensure system users are aware of the possibilities presented by a given technology. Conscious articulation of the expected outcomes associated with these affordances supports analysis of whether users are actualizing the affordances effectively. Identifying bundles of affordances and their dependencies can help explain how interdependencies generate blockages for achieving expected benefits, or highlight external factors that might interfere with actualization. Similarly, surfacing unrecognized affordances may explain unexpected and unintended outcomes. Such analyses can also improve how groups of users jointly actualize either shared or collective affordances.

Finally, the affordance lens enables improvements to the design of IT artifacts and the work practices surrounding those artifacts, as we better understand the bundles of affordances and their interactions that IT artifacts provide to capable users. Overall, Affordance Theory – if appropriately employed – allows researchers to create for managers a new set of levers for solving practical problems.

Acknowledgements

We thank the participants in seminars at Victoria University in Wellington, New Zealand; University of Canterbury in Christchurch, New Zealand; University of Queensland in Brisbane, Australia; the University of the Witwatersrand in Johannesburg, South Africa; and Rhodes University in Grahamstown, South Africa for their helpful feedback and the many stimulating discussions before and after those seminars. We also thank the editors of this volume for the invitation to contribute a chapter, and comments on the early versions. Finally, we acknowledge support from both the Beedie School of Business, Simon Fraser University, and Worcester Polytechnic Institute.

References

Bloomfield, B., Latham, Y. & Vurdubakis, T. (2010). Bodies, technologies and action possibilities: When is an affordance? *Sociology*, (44:3), pp. 415–433.
Boillat, T., Lienhard, K. & Legner, C. (2015). Entering the world of individual routines: The affordances of mobile applications. *Proceedings of the Thirty-Sixth International Conference on Information Systems*, Fort Worth, 2015, pp. 1–18.

Burton-Jones, A. & Gallivan, M. J. (2007). Toward a deeper understanding of system usage in organizations: A multilevel perspective. *MIS Quarterly*, (31:4), pp. 657–679.

Carlsson, S. A. (2010). Design science research in information systems: A critical realist approach. In A. Hevner & S. Chatterjee (Eds.), *Design research in information systems* (pp. 209–233). Integrated Series in Information Systems 22. New York: Springer Science+Business Media, LLC.

Chemero, A. (2003). An outline of a theory of affordances. *Ecological Psychology*, (15:2), pp. 181–195.

Chemero, A. & Turvey, M. (2007). Hypersets, complexity, and the ecological approach to perception-action. *Biological Theory*, (2:1), pp. 23–36.

Fayard, A.-L. & Weeks, J. (2014). Affordances for practice. *Information and Organization*, (24:4), pp. 236–249.

Gaskin, J., Berente, N., Lyytinen, K. & Yoo, Y. (2014). Toward generalizable sociomaterial inquiry: A computational approach for zooming in and out of sociomaterial routines. *MIS Quarterly*, (38:3), pp. 849–871.

Gibson, J. (1977). The theory of affordances. In R.E.S.J. Bransford (Ed.), *Perceiving, acting, and knowing: Toward an ecological psychology* (pp. 67–82). Hillsdale, NJ: Lawrence Erlbaum Associates.

Gibson, J. (1979). *The ecological approach to visual perception*. Boston: Houghton Mifflin.

Glowalla, P., Rosenkranz, C. & Sunyaev, A. (2014). Evolution of IT use: A case of business intelligence system transition. *Proceedings of the Thirty-Fifth International Conference on Information Systems*, Auckland, 2014, pp. 1–19.

Goh, J. M., Gao, G. & Agarwal, R. (2011). Evolving work routines: Adaptive routinization of information technology in healthcare. *Information Systems Research*, (22:3), pp. 565–585.

Gregg, D. G., Kulkarni, U. R. & Vinzé, A. S. (2001). Understanding the philosophical underpinnings of software engineering research in information systems. *Information Systems Frontiers*, (3:2), pp. 169–183.

Hutchby, I. (2001). Technologies, texts and affordances. *Sociology*, (35:2), pp. 441–456.

Jung, Y. & Lyytinen, K. (2014). Towards an ecological account of media choice: A case study on pluralistic reasoning while choosing email. *Information Systems Journal*, (24:3), pp. 271–293.

Krancher, O. & Luther, P. (2015). Software development in the cloud: Exploring the affordances of platform-as-a-service. *Proceedings of the Thirty-Sixth International Conference on Information Systems*, Fort Worth, 2015, pp. 1–19.

Leonardi, P. M. (2011). When flexible routines meet flexible technologies: Affordance, constraint, and the imbrication of human and material agencies. *MIS Quarterly*, (35:1), pp. 147–167.

Leonardi, P. M. (2013). When does technology use enable network change in organizations? A comparative study of feature use and shared affordances. *MIS Quarterly* (37:3), pp. 749–775.

Leonardi, P. M. & Barley, S. R. (2010). What's under construction here? Social action, materiality, and power in constructivist studies of technology and organizing. *Academy of Management Annals*, (4:1), pp. 1–51.

Lindberg, A., Gaskin, J., Berente, N. & Lyytinen, K. (2014). Exploring configurations of affordances: The case of software development. *Proceedings of the Twentieth Americas Conference on Information Systems*, Savannah, 2014, pp. 1–12.

Majchrzak, A., Faraj, S., Kane, G. C. & Azad, B. (2013). The contradictory influence of social media affordances on online communal knowledge sharing. *Journal of Computer-Mediated Communication*, (19:1), pp. 38–55.

Majchrzak, A. & Markus, M. L. (2012). Technology affordances and constraints in management information systems (MIS). In E. Kessler (Ed.), *Encyclopedia of management theory, Vol. 2* (pp. 832–835). Los Angeles, CA: Sage.

Markus, M. L. & Silver, M. (2008). A foundation for the study of IT effects: A new look at DeSanctis and Poole's concepts of structural features and spirit. *Journal of the Association for Information Systems*, (9:10/11), pp. 609–632.

McGrenere, J. & Ho, W. (2000). Affordances: Clarifying and evolving a concept. *Proceedings of Graphics Interface 2000*, Montreal, Quebec, May 15–17.

Michaels, C. F. (2003). Affordances: Four points of debate. *Ecological Psychology*, (15:2), pp. 135–148.

Mingers, J. (2004). Real-izing information systems: Critical realism as an underpinning philosophy for information systems. *Information and Organization*, (14:2), pp. 87–103.

Morgeson, F. P. & Hofmann, D. A. (1999). The structure and function of collective constructs: Implications for multilevel research and theory development. *Academy of Management Review*, (24:2), pp. 249–265.

Norman, D.A. (1988). *The psychology of everyday things*. New York: Basic Books.
Norman, D.A. (1999). Affordance, conventions, and design. *Interactions*, (6:3), pp. 38–42.
O'Mahoney, J. & Vincent, S. (2014). Critical realism as an empirical project. In P.K. Edwards, J. O'Mahoney & S. Vincent (Eds.), *Studying organizations using critical realism* (pp. 1–20). Oxford: Oxford University Press.
Pentland, B., Recker, J. & Wyner, G. (2015). A thermometer for interdependence: exploring patterns of interdependence using networks of affordances. *Proceedings of the Thirty-sixth International Conference on Information Systems*, Fort Worth, 2015, pp. 1–11.
Purao, S. (2013). Truth or dare: The ontology question in design science research. *Journal of Database Management*, (24:3), pp. 51–66.
Robey, D., Anderson, C. & Raymond, B. (2013). Information technology, materiality, and organizational change: A professional odyssey. *Journal of the Association for Information Systems*, (14:7), pp. 379–398.
Robey, D., Raymond, B. & Anderson, C. (2012). Theorizing information technology as a material artifact in information systems research. In P. Leonardi, B. Nardi & J. Kallinikos (Eds.), *Materiality and organizing: Social interaction in a technological world* (pp. 217–236). New York: Oxford University Press.
Seidel, S., Recker, J. & vom Brocke, J. (2013). Sensemaking and sustainable practicing: Functional affordances of information systems in green transformations, *MIS Quarterly*, (37:4), pp. 1275–1299.
Stoffregen, T. (2003). Affordances as properties of the animal-environment system. *Ecological Psychology*, (15:2), pp. 115–134.
Strong, D.M. & Volkoff, O. (2016). *Principles for conducting and evaluating IS research that uses an affordance theory lens*. Working paper.
Strong, D.M., Volkoff, O., Johnson, S.A., Pelletier, L.R., Tulu, B., Bar-On, I., Trudel, J. & Garber, L. 2014. A theory of organization-EHR affordance actualization. *Journal of the Association for Information Systems*, (15:2), pp. 53–85.
Treem, J.W. & Leonardi, P.M. (2013). Social media use in organizations: Exploring the affordances of visibility, editability, persistence, and association. *Communication Yearbook* (36), pp. 143–189.
Tsoukas, H. (1989). The validity of ideographic research explanations. *Academy of Management Review*, (14:4), pp. 551–561.
Turvey, M. (1992). Affordances and prospective control: An outline of the ontology. *Ecological Psychology*, (4:3), pp. 173–187.
Van de Ven, A.H. (1989). Nothing is quite so practical as a good theory. *Academy of Management Review*, (14:4), pp. 486–489.
van Osch, W. & Mendelson, O. (2011). A typology of affordances: Untangling sociomaterial interactions through video analysis. *Proceedings of the Thirty-Second International Conference on Information Systems*, Shanghai, 2011, pp. 1–17.
Volkoff, O. & Strong, D.M. (2013). Critical realism and affordances: Theorizing IT-associated organizational change processes. *MIS Quarterly*, (37:3), pp. 819–834.
Zammuto, R.F., Griffith, T.L., Majchrzak, A., Dougherty, D.J. & Faraj, S. (2007). Information technology and the changing fabric of organization. *Organization Science*, (18:5), pp. 749–762.

PART 3

Managing organisational IS, knowledge and innovation

Introduction

Having discussed the development, adoption and use of information systems (IS) in Part 2, we turn now to a consideration of management issues associated with IS use, together with aspects of innovation and knowledge sharing across organisations. We start with the topic of digital infrastructures and major enterprise systems, and then go on to consider required organisational capabilities and sourcing issues, before considering innovation on the back information technology, aligning IS with strategic imperatives and knowledge sharing. All of these topics are of key concern for organisations and, while treated separately in this Companion, are inter-related and go to make up the range of management concerns that should form the management armoury when it comes to the astute leverage of modern-day information technologies to good effect.

We commence in Chapter 17 with a contribution by Kalle Lyytinen, Carsten Sørensen and David Tilson that considers "Generativity in Digital Infrastructures." The chapter notes the growth in scale and scope of such infrastructures over recent years, with cloud-based services across personal, local and global networks now being commonplace. These highly complex socio-technical systems process, store and transfer data on a global scale and present a significant challenge to management and researchers alike. Thus, in this chapter, Lyytinen, Sørensen and Tilson explore this emerging topic from the standpoint of generativity, which they define as from-within, inherent recursive growth in the diversity, scale, and embeddedness associated with digital infrastructures. Noting a distinction between digital infrastructures and earlier information infrastructures such as telecommunications, they develop a conceptual model that is organised around dimensions that capture the tangible and intangible sources of infrastructural coordination and the social as well as technical nature of infrastructural arrangements. They argue that the tensions inherent in the model "create the properties of emergence and complexity that drive the generativity and growth associated with digital infrastructures." A set of principles that arise from this conception is presented along with a number of challenges that we need to face as our understanding of how generativity emerges and drives the growth of digital infrastructures.

As noted, innovation is a recurring theme in this part of the Companion. Thus, in Chapter 18, means by which such established technologies as enterprise systems can lead to innovation in organisations are considered. Written by Darshana Sedera and Sachithra Lokuge, the chapter notes that, while the advent of enterprise systems established a pathway for organisational innovation, more recent additions to the corporate IT portfolio – such as cloud computing, mobile, wearables and social media – have increased the number of opportunities for organisations to innovate on the back of technology. In discussing these recent phenomena, the authors consider the changing role of enterprise systems in enabling organisational innovation in their IT portfolios.

The ability of organisations to manage their IT portfolios effectively and to gain the best possible advantage from their investment depends crucially on organisational capabilities in this regard. Organisational capability relates to the strategic application of an organisation's competences (Kangas, 1999; Moingeon et al., 1998). Thus, in Chapter 19, Joe Peppard considers digital capability in terms of "scaffolding" and "rewiring." Noting that many organisations continue to struggle "to embrace digital opportunities and rewire themselves as digital organizations," Peppard argues that, while the technology itself plays an important role in digital transformation, building a digital capability is not so much a technology challenge as it is a challenge to harness knowledge to create the organizational knowing to continually optimize the value that can be derived from digital technologies. Given that such knowledge is dispersed across and within organisations, it is difficult to coordinate and integrate – a theme to which we shall return in subsequent chapters, including Chapter 8 in particular. Drawing on the resource-based view (RBV) of the firm (e.g., Barney, 1991; Wernerfelt, 1984) and social capital theory (e.g., Alder & Kwon, 2002; Nahapiet & Ghoshal, 1998; Tsai & Ghoshal, 1998), Peppard presents a scaffold for positioning the digital capability. This scaffold emphasises "the essential role of human action in knowing how to get things done that lies at the heart of a digital capability." The chapter concludes with a number of practice implications for building a digital capability.

Not all capabilities (technological and human) are always found within a particular organisation, and thus, in Chapter 20, we consider "Sourcing Information Technology Services." Written by Mary Lacity, Aihua Yan and Shaji Khan, this chapter reflects on extant research and calls for even more influential work on the sourcing of information technology services. Lacity, Yan and Khan review scholarly research and propose future research directions, based on their coding of 1,170 empirical relationships found in 257 journal articles published between 1992 and 2014. Their findings include the discovery that two types of dependent variables associated with sourcing tend to be studied: IT sourcing *decisions* and IT sourcing *outcomes*. As an outcome of their analysis, the authors develop models of the determinants of these decisions and outcomes: The model of ITO decisions includes 21 independent variables associated with transaction attributes, outsourcing motivations, influence sources, client characteristics and capabilities, relationship characteristics, and environmental variables. The model of ITO outcomes includes 31 independent variables associated with transaction attributes, relational and contractual governance, client and provider capabilities, client characteristics and decision characteristics. Together, these models capture, in a succinct form, the results of a considerable amount of empirical work undertaken over the years, with a view to aiding the management of sourcing relationships, both from a client and a provider perspective. The chapter goes further by helping to answer such enduring societal questions as the potential role of IT sourcing in alleviating poverty, sustaining the environment, mitigating cyber threats and adjusting to further automation.

We return to the innovation theme in Chapter 21, this time in a healthcare setting. Written by Sue Newell and Marco Marabelli, the "power of everyday practices" is brought to the fore in relation to an innovation process focused on encouraging greater coordination across a network of child care organisations dealing with complex care needs. Noting that there are no (formal) hierarchical relationships that can be used to impose the change in such settings, Newell and Marabelli point to the limitations of much of the management of change literature that focuses on the role of senior management teams in strategy making. As such, Newell and Marabelli contribute further to a theme started by Marabelli and Galliers, and Arvidsson and Holmström in Part 2. As noted there, the significant shifts brought about by digitalisation mean that much of the traditional thinking around strategy and innovation needs re-thinking. A practice view of power provides very different insights into what allows innovations to take place as compared to a resource view that assumes power depends on the resources that can be mustered by individuals 'in charge.'[1] Thus, they take a strategy-as-practice perspective to examine the everyday practices of all the stakeholders involved in a process innovation.[2]

Chapter 22 considers another vexed issue that has been the concern of senior executives for many years, namely the issue of aligning IS/IT with the business (e.g., Luftman et al., 2013). Written by Anna Karpovsky and Bob Galliers, the chapter points to the extensive literature on alignment, but considers that the topic's current research trajectory is limited given the concept's predominantly static focus to date. The authors contend that we know little about what it is that organizational actors actually do, on a day-to-day basis, to align IS and related concerns with business imperatives. Thus, they argue for research that goes beyond the abstract macro analysis of alignment processes typical of much of the extant research on the topic, arguing instead for studies that consider the actual micro practices of aligning. They analyse the limited literature that does consider aligning practices and classify the relevant activities that have been identified in the past. This is done with a view to providing insightful contributions to our understanding of aligning as enacted in practice. Arising from this analysis, Karpovsky and Galliers identify important new research themes that they argue need to be addressed if future research on alignment is to become more relevant.[3]

The following chapter, by Philipp Hukal and Ola Henfridsson, considers digital innovation specifically as an emerging area of IS research. The authors discuss certain unique characteristics of digital technology and their implications for innovation, and thus build on some of the material introduced earlier in this part – in Chapters 17 and 19 in particular. Hukal and Henfridsson define digital innovation as "the co-creation of novel offerings through recombination of digital and/or physical components." They view digital innovation as an iterative and open-ended organisational activity, and by doing so, are able to revisit such conventional assumptions concerning innovation as the producer-consumer divide, process-product distinction, and value creation. Noting that our current understanding of innovation is largely rooted in theory aimed at explaining organisational activity in the industrial age, they point to the idea that innovation has been largely based on the Schumpeterian notion (Schumpeter 1934) that "the creation of novel products [arises from] recombining production forces for market-based exchange" focused primarily on the exchange of manufactured goods. Clearly, things have moved on from the industrial age, so the authors go on to highlight the opportunities arising for the IS academy to take "an integrative digital innovation perspective" in its future research agendas.

Our final chapter in Part 3 of the Companion is by Samer Faraj, Karla Sayegh and Linda Rouleau and deals with knowledge management – or rather knowledge *sharing* – in organisations. Titled "Knowledge Collaboration in Organizations: From Information Processing to Social Knowing," the chapter makes the point that organisations have traditionally been conceptualised as information processing systems that must be appropriately coordinated to manage external and internal sources of uncertainty (Tushman & Nadler, 1978, Galbraith, 1973). The authors go on to note that, despite the ubiquity of IS/IT in modern-day organisations, coordination of knowledge work remains problematic. They argue that this is due in part to knowledge being 'sticky' and not easily transferable (Szulanski, 1996), namely: "Actors embedded in different communities of practice bring with them significant differences in problem conceptualizations and interpretive schemes, speak different technical languages and have often disparate vested interests rooted in their expertise." Misunderstandings, incorrect interpretations and attributions, and team conflicts can arise as a result. Thus, Faraj, Sayegh and Rouleau explore these challenges of knowledge sharing and the role of IS/IT in helping to ameliorate these. Topics discussed include, *inter alia*, dialogue, boundary objects, collaborative agreements and brokering roles – as well as how modern technologies are transforming the processes of knowledge co-creation.[4]

Notes

1 See also Marabelli & Galliers (2017), for example.
2 See, for example, Jarzabkowski (2005), Peppard et al. (2014) and Whittington (2006).
3 For a major prior review of the alignment literature see, for example, Chan and Reich (2007).
4 For further related reading see, for example, Star (2010), Star & Griesemer (1989), Starbuck (1992) and Tsoukas (1996).

References

Adler, P.S. & Kwon, S.W. (2002). Social capital: prospects for a new concept, *Academy of Management Review*, 27(1), 17–40.
Barney, J.B. (1991). Firm resources and sustained competitive advantage, *Journal of Management*, 17, 99–120.
Chan, Y.E. & Reich, B. (2007). IT alignment: What have we learned? *Journal of Information Technology*, 22(4), 297–315.
Galbraith, J.R. (1973). *Designing complex organizations*. Boston: Addison-Wesley Longman.
Jarzabkowski, P. (2005). *Strategy as practice: An activity-based approach*. London: Sage.
Kangas, K. (1999). Competency and capabilities based competition and the role of information technology: The case of trading by a Finland-based firm to Russia, *Journal of Information Technology Cases and Applications*, 1(2), 4–22.
Luftman, J., Zadeh, H.S., Derksen, B., Santana, M., Rigoni, E.H. & Huang, D. (2013). Key information technology and management issues 2012–2013: An international study, *Journal of Information Technology*, 28(4): 354–366.
Marabelli, M. & Galliers, R.D. (2017). A reflection on information systems strategizing: The role of power and everyday practices, *Information Systems Journal*, 27(3), 347–366.
Moingeon, B., Ramanantsoa, B, Métais, E. & Orton, J.D. (1998). Another look at strategy–structure relationships: The resource-based view, *European Management Journal*, 16(3), 298–304.
Nahapiet, J. & Ghoshal, S. (1998), Social capital, intellectual capital, and the organizational advantage, *Academy of Management Review*, 23, 242–266.
Peppard, J., Galliers, R.D. & Thorogood, A. (2014). Information systems strategy as practice: Micro strategy and strategizing for IS, *Journal of Strategic Information Systems*, 23(1), 1–10.
Schumpeter, J.A. (1934). *The theory of economic development: An inquiry into profits, capital, credit, interest, and the business cycle*, Harvard Economic Studies 46, Cambridge, MA.
Star, S.L. (2010). This is not a boundary object: Reflections on the origin of a concept, *Science, Technology & Human Values*, 35(5), 601–617.
Star, S.L. & Griesemer, J.R. (1989). Institutional ecology, translations and boundary objects: Amateurs and professionals in Berkeley's Museum of Vertebrate Zoology, 1907–39, *Social Studies of Science*, 19(3), 387–420.
Starbuck, W.H. (1992). Learning by knowledge intensive firms, *Journal of Management Studies*, 29(6), 713–740.
Szulanski, G. (1996). Exploring internal stickiness: Impediments to the transfer of best practice within the firm, *Strategic Management Journal*, 17(S2), 27–43.

Tsai, W. & Ghoshal, S. (1998). Social capital and value creation: The role of intra-firm networks, *Academy of Management Journal*, 41(4), 464–476.

Tsoukas, H. (1996). The firm as a distributed knowledge system: A constructionist approach, *Strategic Management Journal*, 17, 11–25.

Tushman, M.L. & Nadler, D.A. (1978). Information processing as an integrating concept in organizational design, *Academy of Management Review*, 3(3), 613–624.

Wernerfelt, B. (1984). A resource-based view of the firm, *Strategic Management Journal*, 5(2), 171–180.

Whittington, R. (2006). Completing the practice turn in strategy research, *Organization Studies*, 27(5), 613–634.

17
GENERATIVITY IN DIGITAL INFRASTRUCTURES
A research note

Kalle Lyytinen,[1] Carsten Sørensen, and David Tilson

A note to the reader: This chapter advances theoretical discussion of digital infrastructures originated in Hanseth and Lyytinen (2010) and Tilson et al. (2010) by seeking to develop a more comprehensive model of generativity and its drivers. Due to the theoretical and abstract nature of the argument and the coverage of the topics, the chapter is rather dense. Reading the two preceding articles is, therefore, helpful if the reader is not acquainted with the previous arguments.

Introduction

Infrastructures are key elements of modernity whereby nation states create public goods and services that help promote economic growth or other important national goals such as military reach. Infrastructures like railways, highways, post and telecoms, and power grids were therefore initially controlled and regulated by nation states. The growth of these infrastructures during the 19th and 20th centuries triggered the rise of industrial nations, promoted growth and global trade, and ultimately spread prosperity for many. Similarly, the growth of digital infrastructures from their humble beginnings in the 1960s was initially enabled and dictated by the needs of nation states to serve specific military or business goals. The last half century, however, has witnessed accelerating diffusion and growth of digital infrastructures characterized by decreased state control while resulting in higher diversity and scale along with unprecedented complexity.

Digital infrastructures naturally share several salient properties with earlier industrial age infrastructures – like standards-based coordination, shared interfaces, and reliance on modularity as a governing design principle. The development and use of all infrastructures also involves the adaptation and tuning of the infrastructure as it gets embedded in local practices. Yet, the nature of the digital material underlying digital infrastructures sets them apart from the classic infrastructures of modernity (Tilson et al., 2010). Digital infrastructures rely on digitizing all processed material to 1's and 0's and using programmable processors to change the state and behaviour of its parts. They are also semiotic and abstract – the bits can carry diverse meanings about the wider physical and social contexts in which they are embedded, including the behavior of the infrastructure itself. The resulting inherent flexibility of digital representations, the enormous advances in underlying technologies, and ever more sophisticated architectures to store, transmit, and process digital representations has resulted in an enormous, globally distributed socio-technical system that stores (and retrieves), transfers (by directing to specific addresses), and processes (anyway you want) digital data. The growth in the scale and diversity of this infrastructure supersedes that of any earlier non-digital infrastructure. While the early Internet in the late 1970s allowed a few scientists and military experts to send messages and share computing resources, the contemporary merged 'super-infrastructure' of platforms layered over the Internet forms an essential foundation for most socializing, entertainment, business, and public administration in industrialized countries.

Technologies possessing infrastructural properties present unique challenges for understanding the 'grand' issues related to their design, implementation, and use – including how to manage their dynamics, evaluate their value, and regulate their operation. The work by Information Systems (IS) and other scholars has so far revealed multiple important issues related to these topics covering among others: the institutionalization of digital infrastructures (Ciborra et al., 2001; Hanseth and Lyytinen, 2010; Henfridsson and Bygstad, 2013); institutionalization of digital information (Kallinikos, 2007); the dynamics of the initiation and growth of digital infrastructures (Internet) (Abbate, 2000); the public value of digital infrastructures (Internet) (Frischmann, 2012); the control arrangements for digital infrastructures (Internet) (Goldsmith and Wu, 2006); the dynamics of innovation and regulation within digital infrastructures (Lessig, 2000; Lessig, 2002; Lessig, 2006); the control of emerging information industries (Wu, 2010); the impact of demand side economics and associated dynamics of growth in scaling digital infrastructures (Shapiro and Varian, 1998); the control-generativity dialectic of digital infrastructure (Internet) growth (Zittrain, 2008); and the design and management of digital platforms as salient market arrangements enabled by digital infrastructures (Gawer and Cusumano, 2002; Gawer, 2009; Ghazawneh and Henfridsson, 2013; Tiwana, 2014; Eaton et al., 2015; Evans and Schmalensee, 2016; Parker et al., 2016).

This research testifies to the presence of a growing body of important work concerned with the control and growth of digital infrastructures and their evolutionary dynamics. A bulk of this work recognizes that growth patterns within digital infrastructures differ significantly from patterns of their earlier physical counterparts. Earlier research on this topic remains largely descriptive and has neither specifically focused on nor identified *a set of mechanisms* that drive growth. Those that have typically limit their examination to social mechanisms like network effects or technological enablers such as the malleability of the digital material or the specificity of loosely coupled architectures. As yet no work has sought to unify such growth drivers into a more encompassing theoretical framework. No studies have sought to provide a systemic account, founded on principles of complexity and the idea of internal tensions, of how such digital infrastructures as specific socio-technological systems are prone to grow rapidly in scale and scope. This paper seeks to provide an initial, tentative attempt to articulate such a systemic account of generativity in digital infrastructures.

Moreover, further work is needed to deepen our understanding of the proposition that digital infrastructures differ from other digital artefacts in terms of their growth mechanisms (Tilson et al., 2010). On the one hand, digital infrastructures display emerging structural properties such as malleability, which also characterize applications and platforms (Hanseth and Lyytinen, 2010). The main difference appears to be the inherent generativity in scale and scope that emerges from inherent tensions embedded within the socio-technical characteristics of digital infrastructure. This topic was raised in passing in Hanseth and Lyytinen (2010) as a specific feature around how digital infrastructures grow. None of the previous works cited has, however, truly examined the specific sources of generativity that underlie digital technologies with infrastructural characteristics. In the following, we posit that the generativity within digital infrastructures relates to the complex interplay between several dimensions of digital infrastructure:

1 The size and growth of the installed base;
2 The complexity of heterogeneous networks of technologies that can be integrated through gateways and standards;
3 The intangible nature and diversity of anticipatory standards[2] and the wide range of connected actors;
4 The scale and scope of network externalities (both direct and indirect);
5 The open nature of infrastructural resources that can be integrated and deployed;
6 The unbounded change in infrastructural components that take place in both a bottom-up and a top-down fashion.

These critical dimensions are locked in tensions and emerge from the unique phenomena that underlie digital infrastructures. This calls for a characterization of digital infrastructures in terms of paradoxes, which manifests in the emergent, open, unbounded and relational nature of digital infrastructures. Tilson et al. (2010) outline the two paradoxes characterizing digital infrastructures: (1) stability and flexibility; and (2) openness and control. These paradoxes can also be expressed in terms of upward and downward flexibility of related infrastructure components. Digital infrastructures, accordingly, denote a new category of information technology (IT) artefact with distinct properties and associated socio-technical dynamics best described as generativity (Hanseth and Lyytinen, 2010; Tilson et al., 2010). In this essay we expand this argument to a more general case and identify two new paradoxes not presented in Tilson et al. (2010). We advance our argument accordingly and conduct a detailed analysis and theorizing of the inherently generative nature of digital infrastructures as well as its sources of generativity. Generativity is here defined as the capability and related mechanisms for unbounded growth in scale and diversity of the functions and embeddedness of the infrastructure. We show that this growth is a product of recursive, inherent properties of socio-technical constellations that underlie digital infrastructures.

The aim of this chapter is to critically identify and assess 'forces' that shape digital infrastructure growth as a product of four interrelated, yet distinct, paradoxes: (1) fixity vs. variation of the underlying technologies forming the physical base; (2) stability vs. change in architecting of technologies; (3) control vs. autonomy within the socio-economic contexts; and (4) local vs. global arrangements governing the physical embeddedness of the digital infrastructure. By conducting the analysis of these paradoxes and their joint dynamics we strive to demonstrate that balancing and reconciling these tensions produce the generative nature of digital infrastructures (Zittrain, 2006). We also posit that the four combined result in the emergent property of generativity associated with digital infrastructures – that is, the unique relational nature of the digital infrastructures that promotes from within growth of all sorts of relationships in scale and kind composing the infrastructure.

Paradox model of change in digital infrastructures

It is well-known that neither technological nor social determinism can offer plausible explanations of the technological and social change associated with the growth of the scale and scope of digital infrastructures (Tilson et al., 2010). Technological change is not inherently automatic and cannot be predicted solely based on the evolutionary logic of underlying technologies (Arthur, 2009). At the same time, mere social explanations that ignore the nature and effects of technologies in shaping the growth are blind (Arthur, 2009). Thus, plausible explanations need to combine the social and technical which we see as deeply intertwined at multiple levels of analysis. The challenge with this view is that the complexity of the interactions and inseparability of the two makes it difficult to come to grips with and explain how infrastructures emerge and change over time.

In what follows we frame the growth of digital infrastructures as being driven by socio-technical paradoxes which are concerned, for example, with how technological change and its social control are connected during socio-technical change. In the past this approach has proven a viable means when scholars have sought to understand the underlying evolutionary dynamics of digital infrastructures (Tilson et al., 2010; Eaton et al., 2015). The paradoxes recognize some unique characteristics of digital infrastructures. For example, the loosely coupled elements of a digital infrastructure may provide communication, storage, or computational services capable of supporting many possible applications – a property referred to as *upward flexibility*. Similarly, a digital infrastructure element may be able to operate effectively by drawing on the services from among many alternative elements lower in the stack – a property referred to as *downward flexibility*. The Internet Protocol (IP) and related stack offers a great example of both upward and downward flexibility. It provides critical communication services for all Internet applications (upward flexibility) and works well over a diverse range of networking technologies (downward flexibility) (Tilson et al., 2010; Akhshabi and Dovrolis, 2013). The socio-technical analysis of this arrangement suggests paradoxical relationships between distributed and decentralized control as well as between stability and change (Tilson et al., 2010). Next, we elaborate on the idea of tensions, or paradoxes, as a key conceptual lens toward understanding the processes that underlie constant and often tumultuous change in digital infrastructures. The model presented in Figure 17.1 introduces the four key tensions that underlie such change: (1) fixity vs. variety in underlying material; (2) stability vs. change in architectural arrangements; (3) autonomy vs. control in socio-economic contexts; and (4) global vs. local physical embeddedness. These tensions can be arranged in specific relationships between one another along two dimensions that characterize digital infrastructures:

- The first dimension differentiates between the *technological* and *non-technological* aspects of digital infrastructures. Here the non-technological aspects provide the range of contexts (physical, organizational, and wider socio-economic contexts) that surround tangible infrastructure and against which technological change plays out. These non-technical aspects are in their turn reconfigured by such change.
- The second dimension differentiates between the *tangible* and the *intangible* character of digital infrastructures. The *underlying technologies* quadrant represents the arrangements of tangible physical materials and their properties that underpin technologies composing the infrastructure, while the *architected technologies* quadrant captures the intangible 'organizing logics' whereby complex assemblages of the physical and virtual technologies are put together. The *physical context* represents the tangible geographical locations that vary along various dimensions, closely linked to which is the *socio-economic context* that encompasses the full range of social structures of human experience.

The two paradoxical relationships already mentioned by Tilson et al. (2010) – distributed vs. decentralized control (or control vs. autonomy) and stability vs. change – are associated with the quadrants on the intangible side of the model in Figure 17.1. Later we introduce two additional paradoxes, one for each quadrant on the tangible side. These are important in articulating how the abstract semiotic character of digital infrastructures 'decouples' the

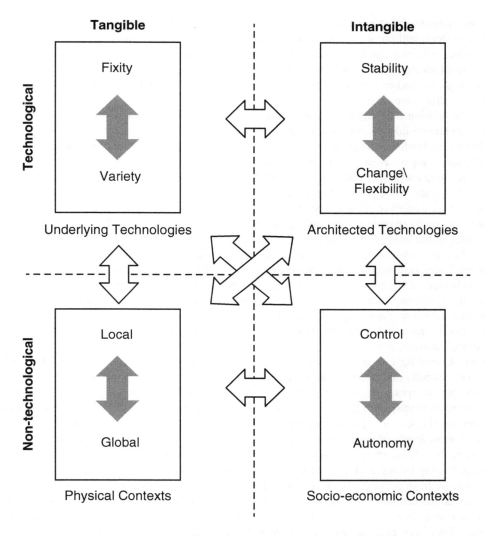

Figure 17.1 Conceptual model of the socio-technical structure of digital infrastructures

infrastructure operations from the underlying physical phenomena and thereby permits increased variation.

Clearly, the model's quadrants are deeply entwined and mutually constitutive. Here, we only make these distinctions among them for analytical purposes to help us tease out the inherent tensions that drive infrastructure growth. Better understanding the interactions within and across the four quadrants and the ways in which the embedded paradoxes become resolved provides a means of getting to grips with the complex dynamics of socio-technical configurations that characterize digital infrastructures. Before exploring these interactions and tensions, we expand upon the content and nature of each quadrant.

As scientists and engineers explore the physical, chemical, electrical, magnetic, optical, quantum, and other phenomena, they learn to harness matter in innumerable ways to serve basic operations that underlie infrastructural operations – in our case to represent, communicate, store, and process digital material as 1's and 0's. For example, engineers can deploy ceramics, silicon crystals, and glass (among many other materials) to create the components of digital electronics and photonics. The *underlying technologies* quadrant represents these tangible, physical materials and their associated attributes and capacities from which tangible infrastructures are created.

The relationships among the components of an infrastructure carry an organizing logic or architecture that governs how the components deliver specific functionality. In traditional physical technologies, the same principle applies. For example, a hammer has a head attached to handle using a wedge or other mechanism to provide the function of hammering. This basic arrangement and associated logic can be altered to better pursue particular objectives (such as more accurate, more powerful hammering, or hammering leaving no traces on surfaces) by varying the materials, shapes, weights, or sizes of the parts and how they relate to one another. We view such organizing logics that guide the composition of architected technologies as the essence of the intangible-technological quadrant of Figure 17.1.

The knowledge encapsulated in these architectures allows the properties of the underlying technologies and the myriad properties of matter to be diligently harnessed to create more complex technological artefacts and to organize them into functional relationships that address specific functional ends. In the case of infrastructure, it is its functions and related operations (such as addressing or storage). For example, the menagerie of electronic component types that harness the electrical, magnetic, optical, and quantum properties of silicon crystals, metals, oxides, ceramics, glass, and other materials are themselves already architected technologies. These in turn have their own properties and interfaces that can be combined and integrated to form circuits that underpin digital technologies that process, store, or transfer bits. These materials, components, circuits, subsystems (such as addressing), and higher systems (such as instruction sets) form layers of hierarchically architected technologies where the expertise at one level does not require the deepest of knowledge about the functions at the other levels. The lowest levels of such organizing logics in digital infrastructures are intimately tied to the tangible character of underlying technologies – something they share with the hammer in the preceding example. But as we move up the architectural hierarchy, the organizing logics shift away from dealing with the physical and tangible even though the related functions and relationships continue to be underpinned by them. We learn to deal, for example, with bits, bytes, instructions, resource scheduling, programming languages, storage systems, communication interfaces, packets, frames, protocols, input/output drivers, standardized encodings for text, audio, images, video, file systems, kernels, multiplexing architectures, databases, operating system services, clients and servers, modules, APIs, web services, applications, virtual machines, cloud services, and so on. The higher we go the greater the power these architected components and related functions offer to the services, applications, and ecosystems that compose the 'observed' infrastructure. The benefit of these functions for individuals and organizations who care about infrastructures is also clearer and more direct. As we move higher the architected technologies are increasingly built around intangible organizing logics and related patterns that offer dedicated functional abstractions for the sort of work these elements or subsystems do for the infrastructures. They also become increasingly *intangible* in that they only remotely assume the presence of the tangible elements at the lower layers but which rarely need to be physically located or identified.[3]

As a result, the foundational, tangible technological elements of digital infrastructures are necessarily analytically separated from the functional technologies manifested in specific infrastructural designs. This mirrors Arthur's (2009) distinction of technology as "assemblages of practices and components," and his distinction between the physical equipment and the logical sequencing of operations in architected technologies.

The *socio-economic context* of a digital infrastructure is the set of relationships among all the actors at various levels who have a potential stake in the operation or development of the infrastructure. At the macro level, it encapsulates the organizations, value chains, industry structures, legal and educational institutions, as well as the relationships among them and or other structures of human experience that matter (such as history or tradition). However, it also includes actors at the group and individual levels like users, developers, content creators, and participants in multi-sided platforms. This broader context holds the prospect for the social and economic support necessary for the advancement and growth of the scope and the scale of digital infrastructure. The incredible variety of the functions and applications that have emerged from digital infrastructures are thus not simply a function of technological abilities. Rather they rely on multiple social arrangements (e.g., governance structures around standards, platforms, and protocols), incubators, and investment communities to support new ideas, as well as institutions that help diffuse the knowledge and skills needed to participate in the use or deployment of the infrastructure. Hence, the growth of digital infrastructures relies critically on actions and agreements among the growing installed base of developers, users, and other stakeholders along with the manner in which such actions are governed.

Finally, the *physical context* of a digital infrastructure is the material world spanning the local and the global use and development sites. At the local level, it includes the tangible geographical locations that vary by climate, material resources, and wealth, as well as their endowments of other infrastructures like road, rail, water, electricity, and telecommunications. This along with the socio-economic context form sets of relationships shaping the technological change and related outcomes locally and globally. Change in the physical context occurs when the infrastructural technologies are adopted, elaborated, and built upon while being embedded into the physical and socio-economic contexts.

The paradoxes underlying generativity and change in digital infrastructures

Having defined the nature of the four quadrants presented in Figure 17.1, we next turn to an examination of the interactions among the quadrants and the critical role of the paradoxes and tensions embedded within them. However, before doing so we must first understand the idea and features of generativity – one essential characteristic of digital infrastructure. Zittrain (2008) highlights five features that underlie generativity: Leverage, Adaptability, Ease of Mastery, Accessibility, and Transferability. The properties of even the simplest human tools relate to achieving some concrete objective and thus they provide *leverage* in achieving some goal and can be *adapted* to a variety of goals. For example, a wooden beam can be used as a lever to move a large rock (leverage), or its sharpness can be used pierce a body (adaptability). *Ease of mastery* can vary along with the difficulty of the objective. Stone working, for example, can involve little more than piling rocks to build a rudimentary barrier or involve years of learning to master the application of centuries of accumulated knowledge to build sophisticated stone structures. *Accessibility* depends on the availability both economically and physically, of essential tools, materials, and information. Finally, *transferability* revolves around the ease with which new knowledge and adaptions created can be conveyed to others and other contexts. All else being equal, increases in any of these factors endow a technology with greater generative potential.

The reason we look at these features is that they help explain in a relatively simple way why digital infrastructures tend to grow in both scope and scale.

- Increasing *Leverage* {Lev}, that is making tasks easier to accomplish, is related to growth in the scale of a technology. All else being equal, easier *Access* {Acc} and *Ease of Mastery* {EoM} promote the growth in scale of a technology that possesses the advantages over alternatives that increasing leverage implies.
- Higher levels of Adaptability {Adpt}, the ease with which a technology "can be built on or modified to broaden its range of uses" (Zittrain, 2008), is by definition related to growth in scope. The upward and downward flexibility associated with appropriately architected digital architectural elements and the abstract digital materiality of 1's and 0's makes this feature particularly pertinent for digital infrastructures. All else being equal, greater endowments of *Access* {Acc}, *Ease of Mastery* {EoM}, and *Transferability* {Tsfr} positively influence the diffusion of innovative adaptations and the likelihood that these adaptations will prompt further innovation and broadening of scope.

For digital infrastructures to have generativity, we need to thus show how the tensions and related dynamics influence each of the five features of generativity. Therefore, in the following analysis the role of each feature in connection to each of the four tensions is noted using the abbreviations {Lev, Adpt, EoM, Acc, Tsfr}. These aspects are coded by drawing on pragmatic assessments based on our own knowledge of the evolution of several digital infrastructures (Tilson and Lyytinen, 2006; Tilson et al., 2006; Tilson, 2008; Tilson et al., 2012; Tilson et al., 2013) and the analytical distinctions captured in Figure 17.1.

Next we examine each of the four quadrants of Figure 17.1 and identify the effects that they can have on one another and the sort of tensions these effects generate with regard to the growth potential of digital infrastructures. It is our contention that it is the playing out of these effects and related tensions that have shaped how digital technologies became infrastructural and evolved so fast, and how social connections at multiple levels became subject to radical reconfiguration. We also identify some of the drivers behind the rapid evolution and show how they are inherent and recursively organized in the very socio-technical configurations of digital infrastructures.

Underlying technologies and the paradox of fixity vs. variety

The primary tension associated with this quadrant is that of *fixity vs. variety*. Individual materials always possess fixed properties and exhibit a range of phenomena with the potential to support variation in usage and application. When incorporated into more complex architected technologies (i.e., those composed of more than one part), the prospect for wider variation in the harnessing of the phenomena becomes possible (although not guaranteed). Yet, the variety of applications and the generativity of these technologies are not simple inherent properties of the technologies. Rather they are relational in nature, depending as they do upon the surrounding technological (architected) and social (governed) contexts.

Even the most ethereal idea of a digital infrastructure must at some point revert to tangible server blades and network switches, which, in turn, can still be approached as complex architected components made up by a plethora of diverse physical elements ending up in individual physical elements possessing specific physical characteristics. Digital artifacts are at the same time objects, yet lack the stability offered by physical objects – they are both complete and can be subjected to further development (Kallinikos et al., 2013, p. 357). An electronic text document serves as a simple example. While a printed page in a book may be provided with annotations, it is clear to any reader what makes the original text different from the annotations. This will not be the same in an electronic word processing document – assuming the annotations are not explicitly marked up. Scaling this up to infrastructural artefacts, we can observe that part of a road system under construction will be officially opened to the public by a ceremonial ribbon-cutting. In contrast, on the Internet, elements are simultaneously under constant reconfiguration and use.

Due to this ambivalent ontology (Yoo, 2012; Kallinikos et al., 2013), the underlying technologies contributing to digital infrastructures provide a higher variety of phenomena to harness. Basically, any underlying technology that can serve to present two (or more) distinct states in a sequence, preserve those states, and carry them out with high predictability will do. Accordingly, the primary paradox associated with this quadrant is that of *fixity vs. variety in underlying technologies that can be harnessed to carry out the basic operations underlying the infrastructure*.

Individual materials possess fixed properties and can exhibit a range of phenomena with the potential to support variation in usage and application of infrastructure operations. Paradoxically, the underlying tangible elements may provide the potential for greatest variety through simple and fixed characteristics. The digital 0–1 switch or logic gate – the most basic component technology for the digital computer – is a case in point. It only performs one function, but facilitates upwards flexibility of unprecedented scale as their configuration by the million or billion provides the sophisticated physical underpinnings of modern digital technologies. These simplest of digital building blocks also possess considerable downward complexity as evidenced by their mapping to ever smaller, cheaper, and faster implementations using increasingly refined understanding of physical materials and the development of more sophisticated fabrication technologies, which themselves rely on expanding knowledge and harnessing of physical phenomena. The pulverization of all aspects known to digital infrastructures into 1's and 0's implies the possibility of a flexible agnostic treatment of the underlying semantics. Any output from any process can become input to any other process, and any service can be served on any part of the infrastructure. While some combinations may be irrelevant, illegal, or impractical, many may be unexpectedly useful. One small example of this is to feed the output from a digital portable camera, for example on a smartphone, to a digital-analogue converter driving a speaker. This can facilitate blind people learning to "see" by listening (Sandhana, 2003). Another example is the hiding of malicious code within otherwise legitimate digital representations like images, apps, web pages, and URLs.

Changes in our understanding of the properties of various sorts of matter will influence change in digital infrastructures in the following ways and determine how we approach the related paradox:

- *Underlying Technologies*: Harnessing the properties of one sort of matter can facilitate the discovery of, or harnessing properties of, other materials (e.g., fire to smelt metals). Over time the properties of metals, plastics, ceramics, glass, and of semiconducting materials, such as silicon, have been particularly important for the development of current digital systems. {Lev, Adpt}[4]
- *Architected Technologies*: The properties of various materials have been used in increasingly sophisticated architected technologies to store, transmit, and process the bit (simplest unit of digital information). Newly understood properties of materials increase the performance and reduce cost (e.g., Moore's law). Such performance improvements and cost reductions (orders of magnitude for digital technologies) make the physical all but

disappear from considerations of what information-based architectures and services are feasible. {Lev, Acc, EoM}
- *Socio-economic Contexts*: Newly discovered or developed capabilities change the economics of existing products and services and make new ones conceivable. The orders of magnitude reductions in the cost of underlying technologies makes digital devices and infrastructure available to a growing proportion of the world's population. {Adpt, Acc, Tsfr}
- *Physical Contexts*: Regions that can supply materials (particularly rare and vital ones) gain wealth. Experience with exploiting the earlier properties of a material can give a physical location a head start on exploiting new ones (e.g., working with glass for other needs helped in development of the optical fiber technology that provides most of the bandwidth for global digital infrastructures). {EoM, Acc, Tsfr}

Architected technologies and the paradox of stability vs. change

When new components become incorporated into increasingly complex architected technologies (i.e., those composed of more than one part), the prospect for wider variation in the harnessing of the phenomena becomes possible, although it is not guaranteed. The architectural arrangements can still be highly fixed and constrain growth. For example, the railway needs to be architected in a way that offers a relatively limited set of functions of moving things from one point to another within a physical network. A large number of underlying components, such as rails, wagons, trains, and their relationships and associated control functions need to be designed to deliver even this expected functionality. Despite the complexity of the connections between the components that make up the railway system, the architected functionality of the infrastructure remains highly restricted due to the limited range of ways in which its components can be functionally related or new components added. Hence, such infrastructures exhibit a relatively stable functional variation due to the limited and fixed range of ways in which components can be combined. For example, the components of railways can be rearranged or related to one another in different ways to transport either goods or people and at different speeds or over diverse routes, but functionality cannot easily be expanded beyond that.

In contrast, due to the ambivalent ontology of digital artifacts (Yoo, 2012; Kallinikos et al., 2013), digital infrastructures facilitate the possibility of both upward and downward flexibility in composing systems, where each such extension can deliver a similar set of desired functions. Accordingly, digital infrastructures offer an immensely wider potential for functional variation with a relatively small set of ways in which the basic components of the infrastructure are connected. In fact, digital infrastructures express a paradoxical design regime where a stable design using a small number of basic abstract components and functions can support a high degree of functional variation largely constrained by the current speed/cost ratio of the underlying behavior or transfer components (such as addressing, enabling a uniform way of representing behaviors, and offering generalized transportation service).

The architectural arrangements of digital infrastructures are, therefore, highly paradoxical and call for dualities as governing explanations rather than simple dualisms (Farjoun, 2010). For architected intangible technologies, the paradox of change denotes digital infrastructures' architectures concurrent reliance on both stability and change. This opposing logic operates across several infrastructural layers and components and seeks to ensure that the infrastructure standards remain stable over time as to allow for enrolling new artefacts, protocols, processes and actors, and at the same time be sufficiently flexible as to allow for unbounded growth in scale and functions. Technical stability of the protocols, interfaces, and data definitions is necessary for new connections to be predictable. Equally, stable social arrangements are necessary to reach agreements on the technical changes facilitating further infrastructure dynamics. Yet, the stability of a digital infrastructure requires extensions within its scope. Architectural flexibility can bolster the infrastructure and related functions, but it can also challenge the stability of social categories and established industrial boundaries. Hence, the paradox of change follows from the architected characteristics of digital infrastructures that will contain heterogeneous, unbounded, shared, and open functions (Hanseth and Lyytinen, 2010). Overall, the change is simultaneously enabled and constrained by the installed base.

The Internet has, for example, relied on a growing number of protocols, middleware elements, new communications equipment, and innovative client devices. This has allowed for dramatic expansion in its scope and scale for more than 50 years. Yet, since its inception all the elements and protocols have been organized in an hourglass 'architectural' shape where the core protocols at the "waist" have remained relatively stable with the IP constituting its enter (Akhshabi and Dovrolis, 2013). This architecture has supported the flexible and unbounded recombination of services and new infrastructural elements upwards and downwards. As a result, the Internet has witnessed dramatic changes in other parts. However, it has proven particularly challenging to reach agreements on the transition from IPv4 to the updated IPv6 necessary to expand the scope of addressable machines and services. This can be expressed as a challenge to align the global standards to local settings. The transition, originally scheduled to finish by 2011, has yet to reach 13% adoption by August 2016 (Curran, 2008; Google, 2016). The convergence of the Internet with the mobile phone toward the iOS and Android ecosystems provides another example where significant tussles around blurring of industry boundaries associated with a reconfiguration of architected technologies resulted in new governance and actor dynamics (Elaluf-Calderwood et al., 2011). The technical ease by which smartphones could become part of the Internet ecosystem resulted in new challenges for mobile operators who had to transition from an architecture and an associated business model based on calls and SMS messages to one based on data charges.

When the organizing logics or architectures become standardized and widely adopted, they become infrastructural. Some level of stability in the architecture is necessary for its widespread adoption and for incorporating additional components and related organizing logics proposed by new entrants. Digital infrastructures are of significant interest to individuals, organizations, and researchers, precisely because of the speed and ease at which they change, and because such change is then manifested in unbounded, evolving, shared, heterogeneous and open set of architectural capabilities (Hanseth and Lyytinen, 2010, p. 6). Overall, the *paradox of change* associated with the intangible-technological quadrant can be

> defined by the opposing logics of stability and flexibility that operate across infrastructural layers and components. On the one hand, digital infrastructures need to be stable to allow 'enrollment' of new artifacts, processes and actors; while on the other it must possess flexibility to allow unbounded growth.
> (Tilson et al., 2010, p. 753)

This is probably the most critical tension in understanding the growth of digital infrastructures. The speed of change in organizing logics in both the technological and social structures around digital infrastructures relies ultimately on the dynamic resolutions of the subtle effects of this paradox.

The organizing logic behind architected technologies allows the properties of underlying technologies to be harnessed to solve a wider range of problems. This is a prime example of the relational nature of how the small number of abstract fixed properties of materials can support a much greater variety in applications (upward flexibility). In this case the fundamental idea of building digital systems around the idea of the bit increases the variety of applications for any material with suitable properties. Beyond this, changes in other organizing logics can in turn precipitate change in each of the four quadrants:

- *Underlying Technologies*: New organizing logics allow the harnessing of more properties of tangible materials and in more elaborate configurations expanding the scale of the infrastructure. For example, the desire for smaller, cheaper, faster, and more power-efficient amplification and switching drove exploration of properties of semiconducting materials, discrete transistors, and ever denser integrated circuits. Better instruments and tools, themselves sophisticated architected technologies, helped in the discovery of new properties and in the synthesis of new materials. {Lev, Adpt}
- *Architected Technologies*: The architectural arrangements above the layers directly involved with physically storing, processing, and communicating bits have little or no connection to the physical manifestations of digital systems. The underlying technologies are abstracted away and impose few constraints on how organizing logics evolve. In particular:
    - Interfaces in architected technologies are now more critical for creating flexibility in interconnecting organizing logics at different layers (e.g., the up/downward flexibility of the Internet Protocol). {Lev, Adpt, EoM}
    - Organizing logics around modularity allow components at one layer to provide capabilities for higher layers and to be supported by different versions of components at lower layers (upward and downward flexibility). Making the interfaces of components/modules open for use by others generates more possibilities for other actors to build upon them. {Lev, Adpt, EoM, Acc, Tsfr}
    - Overall the generic and abstract functions associated with digital infrastructures are stable enough for building upon them, yet flexible enough to be used in ways unimagined by the original designer. {Lev, Adpt, EoM, Acc, Tsfr}
    - The virtual nature of digital products and services makes them more widely available more quickly than physical ones. {Acc, Tsfr}
- *Socio-economic Contexts:* The organizing logics of digital architectures have been observed to influence social contexts in the ways detailed herein and are likely where much of the generativity of digital infrastructures emerge:
    - Widespread infrastructural digitalization breaks down old industry structures underpinned by immiscible mechanical and analog architectures. For example, the smartphone integrated telephony, data services, video, photography, and music, which were previously distinct industries using different vertical technologies for most of the 20th century. {Lev, Adpt, EoM, Acc, Tsfr}
    - Inventors, entrepreneurs, and market organizations can now focus only on a few select parts of the architecture (by abstracting away other parts and constraining the knowledge needed). As a result, organizational and industry structures become more fluid as to mirror architectures that now support higher and more diverse specialization (Baldwin and Clark, 2000). {EoM}

- Finally, some points in architecting digital infrastructures are more critical than others as they provide:
    - Flexibility for others (e.g., Internet protocol) to innovate. {Lev, Adpt, EoM, Acc, Tsfr}
    - Free economic assets (e.g., APIs, app stores, social networks) by commoditizing most parts of the architecture. {Lev, Adpt, EoM, Acc}
    - New useful interfaces for functions that become accessible to others for further innovation. {Lev, Adpt, EoM, Acc, Tsfr}

- *Physical Contexts*: Architected technologies with sufficient flexibility can traverse a wider range of temporal or spatial contexts and increase the user base. At the same time, such 'global' infrastructures remain stable across contexts while permitting local variation. In contrast, the spread of other infrastructures (e.g., roads, rail, electricity, telecommunication) typically make physical contexts more similar and thereby amenable to adopting standardized technologies while diminishing the potential for new trade-offs in the local vs. global tension (discussed later). More modular architectures permitted by digital infrastructures allow more adaptations to local contexts at the edge without disrupting the infrastructure's core. The success of the smartphone offers a good example of this. Each device can be instantiated and continuously adapted to fit individual user preferences – for example, local language settings, the suite of apps installed, and the choice of local telecom operator, while simultaneously maintaining the same functional structure of offering video or picture services, tagging, and the like. {Lev, Adpt, Acc}

Socio-economic contexts and the paradox of control vs. autonomy

The paradox of *control vs. autonomy* captures the potential effects of the relevant political, economic, and institutional actors and actions in shaping the use and growth of the infrastructure. These include universities, markets and market makers, industrial organizations, regulatory bodies, and the legal system. These can all fundamentally shape the development, management, deployment, and control of infrastructural digital technologies and related connections.

As a consequence of the presence of three other paradoxes, it is not possible for any one actor or institution to fully centrally control the digital infrastructure through a design hierarchy (Clark, 1985). The control dynamics that unfold in the socio-economic context create the paradox of *centralized vs. distributed control*, where the strategic actions of a growing pool of heterogeneous actors have the potential to influence the directions of design and use of the infrastructure as a whole. Old analog and physical information infrastructures (e.g., telephony, television, music distribution, and publishing) represented high levels of control by a few dominant actors, stable technological platforms, and the logic of mass markets. These actors could act as gatekeepers for others wishing to distribute content or otherwise innovate (Tilson et al., 2010; Wu, 2010). The combination of new digital technologies can both be a result of harnessing a growing variety of physical phenomena, and as new ways of architecting the functions of the infrastructure results in a highly generative digital infrastructure. This can, for example, be new digital encoding techniques, new optical transmission techniques, growing speed of broadband Internet access, cheap personal computers and digital storage, operating systems, the World Wide Web, and easy access to sophisticated programming environments, to name but a few. Control has been at least partially removed from the gatekeepers and has become contested and distributed – leading to unprecedented levels of innovation at the edge of the infrastructure. At the same time, the incumbents are striving to re-establish control by re-purposing other elements of socio-economic context such as influencing legislation (e.g., battle over net neutrality) or seeking to create new forms of vertical integration (Lessig, 2002; Zittrain, 2008; Wu, 2010) as exemplified by the recent proposed mega-merger between AT&T and Time Warner (Anand, 2016). Those seeking to build additional layers of digital infrastructure functions and services constantly face the implications of this paradox (Gawer and Cusumano, 2002).

The implications of infrastructure change expand further into the policy domain – for example, when platform-based innovations, like Uber in transportation or Airbnb in lodging, change the foundations of economic logic in their related industries. The control dimension also relates to what and how services are provided; data ownership; who controls prevailing standards and related intellectual property; who controls access to critical resources (such as address space or priorities in using the infrastructure); and other aspects of technology susceptible to differences in the preferences and capacities to influence control arrangements.

Indeed, generativity can emerge from the capacity of distributed, autonomous, interdependent actors and institutions to engage in strategic actions toward pivotal aspects of the design and use of digital infrastructures (Zittrain, 2006; Tilson et al., 2010). The actions typically center on control points, which capture key defining relationships that help reach resolutions of tussles around centralized (closed) or decentralized (open) solutions. These tussles ultimately reflect conflicting interests of a growing number of heterogeneous decentralized actors (Tilson et al., 2010; Elaluf-Calderwood et al., 2011). Consider Apple's attempt to fully control its iOS platform by coordinating the matchmaking of iOS app developers and iPhone and iPad users (Eaton et al., 2015). Apple coordinates the sourcing of apps through tools and rules. The tools mainly comprise a Software Development Kit (SDK) and Application Programming Interfaces (APIs) that developers can use to create apps. The rules include an opaque approval process determining whether or not a submitted app is made available, as well as published developer agreements, for example stating that iOS apps must be constructed using Apple's SDK on an Apple Mac computer. Jointly, these make up boundary resources (Ghazawneh and Henfridsson, 2013; Eaton et al., 2015) – tools and rules – facilitating Apple and developers' arm's-length coordination of app development and distribution. Despite Apple's continued insistence on tight centralized control over these boundary resources, the deployment dynamics of the boundary resources have been significantly influenced by unexpected and distributed actions carried out by a variety of strategic organizations and individuals including individual developers, software companies, middleware producers, large platform organizations, and regulators, and even a global public debate facilitated by the blogosphere (Vaast et al., 2013). Such efforts have compelled Apple on several occasions to reconsider the rules governing access to the App Store, and the design and use of tools (Eaton et al., 2015). At the most fundamental level, a small group of people have continued to identify vulnerabilities that allow hackers to circumvent Apple's control and install unapproved apps on so-called jailbroken iOS devices. Another example is Amazon's 'forking' its Fire platform from Google's Android platform by assimilating the most critical elements from Android while replacing other services and components with its own (Amazon Music) or those obtained from third parties such as Nokia's (Karhu, 2017).

Overall, changes in socio-economic context influence digital infrastructure growth and generativity in the following ways:

- *Underlying Technologies*: The economic potential of faster, smaller, cheaper storage, processing, and transmission of bits incents uncovering new properties, synthesizing new materials, and refining the use of known properties. Universities and other research and educational institutions refine such knowledge of materials and their properties as well as propagate it to the pool of practitioners and researchers. Legal systems that protect the fruits of innovation further incent investment in underlying technologies and materials. {Lev, Adpt, EoM, Acc, Tsfr}

- *Architected Technologies*: Fully or partly controlling an architecture and its implementations with infrastructural effects ensures profits and market power (e.g., incumbent telecommunications firms, Apple's device-content ecosystem, or Google's central position in search and advertising). At the same time, social institutions and norms elaborate and refine conditions for creating and deploying architected technologies.

  - The economic potential of better products and services incent elaboration of architectures or creation of new ones as well as the propagation and assimilation of knowledge about architected technologies. {Lev, Adpt, EoM, Acc, Tsfr}
  - Legal means for contract enforcement support effective relationships among component producers and other types of partnership. {Acc, Tsfr}
  - Elaborate supply-chains ensure that materials and components are available for complex architected technologies. {Acc}
  - Varied institutional arrangements for reaching agreements (e.g., de facto or de jure standards) among actors about the meaning of digital representations and the use of interfaces promote the adoption and use of digital technologies {Adpt, EoM, Acc, Tsfr}

- *Socio-economic Contexts*: It is impossible to do full justice to the complex dynamics around social structures across all levels of analysis in a few short paragraphs. Instead, we highlight a few of the factors that have been observed as particularly salient for understanding the growth of digital infrastructures. As shown, digital infrastructures are the product of the interactions among many heterogeneous actors. At a minimum, this includes those who control critical elements of the infrastructure and those who build upon it. For some of the more complex digital infrastructures, many actors playing multiple roles influence generative growth:

  - Commercial organizations both cooperate and compete.
    - Across ecosystems to build larger installed bases and the greater network effects that can determine which become infrastructural. {Acc, Tsfr}
    - Within a particular ecosystem to pursue shared and individual interests, divide profits, and shape future change. {Lev, Adpt, Acc, Tsfr}
  - Control of the use of a digital infrastructure conveys power to those who can build and determine what can be built upon it, that is, how interfaces are defined and changed.
    - Tight centralized control restricts the potential for complementary innovation whereby infrastructure adoption and growth will be limited {−Lev, −Adpt, −Acc, −Tsfr}
    - Distributed control provides more autonomy for others to innovate but risks the reliability and stability of key interfaces. {Lev, Adpt, +/−EoM, Acc, +/−Tsfr}
  - Increased connectivity has the potential to bring actors together for mutual gain and understanding or for engaging in conflicts around tussles. {EoM, Acc, Tsfr}
  - Old legal frameworks can fail to deal adequately with the implications of digital infrastructures. Therefore, leaders of incumbent and new entrants seek to exert influence on laws and regulations. {−Adpt, −Acc, −Tsfr}

- *Physical Contexts*: The diffusion of physical digital infrastructures connects more of the world. The associated adoption and adaptation of social structures globally (e.g., industry models, and ways of reaching agreements about digital meanings) increases the homogeneity in some aspects of physical and digital infrastructures and eases their use (e.g., widely diffused communications technologies). {Lev, Adpt, EoM, Acc, Tsfr}

Physical contexts and the paradox of local vs. global

The physical contexts of digital infrastructures are by definition, as all infrastructures, simultaneously *local and global*. The global aspect of infrastructures implies that infrastructures have the capability to span and grow spatially and temporally across a myriad of contexts. As a result, they cut across and become shared by multiple heterogeneous communities. Digital infrastructures, therefore, possess the power to reach beyond any single event, site, or community (Star and Ruhleder, 1996). By doing so they ultimately connect, and are connected to, innumerable diverse and changing local practices across time and space and thus express shared global characteristics. According to Hanseth and Lyytinen's (2010) definition, this arc of tension between *local and global* is expressed through the shared, open, and evolving aspects of digital infrastructures. Through openness they integrate practices in different times and places, and by doing so they evolve, seemingly ad infinitum. They also never 'die' but only wither as to rise in new forms (Edwards et al., 2007).

The *local* aspect is expressed in the idea that digital infrastructure needs to be localized, that is, embedded in the local context. Star and Ruhleder express this idea succinctly with their notion of embeddedness: "infrastructure is 'sunk' into, inside of, other structures, social arrangements and technologies" (1996, p. 113). Hence, as a physical context, digital infrastructure is not a thing. As Star and Ruhleder eloquently note: it is not *what*, it is *when*. The embedding of an infrastructure occurs when "local practices are afforded by a larger-scale technology, which can then be used in a natural, ready-to-hand fashion" (Star and Ruhleder, 1996, p. 114). During this process a digital infrastructure becomes transparent as local variations of it become folded into changes in practices and organizational processes. This makes the infrastructure an unambiguous 'home' for somebody doing something with it (as a tool).

Overall, digital infrastructures are more capable of varying across local context than analog or physical ones. This is a reflection of the simplicity of the bit and the malleability of software. While the local adoption and adaption of a digital infrastructure to the physical and socio-economic contexts is likely, some of the modular features of digital technologies may make this less of a threat to universality. For example, drivers for peripherals needed in a few locations have no impact on the adoption of an operating system in other contexts.

Adoption of a potentially infrastructural technology across numerous locales increases the user base. This amplifies direct and indirect network effects and increases the likelihood of some digital technologies becoming elements of a global infrastructure. For example, road, rail, air, and water transport infrastructures were first adapted to varied local contexts, and then scaled upwards. The shipping container has simplicity and flexibility of the bit as it was embedded as a global element to local practices (Heins, 2016). Yet, this can only happen when the technology gets adapted to a wide range of physical (and socio-economic) local contexts. Because these contexts vary, so too do the adaptions. Increased variation may in turn require increased control in order to avoid the destruction of the potential for a technology reaching global adoption. However, the control may, in turn, limit adoption across a range of locales needed for global adoption. Hence, the question of local versus global is the key tension in this quadrant (Star and Ruhleder, 1996).

The simultaneity of the local and global presents us with the dualistic, paradoxical nature of infrastructures. Infrastructure becomes both "an engine and a barrier for change; both customizable and rigid; both inside and outside organizational practices" (Star and Ruhleder, 1996, p. 111). Therefore, an infrastructure occurs when the tension between local and global gets resolved and meets at the moment of infrastructural enactment. Designing and managing infrastructures imposes the constant challenge of how to make the global local and how to relate the local to the global while still carrying out the local work. This must happen despite significant variation of local settings and significant time and space distances from the origins of most infrastructural components. The classic idea of change following (planned) top-down design, therefore, rarely works with digital infrastructures. Such approaches face local inertia created by the heterogeneity and large installed base of local practices (Hanseth and Lyytinen, 2010).

Overall, the continuous change in the physical context and the demand for local embedding both generate paradoxical outcomes reflected in all elements of the model:

- *Underlying Technologies*: The local physical context influences which materials are potentially made available and their salient properties, that is, it shapes which problems they help solve. {Lev}
- *Architected Technologies*: Locales provide the possible locations for the adoption of architected technologies and therefore the expansion of the global user base. {Adpt, Acc, Tsfr}
- *Socio-economic Contexts*: The availability of raw materials influences the skills and knowledge developed and the potential for innovation based on them. Highly developed physical contexts provide locations where skills and knowledge accumulate (cities and industry clusters). These become attractive locations for those interested in certain technologies and industries – employers, employees, and investors. Similarly, the ongoing build-up of digital infrastructures permits new ways of sharing and coordinating knowledge, which enables new clusters and contexts of innovation to emerge. The new types of clusters of actors with both strong and weak ties that emerge bridge knowledge and innovative activities across unexpected groups, thereby stimulating and fostering further innovation (Lyytinen et al., 2016). {Adpt, EoM, Acc, Tsfr}
- *Physical Contexts*: The reconfiguration of the local physical context (e.g., expansion of physical infrastructures like transportation and energy) spurs further development of both the physical and digital infrastructures. {Adpt, EoM, Acc, Tsfr}

Toward a model of growth in digital infrastructures

Each of the four quadrants presented in the model (Figure 17.1) carry a paradox. However, we postulate that it is specifically *the interactions among the socio-technical configurations present across the quadrants, and the continuous resolution of the paradoxes creating the inescapable properties of emergence and complexity, that fuel the generativity and growth associated with digital infrastructures*. Stepping through some of the potential influences across the four quadrants as described earlier helps illustrate what is happening in each 'frame' or setting behind the complex dynamics underpinning digital infrastructures. The idiosyncratic sequencing of the decisions of actors, the manifestations of their various influences, and the alternative resolutions of the tensions in each quadrant, lead to the unpredictability and the path dependence observed in the ways digital technologies develop and are deployed and how at the same time the broader socio-technical configuration becomes reshaped.

The consequent dynamic interactions among the quadrants and paradoxes in the model describe the increasing complexity leading to the creation of new types of (socio-technical) relationships and the erosion and death of others. New relationships at one layer are often enabled by new relationships at others (higher or lower, technological and other). For example, in the context of the smartphone, the essential flexibility of the bit as the underlying technology is enabled and provides a basis for the as yet unprecedented flexibility of what can be done with the bits quite literally at hand. These developments are naturally related to the constant elaboration of multiple parallel and often unrelated technologies over decades, intentional and less intentional design decisions, and serendipity. They are also related to the creation of simple and elegant architectures, such as the Von Neumann processor architecture, the content agnostic TCP/IP protocols, the corresponding addressing schemes, and the loosely related stacked set of services. These have provided the stability necessary to facilitate growing flexibility for other functions offered by digital infrastructures. For example, the victory of the smartphone marked a shift from the tight coupling of form and function – from the traditional mobile phone with numbered keys used to dial telephone numbers shown on a small screen, to the loose coupling of a general-purpose touchscreen and the myriad of possible functions supported by millions of apps; from telephone number input to making Super Mario jump around the screen. The smartphone is now a general-purpose computing platform that connects to a growing variety of digital infrastructure services themselves sustained by the presence of scale (billions of users) and scope (the versatility of what one can do with these devices). In this regard, the smartphone-driven innovation arrangement, which centers on a series of related or 'stacked' multi-sided digital platforms, has also become a dominant industry model for innovation following in footsteps of older industries like automotive, manufacturing, shipping, process industries, and so on.

Arranging the infrastructural elements, at least conceptually, as modules interconnecting with one another across layers helps users, developers, and other actors manage the exponential complexity and supports their adoption and adaptation to numerous social and physical contexts. Users can further integrate the digital service offerings on mobile devices to fulfill their specific needs (e.g., finding and booking a restaurant on one app, while finding its location, ordering a car to get there, and paying with others). Due to this property, digital infrastructures "are built on the notion that they are never fully complete, that they have many uses yet to be conceived of, and that the public and ordinary organizational members can be trusted to invent and share good uses" (Zittrain, 2008, p. 43). The smartphone arrangements, for example, are continuously developed with more than two million different apps made available on each of the two main platforms (Android and iOS) since 2009. In the transition from version 8 to 9 of the iOS operating system, Apple reported that over 50% of users globally had transitioned within less than a week (Tracy, 2015).

This begins to explain how the paradox of *fixity vs. variation* interacts with the other paradoxes as the underlying physical engine behind the potential for growth in scope, and thereby also in scale. The paradox of *stability vs. change/flexibility* mostly relates to the extent to which it is possible to realize the potential for variation in scope depending on how it can be reconciled with past architectural decisions and how the inertia related to the design debt or the installed base is manifested. This in turn sets up a potential dynamic in which the changing context fundamentally alters the nature of how the paradox of fixity vs. variation continues to evolve and be resolved through the paradox of *autonomy and control*. Finally, the growth in variation needs to be localized by overcoming challenges of the *local and global* paradox through ongoing local accomplishments in how infrastructure gets embedded. This is continuous tuning. New tensions requiring resolution can arise from any quadrant at any time – with knock-on effects spilling over into the other quadrants. In the case of the smartphone infrastructure, much design-debt is sunk into the notion of individual apps, which are largely unconnected in ways other than simple copy and paste of text from one to the other. The centralized push to convince users to automatically install updates of both operating system and apps – as well as frequently upgrading the phone – pushes the ability to achieve a notion of a constantly changing stability. By orchestrating the supply of complements through boundary resources (tools and rules for coordination at arm's length), Apple both maintains significant centralized control over what supplements are accepted, while facilitating developer autonomy to innovate beyond what Apple would be able to accomplish on its own (Eaton et al., 2015). Subjecting the configuration and day-to-day management of devices and content to a highly automated self-service process allows extensive localization of a global infrastructure where it meets the physical realities.

Concluding remarks

We can summarize key observations of our analysis of the tensions in eight key principles of generativity that apply *only* to digital infrastructures:

1 *Loose coupling to physicality implies generativity*: Digital infrastructures are not fixed to specific materials and related technological foundations and practices. This enables a larger variety of technologies to be harnessed to address specific functional needs related to digital processing, thus increasing the leverage, adaptability, accessibility, and transferability associated with digital infrastructures. It also eases embedding and localization of technologies across use sites.
2 *Modularity implies generativity*: The functional elements of digital infrastructures are more malleable, can be architected in multiple ways, and generally evolve into complex network-like dependency structures. Therefore, digital infrastructures can be architected using more generic and right-sized modular architectures which offer more generativity than mostly hierarchical analog and physical architectures. This positively influences the leverage, adaptability, accessibility, and transferability of digital technologies.
3 *Loose coupling across layers implies generativity*: The loosely coupled, layered way in which digital infrastructures are typically architected offers significant generative potential. In consequence, innovation across different domains and functions can take place independently of the innovations taking place at other layers generating complex wave-like patterns and interactions (see e.g., Lyytinen and Rose, 2003; Adomavicius et al., 2008). This is a different set of dependencies than those found in analog, hierarchical, physical architectures and especially influences adaptability, leverage, and transferability.
4 *Abstractions across domains implies generativity*: Digital architectures and infrastructures offer a wider range of ways of creating generic functional modules that provide greater leverage over multiple domains influencing adaptability, transferability, ease of mastery, and leverage.
5 *Shared stable core functions implies generativity*: Digital infrastructures with a layered architecture can be architected in ways where the guiding, local intelligence is placed at the 'edge of the network' or at the 'top of the stack' while abstracting generic functions related to the primary technological functions (storage, addressing, transfer) to be shared as stable core functions. This layered architecture offers higher generative potential than hierarchical architectures of analog physical infrastructures (Yoo et al., 2010) where functional intelligence is centralized – thus driving accessibility, adaptability, leverage, and ease of mastery.
6 *Systems of intangible standards implies generativity*: Digital infrastructures are built upon systems of intangible standards and definitions in addition to physical technologies. The

intangible nature of key foundational technologies positively influences transfer, adaptability, accessibility, and ease of mastery.
7   *Distributed technical control implies generativity*: Digital infrastructures provide more alternatives to manage or bypass control points and to generate new control points. These differences accrue due to differences in the level of modifiability and re-connectivity between modules and infrastructure components, thereby increasing adaptability, leverage, and transferability.
8   *Digital infrastructures with minimal critical interface points implies generativity*: Digital infrastructures and related architectures only presume stability at critical interfaces (e.g., connection between physical and logical, simple transmission of bits). This allows multiple sets of actors to build upon these foundations over time, that is, build a complex network of peripheral modules around the infrastructure's core, thereby increasing leverage, adaptability, accessibility, transferability, and ease of mastery.

Clearly, this is only an initial clearing of these differentiating principles. We do not know to what extent each influences growth patterns, or how they influence them in combination. Similarly, there are differences in early and late growth, and different patterns may apply only at certain stages and under certain conditions (Hanseth and Lyytinen, 2010). However, the tentative conjectures laid out here can be used to guide future work toward the creation of a general 'theory' of digital infrastructures. These conjectures can then be subjected to testing, validation, and expansion. These principles also suggest specific design actions that are more likely to generate growth in digital infrastructures than others. Due to the limitations of the space, we will not detail them here but leave this as a future exercise.

Our primary focus here is on the need to develop a systemic account of the growth of digital infrastructures and what lies below their observed, stunning, growth patterns. By doing this we also want to engage scholars in the history of technology and economics (Hughes, 1983; David, 1990) or those theorizing around the nature and growth of general technologies (Arthur, 2009) in a shared debate. Indeed, interest in this area is significant and growing across multiple disciplines including Science and Technology Studies (STS), Strategy, Evolutionary Economics, Technology History, and Information Systems. We hope that this chapter offers an alternative, fresh framework to understand the conditions and mechanisms of growth related to these recent poorly understood socio-technical systems. This chapter is primarily a study of the growth of complex socio-technical systems. In this regard it advances the initial ideas presented in Hanseth and Lyytinen (2010), and Tilson et al. (2010) – see also Hanseth (2006). Unlike early studies informed by socio-technical theory, which focused on the internal structuring and stability of socio-technical systems (Trist, 1981), we hope that this chapter invites scholars to also study other growth- and variety-related aspects of large socio-technical arrangements (for a similar argument, see Berente et al., 2016). We also hope that the model outlined in this chapter offers a promising conceptual framework for other IS scholars to continue and deepen the work initiated by Zittrain (2006), and to study specifically the effects of different drivers of generativity on the growth patterns as well as the dynamics of different types of digital infrastructure. During such engagements, we may also need to theorize additional drivers of generativity and/or refine those offered by Zittrain. Similarly, we will need to develop better ways of conceptualizing and measuring different types of tension in addition to determining how to study the balancing of the tensions over time (for an initial attempt see Henfridsson and Bygstad (2013)). In this chapter, we have but glimpsed the presence of the complex interactions among the four types of tensions over time and space.

To understand the dynamics, patterns, and outcomes of such tensions better, we need detailed longitudinal case studies as they can reveal how alternative constellations of mechanisms and drivers influence and are influenced by those balancing actions. We have neither touched the recursive and layered organization of the digital infrastructures across firm, network, industry, and national/global infrastructures. The dynamics and related tensions between those levels forms another important missed element in studying the conditions of growth.

Overall, the saga of digitalization is not over. In fact, we predict that it will reach its climax only in the next two decades when the full potential of the exponential growth of generic information processing power has materialized. We hope that this chapter offers insight into to the challenges we face in trying to make sense of it and point out the intellectual challenges that lie ahead.

Notes

1 Authors are listed in alphabetical order.
2 "Anticipatory standards define "future capabilities for ICTs in contrast to recording and stabilizing existing practices, or capabilities de facto" (Lyytinen et al., 2010, p. 147).
3 This process of virtualization has been a characteristic of digital infrastructures from early virtual memory systems or cache memories, to virtualization of physical addresses to 'logical' IP addresses, to cloud services, to virtualization of data storage, and to virtualizing the network itself.
4 These developments underpin modern digital technologies' increase in usefulness and flexible adoption to a wider range of uses increasing both Leverage {Lev} and Adaptability {Adpt}. We follow similar logics to tag each of the following sections with the associated features of generative systems {Lev, Adpt, EoM, Acc, Tsfr}.

References

Abbate, J. (2000): *Inventing the Internet*. Cambridge, MA: MIT Press.
Adomavicius, G., J.C. Bockstedt, A. Gupta, & R.J. Kauffman (2008): Making sense of technology trends in the information technology landscape: A design science approach. *MIS Quarterly*, vol. 32, no. 4, pp. 779–809.
Akhshabi, S. & C. Dovrolis (2013): The evolution of layered protocol stacks leads to an hourglass-shaped architecture. In *Dynamics on and of complex networks*, Vol. 2, ed. A. Mukherjee, M. Choudhry, F. Peruani, N. Ganguly, & B. Mitra. Heidelberg: Birkhäuser, pp. 55–88.
Anand, B. (2016): AT&T, Time Warner, and what makes vertical mergers succeed. *Harvard Business Review*, October 28. https://hbr.org/2016/10/att-time-warner-and-what-makes-vertical-mergers-succeed
Arthur, W.B. (2009): *The nature of technology: What it is and how it evolves*. New York: Free Press.
Baldwin, C.Y. & K.B. Clark (2000): *Design rules, Vol. 1: The power of modularity*. Cambridge, MA: MIT Press.
Berente, N., K. Lyytinen, Y. Yoo, & J.L. King (2016): Routines as shock absorbers during organizational transformation: Integration, control, and NASA's enterprise information system. *Organization Science*, vol. 27, no. 3, pp. 551–572.
Ciborra, C.U., K. Braa, A. Cordella, B. Dahlbom, A. Failla, O. Hanseth, V. Hepso, J. Ljungberg, E. Monteiro, & K.A. Simon, ed. (2001): *From control to drift: The dynamics of corporate information infrastructures*. New York: Oxford University Press.
Clark, K.B. (1985): The interaction of design hierarchies and market concepts in technological evolution. *Research Policy*, vol. 14, no. 5, pp. 235–251.
Curran, J. (2008): An Internet transition plan: 2070–1721. www.rfc-editor.org/rfc/rfc5211.txt
David, P.A. (1990): The dynamo and the computer: An historical perspective on the modern productivity paradox. *American Economic Review*, vol. 80, no. 2, pp. 355–361.
Eaton, B.D., S. Elaluf-Calderwood, C. Sørensen, & Y. Yoo (2015): Distributed tuning of boundary resources: The case of Apple's iOS service system. *MIS Quarterly: Special Issue on Service Innovation in a Digital Age*, vol. 39, no. 1, pp. 217–243.

Edwards, P., S. J. Jackson, G. C. Bowker, & C. P. Knobel (2007): *Understanding infrastructure: Dynamics, tensions, and design*. Report of a Workshop on "History & Theory of Infrastructure: Lessons for New Scientific Cyberinfrastructures." www.sis.pitt.edu/~gbowker/cyberinfrastructure.pdf

Elaluf-Calderwood, S., B. D. Eaton, J. D. Herzhoff, & C. Sørensen (2011): Mobile platforms as convergent systems: Analysing control points and tussles with emergent socio-technical discourses. In *Recent developments in mobile communications – A multidisciplinary approach*, ed. J. P. Maícas. Intech Open Access Publisher, pp. 97–112. www.intechopen.com/books/recent-developments-in-mobile-communications-a-multidisciplinary-approach/mobile-platforms-as-convergent-systems-analysing-control-points-and-tussles-with-emergent-socio-tech

Evans, D. S. & R. Schmalensee (2016): *The matchmakers: The new economics of multisided platforms*. Boston: Harvard Business Review Press.

Farjoun, M. (2010): Beyond dualism: Stability and change as a duality. *Academy of Management Journal*, vol. 35, no. 2, pp. 202–225.

Frischmann, B. M. (2012): *Infrastructure: The social value of shared resources*. Oxford: Oxford University Press.

Gawer, A., ed. (2009): *Platforms, markets and innovation*. Cheltenham: Edward Elgar.

Gawer, A. & M. A. Cusumano (2002): *Platform leadership: How Intel, Microsoft, and Cisco drive industry innovation*. Boston, MA: Harvard Business School Press.

Ghazawneh, A. & O. Henfridsson (2013): Balancing platform control and external contribution in third-party development: The boundary resources model. *Information Systems Journal*, vol. 23, no. 2, pp. 173–192.

Goldsmith, J. L. & T. Wu (2006): *Who controls the Internet? Illusions of a borderless world*. Oxford: Oxford University Press.

Google. (2016): *IPv6 statistics*. www.google.com/intl/en/ipv6/statistics.html.

Hanseth, O. (2006): *Information technology as infrastructure*. PhD Thesis, Goteborg University.

Hanseth, O. & K. Lyytinen (2010): Design theory for dynamic complexity in information infrastructures: The case of building Internet. *Journal of Information Technology*, vol. 25, no. 1, pp. 1–19.

Heins, M. (2016): *The globalization of American infrastructure: The shipping container and freight transportation*. London: Routledge. 131728237X.

Henfridsson, O. & B. Bygstad (2013): The generative mechanisms of digital infrastructure evolution. *MIS Quarterly*, vol. 37, no. 3, pp. 907–931.

Hughes, T. P. (1983): *Networks of power: Electric supply systems in the US, England and Germany, 1880–1930*. Baltimore: Johns Hopkins University.

Kallinikos, J. (2007): *The consequences of information: Institutional implications of technological change*. Cheltenham: Edward Elgar.

Kallinikos, J., A. Aaltonen, & A. Marton (2013): The ambivalent ontology of digital artifacts. *MIS Quarterly*, vol. 37, no. 2, pp. 357–370.

Karhu, K. (2017): *Managing competitive and cooperative strategizing in open platform ecosystems using boundary resources*. Doctoral Dissertation, Department of Computer Science, Aalto University, Helsinki. http://urn.fi/URN:ISBN:978-952-60-7235-7

Lessig, L. (2000): *Code and other laws of cyberspace*. New York: Basic Books.

Lessig, L. (2002): *The future of ideas: The fate of the commons in a connected world*. New York: Vintage Books.

Lessig, L. (2006): *Code: Version 2.0*. New York: Basic Books.

Lyytinen, K., T. Keil, & V. Fomin (2010): A framework to build process theories of anticipatory information and communication technology (ICT) standardizing. *New Applications in IT Standards: Developments and Progress: Developments and Progress*, p. 147.

Lyytinen, K. & G. M. Rose (2003): The disruptive nature of information technology innovations: The case of Internet computing in systems development organizations. *MIS Quarterly*, vol. 27, no. 4, pp. 557–596.

Lyytinen, K., Y. Yoo, & R. J. Boland Jr (2016): Digital product innovation within four classes of innovation networks. *Information Systems Journal*, vol. 26, no. 1, pp. 47–75.

Parker, G. G., M. W. Van Alstyne, & S. P. Choudary (2016): *Platform revolution: How networked markets are transforming the economy and how to make them work for you*. New York: W. W. Norton.

Sandhana, L. (2003): Blind 'see with sound.' http://news.bbc.co.uk/1/hi/sci/tech/3171226.stm.

Shapiro, C. & H. R. Varian (1998): *Information rules: A strategic guide to the network economy*. Boston: Harvard Business School Press.

Star, S. L. & K. Ruhleder (1996): Steps toward an ecology of infrastructure: Design and access for large information spaces. *Information Systems Research*, vol. 7, no. 1, pp. 111–134.

Tilson, D. (2008): *The interrelationships between technical standards and industry structures: Actor-network based case studies of the mobile wireless and television industries in the US and the UK.* Unpublished Doctoral Dissertation, Case Western Reserve University.

Tilson, D. & K. Lyytinen (2006): The 3G transition: Changes in the US wireless industry. *Telecommunications Policy*, vol. 30, no. 10, pp. 569–586.

Tilson, D., K. Lyytinen, C. Sørensen, & J. Liebenau (2006): *Coordination of technology and diverse organizational actors during service innovation – The case of wireless data services in the United Kingdom.* In the 5th Mobility Roundtable, Helsinki, Finland.

Tilson, D., K. Lyytinen, & C. Sørensen (2010): Digital infrastructures: The missing IS research agenda. *Information Systems Research*, vol. 21, no. 5, pp. 748–759.

Tilson, D., C. Sørensen, & K. Lyytinen (2012): *Change and control paradoxes in mobile infrastructure innovation: The Android and iOS mobile operating systems cases.* In 45th Hawaii International Conference on System Science (HICSS 45), Maui, HI:

Tilson, D., C. Sørensen, & K. Lyytinen (2013): *Platform complexity: Lessons from the music industry.* In 46th Hawaii International Conference on System Science (HICSS 46), Maui, HI.

Tiwana, A. (2014): *Platform ecosystems: Aligning architecture, governance, and strategy.* Waltham, MA: Morgan Kaufmann.

Tracy, A. (2015): Apple says iOS 9 adoption rate is the fastest ever, running on 50% of devices. Accessed: 26/1/2016, www.forbes.com/sites/abigailtracy/2015/09/21/apple-says-ios-9-adoption-rate-is-the-fastest-ever/-53d242bf2727.

Trist, E. (1981): *The evolution of socio-technical systems.* Occasional paper, vol. 2, pp. 1981.

Vaast, E., E. Davidson, & T. Matteson (2013): Talking about technology: The emergence of a new actor category through new media. *MIS Quarterly*, vol. 37, no. 4, pp. 1069–1092.

Wu, T. (2010): *The master switch: The rise and fall of information empires.* New York: Knopf.

Yoo, Y. (2012): Digital materiality and the emergence of an evolutionary science of the artificial. In *Materiality and organizing: Social interaction in a technological world*, ed. P. M. Leonardi, B. Nardi, and J. Kallinikos. Ann Arbor: University of Michigan Press, pp. 134–154.

Yoo, Y., O. Henfridsson, & K. Lyytinen (2010): The new organizing logic of digital innovation: An agenda for information systems research. *Information Systems Research*, vol. 21, no. 4, pp. 724–735.

Zittrain, J. (2006): The generative Internet. *Harvard Law Review*, vol. 119, pp. 1974–2040.

Zittrain, J. (2008): *The future of the Internet: And how to stop it.* London: Allen Lane.

18
THE ROLE OF ENTERPRISE SYSTEMS IN INNOVATION IN THE CONTEMPORARY ORGANIZATION

Darshana Sedera[1] and Sachithra Lokuge[2]

Introduction

Since the 1990s information systems (IS) researchers have investigated the organizations' use of information technology (IT) for innovation (Swanson 1994; Swanson and Ramiller 2004). Contrary to the orthodox view of IT's role as an enabler of innovation, a recent study by Nambisan (2013) suggests that IT could plays an advanced role by triggering innovation in an organization. As such, it is evident that contemporary organizations utilize their IT in novel ways to introduce innovation. Since the 1990s organizations have been presented with enterprise systems (ES), which were promoted as a solution to the dotcom bubble (Ives et al. 2002). Since then, ES has gained a special prominence in organizations in their ability to enable innovations through the introduction of efficient and effective business processes aiding innovation (Sedera et al. 2016; Srivardhana and Pawlowski 2007). Enterprise systems are said to have provided the standardized 'best practices' to organizations, at a time when most were struggling to cope with isolated and heavily individualized business processes (Davenport 2013).

Prior research on the ES highlights the importance of the features and functions of ES for innovation through the lens of absorptive capacity (Srivardhana and Pawlowski 2007), operational flexibility (Karimi et al. 2007), business process improvements (Grover and Segars 2005), productivity (Shang and Seddon 2007) and its stability (Sedera et al. 2016). It is also argued that ES provide a standardized technology platform (Gawer 2009) that allows collaboration of multiple functional units such as accounting, warehousing and production planning and collaborators (Kraemmerand et al. 2003), which facilitate innovation. However, the common view is that the ES is inherently rigid and complex, therefore it hinders the innovation capabilities of an organization (Kharabe et al. 2013; Kharabe and Lyytinen 2012). For example, high resource intensiveness (Murphy and Simon 2002), skill shortage (Srivardhana and Pawlowski 2007), diffusion complexities (Gable et al. 2008; Gorla et al. 2010) and steep organizational learning requirements (Gorla et al. 2010; Saraf et al. 2013) have been shown to restrict the ability of ES to enable innovation. Furthermore, some researchers criticize ES for lacking flexibility (Kharabe et al. 2013; Kharabe and Lyytinen 2012) and lacking long-term value propositions for life cycle–wide innovation (Kemp and Low 2008; McAfee and Brynjolfsson 2008).

At the same time, anecdotal commentary suggests that organizations are innovating with low-cost, flexible and easy-to-access technologies such as cloud computing, mobile, wearables and social media. In this chapter, we refer to these technologies as digital technologies to distinguish the role of ES in facilitating innovation in the IT portfolio. Organizations that utilize digital technologies for innovation have shown much resilience to the changes in the environment and hyper-competition and have demonstrated better connectedness with their business partners (Nylén and Holmström 2015). The availability of these digital technologies has raised new innovation possibilities for new and traditional organizations (Avedillo et al. 2015; Yoo et al. 2012). While the 'green-field' organizations can think of technologies 'from scratch,' such options are not available for the incumbent traditional organizations (Avedillo et al. 2015). Further, for many organizations, an ES is critical for existing operations and also represents the largest single IT investment (Srivardhana and Pawlowski 2007). As such, the traditional organizations must see new ways of combining the digital technologies with their ES. The dipolar nature of digital technologies and the existing ES present a challenge to create a consistent and productive IT portfolio that facilitates innovation. Management consultants call this phenomenon of managing new and old technologies in a single IT portfolio a 'two-speed IT system,' highlighting the distinct nature of the two types of systems.[3] Figure 18.1 depicts the characteristics of the legacy ES and digital technologies. Figure 18.1 also highlights that astute organizations can employ the IT portfolio in which the capabilities of each type of system are matched with weaknesses of other types of systems to create portfolio strategies that provide value to the organization.

The objective of this chapter is to raise a discussion about the changing role of ES in innovation in these dynamic and hyper-competitive times. There is growing consensus among the academics (e.g., Carlo et al. 2014) and practitioners (e.g., PwC 2012) that radical innovations facilitated by enterprise systems are too costly to the organization (Benner and Tushman

Enterprise Systems	Digital Technologies
Rigid	**Flexible**
Enterprise Systems architectures tend to be more rigid than those of digital technologies	
On-premise	**Hosted**
Enterprise Systems tend to be on-premise. Some digital technologies are available as subscription based	
Steep learning	**Ease of learning**
Enterprise Systems are complex and hard to learn. Systems based on digital technologies are easy to learn	
Necessitate substantial change	**Changes are minimal**
Enterprise Systems implementations require substantial changes. Digital technology changes are manageable	
Low trialability	**High trialability**
Trailing an Enterprise System is hard. Much of digital technologies can be trialled with less interventions	
Business process orientation	**Functional orientation**
Enterprise Systems tend to provide process orientation. Digital technologies can focus on functions	
Capital Expenditure	**Operating Expenditure**
Enterprise Systems tend to be a capital expense. Digital technologies can be managed as an operating expense	

Figure 18.1 Comparison of enterprise systems and digital technologies

2003). Similarly, there are equally compelling arguments that incremental innovations of ES may not suit the current dynamic environment (Chang et al. 2014). Moreover, there is potential for the organizations to amalgamate digital technologies with the enterprise system to create better innovation potentials.

A quick word on innovation

The "importance of innovation to organizational competitiveness" has been acknowledged for decades by many scholars (Wolfe 1994, p. 405). According to Schumpeterian creative destruction, organizations that are less adaptive to changes in the dynamic environment are less likely to survive (Abrell et al. 2016; Tushman and Anderson 1986). As such, for the survival in the contemporary competitive world, innovation has become a necessity (Leifer et al. 2000; Lewis et al. 2002; Utterback 1994). Innovation in this book chapter is defined as any idea, practice or material artefact perceived to be new by the relevant unit of adoption (Zaltman et al. 1977). This definition takes into account any idea, artifact or any practice that is not new to the world, but new to the organization that adopts it. As Nambisan (2013, p. 216) says,

> in the last one decade or so, the nature of innovation has undergone considerable change in most industries. Innovation has become much more open, global, and collaborative in nature to involve a diverse network of partners and emphasizing distributed innovation processes.

Further, Yoo et al. (2012, p. 1400) argue that the process of innovation itself has shifted dramatically in recent times owing to the "open, flexible affordances of . . . digital technology," thereby requiring separate investigation.

The role of ES in innovation

Information systems scholars have recognized ES as a strong enabler of innovation (Seddon et al. 2010; Srivardhana and Pawlowski 2007; Van den Bergh and Viaene 2013). According to Allied Market Research, the ES market size is predicted to reach $41.69 billion by 2020, with key players like SAP AG, Oracle Corp. and Microsoft noted as the leading vendors. An enterprise system provides a modular suite of software that allows an organization to run its core business processes. Enterprise systems epitomize features such as process integration, process orientation, process standardization and real-time information (Seddon et al. 2010). According to Panorama Consulting Solutions, a typical average enterprise systems implementation time for mid-sized organization is 14 months and implementation costs could start at several million dollars. Organizations have justified the lengthy implementation times and costs, considering the innate characteristics of integration, real-time information flows and standardization. There is also evidence that ES has enabled organizations to innovate by offering increased knowledge capabilities (Srivardhana and Pawlowski 2007). These packaged ES applications provide benefits such as better corporate governance, consistent and real-time information, and stable and flexible platforms (Davenport 2000b; Gable et al. 2008; Seddon et al. 2010; Sedera and Gable 2010). Furthermore, the implementation of the ES to an organization is often characterized as a radical change to business processes (Bingi et al. 1999; Kraemmerand et al. 2003) and management structures (Sasidharan et al. 2012). However, due to its high resource intensiveness, there is a continuous debate on the long-term innovation value propositions of

ES (Davenport 2000a; Davenport et al. 2004; Dutta et al. 2014; Kemp and Low 2008; McAfee and Brynjolfsson 2008).

The ability and the newness of the information systems deteriorate over time, and as a result, for the survival of the organizations these systems must be upgraded or replaced (Swanson and Dans 2000). Enterprise systems too face the same problem in losing their innovation value propositions over time. However, ES are rarely replaced (Eden et al. 2014), highlighting the need for organizations to innovate using their existing ES. Many organizations using ES rely upon the software vendor for life cycle–wide innovations through upgrades and launch of new products (Chua and Khoo 2011). However, factors like the complexity of upgrades, resource constraints and tiresome continuous change management initiatives have dulled the appetite for organizations to engage in regular software upgrades – therefore compromising the innovation potential. Moreover, the exclusive innovation potential of ES diminishes over time. Research on ES use (e.g., Burton-Jones and Grange 2012; McLean and Sedera 2010) and ES benefits (e.g., Seddon et al. 2010) allude to the necessity for continuously finding new ways of using the ES to facilitate innovation. The aforementioned facets relating to enterprise systems place a growing pressure on organizations, vendors and implementation partners to deliver better solutions, models and approaches that facilitates life cycle–wide innovation (Esteves 2009; Lokuge and Sedera 2014b; Lokuge and Sedera 2014c).

However, ES are inherently considered less flexible systems (Kharabe and Lyytinen 2012). For example, ES was considered 'liquid concrete,' highlighting its inflexibility (Lokuge 2015; Lokuge and Sedera 2014a; *Economist* 2007). Anecdotal commentary suggests that company's reliance on the software vendor for its innovations creates an over-dependency. Such overdependencies on the software vendor for innovations not only takes away the innovation spirit of the organization, but it also dampens the unique solution for individual strategic advantage (Kumar and van Hillegersberg 2000; Kumar et al. 2003). Moreover, obtaining appropriate enterprise systems skills still remains one of the challenging tasks for the organization. The appropriate skills shortage is visible at all levels of the organization; technical, management and operational. Not having the right skills is a major barrier for innovations (Jansen et al. 2006). Considering the challenges that organizations face, enterprise systems vendors now promote open architectures for wider participation of third-party vendors and skills, thus expanding innovation opportunities. Such open technologies have eliminated some of the inflexible architectures and have enhanced openness of enterprise systems (Ceccagnoli et al. 2012). Therefore, ES are now taking a more salient role as a technology platform (Gawer and Cusumano 2012; Schenk 2015). The advanced role of ES as a technology platform is providing an ecosystem of independent software vendors to integrate with the ES, facilitating organizations to innovate (Ceccagnoli et al. 2012; Lokuge and Sedera 2016).

The digital technologies join the IT portfolio

The advent of digital technologies such as cloud computing, wearables, mobile technology, social media and business analytics are said to provide unprecedented opportunities to all organizations in the world. These technologies are easily accessible (Nylén and Holmström 2015), easily maintainable (Chakravarty et al. 2013), can be easily integrated with other technologies (Rai and Tang 2010), are flexible (Nambisan 2013), have a low information processing capability (Nylén and Holmström 2015) and enable reusability (Yoo et al. 2012; Yoo et al. 2010). The ease of use of these technologies has increased the participation of the users in innovation activities (Nylén and Holmström 2015; Zittrain 2006). As such, the innate capabilities of digital technologies provide myriad ways to attain innovation in an organization.

The aforementioned positive affordances of digital technologies provide organizations an opportunity to engage in IT-led innovation with relatively low resource availability (e.g., finance and human capital). These technologies enable organizations with fewer resources to innovate and compete with large organizations in a similar manner (Sedera et al. 2016). Thus, researchers argue that the advent of digital technologies has disrupted the orthodox direct relationship with resource availability and organizational outcomes (Lokuge and Sedera 2014a; Sedera et al. 2016). Furthermore, opportunities to apply these technologies have augmented due to the consumerization of IT, through which IT has become an accessible commodity to the general public to take part in innovations (Carr 2003). Researchers and practitioners accredit these factors to the birth and growth of organizations like Uber, Airbnb and Alibaba.com. Although the distinct characteristics of digital technologies, together with the consumerization of IT, have important practical and theoretical implications for organizations, these technologies need to be effectively integrated with existing technologies in the organization. The diverse nature of these technologies – digital technologies and existing technologies – presents a challenge to create a consistent and productive IT portfolio.

McKenzie consulting company calls this phenomenon of managing new and old technologies in a single IT portfolio 'two-speed IT systems,' highlighting the dipolar nature of the systems. They also highlight that astute organizations can employ the IT portfolio in which the capabilities of each type of system are matched with weaknesses of other types of systems to create portfolio strategies that provide value to the organization. On one side of the two-speed IT, the existing IT portfolio includes legacy systems, dominated by ES. Many scholars praise the capabilities of ES in providing operational flexibility, real-time information and transparency (Seddon et al. 2010). However, as mentioned earlier, high resource intensiveness, the need for continuous vendor-driven upgrades, skill shortages, diffusion complexities and steep organizational learning requirements have been shown to restrict the ability of ES-led legacy applications to innovate in the modern dynamic economies. In addition, some criticize ES for lacking flexibility and lacking long-term value propositions for life cycle–wide innovation.

On the other hand, since the mid-2000s, the advent of cloud computing, wearables, mobile technology, social media and business analytics has presented corporate IT with 'fast-paced' new technologies that have dramatically changed the nature of IT for achieving corporate goals. Fueled by the consumerization of IT, the ability to acquire, learn, deploy, use and manage these systems faster than traditional systems has made these technologies popular with organizations seeking rapid opportunities in the hyper-competitive global markets. In addition, these newer technologies go beyond the conventional boundaries of the traditional corporate IT (Lokuge 2015).

The challenge for an organization is not to endorse one type of system, but to strategically use both the existing systems (slow) and fast digital technologies in combination to create value. Furthermore, no organization has the appetite to dispose of the existing systems, especially ES. Therefore, the two types of systems with seemingly dipolar characteristics (as depicted in Figure 18.1) should be strategically amalgamated to derive true business value. Despite the purported opportunities presented to organizations to develop and employ an IT portfolio that is flexible, dynamic and effective, we see that only very few organizations are successful in changing their IT portfolio to achieve high organizational benefits, with most still struggling to assemble and manage their IT portfolio. Even though management consultants coined the term 'two-speed IT architecture' as a survival mantra for established firms, guidelines on how a two-speed IT portfolio is created are scant. Moreover, the era of two-speed IT is a novel experience, especially to the traditional ones. As such the existing management practices may not work effectively. Therefore, the deployment and management of a two-speed IT portfolio requires fundamental re-thinking.

Considerations for organizations

Having considered the historical and current state of ES, digital technologies and the universal need to innovate, this chapter now presents contextual factors for attaining innovation through a mix of IT in contemporary organizations. These considerations can be enacted as strategies. Then such considerations will lead organizations to innovate better.

Stabilize your enterprise system

The stability of the enterprise systems has been discussed in many academic and practitioner outlets (Avedillo et al. 2015; Sedera et al. 2016). It is commonly agreed that an organization with an enterprise system would undergo a performance dip (Ross and Vitale 2000). Anecdotal commentary suggests that using an enterprise system is a complex phenomenon that impacts the organization in a multitude of ways. Academic studies have characterized the impact of ES in organizations demonstrating that organizations take time to train, learn and adopt the system. This process happens over long periods (Kamhawi and Gunasekaran 2009). The journey with the enterprise systems for the organization with initially steep learning curves (Botta-Genoulaz and Millet 2005; Mandal and Gunasekaran 2003) when they first encounter the system and gradually master the use of it (McAfee 2006; Sun 2012) has been characterized using two life cycle phases. Transiting from the early phase of the ES life cycle to a phase of maturity, namely, from the shakedown to the onward and upward phase (Markus and Tanis 2000), users seem to follow the general characteristics identified in learning theories (Cotteleer and Bendoly 2006; Ranganathan and Brown 2006) by gaining competence over time (Sedera and Dey 2013).

Many argue that the turbulence in the shakedown phase inhibits innovations and that the onward and upward phase is the best time for organizations to seek innovations. As such, the 'mature' organization seeks to ignite innovative actions through initiatives like ES business process improvements (Davenport 2013; Srivardhana and Pawlowski 2007) and ES upgrades (Chua and Khoo 2011). Maturity is a relative term and should not be used as a yardstick to compare organizations. The interpretations of the maturity or the stability of the enterprise system can range from 'a time for continuous improvements,' 'time waiting for the next upgrade' and 'leave it alone forever.'

While there is evidence that such activities like business process improvement initiatives and software upgrades would add value to an organization, many organizations seem to struggle to focus on innovation activities due to continuing disturbances of the software upgrades. For organizations to innovate using enterprise systems and digital technologies, it is best that a state where the inconsistencies are minimum is treated as the state of maturity. Then, instead of perfecting the enterprise system through upgrades and business process initiatives, the organization can start using the digital technologies to innovate. Such an approach will enable an organization to increases its emphasis on innovation through favorable characteristics of digital technologies, rather than perfecting the enterprise system.

Figure 18.2 is derived to create a better understanding of the relationship between the two ES life cycle phases and the levels of innovation. Organizations in the top left quadrant, which are attempting to innovate with enterprise systems at the shakedown phase, will have the

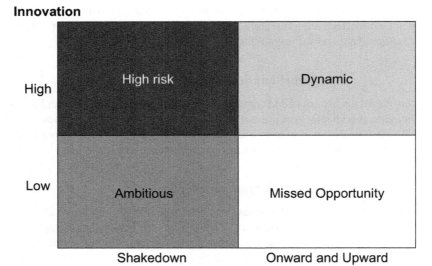

Figure 18.2 Maturity and innovation

highest risks. Researchers alluded to the 'dip in performance' as an ES shock (Ross and Vitale 2000), which indicates characteristics of radical innovations to the organization (Kraemmerand et al. 2003). As such it denotes high risk to the organization. The lower left quadrant demonstrates the continuing innovation attempts at the shakedown phase. Such activities at the shakedown phase will be ambitious and are likely to provide less return on investment. The top right quadrant demonstrates the most favorable scenario, where the rate of innovation is high and the organization is at the onward and upward phase of the life cycle. It is again reminded that the 'maturity' is a relative notion, and once an organization reaches a balanced state, then one should refrain from meddling with the enterprise system. The likelihood that an organization uses digital technologies for innovation together with the mature enterprise system in this quadrant is high. The lower right quadrant highlights an organization with a stable enterprise system, but with low level of innovations. Such organizations miss out on the potential of their enterprise system's stability. These organizations miss out on the potential opportunities to innovate. Perhaps, such organizations should restrict their continuing investments to enterprise systems and focus more on digital technologies.

Recognize ES as a platform

Enterprise systems provide a substantial amount of software features and functions to the organization. The historic discussion of enterprise systems are providing 'best practice' features and functions is a common factor that organizations considered when adopting enterprise systems. There is recent evidence of organizations treating the enterprise system as a platform emerging from the anecdotal commentary. Treating the enterprise system as a technology platform is another way that an organization can facilitate innovations. Such conceptualization will enable organizations to use its base for other applications, processes or technologies to be developed. The enterprise system as a platform has received traction due to its widespread adoption and the emergence of open technology architectures such as the NetWeaver platform interface by SAP (Gawer and Cusumano 2012). An enterprise system is considered a technology platform that allows technologies to be integrated (Tilson et al. 2010). Considering the fundamentals of a platform, Gawer (2009) recognizes the ability of the ES to acts as a building block, allowing other complementary technologies to be integrated (Lokuge et al. 2016; Sedera et al. 2016).

Figure 18.3 provides four views of how organizations can position their innovations against the focus of the software: functional or platform. Commencing from the left panels, the traditional view of an enterprise system emphasizes innovation by adding new features and functionalities. Such an approach is limited, in that an organization attempting innovations by adding software features and functions will have a strong dependence on the enterprise system vendor. This would typically mean that a high rate of innovation would be a costly exercise for the organization. When considering the enterprise system as a platform, the opportunities presented to integrate digital technologies provide an opportunistic environment. However, anecdotal commentary suggests that, even though organizations have the ability to integrate their ES technology platform with digital technologies, they are reluctant to initiate due to risk aversion.

Reduce the vendor-led innovations

When ES were first implemented, there was much focus on maintaining 'vanilla' implementations. In a vanilla implementation, the organization adheres to the way espoused by the software vendor and made it easier for an organization to manage the enterprise system implementation and its subsequent upgrades. A vanilla implementation makes the organization forgo any software customizations to facilitate unique requirements of the organization. Following this approach led to high vendor dependence in traditional ES using organizations. As such, the traditional incumbents of enterprise systems developed a strong reliance on their software vendor and the implementation partner for innovations. However, over time,

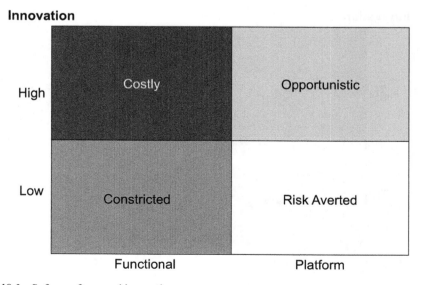

Figure 18.3 Software focus and innovation

organizations have learnt much about the enterprise systems about its implementation and management. Moreover, the ES vendors also have improved the software architectures by making them more flexible and open.

These flexible and open architectures of enterprise systems now allow digital technologies to be connected with ES easily. Moreover, most of the digital technologies are innately vendor agnostic. The digital technologies use common software and data protocols. That means a service of a particular digital technology vendor can be obtained through most other service providers. Moreover, such characteristics like ease of use, ease of learning and the consumerization of IT have led to the creation of a growing network of contributors associated with digital technologies. As such, there are many third-party digital technology–based software applications that are developed to work with ES. The digital technology vendor agnosticism and dynamic contributor network make the scale and speed of innovation much faster compared to that of the ES.

Figure 18.4 provides a conceptual view of the rate of innovation against the continuum of vendor agnosticism. Historically, most organizations prefer the 'vendor-led' innovation approach for their ES initiatives. As such, the enterprise system becomes highly vendor specific. The rate of innovations coming from vendors through software upgrades and optional enhancements is restrained (top left corner). Digital technologies, on the other hand, will enable organizations to become vendor agnostic. This allows the organization to engage with a plethora of vendors beyond the enterprise system vendor for innovations. As such, this will provide opportunities for the organization to develop an aggressive innovation approach.

Decentralized decision-making process

The traditional management structure of enterprise systems tends to be hierarchically topdown, managed by a central entity. Such a management structure was necessary for the organizations to maintain a 'single instance' enterprise system in the organization. However,

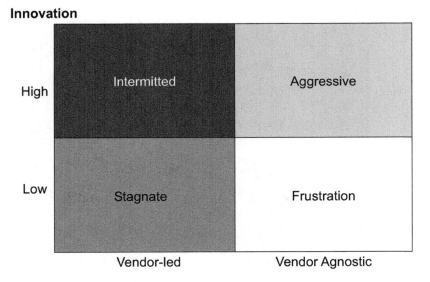

Figure 18.4 Vendor agnosticism and innovation

the centralized decision making in enterprise systems management approach made it nearly impossible to accommodate any changes. Scholars argue that a centralized enterprise systems management approach enabled organizations to increase the emphasis of these mandated systems (Sheu et al. 2004). Moreover, the value-proposition with ES at the beginning of its adoption remained high with high risk of failure. As such, the centralized approach was suitable for organizations.

However, the centralized management approach introduces several substantial barriers to innovation. First, the tight control of the centralized approach introduces local inefficiencies. Centralization can lead to significant delays in decisions that impact executions through ES. For local managers with limited authority, the rapid response time to hyper-competitive market challenges can be a problem. Highly centralized ES initiatives may require local managers to contact remote centralized hosting services in certain situations. Second, poor creativity in relation to ES will emerge as a major issue associated with centralization. An overly top-down organizational approach naturally prohibits creative thinking and innovative ideas from line-of-business levels. On the other hand, a decentralized approach often promotes new product and service ideas conceived by regular employees and conveyed through their managers to the top. When there is a major distance in involvement between centralized leaders and line-of-business employees, there is little motivation for employees to ponder innovations, let alone communicate them internally.

Figure 18.5 demonstrates the scope of innovation for centralized and decentralized management structures. In the centralized management approach, which is typical in most organizations with ES, the organization requires a high level of coordination in order to attain a high rate of innovations. On the other hand, if the organization has a centralized management approach and the rate of innovation is low, then it would seem plausible that the organization is only concerned about the predetermined innovations. Such innovations may not withstand the sudden changes in the market, environment and circumstances. A decentralized management approach is best suitable for a portfolio of ES and digital technologies.

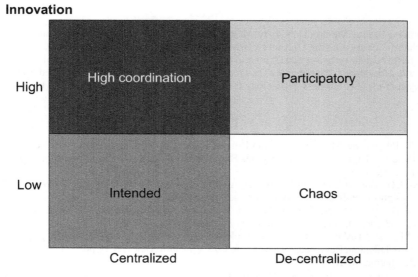

Figure 18.5 Software management approach and innovation

A decentralized approach will enable the organization to include wider participation from a range of participants, from line-of-business to senior managers. Their participation will be informed by the accessibility of digital technologies, knowledge of digital technology gained through common channels and experience with the ES. If such attempts do not lead to a high rate of innovation, then the organization needs to re-think its innovation and management approach.

Final remarks

Enterprise systems are among the most prominent technologies in the 21st century. The advent and proliferation of ES since the late 1990s have changed the entire premise of the corporate IT landscape. Enterprise systems purport to have introduced best practices, integration and process standardization. Overall, there is ample evidence to suggest that the advent of ES provided organizations with new innovation possibilities. However, the role of ES is changing, especially in the past several years. The advent of digital technologies provides the organization with a two-speed IT portfolio to innovate. For organizations to continuously innovate using this two-speed IT portfolio, the changing role of the enterprise system must be well understood. This chapter attempts to contribute to the discussion of the changing role of the enterprise system. It provided four scenarios where ES can work effectively with digital technologies to increase the rate of innovation. For information systems research, the two-speed IT portfolio provides challenges and opportunities. It is the first time that corporate IT is presented with diversity of systems with a plethora of capabilities. The traditional organization will find it challenging to manage and excel with a two-speed IT portfolio by adhering to its traditional strategies. Empirical advice on the changes in the two-speed IT portfolio is scant. Scholars may employ theories like resource-based views (Barney 2001), ambidexterity (Gibson and Birkinshaw 2004) or the theory for organizational readiness for change (Weiner 2009) to explore evidence-based theoretical sound ways to understand how to best employ the two-speed IT portfolio for innovations.

Notes

1 Darshana Sedera, Monash University, Melbourne, Australia. Darshana.sedera@gmail.com.
2 Sachithra Lokuge, Griffith University, Brisbane, Australia. ksplokuge@gmail.com.
3 For further details on two-speed IT, refer to Avedillo, J. G., Begonha, D., & Peyracchia, A. (2015). *Two Ways to Modernize IT Systems for the Digital Era*. Insights & Publications. Retrieved from www.mckinsey.com/insights/business_technology/two_ways_to_modernize_it_systems_for_the_digital_era.

References

Abrell, T., Pihlajamaa, M., Kanto, L., vom Brocke, J., and Uebernickel, F. 2016. "The Role of Users and Customers in Digital Innovation: Insights From B2B Manufacturing Firms," *Information & Management* (53:3), pp. 324–335.
Avedillo, J. G., Begonha, D., and Peyracchia, A. 2015. *Two Ways to Modernize IT Systems for the Digital Era*. Insights & Publications. www.mckinsey.com: McKinsey.
Barney, J. B. 2001. "Is the Resource-Based 'View' a Useful Perspective for Strategic Management Research? Yes," *Academy of Management Review* (26:1), pp. 41–56.
Benner, M. J., and Tushman, M. L. 2003. "Exploitation, Exploration, and Process Management: The Productivity Dilemma Revisited," *Academy of Management Review* (28:2), pp. 238–256.
Bingi, P., Sharma, M. K., and Godla, J. K. 1999. "Critical Issues Affecting an ERP Implementation," *Information Systems Management* (16:3), pp. 7–14.

Botta-Genoulaz, V., and Millet, P.-A. 2005. "A Classification for Better Use of ERP Systems," *Computers in Industry* (56:6), pp. 573–587.

Burton-Jones, A., and Grange, C. 2012. "From Use to Effective Use: A Representation Theory Perspective," *Information Systems Research* (24:3), pp. 632–658.

Carlo, J. L., Gaskin, J., Lyytinen, K., and Rose, G. M. 2014. "Early vs. Late Adoption of Radical Information Technology Innovations Across Software Development Organizations: An Extension of the Disruptive Information Technology Innovation Model," *Information Systems Journal* (24:3).

Carr, N. G. 2003. "IT Doesn't Matter," *Harvard Business Review* (81:5), pp. 41–49.

Ceccagnoli, M., Forman, C., Huang, P., and Wu, D. 2012. "Co-creation of Value in a Platform Ecosystem: The Case of Enterprise Software," *MIS Quarterly* (36:1), pp. 263–290.

Chakravarty, A., Grewal, R., and Sambamurthy, V. 2013. "Information Technology Competencies, Organizational Agility, and Firm Performance: Enabling and Facilitating Roles," *Information Systems Research* (24:4), pp. 976–997.

Chang, W., Franke, G. R., Butler, T. D., Musgrove, C. F., and Ellinger, A. E. 2014. "Differential Mediating Effects of Radical and Incremental Innovation on Market Orientation-Performance Relationship: A Meta-Analysis," *Journal of Marketing Theory and Practice* (22:3), pp. 235–250.

Chua, C.E.H., and Khoo, H. M. 2011. "How Organizations Motivate Users to Participate in Support Upgrades of Customized Packaged Software," *Information & Management* (48:8), pp. 328–335.

Cotteleer, M. J., and Bendoly, E. 2006. "Order Lead-Time Improvement Following Enterprise Information Technology Implementation: An Empirical Study," *MIS Quarterly*, pp. 643–660.

Davenport, T. H. 2000a. "The Future of Enterprise System-Enabled Organizations," *Information Systems Frontiers* (2:2), pp. 163–180.

Davenport, T. H. 2000b. *Mission Critical: Realizing the Promise of Enterprise Systems*. Cambridge, MA: Harvard Business Press.

Davenport, T. H. 2013. *Process Innovation: Reengineering Work Through Information Technology*. Cambridge, MA: Harvard Business Press.

Davenport, T. H., Harris, J. G., and Cantrell, S. 2004. "Enterprise Systems and Ongoing Process Change," *Business Process Management Journal* (10:1), pp. 16–26.

Dutta, A., Lee, H., and Yasai-Ardekani, M. 2014. "Digital Systems and Competitive Responsiveness: The Dynamics of IT Business Value," *Information & Management* (51:6), pp. 762–773.

Economist. 2007. "Liquid Concrete: As Software Shifts to an "On Demand" Model, Can SAP Move With the Times?" *Economist*. www.economist.com.

Eden, R., Sedera, D., and Tan, F. 2014. "Sustaining the Momentum: Archival Analysis of Enterprise Resource Planning Systems (2006–2012)," *Communications of the Association for Information Systems* (35:3), pp. 39–82.

Esteves, J. 2009. "A Benefits Realisation Road-Map Framework for ERP Usage in Small and Medium-Sized Enterprises," *Journal of Enterprise Information Management* (22:1/2), pp. 25–35.

Gable, G. G., Sedera, D., and Chan, T. 2008. "Re-Conceptualizing Information System Success: The IS-Impact Measurement Model," *Journal of the Association for Information Systems* (9:7), pp. 377–408.

Gawer, A. 2009. *Platforms, Markets, and Innovation*. Gloucestershire, UK: Edward Elgar.

Gawer, A., and Cusumano, M. A. 2012. "How Companies Become Platform Leaders," *MIT Sloan Management Review* (49:2), pp. 28–35.

Gibson, C. B., and Birkinshaw, J. 2004. "The Antecedents, Consequences, and Mediating Role of Organizational Ambidexterity," *Academy of Management Journal* (47:2), pp. 209–226.

Gorla, N., Somers, T. M., and Wong, B. 2010. "Organizational Impact of System Quality, Information Quality, and Service Quality," *Journal of Strategic Information Systems* (19:3), pp. 207–228.

Grover, V., and Segars, A. H. 2005. "An Empirical Evaluation of Stages of Strategic Information Systems Planning: Patterns of Process Design and Effectiveness," *Information & Management* (42:5), pp. 761–779.

Ives, B., Valacich, J. S., Watson, R. T., Zmud, R. W., Alavi, M., Baskerville, R., Baroudi, J. J., Beath, C., Clark, T., and Clemons, E. K. 2002. "What Every Business Student Needs to Know About Information Systems," *Communications of the Association for Information Systems* (9:1), p. 30.

Jansen, J.J.P., Van Den Bosch, F.A.J., and Volberda, H. W. 2006. "Exploratory Innovation, Exploitative Innovation, and Performance: Effects of Organizational Antecedents and Environmental Moderators," *Management Science* (52:11), pp. 1661–1674.

Kamhawi, E. M., and Gunasekaran, A. 2009. "ERP Systems Implementation Success Factors: IS and Non-IS Managers' Perceptions," *International Journal of Business Information Systems* (4:6), pp. 688–704.

Karimi, J., Somers, T. M., and Bhattacherjee, A. 2007. "The Impact of ERP Implementation on Business Process Outcomes: A Factor-Based Study," *Journal of Management Information Systems* (24:1), pp. 101–134.

Kemp, M., and Low, G. 2008. "ERP Innovation Implementation Model Incorporating Change Management," *Business Process Management Journal* (14:2), pp. 228–242.

Kharabe, A., and Lyytinen, K. J. 2012. "Is Implementing ERP Like Pouring Concrete Into a Company? Impact of Enterprise Systems on Organizational Agility," in: *Thirty-Third International Conference on Information Systems* (ICIS 2012). Orlando, FL.

Kharabe, A., Lyytinen, K., and Grover, V. 2013. "Do Organizational Competencies Influence How Enterprise Systems Foster Organizational Agility?," in: *International Conference On Information Systems* (ICIS 2013). Milan, Italy.

Klaus, H., Rosemann, M., and Gable, G. 2000. "What Is ERP?" *Information Systems Frontiers* (2:2), pp. 141–162.

Kraemmerand, P., Møller, C., and Boer, H. 2003. "ERP Implementation: An Integrated Process of Radical Change and Continuous Learning," *Production Planning & Control* (14:4), pp. 338–348.

Kumar, V., Maheshwari, B., and Kumar, U. 2003. "An Investigation of Critical Management Issues in ERP Implementation: Empirical Evidence From Canadian Organizations," *Technovation* (23:10), pp. 793–807.

Kumar, K., and van Hillegersberg, J. 2000. "ERP Experiences and Evolution," *Communications of the ACM* (43:4), pp. 22–26.

Leifer, R., McDermott, C. M., O'Connor, G. C., Peters, L. S., Rice, M. P., and Veryzer, R. W. 2000. *Radical Innovation: How Mature Companies Can Outsmart Upstairs*. Boston, MA: Harvard Business School Press.

Lewis, M. W., Welsh, M. A., Dehler, G. E., and Green, S. G. 2002. "Product Development Tensions: Exploring Contrasting Styles of Project Management," *Academy of Management Journal* (45:3), pp. 546–564.

Lokuge, K.S.P. 2015. *Agile Innovation: Innovating With Enterprise Systems*. Queensland University of Technology.

Lokuge, S., and Sedera, D. 2014a. "Deriving Information Systems Innovation Execution Mechanisms," *Australasian Conference on Information Systems* (ACIS 2014), Auckland, New Zealand: AIS Library.

Lokuge, S., and Sedera, D. 2014b. "Enterprise Systems Lifecycle-Wide Innovation," *Americas Conference on Information Systems* (AMCIS 2014), Savannah, Georgia: AIS Library.

Lokuge, S., and Sedera, D. 2014c. "Enterprise Systems Lifecycle-Wide Innovation Readiness," *Pacific Asia Conference on Information Systems* (PACIS 2014), Chengdu, China: AIS Library.

Lokuge, S., and Sedera, D. 2016. "Is Your IT Eco-System Ready to Facilitate Organizational Innovation? Deriving an IT Eco-System Readiness Measurement Model," *International Conference on Information Systems* (ICIS 2016), Dublin, Ireland: AIS.

Lokuge, S., Sedera, D., and Grover, V. 2016. "Thinking Inside the Box: Five Organizational Strategies Enabled Through Information Systems," *Pacific Asia Conference on Information Systems* (PACIS 2016), Chiyai, Taiwan: AIS.

Mandal, P., and Gunasekaran, A. 2003. "Issues in Implementing ERP: A Case Study," *European Journal of Operational Research* (146:2), pp. 274–283.

Markus, L., and Tanis, C. 2000. "The Enterprise Systems Experience – From Adoption to Success," in: *Framing the Domains of IT Management: Projecting the Future Through the Past*, R. W. Zmud (ed.). Cincinnati, OH: Pinnaflex Educational Resources, pp. 173–207.

McAfee, A. 2006. "Mastering the Three Worlds of Information Technology," *Harvard Business Review*, (November), pp. 141–148.

McAfee, A., and Brynjolfsson, E. 2008. "Investing in the IT That Makes a Competitive Difference," *Harvard Business Review* (86:7/8), pp. 98–107.

McLean, E., and Sedera, D. 2010. "The Measurement of Information System Use: Preliminary Considerations," *Americas Conference on Information Systems* (AMCIS), Lima, Peru: AIS.

Murphy, K. E., and Simon, S. J. 2002. "Intangible Benefits Valuation in ERP Projects," *Information Systems Journal* (12:4), pp. 301–320.

Nambisan, S. 2013. "Information Technology and Product/Service Innovation: A Brief Assessment and Some Suggestions for Future Research," *Journal of the Association for Information Systems* (14:4), pp. 215–226.

Nylén, D., and Holmström, J. 2015. "Digital Innovation Strategy: A Framework for Diagnosing and Improving Digital Product and Service Innovation," *Business Horizons* (58:1), pp. 57–67.

PwC. 2012. "How to Drive Innovation and Business Growth: Leveraging Emerging Technology for Sustainable Growth," www.pwc.com/en_US/us/supply-chain-management/assets/pwc-oracle-innovation-white-paper.pdf.

Rai, A., and Tang, X. 2010. "Leveraging IT Capabilities and Competitive Process Capabilities for the Management of Interorganizational Relationship Portfolios," *Information Systems Research* (21:3), pp. 516–570.

Ranganathan, C., and Brown, C. V. 2006. "ERP Investments and the Market Value of Firms: Toward an Understanding of Influential ERP Project Variables," *Information Systems Research* (17:2), pp. 145–161.

Ross, J. W., and Vitale, M. R. 2000. "The ERP Revolution: Surviving vs. Thriving," *Information Systems Frontiers* (2:2), pp. 233–241.

Saraf, N., Liang, H., Xue, Y., and Hu, Q. 2013. "How Does Organisational Absorptive Capacity Matter in the Assimilation of Enterprise Information Systems?" *Information Systems Journal* (23:3), pp. 245–267.

Sasidharan, S., Santhanam, R., Brass, D. J., and Sambamurthy, V. 2012. "The Effects of Social Network Structure on Enterprise Systems Success: A Longitudinal Multilevel Analysis," *Information Systems Research* (23:3/1/2), pp. 658–678.

Schenk, B. 2015. "The Role of Enterprise Systems in Process Innovation," in: *BPM-Driving Innovation in a Digital World*, J.V. Brocke and T. Schmiedel (eds.). Switzerland: Springer, pp. 75–84.

Seddon, P. B., Calvert, C., and Yang, S. 2010. "A Multi-Project Model of Key Factors Affecting Organizational Benefits From Enterprise Systems," *MIS Quarterly* (34:2), pp. 305–328.

Sedera, D., and Dey, S. 2013. "User Expertise in Contemporary Information Systems: Conceptualization, Measurement and Application," *Information & Management* (50:8), pp. 621–637.

Sedera, D., and Gable, G. G. 2010. "Knowledge Management Competence for Enterprise System Success," *Journal of Strategic Information Systems* (19:4), pp. 296–306.

Sedera, D., Lokuge, S., Grover, V., Sarker, S., and Sarker, S. 2016. "Innovating With Enterprise Systems and Digital Platforms: A Contingent Resource-Based Theory View," *Information & Management* (53:3), pp. 366–379.

Shang, S., and Seddon, P. B. 2007. "Managing Process Deficiencies With Enterprise Systems," *Business Process Management Journal* (13:3), pp. 405–416.

Sheu, C., Chae, B., and Yang, C.-L. 2004. "National Differences and ERP Implementation: Issues and Challenges," *Omega* (32:5), pp. 361–371.

Srivardhana, T., and Pawlowski, S. D. 2007. "ERP Systems as an Enabler of Sustained Business Process Innovation: A Knowledge-Based View," *Journal of Strategic Information Systems* (16:1), pp. 51–69.

Sun, H. 2012. "Understanding User Revisions When Using Information System Features: Adaptive System Use and Triggers," *MIS Quarterly* (36:2), pp. 453–478.

Swanson, E. B. 1994. "Information Systems Innovation Among Organizations," *Management Science* (40:9), pp. 1069–1092.

Swanson, E. B., and Dans, E. 2000. "System Life Expectancy and the Maintenance Effort: Exploring Their Equilibration," *MIS Quarterly* (24:2), pp. 277–297.

Swanson, E. B., and Ramiller, N. C. 2004. "Innovating Mindfully With Information Technology," *MIS Quarterly* (28:4), pp. 553–583.

Tilson, D., Lyytinen, K., and Sørensen, C. 2010. "Research Commentary-Digital Infrastructures: The Missing IS Research Agenda," *Information Systems Research* (21:4), pp. 748–759.

Tushman, M. L., and Anderson, P. 1986. "Technological Discontinuities and Organizational Environments," *Administrative Science Quarterly* (31:3), pp. 439–465.

Utterback, J.M. 1994. *Mastering the Dynamics of Innovation*. Boston, MA: Harvard Business School Press.

Van den Bergh, J., and Viaene, S. 2013. "Process Innovation: Redesigning an Enterprise Backbone System," in: *Enterprise Information Systems of the Future*. Berlin: Springer, pp. 1–17.

Weiner, B. J. 2009. "A Theory of Organizational Readiness for Change," *Implementation Science* (4:1), pp. 67–76.

Wolfe, R. A. 1994. "Organizational Innovation: Review, Critique and Suggested Research Directions," *Journal of Management Studies* (31:3), pp. 405–431.

Yoo, Y., Boland R. J., Jr., Lyytinen, K., and Majchrzak, A. 2012. "Organizing for Innovation in the Digitized World," *Organization Science* (23:5), pp. 1398–1408.

Yoo, Y., Henfridsson, O., and Lyytinen, K. 2010. "The New Organizing Logic of Digital Innovation: An Agenda for Information Systems Research," *Information Systems Research* (21:4), pp. 724–735.

Zaltman, G., Duncan, R., and Holbek, J. 1977. *Innovations and Organizations*. New York: John Wiley & Sons.

Zittrain, J. L. 2006. "The Generative Internet," *Harvard Law Review* (119:7), pp. 1974–2040.

19
DIGITAL CAPABILITY
Scaffolding for rewiring a company for digital

Joe Peppard

Introduction

In recent years, the label of digital has entered the lexicon of management and in many organizations digital has now become a fashionable rallying cry. Digital is simultaneously a technology, an objective, a threat, an opportunity, a workplace and a lifestyle. For some organizations, it is enabling new business models. For others, it offers a new way of engaging with customers. For many more, it represents an entirely different way of doing business and working with ecosystem partners. Organizations are building digital strategies and deploying and provisioning digital technologies. One certainty in today's environment is that most could not survive for very long today without their digital systems; indeed for some, technology provides the source of their competitive advantage while, more often than not, it is a necessity just to survive and avoid being disadvantaged.

As they embark on so-called digital transformation journeys, many companies are struggling to embrace digital opportunities and rewire themselves as digital organizations. While technology can be a constraint as well as an enabler of strategy and organizational agility, being digital is not a technology challenge but one of *knowing how* to get things done. Let's assume that an organization moves all its IT infrastructure, applications and services "off premise" and into "the cloud."[1] It does not now follow that the requirement to build a digital strategy, seek innovative digital opportunities, design the organization's architecture, prioritize and make digital investment decisions, or run projects and programs to implement digital strategies all suddenly disappear. As in the past, these requirements are all still paramount, together with the need to define a sourcing strategy, specify service expectations, assess, select and negotiate with vendors, achieve integration across multiple cloud providers and manage the delivery of myriad services. What all these functions have in common is that they are intellectual endeavors requiring the application of knowledge. Moreover, this knowledge is not located in any one organizational unit; rather, it is dispersed across the organization and requires coordination and integration to create "the knowing how to get things done" for these functions to manifest themselves. Having this knowing how is the objective of a digital capability.

In this chapter we introduce the scaffold for a digital capability. We first develop the arguments that embracing digital is a knowledge-based quest, and as this knowledge is distributed across an organization it presents a challenge for its coordination and application.

Furthermore, we argue that the essence of embracing digital is not to manage technology *per se* but to manage for the delivery of value from the capabilities of technology. Having presented its theoretical underpinnings, we first propose scaffolding upon which to hang the elements that make up a digital capability. We then explore how this "knowing how" is achieved. The chapter concludes with suggestions as to how organizations can begin the process of building a digital capability.

From managing technical artifacts to harnessing distributed knowledge

When computers first entered organizations, the expectation for them was limited to the automation of repetitive tasks through the processing of data. This objective was eloquently captured with the label attached to this quest: electronic data processing, or EDP for short. Primarily concerned with payroll and some accounting tasks, computers were seen as improving efficiency and cutting costs. Those organizations that could afford a computer established a separate unit (typically referred to as the computer or EDP department), staffed by technologists, whose job it was to keep this machine running. These professionals had the knowledge, skills and experience to maintain the hardware and software. As early computers were both physically large as well as being expensive to purchase, the majority of organizations availed of the services of computer bureaus, purchasing time share. This usually necessitated physically bringing punched cards and magnetic tape containing the data to be processed to the bureau; indeed, this can be considered as the forerunner to today's outsourcing practices. However, and this is the key point, the role of technology was very much peripheral to the core activities of the organization.

But this all changed in the early 1970s. As technology advanced and computers became more affordable, there was increasing use by organizations of "on premise" technology, with many purchasing their own computers, building data centers[2] and deploying packaged software. With the emergence of the personal computer (PC) and networking offering connectivity between devices, corporate computing was given a massive boost in the 1980s. As an inflection point, it also signaled a shift away from solely investing in technology for efficiency objectives to proactively seeking opportunities for competitive advantage. The role of technology had fundamentally changed, and this was accelerated with the opening up of the Internet for commercial activity in the early 1990s and, more recently, with the emergence of smartphones, cloud computing and the Internet of Things (IoT). Yet this shift is not generally reflected in how the majority of organizations choose to manage IT.

In much of the literature, the dominant practice is to objectify IS (in fact, "IS" and "IT" are generally used interchangeably), portraying it as data, information (sometimes knowledge), systems, hardware, software (including licenses), contracts, staff and associated costs (e.g., development, maintenance). As such, it is depicted as something – essentially artifacts – that can be directly manipulated. Even with outsourcing, the decision is typically framed as deciding what activities and resources should be sourced externally; the outcome of any decision to outsource is characterized as managing contracts, the supply of services (i.e., through service level agreements, service catalogues, and change requests), and relationships. It is likely that this logic sees organizations maintain an IS unit as a separate organizational entity, the assumption being that IS, as an objective construction, is manageable from within this structure. Importantly, what it suggests is that everything to be managed can be ring-fenced and contained within clear organizational boundaries. This unit can then be assigned a head (i.e., the CIO), given resources and a mandate that is often framed as optimizing or maximizing a return from any spend, all of course within an acceptable level of risk.

Moreover, the concept of "IT management" (IT eventually replacing the label "computer") dates back to an era when computers were large, complex and expensive, requiring specialist facilities and knowledge, where the key challenge for IT professionals was to keep the computer functioning. The practice of IT management thus became associated with the activities to keep the machine working, with requirements evolving over time to encompass the design and implementation of systems and the provision and presentation of information. And while the concept of information systems (as opposed to IT) management is now in common use, the tasks ascribed to IS management have expanded to include IS/IT strategy formulation and execution, innovation, IT service management, IT implementation, project management, managing software development projects, protecting information assets, technology and service procurement, vendor management and, in many cases, the delivery of expected benefits from IT investments.

In fact, the notion of IS (or IT) management is tautological, equating to the management of IS (or IT)! It conjures up the notion that ontologically, information systems are something that can actually be managed. Perhaps this is why leadership teams that are disappointed with the perceived return from their IT investments instigate programs to improve the performance of their IS organization; the assumption being that this is where the genesis of this problem lies (after all, this is the organizational unit responsible for IS (or IT)). Indeed, studies reporting on such initiatives typically begin with this proposition (Peppard, forthcoming). For example, Cross et al.'s (1997) presentation of the transformation of the IS organization at British Petroleum noted that "the IT function of the exploration and production division of British Petroleum Company set out to transform itself in response to a severe economic environment and poor internal perceptions of IT performance" – the ultimate sanction being to outsource the function, or parts of it, to a third party.

If we take a contrasting perspective, where the managerial challenge is not to manage IS (or IT) per se, but to generate value from IS – note that we are not specifying what this value is other than have a positive impact on organizational performance – then a somewhat different agenda emerges. This viewpoint accommodates IS in organizations as a situated and socially constructed phenomenon, questioning the very nature of what is sought to be managed.[3] Specifically, it proposes that IS is not a "thing" or set of "things" that can be managed or manipulated directly but that generating value from IS is a multifaceted and complex challenge. It necessitates understanding how technology impacts industry and competitive dynamics, identifying strategic opportunities, assessing and assimilating technological innovations, deriving new technology-enabled business models and organizational blueprints, prioritizing investment opportunities, managing IT-enabled change, deploying appropriate technology, steering IT projects, managing risk, selecting and managing vendors, exploiting investments in technology, ensuring appropriate usage of information systems, creating the environment for staff to embrace the right behaviors and values to work with information, and ensuring that the value delivered from any application of IT is captured by the organization. All related activities, practices and processes cannot happen within the confines of a separate organizational unit, labeled the IS organization, but are pervasive organization-wide concerns and endeavors.

Moreover, all these activities and related practices are underpinned by the application of knowledge, knowledge that is distributed across the organization. Software applications themselves are the automation of organizational knowledge[4] that is made explicit and embedded in workflows that capture algorithmic logic. In fact, technical infrastructures are the embodiment of knowledge, knowledge that has been deployed by systems and solutions architects, software developers, networking experts and so forth in its design and construction. Maintaining this legacy also requires knowledge, and while much of this knowledge will be primarily technical, some knowledge of business imperatives will also be required – for example, making the decision as to whether to decommission an application will depend on whether it is required by the business. Outsourcing arrangements can be similarly viewed as having a basis in knowledge (Kotlarsky et al., 2007); indeed, many organizations argue that they have outsourced their IT to an external service provider (ESP) or vendor, as it will provide them with access to knowledge that they do not currently possess. The challenge in generating value from IS can therefore be framed as one concerned with coordinating and integrating this knowledge to create organizational knowing, knowing how to get things done.

Yet, managing IT (or IT management) has never really been about technology anyway. It has always been a knowledge-oriented undertaking. Even in the 1960s and '70s, keeping complex mainframe computer systems functioning required specialized knowledge, most of it of a technical nature. And, when this was the only requirement, this knowledge was probably best housed within a separate organizational unit. Importantly, it was all under the jurisdiction and control of a single individual with a clear responsibility. Keeping technology functioning is not analogous to the delivery of value from technology; this challenge is much broader in scope.

The perspective of knowledge subscribed to in the foregoing discourse is that it is a social construct and "embodied" (Blackler, 1995) rather than an objectively definable commodity. As such, it is disseminated and legitimated within organizations through an ongoing process of interaction among individuals. Communication therefore plays a key role, with language itself similarly embodied in character. It is through these interactions taking place at multiple levels and among multiple employees that this knowing is developed. Organizational knowing can be seen as "an ongoing social accomplishment, constituted and reconstituted as actors engage the world in practice" (Orlikowski, 2002, p. 249). This knowing is at the heart of the digital capability.

Thus, what is being claimed is that the necessary knowledge underpinning this knowing to deliver value from digital is distributed throughout the organization (Peppard, 2007). Crucially, it is not located solely in a separate IS unit and under the jurisdiction of the CIO. In fact, much of this knowledge is under the control of other C-level executives. This is why, for example, it has been stressed as being of crucial importance for the CIO to build relationships with these executives – to ease access to knowledge resources under their control. If not, access to this knowledge will be difficult, if not impossible. Even with access, the organization must have the capability to coordinate and integrate this knowledge (Grant, 1996). This requires not just having a personal network providing access to knowledge, but also demands that trust, shared understanding and cooperation exist between parties for collective action to happen. Moreover, interactions via conversations play a central role, but this requires the ability to represent the knowledge of others. The not unreasonable assumption is that if all necessary knowledge cannot be harnessed, organizational knowing will be weak and it will be unlikely that value from digital will be optimized.

Digital can be seen as an umbrella term for both IS and IT, having both technological and information and system components (Peppard and Ward, 2016). A digital capability can be characterized as an organization's ability to continually generate value from information, systems and technology (Peppard and Ward, 2004). All organizations require a digital capability even if an organization makes the strategic choice not to seek competitive advantage by being an early adopter of new technology. As technology, via its information handling capabilities, permeates all activities and areas of an organization, having a digital capability becomes a necessity. Building a digital capability is not about constructing a technological infrastructure; rather it is a challenge about creating organizational knowing.

Figure 19.1 Schematic of hierarchy for digital capability

The theoretical underpinnings of a digital capability

To provide a theoretical underpinning for the digital capability we draw on the resource-based view (RBV) of the firm that has emerged from the strategic management discipline. This theory points to the importance of internal firm-specific factors in explaining variations in the performance of organizations, particularly over a period of time (Barney, 1986a, 1986b, 1991, 2001; Cool and Schendel, 1988; Hansen and Wernerfelt, 1989; Rumelt, 1991; Wernerfelt, 1984). A basic assumption of the RBV is that resources (i.e., technology, knowledge, skills) are distributed heterogeneously across organizations (Barney, 1991).[5] The theory argues that it is processes of resource accumulation and deployment that lead to idiosyncratic endowments of proprietary "assets" (Collis and Montgomery, 1995; Dierickx and Cool, 1989; Peteraf, 1993; Prahalad and Hamel, 1990; Wernerfelt, 1984) which may contribute to sustainable competitive advantage (Teece et al., 1997). These assets are typically referred to as competences.[6] While RBV is ostensibly a theory of competitive advantage,[7] it can also be useful when exploring firms at an individual level and how they harness resources to get things done.

Central to the RBV perspective is the fact that resources, *per se*, do not create value (Bowman and Ambrosini, 2000; Penrose, 1959); value is created by an organization's ability (or competence) to utilize and mobilize those resources. In the context of generating value from digital, as a cognitive challenge, the critical resource is the knowledge residing in employees or the employees of third-party vendors. Competence represents an organization's ability to deploy combinations of specific resources to accomplish a given task (Amit and Schoemaker, 1993) and is therefore the ongoing knowing that is enacted through the everyday and ongoing work of employees (Orlikowski, 2002). Thus competences are the collective knowing of the organization in initiating or responding to change "that is built into the organization's processes, procedures and systems, and that is embedded in modes of behavior, informal networks and personal relationships" (Collis, 1996, pp. 149–150).

An organizational capability is the strategic application of organizational competences (Kangas, 1999; Moingeon et al., 1998). In the context of digital, the capability is determined by the existence and strength of the underpinning competences. The hierarchy of capability, competences and resources that can be drawn from the RBV literature is illustrated in Figure 19.1.

A reasonable assumption is that these digital competences are generic across all organizations; that is, all organizations require certain know-how to do things and achieve particular outcomes. Of course, how they might choose to build and execute competences can differ. We also assume that the strength of these competences will be determined by the required capability.

A scaffold for the digital capability

Having introduced the theoretical background, this section builds scaffolding for positioning the digital competences that underpin a digital capability. The core pillars of this scaffold are derived from the basic models of alignment positing a relationship between business strategy, the portfolio of technology investments and performance (e.g., Henderson and Venkatraman, 1993). However, most of these models are based on an assumption that in achieving alignment, any expected value (which is usually not defined) will be guaranteed, omitting that it is the actual usage of information in organizational and inter-organizational processes and by humans that ultimately delivers value (Devaraj and Kohli, 2003). Acknowledging this, the three core pillars of the accommodating scaffold for the digital capability are strategy, technology and use (see Figure 19.2).

It is the strategy pillar where the thinking takes place about how technological capabilities[8] will be harnessed both in enabling and shaping corporate and business unit strategies; these capabilities are centered on technology's ability to handle information (i.e., capture, process, manipulation, store, retrieve and present). However, any strategy merely sets out the *intent* – we know that the success rate of IT projects to implement strategic choices is not stellar. The strategy will also accommodate the organization's appetite for risk that determines, to some extent, its willingness to embrace new and emerging technologies. The technology pillar focuses on the required capabilities of the enabling technologies. Use is concerned with utilizing information to positively affect the performance of processes, support decision making and generate insight.

The linkages between the three pillars are important and they are also illustrated in Figure 19.2. In summary, these linkages can be described as follows:

- *Exploration/exploitation*: Information can be leveraged through either its exploration or its exploitation and the strategic intent determines the nature and extent of this. Organizations have traditionally used technology in an exploitative mode, where information is objectified and manipulated and is the essence of using technology to affect the performance of organizational process. Exploration is where data is interrogated to uncover insight, with technologies capabilities augmenting human cognitive processes.
- *Deployment/provisioning*: While technology provides information handling capabilities, this technology can be built and managed in-house, provisioned from external sources, or most likely today, be a combination of both "on premise" and external resources and services.

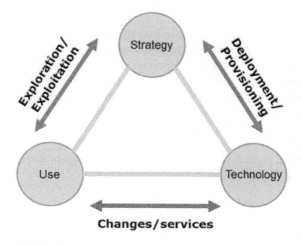

Figure 19.2 Basic scaffolding for a digital capability

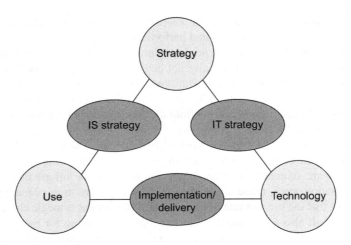

Figure 19.3 The pillars and core domains for digital

- *Changes/services*: It is through programs and projects – devices for implementing the strategic intent – that changes in the organization are shaped and enabled. If managed well, these should lead to the achievement of expected outcomes. These changes in both processes and information use by employees are then sustained by the resultant services delivered by the capabilities of technology.

The objectives of these three linkages are well established and these domains are illustrated in Figure 19.3. The nature and extent of exploration and exploitation is determined by the IS strategy. The IT strategy provides the strategic framework for the supply of technology. The use of information is predicated by, among other issues, the quality of the information system and also how well the data handling capabilities provided by technology are delivered.

The IS strategy essentially articulates how the organization plans to both explore and exploit information. It is concerned with defining the operating model, including both process logic and information flows, determining the extent of information integration and process standardization and the applications (of technology) that will be required to execute the strategy. The IT strategy provides the overall strategic framework for the supply of technology capability. It frames the extent of insourcing and outsourcing. It also addresses issues of security and the protection of information assets. The final domain emphasizes IS and IT strategy implementation and ongoing sustainment of the organization. It defines how programs and projects to implement the strategic intent will be set up and run as well as how the delivery of resultant services, which will sustain these changes (and the realization of the organizational design), will be managed. Best practice program and project management methodologies and processes are often adopted here to deliver in change, such as a new customer management process. Industry standard best practice processes, such as ITIL,[9] are used to assure the quality of IT services.

Digital competences

The three pillars and core domains represent the areas of competence underpinning the digital capability. These six areas are referred to as macro-competences. Using a multi-method

Digital capability: scaffolding

research approach, previous research (Peppard et al., 2000) identified 26 micro-competences distributed around these macro-competences. Over the intervening period, these competences have been refined and the most recent research distinguishes 31 such micro-competences that can be positioned around the scaffolding of the digital capability. These are presented in Table 19.1.

Table 19.1 Macro- and micro-competences definitions

Macro-competence	Micro-competence	Knowing how to...
Crafting strategy	Identify and evaluate the implications of IT-based opportunities as an integral part of business strategy formulation and define the role of digital	
	Business strategy	...ensure that business strategy process identifies the most advantageous uses of information, systems and technology
	Digital innovation	...incorporate the potential of new and emerging technologies in long-term business development
	Investment criteria	...establish appropriate criteria for making decisions on digital investments
	Portfolio management	...optimize the overall value from IS/IT spend ensuring that the portfolio of investments in digital produce the maximum return from resources available within risk parameters
Defining the IS requirement	Translate the business strategy into information, systems and process investments and change plans that match the business priorities (i.e., the IS strategy)	
	IS strategy alignment	...ensure that IS development plans are integrated with organizational and functional strategic plans
	Information quality	...specify data/information quality criteria
	Organization architecture	...determine the overall process and information architecture specifying extent of process standardization and information integration
	Information infrastructure	...identify the information and knowledge needed to achieve strategic and operational objectives
	Business process management	...identify, design, document, monitor and optimize the execution of an organization's processes
	Business improvement	...continually identify opportunities to improve process performance and information availability
Defining the IT capability	Translate the business strategy into long-term information architectures, technology infrastructure and resourcing plans that enable the implementation of the strategy (i.e., the IT strategy)	
	Infrastructure design and development	...define and design information, application and technology architectures and organization structures and processes to manage resources
	Capacity forecasting and planning	...model and forecast the capacity required by the organization to meet demands for IT services, infrastructure, facilities and people
	Technology analysis	...establish criteria and processes to evaluate supply options and contracts with suppliers
	Sourcing strategies	...establish criteria and processes to evaluate supply options and contracts with suppliers

(Continued)

Table 19.1 (Continued)

Macro-competence	Micro-competence	Knowing how to...
	Service requirements	...define service arrangements and performance criteria (service levels) to match the business requirements
	Risk	...establish acceptable criteria for IT-related risks
Using information		Realize the benefits intended from the implementation of digital investments through effective use of information, applications and IT services
	Informed decisions	...make fact-based decisions in a given situation
	Generate insights	...uncover new knowledge and understanding from information
	Benefits delivery	...monitor, measure and evaluate the benefits derived from IS investment and use
Delivering change and services		Deploy resources to develop, implement and operate digital business solutions, which exploit the capabilities of technology
	Benefits planning	...explicitly identify expected benefits from digital investments and plan to realize them
	Managing change	...make the business and organizational changes required to maximize planned benefits without detrimental impact on stakeholders
	Applications development	...implement, at an appropriate speed, information, systems and technology
	Service management	...deliver, operate and control IT services offered to users meeting service-level criteria
	Information asset management	...establish and operate processes that ensure data and information meet quality criteria
	Business continuity and security	...provide effective recovery, contingency and security processes to prevent risk of business failure
Supply of technology		Create and maintain an appropriate and adaptable information technology and applications supply chain and resource capacity
	Supplier relationships	...manage contracts and develop value added relationships with suppliers
	Technology standards	...develop and maintain appropriate standards, methods, controls and procedures for the use of IT and associated resources
	Technology/service acquisition	...develop and apply procurement policies and procedures for the organizational acquisition of infrastructure components and specialist technologies/services
	Asset and cost management	...ensure technology, information and application assets are effectively maintained and costs of acquisition and ownership are understood and managed
	IS/IT staff development	...recruit, train and deploy appropriate staff and ensure technical, business and personal skills meet the needs of the organization
	Technology infrastructure management	...manage technical IT infrastructure during all life cycle phases, comprising all transitional activities (build, deploy, and decommission) and operational activities (operate/maintain and continuously improve)

This table describes the six macro-competences as well as defining each of the 31 micro-competences. The macro-competences have been labeled slightly different from Figure 19.3 to make them more evocative of what is being sought. The micro-competences are, in effect, the 31 "knowing how to . . ." competences that capture the organizational knowing that underpins the digital capability.

Leadership and governance

Over the decades, research has stressed the importance of leadership and governance in the success of digital. However, both are often mistakenly seen as competences that organizations should develop. It is our contention that neither is an organizational competence, rather they frame the digital capability (see Figure 19.4). Without the right leadership and support, organizations will struggle to embrace digital opportunities and deliver any expected business outcomes. This leadership must come from not just the CIO but also the whole leadership team (Weill and Ross, 2009). Digital may have technology connotations but is a critical business issue.

Establishing an appropriate governance structure for digital is also vital (Sambamurthy and Zmud, 1999; Schwarz and Hirschheim, 2003; Weill and Ross, 2004; Zmud, 1984). This is because many decisions, previously considered as falling to the IT professional to make (when all knowledge could be corralled into a specific organizational unit), require active business involvement, sometimes even accountability. Consequently, mechanisms are required to ensure coherence in all decisions made in respect of digital, particularly when decision making is both devolved and distributed (Weill, 2004; Weill and Ross, 2004; 2009).

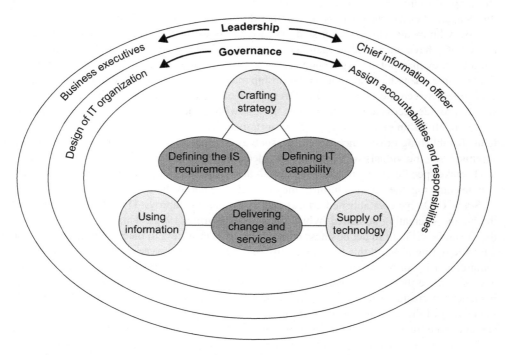

Figure 19.4 Leadership and governance: framing the digital capability

The governance structure should support the behaviors that are deemed necessary in respect of digital and specify clear accountabilities. Governance mechanisms, such as IT steering committees and other cross-function forums, are established to coordinate the consequence of devolvement as well as encourage the involvement of relevant parties in decision-making processes. These forums are operating outside of formal structures – within the so-called informal organization – and are central to creating an environment for knowledge access and integration (Chan, 2002; Preston and Karahanna, 2009; Tan and Gallupe, 2006). While governance structures mandate that decisions traditionally made within the IT unit be devolved out of the remit of the CIO and IT unit altogether and into the realm of business executives, there can be both reluctance and resistance from business executives to assume these new responsibilities. This points to the importance of not just knowledge but also behaviors and values – an issue that we shall address in the next section.

Establishing an IT governance structure is giving tacit recognition that what are often labeled "IT decisions" are essentially decisions that require the coordination and integration of knowledge that can be dispersed across an organization. Even expertise in technologies is also migrating away from IT professionals and becoming more embedded in those with functional responsibility; for example, social media in the marketing organization and analytics and business intelligence (BI) in finance departments. Many applications can now be delivered directly from "the cloud," with end users potentially bypassing corporate infrastructures and, more crucially, the IS organization itself leading to the presence of "shadow IT." With the Internet of Things, there is increasing danger of applications being built outside of an organization's architecture.

Building digital competences

Building the digital competences is an organization-wide endeavor. As emphasized throughout this chapter, the challenge is to bring together those with the relevant knowledge to create the necessary knowing. This is easier said than done. It is worth acknowledging that historically many CIOs have attempted to facilitate access, coordination and integration of knowledge, although they may not always recognize this as the objective of the initiatives they promoted. For example, many have appointed relationship managers as a conduit, facilitating knowledge exchange between the IT unit and different parts of the organization. While such initiatives seek to provide access to knowledge they may, however, not directly impact its integration. In reality, relationship managers typically act as translators of requirements or reporters of problems. Establishing governance structures, such as committees and other cross-organizational forums, bring individuals with relevant knowledge together to debate particular issues related to IT, make specific decisions and have oversight on decisions and outcomes. Yet, even where people come together in such forums, they may choose not to share their knowledge.

Some CIOs have established educational programs to improve IT staffs' knowledge of the business, creating so-called hybrid managers (Skyrme, 1992). This overcomes the fact that it can be difficult to get business engagement, that is, access to their knowledge, with the CIO attempting to build this knowledge inside the IT unit. However, this does not defeat the requirement for business and IT people to cooperate and work together, that is, to integrate and coordinate their knowledge. To this end, education programs for non-IT staff are often instigated to create awareness of digital issues, build digital literacy and highlight their role in delivery of the expected benefits of digital investments. The assumption is that this understanding communication will be forthcoming; usually this requires some priming.

Initiatives like chargeback, where users are "charged" based on the IT resources and services they consume, can serve to foster communications between IT and the business units (Ross et al., 1999). Such communication can generate a rich shared understanding for both parties of the cost and benefits of alternative IT investments and service offerings. Indeed, research shows that a high level of communication between IT and business executives is a direct predictor of alignment of business and IT strategies (Reich and Benbasat, 2000).

Thus, while knowledge is "owned" by the individual, the integration of this knowledge to create knowing and understanding takes place at a collective level: groups and other collective forums, some of which are formal and others informal (Okhuysen and Eisenhardt, 2002). Although specialist knowledge is required to accomplish many tasks in an organization, there are also situations in which individuals with specialized knowledge must represent and integrate their knowledge in a group or other collective to create organizational knowing. As we have seen, this is at the core of a digital capability.

To explore how that might occur, the notion of "social capital" offers an explanation of how distributed knowledge can be harnessed to create organizational knowing. With its origins in sociology, social capital highlights the importance of networks of strong, personal relationships, developed over time, across groups, units and geographies that provide the basis for trust, cooperation and collective action (Alder and Kwon, 2002; Nahapiet and Ghoshal, 1998; Tsai and Ghoshal, 1998). It also emphasizes behaviors. The theory suggests "that actors are motivated by instrumental or expressive needs to engage other actors in order to access other actors' resources for the purpose of gaining better outcomes" (Lin, 2001). In the context of the digital capability, these "resources" are knowledge, and "better outcomes" is the organization knowing contributing to the competences.

Access to knowledge is dependent on an individual's network of contacts and ties as well as the nature and content of the relationship between parties. Recognition of the value of collaboration is based on the ties that people have together with a shared language and cognition to aid mutual understanding. The motivation to share and combine knowledge and collaborate is underpinned by trust and obligations that can be defined by the role and position that individuals have in the organization. Figure 19.5 presents a schematic of this, illustrating that it is through people coming together that knowledge is shared and competences manifest themselves.

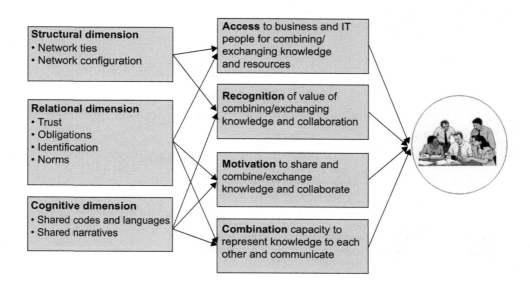

Figure 19.5 Social capital providing the environment for organizational knowing

Figure 19.6 attempts to bring together the earlier discourse about digital competences that draws on the RBV with the preceding discussion on social capital. It illustrates that at the resource level, knowledge resides in people, and that it is through people coming together in social contexts that organizational knowing emerges. Social capital theory can help understand the ingredients that need to be present for this to occur.

In a global reinsurance brokerage where we undertook research, the consequence of a strong digital capability was clearly evident. The company has recognized the value of information and its effective management for its competitive success. The CIO is a member of the board of directors and has a very strong partnership with the CEO. They regularly attend digital conferences together. The CIO is a key player in the business strategy process; one colleague noted, "I think that he is forward-thinking enough to be looking at new technologies and that he is brave enough to take the decision to go with things," and this often means driving the business strategy. A quote from the company's digital strategy document best illustrates how digital is deployed in the company:

> Information systems cannot afford to wait for a clear and detailed specification of "strategy" from the business and customers it is trying to serve. It is more a question of applying IS/IT foresight to the situation, in order to make reasoned assumptions to an appropriate course of action.

There is also a close partnership between the IS unit (and staff in this unit) and the rest of the business. Indeed, this is probably helped, as the CIO is responsible for both IT and the bulk of business operations (the exceptions being marketing and risk management). Roles are clearly specified, particularly in the setup and management of projects and in the delivery of IT services. The philosophy of the IS function was described by one IT manager as "we help you to help yourself," in reference to the fact that they work closely with the business. The company has not set out to develop and nurture the 31 digital competencies explicitly, but they are present. They do provide an explanation of why the company has probably been the most successful player in its industry over the last 20 years and recognized by its peers as being innovative regarding the harnessing of digital.

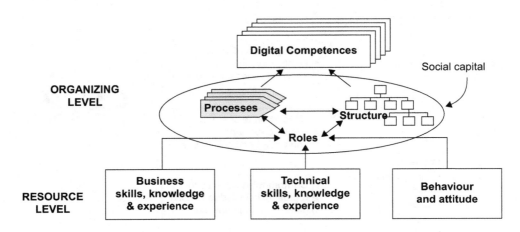

Figure 19.6 Mobilizing resources to create digital competences

Conclusions

Nearly 30 years ago Dearden (1987) predicted the demise of the IT unit in organizations. The basic premise of his arguments were that "users" would soon completely control individual systems and that systems development would be done almost entirely by outside software specialists. However, it is unlikely that he foresaw the tremendous advances in technology and the key role it would play in business and global commerce. Yet while he was right that the IS organization, in its guise at that time, would wither away, he erred by suggesting its demise based largely on arguments focused on technology deployment. Focusing on value generation from IT presents a different conclusion. Rather than withering away, it has become pervasive.

This chapter argues that executives should no longer see the knowledge and the organizational knowing how that required to respond to digital challenges and opportunities as residing in a separate organizational unit under the control of a single individual. Rather, this knowledge is distributed not only across the organization but can also be found in vendors and other third parties, perhaps even customers. The challenge is to coordinate and integrate this knowledge to build the necessary organizational knowing. In this chapter we have suggested that it is achieved by building 31 competences and that these underpin a digital capability. The perspective presented in this chapter emphasizes the essential role of human action in knowing how to get things done that lies at the heart of a digital capability.

While the existence of a strong digital capability may be observable (if not yet measurable), we still do not know precisely the individual knowledge components (perhaps better referred to as the "know-what") of each underpinning competence (the knowing or "know-how"); more research is needed to determine this. Moreover, it is likely that uncovering actual practices will illuminate further the knowing that is enacted through the everyday and ongoing work of employees. Uncovering these practices will demand immersion in study sites.

Notes

1 The colloquial term for cloud computing.
2 Originally they were referred to as servers.
3 Any discourse around this question raises the wider issue as to what IS (both singular and plural) actually is/are and is beyond the scope of this chapter. Interesting insights can be found in Alter (2008), Beynon-Davis (2010); Bryant (2008), Paul (2010) and Lee et al. (2015). For an exposition of the relationship between IS and technology, see some of the recent research on socio-materiality (Orlikowski, 2010; Scott and Orlikowski, 2013; Orlikowski and Scott, 2008; Orlikowski and Iacono, 2001). For extended treatises on what constitutes the IS discipline, see Banville and Landry (1989), Benbasat and Zmud (2003), Somers (2010) and March and Niederman (2012).
4 The view of knowledge that accommodates this is that it can be objectified and made explicit, therefore making it possible "to code" the logic into software programs.
5 It is not our intention to engage in a debate as to whether it is actually a "view" rather than a "theory."
6 The literature is confusing in its usage of the labels "competences" and "capabilities."
7 The RBV has been used by scholars to explore the contribution of IS resources and capabilities to performance and competitive advantage. See, for example, Bhatt and Grover (2005), Bharadwaj (2000), Doherty and Terry (2009) and Wade and Hulland (2004). For seminal research highlighting the role of internal resources in achieving competitive advantage from IS/IT, see Clemons and Row (1991) and Kettinger et al. (1994).
8 To reduce confusion, the use of the label "capabilities" in this instance refers specifically to the *information-handling* capabilities of technology.
9 ITIL is the IT Infrastructure Library and part of the services provides by the UK's Office for Government Commerce (OGC). See *A Code of Practice for IS Service Management*, British Standards Institute, London, 1999.

References

Adler, P. S. and S.-W. Kwon (2002) 'Social capital: Prospects for a new concept,' *Academy of Management Review*, 27(1), 17–40.
Alter, S. (2008) 'Defining information systems as work systems: Implications for the IS field,' *European Journal of Information Systems*, 17, 448–469.
Amit, R. and Schoemaker, P.J.H. (1993) 'Strategic assets and organizational rent,' *Strategic Management Journal*, 14, 33–46.
Banville, C. and Landry, M. (1989) 'Can the field of MIS be disciplined?' *Communications of the ACM*, 32(1), 48–60.
Barney, J. B. (1986a) 'Strategic factor markets: Expectations, luck, and business strategy,' *Management Science*, 42, 1231–1241.
Barney, J. B. (1986b) 'Organizational culture: Can it be a source of sustained competitive advantage?' *Academy of Management Review*, 11, 656–665.
Barney, J.B. (1991) 'Firm resources and sustained competitive advantage,' *Journal of Management*, 17, 99–120.
Barney, J. B. (2001) 'Resource-based theories of competitive advantage: A ten-year retrospective on the resource-based view,' *Journal of Management*, 27, 643–650.
Benbasat, I. and Zmud, R. W. (2003) 'The identity crisis within the IS discipline: Defining and communicating the discipline's core properties,' *MIS Quarterly*, 27(2), 183–194.
Beynon-Davis, P. (2010) 'The enactment of significance: A unified conception of information, systems and technology,' *European Journal of Information Systems*, 19, 398–408.
Bharadwaj, A. (2000) 'A resource-based perspective on information technology and firm performance: An empirical investigation,' *MIS Quarterly*, 24(1), 169–196.
Bhatt, G. D. and Grover, V. (2005) 'Types of information technology capabilities and their role in competitive advantage,' *Journal of Management Information Systems*, 22(2), 253–277.
Blackler, F. (1995) 'Knowledge, knowledge work and organizations: An overview and interpretations,' *Organization Studies*, 16(6), 1021–1046.
Bowman, C. and Ambrosini, V. (2000) 'Value creation versus value capture: Towards a coherent definition of value in strategy,' *British Journal of Management*, 11, 1–15.
Bryant, A. (2008) 'The future of information systems – thinking informatically,' *European Journal of Information Systems*, 17, 695–698.
Chan, Y. E. (2002) 'Why haven't we mastered alignment? The importance of informal organization structure,' *MIS Quarterly Executive*, 2, 97–112.
Clemons, E. K. and Row, M. C. (1991) 'Sustaining IT advantage: The role of structural difference,' *MIS Quarterly*, 15(3), 275–292.
Collis, D.J. (1996) 'Organisational capability as a source of profit,' in B. Moingeon and A. Edmonston, eds., *Organisational Learning and Competitive Advantage*, Sage, London.
Collis, D.J. and Montgomery, C.A. (1995) 'Competing on resources: Strategy in the 1990s,' *Harvard Business Review*, July–August, 118–128.
Cool, K. and Schendel, D. (1988) 'Performance differences among strategic group members,' *Strategic Management Journal*, 9(3), 207–224.
Cross, J., Earl, M. J. and Sampler, J. L. (1997) 'Transformation of the IT function at British Petroleum,' *MIS Quarterly*, 21(4), 401–423.
Dearden, J. (1987) 'The withering away of the IS organization,' *Sloan Management Review*, Summer, 87–91.
Devaraj, S. and Kohli, R. (2003) 'Performance impacts of information technology: Is actual usage the missing link?' *Management Science*, 49(3), 273–289.
Dierickx, I. and Cool, K. (1989) 'Asset stock accumulation and sustainability of competitive advantage,' *Management Science*, 35(12), 1504–1514.
Doherty, N. F. and Terry, M. (2009) 'The role of IS capabilities in delivering sustainable improvements to competitive positioning,' *Journal of Strategic Information Systems*, 18, 100–116.
Grant, R. M. (1996) 'Prospering in dynamically competitive environments: Organizational capability as knowledge integration,' *Organization Science*, 7, 375–387.
Hansen, G. S. and Wernerfelt, B. (1989) 'Determinants of firm performance: the relative importance of economic and organizational factors,' *Strategic Management Journal*, 10, 399–411.
Henderson, J. C. and Venkatraman, N. (1993) 'Strategic alignment: Leveraging information technology for transforming organizations,' *IBM Systems Journal*, 32(1), 4–16.

Kangas, K. (1999) 'Competency and capabilities based competition and the role of information technology: The case of trading by a Finland-based firm to Russia,' *Journal of Information Technology Cases and Applications*, 1(2), 4–22.

Kettinger, W., Grover, V., Guha, S. and Segars, A. H. (1994) 'Strategic information systems revisited: A study in sustainability and performance,' *MIS Quarterly*, 18(1), 31–55.

Kotlarsky, J, Oshri, I., Hillegersberg, J. van and Kumar, K. (2007) 'Globally distributed component-based software development: An exploratory study of knowledge management and work division," *Journal of Information Technology*, 22, 161–173.

Lee, A. S., Thomas, M. and Baskerville, R. L. (2015) 'Going back to basics in design science: From the information technology artefact to the information systems artefact,' *Information Systems Journal*, 25, 5–21.

Lin, N. (2001) *Social Capital: A Theory of Social Structure and Action*, Cambridge University Press, New York.

March, S. T. and Niederman, F. (2012) 'The future of the information systems discipline: A response to Walsham,' *Journal of Information Technology*, 27, 96–99.

Moingeon, B., Ramanantsoa, B, Métais, E. and Orton, J. D. (1998) 'Another look at strategy – structure relationships: The resource-based view,' *European Management Journal*, 16(3), 298–304.

Nahapiet, J. and Ghoshal, S. (1998) 'Social capital, intellectual capital, and the organizational advantage,' *Academy of Management Review*, 23, 242–266.

Okhuysen, G. A. and Eisenhardt, K. (2002) 'Integrating knowledge in groups: How formal interventions enable flexibility,' *Organization Science*, 13(4), 370–386.

Orlikowski, W. J. (2002) 'Knowing in practice: Enabling a collective capability in distributed organization,' *Organization Science*, 13(3), 249–273.

Orlikowski, W. J. (2010) 'The sociomateriality of organizational life: Considering technology in management research,' *Cambridge Journal of Economics*, 34(1), 125–141.

Orlikowski, W. J. and Iacono, C. S. (2001) 'Desperately seeking the 'IT' in IT research: A call to theorizing the IT artefact,' *Information Systems Research*, 12(2), 121–134.

Orlikowski, W. J. and Scott, S. V. (2008) 'Sociomateriality: Challenging the separation of technology, work and organization,' *Annals of the Academy of Management*, 2(1), 433–474.

Paul, R. J. (2010) 'What an information system is, and why it is important to know this,' *Journal of Computing and Information Technology*, 18(2), 95–99.

Penrose, E. T. (1959) *The theory of the growth of the firm*, Wiley, New York.

Peppard, J. (2007) 'The conundrum of IT management,' *European Journal of Information Systems*, 16, 336–345.

Peppard, J. (forthcoming) 'Rethinking the concept of the IS organization,' *Information Systems Journal*.

Peppard, J. and Ward, J. M. (2004) 'Beyond strategic information systems: Towards an IS capability,' *Journal of Strategic Information Systems*, 13, 167–194.

Peppard, J. and Ward, J. M. (2016) *The strategic management of information systems: Building a digital strategy*, 4th ed., Wiley, Chichester.

Peppard, J. W., Lambert, R., and Edwards, C. E. (2000) 'Whose job is it anyway? Organizational information competencies for value creation,' *Information Systems Journal*, 10(4), 291–323.

Peteraf, M. A. (1993) 'The cornerstones of competitive advantage,' *Strategic Management Journal*, 14(3), 179–191.

Prahalad, C. K. and Hamel, G. (1990) 'The core competence of the corporation,' *Harvard Business Review*, May–June, 79–91.

Preston, D. and Karahanna, E. (2009) 'How to develop a shared vision: The key to strategic alignment,' *MIS Quarterly Executive*, 8(1), 1–8.

Reich, B. H. and Benbasat, I. (2000) 'Factors that influence the social dimension of alignment between business and information technology objectives,' *MIS Quarterly*, 24(1), 81–113.

Ross, J., M. Vitale and Beath, C. (1999) 'The untapped potential of IT chargeback,' *MIS Quarterly*, 23(2), 215–23.

Rumelt, R. P. (1991) 'How much does industry matter?' *Strategic Management Journal*, 12(3), 167–185.

Sambamurthy, V. and Zmud, R. (1999) 'Arrangements for information technology governance: A theory of multiple contingencies,' *MIS Quarterly*, 23(2), 261–290.

Schwarz, A. and Hirschheim, R. (2003) 'An extended platform logic perspective of IT governance: Management perceptions and activities of IT,' *Journal of Strategic Information Systems*, 12, 129–166.

Scott, S. V. and Orlikowski, W. J. (2013) 'Sociomateriality – taking the wrong turning? A response to Mutch,' *Information and Organization*, 23, 77–80.

Somers, M. J. (2010) 'Using the theory of the professions to understand the IS identity crisis,' *European Journal of Information Systems*, 19, 382–388.

Skyrme, D. (1992) 'From hybrids to bridge building,' *Research and Discussion Papers*, RDP92/1, Oxford Institute of Information Management, Templeton College, Oxford.

Tan, F. and R. B. Gallupe (2006) 'Aligning business and information systems thinking: A cognitive approach,' *IEEE Transactions on Engineering Management*, 53(2), 223–237.

Teece, D. J., Pisano, G. and Shuen, A. (1997) 'Dynamic capabilities and strategic management,' *Strategic Management Journal*, 18, 509–533.

Tsai, W. and Ghoshal, S. (1998) 'Social capital and value creation: The role of intra-firm networks,' *Academy of Management Journal*, 41(4), 464–476.

Wade, M. and Hulland, J. (2004) 'The resource-based view and information systems research: Review, extension, and suggestions for further research,' *MIS Quarterly*, 28(1), 107–142.

Weill, P. (2004) 'Don't just lead, govern: How top-performing firms govern IT,' *MIS Quarterly Executive*, 3(1), 1–17.

Weill, P. and Ross, J. (2004) *IT governance: How top performers manage IT decision rights for superior results*, Harvard Business School Press, Boston, MA.

Weill, P. and Ross, J. (2009) *IT savvy: What top executives must know to go from pain to gain*, Harvard Business School Press, Boston, MA.

Wernerfelt, B. (1984) 'A resource-based view of the firm,' *Strategic Management Journal*, 5, 171–180.

Zmud, R. W. (1984) 'Design alternatives for organizing information systems activities,' *MIS Quarterly*, 8(2), 79–93.

20
SOURCING INFORMATION TECHNOLOGY SERVICES
Past research and future research directions

Mary Lacity, Aihua Yan, and Shaji Khan

Introduction

Information technology (IT) sourcing is the sourcing of IT services, including application development, application support, systems integration, data management, data center management, telecommunications and network management, and distributed computing services (Lacity et al. 2017). In its simplest conceptualization, an *IT sourcing decision* entails the fundamental "make or buy" decision (Williamson 1975), which results in insourcing or outsourcing of IT services. In reality, sourcing options are more complex; IT sourcing decisions may result in several types of "make" decisions, including insourcing to the internal IT function (e.g., Hirschheim and Lacity 2000), creating shared IT services across organizational units (e.g., McKeen and Smith 2011), offshoring to a client-owned captive center (e.g., Oshri and Van Uhm 2012), or bringing a previously outsourced IT service back in-house, that is, backsourcing (e.g., Veltri et al. 2008). IT sourcing decisions may result in several types of "buy" decisions by outsourcing to a domestic provider (e.g., Pearce 2014), outsourcing to an offshore provider (e.g., Poston et al. 2010), multi-sourcing to several providers (e.g., Su and Levina 2011), or outsourcing to a rural-based provider (Lacity et al. 2010b). In its simplest conceptualization, *IT sourcing outcomes* result in "success" or "failure." In reality, outcomes are multi-faceted and include outcomes associated with organizational performance, strategic enablement of business objectives, IT costs, service quality, service responsiveness, scalability, and user satisfaction, to name some common outcome measures (e.g., Agarwal et al. 2006; Agrawal and Haleem 2013; DiRomualdo and Gurbaxani 1998; Goo et al. 2009; Grover et al. 1996; Lee et al. 2004; Saunders et al. 1997).

During the last few decades, researchers have dealt with this complexity by examining many types of IT sourcing decisions and outcomes. What did we learn from all this academic work? There is great value in conducting a literature review that finds a succinct way to summarize findings across studies, and indeed prior literature reviews summarized the information technology outsourcing (ITO) research in terms of research methods used (Dibbern et al. 2004), theories used (Dibbern et al. 2004; Mahnke et al. 2005), critical success factors (Fjermestad and Saitta 2005), and the most influential articles and researchers (Alsuairi and Dwivedi 2010). The most comprehensive review of empirical findings on the sourcing of IT services was published in Lacity et al. (2010). In that article, we analyzed 365 empirical findings on the determinants of ITO decisions and 376 empirical findings on the determinants of outcomes from 164 quantitative and qualitative articles published between 1992 and the first quarter of 2010. In this update, we examined new empirical IT sourcing articles across 66 academic journals, bringing the total research base to 540 empirical findings pertaining to ITO decisions and 630 empirical findings pertaining to ITO outcomes. These two models serve as robust foundations on what we know to date on ITO decisions and outcomes. ITO researchers can be proud of this body of research as it clearly informs the practice of outsourcing by helping clients with ITO decisions and by helping both clients and providers better manage outsourcing relationships (Lacity et al. 2009).

After presenting the empirical results, we switch perspectives to *future* research. Here we aim to further challenge ourselves as IS scholars to do even more impactful research going forward. In Lacity et al. (2016), we proposed a few rather audacious future research directions. We revisit four in this chapter.

Sourcing remains an important issue to study, in part, because the market continues to grow in size. Gartner, for example, estimated that global ITO was worth $281 billion in 2015 and $424 billion in 2014, with a compound annual growth rate of 4.4%.[1] Another consulting firm, Horses for Sources, sized the 2013 ITO at $648 billion.[2] This spend must be managed well, not only from the client and provider perspectives, but from the vantage point of being global citizens in a world with limited resources.

IT sourcing decisions and outcomes: past research

This chapter serves as an update of Lacity et al. (2010) by adding new findings up through 2014. We present the combined results of a massive review and coding of the ITO empirical findings spanning 23 years of research from 1992 until 2014. In total, we coded 257 articles from 66 refereed journals (see Table 20.1). The most frequent outlets were the *Journal of Management Information Systems* with 16 empirical articles, *Information & Management* (15 articles), *MIS Quarterly* (13 articles), *Information Systems Research* (11 articles), and *Sloan Management Review* (11 articles). Across the 23 years of research, we coded 118 empirical articles that used a qualitative method (e.g., interviews and case studies), 126 articles that used a quantitative method (e.g., surveys and archival data), and 13 mixed-methods papers that used both qualitative and quantitative methods. We coded a total of 1,179 empirical relationships between independent variables (IV) and dependent variables (DV) across the 257 articles. We sorted the relationships by DV type, either ITO decision or ITO outcome. The full data set comprises 540 relationships pertaining to ITO decisions and 630 relationships pertaining to ITO outcomes.

We coded the nature of the relationships between study IV and DV variables using the method used in Jeyaraj et al. (2006), Lacity et al. (2010; 2011; 2016) and Schneider and Sunyaev (2016). A positive "significant" relationship was coded as "+1," a negative relationship was coded as "−1," and a "not significant" relationship was coded as "0." The code "M" was used to indicate a relationship that "mattered." The "M" code was needed because some significant relationships were categorical (i.e., not ordinal, interval, or continuous), but a relationship clearly mattered between the independent and dependent variable. For example, Langer et al. (2014) found that project type (maintenance vs. new development) had significantly different effects on offshoring project success in terms of client satisfaction. The relationship between transaction type and offshore outsourcing success was therefore coded as "M" for "mattered" (Lacity et al. 2016). In essence, the method uses a voting scheme that gives equal weight to each finding (Lee 2016). The scheme allows for the coding of both qualitative and

Table 20.1 Empirical articles used in review

L = *Qualitative article;* T = *Quantitative article,* M = *mixed methods*

	L	T	M	Tot		L	T	M	Tot
1. Academy of Management Jrnl		1		1	24. Information Systems Frontiers	6	4		10
2. California Management Review	2			2	25. Information Systems Jrnl	3			3
3. Communications of the ACM	4	6		10	26. Information Systems Management	4	2		6
4. Communications of the AIS	7	2		9	27. Information Systems Research		11		11
5. Computers & Operations Research	1	1		2	28. Information Technology & People		1	1	2
6. Computers & Security			1	1	29. Information Technology Management	1			1
7. Decision Sciences		4		4	30. Int'l Jrnl Production Economics	1			1
8. Decision Support Systems	1	1		2	31. Int'l Jrnl Accounting Information Systems		3		3
9. E-Service Jrnl		1		1	32. Int'l Jrnl Business and Management		1		1
10. European Jrnl of IS	4	2		6	33. Int'l Jrnl Information Management	5	3	2	10
11. European Jrnl of OR	1			1	34. Int'l Jrnl Innovation Management	1			1
12. European Management Jrnl	1			1	35. Int'l Jrnl of Management		3		3
13. Expert Systems	1			1	36. Jrnl of Applied Business Research		1		1
14. Harvard Business Review	2	1		3	37. Jrnl of Computer Information Systems	1	5		6
15. Health Care Management Science		1		1	38. Jrnl of Electronic Commerce in Orgs	1			1
16. Human System Management		1		1	39. Jrnl of Global Information Management	3			3
17. IEEE Transactions on Engineering Management	4	4		8	40. Jrnl of Global Information Technology Management	3	2		5
18. Industrial & Corporate Change	1			1	41. Jrnl of High Technology Management Research		1		1
19. Industrial Management & Data Systems	1	1		2	42. Jrnl of Information Systems		1		1
20. Industrial Marketing Management		1		1	43. Jrnl of Information Systems and Technology Management	1			1
21. Information & Management	4	11		15	44. Jrnl of Information Technology	10	5		15
22. Information and Software Technology	2	1		3	45. Jrnl of Information Technology Case and Application Research	2	3	1	6
23. Information Resources Management Jrnl		1	1	2	46. Jrnl of IT Theory and Application	1			1

(*Continued*)

Table 20.1 (Continued)

L = Qualitative article; T = Quantitative article, M = mixed methods

	L	T	M	Tot		L	T	M	Tot
47. Jrnl of Int'l Business Studies	1			1	57. MIS Quarterly Executive	9		1	10
48. Jrnl of Int'l Management Studies	1			1	58. Omega		1		1
49. Jrnl of Management Information Systems	4	12		16	59. Organizacija		1		1
50. Jrnl of Management Research	1			1	60. Organization Science	2	2		4
51. Jrnl of Operations Management	1	1		2	61. Production & Operations Management		1		1
52. Jrnl of Strategic Information Systems	2	3		5	62. Project Management Jrnl	1	1		2
53. Jrnl of Systems Management		1		1	63. Sloan Management Review	9		2	11
54. Jrnl of the Association for Information Systems		2		2	64. Strategic Management Jrnl		3		3
55. Management Science		3		3	65. Strategic Outsourcing: An Int'l Jrnl	5		2	7
56. MIS Quarterly	4	7	2	13	66. Technology Analysis & Strategic Management	1			1
					TOTALS	**118**	**126**	**13**	**257**

quantitative empirical findings. Significance was determined at $p < .05$ for quantitative studies and by strong arguments by authors for qualitative studies.

The three authors coded articles individually and met weekly to discuss their codes. Once consensus was achieved for each IV, DV, and the relationship between them, we recorded that relationship into our master database. After the first round of coding was completed, the third author then manually examined the codes to identify inconsistent codes and/or data entry errors. Any issues raised were resolved with input from all authors.

To extract the major determinants of ITO decisions and outcomes, we followed the decision rules from prior reviews to extract the most robust findings of IVs that have been repeatedly examined and produced consistent results (Jeyaraj et al. 2006; Lacity et al. 2010; 2011; 2016; Schneider and Sunyaev 2016). In terms of *multiple examinations*, we replicated the decision rule to extract the relationships that have been examined by researchers at least five times. In terms of *consistent results*, we also replicated the decision rule to extract variables in which at least 60% of the evidence was consistent. This minimum threshold ensures that more than half the evidence produced the same finding. These rules are admittedly arbitrary, but other authors may rerun the analyses using different decision criteria.

In all, we extracted 21 determinants of ITO decisions and 31 determinants of ITO outcomes that were repeatedly examined (at least five times) and produced consistent results (at least 60%). We organized the 21 IVs into a model of ITO decisions that include categories of independent variables associated with transaction attributes, outsourcing motivations, influence sources, client characteristics and capabilities, relationship characteristics, and environmental variables (see Figure 20.1). The model of ITO outcomes includes 31 independent variables associated with transaction attributes, relational and contractual governance, client and provider capabilities, client characteristics, and decision characteristics (see Figure 20.2).

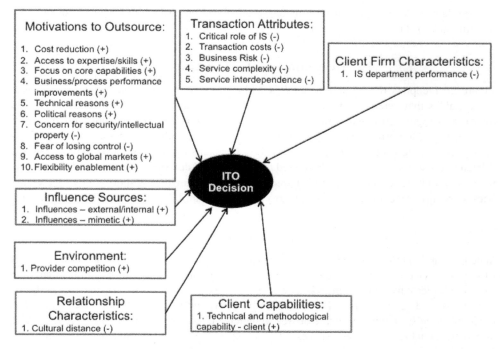

Figure 20.1 Independent variables that determine ITO decisions

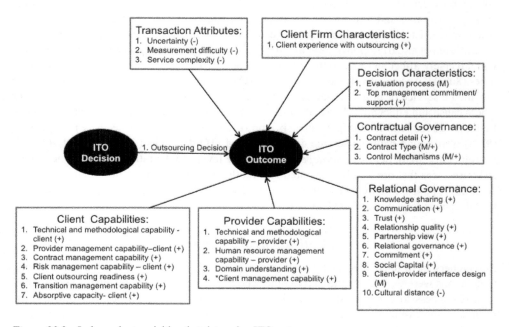

Figure 20.2 Independent variables that determine ITO outcomes

Determinants of ITO decisions

Figure 20.1 depicts the 21 significant IVs within the seven broad categories of independent variables that determine ITO decisions. A positive relationship between an IV and ITO decision in Figure 20.1 means that the IV was positively related to "outsourcing" decisions of some kind (domestic outsourcing, offshore outsourcing, multisourcing, or rural sourcing). A negative relationship between an IV and ITO decisions means that the IV was negatively related to outsourcing or positively related to "insourcing" decisions of some kind (insourcing to an internal IT function, internal IT shared services, client-owned offshore captive centers, or backsourcing). We explain each IV category and significant IVs within it in the next section.

Transaction attributes

When researchers investigated transaction attributes, they explored how the generic attributes of the IT service affected ITO decisions. We uncovered five transaction attributes that were examined at least five times and produced consistent results: (1) the critical role of IS, (2) transaction costs, (3) business risk, (4) service complexity, and (5) service interdependence. The *critical role of IS* is defined as "the degree to which a client organization views the IS service as a critical enabler of business success" (Lacity et al. 2010, p. 423). This variable was examined 17 times, and 12 times (71%) it was found to be negatively associated with IT outsourcing decisions. This finding indicates that clients more frequently insourced IT services that were perceived as critical to business success. *Transaction costs* are defined as "the effort, time, and costs incurred to search, create, negotiate, monitor, and administrate a contract between a client and provider" (Lacity et al. 2010, p. 427; e.g., Levina and Su 2008). Transaction costs were examined 13 times and found to be negatively associated with ITO decisions 11 times (85%), which is consistent with transaction cost economics (Williamson 1991; e.g., Dibbern et al. 2012; Gefen et al. 2011; Gonzalez et al. 2010). *Business risk* is "the probability than an action will adversely affect an organization" (Lacity et al. 2010, p. 422). Examined five times, four times (80%) it was negatively associated with ITO decisions. *Service complexity* is "the degree to which a service or project requires compound steps, the control of many variables, and/or where cause and effect are subtle and dynamic" (Lacity et al. 2016, p. 43; e.g., Ventovuori and Lehtonen 2006; Penfold 2009). Among six empirical examinations, five negative relationships (83%) were found between service complexity and ITO decisions (e.g., Aubert et al. 2012; Poston et al. 2010). *Service interdependence* is "the level of integration and coupling among tasks; services that are highly integrated are tightly coupled and difficult to detach" (Lacity et al. 2016, p. 43). Examined five times, it was always found to be negatively associated with ITO decisions (e.g., Susarla et al. 2010).

Motivations to outsource

Researchers have uncovered many motivations behind IT sourcing decisions. Ten sourcing motivations were examined at least five times and produced consistent results: (1) cost reduction, (2) access to expertise/skills, (3) focus on core capabilities, (4) business/process performance improvement, (5) technical reasons, (6) political reasons, (7) concern for security/

intellectual property, (8) fear of losing control, (9) access to global markets, and (10) flexibility enablement. *Cost reduction,* "a client organization's need or desire to reduce the costs of providing an IT service" (Lacity et al. 2010, p. 423), was examined 50 times and 47 times (94%) it was positively associated with ITO decisions (e.g., Beverakis et al. 2009). Overall, costs are an important driver of sourcing decisions, but clearly not the only motive, because nine other motives were also repeatedly found to be significant. A client organization's desire or need to *access provider skills/expertise* was examined 25 times, and 23 times (92%) it was positively associated with ITO decisions (e.g., McLellan et al. 1995). There is also strong evidence that clients wished to *focus on core capabilities,* which led to the outsourcing of presumably non-core capabilities (e.g., Currie and Seltsikas 2001; Premuroso et al. 2012). Clients were also motivated by *business/process performance improvement,* "a client organization's desire or need to improve the performance of the client's business, processes, or capabilities" (Lacity et al. 2010, p. 422). Examined 18 times, it was always found to positively motivate ITO decisions. *Technical reasons* are "a client's desire or need to engage in an outsourcing relationship in order to gain access to leading edge technology available through providers" (Lacity et al. 2010, p. 427). Examined 10 times, it was always found to positively motivate ITO decisions. *Political reasons,* a "client's desire to use an outsourcing decision to promote a personal agenda" (Lacity et al. 2010, p. 426), was examined eight times and found five times (63%) to be a significant factor motivating ITO decisions (e.g., Hall and Liedtka 2005; Gonzalez et al. 2010). *Concern for security/intellectual property,* "a client organization's concerns about security of information, transborder data flow issues, and protection of intellectual property" (Lacity et al. 2016, p. 38) was examined seven times and five times (71%) it was negatively associated with ITO decisions (e.g., Sobol and Apte 1995; Wullenweber et al. 2008). *Fear of losing control over the IT service* was negatively associated with outsourcing seven out of the nine times (78%) it was examined (e.g., Bhagwatwar et al. 2011; Patane and Jurison 1994). A client organization's desire or need to gain *access to global markets* by outsourcing to providers in those markets was another robust finding (Lacity et al. 2016; e.g., Premuroso et al. 2012), with six empirical examinations all positively related to outsourcing. Finally, *flexibility enablement,* "a client organization's desire or need to increase the flexibility of the use and allocation of resources for IT services" (Lacity et al. 2016, p. 40), was examined six times and it was always found to be an important driver of ITO decisions (e.g., Ceci and Masciarelli 2010).

Influence sources

Within the broad category of influence sources, two independent variables were repeatedly examined and found to be positively associated with outsourcing decisions: (1) external and internal influences and (2) mimetic influences. *External and internal influences* are defined as "the combination of external media, provider pressure, and internal communications at the personal level among manager(s) in charge of a sourcing decision" (Lacity et al. 2010, p. 424). Examined six times, it was always found to influence ITO decisions. *Mimetic influences* "arise from the perception that peer organizations are more successful and by modeling behavior based on peer behavior, the mimicking organization aims to achieve similar results" (Lacity et al. 2010, p. 424). Mimetic influences were found to be positive and significant determinants of IT outsourcing decisions four of the five times it was examined (e.g., Ang and Cummings 1997; Loh and Venkatraman, 1992). From the theory of institutional isomorphism (DiMaggio and Powell 1991), mimetic influences were the only influence source that was repeatedly examined; coercive and normative influences were only studied one time each.

Client firm characteristics

Are certain types of clients more likely to make particular sourcing decisions for IT services than others? One client firm characteristic produced consistent results after repeated examinations: prior IS department performance. *Prior IS department performance* was typically measured as an organizational members' perceptions of the IT function's performance or competence in the past (e.g., Beulen and Ribbers 2003; Pinnington and Woolcock 1995). Examined 16 times, 11 times (69%) it was negatively related to ITO decisions, meaning the worse the IS department's past performance, the more likely it was to be outsourced.

Client capabilities

How do a client's capabilities affect ITO decisions? Only one independent variable – a client's technical and methodological capability – was examined enough times and produced consistent results to be included in Figure 20.1. A *client's technical and methodological capability* is defined as "a client organization's level of maturity in terms of technical or process related standards, and best practices" (Lacity et al. 2016, p. 38). Examined five times, five times it was found that higher levels of a client's technical and methodological capability were associated with outsourcing (e.g., Bardhan et al. 2007; Dedrick et al. 2011). This finding seems to contradict the finding that client firms outsourced for "technical reasons," but maturity is related to processes, not specific technologies.

Relationship characteristics

As a broad category, relationship characteristics examine the features of a particular client-provider pair. Only one independent variable, *cultural distance*, defined as "the extent to which the members of two distinct groups differ on one or more cultural dimensions" (Lacity et al. 2010, p. 423), was examined five times and four times it was negatively associated with ITO decisions. It seems that substantial cultural differences deter clients from outsourcing or influence their selection of offshore destinations (e.g., Gefen and Carmel 2008).

Environment

As a broad category, environmental factors are factors that "exist in the external environment for which parties have little control, such as the level of competition and public opinion about outsourcing/offshoring, that can affect sourcing outcomes for clients or providers" (Lacity et al. 2016, p. 22). Only one independent variable, *provider competition*, defined as "the presence of multiple, reputable and trustworthy service providers which can provide a range of choices for the clients" (Lacity et al. 2016, p. 42), produced enough consistent results to be included in Figure 20.1. Examined six times, four times (67%) it was positively associated with ITO decisions (e.g., Fisher et al. 2008; Levina and Su 2008). High levels of provider competition keeps prices at market value and gives clients more choices at the initial decision and may help clients switch providers if the incumbent performs poorly.

Determinants of ITO decisions

Figure 20.2 depicts the 31 significant IVs within the seven broad categories of independent variables that determine ITO outcomes. A positive relationship between an IV and ITO decision in Figure 20.2 means that the IV was positively related to ITO outcomes of some kind (cost savings, better IT service, better organizational performance, etc.). A negative relationship between an IV and ITO outcomes means that the IV was negatively related to ITO outcomes (cost increases, worse IT service, worse organizational performance, etc.).

Transaction attributes

Researchers have studied transaction attributes to determine whether outsourcing certain types of transactions were more or less likely to result in positive outcomes. Overall, (1) uncertainty, (2) measurement difficulty, and (3) service complexity were negatively and significantly related to ITO outcomes. *Uncertainty* is defined as "the degree of unpredictability or volatility of future states as it relates to the definition of IT requirements, emerging technologies, and/or environmental factors" (Lacity et al. 2010, p. 427; Williamson 1991; e.g., Poppo and Zenger 2002; Aubert et al. 2004). Of the 20 times uncertainty was studied, 14 times (70%) researchers found that uncertainty adversely affected ITO outcomes (e.g., Barthélemy 2001). *Measurement difficulty*, "the degree of difficulty in measuring performance of exchange partners in circumstances of joint effort, soft outcomes, and/or ambiguous links between effort and performance" (Lacity et al. 2010, p. 425; e.g., Eisenhardt 1989), was examined nine times and was found to adversely affect ITO outcomes six times (67%) (e.g., Poppo and Zenger 2002). *Service complexity*, "the degree to which a service or project requires compound steps, the control of many variables, and/or where cause and effect are subtle and dynamic" (Lacity et al. 2016, p. 43; e.g., Ventovuori and Lehtonen 2006; Penfold 2009), was examined five times and was found to adversely affect ITO outcomes four times (80%).

Contractual governance

Contractual governance is the formal, written rules that govern client-provider relationships (Lacity et al. 2016). Three IVs were repeatedly tested with consistent results: (1) contract detail, (2) contract type, and (3) control mechanisms. *Detailed contracts* that defined the scope of services, prices, service levels, and responsibilities of both parties and prescribed how parties would adapt to changes in character, volume, or market best practices had better outsourcing outcomes than contracts with fewer details (e.g., Pinnington and Woolcock 1995; Poppo and Zenger 2002). Contract detail was positively related to ITO outcomes in 15 of the 19 times it was examined (79%). *Contract type* is a term denoting different forms of contracts used in outsourcing. Examples from the ITO literature include customized contracts, fixed price contracts, time and materials contracts, fee-for-service contracts, and partnership-based contracts (Lacity et al. 2010). Contract type mattered or was positively related to ITO outcomes 16 of the 21 times (76%) it was examined (e.g., Gopal et al. 2003). *Control mechanisms* are certain means or devices a controller uses to promote desired behavior (Lacity et al. 2016). Some ITO researchers assessed the *types* of controls while other researchers assessed the *number* of controls. Considering the evidence from both, control mechanisms mattered or were positively related to ITO outcomes in 9 out of the 10 times it was examined.

Relational governance

Relational governance comprises the informal rules used to manage client-provider relationships. In scholarly works we reviewed, ten IVs were repeatedly examined and produced consistent results: (1) knowledge sharing, (2) communication, (3) trust, (4) relationship quality,

(5) partnership view, (6) relational governance (generic IV), (7) commitment, (8) social capital, (9) interface design, and (10) cultural distance. *Knowledge sharing*, "the degree to which clients and providers share and transfer knowledge" (Lacity et al. 2016, p. 40) was examined 23 times and was positively related to ITO outcomes 21 times (91%). *Communication*, "the degree to which parties are willing to openly discuss their expectations, directions for the future, their capabilities, and/or their strengths and weaknesses" (Lacity et al. 2010, p. 423; e.g., Klepper 1995), was examined 14 times and was always positively related to ITO outcomes. *Trust*, "the confidence in the other party's benevolence" (Lacity et al. 2010, p. 427; e.g., Dibbern et al. 2008) was examined 16 times and was positively related to ITO outcomes 13 times (81%) (e.g., Sabherwal 1999). *Relationship quality*, "the quality of the relationship between a client and provider," was found to positively affect ITO outcomes five out of six times (83%). A *partnership view*, defined as "a client organization's consideration of suppliers as trusted partners rather than as opportunistic vendors" (Lacity et al. 2010, p. 426; e.g., Saunders et al. 1997; Kishore et al. 2003) also positively affect ITO outcomes five out of six times (83%). Within the broad category of "relational governance" there is a general independent variable that is also called *relational governance*. This is because some studies measured an independent variable that was simply called relational governance (e.g., Srivastava and Teo, 2012). Examined 11 times, relational governance positively affected sourcing outcomes 9 times (82%). *Social capital* is "the sum of the actual and potential resources embedded within, available through and derived from the network of relationships" (Lacity et al. 2016, p. 43; e.g., Nahapiet and Ghoshal 1998). Higher values of social capital were positively related to higher values of ITO decisions in four of the five times (80%) it was examined. *Client/provider interface design* is the planned structure on where, when, and how client and provider employees work, interact, and communicate (Lacity et al. 2010; e.g., Rottman and Lacity 2006). Studied eight times, six times (75%) client/provider interface design mattered. *Cultural distance* hurt ITO outcomes, but this, in theory, could be offset with higher levels of a cultural distance management capability (Lacity et al. 2016).

Provider capabilities

Which provider capabilities contribute to positive outsourcing outcomes? The four most frequently studied and most important provider firm capabilities were (1) technical and methodological capability, (2) human resource management capability, (3) domain understanding, and (4) client management capability. The provider's *technical and methodological capability* in terms of technical or process related standards, including the Capability Maturity Model (CMM), Capability Maturity Model Integrated (CMMI), and the Information Technology Infrastructure Library (ITIL) and best practices such as component reuse (e.g., Davenport 2005, Rottman and Lacity 2006; Kotlarsky et al. 2007), was found to affect outcomes positively in 15 out of 17 examinations (88%). A provider's *human resource management capability*, the "ability to identify, acquire, develop, and deploy human resources to achieve both provider's and client's organizational objectives" (Lacity et al. 2010, p. 424), was found to positively and significantly affect client outcomes 12 of the 16 times (75%) it was examined. *Domain understanding* is the extent to which a provider has prior experience and/or understanding of the client organization's business and technical contexts, processes, practices, and requirements (Lacity et al. 2016; e.g., Clark et al. 1995; Gopal et al. 2002), and was positively related to ITO outcomes in four out of six examinations (67%). The general *client management capability*, defined as "the extent to which a provider organization is able to effectively manage client relationships" (Lacity et al. 2010, p. 423) was always found to positively affect ITO outcomes in nine examinations.

Client capabilities

Which client capabilities contribute to positive outsourcing outcomes? Seven client capabilities were frequently studied and found to be important determinants of ITO outcomes. Clients with strong capacities in (1) technical and methodological, (2) provider management, (3) contract management, (4) risk management, (5) outsourcing readiness, (6) transition management, and (7) absorptive capacity capabilities had better ITO outcomes compared to clients with weak or immature capabilities. A client's *technical and methodological capability* was an important determinant in both ITO decisions and ITO outcomes. Examined 12 times, it positively affected ITO outcomes nine times (75%). We also see that the technical and methodological capability was needed by both parties in order to deliver good outcomes (see provider capabilities). Clients must become good at managing providers by shifting their capabilities from managing resources and processes to managing inputs and outputs. The *provider management capability* was examined 14 times and was always found to significantly ITO outcomes. Clients also need a strong *contract management capability* to effectively bid, select, and negotiate effective contracts with providers (e.g., Feeny and Willcocks 1998). Examined 11 times, it always positively affected ITO outcomes. A client also needs to be able to identify, rate, and mitigate potential risks associated with outsourcing (*risk management capability*) (e.g., Smith and McKeen 2004), as evidenced by the five times out of seven (71%) that it positively affected ITO outcomes. Clients needed to be *ready to outsource* by having realistic expectations and a clear understanding of internal costs and services compared to outsourced costs and services, as supported by all 12 empirical examinations. *Transition management capability*, defined as "the extent to which a client organization effectively transitions services to or from outsourcing providers or integrates client services with provider services" (Lacity et al. 2016, p. 44), was examined six times and always positively affected ITO outcomes. Finally, a client's *absorptive capacity*, the ability to scan, acquire, assimilate, and exploit valuable knowledge, was significant in four out of five examinations (80%) (e.g., Lee 2001; Lin et al. 2007).

Client firm characteristics

Are certain types of clients more likely to get better outsourcing outcomes for IT services than others? One client firm characteristic produced consistent results after repeated examinations: *client experience with outsourcing*. Prior IT outsourcing experience of clients was associated with better outcomes in five out of six examinations (83%) (e.g., Barthélemy, 2001; Gopal et al., 2003).

Decision characteristics

The way clients made ITO decisions also mattered in that the (1) provider evaluation process and (2) top management support affected ITO outcomes. The **evaluation process** for evaluating and selecting providers mattered in seven out of eight examinations (88%) (e.g., Kern et al., 2002; Lacity and Willcocks 1998). *Top management commitment/support*, defined as "the extent to which senior executives provide leadership, support, and commitment to outsourcing" (Lacity et al. 2010, p. 427), was positively related in all six examinations (e.g., Baldwin et al. 2001; Koh et al. 2004).

ITO decision

Finally, we report that client organizations that decided to outsource IT services reported positive outcomes in 63% of findings. In the past, this metric has been called the ITO "batting average" (Lacity et al. 2016). Essentially this tells us that ITO outsourcing led to good outcomes more often than not, but success is not guaranteed. The variability in outcomes is explained largely by the variation in the other 30 IVs that determined outcomes.

Impactful future research opportunities

What are promising areas for future research? As further contributions to "normal science" (Kuhn 1970), IS scholars may continue to help clients with ITO decisions and to help clients and providers successfully manage ITO relationships by continuing to study the determinants of ITO decisions and outcomes. We made specific recommendations in these areas in Lacity et al. (2016). For example, we called for more empirical studies on:

- *Innovation in ITO delivery*: How can clients incentivize IT service providers to deliver innovations beyond the standard service levels agreed to in contracts?
- *Environmental factors*: How do environmental factors affect ITO decisions and outcomes? We need studies to better understand how shifts in political regimes affect offshoring decisions. We know very little about how public opinion on outsourcing/offshoring affects sourcing decisions and outcomes for clients or providers, despite the media filling the airwaves with politicians espousing the evils of worker visa programs and sending jobs out of a country.
- *Client and provider capabilities*: While we have a good understanding of client capabilities and provider capabilities as independent sets of capabilities, we do not have a good understanding of how they affect each other. What really determines whether outsourcing results in capabilities lost or capabilities gained for each party?
- *Pricing models*: While there are many studies that examine the determinants and effects of fixed-price versus time and materials contracts, we have little understanding about other pricing models like utility pricing, gainsharing, and outcome-based pricing.

Beyond "normal science" contributions, what research might be truly impactful? In Lacity et al. (2016), we proposed some rather audacious future research directions. Here we revisit four questions sought to elevate the research agenda from client and provider perspectives to societal issues.

What roles do sourcing clients and providers have in uplifting marginalized populations around the world?

According to the US Census Bureau, world population exceeded seven billion people in 2012. The World Bank estimated that 80% of the world's population – 5.6 billion people – were below the poverty line, living on less than $10 per day. In 2011, 2.2 billion people lived in extreme poverty, living on less than $2 per day.[3] Caring leaders from the sourcing community realize that all the spending that occurs in sourcing can help alleviate poverty by employing marginalized populations to provide business services. The Global Sourcing Council,[4] for example, was created as a non-profit organization to help organizations source goods and services by uplifting humanity through jobs while protecting the environment.

In the academic community, there are several researchers beginning to study how sourcing clients and providers alleviate poverty through meaningful work. This research stream is called "impact sourcing" and it is defined as "the practice of hiring and training marginalized individuals to provide information technology, business process, or other digitally enabled services who normally would have few opportunities for good employment" (Carmel et al. 2014, p. 397). Impact sourcing may employ as many as 561,000 people and may generate as much as $20 billion worldwide (Accenture 2012; Avasant/Rockefeller Foundation 2012; Everest Group 2014; Monitor Group/Rockefeller Foundation 2011). The small amount of research that does exist provides case studies on companies aiming to help such varied marginalized populations as the poor, Native American tribes, ultra-orthodox Jewish women who are not allowed to work with men, and prisoners, of whom there are six million worldwide (e.g., Gino and Staats 2012; Heeks 2012; Heeks and Arun 2010; Lacity et al. 2012). More research on impact sourcing is needed to convince customers of the value of such services and to inspire other entrepreneurs and established service providers to pursue social missions.

What roles do sourcing clients and providers have in sustaining the planet?

Environmental sustainability is the idea that human survival and well-being depends on the natural environment. Over-population, depletion of natural resources, pollution, and nuclear proliferation are all serious threats to environmental sustainability (Rosa et al. 2010). Companies that source IT services certainly affect the environment through power consumption in data centers, employees' global travel, consumption of water, and disposal of e-waste, to name a few (Babin and Nicholson 2011). One way that companies can protect the environment is to meet standards set by such organizations as the Global Reporting Initiative, the Carbon Disclosure Project, the UN Global Compact and the ISO environmental and social responsibility standards. Babin and Nicholson (2011) assessed the environmental maturity of 19 major ITO and Business Process Outsourcing (BPO) providers, and found that Accenture, Infosys, TCS, Wipro, and HP had the most mature sustainability profiles. Beyond this isolated study, we did not find any empirical research that assessed how sourcing clients and providers specifically help or hurt the physical environment. This is perhaps because environmental sustainability is usually not an isolated goal, but rather part of a three-pronged approach known as corporate social responsibility (CSR). CSR aims to simultaneously balance economic, social, and environmental objectives (Porter and Kramer 2006; 2011). A few academic researchers have begun to study CSR capabilities of both sourcing clients and providers (Babin 2008; Babin et al. 2011; Babin and Nicholson 2009; 2012; Li et al. 2014; Madon and Sharanappa 2013). Clearly, more work is needed.

What are the implications of threats to cybersecurity on sourcing and vice versa?

Arguably, cybersecurity is currently one of the most critical issues facing individuals, organizations, governments, and society (Hoffman et al. 2015), as evidenced by yet another year filled with a spate of spectacular data breaches.[5] An interesting stream of work has recently emerged that examines the outsourcing of information security management (i.e., managed security services) (e.g., Cezar et al. 2014). While studying managed security services as another type of business service being outsourced is certainly important, we believe there are at least two other aspects that deserve urgent attention. First, given most, if not all, business services are IT-enabled and IT services are a major portion of outsourced business services (Lacity et al. 2010; 2011), it appears critical to better understand the impacts of outsourcing of business services on organizational security postures, exposure to cyber threats, and their abilities to effectively manage information security. For example, Reitzig and Wagner (2010) argue that as organizations outsource upstream activities, they face the possibility of losing knowledge on conducting downstream activities through the mechanism of "forgetting by outsourcing vertically related activities" (p. 1196). As organizations continue to disintegrate value chains via globally dispersed service providers, do they risk "forgetting" how to effectively manage information security in the process? On the other hand, how does increased management focus on cybersecurity shape outsourcing decisions and management of outsourced services?

Second, as both the breadth and depth of outsourcing of business services increase, how can organizations effectively build security into the outsourcing process? How can they effectively stipulate security-related expectations in outsourcing contracts, and more importantly govern and monitor outsourcing relationships to ensure security and compliance? While the first set of issues may be more difficult to address empirically, we believe that outsourcing practice can benefit immensely from research-based guidance on these complex and murky issues.

How will service automation affect workers around the globe?

In 2014, Brynjolfsson and McAfee published a best-selling book called *The Second Machine Age*. They argued that the "first" machine age occurred during the Industrial Revolution when machines replaced humans doing physical labor. During the "second" machine age – the age happening now – machines are increasingly replacing humans doing highly perceptional tasks (like driving cars) and highly cognitive tasks (like designing financial portfolios to balance risk). According to the authors, some of the positive consequences will be an explosion in the variety and volume of consumption. One huge unanswered question relates to the nature of work: as computers increasingly take over jobs, what work will humans do? This question has been splattered on the covers of such publications as the *Harvard Business Review* (Davenport and Kirby 2015; Reeves et al. 2015; Frick 2015), the *Atlantic* (Thompson 2015), and the *Wall Street Journal* (Davenport and Iyer 2015).

In the sourcing industry, we are certainly witnessing the shift from labor to automation for the provisioning of business services. Consider these bellwether events:

- In September 2014, Wipro announced it will reduce headcount by one-third over the next three years because of disruptive technologies like automation and artificial intelligence.[6]
- In December 2014, Frank Casale launched the Institute of Robotic Process Automation (IRPA) in New York City.[7] In his keynote speech at the event, Casale, also the founder of The Outsourcing Institute[8] in 1993, said he launched the IRPA because he saw that automation technology was going to be the next game changer in outsourcing.
- In May 2015, The REVAmerica conference,[9] designed to build a vibrant business services industry in the United States, presented a panel on why robotic process automation (RPA) is great for American jobs.
- In June 2015, The WorldBPO Forum[10] and the National Outsourcing Association[11] added keynotes and panel discussions on RPA to their agendas.

- In July of 2015, the IAOP launched a chapter dedicated to RPA.[12] One major Indian provider estimated that going forward, 70% of its IT services would be automated and 30% would be labor based.
- During 2014–2015, the major sourcing advisors started developing RPA practices, including the Everest Group, Alsbridge, HfS, KPMG, and ISG.

The research questions are daunting. If ITO services will be increasingly provided by technology, what happens to countries with labor arbitrage advantages? For example, what will happen to India's middle class, which was largely built on this sector? Will automation lead to more reshoring back to high-cost destinations? Will opportunities to uplift marginalized populations by employing them in the services sector diminish? Bringing all these research issues together, we ask: how can sourcing clients, providers, and advisors protect jobs, protect the environment, and ensure security in an increasingly automated world?

Conclusion

We aimed to accomplish two goals with this chapter. First, we aimed to succinctly review the entire empirical record on the determinants of ITO decisions and ITO outcomes. While the chapter presented the findings at the detailed level of specific IVs, we conclude by abstracting the 23 years of empirical research to the categories of determinants in Figure 20.3. This figure represents our collective learning on ITO. There is something immensely elegant and gratifying to depict over 1,170 findings in such a simple picture. Second, we aimed to inspire ourselves and our colleagues with ambitious goals for future research by proposing studies on the role of IT sourcing in addressing poverty, environmental sustainability, security, and the nature of human work in the age of software robots.

The key empirical findings suggest that client organizations clearly had a rich set of motives driving ITO sourcing decisions in addition to *cost savings*, including the desire to *improve*

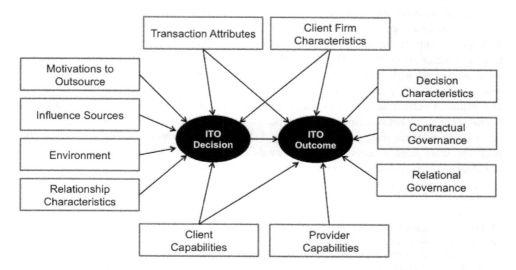

Figure 20.3 Categories of independent variables that determine ITO decisions and ITO outcomes

performance and to increase *flexibility*. Many clients pursued outsourcing as part of a strategy to *focus in-house staff* on critical services. Clients also used outsourcing to *access a provider's expertise, technical assets*, and *global markets*. When clients *feared losing control* of the IT service or *feared security or intellectual property* leakages, they tended to select insourcing options. When making sourcing decisions, client organizations also considered a number of transaction attributes that hindered outsourcing and favored insourcing, like high *transaction costs*, high *business risks*, and high *service complexity* and *interdependence*. Clients tended to also insource IT services deemed *critical to the business*. Client decisions were *influenced by a number of external and internal sources* and tended to outsource when they perceived other competitors were successful in doing so, thereby hoping to *mimic* their competitors' success. Clients felt more confident outsourcing services when they themselves had *mature technical and methodological capabilities*. Clients were also more likely to outsource when they perceived a high level of *provider competition*, perhaps to avoid lock-in or to get a competitive price, but clients tended to avoid selecting providers that were deemed to have a wide *difference in culture*.

On the determinants of ITO outcomes, the empirical evidence suggested that sourcing decisions were also complex, as demonstrated by the 31 significant independent variables that were found repeatedly to influence sourcing outcomes. Client organizations struggled to get good sourcing outcomes when transactions had high levels of *uncertainty, measurement difficulty*, or *service complexity* or when the client organizations had little *prior experience with outsourcing*. Capabilities were also important determinants of sourcing outcomes. Clients with strong *technical and methodological, provider management, contract management, risk management, transition management*, and *absorptive capacity capabilities* had better sourcing outcomes compared to clients with weak or immature capabilities. Also, clients needed to be *ready to outsource* by having realistic expectations and a clear understanding of internal costs and services compared to outsourced costs and services. Provider capabilities were also important; providers with strong *technical and methodological, human resource management, domain understanding*, and *client management capabilities* produced better outcomes for clients and for themselves compared to providers with weak capabilities. Contractual and relational governance were powerful influencers on sourcing outcomes. When clients signed *detailed contracts* and used more *control mechanisms*, they experienced better sourcing outcomes compared to clients with loose contracts and fewer controls. *Contract type* also influenced outcomes in that fixed-price contracts had different effects on risks, success, and financial performance than time and materials contracts. Higher levels of the following relational governance variables were associated with better sourcing outcomes: *knowledge sharing, communication, trust, relationship quality, partnership view, commitment*, and *social capital*. The *interface design* also mattered – clients and providers need to actively design how the parties will work together. *Cultural distance* hurt sourcing outcomes, but this, in theory, could be offset with higher levels of a cultural distance management capability. Like most organizational decisions, outsourcing decisions were more successful when the *evaluation process* was extensive and when *senior management was committed* and supportive of the decision.

Notes

1 http://auriga.com/blog/outsourcing-industry-experts-gathered-in-the-city-of-the-eternal-spring/.
2 www.horsesforsources.com/hfs-index-q12013_02221.
3 www.globalissues.org/article/26/poverty-facts-and-stats; www.worldbank.org/en/topic/poverty/overview.
4 www.gsc.clubexpress.com/.
5 2015 Verizon Data Breach Investigations Report, www.verizonenterprise.com/DBIR/2015/.
6 Times of India, December 2014.

7 www.irpanetwork.com/.
8 www.outsourcing.com.
9 www.revamerica.com/program/.
10 www.worldbpoforum.com/conference_agenda_2015.aspx.
11 www.noa.co.uk/events/noa-symposium/.
12 www.iaop.org/content/23/162/4295.

References

Accenture (2012). *Exploring the Value Proposition From Impact Sourcing: The Buyer's Perspective*, available at www.accenture.com/us-en/Pages/insight-exploring-value-proposition-impact sourcing.aspx.

Agarwal, M., Kishore, R. and Rao, H. R. (2006). Market Reactions to E-Business Outsourcing Announcements: An Event Study, *Information & Management* 43: 861–873.

Agrawal, P. and Haleem, A. (2013). The Impact of the Outsourcing of IT on Firm Performance: An Empirical Study, *International Journal of Management* 30(3): 121–139.

Alsuairi, M. and Dwivedi, Y. (2010). A Multi-Disciplinary Profile of IS/IT Outsourcing Research, *Journal of Enterprise Information Management*, 23(2): 215–258.

Ang, S. and Cummings, L. (1997). Strategic Response to Institutional Influences on Information Systems Outsourcing, *Organization Science* 8(3): 235–256.

Aubert, B.A., Houde, J.F., Patry, M. and Rivard, S. (2012). A Multi-Level Investigation of Information Technology Outsourcing, *Journal of Strategic Information Systems* 21(3): 233–244.

Aubert, B.A., Rivard, S. and Patry, M. (2004). A Transaction Cost Approach to Outsourcing Behavior: Some Empirical Evidence, *Information & Management* 41: 921–932.

Avasant/Rockefeller Foundation (2012). *Incentives & Opportunities for Scaling the "Impact Sourcing" Sector, 2012*. Corporate report by Avasant consultancy, available at www.rockefellerfoundation.org/news/publications/incentives-opportunities-scaling

Babin, R. (2008). Assessing the Role of CSR in Outsourcing Decisions, *Journal of Information Systems Applied Research* 1: 1–14.

Babin, R., Briggs, S. and Nicholson, B. (2011). Emerging Markets Corporate Social Responsibility and Global IT Outsourcing, *Communications of the ACM* 54(9): 28–30.

Babin, R. and Nicholson, B. (2009). Corporate Social and Environmental Responsibility in Global IT Outsourcing, *MIS Quarterly Executive* 8: 123–132.

Babin, R. and Nicholson, B. (2011). How Green Is My Outsourcer? Measuring Sustainability in Global IT Outsourcing, *Strategic Outsourcing: An International Journal* 4(1): 47–66.

Babin, R. and Nicholson, B. (2012). *Sustainable Global Outsourcing: Achieving Social and Environmental Responsibility in Global IT and Business Process Outsourcing*, Palgrave Macmillan, London.

Baldwin, L., Irani, Z. and Love, P. (2001). Outsourcing Information Systems: Drawing Lessons From a Banking Case Study, *European Journal of Information Systems* 10: 15–24.

Bardhan, I., Mithas, S. and Lin, S. (2007). Performance Impacts of Strategy, Information Technology Applications, and Business Process Outsourcing in US Manufacturing Plants, *Production and Operations Management* 16(6): 747–762.

Barthélemy, J. (2001). The Hidden Costs of IT Outsourcing, *Sloan Management Review* 42(3): 60–69.

Beulen, E. and Ribbers, P. (2003). International Examples of Large-Scale Systems Theory and Practice: A Case Study of Managing IT Outsourcing Partnerships in Asia, *Communications of the AIS* 11: 357–376.

Beverakis, G., Dick, G. and Cecez-Kecmanovic, D. (2009). Taking Information Systems Business Process Outsourcing Offshore: The Conflict of Competition and Risk, *Journal of Global Information Management* 17(1): 32–48.

Bhagwatwar, A., Hackney, R. and Desouza, K. C. (2011). Considerations for Information Systems "Back-sourcing": A Framework for Knowledge Re-Integration, *Information Systems Management* 28(2): 165–173.

Carmel, E., Lacity, M. and Doty, A. (2014). The Impact of Impact Sourcing: Framing a Research Agenda. In: *Information Systems Outsourcing: Towards Sustainable Business Value*, Hirschheim, R., Heinzl, A. and Dibbern, J. (eds.), pp. 397–430. Springer, Heidelberg.

Ceci, F. and Masciarelli, F. (2010). A Matter of Coherence: The Effects of Offshoring of Intangibles on Firm Performance, *Industry & Innovation* 17(4): 373–392.

Cezar, A., Cavusoglu, H. and Raghunathan, S. (2014). Outsourcing Information Security: Contracting Issues and Security Implications, *Management Science* 60(3): 638–657.

Clark, T. D., Zmud, R. and McCray, G. (1995). The Outsourcing of Information Services: Transforming the Nature of Business in the Information Industry, *Journal of Information Technology* 10(4): 221–237.

Cullen, S., Seddon, P. and Willcocks, L. (2005). Managing Outsourcing: The Life Cycle Imperative, *MIS Quarterly Executive* 4(1): 229–246.

Currie, W. L. and Seltsikas, P. (2001). Exploring the Supply-side of IT Outsourcing: Evaluating the Emerging Role of Application Service Providers, *European Journal of Information Systems* 10: 123–134.

Davenport, T. (2005). The Coming Commoditization of Processes, *Harvard Business Review* 83(6): 101–108.

Davenport, T. and Kirby, J. (2015). Beyond Automation: Augmentation, *Harvard Business Review* 93(6): 58–65.

Davenport, T. and Iyer, B. (2015). Bringing Outsourcing Back to Machines, *Wall Street Journal*, July 1, 2015: http://blogs.wsj.com/cio/2015/07/01/bringing-outsourcing-back-to-machines/.

Dedrick, J. Carmel, E. and Kraemer, K. L. (2011). A Dynamic Model of Offshore Software Development, *Journal of Information Technology* 26(1): 1–15.

Dibbern, J., Chin, W. and Heinzl, A. (2012). Systemic Determinants of the Information Systems Outsourcing Decision: A Comparative Study of German and United States Firms, *Journal of the Association for Information Systems* 13(6): 466–497.

Dibbern, J., Goles, T., Hirschheim, R. and Jayatilaka, B. (2004). Information Systems Outsourcing: A Survey and Analysis of the Literature, *ACM SIGMIS Database* 35(4): 6–102.

Dibbern, J., Winkler, J. and Heinzl, A. (2008). Explaining Variations in Client Extra Costs Between Software Projects Offshored to India, *MIS Quarterly* 32(2): 333–366.

DiMaggio, P. and Powell, W. (1991). The Iron Cage Revisited: Institutional Isomorphism and Collective Rationality in Organizational Fields. In: *The New Institutionalism in Organizational Analysis*, Powell, P. and DiMaggio, W. (eds.), pp. 63–82. University of Chicago Press, Chicago.

DiRomualdo, A. and Gurbaxani, V. (1998). Strategic Intent for IT Outsourcing, *Sloan Management Review* 39(4): 67–80.

Eisenhardt, K. (1989). Agency Theory: An Assessment and Review, *Academy of Management Review* 14(1): 57–76.

Everest Group (2014). *The Business Case for Impact Sourcing*, available at www.everestgrp.com/2014-09-the-business-case-for-impact-sourcing-sherpas-in-blue-shirts-15662.html.

Feeny, D. and Willcocks, L. (1998). Core IS Capabilities for Exploiting Information Technology, *Sloan Management Review* 39(3): 9–21.

Fisher, J., Hirschheim, R. and Jacobs, R. (2008). Understanding the Outsourcing Learning Curve: A Longitudinal Analysis of a Large Australian Company, *Information Systems Frontiers*, 10: 165–178.

Fjermestad, J. and Saitta, J. (2005). A Strategic Management Framework for IT Outsourcing: A Review of the Literature and the Development of a Success Factors Model, *Journal of IT Case and Application Research* 7(3): 42–60.

Frick, W. (2015). When Your Boss Wears Metal Pants, *Harvard Business Review* 93(6): 84–89.

Gefen, D. and Carmel, E. (2008). Is the World Really Flat? A Look at Offshoring at an Online Programming Marketplace, *MIS Quarterly* 32(2): 367–384.

Gefen, D., Ragowsky, A., Licker, P. and Stern, M. (2011). The Changing Role of the CIO in the World of Outsourcing: Lessons Learned From a CIO Roundtable, *Communications of the AIS* 28(15): 233–242.

Gino, F., and Staats, B. (2012). The Microwork Solution, *Harvard Business Review*, 90: 92–96.

Gonzalez, R., Gasco, J. and Llopis, J. (2010). Information Systems Outsourcing: An Empirical Study of Success Factors, *Human System Management* 29(3): 139–151.

Goo, J., Kishore, R., Rao, H. R. and Nam, K. (2009). The Role of Service Level Agreements in Relational Management of Information Technology Outsourcing: An Empirical Study, *MIS Quarterly* 33(1): 1–28.

Gopal, A., Mukhopadhyay, T. and Krishnan, M. (2002). The Role of Software Processes and Communication in Offshore Software Development, *Communications of the ACM* 45(4): 193–200.

Gopal, A., Sivaramakrishnan, K., Krishnan, M. and Mukhopadhyay, T. (2003). Contracts in Offshore Software Development: An Empirical Analysis, *Management Science* 49(12): 1671–1683.

Grover, V., Cheon, M. and Teng, J. (1996). The Effect of Service Quality and Partnership on the Outsourcing of Information Systems Functions, *Journal of Management Information Systems*, 12(4): 89–116.

Hall, J. and Liedtka, S. (2005). Financial Performance, CEO Compensation, and Large-Scale Information Technology Outsourcing Decisions, *Journal of Management Information Systems* 22(1): 193–222.

Heeks, R. (2012). The Research Agenda for IT Impact Sourcing, blog. *ICTs for Development*, Web paper from http://ict4dblog.wordpress.com/2012/05/06/the-research-agenda-for-it-impact-sourcing/.

Heeks, R. and Arun. S. (2010). Social Outsourcing as a Development Tool: The Impact of Outsourcing IT Services to Women's Social Enterprises in Kerala, *Journal of International Development* 22: 441–454.

Hirschheim, R. and Lacity, M. (2000), Information Technology Insourcing: Myths and Realities, *Communications of the ACM*, 43(2): 99–108.

Hoffman, C., Khan, S.A. and Mirchandani, D. (2015). Developing an Interdisciplinary Cybersecurity Program in the Business School: Reflections and a View to the Future, *Regional Business Review* 34: 51–55.

Jarvenpaa, S. and Mao, J. (2008). Operational Capabilities Development in Mediated Offshore Software Service Models, *Journal of Information Technology* 23(1): 3–17.

Jeyaraj, A., Rottman, J. and Lacity, M. (2006). A Review of the Predictors, Linkages, and Biases in IT Innovation Adoption Research, *Journal of Information Technology*, 21(1): 1–23.

Kern, T., Willcocks, L. and Van Heck, E. (2002). The Winners Curse in IT Outsourcing: Strategies for Avoiding Relational Trauma, *California Management Review* 44(2): 47–69.

Kishore, R., Rao, H.R., Nam, K., Rajagopalan, S. and Chaudhury, A. (2003). A Relationship Perspective on IT Outsourcing, *Communications of the ACM* 46(12): 87–92.

Klepper, R. (1995). The Management of Partnering Development in I/S Outsourcing, *Journal of Information Technology* 10: 249–258.

Koh, C., Ang, S. and Straub, D. (2004). IT Outsourcing Success: A Psychological Contract Perspective, *Information Systems Research* 15(4): 356–373.

Kotlarsky, J., Oshri, I., van Hillegersberg, J. and Kumar, K. (2007). Globally Distributed Component-Based Software Development: An Exploratory Study of Knowledge Management and Work Division, *Journal of Information Technology* 22(2): 161–173.

Kuhn, T. (1970). *The Structure of Scientific Revolutions*, University of Chicago Press, Chicago.

Lacity, M., Khan, S. and Yan, A. (2016). Review of the Empirical Business Services Sourcing Literature: An Update and Future Directions, *Journal of Information Technology*, 31(2):1–60.

Lacity, M., Khan, S. and Yan, A. (2017). Review of 23 Years of Empirical Research on Information Technology Outsourcing Decisions and Outcomes. Submitted to HICSS.

Lacity, M., Khan, S., Yan, A. and Willcocks, L. (2010). A Review of the IT Outsourcing Empirical Literature and Future Research Directions, *Journal of Information Technology* 25(4): 395–433.

Lacity, M., Khan, S. and Willcocks, L. (2009). A Review of the IT Outsourcing Literature: Insights for Practice, *Journal of Strategic Information Systems* 18: 130–146.

Lacity, M., Rottman, J. and Carmel, E. (2012). *Emerging ITO and BPO Markets: Rural Sourcing and Impact Sourcing*, IEEE Readynotes, IEEE Computer Society.

Lacity, M., Rottman, J. and Khan, S. (2010b). Field of Dreams: Building IT Capabilities in Rural America, *Strategic Outsourcing: An International Journal* 3(3): 169–191.

Lacity, M., Solomon, S., Yan, A. and Willcocks, L. (2011). Business Process Outsourcing Studies: A Critical Review and Research Directions, *Journal of Information Technology* 26(4): 221–258.

Lacity, M. and Willcocks, L. (1998). An Empirical Investigation of Information Technology Sourcing Practices: Lessons From experience, *MIS Quarterly* 22(3): 363–408.

Lacity, M., Yan, A. and Khan, S. (2017). *Review of 23 Years of Empirical Research on Information Technology Outsourcing Decisions and Outcomes*. Submitted to Hawaii International Conference on System Sciences.

Langer, N., Slaughter, S.A. and Mukhopadhyay, T. (2014). Project Managers' Practical Intelligence and Project Performance in Software Offshore Outsourcing: A Field Study, *Information Systems Research*, 25(2): 364–384.

Lee, A. (2016). A Commentary: Theory Appropriation and the Growth of Knowledge, *Journal of Strategic Information Systems* 25(1): 68–71.

Lee, J. (2001). The Impact of Knowledge Sharing, Organizational Capability and Partnership Quality on IS Outsourcing Success, *Information & Management* 38: 323–335.

Lee, J., Miranda, S. and Kim, Y. (2004). IT Outsourcing Strategies: Universalistic, Contingency, and Configurational Explanations of Success, *Information Systems Research* 15(2): 110–131.

Levina, N. and Su, N. (2008). Global Multisourcing Strategy: The Emergence of a Supplier Portfolio in Services Offshoring, *Decision Sciences* 39(3): 541–570.

Li, Y., Zhao, X., Shi, D. and Li, X. (2014). Governance of Sustainable Supply Chains in the Fast Fashion Industry, *European Management Journal* 32(5), 823–836.

Lin, C., Pervan, G. and McDermid, D. (2007). Issues and Recommendations in Evaluating and Managing the Benefits of Public Sector IS/IT Outsourcing, *Information Technology & People* 20(2): 161–183.

Lioliou, E., Zimmermann, A., Willcocks, L. and Gao, L. (2014). Formal and Relational Governance in IT Outsourcing: Substitution, Complementarity and the Role of the Psychological Contract, *Information Systems Journal* 24(6), 503–535.

Loh, L. and Venkatraman, N. (1992). Diffusion of Information Technology Outsourcing: Influence Sources and the Kodak Effect, *Information Systems Research* 3(4): 334–358.

Madon, S. and Sharanappa, S. (2013). Social IT Outsourcing and Development: Theorising the Linkage, *Information Systems Journal* 23(5), 381–399.

Mahnke, V., Overby, M. L. and Vang, J. (2005). Strategic Outsourcing of IT Services: Theoretical Stock-taking and Empirical Challenges, *Industry and Innovation* 12(2): 205–253.

McKeen, J. and Smith, H. (2011). Creating IT Shared Services, *Communications of the AIS* 29(34): 645–656.

McLellan, K., Marcolin, B. and Beamish, P. (1995). Financial and Strategic Motivations Behind IS Outsourcing, *Journal of Information Technology* 10: 299–321.

Monitor Group/Rockefeller Foundation (2011). *Job Creation Through Building the Field of Impact Sourcing*. Corporate Report by Monitor Consultancy, Retrieved from Monitor Group/Rockefeller Foundation from www.deloitte.com/view/en_US/us/Services/consulting/Strategy-Operations/strategy-consulting/index.htmRootchange.org.

Nahapiet, J. and Ghoshal, S. (1998). Social Capital, Intellectual Capital, and the Organizational Advantage, *Academy of Management Review* 23(2): 242–265.

Oshri, I. and Van Uhm, B. (2012). A Historical Review of the Information Technology and Business Process Captive Centre Sector, *Journal of Information Technology* 27(4): 270–284.

Palvia, P., King, R., Xia, W. and Jain Palvia, S. (2010). Capability, Quality, and Performance of Offshore IS Vendors: A Theoretical Framework and Empirical Investigation, *Decision Sciences* 41(2): 231–270.

Patane, J. R. and Jurison, J. (1994). Is Global Outsourcing Diminishing the Prospects for American Programmers? *Journal of Systems Management* 45(6): 6–10.

Pearce, J. A. (2014). Why Domestic Outsourcing is Leading America's Reemergence in Global *Manufacturing, Business Horizons* 57(1): 27–36.

Penfold, C. (2009). Off-Shored Services Workers: Labour Law and Practice in India, *Economic and Labour Relations Review* 19(2): 91–106.

Pinnington, A. and Woolcock, P. (1995). How Far Is IS/IT Outsourcing Enabling New Organizational Structure and Competences? *International Journal of Information Management* 15(5): 353–365.

Poppo, L. and Zenger, T. (2002). Do Formal Contracts and Relational Governance Function as Substitutes or Complements? *Strategic Management Journal* 23: 707–725.

Porter, M. and Kramer, M. (2006). Strategy and Society: The Link Between Competitive Advantage and Corporate Social Responsibility, *Harvard Business Review* 84(12): 78–92.

Porter, M. and Kramer, M. (2011). Creating Shared Value, *Harvard Business Review* 89(1/2): 62–77.

Poston, R., Simon, J. and Jain, Radhika. (2010). Client Communication Practices in Managing Relationships With Offshore Vendors of Software Testing Services, *Communications of the AIS* 27(9): 129–148.

Premuroso, R., Skantz, T. and Bhattacharya, S. (2012). Disclosure of Outsourcing in the Annual Report: Causes & Market Returns Effects, *International Journal of Accounting Information Systems* 13(4): 382–402.

Qu, W. G., Oh, W. and Pinsonneault, A. (2010). The Strategic Value of IT Insourcing: An IT-Enabled Business Process Perspective, *Journal of Strategic Information Systems* 19(2): 96–108.

Reeves, M., Zeng, M., and Venjara, V. (2015). The Self-Tuning Enterprise: How Alibaba Uses Algorithmic Thinking, *Harvard Business Review* 93(6): 66–75.

Reitzig, M. and Wagner, S. (2010). The Hidden Costs of Outsourcing: Evidence From Patent Data, *Strategic Management Journal* 31(11): 1183–1201.

Rosa, E., Diekmann, A., Dietz, T., and Jaeger, C. (2010). *Human Footprints on the Global Environment*, MIT Press, Cambridge. Available at: https://mitpress.mit.edu/sites/default/files/titles/content/9780262512992_sch_0001.pdf

Rottman, J. and Lacity, M. (2006). Proven Practices for Effectively Offshoring IT Work, *Sloan Management Review* 47(3): 56–63.

Sabherwal, R. (1999). The Role of Trust in Outsourced IS Development Projects, *Communications of the ACM* 42(2): 80–86.

Saunders, C., Gebelt, M. and Hu, Q. (1997). Achieving Success in Information Systems Outsourcing, *California Management Review* 39(2): 63–80.

Schneider, S. and Sunyaev, A. (2016). Determinant Factors of Cloud-Sourcing Decisions: Reflecting on the IT Outsourcing Literature in the Era of Cloud Computing, *Journal of Information Technology* 31(1): 1–31.

Smith, H. and McKeen, J. (2004). Developments in Practice XIV: IT Outsourcing – How Far Can You Go? *Communications of the AIS* 14(1): 508–520.

Sobol, M. and Apte, U. (1995). Domestic and Global Outsourcing Practices of America's Most Effective IS Users, *Journal of Information Technology* 10: 269–280.

Srivastava, S. and Teo, T. (2012). Contract Performance in Offshore Systems Development: Role of Control Mechanisms, *Journal of Management Information Systems* 29(1): 115–158.

Su, N. and Levina, N. (2011). Global Multisourcing Strategy: Integrating Learning From Manufacturing Into IT Service Outsourcing, *IEEE Transactions on Engineering Management* 58(4): 717–729.

Susarla, A., Barua, A. and Whinston, A. (2010). Multitask Agency, Modular Architecture, and Task Disaggregation in SaaS, *Journal of Management Information Systems* 26(4): 87–117.

Thompson, D. (2015). A World Without Work, *Atlantic Monthly* 316(1): 51–61.

Veltri, N., Saunders, C. and Kavan, C. (2008). Information Systems Backsourcing: Correcting Problems and Responding to Opportunities, *California Management Review* 51(1): 50–76.

Ventovuori, T. and Lehtonen, T. (2006). Alternative Models for the Management of FM Services, *Journal of Corporate Real Estate* 8(2): 73–90.

Williamson, O. (1975). *Markets and Hierarchies: Analysis and Antitrust Implications*, Free Press, New York.

Williamson, O. (1991). Comparative Economic Organization: The Analysis of Discrete Structural Alternatives, *Administrative Science Quarterly* 36(2): 269–296.

Wullenweber, K., Beimborn, D., Weitzel, T. and Konig, W. (2008). The Impact of Process Standardization on Business Process Outsourcing Success, *Information Systems Frontiers* 10(2): 211–224.

21
INNOVATION IN HEALTHCARE SETTINGS
The power of everyday practices

Marco Marabelli and Sue Newell

Introduction

Coordinating the practices of different healthcare professionals is very important, particularly when dealing with life-threatening situations such as in the ER (emergency room), or when healthcare workers deal with severely ill patients who need speedy diagnoses (Kaelber and Bates 2007). This coordination is especially crucial when patients have multiple diseases that require several different interventions (Abraham and Reddy 2008). Doctors and nurses may well be undertaking interdependent activities, which is challenging when health workers have different backgrounds, knowledge and approaches to problem solving and yet are required to coordinate their practices in providing services to patients, families, carers and communities (Gittell et al. 2013; WHO 2010). This issue becomes even more complex when the parties involved do not all sit within the same organization. For example, medical staff in a hospital may need to coordinate not only with other clinicians in the same healthcare facility (or at least the same healthcare organization) but also with professionals in other healthcare-related and social organizations, like social services, independent physicians, psychologists and schools.

It is precisely this type of broader networked coordination that is the focus of many current innovation projects in healthcare settings. For example, the problem of 'bed-blocking' is related to the lack of coordination between hospitals and social service agencies, leading to the situation where, for example, an elderly patient has to remain in a (scarce) hospital bed because the preparations for moving her to a residential home have not been completed in a timely fashion. Many innovation initiatives are geared toward facilitating better coordination across a network of organizations and professional groups in order to improve the efficiency and effectiveness of healthcare service delivery. Yet, as we will discuss, in networked settings, improving coordination requires more than a directive to each party to 'work together' because there are no hierarchical power relations that can impose direction (Swan and Scarbrough 2005). Moreover, a lack of physical proximity can increase the problems of coordination (Ardichvili et al. 2003; Whittington et al. 2009).

Innovations that improve healthcare coordination require that those involved mobilize knowledge and change practices (Currie and White 2012; Kimble et al. 2010; Scarbrough et al. 2014). Given the challenges that using hierarchical power in network settings poses, we focus on the power and knowledge of everyday practices because this helps to understand "the political nature of networking and knowledge management practices undertaken by various interest groups" (Hislop et al. 2000, p. 401). Thus, in this chapter we concentrate on the role of knowledge/power in the success of innovation projects focused on changing practices to improve coordination in the networked healthcare setting. Moreover, informed by the strategy-as-practice (SAP) literature, we acknowledge the relevance of human as well as material agencies (thus, people and 'things,' such as a medical sheet, a document and a presentation) in practices associated with change. We aim, therefore, to address the following research question: what power do everyday social and material practices have in strategic innovation initiatives in networked healthcare settings?

We address our research question using longitudinal and qualitative data collected in a healthcare network in Canada. We found that everyday practices play a key role in fostering innovation in healthcare contexts. In particular, we identified three distinct practices that emerged from our data analysis: talk, text and things. These practices, albeit analyzed individually, are interlocked with each other and 'have' power – they help promoting changes in the healthcare settings that we examined, and ultimately supported changes leading to innovation (here related to improving coordination and communication across carers).

The remainder of this chapter is structured as follows. We begin by providing a theoretical background before outlining our research methods. We go on to present and analyze our findings before discussing them in light of prior literature. We conclude the paper with a consideration of the implications of our study – for theory and practice.

Background literature

The creation of innovative practices (changing how people do things in ways that deviate from their daily tasks/activities) is generally challenging. In healthcare settings, clinicians (i.e., doctors and nurses) are particularly reluctant to change their everyday practices because they typically receive very technical training and 'learn' how to do things in ways that they believe are optimal (Hall 2005; Reese and Sontag 2001). Consequently, change agents (generally visionary physicians, researchers or healthcare managers) need to act strategically to convince (other) clinicians that it is even worth trying to adopt a new practice.[1] The challenges (and associated benefits) of these healthcare changes are often considered strategic.

To this end, strategy has often been conceptualized as a grand vision – to do something different – which is formally planned by the top executive team and then executed by others lower in the management hierarchy (e.g., Prahalad and Hamel 1994). While planning by a top executive team may be important to study, the SAP literature suggests that strategy is a much more messy process than this, and indicates that rather than focusing on the planning of the top executive team, we can learn more from looking at the everyday practices of the range of stakeholders (practitioners) involved in the context of interest, here an innovation project around improving coordination through networking. From the SAP perspective, strategy is studied as an emergent process (formation and execution) where strategy is constantly unfolding in the flow of practices as undertaken by practitioners (e.g., Jarzabkowski 2005; Whittington 2006). In this perspective, knowledge is central, but it is more than simply knowledge held by senior managers who use it to direct activities; in the SAP perspective, knowledge is more complex (and fluid) than this.

Given our interest to examine everyday practices, in this chapter we consider healthcare innovation using the SAP view of strategy, and integrate it with power, a construct that is relevant to accomplish changes (Hardy 1996; Hardy and Thomas 2014) and that has often been studied together with knowledge because, as Foucault (1980) argues, power emerges through social processes underpinning the negotiation of knowledge.

Foucault departs from the (traditional and Weberian) idea that power is owned by individuals or groups who use it as an instrument of coercion and moves toward a view where power is seen as diffused rather than concentrated. Drawing on Foucault, Latour (1986) provides a useful example that contrasts the Weberian view of power (power as a resource) with the perspective we take in this chapter, which implies that power emerges through everyday (social and material) practices. For Latour, an order, a claim or an artifact (described as a token) can be proposed by a powerful individual (or group), and the token, according to the inertia principle, will move in the direction given by the powerful actor (the actor with resource power) as long as there are no obstacles (e.g., frictions or resistances). In this exercise of power (the 'diffusion' model according to Latour), the order (or the token) does not need to be explained, and the greater the strength with which the token is delivered, the more the token will travel and overcome resistances. However, ultimately the token will encounter resistance and this will slow down the order's pace of impact so that the original force (power) is reduced. In contrast, power can be seen as performative, and this relates to the idea that the spread of the token "is in the hands of people" (Latour 1986, p. 267). Its displacement is not caused by the initial impetus (i.e., it is not dependent on the resources of the person attempting to make the change), because the token here has no impetus; instead, it is the energy given to the token by people who keep it going. In this context, the token is not a 'mandatory' order, but is something that people reshape, by "modifying it, or deflecting it, or betraying it, or adding to it, or appropriating it" (Latour 1986, p. 267). Latour calls this way to understand power a 'translation' model, because power relates to social processes where the order is negotiated rather than 'executed' (or spread). Given that mandates are likely to face significant resistance in network settings, because there is not a single authority to 'push' the strategy across the network, we need to examine how the strategy to innovate spreads through everyday translation practices in the focal context.

In this chapter we use this idea of *translation* to examine how innovation practices unfold. In doing this we illustrate how power is not a 'tool' that is used to accomplish long-term planned innovation projects (Weberian way) but, instead, power is action, therefore practice itself – being embedded in the everyday micro-level actions of practitioners. We next turn to describing our fieldwork.

Context and methods

The case focuses on a pilot innovation project, which was set up to improve coordination of care for children with complex care needs at the Canadian hospital, Dooly, and between Dooly and other (external) healthcare agencies such as social services. While the need to improve healthcare coordination at Dooly emerged in 2008, the project analysis and bidding process (and approval) took two years. On April 1, 2010, the pilot was granted funds and a partnership was established involving the hospital and three agencies. The partnership created with the pilot project implies that all four organizations involved in this healthcare network have the same decision-making 'rights,' through representatives of each partner. The funding originated from a surplus of one of the three agencies of the partnership.

Children with complex care needs were defined as children with multiple and life-threatening diseases who need to be seen by several specialists. The necessity to improve healthcare coordination for this group emerged in 2008, when some families of these children pointed out that the different physicians (specialists) who were taking care of their child did not exchange

Innovation in healthcare settings

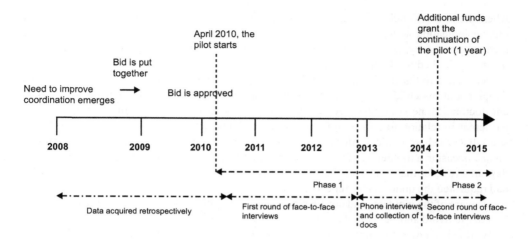

Figure 21.1 Time line of events and data collection at Dooly

crucial medical knowledge with each other. As a result, the families were often overwhelmed and emotionally drained because it fell to them to coordinate the care of their child. Additionally, the external agencies (e.g., social services) were not always aware of each child's most recent health issues, and this too posed health risks. Further, the hospital did not receive the most recent updates – from school or social service agencies – about the children's social/psychological conditions. The project started in April 2010, with 20 children being enrolled in the pilot. A nurse dedicated to the project (nurse coordinator) and a project manager were hired, and one of the hospital doctors, who was already taking care of children with complex needs, undertook the role of full-time responsible physician. In spring 2014 (second phase), additional funds made it possible to add resources: an additional nurse (full-time) and three physicians (one full-time and two part-time) were hired. This allowed them to enroll 20 additional children (see Figure 21.1 for time line of key events).

Fieldwork was undertaken longitudinally (September 2010–April 2015) *in situ* and retrospectively (2008–2010, including the review of documents), adopting an interpretive qualitative approach (Walsham 1993; 2006). Figure 21.1 synthesizes the various phases of our fieldwork.

Findings

From conception to the start of the pilot innovation project (2008–2010)

Dooly hosted a family forum that gave parents the opportunity to share their experiences and feelings about their child's care. Families used the forum to highlight coordination problems they had experienced both within the hospital (specialists not sharing information) and between the hospital and the other agencies. Examples brought up in this forum included a mother recalling that she had to head to the hospital three days in a row, to have her child undertake the same test, but for three different specialists (the physicians were not sharing the information about tests needed); a foster mother pointing to the difficulty she experiences when she needs to talk to a specialist about what another specialist said, about her child; a mother indicating how she was not listened to when taking her child to the ER because of a medical emergency, with the outcome that there was a delay in deciding about treatment while the doctor looked up the medical record; and a father telling how he had put together a short binder related to his child's health (he calls it a 'cheat sheet') in order to help him remember things about his child's diagnoses and treatments when trying to communicate with different doctors. Some specialists seemed relatively sympathetic to the families' complaints, in particular in relation to sharing information with colleagues, but all prior attempts to 'force' specialists to share clinical information about patients had been unsuccessful. For example, on one occasion a mother had formally complained that she had had to go to the hospital three days in a row for the same test. The chief pediatric consultant had rebuked the specialist who had requested the unnecessary repeat test, and for a short while this specialist (and others who were aware of the incident) had notified other doctors about the tests that they were prescribing in order to avoid another complaint about wasted resources.

While this order to improve coordination did not last, those healthcare professionals involved in the forum were moved by the emotional content of many of the families' stories and decided to try and do something about the poor coordination that they were hearing about. One initial activity that was instigated was to sponsor a master's student to undertake a research project examining how coordination in healthcare had been approached in other contexts and with what effects. Another activity that emerged was that a core 'team' (six in total, three from Dooly and three from three other healthcare agencies) involved in the care of the children began to informally meet (including dinners) to discuss how to help the families. In these discussions of what would help, they identified how they would need additional resources to improve coordination and so they decided to put together a proposal to bid for money. They informally approached the CEO who initially was not supportive of the need for a project, especially because resources were tight at Dooly. The core team then, on the one hand, used the evidence produced from the master's thesis to convince the CEO, and on the other hand, decided that it could be worth seeking external funds. In early 2008 the core team put together an eight-page letter addressed to the CEO where they formally asked him to co-sign a bid for obtaining funds to start a pilot innovation project. This time the CEO agreed to advocate for the creation of a pilot and a year and a half later the bid was accepted (effective April 1, 2010) and steering and advisory committees were created. The steering committee includes Dooly's CEO and the CEOs of the other agencies, plus the responsible physician and a project supervisor (vice president of academic affairs at Dooly). The advisory committee includes the individuals who bid for the project (core team) plus two family members, representative of the 'voice' of the many families in the family forum.

The pilot project (April 1, 2010–April 1, 2015)

The pilot had its official start on April 1, 2010. The families soon perceived the benefits of improved coordination. The responsible physician arranged formal meetings to present to her colleagues why improving coordination was important. This involved a PowerPoint presentation, which included evidence about improved coordination (e.g., taken from the master's dissertation) as well as more personal anecdotes from families. Following these formal meetings, the responsible physician took action to improve communication on a more permanent basis. She did this not by imposing strict, mandatory 'rules' for the specialists (who would probably resist); instead, she was able to persuade the specialists of the relevance of each of them having a holistic view of each case. So, she arranged case meetings for each child, where all the specialists involved share their expertise, opinions, test results, and the like. While previous attempts to 'force' doctors to share information had not lasted, these case meetings quickly became established practice.

Families attended these case meetings. However, for them, what made more of a difference was being able to contact the nurse coordinator, whose main role was to act as the interface between the hospital, the families and external agencies. The nurse coordinator reports directly to the responsible physician, from whom she receives the most recent updates about each of the 20 children enrolled in the pilot. The nurse coordinator calls, on average, each family at least once a week – often just to check to see how the child is doing, sometimes to share a lab result or to ask families to take the child to the hospital. The families contact the nurse coordinator about once a week too. Most often contact is made via email, the main reason being that the families need to a refill a prescription. Other times, phone calls are made because of a 'quasi-emergency,' when the child does not feel well and the family struggles with whether or not a visit to ER is required. In these situations, generally, the nurse coordinator immediately contacts the responsible physician, and, if necessary, the responsible physician checks with the specialist(s), and feedback is provided to the family within minutes, avoiding needless trips to Dooly. The project manager supervises these processes, coordinates the advisory committee meetings, and is in constant contact with the families to gather feedback that is then shared with the nurse and the responsible physician.

Aside from these new staff roles and processes, the main ambition of the pilot innovation project had been to create an ad-hoc electronic medical record (EMR) to allow the sharing of the children's medical records across the network of organizations involved. This is because the evidence (e.g., produced by the dissertation) had suggested that such systems were vital components of improved coordination. In fact, in 2010 the hospital already had electronic records where most clinical information about patients was stored. However, different units had their own systems, and this represented a barrier to coordination even within the hospital. The external agencies did not have any type of EMR. Once the pilot project team started to look at implementing something to allow electronic sharing of medical records across the network, they soon realized that it was not feasible:

> So originally I think the goal for our project was to have an electronic record but because of funding we couldn't develop that, it was too expensive and too time-consuming.
>
> (Project Manager)

After some deliberation, the advisory board came up with the idea of developing a single point of care (SPOC). The SPOC was based on the one father's practice of using a 'cheat sheet.' The SPOC is a short (two-page) medical sheet that synthesizes the most relevant information about each child in the pilot. As the nurse coordinator explains, the SPOC works as follows:

> Every family after they had their first intake visit would come back to what we call the family focused team meeting. So at that meeting we would say this is who your family coordinator is, we would present them with that [cheat sheet] document, that summary of their child. And we developed a medical roadmap that looked over their child's care over a year and said okay, every three months this needs to happen, every six months this needs to happen, every year . . . So they had something visually they

could follow and make sure that nothing got missed. Because we didn't want to just take away all of their empowerment, we wanted to be able to give them documents that facilitated making things easier for them, not necessarily do everything for them. So they could look and say oh yeah, he's due for blood work in the next month, let me remember that.... The binder was supposed to also help communication between specialists and between the community and [Dooly]. So dieticians could write notes in that and then they could bring it to the GI and say the dietician wrote this.

The nurse coordinator updates the SPOC when a change in a child's condition occurs. The SPOC is then handed to the families, so they can bring it to different specialists, and if needed, to ER – even in other hospitals. The SPOC is also sent via fax or email to the external agencies (providing coordination across the network). The SPOC is designed to include only relevant (e.g., life-threatening) information about the child, and in a way that is specific enough to be meaningful for doctors, but easily understandable by non-clinicians (the families and other non-medical agencies like schools). The families quickly started to use the SPOC and found it very helpful, giving them legitimacy when they were discussing their child's illness with a professional, because "it was signed by a doctor, not by a mum" (mother of a child involved in the pilot).

The SPOC was also well received by the external agencies involved. Prior to the start of the pilot there had been attempts to promote communication between Dooly and the external agencies, but these attempts were unsuccessful because they were very poorly organized. However, now, with additional resources (in particular the nurse coordinator) and a joint plan created at the advisory committee level and constantly revised to overcome challenges and 'make things happen' (e.g., the creation of the SPOC in place of a 'real' EMR), they were able to dramatically improve communication and coordination at Dooly between specialists as well as across the partnership (Dooly and the agencies) and with the families.

A second phase of the innovation pilot was granted in 2014. This was based on surplus funds from the agencies involved. This second phase allowed the enrollment of 20 more children and the associated new doctors and nurses to support the project. The families continued to use the family forum to advocate for turning the pilot into a program, providing evidence of how the project has helped them. For instance, we interviewed a mother of a child involved in the pilot, who highlights the difference that it made for her and her son:

> Before the [Pilot Project] it was like if I was in a business, you know, I wouldn't be the only person having to do all that work. You would have a manager, and you would have secretaries, you would have clerks, you would have a whole system of people and I before the project didn't have that, you know, so what would happen before the project would only be related to how much energy I had or what his health is, and so that I could only advocate so far to make things happen, you know. But now all doctors work together to talk about how it's going to work and who's going to take responsibility for pieces of making it work. It's not just a nice touchy-feely, this is a good idea, see you all later, but it's more okay, who's going to be responsible for which pieces and for somebody took notes about it, you know, so each doctor has access to those notes and is accountable, and again it's not left to me to run to a doctor and say well, you did do that part, you didn't do that part.

At the end of 2014, the new Dooly CEO was actively trying to convince the provincial government that the innovation at Dooly should become a permanent program with provincial-level funding. There are several pilot projects in Canada that are good candidates to become programs, but funds are limited, and being able to influence relevant decision makers in government can make the difference. Given this, the CEO was actively involved in trying to convince the province of the merits of this program. He was doing this by sending to the province 'official' documents that reflect the success of the pilot and by giving presentations about the innovation. The CEO has drawn on an independent study conducted by an external university that shows that the pilot has substantially improved service delivery. This university study concluded that most families indicate that their workload in managing their child's health is dramatically reduced, while their child receives better support. Interestingly, an internal evaluation study conducted by the research center at Dooly was less conclusive, because using a quantitative approach it had been unable to identify any measurable improvements for the children's health or the hospital efficiency. This evaluation study is not part of the case that the CEO is using to get funding for a program. The outcome of this CEO work is not known at the time of writing, but as one interviewee mentioned – "he (the CEO) knows people, a lot of people [and] this will hopefully help us, otherwise the families will feel that we've abandoned them."

Analysis and discussion

The Dooly case illustrates the myriad everyday practices that both create a strategic innovation initiative and sustain its momentum over time. It shows that senior management were not the instigators of the innovation in this case; rather it was the families – those one might assume would be 'bottom of the pile' in terms of the power they could wield across a complex healthcare network. Moreover, the case highlights practices involving talk, text and things, and their power to mobilize knowledge that supports innovations in practices (see Table 21.1). Of course, many practices contain talk, text and things, so this distinction is for analytical purposes only.

The table illustrates how everyday practices involving talk, text and things have power to mobilize knowledge in a strategic innovation initiative. This resonates with the SAP view of how strategy happens, but there are several points in our analysis that require additional consideration.

The power of talk

First, the role of emotions in practices involving talk that has power to influence future action is highlighted in our analysis. The stories of the families (both before – horror – and after – relief) are passionate, and it is their emotional intensity that helps to feed the existing narrative that improving knowledge sharing among healthcare professionals in the network can positively affect coordination to benefit sick children. These emotional narratives were repeated in a variety of settings to build and sustain momentum for the innovation. For example, the CEO saw the power of these narratives, incorporating family stories in his negotiations with the province (in presentations and speeches). Thus, our case clearly illustrates that the 'pathos' that accompanied the families' stories strongly affected those who were initially skeptical about supporting the pilot innovation project or later engaging with the province to turn the pilot into a long-term program.

Second, we observe the power of talk in informal face-to-face meetings (Balogun and Johnson 2005). For instance, informal meetings (including dinners) among those from the different organizations who were all supportive of the proposed innovation strategy were important

Table 21.1 The power of ongoing practices

Practice	Power of Practice
Talk	
Stories, anecdotes and narratives told by the families at the family forum illustrate the problems with the existing situation. These stories have significant emotional content: the parent losing a job; the parent trying desperately to get an ER doctor to listen to what they know about their child's problems but being ignored.	Emotional content of the stories leads those who listen to empathize with the plight of the families and want to do something to help them. Such emotional content is a well-known tactic, used for example in campaigns to get the public to donate to worthy causes.
Holding informal face-to-face meetings among those supportive of the initiative (e.g., dinners between the 'core team,' prior to 2010). The advocates discuss why the innovation would be helpful and develop short-term tactics for supporting the innovation – e.g., the SPOC, as a 'patch' because they were not able to create an EMR.	Talking with others supportive of the initiative helps to reinforce the 'rightness' of the innovation being promoted without opposition. This helps to keep the momentum of the initiative going and builds consensus among the core team members.
Informal meetings are held between the responsible physician and the specialists. The aim of these meetings is to have the specialists understand the relevance of sharing patients' information.	The responsible physician's reputation plays a key role in having the specialists take her seriously. This is also reinforced by the fact that she provides support to her claims using evidence from the literature.
Text	
Writing a dissertation on the basis of literature showing how coordination improvements can produce benefits for both patients/families and the hospital.	In the field of medicine there is a strong tradition of ensuring that diagnostic and treatment protocols comply with existing 'best practice' evidence. This helped legitimate the project, e.g., by convincing the skeptical first CEO to support the project funding bid.
PowerPoint presentations delivered during formal meetings, which use evidence from the literature and the family stories (e.g., meetings in Dooly where the pilot project is presented).	PowerPoint slides used during presentations helped to give the message durability, so that the text could continue to influence after the meeting. Moreover, slides generally embed metaphors and figures that create links to concepts, and these have symbolic power.
Crafting official documents: the core team writes a long letter to ask the commitment of the first CEO; the second CEO writes to the province.	These official documents provide a durable commitment to the project that is difficult to subsequently renounce. Talk can be denied, but it is more difficult to deny what is written down and circulated to many.
Conducting and presenting results of evaluation studies: an evaluation study undertaken by the hospital was not able to prove that the project was successful because of the small number of children involved. A second independent qualitative study, which involved interviews with the families, demonstrated the benefits of the pilot.	The CEO decided to use only the study that provided supporting results in the materials he presented to the province. Again, the text is important because it provides the evidence base, not simply for the effectiveness of this sort of initiative but for this specific initiative.

Practice	Power of Practice
Things Initially the core team attempted to create a shared EMR, but this was thwarted by a lack of funds and time. The core team then devised a new, paper-based system that would allow those involved to share information. While this SPOC was circulated to the network of organizations involved, it was the families that were the carriers of the SPOC, having a vested interest in ensuring that the health and social care professionals involved were kept fully informed about their child's problems, diagnoses and treatments.	An EMR is the established way of improving coordination across healthcare professionals – the literature review evidenced its importance. The inability to create a shared EMR could thus have stalled the project. However, those involved found a work-around to the problem by creating the paper-based information system. It is important to note that while the SPOC is also a text and has durability, its importance goes beyond merely reinforcing support for the initiative. Rather, the SPOC itself carries information between specialists involved and is constantly updated and signed-off (by a doctor, not a mum). The SPOC, thus, plays a symbolic role by legitimizing certain practices, e.g., when it is handed to a healthcare professional by a parent.

in keeping the initiative live in the early days, before funding was secured. Clearly mobilizing knowledge to improve coordination involved several changes of current practices across the network. Our case shows that such strategic initiatives require significant work, and that this can be made easier when those involved talk together and reinforce the reasons for their engagement.

Another example of the power of talk was shown in the informal meetings between the responsible physicians and the specialists – these led to huge improvements in terms of knowledge mobilization within Dooly. The responsible physician was able to use evidence to legitimate her assertions about the importance of improved coordination, for example, by highlighting evidence of healthcare improvements because of the willingness of doctors to share patient information. Importantly, however, interviewees indicated that it was not simply what she said that was important, it was also who was saying it. Thus, the responsible physician had been working at Dooly for several years and was well respected – and this helped to legitimate what she said. In conclusion, the power of talk was relevant for initiating the strategic innovation initiative, and more importantly talk continued to be important in sustaining the initiative through knowledge mobilization. However, practices at Dooly did not involve just talk. For instance, text played a key role in legitimizing the pilot project, as we explain next.

The power of text

At Dooly, text was used by those who advocated for the pilot project to legitimize the initiative. Creating formal documents and PowerPoint presentations based on 'evidence' highlighted that the initiative could be (master's student's dissertation) and was (external university study) successful. It is clear that talk and text are related, because texts are often powerful when they are used in talk (e.g., see later discussion of PowerPoint presentation). However, texts have a durability that talk does not have. Ancient Romans used to say that "*verba volant, scripta manent"* – by this suggesting that spoken words (*verba*) can easily be forgotten (*volant*), while written documents (*scripta*) can be conclusive in public matters, because of their 'durable' nature (*manent*). Legitimizing the initiative with text (something 'concrete' that can be reviewed at any time) was used by the advocates of the initiative to embed evidence of the benefits of the pilot project in a written (and durable) format. For example, official documents (e.g., the master's dissertation) provided evidence from the literature about the relationship between knowledge mobilization, coordination and improvement of healthcare. Given the importance of evidence-based practice in healthcare, it is not surprising that this textual evidence was drawn upon in many different practices to help promote and maintain the pilot project. Thus, the results of the dissertation were included in an official letter addressed to the CEO, by which the core team aimed to gain support for the changes they wanted to introduce, as well as in subsequent PowerPoint presentations at various meetings.

PowerPoints, along with other official documents and emails, were also the means used by the CEO negotiated with the province to grant the pilot long-term funding. He uses 'all sort of internal data, evidence from the community, families feelings' in his presentations to feed the narrative that the pilot project leads to improvements on several fronts. In the case of the CEO and the province, the former is trying to convince a higher-level entity (the province) that a change (long-term funds granted to the pilot) be undertaken. The CEO uses PowerPoint presentations, which have a durability that talking alone does not. For instance, presentations can be accessed and reviewed after a presentation (often PowerPoint handouts are distributed to the audience for this very purpose). Interestingly, the CEO's presentations were not just based on text. Other elements include images (e.g., representing together the logos of the four organizations involved in the partnership) that have symbolic power (in this case providing a sense that the four organizations are working together and have a shared sense of purpose indicating that the network is cohesive). Representing the journey of the pilot with a graphical image to illustrate the timeline is another example that suggests how the pilot has built legitimacy over time. In sum, creating official documents and PowerPoint presentations are illustrative of the power of text that helped to give legitimacy to the innovation project.

The power of things

The SPOC is an object (thing) that is created with input from numerous people and signed off on by a doctor. The SPOC can be described as a material agent because it has agency – has power to affect practice – in its own right when it is used by various individuals at Dooly, by the external agencies and by the families. Moreover, during its use, the SPOC was modified several times – for instance by adding and removing fields that, through practice, were found to be more or less important for sharing information in a professional (for specialists), synthetic (for ER doctors), yet understandable way (by non-clinicians, i.e., families). This clearly illustrates how the SPOC gained power through use and recalls Latour's translation model. The spread of Latour's 'token' (in this case the SPOC) "is in the hands of people" (Latour 1986, p. 267), and the energy that gives it power (initially, the adoption of the SPOC by the external agencies, for instance) lies in its use and appropriation by different actors, who make changes (reshaping it, when needed), but in so doing they preserve the essence of it (that it is understandable in different ways). Moreover, the SPOC allows for effective communication between Dooly and the agencies, and between the specialists and the families. Namely it maintains its main functionality and this is consistent with Star and Griesemer's (1989) definition of boundary objects that, albeit 'plastic,' are also "robust enough to maintain a common identity across sites" (Star and Griesemer 1989, p. 393). The SPOC, therefore, allows local understandings to be reframed in different 'sites' of practice by different practitioners. Similar to the PowerPoint presentations, the SPOC does not simply play a role in creating common understanding that allows coordinated actions; it also plays a symbolic role, and has power because it legitimizes certain practices for those involved (Swan et al. 2007).

In conclusion, the SPOC's ability to mobilize knowledge across the network is an example of how boundary objects are 'things' with their own agency – they can gain power in their own right. Moreover, it is interesting to note that the SPOC reflects the emergent and unpredictable nature of innovation, as it occurs in practice. The SPOC is nothing but a paper-based way to mobilize knowledge across the Dooly network, and represented a 'patch,' or better a work-around to circumvent the (emergent) problems associated with the impossibility of creating an EMR (initial plan). Here we first show that the SPOC enables knowledge mobilization (quite a radical change, as before the SPOC the healthcare network had struggled for years because of the lack of knowledge mobilization). Second, and probably more importantly, we argue that the SPOC was not just a 'tool' that empowered individuals (e.g., the families). Instead, the SPOC was a boundary object (Star and Griesemer 1989) with agency that gained increased power over time – namely, it was not used as a tool to support an innovation but instead was an emergent element of innovating itself (as a human practitioner can be).

Conclusions and implications

In this chapter we demonstrated that it takes myriad everyday practices (including talk, text and things) to 'make things happen' in network settings. These practices involve a range of practitioners, not just senior executives, as much of the existing strategy literature focuses on. Two examples are (1) the involvement of the 'end users' (in our case, the families) that were fully engaged in strategic practices that promoted knowledge mobilization, which eventually occurred not just between healthcare agencies, but also from and to those who were in receipt of the care; and (2) the emergence of the SPOC as a boundary object gaining power on its own right. Therefore, the main contribution of this chapter focuses on the power of everyday practices to promote innovation. In our healthcare context we found that social and material practices *do* embed power, which can promote innovation. The practitioners in our healthcare network were all engaged in making decisions – jointly – with a view to improving the healthcare of the children.

We therefore contribute to the literature by illustrating the relevance of accounting for the power of different types of practice and practitioners (including end users and material objects) in network settings. Moreover, we were able to show how Latour's translation model of power fits with strategizing in the sense of allowing us to understand how innovation happens in networks settings, with talk, text and things all involved in this translation process.

Finally, we highlighted the power of 'pathos' that unfolds through practice. We found that passion and emotion in advocating for some kind of innovation – especially by the parents during the family forum sessions – had a strong influence, for instance with the CEO. In sum, it is important to consider emotional talk as a form of power in its own right. This leaves a question for future research about whether such emotional talk can be 'made up' to provide additional power for a narrative.

Note

1 To this end, please refer to the several studies illustrative of the difficulties associated with the introduction of EMR systems in hospitals: Cresswell et al. (2014), Middelton et al. (2013) and Miller and Sim (2004).

References

Abraham, J., and Reddy, M. C. 2008. "Moving Patients Around: A Field Study of Coordination Between Clinical and Non-Clinical Staff in Hospitals," *Proceedings of the 2008 ACM Conference on Computer Supported Cooperative Work*: ACM, pp. 225–228.

Ardichvili, A., Page, V., and Wentling, T. 2003. "Motivation and Barriers to Participation in Virtual Knowledge-Sharing Communities of Practice," *Journal of Knowledge Management* (7:1), pp. 64–77.

Balogun, J., and Johnson, G. 2005. "From Intended Strategies to Unintended Outcomes: The Impact of Change Recipient Sensemaking," *Organization Studies* (26:11), pp. 1573–1601.

Currie, G., and White, L. 2012. "Inter-Professional Barriers and Knowledge Brokering in an Organizational Context: The Case of Healthcare," *Organization Studies* (33:10), pp. 1333–1361.

Foucault, M. 1980. *Power/Knowledge: Selected Interviews and Other Writings, 1972–1977*. New York: Pantheon.

Gittell, J.H., Godfrey, M., and Thistlethwaite, J. 2013. "Interprofessional Collaborative Practice and Relational Coordination: Improving Healthcare Through Relationships," *Journal of Interprofessional Care* (27:3), pp. 210–213.

Hall, P. 2005. "Interprofessional Teamwork: Professional Cultures as Barriers," *Journal of Interprofessional Care* (19:S1), pp. 188–196.

Hardy, C. 1996. "Understanding Power: Bringing About Strategic Change," *British Journal of Management* (7:S1), pp. S3–S16.

Hardy, C., and Thomas, R. 2014. "Strategy, Discourse and Practice: The Intensification of Power," *Journal of Management Studies* (51:2), pp. 320–348.

Hislop, D., Newell, S., Scarbrough, H., and Swan, J. 2000. "Networks, Knowledge and Power: Decision Making, Politics and the Process of Innovation," *Technology Analysis & Strategic Management* (12:3), pp. 399–411.

Jarzabkowski, P. 2005. *Strategy as Practice: An Activity-Based Approach*. London: Sage.

Kaelber, D.C., and Bates, D.W. 2007. "Health Information Exchange and Patient Safety," *Journal of Biomedical Informatics* (40:6), pp. S40–S45.

Kimble, C., Grenier, C., and Goglio-Primard, K. 2010. "Innovation and Knowledge Sharing Across Professional Boundaries: Political Interplay Between Boundary Objects and Brokers," *International Journal of Information Management* (30:5), pp. 437–444.

Latour, B. 1986. "The Powers of Association," in *Power, Action and Belief: A New Sociology of Knowledge?*, J. Law (ed.). London: Routledge & Kegan Paul, pp. 264–280.

Prahalad, C.K., and Hamel, G. 1994. "Strategy as a Field of Study: Why Search for a New Paradigm?," *Strategic Management Journal* (15:S2), pp. 5–16.

Reese, D.J., and Sontag, M.-A. 2001. "Successful Interprofessional Collaboration on the Hospice Team," *Health & Social Work* (26:3), pp. 167–175.

Scarbrough, H., Sarah, E., Daniela, D.A., Marabelli, M., Newell, S., Powell, J., and Swan, J. 2014. "Networked Innovation in the Health Sector: Comparative Qualitative Study of the Role of Collaborations for Leadership in Applied Health Research and Care in Translating Research Into Practice," *Health Services and Delivery Research* (2:13).

Star, S.L., and Griesemer, J.R. 1989. "Institutional Ecology, Translations' and Boundary Objects: Amateurs and Professionals in Berkeley's Museum of Vertebrate Zoology, 1907–39," *Social Studies of Science* (19:3), pp. 387–420.

Swan, J., Bresnen, M., Newell, S., and Robertson, M. 2007. "The Object of Knowledge: The Role of Objects in Biomedical Innovation," *Human Relations* (60:12), pp. 1809–1837.

Swan, J., and Scarbrough, H. 2005. "The Politics of Networked Innovation," *Human Relations* (58:7), pp. 913–943.

Walsham, G. 1993. *Interpreting Information Systems in Organizations*. Chichester: Wiley.

Walsham, G. 2006. "Doing Interpretive Research," *European Journal of Information Systems* (15:3), pp. 320–330.

Whittington, K.B., Owen-Smith, J., and Powell, W.W. 2009. "Networks, Propinquity, and Innovation in Knowledge-Intensive Industries," *Administrative Science Quarterly* (54:1), pp. 90–122.

Whittington, R. 2006. "Completing the Practice Turn in Strategy Research," *Organization Studies* (27:5), pp. 613–634.

WHO. 2010. *Framework for Action on Interprofessional Education & Collaborative Practice*. Geneva: World Health Organization.

22
ALIGNING IN PRACTICE[1]

Anna Karpovsky[2] *and Robert D. Galliers*

Introduction

IT/IS-business alignment[3] has been a topic of considerable attention for over three decades (e.g., Chan and Reich, 2007; McLean and Soden, 1977). Alignment has been consistently rated as a top ten IT management concern (Luftman et al., 2013). Conceptually, alignment has been defined variously as the degree of fit and integration between an organization's business strategy, IS strategy, business structure (and/or business processes), and IT infrastructure (Chan and Reich, 2007; Galliers, 2006; Henderson and Venkatraman, 1993). A common theme has been the argument that alignment leads to a more focused and strategic use of IT (Chan et al., 2006), and that those organizations that are able to successfully align their business and IS/IT tend to perform better than their counterparts (e.g., Chan et al., 1997; Kearns and Lederer, 2003).

Nuanced accounts of alignment have appeared. It has been argued that alignment is infeasible if the business strategy is unclear, and the difficulty of matching a relatively fixed set of IT assets to constantly changing business imperatives has also been noted (Galliers, 2004). Others argue that IT should challenge and transform the business, not simply align with it (e.g., Chan and Reich, 2007), while others still criticize the alignment literature for being too conceptual and not reflecting actual practice (Ciborra, 1997). Normative approaches are argued to not account for organizations as organic, dynamic and ambiguous aggregates, with relationships that are parallel and simultaneous (e.g., Tsoukas, 1994), requiring a refocusing on the practices and activities of *aligning* as opposed to alignment per se (Karpovsky and Galliers, 2015; Wilson et al., 2013). Further, empirical results are argued to be lacking in precision, with the resultant models being prone to subjectivity (Avison et al., 2004).

To reflect on the state of the alignment research, we embarked on a study of the extant literature. We aimed to determine what we currently know about aligning practice with a view of developing a framework to describe actions that constitute aligning. We argue that alignment research requires greater focus on organizational actors' day-to-day aligning activities. A contribution of this chapter is a delineation of a set of aligning activities that serve as a base for future research about the mechanisms actors use to align IS with ongoing processes and strategic imperatives.

The chapter is structured to provide context for our study before discussing the research method adopted and our findings. In the next section, we present a brief review of the extant literature that views alignment as a dynamic process. In the subsequent section, we provide a discussion of the method we employed in our analysis of those cases that report on the actual activities associated with alignment. We go on to report on our findings and conclude with a discussion of a future research agenda.

An overview of the literature on alignment as a dynamic process

In line with some earlier studies, we conceptualize alignment not as a static end-state but as a continuous, ongoing process of *aligning* involving a series of activities resulting in adjustments in various dimensions and across various organizational levels. Some of the prior research suggests that the alignment process represents a continuous synchronization (Smaczny, 2001) or integration by the organization of various technological, organizational, and relational dimensions (Fuchs et al., 2000). Rondinelli et al. (2001) suggest that organizations should continuously readjust and realign four sets of strategic components: business strategy, market penetration decisions, management processes, and structures. For others (e.g., Sabherwal et al., 2001), although the alignment process retains its dynamic nature, it is effectuated on an ad hoc or punctuated rather than continuous basis, depending upon the evolutionary phases experienced by the organization concerned as well as the evolution of its business environment: organizations may experience relatively long periods of minor, evolutionary strategic change, and relatively short periods of sweeping, revolutionary strategic change.

A number of process models of alignment have arisen from this line of research. For example, the "Strategic Alignment Maturity Model" (SAMM) (Luftman, 2000) posits that, as organizations pursue the goal of strategic alignment, alignment moves through the following process stages: (1) initial, ad-hoc; (2) committed; (3) established, focused; (4) improved, managed; and (5) optimized. Luftman argues that the greatest benefit to an organization is found when strategic alignment is an optimized process. Thus, the SAMM explores the "maturity" of strategic alignment and focuses not on the *goal of* alignment, but on developing processes that will enable *ongoing* alignment. Peppard and Breu (2003) propose a co-evolutionary model to describe how IS strategies 'co-adapt' with business strategies, where each is considered distinct yet mutually influencing. Additionally, Hirschheim and Sabherwal (2001) suggest that organizations seek alignment through incrementalism – changing one or more components of alignment, then changing some other, and occasionally reversing earlier changes.

Several specific steps and subprocesses have been suggested to foster movement toward alignment. These include evaluating the performance of senior executives, in part by noting their innovative use of IT; allowing IT to provide innovative ideas that will shape the business; embedding IT in multiple departments and business processes; using IT to provide strategic flexibility to the business; giving the CIO visibility among the senior executives; and encouraging IT executives to collaborate with business unit and regional managers to develop new capabilities (Agarwal and Sambamurthy, 2002). Additionally, Kearns and Lederer (2003) propose two specific processes associated with key actors that contribute to strategic alignment: the CEO participating in IS/IT planning, and the CIO participating in business planning. Although the identification of these processes provides insight into means of achieving alignment, it appears that while these processes are a necessary condition they may not be sufficient. A comprehensive, multifaceted conceptualization of strategic alignment appears still to be missing.

From macro processes to micro practices

While we, thus, have a good understanding of alignment processes as a result of this line of research, we nonetheless know little about what managers and other actors actually *do* in their day-to-day activities to achieve alignment (Campbell, 2005). In order to fill this gap, we extend the conceptualization of alignment from not only something that an organization *attains* to something that an organization *does*: as "a pattern in a stream of goal-oriented activity over time" (Jarzabkowski, 2005: 40). From this perspective, we differentiate ourselves from the (macro) process perspective on alignment by focusing on micro processes, activities, and practices (cf. Peppard et al., 2014; Whittington, 2014).

While the process stream of research considers alignment at various levels of an organization, it tends to focus primarily on the organizational or strategic business unit (SBU) level, with the associated unit of analysis being the sequence of 'high-level' organizational events that take place within a period of adjustment. In contrast, we take an activity-based view of aligning practice where activity is the unit of analysis and is associated with the actions of and around organizational actors. Consequently, we view aligning practice broadly as *all organizational actors' activities that may contribute to tightening links between IT and business across an organization*. Taking this extended conceptualization of aligning practice, we reviewed the alignment literature to derive a set of activities based on published cases. Before presenting our findings, we briefly discuss the research method employed.

Research approach

To obtain an overview of the alignment literature, using a structured methodology (Webster and Watson, 2002), we reviewed over 9,000 articles from the IS, strategic management, and management literatures concerned with ISS and related topics (Karpovsky et al., 2014). To narrow our search, we conducted screening of articles in three rounds and used the following criteria to code: (1) the word "alignment" appears in the title or keywords, or (2) the body of the article discusses or mentions alignment-related themes. Then we looked for articles that (1) reported an instance of alignment, (2) reported organizational actions and actors' activities, and (3) provided a rich description of the events.

Findings

We identified 37 articles that discussed alignment activities in some detail. Appendix 1 lists all the case sources.

An iterative analytical technique was used to develop the categorization of aligning activities. The preliminary working themes were constructed through a process of abstracting and generalizing (Strauss, 1987). Coding took the form of a thematic content analysis of the case materials (cf. Mostyn, 1985). The categories were interpreted and reconstructed in light of existing alignment themes (e.g., De Haes and Van Grembergen, 2009; Valorinta, 2011). The final list is presented in Table 22.1.

Two basic conceptual distinctions helped us to organize how the different aspects of aligning have been considered in previous research – the *focus* and the *purpose* of the aligning activity. In terms of *focus*, the alignment literature has widely acknowledged a distinction between two dimensions of alignment: social and intellectual (Chan and Reich, 2007). The social dimension refers to factors such as the choice of actors, their degree of involvement, and

Table 22.1 Aligning activities: coding and categorization

Aligning Activity Code	Aligning Activity Category	Illustration	Metaphor
New governance structure Transformation Turnaround Restructuring IT organization Outsourcing Reward system Integration	RECONFIGURING	"The Board interpreted events as raising a new contingency, requiring a structure that would enable managers to use the information the system now provided, and so in 1992 they gave those managing the five geographical division greater autonomy" (Boddy and Paton, 2005: 147). "To support the new direction for Information Systems, Johnson created three new organisational structures. First, a group of senior executives and two independent external consultants met bimonthly as the Information Services Executive Committee. Although the CEO sponsored this meeting, McKean chaired it. The Information Services Executive Committee's purpose was to focus on business issues and ensure that the top team was committed to and satisfied with the projects delivered on their behalf" (Thorogood et al., 2004: 131).	Aligning as Translation
New system development Business-focused IT	DEVELOPING	"SDMC applied IT applications to production scheduling and mold designing, intending to reduce operational costs and improve new product development capabilities" (Wang et al., 2011: 424). "An analysis of RED transactions of a department yielded missing applications and application features . . . The BIOS committee, made up of the departmental directors and account managers, now had objective information with which to prioritize the portfolio" (Rannath and Landsbergen, 2005: 62).	
User/IT relationship IT-business communication Top management involvement CIO/CEO relationship IS/business partnership Culture change IT training Human resource management/training Reinforcing Strengthening	STRENGTHENING	"Management interpreted key contingencies in the context as requiring them to plan and implement a system which would implement the founder's strategic vision for an EPOS system. This closely matched the manual procedures, and staff interpreted the change as reinforcing the existing (effective) alignment between them and their work. It enabled centralization and allowed depot managers to concentrate on customers" (Boddy and Paton, 2005: 146). "Johnston brought in Chris James to develop relationships with strategic business partners and to act as the account manager, representing IS to the business. James was responsible for managing relationships with strategic partners, primarily Aspect Computing, and for managing relationships with other business units such as the laboratory and Water Services" (Thorogood et al., 2004: 131). "Key personnel were sent to training seminars to learn and master the essence of the balanced scorecard theory and techniques" (Huang and Hu, 2007: 176).	Aligning as Integration

SIGNALING	New position New appointment IT location	"A few years before the project, the former president had retired, and a new one was employed with the task of organizational and managerial restructuring and modernization of the entire organization" (Simonsen, 1999: 10). "The physical location of the IT division in isolation from the Retail division was symbolic of the general estrangement in working relationships. The image that the business had of IT was that 'IT people don't move around, they just sit in X' (Managing Director, Retail Finance) and they have different agendas and 'just want to be told what needs to be done' (Manager, Group Development)" (Coughlan et al., 2005: 311)/	Aligning as Adaptation
EVALUATING	Success measures Reactive response Separation of information/ technology management Clarifying objectives Scanning emerging technologies External factors Review Prioritization	"Many private firms and large international logistics firms entered the business area where AMY operated after China's accession into the WTO, which led to a more competitive environment. The oversupply of mechanical and electrical products strengthened the bargaining power of customers and altered the industrial structure. In this environment, AMY's inefficient traditional sales management led to excessive overstock. In 1999, AMY lost over 40 million RMB because of overstock" (Wang et al., 2011: 423). "Following a consulting firm's report in 1993, the CEO and the other senior managers began recognizing the need for major changes to respond to several international companies' entry into Australia" (Hirschheim and Sabherwal, 2001: 95). "Many customers placed orders without fulfilling their promise to make the payment, creating lots of unpaid accounts receivable" (Wang et al. 2011: 426).	
NEGOTIATING	Resistance to change Meetings Politics Learning the business Organizational learning	"One library visited was one of their largest single customers. They had only 1 or 2 booking requests per day. In this situation, they viewed the telephone as the relevant technology for ordering films and videos. They would resist paying for equipment for an on-line connection and for the training of their staff to use the booking system that the Film Board had in mind" (Simonsen, 1999: 13).	Aligning as Experience
LEARNING		"In the past few years, our sales income and profit went down sharply. We should find some ways to stop this. We realized that we need good integrated computer systems, and we couldn't follow the way we walked along before" (Wang et al., 2011: 424).	
DECISION MAKING	Decision making	"The value of IT was questioned by many academics and executives at that time. Some consultants and IT professionals suggested this B2B project be delayed because they thought the investment was too high, while the chance of success was rather slim" (Wang et al., 2011: 426).	

		Focus	
		Tools	Actors
Purpose	Deliberate	**ALIGNING AS TRANSLATION** (developing; reconfiguring)	**ALIGNING AS INTEGRATION** (strengthening; signaling)
	Emergent	**ALIGNING AS ADAPTATION** (evaluating)	**ALIGNING AS EXPERIENCE** (negotiating; decision-making; learning)

Figure 22.1 Aligning: an analytical framework

the methods and modes of communication and decision making (Reich and Benbasat, 2000). The focus is on the *actors* and their actions and cognitions. Conversely, intellectual alignment refers to the degree to which the business strategy and the IS strategy are congruent (Kearns and Lederer, 2000). The focus is on a set of *tools* – methodologies, techniques, technology, plans, and data used in the form(ul)ation of alignment. In terms of *purpose*, aligning actions can be *deliberate* or *emergent*. *Deliberate* actions have a planned outcome and are performed in a methodical and intentional manner. *Emergent* actions have an evolving, sometimes unintended and unpredictable outcome and are performed in a more spontaneous manner.

Combining the two dimensions yields a 2 × 2 matrix that locates four metaphors that can be used to describe aligning as: *experience, integration, translation,* and *adaptation* (see Figure 22.1). Aligning as experience and aligning as integration represent a set of activities primarily involving human dynamics; however, while integration activities are characterized as deliberate and instrumental in nature, aligning as experience suggests a set of evolving activities that emerge from unplanned or unintended situations. Similarly, both aligning as translation and aligning as adaptation suggest activities that involve generation and execution of plans and other intellectual imperatives, but the purpose of these activities differs. While translation is anticipated action, adaptation is more unpredicted and evolving. The sections that follow expand on each of these types of activity and provide illustrative examples from the analyzed case studies.

Aligning as adaptation

We identified a number of activities as aspects of adaptation. These activities are mainly focused on *tools* as it is necessary to determine whether a new system needs to be implemented or enhanced. These actions emerge as a result of the advent of new conditions that are not necessarily foreseeable or cannot be easily planned for. Some form of improvisation might be evident here. The nature of these activities is, therefore, *emergent* with a main focus on *tools*.

Given the need to be aware of the new conditions, tools are applied in continuously EVALU-ATING the environment and ascertaining how technology can support or enable future operations. About half of articles in our final set report on some form of evaluation of the internal and/or external environment. Evaluating practices are usually reported as something that happens before aligning processes are themselves enacted. Examples include when an organization evaluates its context or seeks to clarify its objectives or business focus (e.g., Sillince and Frost, 1995; Simonsen, 1999), scans emerging technologies (e.g., Tarafdar and Qrunfleh, 2009), or prioritizes applications and application features (e.g., Dutta, 1996; Ramnath and Landsbergen, 2005) prior to any change process taking place. Further, evaluation of the strategic focus might reveal contradictions in the overall organizational strategy and might indicate new system needs (Simonsen, 1999).

Aligning as translation

Achieving alignment has traditionally been seen as a part of a CIO's duties, typically involving communication and strategy translation at executive levels (Sabherwal et al., 2001). A number of studies suggest that business and IT 'speak' a different language (e.g., Bassellier and Benbasat, 2004; Rosenkranz et al., 2013), and aligning would thus need to involve IT personnel understanding business needs and rendering these into IT solutions. These translations involve *intentionality*: clarifying existing strategies; prioritizing projects; formulating and implementing plans; applying a set of planning methodologies; and consequently, capturing, through the use of *tools*, planning methodologies or systems.

Developing a new system is a common activity of translating that aims to find new IS solutions to align with what may often be a new strategic imperative. In certain cases, developing entails the consolidation or rebuilding of systems or services rather than implementing a completely new technology (e.g., Sauer and Willcocks, 2003). Nonetheless, developing is *tools*-focused and is based on *deliberate* approaches to system implementation. More than half of the articles describe the development of a new system. For example, Vayghan et al. (2007) report that IBM developed and deployed data solutions for its customers as well as within IBM itself as part of their transformation. Dutta (1996) reports on the creation of NovaRede – a new distribution network, with small branches enabled by new IT infrastructure in a Portuguese bank, while Ives et al. (1993) describe challenges of development of a worldwide financial reporting system, an inventory management system, and a new customer profitability analysis system in a multinational company.

Reconfiguring activities also classify as translation-related actions as they also focus on *intellectual* aspects of aligning such as structures and arrangements. Reconfiguring refers to activities related to such restructuring actions as a change in the governance and management of IT including outsourcing. Restructuring governance and the IT function is the most commonly observed action. For example, Sauer and Willcocks (2003) report on Oracle changing country managing directors' performance measures so that they would be more cost-conscious, with the IT function becoming centralized – as a corporate entity – rather than being country-based as was previously. Similarly, Boddy and Paton (2005) describe the introduction of divisions with profit responsibilities in a chain of roadside vehicle repair depots. Outsourcing is also a major activity when it comes to aligning. Dutta (1996) describes an organization that had outsourced its IT and had to create a technical oversight group and a 20-person team to coordinate with the vendors.

Aligning as integration

The alignment literature recognizes that open and effective exchanges and interactions help IT and business work well together (Brown and Ross, 1996). We found a number of *deliberate* activities that focused on integrating IT/business planning by bringing IT and business functions or tasks closer together to strengthen the communication, understanding, and perspectives between them. These activities revolve around *actors* and the necessary steps needed to develop a unified entity in an effort to enable alignment to take place.

We classified *strengthening* activities in terms of aligning as integration because, similar to aligning as translation, these are actions stimulated by *deliberate* procedures. Unlike aligning as translation, these activities are focused on bringing IT and business *people* together and enabling a smoother process of mutual understanding and appreciation, invoking the social dimension of alignment discussed earlier. Primarily, these involve the strengthening of relationships between various organizational groups. To illustrate, some studies consider "joint" language – to improve the quality of communication between business and IS (e.g., Powell and Powell, 2004). Sauer and Willcocks (2003) suggest advocacy on the part of CIOs in helping their senior business colleagues to become more sensitive to the challenges associated with designing and managing technology platforms. User participation has also been reported as a means of strengthening aligning processes. Dutta (1996) describes how users submitted new software development proposals to business groups who then channeled these proposals to user committees. Training, with respect to both IT for non-IT personnel, and with respect to business issues for IT personnel, has also been reported as a practice that might strengthen alignment – both in terms of the process and the outcome. For example, Chan (2002) reports on information sessions and technology demonstrations. Coughlan et al. (2005) consider the acquisition of "hybrid skills" and Martinez (1995) highlights the skills necessary for large project management.

Another set of activities classified as integration is *signaling*. These activities are *people-focused* because they might affect and reshape actors' views or attitudes and might involve changes in roles. For example, a number of cases highlight the establishment of a new position (e.g., Chen et al., 2008; Grant, 2003) or, more commonly, a new appointment to an existing position (e.g., Johnston and Yetton, 1996). To illustrate, Sabherwal et al. (2001) report on the establishment of a new IS director position at an equipment sales company. The position was created to signal the strategic role of IS, however, it was discontinued later as the perceived importance of IS diminished – a further signal. The location of the IT division has also been found to be symbolic of working relationships and, ultimately, (mis)alignment between IT and organizational priorities (e.g., Coughan et al., 2005).

Aligning as experience

A number of reported activities focused specifically on *individuals* and their actions. These actions are indicative of the *emergent* nature of organizing practice. *Negotiating* – political activities in general – is commonplace in organizational life, and aligning is no different in this regard. A number of studies touch on the issue of organizational politics and external political pressures. For example, Sillince and Frost (1995) describe IS-related reforms in primary care that were pushed through to head off political opposition by the medical professionals. This case was contrasted with another concerned with the work of the national police force. Here, Sillince and Frost note that politicians did not want to be "saddled" with a reputation for having shaped the police force – not wanting "to be remembered as having reinforced European federalism" (Sillince and Frost, 1995: 113). Authors make the point that, in a different political situation, different organizational practices would likely be apparent. The reduced – or absent – pressure impacted aligning practice, as the police force was able to be more flexible in making IS-related decisions and thus – potentially at least – to be in a better position to align its practices.

Illustrations of negotiating can also be found in the private sector. For example, Dutta (1996) reports on an instance of negotiating when a list of proposed IS projects was assembled from a number of user groups. Conflicts arose as the IT users' committee had to determine relative priorities of the proposals.

A process of LEARNING is inherent in aligning practices. We considered those learning activities that are *actor-focused* and address the process of intuiting and interpreting. This process is *emergent* and distinctive from the strengthening activities which are associated with training and are *deliberate* in nature. Learning concerns, for example, the creation of novel insights; building actions based on experience, and developing business awareness (Bontis et al., 2002), are evolving. Salmela and Ruohonen (1992) observed learning to be the single most important aspect of aligning, where organizational members continuously learn to focus on IS as an opportunity for organizational change. Conversely, it has been reported that IT personnel should learn more about the business to facilitate alignment. Chen et al. (2008) provide the example of IT staff expending considerable effort to understand the manufacturing process of a semiconductor company.

Aligning will ultimately involve decisions that *actors* must make concerning IS/IT and business functions. *Decision making* is a social activity undertaken by individuals within organizations. Such activities are also *emergent* in nature as decisions need to be made as issues arise. Hirschheim and Sabherwal (2001) describe how a new CEO makes a decision to shift centralized IS to a more distributed form in a company that changed its strategy to one focusing more on efficiency. A number of studies report specifically on decisions made by the CEO, with or without discussion or agreement with those responsible for IT (e.g., Dutta, 1996; Sabherwal et al., 2001; Sauer and Wilcocks, 2003). Wang et al. (2011) show how conservatism and culture can have an impact on the decisions made. Overall, we found few cases of decision-making practices.

Discussion: a research agenda for aligning in practice

Our extension of prior conceptualizations of alignment as aligning practice, consisting of aligning activities, allows for a more holistic treatment of alignment at multiple organizational levels and across multiple dimensions, as called for by Chan and Reich (2007). Such a conceptualization allows alignment research to move away from studies that focus solely on the antecedents, enablers, and inhibitors of alignment, to research that focuses on the activities of aligning where actors *do* 'aligning.' When alignment is thought of primarily as an outcome of a macro-level process, consisting of phases and stages, knowledge of the rich and complex ways in which actors translate, adapt, integrate, experience, and thus 'make' alignment happen, is limited.

A contribution of this chapter has the introduction of a framework (Figure 22.1), which shifts alignment discourse away from characterizations of alignment or misalignment toward an understanding of how actors are engaged in the practice of aligning and what types of activities are involved in that practice. The categorization of activities that emerges is a resource to guide future empirical research. We do not claim that our list of aligning activities is exhaustive; rather, it represents an illustration of what is known or what can be inferred from current research. We anticipate that future research will reveal and explicate other relevant activities.

Suggestions for future research

We conclude that the majority of the literature considers the alignment process as following prescribed methodologies, assuming rational decision making, and is often sequential in nature. A focus on activities suggests instead that aligning practice is more organic in nature, being subject to political and interpretive influences (Jarzabkowski, 2003). One implication of this view is that studying processes and actors independently may be less analytically useful than has been assumed. While aligning as adaptation and translation presumes intellectual-level activities materializing at the level of plans and objectives, it is through the individual use and creation of these tools, and amid individual actions of actors, that aligning happens. Conversely, while aligning as integration and experience both involve individual actions and interactions, it is the actions and interactions that also occur in relation to the usage of tools that constrain and/or enable these actions. As such, aligning activities are interrelated and inseparable in practice. If one considers activities inherent in the practices of aligning around strategies and plans, one needs to acknowledge the role of social actors and their actions. Thus, in order to understand and facilitate aligning, examination is needed not only of specific tools or actors, but also the rich interactions within which people and things are engaged in doing 'alignment work.'

Taking the perspective on alignment as aligning practice allows us to unite the social and intellectual dimensions of alignment. In particular, a consideration of the recursive loops between the social and the intellectual could provide an integrated understanding of how actors mobilize tools and how tools can assemble actors to attain alignment outcomes. Therefore, one avenue of research might be to study the use of alignment tools in practice. While we know about the tools available in aligning practice – the methodologies and approaches used in 'translations' – we do not yet know the precise nature of the 'tools' the practitioners actually use, nor how they use them. For example, while such tools as balanced scorecards (Huang and Hu, 2007), Andersen Consulting's Method-1 (Lederer and Gardiner, 1992), IBM's Business Systems Planning (BSP) (Zachman, 1982), Information Engineering (Martin and Leben, 1989), and Total Information Systems Management (Osterle et al., 1993) have been introduced, studies suggest that practitioners ignore or modify them, or develop their own methods (e.g., Teubner, 2007). Potential research questions would relate to, for example: (1) How are alignment tools applied in practice? (2) Which tools are utilized and in which context? (3) Are they used in ways in which they were intended? (4) Are the plans and strategies followed mechanistically or used as a guideline in practice? (5) Do tools evolve over the period of aligning and, if so, how do they evolve?

In addition, the strategy-as-practice literature uncovers various impacts of tools such as PowerPoint presentations (e.g., Kaplan, 2011) and social media (e.g., Huang et al., 2013) on strategy formation. Can the use of such tools also be observed in aligning practice? Do aligning practices differ from other organizational practices previously studied? From the literature we have analyzed, it becomes clear that, while we are starting to understand something of the activities involved in the process of aligning, what is still missing are studies on this "internal life of a process" (Brown and Duguid, 2000: 94).

The lack of focus on micro processes is evident from the relative scarcity of literature on, for example, decision-making activities and politics involved in aligning. Actors make various decisions in relation to business processes and associated IS, and therefore, decision making becomes central to aligning. Decisional factors such as the motivating reason(s) behind the drive toward achieving strategic alignment can shape the process of its achievement (Negoita et al., 2013). However, there is little discussion of decision making in the practices associated with aligning. Understanding these practices is crucial in helping practitioners deal with the challenges associated with aligning. The extant alignment literature usually considers the decisions made "in terms of actions taken, the resources committed, or precedents set" (Mintzberg et al., 1976: 246), but not how these decisions emerge or what the implications might be.

Further, we know from prior research that decision making is infused with politics (Eisenhardt and Bourgeois, 1988); however, the alignment literature rarely considers the contestation and dialogue involved. It goes without saying that negotiating is part of organizational life – and this includes aligning activity, given that it involves multiple organizational members with a variety of personal as well as collective agendas. Echoing the recent call for the incorporation of the concept of power into the study of IS strategizing (Marabelli and Galliers, 2017), we suggest a greater focus on power in future research on aligning practice. For example, researchers should revisit the discussion on the role of CIOs (e.g., Gerow et al., 2012; Karpovsky and Galliers, 2013, Preston et al. 2008) and consider the influential role these executives might play in aligning practice.

The framework that we introduced herein may prove to be a useful starting point on which to base such investigations. We argue for going beyond simply explaining organizational activities that are considered to be part of aligning by also focusing simultaneously on activities at multiple levels beyond the level of the organization. As can be observed from Appendix 1, which lists all the articles considered in order of the number of categories of activities observed, only a few studies have captured the full set of proposed categories. We argue that it is through the focus on day-to-day activities that we will better be able to present a more comprehensive picture of aligning practice. Once we have this better understanding of aligning activities, and the actors involved, we would be in a better position to consider micro processes of aligning, the tools used in aligning, and the unconscious actions that are performed by 'alignment actors.'

An expanded range of research methods is necessary to pursue this research agenda.[4] Our view of aligning as practice suggests different units of analysis for research. That is, alignment scholars would not only center on the organization as a uniform whole, but also consider decisions, individuals, groups, projects, and tools. To undertake this program of research, a wider range of research methods may need to be employed. Current work in the strategy-as-practice domain is dominated by observational field studies (e.g., Kaplan and Orlikowski, 2013). If our intention is to comprehend practices, there is little or no substitute for spending time in the field observing actors engaged in their daily work-related activities (Jarzabkowski and Kaplan, 2014). A difficulty in undertaking such research, however, is that it is challenging to determine, *a priori*, which of the activities and interactions are related to aligning practice (Bechky, 2008). Consequently, going into the field to observe actors 'do' aligning work requires being in the right context at the right time (Jarzabkowski and Kaplan, 2014). To capture aligning as it unfolds doubtless requires longitudinal study (e.g., Pettigrew, 1990). In addition, combining approaches might be valuable. Different approaches focus attention on different aspects of the object of study, thereby providing a richer, more complete picture (Mingers, 2003). Interviews and surveys are valuable supplements (Jarzabkowski and Kaplan, 2014).

There are a number of potential extensions to our findings that could be explored in future research. These include examining a broader range of contexts, actors, and their aligning activities. Our focus in this study has been on those aligning activities that have been reported in existing, published cases in the academic literature. We might suppose, however, that there are activities and actors that have not thus far been reported upon that might well reflect additional aligning practices. For example, while Grant (2003) reports on such aligning activities as restructuring, hiring, and outsourcing, who was involved, and how they went about these tasks remains unclear. In many cases, we have yet to know who are the 'alignment practitioners' and what they actually do to align organizational processes, structures, and functions. Similarly, Roepke et al. (2000) present an account of 3M's alignment initiatives, and in particular, their IT management development programs. However, the case fails to account for the manner in which employees' attitudes changed over time.

Most alignment research has focused on aggregate classes of actors (e.g., 'top management,' 'IS management,' 'middle management'), and has attributed specific activities to these archetypes. Consequently, the description of activities performed by these aggregate actor classes becomes abstracted, and somewhat distant from the everyday activities of any individual actor.

We suggest a research agenda that focuses on a wider range of individual actors and their everyday work practices in interaction with others. We further suggest that 'external' actors (i.e., those outside of the organization concerned), with whom 'internal' alignment practitioners interact, should also be studied in ongoing studies of aligning practice. We found only a very few external groups to have been considered thus far. Sillince and Frost (1995) incorporate the role of politicians with respect to the aligning practice of public sector organizations. Consultants and researchers – the latter partially playing the role of consultants as well in action research studies – have been considered in certain studies (e.g., Powell and Powell, 2004; Salmela and Ruohonen, 1992). The strategy literature indicates that 'strategy gurus' and business media actors play important roles in organizational activities (e.g., Clark and Greatbatch, 2002) and, consequently, should be studied in the context of aligning.

Lastly, future research should consider a wider range of contexts. For example, not-for-profit organizations (charity or service organizations) might have a different set of approaches to goal specification and assessment (Newman and Wallender, 1978), methods of performance measurement (Kanter and Summers, 1987) and marketing and competitive practices (Rangan et al., 1996). Consequently, this sector could provide a fruitful setting for comparing the set of aligning activities taking place. Studying these and other related settings and novel sets of actor groups might hold promise.

Implications for managers

Alignment research has provided managers with a number of methodologies (e.g., Huang and Hu, 2007; Lederer and Gardiner, 1992; Zachman, 1982). However, it has been argued that such tools should not be mechanistically applied in practice, but rather used as means for surfacing assumptions, questioning interests (e.g., Galliers and Sutherland, 1991). Methods are often talked of in terms of the "instrumental mode" (Astley and Zammuto, 1992: 453) of contributing managerial techniques, often associated with the notion of "best practices." Yet, in practice, methods are not operationalized precisely as they are designed. For example, IS/IT plans do not typically describe how IT and business personnel have to interact to put these plans into action, and formal conventions often play only a minor part in the interactions between business and IT (Chan, 2002). Recognizing the range of aligning activities involved in practice, such as the ones identified in our study, should allow managers to realize and prepare themselves for unforeseen challenges in alignment.

Concluding remarks

The intention of this chapter has been to serve as a catalyst for a broader and richer agenda for alignment research. We believe that this is an important research topic as it goes to the very essence of the strategic value of IT in organizations and develops a link between business and IT-related issues. The categories of aligning activities that have been described here are somewhat nuanced, but introduce a new departure for research in this domain. Specifically, we propose a subtle shift of focus from the alignment process to aligning practice, with emphasis being placed on day-to-day activities rather than abstract phases. We argue this point of departure can help alignment research to become more relevant to practice, as called for by Arvidsson et al. (2014) and to practitioners – the people who 'do' aligning. The research agenda we outline recognizes trends in other fields, such as in strategic management (cf. Whittington, 2014), and encourages IS researchers to respond by increasing their theoretical and empirical efforts with respect to aligning *practice*.

Notes

1 The chapter is based on Karpovsky, A. and Galliers, R. D. (2015) Aligning in practice: From current cases to a new agenda, *Journal of Information Technology* 30(2): 136–160.
2 Correspondence: Anna Karpovsky, Boston University, Questrom School of Business, 595 Commonwealth Ave, Boston, MA 02215, USA. Email: akarpovs@bu.edu
3 Hereinafter, we shall use the simple term "alignment."
4 Cf. Galliers and Land (1987) for a taxonomy of IS research approaches and Mingers (2003) for mixed method research.

References

Agarwal, R. and Sambamurthy, V. (2002) Principles and models for organizing the IT function, *MIS Quarterly Executive* 1(1): 1–16.
Arvidsson, V., Holmström, J. and Lyytinen, K. (2014) Information systems use as strategy practice: A multi-dimensional view of strategic information system implementation and use, *Journal of Strategic Information Systems* 23(1): 45–61.
Astley, W. G. and Zammuto, R. F. (1992) Organization science, managers, and language games, *Organization Science* 3(4): 443–460.
Avison, D., Jones, J., Powell, P. and Wilson, D. (2004) Using and validating the strategic alignment model, *Journal of Strategic Information Systems* 13(3): 223–246.
Bassellier, G. and Benbasat, I. (2004) Business competence of information technology professionals: Conceptual development and influence on IT-business partnerships, *MIS Quarterly* 28(4): 673–694.
Bechky, B. A. (2008) Analyzing artifacts: Material methods for understanding identity, status, and knowledge in organizational life, in D. Barry and H. Hansen (eds.) *The Sage Handbook of New Approaches in Management and Organization*, Sage: Thousand Oaks, CA, pp. 98–110.
Boddy, D. and Paton, R. (2005) Maintaining alignment over the long-term: Lessons from the evolution of an electronic point of sale system, *Journal of Information Technology* 20 (3): 141–151.
Bontis, N., Crossan, M. M. and Hulland, J. (2002) Managing an organizational learning system by aligning stocks and flows, *Journal of Management Studies* 39(4): 437–469.
Brown, C. V. (1997). Examining the emergence of hybrid IS governance solutions: Evidence from a single case site, *Information Systems Research*, 8(1), 69–94.
Brown, C. V. and Ross, J. W. (1996) The information systems balancing act: Building partnerships and infrastructure, *Information Technology and People* 9(1): 49–62.
Brown, J. S. and Duguid, P. (2000) *The social life of information*, Boston: Harvard Business School Press.
Brown, J. S. and Duguid, P. (2001) Knowledge and organization: A social-practice perspective, *Organization Science* 12(2): 198–213.
Campbell, B. (2005) Alignment: Resolving ambiguity within bounded choices, in *PACIS* (Bangkok, Thailand). 1–14.
Chan, Y. E. (2002) Why haven't we mastered alignment? The importance of the informal organization structure, *MIS Quarterly Executive* 1(2): 97–112.
Chan, Y. E., Huff, S. L., Barclay, D. W. and Copeland, D. G. (1997) Business strategic orientation, information systems strategic orientation, and strategic alignment, *Information Systems Research* 8(2): 125–150.
Chan, Y. E. and Reich, B. (2007) IT alignment: What have we learned? *Journal of Information Technology* 22(4): 297–315.
Chan, Y. E., Sabherwal, R. and Thatcher, J. (2006) Antecedents and outcomes of strategic IS alignment: An empirical investigation, *IEEE Transactions on Engineering Management* 53(1): 27–47.
Chen, R. S., Sun, C. M., Helms, M. M. and Jih, W. J. (2008) Aligning information technology and business strategy with a dynamic capabilities perspective: A longitudinal study of a Taiwanese semiconductor company, *International Journal of Information Management* 28(5): 366–378.
Ciborra, C. U. (1997) De profundis? Deconstructing the concept of strategic alignment, *Scandinavian Journal of Information Systems* 9(1): 67–82.
Clark, T. and Greatbatch, D. (2002) Collaborative relationships in the creation and fashioning of management ideas: Gurus, editors and managers, in M. Kipping and L. Engwall (eds.) *Management consulting: Emergence and dynamics of a knowledge industry*, Oxford: Oxford University Press, pp. 127–145.

Cook, S. D. and Brown, J. S. (1999) Bridging epistemologies: The generative dance between organizational knowledge and organizational knowing, *Organization Science* 10(4): 381–400.

Coughlan, H., Lycett, M. and Macredie, R. D. (2005) Understanding the business-IT relationship, *International Journal of Information Management* 25(4): 303–319.

De Haes, S. and Van Grembergen, W. (2009) An exploratory study into IT governance implementations and its impact on business/IT alignment, *Information Systems Management* 26(2): 123–137.

Dutta, S. (1996) Linking IT and business strategy: The role and responsibility of senior management, *European Management Journal* 14(3): 255–268.

Eisenhardt, K. M. and Bourgeois, L. J. (1988) Politics of strategic decision making in high-velocity environments: Toward a midrange theory, *Academy of Management Journal* 31(4): 737–770.

Feurer, R., Chaharbaghi, K., Weber, M., & Wargin, J. (2000). Aligning strategies, processes, and IT: A case study. *IEEE Engineering Management Review*, 28(3), 81–91.

Fuchs, P. H., Miffin, K. E., Miller, D. and Whitney, J. O. (2000) Strategic integration, *California Management Review* 42(3): 118–129.

Galliers, R. D. (2004) Reflections on information systems strategizing, in C. Avgerou, C. Ciborra and F. Land (eds.) *The social study of information and communication technology*, Oxford: Oxford University Press, pp. 231–262.

Galliers, R. D. (2006) On confronting some of the common myths of information systems strategy discourse, in R. Mansell, C. Avgerou, D. Quah and R. Silverstone (eds.) *The Oxford handbook of information and communication technologies*, Oxford: Oxford University Press, pp. 225–243.

Galliers, R. D. and Land, F. F. (1987) Viewpoint: Choosing appropriate information systems research methodologies, *Communications of the ACM* 30(11): 901–902.

Galliers, R. D. and Sutherland, A. R. (1991) Information systems management and strategy formulation: The 'stages of growth' model revisited, *Journal of Information Systems* 1(2): 89–114.

Gerow, J. E., Grover, V. and Thatcher, J. (2012) "Power and politics: Do CIOs have what it takes to influence the executive team's commitment to IT Initiatives?" in *AMCIS Proceedings*, Paper 1.

Grant, G. G. (2003) Strategic alignment and enterprise systems implementation: The case of Metalco, *Journal of Information Technology* 18(3): 159–175.

Gregor, S., Hart, D., & Martin, N. (2007). Enterprise architectures: enablers of business strategy and IS/IT alignment in government, *Information Technology & People*, 20(2): 96–120.

Hackney, R., & Little, S. (1999). Opportunistic strategy formulation for IS/IT planning, *European Journal of Information Systems*, 8(2), 119–126.

Henderson, J. C. and Venkatraman, N. (1993) Strategic alignment: Leveraging information technology for transforming organizations, *IBM Systems Journal* 32(1): 4–16.

Hirschheim, R. and Sabherwal, R. (2001) Detours in the path toward strategic information systems alignment, *California Management Review* 44(1): 87–108.

Huang, C. D. and Hu, Q. (2007) Achieving IT-business strategic alignment via enterprise-wide implementation of balanced scorecards, *Information Systems Management* 24(2): 173–184.

Huang, J., Baptista, J. and Galliers, R. D. (2013) Reconceptualizing rhetorical practices in organizations: The impact of social media on internal communications, *Information & Management* 50(2–3): 112–124.

Ives, B., Jarvenpaa, S. L. and Mason, R. O. (1993) Global business drivers: Aligning information technology to global business strategy, *IBM Systems Journal* 32(1): 143–161.

Jarzabkowski, P. (2003). Strategic practices: An activity theory perspective on continuity and change, *Journal of Management Studies*, 40(1): 23–55.

Jarzabkowski, P. (2005) *Strategy as practice: An activity-based approach*, SAGE.

Jarzabkowski, P. and Kaplan, S. (2014) Strategy tools-in-use: A framework for understanding "technologies of rationality" in practice, *Strategic Management Journal*. doi:10.1002/smj.2270.

Johnston, K. D. and Yetton, P. W. (1996) Integrating information technology divisions in a bank merger fit, compatibility and models of change, *Journal of Strategic Information Systems* 5(3): 189–211.

Kanter, R. M. and Summers, D. V. (1987) Doing well while doing good: Dilemmas of performance measurement in nonprofit organizations and the need for a multiple-constituency approach, in W. W. Powell (ed.) *The nonprofit sector*, New Haven, CT: Yale University Press, pp. 220–236.

Kaplan, S. (2011) Strategy and PowerPoint: An inquiry into the epistemic culture and machinery of strategy making, *Organization Science* 22(2): 320–346.

Kaplan, S. and Orlikowski, W. J. (2013) Temporal work in strategy making, *Organization Science* 24(4): 965–995.

Karpovsky, A. and Galliers, R. D. (2013) Sources of power and CIO influence and their impact: An explorative survey, in *Proceedings: 34th International Conference on Information Systems*, Milan, Italy, December 16–18.

Karpovsky, A. and Galliers, R. D. (2015) Aligning in practice: From current cases to a new agenda, *Journal of Information Technology* 30(2): 136–160.

Karpovsky, A., Hallanoro, M. and Galliers, R. D. (2014) The process of information systems strategizing: Review and synthesis, in H. Topi and A. Tucker (eds.) *The CRC handbook of computing, 3rd ed. Vol. II: Information systems and information technology*, London: Chapman & Hall/CRC, pp. 66-1–66-28.

Kearns, G. S. and Lederer, A. L. (2000) The effect of strategic alignment on the use of IS-based resources for competitive advantage, *Journal of Strategic Information Systems* 9(4): 265–293.

Kearns, G. S. and Lederer, A. L. (2003) A resource-based view of strategic IT alignment: How knowledge sharing creates competitive advantage, *Decision Sciences* 34(1): 1–29.

Lacity, M. C., Khan, S. A. and Willcocks, L. P. (2009) A review of the IT outsourcing literature: Insights for practice, *Journal of Strategic Information Systems* 18(3): 130–146.

Lederer, A. L. and Gardiner, V. (1992) The process of strategic information planning, *Journal of Strategic Information Systems* 1(2): 76–83.

Luftman, J. (2000) Assessing business-IT alignment maturity, *Communications of the Association for Information Systems* 4(14): 1–50.

Luftman, J., Zadeh, H. S., Derksen, B., Santana, M., Rigoni, E. H. and Huang, D. (2013) Key information technology and management issues 2012–2013: An international study, *Journal of Information Technology* 28(4): 354–366.

Marabelli, M. and Galliers, R. D. (2017). A reflection on information systems strategizing: the role of power and everyday practices, *Information Systems Journal*, 27(3): 347–366.

Martin, J. and Leben, J. (1989) *Strategic information planning methodologies*. Upper Saddle River, NJ: Prentice-Hall.

Martinez, E. V. (1995) Successful reengineering demands IS/Business partnerships, *Sloan Management Review* 36(4): 51–60.

McKenney, J. L., Mason, R. O., & Copeland, D. G. (1997). Bank of America: The crest and trough of technological leadership, *MIS Quarterly*, 321–353.

McLean, E. and Soden, J. (1977) *Strategic planning for MIS*, New York: John Wiley & Sons.

Mehta, M. and Hirschheim, R. (2007) Strategic alignment in mergers and acquisitions: Theorizing IS integration decision making, *Journal of the Association for Information Systems* 8(3): 143–174.

Merali, Y., Papadopoulos, T. and Nadkarni, T. (2012) Information systems strategy: Past, present, future? *Journal of Strategic Information Systems* 21(2): 125–153.

Mingers, J. (2003) The paucity of multimethod research: A review of the information systems literature, *Information Systems Journal* 13(3): 233–249.

Mintzberg, H., Raisinghani, D. and Theoret, A. (1976) The structure of "unstructured" decision processes, *Administrative Science Quarterly* 21(2): 246–275.

Mostyn, B. (1985) The content analysis of qualitative research data: A dynamic approach, in M. Brenner, J. Brown and D. Cauter (eds.) *The research interview*, London: Academic Press, pp. 115–145.

Negoita, B., Lapointe, L. and Pinsonneault, A. (2013) Achieving strategic alignment: A decision-making perspective, in *34th International Conference on Information Systems*, Milan, Italy.

Newman, W. H. and Wallender, H. W. (1978) Managing not-for-profit enterprises, *Academy of Management Review* 3(1): 24–31.

Osterle, H., Brenner, W. and Hilbers, K. (1993) *Total information systems management: A European approach*, Chichester: John Wiley & Sons.

Peak, D., & Guynes, C. S. (2003a). Improving information quality through IT alignment planning: A case study, *Information Systems Management*, 20(4): 22–29.

Peak, D., & Guynes, C. S. (2003b). The IT alignment planning process. *Journal of Computer Information Systems*, 44(1): 9–15.

Peppard, J. and Breu, K. (2003) Beyond alignment: A coevolutionary view of the information systems strategy process, in *Twenty-Fourth International Conference on Information Systems*, Seattle, pp. 743–750.

Peppard, J., Galliers, R. D. and Thorogood, A. (2014) Information systems strategy as practice: Micro strategy and strategizing for IS, *Journal of Strategic Information Systems* 23(1): 1–10.

Pettigrew, A. M. (1990) Longitudinal field research on change: Theory and practice, *Organization Science* 1(3): 267–292.

Powell, J. and Powell, P. (2004) Scenario networks to align and specify strategic information systems: A case-based study, *European Journal of Operational Research* 158(1): 146–172.

Preston, D. S., Chen, D. and Leidner, D. E. (2008) Examining the antecedents and consequences of CIO strategic decision-making authority: An empirical study, *Decision Sciences* 39(4): 605–642.

Ramnath, R. and Landsbergen, D. (2005) IT-enabled sense-and-respond strategies in complex public organizations, *Communications of the ACM* 48(5): 58–64.

Rangan, V. K., Karim, S. and Sandberg, S. K. (1996) Doing better at doing good, *Harvard Business Review* 74(3): 42–51.

Reich, B. and Benbasat, I. (2000) Factors that influence the social dimension of alignment between business and information technology objectives, *MIS Quarterly* 24(1): 81–113.

Rondinelli, D., Rosen, B. and Drori, I. (2001) The struggle for strategic alignment in multinational corporations: Managing readjustment during global expansion, *European Management Journal* 19(4): 404–416.

Roepke, R., Agarwal, R. and Ferratt, T. W. (2000) Aligning the IT human resource with business vision: The leadership initiative at 3M, *MIS Quarterly* 24(2): 327–353.

Rosenkranz, C., Charaf, M. C. and Holten, R. (2013) Language quality in requirements development: Tracing communication in the process of information systems development, *Journal of Information Technology* 28(3): 198–223.

Sabherwal, R., Hirschheim, R. and Goles, T. (2001) The dynamics of alignment: Insights from a punctuated equilibrium model, *Organization Science* 12(2): 179–197.

Salmela, H. and Ruohonen, M. (1992) Aligning DSS development with organization development, *European Journal of Operational Research* 61(1–2): 57–71.

Sauer, C. and Willcocks, L. (2003) Establishing the business of the future: The role of organizational architecture and information technologies, *European Management Journal* 21(4): 497–508.

Sillince, J.A.A. and Frost, C.E.B. (1995) Operational, environmental and managerial factors in non-alignment of business strategies and IS strategies for the police service in England and Wales, *European Journal of Information Systems* 4(2): 103–115.

Simonsen, J. (1999) How do we take care of strategic alignment? Constructing a design approach, *Scandinavian Journal of Information Systems* 11(2): 51–72.

Sledgianowski, D., & Luftman, J. (2005). IT-business strategic alignment maturity: A case study. *Journal of Cases on Information Technology (JCIT)*, 7(2): 102–120.

Smaczny, T. (2001) Is an alignment between business and information technology the appropriate paradigm to manage IT in today's organisations? *Management Decision* 39(10): 797–802.

Strauss, A. L. (1987) *Qualitative analysis for social scientists*, Cambridge: Cambridge University Press.

Tarafdar, M. and Qrunfleh, S. (2009) IT-business alignment: A two-level analysis, *Information Systems Management* 26(4): 338–349.

Teubner, R.A. (2007) Strategic information systems planning: A case study from the financial services industry, *Journal of Strategic Information Systems* 16(1): 105–125.

Thorogood, A., Yetton, P., Vlasic, A. and Spiller, J. (2004) Raise your glasses – the water's magic! Strategic IT at SA Water: A case study in alignment, outsourcing and governance, *Journal of Information Technology* 19(2): 130.

Tsoukas, H. (1994) *New thinking in organizational behavior*, Oxford: Butterworth-Heinemann.

Valorinta, M. (2011) IT alignment and the boundaries of the IT function, *Journal of Information Technology* 26(1): 46–59.

Van Grembergen, W., Saull, R., & De Haes, S. (2003). Linking the IT balanced scorecard to the business objectives at a major Canadian financial group, *Journal of Information Technology Case and Application Research*, 5(1): 23–50.

Vayghan, J., Garfinkle, C., Walenta, D., Healy, D. and Valentin, Z. (2007) The internal information transformation of IBM, *IBM Systems Journal* 46(4): 669–683.

Wang, N., Xue, Y., Liang, H. and Ge, S. (2011) The road to business-IT alignment: A case study of two Chinese companies, *Communications of the Association for Information Systems* 28(1): 415–436.

Webster, J. and Watson, R. (2002) Analyzing the past to prepare for the future: Writing a literature review, *MIS Quarterly* 26(2): 13–23.

Weiss, J. W. and Thorogood, A. (2011) Information technology (IT)/business alignment as a strategic weapon: A diagnostic tool, *Engineering Management Journal* 23(2): 30–41.

Whittington, R. (2014) Information systems strategy and strategy-as-practice: A joint agenda, *Journal of Strategic Information Systems* 23(1): 87–91.

Wijnhoven, F., Spil, T., Stegwee, R., & Fa, R.T.A. (2006). Post-merger IT integration strategies: An IT alignment perspective, *Journal of Strategic Information Systems*, 15(1): 5–28.

Wilson, A., Baptista, J. and Galliers, R. D. (2013) Performing strategy: Aligning processes in strategic IT, in *34th International Conference on Information Systems*, Milan, Italy, pp. 15–18.

Zachman, J.A. (1982) Business systems planning and business information control study: A comparison, *IBM Systems Journal* 21(1): 31–53.

Appendix 1
CASE SOURCES

Article	Reconfiguring	Decision-making	Negotiating	Signaling	Evaluating	Strengthening	Learning	Developing	Topics covered
McKenney et al. (1997)	x	x	x	x	x	x	x	x	8
Coughlan et al. (2005)	x		x	x	x	x	x	x	7
Wang et al. (2011)	x		x	x	x	x	x	x	7
Dutta (1996)	x		x	x	x	x		x	6
Mehta and Hirschheim (2007)	x	x	x	x		x		x	6
Sillince and Frost (1995)	x		x		x		x	x	5
Chen et al. (2008)	x			x		x	x	x	5
Martinez (1995)	x		x	x		x		x	5
Johnston and Yetton (1996)	x		x	x	x			x	5
Weiss and Thorogood (2011)	x			x	x	x		x	5
Ramnath and Landsbergen (2005)	x				x		x	x	4
Salmela and Ruohonen (1992)			x		x		x	x	4
Gregor et al. (2007)	x				x	x		x	4
Thorogood et al. (2004)	x			x		x		x	4
Chan (2002)	x					x	x	x	4
Simonsen (1999)			x		x	x		x	4
Tarafdar and Qrunfleh (2009)		x			x	x		x	4
Hirschheim and Sabherwal (2001)	x			x				x	3
Huang and Hu (2007)					x	x		x	3
Powell and Powell (2004)					x	x		x	3
Sauer and Willcocks (2003)	x	x				x			3
Vayghan et al. (2007)	x					x		x	3
Ives et al. (1993)				x	x			x	3
Sledgianowski and Luftman (2005)	x			x		x			3

Study						Total
Van Grembergen et al. (2003)	x				x	3
Sabherwal et al. (2001)	x	x	x			3
Huang and Hu (2007)	x		x			3
Peak and Guynes (2003a)			x	x		3
Avison et al. (2004)			x		x	2
Boddy and Paton (2005)	x			x		2
Grant (2003)	x	x				2
Roepke et al. (2000)	x		x			2
Peak and Guynes (2003b)			x		x	2
Feurer et al. (2000)			x	x		2
Hackney and Little (1999)					x	1
Brown (1997)	x					1
Wijnhoven et al. (2006)				x		1

23
DIGITAL INNOVATION – A DEFINITION AND INTEGRATED PERSPECTIVE

Philipp Hukal and Ola Henfridsson

Introduction and goal

Over the last decade, digital innovation has gained considerable popularity as a topic in the field of information systems and beyond. In view of a growing yet nascent body of literature, it seems timely to integrate existing work into a perspective that allows interesting ways forward. This chapter seeks to do this.

Dealing with innovation in a management information systems (MIS) reader, a possible starting-point could have been the seminal work of Burt Swanson on information systems innovation (Swanson 1994) and its further developments (Lyytinen and Rose 2003). Swanson's work has had significant influence on IS innovation work (cf. Fichman 2004). However, rather than making information systems innovation the starting point, we decided to contrast digital innovation with ideas tractable to the Industrial Revolution and production of physical goods (cf. Svahn and Henfridsson 2012). This decision is consistent with recent work on digital innovation (Henfridsson et al. 2014; Svahn 2012; Yoo et al. 2010, 2012), where such innovation is compared and contrasted with the innovation logics of industrial organization rather than IS innovation. The integration of digital technology into the very heart of the services and products of our age has simply made this comparison increasingly relevant.

Our current understanding of innovation is largely rooted in theory aimed at explaining organizational activity in the industrial age. Broadly speaking, innovation is depicted as the creation of novel products by recombining production forces for market-based exchange (Schumpeter 1934/1983). Central to this industrial view of innovation is the transformation of physical matter into manufactured goods. No wonder that significant streams of research on industrial organization (see Langlois 2007) and competitive strategy (see Porter 1980) are based on the idea of producing and exchanging manufactured goods.

Three assumptions underpin such an understanding of innovation (Lusch and Nambisan 2015; Ng and Smith 2012). (1) *Producer–consumer divide*: the parties of the transaction are clearly demarcated. Economic exchange of tradable goods is realized between producing and consuming parties. (2) *Product–process innovation distinction*: product and process innovation are clearly separated. While product innovation is about generating new outcomes, process innovation is about building new methods. (3) *Innovation as deliberate organizational activity*: innovation is viewed as a plannable and controllable organizational process. Indeed, "the organization is the epicenter of innovation activity and the natural container of innovation capability" (Svahn and Henfridsson 2012; p. 3348). As such, innovation processes are typically considered as linear including distinct steps for facilitating and planning (Godin 2006). Governed by basic principles of hierarchical control and division of labor, innovation is subject to managerial planning and executing activity aimed at successful commercialization of a novel product, or adopting a new process. Dominated by intra-organizational perspectives on the creation, commercialization, and implementation of information technology, innovation research in information systems has also been influenced by these ideas (Fichman et al. 2014).

Defining digital innovation

We define "digital innovation" as *the co-creation of novel offerings through the recombination of digital and/or physical components*. In what follows, we detail core aspects of digital innovation: digital technology, recombination, and value co-creation.

Digital technology

The properties of digital technology are imperative to the current understanding of digital innovation (Boland et al. 2007; Lee and Berente 2012; Yoo et al. 2010). There are at least three properties with specific implications for organization and innovation (Yoo et al. 2010). First, digital technology involves homogenizing data. Once digitized, information in digital form (bits) can be stored and transmitted irrespective of its content type by any device with computing capabilities. Second, digital technology is re-programmable. Digital bits are editable at any point in time, making digital technology malleable to changes through interaction by both human and non-human actors such as other technologies. Third, digital technology is needed to create digital innovations. In other words, digital technology is characterized by self-reference, that is, it is both the result of and the basis for developing new digital technologies.

The properties of digital technology afford new forms of organizing that are central to the creation of novel offerings. While digitization describes changes on the artefact level, digitalization summarizes the widespread utilization of digital technology on a collective level. Both developments induce dynamic evolution of digital technologies. Digitization shapes the attributes of digital technology in an integrative way, enabling diverse artefacts to interoperate on the basis of digital information. Digitalization helps shaping digital infrastructures, that is, the collection of connected, unbounded, and evolving socio-technical systems that render organizational activity (Hanseth and Lyytinen 2010; Henfridsson and Bygstad 2013; Tilson et al. 2010). As the aggregate of the technologies they employ, digital infrastructures are subject to dynamic changes due to the interactivity and malleability of their constituent parts. If successful, the installed base of digital infrastructures grows and integrates technologies further, spawned by positive feedback.

Another useful way to think about the role of digital technology in digital innovation activities is to distinguish between *operant* and *operand* resources (Lusch and Nambisan 2015; Lyytinen et al. 2016; Nambisan 2013). As an operand resource, digital technology acts as means to an end and facilitates purposeful activity. In contrast, as an operant resource, digital technology is deployed as a purpose in and of itself. Lusch and Nambisan (2015) uses the example of the creation of a network: on the one hand, digital technology serves as facilitator as it enables the connection of various components, thus contributing to form a network in the first place. On the other hand, the amalgam of the connected technology components forms an artefact itself. Hence the resulting network serves a purpose on its own. The role of digital technology in digital innovation thus varies depending on whether components enable an innovation, or are themselves forming the innovative composition.

Recombination

Another important aspect of digital innovation is recombination. In most cases, digital architecture facilitates recombination. It supports three dynamics:

1   The separation of form and function
2   The separation of content and medium
3   Generativity

First, recombination benefits from the separation of form and function (Yoo et al. 2010). In contrast to physical objects, digital technology allows alterations of functionality after production. Digital artefacts can be re-programmed so that the same underlying form delivers new functionality. This is possible because the semiotic functional logic is independent of the physical device executing it (Yoo et al. 2010, p. 726). For instance, developing, installing, and executing a new application for heart rate monitoring on a smartphone adds new functionality without changing the underlying device. In contrast, physical objects are characterized by a tight coupling between the functions of the object and its physical composition. For instance, the function of a chair would typically be to offer comfortable seating, and the extent to which a particular chair delivers toward that function depends on its physical implementation. If someone wishes to change the function of the chair (e.g., from comfortable seating to ladder-like functionality) after it has been produced, this would involve changes to the actual chair. In other words, in physical objects, form and function are tightly integrated.

Second, recombination is also enabled by the separation of medium and content (Yoo et al. 2010). Due to the homogenous character of digital data, content can be stored, transferred, changed, accessed, or deleted on a single medium. And almost any device with computing capability can be utilized to handle digital information. For instance, a smartphone serves as an excellent medium for consuming news, music, and photographs, and other type of content. In contrast, with analogue data, news used to be tightly integrated with its medium, the printed newspaper; music was reliant on dedicated players and physical storage (such as the vinyl record); and photographs relied on scrapbooks or other physical distribution methods. The separation of medium and content has profound consequences for businesses, where all examples previously mentioned belong to an industry that has been a target for significant disruption.

Finally, generativity is fueled by both separations briefed earlier. It is also amplified by the self-referential character of digital technology. Indeed, embedded in vast networks of connected devices, newly created components of digital technology are both the result of and the basis for recombination. Heterogeneous and distributed interaction with technology thereby regularly results in non-obvious recombinant outcomes – a behavior referred to as *generativity*. Generativity denotes novel unanticipated outcomes of interaction with digital technology beyond the initial design, often without deliberate planning and in absence of direct control through the originator of the initial technology (cf. Wareham et al. 2014). A popular example of highly generative digital technology is the Internet. By enabling interaction with its components, the Internet's design and architecture led to the creation of novel applications and features way beyond the initial intent. Influential to the debate of generativity in the information systems domain is Zittrain's work on the generative pattern of the Internet's development (Zittrain 2008). Most current scholarly work considers generativity pivotal to the dynamics of digital innovation as the notion of innovation through diverse and unforeseen interaction offers an insightful lens. Focal to the ongoing discourse in information systems is the identification of mechanisms that trigger generativity while maintaining sufficient control for organizations (see Hanseth and Lyytinen 2010; Henfridsson and Bygstad 2013; Tilson et al. 2010; Yoo 2013).

Value co-creation

Digital innovation alters the way that value is generated by organizations. Dominated by industry organization economics and strategic management, value in scholarly literature is typically depicted as the value-of-exchange of a product and thus expressed in monetary terms (Ng and Smith 2012). As such value is traditionally assumed to be created through transformation of physical matter by firm activity and captured as the difference between costs of a good and a customer's willingness to pay (e.g., Brandenburger and Stuart 1996; Porter 1985). However, the view of value creation as a function of production and transaction has its limitations in digital innovation.

As a cornerstone of most digital innovation studies, value is subject to co-creation by networks of actors. Rather than unilaterally created, value is offered via propositions to other actors (Lusch and Nambisan 2015; Vargo and Lusch 2004). Digital technology capabilities increase the density of the core resource needed for digital innovation: digitally stored information. The dynamics of digitalization and digitalization in the same time increase liquefaction of information. As a result, information resources are widely accessible and available for resource integrating activity across actors to configure novel digital services (Lusch and Nambisan 2015). In contrast to understanding of value as value-in-exchange, the service-dominant view conceives of it as *perceived value-of-use* for an organization: resources, services or relations hold value-of-use as they represent a potential benefit for an actor detached from but transferrable to monetary terms (Ng and Smith 2012).

Three characteristics qualify a view on value in digital innovation. First, value is *contextual* as it is detached from the price of an exchange. Instead, valuation is the context-dependent assignment of perceived value-in-use by actors of economic exchanges when utilizing a resource (Lepak et al. 2007). Second, value is *relational* as it derived through continuous relation among actors rather than isolated transactions (Ng and Briscoe 2012). Third, value is *interactional*; actualizing relations, value is proposed, created, and captured through interaction among diverse actors (Lusch and Nambisan 2015; Ng and Smith 2012).

In sum, the value of digital innovations does not equate to monetary value of the resulting offering. Rather, in absence of direct monetary exchanges, value co-creation entails the integration of resources that hold value-in-use for one party as the recombination of a resource enables offering additional value when embedded in a digitally enabled exchange of services. Implied by the recombination of technology components, the aggregate value of a digital innovation is thus not the result of isolated "value-adding" activities through focal organizations. Instead, value is generated through co-creation processes aggregating recombinant technology components by interacting with diverse resources and often across firm boundaries. The shifts in the logics of the value that digital innovations offer, create, and capture, as well as the dynamic that spreads these activities across organizations, merits a reflection of value and value generation. Most digital innovations encompass a multiplicity of values attached to its various components and functions. As not every resource is uniformly valuable to all actors at all points in time value is actualized at the point when a resource is utilized and incorporated into a novel offering (Ng and Smith 2012; Yoo 2015).

Innovation aspects revised

The three core aspects of digital innovation merit a return to the three assumptions underpinning much innovation research:

1. The producer-consumer division is challenged as digital innovations are co-created and shaped by diverse actors (Eaton et al. 2015; Kallinikos et al. 2013; Yoo et al. 2012). Actors in digital innovation often have multiple and simultaneous roles as they are involved in the creation, delivery, and use of a novel offering. For instance, the offerings of social networks rely on significant input and manipulation of users, associated actors, and technologies, where role reversal is common.
2. The product vs. process distinction is less pertinent. Digital innovation challenges the distinction between product and process innovation. Both aspects are subject to constant interaction with digital technology, and digital innovation entangles product and process notions. The composition of functions and features underlies continuous adjustment driven by the attributes of digital technology and the role of editable digital information as the core resource. Digital innovation entails changes to the way outcomes are achieved, and alters the outcome itself. The exchange of services on the basis of digital technology conflates notions of both processes and products due to the operand and operant character of digital resources (see also Lyytinen et al. 2016).
3. Distinct stages as in a controlled, linear organizational process are not clearly discernible in digital innovation. Instead of a discrete sequence of steps, the mechanisms that yield digital innovations are akin to ongoing, multiple iterations. Such iterations are emergent to a degree that makes deliberate process phases unrecognizable. Rather than a stringent process yielding an end result, sufficient iteration eventually culminates in a temporal stabilization of a coherent set of functions that form a service offered at a given point in time. This stabilization, however, is only the basis for the next iteration and refinement of the offering, inducing a new version and potentially extending functionalities by the inclusion of new actors. Without direct control as a tool for management to shape digital innovation processes, the means of organizations to influence or steer digital innovation are altered.

Organizing for digital innovation

A crucial challenge for information systems researchers is the theorization of novel organizational forms and dynamics induced by digital innovation. Digital technology enables connectivity which in turn increases scale, speed, and scope of digital innovation delivered through networks of actors (Lyytinen et al. 2016). In understanding digital innovation, attention is therefore needed toward the supra-organizational structures emerging from the interaction required for the delivery of digital services, such as digital infrastructure and platforms. Because information flows are facilitated via digitally enabled technologies embodying reciprocal connections, innovative ideas are introduced from diverse origins across the network of connected actors (Benkler 2006; Lyytinen et al. 2016). The driving force behind all novel organizational forms is digital technology and the activity it affords. But despite sharing this cause, resulting organizational transformations are non-deterministic and the organizing logic of firms is affected in various ways (see Lyytinen et al. 2016).

Organizing logic

Organizing activity around digital objects and the dynamics they evoke challenges static and tightly coupled forms of organizations. Using the layered-modular architecture (Yoo et al. 2010), we can learn something about organizing for, and business modelling of, digital innovation. In particular, it is clear that innovation is taking place across layers (such as contents, service, network, and device) rather than within the scope of verticals such as industries and organizations. As an example, competitive services can be offered by focusing on one layer only and activating functions in the remaining layers by interacting with external parties. For instance, a smartphone application that operates on the content layer relies on the delivery of other functionalities by drawing on additional information resources such as communication capabilities provided by network carrier (network layer), payment processing (service layer), and input-output functionalities through interface capabilities provided by the phone manufacturer (device layer). Whether as purely digital services or as additional functionality embedded in physical objects, digital information is collected, combined, and contextualized by utilizing diverse technology components from various organizational as well as architectural sources. Within and across layers of digital architecture, information handling processes are enabled between various modules by integrating information resources. As actors rarely cover activity across all layers necessary to deliver a service, the continuous, iterative process of recombination of components across actors is vital to the configuration of the digital offering. Changes affecting the design of digital service offerings are hence highly dynamic (Lyytinen et al. 2016; Yoo et al. 2010). Changes to offerings are introduced in such a way that continuous transfiguration renders digital objects as perpetually in the making (Kallinikos et al. 2013) and incomplete by design (Garud et al. 2008). As indicated by the description of digital technology's attributes, design in digital innovation is bi-directional: every offering is the result of complex recombination processes and at the same time invites recombination of its own components that might eventually alter the offering in return.

Digital components introduced to product and service architectures thereby induce and manage increasing product complexity. In a study of an automotive manufacturer, Lee and Berente (2012) demonstrate how digitally controlled components span multiple functions and in turn produce digital information able to be used for novel functions, controls, and use (Lee and Berente 2012). Digital components do not merely take the place of analogue parts, but enable new possibilities: through their computational characteristics, digital components monitor and regulate subsystems in a variety of ways, to process data in real time quickly and reliably, and to link otherwise decoupled subsystems so that these subsystems become responsive to each other (Lee and Berente 2012). This in turn influences the evolution of complex, digitally enabled systems that form the basis of novel digital offerings.

These dynamics also result in constant adaptions of a firm's business model as the dominant logic of offering, creating, and capturing value (Chesbrough 2010). Driven by complex and changing interactions with other parties, redefining the business model is required when configurations of activity and revenue streams are adjusted to deliver a digitally enabled offering (see e.g., Jonsson et al. 2008; Nylén and Holmström 2015). The balance of the activity that an organization performs and the activities that are remunerated are diverging due to the intricate collaborations that digital technology afford. While enabling and reacting to new constellations is imperative to deliver digital innovations it also constantly alters the firm's organizing and business logics.

Growth and scaling

Digitally enabled organizing logics also alter how core dynamics such as organizational growth and scaling of activity plays out in digital innovation. For instance, digital technologies surrogate the build-up of organizational practices needed in transition and growth phases of organizations. They enable the orchestration of organizational functions and roles through the connection with external providers as a network of actors delivers a service. Additional actors are brought in to orchestrate the offering of novel services in the absence of capabilities needed for the actor initiating the offering. This is especially valuable to early-stage organizations as the exploitation of digital capabilities allows the immediate leap from idea generation to idea delivery without building up all needed capabilities incrementally (Tumbas et al. 2015). The bridging of full organizational capabilities through leverage of digital technologies helps releasing novel services using technologies existing outside the organization, effectively surrogating capabilities that then do not have to exist internally. For example, consider how web-based application programming interfaces extend an organization's capability base by tapping into an infrastructure of existing digital technologies. Erecting de-facto organizational capabilities by orchestrating digital technology preempts the resource intensive building of similar capabilities organically. In later stages organizations often do not replace these de-facto capabilities, but rather incorporate them in the efforts needed for subsequent growth. Compositions of digital technologies across firm boundaries thus become elemental to organizational structure and the initial orchestration of services defines the factual organizational design in retrospective (see Tumbas et al. 2015). As a result, organizations embedding digital technologies in early growth stages mature while being deeply rooted in digital infrastructures, less limited to organizational boundaries than by loosely defined spheres in which activity is orchestrated through technology use.

Beyond organizational maturation, the dynamics of digital technology use also affect how organizations are able to scale their activity. Organizations utilizing the dynamics enabled by the interplay of digital technology components can grow near exponentially by relying on instantaneous exchange of digital information. Abandoning limitations arising from the transformation of physical matter, operation on the basis of newly created information resources, rapid deployment of digital product prototypes, and incorporation of immediate feedback into new organizational formation are indicated as key advantages of digital innovation for ventures seeking to scale rapidly (Huang et al. 2017). Exploiting positive feedback dynamics can also result in generative developments and help grow the entire network of actors involved in the realization of a digital offering (Henfridsson and Bygstad 2013).

Management and control

Digital innovation exhibits a new form of control. Rather than firm-centric control, the locus of control is shifted toward supra-organizations such as platforms. Challenging firm-centric control, platform-centric control routinely transcends firm boundaries and locates digitally enabled interaction possibilities that defy functional division (Svahn et al. 2015). In the platform setting, control is enacted through configuration and reconfiguration of digital resources, typically with the aim to stimulate vibrant and generative innovation while protecting the integrity of the platform (Gawer and Cusumano 2014; Ghazawneh and Henfridsson 2013; Tiwana et al. 2010;

Yoo et al. 2012). For instance, Apple's governance of the iOS platform (including App Store) involves reconfiguration of the framework that guide third-party developers' interaction with platform resources. One key challenge in such governance is the balancing act of enabling and constraining activity by means of technology design in shared domains of supra-organizations (Hanseth and Lyytinen 2010; Lyytinen et al. 2016; Tilson et al. 2010). Successful balancing involves appropriate design of interface capabilities and careful determination of what and how resources are available for interaction (Ghazawneh and Henfridsson 2013). Managerial control as (re)configuration governs the complex interdependencies arising from the creation of novel digital offerings (Tiwana et al. 2010; Wareham et al. 2014; Woodard 2008).

Conclusion

This chapter presents digital innovation as a new mode of creating novelty in business. The newness of digital innovation compared to its traditional manufacturing counterpart lies in three aspects of its definition: the unique properties of digital technology, massive recombination, and value co-creation. While these central aspects of digital innovation are indeed discussed in the emerging literature, however, our chapter represents an attempt to integrate them within a single definition. In doing so, we also speculate on the consequences for anyone interested in organizing digital innovation by highlighting changes in organizing logics, growth and scaling, and management and control.

In going forward, there is little doubt that digital technology will play a significant role in how innovation is shaped. The most notable and profound element in this shaping might be the challenges to the individual firm as the entity for innovation. As traditional boundaries are reshaped by increasingly non-linear and complex inter-dependencies, it makes sense to examine both emerging supra-organizational forms and new market mechanisms following in the aftermath of digital innovation. In this regard, information systems researchers studying digital innovation have both the privilege and the responsibility to continue examining an intellectually challenging and rewarding area of research.

References

Benkler, Y. 2006. *The Wealth of Networks – How Social Production Transforms Markets and Freedom*, New Haven and London: Yale University Press.

Boland, R. J., Lyytinen, K., and Yoo, Y. 2007. "Wakes of Innovation in Project Networks: The Case of Digital 3-D Representations in Architecture, Engineering, and Construction," *Organization Science* (18:4), pp. 631–647.

Brandenburger, A. M., and Stuart, H. W. 1996. "Value-Based Business Strategy," *Journal of Economics & Management Strategy* (5:1), pp. 5–24.

Chesbrough, H. 2010. "Business Model Innovation: Opportunities and Barriers," *Long Range Planning* (43), pp. 354–363.

Eaton, B., Elaluf-Calderwood, S., Sorensen, C., and Yoo, Y. 2015. "Distributed Tuning of Boundary Resources: The Case of Apple's iOS Service System," *MIS Quarterly* (39:1), pp. 217–243.

Fichman, R. G. 2004. "Going Beyond the Dominant Paradigm for Information Technology Innovation Research: Emerging Concepts," *Journal of the Association for Information Systems* (5:8), pp. 314–355.

Fichman, R. G., Santos, B. L. Dos, and Zheng, Z. 2014. "Digital Innovation as a Fundamental and Powerful Concept in the Information Systems Curriculum," *MIS Quarterly* (38:2), pp. 329–353.

Garud, R., Jain, S., and Tuertscher, P. 2008. "Incomplete by Design and Designing for Incompleteness," *Organization Studies* (29:3), pp. 351–371.

Gawer, A., and Cusumano, M. 2014. "Industry Platforms and Ecosystem Innovation," *Journal of Product Innovation Management* (31:3), pp. 417–433.

Ghazawneh, A., and Henfridsson, O. 2013. "Balancing Platform Control and External Contribution in Third-Party Development: The Boundary Resources Model," *Information Systems Journal* (23:2), pp. 173–192.

Godin, B. 2006. "The Linear Model of Innovation: The Historical Construction of an Analytical Framework," *Science, Technology & Human Values* (31:6), pp. 639–667.

Hanseth, O., and Lyytinen, K. 2010. "Design Theory for Dynamic Complexity in Information Infrastructures: The Case of Building Internet," *Journal of Information Technology* (25:1), pp. 1–19.

Henfridsson, O., and Bygstad, B. 2013. "The Generative Mechanisms of Digital Infrastructure Evolution," *MIS Quarterly* (37:3), pp. 907–931.

Henfridsson, O., Mathiassen, L., and Svahn, F. 2014. "Managing Technological Change in the Digital Age: The Role of Architectural Frames," *Journal of Information Technology* (29:1), pp. 27–43.

Huang, J., Henfridsson, O., Liu, M. J., and Newell, S. (2017). "Growing on Steroids: Rapidly Scaling the User Base of Digital Ventures Through Digital Innovation," *MIS Quarterly*, (41:1), 301–314.

Jonsson, K., Westergren, U. H., and Holmström, J. 2008. "Technologies for Value Creation: An Exploration of Remote Diagnostics Systems in the Manufacturing Industry," *Information Systems Journal* (18:3), pp. 227–245.

Kallinikos, J., Aaltonen, A., and Marton, A. 2013. "The Ambivalent Ontology of Digital Artifacts," *MIS Quarterly* (37:2), pp. 357–370.

Langlois, R. N. 2007. "The Entrepreneurial Theory of the Firm and the Theory of the Entrepreneurial Firm," *Journal of Management Studies* (44:7), pp. 1107–1124.

Lee, J., and Berente, N. 2012. "Digital Innovation and the Division of Innovative Labor: Digital Controls in the Automotive Industry," *Organization Science* (23:5), pp. 1428–1447.

Lepak, D. P., Smith, K. G., and Taylor, M. S. 2007. "Value Creation and Value Capture: A Multilevel Perspective," *Academy of Management Review* (32:1), pp. 180–194.

Lusch, R. F., and Nambisan, S. 2015. "Service Innovation: A Service-Dominant Logic Perspective," *MIS Quarterly* (39:1), pp. 155–176.

Lyytinen, K., and Rose, G. M. 2003. "The Disruptive Nature of Information Technology Innovations: The Case of Internet Computing in System Development Organizations," *MIS Quarterly* (27:4), pp. 557–596.

Lyytinen, K., Yoo, Y., and Boland, R. J. 2016. "Digital Product Innovation Within Four Classes of Innovation Networks," *Information Systems Journal*, pp. 47–75.

Nambisan, S. 2013. "Information Technology and Product/Service Innovation: A Brief Assessment and Some Suggestions for Future Research," *Journal of the Association for Information Systems* (14:Special Issue), pp. 215–226.

Ng, I.C.L., and Briscoe, G. 2012. "Value, Variety and Viability: New Business Models for Co-creation in Outcome-Based Contracts," *International Journal of Service Science, Management, Engineering, and Technology* (3:3), pp. 26–48.

Ng, I.C.L., and Smith, L. 2012. "An Integrative Framework of Value," *Review of Marketing Research* (9: Special Issue-Toward a Better Understanding of the Role of Value in Markets and Marketing), pp. 207–243.

Nylén, D., and Holmström, J. 2015. "Digital Innovation Strategy: A Framework for Diagnosing and Improving Digital Product and Service Innovation," *Business Horizons* (58), pp. 57–67.

Porter, M. E. 1980. *Competitive Strategy: Techniques for Analyzing Industries and Competitors*, New York: Free Press.

Porter, M. E. 1985. *Competitive Advantage: Creating and Sustaining Superior Performance*, New York: Collier Macmillan.

Schumpeter, J.A. 1934/1983. *The Theory of Economic Development*, New Brunswick/London: Transaction.

Svahn, F. 2012. *Digital Product Innovation: Building Generative Capability Through Architectural Frames*, University of Umeå, Sweden.

Svahn, F., and Henfridsson, O. 2012. "The Dual Regimes of Digital Innovation Management," *2012 45th Hawaii International Conference on System Sciences*, IEEE, pp. 3347–3356.

Svahn, F., Lindgren, R., and Mathiassen, L. 2015. "Applying Options Thinking to shape Generativity in Digital Innovation: An Action Research Into Connected Cars," in *Proceedings of the Annual Hawaii International Conference on System Sciences*, pp. 4141–4150.

Swanson, E. B. 1994. "Information Systems Innovation Among Organizations," *Management Science* (40:9), pp. 1069–1092.

Tilson, D., Lyytinen, K., and Sørensen, C. 2010. "Research Commentary – Digital Infrastructures: The Missing IS Research Agenda," *Information Systems Research* (21:4), pp. 748–759.

Tiwana, A., Konsynski, B., and Bush, A. A. 2010. "Research Commentary – Platform Evolution: Coevolution of Platform Architecture, Governance, and Environmental Dynamics," *Information Systems Research* (21:4), pp. 675–687.

Tumbas, S., Seidel, S., Berente, N., and Vom Brocke, J. 2015. "The 'Digital Façade' of Rapidly Growing Entrepreneurial Organizations," in *Proceedings of the 36th International Conference on Information Systems (ICIS)*, pp. 1–19.

Vargo, S. L., and Lusch, R. F. 2004. "Evolving to a New Dominant Logic for Marketing," *Journal of Marketing* (68:January), pp. 1–17.

Wareham, J., Fox, P. B., and Cano Giner, J. L. 2014. "Technology Ecosystem Governance," *Organization Science* (25:4), pp. 1195–1215.

Woodard, C. J. 2008. "Architectural Control Points," in *DESRIST – International Conference on Design Science Research in Information Systems and Technology*, Georgia, pp. 1–6.

Yoo, Y. 2013. "The Tables Have Turned: How Can the Information Systems Field Contribute to Technology and Innovation Management Research," *Journal of the Association for Information Systems* (14:5), pp. 227–236.

Yoo, Y. 2015. "Design in the Generative Economy," *Research-Technology Management* (58:2), pp. 13–20.

Yoo, Y., Boland, R. J., Lyytinen, K., and Majchrzak, A. 2012. "Organizing for Innovation in the Digitized World," *Organization Science* (23:5), pp. 1398–1408.

Yoo, Y., Henfridsson, O., and Lyytinen, K. 2010. "The New Organizing Logic of Digital Innovation: An Agenda for Information Systems Research," *Information Systems Research* (21:4), pp. 724–735.

Zittrain, J. 2008. *The Future of the Internet – and How to Stop It*, New Haven: Yale University Press.

24
KNOWLEDGE COLLABORATION IN ORGANIZATIONS
From information processing to social knowing

Samer Faraj, Karla Sayegh and Linda Rouleau

Introduction

The accumulation, sharing, transfer, transformation and co-creation of knowledge remains a central focus of management research because it entails the study of how innovation is performed in organizations. Early contingency theorists conceived of organizations as information processing systems whose primary purpose was to manage multiple sources of uncertainty stemming from task complexity, task interdependence, task environment and interunit dependencies (Galbraith, 1977; Tushman & Nadler, 1978). The way to do this was through the acquisition and consumption of information to bridge the gap between the information processed and the information needed to meet complex task requirements. As uncertainty increased, so did the need for increased amounts of information (Huber, O'Connell, & Cummings, 1975). Increased amounts of information meant that an organization must raise its information processing capacity. Effective information processing capacities required "the collection of appropriate information, the movement of information in a timely fashion, and its transmission without distortion" (Tushman & Nadler, 1978, p. 617). Thus, a fit needed to be maintained between information processing needs and capacity. This information processing perspective dovetailed nicely with the computerization and communication investment wave that transformed most organizations during the '80s and '90s. Today, most organizations have reached a level of IT capability and sophistication that effectively supports a very high level of information sharing and processing. Almost all organizational processes have been automated and substantially informated and the problem of collecting and disseminating "the right information to the right people at the right time" has been largely resolved (Zuboff, 1988). In sum, organizations have successfully heeded the call of the information processing perspective.

Yet, despite the current pervasiveness of information technologies within organizations and the availability of infinite amounts of information at the individual's fingertips, the transfer of knowledge across groups, units and/or boundaries of any kind within and across organizations remains an ongoing challenge (Bechky, 2003; Dougherty, 1992; Majchrzak, More, & Faraj,

2012). This is because knowledge has a predominantly tacit dimension that is "sticky" and not easily transferable (Nonaka, 1994; Szulanski, 1996). Actors embedded in different communities of practice (Lave & Wenger, 1991) bring with them significant differences in problem conceptualizations and interpretive schemes (Dougherty, 1992), speak different technical languages and have often disparate vested interests rooted in their expertise (Carlile, 2004). For these reasons, knowledge transfer processes can result in misunderstandings, incorrect interpretations and attributions, and team conflicts. Knowledge work therefore entails elaborate social processes that are messy and emergent.

This chapter explores the evolution, challenges and mechanisms underlying what we call knowledge collaboration processes. Broadly speaking, we define knowledge collaboration as the sharing, transfer, accumulation, transformation and co-creation of knowledge. We discuss its history and evolution as well as the mechanisms that enable and constrain it. We also focus on the role of technology in heralding new forms of knowledge work in the context of online communities. In particular, we examine the potential of these generative spaces in co-creating new knowledge and propelling open innovation. Lastly, we propose new research directions for knowledge collaboration research.

From "information processing" to "social knowing": a brief history

For more than half a century, management scholars have pondered problems of organizing and coordinating. Herbert Simon's early work on human cognitive limits directed attention toward the study of how best to organize. Organizations were conceptualized as elaborate systems that overcame the individual's bounded rationality and limits to information processing and decision making (March & Simon, 1958) through formal working arrangements. These included hierarchy, rules, roles, task partitioning and scheduling, to name a few. By focusing attention on these building blocks and how they fit together, Simon's work opened the door to what came to be known as contingency theory. The central premise of this theory was that the most effective method of organizing is contingent on some attributes of an organization's internal and external environment (Lawrence & Lorsch, 1967a). Foremost among these attributes was uncertainty (Galbraith, 1977; Huber et al., 1975).

Uncertainty limited the organization's ability to preplan or make decisions about tasks in advance of their execution (Galbraith, 1973). The thinking was that the more uncertain a task, the more the information that needed processing among actors performing the task (Galbraith, 1973). In this tradition, the organization came to be seen as an open social system that must deal with work-related uncertainty through information processing capacity. The effectiveness of an organization's information processing capacity was dependent on its organization structure and the coordination and control mechanisms used in it (Galbraith, 1973; Tushman, 1977; Tushman & Nadler, 1978). These structures and mechanisms varied in cost, complexity and the ability to handle consequential events that could not be anticipated or planned for in advance (Galbraith, 1973; Tushman & Nadler, 1978).

In integrating subtasks around the completion of the global task, organizations could either (a) reduce uncertainty or (b) increase capacity to process information with cost and performance trade-offs. For example, the use of slack resources (e.g., time, budget, staff and inventories) provided one way to reduce the amount of interdependence between subunits (Cyert & March, 1963; March & Simon, 1958), a considerable source of uncertainty. Alternatively, the organization could enhance its capacity to process information by, for example, investing in information systems. Information systems were thought to reduce the burden on communication channels in the hierarchy. By equipping actors with computing resources, information could be more readily collected, transmitted, processed and disseminated without distortion (Galbraith, 1973).

Thus, the problem of organizing from the information processing perspective was one of selecting from appropriate *structural* arrangements that permitted coordinated action across a multitude of interdependent roles. The consensus was that high performing units facing complex interdependence with other areas should utilize more complex coordination and control mechanisms. For example, organismic structures with highly connected communication networks of individuals provided the opportunity for feedback and error correction and for the synthesis of different points of view (Tushman & Nadler, 1978). This coordination by feedback (March & Simon, 1958) and mutual adjustment (Thompson, 1967) implied that as tasks increased in uncertainty, complexity and interdependence, coordination through hierarchy and impersonal programming alone was largely insufficient (Van de Ven, Delbecq, & Koenig, 1976). In sum, the essence of organizing involved a choice among a feasible set of *structural* alternatives to most effectively deal with their information processing requirements.

In its quest to bridge the gap between the "information processed" and "the information required to perform complex tasks," the information processing view tended to equate information with knowledge (Newell & Simon, 1972). The implicit assumption was that the actual "transfer" of information was not problematic once *appropriate structures* were in place. Information was conceived as a monolithic "thing" that was collected and transmitted from one individual to another largely unchanged. For example, Tushman and Nadler (1978) define information as "data which are relevant, accurate, timely and concise" (p. 614) and must effect a change in knowledge. Although information processing involves "the gathering, interpreting, and synthesis of information in the context of organizational decision making" (Tushman & Nadler, 1978), how this process is done and how it translates into knowledge remained unexplored. The distinction between knowledge and information was left unaddressed. As per the information processing view, task uncertainty and complexity could simply be managed with administrative arrangements or information infrastructure that increase the amounts of information the organization can digest.

In the early 1990s, a growing group of scholars began to question this view. First, the advent and prevalence of technologies that were, according to the information processing perspective, a compelling way to increase information processing capacity, did not resolve key challenges associated with knowledge work. Second, contrary to prevailing views that teams were best deployed as inter-unit coordination mechanisms (Galbraith, 1973), teams became prevalent as basic modes of organizing work within units. Further, even when teams were deployed in situations where task uncertainty and complexity were high across groups, units and/or boundaries, knowledge integration remained challenging (Dougherty, 1992; Nonaka, 1994; Weick & Roberts, 1993). These findings shifted scholarly attention away from formal, structural mechanisms toward a deeper understanding of the social processes behind knowledge transfer and sharing. Previous to this shift, informal social processes were merely regarded as the messy remainders of more formal coordinating arrangements.

Knowing in organizations: a shift from structural to social mechanisms

The difficulty of transferring knowledge, the tacit nature of knowledge and its stickiness have been pivotal in rethinking what knowledge means and how it is coordinated in organizations (Nonaka, 1994; Nonaka & Von Krogh, 2009; Polanyi, 1967; Szulanski, 1996). Although the nature of knowledge has long preoccupied philosophers and sociologists of science, management scholars have only turned their attention to knowledge in the last two decades. This is because knowledge diversity and knowledge-based organizing came to be known as the core to firm growth, innovation and competitive advantage (Kogut & Zander, 1992; Leonard-Barton, 1995; Starbuck, 1992). At the same time, structural arrangements alone were inadequate in addressing coordination breakdowns associated with knowledge work (Faraj, Sproull, Constant, & Kiesler, 2000).

Adding to the challenges of engaging with a knowledge perspective, understanding knowledge and its role in organizations is dependent on the ontology that is adopted. A substantialist ontology, shared by proponents of the information processing view, underlies the "economistic" perspective. Knowledge in this view is seen as something that can be abstracted and represented in codified form. It is acquired and synthesized through cognitive processes and is generally regarded as a static, embedded capability or stable disposition of actors. Consequently, it can be considered an independent resource exchangeable in the marketplace. This notion finds its roots with Simon:

> All the aspects of knowledge – its creation, its storage, its retrieval, its treatment as property, its role in the functioning of societies and organization – can be (and have been) analyzed with the tools of economics. Knowledge has a price and a cost of production; there are markets for knowledge, with their supply and demand curves, and marginal rates of substitution between one form of knowledge and another.
> (Simon, 1999, quoted in Duguid, 2005, p. 3)

This conception of knowledge has also been characterized as "taxonomic" (Tsoukas, 1996) proposing that organizations have different "types" of knowledge. Researchers in this domain develop "different classifications and use these to examine the various strategies, routines, and techniques through which different types of knowledge are created, codified, converted, transferred, and exchanged" (Orlikowski, 2002, p. 250) and relate them to organizational performance.

An alternative ontology posits that knowledge is relational (Emirbayer, 1997) and thus primarily existing in the social realm. From this lens, knowledge is constituted in and through situated connections and interactions that are emergent and subject to change. Knowledge or "knowing" is dynamic, predominantly tacit, context dependent and emerging from interactions (sayings and doings) and relations in particular situations and times. It is deeply rooted in action, commitment and involvement in a specific context and requires a substantial investment in time and resources to develop, becoming part and parcel of an actor's professional/occupational identity (Carlile, 2002).

Although knowledge has a universal, explicit component, its stickiness derives from its tacit dimension (Nonaka, 1994; Nonaka & Von Krogh, 2009; Polanyi, 1966; Szulanski, 1996). The distinction between the explicit and the tacit can be understood through the simple example of playing tennis. Reading a tennis manual results in the accumulation of "knowing-that" which confers the ability to talk a good game, but not necessarily to play one. For this reason, knowledge necessarily entails a "doing" or practice component, which is fundamentally social. To extend the tennis analogy further, playing tennis involves an opponent, communication through tennis moves, sharing tactics and practicing them, watching experts in action and speaking a common language with other tennis players. This "procedural knowledge" (Anderson, 1984) accumulates and changes over time with practice and becomes very difficult to articulate and codify in its entirety to, say, a hockey player, someone new to the game of tennis. So the key to acquiring tacit knowledge is some form of shared experience that allows people to partake in one another's thinking and acting process through social actions and interactions. Nonaka refers to the process of transferring tacit knowledge through shared practice as "socialization" (Nonaka, 1994). According to Nonaka (1994), "the mere transfer of information will often make little sense if it is abstracted from embedded emotions and nuanced contexts that are associated with shared experience" (p. 19). As such, tacit knowledge implies the participation in an activity system or community of practice, about which *participants share understandings* concerning what they are doing and what that means in their lives and for their communities (Lave & Wenger, 1991). To know is therefore to *experience*. The irony

Table 24.1 Synthesis of approaches to knowledge collaboration

	Information Processing	Social Knowing
Primary concern	Managing task uncertainty	Overcoming knowledge differences
Key complication	Task interdependencies	Knowledge and skill interdependencies
Purpose	To accomplish complex tasks	To co-create new knowledge
Conception of knowledge	Knowledge can be made explicit, represented in a universally accessible form and transferred as information	Knowing is sticky, contextualized, always in the making and often cannot be adequately represented as information
Coordination mechanisms emphasized	Pre-specified, formal, structured	Improvisational and emergent, Informal social interactions over time
Organizational emphasis	Designing appropriate information processing infrastructure Structural mechanisms	Social processes
Managing complexity	Developing tight communication networks Mutual feedback and adjustment	Achieving common ground Traversing or transcending semantic, syntactic and pragmatic boundaries
Ontology	Substantialist Realist	Interpretivist Relational
Theoretical traditions	Contingency theory Functionalism Managerialism	Communities of practice Practice perspective Phenomenology Pragmatism
Dominant research methods	Deductive	Inductive
Purpose of technology	Provide each decision maker with the right information at the right time	Connect with the right experts, encourage participation and facilitate distributed dialoguing and work display
Focal technologies	Resource planning, decision support, data analytics, customer relationships, control, e-business, etc.	Platforms that expose expertise, provide connectivity and facilitate conversation, work display and other exchanges involving complex knowledge and expertise

is that the very process of deep engagement required for knowing in one's community actually hinders the integration of knowledge across communities (Boland & Tenkasi, 1995; Carlile, 2002), particularly when both knowledge and the resolution of differences are at stake.

Carlile (2004) describes a scenario in an automotive company where actors from various engineering groups – vehicle styling, engine/powertrain, climate control and safety, each specializing in different types of automotive engineering work – are brought together for the first time to develop a competitive vehicle prototype in a finite time frame. Each team member, representing a different occupational group in the organization, has different levels of experience, terminologies, mental models, tools and incentives with respect to the team task. Team members must also depend on one another to deliver the new product. While the styling group strives to create a distinctive-looking vehicle for competitive positioning, the engine/powertrain group aims to build the most efficient and most powerful engine possible. Yet, an engine's power may interfere with a sleek vehicle look because of a protruding hood. How (and how well) these knowledge differences and dependencies are translated, transferred, managed and/or transformed is of crucial importance in the co-generation of new knowledge, the latter being associated with innovation and competitiveness (Carlile, 2004; Faraj & Xiao, 2006; Kellogg, Orlikowski, & Yates, 2006; Okhuysen & Bechky, 2009). This process is what we refer to as knowledge collaboration. In the following section, we explore the process in depth, synthesizing the current thinking with a view to proposing future directions for the research conversation. See Table 24.1 for a synthesis of the evolution in knowledge perspectives on organizing.

Knowledge collaboration in organizations: social mechanisms

Knowledge collaboration is defined broadly as the sharing, transfer, accumulation, transformation and co-creation of knowledge (Faraj, Jarvenpaa, & Majchrzak, 2011). Because the process requires that domain-specific knowledge be translated and transformed across boundaries, it entails the proactive development of a shared understanding, collective common ground or common knowledge so that task- and role-related actions and needs of others can be better understood and anticipated (Bechky, 2003; Carlile, 2002; Carlile, 2004; Hargadon & Bechky, 2006; Okhuysen & Bechky, 2009; Rico, Sánchez-Manzanares, Gil, & Gibson, 2008; Tsoukas, 2009). Recent scholarship has explored a variety of social mechanisms that explain how common ground is developed and how knowledge co-creation unfolds. These include dialogic approaches (Faraj & Xiao, 2006; Tsoukas, 1996), boundary objects (Bechky, 2003; Carlile, 2002; Nicolini, Mengis, & Swan, 2012), collaborative agreements (Kellogg et al., 2006; Majchrzak et al., 2012) and brokering roles (Klein, Ziegert, Knight, & Xiao, 2006; Valentine & Edmondson, 2014) to name a few.[1] In the following section, we explore the key insights and limitations of these mechanisms in coordinating knowledge across boundaries.

Dialogic approaches

In situations involving temporary teams, participants use dialogic contestation to deal with the unexpected. For example, in role-based teams performing high reliability, time-sensitive work, dialogue is used to improvise in order to avoid fatal errors and costly failures (Faraj & Xiao, 2006). The improvisational talk and action involving impromptu adaptation to execute a novel "production" (Bechky & Okhuysen, 2011) is an emergent form of *in situ* learning that engenders the mindfulness required to perform in these settings (Weick & Sutcliffe, 2007; Weick & Roberts, 1993).

In situations involving longer-term work arrangements, face-to-face dialogue plays a different role. Boland and Tenkasi (1995) observed that a vital element in bridging across community boundaries is to deeply engage with the assumptions of other communities in a process of conversational interaction referred to as perspective taking. Two reasons explain why conversation is vital to deep-knowledge sharing. First, face-to-face "talk" is core to building interpersonal relationships. Interpersonal relationships are built over time through *relational engagement*, a stylistic dialogic approach whereby team members not only convey substance but also "an attitude or orientation to the kind of relationship" one has or seeks with his/her conversational partner (Tsoukas, 2009, p. 944). As a less calculative mode of engagement, a relational approach generates trust and a positive team affect, usually resulting in increased interpersonal interaction (Boland & Tenkasi, 1995). Over time, trust builds an atmosphere that encourages "risk-taking," thoughtful dialogic contestation or resistance and a healthy amount of task conflict leading to a motivational climate for collaboration and positive team outcomes (Edmondson, 1999; Jehn, Northcraft, & Neale, 1999; Möllering, 2001; Thomas, Sargent, & Hardy, 2011). Because expertise is highly invested and at stake in cross-disciplinary work (Carlile, 2004), the relational engagement that is associated with both cognitive and affective trust (McAllister, 1995) facilitates the traversal of more pragmatic boundaries (Carlile, 2004).

Second, talk engenders reflexivity. The latter prompts the co-generation of new insights through new ways of framing and reframing issues in the process elaborating and refining vocabulary, instruments and theories related to the task at hand (Tsoukas, 2009). In hearing our own thoughts, attempting to understand the other through talk, and in taking turns in dialogue, we can better know the meaning of what we say (Weick & Kiesler, 1979). In other words, actors better understand their own utterances in light of the other's responses to them. This generates new and different thoughts that actors could not come up with alone and enables them to take distance from their own thoughts. Distance taking from one's own thought world and customary ways of acting frees actors from its cognitive confines, thereby allowing for fresh thinking, unexpected insight and new ideas and understandings to emerge (Tsoukas, 2009).

Dialogic approaches (talk, conversation) are critical to interpersonal cooperation but they do not capture the entirety of organizational work. Much of work activity in post-bureaucratic organizations is accomplished in and through objects and material arrangements (Star, 2010). In particular, the theorization of the boundary object as facilitating knowledge transformation has received much attention.

Boundary objects

Boundary objects are flexible epistemic artifacts that "inhabit several intersecting social worlds and satisfy the information requirements of each of them" (Star & Griesemer, 1989, p. 393). Because they are anchored in and meaningful across these worlds, they create the conditions for collaboration while, "by way of their interpretive flexibility, not requiring *deep sharing*" (Nicolini et al., 2012, p. 619). Bechky (2003) showed how a machine transformed knowledge between engineers, technicians and assemblers on a production floor. Transformation occurred when a member of one community came to understand how knowledge from another community fit within the context of his own work, enriching and altering what he knew. Revised understandings based on this new knowledge enabled him to see his own world in a new light. Misunderstandings that arose were reconciled through the use of *tangible definitions* to co-create common ground: that is, physically demonstrating the problem on the machine itself. The creation of common ground allowed the groups to "re-contextualize local understandings" (Bechky, 2003, p. 321).

The potential of the boundary object to make visible and explicit differences and dependences between occupational groups is crucial (Carlile, 2002). This is because a representation of these differences and dependencies facilitates the establishment of shared meaning and clarifies the knowledge that is at stake for each group (Carlile, 2002; Carlile, 2004). Only when this happens can the groups begin to negotiate a novel co-generated solution.

Although the boundary object itself was very insightful at the time of its introduction, it does not address several important considerations (Nicolini et al., 2012; Star, 2010; Whyte & Harty, 2012). First, the term "interpretive flexibility" almost implies that boundary objects are neutral lumps to which people assign meaning and around which people organize. In reality, objects are always already imbued with value in the social milieu in which they are situated and can "push back" (D'Adderio, 2011). So, in order to better understand deeply how objects are implicated in the set-up of social relations, we need a "theory" that better captures how the setup of the focal context shapes the roles a boundary object takes on.

Second, the collaborative value or meaning of the boundary object lies not in the object itself but occurs in its relation with other implicated objects and human actions in a focal context (Faraj & Azad, 2012). For example, the machine's collaborative potential in Bechky's (2003) example could only be actualized through the actor "tangibly defining" or physically demonstrating the problem. This intersection of material and human agencies is not adequately addressed in studies of boundary objects. Nicolini et al. (2012) alludes to this by dimensionalizing the drives and motivations objects provide to support cross-disciplinary collaboration. For example, epistemic objects always reflect a "lack" to people acting on them as they are a symbol of insufficiency or "incomplete work" (Knorr-Cetina, 1997). This ongoing representation of "lack" appeals to the human nature of wanting to improve/fix/complete. The desire and attachment created by this lure begins to dissolve boundaries and create mutual dependencies. Therefore, the materiality of the object foregrounded in Nicolini's analysis derives from "action potential" not from a sense of prefabricated "stuff or thingness" (Star, 2010). This is very much in line with the lens of affordances currently prevalent in studies of technology and organizing (Faraj & Azad, 2012; Hutchby, 2001; Zammuto, Griffith, Majchrzak, Dougherty, & Faraj, 2007). Objects play a far more active role than simply being passive enablers of knowledge translation and this needs further theoretical elaboration. For example, some studies have shown how objects can alter and shape role relations (Barrett, Oborn, Orlikowski, & Yates, 2012; Tuertscher, Garud, & Kumaraswamy, 2014) and reconstitute the very structures that shape organizations (Barley, 1986).

Collaborative agreements

Another social mechanism that has emerged in the context of fast-paced, time-sensitive knowledge work is what we call the collaborative agreement. Collaborative agreements are temporary understandings aimed at suspending knowledge differences in order to move work forward. By creating these temporary understandings, individuals often circumvent deep-knowledge sharing and its potential to create interpersonal conflict that erodes relationships. Instead, individuals choose to transcend knowledge differences by creating temporary, logical agreements to move forward based on a shared understanding.

For example, Kellogg et al. (2006) found that members of different occupational groups in an ad agency did not attempt to exchange deep knowledge to establish shared understanding; instead, they created a "trading zone" whereby display practices (making their work and the progress of their work visible), representation practices (making their work legible to each other) and assembly practices (reusing, revising and aligning their work products) were used to create a "collage of loosely coupled contributions" (p. 38). Majchrzak et al. (2012) also found that instead of engaging in deep knowledge exchange, cross-functional team members working on part-time projects transcended knowledge differences by voicing idea fragments aimed at building a landscape of thoughts (akin to brainstorming), co-creating a framework or scaffold to develop a collective team orientation and engaging in generative non-confrontational dialoguing around the scaffold. As time elapsed and interactions increased, team members moved the scaffold aside in a sustained effort at problem-solving. Faraj and Xiao (2006) also found that trauma care anesthesiologists, nurses and surgeons working with unpredictable urgent patient cases, in conditions of high load uncertainty and under very tight time frames, co-developed treatment solutions through the use of protocols which acted as legitimate "ground rules" to create a truce.

Interestingly, we know very little about whether and how these provisional settlements evolve into more taken for granted routines or working arrangements and with what consequences. What we do know is that working arrangements emerge out of everyday *improvising*. Improvising involves accommodations to and experiments with the everyday contingencies, breakdowns, exceptions, opportunities and unintended consequences as we encounter them (Feldman & Orlikowski, 2011; Tsoukas & Chia, 2002). Yet, how this temporal process unfolds and transforms into taken-for-granted practices remains elusive.

Brokering roles

In work involving cross-disciplinary expertise, roles, both formal and informal, serve as crucial collaborative mechanisms but with very different consequences. Formal roles were classically touted for their staffing flexibility and administrative efficiency because they structured individuals' interactions with one another in the absence of interpersonal familiarity. In high reliability settings requiring expertise, roles allow collaboration to be de-individualized (Klein et al., 2006). They also delineate expertise, jurisdictions and responsibility so that anyone in a particular role will know her individual responsibilities and interdependencies with those in other roles, even in the absence of previous joint work experience. This is important in enabling coordination. For example, roles on separate trauma teams of medical professionals allow for what Faraj and Xiao (2006) call "plug and play teaming." This is important because roles in these "improvisational organizational units" actually enable non-programmed cross-boundary coordination in dynamic settings. Klein et al. (2006) also demonstrated that de-individualized, hierarchical roles in temporary trauma teams allow for dynamic delegation. This is a form of shared leadership where senior leaders actively and repeatedly delegate to and subsequently withdraw the active role leadership from more junior leaders of the team. Dynamic delegation thus enabled teams to perform reliably while also building their amateur team members' skills (Klein et al., 2006).

Informal, non-hierarchical roles, on the other hand, are not planned or prespecified in advance and emerge over time as collaborators interact with one another. Although informal roles can take on many forms, one of particular importance to knowledge collaboration involves brokering between members from different thought worlds. This type of boundary work manifests itself along two dimensions. The first dimension entails the active creation of opportunities for team socialization in order to foster the affective and cognitive trust necessary to bring expertise to bear, work through differences and achieve common ground. The second dimension involves the use of process, meaning and social power to defend or buffer and reinforce the boundaries of the social space in which the team collaborates in order to allow for the delicate and often tenuous process of knowledge co-creation to unfold (Faraj & Yan, 2009).

Originally identified as coordination integrators (Lawrence & Lorsch, 1967b), these brokers often engage with others by aligning interests through clarity and simplification to link focal initiatives to issues of importance to and business priorities of team members in effect finding common ground (Balogun, Gleadle, Hailey, & Willmott, 2005; Rouleau & Balogun, 2011). In so doing, they use relevant, interesting and plausible narratives coupled with arguments that are logical, coherent, consistent and non-contradictory (Boland Jr & Tenkasi, 1995). Meanings are effectively altered as these brokers frame their ideas in language or through a metaphor the other can relate to, facilitating the shared understanding of that idea. In the process, the implicit assumptions of the other are surfaced and delicately questioned. It is in this manner that these brokers "perform the conversation" (Rouleau & Balogun, 2011). They therefore bridge knowledge differences by consciously or unconsciously leveraging their capacity for perspective taking to perform delicate "sensemaking work." They take the time to learn the schemas, scripts and socio-cultural dynamics of their epistemic counterparts early on in the relationship through increased conversational interactions. They use these conversational opportunities to understand the "other's" language and socio-cultural systems through language (the target is comfortable with), representations and boundary objects that inhabit their social worlds. The counterparty feels "related to" and the broker becomes accustomed to his/her community's practice norms (Rouleau & Balogun, 2011).

These brokering roles often transform with time and morph into models of shared leadership that are expertise rather than hierarchy-based. Teulier and Rouleau (2013) studied the "translation" practices through which managers and their collaborators from leading firms in the French public works and civil engineering sector make sense of a three-dimensional (3D) design software for the whole sector. By forming a study group in which they familiarize themselves with others through intensive working and writing sessions, industrial visits and so on they use their abilities, connections and their craft knowledge to make sense of a new technology across organizational boundaries. Collaborators in such arrangements nature hold one another accountable in spite of status differences. They also engage in ongoing and generative communication and updating occasioned by propinquity to co-create new knowledge (Tsoukas, 2009).

Although broker roles are enabling, formal roles can limit knowledge collaboration in a variety of ways. For example, if people in the role structure are not collectively responsible for their work, they may focus on individual role responsibilities at the expense of overall work. Also, role occupants may not easily find and communicate with interdependent partners in large groups and there is a tendency the role groups will function as divisive "in-groups" (Valentine & Edmondson, 2014).

The generative promise of the online community

There is a growing interest among IS researchers in the phenomenon of generativity. Generativity is a label that is often affixed to technology and has been most saliently used to characterize digital platforms. A platform is described as generative because it allows different types of actors, typically seller-buyer or consumer-producer pairs, to connect with one another, self-organize and co-create novel solutions. The economic and relational value created by these network effects is superior to that of a traditional value chain because of the unexpected synergies that take place between all the platform participants (Parker, Van Alstyne, & Choudary, 2016). The digital platform is therefore ascribed the generativity label because the underlying technology is malleable, rapidly modifiable and easy to connect to through APIs and other interfaces thereby sustaining a large population of interacting users (Lyytinen, Yoo, & Boland Jr, 2016; Yoo, Boland Jr, Lyytinen, & Majchrzak, 2012; Zittrain, 2008).

We believe that the attribution of generativity to platforms conceals the crucial role played by the online communities (OCs) that inhabit them. While digital platforms host large populations of interacting participants, it is too simplistic and reifying to reduce the rich community dynamics to a by-product of the digital platform. In short, the digital platform cannot be generative in itself, but rather, is propelled by a powerful form of online sociality that enables knowledge flows among participants. This is what makes the OC distinctive as a nexus and "site" of knowledge collaboration. The sociality lends itself to the generative remixing and recombination of knowledge flows on an unprecedented scale. In this regard, the technology can facilitate knowledge collaboration by creating new interaction possibilities and "spaces" for distributed workers who would otherwise face challenges in sharing information and working across boundaries (Beane & Orlikowski, 2015; Jarzabkowski, Le, & Feldman, 2012; Kellogg et al., 2006; Nicolini, 2011). Thus, OCs offer unique collaborative advantages, primarily because they facilitate the four knowledge collaboration mechanisms prevalent in traditional organizations: dialogic practices, boundary objects, collaborative agreements and brokering roles.

First, dialogic exchanges are accelerated in the OC. Because OCs lack the formal hierarchy and controls found in traditional organizational settings, human contribution and collaboration is somewhat freed of social conventions, ownership disputes, and legal constraints. The attenuation of such structural factors, when coupled with enabling platforms creates the possibility of unconstrained knowledge recombination, a degree of innovative collaboration rarely seen in more traditional organizational structures (Faraj et al., 2011). By creating a "space" for contribution that is free of the social norms and constraints that limit unencumbered idea-sharing in traditional contexts, OCs allow for the development of swift trust (Faraj, Von Krogh, Monteiro, & Lakhani, 2016). This swift trust emerges online because community interactions tend to be less calculative or concerned with impact on social relations or organizational politics. In a sense, the weak social context cues encourage participants to engage in more open dialogue. Conversations are likely to be initiated more liberally and with increased frequency. Because contextual details are especially important to situated knowledge work and messages can only be interpreted in relation to other texts or what is already known, participants who post questions are likely to include a variety of relevant information in their posts to communicate a certain question or issue more effectively (Kudaravalli & Faraj, 2008). This prepares the ground for subsequent dialogue while generating interest. The sustained multi-member back-and-forth dialogue that ensues is crucial to the development of the common ground necessary to transcend knowledge boundaries.

Second, the technology supporting the OC can facilitate the representation of boundary objects (e.g., plans, drawings, prototypes, wiki-type entries, trade-off methods) in digital format that is easily shareable. Such representation can be annotated and discussed by large numbers of individuals independent of time zone differences and geographic distance. Digitally represented boundary objects can also provide more effective representation of the input and interests of the various players and thus avoid any unnecessary political struggles down the line. In short, technology can facilitate the negotiation of meaning and the negotiation of differences.

Third, technology can support the emergence and evolution of collaborative agreements. Given the absence of strong social and organizational structures, collaborative agreements play an essential role in sustaining knowledge exchange in the OC. They do so by allowing members to rapidly create FAQs, rules of engagement, guidelines, and membership criteria. Specifically, technology can facilitate the coordination and integration of knowledge by embedding in software the rules for who can contribute to repositories or update the shared work (e.g., version control in open source projects). In addition, reputation systems and moderation roles and responsibilities help reinforce these collaborative agreements.

Fourth, brokering roles are very salient in the OC to compensate for the lack of formal structures. One brokering role may be to bridge with other communities with the purpose of bringing back resources to the focal OC (Dahlander & Frederiksen, 2012). Another is to suppress negative dynamics (e.g., intervene in flame wars) or patrol the OC's boundaries to keep it focused on the agreed-upon topic (e.g., reprimand invaders, remind others of etiquette or intervene when content is clearly inappropriate). Furthermore, the brokering role can involve helping activities aimed at encouraging further engagement and contribution by others in the OC. An important attribute of emerging leaders in a brokering role is that they exhibit communication clarity and can relate to members of engaged OC with more ease (via shared vocabulary and meanings) (Johnson, Safadi, & Faraj, 2015). Overall, these roles are emergent and constantly morphing as per the needs and demands of the community. Additionally, technology provides support for all forms of brokering roles by surfacing and curating new knowledge or by providing rights and privileges for those who are good citizens (e.g., moderator status).

In sum, OCs are emerging as generative spaces where novel forms of knowledge collaboration are unfolding and creating an altered sociality that we have yet to understand deeply. Thus far, what we do know is that the sharing, transformation and co-creation of knowledge is critical to the sustainability of OCs as individuals share and combine their knowledge in ways that benefit them personally, while contributing to the community's overall value (Dahlander & Frederiksen, 2012; Faraj et al., 2011). Yet, despite the importance of knowledge sharing and co-creation in OCs, we know little about how this happens (von Krogh & von Hippel, 2006). A deeper understanding of how accelerated knowledge combination, recombination and integration processes unfold in OCs lies at the heart of new ways of innovating. From this perspective, technology has a leading role to play in facilitating participation and improving the flow of knowledge. Digital platforms can make it easy to seek out like-minded others, sustain the sharing of partial knowledge and facilitate the easy remixing of others' contributions. Through a badge and rating system (also known as gamification), the platform can sustain a history of engagement that allows members to recognize those with higher status or in position of expertise. Further, with the preservation of digital traces (previous contributions and interactions), the knowledge production process is made visible; facilitating the learning of interested others.

What makes the OC of particular interest to scholars of knowing and organizing is its ability to harness human knowledge and innovative potential in new and interesting ways. OCs are increasingly being identified as alternate forms of organizing and innovating. Interestingly, knowledge collaboration in them occurs often despite the absence of the deep social relationships, which are deemed crucial to knowledge transformation and co-creation in traditional organizational contexts (Boland & Tenkasi, 1995; Carlile, 2004; Tsoukas, 2009). That said, OCs create a "generative space partially disembodied from typical structural mechanisms and unencumbered by the social shadows of past and future" (Faraj et al., 2011, p. 2). They also exhibit a strong work ethos, collective work understandings and standards of performance. This is why we suggest that the term "generativity" be reserved for social interactions taking place in the OC. While the OC is clearly empowered and enabled by the affordances of the platform, the essential aspect is the existence of a large group of participants who believe in the goals of the collectivity and who display a level of sociality that enables the sharing, combination and remixing of knowledge.

How expertise is recognized, knowledge integrated and value generated are important issues to understand if we are to examine how innovation unfolds in OCs. These communal spaces where participants the world over come together in the pursuit of open and collaborative innovation have the potential to transform how people and organizations harness human talent to solve pressing problems of any kind. But because many knowledge OCs are utilitarian in nature and have voting and gaming mechanisms as centerpieces of their design to help users identify the trustworthiness and accuracy of the content provided, strong social ties are unlikely to develop. This provides little means by which to translate and transfer knowledge across boundaries (Bechky, 2003; Carlile, 2004). Because communication clarity increases the likelihood of leadership in OCs (e.g., becoming moderator) (Johnson et al., 2015), it makes sense that experts will relate to members of their "conversation" with more ease (via shared vocabulary and meanings). If epistemological boundaries remain very salient in OCs, are OCs realizing their full innovative potential? This opens up a new research agenda on whether OCs are truly innovative, and if so, how they afford users new ways of transforming knowledge absent the formation of strong social ties.

Conclusion and implications

Research has shown that innovation happens at the intersection of diverse disciplines and world views when actors are able to distance themselves from their own paradigms, approach new problems through collective shared understandings and transform existing knowledge. For a variety of reasons we discuss in this chapter, this process of knowledge collaboration is fraught with challenges. Management and organization scholars have spent the last two and half decades gaining a deeper theoretical understanding of how this process unfolds in traditional organizational settings. With the rapid and pervasive advent of transformational information technologies, scholars have called for in-depth empirical investigations of how technology and organizing are mutually shaping and with what consequences. One emerging theoretical lens has directed attention toward the material in studies of social practice. The idea is to examine how materiality can alter and reconstitute human action and vice versa in an ongoing process of "becoming."

In traditional organizations employing pervasive technologies, we have made significant headway in theorizing the role technology. Organization scholars are now paying attention to the material, and technology is leading the charge in terms of the phenomenon of interest. Yet, we still know very little about how the material shapes the process of knowledge collaboration. Other phenomena such as space, our bodies, infrastructure and other "equipment" (Heidegger, 1962) involved in a collective skillful performance remain underexplored, particularly in understanding how knowing shapes and is shaped by the material. For example, because human sayings and doings or *praxis* is central to the creation and recreation of social realities, at the most basic level, *praxis* takes place in and through our situated bodily movements in space and time. So for the social being, the body in its surroundings serves as the primary conduit of engaged agency (Sanders, 1999). Because interaction in practice, broadly speaking, explains in large part *how* we come to know (Lave & Wenger, 1991), the body and the equipment it enrols cannot but be foregrounded in studies of knowing. Yet, to say that we "create knowing as we do what we do in our everyday communities" in and through a nexus of interconnected practices (Nicolini, 2011, p. 603; Schatzki, Knorr-Cetina, & von Savigny, 2001) takes for granted the body's involvement but does not explain exactly how it is implicated in *knowing*. In traditional organizational settings, how material enactments shape the process of knowledge collaboration remains a vital, underexplored area of inquiry.

Empirically, this "relational" inquiry poses methodological challenges that are well-documented (Langley, 1999; Langley, Smallman, Tsoukas, & Van de Ven, 2013). Studies of this nature involve prolonged (often multi-year) in-depth longitudinal engagement in field settings that seldom "stabilize" (from a relational ontological perspective). In addition, because material arrangements do not visibly do the "acting," they often go unnoticed unless they are "yanked" or dramatically altered. Identifying extreme information-rich cases that expose the taken-for-granted role of materiality becomes key to rich theorizing.

In alternate forms of organizing involving online communities, how ideas are shared, combined, recombined and transformed over time remains largely uncharted. One helpful way to direct this research agenda is to compare these communities with more traditional organizational contexts. A hallmark of OCs, for example, is that they bring together people with no preexisting social ties. In traditional contexts, innovation is more likely to occur when people from different epistemologies can transcend and reconcile their differences through social processes. In utilitarian, knowledge-focused OCs or open crowdsourcing contexts, it is unclear what role deep social ties have in shaping the knowledge recombination trajectories of open innovating. This is because actors have no prior social ties and fleeting, expertise-focused interactions borne out of gamification incentives provide little mechanisms for interpersonal ties to develop.

The challenge in studying OC phenomena is not one of access. In fact, the research lure of unfettered data access can be misleading and result in what some have termed "light post research." The ability to scrape and acquire large swathes of data has eroded "analysis barriers." Data mining, cleaning and sorting is becoming increasingly commoditized and outsourceable, particularly to computer scientists. The challenge for social scientists will be to make sense of the formidable amounts of real-time "trace data." This can only be done through focused, rigorous analysis aimed at answering pressing research questions through in-depth theorizing. Where scholars of organizing and technology can play a pivotal role is in understanding *how* people share, transfer and transform knowledge in and through OCs that do not rely on the formation of interpersonal relationships. Is this a new form of sociality that propels innovating, or are OCs far from realizing their innovative potential? What are the consequences of these potential findings for collaborative affordances of OCs and post-bureaucratic organizations? The answers to these questions have the potential to transform what we know about how new knowledge is co-created and how innovating unfolds in these novel contexts.

Note

1 This is by no means an exhaustive list of knowledge coordination mechanisms. Routines, rules and protocols, for example, are intentionally omitted because they were classically conceptualized as more "planned" forms of coordination.

References

Anderson, J.R. 1984. Cognitive Psychology. *Artificial Intelligence*, 23(1): 1–11.
Balogun, J., Gleadle, P., Hailey, V.H., & Willmott, H. 2005. Managing Change Across Boundaries: Boundary-Shaking Practices. *British Journal of Management*, 16(4): 261–278.
Barley, S.R. 1986. Technology as an Occasion for Structuring: Evidence from Observations of CT Scanners and the Social Order of Radiology Departments. *Administrative Science Quarterly*, 31(1): 78–108.
Barrett, M., Oborn, E., Orlikowski, W.J., & Yates, J. 2012. Reconfiguring Boundary Relations: Robotic Innovations in Pharmacy Work. *Organization Science*, 23(5): 1448–1466.
Beane, M. & Orlikowski, W. 2015. What Difference Does a Robot Make? The Material Enactment of Distributed Coordination. *Organization Science*, 26(6): 1553–1573.
Bechky, B.A. 2003. Sharing Meaning Across Occupational Communities: The Transformation of Understanding on a Production Floor. *Organization Science*, 14(3): 312–330.

Bechky, B. A. & Okhuysen, G. A. 2011. Expecting the Unexpected? How SWAT Officers and Film Crews Handle Surprises. *Academy of Management Journal*, 54(2): 239–261.

Boland, R. J. & Tenkasi, R. V. 1995. Perspective Making and Perspective Taking in Communities of Knowing. *Organization Science*, 6(4): 350–372.

Carlile, P. R. 2002. A Pragmatic View of Knowledge and Boundaries: Boundary Objects in New Product Development. *Organization Science*, 13(4): 442–455.

Carlile, P. R. 2004. Transferring, Translating, and Transforming: An Integrative Framework for Managing Knowledge Across Boundaries. *Organization Science*, 15(5): 555–568.

Cyert, R. M. & March, J. G. 1963. *A Behavioral Theory of the Firm*. Englewood Cliffs, NJ: Prentice-Hall.

D'Adderio, L. 2011. Artifacts at the Centre of Routines: Performing the Material Turn in Routines Theory. *Journal of Institutional Economics*, 7(Special Issue 2): 197–230.

Dahlander, L. & Frederiksen, L. 2012. The Core and Cosmopolitans: A Relational View of Innovation in User Communities. *Organization Science*, 23(4): 988–1007.

Dougherty, D. 1992. Interpretive Barriers to Successful Product Innovation in Large Firms. *Organization Science*, 3(2): 179–202.

Duguid, P. 2005. "The Art of Knowing": Social and Tacit Dimensions of Knowledge and the Limits of the Community of Practice. *Information Society*, 21(2): 109–118.

Edmondson, A. C. 1999. Psychological Safety and Learning Behavior in Work Teams. *Administrative Science Quarterly*, 44(2): 350–383.

Emirbayer, M. 1997. Manifesto for a Relational Sociology. *American Journal of Sociology*, 103(2): 281–317.

Faraj, S. & Azad, B. 2012. The Materiality of Technology: An Affordance Perspective. In P. M. Leonardi, B. Nardi & J. Kallinikos (Eds.), *Materiality and Organizing: Social Interaction in a Technological World*: 237–258. Ann Arbor: University of Michigan Press.

Faraj, S., Jarvenpaa, S. L., & Majchrzak, A. 2011. Knowledge Collaboration in Online Communities. *Organization Science*, 22(5): 1224–1239.

Faraj, S., Sproull, L. S., Constant, D., & Kiesler, S. 2000. Coordinating Expertise in Software Development Teams. *Management Science*, 46(12): 1554–1568.

Faraj, S., Von Krogh, G., Monteiro, E., & Lakhani, K. R. 2016. Online Community as Space for Knowledge Flows. *Information Systems Research*.

Faraj, S. & Xiao, Y. 2006. Coordination in Fast-Response Organizations. *Management Science*, 52(8): 1155–1169.

Faraj, S. & Yan, A. 2009. Boundary Work in Knowledge Teams. *Journal of Applied Psychology*, 94(3): 604–617.

Feldman, M. S., & Orlikowski, W. J. 2011. Theorizing Practice and Practicing Theory. *Organization Science*, 22(5): 1240–1253.

Galbraith, J. R. 1973. *Designing Complex Organizations*. Boston, MA: Addison-Wesley Longman.

Galbraith, J. R. 1977. *Organizational Design*. Reading, MA: Addison-Wesley.

Hargadon, A. B. & Bechky, B. A. 2006. When Collections of Creatives Become Creative Collectives: A Field Study of Problem Solving at Work. *Organization Science*, 17(4): 484–500.

Heidegger, M. 1962. *Being and Time*. Oxford: Basil Blackwell.

Huber, G. P., O'Connell, M. J., & Cummings, L. L. 1975. Perceived Environmental Uncertainty: Effects of Information and Structure. *Academy of Management Journal*, 18(4): 725–740.

Hutchby, I. 2001. Technologies, Texts and Affordances. *Sociology*, 35(2): 441–456.

Jarzabkowski, P., Le, J. K., & Feldman, M. S. 2012. Toward a Theory of Coordinating: Creating Coordinating Mechanisms in Practice. *Organization Science*, 23(4): 907–927.

Jehn, K. A., Northcraft, G. B., & Neale, M. A. 1999. Why Differences Make a Difference: A Field Study of Diversity, Conflict and Performance in Workgroups. *Administrative Science Quarterly*, 44(4): 741–763.

Johnson, S. L., Safadi, H., & Faraj, S. 2015. The Emergence of Online Community Leadership. *Information Systems Research*, 26(1): 165–187.

Kellogg, K. C., Orlikowski, W. J., & Yates, J. 2006. Life in the Trading Zone: Structuring Coordination Across Boundaries in Post-Bureaucratic Organizations. *Organization Science*, 17(1): 22–44.

Klein, K. J., Ziegert, J. C., Knight, A. P., & Xiao, Y. 2006. Dynamic Delegation: Shared, Hierarchical, and Deindividualized Leadership in Extreme Action Teams. *Administrative Science Quarterly*, 51(4): 590–621.

Knorr-Cetina, K. 1997. Sociality With Objects: Social Relations in Post-Social Knowledge Societies. *Theory Culture and Society*, 14: 1–30.

Kogut, B. & Zander, U. 1992. Knowledge of the Firm, Combinative Capabilities, and the Replication of Technology. *Organization Science*, 3(3): 383–397.

Kudaravalli, S. & Faraj, S. 2008. The Structure of Collaboration in Electronic Networks. *Journal of the Association for Information Systems*, 9(10/11): 706.

Langley, A. 1999. Strategies for Theorizing From Process Data. *Academy of Management Review*, 24(4): 691–710.

Langley, A., Smallman, C., Tsoukas, H., & Van de Ven, A. H. 2013. Process Studies of Change in Organization and Management: Unveiling Temporality, Activity and Flow. *Academy of Management Journal*, 56(1): 1–13.

Lave, J. & Wenger, E. 1991. *Situated Learning: Legitimate Peripheral Participation*: Cambridge: Cambridge University Press.

Lawrence, P. & Lorsch, J. 1967a. *Organization and Environment*. Hayward, IL: Irwin Press.

Lawrence, P. & Lorsch, J. 1967b. Differentiation and Integration in Complex Organizations. *Administrative Science Quarterly*: 1–47.

Leonard-Barton, D. 1995. *Wellsprings of Knowledge: Building and Sustaining the Sources of Innovation*. Cambridge, MA: Harvard Business Press.

Lyytinen, K., Yoo, Y., & Boland Jr, R. J. 2016. Digital Product Innovation With Four Classes of Innovation Networks. *Information Systems Journal*.

Majchrzak, A., More, P. H., & Faraj, S. 2012. Transcending Knowledge Differences in Cross-Functional Teams. *Organization Science*, 23(4): 951–970.

March, J. G. & Simon, H. A. 1958. *Organizations*. Oxford, England: Wiley.

McAllister, D. J. 1995. Affect- and Cognition-Based Trust as Foundations for Interpersonal Cooperation in Organizations. *Academy of Management Journal*, 38(1): 24–59.

Möllering, G. 2001. The Nature of Trust: From Georg Simmel to a Theory of Expectation, Interpretation and Suspension. *Sociology*, 35(2): 403–420.

Newell, A. & Simon, H. A. 1972. *Human Problem Solving*. Englewood Cliffs, NJ: Prentice-Hall.

Nicolini, D. 2011. Practice as the Site of Knowing: Insights from the Field of Telemedicine. *Organization Science*, 22(3): 602–620.

Nicolini, D., Mengis, J., & Swan, J. 2012. Understanding the Role of Objects in Cross-Disciplinary Collaboration. *Organization Science*, 23(3): 612–629.

Nonaka, I. 1994. A Dynamic Theory of Organizational Knowledge Creation. *Organization Science*, 5(1): 14–37.

Nonaka, I. & Von Krogh, G. 2009. Perspective-Tacit Knowledge and Knowledge Conversion: Controversy and Advancement in Organizational Knowledge Creation Theory. *Organization Science*, 20(3): 635–652.

Okhuysen, G. A. & Bechky, B. A. 2009. Coordination in Organizations: An Integrative Perspective. *Academy of Management Annals*, 3(1): 463–502.

Orlikowski, W. J. 2002. Knowing in Practice: Enacting a Collective Capability in Distributed Organizing. *Organization Science*, 13(3): 249–273.

Parker, G., Van Alstyne, M., & Choudary, S. 2016. *Platform Revolution*. New York: W. W. Norton.

Polanyi, M. 1966. *The Tacit Dimension*. London: Routledge & Kegan Paul.

Rico, R., Sánchez-Manzanares, M., Gil, F., & Gibson, C. 2008. Team Implicit Coordination Processes: A Team Knowledge-Based Approach. *Academy of Management Review*, 33(1): 163–184.

Rouleau, L. & Balogun, J. 2011. Middle Managers, Strategic Sensemaking, and Discursive Competence. *Journal of Management Studies*, 48(5): 953–983.

Sanders, J. T. 1999. Affordances: An Ecological Approach to First Philosophy. In G. Weiss & H. Haber (Eds.), *Perspectives on Embodiment: The Intersections of Nature and Culture*: 121–142. London: Routledge.

Schatzki, T. R., Knorr-Cetina, K., & von Savigny, E. 2001. *The Practice Turn in Contemporary Theory*. London: Routledge.

Simon, H. A. 1999. The Many Shapes of Knowledge. *Revue d'économie industrielle*, 88(1): 23–39.

Star, S. L. 2010. This Is Not a Boundary Object: Reflections on the Origin of a Concept. *Science, Technology & Human Values*, 35(5): 601–617.

Star, S. L. & Griesemer, J. R. 1989. Institutional Ecology, Translations' and Boundary Objects: Amateurs and Professionals in Berkeley's Museum of Vertebrate Zoology, 1907–39. *Social Studies of Science*, 19(3): 387–420.

Starbuck, W. H. 1992. Learning by Knowledge Intensive Firms. *Journal of Management Studies*, 29(6): 713–740.

Szulanski, G. 1996. Exploring Internal Stickiness: Impediments to the Transfer of Best Practice Within the Firm. *Strategic Management Journal*, 17(S2): 27–43.

Teulier, R. & Rouleau, L. 2013. Middle Managers' Sensemaking and Interorganizational Change Initiation: Translation Spaces and Editing Practices. *Journal of Change Management*, 13(3): 308–337.

Thomas, R., Sargent, L.D., & Hardy, C. 2011. Managing Organizational Change: Negotiating Meaning and Power-Resistance Relations. *Organization Science*, 22(1): 22–41.

Thompson, J.D. 1967. *Organizations in Action*. New York: McGraw-Hill.

Tsoukas, H. 1996. The Firm as a Distributed Knowledge System: A Constructionist Approach. *Strategic Management Journal*, 17(Winter): 11–25.

Tsoukas, H. 2009. A Dialogical Approach to the Creation of New Knowledge in Organizations. *Organization Science*, 20(6): 941–957.

Tsoukas, H. & Chia, R. 2002. On Organizational Becoming: Rethinking Organizational Change. *Organization Science*, 13(5): 567–582.

Tuertscher, P., Garud, R., & Kumaraswamy, A. 2014. Justification and Interlaced Knowledge at ATLAS, CERN. *Organization Science*, 25(6): 1579–1608.

Tushman, M.L. 1977. Special Boundary Roles in the Innovation Process. *Administrative Science Quarterly*: 587–605.

Tushman, M.L. & Nadler, D.A. 1978. Information Processing as an Integrating Concept in Organizational Design. *Academy of Management Review*, 3(3): 613–624.

Valentine, M.A. & Edmondson, A.C. 2014. Team Scaffolds: How Mesolevel Structures Enable Role-Based Coordination in Temporary Groups. *Organization Science*, 26(2): 405–422.

Van De Ven, A.H., Delbecq, Andre L., & Koenig, R. 1976. Determinants of Coordination Modes within Organizations. *American Sociological Review*, 41(2): 322–338.

von Krogh, G. & von Hippel, E. 2006. The Promise of Research on Open Source Software. *Management Science*, 52(7): 975–983.

Weick, K.E. & Kiesler, C.A. 1979. *The Social Psychology of Organizing*. New York: Random House.

Weick, K.E. & Roberts, K.H. 1993. Collective Mind and Organizational Reliability: The Case of Flight Operations on an Aircraft Carrier Deck. *Administrative Science Quarterly*, 38(3): 357–381. doi:10.2307/2393372

Weick, K.E. & Sutcliffe, K.M. 2007. *Managing the Unexpected*. Hoboken, NJ: Jossey-Bass.

Whyte, J. & Harty, C. 2012. Socio-material Practices of Design Coordination: Objects as Plastic and Partisan. In P.M. Leonardi, B.A. Nardi & J. Kallinikos (Eds.), *Materiality and Organizing: Social Interaction in a Technological World*: 196–212. Oxford: Oxford University Press.

Yoo, Y., Boland Jr, R.J., Lyytinen, K., & Majchrzak, A. 2012. Organizing for Innovation in the Digitized World. *Organization Science*, 23(5): 1398–1408.

Zammuto, R.F., Griffith, T.L., Majchrzak, A., Dougherty, D.J., & Faraj, S. 2007. Information Technology and the Changing Fabric of Organization. *Organization Science*, 18(5): 749–762.

Zittrain, J.L. 2008. *The Future of the Internet – And How to Stop It*. New Haven: Yale University Press: Yale University Press.

Zuboff, S. 1988. *In the Age of the Smart Machine: The Future of Work and Power*. New York: Basic Books.

PART 4

IS in society and a global context
Emerging – and continuing – issues and controversies

Introduction

As IT is becoming more ubiquitous and permeating every aspect of society, organisations, work, entertainment, education and everyday life, considerations of its impacts and implications are becoming increasingly critical. IT is often behind the most ingenious and societally beneficial innovations (e.g., peer-to-peer microloans), the facilitator of the darkest instincts of human nature (cyberbullying, revenge porn, online hate speech and racism), as well as the frequent unintended mess-ups in between (e.g., mistaken collective identification of terrorism suspects online, such as in the case of Boston Marathon bombing). The IS field has much to contribute to the investigation of such topics, but is not always perceived as the thought leader (see also Chapter 31 by Ning Su, John King and Jonathan Grudin). With that in mind, we have compiled in Part 4 an exciting array of thought-provoking, novel and trend-setting articles that we hope can blaze the way for the field to thrive and lead in the turbulent transformational times ahead.

The theme of datification, big data and the power of analytics is picked up and developed by Stella Pachidi and Marleen Huysman in their chapter on how more data and analytics insights can make organisations smarter, but also lead to new kinds of breakdowns in learning. For example, by relying too much on analytics, organisations risk becoming path dependent and bounded by their very own information-producing devices, leading to superstitious learning. Importantly, in the age of data abundance where intelligent, rational and informed decision making is the norm, Stella and Marleen remind us that organisations may also need "technologies of foolishness" – to experiment with outliers, deviate from the norm and foster creativity.

We continue with Chapter 26 by Sue Newell and Marco Marabelli, who set the scene with a discussion of one of the major trends in society and businesses that is both enthusiastically embraced and highly controversial: algorithmic decision making. Datification of everything (Brynjolfsson and McAfee, 2014) has resulted in a situation where smart algorithms guide our lives often without us knowing or noticing; algorithms personalise and predict everything from our news consumption, insurance payments and loan offers to our medical needs and career trajectories (Ha-Thuc et al., 2016; Schildt, 2016; Ziewitz, 2016). Sue and Marco highlight how privacy concerns and discrimination are two of the important negative side effects of this state of affairs and suggest a way forward that does not rely purely on top-down regulation and legal protections, but also on bottom-up consumer behaviour that through demand and supply can prioritise privacy and fairness among consumers and service providers.

From the world of ubiquitous IT, we then move to two chapters examining the persistent inequalities haunting the digital revolution. First, Maria Skaletsky, James Pick, Avijit Sarkar and David Yates offer an up-to-date overview of the various digital divides characteristic to both developed and developing countries. Inequalities are not just related to material resources such as infrastructure and access to computers and the Internet, but also to the differences in digital skills and degree of technology use. While some kinds of digital divides (e.g., in terms of access) are diminishing, new kinds of divides appear as the economy, work and labour are digitally transformed. For example, as highlighted in the chapter, crowdworking platforms provide paid labour and flexibility to tech-savvy workers in developing countries, but still marginalise those who are unemployed and with lower educational levels because of the power imbalance between the crowdworkers and job providers (see also Deng et al., 2016). Chrisanthi Avgerou and Atta Addo (Chapter 28) continue the investigation by critically reflecting on the socio-economic benefits that ICT innovations have had in developing countries. They highlight the danger of expectations and predictions that build on technologically deterministic thinking that sees such benefits as deriving from technological potential alone. Rather, they advocate for the consideration of complex relationships between technological potential and the social actors that use the technologies, as well as the broader socio-technical structures in which these actors are embedded.

The divides, inequalities and unintended negative consequences associated with digital transformation are not the only challenges facing society and the IS field. Two of the key challenges increasingly discussed in both academic and practitioner literature relate to those of digital technology, work and labour, and digital technology and the economy. Accordingly, we have included two insightful chapters on these topics.

Changes in the nature of work and labour are at the forefront of the challenges policymakers and academics foresee in the next decades (Cappelli and Keller, 2013; Forman, King and Lyytinen, 2014). Concerns include, for example, automation-induced unemployment (Frey and Osborne, 2017) and widespread experiences of technostress and dissatisfaction at work (Ayyagari et al., 2011; Tarafdar et al., 2007). As Carsten Sørensen points out in Chapter 29, the challenges are exacerbated by the complex dynamics between what he calls computing in the small, computing in the large and computing at scale. While computing in the small (e.g., constant connectivity through smartphones) has introduced many paradoxes for the individual worker (Mazmanian et al., 2013), such changes are not independent from larger-scale dynamics. For example, as described by Carsten, in the digital age data from a motion tracker on someone's arm (computing in the small) can easily be combined with other digital behavior patterns, informing novel workforce optimisation tools (computing in the large). Such digital dynamics raise much broader questions concerning individual privacy, ownership of data, the distribution of effort and rewards, and the general marketisation of individuals, in what has been characterised as surveillance capitalism (computing at scale) (Zuboff, 2015). The changes digitalisation is introducing to the economy as a whole (computing at scale) is further developed and examined by Roman Beck in Chapter 30. In particular, Roman takes a closer look at blockchain technology – often touted as a game-changer, particularly in the financial industry. Roman explains how blockchain is more than just the technology underlying Bitcoin, but may through its fundamental principles as a distributed ledger system become the operation system of the service economy, providing the governance structure, enforceability of business logics, and accountability of the connected service systems, thereby minimising the need for inter-organisational trust. On an individual level, it may also provide ways to decentralise ownership of data and for individuals to manage and retain control over any transactions with their data (Zyskind and Nathan, 2015). Coming back to Sue and Marco's Chapter 26, blockchain may just be the technology to facilitate the sought-after bottom-up consumer behaviour that through demand and supply can prioritise privacy and fairness among consumers and service providers. Yet, heeding Chrisanthi and Atta's warnings, the potential does not guarantee the outcome. Much work remains to be done by IS scholars to drive this positive impact.

We end Part 4 – and the book – with an imaginative, scary and magical chapter by Ning Su, John Leslie King and Jonathan Grudin. Reflecting on the state of the IS field, Ning, John and Jonathan summon the army of the Undead to help drive across the point that we – as the scholars who make up the Information Systems field – should strive for more than just staying alive. They consider some of the metaphorical Frankensteins, vampires and zombies haunting the field (the rigour–relevance debate that just refuses to die being one of them) and set forth a few ideas on how the field could move past the liminal zone between life and death toward truly thriving. The path is neither easy nor clear, but we have the rather immodest hope that this book, and its collection of "very much alive" papers, can provide some guidance.

References

Ayyagari, R., Grover, V., & Purvis, R. (2011). Technostress: Technological antecedents and implications. *MIS Quarterly, 35*(4), 831–858.

Brynjolfsson, E., & McAfee, A. (2014). *The second machine age: Work, progress, and prosperity in a time of brilliant technologies*. New York: W. W. Norton.

Cappelli, P., & Keller, J.R. (2013). Classifying work in the new economy. *Academy of Management Review, 38*(4), 575–596.

Deng, X., Joshi, K.D., & Galliers, R.D. (2016). The duality of empowerment and marginalization in microtask crowdsourcing: Giving voice to the less powerful through value sensitive design. *MIS Quarterly, 40*(2), 279–302.

Forman, C., King, J.L., & Lyytinen, K. (2014). Special section introduction – information, technology, and the changing nature of work. *Information Systems Research, 25*(4), 789–795.

Frey, C.B., & Osborne, M.A. (2017). The future of employment: How susceptible are jobs to computerisation? *Technological Forecasting and Social Change, 114*, 254–280.

Ha-Thuc, V., Xu, Y., Kanduri, S.P., Wu, X., Dialani, V., Yan, Y., . . . & Sinha, S. (2016). Search by ideal candidates: Next generation of talent search at LinkedIn. In *Proceedings of the 25th International Conference Companion on World Wide Web* (pp. 195–198).

Mazmanian, M., Orlikowski, W.J., & Yates, J. (2013). The autonomy paradox: The implications of mobile email devices for knowledge professionals. *Organization Science, 24*(5), 1337–1357.

Schildt, H. (2016). Big data and organizational design – the brave new world of algorithmic management and computer augmented transparency. *Innovation: Organization & Management*, advanced online publication, 1–8.

Tarafdar, M., Tu, Q., Ragu-Nathan, B.S., & Ragu-Nathan, T.S. (2007). The impact of technostress on role stress and productivity. *Journal of Management Information Systems, 24*(1), 301–328.

Ziewitz, M. (2016). Governing algorithms myth, mess, and methods. *Science, Technology & Human Values, 41*(1), 3–16.

Zuboff, S. (2015). Big other: Surveillance capitalism and the prospects of an information civilization. *Journal of Information Technology, 30*(1), 75–89.

Zyskind, G., & Nathan, O. (2015). Decentralizing privacy: Using blockchain to protect personal data. In *Security and Privacy Workshops (SPW), 2015 IEEE* (pp. 180–184). IEEE.

25
ORGANIZATIONAL INTELLIGENCE IN THE DIGITAL AGE
Analytics and the cycle of choice

Stella Pachidi and Marleen Huysman

Introduction

Analytics is said to be the key for organizational success in the digital era (Davenport and Harris 2007), helping organizations transition from myopic to holistic (Winig 2016), become smarter (Davenport, Harris, and Morison 2010) and gain competitive advantage (Ransbotham, Kiron, and Prentice 2015). While this sounds promising enough to put analytics on the top of CIOs' agendas (Forni 2016) and to awaken the interest of researchers in the field of information systems (Chen et al. 2012) and management (George, Haas, and Pentland 2014), some prudence may be necessary before we all jump on the bandwagon bringing us straight to a data-driven wonderland. It is generally accepted that analytics, even though perhaps at a more mature stage, will be here to stay (Ghoshal, Menon, and Sarkar 2015). This implies a call to academics, to be more reflective about how the topic is studied and first of all to unpack assumptions that have given boost to its present popularity; in particular: *does analytics indeed make organizations more intelligent?*

Going back to the behavioral theory of the firm (Cyert and March 1963) may help us in this inquiry. The behavioral theory of the firm has an enormous influence in the field of organizational intelligence, in particular through decision making and organizational adaptation. From this theoretical perspective, organizational intelligence has been related with making choices through two fundamental processes: rational calculation of alternatives and their consequences to choose the optimal alternative, and learning from past experience to choose among present alternatives (March and Olsen 1975). These two processes take place by processing information gathered internally in the organization and from the external environment. Rationality entails acting based on a thorough examination of alternatives and their consequences, which is done by gathering information, while organizational learning (i.e., modifying rules and actions) based on past experience (March and Olsen 1975) is used to replace or to augment the search for information while pursuing intelligent organizational action. Rational choice making as well as organizational learning involve inferences from information, and may therefore be imperfect if organizations are bounded by cognitive limits, time available to search for the information and so forth (Levinthal and March 1993; March 1994; Simon 1976). Analytics is believed to reduce such boundedness by supporting a complete examination of the choice alternatives and their consequences and in making sense of past actions and their consequences, due to the information processing capabilities that it offers (Clark et al. 2007; Davenport 2009; Winig 2016). Thus, analytics is assumed to make organizations more intelligent by increasing rational action and adaptation to the environment based on past experiences.

We will investigate this assumption by using the cycle of choice framework as it has been developed by March and Olsen (1975). The framework is based on the ideal situation of full rationality and unboundedness in which intelligent organizations learn by making choices following a closed cycle of connections between the beliefs held by individuals, the individual behavior, the organizational choices and the responses from the environment. However, given that information is seldom complete, difficult to interpret and often distorted, the steps that organizations take to learn are often broken down, which results in organizations learning in a bounded and irrational way. If indeed analytics makes organizations more intelligent, this would mean that the use of analytics helps fixing the breaks in the cycle of choice. In this chapter, we take a closer look at this assumption.

The technology of analytics

With the term *analytics* we refer to the set of practices, skills, techniques and technologies, such as analyzing past behavior, predictive modeling and optimization, which are employed by organizations to extract actionable insights from data and steer decisions and actions (Bose 2009; Davenport and Harris 2007; Davenport et al. 2010). A common example of using analytics is the employment of market basket analysis (Kumar and Rao 2006) by Walmart, with the goal to learn from the purchase behavior of customers and to improve their sales promotions, store design and so forth.

The vast development and use of various information systems and the increased digitization have significantly increased the amount of data that is available to organizations (McAfee and Brynjolfsson 2012; Constantiou and Kallinikos 2014). Unavoidably, analytics has been established as one of the most influential technologies in our era (Luftman et al. 2015), as it is considered indispensable to leverage the value of big data (Chen, Chiang, and Storey 2012) and to make organizations survive and succeed in highly competitive and constantly changing environments (Davenport and Harris 2007). Most enthusiasm has concentrated on the argument that analytics helps organizations become more intelligent (Clark, Jones, and Armstrong 2007; Davenport et al. 2010; Kiron, Shockley, Kruschwitz, Finch, and Haydock 2012), and transform their ways of acting from myopic and reactive to holistic and proactive (Winig 2016). Some criticism has been expressed regarding organizations investing in analytics yet failing to transform their organizational processes and to act based on the data analytics insights, for example, because of lacking management support, or insufficient appropriate skills and understanding for how to use analytics, or unsupportive organizational culture (Ransbotham et al. 2015). Nevertheless, the assumption is that if organizations overcome such barriers, they will be able to make better informed decisions and learn from their past experience more effectively, and thus become more intelligent and succeed with analytics (Davenport and Harris 2007; Petrini and Pozzebon 2009).

Analytics is closely related to decision support systems (Arnott and Pervan 2014), which include techniques for providing an automated solution to a certain problem with a specified set of data and a specific model. It is also closely related to business intelligence (Chen et al. 2012), which focuses on techniques for accessing, reporting and monitoring information. The main difference with those (older) technologies is that analytics includes more fine-tuned data mining techniques customized to analyze various problems, to explain why things are happening in a certain way and to project what will happen next (Sharma, Reynolds, Scheepers, Seddon, and Shanks 2010).

The study of analytics in organizations necessitates also studying the use of algorithms that are either included in commercial software packages such as SAS or custom-made by data analysts in order to query, construct, preprocess and analyze the datasets. Acting based on analytics is related to an algorithmic way of managing the organization (Newell and Marabelli 2015), that is, sense-making, making choices and acting while adhering to the outcomes of algorithms. Such algorithms are often black-boxed, in the sense that they encapsulate the knowledge frames of the analysts that are not shared with the rest of the organization (Pollock and Williams 2011). As a result, organizational members have to sense-make through representations (created by the algorithms included in the analytics code), and to follow actions based on analytics insights, without fully understanding how those representations and insights were created.

The technology of analytics brings along the need for new skills in the organization. It has even necessitated the new profession of "data scientist" (Davenport and Patil 2012), that requires highly analytical skills and the ability to extract the correct datasets and to apply the appropriate techniques with the goal to find patterns in the data. To succeed in analytics, organizations need to employ a variety of skills (Bose 2009) including data management, technology, statistical modeling and analytical, business knowledge and communication skills.

Analytics and the cycle of choice

In *Behavioral Theory of the Firm*, Cyert and March (1963) view organizations as intendedly rational systems; that is, organizations tend to learn and adapt their behavior based on past experience and experience of others (Levitt and March 1988). Building on this notion, March and Olsen (1975) introduced a model of "complete cycle of organizational choice" (p. 149), to analyze organizational learning by adaptation. The model assumes that ideally organizations can act as fully rational and make decisions based on "perfect" information. Specifically, the rational cycle of choice assumes that (1) individuals make interpretations based on complete information about the environment, (2) changes in individual actions follow from adapting fully to these changes in interpretations, (3) organizational actions are informed by these individual actions, and (4) actions of the environment in turn are assumed to be reactions to these changed organizational actions.

Let us introduce here an example of organizational learning that we will use in the rest of our analysis. Telecom is a telecommunications organization serving businesses with telephony and Internet services. The sales department of Telecom performs business-to-business sales by employing account managers. An account manager serves a set of business customers by being in frequent contact with them and making sure they are offered the portfolios that fit their needs. In the ideal situation, organizational learning in Telecom would take place while performing full cycles of choice: each account manager would have complete information and could fully understand why certain customers churn to competitors, while others retain or even upgrade their contacts. This individual understanding would inform the way each account manager approaches the customers, as well as the pricing, portfolio roadmapping, marketing and other strategic activities that Telecom performs. The organizational actions would eventually influence a response from the customers (e.g., ordering a new portfolio), and this would feed back to the individual understanding of the account managers, and the cycle would continue.

However, adapting to experience based on "perfect" information is highly problematic, as organizations face bounded rationality (March & Simon, 1958). For example, in the case

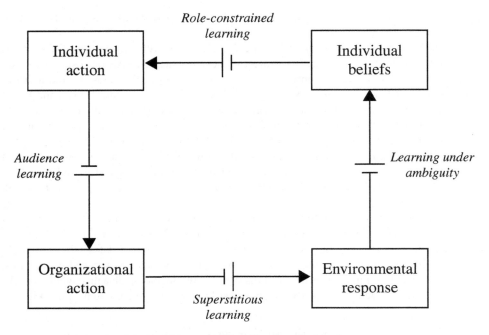

Figure 25.1 The cycle of choice with organizational learning dysfunctions

of Telecom, it is often hard to have complete information to understand the way its business customers behave, because there are various factors that influence a company's telecom and IT choices. March and Olsen (1975) consider several instances of incomplete learning, in which information processing is ambiguous. These cases of dysfunctional learning (Kim 1993) are represented by breakdowns in the cycle and include role-constrained learning, audience learning, superstitious learning and learning under ambiguity. The cycle with the breakdowns is depicted in Figure 25.1.

The breakdowns in the cycle of choice emerge because the organizations often face difficulties in acquiring or understanding information perfectly. Because analytics helps analyze vast amounts of data and produces valuable insights, it can be assumed that analytics may help reduce the occurrence of breakdowns in the cycle, and consequently make organizations more intelligent. In the next paragraphs, we unpack this assumption by investigating each case of dysfunctional learning, to examine whether analytics will help avoid the dysfunctions, or whether it may create new ones.

Learning under ambiguity

Learning under ambiguity happens when individuals learn and modify their understanding while being faced with ambiguity about what happened in the environment (March and Olsen, 1975). Individuals change their views and beliefs but without fully understanding what happened or why it happened. The modified beliefs drive their individual actions, which then influence organizational actions. Consequently, the organization learns and adapts its behavior under ambiguity.

As analytics provide visualization capabilities and multidimensional analysis, they may support making sense of the environment (Chung et al. 2005), and therefore help reduce uncertainty in individual and organizational actions (Clark et al. 2007). In the example of Telecom, using analytics in sales could help account managers have a more complete view about their customers' behavior, actions and preferences, and learn what approaches and actions are needed to keep them from churning to competitors, and to increase sales.

However, analytics may have a reverse effect if individuals rely too much on analytics: while in today's world the problems of computer illiteracy are gone, a new illiteracy is emerging, one that can be called algorithmic illiteracy: even if organizational members know how to use digital tools, they often remain unaware of the algorithms that are encapsulated in them. This could limit their interpretation of analytics insights. Getting lost in the translation of analytics insights into action yields learning under ambiguity.

Next to that, by creating an analytical model, people tend to treat it later as "objective" information, while there is a lot of subjectivity in the way models are constructed. However, quantitative methods also have their limits (Phillips 2003; Yoo 2015). "The factors that enter decision making are often so numerous and complex as well as individual specific that it is hard to conceive of a probability space large enough to capture all of the determining factors accurately" (Phillips 2003: C39). The algorithms for collecting, processing and analyzing the data are most often not created by the individuals who act upon them. This means that they may not encapsulate their own beliefs and experiences, but instead include rules based on the beliefs and biases of the data scientist who developed them (Nature Publishing Group 2016). By making sense of the environment only through data representations, individuals' own mental representations are eventually altered and their capacity to learn is reduced (Constantiou and Kallinikos 2014). Think of the example of Telecom's sales department: the analytics algorithms often do not capture the personal relationship between account managers and their customers, while this is an important source for understanding customer behavior better. In that case, if account managers relied too much on the analytics, they would learn under ambiguity – even though they may not be aware of it. Overall, if organizations use analytics yet treat it as a black box, learning under ambiguity may increase, and may cause severe long-term consequences.

Role-constrained learning

Role-constrained learning occurs when the link between individual beliefs and actions is broken down (March and Olsen 1975). That is to say, individuals learn and change their beliefs and interpretations, but they are constrained in modifying their individual behavior accordingly, because of their role descriptions, rigid bureaucratic rules, and standard operating procedure. Still, the organization in general learns, without knowing that the knowledge of individuals is different from what they put in action. This case of dysfunctional learning often results in organizational inertia. Let us go back to the example of Telecom and its sales department: account managers have direct contact with their customers and can therefore see what problems they face, when their preferences change and why this happens. Ideally, this should entail changing the services and prices that they offer to their customers, in order to make sure the customers remain satisfied and do not churn to a competitor. However, if the organization is organized in silos, most probably the account manager's job description does not allow for influencing how the offered services are structured into portfolios, or how they are priced. In that case, account managers realize that they need to change the way they serve their customers' needs, yet they are bounded in doing so. The individual has learned but cannot put this learning in action and thus limits the potential for the organization to adapt to individual local and situated experiences.

Analytics may help reduce role-constrained learning because it is expected to increase organizational agility and help fight inertia by providing timely information to the organization on how rules and routines need to be adapted (Davenport 2014). In a data-driven culture, if we assume that individual learning takes place with the help of analytics, the organization will be willing to adjust its structure, roles description and operating procedures to reflect the changes recommended by the analytics insights. In that case, individual learning can be better aligned with individual actions and further influence the organizational actions. In the example of Telecom, we could assume that using analytics to analyze the customers would inform the organization that the account managers need to have more flexibility in the way they serve the customers the offers that they make to them, and would allow them to provide more customized portfolios.

On the other hand, by relying too much on analytics, a reversed situation might happen in which role-constrained learning is reinforced. If individuals are expected to act solely based on analytics, they may not be able to apply their intuition and beliefs drawn from their personal experience. Undoubtedly, the importance of intuition and personal judgment cannot be underestimated, especially in today's complex, uncertain and volatile environments (Abbasi, Sarker, and Chiang 2016; Constantiou and Kallinikos 2014). With the expansion of big data and analytics technologies, it becomes highly challenging for organizations to balance data with intuition, while it also raises questions of accountability. For example, there can be several cases when individuals are expected to act based on analytics, but their intuition suggests taking a different course of action. Also, this could have a long-term impact on the individual knowledge, because the individual stops learning through direct experience. Even if analytics helps avoid one type of role-constrained learning, other types of role-constrained learning open up if organizations act fully based on the data analytics insights.

Audience learning

Audience learning occurs when individual action is not adopted or integrated by the organization (March and Olsen 1975). While individuals change their actions based on what they learned, this learning does not affect organizational learning. In the example of Telecom's sales department, one account manager may see that a specific portfolio does not represent most customers' needs, and therefore focus on selling other portfolios. The account manager realizes that the organization is investing too much on a portfolio that is unsuccessful. However, due to the lower hierarchical status and the political interests of several managers who are at stake, the account manager cannot persuade the marketing department to change the portfolio's structure. Although learning has occurred on the individual level, the organization does not change anything. Next to being unable to influence management, it can also be just management itself that is blind to what is really happening on the work floor causing individual action to be disconnected from the organizational action.

Analytics can help overcome audience learning in a number of ways: individuals can use analytics to justify their actions to others. In a data-driven culture, analytics insights can be viewed as the objective information that bridges different viewpoints and brings more agreement in the organization (Davenport et al. 2010). In this way, individuals can influence organizational action by providing the figures that support their arguments and actions. Furthermore, analytics increases transparency in organizations (Fitzgerald 2016) by providing not only an analysis of what has happened in the past or what is happening in real time, but also by creating anticipation of what is likely to occur in the future (Hansen and Flyverbom 2015).

Nevertheless, analytics can also stimulate audience learning. First, it can easily be the case that people choose to use numbers and figures only when this data is aligned with the actions that they want to take (McAfee and Brynjolfsson 2012). This is an example of "action rationality" (Brunsson 1982); people perform an action and later make a decision to justify the action. Individuals may choose to use the type of analysis that shows a pattern between an action and a reaction, but in practice they try to cover up the action that they would have performed anyway for other reasons. In the example of Telecom, account managers may choose to use analytics only when the sales predictions match with the approach that they wanted to take, and omit mentioning analytics insights that indicated collaborating with different partners, or contacting customers with whom they do not have a friendly relationship. In addition, people may even start playing numbers games and distorting the data that is stored in the information systems, in order to influence the analytics results so that they fit with their actions (Pachidi, Huysman and Berends 2016). For example, the account managers of Telecom may distort the figures regarding their sales opportunities, in order to get their bonuses easier. If the higher management of Telecom is blinded by using analytics to run the organization by numbers, they may remain unaware of the numbers games and introduce a bonus structure that does not correspond to the real sales actions of the account managers.

Superstitious learning

Superstitious learning occurs when information about the causes of environmental changes is incomplete yet the organization assumes that environmental actions are reactions to their own actions (March and Olsen 1975; Levitt and March 1988). Superstitious learning thus can also be referred to as egocentric learning: organizations adapt to a false interpretation of environmental changes because they do not take exogenous causes of environmental changes into account. In the example of Telecom, the management of Telecom believed that the significant increase in sales was driven by their increased investments in marketing and customer relationship management, and overlooked the fact that small-to-medium enterprises were paying for their services because the economy was good. After a financial crisis, Telecom suffered from significant losses, because their small to medium business customers churned to competitors with lower prices, despite the competitors' lack in marketing and customer relationship management.

Many studies have shown the effectiveness of analytics to provide valid insights from the analysis of data from the environment (Lilien, Rangaswamy, Van Bruggen, and Starke 2004; Tremblay, Fuller, Berndt, and Studnicki 2007). By providing more information regarding what is happening in the market, how competitors are behaving and how customers react, analytics has the potential to limit superstitious learning. For example, analytics can be used in the healthcare domain: association rule mining on electronic health records has proved to be effective for identifying relevant and accurate associations between symptoms, diseases and treatments (Chen et al. 2012).

However, too heavy reliance on analytics could also reinforce superstitious learning. If the organization keeps using analytics solely to understand what organizational actions caused an environmental response and adapt accordingly, they may start focusing only on actions that have proved to be successful. Behaviors, patterns and discriminations that are inscribed in the analytics algorithms (Newell and Marabelli 2015) will be reinforced, while other patterns and parameters will be ignored (Yoo 2015). Next to that, it does not seem possible that analytics can capture all aspects of the environment. It is possible that certain types of patterns are not coded into algorithms. For example, in the case of Telecom, if the organization relies only on analytics to understand the changes in sales, they may ignore tacit information that cannot be coded into the algorithms, such as the plans of the customers to expand their businesses to new locations. Thus, by relying too much on analytics, organizations risk becoming path dependent, egocentric and bounded by their very own information-producing devices.

Organizational intelligence by analytics: closing the cycle or keeping it open?

In this chapter we have taken a more reflective approach toward analytics, in order to examine the taken-for-granted assumption that it reduces organizations' boundedness by facilitating better information to make choices and learn from it. Organizations are embracing analytics as if it is the holy grail of perfect information that will reduce uncertainty and increase rationality in their decisions and improve their learning (Clark et al. 2007), seduced by the lure to being perfectly rational (Cabantous and Gond 2011). However, as organizations use analytics to act and learn more rationally, they run the risk of becoming even more bounded. We returned to the roots of the conversation on using technologies of rationality in order to improve learning from past experiences. For this, we revisited the cycle of choice framework developed by March & Olsen (1975), which is helpful to analyze learning from experience and its tendency to dysfunction as a result of making adaptations to imperfect information about individual beliefs and individual actions, the organizational actions and the responses from the environment. We argued that even though the use of analytics can indeed improve decision making, in case organizations rely too much on analytics, those dysfunctions in learning will be reinforced or reappear in different ways. This is the lure of analytics: while organizations think that by using analytics they become unbounded, they risk becoming even more bounded. A summary of our analysis is provided in Table 25.1.

Whether analytics increases or decreases organizational intelligence, it is questionable anyway why we would want to develop organizations that learn perfectly and act fully rationally. Acting based on analytics by definition entails employing a technology of rationality, i.e., acting upon a model-based assessment of the likelihoods of possible future ends and of pre-established preferences among those ends (March 2006). However, in order to innovate and to survive in highly volatile environments, organizations also need to apply technologies of foolishness (March 1988), i.e., being open to new alternatives by employing playfulness, trial and error, and improvisation. Acting irrationally can sometimes lead to great outcomes for the organization. The organization needs to have some Don Quixotes, the people who may seem crazy by deviating from the expected behavior and remaining open to unexpected consequences (March and Weil 2009). By acting solely based on analytics in the hope to close the learning cycle, organizations risk losing the occurrence of outliers to learn from, the success of the unexpected, the plurality of different viewpoints, the generous insights by Steve Jobs and all other less-known Don Quixotes out there. Thus, not only should organizations reduce their high expectations regarding what analytics brings to organizational intelligence, it would be smart to include technologies of foolishness when engaging in learning. To cite March: "Individuals and organizations need ways of doing things for which they have no good reason. Not always. Not usually. But sometimes. They need to act before they think" (March 1988: 259). Hence, even though with the use of analytics the cycle of choice can be closed to a certain degree, aiming for a closed circle would be counterproductive.

Table 25.1 The effect of analytics on organizational learning dysfunctions

Organizational learning dysfunction	Definition	How analytics can close the cycle of choice	How analytics can break down the cycle of choice
Learning under ambiguity	Individuals learn and modify their understanding while being faced with ambiguity about what happened in the environment.	Analytics helps make sense of the environment, e.g., through visualization techniques and multidimensional analysis.	Relying too much on analytics while treating it as black box results in more ambiguity, as the mental representations of individuals are ignored.
Role-constrained learning	Individuals learn and change their beliefs and interpretations, but they are constrained in modifying their individual behavior accordingly, because of rigid role descriptions, bureaucratic rules and standard operating procedures.	Analytics may help reduce role-constrained learning, because it is expected to increase organizational agility and help fight inertia, by providing timely information to the organization on how rules and routines need to be adapted.	If individuals are expected to act solely based on analytics, they may not be able to apply their intuition and beliefs, and eventually stop learning through direct experience.
Audience learning	Audience learning occurs when individual action is not adopted or integrated by the organization.	Individuals can use analytics to justify their actions to the organization, while analytics also increases transparency regarding what is happening on the work floor.	Organizational members may use analytics only when the data is aligned with the actions that they want to take, or may even play numbers games. Management can be blinded by analytics and overlook what actually happens on the work floor.
Superstitious learning	Information about the causes of environmental changes is incomplete yet the organization assumes that these changes are caused by its own actions.	By providing more information regarding what is happening in the market, how competitors are behaving and how customers react, analytics has the potential to limit superstitious learning.	By relying too much on analytics, organizations risk becoming path dependent and bounded by their very own information-producing devices.

One thought before closing this chapter concerns our choice to use the cycle of Choice (March and Olsen 1975) as an analytical framework while thinking about analytics. This framework corresponds to the most popular assumption taken by the proponents of analytics, regarding making organizations more intelligent. Analyzing historical data collected from internal and external (to the organization) information systems is assumed to increase rationality and learning from experiences, and thus to perform complete cycles of choice. It was useful to examine whether this is true, in order to be more reflective about the enthusiasm by scholars and practitioners in advocating analytics as the holy grail to achieving organizational intelligence. We found the cycle a useful analytical framework for scholars and practitioners to think about analytics, and we believe that it could be revisited and used as a framework to think about other similar technologies. Further than that, revisiting this old framework brings back the never-ending discussions regarding rationality and foolishness in organizations, and the balance between exploration and exploitation. It refreshes the conversation on the information processing perspective, which has become taken-for-granted in achieving organizational success.

Our analysis questions basic assumptions regarding why and how information systems should be used in organizations, and serves as a reminder that we need to develop technologies that not always make us smarter, but also afford some foolishness. Acknowledging that we do not want to fully close the circle of choice, we hope to see future research investigating how technologies such as analytics and big data, so far approached with the goal to increase rationality, could increase creativity and innovation. For example, scholars should consider how we could use data mining techniques to experiment with the outliers, or how we could use big data to play with novel, unanticipated insights (George et al. 2014; Pentland 2014). We hope that our reflection triggers the readers to stop thinking about analytics solely as the means to organizational intelligence. Instead, it is time to explore how analytics can make organizations more rational but also more foolish.

References

Abbasi, A., Sarker, S., and Chiang, R.H.L. 2016. "Big data research in information systems: Toward an inclusive research agenda," *Journal of the Association for Information Systems* (17:2), pp. i–xxxii.

Arnott, D., and Pervan, G. 2014. "A critical analysis of decision support systems research revisited: The rise of design science," *Journal of Information Technology* (29), pp. 269–293.

Bose, R. 2009. "Advanced analytics: Opportunities and challenges," *Industrial Management & Data Systems* (109:2), pp. 155–172.

Brunsson, N. 1982. "The Irrationality of action and action irrationality: Decision ideologies and organisational actions," *Journal of Management Studies* (19:1), pp. 29–44.

Cabantous, L., and Gond, J.-P. 2011. "Rational decision making as performative praxis: Explaining rationality's Éternel Retour," *Organization Science* (22:3), pp. 573–586.

Chen, H., Chiang, R.H.L., and Storey, V.C. 2012. "Business intelligence and analytics: From big data to big impact," *MIS Quarterly* (36:4), pp. 1165–1188.

Chung, W., Chen, H., and Nunamaker, J.F. 2005. "A visual framework for knowledge discovery on the Web: An empirical study of business intelligence exploration," *Journal of Management Information Systems* (21:4), pp. 57–84.

Clark, T., Jones, M., and Armstrong, C. 2007. "The dynamic structure of management support systems: Theory development, research focus, and direction," *MIS Quarterly* (31:3), pp. 579–615.

Constantiou, I.D., and Kallinikos, J. 2014. "New games, new rules: Big data and the changing context of strategy," *Journal of Information Technology* (30:1), pp. 44–57.

Cyert, R.M., and March, J.G. 1963. *The behavioral theory of the firm*. Upper Saddle River, NJ: Prentice-Hall, Vol. 1.

Davenport, T.H. 2009. "Make better decisions," *Harvard Business Review* (87:11), pp. 117–123.

Davenport, T.H. 2014. "How strategists use 'big data' to support internal business decisions, discovery and production," *Strategy & Leadership* (42:4), pp. 45–50.

Davenport, T. H., Harris, J. G., and Morison, R. 2010. *Analytics at work: Smarter decisions, better results.* Boston, MA: Harvard Business School Press.

Davenport, T. H., and Harris, J. 2007. *Competing on analytics: The new science of winning.* Boston, MA: Harvard Business School Press.

Davenport, T. H., and Patil, D. J. 2012. "Data scientist: The sexiest job of the 21st century," *Harvard Business Review* (October), pp. 70–76.

Fitzgerald, M. 2016. "Better data brings a renewal at the Bank of England," *MIT Sloan Management Review* (57471), pp. 1–16.

Forni, A. A. 2016 "Gartner identifies the top 10 strategic technology trends for 2017," press release, October 18, 2016. Retrieved from www.gartner.com/newsroom/id/3482617.

George, G., Haas, M. R., and Pentland, A. 2014. "Big data and management," *Academy of Management Journal* (57:2), pp. 321–326.

Ghoshal, A., Menon, S., and Sarkar, S. 2015. "Recommendations using information from multiple association rules: A probabilistic approach," *Information Systems Research* (26:3), pp. 523–551.

Hansen, H. K., and Flyverbom, M. 2015. "The politics of transparency and the calibration of knowledge in the digital age," *Organization* (22:6), pp. 872–889.

Kim, D. H. 1993. "The link between individual and organizational learning," *Sloan Management Review* (35:1), pp. 37–50.

Kiron, D., Shockley, R., Kruschwitz, N., Finch, G., and Haydock, M. 2012. "Analytics: The widening divide," *MIT Sloan Management Review* (53:2), pp. 1–22.

Kumar, N., and Rao, R. 2006. "Using basket composition data for intelligent supermarket pricing," *Marketing Science* (25:2), pp. 188–199.

Levinthal, D. A., and March, J. G. 1993. "The myopia of learning," *Strategic Management Journal* (14:2), pp. 95–112.

Levitt, B., and March, J. 1988. "Organizational learning," *Annual Review of Sociology* (14), pp. 319–340.

Lilien, G. L., Rangaswamy, A., Van Bruggen, G. H., and Starke, K. 2004. "DSS effectiveness in marketing resource allocation decisions: Reality vs. perception," *Information Systems Research* (15:3), pp. 216–235.

Luftman, J., Derksen, B., Dwivedi, R., Santana, M., Zadeh, H. S., and Rigoni, E. 2015. "Influential IT management trends: an international study," *Journal of Information Technology* (30:3), pp. 293–305.

March, J. G. 1988. "Technology of foolishness," in *Decisions and organizations*, J. G. March (ed.), Oxford: Blackwell, pp. 253–265.

March, J. G. 1994. *A primer on decision making.* New York: Free Press.

March, J. G. 2006. "Rationality, foolishness, and adaptive intelligence," *Strategic Management Journal* (27:3), pp. 201–214.

March, J. G., and Olsen, J. P. 1975. "The uncertainty of the past: Organizational learning under ambiguity," *European Journal of Political Research* (3), pp. 147–171.

March, J. G., and Simon, H. A. 1958. *Organizations.* New York: Wiley.

March, J. G., and Weil, T. 2009. *On leadership.* New York: John Wiley & Sons.

McAfee, A., and Brynjolfsson, E. 2012. "Big data: The management revolution," *Harvard Business Review* (90:10), pp. 60–68.

Nature Publishing Group, 2016. "More accountability for big-data algorithms," Editorial, *Nature* (537), pp. 449.

Newell, S., and Marabelli, M. 2015. "Strategic opportunities (and challenges) of algorithmic decision-making: A call for action on the long-term societal effects of 'datification,'" *Journal of Strategic Information Systems* (24:1), pp. 3–14.

Pachidi, S., Huysman, M., and Berends, H. 2016. "Playing the numbers game: Dealing with transparency," in *Proceedings of International Conference on Information Systems (ICIS) 2016*, Dublin, Ireland.

Pentland, A., 2014. *Social physics: How good ideas spread – the lessons from a new science.* New York: Penguin.

Petrini, M., and Pozzebon, M. 2009. "Managing sustainability with the support of business intelligence: Integrating socio-environmental indicators and organisational context," *Journal of Strategic Information Systems* (12:4), pp. 178–191.

Phillips, P.C.B. 2003. "Laws and limits of econometrics," *Economic Journal* (113:486), pp. C26–C52.

Pollock, N., and Williams, R. 2011. "Who decides the shape of product markets? The knowledge institutions that name and categorise new technologies," *Information and Organization* (21:4), pp. 194–217.

Ransbotham, S., Kiron, D., and Prentice, P. K. 2015. "Minding the analytics gap," *MIT Sloan Management Review* (56480:Spring), pp. 63–68.

Sharma, R., Reynolds, P., Scheepers, R., Seddon, P. B., and Shanks, G. 2010. "Business analytics and competitive advantage: A review and a research agenda," in *Proceedings of the 2010 Conference on Bridging the Socio-Technical Gap in DSS – Challenges for the Next Decade: DSS 2010*. Amsterdam, NL: IOS Press, pp. 187–198.

Simon, H.A. 1976. *Administrative behavior. A study of decision-making processes in administrative organization*, 3rd ed. London, UK: Free Press, Collier Macmillan.

Tremblay, M., Fuller, R., Berndt, D., and Studnicki, J. 2007. "Doing more with more information: Changing healthcare planning with OLAP tools," *Decision Support Systems* (43), pp. 1305–1320.

Winig, L. 2016. "GE's big bet on data and analytics," *MIT Sloan Management Review* (57380).

Yoo, Y. 2015. "It is not about size: A further thought on big data," *Journal of Information Technology* (30:1), pp. 63–65.

26
DATIFICATION IN ACTION
Diffusion and consequences of algorithmic decision-making[1]

Sue Newell and Marco Marabelli

Introduction

The last decade has witnessed the widespread diffusion of digitized objects that capture data about the minutiae of our everyday lives (Hedman et al. 2013). These digitized objects are everywhere – a phenomenon described as ubiquitous computing (Nolan 2012). The data trail we leave is increasingly used by companies to target and personalize information, products and services, based on developing algorithms that can make predictions about individuals by recognizing complex patterns in huge data sets compiled from multiple sources. For example, some car insurance companies now provide customers with on-board diagnostic (OBD) devices equipped with a GPS and sensor technology that captures many aspects of driving style. These data are then used by insurance companies in their decision-making, based on developing algorithms that can predict whether a person is a safe or risky driver and so more or less likely to have an accident; personalized insurance premiums are then set based on these data-driven predictions.

Similarly, data collected from social media platforms is used to gauge users' opinions on products and services, political views, interests, hobbies and the like. These data are then processed by algorithms that are used to prioritize certain contents that are made available to different people. In other words, algorithms 'decide' if we are a driver at risk of accidents and whether we like to see, on our news feeds, a Walmart cold-cure advertisement, a request to sign a change.org petition or our former high school mate's pictures of her newborn son.

When the phenomenon of datification (everyone and everything is, or at least can be turned into, data) started, almost a decade ago, it was introduced into our everyday lives in a subtle way (no one told us about it) and most individuals found algorithmic decision-making a good way to save money (if we refer to insurance companies) or to have 'likable' content readily available on social media. More recently, academics, the media and governments (lawmakers, and more generally politicians) have highlighted potential societal consequences associated with algorithmic decision-making. In this chapter, we focus on privacy issues and discriminations. We illustrate that data-driven decision-making poses social and ethical issues because there can be a difference between how *business* is benefiting and how *society* is benefiting – or otherwise. Interestingly, the MIS (management information systems) literature is not very rich in this regard and often relies on sources from neighbor literatures such as sociology (see for instance David Lyon's project at Queen's University, www.sscqueens.org/people/david-lyon). Therefore, we take this opportunity to expand on this body of research while contributing to the MIS literature.

Later we illustrate how datification can lead to more or less intended consequences for individuals, businesses and the wider society. We do so by first identifying two key sources of data (social software and sensors) and second by providing examples and discussing a variety of consequences. We then propose that all stakeholders involved (individuals, businesses and lawmakers) should contribute by promoting the adoption, use and exploitation of emerging technologies (and associated data analytics opportunities) while mitigating side effects.

Sources of data and algorithmic decision-making

Social software

One important source of data that companies are increasingly using for decision-making comes from various types of social software platforms that enable interactions among many distributed people (Yuan et al. 2013). Organizations are using such platforms to tap into the 'wisdom of the crowd' (Martinez and Walton 2014) and so enable fast and effective open innovation (Chesbrough and Garman 2009). Examples include using contests to stimulate contributions (Boudreau 2012), especially if 'solver brokers' are used to orchestrate this crowdsourcing (Feller et al. 2012). This type of crowdsourcing is based on actual data and information that are provided by individuals. The literature has shown that the IT (information technology) platform used for encouraging such contributions can not only enable but can also shape the content (if appropriately designed), thereby encouraging the types of contributions for which a firm is looking (Majchrzak and Malhotra 2013).

Social media platforms are also being used to comment on an organization's products and services (e.g., in the form of reviews or comments on sites like Amazon and TripAdvisor). Such reviews have been found to influence what stakeholders (and in particular customers or potential customers) feel they know about a firm's products or services – more so than a firm's own market-generated content that only attempts to inform customers about the benefits of their products and services (Goh et al. 2013). This use of social media suggests that corporations need to strategically identify ways to respond to this user-generated content in order to limit any damage that may arise from bad reviews. More importantly from the perspective of this chapter, we note that it is the corporations themselves that provide the platforms and social media applications, and it is these IT artifacts that can have a dark side in their use. Examples include various types of problems associated with Internet addiction and loss of contact with reality (Leung 2004), review manipulation (Scott and Orlikowski 2012), predatory activity and defaming someone's reputation – all of which lead to various forms of individual and ultimately societal harm.

In sum, these social media technologies (which make up a significant part of the ubiquitous computing environment), can affect individuals, organizations and society – either positively or negatively – depending on the strategies that corporations adopt in their design and functionality. Thus, we posit that undertaking research to assess these societal harms, so that corporations can be held responsible and citizens become more aware, can potentially be very useful, and is in line with recent calls for MIS scholars to take a greater interest in the societal issues associated with new technologies (Loebbecke and Picot 2015; Marabelli et al. 2017; Newell and Marabelli 2015).

More importantly, aside from those data explicitly contributed by users in this era of ubiquitous computing, there is also the data trail left by social software applications (e.g., locational information) as well as from other devices that increasingly now have tracking and sensing software in them so that "the digital artifacts will be able to remember where they were, who used them, the outcomes of interactions, etc." (Yoo 2010, p. 226). As Mcafee and colleagues (2012, p. 5) state, "each of us is now a walking data generator." It is this data trail that provides the opportunity for organizations to move to data-driven decision-making, which McAfee and colleagues argue, is superior to traditional 'HiPPO' (highest-paid person's opinion) decision-making. Algorithmic decision-making, these authors argue – here defined as an algorithm's 'power' to lead (instead of simply influence) decisions or even to act autonomously and make automatic decisions on behalf of human beings – is often *superior* to human judgment-based decisions given all its inherent biases. In this chapter we question this assumption.

Data-driven or algorithmic decision-making is based on collecting large quantities of data from the tracking software that is now built in to the applications and devices that we use in our daily lives and then developing algorithms that make a selection in order to model a particular phenomenon of interest (Brynjolfsson and McAfee 2014). These algorithms can predict particular outcomes, as with the numbers of Facebook friends being used to predict a person's credit risk (www.google.com/patents/US8560436). Data can, then, be used to track general trends (big data) as well as the minutiae of an individual's everyday life (little data).

Big and little data, in our opinion, represent the old and the new aspects of using computers with high speed and capacity to process a vast amount of data – namely, what in 2001 Gartner defined as "big data" (http://blogs.gartner.com/doug-laney/files/2012/01/ad949-3D-Data-Management-Controlling-Data-Volume-Velocity-and-Variety.pdf). Little data is of course an extension of big data supported by new technologies, in that it is because of the availability of such extensive amounts of data, which can be processed quickly, that we can access the minutiae of people's everyday life.

Big data analytics, therefore, is very similar to the more familiar (and less sexy) business intelligence (Chen et al. 2012; Golfarelli et al. 2004; Watson and Wixom 2007). Little data is data collected through digital traces (Hedman et al. 2013) from crowd applications or sensors included in devices that individuals carry or use and that record (and in some cases transmit to data centers) information related to people's whereabouts (locator-based or GPS-equipped sensors) and even more sensitive information such as health data (heartbeat, blood pressure etc.) through wearable devices. All these pieces of information collected on a personal basis (little data) deserve particular attention because companies are able to profile specific individuals, and by using computing capacity they can collect and analyze extremely granular information (Munford 2014). We next provide an example of the use (and misuse) of big and little data in Facebook, which had over a billion users in summer 2016.

The case of Facebook's news feeds, and its potential consequences

Social software allows various types of analyses suggesting trends. For instance, Facebook Likes are able to shed light on individuals' personality traits, political views, sexual orientation and other behavioral characteristics (Ross et al. 2009; Youyou et al. 2015). These data are used in an aggregate way, for instance, to suggest that people, over the summer, are less stressed or that a particular geographical region is dominated by liberal (or conservative) ideas. This relates to big data and might be helpful to identify general trends. In November 2016, conversation analysis (news feeds) of over four million Facebook profiles led to predictive results associated with the US general election that were more accurate than traditional polling techniques (https://medium.com/@erinpettigrew/how-facebook-saw-trump-coming-when-no-one-else-did-84cd6b4e0d8e#.d92cvk1vj). Little data, instead, aims to profile specific individuals (with privacy consequences), as we explain next.

Algorithms, it is now well-known (www.nytimes.com/2016/05/19/opinion/the-real-bias-built-in-at-facebook.html?_r=0), manage how our Facebook's news feeds are populated. For instance, we may see many posts about the newest iPhone and assume that many of our Facebook friends are posting articles about it. However, the frequency with which we see these posts may be partially due to us having clicked an advert related to the specific smartphone: Facebook's algorithm decides that we are interested in such technology and then shows us others' posts that are related to the newest iPhone. A consequence of such use of algorithms by corporations to decide for the consumer the posts, news or advertising that they are exposed to is that it may lead to a slow and often subtle manipulation of consumers' worldviews as well as to new forms of discrimination. Simply, what is presented to the reader is decided by an algorithm – tapping in to prior searches – and is not based on an explicit personal choice, a phenomenon that can be described as uninformed control (Newell and Marabelli 2015). An example of uninformed control by a corporation that produces worrisome ethical issues is found in the account presented by Eli Pariser, who during a TEDX presentation pointed out that

> Facebook was looking at which links I clicked on, and it was noticing that I was clicking more on my liberal friends' links than on my conservative friends' links. And without consulting me about it, it had edited them [conservative friends' links] out. They disappeared.
>
> (Pariser 2011)

In the longer term, this manipulation by corporations of what the consuming public is exposed to – exposing us only to things that we like (or the things that an algorithm assumes we like) – may produce societal changes. For instance, our exposure to online diversity will be reduced (as in the example of removing conservatives' links). More recently, Greg Marra, a Facebook engineer argued, "We think that of all the stuff you've connected yourself to, this is the stuff you'd be most interested in reading," explaining further that an algorithm monitors 'thousands and thousands' of metrics to decide what we should see on our Facebook page. These metrics include what device we use, how many comments or 'Likes' a story has received and how long readers spend on each article/post. The assumed goal, as a *New York Times* article suggests, is that companies are using this algorithmic approach to decision-making "to identify what users most enjoy" (www.nytimes.com/2014/10/27/business/media/how-facebook-is-changing-the-way-its-users-consume-journalism.html?_r=0). However, this also indicates that this practice of showing us only things that 'fit' with our little data profile, limits our choices, and might inhibit our capacity to make informed decisions (on what we buy and even what we think). Moreover, algorithms are monitored against "intensity of use" (Bode 2012), a metric used by Facebook to measure users' response to specific reorganization of the news feeds. Therefore 'evidence' emerging from little data is turned into trends (big data).

These strategies exploit the potential of little data, which is collected by observing individuals' behaviors. These data analysis practices are leading to citizens (i.e., all of us who 'surf the web') being exposed to less and less diversity online. A potential consequence is that we may become less tolerant to diversity in our real life, meaning we may be less able to listen to someone who thinks differently (e.g., a Republican, in Pariser's example). Moreover, there may be other, more dangerous consequences in the long term that are associated with race-diversity intolerance and the increased exploitation of the vulnerable. For example, in relation to the latter issue, if algorithms work out who is less capable of making good financial decisions, personalized adverts can then be sent persuading these people to take out risky loans, or high-rate instant credit options, thereby exploiting their vulnerability. The strategic use of our own data by corporations to personalize our Internet, in other words, is just another and potentially more pernicious way of allowing discrimination – pernicious because the only person who has access to the outcomes of the discrimination is the individual being discriminated against (who is often not aware of the fact that they are exposed to discriminatory information; uninformed control), making it easy for unscrupulous businesses to use personalization in a way that harms the vulnerable.

In conclusion, big and little data analytics can be successfully used to process user-generated contents in social media settings. In this example, it seems that little data might be more harmful because it poses privacy issues. As we illustrate next, however, in other contexts little data might be able to overcome discriminations, which are based on algorithmic decision-making deriving from the analysis of vast amounts of data (big data).

Sensors

Ubiquitous computing can protect citizens, for example, when prisoners are released but are required to wear a tracking ankle bracelet. These systems are aimed at improving the overall security of our society, with the sensor acting as a deterrent for prisoners to escape or commit a crime when they are on parole. Other instances where security is enhanced by ubiquitous computing is in the capacity of sensors to trace a stolen device, or a kidnapped child, as in the case that occurred in September 2013 in Texas, where the Houston police were able to trace the whereabouts of a kidnapper by tracing his iPad that he had with him in his car (http://abc13.com/archive/9242256/). A similar example relates to police authorities being able to detect a crime because it is all 'caught on tape,' for example with sensor-activated security cameras.

All these examples of companies and government agencies using sensor technology to protect citizens come at some costs in terms of individuals' privacy. In terms of locating a lost smartphone, it has to be the user who, deliberately, accepts giving up her/his (right of) privacy by activating the 'Find my iPhone' option (e.g., https://itunes.apple.com/us/app/find-my-iphone/id376101648?mt=8). However, in some circumstances one's use of social software applications affects others' privacy, as for example, for people who are tagged in somebody's Facebook profile without them knowing. Perhaps not surprisingly, privacy advocates have argued that in these types of exchanges consumers are justified in expecting that the information they share remains private among those to whom it was originally disclosed, dependent on users' risk perceptions, rather than shared with third parties who may subsequently behave opportunistically (Gerlach et al. 2015).

Nevertheless, the exponential diffusion of tracking software embedded in social networks such as Facebook and the sensors in many other digital devices leads us to think that it will be hard for organizations (or governments) to regulate how individuals use technologies that enable tracking responsibly (i.e., in a way that balances security and privacy). However, several lawmakers in the US agree that police officers should wear cameras after recent cases involving police officers' improper use of force. Here, a sensor technology would be employed but would not actually generate big data, because the camera records would be reviewed only in particular circumstances. This and other types of sensor are pervasive (and invasive), and the data (e.g., the camera records) would be stored. In such circumstances, we do not know whether in the future somebody will develop an algorithmic-based decision system to analyze the data (e.g., to assess the performance of police officers).

It is, thus, clear that ubiquitous computing can be harmful to individuals' privacy while justified by corporations and governments in the name of public security (e.g., protecting citizens). This in turn raises social issues when, for example, algorithms determine that particular categories of people (based on e.g., race, income, job) are more likely to commit a crime, and would, therefore, be subjected to higher levels of policing and potentially also face more discrimination in other areas (e.g., obtaining a loan or finding a job). This emerging and very under-studied phenomenon relates to the formation of people's beliefs on the basis of big data analytics (boyd and Crawford 2012; LaValle et al. 2011).

Overall, data collected through sensor technologies, like these collected through social software might have relevant (and somewhat worrying) consequences, at the individual as well as the societal level. In some cases, the use of little data can virtually avoid discriminations by moving from the 'trend approach' (which generalizes, sometimes at the expense of minorities) to the 'individual approach.' People are held accountable for their own (individual) behaviors as it is the case of sensor devices (OBD) that monitor a car's speed, usage of brakes, horn, lights and so forth (www.onstar.com). Automotive insurance companies such as Progressive (www.progressive.com) adopt these technologies to identify 'good' and 'bad' drivers that would be charged differently. This, however, raises a different 'dark side.' An example is provided next.

The case of Progressive

Insurance companies have long been able to use police statistics to discriminate (Lemaire 2012). For instance, the industry charges men higher premiums because the data indicates they drive less safely. Such data-driven decision-making has been questioned because it can go against the ethical principle of equal or fair treatment. This is exemplified in a recent case in the EU, where insurers are required to no longer use statistical evidence about gender differences to set premiums. Thus, despite the fact that gender differences are clear from the data (e.g., young male drivers are 10 times more likely to be killed or injured than those – of both sexes – over the age of 35; women live, on average, longer than men), it is considered to be discriminatory (following an EU ruling that came into effect in December 2012) to use this trend evidence to differentiate premiums (e.g., car insurance or actuarial rates) for men and women. The point about this change in the law was that it was considered to be discriminatory because while young men in general, for example, may drive more recklessly and so be more prone to accidents, an individual young man may not and would therefore be discriminated against when insurers set premiums based on group trends observable in collective data.

In contrast to these trends, the introduction of sensors in the form of small devices connected to a car's computer, capable of recording and analyzing an insured's driving style (little data), can overcome trend-based discriminations. By using sensor data, the insurer would not be setting premiums based on the general trends in accident rates between groups, but instead would base their calculations on the actual driving habits of an individual. However, if little data is more 'objective' in terms of discriminations made by corporations, it nevertheless poses ethical issues, because of the observed or potential social consequences, in particular those associated with privacy. We elaborate on the positive and negative consequences of employing big and little data with respect to privacy and discriminations next.

Big and little data: avoiding discriminations and preserving privacy

As we have illustrated, while the central focus of data analytics rests on the identification of broad trends within one or more datasets, with sensors datification can be used in a more benign sense (and algorithmic decision-making processes act accordingly) in regard to at least two aspects. First, with OBD devices issues associated with the high rate of accidents are no longer linked with individual characteristics (i.e., trends). Instead, individual-level analysis of sensors moves away from contextual variables (when we use cars) such as driving hours (night/day) (when 'statistically' most incidents occur), and instead examines whether a specific driver has (or has not) incidents at night. In addition, this analysis focuses on whether individual's driving behaviors might lead to accidents. These behaviors might include speeding up, using breaks very frequently and similar things. These behaviors *may* lead to accidents, as someone could be a very skilled driver (or simply a lucky driver) and break speed limits without harming herself or others. However, focusing on individuals provides information which is at least less discriminating than the blind application of general trends. The general trend would be associated with the belief that driving at night equates to having more accidents (true, but only statistically). Examining little data will tell if specific night drivers are also more reckless (at night there is less traffic so people tend to drive faster, but not all people do so).

It is also important to note that collecting little data – the minutiae of private citizens' lives – should *always* imply that those monitored are aware of it. This awareness, we argue, cannot be dealt with by businesses simply producing very long and complex 'terms and conditions' that only expert lawyers can fully understand. Businesses aim to collect data in exchange for services offered, whether they relate to the possibility to rejoin with former classmates 'for free,' by accessing a very expensive IT infrastructure (Facebook) or to benefit from a discount on their yearly car insurance premium. However, the "data generators" (McAfee et al. 2012) need to be fully aware that their actions will have consequences, and these consequences might well go beyond the ads they will see on social media or a change in the monthly rate of their car insurance.

Current laws and regulations mandate that companies disclose how user data is handled and stored (transparency). However, the emergence of new technologies is happening faster than the lawmakers' ability to protect consumers. Therefore some argue that it is businesses that should protect their current and potential customers by acting ethically (McGinn 2015). Moreover, regulations can be circumvented. For example, in terms of transparency social media companies should detail what they do, when they capture digital traces, and ensure that every user will be reasonably aware of what is going on with her/his data. This can be described as 'enforced transparency' because it is not enough that businesses provide long statements about the details of their data collection and analysis; these statements need to be accessible to all users (simple language) and synthetic (can be read in a few minutes), and businesses should ensure that users understand what is going on with their data.

Other privacy issues that can emerge from the collection (but more important the use) of little data relates to the potential data sharing between companies. Part of this process is associated with the previous discussed 'awareness,' whereby companies apply enforced transparency to all their users/customers. Now, we have the possibility to log in to new services (TripAdvisor, Yelp, Instagram) using our Facebook profile, so we don't have to fill out a new form, yet the new business (very briefly) tells us that they will be able to access our Facebook friends' information, our 'about' area of our profile, our Likes and so forth. This practice is legal, but is also a subtle way to allow inter-company data exchange; users have to decide whether to spend 5–10 minutes to create a new profile (e.g., on TripAdvisor) or just log in automatically (as new users) with their existing Facebook credentials. Other even more subtle ways businesses can exchange little data about individuals can be found in the use of tracking cookies, which are those text files that document our Internet behaviors and enable quick access to our email, bank account and so forth (our computer 'remembers' websites and username autofill becomes possible), but that, for instance, let Facebook know that we have just searched for flu drugs because we feel sick. In turn, Facebook can customize our ads accordingly. Here, too, transparency is applied but not explicitly enough, one example being the somewhat ambiguous messages that appears on tracking cookies-based websites, where we are told that in order to access all the functionalities of a portal our cookies will be enabled (and, by the way, we are not told about what enabling cookies implies).

Finally, little data can be collected in ways that might determine the conditions/rates (or even prevent the eligibility) to access services such as healthcare. For instance, at the time of writing, 19 million Americans use Fitbit,[2] which is somewhat connected with a data center. The data center allows Fitbit users to receive text messages (or SMS) on their wearable device, analyze calorie-burn activities and workout progress and save their results (http://expandedramblings.com/index.php/fitbit-statistics/). However, one might wonder whether (or how) all this personal information is systematically stored (and protected), and if so, for how long. In the US, healthcare providers (i.e., HMOs, or health maintenance organizations) would certainly be interested in knowing more about people's physical conditions, how much they work out, what their average heart rate is and so forth. This information can well be used by researchers to predict vascular diseases and other pathologies. Here it is interesting to see the intersection between little data, which is collected at a personal level and enjoyable by their owners (the walking/running/sleeping data generators, in the case of Fitbit) and big data, which can actually help improve people's health by increasing our knowledge on root causes of diseases. Recording people's vitals for long periods of time might help (using big data) identify relationships between behaviors, vitals such as heart rate and blood pressure, and particular diseases. However, the sharing of these results at the individual level might prevent people's access to basic medical care for the very same reason should, for example, Fitbit personal data become accessible by HMOs.

In sum, in general terms discrimination relates to big data (decisions based on trends) while privacy issues are more associated with little data (invasion of one's personal sphere). However, big and little data concerns also overlap. For instance, in the automotive insurance industry and OBDs, the monetization of privacy (Acquisti 2012) is about little data being used to (potentially) discriminate against individuals with poor financial capacity; these individuals might not be willing to be monitored (so they would not want to sign-off on having an ODB installed on their cars). However, they might have to give up their privacy (and thus they will accept to be monitored) because they would not be able to afford car insurance otherwise. In terms of how far big data analytics might violate one's privacy, examples relate mostly to data leaks (Markus 2016) and the fact that the data that is collected today will probably be stored somewhere for an unlimited amount of time, while laws in place that now protect these data might change (Chen et al. 2012).

A call for action: the joint efforts of individuals, businesses and lawmakers

The societal concerns previously examined apply to both big and little data, and it is not likely that laws and regulations will be able to keep up with the fast pace of the evolution of emerging technologies. It seems, therefore, obvious that we need to rely mostly on the ethical practices of businesses first, rather than expect that specific laws will regulate digital contexts in a timely manner (Stone-Gross et al. 2013). This, however, might be hard to achieve; businesses operate in a global environment. The challenges associated with setting up privacy and discrimination policies that are compliant with country-specific laws, norms and cultures might lead the businesses themselves to circumvent these problems. Companies might attempt to manage data (collection, analysis and implementation of decision-making outcomes) in very standardized ways, by using domestic laws in foreign countries. Global companies such as Google and Yahoo have been doing this over the past decade (Rosen 2012).

It is nevertheless worth noting that foreign laws can also be utilized by businesses to grant customers privacy even when local laws would not do this. For instance, in summer 2016 the Second Circuit Court of the United States ruled that Microsoft Corporation has no obligation to turn in customers' emails to authorities when these data (emails) reside in countries where privacy regulations do not enforce providers to do so (Ireland, in this case; www.forbes.com/sites/insider/2016/08/02/the-microsoft-warrant-case-unintended-consequences-of-the-second-circuits-ruling/#d7bd5e34e44d). We will therefore need to rely on businesses embracing ethical values. It is, however, worrying that, as recent studies illustrate (e.g., Markus 2016) companies' decision-makers as well as the data scientists involved in 'setting up' algorithms are not always well prepared to deal with the consequences of datification ethically, because education systems worldwide do not cover these ethical issues (Pearson and Wegener 2013). Nor are specific organizational roles currently in place in most companies that have the specific task to consider the ethical implications of big data policies (Carey 2015).

We thus argue that individual citizens' behaviors are also relevant to ensure that businesses first and laws and regulations second preserve privacy rights while avoiding discrimination (thus, using big and little data responsibly). Their contribution is key because citizens are also customers (or consumers) and users of a variety of social media and their sensitivity to privacy, therefore their rejection of discriminating behaviors, might affect the conduct of those who provide these services (businesses). For instance, it is in the interest of social media platforms/companies to articulate clear privacy rules (not simply to obey the law), because this makes users feel 'safe' (Madden 2012). Similarly, automotive insurance companies such as Progressive highlight the strong level of security of their data storage, and point to how relevant it is for them to collect individuals' data to avoid unfair treatments. National and international laws and regulations are relevant as well. Albeit these laws generally follow (and do not precede) the opportunities and threats of emerging technologies, they need to be in place to allow citizens (and businesses) to appeal, should at some point opportunistic behaviors surface.

In other words, we argue that privacy and discrimination are among the most prominent red flags associated with little and big data, respectively. Individuals have the power (and responsibility) to potentially avoid using certain services or taking advantage of financial benefits; businesses should embrace a culture of ethical behaviors associated with 'datification'; and lawmakers should ensure, in a timely fashion, that big data analytics (and the emerging little data issues) advance knowledge discovery and well-being (for instance to the extent to which Fitbit devices can collect information that help improve prevention and treatment), while protecting individuals' privacy and minimizing discrimination. Figure 26.1 illustrates that privacy issues, on the one hand, (generally) emerge through the use of little data, which focuses on the minutiae of people's life, at the individual level. Discriminations, on the other hand, might occur when big data findings are generalized (e.g., are assumed true for everyone). Areas of overlap involve monetizing privacy through little data that is a form of financial discrimination. In a similar way, data leaks jeopardize privacy while exposing

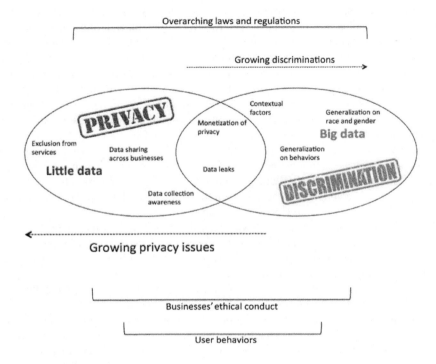

Figure 26.1 Privacy and discrimination in the big and little data era

people's past behaviors, which again leads to potential discriminations. Privacy and discrimination issues, we argue, should be addressed collectively by the three main stakeholders involved: individuals, businesses and lawmakers.

Concluding remarks

Datification – turning the minutiae of our lives into data – is growing very rapidly, as an IT-related societal phenomenon. This phenomenon is clearly not fully controllable. The fast-paced evolution of portable, wearable devices poses concerns. These devices have the ability to take pictures in public places, involving car license plates, people's personal details, images of minors and the like. All these contents can be posted on social media in real time. This makes it difficult for lawmakers to enforce regulations that prohibit capturing particular details of our private life. Moreover, current technologies are able to store likely infinite data streams, therefore anything that has been streamed is potentially retrievable either from official sources or from the underground Internet. To this end, in this chapter we have identified two major issues: privacy and discrimination. Other, even more relevant issues that stem from (but also go beyond) privacy and discrimination deserve careful examination. For instance, ubiquitous computing (privacy) allows algorithms to 'assist' people in their everyday activities. This phenomenon can restrict our exposure to news and information that is not aligned with our interests as determined by previously monitored activities (e.g., when an Internet search provides a list of 'hits' that is dependent on our past searches; see TED video by Eli

Pariser (2011). Taking this further, manipulating what we see and do could affect our ability to learn. For instance, algorithm-based GPS systems that suggest the best route to our desired destination might save us time (because they identify the fastest route with respect to current traffic). However, in the long term they might inhibit our ability to make decisions on our own, should the GPS stop working. Or again, using the car example, our cars can now brake for us in the face of a hazard, potentially restricting our ability to know when and how hard we should be braking in different situations, a problem if the technology were to go wrong.

Another important issue that needs to be investigated, here related to discriminations, is about the potential loss of job opportunities. While we have shown that algorithm-based trends might negatively affect 'minorities' (e.g., good 'night drivers'), the same algorithms have the ability to assert that people with specific characteristics are not fit for certain jobs. For instance, analyzing our social media networks (according to an algorithm) can determine whether we will pay off a loan (http://money.cnn.com/2013/08/26/technology/social/facebook-credit-score/). Therefore, algorithmic decision-making will veto hiring potential creative talents because they are 'judged' as unreliable by an algorithm. There is also the broader issue of how many jobs will remain once so many jobs or tasks within jobs are taken over by 'intelligent systems.'

In sum, current and emerging issues bring to the surface the urgency to take the widespread diffusion of big/little data (and associated algorithms) very seriously. According to our analysis it does not seem realistic to expect that specific laws can fully (and timely) regulate (or enforce) what people (whether they are private citizens or business managers) can or can't do in terms of exploiting social software and sensors. Therefore, we have suggested a joint approach where the main actors involved each take responsibility for their *doings*. Opportunities concerning knowledge creation and sharing, and innovation offered by emerging technologies (e.g., exploring the opportunities of big/little data) need to be pursued. At the same time, mitigating the dark side of datification should be an imperative for all parties involved.

Our call for action aims to encourage very focused and addressed research on the challenges and opportunities of big and little data seen from different perspectives (end users, businesses, legislators, society as a whole). Only by examining these issues from different angles will a joint effort toward progress be possible. Addressing these relevant societal problems will necessarily imply interdisciplinary research with strong practical implications. We thus encourage collaboration between scholars from various fields and between academia, industry and government, aimed at carrying out constructive and informative discussions around the present threats/opportunities and the future challenges emerging from the increasing datification of everybody's lives.

Notes

1 This chapter builds on and significantly extends earlier work published in Newell, S., & Marabelli, M. (2014). *The crowd and sensors era: opportunities and challenges for individuals, organizations, society, and researchers*. ICIS 2014, http://aisel.aisnet.org/icis2014/proceedings/EBusiness/3/
2 www.fitbit.com

References

Acquisti, A. 2012. "Nudging Privacy: The Behavioral Economics of Personal Information," in *Digital Enlightenment Yearbook 2012*, J. Bus, M. Crompton, M. Hildebrandt and G. Metakides (eds.). Amsterdam, Netherlands: IOS Press, pp. 193–197.

Bode, L. 2012. "Facebooking It to the Polls: A Study in Online Social Networking and Political Behavior," *Journal of Information Technology & Politics* (9:4), pp. 352–369.

Boudreau, K. J. 2012. "Let a Thousand Flowers Bloom? An Early Look at Large Numbers of Software App Developers and Patterns of Innovation," *Organization Science* (23:5), pp. 1409–1427.

boyd, d., and Crawford, K. 2012. "Critical Questions for Big Data: Provocations for a Cultural, Technological, and Scholarly Phenomenon," *Information, Communication & Society* (15:5), pp. 662–679.

Brynjolfsson, E., and McAfee, A. 2014. *The Second Machine Age: Work, Progress, and Prosperity in a Time of Brilliant Technologies*. New York: W. W. Norton.

Carey, P. 2015. *Data Protection: A Practical Guide to UK and EU Law*. Oxford, UK: Oxford University Press.

Chen, H., Chiang, R. H., and Storey, V. C. 2012. "Business Intelligence and Analytics: From Big Data to Big Impact," *MIS Quarterly* (36:4), pp. 1165–1188.

Chesbrough, H. W., and Garman, A. R. 2009. "How Open Innovation Can Help You Cope in Lean Times," *Harvard Business Review* (87:12), pp. 68–76, 128.

Feller, J., Finnegan, P., Hayes, J., and O'Reilly, P. 2012. "'Orchestrating' Sustainable Crowdsourcing: A Characterisation of Solver Brokerages," *Journal of Strategic Information Systems* (21:3), pp. 216–232.

Gerlach, J., Widjaja, T., and Buxmann, P. 2015. "Handle With Care: How Online Social Network Providers' Privacy Policies Impact Users' Information Sharing Behavior," *Journal of Strategic Information Systems* (24:1), pp. 33–43.

Goh, K.-Y., Heng, C.-S., and Lin, Z. 2013. "Social Media Brand Community and Consumer Behavior: Quantifying the Relative Impact of User-and Marketer-Generated Content," *Information Systems Research* (24:1), pp. 88–107.

Golfarelli, M., Rizzi, S., and Cella, I. 2004. "Beyond Data Warehousing: What's Next in Business Intelligence?," *Proceedings of the 7th ACM International Workshop on Data Warehousing and OLAP*: ACM, pp. 1–6.

Hedman, J., Srinivasan, N., and Lindgren, R. 2013. "Digital Traces of Information Systems: Sociomateriality Made Researchable," *Proceedings of the 34th International Conference on Information Systems*, Milan, Italy.

LaValle, S., Lesser, E., Shockley, R., Hopkins, M. S., and Kruschwitz, N. 2011. "Big Data, Analytics and the Path From Insights to Value," *MIT Sloan Management Review* (52:2), p. 21.

Lemaire, J. 2012. *Bonus-Malus Systems in Automobile Insurance*. New York: Springer Science & Business Media.

Leung, L. 2004. "Net-Generation Attributes and Seductive Properties of the Internet as Predictors of Online Activities and Internet Addiction," *CyberPsychology & Behavior* (7:3), pp. 333–348.

Loebbecke, C., and Picot, A. 2015. "Reflections on Societal and Business Model Transformation Arising from Digitization and Big Data Analytics: A Research Agenda," *Journal of Strategic Information Systems* (24:3), pp. 149–157.

Madden, M. 2012. "Privacy Management on Social Media Sites," PEW Internet Report, pp. 1–20.

Majchrzak, A., and Malhotra, A. 2013. "Towards an Information Systems Perspective and Research Agenda on Crowdsourcing for Innovation," *Journal of Strategic Information Systems* (22:4), pp. 257–268.

Marabelli, M., Hansen, S., Newell, S., and Frigerio, C. 2017. "The Light and Dark Side of the Black Box: Sensor-Based Technology in the Automotive Industry," *Communication of the AIS*.

Markus, M. L. 2016. "Obstacles on the Road to Corporate Data Responsibility," in *Big Data Is Not a Monolith: Policies, Practices, and Problems*, C. R. Sugimoto, H. R. Ekbia and M. Mattioli (eds.). Cambridge, MA: MIT Press, pp. 143–162.

Martinez, M. G., and Walton, B. 2014. "The Wisdom of Crowds: The Potential of Online Communities as a Tool for Data Analysis," *Technovation* (34:4), pp. 203–214.

McAfee, A., Brynjolfsson, E., Davenport, T. H., Patil, D., and Barton, D. 2012. "Big Data: The Management Revolution," *Harvard Business Review* (90:10), pp. 61–67.

McGinn, R. 2015. *The Ethically Responsible Engineer: Concepts and Cases for Students and Professionals*. New Jersey: John Wiley & Sons.

Munford, M. 2014. "Rule Changes and Big Data Revolutionise Caterham F1 Chances," *The Telegraph*.

Newell, S., and Marabelli, M. 2015. "Strategic Opportunities (and Challenges) of Algorithmic Decision-Making: A Call for Action on the Long-Term Societal Effects of 'Datification,'" *Journal of Strategic Information Systems* (24:1), pp. 3–14.

Nolan, R. L. 2012. "Ubiquitous IT: The Case of the Boeing 787 and Implications for Strategic IT Research," *Journal of Strategic Information Systems* (21:2), pp. 91–102.

Pariser, E. 2011. *The Filter Bubble: What the Internet Is Hiding From You*. Penguin UK.

Pearson, T., and Wegener, R. 2013. "Big Data: The Organizational Challenge," Available at www.bain.com/images/bain_brief_big_data_the_organizational_challenge.pdf (Last time accessed August 17 2016).

Rosen, J. 2012. "The Right to Be Forgotten," *Stanford Law Review Online* (64), p. 88.

Ross, C., Orr, E. S., Sisic, M., Arseneault, J. M., Simmering, M. G., and Orr, R. R. 2009. "Personality and Motivations Associated With Facebook Use," *Computers in Human Behavior* (25:2), pp. 578–586.

Scott, S. V., and Orlikowski, W. J. 2012. "Great Expectations: The Materiality of Commensurability in Social Media," in *Materiality and Organizing: Social Interaction in a Technological World*, P. M. Leonardi, B. A. Nardi and J. Kallinikos (eds.). Oxford: Oxford University Press, pp. 113–134.

Stone-Gross, B., Abman, R., Kemmerer, R. A., Kruegel, C., Steigerwald, D. G., and Vigna, G. 2013. "The Underground Economy of Fake Antivirus Software," in *Economics of Information Security and Privacy*. Springer, pp. 55–78.

Watson, H. J., and Wixom, B. H. 2007. "The Current State of Business Intelligence," *Computer* (40:9), pp. 96–99.

Yoo, Y. 2010. "Computing in Everyday Life: A Call for Research on Experiential Computing," *MIS Quarterly* (34:2), pp. 213–231.

Youyou, W., Kosinski, M., and Stillwell, D. 2015. "Computer-Based Personality Judgments Are More Accurate Than Those Made by Humans," *Proceedings of the National Academy of Sciences* (112:4), pp. 1036–1040.

Yuan, Y. C., Zhao, X., Liao, Q., and Chi, C. 2013. "The Use of Different Information and Communication Technologies to Support Knowledge Sharing in Organizations: From E-Mail to Micro-Blogging," *Journal of the American Society for Information Science and Technology* (64:8), pp. 1659–1670.

27
DIGITAL DIVIDES
Past, present, and future

Maria Skaletsky,[β] James B. Pick,[δ] Avijit Sarkar,[δ] and David J. Yates[β]

Introduction

Digital divides refer to differences in access to and purposeful use of information systems and technologies by people, or by social or political units such as cities, states, and nations. As computing became more widespread in the late 20th century, government and academic awareness of a variety of digital divides commenced, as illustrated by the early studies of the US National Telecommunications and Information Administration (NTIA 1995–1999), international agencies (ITU 1997–2016; World Bank 1982–2016; WEF 2004–2016), by early researchers (Hargittai 1999; Robison and Crenshaw 2002–2003), and by the recognition of the global information society (Castells 1996–1998).

In the 1990s, some national governments recognized the need to support digital access for their citizens. For example, Estonia, which established its independence from the Soviet Union in 1991, set attainment of widespread information technology as a national goal. With investment and support from its high-tech neighbor, Finland, Estonia steadily built up societal information and communication technologies (ICTs) knowledge and skills over several years through education, training, and government initiatives during successive administrations (WEF 2007, 81–90). The nation's first prime minister, Mart Laar, placed information technology as a unifying theme to advance the small nation and went as far as making the declaration that the Internet is a basic human right (WEF 2007). By continually reaching for very high goals over the next 15 years and through successive administrations, the nation moved up to achieve a high world ranking in its national use of ICTs, including the Internet. Another example of a nation that set high ICT-based goals early on throughout its society was Singapore (WEF 2015). The leaders of the nation have sought since the 1990s to advance Singapore by infusing information technology throughout its society to become an "intelligent island" (Warschauer 2001).

This chapter introduces the concepts of the digital divide, considers the evolution of its concepts and definitions, describes the different units of analysis, specifies their measurement and sources of data, describes several digital divide theories, indicates major determinants of digital divides, and discusses the evolution of concerns from access, to utilization, to productive outcomes of use. Digital divides worldwide will be illustrated by emphasizing major continental regions. At the national level, a more detailed comparison will be made of changes in digital divides within the United States and within the Russian Federation. The chapter will conclude by considering the goal of an inclusive and fair digital society (United Nations 2001; DiMaggio et al. 2004), how this relates to basic human rights, and the journey from digital access to usage and positive outcomes. The question of whether trends in digital divides are narrowing or widening, a newly emerging digital divide in big data, digital natives, and the question of how digital inclusion supports education (Warschauer and Matuchniak 2010) will also be discussed.

Digital divides are regarded by many observers, and by us in this chapter, as complex and evolving phenomena, which have multiple dimensions, measurements, units of analysis, and relationships with society and the economy (Barzilai-Nahon 2006; James 2008; van Dijk and Hacker 2003). An observer who has particularly pointed to the complexity of the digital divide concept (van Dijk 2005) posits a complex model that is permeated by inequalities. Personal characteristics such as age, intelligence, and personality lead to unequal availability of mental, social, and cultural resources, which in turn results in differential access. ICT access impacts the society, economy, culture, and politics, which leads to unequal positions in education, the workforce, and national leadership, which complete a feedback loop by influencing resource availability. Another loop impacting this access loop involves the capacities of ICTs and the associated skills to use them (van Dijk 2013). This model has the complexity that we feel is appropriate in viewing digital divides, yet, the model is so large that it can be difficult to operationalize and validate.

The complexity of these phenomena is also reflected in the wide variety of tools to analyze digital divides. Metrics that can be used range from those of infrastructure access, to affordability, utilization, social and government support or constraints, and socio-demographic factors, which amount to over 30 basic types of metrics (Barzilai-Nahon 2006). A comprehensive index of all such metrics is probably not achievable or useful, but rather a more specific set of metrics can be applied given a unit of analysis, cultural context, and specific purpose of a study.

Finally, the digital divide phenomenon is rendered complex because divides are evolving over time from access divides, to usage divides, and to inequalities in outcomes (DiMaggio et al. 2004; van Dijk 2013; Warschauer and Matuchniak 2010). In the 1990s and early 2000s, there were very large gaps among socio-economic groups in access to ICTs (NTIA 1998, 1999), but in the 2000s as access gaps narrowed, at least in developed nations, studies shifted to emphasizing usage of technologies (WEF 2011, 3–32; van Dijk 2012). Recently, as usage gaps have narrowed, studies have started to have a principal focus on outcomes of use. The outcomes include improved learning, economic productivity, social connectedness, professional skills, political engagement, and access to information. We can expect that this thrust will continue, and we give it attention in the chapter.

In digital divide studies, often the challenge of social inclusiveness in digital access and use appears. In the United States, although many divides are closing (NTIA 2014), parts of US society do not have basic digital access and use. Thus, social and political inclusion becomes a policy issue, that is, how to bring the fruits of using contemporary digital technologies to the underserved, who include the elderly, certain racial and ethnic minorities, and the impoverished. Because digital divides are very complex, solutions to expand inclusiveness are also complicated.

This chapter will proceed to examine many of these concepts and issues by next turning to analyze global digital divides.

Global digital divides

An important determinant of digital divides is the affordability of the hardware, software, and services that make up ICTs. Many people in developed countries therefore take for granted access to and use of telecommunication and Internet services. Such individuals live and work in a well-connected information society with universal availability of ICTs. A global analysis of contemporary digital divides, however, paints a much more variegated picture (Chinn and Fairlie 2007; Hilbert 2011; Pick and Sarkar 2015; UN 2015b).

Measuring global digital divides

Many measures of digital divides assess the extent to which ICTs have been adopted by individuals, households, schools, and other organizations in different countries. The diffusion, adoption, and affordability of ICTs is measured and tracked by several organizations.

The International Telecommunication Union (ITU) maintains and extends international cooperation "for the improvement and rational use of telecommunications of all kinds" and publishes current and historical data for many measures of digital divides, some of which are listed in Table 27.1.

The World Bank compiles national data on financial aspects of ICTs. For example, it tracks telecommunications revenue and investment and also ICT imports and exports. It also tracks the aggregate size of the Web using the number of secure Internet servers online as the indicator (World Bank 2015a, 2016). Whereas the ITU, UNESCO, and World Bank measure digital divides in very broad contexts, the World Economic Forum (WEF) does so in the context of an economic, social, and political framework. The WEF (2016) organizes measures of digital divides into four areas, namely environment (business and government), readiness (infrastructure, affordability, and skills), usage, and impact (economic and social), each with multiple indicators. Additionally, Internet World Stats (www.internetworldstats.com) is a non-governmental website that publishes social media (Facebook and Twitter) usage data.

Because most measures of digital divides revolve around individual choice, capability, and usage, it is helpful to consider a theory that integrates these factors. In the language of van

Table 27.1 Measures of digital divides tracked by the United Nations (UN) sources

In UN Millennium Development Goals (MDGs)	Fixed-telephone subscriptions per 100 inhabitants
	Mobile-cellular telephone subscriptions per 100 inhabitants
	Internet use as the percentage of individuals using the Internet (also in UN SDGs
Tracked by ITU and WEF	Computer access as proportion of households with a computer
	Proportion of households with Internet access
In UN Sustainable Development Goals (SDGs)	Percentage of population covered by a mobile network, by technology
	Proportion of individuals who own a mobile telephone, by gender
	Fixed-broadband subscriptions per 100 inhabitants, by access speed
	Proportion of schools with access to (1) computers and (2) the Internet for teaching
	Proportion of individuals with ICT skills, by type of skill

Source: ITU (2015a, 2016a); UN (2015a, 2015b).

Dijk's (2013) *resources and appropriation theory* (pp. 32–35), purchasing a subscription, for example, to a broadband service, is an appropriation of a digital technology. Van Dijk considers each appropriation of an ICT to be based on four distinct but related kinds of access: motivational, physical and material, digital skills, and usage, as shown in Figure 27.1.

> To appropriate a new technology one should first be motivated to use it. When sufficient motivation is developed one should be able to acquire physical access to a computer, the Internet or another digital medium. Additionally, one needs the material resources to keep using the technology that consist of peripheral equipment, software, ink, paper, subscriptions, and so on. Having physical and material access does not automatically lead to appropriation of the technology as one first has to develop several skills to use the medium concerned. The more these skills are developed the more appropriate use can be made of the technology in several applications. The concept of usage can be measured, among others by the observation of the frequency of usage and the number and diversity of applications.
>
> (van Dijk, 2013, 34)

This chapter measures the access divide of ICTs – globally, nationally, and regionally – in terms of the number of subscriptions as well as the proportion of individuals or households. Later in the chapter, we discuss a shift in the digital divide discourse away from access and use and toward social, economic, and environmental outcomes such as those articulated in the UN Sustainable Development Goals (UN 2015b).

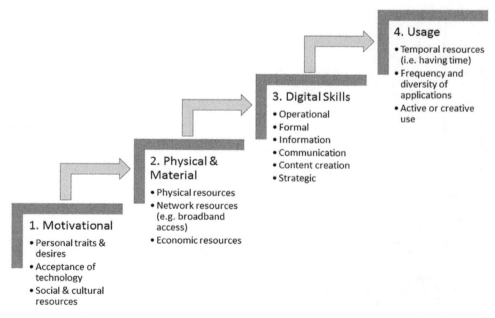

Figure 27.1 Four successive types of access in the appropriation of an ICT
Source: Adapted from van Dijk (2012, 2013).

Evolution of global digital divides

The term "digital divide" is used both in the singular and plural. Within the broad array of current definitions, the term was first used in the singular by Lloyd Morrisett to describe a divide between the information "haves" and "have-nots" (Compaine 2001). As the term came into common use, it became both a motivator for and a target of policy agendas (Selwyn 2004). Before the turn of the century, attention on digital divides focused mostly on access to ICTs and their relationship to economic development and education (UN 2001; Warschauer 2004). Subsequently, scholars began to grasp the complexity of understanding digital divides in the large (Norris 2001) and also their dynamic nature (van Dijk and Hacker 2003). It is therefore not surprising that in their latest report, the ITU (2015a) uses 61 "core" variables to measure global digital divides and their many interrelated dimensions. Furthermore, as the United Nations prepares to track global progress toward its Sustainable Development Goals, several targets highlight the important role that access to ICTs, the skills to use them, and their productive use play in leveraging the full potential of ICTs for sustainable development.

Figure 27.2 shows to what extent specific global digital divides are narrowing over time. Since 2000, the adoption of mobile-cellular services has followed the well-known S-shaped curve predicted by the *diffusion of innovations* theory (Rogers 2003). The quality and per capita distribution of mobile-cellular subscriptions, however, vary greatly. Between countries and regions, the voice quality and the reliability of message delivery are uneven. Furthermore, aggregated statistics like those shown in Figure 27.2 mask the fact that affluence and cultural factors can yield subscription ratios that vary greatly in different countries (UN 2015a). While not shown in this figure, the number of fixed-telephone subscriptions peaked at about 19.4 (per

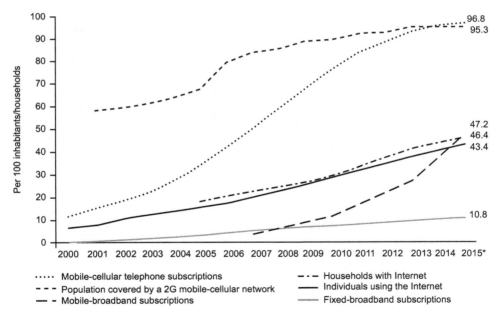

Figure 27.2 Global changes in ICT adoption, 2000–2015
Source: ITU (2015a).

100 inhabitants) in 2005 (ITU 2014b) and has been declining since then due to fixed-mobile substitution and to the higher cost of maintaining fixed-line infrastructure.

The global adoption of mobile-cellular subscriptions is perhaps the most significant bridge across the many digital divides since the advent of computing in the 1940s. In contrast, the sluggish adoption of fixed-broadband services highlights a significant and continuing global digital divide, which like most such divides is greatest between developed and developing countries (Norris 2001; van Dijk 2005). This divide is mostly due to the high capital costs of building broadband infrastructure and high labor costs to deploy fixed-broadband services.

What makes digital divides in aggregate a more challenging problem than any single divide is that these divides often travel together. Moreover, in early stages of development new ICTs may reinforce or even widen existing economic, political, and social inequalities between the haves and have-nots (Guillén and Suárez 2005; NTIA 1999). As the Internet emerged as a new technology in the 1990s, residents of the wealthiest nations were appropriating second-generation cellular phones at the same time (Gruber and Verboven 2001). Recent longitudinal analysis (Hilbert 2016) suggests that this pattern is repeating as optical fiber-based fixed-broadband is being adopted concurrently with fourth- and fifth-generation mobile services that include mobile-broadband, but almost exclusively in high-income countries as of this writing. It is therefore important to think of van Dijk's four types of access, illustrated in Figure 27.1, as repeating for each new or next generation technology and also sometimes at work in parallel, for example, for distinct types of access such as fixed- and mobile-broadband today (Lee, Marcu, and Lee 2011).

Current and future global divides

It is important to understand and visualize global digital divides and how they change over time (Pick and Sarkar 2015; Skaletsky, Soremekun, and Galliers 2014), even if it is difficult to understand the divides themselves, their causes, their effects, and their interrelationship at every level of detail (Hilbert 2011). Figure 27.3 shows that in 2014, Internet use was very

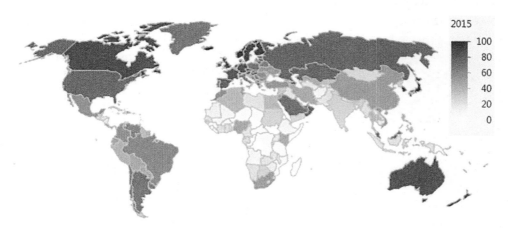

Figure 27.3 Internet users in 2014 (% of population)
Source: ITU (2015a).

high in North America, Europe, and Australia, but quite low in African nations in which less than 10% of the population regularly uses the Internet. Africa also exhibits lower levels of adoption of mobile-cellular technology on average (see Figure 27.4), however, some countries (e.g., Libya, Mali, Gabon, Botswana, and South Africa) have demonstrated "leapfrogging," in which mobile-cellular services have been adopted at levels that exceed those in more developed and affluent countries. South America, Europe, and Australia appear to have high numbers of mobile subscriptions, however more interesting comparisons occur across continental boundaries. Specifically, Figure 27.4 highlights there are some countries that have a very high number of mobile subscriptions, some of which are expected (e.g., Uruguay, Italy, Austria, Kuwait, UAE, and Australia) and some of which are unexpected (e.g., Suriname, Argentina, Jordan, Saudi Arabia, Oman, Kazakhstan, and the Russian Federation) (ITU 2015a, ITU 2016c).

Mobile-broadband services combine the benefits of mobility, voice, and messaging, as well as access to many web-based and mobile applications (ITU 2014b).

Figure 27.4 Mobile-cellular subscriptions per 100 inhabitants in 2014
Source: ITU (2015a).

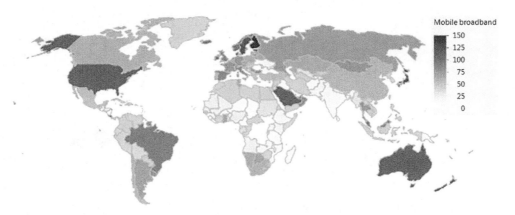

Figure 27.5 Mobile-broadband subscriptions per 100 inhabitants in 2015
Source: ITU (2016b).

Africa again exhibits lower levels of adoption of this mobile technology on average (see Figure 27.5). Only some African countries (Tunisia, Ghana, Namibia, Botswana, and South Africa) have adoption levels that approach the worldwide average. Again, more interesting comparisons occur across continental boundaries. Specifically, this figure highlights there are only some countries that have very high per capita levels of mobile-broadband subscriptions; namely, the Nordic countries, Estonia, the United States, Kuwait, Saudi Arabia, Bahrain, Singapore, South Korea, Japan, Australia, and New Zealand.

Overall progress toward bridging global digital divides has been mixed. Figure 27.4 shows that of the over seven billion people that have mobile-cellular subscriptions in 2015, many are living in affluent countries in which the number of subscriptions per person is greater than two. This good news is offset by the bad news that a greater number are living in poorer countries where there is less than a subscription per person, even though 95% of the world's population is covered by a mobile-cellular signal (UN 2015a). The adoption of this mobile technology has happened quickly in historical terms, as shown in Figure 27.2; however, less than three-quarters of a billion people subscribed to mobile services in 2000. A similar uneven per capita distribution of Internet use is illustrated in Figure 27.3. In aggregate, however, Internet use by the world's population has grown from just over 6% in 2000 to 43% in 2015. As a result, 3.2 billion people were linked to a global network of content and applications at this time (UN 2015a). One reason that Internet use has progressed more slowly than mobile phone use is that using the Internet requires greater literacy and superior digital skills (van Dijk 2005).

As old digital divides are bridged, new digital divides emerge. For example, as mobile- and fixed-broadband are being adopted more widely, bandwidth digital divides and their importance are emerging (Hilbert 2016). Although Barzilai-Nahon (2006) and others argue against over-emphasizing bandwidth as an important digital divide, recent studies remind us that greater bandwidth promotes more productive use of ICTs by increasing access to the number and diversity of applications and often providing a richer user experience.

Regional digital divides

Since the start of the new millennium, ICTs have catalyzed the fourth industrial revolution (WEF 2016). During the period 2000–2015, adoption and use of ICTs worldwide increased across the board, with the exception of fixed-telephone subscriptions. For example, the global growth in mobile-cellular adoption reflects rapid deployment of mobile infrastructure and concomitant improvements in network coverage. Multiple subscriptions per person in wealthier countries, however, in part explains the quintupling of such subscriptions since 2000 (see Figure 27.2). Leveraging similar but more advanced technologies, growth in mobile-broadband is more recent. This is due to increasing availability and declining pricing of mobile-broadband networks, especially in developing nations (Rouvinen 2006), and to rapid adoption of smart devices, mostly in developed nations (ITU 2016a). While mobile-broadband is projected to bridge affordability and connectivity divides, it is being used as a complementary technology (to fixed-broadband) in more affluent countries while being adopted more gradually in poorer countries as an affordable substitute (ITU 2016b).

The growth in household personal computer adoption since 2005 has been outpaced by the near tripling of both proportions of individuals using the Internet and of households with Internet access at home. Available data from the ITU indicate that nearly half of the global population is expected to have cyber-connectivity in 2016. ICT data also point to the fact that increasing cyber-connectivity is being spurred by the explosion of mobile-cellular subscriptions and mobile-broadband availability, indicating a shift away from reliance on a computer to obtain access to the Internet.

Closer examination of subscriptions to ICT services and ICT usage patterns, however, demonstrate significant digital divides between world regions. The gaps between the developed and developing world in terms of leading ICT indicators such as Internet, mobile-cellular, broadband (both fixed and mobile) remain stark, as shown in Figure 27.6. In 2015, mobile-cellular subscriptions in the developing world lagged those in the developed world by almost 32 per 100 inhabitants. Moreover, this gap has persisted at over 30 subscriptions per 100 inhabitants between the developed and developing nations since 2012. Broadband subscriptions also paint a similar picture, with fixed- and mobile-broadband subscriptions per capita in developing nations lagging behind those in developed nations by a factor of approximately 4.0 and 2.5, respectively, in 2015. Encouragingly, the gap in percentage of individuals using the Internet has shrunk somewhat between developing and developed countries since 2010. In 2016, per capita Internet access in the developing world is projected to be approximately half of the developed world (81% individuals using the Internet in developed nations compared to 40+% in the developing world) (ITU 2015a).

Digital divides between developed and developing countries are often echoed in disparities in the adoption and diffusion of ICTs among the major continental regions of the world. While Internet users and mobile-cellular subscribers in the Asia-Pacific region far outnumber their peers in Europe and the Americas due to a large population base of such users in China and India, per capita penetration of the Internet is half of that in Europe, as shown in Figure 27.7. However, the world region most afflicted by poor ICT connectivity is Africa, which lags significantly behind Europe, the Americas, and also the Asia-Pacific in all forms of ICT adoption.

Digital divides are often symptoms of economic, social, and technological divides. For example, in 2015 only 22.5% of African individuals had Internet connectivity compared to 62.2% in

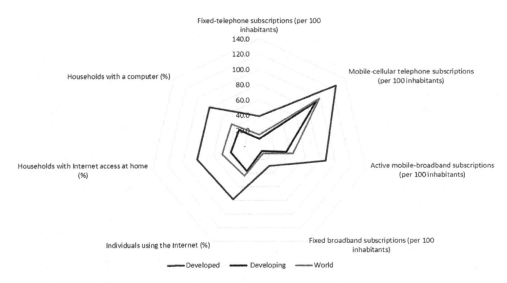

Figure 27.6 Digital divides in developed vs. developing countries, 2015
Source: ITU (2016c).

Digital divides: past, present, and future

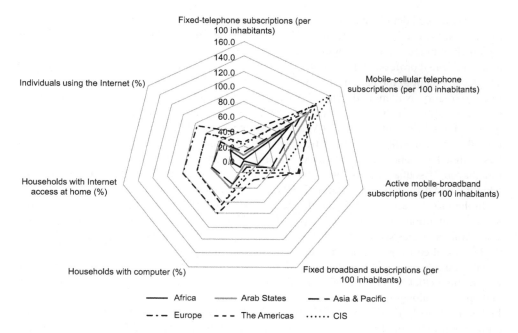

Figure 27.7 ICTs in ITU world regions in 2015
Source: ITU (2016c).

the Americas. Encouragingly however, giant strides have been made in Africa recently; since 2010, mobile-cellular subscriptions have grown from 45 per 100 inhabitants (2010) to nearly 81 projected subscriptions in 2016. Similarly Internet penetration has more than doubled from almost 10% to 22.5% of total population in 2015. Fixed-broadband subscriptions continue to lag in African nations compared with the Asia-Pacific and with developed and industrialized Western economies, suggesting an infrastructural malaise (Fuchs and Horak 2008).

Over the years, demographic and socio-economic factors such as age, gender, race and ethnicity, income, and educational attainment, as well as geographic location (urban versus rural) have been associated with disparities in adoption and diffusion of ICTs in many parts of the world (Pick and Sarkar 2015). Gaps in Internet adoption and use stemming from disparities in income and education are as geography-invariant in modern, industrialized Western economies as in poverty-stricken, socio-economically challenged nations in the African continent (Warf 2013).

European nations for the most part are considered as leaders, with high GDP per capita and the availability of a skilled workforce due to high per capita human resources in science and technology acting as catalysts in their adoption and use of ICTs, especially the Internet (European Union 2015; Vicente and López 2011). Regional unemployment, however, imposes challenges in bridging ICT disparities in Europe, and so do non-English speaking populations in eastern and southern parts of Europe compared to northern and western Europe (Vicente and López 2011; Warf 2013). Much of Europe is aging; in fact, nine out of the 10 most aged nations worldwide in 2012 are European (UN Statistics Division 2016); therefore many of Europe's ICT challenges stem from an aging population.

Infrastructural deficiencies also continue to engender challenges in bridging digital divides in many parts of Asia, including India. However in both China and India, nationally and internationally reputed centers of higher education have contributed to the ready availability of a highly educated professional, scientific, and technical workforce, contributing to rapid growth and development in the nations' hardware, software, and knowledge-services sectors, respectively (Gregory, Nollen, and Tenev 2009). This helps bridge digital divides in the two most populous nations of the world (Pick and Sarkar 2015, chaps. 5, 6). Additionally, consistent with findings in recent literature (Agarwal, Animesh, and Prasad 2005; Chen 2013), social capital – often manifesting itself in tight, socially knit communities such as cooperative societies founded and operated on the basis of agrarian cooperation (Prakash and De' 2007; Veeraraghavan, Yasodhar, and Toyama 2009) in rural areas – has been found to be associated with adoption and diffusion of ICTs in India (Pick, Nishida, and Sarkar 2014).

In the broader context of digital divides, the role of Internet censorship has received considerable attention in the literature. Apart from China, Central Asian nations such as Kazakhstan, Arab countries such as Saudi Arabia, and minuscule Internet penetration in sub-Saharan Africa has often been associated with various levels of censorship that enfeeble civil society and discourage open and free dissemination of information (Warf 2013). Unsurprisingly, one recent study (Pick and Sarkar 2015, chap. 9) has documented the strong association of societal openness along with urbanization and industrial activity in the manufacturing sector with higher levels of ICT adoption in African nations. Another finding that has gained prominence with regard to digital divides in Africa counters the argument that neoliberal policies encouraging market liberalization, deregulation, and privatization are part of the solution to bridge digital divides in less prosperous, developing parts of the world including sub-Saharan Africa. Older studies (e.g., Fuchs and Horak 2008; Heeks 2002) have provided exemplary cases of Internet use founded on the principles of bridging economic disparities and social inequities in which technology is conceptualized and used to solve human problems with clearly articulated development goals in traditionally impoverished settings.

An example of the pluses of societal openness is the success in Bangladesh of Dnet, a not-for-profit social enterprise that works with rural, impoverished communities to provide access to information, healthcare, education, and employment using ICTs to provide pathways for social and economic empowerment. Like many less developed and highly populous nations, the voice and messaging digital divides in Bangladesh are marked by a patriarchal society resulting in deep-rooted gender-based discrepancies in access to education, employment, and technology, infrastructural challenges in the telecommunications sector, and consequent "leapfrogging" stemming from availability of cheap mobile devices and calling plans, which contrast with a sparser, less reliable fixed-phone network. Over the past decade, Dnet has hired and equipped rural Bangladeshi women with mobile phones and trained them as "mobile info-ladies" who are employed at Dnet's helpdesk. The info-ladies would assist their untrained rural peers in connecting and communicating with experts such as doctors, lawyers, and specialists in healthcare, education, agriculture, and other fields. Dnet also conducted research that ultimately led to the creation of a knowledge repository database and search engine in the local Bengali language, thus providing access to valuable information that would otherwise prove illusive to the socially disconnected, often uneducated rural poor. This and other social empowerment initiatives facilitated by ICTs are highlighted by the Broadband Commission for Sustainable Development (Broadband Commission 2016).

Whereas this chapter focuses mostly on the relationship between economic and social factors and digital divides (e.g., van Dijk 2005; Warschauer and Matuchniak 2010), technological divides cannot be ignored (e.g., Gulati and Yates 2012). In other words, while the focus on education, digital skills and usage is important, technological divides are also critical in defining

> the questions of who (e.g. divide between individuals, countries, etc.), with which kinds of characteristics (e.g. income, geography, age, etc.), connects how (mere access or effective adoption), to what (e.g. phones, Internet, digital TV, etc.). Different constellations in these four variables lead to a combinatorial array of choices to define the digital divide.
>
> (Hilbert 2011, 715)

Hilbert (2016) further argues that traditional approaches of measuring digital divides are inadequate, and need to be expanded to recognize the extent and quality of an individual's foray into cyberspace. Accordingly, computer storage capacity and network bandwidth represent additional dimensions of digital inequality. Such developments reflect an expanded research opportunity to focus on newly emerging computing and network capabilities that underlie ICT usage and outcomes.

Digital divides in the United States

The United States, as one of the most populous, geographically vast, and diverse nations worldwide is also a world leader in the access to and use of ICTs. In 2014, the United States was ranked 15th worldwide in terms of the International Telecommunication Union's ICT Development Index, a gain of one position since 2010 (ITU 2015a). In fact, since the turn of the millennium, US household adoption of computers, Internet, and broadband have all increased consistently as documented in a series of reports of the National Telecommunications and Information Administration (NTIA 2011–2013). These reports paint a picture of diminishing digital divides, with computer, Internet, and broadband adoption all exceeding 70% household adoption by 2013, as shown in Figure 27.8 (NTIA 2014).

From Figure 27.8, it is evident that the growth in broadband adoption since 2000 steadily increased and caught up with computer and Internet adoption in the household by 2012–2013.

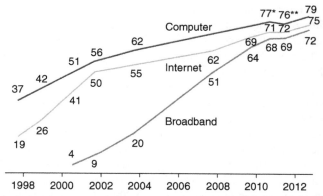

* Includes handheld devices such as smartphones and tablets (2010 only).
** Includes tablets but not smartphone (2011-2012).

Figure 27.8 Household adoption of computer, internet, and broadband (% of households), 1997–2012

Part of this impressive growth can be attributed to the development of the National Broadband Plan in 2008–2010 in the aftermath of the housing market crash and economic recession in the United States. The development of such a plan was based on the contention that improved access to broadband provides the foundation for economic growth, employment opportunities, global competitiveness, and a better quality of life. Since 2007, home broadband use has increased, with the most dramatic increase (from 32% in 2007 to 47% in 2012) in the 65 and older age group. This is encouraging because age is one of several factors that continues to impede a uniformly networked society in the United States.

Among other ICTs, computer and Internet adoption in the household continue to increase, with adoption levels approaching 80% of US households in 2016. Despite steady gains in Internet connectivity, disparities continue to persist, with low user interest in cyber-connectivity, concerns stemming from affordability, and lack of a computer – in that order – being the primary deterrents (NTIA 2014).

The NTIA in its recent reports has begun to focus on the mobile Internet. In 2000, mobile Internet subscriptions numbered fewer than 40 per 100 inhabitants in the United States, much lower compared to developed peers such as the United Kingdom, where the corresponding number exceeded 70. Since then, however, mobile subscriptions have steadily increased in the United States to almost 118 mobile-cellular subscriptions per 100 inhabitants in 2014 (ITU 2015a). As broadband availability has improved and smartphones have become ubiquitous, mobile devices and tablets rather than personal computers have provided alternative pathways to Internet connectivity to the US consumer (NTIA 2014). While mobile phone use has become widespread even among traditionally disadvantaged groups such as low-income families and people with disabilities, use of applications on mobile phones has varied significantly based upon educational attainment, income, population density, and other factors. In fact, US digital divides (NTIA 2014), irrespective of the type of ICT, are associated with demographic, socio-economic, and social connectivity factors.

Individual digital divides in the United States

Prior studies found socio-economic differences in the rates of use of ICTs (Fairlie 2004; Martin 2003), with those who are less educated, have lower income, minorities, and women having lower rates of use.

The difference in Internet use in the United States by gender was quite low in 2000, with 54% of men and 50% of women using the Internet. This difference shrunk to about 2% beginning in 2005 and closed in 2014 (see Figure 27.9). While more extensive research is required to assess whether there is a larger difference between genders when controlling for income, education, and other demographic characteristics, these numbers reassure us that there is no significant gender divide in Internet use in the United States.

The patterns of Internet use for people in different age, education and income groups are very similar. Those who are younger, more educated, and have higher income use the Internet at higher rates. Even though differences in Internet use by people in different age groups has decreased over time, it remains present and quite large (see Figure 27.10). While the difference between Internet users ages 18–29 and 30–49 has almost closed (96% and 93% in 2015), older age groups still lag behind, especially those 65 and older. However, the 65 and older group had the highest rate of increase in Internet users from 2000 to 2015, with the number of users increasing from 14% to 58%.

A similar pattern is seen in Internet use by people with different educational and income levels. Those with the highest levels of income and education have the highest rates of Internet

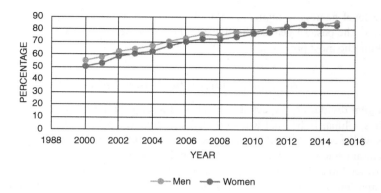

Figure 27.9 Internet use in the United States by gender
Source: Pew Research Center.

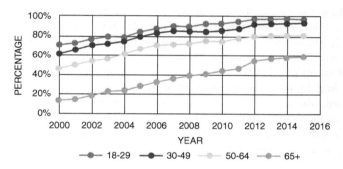

Figure 27.10 Internet use in the United States by age
Source: Pew Research Center.

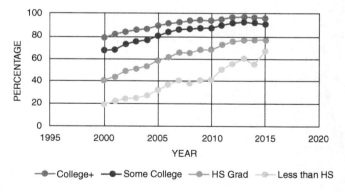

Figure 27.11 Internet use in the United States by education level
Source: Pew Research Center.

use (see Figure 27.11). However, the rate of Internet use among those with the lowest level of education and income has risen at the highest rate from 2000 to 2015.

We conclude that digital divides in the United States among individuals in different socio-economic groups still exist, with those who are younger and those having a higher educational

Maria Skaletsky et al.

and income level achieving higher rates of Internet use. However, gaps have consistently decreased over the past 15 years, with those in the oldest, least educated, and lowest income groups making the most progress.

Regional divides in the United States

Regional digital divides are expected to be present in large and diverse countries such as the United States, China, India, and Russia. In 2003, US states with the highest percentages of households with a computer and Internet were concentrated in the Northeast, West Coast, and Rocky Mountain states. States in the Midwest and the Rust Belt reported moderate levels of computer ownership and Internet access. States with the lowest rates of household adoption of computers and Internet access were in the rural South, an area acknowledged as a laggard in adoption and diffusion of ICTs (NTIA 2014; Pick, Sarkar, and Johnson 2015).

Figures 27.12 and 27.13 depict the states in 2013 by percentage of population living in households with a computer and households with a high-speed Internet connection, respectively. Interestingly, the geographic distribution of percent of people living in a household with a computer in 2013 is almost identical to the percent of households with a computer in 2003, as shown in Figure 27.12. The states with the highest and the lowest rates mostly remained the same. Overall progress was achieved between 2003 and 2013, however; the gap between states with the highest and lowest levels of computer ownership in the household decreased from 25.3% in 2003 to 14.9% in 2013, indicating a narrowing of the Internet digital divide. A narrowing of the high-speed Internet digital divide can also be observed by comparing Figures 27.11 and 27.13.

Broadband adoption patterns in US states (see Figure 27.16) largely mirror the geographic distributions of high-speed Internet adoption and computer use. Computer ownership, high-speed Internet, and broadband digital divides in US states follow an urban–rural divide,

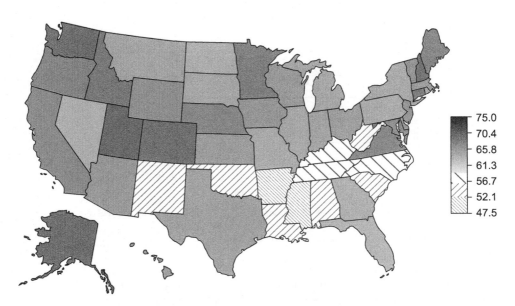

Figure 27.12 Households with a computer (% of households) in US states in 2003
Source: US Census Bureau, Current Population Survey, October 2003.

Digital divides: past, present, and future

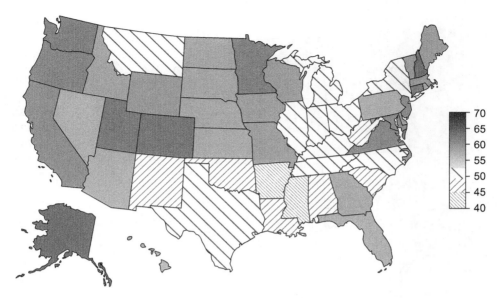

Figure 27.13 Households with Internet access (% of households) in US states in 2003
Source: US Census Bureau, Current Population Survey, October 2003.

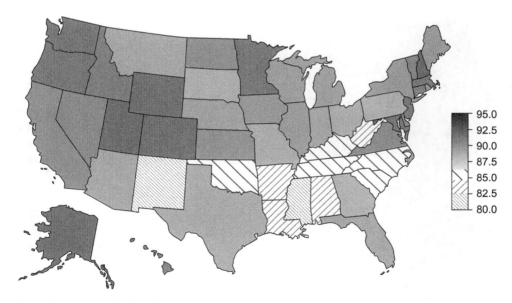

Figure 27.14 Households with computers in US states in 2013
Source: US Census Bureau, American Community Survey, 2013.

indicating that where people live often dictates the availability of and access to ICTs. Traditionally rural states and regions of the country have experienced slower and less extensive buildout of network infrastructure (NTIA 2014) indicating that infrastructural issues persist as impediments to bridging digital divides in the United States.

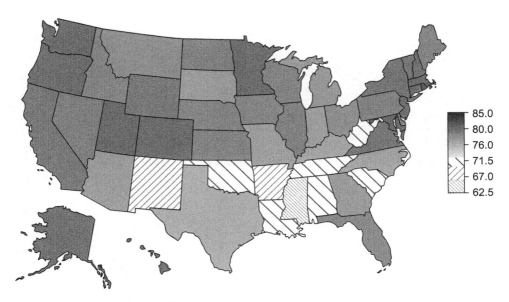

Figure 27.15 Households with high-speed Internet access in 2013

Source: US Census Bureau, American Community Survey, 2013.

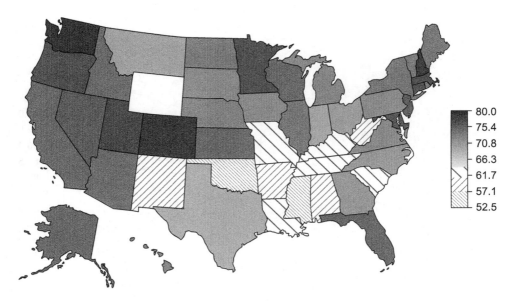

Figure 27.16 Broadband adoption in US states in 2013: percent of households using broadband in areas where broadband is available

Source: NTIA (2014); the data for WY are missing.

An exception to this rule is the narrowing of the gap in mobile-cellular adoption in US states. As evident from Figure 27.17, at least half of the households in states in the rural South are wireless-only households, indicating possible infrastructural deficiencies with respect to

Digital divides: past, present, and future

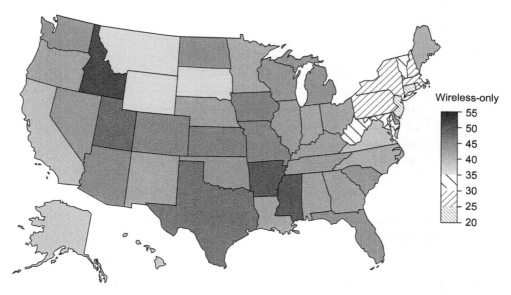

Figure 27.17 Wireless-only households in US states in 2012
Source: NTIA (2014); the data for MT, SD, and WY are missing.

fixed-line technologies. Nonetheless, a recent NTIA (2014) report provides evidence that mobile phones are becoming more common among historically disadvantaged groups and adoption gaps are diminishing across demographic and socio-economic groups, indicating a narrowing of the mobile digital divide in the United States.

We conclude this section by observing that recent research indicates that social interactions and connectedness of individuals and communities, which is often measured by social capital, is positively associated with adoption and diffusion of ICTs in the United States at the individual (Chen 2013), and also the state level (Pick, Sarkar, and Johnson 2015). Social capital in this context represents the extent of an individual's social and intellectual interactions in their communities. This reiterates the fact that a digital divide is not simply the difference between digital haves and have-nots, but rather it is multidimensional and multilayered.

Digital divides in Russia

Given the great progress achieved in access to and use of information and communication technologies in recent years, Russia can be considered a success story. Access to ICTs in Russia expanded significantly over the past several years. The proportion of households with Internet access increased from 48% in 2010 to almost 74% in 2014, while the proportion of households with personal computers increased from 55% to 75% during the same period (see Figure 27.18). The number of fixed-broadband subscriptions per 100 people increased from 1.1 in 2005 to 17.45 in 2014, while the number of mobile phone subscriptions per 100 people increased from 2.2 in 2000 to 155.1 in 2014 (World Bank 2015a). These significant improvements in access to ICTs improved Russia's position relative to those of other countries. Despite the current recession and economic difficulties, Russia's Networked Readiness Index global rank improved to 41 in 2015, up from 77 in 2010 (WEF 2011, 2016).

Maria Skaletsky et al.

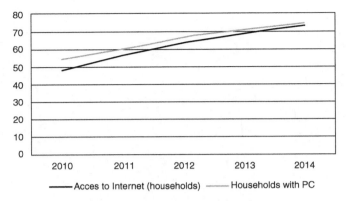

Figure 27.18 Household access to PCs and Internet in Russia, 2010–2014
Source: ROSSTAT (2015a).

A variety of data on ICT access and use, both at the individual and regional levels in Russia is collected and made available. The Russian Federal Agency of National Statistics (ROSSTAT)[1] has been conducting annual living standards surveys of Russian households since 2005. Another source of data is the Russian Longitudinal Monitoring Survey (RLMS),[2] a comprehensive living standards survey covering every year from 1992 to 2015. Both sources include data on access to ICTs, such as personal computers and the Internet, and also on the purpose of Internet use.

Despite the progress made in access to ICTs overall, there are significant inequalities among some demographic groups based upon age, ethnicity, gender, and extent of urbanization, as well as among regions.

Individual digital divides in Russia

As in the United States, there is a significant difference in the use of Internet by people in different age groups. Figure 27.19 shows that while 60.7% of the Russian population used the Internet in 2014, only 28.5% of those older than 55 used the Internet compared to 81.2% of those 18 to 35 years old. This is consistent with Internet usage patterns in many other nations where cyber-connectivity of older populations lags significantly behind that of their younger counterparts.

Another significant divide in Internet use is between urban and rural areas, as shown in Figure 27.20. While the extent of Internet use for those in urban areas was 65.6%, usage in rural areas was only 46%. The main reason for this difference is the very high cost of providing fixed Internet access to remote rural areas (Deviatko 2013). The most dramatic difference between Internet use in rural and urban areas was in the older group – 48% fewer of the older population in rural areas used the Internet compared to the same age group in urban areas.

While there is no significant gender difference in use of the Internet overall and in rural areas, Skaletsky (2013) found a significant gender-based difference in urban areas. While further investigation is needed to draw conclusions about the reasons for this difference, it might be attributed to the fact that fewer technical employment positions are held by women. It is therefore possible that the inequality in use of ICTs between men and women in urban areas is a symptom of a larger problem of employment inequality. Skaletsky (2013) also found a

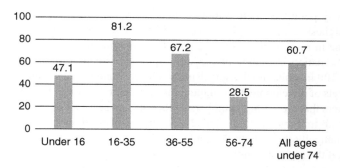

Figure 27.19 Internet use by age in 2014
Source: ROSSTAT (2015a).

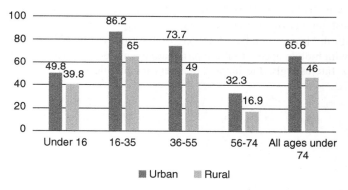

Figure 27.20 Internet use by urban and rural population in 2014
Source: ROSSTAT (2015a).

significant difference in levels of technology use among people of different ethnicities, with those of Russian ethnicity having higher levels of Internet use, compared to the minorities. Thus, an ethnic divide is also reflected within the regional digital divides in Russia.

Regional divides in Russia

Regional digital divides present significant problems in large countries, such as China, India, and Russia. Russia presents an interesting case because not only is it the largest country in the world in terms of land area, spanning 6.6 million square miles and 11 time zones, but it is also ethnically diverse. Russia's population includes over 185 ethnic groups, 26 of which are concentrated in national republics. Overall, there are 85 different regions within Russia. The 2013–2014 report of the composite Index of Readiness for the information society shows that while the difference in the readiness index, as well as all of the sub-indices, among Russian regions has decreased over time, it still remains extremely high (Institute of Development of Information Society 2015). The highest value of the index in 2013–2014 was 0.693 in Moscow, which is 2.3 times higher than the lowest value of 0.302 for the Republic of Dagestan, located in the North Caucasus region. This region has a very ethnically diverse population, with more than 30 languages spoken.

While densely populated metropolitan regions such as Moscow and St. Petersburg enjoy some of the highest levels of digital development in the country, small population centers, especially those in rural areas, lag far behind. For example, the Moscow and St. Petersburg regions lead the nation in mobile phone subscriptions per capita in 2000, as shown in Figure 27.21 (per 100 inhabitants). Unsurprisingly, Moscow and St. Petersburg have experienced the highest levels of development throughout the history of the Soviet Union and Russian Federation as centers that attract high numbers of tourists and serve as showcases of the country.

As evident from Figures 27.21 and 27.22, the number of mobile phone subscriptions increased dramatically throughout Russia by 2014. However, the Moscow and St. Petersburg regions still had the highest number of subscriptions. Figure 27.22 shows that some regions, particularly in the eastern and northern part of the country such as the Yamalo-Nenetskiy Autonomous Region and Magadanskaya Oblast, among others, made significant progress, while many regions remained far behind.

The difference between the regions with the highest and the lowest levels of digital development is very high. The number of mobile phone subscriptions per 100 people in the city with the highest number of subscriptions (St. Petersburg) was three times higher than that in the region with the lowest number (Republic of Ingushetiya) in 2014. Differences between the numbers with mobile access to the Internet are even more dramatic between regions (see Figure 27.23). Interestingly, the highest numbers for mobile Internet use, besides Moscow

Figure 27.21 Number of mobile subscriptions per 100 people in 2000
Source: ROSSTAT (2012).

Figure 27.22 Number of mobile subscriptions per 100 people in 2014 (excluding St. Petersburg)
Source: ROSSTAT (2015b).

Figure 27.23 Number of active mobile subscriptions using the Internet per 100 people in 2014
Source: ROSSTAT (2015b).

and a few other regional centers in the western part of the country, appear to be in the eastern regions.

Regions that are homes to various ethnic minority groups are among those with the lowest levels of both mobile phone and Internet use. Many of those regions, especially those in the Caucasus region, in the far southwest of the nation, had not only some of the lowest levels of digital development, but also the lowest levels of change between 2010 and 2014. Of the 20 regions with the lowest levels of mobile phone use in 2014, 15 were regions with a higher ethnic minority population per capita. Some of these regions also had the lowest increase in mobile phone use between 2010 and 2014. Thirteen of the minority republics were also among the 20 regions with the lowest levels of households with Internet access through personal computers in 2014.

While Russia has made significant progress in digital development overall in recent years, and improved its global standing, digital divides remain a problem within the country. Gender, age, and especially ethnic differences remain present in the levels of use of ICTs by different demographic groups. Furthermore, regional differences present a problem, with most less developed regions lagging far behind urban population centers like Moscow and other highly developed parts of the country. In sum, regional digital divides in Russia also reflect an ethnic divide, with regions that are home to a higher concentration of ethnic minorities having lower levels of digital development.

Summary and ways forward

Narrowing divides, international aspirations

Since the emergence of the Internet more than 25 years ago, the role of ICTs in the global information society has vastly expanded. This motivates the need to work harder to bridge current digital divides. Such effort is reflected at the international level as the United Nations has transitioned its focus from the Millennium Development Goals (UN 2015a) to the Sustainable Development Goals (SDGs), which specify goals and targets through 2030 (UN 2015b). Based on needs for economic development, there is also a strong shift in countries toward making broadband policy universal and promoting the adoption of more advanced technologies. For example, of the 196 nations for which the ITU gathers data on ICTs, 151 have a national broadband plan or strategy (ITU 2016b).

Looking to the future, the ITU and UNESCO are jointly tracking an expanded set of social, economic, and ICT-specific goals and targets. For example, the Connect 2020 goals are:

1   Growth – Enable and foster access to and increased use of telecommunications/ICTs;
2   Inclusiveness – Bridge the digital divide and provide broadband for all;
3   Sustainability – Manage challenges resulting from telecommunication/ICT development;
4   Innovation and partnership – Lead, improve, and adapt to the changing telecommunication/ICT environment (www.itu.int/en/connect2020/Pages/default.aspx).

Many of the SDGs are motivated by economic, educational, and other inequalities that remain a significant challenge. Thus, the SDGs argue for social justice and for environmental sustainability. With respect to social inequalities, for example, the Broadband Commission recently stated that conventional approaches to bridging digital divides "will not produce the results needed to connect the remaining offline populations, who are now found in more remote, rural areas, and consisting disproportionately of poorer, minority, less educated, and often female, members of society" (ITU 2016b, 6).

Convergence or divergence in digital divides

As access and use of technologies grows worldwide, it might be assumed that the digital divides will narrow, leading to convergence in measures of the technology intensity between the technology leaders and trailers. It is perhaps a surprise that very detailed studies of convergence versus divergence have mixed results (Hilbert 2016; Kyriakidou, Michalakelis, and Sphicopoulos 2011; Park, Choi, and Hong 2015; Pick and Sarkar 2015; Rath 2016). One explanation is that as older technologies converge or die away, the new technologies introduced refresh or even increase the relative size of the divides. Another explanation might be that the 21st-century aging of the world's population is tending to perpetuate the age-related digital divide (Niehaves and Plattfaut 2014). A study of convergence/divergence in 47 developing and developed nations based on annual data for the first 12 years of this century indicated that the initial divergence in IT development will reach a steady state that is even more diverged (Rath 2016). The drivers of the intensifying divergences were per capita income growth and the urban-to-rural population ratio. It is therefore likely that the shift in emphasis to differences in outcomes due to underlying digital inequalities means that global digital divides (Pick and Sarkar 2015) will persist for years to come.

Divides are not only converging/diverging for nations but also for smaller geographic units such as states, counties, and urban areas, which have been little studied. This opens up challenging areas of research that have large practical implications for regional planning, healthcare, marketing, educational planning, and equity and inclusiveness.

Journey from access to usage to outcomes

The digital divides of the 1990s concerned people and households gaining *access* to what were then relatively new technologies (personal computers, mobile phones, email). By 2015, although the simple use gap has narrowed considerably, another gap of what the users are doing is receiving more attention. For example, if a college-educated person mainly uses the Internet for gaming, but a high school graduate uses it for lifelong learning of career skills, there is a new type of digital gap emerging. Beyond use, an even more contemporary and forward-looking view is to evaluate what the differences are in the *outcomes* of use, that is, on the economy, society, behavior, communication, and politics.

In the 21st century, as the developed world has achieved high penetration rates for personal computers, mobile devices, and Internet access, the prominent digital divide phenomenon is becoming outcomes. This advance in the concept is exemplified by the shift in 2012 in the World Economic Forum's Networked Readiness Index (NRI), a prominent measure of the digital level of nations. The NRI definition remained largely unchanged from 2002–2011 with a focus on usage of traditional technologies, such as mobile phones, personal computers, and the Internet. The definitional change was provoked by the world overflowing with connected technologies, which is termed hyperconnectivity (WEF 2012, 3–34). The WEF responded by reworking the NRI to include four drivers: regulatory and innovation environment; technology readiness; technology usage by people, business, and government; and impacts on the economy and society (WEF 2012). The new NRI is much more complex than its predecessor, with 53 underlying variables. This example reflects the challenge of digital divide outcomes; phenomena that are much more complex and difficult to measure.

Another example of the newly perceived digital divide of outcomes was evident in a review of studies involving digital divides for K–12 schooling in the United States (Warschauer and Matuchniak 2010). The study identified that the older measure of *access* was outmoded for the American 21st-century youth, because nearly all youth had access. Accordingly, scholars shifted to examine *use* of technologies, but although numbers of users could be counted, it was very difficult to understand what school children were doing online, what their IT support and training systems were, and how their in-school versus out-of-school uses varied. Interest has now moved to understanding and measuring technology outcomes, but that has become exceedingly difficult "in part because the goals of teaching with technology are so diverse" and because metrics are not available to measure these outcomes (Warschauer and Matuchniak 2010, 201).

What can we draw from this evolution in digital divide concepts? Outcomes due to underlying digital inequalities will be much more complex to study, yet their practical implications are far greater. There is not the wealth of systematic government data to ground research on outcomes in a common base, but rather multiple smaller research studies will be needed of particular technologies, cultures, applications, and skills. More complex theoretical models will be required, going beyond even the most comprehensive ones in the literature (e.g., van Dijk 2005, 2013). Furthermore, the outcome differences are so great between privileged and deprived communities worldwide that outcomes due to digital divides might persist for many years and call for even more investigation than for earlier digital divides, as well as governmental efforts toward inclusion of the digitally deprived.

Digital natives, big data and emerging digital divides

One of the relatively new phenomena related to the use of ICTs is the notion of "digital natives," the population of young people who have been using ICTs in their daily lives since an early age. Many different definitions of digital natives exist, all of which refer to young people who do not know life without ICTs. Not only do digital natives adopt technologies more easily than older generations, but research suggests that the use of ICTs also has changed the way they think and learn (Prensky 2001). More research is needed to assess the long-term effects of these cognitive changes and ways in which education should adjust to be able to accommodate them. While most research on digital natives concentrates on developed countries, this phenomenon will have the most effect in developing countries (ITU 2013a). The development and adoption of new technologies lead to the emergence of new opportunities and consequently to the new divides. Crowdworking is one example of an emerging use of ICTs leading to a new form of digital divide. Crowdworking, or crowdsourcing, is a virtual marketplace where individuals perform small-scale tasks requested by organizations or other individuals. Some of the examples of crowdworking platforms are Amazon Mechanical Turk, Fiverr, and Microworker. These marketplaces are growing and include workers and job providers from different parts of the world. Workers' compensation varies from a few cents per minute to hundreds of dollars per task. While crowdsourcing offers job opportunities and flexibility to workers, Deng, Galliers and Joshi (2016) discuss the differences in motivation, perceived value, and use of crowdworking platforms by different demographic groups. They find that those who are unemployed and those with lower educational levels are impacted the most by the power imbalance between the crowdworkers and job providers, and thus are marginalized in terms of digital divides.

Another example of a new digital divide is the divide related to the capability to collect, store, and analyze big data. The volume of data available from various sources has increased dramatically in recent years. Big data mining has a variety of business, technological, healthcare, government, and other applications. Knowledge extracted from big data allows predicting customers' behavior, exploring the human genome, creating smart cities with focus on sustainable development, and so forth. The ability to process large volumes of data in real time requires both cutting-edge technological capabilities and analytical skills. Therefore, new divides emerge between organizations that have the ability to extract knowledge from big data and those that do not. The importance of narrowing the looming digital divide in utilization of big data is recognized by the UN Global Pulse initiative (http://unglobalpulse.org) and offers new research avenues. The mission of this initiative is "to accelerate discovery, development and scaled adoption of big data innovation for sustainable development and humanitarian action." The Global Pulse projects include analysis of social media to gain understanding of immunization awareness in India, Pakistan, Kenya, and Nigeria, measuring poverty in Uganda by using satellite images to determine roofs of different materials, used as a proxy for poverty, and using mobile phone data to track population mobility in Senegal, among many other projects.

Author affiliation notes

β Bentley University, Waltham, Massachusetts, USA.
δ University of Redlands, Redlands, California, USA.

Notes

1 www.gks.ru/.
2 www.cpc.unc.edu/projects/rlms-hse.
3 A more comprehensive set of references can be found at http://atc4.bentley.edu/media/Digital_Divide_Chapter_Extended_References.pdf.

References[3]

Agarwal, Ritu, Animesh Animesh, Kislaya Prasad. 2005. "Social interactions and the 'digital divide': Explaining regional variations in Internet use." *Research Paper No. RHS* 06–024.
Barzilai-Nahon, Karine. 2006. "Gaps and bits: Conceptualizing measurements for digital divide/s." *Information Society* 22(5):269–278.

Broadband Commission. 2016. *Doubling digital opportunities: Enhancing the inclusion of women & girls in the information society*. Geneva, Switzerland.

Castells, Manuel. 1996–1998. *The information age* trilogy, Vol. I–III. Malden, MA: Blackwell.

Chen, Wenhong. 2013. "The implications of social capital for the digital divides in America." *Information Society* 29(1):13–25.

Chinn, Menzie, Robert Fairlie. 2007. "The determinants of the global digital divide: A cross-country analysis of computer and internet penetration." *Oxford Economic Papers* 59(1):16–44.

Compaine, Benjamin. 2001. *The digital divide: Facing a crisis or creating a myth?* Cambridge, MA: MIT Press.

Deng, Xuefei, Robert Galliers, K. D. Joshi. 2016. "Crowdworking – A new digital divide? IS design and research implications." European Conference on Information Systems (ECIS) Proceedings, Research Paper No. 148.

Deviatko, Inna. 2013. "Digitizing Russia." In *The digital divide: The internet and social inequality in international perspective*, 118–133. London: Routledge.

DiMaggio, Paul, Eszter Hargittai, Coral Celeste, Steven Shafer. 2004. "From unequal access to differentiated use: A literature review and agenda for research on digital inequality." In *Social inequality*, 355–400. Thousand Oaks, CA: Sage.

European Union. 2015. *Eurostat regional yearbook 2015*. Luxembourg, Luxembourg.

Fairlie, Robert. 2004. "Race and the digital divide." *Contributions to Economic Analysis & Policy* 3(1):1–38.

Fuchs, Christian, Eva Horak. 2008. "Africa and the digital divide." *Telematics and Informatics* 25(2):99–116.

Gregory, Neil, Stanley Nollen, Stoyan Tenev. 2009. *New industries from new places: The emergence of the hardware & software industries in China & India*. Palo Alto, CA: Stanford Economics and Finance Press.

Gruber, Harald, Frank Verboven. 2001. "The evolution of markets under entry and standards regulation – The case of global mobile telecommunications." *International Journal of Industrial Organization* 19(7):1189–1212.

Guillén, Mauro, Sandra Suárez. 2005. "Explaining the global digital divide: Economic, political and sociological drivers of cross-national Internet use." *Social Forces* 84(2):681–708.

Gulati, Girish J., David Yates. 2012. "Different paths to universal access: The impact of policy and regulation on broadband diffusion in the developed and developing worlds." *Telecommunications Policy* 36(9):749–761.

Hargittai, Eszter. 1999. "Weaving the Western Web: Explaining differences in Internet connectivity among OECD countries." *Telecommunications Policy* 23(10):701–718.

Heeks, Richard. 2002. "Information systems and developing countries: Failure, success, and local improvisations." *Information Society* 18(2):101–112.

Hilbert, Martin. 2011. "The end justifies the definition: The manifold outlooks on the digital divide and their practical usefulness for policy-making." *Telecommunications Policy* 35(8):715–736.

Hilbert, Martin. 2016. "The bad news is that the digital access divide is here to stay: Domestically installed bandwidths among 172 countries for 1986–2014." *Telecommunications Policy* 40(6):567–581.

Institute of Development of Information Society. 2015. *Index of readiness for the information society: 2013–2014*. Moscow, Russia.

ITU. 1997–2016. *International Telecommuniation Union, World telecommunication/ICT indicators database*. Geneva, Switzerland.

ITU. 2009a–2016a. *Measuring the information society reports*.

ITU. 2014b. *Final WSIS targets review – Achievements, challenges and the way forward*.

ITU. 2016b. *The state of broadband 2016: Broadband catalyzing sustainable development*.

ITU. 2016c. *ICT facts and figures 2016*. From www.itu.int/en/ITU-D/Statistics/Pages/stat/default.aspx.

James, Jeffrey. 2008. "Evaluating latecomer growth in information technology: A historical perspective." *Technological Forecasting and Social Change* 75(8):1339–1347.

Kyriakidou, Vagia, Christos Michalakelis, Thomas Sphicopoulos. 2011. "Digital divide gap convergence in Europe." *Technology in Society* 33(3):265–270.

Lee, Sangwon, Mircea Marcu, Seonmi Lee. 2011. "An empirical analysis of fixed and mobile broadband diffusion." *Information Economics and Policy* 23(3):227–233.

Martin, Steven. 2003. "Is the digital divide really closing? A critique of inequality measurement in a nation online." *IT & Society* 1(4):1–13.

Niehaves, Björn, Ralf Plattfaut. 2014. "Internet adoption by the elderly: Employing IS technology acceptance theories for understanding the age-related digital divide." *European Journal of Information Systems* 23(6):708–726.

Norris, Pippa. 2001. *Digital divide: Civic engagement, information poverty, and the internet worldwide*. New York: Cambridge University Press.

NTIA. 1995–2000. Falling through the 'net reports. National Telecommunications and Information Administration. Washington, D.C.

NTIA. 2010–2014. Exploring the Digital Nation reports.

Park, Seung Rok, Doo Yull Choi, Pilky Hong. 2015. "Club convergence and factors of digital divide across countries." *Technological Forecasting and Social Change* 96:92–100.

Pick, James, Avijit Sarkar. 2015. *The global digital divides: Explaining change*. Berlin: Springer.

Pick, James, Avijit Sarkar, Jeremy Johnson. 2015. "United States digital divide: State level analysis of spatial clustering and multivariate determinants of ICT utilization." *Socio-Economic Planning Sciences* 49:16–32.

Pick, James, Tetsushi Nishida, Avijit Sarkar. 2014. "Broadband utilization in the Indian states: Socio-economic correlates and geographic aspects." *Management of Broadband Technology Innovation*, 269–296. London: Routledge.

Prakash, Amit, Rahul De.' 2007. "Importance of development context in ICT4D projects: A study of computerization of land records in India." *Information Technology & People* 20(3):262–281.

Prensky, Marc. 2001. "Digital natives, digital immigrants Part 1." *On the Horizon* 9(5):1–6.

Rath, Badri. 2016. "Does the digital divide across countries lead to convergence? New international evidence." *Economic Modelling* 58:75–82.

Robison, Kristopher, Edward Crenshaw. 2002–2003. "Post-industrial transformations and cyberspace: A cross-national analysis of Internet development." *Social Science Research* 31(3):334–363, 32(3):519–524.

Rogers, Everett. 2003. *Diffusion of innovations*. New York: Free Press.

ROSSTAT. 2012. *Russian statistics 2012*. From: www.gks.ru/bgd/regl/b12_13/Main.htm.

ROSSTAT. 2015a. *Russia in figures 2015*. From: www.gks.ru/free_doc/doc_2015/rusfig/rus-15e.pdf.

ROSSTAT. 2015b. *Russian regions: Socio-economic indicators 2015*. From: http://eregion.ru/sites/default/files/upload/report/index-russian-regions-2013-2014.pdf.

Rouvinen, Petri. 2006. "Diffusion of digital mobile telephony: Are developing countries different?" *Telecommunications Policy* 30(1):46–63.

Selwyn, Neil. 2004. "Reconsidering political and popular understandings of the digital divide." *New Media & Society* 6(3):341–362.

Skaletsky, Maria. 2013. *Essays on the digital divide – Explorations through global, national and individual lenses*. Bentley University, http://ezp.bentley.edu/login?url=http://search.proquest.com/docview/1427340691?accountid=8576.

Skaletsky, Maria, Olumayokun Soremekun, Robert Galliers. 2014. "The changing – and unchanging – face of the digital divide: An application of Kohonen self-organizing maps." *Information Technology for Development* 20(3):218–250.

United Nations (UN). 2001. *Human development report 2001*. New York, NY: United Nations.

UN 2015a. *The millennium development goals report 2015*. New York: United Nations.

UN 2015b. *Transforming our world: The 2030 agenda for sustainable development*, A/RES/70/1.

UN Statistics Division. 2016. *Population median age 2012*. From: http://data.un.org/Data.aspx?q=median+age&d=WHO&f=MEASURE_CODE%3aWHS9_88.

van Dijk, Jan A.G.M. 2005. *The deepening divide: Inequality in the information society*. Thousand Oaks, CA: Sage.

van Dijk, Jan 2012. "The evolution of the digital divide: The digital divide turns to inequality of skills and usage." In *Digital enlightenment yearbook*, 57–75. Amsterdam: IOS Press.

van Dijk, Jan 2013. "A theory of the digital divide." In *The digital divide: The internet and social inequality in international perspective*, 29–51. London: Routledge.

van Dijk, Jan, Kenneth Hacker. 2003. "The digital divide as a complex and dynamic phenomenon." *Information Society* 19(4):315–326.

Veeraraghavan, Rajesh, Naga Yasodhar, Kentaro Toyama. 2009. "Warana unwired: Replacing PCs with mobile phones in a rural sugarcane cooperative." *Information and Communication Technologies and Development* 5(1):81–95.

Vicente, María, Ana López. 2011. "Assessing the regional digital divide across the European Union-27." *Telecommunications Policy* 35(3):220–237.

Warf, Barney. 2013. *Global geographies of the internet*. Heidelberg: Springer.
Warschauer, Mark. 2001. "Singapore's dilemma: Control versus autonomy in IT-led development." *Information Society* 17(4): 305–311.
Warschauer, Mark. 2004. *Technology and social inclusion: Rethinking the digital divide*. Cambridge, MA: MIT Press.
Warschauer, Mark, Tina Matuchniak. 2010. "New technology and digital worlds: Analyzing evidence of equity in access, use, and outcomes." *Review of Research in Education* 34(1):179–225.
WEF. 2004–2016. *World Economic Forum global information technology reports*. Geneva, Switzerland.
World Bank. 1982–2016. *World development indicators*. Washington, D.C.: World Bank.
World Bank. 2015a. *The little data book on information and communication technology 2015*. Washington, D.C.: World Bank.

28
THE DEVELOPMENTAL EFFECTS OF THE DIGITAL REVOLUTION

Chrisanthi Avgerou and Atta Addo

Introduction

The discourse on the transformational role of ICT has lately acquired renewed audacity. In a series of lectures on the 'digital revolution' in autumn 2015, Anthony Giddens, an influential contemporary sociologist, outlined a mix of high opportunities and high risks from the "increasingly complex integration of the internet, supercomputers and robotics" that brings about an uncontrollable and unpredictable "transformation of everything." Humanity, he argued, faces a future "between Immortality and Armageddon."[2] Less dramatic, but for that perhaps more effectively attracting attention in policy circles, are the arguments about ICT induced socio-economic transformation that are put forward by economic analysts, journalists and business strategists.[3] These draw attention to nearly worldwide diffusion of computer and mobile communication devices, a huge and increasing stock of software applications available over Internet platforms, big data analytics and machine intelligence. They predict transformations across all aspects of society, most prevalent in economic growth, employment, medicine and security (Schmidt and Cohen 2013). The extent to which these transformative predictions will be realized is debatable. What is certain is that a range of powerful technologies are currently under construction and implementation in several contexts.[4]

Of interest to us in this chapter is the way the current wave of ICT innovation[5] dubbed the digital revolution might affect developing countries. Optimistic predictions envisage a wide range of life-changing benefits, such as mitigation of natural disasters and humanitarian crises (Global Agenda Council on Risk & Resilience 2016), inclusion of the poor in the formal economy (Nilekani et al. 2015), better health through telemedicine (Bonnefoy et al. 2014), improved education by accessing online courses and information and participation in the global high-tech industry.[6] More cautious views acknowledge risks such as 'premature deindustrialization,' that is, the trend of diminishing employment opportunities in manufacturing in developing countries resulting from the use of labour-saving technologies in the advanced industrial economies (Rodrik 2016; United Nations Development Programme 2015).

While the way the digital revolution will affect developing countries to a large extent depends on the course of ICT innovation and its socio-economic consequences in the advanced industrialized countries, a lot depends on the capacity of developing countries themselves to engage with ICT innovation for their socio-economic needs. Our understanding of ICT innovation in developing countries is too limited to support confident predictions of ICT-driven socio-economic development. This is partly because until recently there was not much ICT in developing countries, at least in comparison to industrialized countries. Known as the 'digital divide' problem, the very slow diffusion of computers and Internet connectivity in many parts of the world has attracted a great deal of attention by international development organizations since the 1990s. Policies fostering telecentres that were intended to bring computer facilities and Internet connections in poor communities did not lead to the expected widespread use of Internet services and telecentre enterprises were often short-lived (Madon et al. 2007).

For many people in poor and remote regions, IT devices and Internet connectivity continue to be in short supply. According to ITU data, Internet penetration in least developed areas is only 7%.[7] Optimism increased with the spreading of mobile phones in the last 10 years. By 2015 70% of the lowest fifth of the population in developing countries owned a mobile phone (World Bank 2016). Relatively affordable and widely desirable for personal communication, mobile phones have been taken up without policy interventions, bringing for the first time telecommunication capabilities in regions with no fixed telephone lines. But there are still regions without mobile signals, and broadband speed in most developing countries is far below the speed in advanced industrialized countries while prices of Internet connection and mobile phones are higher. The mobile phones of the poor have only basic functionality of voice and SMS. Smartphones, on which mobile telephony converges with the Internet, are beyond the reach of most people in developing countries and so are the digital business and digital services of the digital revolution.

What technology and technology services are available does matter, and we should not expect developing countries to benefit substantially from the digital revolution without adequate telecommunication infrastructures, advanced ICT artefacts and online services. Nevertheless, we should be able to draw lessons about what it takes to achieve developmental objectives even from the so far limited ICT innovation experience in developing countries. This is what the research field of ICT for development tries to do. Such research is based on the assumption that ICT innovation bears developmental benefits. The validity of this assumption is less obvious than it may appear at first thought because ICT innovation and its effects are part of many other processes of change in the world's socio-economic conditions.

Macro-level analyses of world socio-economic change do not provide a clear view of the impact of ICT in developing countries. It is difficult to disentangle the contribution ICT has made to their changing socio-economic conditions from other contributing factors. In the last three decades extreme poverty has been reduced and the proportion of middle-income families has increased in several regions of the world, most notably South and East Asia and Latin America (Ferreira et al. 2015; United Nations 2016; World Bank Group 2015). But the extent to which ICT, among other changing factors such as social welfare policies or liberalization of trade, has contributed to this global development pattern is hardly known.

We therefore have to cope with large amounts of anecdotal evidence and we need to develop the ability to interpret it. Mass media, the popular press and several documents by international developing organizations and think tanks give myriad examples of how ICT can improve the life of the poor in such vital aspects as income, health, education and contact with the state. Less frequently we read also about failed projects and shattered dreams of making prosperous modern lives out of ICT. Similarly, relevant academic literature has produced contradictory messages from mixed evidence. Research that followed the unfolding of some high-profile major initiatives addressing local needs found disappointing outcomes. Indicatively, the donation of computers to school-age children has questionable effects (Kraemer et al. 2009), and the telemedicine services India offered to Africa remains severely underutilized (Duclos

2016). Overall, weighing existing evidence of ICT diffusion and its socio-economic consequences around the globe, the latest study of ICT diffusion and socio-economic impact by the World Bank (2016) found that expected development benefits remain unfulfilled.

These are disheartening findings for the many advocates of ICT for development. Some policy experts and academics with an active involvement in the diffusion of ICT in developing countries came to doubt the power of ICT to produce expected transformative development effects (Kenny 2006; Toyama 2011). But research has also revealed cases of ICT that surpassed their initial expectations. Kenya's M-Pesa system for micropayments through mobile phones stands out as a case of innovation addressing needs with imaginative solutions feasible under local conditions (Hayes and Westrup 2012; Morawczynski and Miscione 2009; Morawczynski 2009). Studies of M-Pesa shed light on the socio-economic, technical and other peculiarities that enabled the unique success of M-Pesa in Kenya, even as the system struggled to be replicated elsewhere.

The increasingly more ambitious ICT innovation initiatives undertaken by developing countries expose the limits of existing knowledge about the role of ICT and development. For example, the Aadhaar project of electronic identification in India is a large-scale digital infrastructure with potential developmental effects (Nilekani et al. 2015). It is imbued with expectations for inclusion of millions of poor people in rural areas and urban slums in the formal economy and social services. It is too early to derive conclusions on whether such expectations will be met. The various questions concerning the unfolding of ongoing innovation such as Aadhaar exemplify the uncertainty confronting predictions of the developmental potential of digital innovation. Will Aadhaar become a springboard for the inclusion of marginalized poor into a modern country's social services and economic opportunities, or will it leave their lives untouched or even worse off? Will it enable transparency and fairness, or will it become an instrument through which the state will try to meet collective objectives with little concern for fundamental human rights such as individual privacy? Will the existence of an effective electronic identification infrastructure enable further socio-economic innovation that will benefit the poor and marginalized sections of the Indian subcontinent? Can the Aadhaar innovation experience be emulated by other countries and produce similar socio-economic effects?

To address such questions, ICT for development research needs to draw from theory-based analytical approaches for understanding how ICT innovation and socio-economic change occur. The importance of theory has been repeatedly emphasized by scholars of the ICT for Development field (Avgerou 2008; Heeks 2006; Walsham 2013). In this chapter we argue that understanding, explaining and predicting the course and developmental outcomes of ICT innovation in developing countries requires a combination of three foundational theories: theory of technology, theory of action and theory of development. The first two can be drawn from the theoretical debates in the IS field. For the third one, ICT innovation and development researchers need to draw from the interdisciplinary studies of development.

In the following section of this chapter, we will elaborate on theoretical perspectives of technology, action and development. Then, drawing insights from them and using secondary data we will seek to explain the unfolding of Aadhaar so far and attempt to assess its developmental consequences.

Theoretical foundations for ICT and development

The importance of technology is highlighted in many economic models used in research and policy on socio-economic development (see, for example, Porter et al. 2002; Ros 2013). While valuable for attracting attention to technology-enabled change, these are inadequate to cope with the complexity of challenges confronting ICT innovation in the developing world. Some theoretical fallacies plaguing this research and policy field are easy to identify. A common mistake is technology determinism, that is, the tendency to derive socio-economic effects on the basis of what technologies are capable of doing. It is also misleading to think about digital innovation and its impact in developing countries on the basis of assumptions of global technology trajectories with universal socio-economic effects.

Policy makers and managers in developing countries often set ICT innovation goals and initiate institutional reforms that imitate the experience of technologically advanced countries. In such approaches, developing countries are expected to 'catch up' with technological and institutional innovation and participate in the global supply chains of the open world economy (Mansell 2001). Analysts often emphasize norms of good governance and management, regulations and imitation of best practice across national borders. Yet, ICT innovation and its consequences vary substantially around the world because they take place at the meeting point of global influences and local institutions. Assumptions of a uniform trajectory of ICT-induced socio-economic transformations is bound to lead to wrong guidance for practice and wrong predictions.

The challenge for ICT and development research is to develop a theoretical perspective capable of explaining the process of ICT innovation and socio-economic change in relation to relevant contexts. A starting point for a contextual perspective to guide analytical thinking about ICT innovation and potential socio-economic transformation in developing countries is the ongoing theoretical developments in the field of Information Systems. In addition, research on ICT and development needs guidance from theories of development. In a nutshell, we suggest that the study of ICT for development should pay attention to three relationships:

1. The relationship of ICT artefacts or systems with the social actors that shape their functionality and their use, and have their capabilities shaped by them; these can be individuals, formal organizations or communities.
2. The relationship of socio-technical units of innovation with the socio-technical structures within which they are embedded.
3. The relationship of ICT innovation with goals and processes of socio-economic development.

Technology and society

The first relationship refers to a general theory of technology and concerns the causal mechanisms through which technology artefacts, in relation to human action, come to make a difference in social settings. Research by IS scholars in the 1970s challenged technology deterministic views about the impact of computers in organizations and highlighted the importance of the social environment of the capacity of an organization to develop computer applications and achieve expected productivity benefits (Kling 1980; Mumford et al. 1979). On the whole that early research on ICT innovation also rejected social deterministic positions that derive the features and effects of technology from social conditions of their development and use.

Indicatively, scholars endorsing the 'socio-technical design' approach aspired to create a better work environment by designing both technology functions and new work arrangements, in effect calling attention to the interaction of people with ICT artefacts in the context of their work (Land et al. 1980; Mumford et al. 1979). Empirical studies supported arguments that the results achieved by developing computer-based information systems at the workplace can neither be predicted by the material properties of the technologies alone nor by the behavioural traits of workers alone, thus forming the core idea of the socio-technical perspective of

ICT innovation (Markus 1983). It was suggested that it is the interaction of employees with the computerized information systems in their work contexts that produce observed effects, whether positive, such as more productive work practices, or negative, such as resistance to the new technology systems. Markus and Robey proposed the interaction of computer artefacts and human agency as the fundamental causal mechanism of the organizational effects of computers (Markus et al. 1988).

The causality between ICT innovation and social change has been further elaborated in the 1990s by drawing from Science and Technology Studies (STS) in sociology (Howcroft et al. 2004) and more recently with a stream of theoretical debates on socio-materiality (Leonardi et al. 2012). A consensus has been formed regarding the importance of considering ICT innovation and its effects as relationships of the capacity of artefacts to make a difference with the socially embedded capacity of people to act. Attention to technology and human actor relationships is drawn through a variety of concepts, such as actor networks – with technology artefacts assumed actor status – imbrication or entanglement. Their ontological and epistemological differences notwithstanding, all these concepts contribute to a view of the digital revolution as the closely interrelated processes of technology construction and social change, bearing potential for the formation of new socio-material conditions.

Individual action and society

The second relationship is elaborated in theories of action that explicitly or tacitly underpin research in all social sciences. The most common theory of action in economics, management and information systems is a rationalist view according to which calculated decisions of individuals confronted by choices in their everyday life aggregate to form social stability or change (Markus 2004). Various models of technical or rational action provide useful analytical tools for decision makers in management and policy, but they offer an oversimplified perspective of the way people come to act and the way their action leads to change in social collectives such as organizations, communities and states.

Various critiques have been proposed to the limitations of rationalist theories of action. For example, Granovetter (1985) criticized the dominant economic theories for taking for granted the utility 'maximization' effort of individuals and for missing the extent to which economic behaviour is embedded in, and therefore an outcome of, historically formed value choices of social collectives. The most powerful alternative to the rationalist perspective is based on the concept of agency, which refers to capacity to act with the following three fundamental characteristics. First, agency is inextricably related with individuals' experiences as members of social collectives. Second, agency includes capacity for rational, calculative action but also involves acting on moral will, tacit consciousness and impulse. Third, it assumes that action unfolds dynamically as individual actors interpret unfolding situations and readjust the initial plan (Emirbayer et al. 1998).

Several general 'structuration' theories elaborate the relationship of human agency and social structures, assuming that human action shapes social institutions while at the same time they recognize the enabling or constraining effects of social context on human action. The most prominent ones in IS research are Giddens's structuration theory, critical realism, Bourdieu's theory of practice, and the institutional logics variation of organizational institutional theory (Jones et al. 2008; Kvasny et al. 2006; Mingers 2004; Thornton et al. 2012). One of the differences of IS analyses that stems from the adopted structuration theory concerns the breadth of context they consider. For example, a stream of IS research focuses on analyses of situated practice in the micro-context of an organization (Lave et al. 1991; Orlikowski

2000). In contrast, several structurational IS analyses have sought to associate ICT innovation incidents in organizations and their consequences with a broader context of the organization concerned and its social environment (Njihia et al. 2013; Walsham et al. 1999).

The ability to account for a broader context that enables or constrains a process of ICT innovation and is consequently affected by the course and outcomes of innovation is, obviously, of crucial importance in ICT and development research. An important question in such contextual research is how the researcher identifies the relevant context that shapes and is consequently shaped by technology innovation (Avgerou and Madon 2004). The most common approach is to consider the ICT innovation process in relation to the social context of an organization and the country within which the organization is located (Madon 1993; Pettigrew 1985). Sometimes analysis is extended to consider influences from a global context. An alternative approach is indicated by Hayes and Westrup (2011). They suggest the tracing of relevant context empirically by following the connections of actions of individuals and social entities involved in the processes that brought about an innovation. They demonstrate their approach with an analysis of the M-Pesa case. Such approaches, which do not assume a context in terms of predetermined social categories, such as organization and country, are particularly appropriate for studies of ICT innovation that may involve networks of individuals and institutions from across national borders.

One glaring omission in most theories of the relationship of individual and localized action with a broader context is technology. The context tends to be purely social. Thus structurational analyses tend to focus on what individuals do under the influence of power relations, culture and various social norms. They ignore material aspects of social context such as technology infrastructures of electricity, transportation and telecommunications.[8] This is an important limitation in developing countries research, in which the availability of technology and more general material structures taken for granted in most IS research may be missing. Research on ICT innovation in developing countries should study socio-technical actors in relation to socio-technical contexts. Few studies so far pursue such analyses. While many ICT researchers in the field of ICT for development adopt a socio-material perspective of action in micro-settings such as hospitals or business firms, they assume a purely social country and global context. We need to develop theoretical perspectives of context as socio-material; that is, as social institutions sustained by material conditions and intertwined with technology infrastructures.

Development

The third theoretical articulation associates ICT innovation with theories of socio-economic development from which ICT research derives normative ideas about objectives of ICT innovation and explanatory mechanisms about the way development objectives are achieved. Several notions of development are used to identify developing countries as a distinctive category in the social sciences and international policy institutions. Most influential is the notion of development as economic growth, measured by the indicators of gross national product (GNP), income per person (IPP), and income distribution (the Gini coefficient) (Mann 2004). The achievement of economic growth is a central research concern in economics, with several contributing theories (Ros 2013). Each of them suggests different mechanisms for the developmental effects of technology and ICT in particular, albeit the most common view is ICT as a factor of productivity growth.

In its crudest form, the economic growth approach to development associates measures of the diffusion of computers, Internet connections or mobile phones with increases of gross domestic product (GDP) and employment. For example, the authors of the chapter on "The Changing World of Work" in the 2015 Human Development Report quote a study that estimates that "if Internet access in developing countries were the same as in developed countries, an estimated $2.2 trillion in GDP and more than 140 million new jobs – 44 million of them in Africa and 65 million in India – could be generated" (UNDP 2015, p 89). Similarly, Chavoula (2013) derives the following estimate from an econometric analysis: "on average, a 1% increase in mobile telephony users for every 100 people would increase per capita GDP by 0.39%, 0.26% and 0.15% for the upper-middle-, low-middle- and low-income countries, respectively." The validity of such estimates is questionable because research has also showed that there is no straightforward relationship between ICT diffusion and productivity growth; and the productivity puzzle of ICT noticed in the 1980s (Brynjolfsson 1993; Dedrick et al. 2003) continues three decades later (*Economist* 2016). More nuanced economic approaches account also for complementary factors, such as organizational restructuring (Brynjolfsson et al. 2000).

Alternative economic approaches shifted attention to other measures of economic exchange, such as transaction costs (Jensen 2007) and competitiveness (Porter et al. 2002). Importantly, purely economic theories of development accommodated consideration of social institutions to explain economic growth or the lack of it (Ros 2013, chap. 17). But with more complex economic theories the role of ICT in the processes of economic growth is less clear; the way ICT innovation contributes to economic performance of organizations, sectors and countries is multifaceted and marred with uncertainty (Kirkman et al. 2002). Developmental outcomes are anything but straightforward correlations of the diffusion of ICT with economic benefits suggested by parsimonious economic models (Srinivasan et al. 2015). Policy makers have to muddle through models that associate economic growth benefits of ICT with interventions for investment, competitiveness, regulation and structural reforms (World Bank 2016).

Development as economic growth has been criticized as inadequate to represent life conditions that people in developing countries are struggling to improve. Alternative approaches have been proposed throughout the history of post-WWII development ideas and policies (Colclough 2014). At present the most influential alternative approach centres on the notion of 'human development,' which underpins the United Nations Development Programme's (UNDP) Human Development reports, and the UN's initiatives known as Millennium Development Goals and Agenda for Sustainable Development (Millennium Project 2006; UNDP 2016). The notion of human development draws from Amartya Sen's ideas of development as people's freedom to 'lead lives that they value,' known also as the 'capabilities approach' (Sen 1999). Key concepts in Sen's theory are well-being, which refers to a person's 'functionings' (what he/she can do or be) and agency, defined in this theory as the pursuance of what a person values or regards as important. Thus, policies aiming to enhance human development adopt indicators for health, education, work and political freedom. Income indicators are also included but they are understood as means for enlarging people's choices rather than as an end of development.

Sen's capabilities theory has become the preferred theory of development for many researchers in the field of ICT for development studies. Most researchers declare its adoption as a normative intellectual device, that is, to justify objectives to be pursued by ICT innovation. From the perspective of the capabilities theory, conventional topics of information systems research, such as entrepreneurial ICT activities or e-government, are examined for their potential and actual empowering effects for disadvantaged citizen groups (Jimenez and Zheng 2016; Madon 2005). More importantly, by invoking the capabilities approach, ICT for development researchers have broadened the research agenda of the field to study questions that rarely feature in IS research, but considered crucial for human development, such as gender inequalities (Buskens 2010) and education issues (Bass et al. 2013).

Sen's contribution to the critique of development as economic growth created awareness that the choice of development theory is a moral choice. But there are also pragmatic and political implications in this choice, for the study of which the capabilities theory does not provide much guidance. Aspiring to noble goals is not enough to achieve developmental effects. An important pragmatic question in the debate of development approaches is whether the pursuit of economic growth is a prerequisite to achieving human development (Colclough 2014). Politically, the operationalization of development theory in policy action involves conflicts of interests and strategies for domination at the local and global level. ICT for development research often addresses conflicts of interest and power structures that are implicated in the appropriation of ICT for development goals, but it tends to limit such analyses to the local context.

Processes of ICT innovation as well as socio-economic development are to a large extent international and involve influences from globally powerful technology firms and institutional actors. They cannot be adequately studied by focusing only on local community or even national social and political dynamics. A thought-provoking study that considers multiple aspects of the political economy of ICT-driven development is Carmody's (2012) critical study of the developmental role of mobile phones in Africa. The challenge for ICT for development research is to shed light on the local processes of ICT innovation without missing their connection with the dynamics of international industrial economic and political processes.

As researchers on ICT for development become more aware of the importance of drawing from development theory and draws from the field of development studies for the framing of questions and the search for explanation, it would be a mistake to form rigid preferences of development approaches uncritically. The capabilities approach should be subject to critique of the processes of change it addresses and the outcomes it achieves as much as the economic growth approach. Moreover, on its own, a normative theory of development does not provide explanatory power. ICT for development research needs to engage also with the political economy of development and there is a lot to learn from research in the field of development studies.

Operationalizing foundational theories in ICT for development studies

Each of these three abstract theoretical perspectives provides specific guidance for the design of ICT for development research strategies. Theories of technology guide the researcher to clarify what causes what in the interaction of specific technologies with specific individuals as users, technology developers, entrepreneurs and so forth. There is a clear warning from the theoretical debates on technology and social change: avoid deriving conclusions of socio-economic effects either on the basis of what technologies can do alone, or on the basis of the socio-economic conditions of their enactment alone. Examine instead the ways people in their specific circumstances take up technologies and technology services to meet their local needs. Theories of action guide the researcher to trace the circumstances that matter for the specific phenomena they observe and try to explain. They are important for deciding what aspects of the developing country or global context to bring into the analysis as bearing on the socio-technical processes constituting the phenomenon they research. Theories of development help IS researchers to associate ICT innovation with the improvement of life conditions of the poor and marginalized in developing countries. They also guide them to consider how desirable objectives might be achieved amid other local and global dynamics of socio-economic change that may support or inhibit ICT innovation.

In short, foundational theories help the researcher to clarify:

- Which socio-technical ICT entity or phenomenon is the focus of their research (theory of technology);
- What actors, technology infrastructures and institutions, other than those who are immediately involved in working out the ICT innovation under study, influence the course of ICT innovation and its outcomes (theory of action).
- What developmental potential or goals the ICT phenomenon under study aims to achieve (theory of development).

The theoretical perspectives we outlined earlier should be understood as interrelated rather than standing alone: one requires the other to form the basis of an effective explanatory strategy. For example, on its own, the capabilities theory of development does not have much explanatory power of issues regarding ICT and development (Deneulin 2014). It does not explain how ICT innovation occurs or has developmental effects. ICT researchers have to combine this normative view of development with other theories that provide analytical guidance for studying processes of ICT and socio-economic change. But an in-depth understanding of its premises suggests its affinity to structurational theories of action and should be combined with them. A good example of such a theoretical fusion is explicitly undertaken by Kleine (2013), who included the key notions of functionings, capabilities, and agency in a structurational framework, according to which ICT is part of the structures that enable or constrain agency for the achievement of choices leading to human development outcomes.

In the remainder of this chapter we demonstrate this operationalization of abstract theory in an analysis of the Aadhaar project in India. We will attempt to explain its unfolding so far and assess its developmental potential.

The Unique Identification (Aadhaar) Project in India

Background

The Aadhaar project is the world's largest biometric and national identification number project as well as the largest IT project in any government (Dass 2011). 'Aadhaar,' meaning 'foundation' in many Indian languages, was launched by the Unique Identification Authority of India (UIDAI), a national agency created by the Planning Commission of the Indian government in January 2009 to issue a unique identification number to all Indian residents (Government of India Planning Commission 2009). Aadhaar provides each resident with unique identification (UID) consisting of a twelve-digit unique identification number that is linked with their demographic data such as name, date of birth and address, as well as biometric data such as photograph, iris scan and fingerprints.

The data is stored in UIDAI's Central Identities Data Repository (CIDR), and as of July 2016, over 1 billion Aadhaars had been issued (UIDAI 2016), making Aadhaar the world's largest personal data management scheme (Jayashankar and Ramnath 2010). While there might be cards printed by approved registrars or their contracted enrolment agencies, physical cards are not necessary because what matters most is the unique identification number, along with the biometric details of all those enrolled (ET Bureau 2009; News18 2016;

UIDAI (2012a). Any Aadhaar recipient or service provider can verify the UIN through Aadhaar Verification Service (AVS), a user-friendly service available on the website of the UIDAI that provides a simple 'yes' or 'no' to UIN queries. This simple verification process does not relay any personal information captured in the database.

Despite the wide scope of possible Aadhaar uses such as security controls and attendance tracking of workplaces and educational facilities (Indian Council of Agricultural Research 2014; The New Indian Express 2013), various restrictions remain that continue to be politically and legally negotiated between government and relevant groups and interests. At present there are various lawsuits alleging violations of citizens' privacy as well as the use of Aadhaar in sundry government programmes. In March 2016, a controversial new order known as the Aadhaar Bill was approved by the Indian Parliament to provide legal backing for the use of Aadhaar in anti-poverty programmes (Damodaran 2016). The controversy surrounding the bill hinged on the propriety of introducing the bill as a money bill – hence ensuring a less stringent passing by simple majority – and avoiding complex and broad-based debate on its wider merits and implications, particularly for anti-poverty programmes (Economic and Political Weekly, 2016). The 2016 Aadhaar Bill was significant for overcoming a 2013 order by the Supreme Court of India that forbade states from making enrolment in social programmes conditional on Aadhaar registration, because Aadhaar registration was not to be made mandatory.

Obtaining the Aadhaar is currently voluntary, and individuals without existing identity documents may still obtain an Aadhaar when introduced to the issuing agency by an existing enrolee in the scheme (Mahapatra 2015). Table 28.1 shows the UIDAI publication on what Aadhaar is.

Developmental objectives

The government of India spends about $50 billion on direct subsidies (coupons for cooking gas, food items like rice, etc.) every year. Most public and private service providers in India require proof of identity before providing benefits, entitlements or services to citizens and

Table 28.1 What the Aadhaar is

Aadhaar Is	Aadhaar Isn't
1. A 12-digit unique identity for every Indian individual, including children and infants	Just another card
2. Enables identification for every resident Indian	Only one Aadhaar card per family is enough
3. Establishes uniqueness for every individual on the basis of demographic and biometric information	Collects profiling information such as caste, religion and language
4. It is a voluntary service that every resident can avail irrespective of present documentation	Mandatory for every Indian resident who has identification documents
5. Each individual will be given a single unique Aadhaar ID number	An individual can obtain multiple Aadhaar ID numbers
6. Aadhaar will provide a universal identity infrastructure that can be used by any identity-based application (like ration card, passport, etc.)	Aadhaar will replace all other IDs
7. UIDAI will give yes/no answer to any identity authentication queries	UIDAI information will be accessible to public and private agencies

Source: UIDAI (2012b).

residents. Yet, a vast number of India's 1.2 billion people, particularly those living in poverty in India's 6,400 villages, are unable to prove their identity and hence unable to access critical services and social benefits (Nemschoff 2015; Nilekani and Shah 2015).

The stated goal of Aadhaar was to promote socio-economic inclusion by establishing the identity of individuals for targeted delivery of state services and subsidies under various welfare and social schemes of the government (UIDAI 2012b, 2012c). It was proposed as a remedy to leakage and fraud through the incidence of 'ghost names' and duplicate records in the benefits and entitlement systems of the government. It is not a citizenship or entitlement document (Venkatesan 2013), but qualifies as a valid national ID and proof of residence for recipients and could be used to access various government services like utilities, National Rural Employment Guarantee Scheme (NREGS), benefits under the National Social Assistance Programme (NSAP), or subsidized rations of daily necessities like kerosene and food from the Indian Public Distribution System (PDS). It also enables access to social levelling services such as banking and telecom that previously required strict proof of identity (UIDAI 2012b).

Significantly, the Indian government has proposed using Aadhaar in a policy programme it calls the 'JAM Trinity' to effect transformation of current anti-poverty programmes that are believed to be prone to leakage and inefficiencies (JAM stands for Jan Dhan Yojana, Aadhaar, Mobile) (Government of India 2015). Aadhaar – along with mobile phones and Jan Dhan Yojana, a financial inclusion programme to provide bank accounts to each household – is intended as infrastructure to enact a new scheme of direct transfers to entitled beneficiaries. As such, each of the JAM systems rather than being considered in isolation has developmental significance in combination with each other and with an overarching policy goal; Aadhaar, despite not being compulsory for accessing social safety nets, can provide needed identification to obtain and access a bank account through Jan Dhan Yojana. And given the ubiquity of mobile phones, mobile technology can play a critical role by enabling transactions such as receiving notification on transfers and communicating grievances and disputes to relevant authorities for resolution.

Role of IT

Aadhaar technology is suitably viewed as an 'e-infrastructure' in that it is a digital equivalent of conventional infrastructures like telephony and electricity that provide robust, reliable and widely accessible service (Srinivasan and Johri, 2013; Edwards et al. 2009). Aadhaar's database (CIDR) is centralized across data centers and powers several software applications mediated by registrar systems (Figure 28.1). The supported applications include core applications such as (1) an enrolment application for capturing new personal data and (2) authentication application for verifying UIN that are queried. Supporting applications include (1) a fraud detection application for catching fraudulent scenarios, (2) an administration application for user management, access control and reporting, (3) an analytics and reporting application for generating aggregate statistics, (4) an information portal for administrative access for internal users and general responses to public, (5) a contact center application for query and status updates, and (6) a logistics interface application for logistics providers (Computer Weekly 2011; Unique Identification Authority of India (UIDAI) 2012b).

The architecture of Aadhaar was developed according to principles of scalability, openness, security and vendor neutrality (Nemschoff 2015). Because every new enrolment requires authentication and biometric de-duplication across the entire system, every component needs to scale with high amounts of data. Open standards were also necessary to ensure

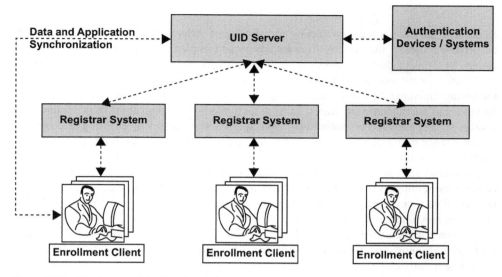

Figure 28.1 Illustration of Aadhaar's architecture
Source: Unique Identification Authority of India (UIDAI) (2012b).

interoperability with other systems such as the registrar systems through APIs linked to the UID server (CIDR). Relatedly, vendor neutrality was necessary to avoid technology lock-in and to ensure that the system worked across any network and device across standard interfaces. In terms of security, the system encrypts all data (using a 2048-bit PKI encryption and tamper detection) and does not store transactional information.

Explaining the unfolding of the Aadhaar project

Given the scope and scale of the Aadhaar project, its implementation was timely and relatively smooth.[9] Its rapid adoption and use are similarly noteworthy given the poor reputation of such large-scale identity projects generally (Davies et al. 2005; Whitley and Hosein 2010). Against the backdrop of generally disappointing narratives of ICTs in the developing country public sector context (Andrews 2013; Heeks 2003; World Bank Group 2011), such atypical unfolding of a large ICT project is worth exploring. Specifically, how do we explain Aadhaar innovation and related socio-economic transformations in relation to the organizational and broader contexts of India? And to what extent might the Aadhaar experience in India be emulable in other developing country contexts as has been proposed by some development actors (Raj and Jain 2016)?

Rather than seeing Aadhaar as a triumph of technological capabilities and what it could achieve universally, we suggest it is an information systems innovation that might be best understood through (I) the relationship of ICT artefacts and systems with the social actors that shape their functionality and their use, and in turn have their capabilities shaped by them, (II) the relationship of socio-technical units of innovation with the socio-technical structures within which they are embedded, and (III) the relationship of ICT innovation with goals and processes of socio-economic development.

(I)

In the Aadhaar case, mutual interaction and shaping of technological artefacts and the social occurred throughout the project, from its design and implementation through use and outcomes. In terms of design, features of the ICT artefacts such as standardization, scalability, openness, security and vendor neutrality were shaped as much by technical requirements as by the social imperative of India's large and growing population, as well as fragmented administrative and bureaucratic structures. In turn, the underlying technical artifacts, features and choices shaped potential organizational applications and processes by enabling or constraining their range of possibilities. Aside the architectural features, the user interfaces such as the Aadhaar Verification System (AVS) have a simple yet robust design and functionality (a search box that returns a 'yes' or 'no' to UIN queries); no doubt shaped in consideration of the limited capabilities of millions of potential users who might belong to India's vast poor, rural, illiterate and unskilled socio-economic segments. Such social impingements on ICT artefacts influence their form and function and recursively affect patterns of adoption, use and outcomes.

Aadhaar's implementation was similarly the result of technical and social interactions such as the use of innovative organizational design – a public–private partnership – whereby the government collaborated with the private sector to overcome technical, quality and human resource constraints. The project was headed by highly capable and proven technology management leadership with relevant private sector experience and keen awareness of public sector and political dynamics (Dhoot and Rajshekar 2014; Klitgaard 2011; Nilekani and Shah 2015). While the government's UID authority handled overall strategy and broader architecture, administrative matters such as procurement and financial planning ran through the government system and technical activities were outsourced to national and international private firms. Aadhaar as a standardized technical infrastructure implementation, in turn, allowed bridging of governmental silos and the creation of ecosystems that foster cross-functional collaboration (Krishnan 2012). For example, Aadhaar enabled its numerous registrars and agencies to clean up and interlink their own databases thereby facilitating a 'big data' paradigm. In addition to the core UIN and biometric data, all operational data was capturable – the time an operator took for each registration, delays, number of repeat attempts and so forth. Aadhaar thereby enabled management through data integration and analytics rather than traditional government approach of data fragmentation and silo ownership.

Finally, in terms of Aadhaar's use and outcomes, its intertwining in the JAM Trinity reveals a complex social and technical entanglement. The intended reform of the current social safety programmes in India into a direct cash transfer programme is not to be seen as a simple technological streamlining of an existing system but as a fundamental socio-technical transformation in which technology is entangled with policy and socio-economic objectives that are themselves fraught with political contention. This entanglement enables a reconfiguration of state–citizen relations as well as relations with financial entities and various services. Hence, eventual transformations enabled by JAM Trinity (of which Aadhaar is a key part) and their consequent outcomes for poverty reduction will not be determined by technology alone but by these complex sets of interactions.

(II)

Beyond the organizational and situated levels where socio-technical change unfolds, it is worth elaborating the broader socio-technical structures within which Aadhaar was embedded. Such broader context had both enabling and constraining effects in their interaction with the socio-technical unit of innovation described. In terms of enablers, the political economy of India, with its need for effective distributive regimes to reach the vast number of poor and socio-economically marginalized, provided a strong impetus for high level political and financial commitment to Aadhaar both with the Indian National Congress (INC) Party that introduced it and the Bharatiya Janata Party (BJP) currently in office (Sanyal 2012; Tewari 2014).

In addition, despite concerns over issues like privacy and civil liberties (*The Economic Times* 2016), the inclusivity and welfare objectives of Aadhaar, as a means for accessing social benefits and economic resources, appears to have gained strong institutional ground amid the high level of poverty and socio-economic marginalization in India. Furthermore, given India's administrative fragmentation, as well as its high level of social, cultural and ethnic heterogeneity and cleavages such as the caste system, Aadhaar appears to have filled a void in forging a 'superordinate' national identity among Indians (Akerlof and Kranton 2010; Klitgaard 2011; Putnam 2007). Finally, India's preeminent position as a global low-cost and high-skill technology hub meant that some of the world's best technologies, technology talent and resources were available and committed to the Aadhaar project at various levels, amid a national socio-political climate that was generally accustomed to and appreciative of technological progress as a symbol of modernity and national pride.

Despite these powerful enablers of Aadhaar innovation, various constraints exist within the broader context. The political economy of India imposes constraints on Aadhaar innovation. For example, while Aadhaar targets the state–citizen interface, a large part of leakage and diversion in anti-poverty programmes is believed to happen *before* that interface, that is, before ration dealers in the PDS and before disbursement agencies in NREGA. Aadhaar has been criticized as being unable to solve this 'real' issue (Ramakumar 2010, Khera 2011a).

Critics of the project have also pointed to privacy and civil liberty concerns as well as the potential of the state to use or abuse the system for 'security' purposes such as surveillance, profiling, tracking and even targeted harassment of political opposition (Bidwai 2010; Jijeesh 2011; PRS Legislative Research 2016). Furthermore, the threat of market intrusion, data breaches, data theft and data losses are said to be real, potentially catastrophic and far outweighing any benefits (Bidwai 2010; Jijeesh 2011; The Center for Internet and Society 2016). Finally, in the particular case of India, while Aadhaar has been advocated as a remedy for socio-economic exclusion, for example, by replacing existing discriminatory identifiers such as the caste system and domicile certificates (*The Hindu* 2016), concerns have been raised about the potential of Aadhaar to exacerbate rather than ameliorate exclusion by making a 'new caste' out of those who opt to not participate or who are unable to participate (Kraktivist 2013). This point about choice and its potential implications is particularly salient considering that many Indians already have one or several other official means of identification and might not see a need for or use the Aadhaar.

On the broader issue of socio-economic exclusion, it has been suggested that Aadhaar is designed to prevent the inclusion of the non-entitled, but is less effective at preventing the exclusion of the entitled, which is seen as a priority by many studies on India's political economy (e.g., Swaminathan 2008, Khera 2011a, 2011b, Sen and Himanshu 2011, Svedberg 2012, Drèze and Khera 2015). In this view, the problem of India's anti-poverty system is that of excluding needy users who are genuinely poor and vulnerable but do not receive entitlements.

(III)

Aadhaar's explicit developmental objective was to promote socio-economic inclusion by establishing the identity of individuals for targeted delivery of state services and subsidies under various welfare and social schemes of the government (UIDAI 2012b, 2012d). A less touted objective was to create infrastructure that would enable other potentially developmental innovations and 'applications' such as an Aadhaar Enabled Bank Account (AEBA) and Aadhaar Enabled Payment System (AEPS) through micro ATMs (UIDAI 2013). From a theoretical standpoint, these objectives evoke both economic and capabilities approaches to understanding development. The economic mechanisms of development at play with Aadhaar appear to be, among others, a reduction in transaction costs of distributive and welfare schemes as well as spill-over effects in innovation and economic participation more broadly,[10] all of which are expected to have positive effects on India's economy and public welfare. The capabilities approach further highlights the economic empowerment and human well-being that Aadhaar potentially facilitates for India's marginalized poor.

In spite of such assumed theoretical pathways to development, developmental outcomes will depend on actual use of the Aadhaar as suggested by our socio-technical perspective on the JAM Trinity initiative. In this vein, the Indian authorities' over-emphasis on metrics of success such as enrolment might be misplaced. It is as yet unclear what the extent and impact of Aadhaar's use is from a development standpoint. Based on a historical perspective of ICT for development, developmental improvements are likely to be contingent (rather than determinate), contextual (rather than general) and emergent (rather than entirely planned) due to the socio-technical nature of ICT innovation and the complex influence of various layers of context. Whether Aadhaar remains transparent and responsive to criticisms such as the potential for privacy and civil liberties violations, abuse by the state for unsanctioned purposes and so on remains to be fully seen. And a fundamental question remains, whether India's developmental problems such as lack of inclusivity and inefficiency in public welfare schemes are at their roots policy induced or technical (Ramakumar 2010). As such, it is far from straightforward to assess the developmental effects of Aadhaar based on its potential alone.

Can the Aadhaar experience be transferred to other countries?

The 'underdocumentation' challenge is not unique to India and poses an obstacle to developmental efforts in many parts of the developing world. The inability to appropriately identify and authenticate citizens in daily socio-economic interactions with the state and private entities such as banks and hospitals impedes rights, entitlements and access to services like education, healthcare, voting, financial services and employment. By contrast, citizens in developed countries are well identified from cradle to grave. Such an "identity gap" inhibits inclusive socio-economic participation (Gelb and Clark 2013). Furthermore, there are several other developmental challenges that are directly linked to underdocumentation, poor identification and authentication. For example, the age-old phenomenon of 'ghost' workers in bureaucracies like those in Africa and elsewhere that causes bloated civil service payrolls and leakages in public expenditure (Zelazny 2012).

In light of our analysis, we take up the question of the extent to which the Aadhaar experience in India will be emulable in other (developing country) contexts, as has been championed by certain development actors (Raj and Jain 2016). We have shown that Aadhaar innovation is not merely a technological feat but involves socio-technical interactions at different levels of context from the local to national, and even global levels. Such socio-technical interactions explain general patterns of ICT outcomes in diverse social and organizational settings but is not necessarily predictive. As such, outcomes of the same ICT system in various organizational settings and national contexts will likely vary and be contingent on the unique socio-technical and contextual factors at play.

This lesson has been frequently supported in various ICT initiatives in developing countries, most recently with the M-Pesa mobile payments system that was unsuccessfully emulated in other countries after its initial runaway success in Kenya (Camner and Sjoblom 2009; Hayes and Westrup 2012). Our socio-technical and contextualist position is by no means groundbreaking but remains at odds, implicitly or explicitly, with the typical technology determinism of various technology solution providers and development actors including major development organizations. It also runs counter to social determinist positions that see technological phenomena as largely the result of social influences and therefore tends to over-emphasize organizational, cultural and structural conditions.

Conclusion

In this chapter we examine the developmental promise of ICT in developing countries in light of the current wave of ICT innovations dubbed the 'digital revolution.' We propose a theoretical approach to study potential implications of the digital revolution for developing countries that combines an understanding of three levels of change: the relationship of ICT artefacts or systems with the social actors that shape their functionality and their use, and have their capabilities shaped by them; the relationship of socio-technical units of innovation with the socio-technical structures within which they are embedded; and the relationship of ICT innovation with goals and processes of socio-economic development. We illustrate such theoretical framing with an analysis of the Unique Identification (Aadhaar) Project in India – an ICT project that exemplifies the current ethos of ICT innovation both in terms of its vast promise and novel reach. We explore an explanation for the unfolding of Aadhaar and its potential implications for development and suggest that although such analysis might provide an informed basis for evaluating implications of the digital revolution in developing countries generally, it does not necessarily predict particular outcomes due to the contingencies of socio-technical interaction and the complex influence of various layers of context.

In the case of the Aadhaar, we venture to envision two possible futures for the innovation. In the first, Aadhaar, through its centrality in the JAM Trinity succeeds in its key goal of enabling fundamental reform of – if not dismantling – current anti-poverty programmes by reconfiguring them into a direct cash transfer programme as proposed by the Indian government. This outcome faces an uphill task, not only because of the potentially significant short-term disruptions and switching costs entailed in making such transition, but importantly because of the political pressures and conflicting interests surrounding it (Mooij 1999; Drèze and Khera 2015).

In the second possible future, Aadhaar fails to achieve its intended grand outcomes and at best achieves some modest outcomes unrelated to the initial plans. Such outcomes will be emergent and the result of complex socio-technical interactions and negotiated compromises that continue to unfold. For example, as the government continues to pursue belated legal underpinnings for the Aadhaar's continuous development and use, much will depend on the outcomes of legal and political negotiations, as well as the buy-in of relevant interests and social groups.

To sound a note of caution on our approach: our elaboration assumes a single case study, by far the dominant research method in the ICT for development arena. But this is not to suggest a methodological or epistemological hegemony in how the implications of the digital revolution in developing countries ought to be studied and understood. Indeed, various challenges remain that might benefit from alternative approaches. Specifically, we need better macro-level analyses of the mechanisms of change and the impact of ICT in developing countries that adequately disentangle the contributions of ICT to changing socio-economic conditions. Other approaches are also needed to synthesize, interpret and make better sense of the copious anecdotal and observational studies that continue to be produced in the area.

Notes

1. From a speech at Durham University, October 22, 2014, "Between Immortality and Armageddon: Living in a High Opportunity, High Risk Society" at www.youtube.com/watch?v=2Dk7lYx4x-s, visited March 31, 2016.
2. See, for example, the attention given to transformative digital innovation at the World Economic Forum in Davos in January 2016, which had 'The Fourth Industrial Revolution' as its central theme: www.weforum.org/agenda/archive/fourth-industrial-revolution, visited April 4, 2016.
3. 'Digital revolution' is a notion that is part of Schumpeterian theory of socio-economic evolution consisting of periods of creative destruction that is driven by technological change. It is juxtaposed with precedent 'industrial revolution' and 'agricultural revolution' (Freeman and Louçã 2002; Perez 1983; Pérez 2004; Schumpeter 1939).
4. We use ICT innovation to refer to the take-up of ICT and the working out of concomitant change in specific social contexts. As such, ICT innovation is synonymous with IS development and socio-organizational change.
5. See the discussions and papers of the World Economic Forum on Africa www.weforum.org/agenda/2016/05/africa-s-digital-revolution-a-look-at-the-technologies-trends-and-people-driving-it, visited July 4, 2016.
6. ITU (2015). ICT Facts and Figures, available at www.itu.int/en/ITU-D/Statistics/Documents/facts/ICTFactsFigures2015.pdf.
7. One exception is actor network theory (ANT), which explains cases of technology innovation by tracing connections of human-technology hybrids. But ANT conflates individual actors and social entities. Its fundamental principle to treat individuals, artefacts and institutions indistinguishably as interacting actors makes it difficult for analysts to identify the enabling or constraining conditions of social institutions and technology infrastructures.
8. Within two years post-implementation, the system had enrolled about 100 million people and was enrolling at a rate of over a million new people per day (UIDAI 2012d, p. 23).
9. An example of innovation spill over is the internet, which emerged out of initially unrelated work by the US government's Defense Advanced Projects Agency (DARPA) (Panel on the Government Role in Civilian Technology 1992).

References

Akerlof, G., and Kranton, R. 2010. *Identity economics: How our identities shape our work, wages, and well-being*, Princeton: Princeton University Press.

Andrews, M. 2013. *The limits of institutional reform in development*, New York, NY: Cambridge University Press.

Avgerou, C. 2008. "Information systems in developing countries: A critical research review," *Journal of Information Technology* (23:3), pp. 133–146. doi:10.1057/palgrave.jit.2000136.

Avgerou, C., and Madon, S. 2004. "Framing IS studies: Understanding the social context of IS innovation," in *The social study of information and communication technology: Innovation, actors, and contexts*, C. Avgerou, C. Ciborra, and F. Land (eds.), Oxford: Oxford University Press, pp. 162–182.

Bass, J., Nicholson, B., and Subrahmanian, E. 2013. "A framework using institutional analysis and the capability approach in ICT4D," *Information Technology & International Development* (9:1), pp. 19–35.

Bidwai, P. 2010. "Why Indians should fear the UID," *Rediff News*.

Bonnefoy, A., and Gionet-Landry, D. 2014. "Humanitarian telemedicine: Potential telemedicine applications to assist developing countries in primary and secondary care," European Space Policy Institute (ESPI).

Brynjolfsson, E. 1993. "The productivity paradox of information technology," *Communications of the ACM* (36:12), pp. 66–77.

Brynjolfsson, E., and Hitt, L. M. 2000. "Beyond computation: Information technology, organizational transformation and business performance," *Journal of Economic Perspectives* (14:4), pp. 23–48.

Buskens, I. 2010. "Agency and reflexivity in ICT4D research: Questioning women's options, poverty, and human development," *Information Technology & International Development* (6), pp. 19–24.

Camner, G., and Sjoblom, E. 2009. "Can the success of M-PESA be repeated? A review of the implementation in Kenya and Tanzania."

Carmody, P. 2012. "The informationalization of poverty in Africa? Mobile phones and economic structure," *Information Technology & International Development* (8:3), pp. 1–17.

The Center for Internet and Society. 2016. "Critique of the Aadhaar Bill 2016," (available at http://cis-india.org/aadhaar-bill-2016; retrieved July 4, 2016).

Chavula, H. K. 2013. "Telecommunications development and economic growth in Africa," *Information Technology for Development* (19:1), pp. 5–23.

Colclough, C. 2014. "Human development as a dominant paradigm: What counts as success?," in *Towards human development: New approaches to macroeconomics & inequality*, G. A. Cornia and F. Stewart (eds.), Oxford: Oxford University Press, pp. 66–85.

Computer Weekly. 2011. "Understanding the UID Aadhaar project and IT's role in its success," *Computer Weekly*.

Damodaran, H. 2016. "Simply put: What is the bill giving 'statutory backing' to Aadhaar about?," *Indian Express*.

Dass, R. 2011. "Unique identification for Indians: A divine dream or a miscalculated heroism?," No. 2011–03–04, 380 015.

Davies, S., Hosein, I., and Whitley, E. 2005. *The identity project: an assessment of the UK Identity Cards Bill and its implications*, London.

Dedrick, J., Gurbaxani, V., and Kraemer, K. L. 2003. "Information technology and economic performance: A critical review of the empirical evidence," *ACM Computing Surveys* (35:1), pp. 1–28.

Deneulin, S. 2014. "Constructing new policy narratives: The capability approach as normative language," in *Towards human development: New approaches to macroeconomics & inequality*, G. A. Cornia and F. Stewart (eds.), Oxford: Oxford University Press, pp. 45–65.

Dhoot, V., and Rajshekar, M. 2014. "Nandan Nilekani impresses Narendra Modi & Arun Jaitley, gets Aadhaar a lifeline," *Economic Times*.

Drèze, J., and Khera, R. 2015. "Understanding leakages in the Public Distribution System," *Economic & Political Weekly* (50:7), 39–42.

Duclos, V. 2016. "The map and the territory: An ethnographic study of the low utilization of a global eHealth network," *Journal of Information Technology* (forthcoming).

Economic and Political Weekly (2016). "Aadhaar as a money bill," *Economic and Political Weekly*, 51(11), p. 9.

The Economic Times. 2016. "Aadhaar appeal grows, downloads go past 40 crore mark," *Economic Times*, New Delhi.

Economist. 2016. "Working hard for the money: There are more explanations than solutions for the productivity slowdown," *Economist*.

Edwards, P. N., Bowker, G. C., Jackson, S. J., and Williams, R. 2009. "Introduction: An agenda for infrastructure studies," *Journal of the Association for Information Systems* (10:5), pp. 364–374

Emirbayer, M., and Mische, A. 1998. "What is agency?," *American Journal of Sociology* (103:4), pp. 962–1023.

ET Bureau. 2009. "Nilekani to give numbers, ministries to issue cards," *Economic Times* (available at http://articles.economictimes.indiatimes.com/2009-07 16/news/28448725_1_ration-cards-pan-cards-biometric; retrieved July 4, 2016).

Ferreira, F., Chen, S., Dabalen, A., Dikhanov, Y., Hamadeh, N., Jolliffe, D., Narayan, A., Prydz, E., Revenga, A., Sangraula, P., Serajuddin, U., and Yoshida, N. 2015. "A global count of the extreme poor in 2012: Data issues, methodology and initial results," No. 7432, *Policy Research Working Paper*, Washington, DC. doi:10.1007/s10888-016-9326-6.

Freeman, C., and Louçã, F. 2002. *As time goes by: From the industrial revolutions to the information revolution*, Oxford: Oxford University Press. doi:10.1093/0199251053.001.0001.

Gelb, A., and Clark, J. 2013. "Identification for development: The biometrics revolution," No. 315, Washington, DC. doi:10.2139/ssrn.2226594.

Gelb, A., and Clark, J. 2013. "Performance lessons from India's Universal Identification Programme," *CGD Policy Paper*.

Global Agenda Council on Risk & Resilience. 2016. "Resilience insights," World Economic Forum.
Government of India Planning Commission. 2009. "Gazette on Constitution of Unique Identification Authority of India (UIDAI)," pp. 1–3.
Government of India. 2015. "Economic survey 2014–2015," Department of Economic Affairs Ministry of Finance, New Delhi (available at: http://indiabudget.nic.in/es2014-15/echapter-vol1.pdf)
Granovetter, M. 1985. "Economic action and social structure: The problem of embeddedness," *American Journal of Sociology* (91:3), pp. 481–510.
Hayes, N., and Westrup, C. 2012. "Context and the processes of ICT for development," *Information and Organization* (22), pp. 23–36.
Heeks, R. 2003. "Most e-government for development projects fail: How can risks be reduced?" 14. Manchester.
Heeks, R. 2006. "Theorizing ICT4D research," *Information Technologies and International Development* (3:3), pp. 1–4.
The Hindu. 2016. "Aadhaar to be linked with caste, domicile certificates," *Hindu*, New Delhi.
Howcroft, D., Mitev, N., and Wilson, M. 2004. "What we may learn from the social shaping of technology approach," in *Social Theory and Philosophy for Information* Systems, J. Mingers and L. Willcocks (eds.), Chichester: John Wiley, pp. 329–371.
Indian Council of Agricultural Research. 2014. "Implementation of the Aadhaar Enabled Biometric Attendance System (AEBAS)," (available at www.icar.org.in/files/MX-M282N_20141126_182641.pdf).
Jayashankar, M., and Ramnath, N. 2010. "UIDAI: Inside the world's largest data management project," *Forbes India* (available at http://forbesindia.com/article/big-bet/uidai-inside-the-worlds-largest-data-management-project/19632/1).
Jensen, R. 2007. "The digital provide: Information (technology), market performance, and welfare in the south Indian fisheries sector," *Quarterly Journal of Economics* (122:3), pp. 879–924.
Jijeesh, P. 2011. *Aadhaar: How a nation is deceived* (2nd ed.), Muvattupuzha: Evees Press.
Jimenez, C., and Zheng, Y. 2016. "A capabilities approach to innovation: A case study of a technology and innovation hub in Zambia," in *Twenty-Fourth European Conference on Information Systems (ECIS)*.
Jones, M. R., and Karsten, H. 2008. "Giddens's structuration theory and information systems research," *MIS Quarterly* (32:1), pp. 127–157.
Kenny, C. 2006. *Overselling the Web?: Development and the Internet*, Boulder, CO: Lynne Reinner.
Kirkman, G. S., Cornelius, P. K., Sachs, J. D., and Schwab, K. 2002. *The global information technology report 2001–2002: Readiness for the networked world*, New York: Oxford University Press.
Kleine, D. 2013. *Technologies of choice? ICTs, development and the capabilities approach*, Cambridge, MA: MIT Press.
Kling, R. 1980. "Social analysis of computing: Theoretical perspectives in recent empirical research," *Computing Surveys* (12:1), pp. 61–110.
Klitgaard, R. 2011. "Designing and implementing a technology-driven public-private partnership," *Innovations Journal* (6:2).
Khera, R. 2011a. "The UID project and welfare schemes," *Economic and Political Weekly* (46:9), 38–44.
Khera, R. 2011b. "Trends in diversion of PDS grain," *Economic and Political Weekly* (46:21), 106–114.
Kraemer, K. L., Dedrick, J., and Sharma, P. 2009. "One laptop per child: vision vs reality," *Communications of the ACM* (52:6), pp. 66–73.
Kraktivist. 2013. "Warning - UID will create a digital caste system: Interview with WikiLeaks activist," *Kraktivist* (available at https://kractivist.wordpress.com/2013/06/01/india-warning-uid-will-create-a-digital-caste-system-aadhaar-aadhar/).
Krishnan, R. 2012. "Aadhaar: A national innovation platform?," *From Jugaad to systematic innovation* (available at http://jugaadtoinnovation.blogspot.co.uk/2012/06/aadhaar-national-innovation-platform.html; retrieved July 12, 2016).
Kvasny, L., and Keil, M. 2006. "The challenges of redressing the digital divide: a tale of two US cities," *Information Systems Journal* (16:1), pp. 23–53.
Land, F. F., Mumford, E., and Hawgood, J. 1980. "Training the Systems Analysts of the 1980s: Four analytical procedures to assist the design process," in *The information systems environment*, L. et al. (eds.), Amsterdam: North-Holland, pp. 239–256.
Lave, J., and Wenger, E. 1991. *Situated learning: Legitimate peripheral participation*, New York: Cambridge University Press.
Leonardi, P. M., Nardi, B. A., and Kallinikos, J. 2012. *Materiality and organizing*, Oxford: Oxford University Press.

Madon, S. 1993. "Introducing administrative reform through the application of computer-based information systems: A case study in India," *Public Administration and Development* (13), pp. 37–48.

Madon, S. 2005. "Evaluating the developmental impact of e-governance initiatives: An exploratory framework," *Electronic Journal of Information Systems in Developing Countries* (15), pp. 1–15.

Madon, S., Reinhard, N., Roode, D., and Walsham, G. 2007. "Digital Inclusion projects in developing countries: processes of institutionalisation," in *IFIP WG9.4 9th international conference "Taking Stock of E-Development,"* C. Wesrup and L. Silva (eds.), Sao Paulo.

Mahapatra, D. 2015. "Aadhaar use will be voluntary, says government," *Times of India*, New Delhi.

Mann, C.L. 2004. "Information technologies and international development: conceptual clarity in the search for commonality and diversity," *Information Technologies and International Development* (1:2), pp. 67–79.

Mansell, R. 2001. "Digital opportunities and the missing link for developing countries," *Oxford Review of Economic Policy* (17:2), pp. 282–295.

Markus, M.L. 1983. "Power, politics and MIS implementation," *Communications of the ACM* (26:6), pp. 430–445.

Markus, M.L. 2004. "Fit for function: Functionalism, neofunctionalism and information systems," in *Social theory and philosophy for information* systems, J. Mingers and L. Willcocks (eds.), Chichester: John Wiley, pp. 27–55.

Markus, M.L., and Robey, D. 1988. "Information technology and organizational change: Causal structure in theory and research," *Management Science* (34:5), pp. 583–598.

Mas, I., and Morawczynski, O. 2009. "Designing mobile money services: Lessons from M-Pesa," *Innovations* (4:2).

Millennium Project. 2006. "Millennium Development Goals: What are they?," (available at www.unmillenniumproject.org/goals/; retrieved July 13, 2016).

Mingers, J. 2004. "Re-establishing the real: Critical realism and information systems," in *Social theory and philosophy for information* systems, J. Mingers and L.P. Willcocks (eds.), Chichester: Wiley.

Mooij, J. 1999. "Food policy in India: The importance of electoral politics in policy implementation," *Journal of International Development* (11:4), pp. 625–636.

Morawczynski, O., and Miscione, G. 2009. "Exploring trust in mobile banking transactions: The case of M-Pesa in Kenya."

Morawczynski, O. 2009. "Exploring the usage and impact of 'transformational' mobile financial services: The case of M-PESA in Kenya," *Journal of Eastern African Studies* (3:3), pp. 509–525. doi:10.1080/17531050903273768.

Mumford, E., and Weir, M. 1979. *Computer systems in work design: The ETHICS method*, London: Associated Business Press.

Nemschoff, M. 2015. "Architecting the world's largest biometric identity system: The Aadhaar experience," *Converge Blog*.

The New Indian Express. 2013. "General education department to implement Aadhaar-based activities," *New Indian Express*.

News18. 2016. "You don't need an Aadhaar smart card because there is no such thing," *News18* (available at www.news18.com/news/tech/you-dont-need-an-aadhaar-smart-card-because-there-is-no-such-card-1228636.html).

Nilekani, N., and Shah, V. 2015. *Rebooting India: Realizing a billion aspirations*, New York: Penguin Books.

Njihia, J.M., and Merali, Y. 2013. "The broader context of ICTD projects: A morphogenetic analysis," *MIS Quarterly* (37:3), pp. 881–905.

Orlikowski, W.J. 2000. "Using technology and constituting structures: A practice lens for studying technology in organizations," *Organization Science* (11:4), pp. 404–428.

Panel on the Government Role in Civilian Technology. 1992. *The government role in civilian technology: Building a new alliance journal of chemical information and modeling* (Vol. 53), Washington, DC: National Academy Press. doi:10.1017/CBO9781107415324.004.

Perez, C. 1983. "Structural change and assimilation of new technologies in the economic and social systems," *Futures* (15:5), pp. 357–375. doi:10.1016/0016–3287(83)90050–2.

Pérez, C. 2004. "Technological revolutions, paradigm shifts and socio-institutional change," in *Globalization, economic development and inequality: An alternative perspective*. E. Reinert (ed.), Cheltenham, UK: Edward Elgar, pp. 217–242. doi:10.1016/S0954–349X (97)00029–5.

Pettigrew, A.M. 1985. "Contextualist research and the study of organisational change processes," in *Research methods in information systems*, E. Mumford, R. Hirschheim, G. Fitzgerald, and A.T. Wood-Harper (eds.), Amsterdam: North-Holland, pp. 53–78.

Porter, M. E., Sachs, J. D., Cornelius, P. K., McArthur, J. W., and Schwab, K. 2002. *The global competitiveness report 2001–2002*, New York: Oxford University Press.

PRS Legislative Research. 2016. "Nine issues to debate in Aadhaar Bill," *Hindu*, New Delhi.

Putnam, R. 2007. "E pluribus unum: Diversity and community in the twenty-first century. The 2006 Johan Skytte Prize lecture," *Scandinavian Political Studies* (30:2), pp. 137–174.

Raj, A., and Jain, U. 2016. "Aadhaar goes global, finds takers in Russia and Africa," *Live Mint* (available at www.livemint.com/Politics/UEQ9o8Eo8RiaAaNNMyLbEK/Aadhaar-goes-global-finds-takers-in-Russia-and-Africa.html; retrieved July 11, 2016).

Ramakumar, R. 2010. "The huge UID Project in India: A sceptical note," in *Ethics and policy of biometrics*, A. Kumar and D. Zhang (eds.), Springer.

Rodrik, D. 2016. "Premature deindustrialization," *Journal of Economic Growth* (21:1), pp. 1–33.

Ros, J. 2013. *Rethinking economic development, growth, and institutions*, Oxford: Oxford University Press.

Sanyal, P. 2012. "PM launches Aadhaar-based direct cash transfers in 51 districts of India," *NDTV*.

Schmidt, E., and Cohen, J. 2013. *The new digital age: Reshaping the future of people, nations and business*, London, UK: John Murray.

Schumpeter, J. 1939. *Business cycles: A theoretical, historical and statistical analysis of the capitalist process* (Vol. 1950), New York: McGraw-Hill Books.

Sen, A. 1999. *Development as freedom*, Oxford: Oxford University Press.

Sen, A., and Himanshu. 2011. "Why not a universal food security legislation?," *Economic & Political Weekly* (46:12), 38–47.

Srinivasan, J., and Burrell, J. 2015. "On the importance of price information to fishers and to economists: Revisiting mobile phone use among fishers in Kerala," *Information Technology & International Development* (11:1), pp. 57–70.

Srinivasan, J., and Johri, A. 2013. "Creating machine readable men: Legitimizing the 'Aadhaar' mega e-infrastructure project in India," in *Proceedings of the Sixth International Conference on Information and Communication Technologies and Development ICTD '13: Full Papers* (Vol. 1) pp. 101–112.

Svedberg, P. 2012. "Reforming or replacing the public distribution system with cash transfers," *Economic and Political Weekly* (47:7), pp. 53–62.

Swaminathan, M. 2008. Programmes to protect the hungry: Lessons from India. *DESA (Department of Economic and Social Analysis) Working Paper* 70.

Tewari, R. 2014. "Aadhaar, DBT get a lifeline, Modi to retain, push UPA schemes," *Indian Express*.

Thornton, P., Ocasio, W., and Lounsbury, M. 2012. *The institutional logics perspective: A new approach to culture, structure, and process*, Oxford: Oxford University Press.

Toyama, K. 2011. "Technology as amplifier in international development," *iconference '11*, pp. 75–82.

UIDAI. 2012b. "Features of the UIDAI model," *Aadhaar Technology* (available at https://uidai.gov.in/aadhaar-technology.html).

UIDAI. 2012c. "Role of biometric technology in Aadhaar enrollment," New Delhi.

UIDAI. 2012d. "What are the expected benefits of Aadhaar authentication?," (available at https://uidai.gov.in/auth.html; retrieved July 4, 2016).

UIDAI. 2013. "Aadhaar services overview," (available at https://resident.uidai.net.in/en_GB/aadhaar-services; retrieved July 12, 2016).

UIDAI. 2016a. "Dashboard summary Aadhaar data," (available at https://portal.uidai.gov.in/uidwebportal/dashboard.do).

UIDAI. 2016b. "Verify Aadhaar," (available at https://resident.uidai.net.in/aadhaarverification; retrieved July 4, 2016).

UNDP. 2015. *Human development report 2015*, New York: United Nations Development Programme.

UNDP. 2016. "A new sustainable development agenda," (available at www.undp.org/content/undp/en/home/sdgoverview.html; retrieved July 13, 2016).

Unique Identification Authority of India (UIDAI). 2012a. "Aapka Aadhaar," (available at https://uidai.gov.in/aapka-aadhaar.html; retrieved July 4, 2016).

United Nations. 2016. "What progress has been made in ending global poverty?," *Sustainable development goals: 17 goals to transform our world* (available at www.un.org/sustainabledevelopment/blog/2015/07/what-progress-has-been-made-in-ending-global-poverty/).

Venkatesan, J. 2013. "Don't tie up benefits to Aadhaar, court tells center," *Hindu*, New Delhi.

Walsham, G. 2013. "Development informatics in a changing world: Reflections from ICTD2010/2012," *Information Technology & International Development* (9:1), pp. 49–54.

Walsham, G., and Sahay, S. 1999. "GIS technology for district-level administration in India: Problems and opportunities," *MIS Quarterly* (23:1), pp. 39–66.
Whitley, E., and Hosein, G. 2010. *Global challenges for identity policies*, London: Palgrave Macmillan.
World Bank. 2016. *World development report 2016: Digital dividends*. Washington, DC: World Bank.
World Bank Group. 2011. *An evaluation of World Bank Group activities in information and communication technologies*, Washington, DC: World Bank.
World Bank Group. 2015. *Ending extreme poverty and sharing prosperity*, Washington, DC: World Bank.
Zelazny, F. 2012. "The evolution of India's UID program: Lessons learned and implications for other developing countries," No. 008.

Acknowledgements

The authors would like to thank Dr. Silvia Masiero for helpful comments on an early draft of the chapter based on her knowledge of the Aadhaar case.

29
BEYOND MOBILE IT
Ubiquitous digitality and work[1]

Carsten Sørensen

Introduction

There is little doubt that the organisational use of information technology has changed since the world first witnessed business use of electronic computing in 1951. Here the Lyons Electronic Office (LEO) signalled the beginning of the mainframe era, where computer technology would provide organisations with an increasing range of capabilities (Caminer et al., 1998). Mainframe computing supported extensive automation of back-office procedures, supply-chain management, management decision making, and much more. The advent of the personal computer in the late 1970s and onwards supported more targeted support for complex data manipulation and analytical insights, for example through spreadsheets. Locally networked personal computers further supported coordination and collaboration between team members within the same physical location. The widespread diffusion of Internet-enabled personal computers during the 1990s further extended collaborative capabilities to globally distributed co-workers. While the Internet in general and the World Wide Web in particular was available on so-called smartphones before the iPhone was launched in 2007, the rapidly spreading smartphones since that year have produced near 100% diffusion of Internet-enabled multi-purpose mobile phones. The Internet of Things brings promises of an even smaller granularity of connected technologies for pleasure and work. The adoption of radio-frequency identification (RFID) technology, home automation, and network connected devices will provide a rich tapestry of devices and standards, but also present the challenge of replicating focus, interoperability, and security through platformisation, which has proven the magic ingredient for the smartphone. The lack of interoperability and security arrangements has so far resulted in both lack of progress and increased security risk (*Economist*, 2014; Gallager, 2016).

The aim of this chapter is to critically discuss this technological development, and in particular relate to the organisational impacts of a range of mobile- and ubiquitous information technologies. The purpose is to place the organisational use of these technologies within a broader context of how computer technologies present opportunities and challenges for both organisations and the academics studying the organisational adoption of the technologies.

This perspective is motivated by the distinct lack of academic engagement in seeking to understand mobile and ubiquitous information technologies in organisational contexts (Sørensen and Landau, 2015). Perhaps it is necessary to reconnect the specific enterprise mobility research agenda to the broader issue of the challenges of making sense of technological choices for digitally enhanced enterprises. Current organisations now have a larger variety of computational capabilities at their disposal than ever before. These range from the tiniest electronic devices to global digital infrastructures, all potentially connected in a variety of device, personal, local, and global network configurations. Whereas organisational computing of the past was characterised by mainframe-centric computation of back-office procedures, this has been expanded to the edges in terms of the artefacts. The central position of a mainframe has been challenged by a shift of focus to the edges of both smaller, more personal devices, and at the other end, the increased reliance on digital platforms and infrastructures. How does this change the way organisations innovate and operate? How we can conceptualise these changes? The chapter synthesises the analysis from a number of past publications, spanning an extensive period of studying enterprise mobility (Sørensen et al., 2008; Sørensen, 2011; Sørensen and Landau, 2015; Sørensen, forthcoming).

The main argument presented here proposes that computational support for organisational activities can be characterised in terms of three main aspects, which will be applied in the analysis of organisational impact. The organisational challenges in creating supportive portfolios of information technology are described in terms of (1) *computing in the small*, which focuses on the intimate links between devices and individuals and their environment; (2) *computing in the large*, which emphasises the increasing importance of digital networking, platforms and infrastructures; and (3) *computing at scale*, which explores the importance of complex processing under digitalisation and the allocation of agency from humans to computational artefacts. The technological and organisational development has provided opportunities for paradoxically shifting organisational decision processes in two directions at the same time, of both more centralised and rule compliant, while at the same time supporting more emerging and fluid decision processes (Sørensen, 2011). The extensive organisational digitalisation can in this manner render organisational decisions subject to similar dynamics as those found in digital infrastructures (Lyytinen et al., Chapter 17 of this volume).

The next section outlines the three analytical dimensions, and the sections after that will each in turn explore one of the dimensions. The final section looks ahead to possible challenges for the digitised enterprise.

Three computing challenges

Given the extensive digitalisation of society in general and organisational processes in particular, and given the significant effects already witnessed, there are many challenges ahead of conceptualising these rapidly changing effects of technological development. Although meeting these challenges requires engaging a variety of related concerns, this chapter focuses specifically on how new forms of digital artefacts enables new forms of synthesis between technical and non-technical concerns within an organisational context. The analysis will be divided into three main sections, each concerned with a particular aspect of the organisational use of computer technology. The first aspect, *computing in the small*, is directly related to increasing miniaturisation and personalisation of computing devices at the edge of networks. This emphasises both individual members of the organisation having direct access to computing wherever they may be, but also to the use of Machine-to-Machine (M2M) technologies without any direct human engagement. The second aspect, *computing in the large*, focuses on the extension of digital networking activities in organisational computing connecting into global networks and digital infrastructures with the associated effects of enabling inter-organisational processes and platformisation. The third aspect explores *computing at scale*, emphasising the growing

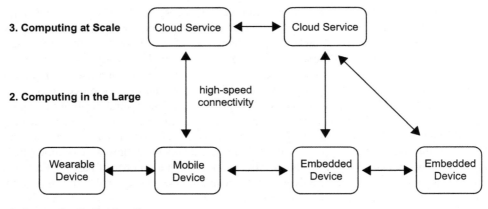

Figure 29.1 Illustration of the common architecture of edge-devices off-loading computational complex tasks through high-speed networking to cloud services

importance of complex digital computational processes leveraging the exponential growth in computing capabilities. These are both data and processing intensive, and will often be carried out in some form of distributed cloud service arrangement, but can also be located within an organisation's data centre, and indeed over time possibly also on edge-devices. This aspect relates to a number of diverse computational processes, including what can be characterised as artificial intelligence (AI).

These three aspects are here treated analytically separately, but are to a large extent in practice interdependent. Figure 29.1 illustrates how these three aspects are related in a common architecture for computation where mobile, wearable, or embedded edge-devices (computing in the small) provide some local processes, but also via high-speed connectivity (computing in the large) off-load complex data processing to cloud services (computing at scale). The diagram in Figure 29.1 is merely a simplified schema, and a range of different and significant more complex architectural schemata will be needed to explain the intricate details of such arrangements in practice.

There are many examples of current services facilitated by this kind of architecture. When iOS users call up Siri and ask, "What is the weather going to be today?," they do so on an iPhone or iPad mobile edge-device carrying out some of the processing. However, the heavy lifting is carried out in large datacenters crunching the question and providing essential parts of delivering the answer. Uber customers and drivers connect to each other through edge-devices, which in turn are linked to cloud-based server farms keeping track of available drivers and customers requesting transportation. When Android app developers and customers match up, this is also conducted through edge-devices that upload and download apps from cloud-based app stores. Each of the three dimensions will be discussed in the following three sections.

Computing in the small

It is often forgotten that the illustrious era of computing began with humans who were characterised as *computers* (Grier, 2005). The efforts of a large number of these human computers were in effect automated first by various mechanical and electro-mechanical computing technologies. The subsequent efforts applying mainframe computing technology resulted in the additional widespread *automation* of a range of other workers' activities as the need for discretionary decisions could be driven out of their work processes, as elegantly characterised by Zuboff (1988). Indeed, there is a close connection between the development of scientific management and the use of a variety of information and communication technologies to exercise organisational control (Beniger, 1986; Yates, 1989; Yates, 2005). However, the organisational use of digital computing also provided opportunities for *informating* remotely distributed workers about circumstances beyond their individual reach with a resulting distributed ability to engage in discretionary decisions (Zuboff, 1988).

The technological development from the mainframe era and onward has further sharpened this duality through further extending the abilities for organisations to codify business processes and stipulate these directly to remote workers, while simultaneously providing individuals with opportunities for discretionary local adaptation of decisions (Sørensen, 2011). Whereas the past very much reflected an either–or situation of either direct supervisory control when co-present, or lack of direct control when distributed, mobile IT enables the two modalities simultaneously. For the executive function, the provision of a rich set of digital data on, for example operations, customers, and logistics, gave rise to increasingly advanced decision support (Culnan, 1987).

The widespread diffusion of mobile and ubiquitous information technologies has emphasised the need for better understanding of decentralised connectivity. Computing in the small has altered our common explanation of life as occurring either at home or at work. Work life and home life will often no longer be completely separate, as Facebook posts can be checked and reposted at work, and work emails can be processed and authored at home. This shift implies that our lives with computing best can be characterised as fluid activities across a variety of contexts or situations, facilitated by distributed connectedness (Kakihara and Sørensen, 2002; Bassoli, 2010; Yoo, 2010). Extensive work within sociology, social geography, and communication studies has explored what has been characterised as "The Mobility Turn" or the "New Mobilities Paradigm" (Urry, 2000; Urry, 2007; Urry, 2008; Sheller and Urry, 2016). There is a series of important monographs and anthologies on the sociology of the mobile phone and mobile communication, relating to, for example, rituals and routines (Ling, 2008); technological ubiquity (Ling, 2012); impact on language (Baron, 2008); maintaining social networks for underprivileged in developing countries (Horst and Miller, 2006); and SMS messaging (Harper et al., 2005). Characteristic for most of this work is generally the lack of specific technological assumptions beyond mobile voice communication and SMS messaging, and very little interest in the world of work. Countering this is the extensive interest in framing social phenomena. At the other end of an imaginary socio-technical scale, the Human-Computer Interaction (HCI) field, and the part of the IS field close to HCI, have explored the design of mobile information technology with little interest in theorising the socio-technical relationships – with a few notable exceptions, such as Dourish's (2001) book on ubiquitous interaction.

Within mainstream IS, only little work has been done with a singular perspective on mobile information technology at work, in terms of both mainstream journal publications (Sørensen and Landau, 2015) or monographs (Sørensen, 2011). There has been no shortage of calls for action, most notably led by Lyytinen and Yoo (Lyytinen and Yoo, 2002a; Lyytinen and Yoo, 2002b; Lyytinen et al., 2004; Yoo, 2010). Yet, these calls have so far largely been ignored within IS with a decline in interest since 2006 (Sørensen and Landau, 2015). The IS field has failed to establish a lasting theoretical narrative related to the widespread mobile information technology and associated practices and ways of organising (Sørensen, 2011), or indeed engage in a rigorous debate on why there is none to be found. While it has been possible to observe the sweeping computation in the small, it has proven difficult to identify a lasting research agenda anchored in this phenomena and in the associated changes to working life.

When considering how to conceptualise computing in the small, a number of observers note that individuals are both faced with, and help create, multi-faceted tensions and paradoxes of social and work situations. Organisational members will often perceive their context as governed by various tensions and paradoxes (Lewis, 2000; Schad et al., 2016). Similarly, their actions with technology can both seek to resolve and enhance such tensions, as members' complex technology performances do not simply map a given performance to a given perceived purpose (Arnold, 2003). Rather, they engage complex, non-linear, technology performances in order to make decisions (Kakihara and Sørensen, 2001; Arnold, 2003). The individual will continuously be immersed in a range of possibly conflicting circumstances and their use of mobile and ubiquitous technological affordances can assist in resolving these, create new contradictions, or simply just engage in performances within paradoxical contexts. In this sense, mobile performances represent challenges to the bureaucratic order of workers as modular, that is, possessing sets of interchangeable skills and operating across distinctly separate spheres (Kallinikos, 2003). Figure 29.2 illustrates a set of possible basic mobile IT affordances from which complex service portfolios can be constructed. As a simple example, a person can concurrently be both fixed (for example as always available through a mobile phone number) and mobile (away from a fixed physical location). A person can engage in complex technology performances rendering them at the same time both busy and available – critically depending on for whom and regarding what. The use of mobile and ubiquitous information technologies does not only shift the spatial and temporal aspects of interaction (where

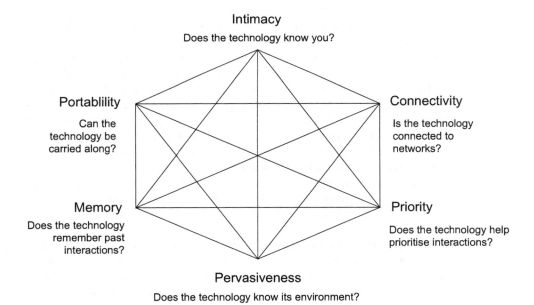

Figure 29.2 Illustration of six categories of affordances related to mobile and ubiquitous computing technologies

Source: Sørensen (2011).

and when), but crucially also the contextual aspects (in what circumstances) (Kakihara and Sørensen, 2002).

Organisational performances with mobile IT can be characterised as the attempts to resolve the tensions emerging from the work context through evoking a variety of affordances (Sørensen, 2011). Figure 29.3 illustrates this and further points toward the dual emergent and planned aspects of such performances. Schedules, plans, routines, procedures, and so forth govern parts of organisational life (Carstensen and Sørensen, 1996; Schmidt and Simone, 1996). However, emerging situations may require unplanned or improvised performances. Figure 29.3 also highlights that a need to balance fluid interaction among members and across the organisation with a need for interactional boundaries to shield from fluidity will be an important context for such mobile performances. It matters how work is organised in terms of creating a collaborative environment facilitating interaction within and limiting outside disturbance (Ciborra, 1996; Perlow et al., 2004).

The diffusion of the mobile phone has reached a saturation point globally, and smartphones may soon reach this level too beyond the developed part of the world. The coming years will likely see the possibilities and challenges of the wider spread of the Internet of Things. It seems clear that these developments along with the smartphone and tablet app stores jointly has provided a highly successful innovation arrangement for further extending computing in the small. However, embedded in the understanding of computing in the small is the challenge of also understanding the related computing in the large.

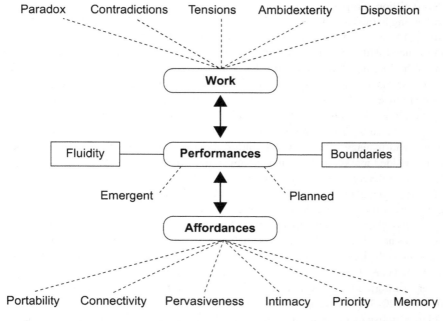

Figure 29.3 Mobile performances occur when individuals apply mobile IT affordances as a means of optimising decisions and actions within a context of contradictory work requirements and situations. Such performances can be both planned and emergent, and seek to optimise appropriate balance between establishing interaction fluidity while managing interactional boundaries.

Source: Sørensen (2011).

Computing in the large

The increasing reliance on distributing and locally networked computing during the 1980s and 1990s facilitated increased digital information flows between different parts of the organisation, and more advanced support for computer-mediated collaboration (Johansen, 1988; Schmidt and Bannon, 1992). Early on, the challenges were significant, as each business unit would implement its own support, thus making it difficult to establish an integrated firm from "islands of automation" (McFarlan et al., 1983). During the 1980s, standardisations emerged for process integration across organisations through Electronic Data Interchange (EDI), in order to engage in electronic markets (Damsgaard, 1996; Ngai and Wat, 2002). The arrival of open Internet protocols and subsequently a variety of XML standards fueled a variety of new innovations of computing in the large, such as corporate intranets (Stenmark, 2002) and open EDI standards (Nurmilaakso, 2008).

When the Internet became available on user-friendly smartphones with end user–managed ecologies of apps, computing in the small and computing in the large entered the most successful alliance so far. While initial slow growth from the first mobile phone call in 1973, mobile telephony grew radically from the 1980s onwards. The billions of daily Facebook users mostly update their news feeds from mobile devices. The mobile technology industry has seen significant changes over a short period of time. From being the world's largest camera manufacturer in 2008 by stealing the crown from a struggling Kodak, Nokia's handset division ended up being first bought by Microsoft, then largely written off in 2015. On the back of the iPhone, Apple, which in 1997 was struggling, became in 2015 the first-ever $700 billion company.

Computing in the large has received some interest beyond the IS community – for example, the study of how the Internet was established (Abbate, 2000); the public value of infrastructures in general with some discussion of the Internet (Frischmann, 2012); the control arrangements on the Internet (Goldsmith and Wu, 2006); a range of issues relating to the dynamics innovation and law in digital infrastructural arrangements (Lessig, 2000; Lessig, 2002; Lessig, 2006); centralised and decentralised control arrangements in the information industries (Wu, 2010); the economics of networked information arrangements (Shapiro and Varian, 1998); the changing of the control-generativity dynamics of the Internet (Zittrain, 2008); and the design, dynamics, and management of digital platforms serving the meeting of different stakeholders in multi-sided market arrangements (Gawer and Cusumano, 2002; Gawer, 2009; Tiwana, 2014; Evans and Schmalensee, 2016; Parker et al., 2016).

While the management literature and beyond has dealt with infrastructures and platforms, the IS field is still attempting to address the question of what is particular about digital infrastructures and platforms compared with their analogue and physical counterparts. The work by several IS academics and groups has studied issues related to computerisation in the large, for example on the institutional character and dynamics of information infrastructures (Ciborra et al., 2001; Hanseth and Lyytinen, 2010; Henfridsson and Bygstad, 2013); the institutional character of information (Kallinikos, 2007); and digital platform dynamics (Ghazawneh and Henfridsson, 2013; Eaton et al., 2015). There is, however, an abundance of challenges for the IS field to establish theoretical constructs and models – for example, related to how the dynamics of digital infrastructures differ from their analogue ones (Tilson et al., 2010), for example, in terms of their generativity (Tilson et al., 2013); the specific characteristics of layered-modular architectures combining modular hardware components and layered software arrangements (Yoo et al., 2010); or how to understand what emerge as the specific characteristics of platforms supporting multi-sided markets and highly distributed innovation arrangements when these platforms are digital (Eaton et al., 2015; de Reuver et al., forthcoming; Lyytinen et al., Chapter 17 in this volume).

The new technological configurations combining computing in the small and computing in the large also challenge what constitutes work and its organisation. The emergence of a variety of types of flexible working is largely enabled by changes in the technological foundation for communicating, collaborating and for distributing activities across time and distance. Such flexible working can provide members of organisations the ability to better organise the separation of home life and working life (Wajcman et al., 2008; Bittman et al., 2009). However, a more radical type of flexibility emerges from a looser coupling between the organisation and its workers. Itinerant workers can engage in contractual arrangements with organisations for short- or long-term engagements. These itinerant workers rely on both employment hubs as mediators, but they may also spend a significant part of their time networking in order to ensure a future stream of work (Nardi et al., 2002; Barley and Kunda, 2004).

The bureaucratic assumption of humans as interchangeable collections of distinct modular capabilities governed by clear distinctions separates tasks and skills from all other aspects of a person, mirrors organisational processes of modularising work tasks, and thus makes these more easily the subject of distribution and recombination (Kallinikos, 2003; Hirst and Humphreys, 2015). The widespread availability of smartphone apps connected to business infrastructures and global Internet communications allows for new reconfigurations of itinerant work taking this modularisation to new global levels. In the so-called gig economy (Sundararajan, 2016), the technology is the main mediator for the piecemeal allocation of tasks and whole projects to a collection of participants gathered for the particular purpose. For companies such as Uber or Airbnb, the digital infrastructure in effect becomes a defining aspect of the organisation as it enables the timely coordination and meshing of tasks and workers to complete these projects. A variety of crowdsourcing and crowdfunding services are supported by both computing in the small and large to source new ideas and funding from a loosely coupled group of globally distributed individuals. Wikipedia is probably the best example of crowdsourcing, and Innocentive.com is one of the oldest crowdsourcing marketplaces for ideas and solutions. Kickstarter.com and Indigogo.com exemplify crowdfunding of new ideas, while Amazon's Mechanical Turk offers an extreme example of crowdsourced activities, also called clickworking. Here, automation renders an ephemeral collection of networked humans into the main part of the computing process. The technology along with increased codification of even complex organisational processes into modular entities support the separation of complex human efforts into ever-smaller constituent modules to be globally distributed to a hyper-specialised workforce for subsequent synthesis into a finished result (Malone et al., 2011).

Computing at scale

The computational capabilities of digital technologies based on the Von Neumann Architecture has increased exponentially the past 50 years in accordance with Gordon Moore's prediction. Moore predicted that the number of components in a specific size integrated circuit would double every 18 months. This doubling has occurred about 34 times since the prediction was made in 1965. It has been argued that this exponential growth of both computational capabilities is now beginning to yield services of a significant different kind than previously, and that the extent, complexity, and sophistication of such services goes beyond our previous imagination (Brynjolfsson and McAfee, 2014). This development has contributed significantly to contemporary computational solutions to problems, which a decade ago seemed impossible to crack. As an example, the Simultaneous Location and Mapping (SLAM) problem was for a long time an unresolved challenge. Even very small children manage to avoid bumping heads into tables through SLAM, but this was a significant challenge for computer-based systems (Wikipedia, 2016). A simple solution was subsequently produced using the Microsoft Kinect consumer games peripheral (Anderson, 2010). This solution was simple as it essentially was based on the rapid technological development of standard consumer technologies for infrared 3D scanning (the Xbox Kinect), and exponentially increasing computational power.

The ability for the scaling of computer capabilities to directly influence organisational processes relates directly to the digitalisation of broad ranges of phenomena both internal and external to organisations. The wholesale digitalisation of nearly all aspect of personal and professional life has accelerated the past decades with complex consequences for industrial, organisational, and individual processes (Kallinikos, 2007). This digitalisation challenges the existing understanding of socio-technical phenomena and is a force to be reckoned with theoretically within IS (Tilson et al., 2010; Yoo et al., 2010; Kallinikos et al., 2013; de Reuver et al., forthcoming). Assumptions that digital arrangements merely display similar dynamic characteristics as analogue counterparts are not tenable.

Once digitised, what previously was bundled can potentially be subjected to unbundling (Hagel and Singer, 1999), leading to the reshaping of what organisational entity is in control and can extract the value. Subsequent re-bundling can lead to a shift in control to a different set of stakeholders than initially. The technical process of digitising is associated with socio-technical processes of digitalisation potentially altering the control dynamics between stakeholders (Tilson et al., 2010). For example, within the music publishing business, digitising resulted in the loosening of traditionally tight couplings between the music storage formats, the processing technologies, and the distribution mechanisms and leading to two waves of restructuring over a short period of time. Music labels could control their intellectual property as it was locked into vinyl discs, only to be played on turntables, and distributed in record stores. The transition to digital CDs initially went very well and grew revenue significantly. However, this early digitisation conducted by intellectual property owners themselves paved the way for wholesale disruption. MP3 compression technology from the Fraunhofer Institute, cheap storage technology, and fast Internet connectivity allowed for peer-to-peer (P2P) music sharing (Goldsmith and Wu, 2006, chap. 7). While the music business, with the help of Apple and others, managed to divert some of the free music download on P2P services to paid downloads, a subsequent rapid shift has made free or subscription-based music streaming the place for companies to compete.

Many of the most innovative services launched can be explained as combinations of the entire stack of computing in the small, large, and at scale. In the previous example, Napster users initially disrupted the music industry business arrangements by enabling end-user computers to become P2P nodes in a file sharing arrangement as illustrated in Figure 29.1. When a Waze driver opens the company's smartphone app, she instantaneously becomes a node in the traffic management system, digitising the position and movement of each of the cars currently on the road with Waze. Such computational complexity of constant updates of the positions of potentially millions of cars across the world can only be managed through combining all three elements (as illustrated in Figure 29.1).

The understanding of computing at scale also relates to the separation and synthesis of human and non-human agency, for example, in terms of technological developments of robotics, artificial intelligence, and automated customer self-service. The future of humanity in general, and of work in particular, under extensive digitalisation, artificial intelligence, and robotics has been explored by a number of authors and commentators. This work has explored, for example, the increasing algorithmification and datification of decisions (Harari, 2016);

the ability to control technology with superhuman intelligence (Bostrom, 2014); the role of human effort under highly digitised and automated technology arrangements (Brynjolfsson and McAfee, 2011; Brynjolfsson and McAfee, 2014); the feasibility, appropriateness, and possible consequences of extensive reliance on automation (Carr, 2014; Lacity and Willcocks, 2016; Willcocks and Lacity, 2016); and the future role of professionals when expertise is being unbundled (Susskind and Susskind, 2015).

The IS tradition has a complex relationship to this development from a past of AI super-optimism. Underwhelmed by the reality of the hype surrounding AI and expert systems in the 1980s, IS researchers do not seem to embrace the fast computational land grabs and translate these into revised understanding of our field.

Challenges ahead

The challenges for both practitioners and academics of navigating computing in the small, in the large, and at scale are significant. Each aspect provides a rich set of complex, and importantly, fast moving socio-technical phenomena to engage with. Each aspect, equally, raises a number of fundamental questions for organisations and academics alike. However, irrespective of the separate challenges, combinations of the three denote a seemingly insurmountable challenge.

For organisations the challenge of digital transformation can indeed seem insurmountable. An incumbent's business arrangement can be subjected to disruption from above, if a global superstar company casts its Sauronic glance on it (*Economist*, 2016), or from below if an emerging competitor overtakes from under the radar (Christensen, 1997). It is expensive, difficult, and risky for large companies to simplify organisational complexity evolved over decades, in order to synthesise computing in the small, in the large, and at scale into new business arrangements. Digital business transformation is deeply concerned with changing what the business does, and how it integrates human and algorithmic processes in new ways. This means that standardised solutions are not likely to emerge in the short term. If they were, these solutions would not be likely to offer significant strategic advantage (Ciborra, 1991). While some organisations will need to wholesale rethink what they do, many may be able to engage rapid efforts to instill innovation agility, for example, by evoking the collective's ability to both keep the wheels turning while at the same time also keep looking ahead for new opportunities (Birkinshaw and Gibson, 2004; O'Reilly and Tushman, 2013)

For academics this is an equally imposing challenge, among others, because the stable unit of analysis, the organisation, is challenged. Furthermore, there seems so far insufficient research within IS on each of these three issues and even less on the combinations. The IS field seems in general to be mostly interested in studying technological phenomena that can be brought to conform with the tried and tested organisation-centric perspective (Sørensen, forthcoming). However, even when studying the organisational arrangements with information technology in the context of one organisation, the technologies and processes will increasingly be linked together across boundaries external to the organisation linking tiny sensors, distributed customer and employee handheld smart devices together with customer apps, business services, and back-end systems – all connected through globally distributed networks and cloud services. The trusted unit of analysis is further being challenged by different socio-technical arrangements, such as digital platforms (de Reuver et al., forthcoming), and digital infrastructures (Tilson et al., 2010). The IS field will, therefore, need to theoretically frame its discourse broader than in terms of the single organisation's use of a limited set of information technology (see Figure 29.4).

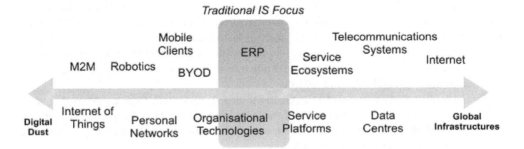

Figure 29.4 The breadth and interconnectedness of organisational technologies span digital dust and global infrastructures – far beyond the traditional IS perspective centered around an organisational locus of information processing

Source: Sørensen & Landau (2015, p. 167).

Complex interactions span from a motion tracker on someone's arm, to this data being combined with other digital behavior patterns, and feeding into global auctions for the person's attention, to informing how this person will be presented with other essential digital services. Such digital dynamics raise much broader questions, for example, of individual privacy, ownership of data, the distribution of effort and rewards, the societal regulation of such global digital processes, and the general marketisation of individuals, in what has been characterised as surveillance capitalism (Zuboff, 2015). There is, within IS, a need to transcend the constructive narrative and seek to engage critically in the broader analysis of societal impact and choice (Aanestad, 2016). As an example, the largely uncritical discussions of the "sharing economy" has so far optimistically talked about removing friction, but not considered the broader framework of capital flows and subsidisation that has facilitated some of these services to outcompete incumbents, or indeed the wider consequences in terms of a race to the bottom of the work force, and shifting importance from labor to capital (Morozov, 2016).

It is important to realise that the forces of computation in the small, in the large, and at scale are touching almost all aspects of life, and challenging all of us to consider the effect and alternative responses (Harari, 2016). The challenges are already significant and can only be met by contextualised critical analyses of opportunities and constraints. These will require better understanding of the fundamentals, and for that we need to consider each humble technological artefact from the RFID chip, to the smartphone, and to global digital infrastructures both as distinct technological phenomena and as integral parts of complex socio-technical and socio-economic assemblages.

Note

1 This chapter draws on, synthesises, and extends upon some of the arguments put forth in (Sørensen, 2011; Sørensen and Landau, 2015; Sørensen, 2017).

References

Aanestad, M. (2016): Porting IS research to the cloud: Keynote at IRIS 39/SCIS 7. http://iris2016.org/keynotes/

Abbate, J. (2000): *Inventing the internet*. Cambridge, MA: MIT Press.

Anderson, C. (2010): Kinect + ROS = Awesome SLAM solution!, Accessed: http://diydrones.com/profiles/blogs/kinect-ros-awesome-slam.

Arnold, M. (2003): On the phenomenology of technology: The "Janus-faces" of mobile phones information and organization. *Information and Organization*, vol. 13, no. 4, pp. 231–256.

Barley, S. R. & G. Kunda (2004): *Gurus, hired guns, and warm bodies: Itinerant experts in a knowledge economy*. Princeton, NJ: Princeton University Press.

Baron, N. S. (2008): *Always on: Language in an online and mobile world*. Oxford: Oxford University Press.

Bassoli, A. (2010): *Living the urban experience: Implications for the design of everyday computational technologies*. PhD Thesis, London School of Economics and Political Science.

Beniger, J. R. (1986): *The control revolution: Technological and economic origins of the information society*. Cambridge, MA: Harvard University Press.

Birkinshaw, J. & C. Gibson (2004): Building ambidexterity into an organization. *Sloan Management Review*, vol. 45, no. 4, pp. 47–55.

Bittman, M., J. E. Brown, & J. Wajcman (2009): The mobile phone, perpetual contact and time pressure. *Work, Employment & Society*, vol. 23, no. 4, pp. 673–691.

Bostrom, N. (2014): *Superintelligence: Paths, dangers*. Oxford: Oxford University Press.

Brynjolfsson, E. & A. McAfee (2011): *Race against the machine*. Lexington, MA: Digital Frontier Press.

Brynjolfsson, E. & A. McAfee (2014): *The second machine age: Work, progress, and prosperity in a time of brilliant technologies*. New York: W. W. Norton.

Caminer, D., J. Aris, P. Hermon, & F. Land (1998): *L.E.O. – The incredible story of the world's first business computer*. London: McGraw-Hill Education.

Carr, N. G. (2014): *The glass cage: Automation and us*. New York: W. W. Norton.

Carstensen, P. & C. Sørensen (1996): From the social to the systematic: Mechanisms supporting coordination in design. *Journal of Computer Supported Cooperative Work*, vol. 5, no. 4, December, pp. 387–413.

Christensen, C. M. (1997): *The innovator's dilemma: When new technologies cause great firms to fail*. Boston, MA: Harvard Business School Press.

Ciborra, C. U. (1991): From thinking to tinkering: The grassroots of strategic information systems. In *Proceedings of the Twelfth International Conference on Information Systems*, New York. University of Minnesota, pp. 283–291.

Ciborra, C. U., ed. (1996): *Groupware and teamwork*. Chichester, United Kingdom: John Wiley & Sons.

Ciborra, C. U., K. Braa, A. Cordella, B. Dahlbom, A. Failla, O. Hanseth, V. Hepso, J. Ljungberg, E. Monteiro, & K. A. Simon, eds. (2001): *From control to drift. The dynamics of corporate information infrastructures*. New York: Oxford University Press.

Culnan, M. J. (1987): Mapping the intellectual structure of MIS, 1980–1985: A Co-citation analysis. *MIS Quarterly*, vol. 11, no. 3, pp. 341–353.

Damsgaard, J. (1996): *The diffusion of electronic data interchange: An institutional and organizational analysis of alternative diffusion patterns*. PhD Dissertation, Aalborg University, Denmark. Document number: R96-2041.

de Reuver, M., C. Sørensen, & R. Basole (Forthcoming): The digital platform: A research agenda. *Journal of Information Technology*, no. Accepted.

Dourish, P. (2001): *Where the action is: The foundations of embodied interaction*. Cambridge, MA: MIT Press.

Eaton, B. D., S. Elaluf-Calderwood, C. Sørensen, & Y. Yoo (2015): Distributed tuning of boundary resources: The case of Apple's iOS service system. *MIS Quarterly: Special Issue on Service Innovation in a Digital Age*, vol. 39, no. 1, pp. 217–243.

Economist (2014): Difference engine: The internet of nothings. *Economist*, May 28th. www.economist.com/blogs/babbage/2014/05/difference-engine-1

Economist (2016): The rise of the superstars. *Economist*, September 17th. www.economist.com/news/special-report/21707048-small-group-giant-companiessome-old-some-neware-once-again-dominating-global

Evans, D. S. & R. Schmalensee (2016): *The matchmakers: The new economics of multisided platforms*. Boston: Harvard Business Review Press.

Frischmann, B. M. (2012): *Infrastructure: The social value of shared resources*. Oxford: Oxford University Press.

Gallager, S. (2016): Double-dip Internet-of-Things botnet attack felt across the Internet. *Ars Technica*, October 21st. http://arstechnica.com/security/2016/10/double-dip-internet-of-things-botnet-attack-felt-across-the-internet/

Gawer, A., ed. (2009): *Platforms, markets and innovation*. Cheltenham: Edward Elgar.

Gawer, A. & M.A. Cusumano (2002): *Platform leadership: How Intel, Microsoft, and Cisco drive industry innovation*. Boston, MA: Harvard Business School Press.

Ghazawneh, A. & O. Henfridsson (2013): Balancing platform control and external contribution in third-party development: The boundary resources model. *Information Systems Journal*, vol. 23, no. 2, pp. 173–192.

Goldsmith, J.L. & T. Wu (2006): *Who controls the Internet?: Illusions of a borderless world*. Oxford: Oxford University Press.

Grier, D.A. (2005): *When computers were human*. Princeton: Princeton University Press.

Hagel III, J. & M. Singer (1999): Unbundling the corporation: What business are you in? Chances are, it's not what you think. *Harvard Business Review*, pp. 133–141.

Hanseth, O. & K. Lyytinen (2010): Design theory for dynamic complexity in information infrastructures: The case of building Internet. *Journal of Information Technology*, vol. 25, no. 1, pp. 1–19.

Harari, Y.N. (2016): *Homo deus: A brief history of tomorrow*. New York: Random House.

Harper, R., L. Palen, & A. Taylor, eds. (2005): *The inside text: Social, cultural and design perspectives on SMS*. Dordrecht, the Netherlands: Springer.

Henfridsson, O. & B. Bygstad (2013): The generative mechanisms of digital infrastructure evolution. *MIS Quarterly*, vol. 37, no. 3, pp. 907–931.

Hirst, A. & M. Humphreys (2015): Configurable bureaucracy and the making of modular man. *Organization Studies*, vol. 36, no. 11, pp. 1531–1553.

Horst, H. & D. Miller (2006): *The cell phone: An anthropology of communication*. Oxford: Berg.

Johansen, R. (1988): *Groupware: Computer support for business teams*. New York and London: Free Press.

Kakihara, M. & C. Sørensen (2001): Expanding the 'mobility' concept. *ACM SIGGROUP Bulletin*, vol. 22, no. 3, pp. 33–37.

Kakihara, M. & C. Sørensen (2002): Mobility: An extended perspective. In *Thirty-Fifth Hawaii International Conference on System Sciences (HICSS-35)*, Big Island Hawaii, ed. R. Sprague Jr. IEEE. www.hicss.org/

Kallinikos, J. (2003): Work, human agency and organizational forms: An anatomy of fragmentation. *Organization Studies*, vol. 24, no. 4, pp. 595–618.

Kallinikos, J. (2007): *The consequences of information: Institutional implications of technological change*. Cheltenham: Edward Elgar.

Kallinikos, J., A. Aaltonen, & A. Marton (2013): The ambivalent ontology of digital artifacts. *MIS Quarterly*, vol. 37, no. 2, pp. 357–370.

Lacity, M. & L. Willcocks (2016): A new approach to automating services. *Sloan Management Review*, vol. 58, no. Fall, pp. 40–49.

Lessig, L. (2000): *Code and other laws of cyberspace*. New York: Basic Books.

Lessig, L. (2002): *The future of ideas: The fate of the commons in a connected world*. New York: Vintage Books.

Lessig, L. (2006): *Code: Version 2.0*. New York: Basic Books.

Lewis, M. (2000): Exploring paradox: Toward a more comprehensive guide. *Academy of Management Review*, vol. 25, no. 4, pp. 760–776.

Ling, R. (2008): *New tech, new ties: How mobile communication is reshaping social cohesion*. Cambridge, MA: MIT Press.

Ling, R. (2012): *Taken for grantedness*. Cambridge, MA: MIT Press.

Lyytinen, K. & Y. Yoo (2002a): Issues and challenges in ubiquitous computing. *Communications of the ACM*, vol. 45, no. 12, pp. 63–65.

Lyytinen, K. & Y. Yoo (2002b): The next wave of nomadic computing: A research agenda for information systems research. *Information Systems Research*, vol. 13, no. 4, pp. 377–388.

Lyytinen, K.J., Y. Yoo, U. Varshney, M. Ackerman, G. Davis, M. Avital, D. Robey, S. Sawyer, & C. Sørensen (2004): Surfing the next wave: Design and implementation challenges of ubiquitous computing. *Communications of the AIS*, vol. 13, Article 40, pp. 697–716. http://cais.aisnet.org/

Malone, T.W., R.J. Laubacher, & T. Johns (2011): The age of hyperspecialization. *Harvard Business Review*, vol. 89, no. 7/8, pp. 56–65.

McFarlan, F. W., J. L. McKenney, & P. Pyburn (1983): The Information archipelago – Plotting a course. Reprint Service, *Harvard Business Review*.

Morozov, E. (2016): Cheap cab ride? You must have missed Uber's true cost. *Guardian*. www.theguardian.com/commentisfree/2016/jan/31/cheap-cab-ride-uber-true-cost-google-wealth-taxation

Nardi, B. A., S. Whittaker, & H. Schwarz (2002): NetWORKers and their activity in intensional networks. *Computer Supported Cooperative Work*, vol. 11, pp. 205–242.

Ngai, E. W. T. & F. K. T. Wat (2002): A literature review and classification of electronic commerce research. *Information & Management*, vol. 39, no. 5, pp. 415–429.

Nurmilaakso, J.-M. (2008): EDI, XML and e-business frameworks: A survey. *Computers in Industry*, vol. 59, no. 4, pp. 370–379.

O'Reilly, C. & M. Tushman (2013): Organizational ambidexterity: Past, present and future. *Academy of Management Perspectives*, vol. 27, no. 4, pp. 324–338.

Parker, G. G., M. W. Van Alstyne, & S. P. Choudary (2016): *Platform revolution: How networked markets are transforming the economy and how to make them work for you.* New York: W. W. Norton.

Perlow, L. A., J. Hoffer Gittell, & N. Katz (2004): Contextualizing patterns of work group interaction: Toward a nested theory of structuration. *Organization Science*, vol. 15, no. 5, pp. 520–536.

Schad, J., M. W. Lewis, S. Raisch, & W. K. Smith (2016): Paradox research in management science: Looking back to move forward. *Academy of Management Annals*, pp. 1–60.

Schmidt, K. & L. Bannon (1992): Taking CSCW seriously: Supporting articulation work. *CSCW*, vol. 1, no. 1–2, pp. 7–40.

Schmidt, K. & C. Simone (1996): Coordination mechanisms: An approach to CSCW systems design. *Computer Supported Cooperative Work: An International Journal*, vol. 5, no. 2–3, pp. 155–200.

Shapiro, C. & H. R. Varian (1998): *Information rules: A strategic guide to the network economy.* Boston: Harvard Business School Press.

Sheller, M. & J. Urry (2016): Mobilizing the new mobilities paradigm. *Applied Mobilities*, vol. 1, no. 1, pp. 10–25.

Sørensen, C. (2011): *Enterprise mobility: Tiny technology with global impact on work.* Palgrave Macmillan. http://enterprisemobilitybook.com/

Sørensen, C. (2017): The curse of the smart machine? Digitalisation and the children of the mainframe. *Scandinavian Journal of Information Systems*, vol. 28, no. 2, Article 3. http://eprints.lse.ac.uk/68996/1/Sørensen_The_curse_of_the_smart_machine_author_2016_LSERO.pdf.

Sørensen, C., A. Al-Taitoon, J. Kietzmann, D. Pica, G. Wiredu, S. Elaluf-Calderwood, K. Boateng, M. Kakihara, & D. Gibson (2008): Enterprise mobility: Lessons from the field. *Information Knowledge Systems Management Journal*, vol. 7, Special Issue on Enterprise Mobility, pp. 243–271.

Sørensen, C. & J. Landau (2015): Academic agility in digital innovation research: The case of mobile ICT publications within information systems 2000–2014. *Journal of Strategic Information Systems*, vol. 24, no. 3, pp. 158–170.

Stenmark, D. (2002): Information vs. knowledge: The role of intranets in knowledge management. In *Thirty-Fifth Hawaii International Conference on System Sciences (HICSS-35), Big Island Hawaii*, ed. R. Sprague Jr. IEEE, pp. 928–937. www.hicss.org/

Sundararajan, A. (2016): The 'gig economy' is coming: What will it mean for work? *Guardian*. www.theguardian.com/commentisfree/2015/jul/26/will-we-get-by-gig-economy

Susskind, R. E. & D. Susskind (2015): *The future of the professions: How technology will transform the work of human experts.* Oxford: Oxford University Press.

Tilson, D., K. Lyytinen, & C. Sørensen (2010): Digital infrastructures: The missing IS research agenda. *Information Systems Research*, vol. 21, no. 5, pp. 748–759.

Tilson, D., C. Sørensen, & K. Lyytinen (2013): Platform complexity: Lessons from the music industry. In *46th Hawaii International Conference on System Science (HICSS 46)*, Maui, HI.

Tiwana, A. (2014): *Platform ecosystems: Aligning architecture, governance, and strategy.* Waltham, MA: Morgan Kaufmann.

Urry, J. (2000): Mobile sociology. *British Journal of Sociology*, vol. 51, no. 1, pp. 185–203.

Urry, J. (2007): *Mobilities*. Cambridge: Polity.

Urry, J. (2008): Moving on the mobility turn. In *Tracing mobilities: Towards a cosmopolitan perspective*, ed. W. Canzler, V. Kaufmann, and S. Kesselring. Aldershot, England: Ashgate, pp. 13–24.

Wajcman, J., M. Bittman, & J. E. Brown (2008): Families without borders: Mobile phones, connectedness and work-home divisions. *Sociology*, vol. 42, no. 4, pp. 635–652.

Wikipedia (2016): Simultaneous localization and mapping. https://en.wikipedia.org/wiki/Simultaneous_localization_and_mapping.

Willcocks, L. P. & M. C. Lacity (2016): *Service automation: Robots and the future of work.* Stratford-upon-Avon: Steve Brookes.

Wu, T. (2010): *The master switch: The rise and fall of information empires.* New York: Knopf.

Yates, J. (1989): *Control through communication: The rise of system in American management.* Baltimore: Johns Hopkins University Press. 0–8018–3757-X.

Yates, J. (2005): *Structuring the information age: Life insurance and technology in the twentieth century.* Baltimore: Johns Hopkins University Press.

Yoo, Y. (2010): Computing in everyday life: A call for research on experiential computing. *MIS Quarterly,* vol. 34, no. 2, pp. 213–231.

Yoo, Y., O. Henfridsson, & K. Lyytinen (2010): The new organizing logic of digital innovation: An agenda for information systems research. *Information Systems Research,* vol. 21, no. 4, pp. 724–735.

Zittrain, J. (2008): *The future of the Internet: And how to stop it.* London: Allen Lane.

Zuboff, S. (1988): *In the age of the smart machine: The future of work and power.* New York: Basic Books.

Zuboff, S. (2015): Big other: Surveillance capitalism and the prospects of an information civilization. *Journal of Information Technology,* vol. 30, no. 1, pp. 75–89.

30
TECHNOLOGY-DRIVEN CHANGES IN THE ECONOMY

Roman Beck

The technology-driven change of work

When Johann Heinrich von Thünen, a German economist of the early 19th century, started to write his first academic book in 1826, he was already 43 years old and a well-established farmer. Von Thünen was intrigued by how the prices for crops together with transport costs define the optimal location of farmland for certain types of agricultural harvest relative to the market where those products are sold. Water canals and a better road system in Prussia made it possible to deliver to larger cities that were not reachable as markets by farmers before. In 1830, von Thünen was awarded an honorary PhD for his achievements for explaining agricultural productivity, revenue streams, and overcoming geographic distances in an agricultural society (Thünen 1826). His theorizing became famous. His Von Thünen circles helped to explain all the production functions, input variables, and cost determinants of value generation in the sourcing of agricultural goods. In other words, he explained the agricultural system of his time. He applied technology in the form of analytics and knowledge to change the economy.

A few decades later, the young Frederik Winslow Taylor started his career as toolmaker and machinist in the booming steel-making industry on the East Coast of the United States. He also had the good fortune to also study engineering through one of the first distance learning offerings at the Stevens Institute of Technology. His credentials allowed him to become the leading engineer in the Midvale Steel Corporation. Industrialization and technologies such as the steam engine allowed manual labor to be in part replaced by machines. This required workers to specialize their skills and to work in the rhythm of steam hammers. Similar to Von Thünen on his farm 50 years earlier in Germany, Taylor did not just organize the shop floor. He understood and optimized processes in an industrial environment. There are other similarities between Von Thünen and Taylor. Like Von Thünen, Taylor published his main academic contribution rather late in his career, just four years before he died. He was also awarded with an honorary PhD. His book, *The Principles of Scientific Management* (Taylor 1911), combined many of his insights, and laid the foundations for job shop scheduling, automation and optimization of industrial workflows, and supply chain management, although those terms were coined after he died. It is not a stretch to claim that Taylor belongs to the group of founding economists who tried to understand and optimize industrial age processes. And again, like Von

Thünen, he had been a practitioner with an academic interest. He understood the industrial system and the implication technology had on the value generation of physical goods.

Today, over 100 years later, economic geography and agriculture economics are not as salient in academe. Nevertheless, we still teach the theories and insights learned from the industrial area more than 150 years ago. Of course, we have refined these theories. Our academic understanding of technology-driven value generation has diversified. Nevertheless, we still draw more or less on theories and ways of thinking developed in the 19th and 20th centuries. Cast in this light, it is not surprising that in the last decade of the last century and the first years of the new century we have been forced to reassess the value of information technology.

The benefits of services and the creation of value in a service society are not as measurable when research and practice rely on dated theories. Alan Greenspan, chairman of the US Federal Reserve Bank between 1987 and 2006, was in office for the 19 years that brought the rise of the Internet and emergence of e-commerce. The United States led technologically and the Fed followed a strategy of cheap money. Yet, investments in the service sector did not adequately materialize in official statistical gross domestic productivity reports. In a March 2001 speech at the Washington Economic Policy Conference of the National Association for Business Economics, Greenspan acknowledged that the new economy created significant challenges. He stated that

> newer technologies and the structure of output they have created have surfaced a set of definitional problems that – although evident in a world of steel, fabrics, and grains – were never on the cutting edge of analysis. I refer, of course, to the age-old problem of defining what we mean by a unit of output and, by extension, what we mean by price.
>
> (Greenspan 2001)

Greenspan referred later in his speech to medical services and the challenges of adequately measuring their value, talking about the challenges of measuring the value generation of intangible services made possible by information technology. Who is going to academically analyze and optimize service systems made possible by information technology? We don't know yet. Even here, Greenspan proved to have great insight. He concluded his speech, "information systems might some day allow statistical agencies to tap into a great many economic transactions on a basis close to real time" in order to understand and optimize those service systems. We will get back to this later.

The Greenspan example illustrates that the question of how one can assesses a new information technology at an early stage that might or might not have serious economic implications remains an open issue. How do we recognize groundbreaking technological shifts and adapt our work processes and academic understanding accordingly? How do we better assess economic changes induced by new technologies? In the following, I will look closer at blockchain, a new technology that may address issues of trust and governance in inter-organizational systems. Blockchain may be the key to unlock the service economy that is characterized by decentralized systems, value creation, and decision making.

Some perspectives on the changing nature of value creation

Humankind has come a long way in the last 200 years of technological development. Technologies have helped us to make our life easier, to generate goods and services, and extend our lives due to medical achievements and better availability of food. From helping us to produce goods to meet daily human needs, technologies increasingly help us to generate services to even further improve our way of life. That became visible in the official statistics: around two-thirds of the gross domestic product (GDP) in developed countries is generated in the service sector.

The transition from agricultural systems to industrial systems toward service systems has been made possible by technology. This has had a deep effect on decision making, institutional governance structures, and processing of goods and information. A service system (a kind of work system) is a combination of information technology and organizational resources designed to deliver services that meet the demand and expectation of customers (Alter 2013). Technology has allowed us to move from centralized manual processing in the agricultural area to centralized automated processing in the industrial age. The first transition from manual to automated processing kept the central, hierarchical element of decision making. The transition from the industrial age to the service age changed not only the processing mode (from automation to virtualization), but also the governance mode, from central and hierarchical to decentralized and distributed. Virtualized processing is a value creation processes that transcends the boundaries of a single firm. The results are not controlled by a single organizational hierarchy. Value generation becomes flexible, done with different partners at different times, possibly geographically dispersed (Kraut et al. 1999).

The service age, having been driven by technology that allows for decentralized and distributed decision making in virtualized value processing networks, is at the heart of contemporary economies characterized by complicated, sometimes complex social-technical service systems that surround us at every moment. We are integrated in communication networks, computer-mediated social networks, integrated billing and payment systems, multi-modal transport systems, smart power grids, and many more systems and infrastructures that support modern life (Beck 2006).

The same interlaced network of integrated service systems can be found in commercial environments, where enterprise resource planning systems, supply chain management systems, financial transaction systems, and many more have to work together in an interactive, automated, or semi-automated way. These systems have grown over several decades, and are dynamic and constantly changing. As maturing systems are decommissioned, new systems are added, older systems are revitalized, and additional functionalities are added to existing systems. This has created a complicated network, a heterogeneous "system of systems" of different age, quality, reliability, and performance. Many of these systems develop their own dynamics. Often, when someone is referring to a system of systems, one is typically talking about the organizational level or a firm that can be understood as a conglomerate (Ackoff 1971).

However, when we view this from a macroeconomic perspective, we talk about inter-organizational "service systems of service systems," which exist outside the legal responsibility and sphere of influence of a single firm. While "system of systems" can mean many things to different people, with "service systems of services systems," I refer to a technology-driven environment that is characterized by operational and legal independence of the connected service systems and their management, and that has to create services on demand in a (globally) distributed, decentralized ecosystem. If that sounds familiar, it is because we witness this on a daily basis in outsourcing projects, shared services deals, virtualization of applications in cloud environments, and so on. The technology-driven service society accelerates interconnectivity and complexity of existing service systems. Individuals play with their smartphones, watch Internet TV, or call friends via voice-over-IP. Companies use integrated service systems for business intelligence to orchestrate complicated service sourcing networks with their vendors. While this is the new normal, properly understanding "service systems of service systems" is increasingly crucial for prudent management of emerging service systems risks. The most prominent service system of service systems is without doubt the Internet. While we got used to the advents and benefits of inter-organizational service systems, we still lack the enforcing mechanisms and governance structures to manage such decentralized systems. But why is that so, and why are we locked into a mindset where hierarchies, central decision making, and top-down strategies play such a dominating role?

From the nature of the firm to a world of individual contractors

Technology has changed how we generate value, but there remains a need for theories that explain the shift toward decentralized, distributed processing of virtualized services. In 1937, Ronald Harry Coase proposed that firms and markets are alternative organizational forms for organizing transactions (Coase 1937). In essence, he wondered why there is not a world of individual contractors. His answer can be found in his publication about the nature of the firm and transaction cost theory: firms exist because there are costs such as searching, negotiating, monitoring, and enforcing required by the market and its price mechanism. In other words, firms were more efficient when goods or services are transferred across separate interfaces between organizations.

Following Coase, Oliver Eaton Williamson postulated that organizations emerge when the coordination of transactions through hierarchies is more advantageous than co-ordination through markets (Williamson 1985). Economic benefits from vertical integration (incorporating a company) arise when internalization comes with lower transactions costs than using the market offers. The more specific a product or service is, the more likely it is that the sourcing is not done via the market, but via collaborations that create products or services within a company. The centerpieces of transaction cost theory are coordination costs, and the choice is between the market and the firm. A third form termed "hybrid" applied to variants that make up elements of markets and hierarchies: collaborations, alliances, or joint ventures of all kinds. However, the sourcing mechanism for hybrids was not clearly specified, the governance structure of hybrid sourcing was difficult to understand, and not consistent with the way that products and services were generated in the 1930s when Coase's theory of the firm was published.

Information technologies have made both markets and hierarchies more efficient, but it is likely that the hybrid form has benefitted most due to improvements in coordination and logistics in inter-organizational settings. Many industry-specific, electronic data interchange (EDI) driven supply chain management examples illustrate this (many in the automobile industry). The net effect of increased use of interconnected IT systems has been to improve hybrid coordination, creating the possibility to source more and more services and products through inter-organizational collaboration. As already mentioned, transaction costs are mainly the costs of coordinating, including costs of information and communication. A lack of trust will increase such costs as the "economic equivalent of friction in physical systems" (Williamson 1985, p. 19). Technical progress and the ongoing diffusion of IT has reduced such frictions to a great extent, allowing organizations to source products and services across time and space.

The last big enabler for value generation and services sourcing was the Internet, allowing hybrid coordination forms at an unprecedented scale. For example, the Internet allowed organizations to turn assets into services, as the sharing economy signifies. However, the sharing economy does not completely capture the emerging economic order. It still represents elements of the old order, the industrial age economy, such as central hierarchies that orchestrate value creation of distributed production. Yet, if we believe that the dawn of the technology-driven service age is characterized by distributed and decentralized decision making in order to generate value in virtualized processes, something important is still missing. We seek the decentralized, hybrid sourcing form. We will get back to what it takes to have a world of individual contractors in the service age, as Coase envisioned. First we must examine the sharing economy as an important but temporary phenomenon of the service economy.

Sharing economy as bridge to the service economy

Many regard the sharing economy as the beginning of the age of the service economy. The sharing economy receives a lot of academic attention, yet at the same time academics seem to struggle how to grasp the nature of sharing economy. The term sharing economy points to economics and indicates something new, but it actually describes something well-known in economics, and not something that became possible only recently because of IT.

From an economic point of view, the so-called sharing economy is about something economists call "club goods." If a good is non-rivalrous, its consumption is not ultimate. It can be recreated for consumption by others. A home or car can be used again and again to provide services, and there is no rivalry if the same service is provided over and over again if there is no significant wear and tear on the assets of production. Multiple individuals can use the same good. The ability to exclude someone is not given in the service, *per se*, but by assignment of property rights (Musgrave 1959, p. 9). Ownership of a house or car is the deciding factor over who uses it. Goods and services characterized by non-rivalry but that are excludable from general use are called club goods. Usually a central institution grants access to the property owned by its members.

Examples of club goods are golf courses or tennis courts owned by clubs – that is where the name comes from. Club members can use the good or service, but must be members of the club and obey the club rules. Registered users of Airbnb and Uber are members of the club. Not all club members know each other, but they must respect the rules. As members they are not strangers to each other, but a group of people connected via a centrally, hierarchically organized IT platform. Technology has enabled making former private goods that are rivalrous in consumption and excludable in use (e.g., my house, my car) a club service. Technology is the central facilitator, allowing use of private goods to be offered as services. One might argue that the scale of Airbnb or Uber makes them unique, but the economic model does not represent a new paradigm or economic innovation. The sharing economy has more in common with the hierarchical, centralized automation of processes of the industrial age than with the distributed, decentralized virtualization of processes associated with the age of service systems. Technology is allowing us to share collectively the cost of owning and maintaining assets. We will now discuss how this is possible and why this truly is a shift.

Blockchain – a technology that might drive the emerging service economy

Blockchain gained prominence with the emergence of Bitcoin in 2009. We still do not understand its potential and impact on the service economy. Blockchain is essentially just what the name says: a chain of blocks. A block contains the data of all transactions related to that block within a period of time, and references to blocks before it. Cryptography goes into creating blocks. The cryptography can differ depending on which blockchain protocol is used, but one can traverse through an entire blockchain and find every transaction ever made, all the way back to the first one, the so-called genesis block. Hashing algorithms are used to make sure that all blocks are well formed and not tampered with. A blockchain keeps itself secure and virtually unbreakable, but is not provided from a single server. It is run on a widespread network of computers as a distributed ledger. All network participants hold all data in the blockchain, and work together to expand it. Blockchain technology can allow for innovative solutions, and might fundamentally change the principle foundations of economic transactions as we know them (Beck et al. 2016).

Blockchain allows to think about transformation from the industrial to the service economy. In principle, blockchain enables building of economic systems that use distributed, decentralized mechanisms to enforce property rights. The *Economist* called the blockchain "the trust machine" that removes economic friction necessary to build, signal, and enforce trust (Economist 2015). Blockchain agreements might make it possible to create systems that, once the start-up issues are resolved, make completing a transaction so different from tradition that it is "trust free." Transaction cost theory says friction costs contain the costs for lack of trust and uncertainty in transaction. If blockchain can bring certainty into transactions once the transaction logic is instantiated as code in the blockchain, contracts can be electronically executed without costs associated with trust. Bitcoin was the first widely heralded blockchain application, but blockchain need not be limited to cryptocurrencies like Bitcoin. Blockchain technologies might be used to implement all kinds of property rights exchanges in economic transactions between individuals and organizations that are trust-free, transparent, and highly secure. Technology might thus eliminate or much diminish the need for interpersonal and inter-organizational trust.

Blockchain burst on the scene in a white paper authored by someone calling himself Satoshi Nakamoto. This is a pseudonym and it is not clear who the real inventor of Bitcoin might be. However, the white paper explained the underlying blockchain technology and how transactions on blockchain work. Suppose somebody wants to transfer money to somebody else. The transaction is represented online as code entry and becomes part of a block of other transaction entries. The block is then shared with every node in the distributed network. If those network nodes approve the transaction, the block is added to the previous blocks, thereby creating a chain of blocks. Together with the rest of the transactions, this provides an irreversible and transparent record of transactions. Nakamoto (2008, p. 3) described the process as:

1. New transactions are broadcasted to all nodes.
2. Each node collects new transactions into a block.
3. Each node works on finding a difficult proof of work for its block.
4. When a node finds a proof of work, it broadcasts the block to all nodes.
5. Nodes accept the block only if all transactions in it are valid and not already spent.
6. Nodes express their acceptance of the block by working on creating the next block in the chain, using the hash of the accepted block as the previous hash.

The simple example illustrates the fundamental features of blockchain.

1. It operates without a central decision maker or hierarchy.
2. It allows independent contractors to interact in a decentralized, distributed environment.
3. It takes care of the secure execution of the transaction.
4. It works as a virtualized service in the background, supporting all kinds of economic transactions.

The principle behind blockchain is the absence of the need to depend on central, hierarchical planning as Von Thünen and Taylor did. The service economy built upon this technology might, for the first time in history, allow decentralized governance of economic transactions that are nevertheless enforceable. This would be fundamentally new. Blockchain could complement and compete with the Internet in decentralizing the world. Central organizing forces such as Airbnb or Uber might not be necessary if the transaction logic can be orchestrated and enforced without a central entity doing this. If blockchain generates real-time information flows of transactions that Alan Greenspan was talking about back in 2001, it will allow for completely new ways to digitally audit economic transactions. Such a paradigm shift could be understood as a system that organizes transactions completely reliably without any human interaction, following rules set in the computer protocol. Such a service economy could be compared with an unstaffed, automatically navigating vessel or a driverless steering car, bringing safely passengers from A to B, completely controlled by a cryptographic protocol that minimizes malicious and accidental exceptions by getting humans out of the loop. It could serve as the backbone of the Internet-of-things, allowing tamper-proof coordination among machines such as drone communication with delivery stations. Transaction costs might be reduced.

Blockchain might enable trustworthiness through third-parties to be replaced by understanding the blockchain technology and the status of transactions. Instead of trusting that a transaction will be conducted as agreed upon, blockchain might enable one to see the status of the transaction and know what is going on. Blockchain could thereby support all kinds of codified agreements: digital assets such as shares, contracts, and stock options that have been traded by conventional means could be implemented as smart contracts on the blockchain.

What the blockchain-enabled decentralized service economy might look like

As explained in the previous section, the Internet and the sharing economy did not support a decentralized, distributed governance of the service economy, which is probably the most fundamental paradigm shift in contrast to the central steering and governance approaches we are used to and theorized about in the past. Blockchain technology now allows for an enforceable governance structure in inter-organizational, decentralized environments. Such a so-called decentralized autonomous organization (DAO) that supports the service economy is a virtual institution, implemented among market participants without being a own legal entity. Such a DAO makes all decisions and transactions visible to the DAO members, making fraudulent behavior such as corruption impossible to hide from others.

A DAO, once established, runs completely autonomously, decentralized, transparent, and secure, providing the operation system and governance structure between legally independent market participants. Such a service economy will run on a cryptographically secured operation system that is not controlled by any market participant, yet it provides the function and services of a trusted third party, which markets typically have to rely on as proxy where trust and enforceability of rules can otherwise not be guaranteed. In other words, a DAO might enable curbing transaction costs involved to setup, maintain, regulate, and supervise the operation of an entrusted third-party organization. Such a self-enforcing economic system allows for trust-free transactions where neither the trust to a counterparty nor the need to trust a third party to enforce transactions is needed. In addition, those transactions and based-upon services are completed according to the rules coded into the blockchain.

Self-enforcing autonomous systems are capable to run or control transactions on autopilot. This is a change from a social-technical system to a technical-social system. In the case of social-technical systems, transactions are run by technical systems autonomously, but all operations are controlled by social systems. In contrast, technical-social systems–based transactions are run by social systems, but all transactions are controlled by technical systems autonomously (as it is the case for blockchain-based DAO) (Quintana Diaz 2014). We do not know yet how exactly those blockchain-supported service systems will look like in all details, but we now have the technology to operate decentral systems in a secure way. But what are the implications for our academic understanding for value creation?

The theories that explain the blockchain-driven service economy

Notice that Von Thünen and Taylor were cited earlier, and no other economists serve as the main protagonists. Before they came up with their famous ideas, they were "everyday" people: Von Thünen was a farmer, and Taylor was a toolmaker and engineer. Yet they were experts in the technologies that changed processing and production of food and physical goods. The service economy depends on information technologies and the creation of services. It should be IT experts who pave the way to a more holistic understanding of the service economy. Through changes in processing information, products and services have moved from manual processing to automation to virtualization. Significant organizational changes have taken place in the more recent transition from industry to service in central to decentralized ownership and decision making.

This shift suggests the limits of traditional business theories that concentrate on central decision making within organization, but not on decentralized, network-coordinated decision making. It is not a stretch to claim that IT experts will provide explanatory economic theories to explain this. Computer scientists and information systems researchers unused to developing insights on the macroeconomic level will find they lack the economic background to understand and categorize these new phenomena in economic terms. The preceding discussion of the sharing economy illustrates this.

Blockchain requires profound understanding. It might not just enable new business models, but could also mark the beginning of a new economy. Understanding it requires people with process and management knowledge, as well as IT, design, and programming backgrounds. The blockchain-supported service economy requires design, technology, and business process understanding from those who wish to build new value creation systems. Information systems can be the discipline that creates new understanding, models, and theories. The IS discipline is at the intersection of IT and business. It creates and explains the emerging service economy and can provide the theories needed to explain the new world, in line with Von Thünen and Taylor.

References

Ackoff, Russell L. (1971). Towards a System of Systems Concepts, *Management Science*, (17:11), pp. 661–671.

Alter, Steven (2013). Work System Theory: Overview of Core Concepts, Extensions, and Challenges for the Future, *Journal of the Association for Information Systems*, (14:2), pp. 72–121.

Beck, Roman (2006). The Network(ed) Economy – The Nature, Adoption, and Diffusion of Communication Standards, Deutscher Universitätsverlag; Wiesbaden, Germany.

Beck, Roman, Stenum Czepluch, Jacob, Lollike, Nicolaj, Malone, Simon (2016). Blockchain – The Gateway to Trust-Free Cryptographic Transactions, in: *Proceedings of the 24th European Conference on Information Systems* (ECIS 2016); İstanbul, Turkey.

Coase, Ronald Harry (1937). The Nature of the Firm, *Economica* (4:16), pp. 386–405.

Economist (2015). Blockchain – The Next Big Thing. Available at: www.economist.com/news/special-report/21650295-orit-next-big-thing [Accessed 21st November 2015].

Greenspan, Alan (2001). The Challenge of Measuring and Modeling a Dynamic Economy. Available at: www.federalreserve.gov/BOARDDOCS/SPEECHES/2001/20010327/default.htm [Accessed 27th July 2016].

Kraut, Robert, Steinfield, Charles, Chan, Alice P., Butler, Brian S., Hoag, Anne (1999). Coordination and Virtualization: The Role of Electronic Networks and Personal Relationship, *Organization Science*, (10:6), pp. 722–740.

Musgrave, R.A. (1959). *The Theory of Public Finance – A Study in Public Economy*, New York: McGraw-Hill Books.

Nakamoto, Satoshi (2008). Bitcoin: A Peer-to-Peer Electronic Cash System. Available at: https://bitcoin.org/bitcoin.pdf [Accessed 26th July 2016].

Quintana Diaz, Josue Manuel (2014). The Merger of Cryptography and Finance – Do Cryptographic Economic Systems Lead to the Future of Money and Payments? Available at SSRN: http://ssrn.com/abstract=2536876

Taylor, Frederick Winslow (1911). *The Principles of Scientific Management*, New York, NY, and London, UK: Harper & Brothers. Available at: www.gutenberg.org/ebooks/6435 [Accessed 26th July 2016].

Thünen, Johann Heinrich von (1826). Der isolirte Staat in Beziehung auf Landwirtschaft und Nationalökonomie. Available at: www.deutschestextarchiv.de/book/show/thuenen_staat_1826 [Accessed 26th July 2016].

Williamson, O.E. (1985). *The Economic Institutions of Capitalism: Firms, Markets, Relational Contracting*, New York: Free Press.

31
STAYING ALIVE
The IS field at the half century mark

Ning Su, John Leslie King, and Jonathan Grudin[1]

Introduction: dating the birth of the IS Field

The academic Information Systems Field (which we call the IS Field) is about at the half century mark. It is difficult to say precisely how old the field is. It is built on traditions that started with unit-record equipment and "business data processing" in the late 19th century. However, most would now agree it did not start until the commercial application of electronic digital computers in the early 1950s. The UK's Lyons Electronic Office, the first commercial application of digital computers, was soon followed by the US's UNIVAC I. Few commercial organizations had adopted this technology by the mid-1950s, but it became important to commerce by the mid-1960s, when International Business Machines (IBM) launched its successful line of 360 computers. The "mainframe" market emerged, and use grew.

The early days were preoccupied companies applying digital computers to commerce. These companies turned to higher education to meet their needs for expertise. The first textbooks appeared in the 1960s. Börje Langefors created an early instructional program at Stockholm University in the mid-1960s, soon followed by Gordon Davis's program at the University of Minnesota and Frank Land's program at the London School of Economics. There was little organized research publication in information systems. Some publication appeared in accounting outlets, but much appeared in computer science outlets such as the US Fall and Spring Joint Computer Conferences, and publications of the Association for Computing Machinery (ACM), the Institute of Electrical and Electronics Engineers (IEEE), and The Institute of Management Sciences (TIMS). Similar venues were used in other countries. There were no dedicated information system research venues in the 1960s.

Nevertheless, research grew along with teaching. An early formal gathering for information systems research was the Technical Committee 8 of the International Federation of Information Processing Societies (IFIP TC8) in 1976. In 1977 an academic journal dedicated to the IS Field, *Management Information Systems Quarterly*, was created at the University of Minnesota. The Information Systems Research Seminar in Scandinavia (IRIS) held its first meeting in 1978. Academic units (e.g., departments) proliferated and the IS Field took shape. In 1980 what became the International Conference on Information Systems (ICIS) started. The Association for Information Systems (AIS), started in the early 1990s. Assuming the IS Field is at least as old as the AIS, and possibly dates back to the beginnings of digital computers, it is between 25 and 65 years old. We use the "start date" for the academic IS Field consisting of both research and teaching, in the mid-1970s. This places the field at about the half century mark.[2]

The IS Field is not very old by academic standards, and still faces many challenges of the "start-up." Not the least of these is uncertainty about whether it will survive. Half a century does not guarantee survival in the academy. Many in the IS Field are part of management schools that are relative latecomers to the academy, most less than a century old (the earliest management schools date from the late 19th century). The IS Field began at about the same time that digital information technology started to change the world. The academy itself is now changing because of information technology and other reasons. The substrate of the IS Field is itself changing, making it difficult to find a natural "place." The IS Field could never develop as academic fields "normally" do because the norms have long been up for grabs.

This chapter is written for people whose knowledge of the IS Field is grounded mostly in the content of this book. It reflects the opinions of the authors and does not attempt a definitive statement beyond that. The IS Field has survived. This is testimony to the importance of the underlying issues, especially the application of digital information technology to human enterprise, and to the intelligence and determination of people in the field. The chapter addresses a sentiment frequently found in assessments: pride in past accomplishments, but concern about the future. By the time this chapter is done, we will have made the argument that the IS Field has accomplished much by "staying alive," but has the opportunity to advance to "really living." The IS Field should take advantage of the opportunity.

Staying alive and The Undead

The "start date" of the IS Field is contemporary with disco. The Bee Gees hit "Stayin' Alive" opened the disco-oriented film *Saturday Night Fever* in 1977. (Both can be found online.) The IS Field "stayed alive" despite frequent encounters with The Undead. We use The Undead as a literary device, examining the IS Field's encounters with The Undead to explore challenges of the field. We also assess what it will take to "really live" as information systems become important throughout organizations. Our pride in past accomplishments is found in the IS Field's energy and excitement. Our concern about the future is grounded in IS programs being eliminated or forcibly merged with other groups. The anxiety of the IS Field might be an indication that the field is on to something big. We think so.

The Undead as a literary thing arises from the definition of what it means to be alive or dead. We first consider this. We then look at the rigor/relevance discussion, the emerging vision of design, and the broader ecology of changes. The IS Field hangs out with The Undead, and in so doing loses vitality. One might say the field spends too much time in whited sepulchres, and is depressed, or at least, puzzled.[3] Perhaps the problem is not the IS Field's familiarity with The Undead, *per se*, but with how the field engages The Undead.

Most living people believe that life is better than the alternative. Yet the living do not have a precise understanding of life. A rudimentary definition says life is a characteristic of physical entities that exhibit biological and self-sustaining processes. Termination of biological functions results in the end of life (death). Yet, the life sciences have abandoned explanations involving a special "life force" or "essence." Viruses and prions (infectious proteins) can kill, but whether they are alive is disputed. To make matters more complicated, life is more than biological. An archaic word for alive is "quick," and the dead are not "quick" by any definition (they do not "go" anywhere). Movement alone cannot be definitive: water moves, but is not alive. To top it off, life is often used metaphorically. Thoreau wrote in 1854 that he went to the woods to live deliberately, to discover what it means to live, to be sure that, at the end of his life, he had lived. For Thoreau, life was a teacher.

The Undead is metaphorical, too. Metaphors can be powerful. Life and death matter to the living (and maybe the dead; we aren't sure). Religious beliefs frequently touch on the life/death distinction. Nevertheless, the topic remains obscure. Living people talk about life and death without knowing *exactly* what they are talking about. This ambiguity extends to academic fields pursued by living people who care about them and try to keep them alive. Previously alive fields (e.g., alchemy) "live on" in other fields (e.g., chemistry). Fields with needed knowledge are often kept alive: the IS Field will probably be kept alive because companies need the knowledge. Even archaic fields such as classical studies in ancient Greek or Latin survive. Technological improvements render knowledge immaterial or salient. It is a metaphor to say that the IS Field is "staying alive." But the notion is not uncommon. Truly dead academic fields are rare, and the number of academic fields has grown dramatically over the last century. The IS Field is not alone.

We recognize the metaphorical pitfalls of the literary device of The Undead. We are trying to capture something as elusive as the definition of life. We use The Undead because it shows value from and for the IS Field. We use the metaphor to articulate two visions for the field. In one the IS Field becomes The Undead, squabbling over a decreasing share of what matters, staying alive only because the topic remains important to external audiences and cannot be killed outright. The other is preferable for us: an IS Field enlivened by proximity to major change, showing leadership and courage as information systems change the world. The idea of being truly alive is itself metaphorical. It cannot be achieved by members of the IS Field scolding each other, any more than depressed people can exhort each other to be happy. Truly living requires *departure* from the existing path. It takes courage.

Three kinds of The Undead

We are primarily concerned with three kinds of The Undead. One is the Frankenstein monster. Henry Frankenstein made a creature out of dead human body parts and brought it to life by the animating force of electricity. ("It's alive!" uttered Henry Frankenstein, played by Colin Clive, in James Whale's 1931 film *Frankenstein*.) The 1818 novel *Frankenstein, or, The Modern Prometheus*, was written by 19-year-old Mary Shelley, daughter of feminist Mary Wollstonecraft and anarchist William Godwin, and wife of poet Percy Bysshe Shelley. She wrote it on a challenge from Lord Byron. The book became a Romantic icon, a cautionary tale as people were starting to realize the terrible power of science to *create* what might or might not be human (Holmes, 2008). Henry Frankenstein was hurt for playing God, and his creature was misunderstood. The problem was in the intentions of people.

A second is the vampire. Bram Stoker's 1897 post-Romantic, Gothic horror novel *Dracula* is an early example. Vampires are immortal unless killed by natural means (e.g., sunlight) or human agency (e.g., a stake through the heart, head torn off). Vampires are basically evil, but not because of normal people who chase them with torches and pitchforks. Science had advanced by the late 19th century, and people were less concerned that too much knowledge would make people evil. Rather, they were concerned with *resident evil* that had to be killed for good. In Stoker's novel, Abraham Van Helsing takes care of the vampires (there were more than one – Dracula was just in charge). The evil was non-human and abroad irrespective of human agency. Vampires could wreak havoc on humans, but humans could (and did) destroy them.

Third is the zombie, a reanimated dead human body that attacks the living. This 20th-century creation originated in magic's triumph over science in Haitian folklore that reanimated bodies through voodoo magic (e.g., W.B. Seabrook's 1929 *The Magic Island*). Subsequently, the genre was scientifically updated. Reanimated zombies now occur through radiation or pathogens (if explained at all), and are seen in cinema (e.g., George Romero's 1968 *Night of the Living Dead* and Mark Forster's 2013 *World War Z*) or television shows like *The Walking Dead*. Zombies are individual people, although often the worse for wear, who return from death as limited-capability humans bent on destroying fully alive humans. Unlike Frankenstein's meddling with the divine, or the vampire's "resident evil," zombies embody the nasty things that humans are capable of.

Interestingly, The Undead are neither dead nor alive. They are kind of dead. Living humans try to make The Undead really dead. Most plots revolve around people trying to truly kill The Undead. Although the authors do not "believe in" The Undead, we suggest that the IS Field embrace them, but not truly kill them. Their manifestation is central to the IS Field. Instead, we suggest that the field learn from The Undead how to move beyond staying alive. We take a quick tour through the rigor/relevance debate, the rise of design, and the broader ecology of the IS Field in this effort.

Rigor/relevance

The rigor/relevance discussion has been going on for a while. Some date it to Keen's 1980 paper on reference disciplines (Keen, 1980), and some to Mason's 1989 piece on the role of experiments in IS research (Mason, 1989). Most start with Keen's 1991 paper. In general it is an either/or choice between academic rigor that stands the test of time, or relevance enough to be useful immediately. The issue is still discussed today, and has become an industry that goes far beyond the IS Field.[4] Education has long cared about the topic (Whitehurst 2008), and teachers can find the right balance of rigor and relevance in their work using the Rigor/Relevance Framework.[5]

Some characterizations of the rigor/relevance debate posits an artificial dichotomy of two classes of stakeholders: scholars and practitioners. This is an old notion: more than 2,000 years ago Aristotle of slave-owning Athens distinguished between the "liberal arts" (subjects for free people that might have no practical utility) and the "servile arts" (practical subjects like medicine or architecture) for slaves. The fight between Liberal Arts and the Professions embodies this. The "trades" (plumber, mechanic, electrician, etc.) remains too "vocational" for four-year colleges, but a lot can happen in 2,000 years. Vocations might eventually rise. When rigor/relevance is a linguistic construction of either/or, it is not really alive but it keeps coming around. It is The Undead, and puts the IS Field 2,300 years in the past – a difficult trick for a field that started with digital computers in the 20th century.

The either/or distinction of rigor/relevance is not very helpful for most IS academics. Proposals that get funded, papers that get accepted, key editorial assignments that get awarded, promotions made in the academy, are all decided by academics with a strong voice for rigor and a weak voice for relevance. IS academics seeking legitimacy listen to other academics. Those seeking relevance look outside the academy. Being rewarded *within the academy* requires publishing papers "on the right things" and "in the right places." Rigor is given preference over relevance. Despite some sympathy for relevance, many academic journal editors reject papers that are insufficiently rigorous. The either/or distinction means that academics go for rigor, while practitioners go for relevance. This splits the community, making it weaker.

Some deny the either/or construct, and say the issue has never really been about rigor *or* relevance, but about rigor *and* relevance. This idea is also older than many realize, and certainly predates the IS Field. In the early 20th century, John Dewey said that much of learning is for practical application, and that rigorous science should serve this end (Dewey, 1929). He felt that the purpose of science is to gain practical knowledge, and that knowing how to *do* science requires practical skills. Donald Stokes captured this idea in his 1997 *Pasteur's Quadrant* framework:

| | | Considerations of Use? | |
		No	Yes
Quest for Fundamental Understanding?	Yes	Pure basic research (e.g., Bohr)	Use-inspired basic research (e.g., Pasteur)
	No		Pure applied research (e.g., Edison)

Stokes' model, like many 2 × 2 representations, favors the "northeast" quadrant: use-inspired basic research of the kind done by Louis Pasteur (hence the book's name). Many have lauded this insight, yet although the book was published decades ago, and many have spoken highly of it, few have done anything to implement its implications. In Stokes's model, those at the intersection of fundamental understanding and practical use contribute most. The old-school either/or construct of rigor/relevance is reinforced.

Pasteur died in 1895, Edison in 1931, and Bohr in 1962. Neither Pasteur nor Edison is "contemporary." Both died before WWII. Yet their experiences correspond with the world today. Edison accomplished many things, including starting the company General Electric, but these were not *academic* things. Edison never won a Nobel Prize (although the rumor that he was considered infuriated some scientists). Bohr did have *academic* accomplishments, including the Nobel Prize. Pasteur never won a Nobel Prize; he died before the prize was established. In Stokes's model academics can contribute to fundamental understanding *and* use, but not to use alone. They can be rigorous *and* relevant, but if forced to choose, they must err on the side of fundamental understanding. Relevance and rigor, or just rigor. The former requires a lot of work. The latter is easier.

Unfortunately, the either/or construct of rigor/relevance is like the Frankenstein monster. While relevance in practice is at the IS Field's origins, those whose academic employment is not secure (i.e., they do not have tenure) see relevance as too costly. As with the Frankenstein monster, they would like to be fully human and engaged with praxis, but this path is foreclosed. Work that starts out in praxis is subjected to a peer review process run by and for academics. These processes can drive out relevance, insisting on rigor, especially if space (e.g., page count) is limited, which it usually is. Editors and reviewers do not hate relevance; they just like rigor more. Many in the IS Field are conditioned to write papers that editors and reviewers like, even if practitioners wonder what to do with the results. While the Stokes model correctly points out that academics *can* focus on praxis and still achieve job security in the academy, in practice few do this. Rigor/relevance with *and* instead of *or* is a cruel hoax for many because it is simply too costly to the individual. The transgressive path of Frankenstein is unwise. If staying alive requires rigor, the community remains split between academics and practitioners.

Few academics hate relevance in our experience, but some academic gatekeepers consider time spent on considerations of use as *wasted* or *stolen from* fundamental understanding. In such cases rigor is reinforced at the cost of relevance. The IS Field loses its *raison d'être*. The problem is not that it becomes too "pure." Rather, it becomes less useful for practitioner patrons who use IS. The academy is a patronage scheme, and many patrons are practitioners. Patrons must benefit or they will not support the academy. Patrons benefit from graduates who can "think outside the box" and do what higher education prepares them for. Patrons also benefit from innovation. Some benefit from far-reaching research in which payoffs do not show up right away. Payoffs 10 or 20 or even 100 years hence have their place. Most understand that the full implications of some research cannot be known at present. Patrons also benefit when academics show that otherwise promising ideas are dead ends. But when relevance becomes difficult to explain, patronage is at risk. There are issues of relevance in every line of academic work. "Pure" research that has no conceivable application treats patrons as a food source – rather like a vampire.

Some relevant work lies outside the academy, but few IS academics show slavish adherence to considerations of use. Highly trained IS academics seldom produce directly the breakthroughs touted by technology companies or the newest techniques recommended by management consultants. However, they test claims and show whether benefits materialize as hoped. They can prevent others from heading down a dead end. They can challenge misleading advertising slogans upended by evidence. They can speak truth to power. Academics should be unafraid to pursue the consequences of new technologies and capabilities, even when they perturb the environment in surprising ways that require venturing into other fields or disciplines. Yet here the problem for the IS Field becomes acute. The academy is highly "stovepiped." Woe betide any IS academic who crosses the boundaries between stovepipes. Most IS academics recognize the sneer followed by the accusatory question, "What are *you* doing here?"

IS academics should be among the first to say, "I am not convinced." However, this poses a conundrum that can be risky to one's academic career. Lewis Branscomb, Chief Scientist for IBM and Chair of the National Science Board, once remarked that a major contribution of research is to show that things that should work do not.[6] This saves everyone time and money. Unfortunately, some grant application reviewers feel being negative is "not rigorous," and some reviewers and editors of respected journals prefer positive findings. In such circumstances, scholars fear they will not be funded or published. They write only about positive results. Positive is tied to "innovation," which is fashionable. Fashion is big in the IS Field. It is also part of the problem.

Oscar Wilde said, "Fashion is a form of ugliness so intolerable that we have to alter it every six months" (Esar, 1949). Fashion is indeed a tempestuous child, but we humor it because it dies so young. This poses a problem for academics. When academics take on fashion, asking what is really new, they often note that almost nothing "changes everything." Yet that new technology "changes everything" is a frequent claim about fashionable innovation. Santayana said those who cannot remember the past are condemned to repeat it (Santayana, 1905), and many in the "innovation" space promote ballyhooed ideas that are just warmed-over versions of what has gone before. Even when dressed up in the fine raiment of smaller semiconductors, such innovations can still be a fraud. Academics in fast-changing fields must live in the uncomfortable territory between the Ecclesiastes (1:9) admonition that there is nothing new under the sun, and Heraclitus's aphorism that you cannot step twice in the same river. Nearly everything is simultaneously a rehash of what has gone before and new in the moment. The academy repays patrons by being methodical, but this is risky business. Academics can seem too hasty when public acceptance is slow, and too conservative when public acceptance is rapid. The happy medium is elusive.

Part of this elusiveness is the misplaced quest for rigor tied to the traditions of natural sciences that prize results reached through theory and experimentation. This is a losing proposition when every organization is different and experiences with IS differ. Natural science experimentation can be difficult to arrange, when it makes sense at all, so many IS academics use statistical testing to show general trends, but this seldom achieves the results of natural science experiments, and infrequently provides practitioners with much they can use. IS researchers who conclude it "all depends," and use contingency theories often get as close to the truth as possible, but some see such work as insufficiently rigorous. The *resident evil* is hegemony of "good" research following traditions of the natural sciences applied to socio-technical issues that require more interpretation.

The problem cannot be resolved. It makes more sense to see rigor/relevance conundrum as *inherent* in the IS Field, as *part* of the field. IS researchers who must choose rigor over relevance because that is what is expected of them must do as their immediate environment requires, irrespective of the fact that demands for rigor can destroy considerations of use. This is especially true if usefulness is *prima facie* evidence of lack of rigor. Such researchers have to accept that separation from relevance makes IS research dull, and such research can be off-putting to patrons. The rigor/relevance conundrum keeps coming back. It is similar to what Roman Catholics call the Mystery of the Faith. It is hard to explain but real to many. It is part of the DNA that gave rise to the field. Many of the field's insights come through explaining the consequences of use.

There is little solid IS research without consideration of use. Socio-technical systems draw their purpose and much of their interest from use. It might be difficult or impossible to persuade academic leaders to treat considerations of use as part of academic contribution. It is also difficult to work in Pasteur's Quadrant. Taking use away from the IS Field cannot be a successful strategy over the long run. However, it can be necessary over the short run. It is not a matter of finding the right balance in the short run. The only way academic researchers in IS Field can win with promotion committees full of scientists and liberal arts scholars who warn against "creeping professionalism" is to not play. To be "rigorous" is to be safe. Preferring rigor over relevance (or vice versa) splits the community and weakens it, but over the long run academic researchers in IS must return to consideration of use. The tension never abates. Seen in this light, rigor/relevance helps to animate the IS Field.

Design

"Design" in the IS Field brings a new dimension to The Undead. Design is aimed at creating organizations, processes, and so forth to produce desired outcomes and mitigate undesired ones in organizations, institutions, markets, and so forth. The design notion in the IS Field emerges from Herbert Simon's influential book, *The Sciences of the Artificial*, built from a set of lectures at the University of California, Berkeley (Simon, 1969; Boland and Collopy, 2004; March and Storey, 2008). Simon distinguished between the natural (as evolved without human agency) and the artificial (shaped by human agency). He made *design science* – the informed and purposeful creation of things that make the artificial desirable for humans – the heart of the sciences of the artificial. The designer develops and shapes information systems for managerial decision making, software prototyping, and managing business processes.

Design has become an attractive way to accommodate "innovation" in the IS Field. The designer shapes human endeavor as the he or she pleases. It is relatively new, emerging since 1990, and especially since 2000. We cite some of the contemporary literature on the idea. Design techniques are used to help forecast technology trends, provide frameworks for text analysis in computer-mediated communication, and create rules for conceptual modeling (Lee et al., 2008; Pries-Heje and Baskerville, 2008; Parsons and Wand, 2008; Adomavicius et al., 2008; Abbasi and Chen, 2008). It has become bifurcated, with one stream aimed at creating artifacts for problem solving (Hevner et al., 2004; March and Smith, 1995; Nunamaker et al., 1990–91), and another aimed at generalizable and abstract design theories (Gregor and Jones,

2007; Markus et al., 2002; Walls et al., 1992). The streams differ in concept, execution, and presentation.

Design research joins description with prescription in the construction of artifacts to achieve rigor and relevance (Gregor and Hevner, 2013). It has stimulated discussion of field and discipline boundaries and contributed to knowledge creation and accumulation through two views of the design process. One is design as rational and rigorous problem solving, essentially Simon's view that shaped disciplines from economics to computer science. Dorst calls Simon's view a "dominant paradigm" of design, fitting sciences and engineering, and encompassing information technology software and hardware (Dorst 2006). Others place greater emphasis on intuition, interaction, experience, and judgment akin to the architecture of the built environment or fashion, closer to art than science (Huppatz 2015).

The rigor/relevance issues are not easily resolved, however. The tension is seen in many higher education institutions that have programs in art and design while granting a design role for engineering. There is disagreement over the "profession" of design. Simon's view makes design a profession in the traditions of engineering, but others disagree. Fashion designer Elsa Schiaparelli called dress design an art rather than a profession (Secrest, 2014). Design reflects opportunities and challenges beyond socially constructed boundaries. The difficulty of classifying art extends to design as evident when people say, "I can't define it but I know what I like." Teaching people to design is also hard. Is design talent, like art talent, resident in the person? If so, training might bring it out or make it more refined, but training cannot make an "unartistic" person into an "artist." Others feel design can be taught, and many are in between. There is not an agreed-on "canon" and teaching design is a hit-or-miss proposition. There is much disagreement over whether everyone above some level of education and/or aptitude can grasp the fundamentals of a design and apply them.

Design in the IS Field is too new to evaluate completely, but some things can be said about it. Its core issue is the power of will. Design tries to make the world as we want it to be, and makes willfulness part of professional identity. Professionals have knowledge, skill, and authority to act, and their actions should be judged only by peers with similar knowledge, skill, and authority. Through willfulness one can design organizations and enterprise, and set the direction of management education. Design proposals arising from the IS Field often look far beyond historic limits.

Design feasts on other areas, works with what is available, and adds value by overcoming constraints and inertia. Design attempts to make things better with the materials at hand while transcending business as usual. Design is not The Undead. It causes observers to realize what they would never have thought of. It is something that living humans can do (dead humans do not design things), but not *every* living human can do good design. Some can, and some cannot. Professional education is predicated on the belief that sufficient preparation makes people with modest talents "good enough" to meet the high demand for talent. "Naturals" – people who "get it" without having professional education – pose a challenge. In the "real world" something "big" might be going on, but it is unclear.

The design perspective ignores the limits that some place on the IS Field. It end-runs the problematic of The Undead, especially as seen in the rigor/relevance debate, by claiming both engineering and artistic traditions. Design leaves the IS Field free to make use of method that leads to rigor, without obliging the field to do so. Design also embraces art, which is notoriously difficult to define precisely. Relevance can appeal to the "art" end of the spectrum. This end-run will fail if academic gatekeepers insist on rigor, and judge rigor by the expectations of the natural sciences. Most universities contain artistic programs and the insistence on the criteria of the natural sciences might be losing power in situations where "it all depends." Few practitioners believe that sustainable solutions to socio-technical problems can be found using only the methods of the natural sciences. The design strategy might help the IS Field move permanently past The Undead, but there is cause for concern as well as for hope.

The major concern with design is that it seems *subjective* in an era when *objectivity* is emphasized. Terms like "design science" or "design research" skirt that part of design that lies in an individual's ability to "see" what is needed and deliver it, but not to eliminate it. Traditions of the natural sciences and much of engineering are against people who "see" in this way, but most scientists and engineers admit to the role of "creativity" in science and engineering work. To the extent that they take positions against those they see as "unfit" by demanding greater rigor, the design strategy cannot prevail. The trick is not to make a frontal assault on rigor: people often harden their positions when they feel threatened. Besides, much of the academy's value to patrons comes from rigor. The legitimate defense of rigor remains important. But when rigor is used as a political weapon it hurts the field over time. The artistic side is a real, if ambiguous, part of design.

Hope springs from the possibility that design will open the IS Field to a more nuanced and fine-grained view of the rigor/relevance debate. The field might embrace the inherent tension of rigor/relevance as part of the role of information systems in social settings. This must happen mostly in the minds of IS researchers, not in the tools of discourse. For the foreseeable future academic publications will require rigor, practitioners will require relevance, and IS academics must be bi-lingual, understanding *all sides* of the issues. Design emphasizes that. The problem is hard. When relevance is marginalized, the vampire returns. Truly living requires embracing the tension inherent in design.

An ecological perspective

Thus far we have attended to Frankenstein's monster and to vampires. What about zombies found in the ecology of the IS Field's evolution? As the foregoing discussion suggests, the IS Field's initial professional affiliation was in other associations. People "specialized" Special Interest Groups, or SIGs.[7] Membership in SIGs has been changing. One such association, the Association for Computing Machinery (ACM), showed membership across more than 30 SIGs dropped from over 100,000 in 1990 to less than 40,000 in 2015. The SIG for Management Information Systems dropped from over 3,000 to less than 300, but ACM membership did not drop appreciably in this time, remaining above 80,000. People in the IS Field might have moved to the Association for Information Systems (AIS) in the early 1990s. By 2007 AIS membership had grown to about 3,600 and in 2016 stood at around 4,300. The number of AIS SIGs grew from six established in 2001 to more than 30 today. The decline of SIG membership in ACM is striking, but does not seem to be represented in the much smaller AIS.

We suspect that the reasons people join associations are changing, leaving zombies in the wake. Research from the IS Field seems to show that information systems are changing human enterprise, and speculation about these changes is rampant. Among other things, there are predictions of driverless vehicles and massive unemployment, not to mention effects from data ("big data," "data science," "analytics," etc.). These speculations might come to pass: there have been changes such as supply-chain management, the "sharing" economy, and crowd-sourcing. Whether the IS Field will capitalize on these changes is as yet unclear, but the origins of the field have caught up with it, raising questions about what "relevance" means. This is seen mostly in changes in the IS Function.

The IS Function arises from a functionalist view of what IS entities in organizations do. Functionalism (often called structural functionalism) in sociology says parts contribute to the whole, which is more than the sum of its parts. Each component plays a part. Parts make the whole. Different parts fulfill different needs and depend on each other. Parts that no longer serve a role die away. This view was originally derived from the study of living organisms. It profoundly shaped the field of management education. Specialists in functions were produced, and many areas of management education grew around this view.

The IS Function emerged to process the organization's information. Its heyday was the "mainframe era" that grew out of electromechanical unit record equipment. Unit record devices and the digital computers that followed were expensive. Organizations created central data processing functions for economies of scale. The advent of stored program computers in central data processing led to the "software" era, and most application software was written in-house. Data communications supported remote job entry (RJE) and remote printing for "batch" jobs. "Interactive" computing emerged through use of terminals connected to the mainframe. The power of central data processing – what became the IS Function – grew. The computers in the "glass house" of the data center might have been powerless compared to today's equipment, but their high costs compelled all or most organizational units to work through the central data processing unit. Central data processing, in turn, came to know at least part of the core business of every unit.

The IS Field emerged to serve the IS Function in the 1970s. Central data processing units needed expert professionals. The academy (increasingly management schools within the academy) came to produce these professionals. As management schools became more "academic," research grew. By the 1980s, central data processing was in decline. Computer technology became more decentralizable through minicomputers and microcomputers that served as terminals to the mainframe *and* as stand-alone computers running spreadsheets and other useful software. By the 1990s computers were connected to internal and external data communication networks like the Internet. The cost of computing fell between 1975 and 1999. Organizational units that could not earlier afford to buy computers did so. Central data processing's power loss accelerated as outsourcing grew. Many "hardware" functions were outsourced, and central data processing often did little more than manage "enterprise systems" and contracts with outsource providers.

The declining cost of computers was only part of the decline of central data processing's power. Starting in the 1980s application software moved out of central data processing, and often out of the organization. Operating system software was still "bundled" with computer purchases (a practice still followed today) and was not a hindrance to decentralization. Application software moved increasingly to packaged software produced by software companies (virtually unknown in the 1960s). Bundles such as Microsoft Office contained most of the software moderately sophisticated microcomputer users needed. Most units, not just central data processing, could buy application software. "Software as a service," or SaaS, continued the migration of application software out of the organization. For many employees, including those outside central data processing, computing became *personal* as well as *organizational*. Computers at home allowed employees to do organizational work at home or to "telecommute."

Many computerized tasks became once again the province of those units that owned the tasks, as opposed to those that controlled data processing. Prior to unit record equipment there was little centralized data processing. Most units had their own data processing expertise. As central data processing grew, units complied as organization policy required. In time, central data processing's power base became dependent on policies that required use of central data processing. Central data processing might try to defend centralization (or re-centralization) by arguing cost saving (usually economies of scale), enforcement of uniformity, and so on. But central data processing never regained the power of its heyday. Renaming central data processing to Information Systems or the Data Processing Manager to Chief Information Officer (CIO) did not change this fact. The IS Function became weaker as people who had never used computers became expert with desktops, laptops, tablets, and mobile devices far more powerful than early mainframe computers, and as software moved outside the organization. IT became more important, but the IS Function became less important.

This ecological change has had important implications for the IS Field. The field was originally launched to meet the workforce needs of the IS Function, and much of "relevance" was tied to the IS Function's power base. As that power base contracted, the IS Field faced new challenges. As IS academics had to meet expectations for academic rigor, irrespective of relevance, they became less interested in relevance at the same time the IS Function was fading as a source for guidance on relevance. To make matters worse, other organizational functions recognized information technology as vital to their long-term prosperity and sustainability and became less interested in having the IS Function play a dominant (or any) role to constrain their destiny. They did not want the IS Function moving into "their" territory, and other functional areas of management education followed suit. Marketing provides a good example. An executive from a large technology company recently told one of this chapter's authors that her company no longer talks much with CIOs. In many cases her company *is* the CIO due to outsourcing. More important, her company spends time with client marketing leaders. The IS Function is no longer at the IS frontier; marketing is. Marketing belongs to marketing, not to IS, and relevance is determined by marketing, not IS.

The *raison d'être* of the IS Field was the praxis from whence it was born. Yet the seat of that praxis, the IS Function, is often decreasingly salient. The IS Field's heroic and well-intentioned efforts to find alternatives may be to no avail because most functions in organizations have their functional counterparts in the academy. For example, health-related IT usually must deal with physicians and others from the health sciences who determine what is relevant. The *academic enterprise* is the problem. It might not work to hitch the IS Field's fortunes to unstable praxis.

Nothing lasts forever, especially on "Internet Time." The IS Function might have given birth to the IS Field, but times change. The IS Field cannot draw much comfort from the academic side that is increasingly hard to predict, especially in management schools that house many in the IS Field. Of more than 500 accredited MBA-granting programs in the United States, perhaps 100 are making money off their full-time MBA programs. Subsidies go to high-performing MBA students to keep rankings up, while full-time programs move toward the undergraduate level and MBA programs move toward fully employed students as fewer students can afford to quit their jobs and return to school. To further complicate things, many of the management fields look *backwards*, while the IS Field must be about the future. About all we can be certain of is that there will be organizations, and information systems will be important. The zombies of the IS Field are tied to a different and disappearing world. Turning away from the IS Field's origins *and* the promise of academic legitimacy presents a major challenge.

Beyond staying alive

This all sounds rather anxious (King and Lyytinen, 2006). The important but difficult thing is to see the bright side captured in this observation: there will be organizations, and information systems will be important. Organizations have been around since humans have been on the scene (an early, detailed account of hierarchy can be found in Exodus 18, written about 4,500 years ago). They will probably be around a while longer. Information systems appear to be changing much, if not *everything*. There is ample evidence that information systems are changing organizations. Academic fields struggle hard to maintain their salience, and functionalist fields founded in professional schools (like management schools) do this all the time. But that does not mean they always succeed.

The IS Field's anxiety does not properly belong with the notion that there will be organizations, or that information systems will be important. It belongs with the likelihood that failing academic constructs encourage the field to live with The Undead instead of really living. The IS Field is an academic enterprise. Is it fair to ask how the IS Field can escape academic constructs? It probably cannot. Yet the *current* constructs need not be the constructs of the future. Earlier we noted that the academy is a patronage scheme. Who are our patrons, and what are they interested in? The IS Field seems smitten with "crowdsourcing." Maybe the IS Field should crowdsource from our patrons. We recognize that this puts great pressure on people who are just joining the academic enterprise, and especially on those who will soon seek security of employment through tenure. This is an artifact of the times in which we live. We are not saying that every aspect of academic life will change. Most change will be on the margins, but marginal change can be a big deal. It is time to rethink the IS Field, learning from The Undead to be more fully alive. Tensions that refuse to go away can guide us.

As strange as it might sound, a source of inspiration for the IS Field is Robert Michels's century-old Iron Law of Oligarchy (Michels, 1915): no matter how democratic a complex social organization might be when started, in time it evolves into an oligarchy ruled by an elite. It is time to start questioning elites. There is false hope in the IS Field emphasizing preservation of the *field* (or even worse, as the *discipline*) – things are changing too fast and too much. Elites benefit even from fields not fully alive. The leadership of the IS Field are no more to blame for this dilemma than are leaders of science who Thomas Kuhn criticized as inherently conservative (Kuhn, 1962). Change does happen, and it is seldom easy in the academy. The academy of the 15th century (when there was no IS Field) could not cope with the challenges of the late 20th century (when the IS Field had emerged). The context of the academy is changing at an accelerating pace. The IS Field's question of what it means to be a "field" (or a "legitimate field") is increasingly difficult to answer because the quest for academic legitimacy began in the 1980s when the norms of academic legitimacy themselves began to change. That change has not abated, and might have accelerated. Information systems affect academic legitimacy, as even a modest glance at various "impact" metrics shows.

Comfortable answers do not take care of uncomfortable questions. Why look at the IS Field to understand the problems *of the IS Field?* We suggest the problems lie in the academy itself. The IS Field was born and grew up in the latter quarter of the 20th century, a fairly stable time for academic fields. However, stable does not mean permanent. The IS Field hitched itself to a star – the tradition of academic legitimacy. This star appeared unchangeable until it fell. The IS Field's roots are in the rapidly evolving digital ecosystem, but they cannot today reside in the heyday of the central data processing function – that world is gone. The new ecosystem is unstable, and the ideal balance between old and new, socio and technical, rigorous and relevant, or whatever dichotomy one chooses, is as elusive as the Golden Mean. Fast change affords opportunities for frame-breaking as well as opportunities to get things wrong. We learn by doing. The IT-centric economy creates speculation about the future. The "important" stakeholders seem to be from the private sector. Or maybe they are from the public sector. Or maybe they are from developed economies. Or maybe they are from emerging markets. Any thesis and antithesis will do in a pinch. All are worthy of discussion as long as there will be organizations and information systems will be important.

To be really alive, the IS Field must recapture the vitality and inherent riskiness of life at the frontier, even as the frontier that gave rise to the field is no more. This might – probably will – require breaking with academic orthodoxy. This is risky, but it is a small price to pay for really living.

Notes

1. Authors are listed in reverse alphabetical order.
2. Hirschheim and Klein's (2011) excellent history says instruction started in the 1960s. We address the academic enterprise of the IS Field, including research that got organized somewhat later. This paper is not primarily about history. For history we defer to Hirschheim and Klein and similar work.
3. See Matthew 23:27 (KJV).
4. A detailed review is beyond this chapter. Searching on <rigor relevance> produces many hits. See King and Lyytinen (2006) for more discussion of this and related issues.
5. As of January 2017, www.leadered.com/our-philosophy/rigor-relevance-framework.php.
6. Remark made to one of the authors of this chapter.
7. Data included here come from the ACM and AIS, a combination of website examination and email correspondence.

References

Abbasi, A. and Chen, H. (2008). "CyberGate: A System and Design Framework for Text Analysis of Computer Mediated Communication," *MIS Quarterly* (32: 4), 811–837.

Adomavicius, G., Bockstedt, J.C., Gupta, A. and Kauffman, R.J. (2008). "Making Sense of Technology Trends in the Information Technology Landscape: A Design Science Approach," *MIS Quarterly* (32: 4), 779–809.

Boland, R.J. and Collopy, F. (Eds.) (2004). "Managing as Design," *Stanford Business Books*.

Dewey, J. (1929). *The Sources of a Science Education*. New York: Liveright.

Dorst, K. (2006). "Design Problems and Design Paradoxes," *Design Issues* (22:3), 4.

Esar, E. (1949). *The Dictionary of Humorous Quotations*. Garden City, NY: Doubleday.

Gregor, S. and Hevner, A.R. (2013). "Positioning and Presenting Design Science Research for Maximum Impact," *MIS Quarterly* (37:2), 337–355.

Gregor, S. and Jones, D. (2007). "The Anatomy of a Design Theory," *Journal of the Association of Information Systems* (8:5), 312–335.

Hevner, A., March, S., Park, J. and Ram, S. (2004). "Design Science in Information Systems Research," *MIS Quarterly* (28:1), 75–105.

Hirschheim, R. and Klein, H.E. (2011) "Tracing the History of the Information Systems Field," in Galliers, R.D and Currie, W.L. (eds.) *The Oxford Handbook of Management Information Systems*. Oxford: Oxford University Press: pp. 16–61.

Holmes, R. (2008). *The Age of Wonder: The Romantic Generation and the Discovery of the Beauty and Terror of Science*. New York: Random House.

Huppatz, D.J. (2015). "Revisiting Herbert Simon's 'Science of Design,'" *Design Issues* (31:2), 29–40.

Keen, P.G.W. (1980) *MIS Research: Reference Disciplines and a Cumulative Tradition*. Minneapolis, MN: ICIS 1980 Proceedings.

Keen, P.G.W. (1991) "Relevance and Rigor in Information Systems Research: Improving Quality, Confidence, Cohesion and Impact," in Nissen, H.E., Klein, H. and Hirschheim, R. (eds.) *Information Systems Research: Contemporary Approaches and Emergent Traditions*. Amsterdam: North-Holland, pp. 27–49.

King, J.L. and Lyytinen, K. (eds.) (2006). *Information Systems: The State of the Field*. London: John Wiley and Sons.

Kuhn, T.S. (1962). *The Structure of Scientific Revolutions*. Chicago: University of Chicago Press.

Lee, J., Wyner, G.M. and Pentland, B.T. (2008). "Process Grammar as a Tool for Business Process Design," *MIS Quarterly* (32:4), 757–778.

Markus, M., Majchrzak, L. and Gasser, L. (2002). "A Design Theory for Systems That Support Emergent Knowledge Processes," *MIS Quarterly* (26:3), 179–212.

March, S. and Smith, G. (1995). "Design and Natural Science Research on Information Technology," *Decision Support Systems* (15), 251–266.

March, S.T. and Storey, V.C. (2008). "Design Science in the Information Systems Discipline: An Introduction to the Special Issue on Design Science Research," *MIS Quarterly* (32:4), 725–730.

Mason, R.O. (1989). "MIS experiments: A pragmatic perspective," in Benbasat, I. (ed) *The Information Systems Research Challenge: Experimental Methods*, Vol. 2. Boston MA: Harvard Business School, pp. 3–20.

Michels, R. (1915) *Political Parties: A Sociological Study of the Oligarchical Tendencies of Modern Democracy*. New York: Free Press.

Nunamaker, J., Chen, M. and Purdin, T. (1990–91). "Systems Development in Information Systems Research," *Journal of Management Information Systems* (7:3), 89–106.

Parsons, J. and Wand, Y. (2008). "Using Cognitive Principles to Guide Classification in Information Systems Modeling," *MIS Quarterly* (32:4), 839–868.

Pries-Heje, J. and Baskerville, R. (2008). "The Design Theory Nexus," *MIS Quarterly* (32:4), 731–755.

Santayana, G. (1905) *Reason in Common Sense, Volume 1 of The Life of Reason*. New York: Charles Scribner's Sons.

Simon, H.A. (1969) *The Sciences of the Artificial*. Cambridge, MA: MIT Press.

Secrest, M. (2014). *Elsa Schiaparelli: A Biography*. New York: Knopf Doubleday.

Walls, J.G, Widmeyer, G.R. and El Sawy, O.A. (1992). "Building an Information System Design Theory for Vigilant EIS," *Information Systems Research* (3:1), 36–59.

Whitehurst, G.J. (2008). *Rigor and Relevance Redux: Director's Biennial Report to Congress*. Washington, DC: U.S. Department of Education.

INDEX

Aadhaar project 452–9; architecture of, illustrated 455; background 452–3; Bill 453; developmental objectives 453–4; Aadhaar Enabled Bank Account (AEBA) 458; Aadhaar Enabled Payment System (AEPS) 458; Aadhaar Verification Service (AVS) 453, 456; IT's role in 454–5; overview of 453; transferring to other countries 458–9; unfolding of, explaining 455–8
absorptive capacity 317
actor-network theory 19
actualization: social forces 237–8; applying 239; arising from user/artifact relation 236; bundles of 235; defined 235; enabling and constraining 239; identifying 237; interaction of 237; level(s) of granularity for 236–7; perceived 238
adaptation, aligning as 346–7
affect in ICT context 122, 166–77; affective concepts 167–9; affective responses toward ICT 170–1; biosignals 175–6; causal relationships during ICT interaction episode 170–1; circumplex model 168; conclusions and future directions 176–7; detection by ICT 171–6; facial signals 173–4; introduction 166–7; neurosignals 175–6; speech signals 174–5; textual signals 172–3
affective computing 97, 171, 174
affective concepts, in ICT 167–9; categorical view 167; dimensional view 167–8
Affective Response Model (ARM) 122, 169–70
affordance lens 157, 234–5, 237–8, 243
Affordance Theory 232–43; adapting, for IS research 234–5; bundles 235; conducting IS research using 241–3; consistency of, with philosophical perspectives 240–1; origins of 232–4; overview 232; principles for using, in IS research 236–8; unresolved issues 238–9
agency: concept of 448; defined 450
Agenda for Sustainable Development 450
Agile Portfolio Management 145
agility: concept of 138; evolution of 138–9; flow and 139–42; future development of 146–7; in IS development 138–48; of IS strategising 210; openness and 145–6; project portfolio management and 142–5; of software development 125, 129–31, 134; value-based measurement of 140
algorithmic decision-making 122, 387, 403–8; *see also* data sources
algorithmic illiteracy 395
aligning/alignment 341–52; as adaptation 346–7; analytical framework of 346; coding, 344–5; coding and categorization 344–5; concept of 204, 341; defined 341; as experience 348–9; findings 343–6; future research, suggestions for 349–52; implications for managers 352; as integration 347–8; introduction 341–2; macro/micro processes 343; overview 342; in practice, research agenda for 349; research approach 343; as translation 347
Allied Market Research 278
Amazon 266
Amazon Mechanical Turk 440, 473
analysis of IS historical studies 14–19; *see also* historiographical paradigms
analytics 391–400; cycle of choice and 393–9; decision support systems related to 392–3; effect of, on organizational learning dysfunctions 398–400; introduction 391–2; overview 392–3; study of 393; technology of 392–3
Android platform 133, 263, 266, 270, 468

505

Apple 266–7, 270–1, 367, 472, 474
Application Programming Interfaces (APIs) 266
architected technologies quadrant 256, 258, 260–5, 267, 269
artificial intelligence (AI) 320, 468, 474
Association for Computing Machinery (ACM) 498
Association for Information Systems (AIS) 5–6, 490–1, 498
audience learning 396–7, 399
autonomic nervous system (ANS) 96

badge and rating system 381
BAPO framework 135
big data 113, 125, 129, 387, 392, 396, 400, 405–8, 410–11, 413, 417, 439–40
biosignals 175–6
Bitcoin 388, 485–6
black hole proposition 49–50, 52–3
blockchain 485–8
boundary objects 376–7
bracketing 35–7
brain-computer interaction (BCI) 97, 100
broadcast social media tools in disasters, effective use of (case study) 158–9
brokering roles 378–9
business intelligence systems in universities, effective use of (case study) 157–8
business process change (BPC) tools 41–3
Business Process Outsourcing (BPO) 319
business risk 312
Business Systems Planning (BSP) 350

Capability Maturity Model (CMM) 316; Capability Maturity Model Integrated (CMMI) 316; theory 450–2
Carbon Disclosure Project 319
case studies: on aligning in practice 346–9; case sources 358–9; data-driven decision-making 408; on digitalization 223; on effective use 157–61; ethnography compared to 86–7; historical 9, 16, 18–19; on innovation in healthcare settings 328–39; on software scaling 131–5; on sourcing IT services 319; on user resistance to IT 189–90
categorical view 167
Central Identities Data Repository (CIDR) 452, 454–5
centralized vs. distributed control paradox 265–6
central nervous system (CNS) 96
circumplex model 168
clickworking 473
client capabilities: ITO decisions and 314; ITO outcomes and 317
client firm characteristics: ITO decisions and 314; ITO outcomes and 317
client management capability 316–17
client/provider interface design 316
client's technical and methodological capability 314
cloud computing 135, 248, 277, 279–80, 291
cognitive neuroscience 94–5, 97, 105
cognitive processes 102–3, 160, 295, 373
cognitive transformation 35–6
collaborative agreements 377–8
collective reflection-in-action 88
commercial off-the-shelf (COTS) vendors 130
communication 316
communities of practice (CoP) 130, 204, 206, 222, 250, 371, 374
competences (macro/micro) 296–9
computational linguistic techniques 173
computational support for organisational activities 466–76; categories of affordances related to 470–1; challenges 467–8; computing at scale 467, 473–5; computing in the large 467, 472–3; computing in the small 467–71; future challenges 475–6; interconnectedness of organisational technologies 475–6; introduction 466–7; organisational performances with mobile IT 471
computing at scale 388, 467, 473–5
computing in the large 388, 467, 472–3
computing in the small 388, 467–71
conceptual reviews 75, 77–8
Connect 2020 438
consistency, in effective use 157
context of discovery see theory building
context of justification see theory testing
contextualization, principle of 89
contingency theory 371, 374
continuous compliance 131–2
contracts: detail 315 contractors, individual 484–5
contractual governance, ITO outcomes and 315
control: vs. autonomy paradox 265–8; digital innovation and 366–7; mechanisms 315, 322, 371–2
corporate social responsibility (CSR) 319
critical research: paradigm 13 critiquing historical evidence 22–3
crowdsourcing 128, 130, 383, 404, 440, 473, 498, 501
culture 43–4; cultural distance 314
Cumulative Flow Diagrams (CFDs) 140
customer relationship management (CRM) 79, 188, 210–11
cybersecurity 319–20
cynicism 192

data analysis, in literature review 79
data sources 404–8; Facebook's news feeds, potential consequences of 405–7; in literature

review 79; sensors 407–8; social software 404–5
datification in action 403–13; data sources and algorithmic decision-making 404–8; discrimination 409–12; ethical practices 410–12; introduction 403–4; privacy issues 409–12
decentralized autonomous organization (DAO) 487–8
decentralized decision-making process 284–6
decision characteristics, ITO outcomes and 317–18
decision-making: activities 345, 349, 358–9; algorithmic 122, 387, 403–8; data-driven 408; in NeuroIS paper classification 102–3; social software platforms for 404–5
decision support systems (DSS): for management decision making 7; related to analytics 392–3
decision tree 74, 77–80; coverage 79; data analysis 79; data source or types of papers 79; focus 77, 79; goal of review with respect to theory 77; illustrated 78; purpose of, summarized 79–80; systematicity and transparency 77
dependent variables 86, 99, 248, 308, 310
deployment/provisioning pillar 295
descriptive reviews 74–5, 77–9
design, in IS Field 496–8
design and action theory 58, 61
design ethnography 113
detection from speech signals 174–5
developing activities 342, 344, 346–7, 358–9
development research, ICT and 447–52; economic growth approach 449–51; foundational theories in, operationalizing for development studies 451–2; individual action and society 448–9; operationalizing foundational theories in 451–2; socio-economic theories 449–51; socio-technical theories 447–8; technology and society 447–8
DevOps 129
dialogical reasoning, principle of 89
dialogic approaches 375–6
diffusion model of power 208–12, 330
digital behavior patterns 388, 476
digital capability 290–303; introduction 290–1; leadership and governance for framing 299–300; from managing technical artifacts to harnessing distributed knowledge 291–3; pillars and core domains for 295–6; resource-based view of 294; scaffold for 294–6; theoretical underpinnings of 294
digital competences 294–302; building 300–2; governance structure for 299–300; leadership structure for 299–300; macro/micro-competences 296–9; mobilizing resources to create 302; scaffolding for positioning 294–6;

social capital providing environment for organizational knowing 301
digital divide(s): 416–40; access to usage to outcomes 438–9; convergence or divergence in 438; digital natives, big data and emerging digital divides 439–40; global 418–23; goals and targets 438; introduction 416–17; measuring 418–19; narrowing, international aspirations for 437–40; problem 445; regional 423–7; in Russia 433–7; in United States 427–33
digital ethnography 111–13
digital infrastructures 253–73; introduction 253–5; model of growth in 269–70; paradoxes 255–69
digital innovation 360–7; core aspects of 364; defining 361–4; digital technology and 361–2; growth and scaling 366; introduction and goal 360–1; logic and, organizing 365–6; management and control 366–7; organizing for 364–6; recombination and 362–3; value co-creation and 363–4
digitalization 218–29; digital strategizing in practice 223–8; introduction 218–19; from IT strategy to digital strategizing 219–22; movements in 219–22; Papermill vignette 224–5, 228; as strategy practice 222–3
digital revolution 444–60; Aadhaar project 452–9; introduction 444–6; theoretical foundations for ICT and development 446–52
digital technology: digital innovation and 361–2; IT portfolio and 279–80
digital transformation 122, 248, 290, 388, 475
disciplinary and methodological foundations of IS: ethnography in IS research 108–18; historical research in IS 5–24; interpretive research 83–90; introduction 1–3; IS as reference discipline 47–54; literature review 73–80; NeuroIS 94–105; philosophy and method 30–45; theory 57–69
discrimination 409–12
domain understanding 316
downward flexibility 255–6, 260, 262, 264

ecological perspective, in IS Field 498–500
ecological psychology 232, 240
economy, technology-driven changes in 481–8; blockchain 485–8; individual contractors 484–5; sharing economy as bridge to service economy 485; value creation 482–4; work 481–2
EDSAC project 6–7
effective use of IT: of broadcast social media tools in disasters (case study) 158–9; of business intelligence systems in universities (case study) 157–8; of electronic health records in community care (case study) 157;

Index

introduction 152; lessons from case studies 160–1; program of research on, map guide to 153–5; of reporting systems in clinical networks (case study) 159–60; research in progress on 155–7; from use to 152–3
egocentric learning 397
electrocardiogram (EKG) 94, 104, 175
electrodermal activity (EDA) 101, 103–4, 175–6
electroencephalography (EEG) 94, 98, 101–4, 175
electronic data processing (EDP) 291; equipment 183
electronic medical record (EMR) 333–4, 336–7, 339; in community care, effective use of (case study) 157
emotion(s): anxiety 169; cues (implicit and explicit) 172–3; lexicon 172; processes 102–3, 175 expressions: in text 172–3; facial 174
enforced transparency 409
Enlightenment paradigm 10–11
enterprise resource planning (ERP) 17, 79, 88, 101–3, 176, 196, 204
enterprise systems (ES): considerations for organizations 281–6; decentralized decision-making process 284–6; digital technologies and IT portfolio 279–80; digital technologies compared to 277; importance of innovation 278; in innovation 276–86; introduction 276–8; maturity and innovation 281–2; as platform 282–3; role of, in innovation 278–9; software focus and innovation 283–4; software management approach and innovation 285; stability of 281–2; vendor-led innovations, reducing 283–4
environment, ITO decisions and 314, 318
ethical practices 410–12
ethnography 3, 40–1, 86–90, 108–18; case study research compared to 86–7; design 113; digital 111–13; in IS research 109–13; mobile 114–15; organizational 110–11; overview 108–9; phenomena in IS 113–17; sensory 115–16; visual 117
evaluating activities 345–7, 358–9
evidence: citation, contradictions in 52; critiquing historical 22–3; primary sources for gathering historical 21–2
explanation theory 58, 61
exploitation, knowledge 208, 210–11
exploration, knowledge 208–11
exploration/exploitation pillar 295
external and internal influences 313
Eye-Fixation Related Potential (EFRP) 103–4
eye-tracking 102–3

Facebook's news feeds, potential consequences of 405–7, 472
Facial Action Coding System (FACS) 173–4
facial electromyography (fEMG) 104, 174
facial signals 173–4
family focused team meeting 333–4
Fitbit 410–11
Fiverr 440
fixity *vs.* variety paradox 260–2
flow: agility and 139–42; defined 140; in ICT 169
Food and Drug Administration (FDA) 127
Frankenstein 492
functionalism 374, 499
functional magnetic resonance imaging (fMRI) 94, 98, 100, 102–4, 175
functional near-infrared spectroscopy (fNIRS) 94, 103–4

galvanometer 94
gamification 381, 383
General Electric (GE) 7
generativity: changes in socio-economic context influencing 266–8; computing in the large 472; defined 255; in digital infrastructures 253–73; features of 259–60, 262, 264–5, 267–9; online communities 379–82; paradoxes underlying 259–69; principles of 271–2; recombination 362–3
gig economy 473
Global Compact 319
Global Pulse projects 440
Global Reporting Initiative 319
global software development (GSD) 130
Google 24, 266–7, 411
Google Scholar 24
gross domestic product (GDP) 425, 450, 483
gross national product (GNP) 449
grounded theory methods (GTMs) 63–4, 67, 74, 79, 87, 154, 156–7
growth, digital innovation and 366

healthcare settings, innovation in (case study) 328–39; analysis and discussion 335–9; background literature 329–30; from conception to start of pilot innovation project (2008–2010) 331–2; conclusions and implications 339; context and methods 330–1; findings 331–5; introduction 328–9; pilot project (April 1, 2010–April 1, 2015) 332–5; power of talk 335–7; power of text 336–8; power of things 337–9; timeline of events and data collection 331
hermeneutic circle, fundamental principle of 89
historical method 6–10; Christian 8; determining patterns of historical facts 23; formulating historical questions 20–1; Greco-Roman 7–8; history of 7–10; overview 6–7; Renaissance 9–10; verisimilitude of Muslim historians 8–9
historical research in IS 5–24; analysis of IS historical studies 14–19; historical method 6–10; historiographical paradigms

10–14; historiography's seven steps 19–24; introduction 5–6
historicism 11–14, 24
historiographical paradigms 10–14; critical 13; Enlightenment 10–11; Marxist 13; postmodern 13–14; Rankean 11–12; Romantic 11; social science 12–13
historiography's seven steps 19–24
homeostasis 96
human-computer interaction (HCI) 101, 103, 233–4, 469
human resource management capability 316
Husqvarna 132–3
hybrid managers 300
hybrid reviews 80
hypothetico-deductive (H-D) approach 2, 7, 23, 38–44, 62–4

IAOP 321
impact sourcing 319
income per person (IPP) 449
independent variables 86, 248, 308, 310–16, 318, 321–2
Indian Parliament 453
Individual Interaction with Information Technology (IIIT) model 169
influence sources, ITO decisions and 313
information and communication technologies (ICTs): access types in appropriation of 419; affect in context of 122, 166–77; to detect affective responses from users 122; development research 447–52; digital divides 416–40; digital revolution 444–60; indigenous adoption of 67; IS domain and 21; socio-economic benefits of 388; in specifying IS domain 21; theoretical foundations for 446–52; users' choices of 166
information systems development (ISD) 138–48; agility and flow 139–42; agility and openness 145–6; agility and project portfolio management 142–5; evolution of agility and agile evaluation in 138–9; future development of agile and open 146–7
Information Systems Field (IS Field) see IS Field
Information Systems Research Seminar in Scandinavia (IRIS) 490
Information Technology Infrastructure Library (ITIL) 316
informed action 155–6, 160–1
Inner Source 129–30, 133
innersourcing 128, 147
innovation: defined 278; digital 360–7; ES in 276–86; future research opportunities 318; in healthcare settings (case study) 328–39; importance of 278; maturity and 281–2; software focus and 283–4; software

management approach and 285; vendor-led, reducing 283–4
Institute of Electrical and Electronics Engineers (IEEE) 490
Institute of Management Sciences, The (TIMS) 490
Institute of Robotic Process Automation (IRPA) 320
integration, aligning as 347–8
intellectual alignment 346
interaction between researchers and subjects, principle of 89
International Business Machines (IBM) 21, 490, 495; Business Systems Planning 350; Watson 125, 173
International Conference on Information Systems (ICIS) 48, 94–5, 490
International Telecommunication Union (ITU) 418, 420, 423–5, 437–8, 445
Internet of Things (IoT) 121, 125, 291, 300, 466, 471
interpreting meaning 33–8; validity of, assessing 38–43
interpretive flexibility 376–7
interpretive research 83–90; ethnography, applicability of 86–7; examples of 87–9; introduction 83–5; manuscripts, evaluating 89–90; meaning in 30–44; nature of 85–6; principles for 89–90
interpretivism 14, 30, 85
iOS platform 263, 266–7, 270–1, 367, 468
iPhone 266, 406–7, 466, 468, 472
IS, development, adoption and use of: affect 166–77; Affordance Theory 232–43; agility in IS development 138–48; digitalization 218–29; introduction 121–3; IT use 152–61; software development 125–35; strategy and strategising 202–12; user resistance to IT 183–99
IS domain, specifying 21
IS Field 490–502; affective concepts in 168–9; design 496–8; ecological perspective 498–500; preservation of 500–2; problems of 501–2; rigor/relevance 493–6; start date of 490–1; Undead 491–3
IS Function 498–500
IS in society and a global context: computational support for organisational activities 466–76; datification in action 403–13; digital divides 416–40; digital revolution, developmental effects of 444–60; economy, technology-driven changes in 481–8; introduction 387–9; IS Field 490–502; organizational intelligence in digital age 391–400
IS strategy and strategising 202–12; concept of 202; diffusion model of power in 208–12; digitalization 218–29; discussion 209–11;

framework 205–6, 208; implications 211–12; introduction 202–12; IS literature and 203; knowledge exploitation in 208, 210–11; knowledge exploration in 208–11; movements in 219–22; organisational tensions and 203–6; overview 203–6; power and practice-based view 206–7; power and strategising 207–9; translation model of power in 208–12

IT management 292–3, 341, 351

ITO batting average 318

ITO decisions, determinants of 312–14; client capabilities 314–15; client firm characteristics 314; environment 314; illustrated 311; influence sources 313; motivations to outsource 312–13; relationship characteristics 314; transaction attributes 312

ITO decisions and outcomes *see* sourcing IT services

ITO outcomes, determinants of 314–18; client capabilities 317; client firm characteristics 317; contractual governance 315; decision characteristics 317–18; illustrated 311; ITO decision 318; provider capabilities 316–17; relational governance 315–16; transaction attributes 315

IT sourcing *see* sourcing IT services

IT use 152–61; effective 152–61; resistance to 183–99

JAM Trinity 454, 456, 458–9

knowledge: diversity 373; exploitation 208, 210–11; exploration 208–11; possession perspective of 206–7; thematic advances in 61–2

knowledge-based organizing 373

knowledge collaboration 370–83; defined 375; generative promise of online community 379–82; implications 382–3; from information processing to social knowing 371–2; introduction 370–1; social mechanisms in 372–9; synthesis of approaches to 374

knowledge sharing: in affordance theory 234; collaborative agreement and 377; defined 316; in IS strategizing 204–5, 207, 211; in online communities 381; in organizational IS 247, 249–50; power of talk and 335, 376; in relational governance 315–16, 322

Kuhnian paradigm 14, 18

leadership and governance 299–300

lean methods: software development 125, 129, 146

learning: activities 345, 348–9, 358–9

learning under ambiguity 394–5, 399; *see also* organizational learning

lexicon-based emotion detection 172

Linguistic Inquiry and Word Count (LIWC) 172

literature review 73–80; conceptual reviews 75, 77–8; concluding remarks 80; critical reviews 75, 77–8; descriptive reviews 74–5, 77–9; focus 77, 79; introduction 73–4; meta-analysis 75–6, 78–9; narrative reviews 74–5, 77–9; qualitative systematic reviews 76–9; realist reviews 76–9; scoping reviews 75, 77–9; theoretical reviews 75–9; types of, choosing 77–80; types of, relevant to IS 74–7; umbrella reviews 76–9

little data 405–13

local *vs.* global paradox 268–9

logic, digital innovation and 365–6

logical positivism 59–60

Lyons Electronic Office (LEO) 7, 22, 466

magnetoencephalography (MEG) 104

management capability 317; type 315, 322

management, digital innovation and 366–7

MANCO 41–3

Marxist paradigm 13

meaning 30–44; discussion 43–4; interpreted, assessing validity of 38–43; interpreting 33–8; overview 30–1; problematizing 31–3

measurement difficulty 315

mentalizing 100

meta-analysis 75–6, 78–9

method *see* philosophy and method

metrics used to manage flow 140–1

Microsoft: Corporation 278, 411, 472; Kinect 474; Office 499; PowerPoint presentations 332, 336–9, 350

Microworker 440

Millennium Development Goals (MDGs) 418, 437, 450

mimetic influences 313

mobile ethnography 114–15

mobile IT, organisational performances with 471

motion tracker 388, 476

multiple interpretations, principle of 89

narrative (telling the story) 23–4

narrative reviews 74–5, 77–9

National Outsourcing Association 320

National Rural Employment Guarantee Scheme (NREGS) 454

National Social Assistance Programme (NSAP) 454

National Telecommunications and Information Administration (NTIA) 416, 427–8, 433

negotiating activities 345, 348, 358–9

Networked Readiness Index (NRI) 439

neuroeconomics 97

neuroergonomics 97

NeuroIS 94–105, 175; affective computing 97; biological foundations and applications

relevant to 96–7; brain-computer interaction 97, 100; cognitive neuroscience 94–5, 97, 105; contributions from neurobiological approaches to 97–100; human neurobiology and 95–6; importance of 97–100; introduction 94–5; measurement instrument, factors with respect to 104–5; methodology 103–5; nervous system and 96; neuroeconomics 97; neuroergonomics 97; neuromarketing 97; neurophysiological tools in 94, 103–5; neuropsychology 97; overview 95–7; paper classification 102–3; papers published dealing with 94, 103; reference disciplines of 96–7; research methodology 103–5; topics 100–3
neuromarketing 97
neurophysiological tools 3, 94, 103–4, 175–6
neuropsychology 97
neurosignals 175–6
news feeds 403, 405–7, 472

object orientation 125
oculometry 94
offshoring 88–9, 110, 130; *see also* sourcing IT services
online communities (OCs) in knowledge collaboration 379–82
open source software (OSS) 125, 130, 133
open-sourcing 128
Oracle Corp. 278, 347
organizational IS: aligning 341–52; digital capability 290–303; digital infrastructures 253–73; introduction 247–50; knowledge collaboration 370–83; sourcing of IT services 307–22
organizational tensions, ISS and 203–6
organizational intelligence in digital age 391–400; *see also* analytics
organizational learning: dysfunctions, cycle of choice with 393–9; audience learning in 396–7, 399; learning under ambiguity in 394–5, 399; role-constrained learning in 395–6, 399; superstitious learning in 397–9
organization: ethnography 110–11; informal 300
organizing for digital innovation 364–6
outsourcing 88–9, 130, 134, 248, 291, 293, 296; *see also* sourcing IT services

Papermill vignette 224–5, 228
paradoxes 259–69; centralized *vs.* distributed control 265–6; control *vs.* autonomy 265–8; fixity *vs.* variety 260–2; importance of 260; local *vs.* global 268–9; model of change 255–9; stability *vs.* change 262–5
paradox model of change 255–9; architected technologies quadrant 256, 258, 260–5, 267, 269; illustrated 257; physical context quadrant 256, 259, 262, 265, 268–9; socio-economic contexts quadrant 255–6, 259, 262, 264–9; underlying technologies quadrant 255–6, 258, 260–2, 264, 266–7, 269
partnership view 316
peer-to-peer (P2P) music sharing 474
perceived affordances 238
perceived ease of use (PEOU) 195
perceived usefulness (PU) 195
peripheral nervous system (PNS) 96
perspective taking 376, 379
phenomenological reduction 35–7, 43
phenomenology 33–4
philosophy and method 30–45; interpreted meaning, assessing validity of 38–43; interpreting meaning 33–8; introduction 30–1; method in the sense of research method 30; problematizing meaning 31–3
physical context quadrant 256, 259, 262, 265, 268–9
plug and play teaming 378
portfolio: agility and project portfolio management 142–5; creating, challenges in 467; digital technologies and 279–80; two-speed 280–1
positivism 14, 44, 59–60, 85, 241
positron emission tomography (PET) 104, 175
possession perspective 206–7
postmodern paradigm 13–14
post-positivism 85
power 206–9; dominance/submissiveness 168; practice-based view 206–7; strategising and 207–11
PowerPoint presentations 332, 336–9, 350
practice-based view, power and 206–7
pragmatic view of theory 58, 60, 62, 69
predicting theory 58, 61
pricing models 318
privacy issues 409–12
problematization 31–3; 75
proclamation/presentation stage 64, 69
Programming Interfaces (APIs) 266
Project Management Office (PMO) 145
provider capabilities, ITO outcomes and 316–17
provider competition 314
provider management capability 317
Public Distribution System (PDS) 454
pull factors 125–6, 135
pupillometry 94, 102–4, 175
push factors 125–6, 135

qualitative systematic reviews 76–9
QUMAS 131–2

radio-frequency identification (RFID) 466
Rankean paradigm 11–12
realist reviews 76–9
received view 60

recombination, digital innovation and 362–3
reconfiguring activities 344, 346–7, 358–9
reference discipline, IS as 47–54; black hole proposition 49–50, 52–3; citation evidence, contradictions in 52; future directions 54; introduction 47; questions, IS scholars to consider different set of 53–4; reasons for 47–9; reframing propositions 52–3; rising star proposition 51–3; subsequent reference discipline discourse 49–54; summarizing 54
reflection-in-action 88, 156–7
relational engagement 376
relational governance 316; ITO outcomes and 315–16
relationship characteristics, ITO decisions and 314
relationship quality 316
remote job entry (RJE) 499
reporting systems in clinical networks, effective use of (case study) 159–60
representational fidelity 154–60
Representation Theory (RT) 153–61
representative coverage 79
research methods: assessing validity of interpreted meaning 38–43; choice of 67–8; ethnography 3, 40–1, 86–90, 108–18; interpreting meaning 33–8; literature reviews as 73–80; method in sense of 30–1; NeuroIS research 94–105; problematizing meaning 31–3
resistance *see* user resistance to IT
resolution 40–1
resource-based view (RBV) 294
reviews 75, 77–8
rigor/relevance, in IS Field 493–6
rising star proposition 51–3
risk management capability 317
robotic process automation (RPA) 320
robotics 132, 320, 444, 474–5
role-constrained learning 395–6, 399
routine workplace resistance 192
Russian Federal Agency of National Statistics (ROSSTAT) 434
Russian Longitudinal Monitoring Survey (RLMS) 434

SAP AG 278
satisfaction, in ICT 168
scaffold for digital capability 294–6
Scaled Agile Framework (SAFe) 144–5
scaling, digital innovation and 366
scaling of software *see* software scaling
Science and Technology Studies (STS) 272, 448
scoping reviews 75, 77–9
search stage 63–5, 69
semantic view of theory 60, 69
sensors 407–8

sensory ethnography 115–16
service complexity 312, 315
service economy 485–7
service interdependence 312
service-oriented architectures (SOA) 128, 135
servitization 129
seven steps of historiography 19–24; critiquing historical evidence 22–3; evidence, primary sources for gathering 21–2; historical questions, formulating 20–1; IS domain, specifying 21; overview 19–20; patterns, determining 23; telling the story (narrative) 23–4; writing the history 24
sharing economy 485
signaling activities 345–6, 348, 358–9
Simultaneous Location and Mapping (SLAM) 473–4
single point of care (SPOC) 333–4, 336–9
skin conductance response (SCR) 175
smartphones 115, 263, 291, 388, 427–8, 445, 466, 471–2, 483
social capital 316
social construction of technology (SCOT) 12–13
socialization 374
social mechanisms in knowledge collaboration: boundary objects 376–7; brokering roles 378–9; collaborative agreements 377–8; dialogic approaches 375–6; limitations of 375–9; shift from structural mechanisms to 372–5
social processes 102–3, 208, 239, 330, 371–2, 374, 383
social science paradigm 12–13
social software 404–5
socio-economic contexts: changes in, influencing digital infrastructure 266–8; paradox of control *vs.* autonomy 265–8; quadrant 255–6, 259, 262, 264–9
socio-technical structure of digital infrastructures 254–7, 260, 269–70
socio-technical theories 447–8
socio-technical unit of innovation 456–7
soft systems methodology (SSM) 87
Software Crisis 1.0 125
Software Crisis 2.0 125–6
software development 125–35; agile methods of 125, 129–31, 134; impediments in 141; introduction 125; methods, future of 128–30; metrics used for understanding and managing flow of work in 140–1; predominant nature of 126–8; principles of 125; pull factors 125–6, 135; push factors 125, 135
Software Development Kit (SDK) 266
software focus and innovation 283–4
software management approach and innovation 285
software product lines (SPL) 125, 129–30, 132, 135

software scaling: Husqvarna case 132–3; illustrated 128; interrelation of dimensions 131; organizations and business domains 130, 133; processes and methods 129–32; products, systems and services 128–9, 132–3; QUMAS case 131–2; research implications 133, 135; scenarios in each dimension 134; service-oriented architectures 128, 135; software product lines 125, 129–30, 132, 135; Sony Mobile case 133
somatic nervous system (SNS) 96
sourcing IT services 307–22; categories of independent variables that determine 321–2; client capabilities 314, 317; client firm characteristics 314, 317; contractual governance 315; cybersecurity and 319–20; decision characteristics 317–18; determinants of decisions 312–14; determinants of outcomes 314–18; empirical articles used in review 309–10; environment 314; future research opportunities 318; influence sources 313; introduction 307–8; motivations to outsource 312–13; past research on 308–12; provider capabilities 316–17; relational governance 315–16; relationship characteristics 314; roles in sustaining the planet 319; roles in uplifting marginalized populations around the world 318–19; service automation 320–1; transaction attributes 312, 315
Special Interest Groups (SIGs) 498
speech emotion recognition 174–5
speech signals 174–5
stability *vs.* change paradox 262–5
status quo bias 189
Strategic Alignment Maturity Model (SAMM) 342
strategic business unit (SBU) 343
strategic planning for information systems (SPIS) 220; *see also* IS strategy and strategising
strategy and strategising *see* IS strategy and strategising
strategy-as-practice 17, 101, 218–26, 283, 329–30, 335
strengthening activities 344, 346–9, 358–9
structural functionalism 499
superstitious learning 397–9
supply-chain management 498
suspicion, principle of 89
Sustainable Development Goals (SDGs) 419–20, 437
syntactic view of theory 60, 69
systematicity, in literature review 77
systems development life cycle 125
Systems of Systems (SoS) 125
system use, resistance to 192

talk, power of 335–7
Technical Committee 8 of the International Federation of Information Processing Societies (IFIP TC8) 490
technological frame of reference (TFR) 160
Technology Acceptance Model (TAM) 189
TELECO 41–3
telling the story (narrative) 23–4
tension/phenomena stage 63–5, 69
tertiary types of evidence synthesis 76
text, power of 336–8
textual signals 172–3
thematic advances in knowledge 61–2
theory 57–69; blockchain explained by 488; building 2, 50, 62, 64–7, 69, 234; capabilities 450–2; definition of different types of 60–2; development reviews 75–9; in digital capability 294; discussion 69; elaboration/research stage 63–5, 69; goal of literature review with respect to 77; introduction 57–8; meaning of 58–62; multiple purposes of 64; perspectives on 60; pragmatic view of 58, 60, 62, 69; proclamation/presentation stage 64, 69; search stage 63–5, 69; semantic view of 60, 69; syntactic view of 60, 69; tension/phenomena stage 63–5, 69; testing 2, 62, 64–5, 67, 69, 75–8; theorizing process 62–5
theory building 2, 50, 62, 64–7, 69, 234
Theory Contribution Canvas 65–9; choice of genre and method 67; completed example of 68; describe the problem and its importance (motivation) 66–7; diagrammatic representation of 68; identify relevant theory and prior knowledge 67–8; overview 65–6; tell the story 69; unfinished workshop demonstration of use of 66
theory development reviews 75–9
theory testing 2, 62, 64–5, 67, 69, 75–8
things, power of 337–9
token 207–9, 330, 338
top management commitment/support 317–18
transaction attributes: as determinant of ITO decisions 312; as determinant of ITO outcomes 315
transaction costs 312
transcranial direct-current stimulation (TDCS) 94
transformed sentence 36
transition management capability 317
translation, aligning as 347
translation model of power 208–12, 330, 338–9
transparency, in literature review 77
trust 316
two-speed IT portfolio 280–1
two-speed IT system 277, 280–1

ubiquitous computing 114, 403–8, 412, 470
umbrella reviews 76–9

uncertainty 315
Undead 491–3; Frankenstein 492; vampire 492; zombie 492–3
underlying technologies quadrant 255–6, 258, 260–2, 264, 266–7, 269
UNESCO 418, 438
uninformed control 406–7
unique identification (UID) 452–3
Unique Identification Authority of India (UIDAI) 452–3; *see also* Aadhaar project
unique identification number (UIN) 452–3
United Nations Development Programme (UNDP) 444, 450
UNIVAC 6–7, 490
upward flexibility 255–6, 260, 262, 264
usage to outcomes, access to 438–9
user resistance to IT 183–99; conceptualizing 191–5; defining 191–2; explaining 184–8; explaining, independently from acceptance 184–8; gaps, identifying 190–1; introduction 183–4; problematizing literature on 195–8; studying resistance and acceptance jointly 188–90

valence 168
value co-creation, digital innovation and 363–4
value creation 482–4
vendor-led innovations, reducing 283–4
verisimilitude of Muslim historians 8–9
visual ethnography 117
voice-over-IP 483

wearable technology 114, 388, 476
Wikipedia 473
work, technology-driven changes in 481–2
work-in-progress (WIP) 140
World Bank 318, 418, 446
WorldBPO Forum 320
World Economic Forum (WEF) 418, 439
World of Warcraft (WoW) 116

Invasive Animals and Plants in Massachusetts Lakes and Rivers

There is a growing demand for appropriate management of aquatic invasive species in lakes and rivers worldwide. This book covers biology, invasion ecology, sightings, and control techniques of 4 invasive animals and 15 invasive plants in Massachusetts lakes and rivers. It provides valuable information on their biological characteristics and potential expansion pathways, as well as monitoring and management, including alternative management tools using updated biological, chemical, and mechanical methods. The book also includes the regulation of invasive species management to allow resource managers, biologists, practitioners, volunteers, and students a better understanding of compliance and enforcement with environmental law. An example of successful management is highlighted for each invasive species.

Invasive Animals and Plants in Massachusetts Lakes and Rivers is the first book to provide comprehensive, systematic coverage and illustrations for both freshwater invasive animals and plants. Although focusing on Massachusetts, it will provide readers with the bigger picture on multiple invasive species, from prevention, early detection, control, ecological restoration, to public education. Natural resource managers in Massachusetts and surrounding states will glean the detailed and valuable information they need to learn and use to prevent and manage freshwater invasive species in the field.

Invasive Animals and Plants in Massachusetts Lakes and Rivers

Lessons for International Aquatic Management

Wai Hing Wong

CRC Press
Taylor & Francis Group
Boca Raton London New York

CRC Press is an imprint of the
Taylor & Francis Group, an **informa** business

First edition published 2023
by CRC Press
6000 Broken Sound Parkway NW, Suite 300, Boca Raton, FL 33487–2742

and by CRC Press
4 Park Square, Milton Park, Abingdon, Oxon, OX14 4RN

CRC Press is an imprint of Taylor & Francis Group, LLC

© 2023 Wai Hing Wong

Reasonable efforts have been made to publish reliable data and information, but the author and publisher cannot assume responsibility for the validity of all materials or the consequences of their use. The authors and publishers have attempted to trace the copyright holders of all material reproduced in this publication and apologize to copyright holders if permission to publish in this form has not been obtained. If any copyright material has not been acknowledged please write and let us know so we may rectify in any future reprint.

Except as permitted under U.S. Copyright Law, no part of this book may be reprinted, reproduced, transmitted, or utilized in any form by any electronic, mechanical, or other means, now known or hereafter invented, including photocopying, microfilming, and recording, or in any information storage or retrieval system, without written permission from the publishers.

For permission to photocopy or use material electronically from this work, access www.copyright.com or contact the Copyright Clearance Center, Inc. (CCC), 222 Rosewood Drive, Danvers, MA 01923, 978–750–8400. For works that are not available on CCC please contact mpkbookspermissions@tandf.co.uk

Trademark notice: Product or corporate names may be trademarks or registered trademarks and are used only for identification and explanation without intent to infringe.

ISBN: 978-1-032-06186-3 (hbk)
ISBN: 978-1-032-06188-7 (pbk)
ISBN: 978-1-003-20110-6 (ebk)

DOI: 10.1201/9781003201106

Typeset in Times
by Apex CoVantage, LLC

Contents

Foreword xiii
Acknowledgments..xv
Disclaimer...xvii
Author Biography xix

Chapter 1 Introduction to Freshwater Invasive Species in Massachusetts.....................1

    Abstract 1
    Introduction 1
    The 19 Invasive Species in MA Lakes and Rivers 1
    Spread of Freshwater Invasive Species 6
    Climate Change on Freshwater Invasive Species 7
    Ecological and Economical Damage...7
    Management 8
    Public Education and Awareness 9
    Prevention..10
    Early Detection and Rapid Response (EDRR)..............................12
    Early Detection and Monitoring..13
    Rapid Response 15
    Control and Containment 15
    Physical Removal 16
    Chemical Treatment 16
    Biological Control 27
    Regulation and Permitting 27
        Regulation...27
        Permitting 28
            Order of Conditions...28
            401 Water Quality Certification (Dredge) 28
            WM 04 Chemical Application License 29
            MESA-associated Permits 29
    Weakness and Strength...30
    References 30

Chapter 2 Asian Clam (*Corbicula fluminea*) 35

    Abstract 35
    Introduction 35
        Ecological Impacts 36
        Economic Impacts 37
    Monitoring and Sightings..37
    Managing Actions 45
        Chemical Treatment...46
        Physical Treatment 46
        Biological Treatment 47
    Success Stories 47
        Benthic Barrier Control of Asian Clams 47
        Dry Ice Study..48
    References 48

Chapter 3	Zebra Mussel (*Dreissena polymorpha*)	51
	Abstract	51
	Introduction	51
	Monitoring and Sightings	57
	Managing Actions	59
	Success Story	62
	References	63
Chapter 4	Chinese Mystery Snail (*Bellamya chinensis*)	69
	Abstract	69
	Introduction	69
	Native and Invasive Range, Mechanisms of Spread	72
	Ecological Impacts	72
	Human Impacts	73
	Monitoring and Sightings	73
	Managing Actions	74
	Chemical Control	74
	Physical Control	78
	Biological (Ecological) Control	79
	Success Story	79
	References	80
Chapter 5	Northern Snakehead (*Channa argus*)	83
	Abstract	83
	Introduction	83
	Native and Invasive Range, Mechanisms of Spread	85
	Ecological Impacts	88
	Human Risks and Benefits	88
	Monitoring and Sightings	89
	Managing Actions	90
	Chemical Control	90
	Physical Control	90
	Biological (Ecological) Control	91
	Success Stories	91
	MacQuilliam Pond, Crofton, Maryland	91
	Ridgebury Lake	92
	References	93
Chapter 6	Hydrilla (*Hydrilla verticillata*)	95
	Abstract	95
	Introduction	95
	Ecological Effects	96
	Economic Impacts	97
	Native and Invasive Range	98
	Vectors of Spread	98
	Monitoring and Sightings	98
	Management	101
	Success Story	103

	Pickerel Pond in Maine	103
	Cayuga Lake and Fall Creek in New York	104
	References	104

Chapter 7 Curly-leaf Pondweed (*Potamogeton crispus*) 107

Abstract 107
Introduction 107
Curly-leaf Pondweed as an Invasive Species 107
    Ecological Impact 109
    Economic Impact 109
    Positive Aspects 109
Monitoring and Sightings 109
Management 112
    Mechanical and Physical Methods 112
    Chemical Methods 130
    Prevention Methods 130
Success Story 131
References 132

Chapter 8 Eurasian Milfoil (*Myriophyllum spicatum*) and Variable Milfoil (*Myriophyllum heterophyllum*) 133

Abstract 133
Introduction 133
Biology of Eurasian Milfoil and Variable Milfoil 133
    Native Range 135
    Invasive Range 135
Ecological Impacts 136
Economic Impacts 136
Monitoring and Sightings 136
Management 138
    Eurasian Milfoil 138
    Variable Milfoil 186
Success Story 186
Conclusion 187
References 187

Chapter 9 Parrot-feather (*Myriophyllum aquaticum*) 189

Abstract 189
Introduction 189
    Native and Invasive Range, Mechanisms of Spread 190
    Ecological and Human Impacts 191
Monitoring and Sightings 193
Managing Actions 193
    Chemical Control 194
    Physical Control 195
    Biological Control 196
        Insect Control Agents 196
        Fish and Mammal Control Agents 197

	Success Story	197
	References	198
Chapter 10	Carolina Fanwort (*Cabomba caroliniana*)	201
	Abstract	201
	Introduction	201
	Basic Biology	201
	Native Range	202
	Invasive Range	202
	Mechanisms/Vectors of Spread	202
	Ecological Impacts	203
	Economic Impacts	203
	Positive Aspects	203
	Monitoring and Sighting Data	203
	Management Options	204
	Success Story	231
	References	231
Chapter 11	European Naiad (*Najas minor*)	233
	Abstract	233
	Introduction	233
	Basic Biology	233
	Native and Invasive Range	234
	Mechanisms/Vectors of Spread	234
	Ecological Impacts	235
	Economic Impacts	236
	Monitoring and Sightings	236
	Managing Actions	236
	Chemical Control	240
	Physical Control	241
	Biological Control	241
	Success Story	241
	References	242
Chapter 12	South American Waterweed (*Egeria densa*)	245
	Abstract	245
	Introduction	245
	Native and Invasive Range	247
	Spread and Impacts	247
	Monitoring and Sightings	249
	Managing Actions	249
	Chemical Control	251
	Physical Control	251
	Biological Control	252
	Success Stories	252
	Chemical Control	252
	Domestic Ducks as Biological Control	253
	References	254

Contents

Chapter 13 Swollen Bladderwort (*Utricularia inflata*) 257
    Abstract 257
    Introduction 257
        Native and Invasive Range 261
        Vectors of Spread 261
        Ecological Impacts 261
        Economic Impacts 261
        Positive Effects 261
    Monitoring and Sightings 262
    Managing Actions 263
        Success Story 264
    Conclusion 265
    References 265

Chapter 14 Water Chestnut (*Trapa natans*) 267
    Abstract 267
    Introduction 267
    Basic Biology 267
    Native Range 268
    Invasive Range 268
    Ecological Impact 269
    Economic Impact 269
    Positive Aspects 269
    Monitoring and Sightings 270
    Management Actions 270
    Physical Control 280
    Biological Control 281
    Chemical Control 281
    Success Story 282
        Connecticut River Watershed 282
    Conclusion 283
    References 284

Chapter 15 Water Hyacinth (*Eichhornia crassipes*) 285
    Abstract 285
    Introduction 285
        Biology 285
        Native and Invasive Range 286
        Mechanisms/Vectors of Spread 287
        Ecological Impacts 287
        Economic Impacts 287
        Utilization of Water Hyacinth 288
    Monitoring and Sightings 288
    Management 290
        Physical 290
        Chemical 290
        Biological 291
    Success Story 291
        Remaining Challenges 292
    References 292

Chapter 16 European Waterclover (*Marsilea quadrifolia* L.) 295
    Abstract 295
    Introduction 295
        Biology 295
        Native and Invasive Range 296
        Mechanisms/Vectors of Spread 297
        Ecological Impacts 298
        Economic Impacts 298
        Positive Aspects 298
    Monitoring and Sightings 298
    Managing Actions 299
    Success Story 301
    References 304

Chapter 17 Yellow Floating Heart (*Nymphoides peltata*) 307
    Abstract 307
    Introduction 307
        Basic Biology 307
        Native Range 307
        Invasive Range 308
    Mechanisms/Vectors of Spread 309
        Ecological Impacts 309
        Economic Impacts 310
    Positive Aspects 310
    Monitoring and Sightings 310
    Managing Actions 310
        Physical Methods 310
        Chemical Methods 312
        Biological Methods 312
    Success Story 313
    Conclusion 313
    References 313

Chapter 18 Common Reed Grass (*Phragmites australis*) 315
    Abstract 315
    Introduction 315
    Monitoring and Sightings 321
    Managing Actions 321
        Chemical Control 321
        Physical Control 324
        Biological Control 326
    General Management Plans 327
    Success Story 328
    References 329
    Appendix A: Latitude and Longitude for Each Waterbody with
        Phragmites australis 331

Contents

Chapter 19 Purple Loosestrife (*Lythrum salicaria*) 337
    Abstract 337
    Introduction 337
        Basic Biology 337
        Ecological and Economic Impacts 340
    Monitoring and Sightings 341
    Managing Actions 373
        Chemical Techniques 373
        Mechanical or Physical Techniques 373
        Biological Techniques 374
    Success Story 375
    References 377

Appendix I   **MassDEP Equipment Decontamination Protocol** 379

Appendix II   **A Guide for Using Hand Pulling and Benthic Barriers to Control Aquatic Invasive Species Pioneer Populations (Modified from MA DCR 2007)** 389

Appendix III   **Literature Research of Chemical Control Methods on 19 Invasive Species** 393

Appendix IV   **Laws and Statutes Pertaining to Aquatic Invasive/Nuisance Species in the New England States and New York** 417

Index 435

Foreword

Invasive Animals and Plants in Massachusetts Lakes and Rivers: Lessons for International Aquatic Management by Dr. Wai Hing (David) Wong contains a unique mix of well-documented information useful to both regional handbooks addressing the diversity of problematic invasive species and the applied aquatic resource management literature. He is a certified lake manager (CLM) and currently the manager for two Massachusetts Department of Environmental Protection Programs: (1) WM04 Herbicide/Pesticide Application Program and (2) 401 Water Quality Certification Program. In his over 20 years of experience in studying aquatic invasive species in North America and Asia, he has been a principal investigator or co-investigator for over 30 projects funded by federal, state, and private entities. He has been a deputy editor and associate editor for BioInvasions Records, Management of Biological Invasions, and Aquatic Invasions.

This volume is a valuable introduction to those working in government agencies, natural resource venues, students, lake associations, concerned citizens and public education by taking advantage of the summaries and introductions to each chapter. Summaries are valuable to those requiring brief overview of the contents. Introductions provide easy access to information regarding the morphological characteristics, biology, and taxonomic status of the aquatic nuisance species found in Massachusetts.

Management professionals, academicians, and researchers will appreciate the details on the biology and autecology of the treated organisms and the recently documented distributions of each species in the state as included in maps and tabular formats. The native ranges and histories of invasions into Massachusetts, along with records accounting potential and actual ecological and economic impacts are provided. Details of agencies monitoring programs, relevant chemical, physical, and biological management strategies, products and case studies illustrating the success or lack of those strategies are presented. Extensive references listed after each chapter will be particularly valuable.

The contents are structured so that individuals in Massachusetts, other states in the United States, or other countries who are interested in one taxon can peruse all the information on that organism that is available in one chapter. Every chapter has an abstract and introduction in addition to the main narrative, therefore redundancies are unavoidable. This work volume will be especially valuable to readers in nearby states since most nuisance aquatic species in Massachusetts have been found in many nearby sates and a few that are not currently encountered or detected in their regions may soon appear there.

Dr. Willard N. Harman, CLM
Distinguished Service Professor
Rufus J. Thayer Chair, Otsego Lake Research
Director, SUNY Oneonta Biological Field Station
5838 State Highway 80
Cooperstown, NY 13326

Acknowledgments

The author appreciates all inspirations from Richard Chase, Laurie Kennedy, and Therese Beaudoin on the initiation and development of this book. This would not be possible without the bountiful efforts on data and other information collection by the Massachusetts Department of Environmental Protection (MassDEP) staff who have done biological surveys at more than 2,000 waterbodies in the Commonwealth of Massachusetts. Invasive species monitoring data are primarily from MassDEP's biannual assessment reports on Massachusetts Integrated List of Waters. Sighting data in this book are also collected by the following agencies and individuals: Massachusetts Department of Conservation and Recreation, Charles River Watershed Association, Mystic River Watershed Association, Nashua River Watershed Association, Wayland Surface Water Quality Committee, Massachusetts Water Watch Partnership at the University of Massachusetts, the US Geological Survey (USGS), US Fish and Wildlife Service (FWS), US Forest Service (USFS), Water Resource Services LLC, Northeast Aquatic Nuisance Species Panel, Illinois Natural History Survey, EBT Environmental Consultants Inc., Metcalf & Eddy, Inc., Baystate Environmental Consultants, Inc. (BEC), Environmental Science Services, Inc. (ESS), as well as residents (with confirmation from an expert in the field), Robert Bertin, Jamie Carr, Mike Lowery, Eileen McGourty, Bob Nuzzo, Matthew Reardon, Jim Straub, and Joy Trahan-Liptak.

The expertise and time from the following reviewers are gratefully acknowledged because their constructive comments and suggestions significantly improved the quality of this book: Dave Adams, Therese Beaudoin, Tobias O Bickel, Cynthia and Jeff Boettner, Carrie Brown-Lima, Greg Bugbee, Timothy Counihan, Joan Deely, Luc Denys, Tom Flannery, Willard Harman, Nathan Harms, Kimberly Jensen, Barbara Kickham, Susan Knight, Chuhua Liu, Paul Lord, Bob Maietta, Catherine McGlynn, Bob McMahon, John McPhedran, Meg Modley, Bob Nuzzo, Susan Pasko, Steven Pearson, Read Porter, Edward Rainer, Lisa Rhodes, Allison Roy, Kara Sliwoski, Amy Smagula, Rosali Smith, Michele Tremblay, Rebecca Urban, Ken Wagner, and Nathan Waltham.

The MassDEP's Michelle Waters-Ekanem Internship Program and the following interns are appreciated because they have assisted the author in field surveys, graphic-making, reference checking, and quality assurance and quality control: Aymane Akobi, Kira Becker, Alexander Carli-Dorsey, Hana Colwell, Rachel Holland, Peifeng Li (Derek), Salome Maldonado, Kristina McAvoy, Davis Miller, Niki Patel, Fionna Pennington, Jonathan Rickwood, Riani Suarez, Ursula Svoboda, Jiahui Wang, Mingkai Zhang, and Yichen Zhang.

In addition, I am grateful to CRC Press' Alice Oven and Shikha Garg whose expertise and advice make this book more attractive!

Finally, I am thankful to my wife, Ting, for her long-time support and understanding for my career development.

Disclaimer

Although findings and conclusions of this book and many activities such as data sources are associated with Masschusetts Department of Environmental Protection and the author himself is currently an employee of Massachusetts Department of Environmental Protection, the views in this book are solely of the author himself and do not reflect the policies of the Massachusetts Department of Environmental Protection.

Author Biography

Dr. Wai Hing Wong (David) is an Environmental Analyst at the Massachusetts Department of Environmental Protection, Rese-arch Associate Professor in State University of New York at Oneonta, and Adjunct Associate Professor in Worcester State University. David's interests and experience include environmental monitoring, biological invasions, risk assessment, eutrophication management, ecological restoration, and the Clean Water Act. He has over 20 years of experience in studying and managing aquatic invasive species in North America and Asia. He has a Ph.D. in Marine Ecology from City University of Hong Kong, and Master and Bachelor degrees in Aquaculture/Fisheries from Ocean University of China. He is a principal investigator or co-investigator for over 30 projects funded by federal, state, and private entities. Since 2011, he has been an associate editor for BioInvasions Records, Management of Biological Invasions, and Aquatic Invasions. He is a reviewer for 29 scientific journals and 12 grant agencies. He has been a member of the federal Aquatic Nuisance Species Task Force Research Subcommittee since 2012 and was the co-chair of Northeastern Aquatic Nuisance Species Panel from 2019 to 2020. Currently, he is managing the following two programs: (1) WM04 Chemical Application Program and (2) 401 Water Quality Certification Program.

1 Introduction to Freshwater Invasive Species in Massachusetts

ABSTRACT

Nineteen invasive species found in 701 Massachusetts lakes/ponds and 142 rivers/streams are briefly described in this chapter. Among the 19 species, the most prevalent is purple loosestrife, found in 387 waterbodies, followed by variable milfoil, fanwort, curly-leaf pondweed, and Eurasian watermilfoil. The least widespread are water hyacinth and northern snakehead, which have only been detected in two waterbodies. Among these 843 waters with confirmed invasive species, the Charles River is home to the most invasive species (9). This book describes the basic biology and potential expansion pathways of these invasive species. It provides alternative management tools using updated biological, chemical, and physical/mechanical methods. And it includes the regulation of invasive species management to allow resource managers, biologists, practitioners, volunteers, and students a better understanding of compliance and enforcement with environmental law. Although this book is about invasive species in Massachusetts lakes and rivers, the contents apply to other New England states, regions of the United States, and beyond where these invasive species have been detected.

INTRODUCTION

An invasive species is defined by a federal advisory committee as a species that is non-native to the ecosystem under consideration and whose introduction causes or is likely to cause economic or environmental harm or harm to human health (NISC 2007; Beck et al. 2008). Harmful invasive species can spread quickly, displacing native species, substantially affecting species richness and community composition, and attaining ecological dominance in many aquatic ecosystems. Therefore, there is a growing global demand for effective management of aquatic invasive species.

Multiple invasive species have been detected in Massachusetts lakes and rivers. For this book, 19 species documented in Massachusetts lakes and rivers are described; species without official documentation, such as the sacred lotus (*Nelumbo nucifera*), Chinese soft-shelled marsh turtle (*Pelodiscus sinensis*), the freshwater jellyfish (*Craspedacusta sowerbii*), or some potential invasive species such as the spiny waterflea (*Bythotrephes longimanus*), are not included. Each subsequent chapter (Chapter 8 covers two milfoil species) is focused on a specific invasive species, in this format: (1) Introduction including basic biological characteristics (e.g., species identification, growth, reproduction, habitat requirements, etc.), native range, invasive pathways, ecological impacts, and economic impacts; (2) sightings where the specific invasive species has been documented; (3) management options, including prevention and control (i.e., chemical, physical, and biological methods); and (4) success story. Although the focus of this book is on invasive species found in Massachusetts lakes and rivers, it will serve other New England states, other regions of the United States, and other countries where similar invasive species occur in their waters.

THE 19 INVASIVE SPECIES IN MA LAKES AND RIVERS

This book covers the biology, invasion ecology, sightings, and control techniques of 4 invasive animals and 15 invasive plants documented in Massachusetts lakes and rivers, including Asian clam (*Corbicula fluminea*), zebra mussel (*Dreissena polymorpha*), Chinese mystery snail (*Bellamya chinensis*), northern snakehead (*Channa argus*), hydrilla (*Hydrilla verticillata*),

DOI: 10.1201/9781003201106-1

curly-leaf pondweed (*Potamogeton crispus*), Eurasian watermilfoil (*Myriophyllum spicatum*), variable milfoil (*Myriophyllum heterophyllum*), parrot-feather (*Myriophyllum aquaticum*), fanwort (*Cabomba caroliniana*), European naiad (*Najas minor*), South American waterweed (*Egeria densa*), swollen bladderwort (*Utricularia inflata*), water chestnut (*Trapa natans*), water hyacinth (*Eichhornia crassipes*), European waterclover (*Marsilea quadrifolia*), yellow floating heart (*Nymphoides peltata*), common reed grass (*Phragmites australis*), and purple loosestrife (*Lythrum salicaria*).

Unlike many other books that focus on one organism (e.g., zebra mussel), one group of organisms (e.g., bivalves), or one subject of a group (i.e., identification of aquatic plants), this book presents valuable information on biological characteristics (such as identification, reproduction, invasion pathways, etc.), monitoring, and management of both invasive animals and plants. Invasive species monitoring and sightings data are primarily documented in MassDEP's biennial Integrated Lists of Waters, as well as reports by other state, federal, and individual entities (see the list in the Preface). In addition, an example of a successful management technique(s) or lesson(s) learned will be highlighted for each invasive species. Therefore, this book can provide readers a comprehensive view of multiple invasive animal/plant species, ranging from prevention, early detection, and control to ecological restoration and public education.

Among the 19 aquatic invasive species found in Massachusetts, the top 5 most widespread (in order of prevalence) are purple loosestrife (found in 379 lakes and rivers), variable milfoil, fanwort, curly-leaf pondweed, and Eurasian watermilfoil. The next most widespread are common reed grass, water chestnut, Chinese mystery snail, Asian clam, and European naiad (Table 1.1). The least "invasive" species are northern snakehead and water hyacinth, which have only been documented in two waterbodies (Table 1.1). This result is similar to a lake survey conducted from 1994 to 2003 that identified the top invasive

TABLE 1.1
Number of Infested Waterbodies of Freshwater Invasive Species in Massachusetts

Invasive Species	Sightings
Purple loosestrife	387
Variable milfoil	245
Fanwort	196
Curly-leaf pondweed	167
Eurasian watermilfoil	115
Water chestnut	114
Reed grass	112
Chinese mystery snail	37
Asian clam	33
European naiad	23
Swollen bladderwort	15
Hydrilla	11
European waterclover	9
South American waterweed	7
Parrot-feather	6
Yellow floating heart	6
Zebra mussel	3
Water hyacinth	2
Northern snakehead	2

Introduction to Freshwater Invasive Species in Massachusetts

TABLE 1.2
Massachusetts Watershed Codes and Names

Code	Watershed Name
11	Hudson: Hoosic River Basin
12	Hudson: Kinderhook River Basin
13	Hudson: Bashbish River Basin
21	Housatonic River Basin
31	Farmington River Basin
32	Westfield River Basin
33	Deerfield River Basin
34	Connecticut River Basin
35	Millers River Basin
36	Chicopee River Basin
41	Quinebaug River Basin
42	French River Basin
51	Blackstone River Basin
52	Ten Mile River Basin
53	Narragansett Bay (Shore) Drainage Area
61	Mount Hope Bay (Shore) Drainage Area
62	Taunton River Basin
70	Boston Harbor (Proper)
71	Boston Harbor: Mystic River Basin and Coastal Drainage Area
72	Charles River Basin
73	Boston Harbor: Neponset River Basin and Coastal Drainage Area
74	Boston Harbor: Weymouth and Weir River Basin and Coastal Drainage Area
81	Nashua River Basin
82	Concord River Basin
83	Shawsheen River Basin
84	Merrimack River Basin and Coastal Drainage Area
91	Parker River Basin and Coastal Drainage Area
92	Ipswich River Basin and Coastal Drainage Area
93	North Shore Coastal Drainage Area
94	South Shore Coastal Drainage Area
95	Buzzards Bay Coastal Drainage Area
96	Cape Cod Coastal Drainage Area
97	Islands Coastal Drainage Area

aquatic species as purple loosestrife, fanwort, the two non-native milfoil species, and common reed grass (Mattson et al. 2004a).

There are more than 4,230 miles of rivers and over 3,000 lakes and ponds located within 33 watersheds (Table 1.2 and Figure 1.1) in Massachusetts.[1] The largest of these waterbodies, Quabbin Reservoir (24,704 acres) and Wachusett Reservoir (4,160 acres) are manmade. The largest natural lake is Assawompset Pond in southern Massachusetts (2,656 acres). At least 843 waterbodies (701 lakes and 142 rivers, Figure 1.1) are known to be infested by at least one invasive species. The Charles River from Hopkinton to Boston is the most affected, with nine invasive species: Asian clam, Chinese mystery snail, curly-leaf pondweed, Eurasian watermilfoil, fanwort, purple

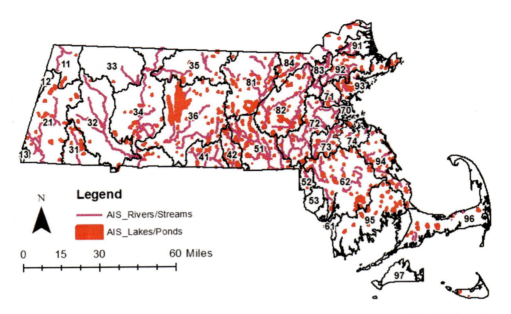

FIGURE 1.1 The 701 lakes/ponds and 142 rivers/streams infested by invasive species within 33 Massachusetts watersheds and drainage areas. (Table 1.1 shows the watershed codes and their corresponding names.)

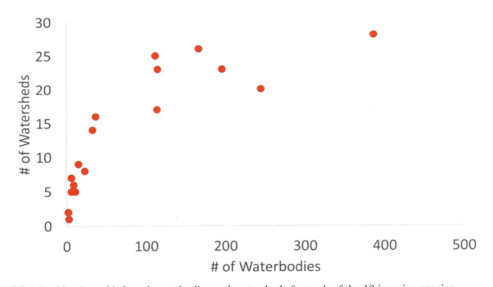

FIGURE 1.2 Number of infested waterbodies and watersheds for each of the 19 invasive species.

loosestrife, variable milfoil, water chestnut, and European waterclover (Table 1.3). Waterbodies with seven and six invasive species are listed in Table 1.3. The Blackstone River watershed has 82 waters infested by invasive species, followed by the Taunton (80 waters), Concord (59 waters), Nashua (58 waters), Connecticut (48 waters), and Chicopee (48 waters) watersheds. It is clear that the more the waterbodies in which an invasive species is detected (Table 1.1), the more watersheds this species has invaded (Figure 1.2).

Since the first invasive species was documented in Massachusetts, the rise of invasive species has occurred in tandem with the rise in population (Figure 1.3). The first documented case of an invasive species in Massachusetts

TABLE 1.3
Massachusetts Waterbodies Mostly Infested by Invasive Species

Waterbody	Asian clam	Chinese mystery snail	Curly-leaf pondweed	Eurasian water milfoil	European naiad	Fanwort	Purple loosestrife	Reed grass	South American waterweed	Swollen bladderwort	Variable milfoil	Water chestnut	European waterclover	Total # of species
Charles River	1	1	1	1	0	1	1	0	0	0	1	1	1	9
Monponsett Pond	0	0	1	1	0	1	1	1	0	1	1	0	0	7
Sudbury River	1	0	1	1	0	1	1	0	0	0	0	1	1	7
White Island Pond	0	0	1	1	1	1	1	1	0	1	0	0	0	7
Bartlett Pond	0	0	1	1	0	1	1	0	0	0	1	1	0	6
Billington Sea	0	0	1	1	0	1	1	1	0	0	1	0	0	6
Blackstone River	1	0	1	0	0	1	1	0	0	0	1	1	0	6
Flint Pond (Blackstone Watershed)	0	0	1	1	1	1	1	0	0	0	1	0	0	6
Fort Meadow Reservoir	1	0	0	1	0	1	1	1	0	0	1	0	0	6
Lake Cochituate	1	0	1	1	0	0	1	0	0	0	1	1	0	6
Lake Quinsigamond	0	1	1	1	0	1	0	0	0	0	1	1	0	6
Lake Rico	0	0	0	1	0	1	1	0	1	1	1	0	0	6
Mill River	0	0	1	0	0	1	1	1	0	0	1	1	0	6
North Pond	0	0	0	0	1	1	1	0	1	1	1	0	0	6
Webster Lake	1	0	1	1	0	1	1	0	0	0	1	0	0	6

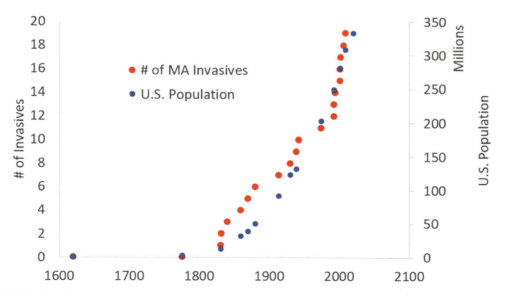

FIGURE 1.3 Number of freshwater invasive species in Massachusetts and US population size (millions).

was purple loosestrife in 1831 (see Chapter 19); freshwater invasive species have been recorded increasingly throughout the state since then (Figure 1.3). On average, from 1800 to 1900, the time period for a freshwater species to be established and detected was 17 years; from 1900 to 2000, that period decreased to 13 years and from 2000 to the present, it again decreased to 4 years. This is consistent with the strong relationship between the spread of invasive species and trade and transportation, i.e., the larger the human population within Massachusetts and the United States, the greater the trade and transportation activities (e.g., commercial and recreational) between waters within the Commonwealth and within the country (see "Spread of Freshwater Invasive Species" section). The latest documented invasive species was the zebra mussel in Laurel Lake in Lee and Lenox in 2009 (see Chapter 3).

SPREAD OF FRESHWATER INVASIVE SPECIES

Historically, trade and transportation have served as the major pathways for the invasion of new territory by invasive species for millennia; in recent decades, the world has entered the era of globalization, a new phase in terms of the magnitude and diversity of biological invasions (Hulme 2009). For coastal waters, the discharge of ballast water and biofouling from ocean-going ships is a major pathway for invasive species (Hewitt et al. 2009; Wan et al. 2021). Much of the ongoing spread of aquatic invasive species to inland waters throughout North America can be attributed to the overland movement of small watercraft (Bossenbroek et al. 2001; Johnson et al. 2001; Leung et al. 2006; Rothlisberger et al. 2010). These boats are usually less than 40 ft (12.2 m) in length, and include vessels such as powerboats, small commercial and recreational fishing boats, sailboats, personal watercraft, canoes and kayaks, and pontoon boats that can be towed overland on trailers (Rothlisberger et al. 2010). Translocation of invasive organisms by boaters can be intentional, but are most often unintentional (see Rothlisberger et al. 2010). These organisms can not only be carried in bilge water, live wells, and bait buckets, but also be entrained on boat exteriors, e.g., entangled on propellers and trailers, or attached to other entangled organisms. The overland transport of small boats is reported to be responsible for the spread of spiny waterflea (MacIsaac et al. 2004; Muirhead and MacIsaac 2005), Eurasian watermilfoil (Buchan and Padilla 2000), and zebra mussels (Schneider et al. 1998; Leung et al. 2004; De Ventura et al. 2016). It has been postulated that the recent large-scale invasion of quagga mussels in the western United States resulting from their introduction to Lake Mead is from bilge water (i.e., bait or live wells) in a boat from the Great Lakes region (Stokstad 2007; Wong and Gerstenberger 2011). During an observational study of 85 boats, it was found that boats and trailers leaving the lakes were three times more likely to be carrying vegetation (as "hitchhikers") than those arriving; these hitchhikers included 13 species of plants and 51 small-bodied organisms (including 28 aquatic animals), and the invasive species Eurasian watermilfoil (*Myriophyllum spicatum*) was among them (Rothlisberger et al. 2010). Therefore, whenever a boat is transported overland from an infested waterway, the possibility exists that invasive species may reach uninfested waterways. The invasion pathway may vary among regions. For example, the major pathways of freshwater invasive species in Europe are aquaculture, the pet/aquarium trade, and stocking activities (Les 2002; Nunes et al. 2015). Aquatic invasive species can also spread by water currents, waterfowl, and other vectors. During invasion, an invasive species at different life stages can be transported such as plant seeds, tubers, buds, rhizomes, fragments, or animal adults and larvae. More information about the potential invasion pathways of each of the 19 species can be found in Chapters 2–19.

Recently, it was found that global online trade plays an increasingly influential role in the potential spread of invasive species, such as the trade of ornamental fish in Brazil (Borges et al. 2021). In addition, the broad-scale patterns of spread may mask considerable variation across regions, time periods, and even entities contributing to invasive species sampling. In some cases, observed temporal shifts in species discovery may be influenced by dramatic fluctuations in the number and spatial extent of individual observations, reflecting the possibility that shifts in sampling effort may obscure underlying rates of species introduction (Mangiante et al. 2018).

After individuals of an invasive species are transported from the source region (their native range) to the recipient region (non-native range), whether the transport is intentional (e.g., plants sold in the aquarium or rain garden trade) or unintentional (e.g., hitchhikers in commercial shipping vessels), establishment occurs if the transported individuals are able to survive and reproduce. The introduced species is considered established if it has formed a reproducing and self-sustaining population. The introduction and establishment transitions in different areas are usually independent of each other, and species that become widely established are successful overall because their introduction has been attempted in many locations, not because of a better establishment capability (García-Berthou et al. 2005). After that, secondary spread can occur in which the species extends its range within the non-native region. Recreational boats in tow between lakes are also a vector of secondary spread of invasive (and native) species among freshwater ecosystems (Muirhead and MacIsaac 2005; Vander Zanden and Olden 2008; Kelly et al. 2013).

CLIMATE CHANGE ON FRESHWATER INVASIVE SPECIES

Hundreds of invasive species are established in the United States (USGS 2020), impacting the United States both ecologically and economically, as shown subsequently (i.e., the section on ecological and economic damage). At the same time, over 11,000 scientists from around the world have declared that, according to clear and unequivocal indicators, the planet is facing a climate emergency (Ripple et al. 2020), given that any of the recent changes observed in the climate are unprecedented in thousands, if not hundreds of thousands, of years (IPCC 2021). For example, O'Reilly et al. (2015) revealed a statistically significant upward trend of 0.34°C per decade in the nighttime surface water temperature in some 300 lakes around the world from 1985 to 2009. As a consequence of the changing climate, invasive species could expand their ranges into the northern US states either through human-mediated pathways or through natural movement. Climate change will influence the likelihood of new species becoming established by eliminating cold temperatures or winter hypoxia that currently limit survival, and by increasing the reservoirs that serve as hot spots for invasive species (Rahel and Olden 2008). Important shifts in species ranges (depending on taxonomic group and scenario in Europe) toward the north and east of Europe are occurring at the unprecedented rate of 14–55 km/decade (Gallardo and Aldridge 2013). In Massachusetts, Asian clams have been detected in the Charles River since 2001 (Colwell et al. 2017). Long-term trend analysis shows that, from 1985 to 2016 (16 years before and after the first sighting of Asian clam in Massachusetts), the winter daily minimal temperature in Massachusetts increased. This higher winter temperature is more conducive to the successful establishment of Asian clams (Chapter 2). Further, the warming trend may be the key factor underlying the recent establishment of Asian clams in the United States north of the 40° latitude line, which is the clams' long-term incipient lower thermal limit (Mattice and Dye 1976). It has been documented that, while the distribution of Asian clams is controlled by both habitat variables (e.g., substrate and pH) and climate variables, climate variables are likely more important than the habitat variables (McDowell et al. 2014). The establishment of Asian clams in Massachusetts further confirms that climate variable is critical in shifting the range of invasive species. Therefore, resource agencies should be aware of and focus on protecting high-risk resource areas to prevent new invasive species invasion amid climate change.

ECOLOGICAL AND ECONOMICAL DAMAGE

Freshwater ecosystems are subject to a large range of anthropogenic threats such as habitat loss and fragmentation, hydrological alteration, climate change, overexploitation, pollution and introduction of alien species (Dudgeon et al. 2006). Biological invasions are responsible for high economic losses to society associated with the monetary expenditures from the management of these invasions. Invasive species have been attributed to a 42% decrease in populations of endangered species in the United States

(Stein and Flack 1997; Wilcove 1998). Many invasive species are also called ecosystem engineers because of the destruction to the waters they invade. Even specific impacts from individual species can be significantly different (see Chapters 2–19 for more information). Invasive species continue to drive major losses in biodiversity and ecosystem function across the globe. Among the most important hazards posed by invasive species, the introduction of such species outside their natural range is widely recognized to be one of the main threats to biodiversity and the second leading cause of animal extinctions (Millennium Ecosystem Assessment 2005). For example, 20% of the 680 species extinctions listed by the International Union for Conservation of Nature (IUCN) are due to invasive species (Clavero and García-Berthou 2005). Understanding the impact of invasive species on extinctions requires the development of more scientific and evidence-based approaches (Gurevitch and Padilla 2004).

Dealing with the effects of invasive species is particularly challenging in marine and freshwater habitats, because the pace at which invaders establish often greatly outstrips the resources available for their eradication (Green and Grosholz 2020). In the United States alone, economic costs are estimated to exceed $120 billion each year (Pimentel et al. 2005). The global cost of aquatic invasive species is conservatively $345 billion, with the majority attributed to invertebrates (62%), followed by vertebrates (28%) and plants (6%). The principal cost is from resource damages (74%) and only 6% of recorded costs were from management (Cuthbert et al. 2021). There is no doubt that the economic cost of invasive species is high and rising worldwide (Diagne et al. 2021).

Estimates of economic costs associated with zebra/quagga mussel infestations of water intake systems in North America range from $100 million to $1 billion per annum (Pimentel et al. 2005; Bidwell 2010). A study was conducted on the economic impacts of invasive quagga and zebra mussels on infrastructure and the economies of nine western states with a focus on the costs, which were mainly associated with mussel establishment prevention strategies and operations and maintenance (O&M) expenditures to control or mitigate mussel-related damages at US Bureau of Reclamation hydropower facilities (Rumzie et al. 2021). Watercraft inspection and decontamination (WID) stations are the primary strategy used to prevent the spread and introduction of dreissenid mussels throughout the West and the 2019 average annual WID budget was approximately $1,605,900. Control cost data collected through a US Bureau of Reclamation survey showed that facilities have spent approximately $10 million in total on preventative control measures since mussel inception (in 2007). Facilities surveyed spend approximately $464,000 annually on increased maintenance, and the total recurring maintenance costs for facilities surveyed were $650,000 per invasive species occurrence; facilities also spend approximately $88,000 in total annually on monitoring (Rumzie et al. 2021).

MANAGEMENT

For the successful prevention/control of invasive species, a management plan must be developed, such as the Massachusetts Department of Conservation and Recreation (MA DCR) aquatic invasive species assessment and management plan (MA DCR 2010). The most efficient approach to controlling the spread of aquatic invasive species is to adopt an integrated management strategy (Henne et al. 2005; Lavergne and Molofsky 2006; Wong and Gerstenberger 2015) which usually includes (1) public education and awareness, (2) prevention, (3) monitoring/early detection and rapid response, (4) control (e.g., physical, chemical, or biological control) and restoration, and (5) regulation.

MA DCR developed decontamination protocols for boaters, to remove aquatic invasive species from boats and trailers before launching in any DCR and Massachusetts Water Resource Authority (MWRA) reservoirs (MA DCR 2010). Another example is invasive species monitoring and mapping which can raise public awareness of the presence of aquatic invasive species in Massachusetts lakes and rivers and keep water users from further spreading them to other waterbodies. The Housatonic River Watershed has been infested by zebra mussels since 2008; as a result, MassDEP developed equipment decontamination protocols for staff conducting water quality and biological monitoring in that watershed (Chase and Wong 2015). Equipment decontamination and gear cleanup are detailed in Appendix I.

PUBLIC EDUCATION AND AWARENESS

Efforts to increase public awareness about the negative impacts of invasive species might increase public support for management actions (Novoa et al. 2017). To increase public awareness of the threats posed by invasive species, appropriate signs and decontamination equipment should be provided at key locations around infested waterbodies to ensure that users are aware of the presence of invasive species, and the need to clean their boats thoroughly before leaving the waterbody. Mapping infested waterbodies in Massachusetts informs local residents and out-of-state travelers of infestations in lakes and rivers (see distribution maps of each invasive species from Chapters 2–19). It is critical to identify and engage stakeholders, such as anglers and other water users, in activities focused on invasive species in their communities. MA DCR has created brochures (Figure 1.4) and booklets to enhance public awareness of aquatic invasive species such as the guide to aquatic plants in Massachusetts (MA DCR 2016). Public awareness and outreach is key in educating all users to clean, drain, and dry their watercraft and equipment to prevent the spread of invasive species in our lakes and rivers. It can also enhance safeguarding invasives-free waters from the introduction of invasive species by facilitating and coordinating actions among federal, state, tribal, and other resource agencies. Finally, maximizing public support and minimizing regional spread are usually weighted much higher than other objectives to reflect decision-maker values; thus, they have greater influence on the overall performance of each alternative in addressing invasive species challenges

FIGURE 1.4 Part of the brochure created by MA DCR for boaters on preventing the spread of invasive species.

for managers while using environmental DNA (eDNA) for early detections and containment alternatives (Sepulveda et al. 2022).

PREVENTION

Prevention refers to both protecting "clean" waterbodies from invasive species and containing invasive species within an infested waterbody and halting their further spread to other waterbodies. One example of a prevention strategy is the decontamination of watercraft and equipment to interrupt the transport pathway of an invasive species (Comeau et al. 2011; DiVittorio 2015; Zook and Phillips 2015). Prevention is an aggressive and proactive approach in minimizing the risk of aquatic invasive species introduction, and is generally regarded as the first line of defense against biological invasion. It is also the best management practice for dealing with any invasive species to avoid ecological impacts and reduce economic costs. More importantly, it has been shown to be far more effective and affordable than dealing with established populations of invasive animals and plants (Scholl 2006): an ounce of prevention is worth a pound of cure. This proactive approach usually includes collecting information about aquatic invasive species, the targeted waterbody ecosystem, early detection (discussed later), education and awareness (discussed earlier), developing a contingency plan and workload, engaging local government and lake community/associations, and funding allocations.

Biological invasions and natural disasters are similar phenomena as both generate enormous environmental damage, with the economic costs of invasions worldwide exceeding that of natural disasters. Although many nations invest in personnel training, disaster preparedness, and emergency response plans for extreme natural hazards (e.g., earthquakes), despite the rarity of such events (Ricciardi et al. 2011), few invest in precautions addressing invasive species (apart from infectious diseases), even though prevention is the most efficient and cost-effective approach to stopping or minimizing the spread of aquatic invasive species among all management options.

Border control and pathway management are the logical priority to prevent the introduction and spread of invasive species. Since the overland movement of small-craft boats is the major contributor for much of the ongoing spread of aquatic invasive species to inland waters throughout North America (see more in "Spread of Freshwater Invasive Species" section), among all management options, drain, clean, and dry watercraft and equipment is the prioritized strategy in prevention. Clean, drain, and dry is a simple three-step process that boaters can follow every time they move from one body of water to another. When boaters take preventive actions every time they leave the water, they can stop the spread of aquatic invasive species. Recently, CD3 Waterless Cleaning Systems are developed as a waterless, free, user-operated cleaning equipment that includes wet/dry vacuum, blower system, tethered hand tools, and lights for watercraft clean, drain, and dry.[2] Before the start of each water quality and biological monitoring season, the Massachusetts Department of Environmental Protection (MassDEP) develops standard operation procedures (SOPs) to prevent potential spread of aquatic invasive species between different waterbodies and/or watersheds (Chase and Wong 2015). MassDEP usually takes multiple approaches for boat and equipment decontamination, such as air-dry, high-pressured wash, or quarantined with disinfectants (Figure 1.5). Since the discovery of zebra mussels in Laurel Lake, MA, in 2009 (see Chapter 3), DCR has set up Watercraft Inspection Stations at Quabbin Reservoir for inspecting, cleaning, and sealing a boat before it enters the Quabbin Reservoir (Table 1.4). Mostly adopted watercraft quarantine methods include flushing (Davis et al. 2016), pressure-washing (Morse 2009; Comeau et al. 2011), rinsing with hot water (Comeau et al. 2015; Kappel et al. 2015), using cleaning agents (Chase and Wong 2015; Davis et al. 2015, 2016), or air-drying (Figure 1.5), even the extent of their efficacy is quite different (Mohit et al. 2021 and references therein). According to a review based on 37 studies to study the efficacy of different quarantine methods, the majority (70.3%) assessed air-drying, followed by hot water (32.4%), household chemicals (16.2%), and pressure-washing (2.7%) (Mohit et al. 2021). The recommended air-drying duration of up to one week produced high mortality (≥90%) among several invertebrate and macrophyte species, although survival was high for certain aquatic

Introduction to Freshwater Invasive Species in Massachusetts

FIGURE 1.5 After sampling in a waterbody, equipment will be air-dried (upper panel) and boat will be cleaned with high-pressured spray (*bottom left*) by MassDEP staff. If more than one waterbody needs to be sampled, gears will be quarantined with chlorine or other disinfectants (*bottom right*). (Photos by W.H. Wong.)

TABLE 1.4
Quabbin Reservoir Boat Decontamination Program at Two Facilities from August 16 to September 26, 2009 (MA DCR 2010)

Facility	# 1 at Belchertown	#2 at Orange	Total
Number of inspections	280	382	662
Number of boats rejected	4	4	8
Total days of activity	12 days	19 days	N/A

snails. Aquatic plant survival and growth were inversely related to water loss (a function of drying time and relative humidity), and short or single fragments were less resistant to air-drying than larger or clustered fragments. Immersion in water ≥50°C for 15 minutes resulted in 100% mortality among mussels, small invertebrates, and some plant species. A higher temperature of 60°C was required for hot water spray applications lasting ≥5 seconds to achieve the same mortality rate among dreissenid mussels (Morse 2009; Comeau et al. 2011). High pressure-washing eliminated significantly more entangled plants and small organisms and seeds than low pressure. Household chemicals such as salt or bleach required specific doses and exposed durations to be lethal to targeted invasive species. The boat cleaning behavior could be significantly improved by changing how boat owners value the perceived costs and benefits of cleaning, as well as by increasing their awareness of the potential negative impacts on aquatic ecosystems caused by non-native species (De Ventura et al. 2017; Golebie et al. 2021). For a specific water district, science-based risk analysis needs to be performed to identify priority invasion pathways for introduction (i.e., watercraft, equipment, retail aquatic plant trade, aquarium, etc.) and species of concern. The most vulnerable waterbodies need to be prioritized for interventions in order for resources to be allocated in the most cost-effective manner.

As mentioned earlier, climate change is also facilitating the spread of invasive species by shifting their ranges. Massachusetts and other northeastern states have been identified as hot spots where up to 100 warm-adapted, range-shifting invasive plants could establish before 2050, it is suggested that only those high-impact species should be prioritized for practically monitoring and management (Rockwell-Postel et al. 2020). For freshwater invasive species such as Asian clams in Massachusetts and beyond (McDowell et al.2014; Colwell et al. 2017), as well as the global distribution and spread of hydrilla (Patrick and Florentine 2021), their ecological and socioeconomic impacts are substantial and should be monitored and prioritized for proactive management (see Chapters 2 and 6 in this book).

EARLY DETECTION AND RAPID RESPONSE (EDRR)

Eradication of the targeted invasive species is the primary goal of the EDRR. EDRR includes biological monitoring and assessment such as eDNA survey, and staff training workshops. A range of capabilities (e.g., risk assessments, monitoring programs, identification support, alert systems, eradication techniques, etc.) are necessary to support effective EDRR (Figure 1.6). EDRR also prioritizes high risk waters that may be invaded by potential invasive species and identifies obstacles and explores opportunities to establish an emergency rapid respond fund, etc. It can respond to new species detections in a timely manner to prevent their establishment and spread to other waterbodies. EDRR is generally necessary to achieve eradication which refers to actions that may be taken to eradicate populations of potentially invasive species that are new to the United States or contain the spread of known invasive species by eradicating satellite populations that could result in range expansions. A template for a decision-making process that incorporates the stages within the EDRR process is described in Figure 1.7.

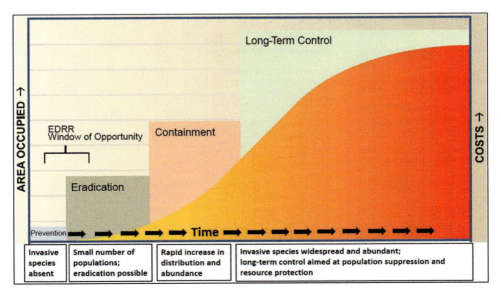

FIGURE 1.6 The invasion curve. (Modified from the U.S. Department of Interior (2016).)

Introduction to Freshwater Invasive Species in Massachusetts

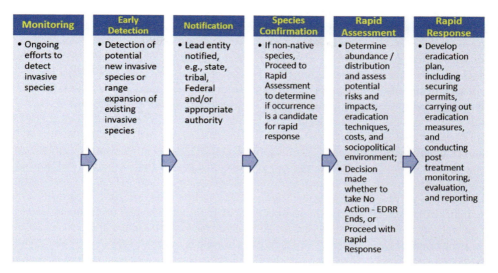

FIGURE 1.7 Depiction of general early detection and rapid response decision-making process. (Modified from U.S. Department of Interior (2016, 2021).)

EARLY DETECTION AND MONITORING

Early detection is the process of surveying for, reporting, and verifying the presence of a non-native species, before the founding population becomes established or spreads so widely that eradication is no longer feasible (U.S. Department of Interior 2016). Early detection can allow for a swift, proactive management response, nipping an infestation in the bud to more successfully and cost-effectively prevent ecological damage (Goldberg et al. 2013, 2016; Trebitz et al. 2017; Sepulveda et al. 2020). In Massachusetts, usually traditional monitoring is applied for species detection and confirmation. For example, MassDEP will add a waterbody to the CWA 303d list if the presence of alive organisms are confirmed (MassDEP 2018). There is growing interest in using environmental DNA (eDNA) methods for monitoring aquatic invasive species. For example, it is found that the frequency of conducting molecular analyses for species identification published from 2012 to 2019 in *BioInvasions Records*, an international journal about invasive species records worldwide, has increased from 4.5% to 25.2% and is expected to further increase with the continuing development of molecular tools (Stranga and Katsanevakis 2021). Therefore, eDNA is specifically described subsequently and should be a priority for future invasive species detection and monitoring.

eDNA is genetic material that is obtained directly from the environment after being shed or excreted by an organism (Thomsen and Willerslev 2014; Eichmiller et al. 2016). Using a variety of techniques, this material can be collected from the field, processed in a lab, and analyzed to uncover the identity of source organisms. The general method for finding the identity of a species based on a DNA sample is called "barcoding." As living things evolve over many generations, different regions of the genome change at different rates, leading to certain regions being more variable than others. Genes controlling respiration and other important cellular processes are more likely to be conserved between individuals of the same species than genes controlling eye color, for example. Some regions, such as the COI gene in animals and the rbcL in plants, are known through experimentation to vary from species to species, but not between individuals of the same species, and so genetic sequences from these regions are useful as "barcodes" to distinguish species based on genetic information (Hajibabaei et al. 2007; Bourlat et al. 2013). Using primers that are designed specially to latch onto these distinct barcode regions, biologists can detect the presence of a species' signature code within a mix of unknown DNA. Once primers have detected a matching segment in the sample, a polymerase chain reaction (PCR) can be used to "amplify" the segment, creating copies at an exponential rate. Conventionally, PCR can be used in this way to detect a target species (Thomsen and Willerslev 2014) by simply answering a yes-or-no question: if the target sequence (i.e., the barcode unique to the target species) is present in the sample, the primers will find it and PCR will proceed, producing a tube full of replicated target DNA; but if the target sequence is absent, PCR will not proceed, resulting in a tube of mostly water. Since PCR primers seek out their target region and make many copies of it, the technique is effective even if there is only a small amount of target DNA in the sample to begin with. Advanced techniques in analyzing eDNA include quantitative PCR (qPCR), high-throughput sequencing, and next-generation sequencing (Zaiko et al. 2018).

eDNA analysis has several advantages over traditional monitoring and sampling methods. Since eDNA samples can be collected from sediment or water, it is logistically simple to collect eDNA during routine water or sediment chemical sampling (Thomsen and Willerslev 2014; Zaiko et al. 2018). eDNA analysis does not require collection of or interaction with any live plants or animals, leading to a non-intrusive sampling process (Thomsen and Willerslev 2014). Identification and detection by eDNA do not require specific expertise of an organism's morphology. This is helpful in cases where it is a challenge to differentiate cryptic invertebrates, plants, or organisms in small, non distinct juvenile stages. (Trebitz et al. 2017; Thomsen and Willerslev 2014). As shown earlier, eDNA analysis can allow for early detection of invasive species, picking up on signs and traces of an organism before the invasive population has become fully established. eDNA analysis is becoming an increasingly powerful tool for ecosystem management, allowing for early detection of invasive species in waterways (Stranga and Katsanevakis 2021). For example, for invasive plants, different binding sites in water samples have been investigated to detect their sightings (Scriver et al. 2015) which include parrot-feather, water hyacinth, and Brazilian waterweed that are found in Massachusetts. For aquatic invertebrates, Thomsen et al. (2011) detected 82% of insect larvae (compared to the results of conventional collection) and Goldberg et al. (2013) successfully detected the invasive New Zealand mud-snail from US field sites. Some others include invasive rusty crayfish (Dougherty et al. 2016), invasive soft-shelled clams (Ardura et al. 2015), and invasive pygmy mussels (Miralles et al. 2016). For fish and other vertebrates, eDNA has been documented in their detection and management (Darling and Mahon 2011; Adrian-Kalchhauser and Burkhardt-Holm 2016; Rey et al. 2018). It is thought that fish and amphibians are easier to detect from environmentally excreted DNA than arthropods or other shelled invertebrates because of the mucus on fish and amphibian skin and its tendency to slough off in the water (Thomsen et al. 2011; Goldberg et al. 2013).

However, the uncertainty associated with eDNA surveillance (Frischer et al. 2012), as well as the lack of robust guidelines and reporting standards for eDNA which has affected the confidence of natural resources managers to apply eDNA results in support of management actions (DFO 2020), makes it challenging to determine appropriate natural resource management responses. Gingera et al. (2017) provided a case study using eDNA as a tool for detecting dreissenid mussels in Lake Winnipeg, Canada, where zebra mussels were first recorded in 2013. They developed two species-specific and one Dreissena-specific qPCR-based eDNA assays designed as a single multiplexed reaction able to identify the presence of zebra mussel and infer the presence of quagga mussel in water samples from at-risk and invaded locations in 2014. This case study demonstrates that eDNA is an early indicator of the presence of zebra mussels. At the same time, there are still critical knowledge gaps for eDNA being recognized as a reliable management tool. For example, when three methods were used to detect the presence of quagga/zebra mussel veligers that cross-polarized light microscopy currently provides the most reliable means (96.3% accuracy) in plankton samples. Imaging flowcytometry was next with 91.7% accuracy, and eDNA was the least reliable (75.8% accuracy) (Frischer et al. 2012). The most prevalent type of error associated with all the methods was false negatives.

The decay of genetic materials might be one of other challenges for eDNA implementation due to uncontrollable environmental factors such as temperature, microbial loads, and pH that can affect eDNA degradation significantly (Lance et al. 2017). Multiple sources of error can give rise to positive detections of eDNA in a sample when that species is not present at the site and acting on an erroneous eDNA inference could result in needless costs (Sepulveda et al. 2022). A structured decision-making process to evaluate appropriate response actions following hypothetical eDNA detections of invasive dreissenid mussel (*Dreissena* spp.) eDNA in Jordanelle Reservoir, Utah, is therefore suggested. This approach needs to communicate and work with decision-makers and stakeholders to identify objectives and discrete management action alternatives, and assess alternative consequences and trade-offs. These alternatives ranged from no action to intensive and expensive control efforts. The alternative identified to most likely satisfy the objectives was delayed containment, where immediate attempts to confirm the eDNA detections using non-molecular sampling techniques were conducted and, regardless of those results, containment efforts were enacted to prevent dreissenid mussel spread to other waterbodies through mandatory watercraft exit inspections shortly thereafter (Sepulveda et al. 2022). Delayed containment had the lowest downside risk, and the highest upside gains relative to other alternative actions would be optimal, regardless of the decision-maker being risk-adverse, risk-neutral, or risk-tolerant. Sensitivity and elasticity analyses demonstrate that it is robust to parameter and outcome uncertainty (Sepulveda et al. 2022).

RAPID RESPONSE

Rapid response is the process that is employed to eradicate the founding population of a non-native species from a specific location (U.S. Department of Interior 2016). Rapid response for eradication of the founding invasive species population alleviates the need for expensive invasive species control programs that would have to be enacted over the long term. Analytics and decision tools will help determine what and when rapid response measures should be taken to find and eradicate potential invasive species before they spread and become harmful ecologically and/or economically. When a potentially invasive species is detected, it is necessary for appropriate decision-makers to employ rapid response. Prevention is obviously the most desirable management option, but often this fails (Cheater 1992; Mattson et al. 2004a). Successful rapid response is contingent on preparedness: having the plans, tools, training, resources etc. in place to mount eradication efforts (U.S. Department of Interior 2016). Therefore, it needs support for response actions and preparedness activities, including intensive monitoring for many taxonomic groups, rapid response training, and tools for containment and eradication such as hand pulling or benthic barriers.

Among the 19 invasive species described in this book, rapid response for eradication is suggested for water hyacinth and northern snakehead because there are only two sightings for each of these two species in Massachusetts. For zebra mussel, even there are three waterbodies infested, but two of them are Housatonic River and Green River, which are not recommended for eradication. Rapid response for eradication can also be implemented to other species to an early infestation in a waterbody. In Massachusetts, MA Department of Conservation and Recreation Lakes and Ponds Program has developed a guide on two different types of manual control techniques rapid response which are suitable for volunteers who wish to implement a rapid response to a small infestation of aquatic invasive species, but they usually are not considered feasible techniques for large-scale infestations (MA DCR 2007). The guide is mainly for two techniques, hand pulling or/and benthic barriers, to potentially eradicate submerged, floating, or emergent aquatic invasive species. More detailed information on the rapid response standard operating procedure is provided in Appendix II.

CONTROL AND CONTAINMENT

While for species in their early invasion stage, rapid response and eradication is prioritized, for widely invaded species whose spread to an extent where eradication is no longer feasible, control and containment is the remaining management option. Habitat and ecosystem restoration such as planting or stocking organisms or improving predator–prey relationships to attain food webs similar to pre-invasion conditions should be conducted since rehabilitation is often necessary to restore ecological processes. Among the 19 invasive species described in this book, the following 17 species are well-established and are recommended for control and containment: purple loosestrife, variable milfoil, fanwort, curly-leaf pondweed, Eurasian watermilfoil, water chestnut, common reed grass, Chinese mystery snail, Asian clam, European naiad, swollen bladderwort, hydrilla, European waterclover, South American waterweed, parrot-feather, yellow floating heart, and zebra mussel (Table 1.1, in the order from most common to least common). Usually a control/contain plan should be developed to evaluate/justify the need for control and the projected consequences of no control and less than full control, as well as potential risk in harming non-target organisms, ecosystems, and the public health. The elimination or reduction in population of aquatic invasive species may promote an increase in indigenous plant and animal diversity and/or edge effect habitat and likely improve wildlife habitat and sever as restoration per Massachusetts Wetlands Protection Act 310 CMR 10.60 (Langley et al. 2004). The cost of the project is critical too in terms of technical feasibility and effectiveness of alternative control strategies and actions. It should be evaluated whether benefits of control, including costs avoided, exceed the costs of the program. Long-term control programs require substantial financial investments in perpetuity. Structuring the plant community to meet clear goals of invasive species management in an ecologically and ethically sound manner is more appropriate, although potentially still quite expensive. While most managers in North America now focus on ongoing containment and suppression interventions, they often lack quantitative guidance from which to set targets and evaluate success. Practical guidelines are recommended for identifying management targets for invasions for which eradication is unfeasible, based on achieving "functional" eradication—defined as suppressing invader populations below levels that cause unacceptable ecological effects—within high-priority locations. Identifying targets for suppression allows managers to estimate the degree of removal required to mitigate ecological impacts and the management resources needed to achieve sufficient control of an invasive species.

Depending on the site to be treated, usually invasive species control involves the use of variable methods which mainly consist of physical removal, chemical treatment, and biological control (Tables 1.5–1.7). Invasive plants should be managed aggressively. Due to the possibility of fragmentation spreading of some species, such as Eurasian watermilfoil, the best treatment is with a selective herbicide unless the growths are extremely localized and amendable to simple physical techniques (hand pulling at low density, benthic barriers at high density). All of the techniques to control plants have their unique advantages and disadvantages (Wagner 2001, 2004; Mattson et al. 2004a) which are summarized in Tables 1.5 (physical removal), 1.6 (chemical treatments), and 1.7 (biological control) in this chapter. Detailed information about these techniques can be found from the Massachusetts' Generic Environmental Impact Report (GEIR), Eutrophication and Aquatic Plant Management (Mattson et al. 2004a), and the accompanying The Practical Guide to Aquatic Plant Management in Massachusetts (Wagner 2004). Although these methods are mainly for aquatic plants, some of these techniques such as benthic barriers or copper treatment can also be used for some invasive animals such as Asian clams or zebra mussels. For more information about control and containment techniques of each specific invasive species, refer to Chapters 2–19 in this book.

PHYSICAL REMOVAL

Physical removal and control techniques are listed in Table 1.5 which includes (1) benthic barriers, (2) dredging, (3) dyes and surface covers, (4) mechanical removal ("harvesting"), and (5) water level control. If harvesting is proposed, the ultimate disposal location of the vegetative spoils should be identified and it should be outside of wetland resource areas or buffer zones (Langley et al. 2004). Plant material decomposition in the water column should be prevented that may result in lower dissolved oxygen.

CHEMICAL TREATMENT

Chemicals used for treating aquatic plants and animals in Massachusetts are listed in Table 1.6. Before each treatment, applicators must apply for a WM04 Chemical Application

TABLE 1.5
Physical Removal and Management Options for Control of Aquatic Invasive Plants

Technique Option	Technique Subdivisions	Mode of Action	Advantages	Disadvantages
Benthic barriers*	(a), (b), or (c) below	• Mat of variable composition laid on bottom of target area, preventing growth • Can cover area for as little as several months or permanently • Maintenance improves results • Usually applied around docks, in boating lanes, and in swimming areas	• Highly flexible control • Reduces turbidity from soft bottom sediments • Can cover undesirable substrate • Can improve fish habitat by creating edge effects	• May cause anoxia at sediment–water interface • May limit benthic invertebrates • Non-selective interference with plants in target area • May inhibit spawning/feeding
	(a) Porous or loose-weave synthetic materials	• Laid on bottom and usually anchored by weights or stakes • Removed and cleaned or flipped and repositioned at least once per year for maximum effect	• Allows some escape of gases which may be generated underneath • Panels may be flipped in place or removed for relatively easy cleaning or repositioning	• Allows some plant growth through pores • Gas may still build up underneath in some cases, lifting barrier from bottom
	(b) Non-porous or sheet synthetic materials	• Laid on bottom and anchored by many stakes, anchors or weights, or by layer of sand • Not typically removed, but may be swept or "blown" clean periodically	• Prevents all plant growth until buried by sediment • Minimizes interaction of sediment and water column	• Gas buildup may cause barrier to float upward • Strong anchoring makes removal difficult and can hinder maintenance
	(c) Improving sediment composition	• Sediments may be added on top of existing sediments or plants • Use of sand or clay can limit plant growths and alter sediment–water interactions • Sediments can be applied from the surface or suction dredged from below muck layer (reverse layering technique)	• Plant biomass can be buried • Seed banks can be buried deeper • Sediment can be made less hospitable to plant growths • Nutrient release from sediments may be reduced • Surface sediment can be made more appealing to human users • Reverse layering requires no addition or removal of sediment	• Lake depth may decline • Sediments may sink into or mix with underlying muck • Permitting for added sediment difficult • Addition of sediment may cause initial turbidity increase • New sediment may contain nutrients or other contaminants • Generally too expensive for large-scale application

(Continued)

TABLE 1.5 (Continued)

Technique Option	Technique Subdivisions	Mode of Action	Advantages	Disadvantages
Dredging	(a), (b), or (c) below	• Sediment is physically removed by wet or dry excavation, with deposition in a containment area for dewatering/disposal • Dredging can be applied on a limited basis, but is most often a major restructuring of a severely impacted system • Plants and seed beds are removed and regrowth can be limited by light and/or substrate limitation	• Plant removal with some flexibility • Increases water depth • Can reduce pollutant reserves • Can reduce sediment oxygen demand • Can improve spawning habitat for many fish species • Allows complete renovation of aquatic ecosystem • May allow for growth of desirable species	• Temporarily removes benthic invertebrates • May create turbidity • May eliminate fish community (complete dry dredging only) • Possible impacts from containment area discharge • Possible impacts from dredged material disposal • Interference with recreation or other uses during dredging • Usually very expensive
	(a) "Dry" excavation	• Lake drained or lowered to maximum extent practical • Target material dried to maximum extent possible • Conventional excavation equipment used to remove sediments	• Tends to facilitate a very thorough effort • May allow drying of sediments prior to removal • Allows use of less specialized equipment	• Eliminates most aquatic biota unless a portion left undrained • Eliminates lake use during dredging
	(b) "Wet" excavation	• Lake level may be lowered, but sediments not substantially dewatered • Draglines, bucket dredges, or long reach backhoes used to remove sediment	• Requires least preparation time or effort, tends to be least cost dredging approach • May allow use of easily acquired equipment • May preserve most aquatic biota	• Usually creates extreme turbidity • Tends to result in sediment deposition in surrounding area • Normally requires intermediate containment area to dry sediments prior to hauling • May cause severe disruption of ecological function • Impairs most lake uses during dredging

Introduction to Freshwater Invasive Species in Massachusetts

	c) Hydraulic (or pneumatic) removal	• Lake level not reduced • Suction or cutterhead dredges create slurry which is hydraulically pumped to containment area • Slurry is dewatered; sediment retained, water discharged	• Creates minimal turbidity and limits impact on biota • Can allow some lake uses during dredging • Allows removal with limited access or shoreline disturbance	• Often leaves some sediment behind • Cannot handle extremely coarse or debris-laden materials • Requires advanced and more expensive containment area • Requires overflow discharge from containment area
Dyes and surface covers		• Water-soluble dye is mixed with lake water, thereby limiting light penetration and inhibiting plant growth • Dyes remain in solution until washed out of system • Opaque sheet material applied to water surface	• Light limit on plant growth without high turbidity or great depth • May achieve some control of algae as well • May achieve some selectivity for species tolerant of low light	• May not control peripheral or shallow water rooted plants • May cause thermal stratification in shallow ponds • May facilitate anoxia at sediment interface with water • Covers inhibit gas exchange with atmosphere and restrict recreation • Cannot be used in waterbodies with an active outlet
Mechanical removal ("harvesting")	(a), (b), (c), (d), or (e) below	• Plants reduced by mechanical means, possibly with disturbance of soils • Collected plants may be placed on shore for composting or other disposal • Wide range of techniques employed, from manual to highly mechanized • Application once or twice per year usually needed	• Highly flexible control • May remove other debris • Can balance habitat and recreational needs	• Possible impacts on aquatic fauna • Non-selective removal of plants in treated area • Possible spread of undesirable species by fragmentation • Possible generation of turbidity
	(a) Hand pulling*	• Plants uprooted by hand ("weeding") and preferably removed	• Highly selective technique	• Labor-intensive • Difficult to perform in dense stands • Can cause fragmentation
	(b) Cutting (without collection)	• Plants cut in place above roots without being harvested	• Generally efficient and less expensive than complete harvesting	• Leaves root systems and part of plant for possible regrowth • Leaves cut vegetation to decay or to re-root • Not selective within applied area

(Continued)

TABLE 1.5 (Continued)

Technique Option	Technique Subdivisions	Mode of Action	Advantages	Disadvantages
	(c) Harvesting (with collection)	• Plants cut at depth of 2–10 ft and collected for removal from lake	• Allows plant removal on greater scale	• Limited depth of operation • Usually leaves fragments which may re-root and spread infestation • May impact lake fauna • Limited selectivity within applied area • More expensive than cutting
	(d) Rototilling	• Plants, root systems, and surrounding sediment disturbed with mechanical blades	• Can thoroughly disrupt entire plant	• Usually leaves fragments which may re-root and spread infestation • May impact lake fauna • Not selective within applied area • Creates substantial turbidity • More expensive than harvesting
	(e) Hydroraking	• Plants, root systems, and surrounding sediment and debris disturbed with mechanical rake, part of material usually collected and removed from lake	• Can thoroughly disrupt entire plant • Also allows removal of stumps or other obstructions	• Usually leaves fragments which may re-root and spread infestation • May impact lake fauna • Not selective within applied area • Creates substantial turbidity • More expensive than harvesting
Water level control	(a) or (b) below	• Lowering or raising the water level to create an inhospitable environment for some or all aquatic plants • Disrupts plant life cycle by desiccation, freezing, or light limitation	• Requires only outlet control to affect large area • Provides widespread control in increments of water depth • Complements certain other techniques (dredging, flushing)	• Potential issues with water supply • Potential issues with flooding • Potential impacts to non-target flora and fauna

(a) Drawdown	• Lowering of water over winter period allows desiccation, freezing, and physical disruption of plants, roots, and seed beds • Timing and duration of exposure and degree of dewatering are critical aspects • Variable species tolerance to drawdown; emergent species and seed bearers are less affected • Most effective on annual to once/three-year basis	• Control with some flexibility • Opportunity for shoreline cleanup/structure repair • Flood control utility • Impacts vegetative propagation species with limited impact to seed-producing populations	• Possible impacts on contiguous emergent wetlands • Possible effects on overwintering reptiles and amphibians • Possible impairment of well production • Reduction in potential water supply and fire fighting capacity • Alteration of downstream flows • Possible overwinter water level variation • Possible shoreline erosion and slumping • May result in greater nutrient availability for algae
(b) Flooding	• Higher water level in the spring can inhibit seed germination and plant growth • Higher flows which are normally associated with elevated water levels can flush seed and plant fragments from system	• Where water is available, this can be an inexpensive technique • Plant growth need not be eliminated, merely retarded or delayed • Timing of water level control can selectively favor certain desirable species	• Water for raising the level may not be available • Potential peripheral flooding • Possible downstream impacts • Many species may not be affected, and some may be benefitted • Algal nuisances may increase where nutrients are available

ᵃBenthic barriers and hand pulling are also introduced in the "Early Detection and Rapid Response" section. See Appendix II for more detailed information.

Source: Modified from Wagner (2001, 2004) and Mattson et al. (2004a).

TABLE 1.6
Major Chemicals for Treating Aquatic Invasive Species in Massachusetts

Major Ingredient	Brand Name	Mode of Action	Advantages	Disadvantages
Fluridone	• AVAST! SC • SONAR SRP • SONAR Q • SONAR PR • SONAR GENESIS • SONAR ONE • SONAR AS • SONAR H4C	• Inhibition of carotenoid biosynthesis at the phytoene desaturase step	• Complete kill of susceptible vegetation • Can be used selectively on certain major invasive species at low doses • Slow death of plants minimizes oxygen demand and nutrient release • Minimal risk of any direct impacts on fauna	• Acts slowly in the aquatic environment; exposure time of up to 90 days needed • Highly diffusive; dilution will limit effectiveness in areas of high flushing activity
Diquat	• REWARD • TRIBUNE	• Interferes with photosynthesis by forming highly reactive and toxic free-radicals, such as peroxide and super oxide, in plant cells	• Effective against a wide variety of species • Relatively rapid kill of targeted vegetation • Can be used for spot treatments; limited drift or impact outside target area	Detriments • Not very selective; kills most species contacted • Does not damage portions of plants with which it does not contact; regrowth from roots is common • Potential for toxicity to fauna, but uncommon in practice
Glyphosate	• GLYPRO • RODEO • AQUAPRO • ACCORD • ROUNDUP CUSTOM	• Inhibition of 5-enolpyruvylshikimate-3-phosphate (EPSP) synthase; EPSP inhibition leads to depletion of the aromatic amino acids tryptophan, tyrosine, and phenylalanine, all needed for protein synthesis or for biosynthetic pathways leading to growth	• Effective on emergent vegetation • Kills entire plant for susceptible species • Selective by area and vegetation type (emergent/floating vs. submergent)	• Ineffective against submergent species • Precipitation (rain) interferes with uptake

Introduction to Freshwater Invasive Species in Massachusetts

Triclopyr	• RENOVATE • RENOVATE OTF • RENOVATE MAXG • RESTORATE • PATHFINDER II • GARLON 3A • GARLON 4 • VASTLAN	• As selective plant growth regulator to induce growth (auxin mimic) while preventing synthesis of essential plant enzymes, resulting in disruption of growth processes	• Complete kill of susceptible vegetation • Can be used selectively on certain major invasive species • Lower necessary exposure time allows for treatment in areas of greater water exchange • Low risk of any direct impacts on fauna	• Lowered oxygen levels are possible as a function of vegetation decay after treatment. • No experience yet with application approaches and control success in Massachusetts
2,4-D	• AQUA-KLEEN • NAVIGATE • PLATOON • DMA 4 • CLEAN AMINE • SCULPIN G	• Absorbed by roots, leaves, and shoots and disrupts cell division throughout the plant	• Complete kill of susceptible vegetation, typically provides multiple years of control for target species • Acts relatively quickly in the aquatic environment; plant death may be delayed, but sufficient uptake occurs within three days • Can be used selectively on certain major invasive species at low doses, and for partial (especially shoreline) lake treatments	• Potential for toxicity to fauna, but a rare occurrence in practice • Use restrictions in or near drinking water supplies (surface or wells) limits application
Endothall	• AQUATHOL-K • AQUATHOL SUPER K • HYDROTHOL • HYDROTHOL 191	• As plant protein phosphatase inhibitor	• Effective against a wide variety of species • Relatively rapid kill of targeted vegetation • Selective; limited drift or impact outside target area	• Not very selective; kills most species contacted • Does not damage portions of plants with which it does not contact; regrowth from roots is common • Potential for toxicity to fauna, but uncommon in practice
Imazapyr	• HABITAT • POLARIS	• It prevents the production of acetolactate synthase and disrupts synthesis of amino acids	• Practically non-toxic (the EPA's lowest toxicity category) to fish, invertebrates, birds and mammals	• Not for use on submersed species • Unlike imazamox, imazapyr does not demonstrate any in-water herbicidal activity

(Continued)

TABLE 1.6 (Continued)

Major Ingredient	Brand Name	Mode of Action	Advantages	Disadvantages
Imazamox	• CLEARCAST	• Inhibition of acetolactate synthase and disrupts synthesis of amino acids	• Low toxicity to animals such as fish, birds, invertebrates, and amphibians, as well as to humans	• Usually limited to monocultural stands of target plants or in areas where selectivity is not a concern
Florpyrauxifen-benzyl	• PROCELLACOR EC	• Action like indole acetic acid (synthetic auxins)	• Non-toxic to fish and birds and has no drinking, fishing or swimming restrictions	• Registered by EPA in 2018 and lots of ongoing studies on it to collect more information
Flumioxazin	• CLIPPER • SCHOONER • REDEAGLE • PROPELLER	• Inhibits photosynthesis, bleaching of the chloroplasts, and cell death	• With a broader spectrum of activity compared to carfentrazone	• The primary breakdown pathway in water is highly dependent on water pH. Under high pH values (> 9), half-life in water is 15–20 minutes. Under more neutral pH values (7–8), half-life in water is around 24 hours
Carfentrazone	• STINGRAY	• Inhibition of protoporphyrinogen oxidase enzyme that is important in chlorophyll synthesis	• Rapid degradation in the aquatic environment, no accumulation in the sediment, low use rates; does not pose a hazard to mammals or other non-target organisms • Provides good selectivity and it will not control comingled non-target plants like pickerelweed or grasses	• Currently very few published literature on the efficacy of carfentrazone against submersed plants
Metsulfuron	• ESCORT XP	• Inhibition of acetolactate synthase (acetohydroxyacid synthase AHAS)	• A potent herbicide active ingredient with a very low use rate	• Do not apply directly to water, or to areas where surface water is present, or to intertidal areas below the mean high water mark

Sodium percarbonate + hydrogen peroxide hydrogen peroxide + peracetic acid sodium percarbonate	• GREEN CLEAN PRO • GREEN CLEAN LIQUID • PHYCOMYCIN • PAK 27	• Damaging cells by oxidation and disruption of cell membranes via the hydroxyl radical • Sodium carbonate peroxyhydrate is transformed into hydrogen peroxide and sodium carbonate in the presence of water	• Hydrogen peroxide residue levels dissipate rapidly and are mostly undetectable at 24 hours	• Undiluted granules should not be allowed to remain in an area where humans or animals may be exposed
Copper	• CUTRINE PLUS • NAUTIQUE • CAPTAIN • CAPTAIN XTR • K-TEA • KOMEEN • SECLEAR • POND BOSS PRO • EARTHTEC • SECLEAR G • HARPOON G • COPPER SULFATE	• The copper ion (copper II) is responsible for the toxicity of all of the formulations • Inhibition of photosynthesis leads to plant death • It may affect nitrogen metabolism	• Rapid kill of susceptible algae • Rapidly eliminated from water column, minimizing prolonged adverse impacts	• Toxic to many non-target organisms • Releases contents of most killed algal cells back into the water column; this may include nutrients, taste and odor compounds, and toxins • Ineffective on some algae; repeated treatments may favor those resistant algae, some of which are major nuisance species • Accumulates in sediments, although long-term impacts may not be severe
Aluminum	• POLYALUMINUM CHLORIDE • SODIUM ALUMINATE • ALUMINUM SULFATE • PHOSCLEAR	• Form a floc that can remove particulates, including algae, from the water column within minutes to hours and precipitate reactive phosphates • Reactions continue at the surface–water interface, binding phosphorus that could otherwise be released from the sediment	• Rapid removal of available phosphorus from the water column • Minimized internal loading of phosphorus • Potential removal of a variety of other contaminants and algae	• Risk of toxicity from aluminum comes from issues with pH due to either poorly buffered water or water with an already lower pH (<6.5). Alkalinization (when pH >8) can also lead to toxicity from aluminum • Limited longevity of effects if external loading is significant

Source: Modified mainly from Wagner (2001, 2004) and Mattson et al. (2004a, 2004b); it also includes information from these references: Durkin (2008, 2012); Glomski et al. (2006); MA DAR and MassDEP 2010, 2014, 2019; McComas (2011); NALMS (2004); Richardson et al. (2008); Sesin et al. (2018); Strid et al. (2018); U.S. EPA (1998); WSSA.

TABLE 1.7
Biological Control Options for Control of Aquatic Invasive Species in Massachusetts

Technique Option	Technique Subdivisions	Mode of Action	Advantages	Disadvantages
Biological introductions	(a), (b), (c), or (d) below	• Fish, insects or pathogens which feed on or parasitize plants are added to system to affect control • The most commonly used organism is the grass carp, but the larvae of several insects have been used more recently, and viruses are being tested	• Provides potentially continuing control with one treatment • Harnesses biological interactions to produce desired conditions • May produce potentially useful fish biomass as an end product	• Typically involves introduction of non-native species • Effects may not be controllable • Plant selectivity may not match desired target species • May adversely affect indigenous species
	(a) Herbivorous fish	• Sterile juveniles stocked at density which allows control over multiple years • Growth of individuals offsets losses or may increase herbivorous pressure. Grass carp are illegal in Massachusetts	• May greatly reduce plant biomass in single season • May provide multiple years of control from single stocking • Sterility intended to prevent population perpetuation and allow later adjustments	• May eliminate all plant biomass, or impact non-target species • Funnels energy into algae • Alters habitat • May escape upstream or downstream • Population control issues
	(b) Herbivorous insects	• Larvae or adults stocked at density intended to allow control with limited growth • Intended to selectively control target species • Milfoil weevil is best known, but still experimental	• Involves species native to region, or even targeted lake • Expected to have no negative effect on non-target species • May facilitate longer term control with limited management	• Population ecology suggests incomplete control likely • Oscillating cycle of control and regrowth • Predation by fish may complicate control • Other lake management actions may interfere with success
	(c) Fungal/bacterial/viral pathogens	• Inoculum used to seed lake or target plant patch • Growth of pathogen population expected to achieve control over target species	• May be highly species specific • May provide substantial control after minimal inoculation effort	• Effectiveness and longevity of control not well-known • Infection ecology suggests incomplete control likely • Largely experimental
	(d) Selective plantings	• Establishment of plant assemblage resistant to undesirable species • Plants introduced as seeds, cuttings, or whole plants	• Can restore native assemblage • Can encourage assemblage most suitable to lake uses • Supplements targeted species removal effort	• Nuisance species may eventually return assemblage • Introduced species may become nuisances

Source: Modified from Wagner (2001, 2004) and Mattson et al. (2004a).

License from Massachusetts Department of Environmental Protection. At the same time, since most of these chemicals are not selective, non-target native species will be impacted, more or less. For example, glyphosate-based herbicides are now the most commonly used herbicides in the world and often promoted as "safe," despite scientific evidence of their harm to all facets of an ecosystem, including the soil, water, and non-target plants, amphibians, reptiles, invertebrates, animals, and humans (Rushton et al. 2016). It is reported that there was a huge invasion of bladderwort to Pierpont Meadow Pond in Dudley and Charlton, MA, about 20 years ago. The floating weed wrapped around docks impeded swimming and boating and was a terrible eyesore. So, yearly chemicals are applied to this lake since then. Lately, residents start to question if there may be a better way than to continue to add chemicals to the lake because they could not see native snails or crawfish in the water anymore which may or may not be a result of the yearly chemical application.[3] Although it is unlikely that snails or crawfish might not be eradicated from this lake because the chemical application permit only allows one-third of the entire lake and half of the littoral zone for chemical application, the negative impacts of accumulative chemical applications should not be overlooked. Therefore, it is important to reiterate that only herbicides products registered for use in Massachusetts through the Department of Agricultural Resources (DFA) may be used in Massachusetts, and then only by licensed applicators with proper permits (except in some water supply cases and ponds with no outlets). An updated list of registered herbicides can be obtained from the Massachusetts Department of Agricultural Resources. Reported chemical control methods on the 19 aquatic invasive species are summarized in Appendix III.

BIOLOGICAL CONTROL

Biological control has the objective of achieving control of plants without introducing toxic chemicals or using machinery. However, any introduction of organisms may have imperceptible impacts on the aquatic community structure and food web. Although still experimental at most times, biological controls may offer effective and low cost controls once properly developed. At the same time, because biological control is one of the most powerful techniques, it must be approached with some caution and respect (Mattson et al. 2004a). For example, water quality can be indirectly impacted by biological control. The most dramatic impacts are from induced grass carp, although not on a consistent basis. Increases in alkalinity, turbidity, and potassium concentrations and significant reductions in dissolved oxygen levels and chlorophyll have all been documented in waters stocked with grass carp (Mitzner 1978; Lembi et al. 1978; Leslie et al. 1987; Mattson et al. 2004a). Since biological controls may provide plant control benefits and represent another tool in addition to physical and chemical controls, interest has grown in biological control methods over the last decades. Various biological control options are listed in Table 1.7. Generally, a full biological survey and study should be conducted to determine what type of manipulation is best suited to achieve the desired goals while minimizing possible adverse impacts. Because of the experimental nature of most biological methods, results are not assured to the same degree as for other methods such as harvesting or herbicide treatment (Mattson et al. 2004a). Therefore, some biological agents for invasive species control, such as the introduction of grass carp to control invasive weeds, are not allowed in Massachusetts (Mattson et al. 2004a).

REGULATION AND PERMITTING

REGULATION

According to the National Sea Grant Law Center, primary responsibility for preventing the spread of invasive species within the United States lies with states and it is the state authority to implement desired management strategies for species and pathways of concern. In Massachusetts, monitoring, control, and management of invasive or native nuisance aquatic species are within the jurisdictions of Massachusetts Department of Conservation and Recreation (DCR), Massachusetts Department of Environmental Protection (DEP), and Massachusetts Department of Fish and Game (DFG). Chemicals used for invasive species treatments must be approved for use by the Massachusetts Department of Agricultural Resource (MA DAR) Pesticide Bureau. The MA laws statutes pertaining aquatic invasive/nuisance species are briefly summarized subsequently in Appendix IV. It is a collection of laws on introduction and possession of fish and other animals, introduction and possession of plants, and prevention and control of invasive plants. More information on statues and laws on aquatic invasive/nuisance species from Massachusetts as well as other New England States and New York can also be found in Appendix IV.

MassDEP provides a guidance for the issuing authority (the Conservation Commission or MassDEP) in the review of aquatic plant management projects proposed to control abundance and distribution of aquatic vegetation under the Wetlands Protection Act Regulations (310 CMR 10) (Langley et al. 2004). Aquatic plant management projects in lakes and ponds subject to the jurisdiction must comply with the general performance standards established for each applicable resource area in the regulations (i.e., 310 CMR 10.54, 10.55, 10.56, 10.57) unless the project is "limited" (310 CMR 10.53(4) or 310 CMR 10.53(3)(l)). If wildlife habitat thresholds described in the general performance standards are exceeded, the requirements of 310 CMR 10.60 for wildlife habitat must be met (e.g., a wildlife habitat evaluation shall be performed). No project may be permitted which will have any adverse effect on specified habitat sites of rare vertebrate or invertebrate species (310 CMR 10.59) (see "Permitting" section).

In Massachusetts, waterbodies infested with an invasive species will be added to the Clean Water Act (CWA) 303d list of impaired or threatened waters during water quality assessments to fulfill the requirements of the Clean Water Act. If an invasive species management project footprint is within an Estimated Habitat of Rare Wildlife or a Priority Habitat of Rare Species area, it will be subject to the Massachusetts Endangered Species Act (MESA) that prevents the "taking" of any rare plant or animal species listed as Endangered, Threatened, or of Special Concern unless specifically permitted for scientific, educational, propagation, or conservative purposes (321 CMR 10.00).

Permitting

Order of Conditions

Whether physical removal/mechanical harvesting, chemical treatment, or biological control, it should fulfill the requirements of Massachusetts Wetlands Protection Act (310 CMR10). Usually, an approval from the local conservation commission is needed. A negative determination of applicability (NDA) may be appropriate if the area to be treated affects less than 5,000 ft^2. A Notice of Intent must be sent to the Conservation Commission with a copy to the Department of Environmental Protection Regional Office. An Order of Conditions (OOC) issued by the local conservation commission may be required for areas greater than 5,000 ft^2 of native vegetation. Non-native vegetation identified on the rapid response usually can be removed without restriction on areal extent (MA DCR 2007).

401 Water Quality Certification (Dredge)

For projects within infested waters may be subject to the jurisdiction of the 401 Water Quality Certification (WQC), conditions on invasive species prevention and decontamination will be provided to avoid the spread of invasive species during construction. For projects involving dredging or disposal of sediment including detritus or biomass of aquatic plants with volumes 100 cubic yards or greater, a 401 WQC must be obtained from MassDEP to ensure that the proposed project is in compliance with existing water quality standards.

There are three categories of water quality certification for dredging: major project, minor project certifications, and Amendment of Certification for Dredging. Major project certification includes the dredging of 5,000 cubic yards or greater, minor dredge project certification includes projects not listed in the major project certification category; and those projects involving dredging less than 5,000 cubic yards but more than 100 cubic yards. If a water quality certification has been issued for a dredging project and the project is subsequently revised, the certification is not valid. An amended certification may be requested for project modifications, such as changes in the dredging area, dredged material volume, or construction methods for dredging or disposal. In addition, a change in one or more of the special conditions of certification may be allowed through an amended certification. The 401 Water Quality Certification applications must be submitted through ePLACE, located at https://eplace.eea.mass.gov/citizenaccess.

WM 04 Chemical Application License

The MassDEP WM04 Chemical Application License grants approval to apply chemicals for the control of nuisance aquatic vegetation in accordance with authority granted to the MassDEP by Massachusetts General Laws c. 111, s. 5E.

Anyone may apply chemicals to bodies of water except under the following conditions: (a) When treatment is undertaken by employees and agents of the Departments of Environmental Protection, Conservation and Recreation, and Fisheries, Wildlife and Environmental Law Enforcement, or of the Reclamation Board, or of related Federal agencies, while in the conduct of their official duties. (b) When treatment is undertaken with algaecide containing copper by a public water system. However, the public water system shall notify the department in writing prior to the application of such algaecides [310 CMR 22.20B(8), the Drinking Water Regulations]. (c) When treatment is undertaken in privately owned (single owner) ponds from which there are no flowing outlets.

What prerequisites should be considered before applying for this permit? (1) Chemical treatments to water using general-use pesticides shall only be performed by an applicator currently licensed by the Massachusetts Department of Agricultural Resources Pesticide Program in the aquatics category. Chemical treatments to Bordering Vegetated Wetlands (310 CMR 10.55(2)(a)) and Salt Marsh (310 CMR 10.32(2)) using general-use pesticides and techniques that ensure chemicals are not applied to water shall only be performed by an applicator currently licensed by the Massachusetts Department of Agricultural Resources Pesticide Program. Chemical treatments using restricted-use pesticides shall only be performed by an applicator currently certified by the Massachusetts Department of Agricultural Resources (MA DAR) Pesticide Program. (2) Chemicals used for treatments must be currently approved for use in the state by the MA DAR Pesticide Bureau. The website listing the approved chemicals is found here: www.mass.gov/herbicides-for-aquaticvegetation-management. (3) A valid Order of Conditions, Negative Determination of Applicability (Wetlands Protection Act), Administrative Consent Order or similar authorization must be obtained prior to the treatment.

What concurrent applications are related to this permit? Since chemical treatments constitute the alteration of wetland resources, a Notice of Intent must be filed in accordance with the Wetlands Protection Act (MGL c. 131, s. 40) and Wetlands Protection Regulations (310 CMR 10.00). The following website can be used to file an application—www.mass.gov/how-to/wm-04-herbicide-application.

MESA-associated Permits

If the proposed project occurs within an Estimated Habitat of Rare Wildlife in the most recent version of the Natural Heritage Atlas, a copy of the Notice of Intent must be submitted to the Natural Heritage and Endangered Species Program (NHESP) within the Massachusetts Department of Fish and Game for review. If the proposed project occurs within a Priority Habitat of Rare Species, the project proponent must submit project plans to the NHESP for an impact determination. An Order of Conditions must be obtained prior to work. In the case of lakes and ponds with rare species, a Conservation and Management Permit likely will be required, or an Alteration Permit if the project is within a formally designated "significant habitat." A Massachusetts Environmental Policy Act (MEPA) review may also be required, depending upon interpretation of the impact thresholds. For biological control, in addition to approval of the Conservation Commission, the importation or liberation of fish or wildlife requires permits from the Division of Fisheries and Wildlife. Generally, native species (native to Massachusetts) do not require extensive testing and quarantine as non-native species do. Introduction of foreign species would require additional testing, approval of Division of Fisheries and Wildlife and Massachusetts Department of Agricultural Resources. It may require quarantine and approval of the federal US Department of Agriculture, Animal Plant Health Inspection Service (USDA-APHIS).

WEAKNESS AND STRENGTH

The sightings data in this book may not be complete due to lack of monitoring efforts (e.g., funding and time). Each chapter just covers sightings using data collected by MassDEP and others before each chapter is drafted. Due to continuous monitoring efforts from MassDEP, MA DCR, and other agencies and institutions, there should be new detection sightings since then but are not included in this book. I hope updated information and new data can be added to future editions of this book. In addition, for some waterbodies that have been treated chemically, physically, or biologically, I am not certain if the targeted invasive species has been eradicated or not due to lack of monitoring data after management activities. Therefore, it is possible that there are no invasive species anymore in a few reported sightings because of management activities, even it is extremely difficult to eradicate an established invasive species population.

Usually, a book either focuses on one organism (e.g., zebra mussel), or one group of organisms (e.g., submerged aquatic plants or bivalves), or just one subject of a group (i.e., identification of aquatic plants). This book provides valuable information on biological characteristics, monitoring, and management of both invasive animals and invasive plants in freshwater systems in Massachusetts. Furthermore, an example of success management is highlighted for each invasive species. Therefore, this book provides readers a bigger picture on multiple invasive animal/plant species from basic biology, prevention, early detection, control, ecological restoration, to public education. This book provides a unique comprehensive, systematic coverage with illustrations for both freshwater invasive animals and plants. Natural resource managers and practitioners usually must handle multiple invasive species in a system. This book will provide detailed and valuable information natural resource managers need to understand and use to prevent and manage freshwater invasive species in the field. Therefore, this book can serve as a field guide for how to identify and respond to invasions for resource managers and practitioners. It can also be a textbook for researchers and college students majoring in ecology, environmental biology, fisheries and wildlife, lake management, environmental science, and environmental study. Although the focus of this book is on Massachusetts lakes and rivers, the method for species identification, data collection, and mapping sightings of aquatic invasive species, as well as control techniques and management strategies can certainly be applied to waterbodies beyond Massachusetts. That is, it can provide valuable lessons for those who are concerned about same invasive animals and plants in a freshwater system (lake or river). Indeed, some success story sites on invasive species management are located in other states/regions/countries. Invasive species know no boundaries and they can come from, spread to, and reestablish in surrounding areas. Therefore, an integrated, strategic approach needs to be taken (Henne et al. 2005; Lavergne and Molofsky 2006; Wong and Gerstenberger 2015) and individuals from local towns, watersheds, regions, states, and even international communities dealing with invasive species need to work together and learn from each other via exchange of information and development of technology (Ding et al. 2006; Wong et al. 2017; Abrahams et al. 2019). Doing so would avoid and/ or minimize ecological and economic impacts from aquatic invasive species in lakes and rivers.

NOTES

1. www.city-data.com/states/Massachusetts-Topography.html
2. See more from www.cd3systems.com/
3. According to an email from Ann Rose, resident at Charlton, MA, to Diane Manganaro, Massachusetts Department of Environmental Protection, dated September 21, 2021.

REFERENCES

Abrahams, B., N. Sitasa, and K.J. Esler. 2019. Exploring the dynamics of research collaborations by mapping social networks in invasion science. *Journal of Environmental Management* 229: 27–37.

Adrian-Kalchhauser, I., and P. Burkhardt-Holm. 2016. An eDNA assay to monitor a globally invasive fish species from flowing freshwater. *PLoS ONE* 11(1): e0147558.

Ardura, A., A. Zaiko, J.L. Martinez, A. Samulioviene, A. Semenova, and E. Garcia-Vazquez. 2015. eDNA and specific primers for early detection of invasive species—A case study on the bivalve rangia cuneata, Currently spreading in Europe. *Marine Environmental Research* 112: 48–55.

Beck, K.G., Z. Kenneth, J.D. Schardt, J. Stone, R.R. Lukens, S. Reichard, J. Randall, A.A. Cangelosi, D. Cooper, and J.P. Thompson. 2008. Invasive species defined in a policy context: Recommendations from the federal invasive species advisory committee. *Invasive Plant Science and Management* 1: 414–421.

Bidwell, J.R. 2010. Range expansion of dreissena polymorpha: A Review of Major Dispersal Vectors in Europe and North America. Backhuys. In: G. Van der Velde, S. Rajagopal, and A. Bij de Vaate (eds). *The Zebra Mussel in Europe*. Leiden: Backhuys, pp. 69–78.

Borges, A.K.M., T.P.R. Oliveira, I.L. Rosa, F. Braga-Pereira, H.A.C. Ramos, L.A. Rocha, and R.R.N. Alves. 2021. Caught in the (Inter)net: Online trade of ornamental fish in Brazil. *Biological Conservation*. DOI: 10.1016/j.biocon.2021.109344.

Bossenbroek, J.M., C.E. Kraft, and J.C. Nekola. 2001. Prediction of long-distance dispersal using gravity models: Zebra mussel invasion of inland lakes. *Ecological Applications* 11: 1778–1788.

Bourlat, S.J., A. Borja, J. Gilbert, M.I. Taylor, N. Davies, S.B. Weisberg, J.F. Griffith, T. Lettieri, D. Field, J. Benzie, F.O. Glöckner, N. Rodríguez-Ezpeleta, D.P. Faith, T.P. Bean, and M. Obst. 2013. Genomics in marine monitoring: New opportunities for assessing marine health status. *Marine Pollution Bulletin* 74(1): 19–31.

Buchan, L.A.J., and D.K. Padilla. 2000. Predicting the likelihood of Eurasian watermilfoil presence in Lakes, A macrophyte monitoring tool. *Ecological Applications* 10: 1442–1455.

Chase, R.F., and W.H. Wong. 2015. *Standard Operating Procedure: Field Equipment Decontamination to Prevent the Spread of Invasive Aquatic Organisms*. Cambridge: Massachusetts Department of Environmental Protection (File # CN 59.6.29 pp).

Cheater, M. 1992. Alien invasion. *Nature Conservancy* 92: 24–29.

Clavero, M., and E. García-Berthou. 2005. Invasive species are a leading cause of animal extinctions. *Trends in Ecology and Evolution* 20(3): 110.

Colwell, H., J. Ryder, R. Nuzzo, M. Reardon, R. Holland, and W.H. Wong. 2017. Invasive Asian clams (*Corbicula fluminea*) recorded from 2001 to 2016 in Massachusetts, USA. *Management of Biological Invasions* 8(4): 507–515.

Comeau, S., R.S. Ianniello, W.H. Wong, and S.L. Gerstenberger. 2015. Boat decontamination with hot water spray: Field validation. In: W.H. Wong, and S.L Gerstenberger (eds) *Biology and Management of Invasive Quagga and Zebra Mussels in the Western United States*. Florida: CRC Press, pp. 161–173.

Comeau, S., S. Rainville, W. Baldwin, E. Austin, S.L. Gerstenberger, C. Cross, and W.H. Wong. 2011. Susceptibility of quagga mussels (*Dreissena rostriformis bugensis*) to hot-water sprays as a means of watercraft decontamination. *Biofouling* 27(3): 267–274.

Cuthbert, R.N., Z. Pattison, N.G. Taylor, L. Verbrugge, C. Diagne, D.A. Ahmed, B. Leroy, E. Angulo, E. Briski, C. Capinha, J.A. Catford, T. Dalu, F. Essl, R.E. Gozlan, P.J. Haubrock, M. Kourantidou, A.M. Kramer, D. Renault, and R.J. Wasserman. 2021. Global economic costs of aquatic invasive alien species. *Science of the Total Environment*. DOI: 10.1016/j.scitotenv.2021.145238.

Darling, J.A., and A.R. Mahon. 2011. From molecules to management: adopting DNA-based methods for monitoring biological invasions in aquatic environments. *Environmental Research* 111: 978–988.

Davis, E.A., W.H. Wong, and W.N. Harman. 2015. Distilled white vinegar (5% acetic acid) as a potential decontamination method for adult zebra mussels. *Management of Biological Invasions* 6(4): 423–428.

Davis, E.A., W.H. Wong, and W.N. Harman. 2016. Livewell flushing to remove zebra mussel (driessena polymorpha) veligers. *Management of Biological Invasions* 7(4): 399–403.

De Ventura, L., N. Weissert, R. Tobias, K. Kopp, and J. Jokela. 2016. Overland transport of recreational boats as a spreading vector of zebra mussel dreissena polymorpha. *Biological Invasions* 18: 1451–1466.

De Ventura, L., N. Weissert, R. Tobias, K. Kopp, and J. Jokela. 2017. Identifying target factors for interventions to increase boat cleaning in order to prevent spread of invasive species. *Management of Biological Invasions* 8(1): 71–84.

DFO. 2020. Advice on the Use of Targeted Environmental DNA (eDNA) Analysis for the Management of Aquatic Invasive Species and Species at Risk. DFO Can. Science Advisory Secretariat. Science Advisory Report. 2020/058.

Diagne, C., B. Leroy, A.C. Vaissière, R.E. Gozlan, D. Roiz, I. Jarić, J.M. Salles, C.J.A. Bradshaw, and F. Courchamp. 2021. High and rising economic costs of biological invasions worldwide. *Nature* DOI: 10.1038/s41586-021-03405-6.

Ding, J.Q., R. Reardon, W.D. Fu, Y. Wu, H. Zheng. 2006. Biological control of invasive plants through collaboration between China and the United States of America: A perspective. *Biological Invasions* 8(7): 1439–145.

DiVittorio J. 2015. Equipment Inspection and Cleaning: The First Step in an Integrated Approach to Prevent the Spread of Aquatic Invasive Species and Pests. In W.H. Wong, and S.L. Gerstenberger (eds.). *Biology and Management of Invasive Quagga and Zebra Mussels in the Western United States*. London: CRC Press, pp. 225–246.

Dougherty, M.M., E.R. Larson, M.A. Renshaw, C.A. Gantz, S.P. Egan, D.M. Erickson, and D.M. Lodge. 2016. Environmental DNA (eDNA) detects the invasive rusty crayfish *Orconectes rusticus* at low abundances. *Journal of Applied Ecology* 53(3): 722–732.

Dudgeon, D., A.H. Arthington, M.O. Gessner, Z.-I. Kawabata, D.J. Knowler, C. Leveque, R.J. Naiman, R.A.H. Prieur, D. Soto, M.L.J. Stiassny, and C.A. Sullivan. 2006. Freshwater biodiversity: Importance, threats, status and conservation challenges. *Biological Reviews* 81: 163–182.

Durkin, P.R. 2008. *Fluridone: Human Health and Ecological Risk Assessment Final Report. Submitted to Paul Mistretta, USDA/Forest Service*. Atlanta, GA: Southern Region, p. 115.

Durkin, P.R. 2012. Aminocyclopyrachlor: Human Health and Ecological Risk Assessment Final Report. Submitted to Dr. Harold Thistle, USDA Forest Service Forest Health Technology Enterprise Team. Morgantown, WV, 26505.212 p.

Eichmiller, J.J., S.E. Best, and P.W. Sorensen. 2016. Effects of temperature and trophic state on degradation of environmental DNA in lake water. *Environmental Science & Technology* 50: 1859–1867.

Frischer, M.E., K.L. Kelly, and S.A. Nierzwicki-Bauer. 2012. Accuracy and reliability of dreissena spp. Larvae detection by cross-polarized light microscopy, Imaging flow cytometry, and polymerase chain reaction assays. *Lake and Reservoir Management* 28(3):265–276.

Gallardo B., and D.C. Aldridge. 2013. Evaluating the combined threat of climate change and biological invasions on endangered species. *Biological Conservation* 160: 225–233.

García-Berthou, E., C. Alcaraz, Q. Pou-Rovira, L. Zamora, G. Coenders, and C. Feo. 2005. Introduction pathways and establishment rates of invasive aquatic species in Europe. *Canadian Journal of Fisheries and Aquatic Sciences* 62: 453–463.

Gingera, T.D., R. Bajno, M.F. Docker, and J.D. Reist. 2017. Environmental DNA as a detection tool for zebra mussels *Dreissena polymorpha* (Pallas, 1771) at the forefront of an invasion event in Lake Winnipeg, Manitoba, Canada. *Management of Biological Invasions* 8: 287–300.

Glomski, L.A.M., A.G. Poovey, and K.D. Getsinger. 2006. Effect of carfentrazone-ethyl on three aquatic macrophytes. *Journal of Aquatic Plant Management* 44(1): 67–69.

Goldberg, C.S., A. Sepulveda, A. Ray, J. Baumgardt, and L.P. Waits. 2013. Environmental DNA as a new method for early detection of New Zealand mudsnails (*Potamopyrgus antipodarum*). *Freshwater Science* 32(3): 792–800.

Goldberg, C.S., C.R. Turner, K. Deiner, K.E. Klymus, P.F. Thomsen, M.A. Murphy, S.F. Spear, A. McKee, S.J. Oyler-McCance, R.S. Cornman, M.B. Laramie, A.R. Mahon, R.F. Lance, D.S. Pilliod, K.M. Strickler, L.P. Waits, A.K. Fremier, T. Takahara, J.E. Herder, and P. Taberlet. 2016. Critical considerations for the application of environmental DNA methods to detect aquatic species. *Methods in Ecology and Evolution* 7(11):1299–1307.

Golebie, E., C.J. van Riper, C. Suski, and R. Stedman. 2021 Reducing invasive species transport among recreational anglers: The importance of values and risk perceptions. *North American Journal of Fisheries Management*. DOI:10.1002/nafm.10696.

Green, S.J., and E.D. Grosholz. 2020. Functional eradication as a framework for invasive species control. *Frontiers in Ecology and the Environment*. DOI:10.1002/fee.2277.

Gurevitch, J., and D.K. Padilla. 2004. Are invasive species a major cause of extinctions? *Trends in Ecology and Evolution* 19(9): 470–474.

Hajibabaei, M., G.A.C. Singer, P.D.N. Herbert, and D.A. Hickey. 2007. DNA barcoding: How it complements taxonomy, Molecular phylogenetics and population genetics. *Trends in Genetics* 32(4): 167–172.

Henne, D.C., C.J. Lindgren, T.S. Gabor, H.R. Murkin, and R.E. Roughley. 2005. An integrated management strategy for the control of purple loosestrife *Lythrum salicaria* L. (Lythraceae) in the netley-libau marsh, Southern Manitoba. *Biological Control* 32: 319–325.

Hewitt, C.L., S. Gollasch, and D. Minchin. 2009. The Vessel as a Vector—Biofouling, Ballastwater and Sediments. In: G. Rilov and J.A. Crooks (eds). *Biological Invasions in Marine Ecosystems*. Berlin: Springer, p. 117–131.

Hulme, P.E. 2009. Trade, Transport and trouble: Managing invasive species pathways in an era of globalization. *Journal of Applied Ecology* 46: 10–18.

IPCC (The Intergovernmental Panel on Climate Change). 2021. www.ipcc.ch/2021/08/09/ar6-wg1-20210809-pr/ (Accessed October 14, 2021).

Johnson, L.E., A. Ricciardi, and J.T. Carlton. 2001. Overland dispersal of aquatic invasive species: A risk assessment of transient recreational boating. *Ecological Applications* 11: 1789–1799.

Kappel, M., S.L. Gerstenberger, R.F. McMahon, and W.H. Wong. 2015. Thermal Tolerance of Invasive Quagga Mussels in Lake Mead National Recreation Area. In: W.H. Wong and S.L (eds). *Gerstenberger Biology and Management of Invasive Quagga and Zebra Mussels in the Western United States*. London: CRC Press, pp. 83–93.

Kelly, N.E., K. Wantola, E. Weisz, and N.D. Yan. 2013. Recreational boats as a vector of secondary spread for aquatic invasive species and native crustacean zooplankton. *Biological Invasions* 15: 509–519.

Lance1, R.F., K.E. Klymus, C.A. Richter, X. Guan, H.L. Farrington, M.R. Carr, N. Thompson, D.C. Chapman, and K.L. Baerwaldt. 2017. Experimental observations on the decay of environmental DNA from bighead and silver carps. *Management of Biological Invasions* 8(3): 343–359.

Langley, L., L. Rhodes, and M. Stroman. 2004. *Guidance for Aquatic Plant Management in Lakes and Ponds As It Relates to the Wetlands Protection Act*. Cambridge, MA: Massachusetts Department of Environmental Protection, Wetlands/Waterways Program. Boston, p. 12.

Lavergne, S., and J. Molofsky. 2006. Control strategies for the invasive reed canary grass (*Phalaris arundinacea* L.) in north American wetlands: The need for an integrated management plan. *Natural Areas Journal* 26(2): 208–214.

Lembi, C.A., B.G. Ritenour, E.M. Iverson, and E.C. Forss. 1978. The effects of vegetation removal by grass carp on water chemistry and phytoplankton in Indiana ponds. *Transactions of the American Fisheries Society* 107(1): 161–171.

Les, D. 2002. Non-indigenous aquatic plants: A garden of earthly delight? *LakeLine* 22(2):20–24.

Leslie, A.J. Jr., J.M. Van Dyke, R.S. Hestand, and B.Z. Thompson. 1987. Management of aquatic plants in multi-use lakes with grass carp (*Ctenopharyngodon Idella*). *Lake and Reservoir Management* 3(1): 266–276.

Leung, B., J.M. Bossenbroek, and D.M. Lodge. 2006. Boats, pathways, and aquatic biological invasions: estimating dispersal potential with gravity models. *Biological Invasions* 8: 241–254.

Leung, B., J.M. Drake, and D.M. Lodge. 2004. Predicting invasions: Propagule pressure and the gravity of allee effects. *Ecology* 85: 1651–1660.

MA DAR (Massachusetts Department of Agricultural Resources) and MassDEP (Massachusetts Department of Environmental Protection). 2010. Hydrogen Peroxide, Peracetic Acid and Sodium Percarbonate. www.mass.gov/doc/sodium-carbonate-peroxyhydrate-and-hydrogen-peroxide/download (Accessed August 2, 2021).

MA DAR (Massachusetts Department of Agricultural Resources) and MassDEP (Massachusetts Department of Environmental Protection). 2014. Imazamox. www.mass.gov/doc/imazamox/download (Accessed July 10, 2021).

MA DAR (Massachusetts Department of Agricultural Resources) and MassDEP (Massachusetts Department of Environmental Protection). 2019. Florpyrauxifen-benzyl. www.mass.gov/doc/florpyrauxifen-benzyl/download (Accessed July 22, 2021).

MA DCR (Massachusetts Department of Conservation and Recreation). 2007. *Standard Operating Procedures: Using Hand Pulling and Benthic Barriers to Control Pioneer Populations of Non-Native Aquatic Species A Guide for Volunteers*. Boston, MA: MA DCR, p. 27.

MA DCR (Massachusetts Department of Conservation and Recreation). 2010. *Aquatic Invasive Species Assessment and Management Plan*. Boston, MA: MA DCR, p. 39.

MA DCR (Massachusetts Department of Conservation and Recreation). 2016. A Guide to Aquatic Plants in Massachusetts. Lakes and Ponds Program. P. 32.

MacIsaac, H.J., J.V.M. Borbely, J.R. Muirhead, and P.A. Graniero. 2004. Backcasting and forecasting biological invasions of inland lakes. *Ecological Applications* 14: 773–783.

Mangiante, M.J., A.J.S. Davis, S. Panlasigui, M.E. Neilson, I. Pfingsten, P.L. Fuller, and J.A. Darling. 2018. Trends in nonindigenous aquatic species richness in the united states reveal shifting spatial and temporal patterns of species introductions. *Aquatic Invasions* 13(3): 323–338.

MassDEP (Massachusetts Department of Environmental Protection). 2018. Consolidated Assessment and Listing Methodology (CALM) Guidance Manual for the 2018 Reporting Cycle. Massachusetts Division of Watershed Management Watershed Planning Program. CN455.0.74 p.

Mattice, J.S., and L.L. Dye. 1976. Thermal tolerance of adult Asiatic clam. *Thermal Ecology* 2: 130–135.

Mattson, M.D., P.L. Godfrey, R.A. Barletta, and A. Aiello. 2004a. *Eutrophication and Aquatic Plant Management in Massachusetts: Final Generic Environmental Impact Report*. Cambridge, MA: Commonwealth of Massachusetts, Executive Office of Environmental Affairs Commonwealth of Massachusetts, p. 514.

Mattson, M.D., P.L. Godfrey, R.A. Barletta, and A. Aiello. 2004b. *Eutrophication and Aquatic Plant Management in Massachusetts: Final Generic Environmental Impact Report—Appendices*. Cambridge, MA: Commonwealth of Massachusetts, Executive Office of Environmental Affairs Commonwealth of Massachusetts, p. 181.

McComas, S. 2011. Literature Review on Controlling Aquatic Invasive Vegetation with Aquatic Herbicides Compared to Other Control Methods: Effectiveness, Impacts, and Costs. Blue Water Science, Prepared for: Minnehaha Creek Watershed District. www.clflwd.org/documents/HerbicideLitReviewReport-2011.pdf (Accessed August 16, 2021).

McDowell, W.G., A.J. Benson, and J.E. Byers. 2014. Climate controls the distribution of a widespread invasive species: Implications for future range expansion. *Freshwater Biology* 59: 847–857.

Millennium Ecosystem Assessment. 2005. *Ecosystems and Human Wellbeing: Biodiversity Synthesis.* Washington, DC: World Resources Institute.

Miralles, L., E. Dopico, F. Devlo-Delva, and E. Garcia-Vazquez. 2016. Controlling populations of invasive pygmy mussel (*Xenostrobus secures*) through citizen science and environmental DNA. *Marine Pollution Bulletin* 110(1): 127–132.

Mitzner, L. 1978. Evaluation of biological control of nuisance aquatic vegetation by grass carp. *Transactions of American Fisheries Society* 107(1): 135–145.

Mohit, S., T.B. Johnson, and S.E. Arnott. 2021. Recreational watercraft decontamination: Can current recommendations reduce aquatic invasive species spread? *Management of Biological Invasions* 12(1):148–164.

Morse, J.T. 2009. Assessing the effects of application time and temperature on the efficacy of hot-water sprays to mitigate fouling by dreissena polymorpha (zebra mussels Pallas). *Biofouling* 25: 605–610.

Muirhead, J.R., and H.J. MacIsaac. 2005. Development of inland lakes as hubs in an invasion network. *Journal of Applied Ecology* 42: 80–90.

NALMS (North American Lake Management Society) 2004. *The Use of Alum for Lake Management.* Washington, DC: NALMS, p. 3.

National Invasive Species Council (NISC). 2007. *Training and Implementation Guide for Pathway Definition, Risk Analysis and Risk Prioritization.* National Invasive Species Council Materials, p. 27. https://digitalcommons.unl.edu/natlinvasive/27.

Novoa, A., K. Dehnen-Schmutz, J. Fried, and G. Vimercati. 2017. Does public awareness increase support for invasive species management? Promising evidence across taxa and landscape types. *Biological Invasions* 19(12): 3691–3705.

Nunes, A.L., E. Tricarico, V.E. Panov, A.C. Cardoso, and S. Katsanevakis. 2015. Pathways and gateways of freshwater invasions in Europe. *Aquatic Invasions* 10(4): 359–370.

O'Reilly, C.M., et al. 2015. Rapid and Highly Variable Warming of Lake Surface Waters Around the Globe. *Geophysical Research Letters*. DOI: 10.1002/2015GL066235.

Patrick, A.E.S., and S. Florentine. 2021. Factors affecting the global distribution of hydrilla Verticillata (L. fil.) Royle: A Review. *Weed Research* 61(4): 253–271.

Pimentel, D., R. Zuniga, and D. Morrison. 2005. Update on the environmental and economic costs associated with alien-invasive species in the united states. *Ecological Economics* 52: 273–288.

Rahel, F.J., and J.D. Olden. 2008. Assessing the effects of climate change on aquatic invasive species. *Conservation Biology* 22(3): 521–533.

Rey, A., O.C. Basurko, and N. Rodríguez-Ezpeleta. 2018. The challenges and promises of genetic approaches for ballast water management. *Journal of Sea Research* 133: 134–145.

Ricciardi, A., M.E. Palmer, and N.D. Yan. 2011. Should biological invasions be managed as natural disasters? *BioScience* 61(4): 312–317.

Richardson, R.J., R.L. Roten, A.M. West, S.L. True, and A.P. Gardner. 2008. Response of selected aquatic invasive weeds to flumioxazin and carfentrazone-ethyl. *Journal of Aquatic Plant Management* 46: 154–158.

Ripple, W.J., et al. 2020. World scientists' warning of a climate emergency. *BioScience* 70(1): 8–12.

Rockwell-Postel, M., B.B. Laginhas, and B.A. Bradley. 2020. Supporting proactive management in the context of climate change: prioritizing range-shifting invasive plants based on impact. *Biological Invasions* 22: 2371–2383.

Rothlisberger, J.D., W.L. Chadderton, J. McNulty, and D.M. Lodge. 2010. Aquatic invasive species transport via trailered boats: What Is being moved, Who is moving it, and What can be done. *Fisheries* 35(3): 121–132.

Rumzie, N., R. Christopherson, S. O'Meara, Y. Passamaneck, A. Murphy, S. Pucherelli, and J. Trujillo. 2021. Costs Associated with Invasive Mussels Impacts and Management. Science and Technology Program, Research and Development Office, Final Report No. ST-2021-8142-01. Bureau of Reclamation. Denver, CO, p. 35.

Rushton, S., A. Spake, and L. Chariton. 2016. *The Unintended Consequences of Using Glyphosate (The Main Ingredient in the Herbicide Roundup).* London: Sierra Club, p. 27.

Schneider, D.W., C.D. Ellis, and K.S. Cummings. 1998. A transportation model assessment of the risk to native mussel communities from zebra mussel spread. *Conservation Biology* 12: 788–800.

Scholl, C. 2006. *Aquatic Invasive Species: A Guide for Proactive & Reactive Management.* Wisconsin: Vilas County Land and Water Conservation Department, p. 58.

Scriver, M., A. Marinich, C. Wilson, and J. Freeland. 2015. Development of Species-specific Environmental DNA (eDNA) Markers for invasive Aquatic Plants. *Aquatic Botany* 122: 27–31.

Sepulveda, A.J., N.M. Nelson, C.L. Jerde, and G. Luikart. 2020. Are environmental DNA methods ready for aquatic invasive species management? *Trends in Ecology and Evolution* 35(8): 668–678.

Sepulveda, A.J., D.R. Smith, K.M. O'Donnell, N. Owens, B. White, C.A. Richter, C.M. Merkes, S.L. Wolf, M. Rau, M.E. Neilson, W.M. Daniel, and M.E. Hunter. 2022. Using structured decision making to evaluate potential management responses to detection of dreissenid mussel (Dreissena spp.) environmental DNA. *Management of Biological Invasions* 13.

Sesin, V., R.L. Dalton, C. Boutin, S.A. Robinson, A.J. Bartlett, and F.R. Pick. 2018. Macrophytes are highly sensitive to the herbicide diquat dibromide in test systems of varying complexity. *Ecotoxicology and Environmental Safety* 165: 325–333.

Stein, B.A., and S.R. Flack. 1997. *Species Report Card: The State of U.S. Plants and Animals.* Arlington, VA: The Nature Conservancy, p. 26.

Stokstad, E. 2007. Feared quagga mussel turns up in western United States. *Science* 315: 453–453.

Stranga, Y., and S. Katsanevakis. 2021. Eight years of bioinvasions records: Patterns and trends in alien and cryptogenic species records. *Management of Biological Invasions* 12(2): 221–239.

Strid, A., W. Hanson, A. Cross, and J. Jenkins. 2018. Triclopyr General Fact Sheet; National Pesticide Information Center, Oregon State University Extension Services. npic.orst.edu/factsheets/triclopyrgen.html. (Accessed September 12, 2021).

Thomsen, P.F., J. Kielgast, L.L. Iversen, C. Wiuf, M. Rasmussen, M.T.P. Gilbert, L. Orlando, and E. Willerslev. 2011. Monitoring endangered freshwater biodiversity using environmental DNA. *Molecular Ecology* 21(11): 2565–2573.

Thomsen, P.F., and E. Willerslev. 2014. Environmental DNA—An emerging tool in conservation for monitoring past and present biodiversity. *Biological Conservation* 183: 4–18.

Trebitz, A.S., J.C. Hoffman, J.A. Darling, E.M. Pilgrim, J.R. Kelly, E.A. Brown, W.L. Chadderton, S.P. Egan, E.K. Grey, S.A. Hashsham, K.E. Klymus, A.R. Mahon, J.L. Ram, M.T. Schultz, C.A. Stepien, and J.C. Schardt. 2017. Early detection monitoring for aquatic non-indigenous species: Optimizing surveillance, incorporating advanced technologies, and identifying research needs. *Journal Environmental Management* 202: 299–310.

U.S. Department of the Interior. 2016. *Safeguarding America's Lands and Waters from Invasive Species: A National Framework for Early Detection and Rapid Response.* Washington, DC: U.S. Department of the Interior, p. 55.

U.S. Department of the Interior. 2021. *U.S. Department of the Interior Invasive Species Strategic Plan, Fiscal Years 2021–2025.* Washington, DC: U.S. Department of the Interior, p. 54.

U.S. EPA (Environmental Protection Agency). 1998. EPA Red Facts Triclopyr. https://www3.epa.gov/pesticides/chem_search/reg_actions/reregistration/fs_G-82_1-Oct-98.pdf (Accessed October 5, 2021).

U.S. Geological Survey (USGS). 2020. *Nonindigenous Aquatic Species Database.* Gainesville, FL. https://nas.er.usgs.gov (Accessed October 10, 2020).

Vander Zanden, M.J., and JD. Olden. 2008. A management framework for preventing the secondary spread of aquatic invasive species. *Canadian Journal of Fisheries and Aquatic Sciences* 65: 1512–1522.

Wagner, K. 2001. Chapter 7 Management Techniques Within the Lake or Reservoir. In: C. Holdren, W. Jones, and J. Taggart (eds). *Managing Lake and Reservoirs.* Madison, WI: USEPA/NALMS, pp. 215–306.

Wagner, K. 2004. *The Practical Guide to Lake Management in Massachusetts A Companion to the Final Generic Environmental Impact Report on Eutrophication and Aquatic Plant Management in Massachusetts.* Cambridge, MA: Commonwealth of Massachusetts, Executive Office of Environmental Affairs Commonwealth of Massachusetts. 160 p.

Wan, Z., Z. Shi, A. Nie, J. Chen, and Z. Wang. 2021. Risk assessment of marine invasive species in Chinese ports introduced by the global shipping network. *Marine Pollution Bulletin* 173: 112950.

Wilcove DS, Rothstein D, Bulow J, Phillips Al, Losos E. 1998. Quantifying threats to imperiled species in the United States. *Bioscience* 48: 607–615.

Wong, W.H., and S.L. Gerstenberger. 2011. Quagga mussels in the western United States: Monitoring and management. *Aquatic Invasions* 6(2): 125–129.

Wong, W.H., and S.L. Gerstenberger. 2015. *Biology and Management of Invasive Quagga and Zebra Mussels in the Western United States.* Boca Raton, FL: CRC Press, p. 566.

Wong, W.H., M. Piria, F.P.L. Collas, P. Simonovic, and E. Tricarico. 2017. Management of invasive species in inland waters: Technology development and international cooperation. *Management of Biological Invasions* 8(3): 267–272.

WSSA (Weed Science Society of America). Summary of herbicide mechanism of action according to the Weed Science Society of America (WSSA). https://wssa.net/wp-content/uploads/WSSA-Mechanism-of-Action.pdf (Accessed November 5, 2021).

Zaiko, A., X. Pochon, E. Garcia-Vazquez, S. Olenin, and S.A. Wood. 2018. Advantages and limitations of environmental DNA/RNA tools for marine biosecurity: Management and surveillance of non-indigenous species. *Frontiers in Marine Science* 5: 322 (17 pages).

Zook, B., and S. Phillips. 2015. Uniform Minimum Protocols and Standards for Watercraft Interception Programs for Dreissenid Mussels in the Western United States. In W.H. Wong, and S.L. Gerstenberger (eds). *Biology and Management of Invasive Quagga and Zebra Mussels in the Western United States.* London: CRC Press, pp. 176–204.

2 Asian Clam (*Corbicula fluminea*)

ABSTRACT

Invasive Asian clams (*Corbicula fluminea*) were first recorded in the state of Massachusetts in 2001, in a section of the Charles River running through Watertown. As of 2019, the species has been found in 32 different bodies of water throughout state. All clams have been found in the warmer parts of the state, where water temperatures are above the clams' long-term incipient lower thermal limit; therefore, the increasing abundance of the Asian clam may be a sign and a result of rising temperatures in this region. The map of infested waterbodies created as a result of this project will serve to increase the general public's awareness of the issue as well as aid water resource managers in tracking the extent of infestations in Massachusetts, measures which will be helpful in preventing the further spread of the clams to new waterbodies. This report also describes the biological characteristics and potential invasive pathways of these invasive clams and review alternative management tools to control the species chemically, mechanically, and biologically.

INTRODUCTION

Taxonomic Hierarchy (ITIS 2021)

Kingdom	Animalia
Subkingdom	Bilateria
Infrakingdom	Protostomia
Superphylum	Lophozoa
Phylum	Mollusca
Class	Bivalvia
Subclass	Heterodonta
Order	Veneroida
Superfamily	Corbiculoidea
Family	Corbiculidae
Genus	*Corbicula*

The Asian clam is a small bivalve mollusk. Its light-colored shell often has concentric sulcations, with anterior and posterior lateral teeth that have many serrations (Foster et al. 2019). While light shells are the predominant shell type in the northeast United States, darker morphs can be found in the southwestern United States. This clam is generally less than 50 mm in shell length. In the Columbia River (CR), the zooplankton community of the lower CR is dominated by recently released juvenile *C. fluminea* suspended on turbulent water currents in late summer and early autumn (Dexter et al. 2015; 2020). The Asian clam is also a self-fertilizing hermaphroditic species which can produce up to 570 larvae per day, resulting in more than 68,000 larvae produced per individual per year (McMahon 1999). This enables a single individual to initiate reproduction in isolation and has been shown to lead to rapid reproduction (Gomes et al. 2016). The unique androgenetic reproductive biology of Asian clams where maternal chromosomes are extruded from the fertilized egg as two polar bodies during first meiosis leaves only the male pronucleus present in the egg. However, there is no second meiosis. The male pronucleus becomes the metaphase chromosomes during the first mitosis. Thus, only male genetic material is left in the developing embryo. More detailed androgenetic reproduction in *C. fluminea* can be found from Ishibashi et al. (2003). Suspended newly released juveniles usually settle by the time they reach shell lengths of ≤5 mm using a single byssal thread to attach to hard substratum. However, adults can leave the substratum to be carried long distances downstream over the substratum by water currents to settle in areas of slower water flow. Food availability has been implicated as an important factor to the growth and reproductive capacity of Asian clams in the lower Rhine River, Germany (Viergutz et al. 2012). Temperature can affect individual growth rate (Cataldo and Boltovskoy 1998) as well as clam shell size and body mass (Denton et al. 2012; Rosa et al. 2012). The species has demonstrated a high degree of both physiological and ecological plasticity, making the Asian clam hard to control and manage (Coughlan et al. 2018).

ECOLOGICAL IMPACTS

The Asian clam, *Corbicula fluminea*, is considered to be one of the most ecologically and economically impactful aquatic invasive species in global aquatic ecosystems (Sousa et al. 2008). Over time, *C. fluminea* has spread from its native range in Eastern Asia and Africa to Europe, North America, South America, and other areas of the world. The initial introduction of Asian clams in North America in 1938 is thought to have been due to transoceanic ballast water exchange and use by Chinese immigrants as a food source (Counts 1981; 1986; Sousa et al. 2008). By the 1960s, the Asian clam had spread through the US waterways and reached as far as the Atlantic coast (McMahon and Bogan 2001). Asian clams have now established themselves in the United States above the 40° latitude line, where waters meet their temperature tolerance. The species' invasive success and wide dispersion are mainly owed to its natural characteristics, including rapid growth, early sexual maturity, short life span, high fecundity, extensive dispersal capacities, tolerance to variable environmental variables, and their association with human activities (McMahon 2002; Karatayev et al. 2005; Sousa et al. 2008; Lucy et al. 2012). As shown in Figure 2.1, clams are able to attach to drifting plant materials, shells, or pebbles (Minchin and Boelens 2018). In a field experiment to study survival and growth of captively reared juveniles of four native mussel species in situ exposures at 17 sites in the Rockcastle River system, Kentucky, it is found that growth of these mussels was negatively related with the abundance of Asian clams, but survival rates were not affected (Haag et al. 2021). In recent years, Asian clams continue to infest new waters as a result of human activity, including ballast water transport and discharge, fish bait, release from aquariums, tourism boats (Sousa et al. 2008), and subsequently through natural water dispersal.

Like many other bivalve mollusks such as zebra or quagga mussels (Baker et al. 1998; Wong et al. 2003), Asian clams are suspension feeders that can drastically change the ecosystem.

FIGURE 2.1 An 8-mm clam attached by a byssal thread to drifting plant material retrieved using a dredge (*left*) and a byssal thread of a clam removed from the mesh of a dredge (Minchin and Boelens 2018).

Asian Clam (*Corbicula fluminea*)

Feeding behavior studies of Asian clams demonstrated that adult clams in the Columbia River at the Pacific Northwest selectively feed on flagellates but avoid feeding on cyanobacteria (Bolam et al. 2019). It is also found that *C. fluminea* veligers are associated with cyanobacteria and higher water temperatures in the Columbia River (Hassett et al. 2017). In the Meuse River in Northwest Europe, the filter feeding of Asian clams caused a 70% decrease in phytoplankton abundance, thereby impacting the entire food web (Pigneur et al. 2014). In addition, Asian clams can also perform pedal feeding on benthic microbes such as flagellates, bacteria, and diatoms, even in the presence of abundant prey in the water column (Hakenkamp et al. 2001).

Although Asian clams have many negative impacts, there are also a few positive effects that stem from their presence. Empty shells can be used by other species as shelters, and the clams are a food source for some species at higher trophic levels, such as cyprinid species (e.g., *Barbus* spp. and *Luciobarbus* spp., *Cyprinus carpio* Linnaeus, 1758) and pumpkinseed sunfish *Lepomis gibbosus* (Linnaeus, 1758) (Pereira et al. 2016 and references therein).

Economic Impacts

Asian clams have significantly reduced ecosystem services and caused economic damages. It has been reported to have cost the United States approximately $1 billion per year to control Asian clams since 1980 (Pimentel et al. 2005). This is due to the damage Asian clams cause to equipment, such as water intake pipes, electric power plant cooling systems, and sewage treatment plants (McMahon 2002; Muller and Baur 2011). The ecological damage Asian clams cause is also significant. Asian clams are filter feeders that consume large amounts of microscopic plants and animals, creating more competition for food sources among native, aquatic life (Robinson 2004). Asian clams can reach densities greater than 6,000 clams/m^2 in rivers (Robinson 2004; Sheehan et al. 2014). Such expansive coverage alters the benthic community and has a large impact on macroinvertebrate communities (Coughlan et al. 2018). The clams also sequester a large portion of the available carbon in the water (Muller and Baur 2011). Native unionid mussel species may be threatened with displacement by the Asian clam (Robinson 2004), although this is not always considered to be the case (McMahon and Bogan 2001).

MONITORING AND SIGHTINGS

The Massachusetts Department of Environmental Protection (MassDEP) is committed to protect, enhance, and restore the quality and value of the waters of the Commonwealth with guidance by the Federal Clean Water Act. It works to secure the environmental, recreational, and public health benefits of clean water for the citizens of Massachusetts. As a result, a long-term statewide benthic macroinvertebrate biomonitoring program has been in place since 1973. Benthic community diversity data is one of the indicators used by WPP staff to assess the health of a waterbody. Benthic samples have been collected from 410 different waterbodies statewide. The standard operating procedures, including sampling methodology, species identification, quality control and assurance, can be found in Nuzzo (2003). Sites with Asian clams were mapped as a data layer with ArcGIS® ArcMap 10.1 (ESRI, Redlands, California). Based on MassDEP's own records, Asian clams were only detected from 2 out of the 410 waterbodies statewide (Table 2.1). This ratio (2/410) is low because not every waterbody in the state is part of the benthic biomonitoring program.

To gain a more complete record of Asian clams in Massachusetts, sightings reported by the Massachusetts Department of Conservation and Recreation (Jim Straub, personal communication) and US Geological Survey (USGS) (Foster et al. 2019) staff were also included. The first documented sighting of live Asian clams in Massachusetts was in a section of the Charles River in Watertown, Massachusetts, in 2001 (Foster et al. 2019). In Massachusetts, as of 2016, there were a total of 25 sampling sites from 24 waterbodies with Asian clams known to MassDEP (Colwell et al. 2017). From 2001 to 2018, Asian clams have been found in 33 waterbodies, including 7 rivers and 26 ponds/lakes (Figure 2.2 and Table 2.1). These sightings are within 14 Massachusetts watersheds (Table 2.2 and Figure 2.2). The Asian clam has also been

TABLE 2.1
Latitude and Longitude for Each Waterbody Shown in Figure 2.1 and Source of Report

Site Number	First Year of Presence Report	Waterbody	Longitude	Latitude	Reporting Agency	Source of the Report
1	2001	Charles River	−71.18164	42.36057	MassDEP, USGS	DEP: Charles River Watershed 2002–2006 Water Quality Assessment Report 72-AC-4 CN136.5 April 2008, DEP: 2007018 Benthic Sample ID, USGS 8/22/2016 http://nas.er.usgs.gov/default.aspx
2	2005	Congamond Lakes (Middle Basin)	−72.75593101	42.02495588	MA DCR, USGS	DCR Data from Lakes and Ponds, 2005, and USGS 8/22/2016 http://nas.er.usgs.gov/default.aspx
3	2005	Congamond Lakes (North Basin)	NA	NA	MA DCR	DCR Data from Lakes and Ponds, 2005
4	2005	Congamond Lakes (South Basin)	NA	NA	MA DCR	DCR Data from Lakes and Ponds, 2005
5	2005	Fort Meadow Reservoir	−71.54811073	42.36864846	MA DCR, USGS	DCR: Lakes and Ponds, 2007, USGS 8/22/2016 http://nas.er.usgs.gov/default.aspx
6	2005	Tispaquin Pond	−70.85731719	41.86342594	MA DCR, USGS	DCR: Lakes and Ponds, 2006, USGS 8/22/2016 http://nas.er.usgs.gov/default.aspx
7	2005	Webster Lake	−71.84417968	42.04063346	MA DCR, USGS	DCR: Lakes and Ponds, 2005, USGS 8/22/2016 http://nas.er.usgs.gov/default.aspx
8	2006	East Brimfield Reservoir	−72.13218404	42.11613205	MA DCR	DCR: Lakes and Ponds, 2007, DCR: National Heritage 2006 DFW T. French, DCR: Lakes and Ponds, 2007
9	2006	Long Pond	−70.94455336	41.80145728	MA DCR	DCR: Lakes and Ponds, 2006
10	2007	Fivemile Pond	−72.51066308	42.14168287	MA DCR, USGS	DRC: Lakes and Ponds, 2007, USGS 8/22/2016 http://nas.er.usgs.gov/default.aspx
11	2007	Lake Sabbatia	−71.10816736	41.94456101	MA DCR, USGS	DCR: Lakes and Ponds, 2007, USGS 8/22/2016 http://nas.er.usgs.gov/default.aspx

Asian Clam (*Corbicula fluminea*)

#	Year	Location	Longitude	Latitude	Source	Reference
12	2007	Mashpee Pond	−70.4697269	41.66106628	MA DCR, USGS	DCR: National Heritage 2007 E. Nedeau, USGS 8/22/2016 http://nas.er.usgs.gov/default.aspx
13	2007	Oldham Pond	−70.8364494	42.06641901	MA DCR	DCR: J. Cordeiro 2007
14	2007	Sampson Pond	−70.75012337	41.85070814	MA DCR	DCR: Lakes and Ponds, 2007
15	2007	Winnecunnet Pond	−71.13126679	41.97093302	MA DCR	DCR: National Heritage 2007 E. Nedeau
16	2010	Middle Pond	−70.41564	41.66864	USGS	USGS 8/22/2016 http://nas.er.usgs.gov/default.aspx
17	2010	Norton Reservoir	−71.19718046	41.98368621	USGS	USGS 8/22/2016 http://nas.er.usgs.gov/default.aspx
18	2010	Taunton River	−71.07509	41.9031	USGS	USGS 8/22/2016 http://nas.er.usgs.gov/default.asp
19	2010	Taunton River	−70.95663889	41.93381794	USGS	USGS 8/22/2016 http://nas.er.usgs.gov/default.aspx
20	2013	Bennett Pond	−71.87779605	42.11796353	Individual	Personal communication 2/1/2017, Joy Traha
21	2013	Massapoag Lake	−71.177528	42.103486	Individual	Personal communication 2/1/2017, Joy Traha
22	2014	Nemasket River	−70.94243923	41.93623946	Individual	Personal communication 2/1/2017, Joy Traha
23	2014	Unnamed Forest Park Tributary	−72.56556396	42.07983422	MassDEP	14-C001–05, 14-C008–05
24	2015	Blackstone River	−71.61710088	42.09218317	Individual	Personal communication 2/1/2017, Joy Traha
25	2015	Hamblin Pond	−70.410532	41.663433	Individual	Personal communication 8/31/2016, Ken Wagner
26	2015	Spy Pond	−71.15275255	42.40706673	USGS	USGS 8/22/2016 http://nas.er.usgs.gov/default.aspx
27	2016	Concord River	−71.336	42.479	FWS	Personal communication 11/8/2016 Eileen McGourty, FWS
28	2016	Dudley Pond	−71.374	42.33	Wayland Surface Water Quality Committee	Personal communication, Mike Lowery, Wayland Surface Water Quality Committee, 10/24/2016
29	2016	Lake Cochituate-Carling Basin	−71.370429	42.30029	DCR	Personal communication, Tom Flannery 10/21/2016 DCR

(Continued)

TABLE 2.1 (Continued)

Site Number	First Year of Presence Report	Waterbody	Longitude	Latitude	Reporting Agency	Source of the Report
30	2016	Lake Cochituate-Middle Basin	−71.374753	42.310286	DCR	Personal communication, Tom Flannery 10/21/2016 DCR
31	2016	Sudbury River	−71.394404	42.335319	FWS	Personal communication, 9/6/2016, Eileen McGourty
32	2017	Heart Pond	−71.387734	42.565745	MassDEP	Fish Servey 5/23/2017
33	2018	Whitins Pond	NA	NA	MassDEP	Therese Beaudoin

Asian Clam (*Corbicula fluminea*)

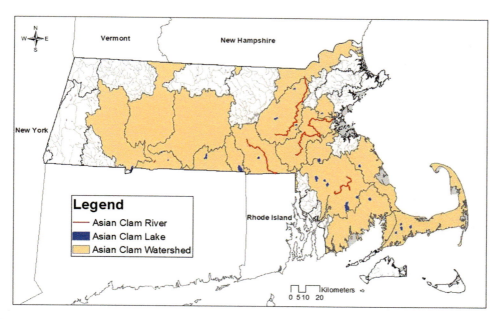

FIGURE 2.2 Distribution map depicting *Corbicula fluminea* in Massachusetts from 2001 to 2018.

recently confirmed in Onota Lake within the Housatonic River Watershed at Pittsfield[1] and Quinsigamond Lake within the Blackstone River Watershed between the City of Worcester and the Town of Shrewsbury.[2] The distribution of Asian clams throughout the state in rivers and ponds and the affected watersheds is also highlighted in Figure 2.2. Most of these waterbodies are in the southern and eastern parts of the state (Figure 2.2). Asian clams were found in both brackish and freshwater sections of the Taunton River (Colwell et al. 2017), signaling dispersion across various types of aquatic habitat. Table 2.1 provides the name of the waterbodies, as well as the latitude and longitude of a sampling site, the agency(s) that reported the sighting, and the more specific report source(s). The figure and table only represent sighting data from during or before the year 2018. Seen as the most widely distributed aquatic nuisance species in the contiguous United States (McMahon and Bogan 2001), Asian clams are an emerging issue for the Northeast states (Lake Champlain Basin Program 2016). The species' presence has recently been detected in other New England states as well. The first infestation of Asian clam in the State of Vermont was in the southwestern part of Lake Bomoseen in the summer of 2016 (Ann Bove, personal communication). In the State of New Hampshire, Asian clams are already present in the lower Merrimack River and in several ponds (New Hampshire Department of Environmental Service 2016). Seen as the most widely distributed aquatic nuisance species in the contiguous United States (McMahon and Bogan 2001), Asian clams are an emerging issue for the Northeast states (Lake Champlain Basin Program 2016).

It is not surprising that the first Asian clam sighting in Massachusetts was in the Charles River. The Charles River is a central feature of Eastern Massachusetts' metropolitan landscape, frequently used recreationally by boaters, swimmers, and anglers. The river is about 129 km (80 miles) long, beginning at an outlet at Echo Lake, Hopkinton, and running through the City of Boston, where it flows into the Atlantic Ocean. The first Asian clam sighting was located in the segment between Watertown Dam and the Boston University Bridge, where boaters and canoers can be found year-round (Table 2.1). Infestations of non-native aquatic species often occur in recreational waterbodies. For example, the first invasion of quagga mussels (*Dreissena rostriformis bugensis*) in the western United States was in the Las Vegas Boat Harbor Marina

TABLE 2.2
Asian Clams Infested Watersheds and Waterbodies in Each Watershed

Watershed	Waterbody
Blackstone	Blackstone River
	Whitins Pond
Boston Harbor: Mystic	Spy Pond
Boston Harbor: Neponset	Massapoag Lake
Buzzards Bay	Sampson Pond
Cape Cod	Ashumet Pond
	Hamblin Pond
	Mashpee Pond
	Middle Pond
	Peters Pond
Charles	Charles River
Chicopee	Fivemile Pond
Concord (SuAsCo)	Concord River
	Dudley Pond
	Fort Meadow Reservoir
	Heart Pond
	Lake Cochituate
	Sudbury River
Connecticut	Unnamed Pond
	Unnamed Tributary
French	Webster Lake
Quinebaug	East Brimfield Reservoir
South Coastal	Oldham Pond
Taunton	Lake Sabbatia
	Long Pond
	Nemasket River
	Norton Reservoir
	Taunton River
	Tispaquin Pond
	Winnecunnet Pond
Westfield	Congamond Lakes, Middle Basin
	Congamond Lakes, North Basin
	Congamond Lakes, South Basin

of Lake Mead (Moore et al. 2015). Lake Mead is ranked as one of the most visited national parks in the United States. The invasive quagga mussel was introduced first into Lake Mead and rapidly spread to other areas of the western United States (McMahon 2011; Wong and Gerstenberger 2011). Likewise, the spread of the Asian clam in Massachusetts may be correlated with the recreational activity of boaters, swimmers, and anglers.

To specifically examine the abundance of the Asian clam in a tributary to Porter Lake (inside Forest Park) in Springfield, MA, samples were collected from four stations along the stream (Colwell et al. 2017). Invasive purple loosestrife (*Lythrum salicaria*) has been found in this lake

Asian Clam (*Corbicula fluminea*)

FIGURE 2.3 An unnamed tributary to Porter Lake in Springfield, Massachusetts. The white spots instream are empty *C. fluminea* shells. (Photos by Wai Hing Wong.)

FIGURE 2.4 Live clams (*left*) and dead empty shells (*right*) collected from sediment (the two photos are not in the same scale). (Photos by W.H. Wong.)

(Kennedy and Weinstein 2000) and there is also an unconfirmed report of invasive curly-leaved pondweed (*Potamogeton cripus*) (Carr and Kennedy 2008). Historically, this lake has very dense growth of aquatic macrophytes (primarily *Ceratophyllum demersum*) and there are floating algal and duckweed mats at the western end (Kennedy and Weinstein 2000). This unnamed tributary drains into Porter Lake, which is a 28-acre freshwater lake. The tributary is small and wadable, with vegetated banks, and black coarse sands being major components of the sediment (Figure 2.3). Both living Asian clams and dead clam shells were found at the sites along the stream (Figure 2.4). The mean density of Asian clams was 6,124 individuals/m^2 (Table 2.3) and the average shell length of clams from the four sites was 6.92, 6.88, 6.44,

TABLE 2.3
Density of Live Asian Clams and Dry Weight of Dead/Broken Shells in an Unnamed Tributary to Porter Lake in Springfield, Massachusetts

Station	Station 1	Station 2	Station 3	Station 4
Density (individuals/m^2)	7,104	6,932	6,416	4,047
Dry dead shell weight (g/m^2)	512.3	159.3	51.7	4.3

Source: From Colwell et al. (2017).

TABLE 2.4
The Size of Asian Clams at Different Stations in an Unnamed Tributary to Porter Lake in Springfield, Massachusetts (Colwell et al. 2017)

Station		Station 1	Station 2	Station 3	Station 4
Shell length (mm)	Mean	6.92	6.88	6.44	6.11
	Standard deviation	2.82	2.72	2.11	1.40
	Maximum	22.64	18.72	15.46	12.69
	Minimum	2.56	3.43	2.49	3.04
Shell height (mm)	Mean	5.83	5.82	5.46	5.16
	Standard deviation	2.41	2.39	1.80	1.20
	Maximum	19.05	15.88	13.64	11.06
	Minimum	2.13	2.89	2.10	2.56

and 6.11 mm, respectively (Table 2.4). The maximum shell length from the four sites was 22.64, 18.72, 15.46, and 12.69 mm, respectively.

This study demonstrates that the infestation of Asian clams in Massachusetts is not as severe as infestations in the southeast states (Foster et al. 2019), but still considerable compared with other locations in the United states. The density from the unnamed tributary to Porter Lake in Springfield, MA, at 6,124 clams/m^2 is moderate compared with densities reported at other sites such as 55 clams/m^2 in Lake Seminole, GA (Patrick et al. 2017), 722 clams/m^2 in Columbia River, OR/WA (McCabe et al. 1997), and more than 10,000 clams/m^2 in New River, VA (Graney et al. 1980). Asian clams that were found upstream were larger and more abundant than those found downstream. Based on the size structure, it is estimated that most Asian clams found at upstream stations are up to 2 years old, while the age of most individuals from the downstream station is about 1 year old (Mouthon 2001). The weight and maximum size of dead clam shells from upstream stations were greater than that from downstream stations. It appears that a few clams reached up to 2 years old in the upstream stations and few, if any, appear to survive beyond the first year of life in the downstream station. This could possibly be attributed to the differences in habitats along this tributary. Asian clams may prefer upstream stations because they are composed of soft mud, unlike downstream sites where the sediments contain hard clays. It also may be that larger individuals are more likely to be displaced downstream during flood events. This may explain the loss of the 2-year-old cohort in the downstream station where the hard clay and coarse sand substrate suggest higher flow rates that could have exposed larger, older clams to being hydrologically transported downstream during flood events (Williams and McMahon 1986). By contrast, the deeper, coarse sand and soft mud substrata of the upstream sites may be indicative of a lower flow regime suggesting that the clams there are less hydrologically disturbed during flood events than the downstream station. To understand the density and size frequency of

Asian clams in other infested waterbodies, and better determine their population dynamics in the Commonwealth of Massachusetts, successive monthly samples from multiple locations should be taken over a period of at least one year (McMahon and Williams 1986).

The distribution of Asian clams is controlled by both habitat variables (e.g., substrate and pH) and climate variables (e.g., minimum temperature ≤2°C in the coldest month) (Mattice and Dye 1976). Invasive clams have typically been found to occur at higher densities in warmer habitats. Almost all Asian clam sightings are in the southern or eastern parts of the state: the warmer the water, the more likely Asian clams can be found. MassDEP has monitored water temperature in five rivers since 2012 where continuous water temperature data were collected every 30 min for each at the five monitoring stations (T1, T2, T3, T4, and T5). Based on data collected from November 1, 2013, to April 24, 2014, Station T1 had significantly lower temperature than Station T2 and T4; while the temperatures of the latter two stations were significantly lower than that of Station T3 and T5 (Analysis of Variance, $P < 0.0001$) (Nuzzo, unpublished data). Stations in the northern or western parts of the state had a lower temperature due to their higher latitude and/or altitude. Overall, the range of Asian clams appears to be expanding northward, given Asian clam sightings in the southern and eastern parts of Massachusetts from 2001 to 2016, as well as recent discoveries of Asian clams in Vermont and New Hampshire. This shift in range corresponds with the general warming trend observed in the Eastern United States.

Warming temperatures have been recorded recently in this region; ice cover has been found to freeze later in the winter with earlier ice breakup in the spring in northeastern lakes (USEPA 2012). In addition, the lowest daily winter temperatures (Blue Hill Observatory, unpublished data) from 1985 to 2000 (specifically, 16 years before Asian clams were found in Massachusetts) were significantly lower than that from 2001 to 2016 (16 years after the first-year Asian clam was confirmed in Massachusetts) which demonstrates that Massachusetts is becoming warmer from 1985 to 2016 (Wilcoxon Two-Sample Test, $N = 2,888$, $P = 0.02$). If trend analysis is used for analyzing the winter daily minimal temperature in Massachusetts from 1985 to 2016, the temperature is increasing (Kendall's Tau Correlation Coefficient, $N = 2,888$, $P = 0.0002$). Therefore, the increasing winter temperature in Massachusetts is highly likely to help Asian clams establish their populations successfully at different waterbodies (Figure 2.2). Climate change is most likely the key reason Asian clams are now able to establish themselves in the United States above the 40° latitude line, as waters now remain above the clams' long-term incipient lower thermal limit (Mattice and Dye 1976). Therefore, the impact of climate change on the distribution of this species in Massachusetts and the northeast region should also be monitored because Asian clams are likely to expand well beyond their present distribution in Massachusetts and the United States (McDowell et al. 2014).

Apart from temperature, calcium concentration in the water is another limiting factor for Asian clam. Bivalve mollusks require calcium for the formation of their shells and calcium is often an important environmental predictor of the presence of freshwater bivalves (McMahon 1996; Lucy et al. 2012). Ferreira-Rodríguez et al. (2017) reported that the growth rates of *C. fluminea* are reduced significantly at lower calcium concentrations. Smith (1993) reported two watersheds, the Hoosic and Housatonic Rivers in Western Massachusetts with favorable conditions for zebra mussels to succeed, while the rest of the Connecticut River Watershed in Central Massachusetts and Eastern Massachusetts were marginally susceptible. So far, zebra mussels are only found in the Housatonic River watershed. However, many Asian clam sightings are found in Central and Southeast Part of Massachusetts. Therefore, Asian clams may be more tolerant than zebra mussels to lower calcium concentrations. This is also in agreement with report from McDowell et al. (2014) that climate variables are likely more important than the habitat variables, although Asian clams can be controlled by both their habitat and climate variables.

MANAGING ACTIONS

The best approach to preventing the spread of aquatic invasive species is an integrated management strategy (Wong and Gerstenberger 2015). An urgent biosecurity requirement is needed to stop or significantly limit the spread of this invasive species. For example, appropriate signage and decontamination equipment should be provided at infested waterbodies for users to be aware of the infestation and the need to clean their boats before leaving the waterbody. Mapping infested waterbodies in Massachusetts, such as the one (Figure 2.2) created in this study, is helpful in keeping local residents and out-of-state travelers aware of the infestations before and after visiting their targeted lakes and rivers, as well as helping resource managers track the expansion or contraction of the infestation. There should be at least four parts to this plan:

1. The primary means by which the species is being spread, whether it is human activity or a natural cause, needs to be identified. The most vulnerable waterbodies also need to be identified in order for resources to be allocated in the most cost-effective manner.
2. A means to slow or stop the spread needs to be created. This would include educational programs to raise public awareness, stricter boating codes, and new legislation (Sousa et al. 2013) to prevent the further spread of Asian clams such as building washing stations at the entrance to susceptible waters.
3. Analysis needs to be completed to determine the ecological and economic impacts of Asian clam infestations of new waterbodies.
4. Finally, a plan for emergency response to an invasion needs to be created (Sousa et al. 2013). This would proactively limit the invasive potential of the species.

The manner of dealing with Asian clams can be both reactive and proactive. Reactive methods of Asian clam control are often more costly than proactive approaches: an example of this would be using a benthic barrier to control their populations (Sousa et al. 2013). Proactive methods target Asian clams in the larval stage, such as with chemical treatments. Proactive methods tend to be more effective and versatile (Sousa et al. 2013). It is more difficult to stop the spread of Asian clams in open waters, where treatment methods are more likely to negatively impact non-target species.

CHEMICAL TREATMENT

Carefully regulated potassium treatments have the potential of eradicating nuisance molluscs while avoiding harm to non-molluscan wildlife and human health (Colwell et al. 2017, Sousa et al. 2013). Chemically innovative means of control such as BioBullets® have also been developed for specific use as molluscicides. These substances are designed to selectively target filter feeders by introducing poison to the water in the form of food particles preferred by molluscans. The poisons are then removed from the water when the molluscs feed, killing the molluscs while theoretically limiting harm to the rest of the aquatic ecosystem (Aldridge et al. 2006). While molluscicides such as these have shown promise in selectively controlling other biofouling organisms, such as the zebra mussel (Aldridge et al. 2006), more testing is required to determine an optimum protocol and dosage for treating Asian clam infestations. Potassium chloride seemed to be more lethal around 100–250 mg/l under hypoxic conditions and the clam mortality rate increased significantly at around 150–900 mg/l with the highest mortality rate resulting from around 450 mg/l under normoxic conditions (Rosa et al. 2015; Densmore et al. 2018). Several other chemicals have been tested which include ammonium nitrate, niclosamide, dimethoate, polyDADMAC, and chlorpyrifos (see more information in Appendix III Literature research of chemical control methods on 19 invasive species). In addition, preliminary experimentation has shown that thyme oil and extracts used for *Eichornia* spp. (water hyacinths) treatment could be employed in controlling Asian clam infestations, but definitive results have not yet been published in support of this theory. There are many other methods and molluscicides that are used to control Asian clam macrofouling of raw water using facilities. Therefore, treatment in raw water facilities may not be suitable for application to open waters (i.e., natural lakes, ponds, rivers, and streams).

PHYSICAL TREATMENT

Depletion of dissolved oxygen induced by the placement of gas-impermeable benthic barriers has been found to be effective on Asian clams in Lake Tahoe (Wittmann et al. 2012) and Lake

George (NY) (Colwell 2017; Sousa et al. 2013), although the strategy is relatively expensive and harmful to non-target benthic organisms. Thermal shock also may be effective in eradicating Asian clams. Treatment of Asian clam infestation using dry ice, hot steam, and open flame (on dry sand substrate) has also been attempted in a controlled setting, and in some cases found to be effective depending on the time and intensity of exposure (Coughlan et al. 2018; Coughlan et al. 2019). Winter lake drawdowns might also be a possible control measure to reduce the population and/or contain them in the deeper area of a lake. However, these methods could also be damaging to non-invasive species and the surrounding ecosystem, and the cost and benefit of their applications should be carefully weighed on a case-by-case basis. Though it is time-consuming, hand removal remains the most safe and effective strategy to combat Asian clam infestations in the interest of avoiding negative effects to other aquatic organisms, especially in the early stage of the infestation. Once established, eradication of Asian clams is often difficult, if not impossible, without destructive impacts to native species and their natural habitats. Therefore, prevention of spread and early detection should be prioritized.

BIOLOGICAL TREATMENT

Biological control agents for *C. fluminea* may be difficult to find or develop, because a predator must be large enough to consume a whole clam and not be limited by clam valve closure or it must have an ability to open the clam's shell valves. It must also not be able to feed extensively on native bivalves and other native species. A study that examined the stomach contents of various fish in Portugal found that only those of *Luciobarbus bocagei*, a species of barbel, contained shells of Asian clams (Pereira et al. 2016). The shells only represented a small portion of the overall diet of the fish, despite high clam abundance in the area. The research team noted that only barbel that were greater than 30 cm in size fed on the clams, perhaps meaning smaller fish avoided the clams as they had a gape limitation. The crayfish *Procambarus clarkia* also was recorded to feed on smaller Asian clams (Pereira et al. 2016). The best biological controls may be parasites or disease organisms that have specifically evolved to infest Asian clams.

SUCCESS STORIES

Due to the Asian clam's physiological and ecological plasticity, many forms of control can achieve a short-term effect. Long-term management can be more difficult to achieve and has led some researchers to investigate other experimental solutions to their management and control. Two case studies for Asian clam control, one conducted in Lake Tahoe, and a second, in the laboratory, are described in the following sections.

BENTHIC BARRIER CONTROL OF ASIAN CLAMS

Gas impermeable benthic barriers made of polyvinyl chloride have typically been used in lakes and ponds for the control of invasive macrophytes, either by smothering them or preventing their access to light. For this reason, the barriers are designed to be gas impermeable, in order to contain nutrient outgassing that results from the large-scale dying and decay of benthic plant life, which would be comparable to the effects of eutrophication if not controlled in this manner (Wittmann et al. 2012). At lake Tahoe, Whittmann et al. (2012) used similar gas-impermeable benthic barriers to create hypoxic to anoxic conditions on the lake floor in an effort to suffocate invasive populations of *C. fluminea*. When the barriers were applied, DO concentrations beneath the barrier dropped to nearly 0 mg/l within 72 hours. Though Asian clams have the documented ability to reduce their metabolism and withstand hypoxic conditions for long periods of time, in particular being more resistant to extended periods of hypoxia than the zebra mussel (*Dreissena polymorpha*) (Ortmann and Grieshaber 2003, Matthews and McMahon 1999), the hypoxia induced by the barrier treatment was sufficient to eliminate the majority of affected Asian clams, significantly reducing their numbers in the area where it was applied. After 120 days under the barrier, the density of *C. fluminea* in the treated area was reduced by nearly 100%, and for one year following the removal of the barrier, the invasive population remained over 90% reduced relative to the control region (Wittmann et al. 2012). While this treatment was, thus, demonstrated to be effective in eradicating molluscs, the effect of the induced hypoxia was not limited to *C. fluminea*: populations of the native pea clam (*Pisidium* spp.) and other benthic organisms were also drastically reduced within the treated area. The long-term effectiveness of the treatment on *C. fluminea* is also not currently known. However, this trial in Lake Tahoe has shown that the use of benthic barriers can be successful in the short-term control of Asian clams if care is taken to select treatment locations with especially dense invasive populations.

Dry Ice Study

Dry ice was used to kill and manage populations of Asian clams in both a laboratory and a simulated setting (Coughlan et al. 2018). Asian clam specimens were gathered from the River Barrow in Ireland and transported to a laboratory. The species was first detected in Ireland in 2010 in the River Barrow, where it was found to have densities of around 9,000 individuals/m^2 in the upper tidal portions of the river (Minchin 2014). It has since spread to additional waterbodies in Ireland. In the laboratory, four different quantities of dry ice were used to test their lethality on Asian clams: 50, 100, 200, and 300 g of 9 mm dry ice pellets. A control group was also created in which no dry ice was applied. Clams were assigned into groups based on their size, with small clams ranging from 8 to 14.9 mm, medium clams from 15 to 20.9 mm, and large clams from 21 to 32 mm. Each dry ice application lasted for a duration of either 1 or 5 minutes. Additionally, several other experimentational variants were performed, such as testing the efficacy of dry ice as a control agent when clams were covered in sediments such as fine gravel or mud. In control groups, survival rates ranged from 87% to 100%, while in groups that were exposed to dry ice, survival ranged from 0% to 100%. Longer exposure times, smaller clam size, and greater amounts of dry ice all resulted in greater clam mortality. The most lethal application was of 300 g of dry ice at a 5-minute exposure, resulting in complete clam mortality across all size ranges (small to large). In the experiments that simulated coverage by various types of sediment, results revealed that dry ice was still effective at inducing mortality, even with increased coverage. The dry ice would bind itself to the clam in the mud or fine gravel and create a frozen layer in which the clam became incapacitated. These results showed the promising potential of dry ice as a control agent for Asian clams, especially at greater quantities of dry ice (300 g) and with longer exposures. It is possible that some non-target species could be affected by dry ice applications, specifically native molluscs and clams. However, if applied correctly in conjunction with a survey of the invaded area, the benefits of dry ice could outweigh the potential negative results. The promising results of this study also may be a window into future control methods of dry ice for other nuisance aquatic species, such as the zebra mussel and quagga mussels (Coughlan et al. 2018). Further testing and experimentation are required to validate to efficacy of dry ice application for controlling Asian clams and dreissenid mussels as well as its potential negative impacts on native, non-target species.

NOTES

1. According to an email from James McGrath, City of Pittsfield, to Tom Flannery and Jim Straub, Massachusetts Department of Conservation and Recreation, dated September 22, 2021.
2. According to an email from Barbara Kickham, Town of Shrewsbury, to David W.H. Wong, Massachusetts Department of Environmental Protection, dated December 21, 2021.

REFERENCES

Aldridge, D.C., P. Elliott, and G.D. Moggridge. 2006. Microencapsulated biobullets for the control of biofouling zebra mussels. *Environmental Science & Technology* 40: 975–979.

Baker, S.M., J.S. Levinton, J.P. Kurdziel, and S.E. Shumway. 1998. Selective feeding and biodeposition by zebra mussels and their relation to changes in phytoplankton composition and seston load. *Journal of Shellfish Research* 17(4): 1207–1213.

Bolam, B.A., G. Rollwagen-Bollens, and S.M. Bollens. 2019. Feeding rates and prey selection of the invasive Asian clam, *Corbicula fluminea*, on microplankton in the Columbia River, USA. *Hydrobiologia* 833(1): 107–123.

Carr, J.W., and L.E. Kennedy. 2008. Connecticut River Basin 2003 Water Quality Assessment Report. Massachusetts Department of Environmental Protection, Division of Watershed Management. Report # 34-AC-2; DWM Control # CN 105.5, 136 pp.

Cataldo, D., and D. Boltovskoy. 1998. Population dynamics of *Corbicula fluminea* (Bivalvia) in the Paraná River Delta (Argentina). *Hydrobiologia* 380(1): 153–163.

Colwell, H., J. Ryder, R. Nuzzo, M. Reardon, R. Holland, and W.H. Wong. 2017. Invasive Asian clams (*Corbicula fluminea*) recorded from 2001 to 2016 in Massachusetts, USA. *Management of Biological Invasions* 8(4): 507–515.

Coughlan, N.E., R.N. Cuthbert, S. Potts, E.M. Cunningham, K. Crane, J.M. Caffrey, F.E. Lucy, E. Davis, and J.T.A. Dick. 2019. Beds are burning: Eradication and control of invasive Asian clam, *Corbicula fluminea*, with rapid open-flame burn treatments. *Management of Biological Invasions* 10(3): 486–499.

Coughlan, N.E., D.A. Walsh, J.M. Caffrey, E. Davis, F.E. Lucy, R.N. Cuthbert, and J.T. Dick. 2018. Cold as Ice: A novel eradication and control method for invasive Asian clam, *Corbicula fluminea*, using pelleted dry ice. *Management of Biological Invasions* 9(4): 463–474.

Counts, C.L. 1981. *Corbicula fluminea* (Bivalvia: Sphaeriacea) in British Columbia. *Nautilus* 95(1): 12–13.

Counts, C.L. 1986. The zoogeography and history of the invasion of the United States by *Corbicula fluminea* (Bivalvia: Corbiculidae). *American Malacological Bulletin* (Special Edition) 2: 7–39.

Densmore, C.L., L.R. Iwanowicz, A.P. Henderson, V.S. Blazer, B.M. Reed-Grimmett, and L.R. Sanders. 2018. An Evaluation of the toxicity of potassium chloride, active compound in the molluscicide potash, on salmonid fish and their forage base. *USGS Science for a Changing World* 1–46.

Denton, M.E., S. Chandra, M.E. Wittmann, J. Reuter, and J.G. Baguley 2012. Reproduction and population structure of *Corbicula fluminea* in an oligotrophic subalpine lake. *Journal of Shellfish Research* 31(1): 145–152.

Dexter, E., S.M. Bollens, and G. Rollwagen-Bollens. 2020. Native and invasive zooplankton show differing responses to decadal-scale increases in maximum temperatures in a large temperate river. *Limnology and Oceanography Letters* 5(6): 403–409.

Dexter, E., S.M. Bollens, G. Rollwagen-Bollens, J. Emerson, and J. Zimmerman. 2015. Persistent vs. ephemeral invasions: 8.5 years of zooplankton community dynamics in the Columbia River. *Limnology and Oceanography* 60(2): 527–539.

Ferreira-Rodríguez, N., I. Fernandez, S. Varandas, R. Cortes, M. Cancela, and I. Pardo. 2017. The role of calcium concentration in the invasive capacity of *Corbicula fluminea* in crystalline basins. *Science of The Total Environment* 580: 1363–1370.

Foster, A.M., P. Fuller, A. Benson, S. Constant, D. Raikow, J. Larson, and A. Fusaro. 2019. *Corbicula fluminea*. USGS Nonindigenous Aquatic Species Database, Gainesville, FL. http://nas.er.usgs.gov/queries/factsheet.aspx?speciesid=92 (Accessed January 7, 2021).

Gomes, C., R. Sousa, T. Mendes, R. Borges, P. Vilares, V. Vasconcelos, L. Guilhermino, and A. Antunes. 2016. Low genetic diversity and high invasion success of *Corbicula fluminea* (Bivalvia, Corbiculidae) (Müller, 1774) in Portugal. *PLoS One* 11(7): e0158108.

Graney, R.L., D.S. Cherry, J.H. Rodgers, and J. Cairns. 1980. The influence of thermal discharges and substrate composition on the population-structure and distribution of the Asiatic clam, *Corbicula fluminea*, in the New River, Virginia. *Nautilus* 94: 130–135.

Haag, W.D., J. Culp, A.N. Drayer, M.A. McGregor, D.E.J. White, and S.J. Price. 2021. Abundance of an invasive bivalve, *Corbicula fluminea*, is negatively related to growth of freshwater mussels in the wild. *Freshwater Biology* 66(3): 447–457.

Hakenkamp, C.C., S.G. Ribblett, M.A. Palmer, C.M. Swan, J.W. Reid, and M.R. Goodison. 2001. The impact of an introduced bivalve (*Corbicula fluminea*) on the benthos of a sandy stream. *Freshwater Biology* 46(4): 491–501.

Hassett, W., S.M. Bollens, T.D. Counihan, G. Rollwagen-Bollens, J. Zimmerman, S. Katz, and J. Emerson. 2017. Veligers of the invasive Asian clam *Corbicula fluminea* in the Columbia River Basin: Broadscale distribution, abundance, and ecological associations. *Lake and Reservoir Management* 33(3): 234–248.

Ishibashi, R., K. Ookubo, M. Aoki, M. Utaki, A. Komaru, and K. Kawamura. 2003. Androgenetic reproduction in a freshwater diploid clam *Corbicula fluminea* (Bivalvia: Corbiculidae). *Zoological Science* 20: 727–732.

ITIS (Integrated Taxonomic Information System). 2021. www.itis.gov/servlet/SingleRpt/SingleRpt#null (Accessed January 28, 2021).

Karatayev, A.Y., L.E. Burlakova, and D.K. Padilla. 2005. *Contrasting Distribution and Impacts of Two Freshwater Exotic Suspension Feeders, Dreissena Polymorpha and Corbicula Fluminea. The Comparative Roles of Suspension-Feeders in Ecosystems, NATO Science Series IV: Earth and Environmental Series*. Dordrecht: Springer, pp. 239–262.

Kennedy, L.E., and M.J. Weinstein. 2000. Connecticut river Basin 1998 Water quality assessment report. Massachusetts Department of Environmental Protection, Division of Watershed Management. Report # 34-AC-1; DWM Control # CN 45, 110 pp.

Lake Champlain Basin Program. 2016. Invasive species task force recommends actions to control invasive Asian Clam in Lake Bomoseen, Vermont. www.lcbp.org/2016/09/invasive-species-task-force-recommends-actions-control-invasive-asian-clam-lake-bomoseen-vt/. (Accessed October 11, 2016).

Lucy, F., A. Karatayev, and L. Burlakova. 2012. Predictions for the spread, population density, and impacts of Corbicula fluminea. *Aquatic Invasions* 7(4): 465–474.

Matthews, M.A., and R.F. McMahon. 1999. Effects of temperature and temperature acclimation in survival of zebra mussels (*Dreissena polymorpha*) and Asian clams (*Corbicula fluminea*) under extreme hypoxia. *Journal of Molluscan Studies* 65: 317–325.

Mattice, J.S., and L.L. Dye. 1976. Thermal tolerance of adult Asiatic clam. *Thermal Ecology* 2: 130–135.

McCabe, G., S.A. Hinton, R.L. Emmett, and B.P. Sandford. 1997. Benthic invertebrates and sediment characteristics in main channel habitats in the lower Columbia River. *Northwest Science* 71: 45–55.

McDowell, W.G., A.J. Benson, and J.E. Byers. 2014. Climate controls the distribution of a widespread invasive species: Implications for future range expansion. *Freshwater Biology* 59: 847–857.

McMahon, R.F. 1996. The Physiological Ecology of the Zebra Mussel, Dreissena polymorpha, in North America and Europe. *American Zoologist* 36(3): 339–363.

McMahon, R.F. 1999. Invasive characteristics of the freshwater bivalve *Corbicula fluminea*. In: R. Claudi, and J.H. Leach (eds). *Nonindigenous Freshwater Organisms: Vectors, Biology, and Impacts*. Boca Raton, FL: Lewis Publishers, pp. 315–343.

McMahon, R.F. 2002. Evolutionary and physiological adaptations of aquatic invasive animals: r selection versus resistance. *Canadian Journal of Fisheries and Aquatic Sciences* 59: 1235–1244.

McMahon, R.F. 2011. Quagga mussel (*Dreissena rostriformis bugensis*) population structure during the early invasion of Lakes Mead and Mohave January-March 2007. *Aquatic Invasions* 6: 131–140.

McMahon, R.F., and A.E. Bogan. 2001. Mollusca: Bivalvia. In: H. Thorp and A.P. Covich (eds). *Ecology and Classification of North American Freshwater Invertebrates* (2nd edition). New York: Academic Press, pp. 331–428.

McMahon, R.F., and C.J. Williams. 1986. A reassessment of growth rate, life span, life cycles and population dynamics in a natural population and field caged individuals of *Corbicula fluminea* (Müller) (Bivalvia:Corbiculacea). *American Malacological Bulletin* (Special Edition) 2: 151–186.

Minchin, D. 2014. The distribution of the Asian clam *Corbicula fluminea* and its potential to spread in Ireland. *Management of Biological Invasions* 5(2): 165–177.

Minchin, D., and R. Boelens. 2018. Natural dispersal of the introduced Asian clam *Corbicula fluminea* (Müller, 1774) (Cyrenidae) within two temperate lakes. *BioInvasions Records* 7(3): 259–268.

Moore, B., G.C. Holdren, S. Gerstenberger, K. Turner, and W.H. Wong. 2015. Invasion by Quagga Mussels (*Dreissena rostriformis bugensis* Andrusov 1897) into Lake Mead, Nevada-Arizona: The first occurrence of dreissenid species in the Western United States. In: W.H. Wong and S.L. Gerstenberger (eds). *Biology and Management of Invasive Quagga and Zebra Mussels in the Western United States*. Boca Raton, FL: CRC Press, pp. 17–31.

Mouthon, J. 2001. Life cycle and population dynamics of the Asian clam *Corbicula fluminea* (Bivalvia: Corbiculidae) in the Saone River at Lyon (France). *Hydrobiologia* 452: 109–119.

Muller, O., and B. Baur. 2011. Survival of the invasive clam *Corbicula fluminea* (Müller) in response to winter water temperature. *Malacologia* 53: 367–371.

New Hampshire Department of Environmental Service. 2016. *Stop Aquatic Hitchhikers! Boating on the Lakes* (2016 ed.). New Hampshire: New Hampshire Department of Environmental Service, pp. 54–55.

Nuzzo, R.M. 2003. *Standard Operating Procedures: Water Quality Monitoring in Streams Using Aquatic Macroinvertebrates*. Worcester, MA: Massachusetts Department of Environmental Protection, Division of Watershed Management, p. 39.

Ortmann, C., and M.K. Grieshaber. 2003. Energy metabolism and valve closure behaviour in the Asian clam *Corbicula fluminea*. *Journal of Experimental Biology* 206: 4167–4178.

Patrick, C.H., M.N. Waters, and S.W. Golladay. 2017. The distribution and ecological role of *Corbicula fluminea* (Müller, 1774) in a large and shallow reservoir. *BioInvasions Records* 6(1): 39–48.

Pereira, J.L., S. Pinho, A. Ré, P.A. Costa, R. Costa, F. Gonçalves, and B.B. Castro. 2016. Biological control of the invasive Asian clam, *Corbicula fluminea*: Can predators tame the beast? *Hydrobiologia* 779: 209–226.

Pigneur, L.M., E. Falisse, K. Roland, E. Everbecq, J.F. Deliège, J.S. Smitz, K.V. Doninck, and J.P. Descy. 2014. Impact of invasive Asian clams, *Corbicula spp.*, on a large river ecosystem. *Freshwater Biology* 59(3): 573–583.

Pimentel, D., R. Zuniga, and D. Morrison. 2005. Update on the environmental and economic costs associated with alien-invasive species in the United States. *Ecological Economics* 52: 273–288.

Robinson, M. 2004. Asian clam: An exotic aquatic species. www.mass.gov/eea/docs/dcr/watersupply/lakepond/factsheet/asian-clam.pdf (Accessed November 1, 2016).

Rosa, I.C., R. Garrido, A. Ré, J. Gomes, J. Peirera, F. Gonçalves, and R. Costa. 2015. Sensitivity of the invasive bivalve *Corbicula fluminea* to candidate control chemicals: The role of dissolved oxygen conditions. *Science of Total Environment* 536: 825–830.

Rosa, I.C., J.L. Pereira, R. Costa, F. Gonçalves, and R. Prezant 2012. Effects of upper-limit water temperatures on the dispersal of the Asian clam *Corbicula fluminea*. *PLoS ONE* 7(10).

Sheehan, R., J.M. Caffrey, M. Millane, P. McLoone, H. Moran, and F. Lucy. 2014. An investigation into the effectiveness of mechanical dredging to remove *Corbicula fluminea* (Müller, 1774) from test plots in an Irish river system. *Management of Biological Invasions* 5(4): 407–418.

Smith, D.G. 1993. The Potential for Spread of the Exotic Zebra Mussel (*Dreissena polymorpha*) in Massachusetts. Report MS-Q-11. Department of Biology, University of Massachusetts Amherst, Massachusetts and Museum of Comparative Zoology, Harvard University, Cambridge, MA. www.mass.gov/eea/docs/dcr/watersupply/lakepond/downloads/zebra-mussel-massdep-ms-q-11.pdf (Accessed June 27, 2018).

Sousa, R., C. Antunes, and L. Guilhermino. 2008. Ecology of the invasive Asian *clam Corbicula fluminea* (Müller, 1774) in aquatic ecosystems: An overview. *Annales de Limnologie—International Journal of Limnology* 44: 85–94.

Sousa, R., A. Novais, R. Costa, and D. Stayer. 2013. Invasive bivalves in fresh water: Impacts from individuals to ecosystems and possible control strategies. *Hydrobiologia* 735: 233–251.

USEPA. 2012. *Climate Change Indicators* (2nd ed.). New York: United States Environmental Protection Agency (USEPA), p. 3.

Viergutz, C., C. Linn, and M. Weitere. 2012. Intra- and interannual variability surpasses direct temperature effects on the clearance rates of the invasive clam *Corbicula fluminea*. *Marine Biology* 159: 2379–2387.

Williams, C.J., and R.F. McMahon. 1986. Power station entrainment of *Corbicula fluminea* (Müller) in relation to population dynamics, reproductive cycle and biotic and abiotic variables. *American Malacological Bulletin* (Special Edition) 2: 99–111.

Wittmann, M.E., S. Chandra, J.E. Reuter, S.G. Schladow, B.C. Allen, and K.J. Webb. 2012. The control of an invasive bivalve, *Corbicula fluminea*, using gas impermeable benthic barriers in a large natural lake. *Environmental Management* 49: 1163–1173.

Wong, W.H., and S.L. Gerstenberger. 2011. Quagga mussels in the western United States: monitoring and management. *Aquatic Invasions* 6: 125–129.

Wong, W.H., and S.L. Gerstenberger. 2015. *Biology and Management of Invasive Quagga and Zebra Mussels in the Western United States*. Boca Raton, FL: CRC Press, p. 566.

Wong, W.H., J.S. Levintion, B.S. Twining, and N. Fisher. 2003. Assimilation of micro- and mesozooplankton by zebra mussels: A demonstration of the food web link between zooplankton and benthic suspension feeders. *Limnology & Oceanography* 48(1): 308–312.

3 Zebra Mussel (*Dreissena polymorpha*)

ABSTRACT

The zebra mussel (*Dreissena polymorpha*), a freshwater bivalve mollusk that was introduced to the Great Lakes in the 1980s, is now thriving in the United States due to its vigorous fecundity, posing threats to native freshwater species. In Massachusetts, the species was first found in 2009 at Laurel Lake and currently is only found in the waters of the Housatonic River basin. This report covers monitoring and sightings of the zebra mussel, as well as alternative management tools to raise awareness to the general public for prevention and to monitor and control (chemical, physical, or biological treatments) of zebra mussels in lakes and rivers.

INTRODUCTION

Taxonomic Hierarchy (ITIS 2021)

Kingdom	Animalia
Subkingdom	Bilateria
Infrakingdom	Protostomia
Superphylum	Lophozoa
Phylum	Mollusca
Class	Bivalvia
Subclass	Heterodonta
Order	Veneroida
Superfamily	Dreissenoidea
Family	Dreissenidae
Genus	*Dreissena*
Species	*Dreissena polymorpha* (Pallas, 1771)

The zebra mussel (*Dreissena polymorpha*) is an invasive freshwater bivalve mollusk in North America which is native to Europe. It has an epifaunal mode of life (Mackie and Schloesser 1996), which usually grows 3.5–5.0 cm in length (Maxwell 1992). They have elongated D-shaped shells with light- and dark-colored bands (Figure 3.1). Due to their genetic and morphological plasticity (as the species name *polymorpha* implies), sometimes the species will have a yellow and brownish color (Feinberg 1979). According to studies from early Soviets, there were five dreissenid species at minimum, based on the discretionary morphological and physiological existence (O'Neill and MacNeill 1991). Like many members of the Class Bivalvia, zebra mussels have byssal threads to attach to nearby surfaces. According to Ekroat et al. (1993), there are two different types of byssal threads: temporary and permanent. Usually, temporary threads range from 1 to 6 threads in a tripod shape, and they are separated from major byssal threads. Permanent threads are clustered together and arranged in rows. The two types of byssal threads differ in numbers, length, thickness, arrangement, and morphology. To calculate the approximate total number of threads, a formula can be applied: number of threads = –8.59 + 19.26* (shell length in mm) (Claudi and Mackie 1994). The dominant constituent of byssal threads is a type of amino acid called DOPA (3, 4-dihydroxyphenyl-alanine) (Rzepecki and Waite 1993). Based on their proclivity to water currents, zebra mussels prefer living in water pipelines and water canals, which can result in decreased water flow and even produce disagreeable flavors in drinking water (Ellis 1978). Lakeshores and riverbanks are preferable sites of colonization for zebra mussels. Due to their high reproductive ability, the species sometimes appears in reef-like mats and can tether themselves to shells of other clams and mussels (Maxwell 1992). Generally, the densities of zebra mussel populations are between 7,000 and 114,000/m² with a standing crop biomass between 0.05 and 15 kg/m² (Thorp and Covich 1991). Colonization of zebra mussels is dependent on light intensity, water temperature, food sources, and many other factors. They usually live in the range of 2–7 meters below the water surface. They sometimes can be found as deep as 50 m (Maxwell 1992). Zebra mussels have a high tolerance to harsh environmental conditions. They prefer living in a temperature range of

FIGURE 3.1 An adult zebra mussel and a zebra mussel bed in Lake Erie. (Left photo by W.H. Wong; right photo by Berkman etal. (1998).)

20–25°C and in water currents ranging from 0.15 to 0.5 m/second. If water temperatures fall below 7°C or above 32°C, with a water current faster than 2 m/second, it will be considered as unsuitable conditions for their growth (Maxwell 1992). A survival threshold value of 12–20 mg/l of calcium is required for the growth of zebra mussels (Neary and Leach 1991). Based on parameters used by Burlakova (1998), a suitable waterbody should have a pH ≥7.5. For marginally suitable conditions, a pH between 7.2 and 7.5 is needed. A pH <7.2 will be considered as unsuitable. Major environmental factors that can limit the survival and/or facilitate the establishment of zebra mussels are summarized in Table 3.1 (Counihan et al. 2018). According to alkalinity or hardness, as well as pH, Smith (1993) reported two watersheds in Western Massachusetts with favorable conditions for zebra mussels to survive and establish sustainable populations: the Hoosic and Housatonic River Basins. The Connecticut River watershed (with the exception of the Millers and Chicopee watersheds) and most of Eastern Massachusetts were moderately to marginally susceptible. The Millers and Chicopee watersheds, the coastal plain of Southeastern Massachusetts, and Cape Cod could not support zebra mussels (Smith 1993).

Usually, a mature female mussel at age 1 or older will produce 30,000–40,000 eggs a year (Maxwell 1992) and up to 1 million eggs during one spawning event (Walz 1978; Sprung 1990). The reproductive cycle highly depends on environmental conditions (see Table 3.1), such as water temperature and plenitude of phytoplankton (Maxwell 1992). Based on O'Neill and MacNeill's (1991) research on Lake Erie, supporting evidence shows that the reproductive rate of zebra mussels can be inhibited by cool water and high turbidity. Zebra mussels fertilize externally, by ejecting sperm and eggs into the surrounding area. After hatching from the fertilized egg, a planktonic veliger larva will float in the water and forage, remaining suspended for about eight to ten days before descending to the substratum (Thorp and Covich 1991). During the larva stage, the veligers can swim and follow the direction of the current to disperse themselves to other waterbodies causing new infestations (Thorp and Covich 1991). After about three weeks, zebra mussels will start to tether themselves to substrate such as cobble, bedrock, debris, boat hulls, water pipes, and breakwaters. Although zebra mussels have a high reproductive rate and are highly active, mortality rates can be as high as 99% or more. Reasons for mortality can be hypoxia, fluctuation of temperature, or failing to find an appropriate substrate (O'Neill and MacNeill 1991; Thorp and Covich 1991). Eventually, they will find a better location to grow and tether themselves via their provisional tiny byssal fibers (Maxwell 1992) and adapt to a sessile lifestyle. Younger zebra mussels are usually between 5 and 10 mm in length (O'Neill and MacNeill 1991; Thorp and Covich 1991). The life span of zebra mussels can vary, with most living up to five to six years (Thorp and Covich 1991). However, O'Neill and MacNeill (1991) argue that the average life span of a zebra mussel is 3.5 years, but occasionally can reach up to 8–10 years if production is less intense. It is also reported that the longevity of zebra mussels varies from 2 to 19 years and it is not clear to what

TABLE 3.1
Risk Categories of Zebra Mussel Invasions under Different Water Quality Parameters

Physical Risk Factor	Minimal Risk	Moderate Risk	High Risk
Calcium concentration	<8 mg/l	8–20 mg/l	>20 mg/l
pH	<7.0 or >9.6	7.0–7.3 or 9.4–9.6	>7.3–<9.4
Mean long-term (≥29 days) summer water temperature	>32°C	31–32°C	<31°C
Minimum temperature for spawning	<14°C	14–16°C	>16°C
Salinity	>5‰	4–5‰	<4‰
Percent full air oxygen saturation at 25°C	<20%	20–30%	>30%
Annual water level variation	No minimal risk	Extensive variation exposing mussels to air and/or submergence in a hypoxic hypolimnion	Relatively constant water levels

extent this variation is caused by biological variability and environmental conditions and what amount of the variation is caused by the methods used to assess age and longevity (Karatayev et al. 2006). Generally, in non-native ranges, the species can sharply increase in population at the early stage of an invasion. However, different long-term trajectories for populations of zebra mussels and other alien species have been illustrated by Strayer and Malcom (2006). In conclusion, rapid growth rate, robust fecundity, relatively short life spans, and the mobility during the larval stage contribute to the aggressiveness of zebra mussels in non-native areas (Maxwell 1992).

The species originated from drainage basins in the Black Sea, Caspian Sea, and Aral Sea in the latter part of the 18th century (Maxwell 1992). After that, zebra mussels settled down firmly around inland waterways of Europe. The zebra mussel was first documented in North America in 1988 in Lake St. Clair (Hebert et al. 1989). However, a recent paper (Carlton 2008) provided convincing evidence that it was present as early as 1986 in Lake Erie (Nalepa and Schloesser 2013). Up to 30,000–40,000 individuals/m^2 were found in the west basin of Lake Erie in 1988. By September 1991, zebra mussels had been reported in most of the Great Lakes. In the same year, the invasion of zebra mussels reached the Hudson River as far south as Catskill, New York (MRB Group 1991). In 1992, the species was reported in Vicksburg, Mississippi, west of Minneapolis, Minnesota, as well as north and east of Quebec. By 1994, the species was found in upper Mississippi, Tennessee, Ohio, and Arkansas (Mackie and Schloesser 1996). In 2008, it was found in the San Justo Reservoir, near Monterrey Bay, California, the first sighting in the western United States (Britton 2015). Recently, another dreissenid mussel, the quagga mussel *Dreissena rostriformis bugensis*, is displacing zebra mussels in the Great Lakes (Mills et al. 1999; Nalepa et al. 2010). It has been documented that Laurentian Great Lakes have been dramatically reengineered by invasive bottom-dwelling dreissenid mussels, especially the quagga mussel which is currently regulating the phosphorus cycling in the invaded Great Lakes (Li et al. 2021). Although quagga mussels and zebra mussels are relatives and share a common native habitat, morphology, lifestyle, life history, and dispersal potential, the former was found to be a better invader than the latter at most spatial scales throughout their invasion history worldwide (Karatayev et al. 2011). Therefore, early detection on quagga mussels and corresponding rapid response actions in Massachusetts are needed to prevent its invasion and establishment.

The invasion pathway of zebra mussels can vary. Among all mechanisms, the planktonic veliger stage should be considered the most effective method of natural spreading. Artificial canals exacerbated the spreading in the former USSR and Britain (Kerney and Morton 1970). Settled mussels that attached to debris may also contribute to the spreading. Moreover, juvenile and adult individuals can be distributed via drifting by water currents (Martel 1993). Some animal-mediated dispersal mechanisms are possible (e.g., turtles, crayfish, and birds, see Carlton 1993); however, anthropogenic mechanisms are thought to be the most common methods of translocating zebra mussels, such as in ballast water used by cargo ships (Mackie and Schloesser 1996), and anchors and anchor lines (McMahon et al. 1991). Not all mechanisms have been verified, especially during the planktonic veliger stage (Nalepa and Schloesser 1993). Recent research shows that over 90% of samples taken from boat live wells/bilges contain five or fewer veligers, which suggests residual water may present a low risk for the spread of this invasive species (Montz and Hirsch 2016); however, Choi et al. (2013) demonstrated a greater likelihood of veliger transport in the residual water of trailered watercraft in favorable conditions when veliger survival times increased with increased level of larval development. Finally, it has been reported that wind-driven currents have an influential effect on the vertical distribution of zebra mussel veligers (Fraleigh et al. 1993). If wind velocities are below 8 km/hour, there will be a manifest depth effect, where 5% of populations are found at depths of 0–2 m. At 2–4 m, 30% of populations have been reported. Finally, 64% have been reported at the depths of 4–6 m (Fraleigh et al. 1993).

Zebra mussels are ecosystem engineers (Nalepa and Schloesser 1993, 2013; Strayer et al. 1999; Karatayev et al. 2002) because they have the potential to change the entire lake or river where they invade (Figure 3.2). Although these invasive mussels may impact ecosystems in different ways, they generally increase water clarity by removing suspended particles (e.g., phytoplankton, debris, silt, and microzooplankton) in the water column (Griffiths 1993, Leach 1993, MacIsaac 1996, Wong et al. 2003). Top-down control on primary production by invasive mussels is mainly due to their efficient filtering behavior (Table 3.2). Since zebra mussels were first discovered in Lake Erie in 1988, chlorophyll-a concentration decreased by 43% in the western basin and 27% in the west-central basin between 1988 and 1989 (Leach 1993). A 20-year (1983–2002) data set shows a downward trend of −0.07 µg/l/year in the central basin of Lake Erie, but no trend was found before the arrival of zebra mussel (Rockwell et al. 2005). In the Hudson River, New York, zebra mussels were found to reduce chlorophyll concentrations by 90% of the pre-zebra mussel level (Caraco et al. 2006). In some areas, such as in Green Bay of Lake Michigan, chlorophyll-a decreased immediately following dreissenid invasion but increased afterward (Qualls et al. 2007, De Stasio et al. 2008). A model of Lake Erie suggests that zebra mussels decreased algal biomass when they first invaded and their population was small (6,000 individuals/m^2). However, when the population grew larger (120,000 individuals/m^2), dreissenid mussels increased non-diatom inedible algae by excreting a large amount of ammonia and phosphate (Zhang et al. 2008). The increased water clarity can then affect other ecosystem components; decreased densities of microalgae result in lower uptake rates for dissolved nutrients from the water column (Nicholls et al. 1999), and benthic algae and plants benefit from increased water clarity (Hecky et al. 2004; Mayer et al. 2013). It is estimated that within the first four to eight years of contact with invasive mussels, Unionidae populations could decrease by 90% (Ricciardi et al. 1998). Generally, there is a strong positive linear relationship between numbers of zebra mussels per unionid and zebra mussel density and there is an overall trend for increased weight of zebra mussels per unionid with increased unionid size during the first ten years subsequent to a zebra mussel invasion; however, the trend decreased ten years after the initial invasion (Lucy et al. 2013). Within the fish communities, planktivorous fish that mainly rely on zooplankton, especially on microzooplankton, may suffer due to food shortage as a result of energy transfer from the pelagic community to the benthic community while benthic feeding fishes may benefit from the establishment of mussels. The influence of invasive mussels on fish vary widely across ecosystems as a function of system morphology, factors that limit primary production, and diets of these fish species (Strayer et al. 2004). In the first decade after zebra mussels arrived at the Hudson River, the biomass of zooplankton and deepwater macrobenthos fell by 50%, while the biomass of littoral macrobenthos rose by 10%. These changes in the forage base were associated

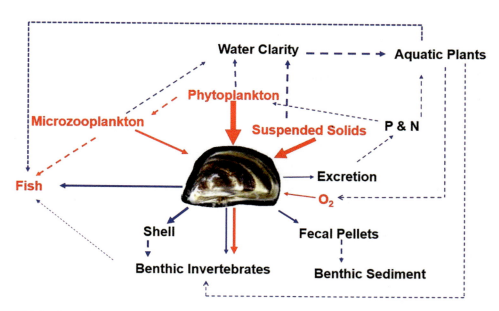

FIGURE 3.2 Potential ecological impacts of zebra mussels on an aquatic ecosystem. Positive (blue font) and negative (red font) effects are diagrammed. Solid and dashed lines represent direct and indirect impacts, respectively. The wider the line, the more profound the impact. Briefly, zebra mussels have potential to reduce the biomass and change the species composition of phytoplankton and zooplankton communities. Decreases in suspended solids and oxygen would increase water clarity. An increase in dissolved inorganic phosphorus and nitrogen would facilitate aquatic plant growth. Benthic production is expected to increase, which would positively impact some fish species. (Modified from Wong et al. (2011).)

with large, differential changes in the abundance, geographic distribution, and growth rates of open water and littoral fish (Strayer et al. 2014). In recent years, populations of zooplankton and deepwater macrobenthos have risen toward pre-invasion levels, while littoral macrobenthos remained unchanged. The analysis of large data sets for young-of-year fishes found no systematic change in the abundance or geographic distribution of either group of fish in the Hudson River, which shows that the ecological effects of a biological invasion may change over time (Strayer et al. 2014). Zebra mussels can also alter the morphological and physical properties of their habitat areas, thereby affecting the availability of resources such as competition on food and space in the food web (Karatayev et al. 1997, Vanderploeg et al. 2002, Hecky et al. 2004). Overall, they are efficient ecosystem engineers that can alter the ecology of a system directly or indirectly (Figure 3.2). The system-wide effect of zebra and/or quagga mussels depends on water mixing rates, lake morphology, and turnover rates. Shortly after initial invasion, as populations increase, both dreissenids will have their largest effects on communities, and most of them will be direct effects. After the initial stage of invasion, impacts are less predictable, and more likely to be caused by indirect effects through changes in the ecosystem (Karatayev et al. 2015).

Economic damage caused by zebra mussels can be serious. Due to their byssal threads, zebra mussels can attach itself to hulls, increasing the weight of the vessel and consumption of fuel, and decreasing speeds. If the veligers or larval mussels are siphoned into engine cooling water intakes, it can overheat the engine and cause damage (Maxwell 1992). Dense mats of zebra mussels can be found on docks, piers, pilings, and ladders, increasing the weight by up to 20–30 pounds/m^2 and eventually sinking the structure due to the heavy colonization (O'Neill and

TABLE 3.2
Filtration Rate of a 15-mm (or 22-mg Total Dry Weight) Zebra Mussel

Mussel	Filtration Rate (ml/h/individual)	Suspended Particle	T (°C)	Reference
Zebra	7.9	*Cryptomonas* sp.	20	(Bunt et al. 1993)
	122.2	Hudson River water	20	(Roditi et al. 1996)
	38.0	*Chlamydomonas reinhardtii*	22	(Berg et al. 1996)
	99.7	*Chlamydomonas reinhardtii*	22	(Berg et al. 1996)
	93.0	*Chlamydomonas* sp.	23	(Horgan and Mills 1997)
	125.0	*Mallomonas* sp.	23	(Horgan and Mills 1997)
	159.5	*Cryptomonas pusilla*	23	(Horgan and Mills 1997)
	167.5	*Cryptomonas ovata*	23	(Horgan and Mills 1997)
	114.0	*Melosira* sp.	23	(Horgan and Mills 1997)
	78.8	*Chroococcus* sp. (globular colony)	23	(Horgan and Mills 1997)
	80.9	*Chroococcus* sp. filaments	23	(Horgan and Mills 1997)
	93.7	Natural assemblage + mixed aglal cultures	20	(Schneider et al. 1998)
	32.3	Clay	16	(Baker et al. 1998)
	63.8	Clay + *Microcystis*	16	(Baker et al. 1998)
	56.3	Clay + *Crucigenia*	16	(Baker et al. 1998)
	47.3	Clay + *Cyclotella*	16	(Baker et al. 1998)
	74.3	*Typha* detritus	16	(Baker et al. 1998)
	90.0	*Typha* detritus + *Microcystis*	16	(Baker et al. 1998)
	61.5	*Typha* detritus + *Crucigenia*	16	(Baker et al. 1998)
	29.6	*Typha* detritus + *Cyclotella*	16	(Baker et al. 1998)
	99.0	*Microcystis*	16	(Baker et al. 1998)
	32.3	*Microcystis* + *Micractinium*	16	(Baker et al. 1998)
	52.5	*Microcystis* + *Crucigenia*	16	(Baker et al. 1998)
	72.0	*Microcystis* + *Thalassiosira*	16	(Baker et al. 1998)
	30.8	*Microcystis* + *Cyclotella*	16	(Baker et al. 1998)
	9.0	*Microcystis* + *Scenedesmus*	16	(Baker et al. 1998)
	66.8	*Crucigenia*	16	(Baker et al. 1998)
	23.3	*Crucigenia* + *Micractinium*	16	(Baker et al. 1998)
	15.4	*Crucigenia* + *Thalassiosir*	16	(Baker et al. 1998)
	5.3	*Thalassiosira*	16	(Baker et al. 1998)
	21.0	*Thalassiosira* + *Cyclotella*	16	(Baker et al. 1998)
	14.3	*Cyclotella*	16	(Baker et al. 1998)
	37.5	*Cyclotella* + *Scenedesmus*	16	(Baker et al. 1998)
	6.0	*Cyclotella* + *Micractinium*	16	(Baker et al. 1998)
	71.6	Lillinonah Reservoir	16–20	(Bastviken et al. 1998)
	74.3	Hudson River + Lillinonah Reservoir (1:1)	16–20	(Bastviken et al. 1998)
	79.4	Hudson River + Lillinonah Reservoir (3:1)	16–20	(Bastviken et al. 1998)
	55.4	Hudson River + Lillinonah Reservoir (1:3)	16–20	(Bastviken et al. 1998)
	41.6	Hudson River + *Microcystis* + *Anabaena*	16–20	(Bastviken et al. 1998)
	42.2	Hudson River + *Microcystis* + *Anabaena* + Seston	16–20	(Bastviken et al. 1998)

Mussel	Filtration Rate (ml/h/individual)	Suspended Particle	T (°C)	Reference
	22–87	*Chlamydomonas*	20	(Baldwin et al. 2002)
	89.0	Suspended sediment	14	(Diggins 2001)
	55.0	Suspended sediment	8	(Diggins 2001)
	155.0	Suspended sediment	14	(Diggins 2001)
	110.0	Suspended sediment	22	(Diggins 2001)
	47.9	*Scenedesmus*	20	(Dionisio Pires et al. 2004)
	89.5	*Scenedesmus + Microcystis*	20	(Dionisio Pires et al. 2004)
	209.5	Cyanobacteria	20	(Dionisio Pires et al. 2004)
	80.0	Detritus	20	(Dionisio Pires et al. 2004)
	112.6	Non-Cyanobacteria phytoplankton	20	(Dionisio Pires et al. 2004)

MacNeill 1991). The shell of the zebra mussel can be sharp enough to cut bare feet. Beach and bathing footgear are used on some of the Great Lakes beaches to protect individuals from the sharp shells (Maxwell 1992). Deceased zebra mussels can generate foul odors. If they die in drinking water pipelines, it can produce unpleasant flavors and cause adverse health effects. Several billion dollars have been spent on facility and infrastructure repair and replacements (Roberts 1990). According to O'Neill (1997), $83 million has been spent on zebra mussel control from 339 facilities in 35 states and 3 provinces, with a mean expenditure of $248,000 per facility (Lovell et al. 2006). Among the expenses, $35,274,020 (51%) has been spent on managing Electric Power Generation and $21,435,610 (31%) has been spent on Water Treatment.

The species is considered as a good candidate for laboratory experiments. Zebra mussels are very easy to collect and they have both epifaunal and sessile life stages (Nichols 1996). For instance, the species has become very valuable due to its contribution to research on ciliary function (Silverman et al. 1996), ion transportation (Horohov et al. 1992), physiological resistance, and capacity adaptations (McMahon et al. 1993; McMahon 1996). It is also a good experimental species for toxicity studies (Roditi et al. 2000a; 2000b).

MONITORING AND SIGHTINGS

Massachusetts Department of Environmental Protection employees have done biological surveys at more than 2,000 waterbodies in Massachusetts since the 1980s. Field sheet quality control, database development, and map construction are under the guidance of the Standard Operating Procedures (SOP). The US Geological Survey (USGS) and other agencies and individuals also contributed to the process of data collection of *D. polymorpha* in Massachusetts (Benson et al. 2019; Wagner 2017). Tools for drafting maps and marking out data layers of sites with *D. polymorpha* were created via ArcGIS® ArcMap 10.1 (ESRI, Redlands, California).

In Massachusetts, adult zebra mussels were first discovered by a Town of Lee employee, Dmitri Consolati, and a lake abutter in Laurel Lake in July of 2009, and confirmed by state officials (Daley 2009). Currently, the Housatonic River Basin is the only watershed infested by zebra mussels (Figure 3.3 and Table 3.3). These waterbodies are located in the western part of the state. Since there are a total of 33 major watersheds in Massachusetts, the percentage of infested watersheds is about 3%.

Laurel Lake has favorable conditions for the growth of zebra mussels with a coarse bottom near the shore and ranging from sand to finer silt further out in deeper waters (Wagner 2017). There is plenty of gravel that is a good habitat for dense younger mussels to attach onto. It is believed that the invasion of Laurel Lake began in 2008 or even earlier. The Lake is the first documented waterbody that is infested by zebra mussels in Massachusetts. There are also other bivalves in Laurel Lake, such as Unionidae mussels and Sphaeriidae (tiny fingernail clams). They are not very common in the lake due to

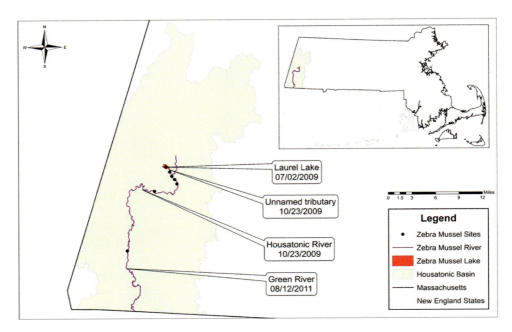

FIGURE 3.3 Distribution map depicting zebra mussel in Massachusetts.

the domination of the zebra mussel (Figure 3.4). The introduction of zebra mussels has placed great stress on native Unionidae populations around the country (see Introduction). The clarity of Laurel Lake ranges from medium to high (4–6.8 m or 13.1–22.3 ft) and the clarity may be improved by zebra mussels' filtering activities. Laurel Lake has been subject to a 3-ft drawdown each winter since 2010–2011 for the control of zebra mussels (and Eurasian watermilfoil) in shallow water. Although greater control is needed and desired, the drawdown has been limited to 3 ft by state regulation. Zebra mussel monitoring at different water depths over six years revealed that populations were denser in shallow water and became sparser as the depth increased (Figure 3.4) (Wagner 2017). Winter drawdowns in this lake have reduced the colonized zone of zebra mussels to depths of lower than 5 ft. This is the result of the desiccation or drying of mussels in the area that is dewatered and/or ice scour and exposure to freezing temperatures for animals exposed above and within an ice zone up to 2 ft below the water line. Deeper drawdowns have been proposed as a potential tool to further manage, and possibly eradicate zebra mussels from Laurel Lake. In Laurel Lake, zebra mussels have been found to depths of 25 ft. It is unlikely that a drawdown could be achieved and maintained to eradicate zebra mussels and the environmental impact to other species and the lake itself would be significant and therefore cannot be ignored. For example, Laurel Lake is home to one of only two populations of the State Endangered Boreal Marstonia snail (*Marstonia lustrica*). Increase of winter drawdown depth will decrease the abundance of Boreal Marstonia snail because highest abundances have been found at depths of 4–6 ft in Laurel Lake.

Amid the arrival of zebra mussels at Laurel Lake, MA DCR developed protocols for watercraft users to fill a Clean Boat Certification Form before launching as well as clean, drain, and dry their boats (MA DCR 2010) to prevent spread of zebra mussels to other waterbodies. Working together with Massachusetts Department of Fish and Game (MA DFG), MA DCR also activated the Massachusetts Interim Zebra Mussel Action Plan to take actions in dealing with invasive mussels mainly in the Housatonic and Hoosic watershed which are highly susceptible to colonization by zebra mussels (Table 3.1). These actions include the following: (1)

Zebra Mussel (*Dreissena polymorpha*)

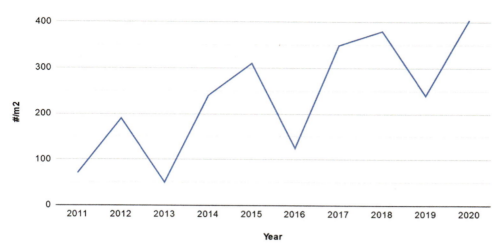

FIGURE 3.4 Dead zebra mussel density in the drawdown zone. For the years 2011–2016, densities of deceased zebra mussels were taken from Wagner (2017). For the years 2017–2020, estimations were provided following the same trend observed between 2011 and 2016. Estimated densities were designed to follow a logistic growth pattern. This was chosen as Wagner states that the substrate in Laurel Lake is a potential limiting factor in the spread of zebra mussels, meaning as the population increases and then decreases cyclically, it may eventually run out of substrate and the population will balance out (i.e., hitting some form of carrying capacity). This theory can be either confirmed or denied through further surveys of deceased zebra mussels during December drawdowns.

Self-certification by users that their boats have not been on waterbodies likely affected by zebra or quagga mussels within the last 30 days, or if they have, that the boats have been properly decontaminated in accordance with the procedures in the plan. Violations of these mandatory requirements are subject to fines and other penalties under OFBA regulations. (2) Extension of the temporary closure of the state boat ramp at Laurel Lake, the one Massachusetts waterbody that has a documented occurrence of zebra mussels to date, until October 15, 2009 (the updated sightings are listed in Table 3.1). (3) Extending the hours of three existing state boat ramp monitors and the addition of a fourth monitor to regularly monitor nine boat ramps in the Hoosic and Housatonic watersheds. (4) Implementation of a robust educational and technical assistance outreach effort designed to facilitate parallel prevention measures by other key stakeholders such as municipalities, lake associations, and recreational users of Massachusetts waterbodies (MA DCR and MA DFG 2009). More systematic zebra mussel management is described subsequently.

MANAGING ACTIONS

Zebra mussels can spread rapidly even though there are many methods to inhibit their colonization of available invasion. Some evidence of biological control methods has been found in Europe. Crayfish are one of the groups that forages on veliger and post-veliger larvae, consuming about 100 mussels per day. However, areas located in deeper lakes with colder water temperatures are not a favorable habitat for crayfish to hunt in. Based on estimations, the loss of zebra mussels due to crayfish predation is only around 5% (Maxwell 1992). There are also some other Eurasian fish species that feed on *D. polymorpha*, such as the European roach or common roach (*Rutilus rutilus*). Reports show that about 90% of the European roach's diet consists of *D.*

TABLE 3.3
List of Town Names and Waterbodies that Contain Zebra Mussels

Town	Waterbody
Great Barrington	Green River
Lee	Housatonic River
	Laurel Lake
	Unnamed tributary
Stockbridge	Housatonic River

polymorpha. Also, *D. polymorpha* consists of on average 97% of the diets of certain species of waterfowl, specifically the common pochard (*Aythya ferina*), tufted duck (*Aythya fuligula*), and Eurasian coot, three species of overwintering diving ducks. Counts of zebra mussel larvae show fluctuations but no upsurge trends have been found, which provides evidence that the equilibrium in those areas is maintained by local predators (Walz 1991). In the Great Lakes, species like carp (*Cyprinidae*), eel (*Anguilliformes*), and sheepshead (*Archosargus*) have found to be promising biological control agents (O'Neill and MacNeill 1991). However, Asian carp itself is an invasive nuisance species and a collaboration of 28 US and Canadian agencies are currently working together to prevent the introduction and establishment of Asian carp in the Great Lakes (Asian Carp Regional Coordinating Committee 2020). Therefore, it is not suggested to introduce any carp species for zebra mussel control in Massachusetts. In an infested reservoir in California, Sweetwater Reservoir, stocking high-density (0.42 or 1.90 fish/m^2) redear sunfish (*Lepomis microlophus*) effectively removed another dreissenid mussel, the quagga mussel in an enclosure (Figure 3.5) and appeared to suppress their growth and recruitment (Wong et al. 2013). Redear sunfish is a species native to the Southeastern United States that has become a popular stocked sportfish in the Southwest. Based upon the experimental results in the Sweetwater Reservoir, biological control of dreissenid mussels with redear sunfish could be an effective approach (Hatcher and McClelland 2015).

Several experiments have been conducted with *Bucephalus polymorphus* to examine effects on *D. polymorpha* (Lajtner et al. 2008) because it is a type of parasite that treats *D. polymorpha* as its first intermediate host (Molloy et al. 1997). However, considering the main impact to mussel gonads is less harmful (Molloy et al. 1997), using *B. polymorphus* as a biological control agent may not be effective. Additionally, a research project by Molloy and Griffin (1991) tested the potential lethality of over 260 different microorganisms on *D. polymorpha* in a laboratory setting over a two-year period and the bacterium *Pseudomonas fluorescens* (*Pf* CL 145A) was found to be an effective biological control agent. Both living and dead cells of *P. fluorescens* are effective in controlling *D. polymorpha*, as well as *D. bugensis* (the quagga mussel). The bacteria can be used within a wide temperature range (5–27°C), which means the agent is far more effective than artificial chemical molluscicides (normally, those copper-based chemical molluscicides can mainly be effective at temperatures above 18°C) (Molloy 2002). Nearly two decades of research on *Pf* CL 145A has led to the development of the first pesticide for the control of invasive zebra (and quagga) mussels, Zequanox® (Rackl and Link 2015). Five case studies from Rackl and Link (2015) (adult mussel control within a hydropower facility, adult mussel control within intake bays at a coal-powered plant, a comparison to chlorine at a drinking treatment facility, a mussel settlement management case within a hydropower facility, and open water treatments in a lake) revealed that Zequanox® can provide greater than 90% control in both flowing and static infrastructure in high volumes of water. Moreover, pilot research at Christmas Lake, Minnesota, has shown some eradication of zebra mussels in that area. By applying several treatments of Zequanox®, no evidence of zebra mussels in an experimental area was found (Smith 2015).

Zebra Mussel (*Dreissena polymorpha*)

FIGURE 3.5 Quagga mussel study design at Sweetwater Reservoir, California. (Photo by Mark Hatcher, Hatcher, and McClelland (2015).)

Due to its tiny size, the value of *D. polymorpha* as a food source is unlikely. The species is also very hard to harvest because of their robust byssal fibers. Toxin bioaccumulation via their filter feeding can be harmful to humans as well (O'Neill and MacNeill 1991). According to many projects in Europe, the former USSR, and North America, it is better to extinguish the species during veliger stage when found in water pipelines, watercrafts, or other infrastructure (Choi et al. 2013; Dalton and Cottrell 2013; Davis et al. 2016; Delrose et al. 2015; DeShon et al. 2016; Moffitt et al. 2016; MRB Group 1991; Watters et al. 2015).

Several physical control methods can be potentially used to help lessen infestations. Strainers and filters can be applied to block the entry of larval, juvenile, and especially adult mussels (Maxwell 1992). The effectiveness is highly dependent on the size of the strainers and filters used. These tools are suggested to be installed at intakes and distribution systems. Scraping is considered very effective in larger conduits, only if the size is wide enough to allow for the use of equipment. However, this method requires high manpower and can be very expensive (O'Neill and MacNeill 1991). Some other methods have also been suggested such as the use of a type of pipe-crawling vehicle (Martin et al. 1991), centrifugal separators (Smythe et al. 1991b), low-voltage electric fields (Smythe et al. 1991a), the use of ultraviolet radiation (Chalker-Scott et al. 1991; Delrose et al. 2015; Stewart-Malone et al. 2015), acoustic energy (Menezes 1991), and coatings (Smithee and Kovalak 1991; Skaja et al. 2015). Periodically flushing water systems with heated water and tap water can be effective and less expensive. For hot water, the temperature should be higher than 37°C (99°F) and flushed through the area for 1 hour to achieve 100% eradication of mussels (O'Neill and MacNeill 1991) and, if it is for water craft decontamination, it is recommended to use 60°C (140°F) for 10 seconds by spraying a target area (Comeau et al. 2011; Comeau et al. 2015; Morse 2009). According to Wagner (2017), partial drawdown is a method that can be applied to reduce biomass of zebra mussels in shallow areas in a waterbody. However, partial drawdowns and/or complete drawdowns will impact all species within the waterbody. The loss of *D. polymorpha* will also cut off the food web of the predatory fish *A. ferina* and *A. fuligula* (Leuven et al. 2014). It is possible that the discharged water may contain some overwinter veligers and larvae that can cause secondary infestations to downstream waterbodies.

There are two main categories of chemical control methods: one is the use of oxidizing agents (chlorine, chlorine dioxide, hydrogen peroxide, potassium permanganate, etc.), the other is the use of toxic chemicals (molluscicides, metallic ions, copper sulfate) to control zebra mussels (Maxwell 1992). Oxidizing agents should not remain in local environments for long periods; therefore, an immediate discharge may be needed (Maxwell 1992). Electrolytically dissolved metal ions can be considered a good method for small conduits that are not easily accessed. The use of chlorine has proved to be an effective control method. However, dechlorination is needed after the application. Concentrations of solutions from 0.25 mg/l to 1.0 mg/l, after two to three weeks of application, results in a 95–100% mortality rate of zebra mussels (O'Neill and MacNeill 1991). One should take proper precautions when applying chlorine treatments to public drinking waters due to the generation of trihalomethanes (THMs) which are potential carcinogens (Cotruvo and Regelski 1989). Acetic acid products (Claudi et al. 2012; Davis et al. 2015a) and potash such as NaCl and/or KCl (Davis et al. 2015b; 2017; Moffitt et al. 2016) are also effective alternative chemicals for zebra mussel control with relatively less side effects under appropriate environmental conditions or when used for watercraft decontamination. Specifically, KCl-based BioBullets® has been developed for specific use in zebra mussel control (Aldridge et al. 2006), which is designed to selectively target filter feeders by introducing poison to the water in the form of food particles preferred by molluscans. Therefore, the poisons are removed from the water when mussels feed and pose minimal impacts to the rest of the aquatic ecosystem (Aldridge et al. 2006). More information about chemical control on zebra mussel and other 18 invasive species can be found in Appendix III. Any chemical used for invasive species control requires a permit from the Massachusetts Department of Environmental Protection.

Among management options, prevention has proved to be the most efficient and cost-effective approach in stopping the spread of aquatic invasive species. The most efficient way to protect the environment from invasive species is integrated management, including prevention and education, early detection, control, ecosystem restoration, and the regulation and enforcement of environmental law (Wong and Gerstenberger 2015). To minimize the spreading of *D. polymorpha*, a combination of treatment methods should be used, which include increasing public awareness of invasive species as part of the integrated management approach. For example, the Massachusetts Department of Environmental Protection has developed and implemented standard operating procedures for internal field equipment decontamination during water quality monitoring in the field to prevent the spread of invasive aquatic organisms (Chase and Wong 2015). Specifically, citizens are strongly encouraged to inspect the hull of boats thoroughly after boating in infested waterbodies, flush hulls with heated water, drawdown wells, and expose the hulls, anchors, and chains under sunlight for drying. Clean, drain, and drying watercraft and experimental equipment and gear is critical to prevent the spread of invasive species from one waterbody to another.

SUCCESS STORY

One form of chemical control that has shown promising results is the application of copper-based pesticides. EarthTec QZ® is a copper-based (5% copper by weight) molluscicide that has been found to kill mollusks at certain concentrations. It is NSF-certified for safe use in drinking water and is approved by the EPA for use to control invasive species of mussels. EarthTec QZ® is a registered herbicide/pesticide in Massachusetts. It has been confirmed that EarthTec QZ® could prevent the settlement of dreissenid mussels (Watters et al. 2015) and it has been applied for eradication of either zebra or quagga mussels in various waterbodies (Hammond and Ferris 2019; Lund et al. 2018). This success story involves the use of EarthTec QZ® to eradicate an invasive population of mussels from a lake in Pennsylvania in 2017.

Billmeyer Quarry is a lake located in Conoy Township, Pennsylvania, with a surface area of 12 ha and a maximum depth of about 35 m in the west basin and 27 m in the east basin (Hammond and Ferris 2019). Billmeyer had become infested with quagga mussels (*Dreissena rostriformis bugensis*), with the first observations being recorded in 2005. Quagga mussels, a relative of the zebra mussel, are an aquatic bivalve mollusk that have also been listed as an invasive species in the United States, causing many of the same issues that the zebra mussel has. The molluscicide was applied to 50% of the lakes surface during each treatment and was allowed for mixing with the remaining waters of the lake naturally. Several cages filled with mussels were placed at various locations and depths around the lake. Treatments were to persist until every preplaced caged mussel was deceased. A total of three treatments occurred, with additional treatments being applied in order to keep the molluscicide at a target concentration of the 0.2 mg/l in the lake. On day 1 of the first treatment occurring in the fall of 2017, 6,245 l of EarthTec QZ® were dispersed at depths of 2, 6, and 9 m. The second treatment, occurring on day 7, dispersed 4,164 l at depths of 2, 6, 18, 21, and 26 m. The third and final treatment, occurring on day 37, dispersed 3,123 l at depths of 9–12 m. Based on historical measurements of water temperature and dissolved oxygen for Billmeyer Quarry, it was estimated that mussels could inhabit depths up to at least 24 m. Treatment methods therefore ensured that the EarthTec QZ® would reach a lethal concentration at that depth.

The first mussels began to die 3 days after the first treatment, with the final mussels dying after 40 days. Samples of plankton were taken several times throughout the study and then examined for the presence of mussel DNA. A sample taken in December of 2017 found very low levels of DNA below the detection limits of the tests used, meaning mussel DNA may have been present in the lake. However, in a sample taken in July 2018, over half a year since the application of the final treatment, no evidence of mussel DNA was found. This suggests that quagga mussels had been completely eradicated in the lake at that time. Future mussel surveys of the lake will be able to verify if this was true. The total cost of the project came out to $109,400, or about $0.06/m^3 treated.

One potential risk that always comes with the use of chemical control agents is spillover deaths of non-target species. In Billmeyer Quarry, large numbers of various fish species were observed prior to the first treatment. The only incident of spillover from the effects of the molluscicide occurred after the second application when ten dead gizzard shad were found floating on the water. Because only one species was affected, it is possible that this species is overly sensitive to copper-based pesticides. It is also possible that, due to the fact that other members of the species were observed to be healthy during other periods of the project, the ten individuals that were killed were exposed to a pocket of a higher concentration of EarthTec QZ®. Another risk that comes specifically with molluscicides is undesired harm to native mollusks. Many native species of mollusks, such as several members of the family Uniondae, are already under great stress due to competition from the zebra and quagga mussels. Therefore, application of harmful molluscicides should be used sparingly in waterbodies inhabited by these native mollusks. In this specific project, the targeted lake had no populations of native mollusks.

The results of this study show that the use of copper-based pesticides such as EarthTec QZ® may be an effective and cost-efficient control agent for eradicating, or at least decreasing, populations of invasive mussels. However, chemical control becomes less effective on larger waterbodies, where the overall cost and needed manpower increase. The amount of chemicals needed to maintain target lethal concentrations would also increase. This makes chemical treatment with copper-based pesticides an effective reactive control agent. Coupled with good preventative measures, such as boat inspections and public education, the spread of invasive mussels in Massachusetts can hopefully be stopped.

REFERENCES

Aldridge, D.C., P. Elliott, and G.D. Moggridge. 2006. Microencapsulated biobullets for the control of biofouling zebra mussels. *Environmental Science & Technology* 40: 975–979.

Asian Carp Regional Coordinating Committee. 2020. *Asian Carp Action Plan for Fiscal Year 2020*. Asian Carp Regional Coordinating Committee, p. 167.

Baker, S.M., J.S. Levinton, J.P. Kurdziel, and S.E. Shumway. 1998. Selective feeding and biodeposition by zebra mussels and their relation to changes in phytoplankton composition and seston load. *Journal of Shellfish Research* 17: 1207–1213.

Baldwin, B.S., M.S. Mayer, J. Dayton, N. Pau, J. Mendilla, M. Sullivan, A. Moore, A. Ma, and E.L. Mills. 2002. Comparative growth and feeding in zebra and quagga mussels (*Dreissena polymorpha* and *Dreissena bugensis*): Implications for North American lakes. *Canadian Journal of Fisheries and Aquatic Sciences* 59: 680–694.

Bastviken, D.T.E., N.F. Caraco, and J.J. Cole. 1998. Experimental measurements of zebra mussel (*Dreissena polymorpha*) impacts on phytoplankton community composition. *Freshwater Biology* 39: 375–386.

Benson, A., D. Raikow, J. Larson, A. Fusaro, A.K. Bogdanoff, and A. Elgin. 2019. *Dreissena polymorpha (zebra mussel)*. https://nas.er.usgs.gov/queries/FactSheet.aspx?speciesID=5 (Accessed November 1, 2019).

Berg, D.J., S.W. Fisher, and P.F. Landrum. 1996. Clearance and processing of algal particle by zebra mussels (*Dreissena polymorpha*). *Journal of Great Lakes Research* 22: 779–788.

Berkman, P.A., M.A. Haltuch, E. Tichich, D.W. Garton, G.W. Kennedy, J.E. Gannon, S.D. Mackey, J.A. Fuller, and D.L. Liebenthal. 1998. Zebra mussels invade Lake Erie muds. *Nature* 393: 27–28.

Britton, D.K. 2015. History of western management actions on invasive mussels. In W.H. Wong and S.L. Gerstenberger (eds). *Biology and Management of Invasive Quagga and Zebra Mussels in the Western United States*. London: CRC Press, pp. 3–14.

Bunt, C.M., H.J. MacIsaac, and W.G. Sprules. 1993. Pumping rates and projected filtering impacts of juvenile zebra mussels (*Dreissena polymorpha*) in Western Lake Erie. *Canadian Journal of Fisheries and Aquatic Sciences* 50: 1017–1022.

Burlakova, L.E. 1998. Ecology of *Dreissena polymorpha* (Pallas) and its role in the structure and function of aquatic ecosystems. [In Russian.] Dissertation. Zoology Institute of the Academy of Science, Minsk, Belarus.

Caraco, N.F., J.J. Cole, and D.J. Strayer. 2006. Top down control from the bottom: Regulation of eutrophication in a large river by benthic grazing. *Limnology and Oceanography* 51: 664–670.

Carlton, J.T. 1993. Dispersal mechanisms of the zebra mussel. In T.F. Nalepa and D.W. Schoesser (eds). *Zebra mussels: Biology, impacts, and control*. London: Lewis/CRC Press, pp. 677–698.

Carlton, J.T. 2008. The zebra Mussel *Dreissena polymorpha* found in North America in 1986 and 1987. *Journal of the Great Lakes Research* 34: 770–773.

Chalker-Scott, L., J.D. Scott, C. Dunning, and K. Smith. 1991. Effect of ultraviolet-B radiation (280–320nm) on survivorship of zebra Mussel Larvae (*Dreissena polymorpha*): A potential control strategy. In Second international Zebra Mussel Research Conference, November 19–22. Rochester, NY, p. 35.

Chase, R.F., and W.H. Wong. 2015. Standard Operating Procedure: Field Equipment Decontamination to Prevent the Spread of Invasive Aquatic Organisms. Massachusetts Department of Environmental Protection. File # CN 59.6.29 pp.

Choi, W.J., S.L. Gerstenberger, R.F. McMahon, and W.H. Wong. 2013. Estimating survival rates of quagga mussel (*Dreissena rostriformis bugensis*) veliger larvae under summer and autumn temperature regimes in residual water of trailered watercraft at Lake Mead, USA. *Management of Biological Invasions* 4(1): 61–69.

Claudi, R., A. Graves, A.C. Taraborelli, R.J. Prescott, and S. Mastitsky. 2012. Impact of pH on survival and settlement of dreissenid mussels. *Aquatic Invasions* 7(1): 21–28.

Claudi, R., and G.L. Mackie. 1994. *Practical Manual for Zebra Mussel Monitoring and Control*. London: Lewis Publishers, p. 227.

Comeau, S., R.S. Ianniello, W.H. Wong, and S.L. Gerstenberger. 2015. Boat decontamination with hot water spray: Field validation. In W.H. Wong and S.L. Gerstenberger (eds). *Biology and Management of Invasive Quagga and Zebra Mussels in the Western United States*. London: CRC Press, pp. 161–173.

Comeau, S., S. Rainville, W. Baldwin, E. Austin, S.L. Gerstenberger, C. Cross, and W.H. Wong. 2011. Susceptibility of quagga mussels (Dreissena rostriformis bugensis) to hot-water sprays as a means of watercraft decontamination. *Biofouling* 27(3): 267–274.

Cotruvo J.A., and M. Regelski. 1989. Issues in developing national primary drinking water regulations for disinfection and disinfection by-products. In: E.J. Calabrese, C.E., Gilbert, and H. Pastids (eds.), *Safe Drinking Water Act: Amendments, Regulations, and Standards*. Chelsea: Lewis Publishers, pp. 57–69.

Counihan, T., W.H. Wong, and R.F. McMahon. 2018. Early detection monitoring for invasive mussels in the Columbia River Basin. Columbia River Basin Dreissenid Mussel Monitoring Forum. October 31, 2018. Boise, ID.

Daley, B. 2009. Invasive mussel found in Bay State lake. Boston Globe. Retrieved from http://archive.boston.com/news/local/massachusetts/articles/2009/07/09/invasive_mussel_found_in_mass_lake/ (Accessed November 1, 2020).

Dalton, L.B., and S. Cottrell. 2013. Quagga and zebra mussel risk via veliger transfer by overland hauled boats. *Management of Biological Invasions* 4(2): 129–133.

Davis, E.A., W.H. Wong, and W.N. Harman. 2015a. Distilled white vinegar (5% acetic acid) as a potential decontamination method for adult zebra mussels. *Management of Biological Invasions* 6(4): 423–428.

Davis, E.A., W.H. Wong, and W.N. Harman. 2015b. Comparison of three sodium chloride chemical treatments for adult zebra mussel decontamination. *Journal of Shellfish Research* 34(3): 1029–1036.

Davis, E.A., W.H. Wong, and W.N. Harman. 2016. Livewell flushing to remove zebra mussel (*Driessena polymorpha*) veligers. *Management of Biological Invasions* 7(4): 399–403.

Davis, E.A., W.H. Wong, and W.N. Harman. 2017. Toxicity of potassium chloride compared to sodium chloride for zebra mussel decontamination. *Journal of Aquatic Animal Health* 30: 3–12.

De Stasio, B.T., M.B. Schrimpf, A.E. Beranek, and W.C. Daniels. 2008. Increased chlorophyll a, phytoplankton abundance, and cyanobacteria occurrence following invasion of Green Bay, Lake Michigan by dreissenid mussels. *Aquatic Invasions* 3: 21–27.

Delrose, P., S.L. Gerstenberger, and W.H. Wong. 2015. Effectiveness of the SafeGUARD ultraviolet radiation system as a system to control quagga mussel veligers (*Dreissena rostriformis bugensis*). In: W.H. Wong and S.L. Gerstenberger (eds). *Biology and Management of Invasive Quagga and Zebra Mussels in the Western United States*. London: CRC Press, pp. 479–485.

DeShon, D.L., W.H. Wong, D. Farmer, and A.J. Jensen. 2016. The ability of scent detection canines to detect the presence of quagga mussel (*Dreissena rostriformis bugensis*) veligers. *Management of Biological Invasions* 7(4): 419–428.

Diggins, T.P. 2001. A seasonal comparison of suspended sediment filtration by quagga (*Dreissena bugensis*) and zebra (*D. polymorpha*) mussels. *Journal of Great Lakes Research* 27: 457–466.

Dionisio Pires, L.M., R.R. Jonker, E. Van Donk, and H.J. Laanbroek. 2004. Selective grazing by adults and larvae of the zebra mussel (*Dreissena polymorpha*): Application of flow cytometry to natural seston. *Freshwater Biology* 49: 116–126.

Ekroat, L.R., E.C. Masteller, J.C. Shaffer, and L.M. Steele. 1993. The byssus of the zebra mussel (Dreissena polymorpha): Morphology, byssal thread formation, and detachment. In: T.F. Nalepa and D.W. Schoesser (eds). *Zebra Mussels: Biology, Impacts, and Control*. London: Lewis/CRC Press, pp. 239–263.

Ellis, A.E. 1978. *British Freshwater Bivalve Mollusca: Keys and Notes for the Identification of Species*. London: Academic Press, p. 109.

Feinberg, H.S. (ed.) 1979. *Simon and Schuster's Guide to Shells.* London: Simon and Schuster, p. 512.

Fraleigh, P.C., P.L. Klerks, G. Gubanich, G. Matisoff, and R.C. Stevenson. 1993. Abundance and settling of zebra mussel (*Dreissena polymorpha*) veligers in western and central Lake Erie. In: T.F. Nalepa, and D.W. Schoesser (eds). *Zebra Mussels: Biology, Impacts, and Control.* London: Lewis/CRC Press, pp. 129–142.

Griffiths, R.W. 1993. Effects of zebra mussels (Dreissena polymorpha) on the benthic fauna of Lake St. Clair. Lewis Publishers. In: T.F. Nalepa, and D.W. Schoesser (eds). *Zebra Mussels: Biology, Impacts, and Control.* London: Lewis/CRC Press, pp. 439–451.

Hammond, H., and G. Ferris. 2019. Low doses of EarthTec QZ ionic copper used in effort to eradicate quagga mussels from an entire Pennsylvania Lake. *Management of Biological Invasions* 10(3): 500–516.

Hatcher, M., and S. McClelland. 2015. Monitoring and control of quagga mussels in sweetwater reservoir. In W.H. Wong and S.L. Gerstenberger (eds). *Biology and Management of Invasive Quagga and Zebra Mussels in the Western United States.* London: CRC Press, pp. 401–424.

Hebert, P.D.N., B.W. Muncaster, and G.L. Mackie. 1989. Ecological and genetic studies on Dreissena polymorpha (Pallas)—A new mollusk in the Great Lakes. *Canadian Journal of Fisheries and Aquatic Sciences* 46: 1587–1591.

Hecky, R.E., R.E.H. Smith, D.R. Barton, S.J. Guildford, W.D. Taylor, M.N. Charlton, and T. Howell. 2004. The nearshore phosphorus shunt: A consequence of ecosystem engineering by dreissenids in the Laurentian Great Lakes. *Canadian Journal of Fisheries and Aquatic Sciences* 61: 1285–1293.

Horgan, M.J., and E.L. Mills. 1997. Clearance rates and filtering activity of zebra mussel (*Dreissena polymorpha*): Implications for freshwater lakes. *Canadian Journal of Fisheries and Aquatic Sciences* 54: 249–255.

Horohov, J., H. Silverman, J.W. Lynn, and T.H. Dietz. 1992. Ion transport in the freshwater zebra mussel, *Dreissena polymorpha*. *Biological Bulletin* 183: 297–303.

ITIS (Integrated Taxonomic Information System). 2021. www.itis.gov/servlet/SingleRpt/SingleRpt#null (Accessed February 8, 2021).

Karatayev, A.Y., L. Burlakova, S. Mastitsky, and D.K. Padilla. 2011. Rates of spread of two congeners, *Dreissena polymorpha* and *Dreissena rostriformis bugensis*, at different spatial scales. *Journal of Shellfish Research* 30(3): 923–931.

Karatayev, A.Y., L.E. Burlakova, and D.K. Padilla. 1997. The effects of *Dreissena polymorpha* (Pallas) invasion on aquatic communities in Eastern Europe. *Journal of Shellfish Research* 16: 187–203.

Karatayev, A.Y., L.E. Burlakova, and D.K. Padilla. 2002. Impacts of zebra mussels on aquatic communities and their role as ecosystem engineers. In E. Leppakoski, S. Gollach, and S. Olenin (eds). *Invasive Aquatic Species of Europe: Distribution, Impacts and Management.* Dordrecht: Kluwer Academic Publishers, pp. 433–446.

Karatayev, A.Y., L.E. Burlakova, and D.K. Padilla. 2015. Zebra versus quagga mussels: A review of their spread, population dynamics, and ecosystem impacts. *Hydrobiologia* 746: 97–112.

Karatayev, A.Y., D.K. Padilla, and L.E. Burlakova. 2006. Growth rate and longevity of *Dkareissena polymorpha* (Pallas): A review and recommendations for future study. *Journal of Shellfish Research* 25: 23–32.

Kerney, M.P., and B.S. Morton. 1970. The distribution of *Dreissena polymorpha*. (Pallas) in Britain. *Journal of Conchology* 27: 97–100.

Lajtner, J., A. Lucić, M. Marušić, and R. Erben. 2008. The effects of the trematode Bucephalus polymorphus on the reproductive cycle of the zebra mussel *Dreissena polymorpha* in the Drava River. *Acta Parasitologica* 53(1): 85–92.

Leach, J.H. 1993. Impacts of zebra mussel (*Dreissena polymorpha*) on water quality and fish spawning reefs in Western Lake Erie. In: T.F. Nalepa and D.W. Schoesser (eds). *Zebra Mussels: Biology, Impacts, and Control.* London: Lewis/CRC Press, pp. 381–397.

Leuven, R., F. Collas, K.R. Koopman, J. Matthews, and G.V. Velde. 2014. Mass mortality of invasive zebra and quagga mussels by desiccation during severe winter conditions. *Aquatic Invasions* 9(3): 243–252.

Li, J., V. Ianaiev, A. Huff, J. Zalusky, T. Ozersky, and S. Katsev. 2021. Benthic invaders control the phosphorus cycle in the world's largest freshwater ecosystem. *Proceedings of the National Academy of Sciences of the United States of America* 118(6): e2008223118. https://doi.org/10.1073/pnas.2008223118.

Lovell, S.J., S.F. Stone, and L. Fernandez. 2006. The economic impacts of aquatic invasive species: A review of the literature. *Agricultural and Resource Economics Review* 35(1): 195–208.

Lucy, F.E., L.E. Burlakova, A.Y. Karatayev, S.E. Mastitsky, and D.T. Zanatta. 2013. Zebra mussel impacts on unionids: A synthesis of trends in North America and Europe. In: T.F. Nalepa and D.W. Schoesser (eds). *Zebra Mussels: Biology, Impacts, and Control.* London: Lewis/CRC Press, pp. 623–646.

Lund K., K.B. Cattoor, E. Fieldseth, J. Sweet, and M.A. McCartney. 2018. Zebra mussel (*Dreissena polymorpha*) eradication efforts in Christmas Lake, Minnesota. *Lake and Reservoir Management* 34(1): 7–20.

MA DCR (Massachusetts Department of Conservation and Recreation). 2010. *Aquatic Invasive Species Assessment and Management Plan.* Boston, MA: MA DCR, p. 39.

MA DCR (Massachusetts Department of Conservation and Recreation) and MA DFG (Massachusetts Department of Fish and Game). 2009. *Massachusetts Interim Zebra Mussel Action Plan.* Cambridge, MA: MA DCR, p. 27.

MacIsaac, H.J. 1996. Potential abiotic and biotic impacts of zebra mussels on the inland waters of North America. *American Zoologist* 36: 287–299.

Mackie, G.L., and D.W. Schloesser. 1996. Comparative biology of zebra mussels in Europe and North America: An overview. *American Zoologist* 36(3): 244–258.

Martel, A. 1993. Dispersal and recruitment of zebra mussels (*Dreissena polymorpha*) in a nearshore area in west-central Lake Erie: The significance of postmetamorphic drifting. *Canadian Journal of Fisheries and Aquatic Sciences* 50: 3–12.

Martin, B., and S.E. Landsberger. 1991. Design of pipe-crawling vehicles for zebra mussel control. In Second international zebra mussel research conference, November 19–22, Rochester, NY, p. 32.

Maxwell, L. 1992. *The Biology, Invasion and Control of the Zebra Mussel (Dreissena polymorpha) in North America.* New York: State University of New York at Oneonta, Biological Field Station, pp. 1–26.

Mayer, C.M., L.E. Burlakova, P. Eklöv, D. Fitzgerald, A.Y. Karatayev, S.A Ludsin, S. Millard, E.L. Mills, A.P. Ostapenya, L.G. Rudstam, B. Zhu, and T.V. Zhukova. 2013. Benthification of freshwater lakes: Exotic mussels turning ecosystems upside down. In: T.F. Nalepa and D.W. Schoesser (eds). *Zebra Mussels: Biology, Impacts, and Control.* London: Lewis/CRC Press, pp. 575–585.

McMahon, R.F. 1996. The physiological ecology of the zebra mussel, *Dreissena polymorpha*, in North America and Europe. *American Zoologist* 36: 339–363.

McMahon, R.F., B.S. Payne, and T. Ussery. 1991. Effects of temperature and relative humidity on desiccation resistance in Zebra Mussels (*Dreissena polymorpha*): Is aerial exposure a viable control option? In Second International Zebra Mussel Research Conference, November 19–22, Rochester, NY.

McMahon, R.F., T.A. Ussery, A.C. Miller, and B.S. Payne. 1993. Thermal tolerance in zebra mussels (*Dreissena polymorpha*) relative to rate of temperature increase and acclimation temperature. In L. Tsou and Y. G. Mussalli (eds). *Proceedings: Third International Zebra Mussel Conference* (EPRI TR-102077). Palo Alto, CA: Electric Power Research Institute, pp. 4-97–4-118.

Menezes, J. 1991. Zebra Mussel control using acoustic energy. In Second International Zebra Mussel Research Conference, November 19–22. Rochester, NY, p. 36.

Mills, E.L., J.R. Chrisman, B. Baldwin, R.W. Owens, R. O'Gorman, T. Howell, E.F. Roseman, and M.K. Raths. 1999. Changes in the Dreissenid Community in the Lower Great Lakes with Emphasis on Southern Lake Ontario. *Journal of Great Lakes research* 25(1): 187–197.

Moffitt, C.M., K.A. Stockton-Fiti, and R. Claudi. 2016. Toxicity of potassium chloride to veliger and byssal stage dreissenid mussels related to water quality. *Management of Biological Invasions* 7(3): 257–268.

Molloy, D.P. 2002. Biological control of Zebra Mussels. In Proceedings of the Third California Conference on Biological Control. University of California, Davis. Division of Research and Collections, New York State Museum, The State Education Department, Albany, NY, pp. 86–94. www.researchgate.net/profile/Daniel_Molloy2/publication/288844393_Biological_control_of_zebra_mussels/links/573d289608aea45ee841a752.pdf (Accessed June 28, 2018).

Molloy, D.P., and B. Griffin. 1991. Biological Control of Zebra Mussels: Screening for the Lethal Microorganisms. In Second International Zebra Mussel Research Conference, Nov. 19–22, 1991, Rochester, NY, p. 30.

Molloy D.P., A.Y. Karatayev, L.E. Burlakova, D.P. Kurandina, and F. Laruelle. 1997. Natural enemies of zebra mussels: Predators, parasites, and ecological competitors. *Reviews in Fisheries Science* 5: 27–97.

Montz, G., and J. Hirsch. 2016. Veliger presence in residual water—Assessing this pathway risk for Minnesota watercraft. *Management of Biological Invasions* 7(3): 235–240.

Morse, J.T. 2009. Assessing the effects of application time and temperature on the efficacy of hot-water sprays to mitigate fouling by *Dreissena polymorpha* (zebra mussels Pallas). *Biofouling* 25(7): 605–610.

MRB Group. 1991. *The Impact of Zebra Mussel Infestations on Public Water Supplies: A Summary Report*. Rochester, NY: MRB Group Engineering, Architecture and Surveying, p. 5.

Nalepa, T.F., D.L. Fanslow, and S.A. Pothoven. 2010. Recent changes in density, biomass, recruitment, size structure, and nutritional state of Dreissena populations in southern Lake Michigan. *Journal of Great Lakes Research* 36(Supplement 3): 19–25.

Nalepa, T.F., and D.W. Schloesser (eds.). 1993. *Zebra Mussels: Biology, Impacts, and Control*. London: Lewis/CRC Press, p. 810.

Nalepa, T.F., and D.W. Schloesser (eds.). 2013. *Quagga and Zebra Mussels: Biology, Impacts, and Control*. London: CRC Press, p. 815.

Neary, B.P., and J.H. Leach. 1991. Mapping the potential spread of the zebra mussel (*Dreissena polymorpha*) in Ontario. *Canadian Journal of Fisheries and Aquatic Sciences* 49: 406–415.

Nicholls, K.H., S.J. Standke, and G.J. Hopkins. 1999. Effects of dreissenid mussels on nitrogen and phosphorus in north shore waters of Lake Erie. In M. Munawar, T. Edsall, and I.F. Munawar (eds.), *State of Lake Erie (SOLE)-Past, Present, and Future*. Leiden: Backhuys Publishers, pp. 323–336.

Nichols, S.J. 1996. Variations in the reproductive cycle of *Dreissena polymorpha*, in North America and Europe. *American Zoologist* 36: 311–325.

O'Neill, C.R., Jr. 1997. Economic impact of Zebra Mussels: Results of the 1995 Zebra Mussel information clearinghouse study. *Great Lakes Res. Review* 3(1): 35–42.

O'Neill, C.R., Jr., and D.B. MacNeill. 1991. The Zebra Mussel (*Dreissena polymorpha*): An unwelcome North American Invader. Sea Grant. Cornell cooperative extension, State New York: University of New York and Coastal Resources Fact Sheet.

Qualls, T.M., D.M. Dolan, T. Reed, M.E. Zorn, and J. Kennedy. 2007. Analysis of the impacts of the zebra mussel, *Dreissena polymorpha*, on nutrients, water clarity, and the chlorophyll-phosphorus relationship in lower Green Bay. *Journal of Great Lakes Research* 33: 617–626.

Rackl, S., and C. Link. 2015. Zequanox®: Bio-based control of invasive Dreissena Mussels. In W.H. Wong and S.L. Gerstenberger (eds). *Biology and Management of Invasive Quagga and Zebra Mussels in the Western United States*. London: CRC Press, pp. 515–535.

Ricciardi, A., R.J. Neves, and J.B. Rasmussen. 1998. Impending extinctions of North American freshwater mussels (Unionoida) following the zebra mussel (*Dreissena polymorpha*) invasion. *Journal of Animal Ecology* 67(4): 613–619.

Roberts, L. 1990. Zebra Mussel invasion threatens U. S. waters. *Science* 249: 1370–1372.

Rockwell, D.C., G.J. Warren, P.E. Bertram, D.K. Salisbury, and N.M. Burns. 2005. The U.S. EPA Lake Erie indicators monitoring program 1983–2002: Trends in phosphorus, silica, and chlorophyll a in the central basin. *Journal of Great Lakes Research* 31(Supplement 2): 23–34.

Roditi, H.A., N.F. Caraco, J.J. Cole, and D.L. Strayer. 1996. Filtration of Hudson River water by the zebra mussel (*Dreissena polymorpha*). *Estuaries* 19: 824–832.

Roditi, H.A., N.S. Fisher, and S.A. Sanudo-Wilhelmy. 2000a. Field testing a metal bioaccumulation model for zebra mussels. *Environmental Science & Technology* 34: 2817–2825.

Roditi, H.A., N.S. Fisher, and S.A. Sanudo-Wilhelmy. 2000b. Uptake of dissolved organic carbon and trace elements by zebra mussels. *Nature* 407: 78–80.

Rzepecki, L.M., and J.H. Waite. 1993. Zebra mussel byssal glue: An unwelcome bond between man and mollusk? *Proceedings: Third International Zebra Mussel Conference*. Pleasant Hill, CA: Electric Power Research Institute, Inc, pp. 2-93–2-107.

Schneider, D.W., S.P. Madon, J.A. Stoeckel, and R.E. Sparks. 1998. Seston quality controls zebra mussel (*Dreissena polymorpha*) energetics in turbid rivers. *Oecologia* 17: 331–341.

Silverman, H., J.W. Lynn, E.C. Achberger, and T.H. Dietz. 1996. Gill structure in zebra mussels: Bacterial-sized particle filtration. *American Zoologist* 36: 373–384.

Skaja, A.D., D. Tordonato, and B. Jo Merten. 2015. Coatings for invasive Mussel control: Colorado river field study. In W.H. Wong and S.L. Gerstenberger (eds). *Biology and Management of Invasive Quagga and Zebra Mussels in the Western United States*. London: CRC Press, pp. 451–466.

Smith, D.G. 1993. The potential for spread of the exotic Zebra Mussel (*Dreissena polymorpha*) in Massachusetts. *Report MS-Q-11*. Department of Biology, University of Massachusetts Amherst, Massachusetts and Museum of Comparative Zoology, Harvard University, Cambridge, Massachusetts. www.mass.gov/eea/docs/dcr/watersupply/lakepond/downloads/zebra-mussel-massdep-ms-q-11.pdf (Accessed June 27, 2018).

Smith, K. 2015. Treatments on Christmas Lake kill off zebra mussels. www.startribune.com/treatments-on-christmas-lake-kill-off-zebra-mussels/300673491/ (Accessed June 28, 2019).

Smithe, R.D., and W.P. Kovalak. 1991. Control of zebra mussels fouling by coatings. In Second International Zebra Mussel Research Conference, November 19–22, Rochester, NY, p. 36.

Smythe, A.G., C.L. Lange, J.F. Doyle, and P.M. Sawyko. 1991b. Application of low voltage electric fields to deter attachment of zebra Mussel to structures. In Second International Zebra Mussel Research Conference, November 19–22. Rochester, NY, p. 34.

Smythe, A.G., C.L. Lange, T.M. Short, and R. Tuttle. 1991a. Application of centrifugal separators for control of zebra mussels in raw water systems. In Second International Zebra Mussel Research Conference, November 19–22, Rochester, NY, p. 33.

Sprung, M. 1990. Costs of reproduction: A study on metabolic requirements of the gonads and fecundity of the bivalve *Dreissena polymorpha*. *Malacologia* 32: 267–274.

Stewart-Malone, A., M. Misamore, S. Wilmoth, A.R. Reyes, W.H. Wong, and J. Gross. 2015. The effect of UV-C exposure on larval survival of the dreissenid Quagga Mussel. *PLoS ONE* 10(7): e0133039.

Strayer, D.L., N.F. Caraco, J.J. Cole, S. Findlay, and M.L. Pace. 1999. Transformation of freshwater ecosystems by bivalves: A case study of zebra mussels in the Hudson River. *Bioscience* 49: 19–27.

Strayer, D.L., K.A. Hattala, and A.W. Kahnle. 2004. Effects of an invasive bivalve (*Dreissena polymorpha*) on fish in the Hudson River estuary. *Canadian Journal of Fisheries and Aquatic Sciences* 61: 924–941.

Strayer, D.L., K.A. Hattala, A.W. Kahnle, and R.D. Adams. 2014. Has the Hudson River fish community recovered from the zebra mussel invasion along with its forage base? *Canadian Journal of Fisheries and Aquatic Sciences* 71: 1146–1157.

Strayer, D.L., and H.M. Malcom. 2006. Long term demography of a zebra mussel (*Dreissena polymorpha*) population. *Freshwater Biology* 51: 117–130.

Thorp, J.H., and A.P. Covich. 1991. *Ecology and Classification of North American Freshwater Invertebrates*. London: Academic Press, Inc, p. 911.

Vanderploeg, H.A., T.F. Nalepa, D.J. Jude, E.L. Mills, K.T. Holeck, J.R. Liebig, I.A. Grigorovich, and H. Ojaveer. 2002. Dispersal and emerging ecological impacts of Ponto-Caspian species in the Laurentian Great Lakes. *Canadian Journal of Fisheries and Aquatic Sciences* 59: 1209–1228.

Wagner, K. 2017. *Laurel Lake Drawdown Summary Report: 2010–2016*. Wilbraham, MA: Water Resource Services, p. 64.

Walz, N. 1978. The energy balance of the freshwater mussel *Dreissena polymorpha* in laboratory experiments and in Lake Constance. 2. Reproduction. *Archiv für Hydrobiologie—Supplement* 55: 106–119.

Walz, N. 1991. New invasions, increase, and ecological equilibrium of *Dreissena Polymorpha* Populations in Central and Southern Europe Lakes and Rivers. In Second International Zebra Mussel Research Conference. November 19–22, Rochester, NY.

Watters A., S.L. Gerestenberger, and W.H. Wong. 2015. Use of a molluscicide on preventing Quagga Mussel colonization. In W.H. Wong and S.L. Gerstenberger (eds). *Biology and Management of Invasive Quagga and Zebra Mussels in the Western United States*. London: CRC Press, pp. 507–513.

Wong, W.H., and S.L. Gerstenberger (eds.). 2015. *Biology and Management of Invasive Quagga and Zebra Mussels in the Western United States*. London: CRC Press, p. 566.

Wong, W.H., S.L. Gerstenberger, M.D. Hatcher, D.R. Thompson, and D. Schrimsher. 2013. Invasive quagga mussels can be attenuated by redear sunfish (*Lepomis microlophus*) in the Southwestern United States. *Biological Control* 64: 276–282.

Wong, W.H., S.L. Gerstenberger, J.M Miller, B. Moore, and C.J. Palmer. 2011. A standardized design for quagga mussel monitoring in Lake Mead, Nevada-Arizona. *Aquatic Invasions* 6(2): 205–215.

Wong, W.H., J.S. Levinton, B.S. Twining, and N. Fisher. 2003. Assimilation of micro- and mesozooplankton by zebra mussels: A demonstration of the food web link between zooplankton and benthic suspension feeders. *Limnology & Oceanography* 48: 308–312.

Zhang, H.Y., D.A. Culver, and L. Boegman. 2008. A two-dimensional ecological model of Lake Erie: Application to estimate dreissenid impacts on large lake plankton populations. *Ecological Modeling* 214: 219–241.

4 Chinese Mystery Snail (*Bellamya chinensis*)

ABSTRACT

Chinese mystery snail (*Bellamya chinensis*) is a freshwater snail native to east and southeast Asia, and invasive in North America. In Massachusetts, this species was first reported in 1914 in the Muddy River, which is part of the Charles River Watershed. Until 2018, it has been found in 37 waterbodies within 16 different watersheds in Massachusetts; however, there has been no formal assessment on the ecological and economic impacts of *B. chinensis*. A comprehensive monitoring plan for *B. chinensis* is needed to better understand their current status and to help curtail their further spread to other waterbodies in Massachusetts and beyond. Information on chemical, physical, and biological control methods are also provided in this report.

INTRODUCTION

Taxonomic Hierarchy (ITIS 2021)

Kingdom	Animalia—animal, animaux, animals
Subkingdom	Bilateria
Infrakingdom	Protostomia
Superphylum	Lophozoa
Phylum	Mollusca—mollusques, molusco, molluscs, mollusks
Class	Gastropoda Cuvier, 1797
Subclass	Prosobranchia Milne-Edwards, 1848
Order	Architaenioglossa
Family	Viviparidae Gray, 1847
Subfamily	Bellamyinae Rohrbach, 1937
Genus	*Cipangopaludina Hannibal*, 1912
Species	*Cipangopaludina chinensis* (Gray 1834)

The Chinese mystery snail (*Bellamya chinensis*)—also known as the black snail, trapdoor snail, or Chinese vivipara—is a species of freshwater snail within the family Viviparidae (Figure 4.1). This species has an inflated shell, and it is large compared to Massachusetts' other freshwater snails, reaching up to 63 mm (2.5 inches) in height, or slightly larger than a golf ball (Figure 4.2). The color of the shell is typically solid olive green to brown and the nacre (inner coloration) of the shell is white to pale blue (Clarke 1981). The aperture of the snail's shell is covered by a reddish operculum.

The specific nomenclatures within and surrounding Viviparidae are not well-determined, and morphological and molecular analyses to this date suggest that groupings within the family and the larger Caenogastropoda clade are paraphyletic, meaning some species have not been correctly placed on the evolutionary tree according to their true relatedness (Lu 2014; Wang et al. 2017). The species known by the common name Chinese mystery snail is referred to by many synonymous genus and species names (*Bellamya chinensis*, *Cipangopaludina chinensis*, *Viviparus malleatus*, and many more names including subspecies designations), as its taxonomic placement has been the subject of debate (USGS 2020). For the purposes of this report, the invasive snail in question will be scientifically referred to as *Bellamya chinensis*.

Despite complexities about the species' placement in Viviparidae, *B. chinensis* are distinct from South America "mystery snails" or "apple snails" in the genus *Pomacea* (family Ampullaridae), which are endemic to South America and have become invasive in China since their introduction in the 1980s, causing agricultural and environmental damage (Yang 2018). Snails in both the genus *Pomacea* and *Bellamya* are commonly sold and distributed as pets for home aquaria and both are often labeled as "mystery snails" in the aquarium trade. Individual snails from both species originating from the home aquarium trade can vary in color and appearance, as they are often selectively bred by hobbyists to achieve certain shell and body colorations. Chinese and

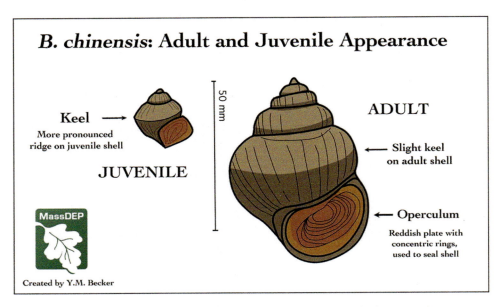

FIGURE 4.1 Adult and juvenile Chinese mystery snail. (Photo by Y.M. Becker.)

South American "mystery snails" are most easily distinguished by the shape of their shell: South American mystery snails have more inflated shells, with a proportionately large body whorl compared to their apical whorls, whereas Chinese mystery snails (*Bellamya*) have more conical shells with more evenly sized whorls (Figure 4.2). *Bellamya* snails are also much more tolerant of cold water than Pomacea apple snails and so they pose a greater threat of invasion to cold Massachusetts waterways.

It is also important to distinguish Chinese mystery snails and banded mystery snails (*Viviparus georgianus*), which are native to North America and can be found from Florida to the St. Lawrence river in Canada (Clench and Fuller 1965). The two species can be difficult to tell apart, since their shells are a very similar shape with only very minute anatomical differences between them. The easiest ways to distinguish these two species are by size and coloration. Banded mystery snails do not grow as large as Chinese mystery snails, the former reaching about 33 mm, only half the maximum size of a fully grown Chinese mystery snail (Figure 4.2). The shells of banded mystery snails also often carry a distinctive banded color pattern, with approximately three evenly spaced dark stripes running along following the spiral of the shell (Clench and Fuller 1965). Chinese mystery snails sometimes possess a striped pattern on their own shells or variations in color, but the stripes on the invasive snails are often not evenly spaced and perpendicular to the shell's spiral, or they may appear as many small pinstripes following the spiral, in contrast to the distinctive three bands found on *V. georgianus*.

North American native *Campeloma* species also have a similar appearance to the Chinese mystery snail, and grow larger than *V. georgianus*, but *Campeloma spp.* tend to have shouldered flattened whorls with a longer, narrower shape to their shells than *Bellamya* (Clench and Fuller 1965), and *Campeloma* snails also have a very wide, flat foot compared to *Bellamya* (visible when alive and active). Juvenile Chinese mystery snails have notably sharper carinae (keel) on their shells than adult snails, which could be used to distinguish juvenile *B. chinensis* from visually similar snails that are smaller at the adult stage (Figure 4.1).

Chinese mystery snails can be found in a variety of freshwater environments, such as lakes, ponds, streams, canals, and roadside ditches (Jokinen 1982). Like other members of the Viviparidae, Chinese mystery snails are

Chinese Mystery Snail (*Bellamya chinensis*)

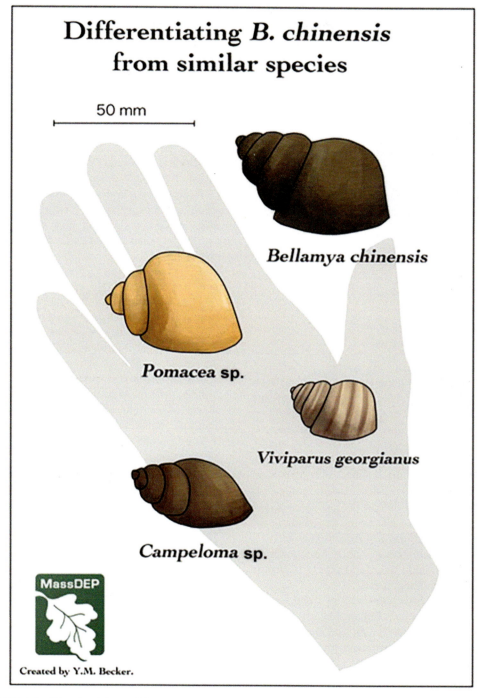

FIGURE 4.2 Visual guide to differentiating *B. chinensis* from visually similar species that may be found in North America (*Pomacea* sp., *Viviparus georgianus*, and *Campeloma* sp.). (Photo by Y.M. Becker.)

ovoviviparous, giving birth to live offspring (Waltz 2008; Martin 1999). Apart from being a viviparous animal (giving live birth) and reproducing sexually (Waltz 2008), it is also dioecious, meaning individual snails are reproductively either male or female. The females can live up to five years, while males can live for three to four years (Jokinen 1982). From the research of Jokinen (1982), it is believed that a female can produce more than 169 embryos over a lifetime. The embryos are usually released as live offspring between June and October, and the snail will spend the winter in the deeper water after reproduction (Jokinen 1982). Chinese mystery snails can tolerate very cold and even freezing water temperatures (Burnett et al. 2018). The snails can live on a variety of different substrate types. They primarily eat by grazing periphyton, but larger adult snails are also capable of filter-feeding (Haak 2015).

Native and Invasive Range, Mechanisms of Spread

Bellamya chinensis is native to Burma, Thailand, South Vietnam, China, Korea, eastern Russia, Japan, Philippines, and Java (Waltz 2008; Kipp 2020). The first documented sighting in the United States was in the Chinese markets in San Francisco in the late 1800s (Wood 1892). The species was most likely first imported as a food source, but were released into freshwater habitats. Since entering natural waterbodies, the invasive range of this species has expanded to many areas in the United States, especially the northeast and the midwest regions (Kipp 2020). In 1914, *B. chinensis* was found in Massachusetts for the first time, in the Muddy River in Boston (Johnson 1915; Kipp 2020).

The spread of *B. chinensis* in some regions of the country has been enhanced by boat access between lakes and rivers, suggesting boating as a vector of dispersion for this species. Experimentation has shown that these snails can survive upward of nine weeks exposed to air, theoretically allowing the snails to cling to the bottoms of boats for long periods of time and travel between bodies of water when the boats are transported by land (Unstad 2013; Havel 2011). Since Chinese mystery snails are also frequently sold as pets for home aquaria, it is possible that they are released outdoors at new locations either accidentally or intentionally by individuals who have purchased them from pet stores.

Ecological Impacts

The influence of Chinese mystery snail on native species has varied among studies. Competition between *B. chinensis* and native snails might depend on the population densities or spatial scale of analysis, and on whether other invasive species or environmental stressors are exerting additional pressure (Johnson et al. 2009; Solomon et al. 2010). A study by Johnson et al. (2009) simulated freshwater ecosystems by building mesocosms stocked with native and invasive species and found that a high density of *B. chinensis* stagnates or decreases the growth of native snail species *Physa gyrina* and *Lymnaea stagnalis*, even leading to the elimination of certain species in the experimental mesocosms when compounded with the presence of the invasive rusty crayfish *Orconectes rusticus*. However, a field survey of 42 lakes published the following year (Solomon et al. 2010) found no increased likelihood of native species loss where *B. chinensis* is present. Twardochleb and Olden (2016) found that when native snail populations are reduced in lakes as a result of human environmental degradation, lakes with introduced populations of *B. chinensis* may be more ecologically stable, as *B. chinensis* could provide molluscivorous predators, including several fish species, with an alternative food source. *B. chinensis* might also serve as food more favorably suited for native crayfish than for invasive crayfish (Olden et al. 2009).

Through examination of water chemistry in their mesocosms and the excretory habits of *B. chinensis*, Johnson et al. (2009) discovered that *B. chinensis* might have an innate ability to sequester or serve as a "sink" for phosphorus, thus raising the N:P ratio of a habitat where it has been introduced. It is generally understood that a high N:P ratio is associated with an oligotrophic ecosystem and a low N:P ratio with a eutrophic one (Downing 1992; Schindler 2008). Atomic nitrogen and phosphorus both are required in a certain proportion for plant and algal growth, and phosphorus is typically the limiting factor in exponential growth. Likewise, reduced phosphorus concentrations lead to reduced algal growth and bloom frequencies (Walker and Havens 1995).

Therefore, the phosphorus sequestering ability of *B. chinensis* may potentially be useful in reversing the effects of eutrophication in heavily polluted waterbodies, though not without the risk of posing as competition to native snail species.

B. chinensis might also serve as a vector for parasites. In the Boston area specifically, *B. chinensis* has been found to carry *Aspidogaster conchiola*, a parasite that begins its life inside mollusks and then moves on to fish (Michelson 1970). *A. conchiola* is not known to be dangerous to humans or to fish in most cases (Petty and Francis-Floyd 2015), but its transmission and spread could have ecological consequences. The role and effects of parasites in an ecosystem are often cryptic and difficult to identify, but worth consideration (Poulin 1999; Hechinger and Lafferty 2005). Certain native parasite species may be less capable of infecting invasive snails, leading to a reduction in their numbers along with the loss of native snail species (Lam 2016).

HUMAN IMPACTS

Some of the parasites spread by Chinese mystery snails can impact human health. Echinostomate parasites (also called flukes or trematodes) have been found to use Chinese mystery snails as hosts (Sohn et al. 2013). These parasites can infect humans if ingested via raw or undercooked mollusks or fish and cause gastrointestinal sickness and damage to the intestines (CDC 2019). Many species of snails, including *B. chinensis*, can also carry *Angiostrongylus cantonensis*, also known as rat lungworm (Chen 1991). *A. cantonensis* affects the central nervous system, typically causing symptoms that last for two to eight weeks, including headaches and nausea. Though serious complications are uncommon, the illness occasionally leads to severe meningitis and even death (CDC 2015). Due to the severity of parasitic illnesses transmitted by gastropods, snails collected from the wild should not be eaten or used as bait (to avoid passing the parasite to fish or birds, which can serve as intermediate or primary hosts and perpetuate their life cycles).

The large number of dead snails or decaying shells on the wrack line at an infested waterbody may diminish the aesthetic value, as observed at heavily infested sites (Bury et al. 2007; Collas et al. 2017). However, these waste shells could have economic and medical value as well: researchers have found that the shells of Chinese mystery snails can be recycled and used for the synthesis of hydroxyapatite, a bioceramic material with important biomedical applications, including bone repair and regeneration (Zhou et al. 2016). Chemical derivatives from the flesh of the Chinese mystery snail could also have biomedical benefits, namely, polysaccharides with anti-inflammatory and anti-angiogenic properties. These compounds could possibly have applications in treating damage caused by immunological disease, or even as a treatment for cancer, blocking the growth of tumors (Xiong et al. 2017; Jiang et al. 2013).

MONITORING AND SIGHTINGS

The invasive species sightings data were collected by the Massachusetts Department of Environmental Protection (MassDEP) and US Geological Survey's non-indigenous aquatic species database (USGS 2020). MassDEP implemented the standard operating procedures, including sampling methodology, species identification, quality control, and quality assurance, during the sample collections and species identification and quantification (Nuzzo 2003). Lake samples collected from 2016 to 2018 were composites of ten littoral zone samples taken at even intervals around each waterbody (so these records convey information about a whole waterbody but not a specific point within the waterbody). Information collected by USGS is from journal articles and the database *Exotic Aquatic Mollusk Collections in the Illinois Natural History Survey*. Sites with *B. chinensis* were mapped as a data layer with ArcGIS® ArcMap 10.1 (ESRI, Redlands, California). This tool is able to pinpoint the infestations and potential for further spreading areas, which can help to inform future decisions and regulations for controlling the spread of this invasive species (Figure 4.3).

B. chinensis was first documented in Massachusetts in Muddy River which is part of the Charles River Watershed in 1914 (Figure 4.3). Currently, there are 37 known waterbodies infested by *B. chinensis* (Tables 4.1 and 4.2) in 16 watersheds in Massachusetts (Table 4.3). The potential economic loss and ecological impact need to be estimated according to different invasive status at different waterbodies. An effective control method should be applied

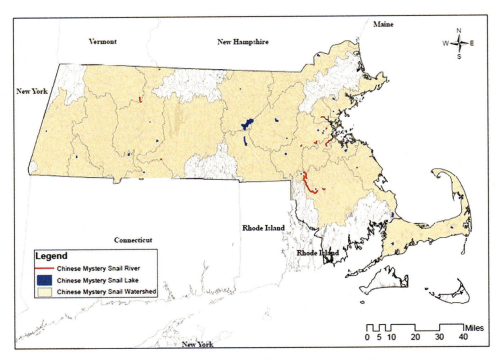

FIGURE 4.3 Map depicting Chinese mystery snail (*Bellamya chinensis*) distribution in Massachusetts.

for the infested waterbody. For waterbodies that have not been invaded or are under the risk of being invaded, prevention measures should be implemented to stop the invasion of the species. More comprehensive monitoring on *B. chinensis* should be developed for a better understanding of their infestation status. This can enhance the public awareness of the presence of invasive mystery snail in Massachusetts lakes and rivers and help to minimize their further spread to other waterbodies in Massachusetts and beyond.

MANAGING ACTIONS

The management of Chinese mystery snail usually includes two major components: prevention and control. Prevention measures usually include boat inspection and decontamination before and/or leaving a waterbody, regulation on trading aquarium pets, and general public education. Early detection and response measures need to be developed to monitor the establishment and spread of *B. chinensis* when it is introduced to new locations. Innovative eDNA (Environmental DNA) analyses have been graded as an effective technique for the early detection of *B. chinensis* and other mollusk species, and this method can also provide an estimate of the quantity of snails (Peñarrubia et al. 2016; Matthews et al. 2017).

The control mainly involves chemical treatment and physical removal, as well as biological control. The best method for controlling Chinese mystery snail populations depends on the region, climate, management budget, regulation restrictions, and other factors.

CHEMICAL CONTROL

Rotenone and copper sulfate are considered by Haak et al. (2014) as two main chemical treatment options to consider for eradicating *B. chinensis*. Rotenone is typically used to eliminate fish, but it is also generally toxic to insects and most invertebrates. In an experiment by Haak et al. (2014), adult Chinese mystery snails were placed in buckets of lake water treated with rotenone (at twice the dosage recommended to kill fish) for 72 hours, after which 100% of the

Chinese Mystery Snail (*Bellamya chinensis*)

TABLE 4.1
Sightings and Report Sources of Infested Waterbodies

Waterbody	Agency	Report_Source	Longitude	Latitude	First Year Reported
Boons Pond	MassDEP	Robert Nuzzo	42.39611	−71.494999	2017
Card Pond	MassDEP	Robert Nuzzo	42.3261883	−73.366693	2016
Charles River		USGS 2020	42.25301	−71.17261	1995
Chicopee River		USGS 2020	42.15583	−72.43295	1997
Coonamessett Pond	MassDEP	Robert Nuzzo	41.6192836	−70.566974	2018
Crystal Lake at 113 Crystal Lake Road, private residence		USGS 2020	42.79965	−71.15197	2017
Emmanuel Pond and the Muddy River		E.H. Michelson, 1970	42.33232	−71.15753	1968
Forest Park Ponds		USGS 2020	42.0736	−72.57345	1986
Forge Pond		USGS 2020	42.27004	−72.46934	2001
Fuller Swamp Brook		USGS 2020	42.53564	−72.61078	1977
Gleason Pond	MassDEP	Robert Nuzzo	42.2865424	−71.412718	2017
Great Herring Pond		USGS 2020	41.79984	−70.55985	2015
Hawes Pond		William James Clench and Samuel L.H. Fuller, 1965	42.063432	−71.297832	1965
Hinckleys Pond	MassDEP	Robert Nuzzo	41.7113503	−70.086067	2018
Indian Head River	MassDEP	Robert Nuzzo			1983
Jamaica Pond		William James Clench and Samuel L.H. Fuller, 1965	42.316764	−71.12033	1965
Lake Quinsigamond		William James Clench and Samuel L.H. Fuller, 1965	42.2709267	−71.75507	1918
Lake Winthrop		USGS 2020	42.1889	−71.42252	1992
Leverett Pond		William James Clench and Samuel L.H. Fuller, 1965	42.329264	−71.113386	1965
Lower Spectacle Pond	MassDEP	Robert Nuzzo	42.163092	−73.11985	2016
Muddy River		William James Clench and Samuel L.H. Fuller, 1965	42.351486	−71.092552	1914
Muddy River		D.S. Dundee, 1974	42.597355	−71.787114	1974
Pauchaug- Louisiana Brook		USGS 2020	42.7185	−72.44828	1978
Peacock Pond		William James Clench and Samuel L.H. Fuller, 1965	41.967404	−71.18278	1965
Pequot Pond	MassDEP	Robert Nuzzo	42.1813088	−72.69846	2016

(Continued)

TABLE 4.1
(Continued)

Waterbody	Agency	Report_Source	Longitude	Latitude	First Year Reported
Pillings Pond		William James Clench and Samuel L.H. Fuller, 1965	42.529872	−71.028671	1965
Pine Tree Brook		USGS 2020	42.25912	−71.08398	1982
Pine Tree Brook and pond		William James Clench and Samuel L.H. Fuller, 1965	42.245099	−71.089495	1965
Pond at Medford		USGS 2020	42.41866	−71.11248	1974
Pond at Mount Hood		William James Clench and Samuel L.H. Fuller, 1965	42.451763	−71.032551	1965
Snake River		USGS 2020	41.96715	−71.12613	1995
Trout Brook		William James Clench and Samuel L.H. Fuller, 1965	42.242137	−71.293625	1965
Turners Pond		William James Clench and Samuel L.H. Fuller, 1965	42.26121	−71.078106	1965
UMass pond		USGS 2020	42.38961	−72.52659	1973
Wachusett Reservoir		USGS 2020	42.40318	−71.68854	1988
Wading River	MassDEP	Robert Nuzzo			2006
Whitmans Pond		William James Clench and Samuel L.H. Fuller, 1965	42.206269	−70.934944	1965

snails survived, suggesting that *B. chinensis* has some resistance to rotenone. In experiments measuring rotenone toxicity on other species of aquatic snails, rotenone was found to cause mortality within hours of exposure at standard dosage (Dalu et al. 2015) and over the course of multiple days at a low dosage (Vehovsky et al. 2007). In Dalu et al.'s (2015) study, several different species of aquatic invertebrates were monitored in a system exposed to rotenone at the typical dosage and timescale recommended to achieve 100% fish mortality. In this experiment, some small aquatic snails such as *Physa acuta* were killed, but the snails did not see as high mortality as other aquatic invertebrates in the study, supporting Haak et al.'s (2014) conclusion that short-term exposure to rotenone is not an effective pesticide treatment for aquatic snails. The long-term effects of rotenone treatment on *B. chinensis* specifically have not been evaluated, but, considering rotenone's toxicity to other forms of aquatic life, long-term application of the pesticide is not likely to be an ecologically sound option.

Copper sulfate, along with other copper compounds, is well-known as a molluscicide, specifically used to eradicate unwanted snails. Copper sulfate's effectiveness in killing Chinese mystery snails has been reported inconsistently in different cases, and its toxicity may depend on the method of exposure (i.e., whether snails ingest the toxic metal or are only exposed to dissolved copper in the water column). Parallel to the rotenone experiment, Haak et al. (2014) exposed adult Chinese mystery snails to copper sulfate solutions in buckets of water, observing the snails over 96 hours. At the end of this experiment, all but one of the snails survived, leading the team to conclude that *B. chinensis* are resistant to copper sulfate. However, there is evidence that copper sulfate is more effective as a molluscicide if it is ingested by snails,

TABLE 4.2
Towns and Infested Waterbodies

Number	Waterbody	Town
1	Boons Pond	Stow
2	Card Pond	West Stockbridge
3	Charles River	Dedham
4	Chicopee River	Wilbraham
5	Coonamessett Pond	Falmouth
6	Crystal Lake at 113 Crystal Lake Road private residence	Haverhill
7	Emmanuel Pond and the Muddy River	Brookline
8	Forest Park Ponds	Springfield
9	Forge Pond	Granby
10	Fuller Swamp Brook	Deerfield
11	Gleason Pond	Framingham
12	Great Herring Pond	Plymouth and Bourne
13	Hawes Pond	Dover
14	Hinckleys Pond	Harwich
15	Indian Head River	Hanover and Hanson
16	Jamaica Pond	Boston
17	Lake Quinsigamond	Worcester
18	Lake Winthrop	Holliston
19	Leverett Pond	Boston
20	Lower Spectacle Pond	Sandisfield
21	Muddy River	Boston
22	Muddy River	Fitchburg
23	Pauchaug-Louisiana Brook	Northfield
24	Peacock Pond	Lexington
25	Pequot Pond	Westfield
26	Pillings Pond	Lynnfield
27	Pine Tree Brook	Milton
28	Pine Tree Brook and pond	Milton
29	pond at Medford	Medford
30	pond at Mount Hood	Melrose
31	Snake River	Norton
32	Trout Brook	Dover
33	Turners Pond	Milton
34	Umass pond	Amherst
35	Wachusett Reservoir	Clinton
36	Wading River	Norton
37	Whitman's Pond	Weymouth

as several studies have found that toxic metal uptake in both land and aquatic snails is greater when the metals are concentrated in soil, sediment, or food rather than dissolved in water (Hoang and Rand 2009; Gomot-de Vaufleury and Pihan 2009; Pang et al. 2012). This would also explain a case in the fall of 2010, where copper sulfate crystals were experimentally applied

TABLE 4.3
Infested Watersheds

Number	Infested Watersheds
1	Blackstone
2	Boston Harbor (Neponset River Basin and Coastal Drainage Area)
3	Cape Cod
4	Charles
5	Chicopee
6	Concord (SuAsCo)
7	Deerfield
8	Farmington
9	Housatonic
10	Connecticut
11	Merrimack
12	Narragansett
13	Nashua
14	South Coastal
15	Taunton
16	Westfield

in two heavily snail-infested bodies of water, successfully killing large numbers of *B. chinensis*. Two ponds in Jackson County, Oregon, were treated with copper sulfate at a dosage of about 2 ppm. Reportedly, over 30,000 dead Chinese mystery snails were retrieved from the ponds within a month as a result of this action, but some live snails were still found, indicating that eradication was not complete. There has also not been any information reported on the broader environmental impact of the copper sulfate treatment, effects on soil or water chemistry, or whether the invasive snail populations have recovered in the decade following 2011, at which point their populations had recovered and required another round of pesticide dosage, according to a local news report (Freeman 2011). Regardless, this story is a sign that copper sulfate treatment is worth consideration as a tool for eradicating *B. chinensis*. Further studies and experimentation are required to learn definitively whether copper compounds can be used to kill Chinese mystery snails, as well as to find the most effective methods and dosages. More information about chemical control on Chinese mystery snail and other 18 invasive species can be found in Appendix III.

PHYSICAL CONTROL

Some physical strategies might be effective in controlling *B. chinensis*, including thermal treatment, manual removal, and hydrologic controls. Hot water treatment has shown potential to be useful against *B. chinensis*. Burnett et al. (2018) tested the thermal tolerance limits of the snail by exposing wild-caught *B. chinensis* to extreme high and low temperature conditions. While they found no lower temperature range, indicating that the snail is well-adapted to cold climates and capable of withstanding freezing cold water, *B. chinensis* was unable to tolerate hot water in the range of 40–45°C. Targeted hot water treatment might therefore be useful as a method of eradicating *B. chinensis*, if more study and experimentation are carried out to find safe and effective implementation. There is also at least one recorded instance of natural *B. chinensis* die-offs occurring following periods of especially hot weather (Haak et al. 2013).

Removal by hand could potentially reduce *B. chinensis* populations; larger adult Chinese mystery snails tend to produce more offspring each season, so selectively removing the largest snails from a waterbody could be a relatively easy task with an outcome of slowing population growth (Haak 2015).

Drawdown or treatments that involve exposing the snails to air for long periods of time seem to be effective against *B. chinensis* juveniles, but not adult snails. In a study by Unstad et al. (2013), adult and juvenile *B. chinensis* snails, along with native snail species, were subjected to desiccation for periods of five to nine weeks at a time. Most of the adult *B. chinensis* snails survived desiccation for as long as nine weeks, while none of the juvenile *B. chinensis* or native snails survived even as long as five weeks. Drawdown treatment therefore might be useful in eradicating juvenile snails (in addition to any native small snail present) but have little effect on adult *B. chinensis*. This study also illuminates the fact that since juveniles of *B. chinensis* cannot tolerate long periods of exposure, there is less evidence to say that juvenile snails are able to be transmitted between waterbodies by attaching to boats and withstanding long trips over land. Watercraft owners might take this into account and note that after storing a boat for a long period of time, adult snails are more likely to remain attached to the hull than juveniles. Physical prevention, targeting the vectors that *B. chinensis* may be using to reach new habitats, could be an effective response to control infestation. These strategies could include encouraging freshwater boaters to drain, dry, and clean their watercraft, checking carefully to ensure that no snails are attached while in transport (Matthews et al. 2017). Educating fish and aquarium owners about invasive species might also prevent introduction of Chinese mystery snails and other aquatic invaders. Pet stores could be asked to distribute informational material instructing against release with the purchase of a known invasive species.

It may also be possible to slow or stop the migration of snails between connected waterbodies by establishing high-velocity currents as boundaries. Some research has found that Chinese mystery snails' movement can be limited by strategic placements of culverts (Rivera 2008). Similarly to the studies on air exposure, larger snails seem more tolerant of high-velocity currents and more capable of moving in spite of them (Rivera 2008). Creating structures that induce high-velocity currents could help control invasion by Chinese mystery snails but could affect other aquatic wildlife that should be considered and mitigated.

BIOLOGICAL (ECOLOGICAL) CONTROL

While *B. chinensis* is a good food source for native and invasive crayfish, possibly being more accessible as prey to native crayfish than to invasive species (Olden et al. 2009), there have been no documented attempts of introducing predators to control Chinese mystery snails and no research seeking to find the effectiveness of biological control on this species.

SUCCESS STORY

So far, no method is known to consistently be effective against *B. chinensis*, and there are no recorded instances of complete or near-total eradication of the species from an ecosystem that has been invaded. However, as already mentioned in the "Chemical Control" section, a period of high mortality was once caused by an applications of copper sulfate in Oregon ponds, according to local press and newsletters (Edwards 2010; Freeman 2010).

In 2009, the Chinese mystery snail was found in two ponds of the Jackson County Sports Park, Oregon, believed to have been released by someone who purchased them through the aquarium trade (Edwards 2010). In the fall of 2010, Oregon Department of Fish and Wildlife (ODFW) detected the new infestation in Klamath County's Lost River, Crane Prairie Reservoir, and Big Butte Pond near Bend, and decided to respond with an experimental chemical treatment in two infested ponds. The more heavily infested pond, with 166 snails/m^2, was dosed with a total of 47.5 pounds of copper sulfate. The pond with a lighter infestation was treated with only 13 pounds. Following the pesticide application, around 30,000 dead snails were collected from the ponds, but live snails were still caught in traps following the application. According to a *Mail Tribune* report, the snails returned the following year, leading ODFW to repeat the pesticide trial with a higher dosage than before (Freeman 2011). In 2011, the sale of Chinese mystery snails was also officially banned in the state of Oregon (ODFW 2011).

Altogether, the chemical treatment caused substantial, but not complete, mortality in the ponds where it was applied. Though this experiment was carried out over ten years ago and is sparsely documented, the circumstances and results of the trial being recorded only in a handful of local news sources, the experiment remains to date the most successful attempted eradication of Chinese mystery snails from a North American waterbody. These results suggest that copper sulfate may be useful in controlling Chinese mystery snail invasions, if applied in solid form at the right dosage, and perhaps combined with other control methods.

REFERENCES

Burnett, J.L., K.L. Pope, A. Wong, C.R. Allen, D.M. Haak, B.J. Stephen, and D.R. Uden. 2018. Thermal tolerance limits of the Chinese mystery snail (*Bellamya chinensis*): Implications for management. *American Malacological Bulletin* 36(1): 140–144.

Bury, J.A., B.E. Sietman, and B.N. Karns. 2007. Distribution of the Non-Native Viviparid Snails, *Bellamya chinensis* and *Viviparus georgianus*, in Minnesota and the First Record of *Bellamya japonica* from Wisconsin. *Journal of Freshwater Ecology* 22(4): 697–703. DOI: 10.1080/02705060.2007.9664830.

Center for Disease Control and Prevention. 2015. Angiostryliasis (also known as *Angiostrongylus* Infection). www.cdc.gov/parasites/angiostrongylus/disease.html (Accessed January 14, 2021).

Center for Disease Control and Prevention. 2019. Echinostomiasis. www.cdc.gov/dpdx/echinostomiasis/index.html (Accessed January 14, 2021).

Chen, E.R. 1991. Current status of food-borne parasitic zoonoses in Taiwan. *Southeast Asian Journal of Tropical Medicine and Public Health* 22: 62–64.

Clarke, A.H. 1981. The freshwater molluscs of Canada. In: *National Museum of Natural Sciences*. Ottawa: National Museums of Canada, p. 447.

Clench, W.J., and S.L.H. Fuller. 1965. The genus *Viviparus* (Viviparidae) in North America. *Harvard Univ. Mus. of Comp. Zool. Occ. Pap* 2(32): 385–412.

Collas, F.P.L., S.K.D. Breedvold, J. Matthews, G. van der Velde, and R.S.E.W. Leuven. 2017. Invasion biology and risk assessment of the recently introduced Chinese mystery snail, *Bellamya (Cipangopaludina) chinensis* (Gray, 1834), in the Rhine and Meuse River basins in Western Europe. *Environmental Sciences* 557: 1–75.

Dalu, T., R.J. Wasserman, M. Jordaan, W.P. Froneman, and O.L.F. Weyl. 2015. An Assessment of the effect of rotenone on selected non-target aquatic fauna. *PLoS One* 10(11): e0142140.

Downing, J.A., and E. McCauley. 1992. The nitrogen: Phosphorus relationship in lakes. *Limnology and Oceanography* 37(5): 936–945.

Dundee, D.S. 1974. Catalog of introduced mollusks of eastern North America (north of Mexico). *Sterkiana* 55: 1–37.

Edwards, R. 2010. Lake Wise: A voice for Quiet Waters. *The Oregon Lakes Association Newsletter*. www.oregonlakes.org/Resources/Documents/Lakewise/2010_Nov.pdf (Accessed May 15, 2020).

Freeman, M. 2010. This snail problem is hardly a mystery. *Mail Tribune*, August 12. https://mailtribune.com/oregon-outdoors/this-snail-problem-is-hardly-a-mystery (Accessed January 26, 2021).

Freeman, M. 2011. Invasive snails return to White City ponds. *Mail Tribune*, May 28. https://mailtribune.com/archive/invasive-snails-make-return-to-white-city-ponds (Accessed January 26, 2021).

Gomot-de Vaufleury, A., and F. Pihan. 2009. Methods for toxicity assessment of contaminated soil by oral or dermal uptake in land snails: Metal bioavailability and bioaccumulation. *Environmental Toxicology* 21(4): 820–827.

Haak, D.M. 2015. Bioenergetics and habitat suitability models for the Chinese mystery snail (*Bellamya chinensis*). University of Nebraska-Lincoln, Nebraska, p. 234.

Haak, D.M., N.M. Chaine, B.J. Stephen, A. Wong, and C.R. Allen. 2013. Mortality estimate of Chinese mystery snail, *Bellamya chinensis* (Reeve, 1863) in a Nebraska reservoir. *Biological Invasions* 2(2): 137–139.

Haak, D.M., B.J. Stephen, R.A. Kill, N.A. Smeenk, C.R. Allen, and K.L. Pope. 2014. Toxicity of copper sulfate and rotenone to Chinese mystery snail (*Bellamya chinensis*). *Management of Biological Invasions* 5: 371–375.

Havel, J.E. 2011. Survival of the Exotic Chinese Mystery Snail (*Cipangopaludina chinensis malleata*) during Air Exposure and Implications for Overland Dispersal by Boats. *Hydrobiologia* 668(1): 195–202.

Hechinger, R.F., and K.D. Lafferty KD. 2005. Host diversity begets parasite diversity: bird final hosts and trematodes in snail intermediate hosts. *Proc Biol Sci* 272(1567): 1059–1066.

Hoang, T.C., and G.M. Rand. 2009. Exposure routes of copper: Short term effects on survival, weight, and uptake in Florida apple snails (*Pomacea paludosa*). *Chemosphere* 76(3): 407–414.

ITIS (Integrated Taxonomic Information System). 2021. www.itis.gov/servlet/SingleRpt/SingleRpt?search_topic=TSN&search_value=18408#null (Accessed September 28, 2021).

Jiang, C., Y. Jiao, X. Chen, X. Li, W. Yan, B. Yu, and Q. Xiong. 2013. Preliminary characterization and potential hepatoprotective effect of polysaccharides from *Cipangopaludina chinensis*. *Food and Chemical Toxicology* 59: 18–25.

Johnson, C.W. 1915. *Viviparus malleatus* Reeve in Massachusetts. *The Nautilus* 29: 35.

Johnson, P.T.J., J.D. Olden, C.T. Solomon, and M.J. Vander Zanden. 2009. Interactions among invaders: community and ecosystem effects of multiple invasive species in an experimental aquatic system. *Oecologia* 159: 161–170.

Jokinen, E.H. 1982. *Cipangopaludina chinensis* (Gastropoda: Viviparidae) in North America, review and update. *Nautilus* 96(3): 89–95.

Jokinen, E.H. 1992. *The Freshwater Snails (Mollusca: Gastropoda) of New York State*. Albany, NY: The University of the State of New York, The State Education Department, The New York State Museum, p. 112.

Kipp, R.M., A.J. Benson, J. Larson, A. Fusaro, and C. Morningstar C. 2020. *Cipangopaludina chinensis* (Gray, 1834): U.S. Geological Survey, Nonindigenous Aquatic Species Database, Gainesville, FL. https://nas.er.usgs.gov/queries/FactSheet.aspx?SpeciesID=1044, Revision Date: 1/15/2020 (Accessed May 13, 2020).

Lake George Association (LGA). n.d. www.lakegeorgeassociation.org/educate/science/lake-george-invasive-species/chinese-mystery-snail/ (Accessed May 13, 2020).

Lam, J. 2016. *Cipangopaludina Chinensis: Effects of Temperatures and Parasite Prevalence*. Notre Dame: University of Notre Dame.

LaRoe, E.T., G.S. Farries, C.E. Puckett, P.D. Doran, and M.J. Mac. 1995. *Our Living Resources: A Report to the Nation on the Distribution, Abundance, and Health of US Plants, Animals, and Ecosystems. US Department of the Interior*. Washington, DC: National Biological Service, pp. 205–209.

Lu, H., L. Du, Z. Li, X. Chen, and J. Yang. 2014. Morphological analysis of the Chinese *Cipangopaludina* species (Gastropoda; Caenogastropoda: Viviparidae). *Zoological Research* 35(6): 510–527.

Martin, S.M. 1999. Freshwater snails (Mollusca: Gastropoda) of maine. *Northeastern Naturalist* 6(1): 39–88.

Matthews, J., F.P.L. Collas, L. Hoop, G. van der Velde, and R.S.E.W. Leuven. 2017. Management approaches for the Alien Chinese mystery snail (Bellamya Chinensis). *Environmental Sciences* 558: 1.

McCann, M.J. 2014. Population dynamics of the non-native freshwater gastropod, *Cipangopaludina chinensis* (Viviparidae): A capture-mark-recapture study. *Hydrobiologia* 730: 17–27.

Michelson, E.H. 1970. *Aspidogaster conchicola* from fresh water gastropods in the USA. *Journal of Parasitology* 56(4): 709–712.

Nuzzo, R.M. 2003. *Standard Operating Procedures: Water Quality Monitoring in Streams Using Aquatic Macroinvertebrates*. Worcester, MA: Massachusetts Department of Environmental Protection, Division of Watershed Management, p. 39.

Olden, J.D., E.R. Larson, and M.C. Mims. 2009. Home-field advantage: Native signal crayfish (*Pacifastacus leniusculus*) out consume newly introduced crayfishes for invasive Chinese mystery snail (*Bellamya chinensis*). *Aquatic Ecology* 43: 1073.

Oregon Department of Fish and Wildlife (ODFW). 2011. Oregon Fish and Wildlife Commission Minutes, February 4, p. 15. www.dfw.state.or.us/agency/commission/minutes/11/08_aug/Approved_Feb%204%202011_Commission%20Minutes_080511.pdf (Accessed January 25, 2021).

Pang, C., H. Selck, S.K. Misra, D. Berhanu, A. Dybowska, E. Valsami-Jones, and V.E. Forbes. 2012. Effects of sediment-associated copper to the deposit-feeding snail, *Potamopyrgus antipodarum:* A comparison of Cu added in aqueous form or as nano- and micro- CuO particles. *Aquatic Toxicology* 106–107: 114–122.

Peñarrubia, L., C. Alcaraz, A. bij de Vaate, N. Sanz, C. Pla, O. Vidal, and J. Viñas. 2016. Validated methodology for quantifying infestation levels of mussels in environmental DNA (eDNA) samples. *Scientific Reports* 6: 39067.

Petty, B.D., and R. Francis-Floyd. 2015. Parasitic Diseases of Fish. *MERCK Manual Veterinary Manual*. www.merckvetmanual.com/exotic-and-laboratory-animals/aquarium-fishes/parasitic-diseases-of-fish (Accessed January 14, 2021).

Poulin, R. 1999. The functional importance of parasites in animal communities: Many roles at many levels? *International Journal for Parasitology* 29(6): 903–914.

Rivera, C.J.R. 2008. Obstruction of upstream migration of the invasive snail Cipangopaludina chinensis by high water currents. In: *Summer UNDERC Project. South Bend*. Notre Dame: University of Notre Dame, Department of Biological Sciences, Galvin Life Sciences Center, p. 13.

Schindler, D.W., R.E. Hecky, D.L. Findlay, M.P. Stainton, B.R. Parker, M.J. Paterson, K.G. Beaty, M. Lying, and S.E.M. Kasian. 2008. Eutrophication of lakes cannot be controlled by reducing nitrogen input: Results of a 37-year whole-ecosystem experiment. *PNAS* 105(32): 11254–11258.

Sohn, W.M., J.Y. Chai, B.K. Na, T.S. Yong, K.S. Eom, H. Park, D.Y. Min, and H.J. Rim. 2013. *Echinostoma macrorchis* in Lao PDR: Metacercariae in *Cipangopaludina* snails and adults from experimentally infected animals. *Korean Journal Parasitol* 51(2): 191–196.

Solomon, C.T., J.D. Olden, P.T.J. Johnson, R.T. Dillon, and M.J. Vander Zanden. 2010. Distribution and Community-level Effects of the Chinese Mystery Snail (*Bellamya chinensis*) in Northern Wisconsin Lakes. *Biological Invasions* 12(6): 1591–605.

Twardochleb, L.A., and J.D. Olden. 2016. Non-native Chinese Mystery Snail (*Bellamya chinensis*) Supports Consumers in Urban Lake Food Webs. *Ecosphere* 7(5): E01293.

U.S. Geological Survey (USGS). 2020. Specimen observation data for *Cipangopaludina chinensis* (Gray, 1834), Nonindigenous Aquatic Species Database, Gainesville, FL, https://nas.er.usgs.gov/queries/CollectionInfo.aspx?SpeciesID=1044&State=MA, (Accessed May 13, 2020).

Unstad, K.M., D.R. Uden, C.R. Allen, N.M. Chaine, D.M. Haak, R.A. Kill, K.L. Pope, B.J. Stephen, and A. Wong. 2013. Survival and behavior of Chinese mystery snails (Bellamya chinensis) in response to simulated water body drawdowns and extended air exposure. *Nebraska Cooperative Fish & Wildlife Research Unit—Sta Publications* 123.

Vehovsky, A., H. Szabó, L. Hiripi, C.J.H. Elliott, and L. Hernádi. 2007. Behavioral and neural deficits induced by rotenone in the pond snail *Lymnaea stagnalis*. A possible model for Parkinson's disease in an invertebrate. *European Journal of Neuroscience* 25(7): 2123–2130.

Walker, W.W., and K.E. Havens. 1995. Relating Algal Bloom Frequencies to Phosphorus Concentrations in Lake Okeechobee. *Lake and Reservoir Management* 11(1): 77–83.

Waltz, J. 2008. *Chinese Mystery Snail (Bellamya chinensis) Review*. Washington, DC: Univ. of Washington.

Wang, J., D. Zhang, I. Jakovlić, and W. Wang. 2017. Sequencing the complete mitochondrial genomes of eight freshwater snail species exposes pervasive paraphyly within the Viviparidae family (Caenogastropoda). *PLoS One* 12(7): e0181699.

Wood, W.M. 1892. *Paludina japonica* Mart. for sale in the San Francisco Chinese markets. *Nautilus* 5: 114–115.

Xiong, Q., H. Hao, L. He, Y. Jing, T. Xu, J. Chen, H. Zhang, T. Hu, Q. Zhang, X. Yang, J. Yuan, and Y. Huang. 2017. Anti-inflammatory and Anti-angiogenic Activities of a Purified Polysaccharide from Flesh of *Cipangopaludina chinensis*. *Carbohydrate Polymers* 176: 152–59.

Yang, Q., S. Liu, C. He, and X. Yu. 2018. Distribution and the origin of invasive apple snails, *Pomacea canaliculata* and *P. maculata* (Gastropoda: Ampulliariidae) in China. *Scientific Reports* 8, 1185.

Zhou, H., M. Yang, M. Zhang, S. Hou, S. Kong, L. Yang, and L. Deng. 2016. Preparation of Chinese mystery snail shells derived hydroxyapatite with different morphology using condensed phosphate sources. *Ceramics International* 42(15): 16671–16676.

5 Northern Snakehead (*Channa argus*)

ABSTRACT

Northern Snakehead (*Channa argus*) is a popular food fish throughout its native distribution in Asia, but an aggressive pest in the United States, where its import has been federally prohibited since 2002. Hardy and prolific, this fish has become especially abundant in Maryland's Potomac River watershed. While the northern snakehead has not yet become established in the state of Massachusetts, fishermen, watershed managers, and citizens alike should remain on guard for appearances of northern snakehead, as an unchecked snakehead population in Massachusetts would be both ecologically damaging and profoundly difficult to reverse. This chapter discusses the basic biology of the northern snakehead, the impacts of its spread in North America, and a range of methods currently in use for monitoring and controlling its populations.

INTRODUCTION

Taxonomic Hierarchy (ITIS 2021)

Kingdom	Animalia
Subkingdom	Bilateria
Infrakingdom	Deuterostomia
Phylum	Chordata
Subphylum	Vertebrata
Infraphylum	Gnathostomata
Superclass	Actinopterygii
Class	Teleostei
Superorder	Acanthopterygii
Order	Perciformes
Suborder	Channoidei
Family	Channidae
Genus	*Channa* Scopoli, 1777
Species	*Channa argus* (Cantor, 1842)

Fish in the family Channidae are commonly called "snakeheads" (Figure 5.1) because of their elongated bodies and wide, flat heads, covered in large scales that are similar in appearance to the epidermal scales on the heads of snakes (Courtenay and Williams 2004). All snakeheads have elongated dorsal and anal fins, small tubular nostrils, and a large mouth full of sharp teeth. Depending on the species, snakeheads are either obligate or facultative airbreathers, meaning they either must regularly swim up to the surface and breathe air (obligate) or they have the ability to supplement water breathing with oxygen from the air (facultative) (Courtenay and Williams 2004). Due to this special adaptation, many snakehead species, including the northern snakehead, are capable of surviving out of the water for several days and can wiggle short distances to new waterbodies (Bressman et al. 2019).

Northern snakehead (*Channa argus*) has become established in several states, benefited by its broad temperature tolerance, ranging from 0°C to >30°C (Kramer et al. 2017). This fish is able to withstand freezing winters by lying dormant under the ice, forgoing eating and even respiration for long periods of time. The northern snakehead is an obligate air breather that thrives in shallow freshwater habitats with aquatic vegetation (Orrell and Weigt 2005; Kramer et al. 2017). It can tolerate slightly saline water, but it cannot live in water with a salinity higher than 10 parts per thousand (Courtenay and Williams 2004; Orrell and Weigt 2005).

Snakeheads, including the northern snakehead, generally reproduce in the summer. Northern snakeheads construct nests by clearing out circular areas of vegetation. The uprooted vegetation is often used above or beside the clearing to form cover for the nest, where females will lay bright yellow-orange eggs (Courtenay and Williams 2004; Landis and Lapointe 2010). Male and female northern snakeheads remain stationed together on or near the nest to guard their offspring. Eggs hatch after one to two days, but parents remain with the young for around four weeks (Qin et al. 2012). The young are reportedly

FIGURE 5.1 Invasive snakeheads in the United States. *From top to bottom:* Northern snakehead (USGS 2003; Cermele 2019; GA DNR 2019; Trammel n.d.), Bullseye snakehead (Randall 2015; RAWWFishing 2017; Everglades CISMA 2018), and Giant snakehead (The Phuket News 2019; Raleigh n.d.).

seen schooling together for a prolonged time after leaving the nest, initially accompanied by a parent (Landis and Lapointe 2010). Northern snakeheads are capable of reproducing multiple times in a year, with female northern snakeheads reportedly bearing up to five separate broods per season (Courtenay and Williams 2004). At 2 years old, a female northern snakehead can lay up to 15,000 eggs (Chesapeake Bay Program n.d.). Larger or older individual fish have been found to produce larger numbers of eggs, and the observed lifespan of the species is 8 years (Qin et al. 2012) or up to 15 years (Susan Pasko, personal communication).

The northern snakehead has a fairly distinctive appearance. It is brown, with dark-colored fins, yellowish-white coloration on the lower part of its body, and large dark-brown blotches covering its sides in a repeating pattern. Like all snakehead species, the northern snakehead has elongated anal and dorsal fins on the bottom and top of its body, and it is covered in large glossy scales (Figure 5.1). Juvenile northern snakeheads appear light yellow-green with translucent fins, but begin to develop adult coloration at around four weeks, at which point they are typically 20 mm long (slightly under 1 inch) (Qin et al. 2012).

Northern snakehead are commonly confused with two fish species indigenous to North America: the burbot (*Lota lota*) and the bowfin (*Amia calva*) (U.S. Fish & Wildlife Service 2003). The burbot is a cod relative that inhabits cold freshwater in North America, Europe, and Asia. Burbot have a similar shape and general appearance to the northern snakehead, but can be easily distinguished from their invasive look-alikes by their slimy skin and lack of visible scales on its body. Burbot also tend to have a less defined, more mottled coloration on their body than snakehead, as well as a split dorsal fin and barbels (whiskers) on its mouth (ADFG n.d.). The bowfin is another visually similar species, common across the eastern United States (Fuller 2021). Bowfin can be distinguished from snakehead in several ways. The body of the bowfin is mostly solid-colored, with faint patterning toward the tail (Figure 5.2) (Fuller 2021). The head of a bowfin is smooth, appearing to lack scales, and male bowfin have a singular eyespot on the base of their tail (TPW n.d.). The most definitive feature that can be used to distinguish bowfin from northern snakehead is the shape and size of fins on the underside of its body: while snakeheads have a very long anal fin, mirroring the dorsal fins on their backs, bowfin have a small, short anal fin. The differences between northern snakehead and these two species are depicted and explained in the guide attached to this report (Figure 5.2).

While the northern snakehead is the highest snakehead species of concern in Massachusetts, on account of New England's climactic suitability for its establishment, there are two species of tropical snakehead that pose a risk of invasion to other areas of the United States. The bullseye snakehead (*Channa marulius*) prefers warmer climates, and so it poses a greater threat to southern states, including Florida, where the species has already established (SPDC 2014). Bullseye snakehead are the largest species of snakehead, capable of growing up to 70 inches (1,800 mm) in length (Courtenay and Williams 2004). They are similar in shape to northern snakehead, but have very different coloration, being a much darker, mostly solid brown or orange color, with some individuals having five or six dull blotches along their sides and sparse white speckles along the posterior edges of the blotches (Figure 5.1). Bullseye snakeheads are named for a distinctive "bullseye" mark on the base of their tails, which appears as a black oval rimmed in bright orange, when it is visible (Figure 5.1). The giant snakehead (*Channa maculata*) is another mostly tropical species of snakehead, which poses an invasion risk primarily to Florida and Hawaii (SPDC 2014). It has a very different appearance to that of the northern snakehead, with bright, almost iridescent-looking yellow-green scales arranged in irregular blotchy or striped patterns interspersed with black across the top of its body. It has a thick, very dark black stripe across the length of its body, and a white underside (Figure 5.1). Juvenile giant snakeheads are light yellow-green, with a red tail and two thin black stripes running the length of the body.

NATIVE AND INVASIVE RANGE, MECHANISMS OF SPREAD

The northern snakehead demonstrates hardiness to a variety of environmental conditions and an ability to spawn in large numbers, increasing its abundance at a rapid rate (Love and Newhard 2018; Kusek 2007). Such characteristics are common to species that travel outside their native range and become invasive. Native to China, Korea, and Russia, the fish was first legally imported to North America for sale in the live food fish market and became established in waterways after unauthorized intentional release (Fuller et al. 2019; SPDC

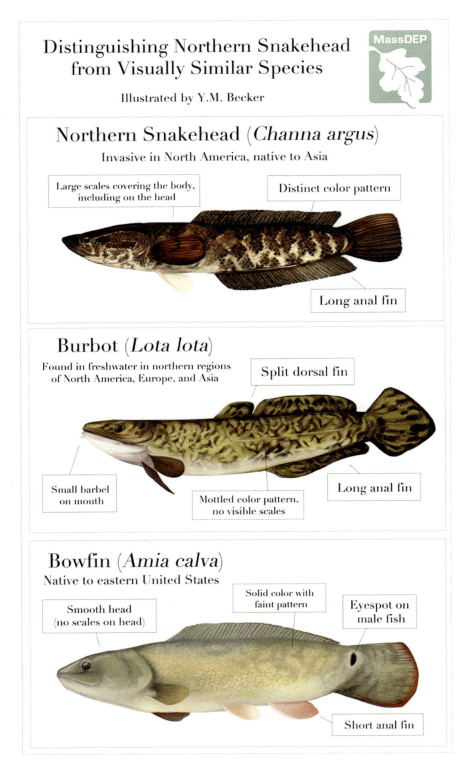

FIGURE 5.2 Invasive snakeheads in the United States. *From top to bottom:* Northern snakehead (USGS 2003; Cermele 2019; GA DNR 2019; Trammel n.d.), Burbot (Schloeffel 2016; Siitari 2018; ADFG n.d.), Bowfin (Knie 2019; Raver n.d.).

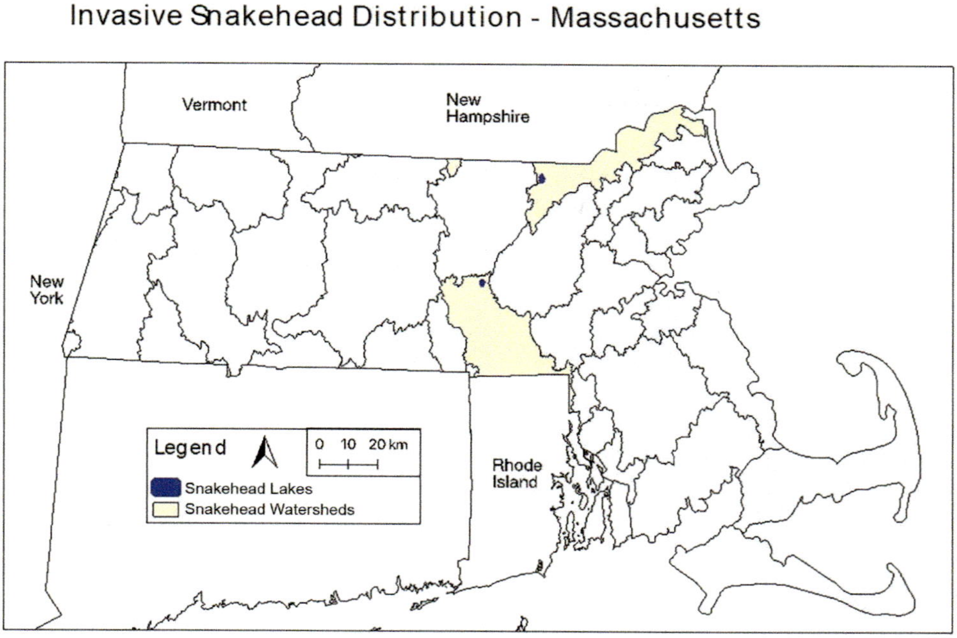

Invasive Snakehead Distribution - Massachusetts

FIGURE 5.3 Distribution map depicting the two waterbodies where northern snakehead (*Channa argus*) has been sighted in Massachusetts.

2014). Other minor contributions to the introduction of northern snakehead include unintentional release during commercial transport of live fish, release associated with the aquarium trade, and release of captive animals as part of religious ceremonies (SPDC 2014).

In 2002, the federal Lacey Act (18 U.S.C. 42) was amended to include all fish in the Channidae family on the list of injurious wildlife. This legislation now prohibits the import and of any snakehead species without a permit, imposing significant fines and a maximum of six months in prison as penalties on those found guilty of injurious wildlife violations (SPDC 2014). Regulation of possession and intrastate transport varies by state. In Massachusetts, it is illegal to own any unpermitted exotic (non-domesticated) wildlife from a species that is not exempt under the conditions of 321 CMR 9.00. Exemption criteria include that "accidental release of the fish . . . will not result in an adverse effect on the ecology of the state," and so possession of snakeheads is therefore illegal in the state of Massachusetts.

The passage and enforcement of state and federal regulations have resulted in fewer introductions of northern snakehead to the United States However, secondary spread from existing established snakehead populations still pose a great threat (SPDC 2014). Introduced northern snakeheads have been sighted in Massachusetts waterways on two different occasions (see "Monitoring and Sightings" section). Once established, a northern snakehead population is capable of rapidly increasing its numbers, as observed in the Potomac River system (Odenkirk and Owens 2011).

The life history of northern snakeheads in their non-indigenous range has in some cases been observed to vary from their typical life history, leading some to assert that snakeheads generally grow larger and faster outside of their native range (Landis et al. 2011). However, a 2014 metanalysis found no difference in northern snakehead growth rates between native and invasive populations, but that growth rates correlate with regional precipitation rates (Rypel 2014). Northern snakeheads may be able to take advantage of high-water or storm events to spread to new waterbodies, and even have the ability to travel overland on account of their air-breathing nature, having been observed to "crawl" slowly over land (Courtenay and Williams 2004; Odenkirk 2018; Bressman et al. 2019). When migrating to new territory through water, snakeheads have a tendency to swim upstream, typically expanding their range in an upstream direction (SPDC 2014). Elevation and precipitation levels may also be predictive factors for risk of northern snakehead invasion (Poulos et al. 2012; Rypel 2014). Middle latitudes (maximum air temperatures of 18–20°C) in the United States are susceptible to its invasion which matches the latitudinal range of its native distribution in China.

A tagging program carried out during 2009–2011 found that the majority (around 90%) of northern snakeheads did not leave the waterbody where they were initially tagged, but the few that did travel were able to travel very far, with one fish being recovered nearly 30 miles upstream (SPDC 2014; Lapointe et al. 2013). The team theorized that the fish could have traveled even further, if they had not been restricted by dams upstream. The majority of movement also seemed to occur in the spring prior to spawning or during high-flow events, and there was no relationship found between movement and fish size or age (SPDC 2014).

ECOLOGICAL IMPACTS

In the Eastern United States, largemouth bass is an ecologically and economically important species, serving as an apex predator in freshwater ecosystems and as a sport-fish commonly sought after by anglers (Ludsin and DeVries 1997; US FWS n.d.). Introduced northern snakeheads pose a potential threat to largemouth bass, as the invaders inhabit a similar ecological niche to native bass, with both species being large, fish-eating ambush predators. Prey availability is thought to be crucial to recruitment (survivability of young past their first year) of largemouth bass, so competition for prey is largely detrimental to young bass (Gutreuter and Anderson 1985). A modeling experiment evaluating the impact of northern snakehead on largemouth bass populations in the Potomac River found that if snakehead expansion continues at its current rate without control measures, largemouth bass abundance could be decreased by 35.5% (Love and Newhard 2012).

Largemouth bass also tend to be sensitive to low water temperatures or reduced dissolved oxygen in water (US FWS n.d.), conditions which northern snakehead is notoriously capable of withstanding (SPDC 2014). Thus, northern snakeheads may have a competitive advantage over largemouth bass following especially harsh winters, or in waterbodies where oxygen is low due to eutrophication, caused by pollution or other environmental stressors. Massachusetts is at a particularly high risk for providing northern snakehead with conditions that favor these advantages: winters in Massachusetts are cold, and eutrophication is a severe issue. Long-term water quality monitoring data has shown that cultural eutrophication (low-oxygen conditions resulting from anthropogenic nutrient pollution) is directly or indirectly linked to 48% of water quality impairments in the state (Wong et al. 2018). However, the long-term data set shows that water chemistry in rivers and streams has been improving over the years, thanks to rigorous protections set in place by the federal Clean Water Act and enforcement by state agencies (Wong et al. 2018). With continued diligence and enforcement of water quality protections, conditions are likely to keep improving with lakes and ponds being prioritized for protection and restoration.

HUMAN RISKS AND BENEFITS

In many parts of Asia, within the fish's native range, northern snakehead is considered an economically important food fish (Wang et al. 2019). In China, specifically, captive cultivation of snakehead produces an annual volume of fish worth the equivalent of US$1.6 billion (Xu et al. 2017). Snakeheads that are collected by fishing from wild or feral populations are also eaten and enjoyed by many anglers. In fact, at the 2018 First International Snakehead Symposium, a large gathering of snakehead-interested researchers and watershed managers, fried snakehead appetizers were served to attendees to demonstrate the quality of the fish as food (Odenkirk 2018).

However, despite snakeheads' value as food in certain settings, they also pose some risks to human livelihood. As discussed in the previous section, northern snakehead has the potential to negatively impact recreational largemouth bass fisheries, which can be detrimental to tourism and to the overall recreational value of an area. Snakeheads also have sharp teeth, and while they are not typically aggressive toward humans, they

TABLE 5.1
Sightings and Report Sources of Infested Waterbodies

Waterbody	Agency	Report_Source	Longitude	Latitude	First Year Reported
Massapoag Pond	MassDEP	USGS NAS Database	−71.496	42.654	2004
Newton Pond	MassDEP	USGS NAS Database	−71.75	42.308	2011

TABLE 5.2
Infested Waterbodies, Towns, and Watersheds

Number	Waterbody	Town_1	Town_2	Watershed
2	Massapoag Pond	Dunstable	Groton/Tyingsborough	Merrimack
1	Newton Pond	Shrewsbury	Boylston	Blackstone

can be defensive of their nesting sites (USGS n.d.a). In Delaware, a young child was once bitten by a juvenile northern snakehead after reaching out to touch it (Howard 2016). Fortunately, the child's injury was not serious, but to avoid these kinds of unpleasant encounters, snakehead should be handled with caution.

MONITORING AND SIGHTINGS

So far, northern snakehead has only been sighted twice in the state of Massachusetts (Figure 5.1 and Table 5.1).[1] The first sighting was in 2004 in Massapoag Pond which is located in north central Massachusetts near the New Hampshire border. The second fish was seen in Newton Pond in Shrewsbury, in central Mass (USGS n.d.b) (Table 5.2). Each sighting was only of a single individual fish, and there is no evidence of northern snakehead reproducing or becoming established anywhere in the state. This is in contrast to nearby states, including Delaware, New York, and Maryland, where established northern snakehead populations are increasingly becoming an issue (SPDC 2014). In order to prevent sporadic individual introductions from going unnoticed and growing into statewide nuisances, it is important to maintain thorough monitoring efforts, paired with investment in public awareness and proactive plans for management in the case that northern snakehead is found.

Attentive monitoring is important to preventing the spread of northern snakehead, since smaller, newer populations are easier to control. Northern snakehead monitoring can be carried out either by conventional, physical surveys or by using newer biological techniques such as environmental DNA (eDNA) analysis. Conventional surveys assessing snakehead populations have involved trapping, netting, and electrofishing to collect snakehead fish where they may be present (Orrell and Weigt 2005; SPDC 2014; Lapointe et al. 2019). Tagging experiments have also been carried out in parts of the United States to track the movement of northern snakehead and the expansion of its invasive range (Lapointe et al. 2013).

Detection by eDNA is another useful method for monitoring northern snakehead, especially useful for passive surveillance over larger areas of concern where conventional surveys are not feasible, or to supplement conventional surveys in measuring the success of control operations. Extensive work has been carried out on elucidating cytochrome oxidase subunit I (COI) gene sequences associated with different species in the Channidae family, so that snakeheads can be identified through DNA barcoding methods used in eDNA analysis (Serrao et al. 2014). eDNA monitoring has recently been used to detect the invasive bullseye snakehead (*C. marulius*) in southern Florida (Hunter et al. 2019). Another surveillance project in 2015 was able to detect northern snakehead by eDNA from the Muskingum River watershed in Ohio, demonstrating the usefulness of molecular screening for monitoring northern snakehead invasion (Simmons et al. 2015).

MANAGING ACTIONS

Demographic models have shown that removal of northern snakehead should occur during pre-spawn periods or prior to juvenile dispersal, since spawning events produce hundreds of new fish (SPDC 2014; Jiao et al. 2009). Eradication also appears to be more successful when it is attempted in confined ponds and lakes, as there are several recorded instances of northern snakehead being completely or almost completely eliminated from lakes (Boesch 2002; Mahon et al. 2016), while cases of treatment within extensive river systems, such as the White River system in Arkansas (SPDC 2014) and in the Potomac River (MDNR n.d.), have been reported to be more difficult and less effective. Since lake and pond infestations are more treatable, and populations within rivers are likely to become established when fish spread into river drainages from nearby ponds, effective preventative management can be achieved through diligent monitoring of lakes and ponds adjacent to large river systems. When northern snakehead is discovered in a pond or a lake, a rapid response is important to prevent the invasive population from growing to an unmanageable extent.

Massachusetts Division of Fisheries and Wildlife has a suite of regulations to prevent importation and liberation of anything vertebrate (321 CMR 2.15 and 4.09). Import permits not only protect natural resources from invasive organisms, but also help to protect them from diseases. All fish, except aquarium trade fish, need a permit and cannot be released to the wild. Even it is exempt from permits to import and possess, aquarium trade fish cannot be released into the wild. In addition, the Massachusetts Endangered Species Act prohibit authorized take; therefore, the general public should be aware that snakeheads cannot be possessed due to its harm to the environment; state agency will not issue permits for taking northern snakehead. Public awareness with regard to those who might eat snakehead and a concerted effort to educate fishermen and women to be on the lookout would be the most effective way of minimizing any intentional or unintentional release. There is currently no established northern snakehead population in Massachusetts, and so it is critical at this stage to invest in strong monitoring and prevention, as well as in raising public awareness to prevent introduction and spread by human means. Snakehead populations grow very quickly, and a population can be most effectively controlled if management is carried out imminently. In order not to be caught off guard by an emergent northern snakehead infestation rapidly propagating and spreading throughout a system, agencies should widely monitor for the presence of northern snakehead, and have a plan in place for a response to be carried out if the invasive fish are detected. Information on effective control methods can be found in the following sections, as well as two case studies describing successful responses to emergent northern snakehead infestations.

CHEMICAL CONTROL

The standard fish poison rotenone has been found to be highly successful in eradicating northern snakehead (Lazur et al. 2011; Nanda et al. 2009). However, rotenone is non-specific and toxic to native species of fish; thus, its use could do more ecological harm than good if applied without caution (Turner et al. 2007; Stinson 2018; Roop and Williams 2020). Ideally, applications of rotenone should be confined to high-density areas of snakehead infestation. Additional practicable precautions to be taken include preemptively capturing and removing native fish to holding tanks, and neutralizing rotenone using potassium permanganate at the end of treatment (Roop and Williams 2020).

Antimycin has not been tested on northern snakehead but is approved for use on other invasive fish species in the United States and could be effective (Abdel-Fattah 2011). Deltamethrin is also found to induce fish tissues damage, oxidative damage, and immunotoxicity (Kong et al. 2021). More information about chemical control on northern snakehead and other 18 invasive species can be found in Appendix III. Before any chemical application, it is required to obtain an aquatic nuisance species control license (BRP WM04 Form) from Massachusetts Department of Environmental Protection.

PHYSICAL CONTROL

Like many other fish, the northern snakehead can be enticed out of the water by a baited hook and a fishing rod. Organized efforts have been carried out in multiple states to collaborate with sport fishermen on the removal of northern snakehead, and to raise public awareness of the risks invasive snakeheads pose to the integrity of native freshwater fisheries. As recreational fish harvest has caused depression of fish biomass for many species in the past, employing sport fishermen to remove invasive fish has the potential to be a strong supplementary method of population control (SPDC 2014).

In the state of Maryland, where northern snakehead invasion is most severe, there have been several campaigns initiated to incentivize snakehead sport fishing. Maryland's Department of Natural Resources (MDNR) holds an annual Snakehead Contest—an event where local anglers compete to catch the biggest snakehead. In 2019, MDNR reported 107 participants in the Snakehead Derby, and 25 northern snakeheads caught in within 6 hours (MDNR 2019). As another incentive program, MDNR once held a photo raffle, where anglers entered photos of caught and killed northern snakehead for a chance to win prizes, such as Bass Pro Shops gift cards or free sport fishing licenses (SPDC 2014).

While these kinds of public outreach campaigns have been valuable in raising awareness of invasive fish and aiding removal efforts, there are risks to encouraging snakehead harvest with incentives. If bounties placed on snakeheads are significant enough to generate a large profit, or even if the entertainment value of snakehead capture is realized, well-intentioned control efforts could create pressure to sustain snakehead populations or introduce them into new areas, rather than to eliminate them (Pasko and Goldberg 2014). Fishermen might be incentivized to cultivate snakehead on their own to continue profiting from bounties or release them to the wild in order to populate a favorite fishing spot. On account of careful planning and consideration, no known case of intentional release thus far has been motivated by the desire to profit from incentives (SPDC 2014).

It is also possible to physically remove snakeheads from the water using electrofishing, netting, or trapping, but physical removal alone is unlikely to fully remove northern snakehead from an area (SPDC 2014). Electrofishing may also be less effective in collecting juvenile or smaller fish (Cohen and MacDonald 2016).

BIOLOGICAL (ECOLOGICAL) CONTROL

There is no known method of biological control that can be used on northern snakehead. As an apex predator in the fish food web, the northern snakehead has few underwater predators. However, piscivorous birds such as osprey (*Pandion haliaetus*) and great blue heron (*Ardea herodias*) have been observed to feed on northern snakehead in the Potomac River system (Lapointe et al. 2019). Northern snakeheads may be especially vulnerable to bird predation due to their biological obligation to rise to the surface of the water and sip air, placing them visibly within reach of birds (Lapointe et al. 2019). Additionally, eastern mosquitofish (*Gambusia holbrooki*) have been observed in the wild feeding on northern snakehead fish eggs and fry in large numbers, a single mosquitofish eating 60 eggs and fry within a short span of time (Landis and Lapointe 2010). Though there is currently no known means of biological control for northern snakehead, conserving and restoring habitat for native herons, osprey, and mosquitofish could be a useful, low-impact way to keep snakehead populations under control and mitigate the ecological effects caused by the invader.

SUCCESS STORIES

MACQUILLIAM POND, CROFTON, MARYLAND

In spring of 2002, an angler caught an 18-inch long northern snakehead from MacQuilliam Pond, a small pond in Crofton, Maryland, located on private property beside a strip-mall (MDNR 2019, n.d.; The Washington Times 2002). The identification of the fish was confirmed by an expert, and several more snakeheads, including juveniles, were found in the same pond. Maryland Department of Natural Resources (MDNR) began monitoring the population with electrofishing surveys. The first survey caught over 100 young-of-the-year northern snakeheads, confirming MacQuilliam Pond to be home to the first established, reproductive population of northern snakehead in the United States (Boesch 2002; SPDC 2014). Investigations by Maryland Natural Resources Police found the source of the infestation to have been a resident, who admitted to having released a pair of 12–14-inch snakehead fish into the pond a couple of years earlier, after the fish outgrew his home aquarium (Boesch 2002; Kobell 2002). The original purpose for this resident to buy the fish was to serve to a sick sister who believed to have medicinal properties (Susan Pasko, personal communication).

Amid urgent concerns that the invasive population would expand into the nearby Little Patuxent River, and somewhat tense negotiations with the pond's owners, eradication efforts finally began (The Washington Times 2002). In September 2002, MacQuilliam Pond was treated with rotenone, a fish poison. Herbicides were also applied to the pond, in an effort to reduce refuge area for the fish and to lower the oxygen content of the pond. Sandbags and silt fences were employed around the periphery of the pond to prevent any fish from escaping over land in the case of heavy rain (Boesch 2002).

During the eradication process, over 1,200 dead snakeheads were recovered. Though MDNR officials had expected the rotenone treatment to kill all of the native fish in the pond and had planned to restock the pond with native fish after the fact to mitigate the ecological damage, it was found that some indigenous species, including bluegills, eels, and pickerel, had survived the poisoning in small numbers (Kiehl 2002). Thanks to the MDNR's swift and aggressive treatment of the snakehead invasion, northern snakeheads have not been sighted in MacQuilliam Pond since 2002. However, separate introductions in the state of Maryland have resulted in widespread established populations of northern snakehead throughout the Potomac and Patuxent river watersheds today that are incredibly difficult to manage, highlighting the importance of early, targeted, preventative responses such as these to control emerging snakehead populations.

Ridgebury Lake

In 2008, northern snakehead fish were collected from Ridgebury Lake, a lake in New York State which drains into a tributary of the Hudson River. The fish were discovered in the spring of 2008, and that summer, Ridgebury Lake and several adjacent ponds in the Catlin Creek drainage area were treated with rotenone. Over 200 dead snakeheads were recovered following treatment, and most were juveniles, indicating that the population was established and reproducing. Treatment was repeated in select ponds the following year in 2009, and subsequent monitoring did not detect any northern snakehead in the area, leading managers to believe that the populations were successfully eradicated (SPDC 2014). To gain more information and to improve their certainty of the snakeheads' eradication, the New York State Department of Environmental Conservation (NYSDEC) worked in collaboration with a team from Central Michigan University (CMU) to begin environmental DNA (eDNA) monitoring in 2012 (SPDC 2014; Wegleitner and Mahon 2014). The sampling protocol was refined, updated, and repeated several times over the course of three years following the eradication efforts (Mahon et al. 2016).

Originally, 308 field samples were collected from the Catlin Creek drainage and 525 from the Erie Canal Corridor (ECC), the large artificial canal system connecting the Great Lakes, the Lake Champlain Basin, and the Mohawk–Hudson River Basin (Mahon et al. 2016). Using species-specific primers and standard PCR, the team from CMU found that none of the samples tested positive for the presence of northern snakehead eDNA. In 2014, after improving filtration and extraction efficiency and changing to a more sensitive method for screening results, digital droplet PCR (ddPCR), Mahon et al. (2016) collected another 294 and 725 samples from the Catlin Creek drainage and ECC, respectively. While once again there were zero positive detections from the ECC, three of the samples from the Catlin Creek drainage returned positive for snakehead eDNA. A memo was sent to the NYSDEC detailing the locations of each positive detections on maps with conclusions and recommendations. Sampling was repeated again in 2015 and this time returned no positive eDNA snakehead detection (Mahon et al. 2016).

This case provides an example for advanced monitoring techniques being used in conjunction with chemical control to ensure successful management of invasive species in vulnerable, highly connected waterways. The CMU team were able to monitor a large, high-risk area, pinpoint the precise location of any emergent evidence for the species' presence, and confirm that northern snakehead was prevented from actively expanding its range into the Hudson River (Mahon et al. 2016).

NOTE

1 According to a comment from Susan Pasko, a recent third sighting has been confirmed in the Canton Reservoir on August 27, 2021. This new infestation site is not mapped in this chapter.

REFERENCES

Abdel-Fattah, S. 2011. *Aquatic Invasive Species Early Detection and Rapid Response- Assessment of Chemical Response Tools*. International Joint Commission, Great Lakes Regional Office, p. 104.

Alaska Department of Fish and Game (ADFG). n.d. Burbot (*Lota lota*) species profile. www.adfg.alaska.gov/index.cfm?adfg=burbot.main (Accessed May 13, 2021).

Boesch, D. 2002. Snakehead Scientific Advisory Panel First Report to the Maryland Secretary of Natural Resources. https://msa.maryland.gov/megafile/msa/speccol/sc5300/sc5339/000113/004000/004189/unrestricted/20071038e.pdf. (Accessed May 7, 2021).

Bressman, N.R., J.W. Love, T.W. King, C.G. Horne, and M.A. Ashley-Ross. 2019. Emersion and Terrestrial Locomotion of the Northern Snakehead (*Channa argus*) on Multiple Substrates. *Integrative Organismal Biology* 1(1): obz026.

Cermele, J. 2019. Is the snakehead epidemic happening all over again? www.fieldandstream.com/is-snakehead-epidemic-happening-all-over-again/ (Accessed May 20, 2021).

Chesapeake Bay Program. n.d. Northern snakehead. www.chesapeakebay.net/discover/field-guide/entry/northern_snakehead#:~:text=Reproduction%20and%20Life%20Cycle,nest%2C%20which%20both%20parents%20guard.&text=After%20that%2C%20they%20feed%20mostly,small%20crustaceans%20and%20fish%20larvae (Accessed May 13, 2021).

Cohen, M.K., and J.A. MacDonald. 2016. Northern Snakeheads in New York City. *Northeastern Naturalist* 23(1): 11–24.

Courtenay, W.R., and J.D. Williams. 2004. *Snakehead (Pisces, Channidae)—A biological synopsis and risk assessment*. New York: U.S. Geological Survey Circular 1251, p. 143.

Everglades Center for Invasive Species and Ecosystem Health (CISMA). 2018. Bullseye Snakehead (Channa marulius). www.evergladescisma.org/the-dirty-dozen/bullseye-snakehead/ (Accessed May 20, 2021).

Fuller, P.L. 2021. *Amia calva* Linnaus, 1766. USGS Nonindigenous Aquatic Species Database, Gainesville, FL. https://nas.er.usgs.gov/queries/FactSheet.aspx?SpeciesID=305. (Accessed May 13, 2021).

Fuller, P.L., A.J. Benson, G. Nunez, A. Fusaro, and M. Neilson. 2019. *Channa argus* (Cantor, 1842). USGS Nonindigenous Aquatic Species Database, Gainesville, FL. https://nas.er.usgs.gov/queries/factsheet.aspx?speciesid=2265. (Accessed May 7, 2021).

Georgia Department of Natural Resources (GA DNR). 2019. Two juvenile northern snakehead fish that were caught in a pond in Gwinnett County, Ga. Via www.nytimes.com/2019/10/10/us/snakehead-fish-georgia.html. (Accessed May 20, 2021).

Gutreuter, S.J., and R.O. Anderson. 1985. Importance of Body Size to the Recruitment Process in Largemouth Bass Populations. *Transactions of the American Fisheries Society* 114(3): 314–327.

Howard, B.C. 2016. Fishermen Battle Invasive 'Frankenfish' Snakeheads. *National Geographic*. www.nationalgeographic.com/animals/article/160317-snakeheads-potomac-river-chesapeake-bay-invasive-species-fish?loggedin=true. (Accessed May 7, 2021).

Hunter, M., P. Schofield, G. Meigs-Friend, M. Brown, and J. Ferrante. 2019. Environmental DNA (eDNA) detection of non-native bullseye snakehead in southern Florida. *American Fisheries Society*. p. 21.

ITIS (Integrated Taxonomic Information System). 2021. www.itis.gov/servlet/SingleRpt/SingleRpt?search_topic=TSN&search_value=166680#null (Accessed April 15, 2021).

Jiao, Y., N.W.R. Lapointe, P.L. Angermeier, and B.R. Murphy. 2009. Hierarchical demographic approaches for assessing invasion dynamics of non-indigenous species: An example using northern snakehead (*Channa argus*). *Ecological Modelling* 220(13–14): 1681–1689.

Kiehl, S. 2002. Hobbyist freed snakeheads in Md. Pond. *The Baltimore Sun*. www.baltimoresun.com/bal-te.md.snakehead-12jul12-story.html (Accessed May 7, 2021).

Knie, A. 2019. Jurassic Park: The Hunt for Jersey Bowfin. www.thefisherman.com/article/jurassic-park-the-hunt-for-jersey-bowfin/ (Accessed May 20, 2021).

Kobell, R. 2002. Snakehead extermination approved. *The Baltimore Sun*. www.baltimoresun.com/maryland/bal-md.snakehead16aug16-story.html (Accessed May 7, 2021).

Kong, Y, M. Li, X. Shan, G. Wang, and G Han. 2021. Effects of deltamethrin subacute exposure in snakehead fish, Channa argus: Biochemicals, antioxidants and immune responses. *Ecotoxicology and Environmental Safety* 209: 111821.

Kramer, A.M., G. Annis, M.E. Wittmann, W.L. Chadderton, E.S. Rutherford, D.M. Lodge, L. Mason, D. Beletsky, C. Riseng, J.M. Drake. 2017. Suitability of Laurentian Great Lakes for invasive species based on global species distribution models and local habitat. *Ecosphere* 8(7): e01883.

Kusek, J.L. 2007. Fishing for a solution: How to prevent the introduction of invasive species such as the snakehead fish. *Penn State Environmental Law Review* 15(2): 331–354.

Landis, A.M.G., and N.W.R. Lapointe. 2010. First record of a Northern Snakehead (*Channa argus* Cantor) Nest in North America. *Northeastern Naturalist* 17(2): 325–332.

Landis, A.M.G., N.W.R. Lapointe, and P.L. Angermeier. 2011. Individual growth and reproductive behavior in a newly established population of northern snakehead (*Channa argus*), Potomac River, USA. *Hydrobiologia* 661: 123–131.

Lapointe, N.W.R., J.S. Odenkirk, and P.L. Angermeier. 2013. Seasonal movement, dispersal, and home range of Northern Snakehead *Channa argus* (Actinopterygii, Perciforms) in the Potomac River catchment. *Hydrobiologia* 701: 73–87.

Lapointe, N.W.R., R.K. Saylor, and P.L. Angermeier. 2019. Diel Feeding and Movement Activity of Northern Snakehead. *American Fisheries Society Symposium* 89: 14.

Lazur, A., S. Early, and J.M. Jacobs. 2011. Acute toxicity of 5% rotenone to Northern Snakeheads. *North American Journal of Fisheries Management* 26(3): 628–630.

Love, J.W., and J.J. Newhard. 2012. Will the expansion of Northern Snakehead negatively affect the fishery for largemouth Bass in the Potomac River (Chesapeake Bay)? *North American Journal of Fisheries Management* 32: 859–868.

Love, J.W., and J.J. Newhard. 2018. Expansion of Northern Snakehead in the Chesapeake Bay Watershed. *Transactions of the American Fisheries Society* 147: 342–349.

Ludsin, S.A., and D.R. DeVries. 1997. First-year recruitment of largemouth bass: the interdependency of early life stages. *Ecological Applications* 7: 1024–1038.

Mahon, A.R., W.L. Chadderton, and A. Tucker. 2016. Final Report—Assessing Erie canal corridor invasion risk using environmental DNA. Institute for Great Lakes Research, Department of Biology, Central Michigan University, p. 43.

Maryland Department of Natural Resources (MDNR). 2019. Freedom and fishing Snakehead Derby. https://dnr.maryland.gov/fisheries/Pages/snakehead_derby.aspx (Accessed May 7, 2021).

Maryland Department of Natural Resources (MDNR). n.d. Northern Snakehead. https://dnr.maryland.gov/fisheries/pages/snakehead.aspx. (Accessed May 7, 2021).

Nanda, N.B.P., P.C. Das, and J. Jena. 2009. Use of rotenone as piscicide: Toxicity levels in a few common freshwater predatory and weed fishes. *Journal of Applied Aquaculture* 21(4): 241–249.

Odenkirk, J.S. 2018. The first international Snakehead symposium: News from the front(s). *Fisheries* 44: 123–128.

Odenkirk, J.S., and S. Owens. 2011. Expansion of a Northern Snakehead population in the Potomac River system. *Transactions of the American Fisheries Society* 136(6): 1633–1639.

Orrell, T.M., and L. Weigt. 2005. The Northern Snakehead *Channa argus* (Anabantomorpha: Channidae), a non-indigenous fish species in the Potomac River, U.S.A. *Proceedings of the Biological Society of Washington* 118(2): 407–415.

Pasko, S., and J. Goldberg. 2014. Review of harvest incentives to control invasive species. *Management of Biological Invasions* 5(3): 263–277.

Poulos, H.M., B. Chernoff, P.L. Fuller, and D. Butman. 2012. Ensemble forecasting of potential habitat for three invasive fishes. *Aquatic Invasions* 7(1): 59–72.

Qin, J., B. Cudmore, and B. Schroeder. 2012. *Channa argus* (northern snakehead). *CABI Invasive Species Compendium.* www.cabi.org/isc/datasheet/89026 (Accessed May 13, 2021).

Raleigh, S. n.d. Giant Snakehead (Channa micropeltes). https://dreamlake-fishing.com/fish-species-of-thailand/giant-snakehead-channa-micropeltes/ (Accessed May 20, 2021).

Randall, Z. 2015. Channa marulius (Hamilton 1822) family channidae. *Florida Museum Ichthyology Collection.* www.floridamuseum.ufl.edu/discover-fish/florida-fishes-gallery/bullseye-snakehead/ (Accessed May 20, 2021).

Raver, D. n.d. Arkansas Game and Fish Commission. www.uaex.edu/environment-nature/ar-invasives/invasive-animals/invasive-fish.aspx (Accessed May 20, 2021).

RAWWFishing. 2017. Fishing for big Bullseye Snakeheads in South Florida with topwater frogs. www.youtube.com/watch?v=a-fOjLc8ktoA (Accessed May 20, 2021).

Roop, J., and A. Williams. 2020. First record of occurrence and genetic characterization of a population of northern snakehead *Channa argus* (Cantor, 1842) in Georgia, USA. *BioInvasions Records* 9: 842–852.

Rypel, A.L. 2014. Do invasive freshwater fish species grow better when they are invasive? *Oikos* 123: 279–289.

Schloeffel, A.R. 2016. A Burbot at the ground of Lake Walchensee, Germany (Bavarian). https://commons.wikimedia.org/wiki/File:Tr%C3%BCsche_Walchensee.jpg (Accessed May 20, 2021).

Serrao, N.R., D. Steinke, and R.H. Hanner. 2014. Calibrating snakehead diversity with DNA barcodes: Expanding taxonomic coverage to enable identification of potential and established invasive species. *PLoS One* 9(6): e99546.

Siitari, K. 2018. New Kootenai River burbot fishery opens for anglers on Jan. 1. https://idfg.idaho.gov/blog/2018/12/kootenai-river-burbot-fishery-open-january-1 (Accessed May 20, 2021).

Simmons, M., A. Tucker, W.L. Chadderton, C.L. Jerde, and A.R. Mahon. 2015. Active and passive environmental DNA surveillance of aquatic invasive species. *Canadian Journal of Fisheries and Aquatic Sciences* 73(1): 76–83.

Snakehead Plan Development Committee (SPDC). 2014. National Control and Management Plan for Members of the Snakehead Family (Channidae), p. 80.

Stinson, H. 2018. The Northern Snakehead, *Channa argus*, as an invasive species. *Eukaryon* 14: 101–102.

Texas Parks & Wildlife (TPW). n.d. Bowfin vs. Snakeheads: Distinguishing features. https://tpwd.texas.gov/huntwild/wild/species/exotic/snakehead_bowfin.phtml (Accessed May 13, 2021).

The Phuket News. 2019. Fish the Exotic: Catching the Giant Snakehead. www.thephuketnews.com/fish-the-exotic-catching-the-giant-snakehead-69909.php. (Accessed May 20, 2021).

The Washington Times. 2002. Pond owner says no to snakehead plan. www.washingtontimes.com/news/2002/aug/8/20020808-035835-2594r/ (Accessed May 7, 2021).

Trammel, S. n.d. Northern Snakehead. Via https://nature.mdc.mo.gov/discover-nature/field-guide/snakeheads (Accessed May 20, 2021).

Turner, L., S. Jacobson, and L. Shoemaker. 2007. Risk Assessment for Piscicidal Formulations of Rotenone. Compliance Services International, p. 104.

U.S. Fish & Wildlife Service. 2003. Recognizing Northern Snakehead. www.fws.gov/fisheries/ans/pdf_files/Recognizing_Snakeheads.pdf (Accessed May 13, 2021).

U.S. Fish & Wildlife Service (US FWS). n.d. Largemouth Bass. *Fish and Aquatic Conservation.* www.fws.gov/fisheries/freshwater-fish-of-america/largemouth_bass.html (Accessed May 7, 2021).

USGS. 2003. Northern snakehead (Channa argus). Via https://en.wikipedia.org/wiki/Northern_snakehead#/media/File:Northern_snakehead.jpg. (Accessed May 20, 2021).

USGS. n.d.a. Can snakehead fish harm humans? *Biology and Ecosystems.* www.usgs.gov/faqs/can-snakehead-fish-harm-humans?qt-news_science_products=0#qt-news_science_products (Accessed May 7, 2021).

USGS. n.d.b. Nonindigenous Aquatic Species (NAS). *Channa argus.* https://nas.er.usgs.gov/queries/CollectionInfo.aspx?SpeciesID=2265&State=MA (Accessed May 10, 2021).

Wang, L., N. Xie, Y. Shen, B. Ye, G. Yue, and X. Feng. 2019. Constructing high-density genetic maps and developing sexing markers in Northern Snakehead (*Channa argus*). *Marine Biotechnology* 21: 348–358.

Wegleitner, B., and A.R. Mahon. 2014. Evaluation of eradication success of Northern Snakehead in the Catlin Creek Drainage, NY using environmental DNA. *American Fisheries Society 144th Annual Meeting.*

Wong, W., J.J. Dudula, T. Beaudoin, K. Groff, W. Kimball, and J. Swigor. 2018. Declining ambient water phosphorus concentrations in Massachusetts' rivers from 1999 to 2013: Environmental protection works. *Water Research* 139: 108–117.

Xu, J., C. Bian, K. Chen, G. Liu, Y. Jiang, Q. Luo, X. You, W. Peng, J. Li, Y. Huang, Y. Yi, C. Dong, H. Deng, S. Zhang, H. Zhang, Q. Shi, and P. Xu. 2017. Draft genome of the Northern snakehead, *Channa argus*. *GigaScience* 6(4): gix011.

6 Hydrilla (*Hydrilla verticillata*)

ABSTRACT

Hydrilla (*Hydrilla verticillata*) is among the most troublesome invasive aquatic plants in many southern states and has recently become established in Massachusetts. The plant crows out native vegetation, harms fisheries, limits recreation, impedes navigation, and reduces property values. Hydrilla is a relatively new introduction to Massachusetts with the first recorded sighting at Long Pond in Cape Cod in 2001. Currently, there are 11 waterbodies infested by hydrilla in Massachusetts. Hydrilla can reproduce and spread in different ways: through fragmentation, turions, tubers, and possibly seeds. Management practices are summarized in this chapter: manual (diver-assisted suction harvesting), mechanical (e.g., drawdowns), biological (e.g., triploid grass carp and some insects), and chemical (e.g., endothall and fluridone) treatments. The documented distribution of invasive hydrilla in Massachusetts' lakes and rivers will allow the general public to become aware of the presence of this invasive species and minimize unintentional transportation and spread of this invasive species to other waterbodies.

INTRODUCTION

Taxonomic Hierarchy (ITIS 2021)

Kingdom	Plantae
Subkingdom	Viridiplantae
Infrakingdom	Streptophyta
Superdivision	Embryophyta
Division	Tracheophyta
Subdivision	Spermatophytina
Class	Magnoliopsida
Superorder	Lilianae
Order	Alismatales
Family	Hydrocharitaceae
Genus	*Hydrilla*
Species	*Hydrilla verticillata* (L.f.) Royle

The invasive hydrilla, also known as Florida elodea and waterthyme, is native to tropical and subtropical areas of Eurasia and Africa and was introduced into the United States in Florida during the 1950s as an aquarium plant (Langeland 1996; Crow and Hellquist 2006; Jacono et al. 2020). It quickly spread after being improperly disposed of into native waterbodies and is now found in 28 states (Jacono et al. 2020). Two genetically and morphologically different biotypes of hydrilla exist: monoecious and dioecious (True-Meadows et al. 2016; Jacono et al. 2020; Tippery et al. 2020). The female and male reproductive organs of dioecious hydrilla are found on different plants, while monoecious hydrilla plants have both sets of reproductive organs (Cook and Lüönd 1982). In the United States, dioecious hydrilla is generally found in the south, while monoecious hydrilla is usually in the north but can be found north of South Carolina (Jacono et al. 2020). A new strain of hydrilla has been recently documented in the Connecticut River from Agawam, MA, to southern Connecticut. It appears more robust but lacks tubers.

Hydrilla is a submersed perennial herb that is adaptable, aggressive, and extremely competitive (Figure 6.1). It is found in freshwater lakes, ponds, rivers, impoundments, and canals. Hydrilla grows submerged, rooted to the bottom of waterbodies with long stems that grow toward the surface where it expands horizontally, forming dense mats (Langeland 1996; Jacono et al. 2020). It can flourish in any freshwater environment and can grow in both low- and high-nutrient conditions. Hydrilla can be found at depths of more than 20 ft, can withstand very low-light conditions. Its leaves are pointed and arranged in whorls of three to eight, ranging from 6–20 mm long and 2–4 mm wide (Figure 6.1). They have serrated margins with sharp teeth, and have spines or glands underneath the reddish midrib. Stems can grow up to 9 m in length. Female flowers can be identified by three whitish sepals and three translucent petals that are

FIGURE 6.1 Hydrilla. (Photos by Summer Stebbins.)

10–50 mm long, 4–8 mm wide, and float on the surface of the water. Male flowers can be identified by three whitish or reddish petals that are about 2 mm long and have three stamen. The female flowers extend via a long stalk to float on the water surface. The male flowers, on the other hand, detaches from the plant and unfold the petals on the surface, where the anthers will then dehisce explosively and release the pollen to fertilize the female flowers. Flowers are rarely observed in New England. Hydrilla reproduces in four ways: fragmentation, tubers, turions, and through seed dispersal. Fragmentation is the most common form of reproduction for hydrilla (Langeland 1996; Jacono et al. 2020). The biology of turion production is comprehensively reviewed by Netherland (1997). A fragment of hydrilla that contains only a single whorl has nearly a 50% chance of sprouting a new plant. Tubers of hydrilla are found at the end of the plant's rhizomes as deep as 30 cm in the sediment, are 5–10 mm long, and are often an off-white or yellowish color (Figure 6.2). They are highly resistant to various control methods, surviving for years in undisturbed sediment and leading to reintroductions years after treatment has stopped. Some genotypes do not appear to produce tubers—the hydrilla recently found in the Connecticut River is a new genotype (Tippery et al. 2020) which does not produce tubers (Greg Bugbee, personal communication). Turions of hydrilla are small buds that fall from the plant (Figure 6.2) and sit on the sediment, and they are 5–8 mm long, with a shiny dark green appearance. Hydrilla grows optimally at 20–27°C in the United States.

Ecological Effects

Hydrilla displaces native species in the plant community, such as native pondweed. The dense mats block sunlight and inhibit the growth of some native species such as eelgrass (Langeland 1996). Hydrilla can grow up to an inch per day and can absorb carbon from the water more effectively than can other aquatic plants (Cornell Cooperative Extension 2019). Hydrilla can also change the chemical and physical composition of lakes by decreasing the dissolved oxygen within waterbodies, reducing water flow, and causing flooding and damage to canal banks (Langeland 1996). Decomposing hydrilla releases nutrients that can accelerate eutrophication and degrade water quality. Stratification of the water column can also occur resulting in fish kills in lakes that have populations of hydrilla (Jacono et al. 2020).

Hydrilla may indirectly impact other species. A survey of three Brazilian reservoirs found the

FIGURE 6.2 Hydrilla tubers (white) and turions (green) and Connecticut River hydrilla aboveground vegetative turion development. (Left photo by Lyn Gettys; right photo by Mark (Heilman 2020).)

invasive bivalve *Limnoperna fortunei* became a problem because hydrilla provided better biomass for attachment compared to native macrophytes (Michelan et al. 2014). In addition, a toxic cyanobacterium, *Aetokthonos hydrillicola*, growing on hydrilla leaves causes a fatal neurological disease in birds that consume it, avian vacuolar myelinopathy (AVM) (Bidigare et al. 2009). It was originally hypothesized that a neurotoxin produced by the cyanobacterium and then ingested by birds was the underlying cause of illness (Williams et al. 2007). Recent research has confirmed that a neurotoxin, aetokthonotoxin (AETX), produced by the cyanobacterium (*A. hydrillicola*) not only affects birds, but also fish and invertebrates (Breinlinger et al. 2021). Fish and waterfowl are exposed to the toxin when they consume hydrilla. The toxin moves up the food chain and afflicts bald eagles. Deaths of bald eagles have been reported in areas of dense *H. verticillata* and *A. hyrillicola* populations (Breinlinger et al. 2021). The cyanobacterium produces the toxin from a bromide solution that likely enters the environment from power plants or other anthropogenic sources as well as diquat dibromide treatments to control hydrilla and other nuisance aquatic vegetation (Stokstad 2021). The toxin is found to be highly potent even at low levels (Pelletier et al. 2019) and mammals may also be susceptible.

Although hydrilla is an invasive species, it may have some beneficial aspects. The plant can provide habitat for fish and wildlife, especially for some animals' early life stages. It is very difficult to maintain the ideal abundance of hydrilla in the habitat. Maintenance of hydrilla could also have a positive effect in some other ways. The main management method of hydrilla has been chemical herbicides, but alternative methods, such as the use of harvester machines for biogas, benefit compost production (Evans and Wilkie 2010). However, use of harvesters is not recommended for hydrilla control because of fragmentation which may facilitate the spread of hydrilla to other waters.

Economic Impacts

Hydrilla has been responsible for many different economic impacts in multiple states. In the states of Massachusetts, Maine, New York, Connecticut, and Florida, hydrilla has inhibited water recreation and angling water quality, flood control, and tourism can also be heavily impacted (Langeland 1996; 2016). Maine has spent close to $200,000 on control in one inland lake and New York is currently spending more than $1 million each year to control several large-scale hydrilla infestations with the aid of US Army Corps of Engineers and many local stakeholders (NEANS 2021). Langeland (1990) reported that the annual control cost to manage 7,600 ha of hydrilla in Florida exceeds $5 million. Hydroelectric power generation is also hindered by fragmented plant material that builds up on trash racks and clogs intakes. For example, during 1991, hydrilla at Lake Moultrie, South Carolina, shut down the St. Stephen powerhouse operations for seven weeks resulting in $2,650,000 of expenses due to repairs, dredging, and fish loss. In addition, during this repair period, there was an estimated $2,000,000 loss in power generation for the plant (Balciunas et al. 2002).

NATIVE AND INVASIVE RANGE

Hydrilla is native to Asia, Africa, and Australia. Specifically, the monoecious strain of hydrilla is thought to originate in Korea, while the dioecious strain is most likely from the Indian subcontinent (Tippery et al. 2020). Hydrilla has been an emerging invasive species that has been slowly invading Massachusetts. It has also been found to be invasive in Maine, Connecticut, New York, New Jersey, Pennsylvania, Maryland, and Florida, as well as many other states (USDA National Invasive Species Information Center 2019). It is the most abundant aquatic plant in Florida public waters (Schardt 1994). A specimen of hydrilla collected at Mystic, Connecticut, in 1989 is the first authenticated record of hydrilla in New England, but it was unnoticed previously because of its misidentification as the South American waterweed (aka Brazillian waterweed, *Egeria densa*) (Les et al. 1997). A new strain of hydrilla has been recently documented in the Connecticut River from Agawam, MA, to southern Connecticut. It has spread rapidly with nearly 900 acres documented (Bugbee and Stebbins 2021).

VECTORS OF SPREAD

Because hydrilla can propagate from fragments, turions, tubers, and seeds, it can spread rapidly to other aquatic habitats. Turions are overwintering buds found where leaves attach to stems. They may break off and be carried by the current to new locations where they can settle, overwinter, and grow into new plants. Tubers are the p, otato-like reproductive structures that form on the roots of hydrilla plants each fall and allow the plants to store energy and regenerate the in following spring or in future seasons. The newly discovered hydrilla strain poses a severe risk to the entire northeast region. Already occurring in the river in Massachusetts, the strain could easily spread into the portions of the river in Vermont and New Hampshire, as well as lakes, ponds, and other rivers throughout the Northeast. In Massachusetts, the Connecticut River has been surveyed at Agawam section and no turions or tubers have been found on any of the hydrilla plants (James Straub 2019, email communication). Nor have tubers been found in the Connecticut River within the boundaries of Connecticut (Greg Bugbee 2019, personal communication).

Hydrilla fragments can spread by attaching to kayaks or boats, trailers, or fishing equipment. The 2019 and 2020 surveys by the Connecticut Agricultural Experiment Station revealed 842 acres of hydrilla in the main channel of Connecticut River from Agawam, MA, downstream to its mouth at Long Island Sound (Bugbee and Stebbins 2021). Based on knowledge of boater movement, the Northeast Aquatic Nuisance Species (NEANS) Panel members have determined that the infestation poses a high risk of spread to other waterways throughout the northeastern United States (NEANS 2020). For example, before boating at Lake George, New York, the last stop for many boaters is the Connecticut River (Table 6.1). These data reinforce the urgency of preventing hydrilla from leaving the Connecticut River (Heilman 2020). In addition to boater movement, waterfowls are vectors with tubers that are regurgitated, not defecated, being viable (Joyce et al. 1980).

MONITORING AND SIGHTINGS

Hydrilla grows rapidly in many waterbodies throughout the United States (Poovey and Getsinger 2010) with multiple infestations confirmed in Massachusetts (Table 6.2). Location and distribution data have been collected from the Massachusetts Department of Environmental Protection (MassDEP) and the Department of Conservation and Recreation (DCR) and mapped using Geographic Information Systems (GIS) to aid in future decisions regarding waterbodies of Massachusetts (Figure 6.3).

GIS-produced maps will also inform the development of regulations that involve efforts to limit the spread of this aquatic invasive species. Hydrilla is a very aggressive invasive species and therefore can spread throughout Massachusetts in a relatively

Hydrilla (*Hydrilla verticillata*)

TABLE 6.1
New York State Department of Environmental Conservation Boat Stewardship Inspection Program Locations/Events Citing Connecticut River as Last Waterbody Visited in 2020

Waterbody Name	Inspections	Waterbody Name	Inspections
Lake George	143	Cayuga Lake	1
Lake Champlain	42	Indian Lake	1
Hudson River	4	Lake Kushaqua	1
Fulton Chain Lakes	3	Lake Placid	1
Great Sacandaga Lake	3	Lake Pleasant	1
Second Pond	3	Mohawk River	1
Canada Lake	2	Oneida Lake	1
Long Lake	2	Otisco Lake	1
Saratoga Lake	2	Round Lake	1
Cayuga Lake	1	Salmon River	1
Indian Lake	1	Seneca Lake	1
Lake Kushaqua	1	Skaneateles Lake	1
		Others	23

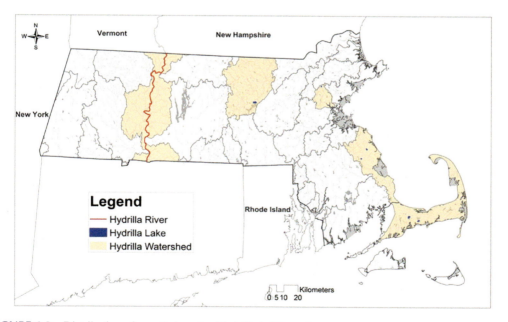

FIGURE 6.3 Distribution of aquatic invasive Hydrilla in Massachusetts.

short period of time (Table 6.2). Hydrilla is a relatively new introduction to Massachusetts and was first identified in Long Pond in Cape Cod in 2001 but reported in the Cape Cod Water Quality Assessment report in 2002 (Table 6.2) (Mattson et al. 2004). Currently, there are 11 waterbodies in Massachusetts (Figure 6.3 and Table 6.2) infested with hydrilla. The sighting at Agwam is the first town north of the Connecticut–Massachusetts state line within the Connecticut River. These waterbodies are distributed in five major Massachusetts watersheds or drainage basins: Cape Cod, South Coast, Boston Harbor (Mystic River), Connecticut River, and Nashua River.

TABLE 6.2
List of Waterbodies with Invasive Hydrilla

Waterbody	Agency	Report Source	Longitude	Latitude	First Year Reported
Long Pond	MassDEP	Cape Cod Watershed Water Quality Assessment Report. CN 50.0			2002
Hobomock Pond	DCR	DCR Data from Lakes and Ponds, September 2008 MR			2008
Mystic Lake	MassDEP	Cape COD Coastal Drainage Areas 2004–2008 Surface Water Quality Assessment Report 96-AC-2 CN 171.0, May 2011			2011
Coachlace Pond	DCR	Jamie Carr	−71.697104	42.413367	2016
South Meadow Pond (East Basin)	DCR	Jamie Carr	−71.705732	42.415348	2016
South Meadow Pond (West Basin)	DCR	Jamie Carr	−71.713092	42.414889	2016
Mossy Pond	DCR	Jamie Carr	−71.701034	42.417156	2016
Connecticut River	DCR	*Hydrilla verticulata* and *Trapa natans* Survey on the Connecticut River, November 2018	−72.610896	42.038974	2018
Connecticut River	DCR	*Hydrilla verticulata* and *Trapa natans* Survey on the Connecticut River, November 2018	−72.610888	42.038902	2018
Connecticut River	DCR	*Hydrilla verticulata* and *Trapa natans* Survey on the Connecticut River November 2018	−72.610781	42.038236	2018
Connecticut River	DCR	*Hydrilla verticulata* and *Trapa natans* Survey on the Connecticut River, November 2018	−72.610799	42.038232	2018
Connecticut River	DCR	*Hydrilla verticulata* and *Trapa natans* Survey on the Connecticut River, November 2018	−72.610494	42.036364	2018
Connecticut River	DCR	*Hydrilla verticulata* and *Trapa natans* Survey on the Connecticut River, November 2018	−72.610769	42.036247	2018
Connecticut River	DCR	*Hydrilla verticulata* and *Trapa natans* Survey on the Connecticut River, November 2018	−72.610425	42.035436	2018
Connecticut River	DCR	*Hydrilla verticulata* and *Trapa natans* Survey on the Connecticut River, November 2018	−72.610353	42.034750	2018
Connecticut River	DCR	*Hydrilla verticulata* and *Trapa natans* Survey on the Connecticut River, November 2018	−72.610691	42.034287	2018
Connecticut River	DCR	*Hydrilla verticulata* and *Trapa natans* Survey on the Connecticut River, November 2018	−72.610805	42.034108	2018
Magoun Pond	DCR	Vanessa Curran			2019
Oakman Pond	DCR	Vanessa Curran			2019
Lower Woburn Street Pond	DCR	Vanessa Curran	−71.143992	42.522064	2019

FIGURE 6.4 Informational sign to prevent spread of Hydrilla (northeastans.org).

MANAGEMENT

In Massachusetts, waterbodies infested with hydrilla are, or will be, included in the 303d list of impaired or threatened waters during water quality assessments, fulfilling the requirements of the Clean Water Act. For projects within infested watersheds subject to the jurisdiction of the 401 Water Quality Certification, conditions on invasive species prevention and decontamination are required. In addition, water quality monitoring gear and watercraft used in these infested watersheds shall be decontaminated before being used in other watersheds to prevent the potential spread of invasive hydrilla.

Prevention and early detection are critical for minimizing the further spread of hydrilla. Voluntary prevention and detection efforts rely on education and outreach to change behavior and foster stewardship. For instance, the NEANS Panel has made hydrilla informational signs that are used by Massachusetts and other New England states to encourage recreationists to report potential hydrilla infestations (Figure 6.4). If reports are made while the infestations cover a small area, there is often a greater likelihood of control or even eradication.

Many different management and control methods have been tested in different waterbodies. Treatments to control monoecious hydrilla are generally the same as for dioecious hydrilla, with chemical control and grass carp generally being the most effective (True-Meadows et al. 2016). Research on management of the monoecious biotype is more limited than dioecious. Monoecious hydrilla active management should begin several weeks after tubers first sprout, or as soon as possible after discovery of new infestations. However, new infestations of monoecious hydrilla are often not detected until much later in the season, when shoot growth reaches the surface of the waterbody, which increases the level of difficulty to achieve control.

Triploid grass carp (*Ctenopharyngodon idella* Val.) are an effective biological control agent for hydrilla (Sutton 2019). However, biological control by grass carp is not being considered for the Connecticut River hydrilla infestations due to the large river size, connectivity to other waters, and the inability to prevent carp from escaping to tributaries (NEANS 2020). Moreover, it is recently demonstrated that management of hydrilla using grass carp may result in unintended consequences. For example, after stocking triploid grass carp, applying herbicide, and planting native macrophyte in experimental ponds infested with hydrilla, some native plants were impacted. In addition, a secondary expansion and infestation of invasive Asian clams was also observed because grass carp ate much of the aquatic vegetation resulting in approximately 60–90% bare, benthic substrate in the experimental ponds which was ideal habitat for the clams (Holbrook et al. 2020). More than two dozen non-US species of insects or pathogens have been considered as potential biological control agents for hydrilla (Balciunas et al. 2002). Laboratory and field data have been gathered to gain approval for release of two weevils and two leaf-mining flies. Although none of these four insects were strictly monophagous, hydrilla was greatly preferred, and the risk to the few other alternative hosts was considered minimal. For example, the tuber feeding weevil (*Bagous affinis*) and the Indian leaf-mining fly (*Hydrellia pakistanae*) have been used for biological control of hydrilla in Florida. The leaf-mining fly was first released in the United States during October 1987 as a potential agent for the biological control of hydrilla and as of 1997, nearly 3 million individuals have been released at more than 25 separate locations in Florida and other states in southeastern United States (Center et al. 1997). Permanent establishment at many locations is attributed to modifications of rearing and release procedures that considered the biology of the agent in relation to various habitat characteristics.

Herbicide such as endothall and fluridone have been successful for hydrilla management. Endothall has been used to control submersed aquatic plants since 1960, providing broad-spectrum control of aquatic weeds by disrupting plants' photosynthesis activities (Ortiz et al. 2019). Although endothall is considered a contact herbicide, many field observations suggest that it might have systemic activity (Ortiz et al. 2019). Because the efficacy to roots, turions, and tubers is poor, long-term control takes many annual applications. Fluridone has been used in New York and other parts of the United States to control hydrilla. It is a systemic herbicide that is absorbed through the roots of the plant and also disrupts photosynthesis. Netherland and Getsinger (1995) suggest the following treatment strategy for fluridone to adequately control hydrilla: an initial treatment of >10 mg/l of fluridone is applied, followed by long-term maintenance of doses lower than 10 mg/l. These herbicides need to be applied repeatedly for several consecutive seasons until the tuber bank in the sediment is exhausted. Diquat- and copper-based herbicides have also been used to control hydrilla (Mattson et al. 2004). Deciding which control method to use is based on the budget of the project and the waterbodies to be protected. Whichever method is chosen, it should be used in conjunction with other preventive measures such as watercraft inspections and proper signage at high-risk waterbodies (NEANS 2020). Additionally, an adaptative management plan, including prevention, early detection, monitoring, control, and restoration, is needed. Using the outcomes of each season's monitoring to assess effectiveness and make informed changes to future management plans is a key part of the adaptive management necessary to controlling hydrilla. Before chemical is applied in Massachusetts waters, it is required to obtain an aquatic nuisance species control license (BRP WM04 Form) from Massachusetts Department of Environmental Protection.

True-Meadows et al. (2016) summarized herbicide treatments on hydrilla and found that diquat and endothall (both dipotassium and monoamine salts) produced similar results on both US biotypes. Diquat and endothall are often more successful when applied early to mid-June, when there is less dense monoecious hydrilla biomass. A second application can be applied in mid-August if regrowth occurs. A concentration of 0.25 mg/l diquat for two days is lethal to both monoecious and dioecious hydrilla; endothall is effective on monoecious hydrilla, but appropriate exposure times and doses must be met (Hofstra and Clayton 2001; Poovey and Getsinger 2010). Fluridone controls monoecious hydrilla and reduces tuber density over time (Nawrocki 2011). However, after years of repetitive fluridone treatments within Florida, fluridone-resistant dioecious hydrilla has been documented (Michel et al. 2004; Giannotti et al. 2014). Mutations of the phytoene desaturase gene at codon 304 have been shown to confer fluridone resistance in dioecious hydrilla (Benoit and Les 2013). Utilizing different herbicides over a season with different modes of action is expected to reduce the possibility of resistance emerging within a population. To date, resistance has only been documented in dioecious hydrilla, but there is no evidence that monoecious hydrilla cannot develop resistance (Arias et al. 2005). As described previously, the occurrence of AVM has been linked to the cyanobacterium growing on hydrilla and the cause is the toxin AETX biosynthesis which relies on the availability of bromide (Breinlinger et al. 2021). As of 2022, no VM has been documented in any Massachusetts waterbody, even though bromide product such as Tribune or Reward has been permitted by MassDEP. It remains to be seen if there are any elevated bromide levels in waters of Massachusetts because of anthropogenic and geologic sources (Breinlinger et al. 2021).

More information about chemical control on hydrilla and other 18 invasive species can be found in Appendix III. Any chemical used for invasive species control requires the WM04 Chemical Application License from the Massachusetts Department of Environmental Protection.

Mechanically, hydrilla can be controlled by dredging, drawdowns, diver-assisted suction harvesting (DASH), or through benthic barriers for very small populations. For effective dredging management for hydrilla, it is critical to remove the entirety of the patch to prevent fragmentation and leaving behind tubers. Dredge spoils will need to be transported off-site and deposited at a safe location far from any waterbodies.

Hand harvesting with a vacuum hose is also a standard removal process for aquatic plants such as Eurasian watermilfoil (*Myriophyllum spicatum*) and is used for small infestations. Benthic barriers, while effective for smaller areas, are not useful for eradication and are not effective in flowing waters (NEANS 2020). Mechanical control is therefore usually not recommended for hydrilla management because of the fragmentation that occurs, regrowth form tubers and turions, the cost, and other negative impacts (True-Meadows et al. 2016). The Connecticut River hydrilla may be an exception because the unique strain does not produce tubers.

Based on molecular phylogenetics, a different strain of hydrilla has been found in a portion of the Connecticut River in Hartford County, Connecticut. It represents a novel introduction likely from northern Eurasia (Tippery et al. 2020). Therefore, genetic analysis of Massachusetts hydrilla is recommended as different management actions could be necessary. In addition, because certain strains of hydrilla have become resistant to fluridone (Michel et al. 2004), it is recommended that low concentrations of herbicides and/or a possible combination of herbicides be used to reduce the likelihood of resistance developing. Consistent long-term monitoring will enable managers to quickly detect and track any plants that have survived herbicide treatment. Intermediately and highly resistant phenotypes of hydrilla were found to need three to seven times more fluridone to control properly, which could impact project budgets and increase risk of non-target impacts. It is suggested that fragments of plants with the resistance mutation left over from previous fluridone treatments may produce new plants and spread into new waterbodies (Michel et al. 2004; Tippery et al. 2020). Because of this, it is critical to ensure no fragments of hydrilla remain when treating a waterbody.

SUCCESS STORY

PICKEREL POND IN MAINE

Maine confirmed the state's first known infestation of *Hydrilla verticillata* in 2002. When discovered in the 52-acre Pickerel Pond, Limerick,

Maine, the infestation was well-established, with an average depth of 16 ft and many areas exceeded 60–70% cover. The Maine Department of Environmental Protection (MDEP) estimated the population to be at least 4 years old. The initial objective of MDEP's response was to prevent infestation of other waters. The response measures included outlet screens to limit downstream migration, restrictions on boat access, public outreach to landowners, tuber bank and plant monitoring, herbicide treatments with fluoridone brand name Sonar, and annual dive surveys. After two years of herbicide treatment, MDEP determined to attempt eradication and continued annual treatments of fluoridone for a total of nine consecutive years (2003–2011). No hydrilla was found during the two years of herbicide treatment (2010 and 2011). In 2012, the first year without herbicide treatment, one plant was found during an annual diver survey. Continued annual diver surveys 2013–2017 resulted in no detection of hydrilla (personal communication with John McPhedran, March 17, 2022).

Cayuga Lake and Fall Creek in New York

There have been some successful instances of controlling hydrilla in the State of New York. For example, hydrilla was first discovered in Cayuga Lake and Fall Creek in New York in 2011. A massive coordinated rapid response effort, carried out by local and state agencies, researchers, and community groups, revealed that 166 acres of the Cayuga Inlet was infested with hydrilla. The Local Cayuga Lake Hydrilla Task Force was formed to oversee the herbicide treatment process and annual monitoring. At the Cayuga Inlet, chemical treatments (fluridone and endothall) were part of the long-term plan to eradicate hydrilla from Cayuga Lake beginning in 2012. In 2018, there were no observations of hydrilla and therefore no chemical treatment needed to be continued. While invasive hydrilla is an ongoing problem, success stories like this help others learn how to eradicate these aquatic invasive species in order to maintain the quality of different waterbodies (Fighting Hydrilla in the Cayuga Lake Watershed, cce-tompkins.org/ accessed November 10, 2020).

Using the Cayuga Inlet as an example and led by the Northeast Aquatic Nuisance Species Panel (NEANS), several New England states and US Army Corps of Engineers are working together on monitoring and managing the hydrilla recently confirmed in the Connecticut River (NEANS 2020; Tippery et al. 2020). It is not too late to prevent the spread of hydrilla into additional states and control it in select locations in the Connecticut River. Most importantly, the Connecticut River Hydrilla Management Plan can be used as a template for control efforts for hydrilla in other states or for other aquatic invasive plants in Massachusetts.

REFERENCES

Arias, R.S., M.D. Netherland, B.E. Scheffler, A. Puri, and F.E. Dayan. 2005. Molecular evolution of herbicide resistance to phytoene desaturase inhibitors in *Hydrilla verticillata* and its potential use to generate herbicide-resistant crops. *Pest Management Science* 61(3): 258–268.

Balciunas, J.K., M.J. Grodowitz, A.F. Cofrancesco, and J.F. Shearer. 2002. Hydrilla. In F.V. Driesche, B. Blossey, M. Hoodle, S. Lyon, and R. Reardon (eds). *Biological Control of Invasive Plants in the Eastern United States*. United States Department of Agriculture Forest Service. Forest Health Technology Enterprise Team. Morgantown, West Virginia. FHTET-2002–04.91–114 pp.

Benoit, L.K., and D.H. Les. 2013. Rapid identification and molecular characterization of phytoene desaturase mutations in fluridone-resistant hydrilla (*Hydrilla verticillata*). *Weed Science* 61(1): 32–40.

Bidigare R.R., S.J. Christensen, S.B. Wilde, and S.A. Banack. 2009. Cyanobacteria and BMAA: Possible linkage with avian vacuolar myelinopathy (AVM) in the south-eastern United States. *Amyotrophic Lateral Sclerosis* 10: 71–73.

Breinlinger, S., T.J. Phillips, B.N. Haram, J. Mareš, J.A. Yerena, P. Hrouzek, R. Sobotka, W.M. Henderson, P. Schmieder, S.M. Williams, J.D. Lauderdale, H.D. Wilde, W. Gerrin, A. Kust, J.W. Washington, C. Wagner, B. Geier, M. Liebeke, H. Enke, T.H.J. Niedermeyer, and S.B Wilde. 2021. Hunting the eagle killer: A cyanobacterial neurotoxin causes vacuolar myelinopathy. *Science*, 371(6536): 1335.

Bugbee, G.J., and SE. Stebbins. 2021. *Connecticut River Middle and Upper Sections East Haddam, CT to Agawam, MA: Invasive Aquatic Vegetation Survey Hydrilla Overwintering and Spread Management Options*. New Haven, CT: The Connecticut Agricultural Experiment Station, p. 115.

Center, T.D., M.J. Grodowitz, A.F. Cofrancesco, G. Jubinsky, E. Snoddy, and J.E. Freedman. 1997. Establishment of *Hydrellia pakistanae* (Diptera: Ephydridae) for the biological control of the submersed aquatic plant *Hydrilla verticillate* (Hydrocharitaceae) in the Southeastern United States. *Biological Control* 8(1): 65–73.

Cook, C.D.K., and R. Lüönd. 1982. A revision of the genus Hydrilla (Hydrocharitaceae). *Aquatic Botany* 13: 485–504.

Cornell Cooperative Extension. Ecological impacts of hydrilla. http://erie.cce.cornell.edu/invasive-species/ecological-impacts-of-hydrilla. (Accessed October 11, 2019).

Crow, G.E., and C.B. Hellquist. 2006. *Aquatic and Wetland Plants of Northeastern North America, Volume II: A Revised and Enlarged Edition of Norman C. Fassett's A Manual of Aquatic Plants, Volume II: Angiosperms: Monocotyledons* (Vol. 2). Madison, WI: University of Wisconsin Press.

Evans, J.M., and A.C. Wilkie. 2010. Life cycle assessment of nutrient remediation and bioenergy production potential from the harvest of hydrilla (Hydrilla verticillata). *Journal of Environmental Management*, 91(12): 2626–2631.

Giannotti, A.L., T.J. Egan, M.D. Netherland, M.L. Williams, and A.K. Knecht. 2014. Hydrilla shows increased tolerance to fluridone and endothall in the winter park chain of lakes: considerations for resistance management and treatment options. https://conference.ifas.ufl.edu/aw14/Presentations/Grand/Thursday/Session%209A/0850%20Giannotti.pdf (Accessed January 29, 2021).

Heilman, M. 2020. *Technical Perspectives on Connecticut River Hydrilla Infestation and Its Potential Future Management*, p. 6.

Hofstra, D.E., and J.S. Clayton. 2001. Evaluation of selected herbicides for the control of exotic submerged weeds in New Zealand: I The use of endothall, triclopyr and dichlobenil. *Journal of Aquatic Plant Management* 39: 20–24.

Holbrook, D.L., A.N. Schad, G.O. Dick, L.L. Dodd, and J.H. Kennedy. 2020. Invasive bivalve establishment as a secondary effect of eradication-focused nuisance aquatic plant management. *Lake and Reservoir Management* 36(4): 423–431.

ITIS (Integrated Taxonomic Information System). 2021. www.itis.gov/servlet/SingleRpt/SingleRpt?search_topic=TSN&search_value=38974#null (Accessed January 28, 2021).

Jacono, C.C., M.M. Richerson, H. Morgan, and I.A. Pfingsten. 2020. *Hydrilla verticillata (L.f.) Royle: U.S. geological survey, nonindigenous aquatic species database*. Gainesville, FL. https://nas.er.usgs.gov/queries/FactSheet.aspx?speciesID=6.

Joyce, J.C., W.T. Haller, and D.E. Colle. 1980. Investigation of the presence and survivability of hydrilla propagules in waterfowl. *Aquatics* 2: 10–14.

Langeland, K.A. 1990. Hydrilla (*Hydrilla verticillata* (L.f.) Royle): A continuing problem in Florida waters. University of Florida Coop. Extension Service Circular No. 884. University of Florida, Gainesville, FL.

Langeland, K.A. 1996. *Hydrilla verticillata* (LF) Royle (Hydrocharitaceae), "the perfect aquatic weed". *Castanea* 61(3): 293–304.

Langeland, K.A. 2016. Hydrilla Management in Florida Lakes. https://edis.ifas.ufl.edu/ag370.

Les, D.H., L.J. Mehrhoff, M.A. Cleland, and J.D. Gebal. 1997. *Hydrilla verticillata* (Hydrocharitaceae) in Connecticut. *Journal of Aquatic Plant Management* 35: 10–14.

Mattson, M.D., P.J. Godfrey, R.A. Barletta, and A. Aiello. 2004. Eutrophication and aquatic plant management in Massachusetts. Final Generic Environmental Report. In: K.J. Wagner (ed.), *Department of Environmental Protection and Department of Conservation and Recreation, EOEA Commonwealth of Massachusetts*. Cambridge, MA: EOEA.

Michel, A., R.S. Arias, B.E. Scheffler, S.O. Duke, M. Netherland, and F.E. Dayan. 2004. Somatic mutation-mediated evolution of herbicide resistance in the nonindigenous invasive plant hydrilla (*Hydrilla verticillata*). *Molecular Ecology* 13(10): 3229–3237.

Michelan, T.S., M.J. Silveira, D.K. Petsch, G.D. Pinha, and S.M. Thomaz. 2014. The invasive aquatic macrophyte *Hydrilla verticillata* facilitates the establishment of the invasive mussel *Limnoperna fortunei* in Neotropical reservoirs. *Journal of Limnology* 73(3): 598–602.

Nawrocki, J.J. 2011. Environmental and Physiological Factors Affecting Submersed Aquatic Weed Management. Master's thesis. North Carolina State University. http://repository.lib.ncsu.edu. (Accessed January 29, 2021).

Netherland, M.D. 1997. Turion ecology of hydrilla. *Journal of Aquatic Plant Management* 35: 1–10.

Netherland, M.D., and K.D. Getsinger. 1995. Laboratory evaluation of threshold fluridone concentrations under static conditions for controlling hydrilla and Eurasian watermilfoil. *Journal of Aquatic Plant Management* 33: 33–36.

Northeast Aquatic Nuisance Species Panel (NEANS). 2020. *Connecticut River Hydrilla Control Project Five-Year Management Plan*. Penacook, NH: NEANS.

Northeast Aquatic Nuisance Species Panel (NEANS). 2021. *A Letter to Coalition of Northeast Governors, Northeast Committee on the Environment*. Penacook, NH: NEANS.

Ortiz, M.F., S.J. Nissen, and C.J. Gray. 2019. Endothall behavior in Myriophyllum spicatum and Hydrilla verticillate. *Pest Management Science* 75(11): 2942–2947.

Pelletier, A.R. 2019. Trophic Transfer of a Novel Cyanotoxin in Fishes. Masters of Science thesis, The University of Georgia, Athens.

Poovey, A.G., and K.D. Getsinger. 2010. Comparative Response of Monoecious and Dioecious Hydrilla to Endothall. *Journal of Aquatic Plant Management* 48: 15–20.

Schardt, J. 1994. 1994 Florida aquatic plant survey report. Florida Department of Environmental Protection, Bureau of Aquatic Plant Management, Tallahassee, Florida.

Stokstad, E. 2021. Mysterious eagle killer identified. *Science* 371(6536): 1298–1298.

Sutton, D.L., V.V. Vandiver, and J.E. Hill. 2019. *Grass Carp: A Fish for Biological Management of Hydrilla and Other Aquatic Weeds in Florida*. Gainesville: University of Florida.

Tippery, N.P., G.J. Bugbee, and S. Stebbins. 2020. Evidence for a genetically distinct strain of introduced *Hydrilla verticillata* (Hydrocharitaceae) in North America. *Journal of Aquatic Plant Management* 58: 1–6.

True-Meadows, S., E.J. Haug, and R.J. Richardson. 2016. Monoecious hydrilla—A review of the literature. *Journal of Aquatic Plant Management* 54: 1–11.

USDA National Invasive Species Information Center. 2019. Hydrilla. www.invasivespeciesinfo.gov/profile/hydrilla (Accessed September 9, 2019).

Williams, S.K., J. Kempton, S.B. Wilde, and A. Lewitus. 2007. A novel epiphytic cyanobacterium associated with reservoirs affected by avian vacuolar myelinopathy. *Harmful Algae* 6(3): 343–353.

7 Curly-leaf Pondweed (*Potamogeton crispus*)

ABSTRACT

In the early 1840s, the invasive species curly-leaf pondweed was first introduced into Philadelphia, Pennsylvania. Following this occurrence, in the 1880s, the curly-leaf pondweed was detected in Spy Pond, Arlington, Massachusetts. The sightings of invasive curly-leaf pondweed in Massachusetts' lakes and rivers have increased to include 167 waterbodies. These sightings were mapped to gain a spatial understanding of the status of this species in Massachusetts lakes and rivers with the goal of increasing public awareness of this invasive species to minimize its spread. In addition, this document provides an overview of the management methods such as mechanical and chemical treatments of curly-leaf pondweed.

INTRODUCTION

Taxonomy Hierarchy (ITIS 2021)

Kingdom	Plantae
Subkingdom	Viridiplantae
Infrakingdom	Streptophyta
Superdivision	Embryophyta
Division	Tracheophyta
Subdivision	Spermatophytina
Class	Magnoliopsida
Superorder	Lilianae
Order	Alismatales
Family	Potamogetonaceae
Genus	*Potamogeton* L.
Species	*Potamogeton crispus* L.

Curly-leaf pondweed (*Potamogeton crispus*) (Figure 7.1) has several common names such as curly-leaf pondweed, crispy-leaved pondweed, crisped pondweed, and curly pondweed (MA DCR 2002, 2015; Bugbee et al. 2015). Curly-leaf pondweed is a perennial submergent herbaceous aquatic plant that can grow longer than 4 m (GISD 2006). The sessile, serrated, oblong leaves can grow up to 7.6 cm (3 inches) long with clear veining on the surface (MA DCR 2002). The leave edges are serrated which helps distinguish them from other pondweeds (Acy 2019). The leaves are light to dark green, and sometimes have a reddish hue (Mikulyuk and Nault 2009). There are usually three to five veins on a prominent midvein. Stems of curly-leaf pondweed are flat and arranged in a spiral. Flowers of the plant are small and have four petal-shaped lobes that produce small reddish-brown fruits each year.

Curly-leaf pondweed can survive in a wide range of conditions, but grows well in waters that are alkaline, and brackish, and highly eutrophic conditions. Curly-leaf pondweed thrives in low-light and cooler temperature conditions (Mikulyuk and Nault 2009).

Yet another characteristic aids this invasive species, as it can reproduce quickly by rhizomatic spread and vegetative propagules called turions (Mikulyuk and Nault 2009). Turions are produced in the late spring. They will be dormant throughout the winter. The plant will begin to germinate and grow slowly until the following spring when rapid growth and turion production occurs (Figure 7.1, right panel). Curly-leaf pondweed dies back in early summer and when it is no longer a nuisance. Due to this uncommon growing cycle, curly-leaf pondweed avoids competition from other species. As summer ends, water temperatures cool down which creates prefect conditions for turion germination. Germination rates are very high according to lab experiments (100%) and field experiments (>60%) (Yeo 1966; Bolduan et al. 1994).

CURLY-LEAF PONDWEED AS AN INVASIVE SPECIES

Curly-leaf pondweed is a nonnative submersed macrophyte that inhabits temperate areas in North America, southern South America,

FIGURE 7.1 Curly-leaf pondweed (*left*) and turions (*right*). (Left photo by Greg Bugbee; right photo by Summer Stebbins.)

FIGURE 7.2 Abundant curly-leaf pondweed in Crystal Lake, Connecticut. (Photo by Greg Bugbee.)

and New Zealand (Kaplan and Fehrer 2004). It can be found in rivers, freshwater lakes, wetlands, estuaries, ponds, and even ditches (Figure 7.2). In North America, the first verified identification was in Philadelphia, PA, in 1841–1842 (Stuckey 1979). By the 1880s, it had spread to Massachusetts and New York (Bolduan et al. 1994). Though accidental introduction is likely to have occurred, curly-leaf pondweed may have been introduced intentionally as it can serve as habitat and provide food for native wildlife (Stuckey 1979). Because this plant spreads mainly through turion germination, even a small fragment of curly-leaf pondweed with attached turions could have been unintentionally transported by boat. Since this plant is highly competitive and aggressive, it may displace native species and disrupt the habitat of waterbodies. Curly-leave pondweed is listed as a prohibited plant species that is banned from the trade in Massachusetts.

Ecological Impact

Curly-leaf pondweed can dominate aquatic plant communities and threaten native *Potamogeton* species. For example, the native *P. ogdenii* in New England, New York, and Canada was outcompeted by curly-leaf pondweed (Tomaino 2004). It has also been found that curly-leaf pondweed can accumulate metals from sediments via their roots and rhizomes. A decomposition experiment on curly-leaf pondweed fragments discovered an increase in the concentrations of Al, Cd, Cr, Fe, Mn, and Pb (Deng et al. 2015). It should be noted that the application of phytoremediation by submerged macrophytes could give a chance for subsidiary pollution during the decomposition of curly-leaf pondweed. Additionally, during July, curly-leaf pondweed becomes senescent. The decay of the large volume of organic matter can deplete oxygen in the water and addition of nutrients, which may result in the death of some native organisms and algal blooms (MA DCR 2002).

Economic Impact

Curly-leaf pondweed can decrease native plant diversity and deplete oxygen in the water causing the death of organisms. This can negatively impact local and regional economics as curly-leaf pondweed can degrade recreational activities such as fishing, boating, and swimming. For example, curly-leaf pondweed forms dense "mat like," monotypic stands that inhibit navigation, block boat docks, and clog water (Poovey 2008). In addition, high densities of curly-leaf pondweed and resulting algal blooms can damage the aesthetic value of waterbodies and reduce real estate values, tourism, and recreation (IL DNR 2009; Jensen 2009; WI DNR 2012). Furthermore, the cost for controlling of curly-leaf pondweed can range from less than $100 to greater than $1,000 to treat a one-acre pond (Washington State Noxious Weed Control Board 2004; Swistock 2021).

Positive Aspects

Despite the deleterious effect of curly-leaf pondweed, there are some beneficial aspects that it provides. First, curly-leaf pondweed is a good indicator of waterbody eutrophication (Cao and Wang 2007). In addition, the absorption process by the plant can help purify water (Wu et al. 2009). Because of this, it can be applied as a purifier for industrial aqueous waste which could reduce the need for chemical treatment (Hafez et al. 1992; Hafez et al. 1998). Several reports have shown that the impact on the native plant community could be overestimated as curly-leaf pondweed dominates the ecosystem during the winter and spring, when most plants are less prominent (Bolduan et al. 1994). It is also reported that curly-leaf pondweed is a good source of carotenoids (Ren and Zhang 2008) with medicinal and cosmetics properties, including antioxidation, tumor reduction, and immunity-regulation (Ren and Zhang 2008; Mikulyuk and Nault 2009; Du et al. 2015).

MONITORING AND SIGHTINGS

The data in this report were collected by MassDEP staff during field visits and recorded in field sheets. Field sheet quality control, database development, and map construction are under the guidance of the MassDEP Standard Operating Procedures (SOP). Massachusetts Department of Conservation and Recreation (MA DCR), the College of the Holy Cross, the United States Geological Survey (USGS), and individual researcher Joy Trahan-Liptak also contributed to the process of data collection of curly-leaf pondweed in Massachusetts. Tools for drafting the map and marking out data layers of sites with curly-leaf pondweed were created via ArcGIS® ArcMap 10.1 (ESRI, Redlands, California).

Curly-leaf pondweed was found in many lakes and rivers in Massachusetts (Tables 7.1 and 7.2).

TABLE 7.1
List of Town Names and Waterbodies that Contain *Potamogeton crispus*

Town	Waterbody	Town	Waterbody
Amesbury	Powwow River	Marlborough	Assabet River
Amherst	Fort River		Hager Pond
Andover	Gravel Pit Pond	Mashpee	Quashnet River
	Shawsheen River	Maynard	Assabet River
Arlington	Spy Pond	Medfield	Charles River
Ayer	Bowers Brook	Milford	Charles River
	Flannagan Pond	Millbury	Kettle Brook
	Grove Pond		Woolshop Pond
Barnstable	Middle Pond	Milton	Pine Tree Brook
Barre	Ware River		Russell Pond
Becket	Center Pond	Monterey	Lake Buel
Bedford	Concord River		Lake Garfield
	Shawsheen River		Stevens Pond
Belchertown	Swift River	Natick	Charles River
Belmont	Clay Pit Pond		Dug Pond
Berlin	North Brook		Fisk Pond
Blackstone	Blackstone River		Lake Cochituate
Bolton	Still River		Nonesuch Pond
Boston	Muddy River	New Bedford	Sassaquin Pond
	Neponset River	New Marlborough	York Lake
Boxford	Baldpate Pond	Norfolk	Mill River
Braintree	Monatiquot River	North Adams	Windsor Lake
Brimfield	Quinebaug River	North Attleborough	Ten Mile River
Brookfield	Dunn Brook	Northampton	Connecticut River
Cambridge	Charles River	Northborough	Assabet River
	Fresh Pond		Bartlett Pond
	Little Fresh Pond		Little Chauncy Pond
Canton	Massapoag Brook	Northbridge	Fish Pond
Chelmsford	Newfield Pond	Norton	Wading River
Cheshire	Cheshire Reservoir (Middle Basin)	Norwood	Neponset River
	Cheshire Reservoir (North Basin)	Orange	Millers River
Clinton	Mossy Pond	Otis	Benton Pond
	Coachlace Pond	Palmer	Chicopee River
	South Meadow Pond (East Basin)		Quaboag River
	South Meadow Pond (West Basin)		Ware River
Cohasset	Lily Pond	Pembroke	Stetson Pond
Concord	Assabet River	Pepperell	Nashua River
	Concord River	Petersham	East Branch Fever Brook
	Sudbury River	Pittsfield	Onota Lake
Deerfield	Connecticut River	Plymouth	Beaver Dam Brook
Dennis	Chase Garden Creek		Billington Sea

Curly-leaf Pondweed (*Potamogeton crispus*)

Town	Waterbody	Town	Waterbody
	Quivett Creek		Town Brook
Douglas	Manchaug Pond		Unnamed Tributary
Dover	Charles River		White Island Pond(East Basin)
Dracut	Beaver Brook	Plymouth	White Island Pond(West Basin)
	Long Pond	Richmond	Richmond Pond
Dudley	French River	Rochester	Leonards Pond
Dunstable	Massapoag Pond	Royalston	Priest Brook
Egremont	Mill Pond	Salisbury	Smallpox Brook
	Prospect Lake	Sheffield	Mill Pond
Erving	Millers River	Shirley	Nashua River
Essex	Chebacco Lake		Squannacook River
Falmouth	Childs River	Shrewsbury	Lake Quinsigamond
	Unnamed Tributary	Southborough	Sudbury Reservoir
Framingham	Cochituate Brook	Southwick	Congamond Lakes(Middle Basin)
	Eames Brook		Congamond Lakes(North Basin)
	Farm Pond		Congamond Lakes(South Basin)
	Sudbury River	Spencer	Sevenmile River
Gill	Barton Cove	Springfield	Porter Lake
Grafton	Flint Pond	Stockbridge	Lily Brook
	Quinsigamond River		Stockbridge Bowl
Great Barrington	Green River	Stow	Assabet River
	Mansfield Pond	Sturbridge	Breakneck Brook
Groton	Cow Pond Brook	Sudbury	Carding Mill Pond
	Nashua River		Grist Mill Pond
Halifax	Monponsett Pond		Hop Brook
	Stetson Brook		Sudbury River
Hanover	Forge Pond	Sutton	Welsh Pond
Hanson	Reservoir	Tyngsborough	Lake Mascuppic
Harvard	Mirror Lake	Uxbridge	West River
	Robbins Pond		Rice City Pond
Harwich	Hinckleys Pond	Wakefield	Lake Quannapowitt
Hingham	Weir River	Walpole	Neponset River
Holyoke	Connecticut River	Ware	Ware River
	Lake Bray	Watertown	Charles River
Hudson	Assabet River	Wayland	Dudley Pond
Ipswich	Turner Hill Country Club Pond		Lake Cochituate
Kingston	Jones River		Sudbury River
Lancaster	Cranberry Pond	Webster	Webster Lake
	Fort Pond	Wellesley	Charles River
	White Pond	Wendell	Whetstone Brook
Lanesborough	Cheshire Reservoir(South Basin)	West Brookfield	Quaboag River
	Pontoosuc Lake	West Stockbridge	Card Pond
Lee	Goose Pond Brook		Shaker Mill Pond
	Laurel Lake	Westfield	Pequot Pond

(Continued)

TABLE 7.1
(Continued)

Town	Waterbody	Town	Waterbody
Littleton	Long Pond	Westford	Forge Pond
	Mill Pond		Nabnasset Pond
	Spectacle Pond		Stony Brook
Lowell	Concord River	Winchendon	Millers River
Lunenburg	Catacoonamug Brook		Otter River
	Lake Whalom	Winchester	Upper Mystic Lake
Lynn	Flax Pond	Woburn	Horn Pond
Mansfield	Rumford River	Wrentham	Crocker Pond
	Wading River		Mirror Lake

Curly-leaf pondweed was first observed at Spy Pond, Arlington, Massachusetts in 1880 (see Stuckey 1979). From 1994 to 2016, MassDEP employees have surveyed 2,050 waterbodies in Massachusetts. During this period, curly-leaf pondweed was found in 132 rivers and lakes in Massachusetts (Figure 7.3) among the 2,050 waterbodies investigated. Out of the 132 waterbodies, 64 are rivers (3.0%), 67 are lakes (3.0%), and 1 is an estuary (<0.1%). These numbers do not represent curly-leaf pondweed in wetlands and the sampling is not randomly designed. In addition, the detection ratio (132 out of 2,050 waterbodies based on map information) likely underestimates the presence of curly-leaf pondweed in Massachusetts because many of the observations occurred during the summer after curly-leaf pondweed senesced. If data from other agencies and organizations (MA DCR, the College of the Holy Cross, USGS and biologist Joy Trahan-Liptak) are counted, there are a total of 163 lakes and rivers within 26 watersheds in Massachusetts that contain curly-leaf pondweed. Most of these waterbodies are in the northern and eastern parts of the state (Figure 7.3). Since there are 33 major watersheds in Massachusetts, the percentage of invasive watersheds is about 79%.

MANAGEMENT

MECHANICAL AND PHYSICAL METHODS

Mechanical and physical removal methods, such as cutting at the surface of the sediment, have proved to be efficient as well as overwinter drawdowns and shallow dredging are equivocal, but some research has shown no serious impact on this species (Mikulyuk and Nault 2009; Nichols and Shaw 1986). This may suggest that there are many limits to mechanical removal methods. For example, drawdowns are not species-selective and pose as threat to local native species by interrupting reproductive cycles. In addition, hand removal serves as an effective technique but is laborious and time-consuming.

Physical barriers using plastics and other materials can be applied to control *P. crispus*. Barrier blocks (anchored on the sediment) may be used to block sunlight and upward growth of the plant which can limit the development of curly-leaf pondweed. Materials used to construct physical barriers vary. Jute is a natural plant used to construct barriers. It is relatively inexpensive and can naturally decay. Due to its permeability, sunlight can transmit through jute, having a reduced impact on benthic fauna compared to other materials (Caffrey et al. 2010). Even so, jute is limited in controlling *P. crispus* because it does not target long-lived propagules (Caffrey et al. 2010). Similarly, fiberglass and polyethylene fabrics can also be used for management via shading sunlight. But due to its buoyancy, the *P. crispus* can move and billow the barrier from natural waves. As a result, sedimentation of *P. crispus* can occur above the barrier and allow for the regrowth of new individuals. Therefore, annual removal and deployment of barriers is needed to help reduce the infestation (Barr and Ditomaso 2014). Another method used to control involves rubber bottom barriers which is an impermeable material used to block sunlight. Due to its impermeability, gas

TABLE 7.2
Latitude and Longitude for Each Waterbody in Figure 7.3

Waterbody	Agency	Report Source	Longitude	Latitude	First Year Reported
Spy Pond	USGS	USGS 4/24/2017 http://nas.er.usgs.gov/default.aspx	−71.155600	42.407900	1943
Spy Pond	USGS	USGS 4/24/2017 http://nas.er.usgs.gov/default.aspx	−71.155600	42.407900	1943
Fresh Pond	USGS	USGS 4/24/2017 http://nas.er.usgs.gov/default.aspx	−71.149000	42.384300	1943
Fresh Pond	USGS	USGS 4/24/2017 http://nas.er.usgs.gov/default.aspx	−71.149000	42.384300	1943
Fresh Pond	USGS	USGS 4/24/2017 http://nas.er.usgs.gov/default.aspx	−71.149000	42.384300	1943
Fresh Pond	USGS	USGS 4/24/2017 http://nas.er.usgs.gov/default.aspx	−71.149000	42.384300	1943
Fresh Pond	USGS	USGS 4/24/2017 http://nas.er.usgs.gov/default.aspx	−71.149000	42.384300	1943
Fresh Pond	USGS	USGS 4/24/2017 http://nas.er.usgs.gov/default.aspx	−71.149000	42.384300	1943
Fresh Pond	USGS	USGS 4/24/2017 http://nas.er.usgs.gov/default.aspx	−71.149000	42.384300	1943
Sudbury River	USGS	USGS 4/24/2017 http://nas.er.usgs.gov/default.aspx	−71.358400	42.465100	1943
Mill Pond	USGS	USGS 4/24/2017 http://nas.er.usgs.gov/default.aspx	−73.423300	42.157600	1972
Lake Buel	MassDEP	Housatonic River Watershed 2002 Water Quality Assessment Report 21-AC-4 CN141.5, September 2007	−73.275920	42.169491	1972
Lake Buel	USGS	USGS 4/24/2017 http://nas.er.usgs.gov/default.aspx	−73.274600	42.169500	1972
Fisk Pond	DCR	DCR Data from Lakes and Ponds, 2008	−71.368351	42.281982	1972
Fisk Pond	USGS	USGS 4/24/2017 http://nas.er.usgs.gov/default.aspx	−71.367800	42.283400	1972
Fisk Pond	USGS	USGS 4/24/2017 http://nas.er.usgs.gov/default.aspx	−71.367800	42.283400	1972
Mill Pond	USGS	USGS 4/24/2017 http://nas.er.usgs.gov/default.aspx	−73.370600	42.123300	1972
Stockbridge Bowl	USGS	USGS 4/24/2017 http://nas.er.usgs.gov/default.aspx	−73.318300	42.334800	1972
Flint Pond	College of the Holy Cross	From Robert Bertin	−71.725087	42.241352	1995
Lake Quinsigamond	College of the Holy Cross	From Robert Bertin	−71.749052	42.256062	1995
Lake Quinsigamond	College of the Holy Cross	From Robert Bertin	−71.749052	42.256062	1995

(Continued)

TABLE 7.2 (Continued)

Waterbody	Agency	Report Source	Longitude	Latitude	First Year Reported
Lake Quinsigamond	MassDEP	Blackstone River Basin 1998 Water Quality Assessment Report 51-AC-1 48.0, May 2011	−71.749052	42.256062	1995
Lake Quinsigamond	USGS	USGS 4/24/2017 http://nas.er.usgs.gov/default.aspx	−71.755100	42.271000	1995
Cheshire Reservoir, South Basin	MassDEP	Hudson River Basin 1997 Water Quality Assessment Report 11/12/13-AC-1 15.0, January 2000	−73.198397	42.515411	1997
Cheshire Reservoir, South Basin	DCR	DCR Data from ACT, GeoSyntec EM-ACT W-A. Madden FEW	−73.198397	42.515411	1997
Manchaug Pond	MassDEP	Blackstone River Basin 1998 Water Quality Assessment Report 51-AC-1 48.0, May 2011	−71.775873	42.098745	1998
Woolshop Pond	MassDEP	Blackstone River Basin 1998 Water Quality Assessment Report 51-AC-1 48.0, May 2011	−71.748620	42.195842	1998
Newfield Pond	MassDEP	Merrimack River Basin 1999 Water Quality Assessment Report 84-AC-1 52.0, November 2001	−71.389923	42.633784	1999
Long Pond	MassDEP	Merrimack River Basin 1999 Water Quality Assessment Report 84-AC-1 52.0, November 2001	−71.370878	42.692695	1999
Massapoag Pond	MassDEP	Merrimack River Basin 1999 Water Quality Assessment Report 84-AC-1 52.0, November 2001	−71.496539	42.648508	1999
Spectacle Pond	MassDEP	Merrimack River Basin 1999 Water Quality Assessment Report 84-AC-1 52.0, November 2001	−71.516164	42.564009	1999
Spectacle Pond	Individual	From Joy Trahan-Liptak	−71.516164	42.564009	1999
Lake Mascuppic	MassDEP	Merrimack River Basin 1999 Water Quality Assessment Report 84-AC-1 52.0, November 2001	−71.384182	42.677679	1999
Forge Pond	MassDEP	Merrimack River Basin 1999 Water Quality Assessment Report 84-AC-1 52.0, November 2001	−71.489933	42.574972	1999
Gravel Pit Pond	MassDEP	Shawsheen River Watershed 2000 Water Quality Assessment Report 83-AC-2 86.0, July 2003	−71.160460	42.672206	2000

Curly-leaf Pondweed (*Potamogeton crispus*)

Lake Cochituate	USGS	USGS 4/24/2017 http://nas.er.usgs.gov/default.aspx	−71.369000	42.314100	2000
Concord River	MassDEP	SuAsCo Watershed 2001 Water Quality Assessment Report 82-AC-1 CN 92.0, August 2005	−71.308410	42.513430	2001
Clay Pit Pond	USGS	USGS 4/24/2017 http://nas.er.usgs.gov/default.aspx	−71.164500	42.394000	2001
Muddy River	USGS	USGS 4/24/2017 http://nas.er.usgs.gov/default.aspx	−71.092600	42.351500	2001
Charles River	USGS	USGS 4/24/2017 http://nas.er.usgs.gov/default.aspx	−71.120400	42.369400	2001
Charles River	USGS	USGS 4/24/2017 http://nas.er.usgs.gov/default.aspx	−71.089100	42.356900	2001
Unnamed Pond	USGS	USGS 4/24/2017 http://nas.er.usgs.gov/default.aspx	−71.154800	42.389200	2001
Lily Pond	MassDEP	South Shore Coastal Watersheds 2001 Water Quality Assessment Report 94-AC-2 CN 93.0, March 2006	−70.815914	42.224638	2001
Assabet River	USGS	USGS 4/24/2017 http://nas.er.usgs.gov/default.aspx	−71.358500	42.465100	2001
Concord River	USGS	USGS 4/24/2017 http://nas.er.usgs.gov/default.aspx	−71.358300	42.460000	2001
Sudbury River	USGS	USGS 4/24/2017 http://nas.er.usgs.gov/default.aspx	−71.358400	42.465100	2001
Connecticut River	USGS	USGS 4/24/2017 http://nas.er.usgs.gov/default.aspx	−72.556500	42.511100	2001
Prospect Lake	Individual	From Joy Trahan-Liptak	−73.451860	42.195137	2001
Prospect Lake	MassDEP	Housatonic River Watershed 2002 Water Quality Assessment Report 21-AC-4 CN141.5, September 2007	−73.451860	42.195137	2001
Prospect Lake	USGS	USGS 4/24/2017 http://nas.er.usgs.gov/default.aspx	−73.452100	42.195500	2001
Eames Brook	MassDEP	SuAsCo Watershed 2001 Water Quality Assessment Report 82-AC-1 CN 92.0, August 2005	−71.433687	42.287723	2001
Farm Pond	MassDEP	SuAsCo Watershed 2001 Water Quality Assessment Report 82-AC-1 CN 92.0, August 2005	−71.426726	42.281553	2001
Sudbury River	USGS	USGS 4/24/2017 http://nas.er.usgs.gov/default.aspx	−71.419100	42.312300	2001
Forge Pond	MassDEP	South Shore Coastal Watersheds 2001 Water Quality Assessment Report 94-AC-2 CN 93.0, March 2006	−70.880004	42.106224	2001
Connecticut River	USGS	USGS 4/24/2017 http://nas.er.usgs.gov/default.aspx	−72.599500	42.212300	2001
Connecticut River	USGS	USGS 4/24/2017 http://nas.er.usgs.gov/default.aspx	−72.602400	42.212800	2001
Connecticut River	USGS	USGS 4/24/2017 http://nas.er.usgs.gov/default.aspx	−72.599800	42.195700	2001
Connecticut River	USGS	USGS 4/24/2017 http://nas.er.usgs.gov/default.aspx	−72.602400	42.212600	2001

(*Continued*)

TABLE 7.2 (Continued)

Waterbody	Agency	Report Source	Longitude	Latitude	First Year Reported
Pontoosuc Lake	MassDEP	Housatonic River Watershed 2002 Water Quality Assessment Report 21-AC-4 CN141.5, September 2007	−73.248769	42.496022	2001
Pontoosuc Lake	DCR	DCR Data from Lakes and Ponds, 2008	−73.248769	42.496022	2001
Pontoosuc Lake	USGS	USGS 4/24/2017 http://nas.er.usgs.gov/default.aspx	−73.248800	42.496200	2001
Pontoosuc Lake	USGS	USGS 4/24/2017 http://nas.er.usgs.gov/default.aspx	−73.241100	42.503000	2001
Mill Pond	USGS	USGS 4/24/2017 http://nas.er.usgs.gov/default.aspx	−71.502800	42.535300	2001
Hager Pond	MassDEP	SuAsCo Watershed 2001 Water Quality Assessment Report 82-AC-1 CN 92.0, August 2005	−71.487758	42.349036	2001
Assabet River	MassDEP	SuAsCo Watershed 2001 Water Quality Assessment Report 82-AC-1 CN 92.0, August 2005	−71.442206	42.438442	2001
Lake Cochituate	MassDEP	05-G016-02	−71.367725	42.304477	2001
Lake Cochituate	Individual	From Joy Trahan-Liptak	−71.371426	42.305669	2001
Lake Cochituate	MassDEP	SuAsCo Watershed 2001 Water Quality Assessment Report 82-AC-1 CN 92.0, August 2005	−71.371426	42.305669	2001
Lake Cochituate	DCR	DCR Data from Lakes and Ponds, 2003	−71.371426	42.305669	2001
Lake Cochituate	MassDEP	SuAsCo Watershed 2001 Water Quality Assessment Report 82-AC-1 CN 92.0, August 2005	−71.371867	42.300575	2001
Lake Cochituate	Individual	From Joy Trahan-Liptak	−71.369349	42.288313	2001
Lake Cochituate	DCR	DCR Data from Lakes and Ponds, 2004	−71.367055	42.289488	2001
Lake Cochituate	MassDEP	SuAsCo Watershed 2001 Water Quality Assessment Report 82-AC-1CN 92.0, August 2005	−71.367055	42.289488	2001
Connecticut River	USGS	USGS 4/24/2017 http://nas.er.usgs.gov/default.aspx	−72.611200	42.332000	2001

Curly-leaf Pondweed (*Potamogeton crispus*)

Location	Source	Reference	Longitude	Latitude	Year
Assabet River	MassDEP	SuAsCo Watershed 2001 Water Quality Assessment Report 82-AC-1CN 92.0, August 2005	−71.625763	42.333629	2001
Bartlett Pond	MassDEP	SuAsCo Watershed 2001 Water Quality Assessment Report 82-AC-1CN 92.0, August 2005	−71.618375	42.317914	2001
Little Chauncy Pond	College of the Holy Cross	From Robert Bertin	−71.617285	42.306107	2001
Little Chauncy Pond	MassDEP	SuAsCo Watershed 2001 Water Quality Assessment Report 82-AC-1CN 92.0, August 2005	−71.617285	42.306107	2001
Onota Lake	Individual	From Joy Trahan-Liptak	−73.281319	42.470479	2001
Onota Lake	MassDEP	Housatonic River Watershed 2002 Water Quality Assessment Report 21-AC-4 CN141.5, September 2007	−73.281319	42.470479	2001
Onota Lake	DCR	DCR Data from Lakes and Ponds, 2008	−73.281319	42.470479	2001
Onota Lake	USGS	USGS 4/24/2017 http://nas.er.usgs.gov/default.aspx	−73.281300	42.469800	2001
Onota Lake	USGS	USGS 4/24/2017 http://nas.er.usgs.gov/default.aspx	−73.282600	42.471000	2001
Richmond Pond	Individual	From Joy Trahan-Liptak	−73.324741	42.415098	2001
Richmond Pond	Individual	From Joy Trahan-Liptak	−73.324741	42.415098	2001
Richmond Pond	MassDEP	Housatonic River Watershed 2002 Water Quality Assessment Report 21-AC-4CN141.5, September 2007	−73.324741	42.415098	2001
Richmond Pond	USGS	USGS 4/24/2017 http://nas.er.usgs.gov/default.aspx	−73.325500	42.414500	2001
Richmond Pond	USGS	USGS 4/24/2017 http://nas.er.usgs.gov/default.aspx	−73.325000	42.415500	2001
Lily Brook	USGS	USGS 4/24/2017 http://nas.er.usgs.gov/default.aspx	−73.299400	42.335500	2001
Assabet River	MassDEP	06-A027-03	−71.508442	42.411634	2001
Assabet River	MassDEP	SuAsCo Watershed 2001 Water Quality Assessment Report 82-AC-1CN 92.0, August 2005	−71.490454	42.418232	2001
Carding Mill Pond	MassDEP	SuAsCo Watershed 2001 Water Quality Assessment Report 82-AC-1CN 92.0, August 2005	−71.465805	42.362001	2001
Grist Mill Pond	MassDEP	SuAsCo Watershed 2001 Water Quality Assessment Report 82-AC-1CN 92.0, August 2005	−71.479147	42.355473	2001
Sudbury River	MassDEP	06-A006-07	−71.364671	42.396351	2001
Dudley Pond	MassDEP	SuAsCo Watershed 2001 Water Quality Assessment Report 82-AC-1CN 92.0, August 2005	−71.372274	42.330103	2001

(*Continued*)

TABLE 7.2 (Continued)

Waterbody	Agency	Report Source	Longitude	Latitude	First Year Reported
Card Pond	USGS	USGS 4/24/2017 http://nas.er.usgs.gov/default.aspx	−73.366800	42.326700	2001
Shaker Mill Pond	MassDEP	Housatonic River Watershed 2002 Water Quality Assessment Report 21-AC-4 CN141.5, September 2007	−73.370704	42.339862	2001
Shaker Mill Pond	DCR	DCR Data from National Heritage 2005	−73.370704	42.339862	2001
Shaker Mill Pond	USGS	USGS 4/24/2017 http://nas.er.usgs.gov/default.aspx	−73.369100	42.338100	2001
Pequot Pond	MassDEP	Westfield River Watershed 2001 Water Quality Assessment Report 32-AC-CN 090.0, April 2005	−72.693713	42.184005	2001
Chebacco Lake	MassDEP	North Shore Coastal Watersheds 2002 Water Quality Assessment Report 93-AC-2 CN 138.5, March 2007	−70.811152	42.611984	2002
Mansfield Pond	MassDEP	Housatonic River Watershed 2002 Water Quality Assessment Report 21-AC-4 CN141.5, September 2007	−73.367856	42.203242	2002
Goose Pond Brook	MassDEP	Housatonic River Watershed 2002 Water Quality Assessment Report 21-AC-4 CN141.5, September 2007	−73.226149	42.294173	2002
Laurel Lake	MassDEP	Housatonic River Watershed 2002 Water Quality Assessment Report 21-AC-4 CN141.5, September 2007	−73.269335	42.325463	2002
Laurel Lake	USGS	USGS 4/24/2017 http://nas.er.usgs.gov/default.aspx	−73.269400	42.325600	2002
Flax Pond	MassDEP	North Shore Coastal Watersheds 2002 Water Quality Assessment Report 93-AC-2 CN 138.5, March 2007	−70.951436	42.482703	2002
Lake Garfield	MassDEP	Housatonic River Watershed 2002 Water Quality Assessment Report 21-AC-4 CN141.5, September 2007	−73.197211	42.182427	2002
Lake Garfield	DCR	DCR Data from Lakes and Ponds, 2004	−73.197212	42.182427	2002
Stevens Pond	MassDEP	Housatonic River Watershed 2002 Water Quality Assessment Report 21-AC-4 CN141.5, September 2007	−73.270578	42.180077	2002
Dug Pond	MassDEP	Charles River Watershed 2002–2006 Water Quality Assessment Report 72-AC-4 CN136.5, April 2008	−71.364385	42.276312	2002
Nonesuch Pond	MassDEP	Charles River Watershed 2002–2006 Water Quality Assessment Report 72-AC-4 CN136.5, April 2008	−71.329177	42.324990	2002

Curly-leaf Pondweed (*Potamogeton crispus*)

Lake Quannapowitt	MassDEP	North Shore Coastal Watersheds 2002 Water Quality Assessment Report 93-AC-2 CN 138.5, March 2007	−71.078556	42.514938	2002
Mirror Lake	MassDEP	Charles river watershed 2002–2006 water quality Assessment report 72-AC-4 CN136.5, April 2008	−71.325293	42.088039	2002
Flannagan Pond	MassDEP	Nashua River Watershed 2003 Water Quality Assessment Report 81-AC-4 CN107.5, August 2008	−71.567523	42.557947	2003
Grove Pond	MassDEP	Nashua River Watershed 2003 Water Quality Assessment Report 81-AC-4 CN107.5, August 2008	−71.584489	42.552566	2003
Center Pond	DCR	DCR Data from Lakes and Ponds, 2003	−73.068746	42.296718	2003
Barton Cove	MassDEP	Connecticut River Basin 2003 Water Quality Assessment Report 34-AC-2 CN 105.5, October 2008	−72.539479	42.605090	2003
Robbins Pond	MassDEP	Nashua River Watershed 2003 Water Quality Assessment Report 81-AC-4 CN107.5, August 2008	−71.604653	42.537585	2003
Lake Bray	MassDEP	Connecticut River Basin 2003 Water Quality Assessment Report 34-AC-2 CN 105.5, October 2008	−72.616671	42.266660	2003
Lake Whalom	College of the Holy Cross	From Robert Bertin	−71.740747	42.574132	2003
Lake Whalom	MassDEP	Nashua River Watershed 2003 Water Quality Assessment Report 81-AC-4 CN107.5, August 2008	−71.740747	42.574132	2003
Porter Lake	MassDEP	Connecticut River Basin 2003 Water Quality Assessment Report 34-AC-2CN 105.5, October 2008	−72.563919	42.073505	2003
Baldpate Pond	MassDEP	Parker River Watershed And Coastal Drainage Area 2004–2008 Water Quality Assessment Report 91-AC-3CN 173.0, March 2010	−71.002371	42.698258	2004
Baldpate Pond	DCR	DCR Data from National Heritage 2004	−71.002371	42.698258	2004
Baldpate Pond	DCR	DCR Data from Lakes and Ponds, 2004	−71.002371	42.698258	2004
Russell Pond	MassDEP	Neponset River Watershed 2004 Water Quality Assessment Report 73-AC-1CN170.4, February 2010	−71.073487	42.236256	2004
Nabnasset Pond	MassDEP	Merrimack River Watershed 2004–2009 Water Quality Assessment Report 84-AC-2 CN179.5, January 2010	−71.426779	42.616987	2004
Upper Mystic Lake	MassDEP	Mystic River Watershed And Coastal Drainage Area 2004–2008 Water Quality Assessment Report 71-AC-2 CN170.2 March 2010	−71.148968	42.437293	2004

(*Continued*)

TABLE 7.2 (Continued)

Waterbody	Agency	Report Source	Longitude	Latitude	First Year Reported
Horn Pond	MassDEP	Mystic River Watershed And Coastal Drainage Area 2004–2008 Water Quality Assessment Report 71-AC-2CN170.2, March 2010	−71.156593	42.468702	2004
Horn Pond	DCR	DCR Data from Lakes and Ponds, 2004	−71.156593	42.468702	2004
Ware River	MassDEP	05-L002–02	−72.064555	42.391214	2005
Ware River	MassDEP	07-K003–02	−72.064555	42.391214	2005
French River	MassDEP	09-P004–05	−71.885074	42.050945	2005
French River	MassDEP	05-M004–04	−71.885074	42.050945	2005
French River	MassDEP	07-M003–04	−71.885074	42.050945	2005
French River	MassDEP	08-N004–04	−71.885074	42.050945	2005
Sudbury River	MassDEP	06-A034–04	−71.394984	42.338646	2005
Mirror Lake	MassDEP	05-G002–01	−71.609790	42.526149	2005
Fort Pond	MassDEP	05-G001–02	−71.688092	42.523470	2005
Millers River	MassDEP	05-H011–06	−72.341352	42.598155	2005
Millers River	MassDEP	05-H013–06	−72.341352	42.598155	2005
Leonards Pond	MassDEP	05-R003–02	−70.804664	41.750263	2005
Congamond Lakes (Middle Basin)	DCR	DCR Data from Lakes and Ponds, 2005	−72.758734	42.028944	2005
Congamond Lakes (North Basin)	DCR	DCR Data from Lakes and Ponds, 2005	−72.753275	42.045111	2005
Congamond Lakes (South Basin)	DCR	DCR Data from Lakes and Ponds, 2005	−72.764429	42.013980	2005
West River	MassDEP	05-K005–03	−71.601117	42.100361	2005
West River	MassDEP	06-G005–03	−71.601117	42.100361	2005
West River	MassDEP	07-J003–03	−71.601117	42.100361	2005
West River	MassDEP	07-J005–03	−71.601117	42.100361	2005

Curly-leaf Pondweed (*Potamogeton crispus*)

West River	MassDEP	08-K003-04	-71.601117	42.100361	2005
West River	MassDEP	08-K005-04	-71.601117	42.100361	2005
West River	MassDEP	09-L003-04	-71.601117	42.100361	2005
West River	MassDEP	09-L004-04	-71.601117	42.100361	2005
West River	MassDEP	10-F002-04	-71.601117	42.100361	2005
West River	MassDEP	11-F004-04	-71.601117	42.100361	2005
West River	MassDEP	12-E001-04	-71.601117	42.100361	2005
West River	MassDEP	12-E003-04	-71.601117	42.100361	2005
West River	MassDEP	12-E004-04	-71.601117	42.100361	2005
West River	MassDEP	05-K003-03	-71.601117	42.100361	2005
West River	MassDEP	05-K004-03	-71.601117	42.100361	2005
West River	MassDEP	06-G003-03	-71.601117	42.100361	2005
West River	MassDEP	06-G004-03	-71.601117	42.100361	2005
West River	MassDEP	07-J004-03	-71.601117	42.100361	2005
West River	MassDEP	08-A040-06	-71.601117	42.100361	2005
West River	MassDEP	08-K002-04	-71.601117	42.100361	2005
West River	MassDEP	08-K004-04	-71.601117	42.100361	2005
West River	MassDEP	08-K007-04	-71.601117	42.100361	2005
West River	MassDEP	13-G003-04	-71.601117	42.100361	2005
Ware River	MassDEP	05-L003-04	-72.285755	42.238726	2005
Ware River	MassDEP	09-M004-04	-72.285755	42.238726	2005
Ware River	MassDEP	10-G003-04	-72.285755	42.238726	2005
Ware River	MassDEP	10-G004-04	-72.285755	42.238726	2005
Ware River	MassDEP	12-F004-04	-72.285755	42.238726	2005
Ware River	MassDEP	06-H004-04	-72.285755	42.238726	2005
Ware River	MassDEP	06-H005-04	-72.285755	42.238726	2005
Ware River	MassDEP	07-K004-04	-72.285755	42.238726	2005
Ware River	MassDEP	07-K005-04	-72.285755	42.238726	2005
Ware River	MassDEP	08-L001-04	-72.285755	42.238726	2005

(Continued)

TABLE 7.2 (Continued)

Waterbody	Agency	Report Source	Longitude	Latitude	First Year Reported
Ware River	MassDEP	08-L004-04	-72.285755	42.238726	2005
Ware River	MassDEP	08-L005-04	-72.285755	42.238726	2005
Ware River	MassDEP	08-L006-04	-72.285755	42.238726	2005
Ware River	MassDEP	08-L007-04	-72.285755	42.238726	2005
Ware River	MassDEP	12-F005-04	-72.285755	42.238726	2005
Sudbury River	MassDEP	05-J004-02	-71.397364	42.325435	2005
Sudbury River	MassDEP	06-F004-02	-71.397364	42.325435	2005
Sudbury River	MassDEP	09-N004-02	-71.397364	42.325435	2005
Sudbury River	MassDEP	09-N005-02	-71.397364	42.325435	2005
Webster Lake	MassDEP	05-G014-01	-71.848724	42.054350	2005
Whetstone Brook	MassDEP	05-H011-05	-72.361166	42.594057	2005
Whetstone Brook	MassDEP	05-H013-05	-72.361166	42.594057	2005
Crocker Pond	MassDEP	Taunton River Watershed Water Quality Assessment Report 62-AC-1 CN 94.0, December 2005	-71.294789	42.067691	2005
Nashua River	MassDEP	10-K002-05	-71.593150	42.626477	2006
Nashua River	MassDEP	11-K003-05	-71.593150	42.626477	2006
Nashua River	MassDEP	06-L005-05	-71.593150	42.626477	2006
Nashua River	MassDEP	09-R003-05	-71.593150	42.626477	2006
Nashua River	MassDEP	12-J004-05	-71.593150	42.626477	2006
Nashua River	MassDEP	13-L003-04	-71.593150	42.626477	2006
Assabet River	MassDEP	06-A027-01	-71.586136	42.380309	2006
Assabet River	MassDEP	06-A015-08	-71.586136	42.380309	2006
Jones River	MassDEP	06-C013-05	-70.734114	41.990752	2006

Curly-leaf Pondweed (*Potamogeton crispus*)

Wading River	MassDEP	06-B020-03		42.018856	-71.266702	2006
Assabet River	MassDEP	06-A015-07		42.346501	-71.614603	2006
York Lake	MassDEP	06-E013-01		42.095690	-73.181588	2006
Assabet River	MassDEP	07-L004-01		42.304853	-71.628451	2006
Assabet River	MassDEP	09-N004-01		42.304853	-71.628451	2006
Assabet River	MassDEP	09-N005-01		42.304853	-71.628451	2006
Assabet River	MassDEP	10-H002-01		42.304853	-71.628451	2006
Assabet River	MassDEP	12-G004-01		42.304853	-71.628451	2006
Assabet River	MassDEP	13-I004-01		42.304853	-71.628451	2006
Assabet River	MassDEP	06-F004-01		42.304853	-71.628451	2006
Assabet River	MassDEP	08-M003-01		42.304853	-71.628451	2006
Wading River	MassDEP	06-B020-06		41.951851	-71.223728	2006
Benton Pond	MassDEP	06-E015-02		42.183490	-73.043922	2006
Nashua River	MassDEP	Nashua River Watershed 2003 Water Quality Assessment Report 81-AC-4 CN107.5, August 2008		42.630111	-71.607427	2006
Town Brook	MassDEP	06-C001-04		41.954362	-70.663983	2006
Town Brook	MassDEP	06-C006-04		41.954362	-70.663983	2006
Town Brook	MassDEP	06-C013-04		41.954362	-70.663983	2006
Town Brook	MassDEP	06-C015-04		41.954362	-70.663983	2006
Unnamed Tributary	MassDEP	06-C013-03		41.926027	-70.613532	2006
Sudbury Reservoir	College of the Holy Cross	From Robert Bertin		42.321064	-71.510778	2006
Hop Brook	MassDEP	06-A025-05		42.357086	-71.403137	2006
Hop Brook	MassDEP	06-A034-05		42.357086	-71.403137	2006
Quinsigamond River	MassDEP	12-E003-02		42.230538	-71.708092	2007
Quinsigamond River	MassDEP	07-J003-05		42.230538	-71.708092	2007
Green River	MassDEP	07-D017-09		42.231769	-73.354869	2007
Charles River	MassDEP	07-A010-06		42.210062	-71.351725	2007
Charles River	MassDEP	07-A014-01		42.147718	-71.513910	2007
Charles River	MassDEP	07-A019-01		42.147718	-71.513910	2007

(Continued)

TABLE 7.2 (Continued)

Waterbody	Agency	Report Source	Longitude	Latitude	First Year Reported
Charles River	MassDEP	07-A011–05	−71.325382	42.264400	2007
Ten Mile River	MassDEP	07-R014–05	−71.328462	41.982719	2007
Nashua River	MassDEP	12-J004–04	−71.567765	42.669687	2007
Nashua River	MassDEP	07-P005–04	−71.567765	42.669687	2007
Smallpox Brook	MassDEP	07-G013–10	−70.864659	42.850044	2007
Smallpox Brook	MassDEP	07-G023–10	−70.864659	42.850044	2007
Smallpox Brook	MassDEP	07-G027–10	−70.864659	42.850044	2007
Squannacook River	MassDEP	07-P004–03	−71.643810	42.620942	2007
Charles River	MassDEP	07-A017–01	−71.190333	42.365145	2007
Charles River	MassDEP	10-D005–05	−71.264030	42.326259	2007
Millers River	MassDEP	10-J002–05	−72.093055	42.672322	2007
Millers River	MassDEP	12-J004–05	−72.093055	42.672322	2007
Millers River	MassDEP	07-N004–05	−72.093055	42.672322	2007
Fort River	MassDEP	08-C015–06	−72.520655	42.355650	2008
Bowers Brook	MassDEP	08-G015–08	−71.574278	42.551830	2008
Bowers Brook	MassDEP	08-G028–08	−71.574278	42.551830	2008
Bowers Brook	MassDEP	08-G032–08	−71.574278	42.551830	2008
Still River	MassDEP	08-B005–09	−71.645563	42.455860	2008
Still River	MassDEP	08-G015–04	−71.645563	42.455860	2008
Still River	MassDEP	08-G015–05	−71.632431	42.469172	2008
Still River	MassDEP	08-G003–05	−71.632431	42.469172	2008
Still River	MassDEP	08-G028–05	−71.632431	42.469172	2008
Still River	MassDEP	08-G032–05	−71.632431	42.469172	2008
Dunn Brook	MassDEP	08-B021–08	−72.078248	42.215406	2008
Dunn Brook	MassDEP	08-B002–08	−72.078248	42.215406	2008

Curly-leaf Pondweed (*Potamogeton crispus*)

Dunn Brook	MassDEP	08-B005-08	−72.078248	42.215406	2008
Dunn Brook	MassDEP	08-B032-08	−72.078248	42.215406	2008
Millers River	MassDEP	09-Q004-01	−72.437840	42.597511	2008
Millers River	MassDEP	12-I005-01	−72.437840	42.597511	2008
Millers River	MassDEP	08-P005-01	−72.437840	42.597511	2008
Catacoonamug Brook	MassDEP	08-G031-03	−71.698654	42.566806	2008
Unnamed Tributary	MassDEP	08-A032-06	−71.787751	42.205410	2008
Unnamed Tributary	MassDEP	08-A026-09	−71.787751	42.205410	2008
Chicopee River	MassDEP	08-B016-05	−72.374590	−72.374590	2008
Ware River	MassDEP	08-B019-07	−72.349834	42.191558	2008
Ware River	MassDEP	08-B033-07	−72.349834	42.191558	2008
East Branch Fever Brook	MassDEP	08-B038-03	−72.245617	42.462583	2008
Beaver Dam Brook	MassDEP	08-F009-02	−70.562879	41.923020	2008
Billington Sea	MassDEP	08-F005-01	−70.681001	41.934830	2008
Unnamed Tributary	MassDEP	08-F005-03	−70.673333	41.926684	2008
Priest Brook	MassDEP	12-I003-04	−72.115037	42.682797	2008
Priest Brook	MassDEP	08-P003-04	−72.115037	42.682797	2008
Priest Brook	MassDEP	08-P004-04	−72.115037	42.682797	2008
Priest Brook	MassDEP	10-I002-04	−72.115037	42.682797	2008
Nashua River	MassDEP	08-G028-11	−71.609769	42.578124	2008
Sevenmile River	MassDEP	08-B002-02	−72.008446	42.249995	2008
Sevenmile River	MassDEP	08-B005-02	−72.008446	42.249995	2008
Quaboag River	MassDEP	08-B002-09	−72.149374	42.228702	2008
Neponset River	MassDEP	09-B010-05	−71.086582	42.269342	2009
Neponset River	MassDEP	09-B012-16	−71.086582	42.269342	2009
Monatiquot River	MassDEP	09-C008-05	−70.980501	42.220580	2009
Massapoag Brook	MassDEP	09-B011-05	−71.145895	42.152208	2009

(Continued)

TABLE 7.2 (Continued)

Waterbody	Agency	Report Source	Longitude	Latitude	First Year Reported
Chase Garden Creek	MassDEP	09-D011-16	−70.200558	41.736337	2009
Quivett Creek	MassDEP	09-D001-12	−70.145314	41.743271	2009
French River	MassDEP	09-P004-04	−71.884182	42.024699	2009
Childs River	MassDEP	09-D007-04	−70.524925	41.593138	2009
Childs River	MassDEP	09-D011-04	−70.524925	41.593138	2009
Childs River	MassDEP	09-D014-04	−70.524925	41.593138	2009
Unnamed Tributary					
Stetson Brook	MassDEP	09-D014-03	−70.563034	41.585417	2009
Stetson Brook	MassDEP	09-G005-03	−70.836605	42.014395	2009
Stetson Brook	MassDEP	10-B009-01	−70.836605	42.014395	2009
Stetson Brook	MassDEP	12-B002-02	−70.836605	42.014395	2009
Stetson Brook	MassDEP	11-B006-03	−70.836605	42.014395	2009
Stetson Brook	MassDEP	12-B006-02	−70.836605	42.014395	2009
Stetson Brook	MassDEP	13-B005-03	−70.836605	42.014395	2009
Stetson Brook	MassDEP	13-B008-02	−70.836605	42.014395	2009
Stetson Brook	MassDEP	14-B002-03	−70.836605	42.014395	2009
Stetson Brook	MassDEP	14-B004-02	−70.836605	42.014395	2009
Stetson Brook	MassDEP	14-B006-02	−70.836605	42.014395	2009
Stetson Brook	MassDEP	15-B004-03	−70.836605	42.014395	2009
Weir River	MassDEP	13-C024-06	−70.859106	42.242234	2009
Weir River	MassDEP	09-C005-03	−70.872251	42.234586	2009
Weir River	MassDEP	09-C014-03	−70.872251	42.234586	2009
Weir River	MassDEP	09-C017-03	−70.872251	42.234586	2009
Weir River	MassDEP	09-C014-02	−70.859055	42.242575	2009
Concord River	MassDEP	09-N003-05	−71.302846	42.641726	2009

Curly-leaf Pondweed (*Potamogeton crispus*)

Quashnet River	MassDEP	09-D007-06	−70.500578	41.617753	2009
Pine Tree Brook	MassDEP	09-B011-14	−71.072817	42.269480	2009
Fish Pond	MassDEP	09-G010-01	−71.687954	42.120918	2009
Neponset River	MassDEP	09-B005-02	−71.185944	42.171871	2009
Neponset River	MassDEP	09-B010-02	−71.185944	42.171871	2009
Neponset River	MassDEP	09-B011-02	−71.185944	42.171871	2009
Welsh Pond	MassDEP	09-G009-02	−71.789985	42.150633	2009
Neponset River	MassDEP	09-B006-01	−71.255889	42.147119	2009
Neponset River	MassDEP	09-B005-01	−71.255889	42.147119	2009
Shawsheen River	MassDEP	10-D015-08	−71.167895	42.617047	2010
Middle Pond	MassDEP	10-B006-05	−70.415504	41.668707	2010
Shawsheen River	MassDEP	10-D003-05	−71.244712	42.517079	2010
Swift River	MassDEP	10-G004-03	−72.332761	42.267975	2010
North Brook	MassDEP	10-D007-03	−71.650556	42.412294	2010
Unnamed Tributary	MassDEP	10-D005-06	−71.395881	42.319815	2010
Hinckleys Pond	MassDEP	10-B006-02	−70.083929	41.709592	2010
Cranberry Pond	College of the Holy Cross	From Robert Bertin	−71.643570	42.503270	2010
Quinebaug River	MassDEP	11-T009-08	−72.148597	42.106759	2011
Sassaquin Pond	MassDEP	11-B011-01	−70.948919	41.735321	2011
Quaboag River	MassDEP	11-G004-05	−72.263543	42.181430	2011
White Island Pond (West Basin)	MassDEP	11-B002-02	−70.627556	41.809994	2011
White Island Pond (West Basin)	MassDEP	14-B003-02	−70.627556	41.809994	2011

(*Continued*)

TABLE 7.2 (Continued)

Waterbody	Agency	Report Source	Longitude	Latitude	First Year Reported
Breakneck Brook	MassDEP	11-D024-04	-72.097147	42.042161	2011
Otter River	MassDEP	11-T005-09	-72.094246	42.633838	2011
Monponsett Pond	MassDEP	12-B002-04	-70.836781	42.001467	2012
Monponsett Pond	MassDEP	14-B004-05	-70.836781	42.001467	2012
Monponsett Pond	MassDEP	15-B007-02	-70.836781	42.001467	2012
Monponsett Pond	MassDEP	13-B008-05	-70.836781	42.001467	2012
Turner Hill Country Club Pond	Individual	From Joy Trahan-Liptak	-70.885150	42.662809	2012
Rumford River	MassDEP	13-C045-03	-71.213447	42.005027	2013
White Island Pond (East Basin)	MassDEP	13-B004-01	-70.617531	41.809183	2013
White Island Pond (East Basin)	MassDEP	14-B003-01	-70.617531	41.809183	2013
Long Pond	Individual	From Joy Trahan-Liptak	-71.470250	42.530021	2014
Windsor Lake	USGS	USGS 4/24/2017 http://nas.er.usgs.gov/default.aspx	-73.092600	42.687100	2014
Rice City Pond	Individual	From Joy Trahan-Liptak	-71.622465	42.100003	2014
Rice City Pond	Individual	From Joy Trahan-Liptak	-71.622465	42.100003	2014
Powwow River	MassDEP	15-C017-05	-70.961591	42.865929	2015
Shawsheen River	MassDEP	15-C022-01	-71.150971	42.652195	2015

Curly-leaf Pondweed (*Potamogeton crispus*)

Location	Source	ID/Notes	Longitude	Latitude	Year
Blackstone River	Individual	From Joy Trahan-Liptak	−71.553560	42.015699	2015
Beaver Brook	MassDEP	15-C013-07	−71.326335	42.668178	2015
Cow Pond Brook	MassDEP	15-C013-01	−71.506158	42.629730	2015
Monponsett Pond	MassDEP	15-B007-01	−70.845254	42.004596	2015
Reservoir	MassDEP	15-B006-02	−70.852628	42.029884	2015
Mill River	MassDEP	15-C024-02	−71.365440	42.121769	2015
Stetson Pond	MassDEP	15-B003-01	−70.826111	42.028496	2015
Stetson Pond	MassDEP	15-B010-01	−70.826111	42.028496	2015
Stony Brook	MassDEP	15-C013-02	−71.447571	42.597591	2015
Stony Brook	MassDEP	15-C023-02	−71.447571	42.597591	2015
Mossy Pond	DCR	From Jamie Carr	−71.701034	42.417156	2016
Coachlace Pond	DCR	From Jamie Carr	−71.697104	42.413367	2016
South Meadow Pond (East Basin)	DCR	From Jamie Carr	−71.705732	42.415348	2016
South Meadow Pond (West Basin)	DCR	From Jamie Carr	−71.713092	42.414889	2016
Charles River	Individual	From Joy Trahan-Liptak	−71.264994	42.257320	2016
Cheshire Reservoir, Middle Basin	DCR	DCR Data from ACT, GeoSyntec EM-ACT W-A. Madden FEW	−73.191871	42.531451	NA
Cheshire Reservoir, North Basin	DCR	DCR Data from ACT, GeoSyntec EM-ACT W-A. Madden FEW	−73.173964	42.547317	NA
White Pond	College of the Holy Cross	From Robert Bertin	−71.716035	42.513314	NA

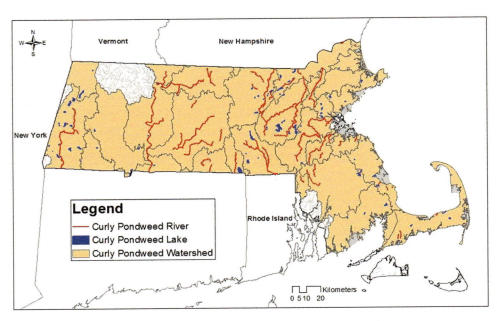

FIGURE 7.3 Distribution map depicting *Potamogeton crispus* in Massachusetts.

released by benthic aquatic organisms can accumulate and dislodge barriers overtime (Barr and Ditomaso 2014). Though benthic barriers need to be routinely maintained to holdfast in their positions, can be expensive, accumulate chemical compounds, and cause the undesired result of chemical pollution to downstream areas, benthic barriers are effective at controlling *P. crispus*. Even so, this method alone is not as effective as combining multiple methods to better manage *P. crispus* outbreaks (Barr and Ditomaso 2014).

CHEMICAL METHODS

Chemical methods may be used to treat curly-leaf pondweed. Endothall, diquat, and fluridone are three effective herbicides (MA DCR2002; Skogerboe and Getsinger 2002; Belgers et al. 2007). Greatest success occurs when herbicides are applied early mid-April–early May before turions are produced (Poovey et al. 2002; Johnson et al. 2012; Bugbee et al. 2015). State permits for herbicides are needed and applications are not suitable to all infestations. Recently, a new treatment method using acetic acid was introduced (Barr and Ditomaso 2014). Acetic acid ($C_2H_4O_2$) is produced by microorganisms naturally in wetland soil. Ultimately, acetic acid, which degrades to carbon dioxide in aquatic systems, can slow down growth and seed production of invasive species. It is suggested that acetic acid can be combined with benthic barriers to perform as a small-volume high-concentration chemical. More information about chemical control on curly-leaf pondweed and other 18 invasive species can be found in Appendix III. It is important to note that the Massachusetts Department of Environmental Protection requires an aquatic nuisance species control license (BRP WM04 Form) before chemical application.

PREVENTION METHODS

Prevention is an efficient and cost-effective approach to stopping the spread of aquatic invasive species. Strategies include boat washing stations, draining water from watercrafts, and disposing of unused bait (Minnesota Department of Natural Resources n.d.). Integrating prevention, education, early detection, control, ecosystem restoration, and environmental law regulation and enforcement will yield the greatest success in protecting waterbodies from invasive species (Wong and Gerstenberger 2015). Public educational programs are important to spread awareness of the impacts and distribution of invasive species. This will facilitate the reporting of new infestations and implementing early season treatment as it is efficient in controlling turion production. Installation of fragment nets and screens is also effective in preventing the spread of *P. crispus* and reducing human-mediated spreading (Mikulyuk and Nault 2009).

So far, no reports on complete eradication of curly-leaf pondweed have been found (Mikulyuk and Nault 2009).

SUCCESS STORY

As stated in the "Managing Actions" section, several herbicides can be an effective tool for the management of *P. crispus*. In this section, two examples of the application of endothall-based herbicides are described which show promising results at reducing the presence of curly-leaf pondweed in targeted and lake wide areas.

The first study occurred in 1999 in a controlled setting consisting of 21 tanks that had curly-leaf pondweed growing in them (Poovey et al. 2002). Prior to this study, herbicide applications mainly occurred in late spring or early summer after turions had already developed. These types of applications were effective at reducing plant biomass but were not effective at long-term management and reducing turion production. It was theorized that applying herbicides in the spring, when water temperature is cooler, could result in more effective long-term control of the invasive plant. Applying herbicides during this time would prove less harmful to native aquatic plants which are generally less active in the spring. Therefore, the treatments often occurred in March, April, and May. Diquat and endothall were applied to the tanks in different rates depending on the ambient temperature. Treatment evaluations were based on recorded plant biomass (the shoots and roots of the plant), turion numbers, and a visual assessment of the plants. Tanks that were treated with diquat showed a shoot biomass decrease of 60% and a root and rhizome decrease of 70% compared to a control tank that received no treatment. Turion numbers decreased by more than 85%. Tanks that were treated with endothall showed a shoot biomass decrease ranging from 60% to 90% and a root and rhizome decrease ranging from 60% to >90% depending on the temperature. Turion numbers decreased by 55% to >90% depending on the temperature. Poovey et al. suggested the use of short exposure of diquat in spring to reduce plant biomass and turion production, and endothall for larger areas, such as a whole lake treatment. The results showed that utilizing endothall-based herbicides in cooler waters during spring could result in a form of long-term control for curly-leaf pondweed.

A second study occurred between 2006 and 2009 in nine lakes in Minnesota. Treatments occurred in the early spring of each year and consisted of low doses of herbicide (Johnson et al. 2012). Treatments continued for up to five consecutive years. Three additional lakes were identified and left untreated to serve as a control. Of the nine lakes, eight were treated exclusively with endothall, and the remaining lake was treated with fluridone between 2005 and 2007. This remaining lake was then treated with endothall between 2008 and 2009 to allow for the recovery of native plants which had declined due to the fluridone. In this case, a fluridone mixture was dispersed across the entire lake. The endothall treatments were spot treatments, i.e., targeted to specific areas of each lake where curly-leaf pondweed had been identified. Surveys were conducted in each lake to assess the frequency of *P. crispus*, measure plant biomass, and record the number of turions. Results showed that lake wide, early season treatments of both endothall and fluridone had a substantial effect on reducing the frequency of curly-leaf pondweed on a year-to-year basis. Plant biomass also saw a reduction in treated lakes versus the control lakes. Additionally, in lakes that received a treatment, no dense matts of curly-leaf pondweed were observed on the water's surface. Turion production was also greatly reduced as an effect of the herbicide treatments, with >99% reduction in treated lakes when compared to control lakes. There was noticeable variability in the three metrics between certain years, most likely due to differences in climatic conditions.

These results coincide with those of Poovey et al. (2002) implying that treating lakes in early spring in cool water conditions can reduce the biomass of plants and lead to long-term management and control through a reduction in turion production. This approach could also present a lower risk to local aquatic species, which are less active during early spring. Additionally, Johnson et al. (2012) found this treatment approach can work at a lake-wide level, and not just at a localized level within a given waterbody.

Endothall-based herbicide treatments alone will not solve the curly-leaf pondweed issue. Instead, it is necessary to take an integrative and adaptive management approach that utilizes prevention, early season herbicide treatments, and public education. This can help reduce the abundance of curly-leaf pondweed and other invasive aquatic plant species in Massachusetts.

REFERENCES

Acy, C. 2019. AIS spotlight—Curly Leaf Pondweed: The Aquatic LASAGNA plant? *Fox-Wolf Watershed Alliance*. https://fwwa.org/2019/01/23/ais-spotlight-curly-leaf- pondweed/ (Accessed July 3, 2021).

Barr, T.C.III., and J.M. Ditomaso. 2014. Curly leaf pondweed (*Potamogeton crispus*) turion control with acetic acid and benthic barriers. *Journal of Aquatic Plant Management* 52: 31–38.

Belgers, J.D.M., R.J. Van, Lieverloo., L.J.T. Van Der, Pas., and P.J. Van Der, Brink. 2007. Effects of the herbicide 2,4-D on the growth of nine aquatic macrophytes. *Aquatic Botany* 86: 260–268.

Bolduan, B.R., G.C. Van Eeckout, H.W. Quade, and J.E. Gannon. 1994. *Potamogeton crispus*– the other invader. *Lake and Reservoir Management* 10(2): 113–125.

Bugbee, G.J., J.A. Gibbons, and M. June-Wells. 2015. Efficacy of single and consecutive early-season diquat treatments on curlyleaf pondweed and associated aquatic macrophytes: A case study. *Journal of Aquatic Plant Management* 55: 171–177.

Caffrey, J.M., M. Millane, S. Evers, H. Moran, and M. Butler. 2010. A novel approach to aquatic weed control and habitat restoration using biodegradable jute matting. *Aquatic Invasions* 5: 123–129.

Cao, Y., and G. Wang. 2007. Effects of submersed plant *Potamogeton crispus* on suspended mud and sand. *Journal of Ecology and Rural Environment* 23(1): 54–56.

Deng, H., J. Zhang, S. Chen, L. Yang, D. Wang, and S. Yu. 2015. Metal release/accumulation during the decomposition of *Potamogeton crispus* in a shallow macrophytic lake. *Journal of Environmental Sciences* 42: 71–78.

Du, Y., J. Feng, R. Wang, H. Zhang, and J. Liu. 2015. Effects of flavonoids from *Potamogeton crispus* L. on proliferation, migration, and invasion of human ovarian cancer cells. *PLoS One* 10(6). doi: 10.1371/journal.pone.0130685

GISD (Global Invasive Species Database). 2006 Species profile: *Potamogeton crispus*. www.iucngisd.org/gisd/species.php?sc=447 (Accessed July 7, 2017).

Hafez, M.B., N. Hafez, and Y.S. Ramadan. 1992. Uptake of cerium, cobalt, and cesium by *Potamogeton crispus*. *Journal of Chemical Technology and Biotechnology* 54: 337–340.

Hafez, N., S. Abdalla., and Y.S. Ramadan. 1998. Accumulation of phenol by *Potamogeton crispus* from aqueous industrial waste. *Bulletin of Environmental Contamination and Toxicology* 60: 944–948.

IL DNR (Illinois Department of Natural Resources). 2009. Aquatic invasive species: Curlyleaf pondweed. www.in.gov/dnr/files/CURLYLEAF_PONDWEED.pdf.

ITIS (Integrated Taxonomic Information System). 2021. www.itis.gov/servlet/SingleRpt/SingleRpt?search_topic=TSN&search_value=3 9007#null (Accessed January 29, 2021).

Jensen, D. 2009. Curlyleaf pondweed (Potamogeton crispus). www.seagrant.umn.edu/ais/fieldguide#curlyleaf.

Johnson, J.A., A.R. Jones, and R.M. Newman. 2012. Evaluation of lake wide, early season herbicide treatments for controlling invasive curly leaf pondweed (*Potamogeton crispus*) in Minnesota lakes. *Lake and Reservoir Management*, 28(4): 346–363.

Kaplan, Z., and J. Fehrer. 2004. Evidence for the hybrid origin of *Potamogeton* x *cooperi* (Potamogetonaceae): Traditional morphology-based taxonomy and molecular techniques in concert. *Folia Geobotanica* 39: 431–453.

MA DCR (Massachusetts Department of Conservation and Recreation). 2002. Curly-leaved Pondweed: An Invasive Aquatic Plant. www.mass.gov/eea/docs/dcr/watersupply/lakepond/factsheet/curly-leaved- pondweed.pdf (Accessed May 10, 2017).

MA DCR (Massachusetts Department of Conservation and Recreation). 2015. A Guide to Aquatic Plants in Massachusetts, p. 32. www.mass.gov/doc/dcr-guide-to-aquatic-plants-in- massachusetts/download

Mikulyuk, A., and M.E. Nault. 2009. Curly-leaf Pondweed (*Potamogeton crispus*): A Technical Review of Distribution, Ecology, Impacts, and Management. Wisconsin Department of Natural Resources Bureau of Science Services, PUB-SS-1052 2009. Madison, Wisconsin, USA.

Minnesota Department of Natural Resources. n.d. Curly-leaf pondweed *(Potamogeton crispus)*. www.dnr.state.mn.us/invasives/aquaticplants/curlyleaf_pondweed.html (Accessed December 1, 2020).

Nichols, S.A., and B.H. Shaw. 1986. Ecological life histories of the three aquatic nuisance plants, *Myriophyllum spicatum*, *Potamogeton crispus* and *Elodea canadensis*. *Hydrobiologia* 131: 3–21.

Poovey, A. 2008. *Curlyleaf pondweed (Potamogeton crispus L.)*. Washington, DC: Department of Washington Education.

Poovey, A.G., J.G. Skogerboe, and C.S. Owens. 2002. Spring treatments of diquat and endothall for curly leaf pondweed control. *Journal of Aquatic Plant Management* 40: 63–67.

Ren, D., and S. Zhang. 2008. Separation and identification of the yellow carotenoids in *Potamogeton crispus* L. *Food Chemistry* 106: 410–414.

Skogerboe, J.G., and K.D. Getsinger. 2002. Endothall species selectivity evaluation: northern latitude aquatic plant community. *Journal of Aquatic Plant Management* 40: 1–5.

Stuckey, R.L. 1979. Distributional history of *Potamogeton crispus* (curly pondweed) in North America. *Bartonia* 46: 22–42.

Swistock, B. 2021. Curly-leaf pondweed. https://extension.psu.edu/curly-leaf-pondweed (Accessed July 2, 2021).

Tomaino, A. 2004. *Potamogeton crispus*: U.S. invasive species impact rank (i-rank). NatureServe, Arlington, VA. www.natureserve.org/explorer (Accessed May 17, 2017).

Washington State Noxious Weed Control Board. 2004. Written findings of the Washington State Noxious Weed Control Board. May 11. www.nwcb.wa.gov/images/weeds/Potamogeton-crispus-2004.pdf (Accessed May 11, 2017).

WI DNR (Wisconsin Department of Natural Resources). 2012. Curly-leaf pondweed (Potamogeton crispus). http://dnr.wi.gov/topic/invasives/fact/curlyleafpondweed.html. (Accessed April, 2013).

Wong, W.H., and S.L. Gerstenberger. 2015. *Biology and Management of Invasive Quagga and Zebra Mussels in the Western United States*. Boca Raton, FL: CRC Press, p. 566.

Wu, J., S. Cheng, W. Liang, F. He, and Z. Wu. 2009. Effects of sediment anoxia and light on turion germination and early growth of Potamogeton crispus. *Hydrobiologia* 628(1): 111–119.

Yeo, R.R. 1966. Yield of propagules of certain aquatic plants. *Weeds* 14: 110–113.

8 Eurasian Milfoil (*Myriophyllum spicatum*) and Variable Milfoil (*Myriophyllum heterophyllum*)

ABSTRACT

Eurasian milfoil (*Myriophyllum spicatum*) and variable milfoil (*Myriophyllum heterophyllum*) are among the most prevalent aquatic invasive species known to occur in Massachusetts waters. These species can become established rapidly once introduced to a new waterbody and are costly to control. As of this writing, there are 115 reported waterbodies infested by Eurasian milfoil and 245 sightings for variable milfoil in Massachusetts. In addition to these two invasive milfoil species, many unidentified (unverified) milfoil species have yet to be categorized as either a native or an invasive milfoil. Therefore, a more comprehensive monitoring of invasive milfoils is needed to increase public awareness, which can be useful in minimizing the spread of invasive milfoils in Massachusetts. Chemicals (fluridone, 2,4-D, florpyrauxifen-benzyl, and triclopyr), physical controls (e.g., lake drawdown and diver-assisted or hand harvest), and biological methods (e.g., American native weevil) are used to manage populations of invasive milfoil species once they become established.

INTRODUCTION

Taxonomy Hierarchy (ITIS 2021)

Kingdom	Plantae
Subkingdom	Viridiplantae
Infrakingdom	Streptophyta
Superdivision	Embryophyta
Division	Tracheophyta
Subdivision	Spermatophytina
Class	Magnoliopsida
Superorder	Saxifraganae
Order	Saxifragales
Family	Haloragaceae
Genus	*Myriophyllum* L.
Species	*Myriophyllum spicatum* L.
Species	*Myriophyllum heterophyllum* Michx. for variable milfoil

BIOLOGY OF EURASIAN MILFOIL AND VARIABLE MILFOIL

There are several milfoils found in Massachusetts: Eurasian milfoil (invasive, aka Eurasian water-milfoil), variable milfoil (invasive, aka variable-leaf milfoil), and low-watermilfoil (*Myriophyllum humile*, a native species) (Figure 8.1). Other native milfoil species, such as *Myriophyllum farwellii*, has also been reported in Massachusetts (Crow and Hellquist 2000). The Eurasian milfoil is a rooted, submerged invasive aquatic plant. This plant has thin stems which can appear either green, brown, or pinkish white and grow 1–3 m in length (Aiken et al. 1979). As the stem moves away from the main growth of the plant, it becomes thinner. Its feathered leaves are blunt-ended and olive green, which are arranged in whorls of three to six (typically four) with gaps of about an inch or more between leaf whorls. Each leaf has 12 or more leaflets per side (Figures 8.2 and 8.3). The flower stalks of Eurasian milfoil grow above the water, and have feather-like bracts that are distinctive. The flowers of Eurasian milfoil, which are small and yellow in color, have four parts and rise 5–10 cm above the surface of the water (Aiken et al. 1979).

Similarly, the variable milfoil is a rooted, submerged invasive plant. The variable milfoil has multiple feather-like leaves that grow 2–4.5 cm long in whorls of four to six around the thick and red stems, giving the plant a resemblance to a "raccoon tail" (Howard 2020) with rounded tips (Figures 8.2 and 8.3). In mid to late summer, the flower stalk of variable milfoil protrudes above the water, with small distinct green bracts on it that are football shaped with toothed edges.

Eurasian and variable milfoil are fairly distinguishable from the native low watermilfoil.

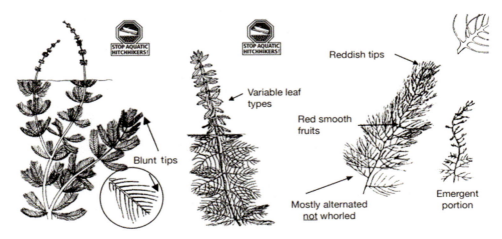

FIGURE 8.1 Eurasian milfoil (*Myriophyllum spicatum*) (*left*), variable milfoil (*Myriophyllum heterophyllum*) (*middle*), and low-watermilfoil (*Myriophyllum humile*) (*right*) (Department of Conservation and Recreation MA 2016).

FIGURE 8.2 Leaves of Eurasian watermilfoil *Myriophyllum spicatum* (*left*) and variable milfoil *Myriophyllum heterophyllum* (*right*). (Photos taken by W. H. Wong.)

Low watermilfoil has stems with limp leaves. In addition, some of these native species have smooth reddish, brownish, or greenish fruits in the axils of their submerged leaves. Low watermilfoil may appear red-tipped with tiny green lobed leaves appearing above the water surface when emergent (Robinson 2002a, 2002b; MA DCR 2016). Because of this, some species of milfoil may be confused with Eurasian milfoil. Even so, invasive Eurasian milfoil can be identified through their leaflet pairs which are usually more than 14, while native species have fewer than 14 pairs (Aiken 1981; Pfingsten et al. 2021). Native milfoils also often have leaves that are staggered along the stem, whereas the invasive milfoils more often have leaves that whorl around the main stem. Additionally, some native species of milfoil produce turion buds (overwintering buds) at the stem tips, while invasive Eurasian milfoil does not. Identification of native milfoils can be tricky, and requires some taxonomic knowledge, and still often genetic verification of the plant if there are no flower stalks or nutlets present.

Like most invasive species, Eurasian milfoil and variable milfoil can grow in various waterbodies as they can tolerate a wide range of temperature, pH, water chemistry, and water nutrient conditions. Both species reside in still or slow-moving waterbodies. However, the

FIGURE 8.3 Stems of Eurasian watermilfoil *Myriophyllum spicatum* (*left*) and variable milfoil *Myriophyllum heterophyllum* (*right*). (Photos taken by W.H. Wong.)

preferences on water chemistry conditions of Eurasian milfoil and variable milfoil are different. Eurasian milfoil is more often found in alkaline waters (pH >7), while variable milfoil is more often found in acidic waters (pH <6.5) (Robinson 2002a; Robinson 2002b). Between a pH of 6 and 7, both species may co-mingle. In terms of their reproductive methods, Eurasian milfoil can reproduce by stem fragmentation and seeds. Over 50% of its plant fragments can resprout, potentially leading to the production of a new plant. Generally, variable milfoil reproduces through fragmentation, rhizome division, budding, and seeds. Stem fragments of the milfoils may attach to boats and other recreational gear, moving plants to other sites. If the watercraft is trailered to another body of water, those hitchhiking fragments can be introduced and become established. Additionally, several hybrids between variable milfoil and native species have been identified. These aggressive hybrid lineages have been found in Connecticut and reproduce vegetatively (Thum and Lennon 2006).

NATIVE RANGE

Eurasian milfoil and variable milfoil are non-native plants in Massachusetts. Eurasian milfoil is a native plant to Europe, Asia, and North Africa (Robinson 2002b). Variable milfoil is native to Southeast and Midwest of the United States (Howard 2020).

INVASIVE RANGE

Both Eurasian milfoil and variable milfoil are on the Massachusetts Prohibited Plants List as they threaten the well-being of ecosystems. Currently, both species are banned from the trade in Massachusetts. The first introduction of the Eurasian milfoil is unknown. Even so, Eurasian milfoil was first observed in North America during the 1800s in New York and Virginia. Since then, this invasive milfoil has been observed in many northern states (Smith and Barko 1990; New York Invasive Species Information 2019).

Variable milfoil is native to many US states but invasive to New England. The first variable milfoil sighting in New England was recorded in 1932 in Bridgeport, Connecticut (Cameron and Wallhead 2004). Since then, variable milfoil can be found in all New England states with recent documentation of variable growth in Vermont (MaineVLMP 2009; VT DEC 2022). It is believed that variable milfoil was introduced to New England by fragments attached to a boat or an aquarium release (Isabel 2011).

ECOLOGICAL IMPACTS

Invasive milfoils have a significant impact on the well-being of native ecosystems. Milfoils can form dense mats in the water column, which can extend to the water surface in as much as 15 ft of water. These mats of invasive milfoil may hinder the water flow, harming other plants and aquatic animals. In addition, the mats can intercept sunlight, which limits native plant growth and alters the chemistry of the water column and sediment (Eiswerth et al. 2000). Invasive milfoils also impact water quality as it increases the nutrient load and temperature, reducing dissolved oxygen. These factors can make the ecosystem less suitable for native species as the removal of native plants threatens both the food source and habitats of native fish and mammals (Eiswerth et al. 2000). This can lead to non-native plants occupying waterbodies, displacing native plants, which can cause fish and other aquatic animals that rely on native plants to relocate or perish, reducing biodiversity.

ECONOMIC IMPACTS

Invasive milfoil infestations can be damaging to local economies, impacting the quality of recreational services, aquaculture, agriculture, and electricity and decreasing property values. Their dense mats, as mentioned earlier, have inhibited boating and fishing as these milfoil mats clog waterways (Invasive Eurasian Watermilfoil 2021). In addition, as a study in Maryland found, invasive milfoil threatens water quality and recreation/industry of fishing, crabbing, oyster production, and clam harvesting (Bayley et al. 1968). Eurasian milfoil can also impact provisioning services such as agriculture and electricity generation by reducing water circulation in irrigation projects and blocking water intakes in power plants (Eiswerth et al. 2000). Furthermore, Olden and Tamayo (2014) found a 19% decline in mean shoreline property sales caused by Eurasian milfoil invasions. Additionally, removing invasive milfoil can be costly as work done by "professional operations range from $100 to $500 per acre" (equivalent to about $400 to $1,200 nowadays) (Rapid Response Plan for Eurasian Watermilfoil n.d.).

MONITORING AND SIGHTINGS

Data about the presence of invasive milfoils in each waterbody were collected by and from a variety of sources, including the Massachusetts Department of Environmental Protection (MassDEP), the Massachusetts Department of Conservation and Recreation (MA DCR), MassDEP Water Quality Assessment Reports, field surveys, personal communications, and EBT Environmental Consults, Inc. Standard operating procedures, including sampling methodology, species identification, and quality control and assurance, were implemented for samples collected by MassDEP (Chase and Wong 2015; MassDEP 2021). Data from other agencies were confirmed by experts. Sites with Aquatic Invasive Species (AIS) were mapped as a data layer with ArcGIS® ArcMap 10.1 (ESRI, Redlands, California).

This chapter mainly addresses the sightings of Eurasian milfoil and variable milfoil. Other unknown milfoil species that were not recognized/hardly distinguishable in Massachusetts waterbodies were documented as "unidentified milfoil." Therefore, characteristics, impacts, and control methods of unidentified milfoil are not discussed in this report because their identification is unknown. The reports and surveys of milfoil locations in Massachusetts have been mapped using Geographic Information Systems (GIS) (Figure 8.4). If regular surveys are conducted to map infestations in the field, GIS can be used to track the spread of invasive milfoils (Figures 8.5–8.8) over time. The map can help to inform future decision-making concerning bodies of water or regulations that could limit the spread of these aquatic invasive species.

Eurasian milfoil and variable milfoil are very aggressive invasive species, and therefore can spread in a short time throughout Massachusetts (Table 8.1). Currently, there are 115, 245, and 32 waterbodies (Tables 8.1 and 8.2) infested by Eurasian milfoil (Figure 8.5), variable milfoil (Figure 8.6), and unidentified milfoil (Figure 8.8), respectively. For these infested waterbodies, 304 are lakes and 32 are rivers. Among these lakes, there are 104 with Eurasian milfoil and 219 with variable milfoil. Meanwhile, 28 lakes were found to support both invasive milfoil species. Among infested rivers, there are 11 and 26 rivers with

Eurasian Milfoil and Variable Milfoil

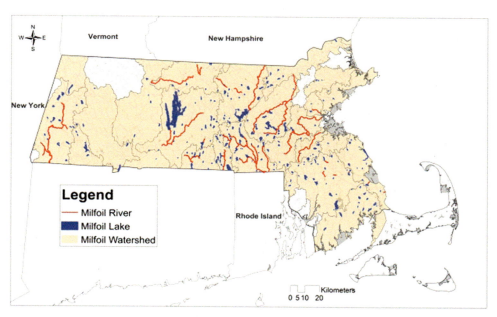

FIGURE 8.4 Distribution map depicting Eurasian milfoil, variable milfoil, and unidentified milfoil in Massachusetts.

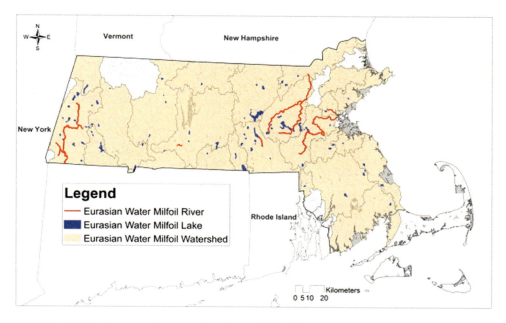

FIGURE 8.5 Distribution maps depicting Eurasian milfoil in Massachusetts.

Eurasian milfoils and variable milfoils. Two rivers were found to have both species. Most watersheds in Massachusetts have been infested by these invasive milfoils, except the following watersheds: Kinderhook River, Bashbish River, Deerfield River, Parker River, Shawsheen River, Narragansett Bay, Cape Cod, and Islands (Figure 8.7 and Table 8.3). While Eurasian milfoil is found statewide (Figure 8.5) and both invasive milfoil species can comingle (Figure 8.7),

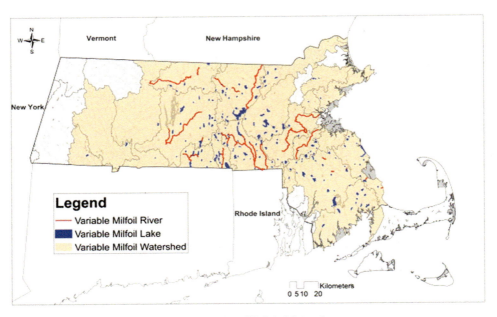

FIGURE 8.6 Distribution maps depicting variable milfoil in Massachusetts.

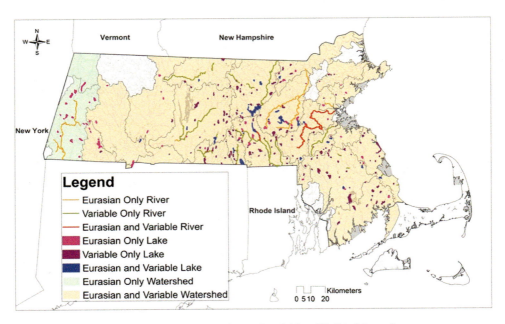

FIGURE 8.7 Distribution maps depicting Eurasian and variable milfoil in Massachusetts.

variable milfoil is mostly detected from eastern to central Massachusetts (Figure 8.6) where waters are relatively lower in pH, alkalinity, or hardness (Smith 1993). This is in agreement with the statement that variable milfoil is often growing in acidic waters (Robinson 2002a; 2002b).

MANAGEMENT

EURASIAN MILFOIL

Many methods have been tested for controlling Eurasian milfoil, including physical, chemical, and biological methods. Physical methods

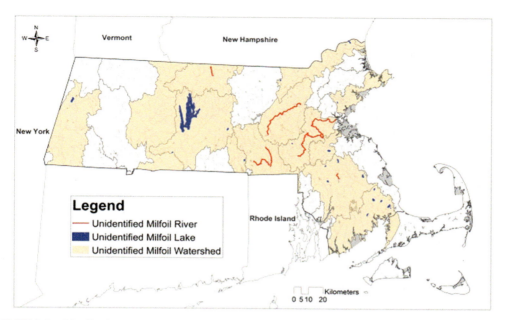

FIGURE 8.8 Distribution maps depicting unidentified milfoil in Massachusetts.

include diver-assisted and hand harvesting, drawdowns, and benthic barriers. Harvesting can effectively reduce small or low-density Eurasian milfoil populations. Because spread of this species occurs by stem pieces, roots, and seeds, harvesting can also cause spread if plant fragments are not carefully managed during harvest events. Fragments may also spread by becoming entangled on boats that are trailered to other bodies of water. Eurasian milfoil fragments are hearty and can survive periods of desiccation while they are transported and unintentionally introduced to a new body of water. Therefore, mechanical harvesting is usually not recommended for plants like milfoil, where fragmentation can be a significant problem by drafting to other sites within the same waterbody or by attaching to boats that can infest other waters. Diver-assisted suction harvesting removes Eurasian milfoil by hand pulling plants and their roots from the bottom sediments. The diver is equipped with a vacuum system on a pontoon boat, and as plants are hand harvested, they are fed up the vacuum tube to a top-side containment method for later disposal. This method can achieve a substantial reduction in milfoil biomass, while having minimal impact on native plants because the diver may select which plants to harvest. However, it cannot eliminate large-scale or even locally dense milfoil populations in a short time, and requires constant maintenance (Eichler et al. 1994). Similarly, drawdown is a helpful method for removing the rooted plants by lowering the water level. However, it can only be effective when sediments are completely dry or when sediments and plants are removed (Dutartre et al. 2006; Scheers 2016). In addition, to reduce impacts to non-target plants and animals during the growing season, drawdowns are conducted in fall and winter in Massachusetts (Mattson et al. 2004). It is also needed to account for those species that burrow or settle for the winter, and drawdown should be timed and staged to allow for these species to adapt before they become dormant for the season. Following this method, benthic barriers are a control method that limits the plant's growth by creating a cover of clay, silt, sand, or gravel. Benthic barrier covers are usually semipermeable or impermeable "blankets" that are placed over the sediments and held in place with weights or re-bar. Benthic barriers that are fabric can be temporary and removed when plants are controlled. These barriers have been proposed by Massachusetts authorities and are most effective in small areas (such as

TABLE 8.1
Latitude and Longitude for Each Waterbody in Figure 8.1

Table 8.1a Eurasian Milfoil

Waterbody	Agency	Report Source	Longitude	Latitude	First Year Reported
Ashmere Lake	MassDEP	MassDEP/WPP 303d List 2012 extract			
Assabet River	MassDEP	Field Survey 06/26/2017 Wong, Li	−71.449741	42.432064	
Assabet River	MassDEP	13-I005–03	−71.449741	42.432064	
Assabet River	MassDEP	11-H004–03	−71.449741	42.432064	
Assabet River	MassDEP	08-M004–03	−71.449741	42.432064	
Assabet River	MassDEP	06-F005–03	−71.449741	42.432064	
Assabet River	MassDEP	06-F004–03	−71.449741	42.432064	
Assabet River	MassDEP	Field Survey 06/26/2017 Wong, Li	−71.474722	42.423178	
Assabet River	MassDEP	06-A018–04	−71.474722	42.423178	
Assabet River Reservoir	MassDEP	MassDEP/WPP 303d List 2012 extract			
Assabet River Reservoir	College of the Holy Cross	Robert Bertin	−71.646010	42.263618	
Bartlett Pond	MassDEP	MassDEP/WPP 303d List 2012 extract			
Bartons Cove	MassDEP	MassDEP/WPP 303d List 2012 extract			
Bartons Cove	Individual	Joy Trahan-Liptak	−72.537734	42.605267	
Beaver Lake	MassDEP	MassDEP/WPP 303d List 2012 extract			
Benton Pond	MassDEP	MassDEP/WPP 303d List 2012 extract			
Benton Pond	MassDEP	Field Survey 06/20/2017 Wong, Li	−73.043922	42.183490	2006
Benton Pond	MassDEP	06-E015–02	−73.043922	42.183490	2006
Berkshire Pond	MassDEP	MassDEP/WPP 303d List 2012 extract			
Big Bearhole Pond	MassDEP	Taunton River Watershed Water Quality Assessment Report 62-AC-1 CN 94.0, December 2005			
Big Bearhole Pond	DCR	DCR Data from Lakes and Ponds, 2002			
Big Bearhole Pond	DCR	DCR Data from Lakes and Ponds, 2007			
Big Bearhole Pond	DCR	DCR Data from Lakes and Ponds, 2008			
Billington Sea	MassDEP	08-F007–05	−70.681001	41.934830	
Buffumville Lake	College of the Holy Cross	Robert Bertin	−71.914557	42.127838	

Waterbody	Agency	Report Source	Longitude	Latitude	First Year Reported
Buffumville Lake	College of the Holy Cross	Robert Bertin	−71.914557	42.127838	
Center Pond	MassDEP	MassDEP/WPP 303d List 2012 extract			
Center Pond	DCR	DCR Data from Lakes and Ponds, 2003			
Charles River	MassDEP	MassDEP/WPP 303d List 2012 extract			
Charles River	Individual	Joy Trahan-Liptak	−71.264994	42.257320	
Charles River	MassDEP	Field Survey 6/26/2017 Wong, Li	−71.190333	42.365145	2007
Charles River	MassDEP	07-A023–01	−71.190333	42.365145	2007
Charles River	MassDEP	07-A017–01	−71.190333	42.365145	2007
Charles River	MassDEP	Field Survey 6/26/2017 Wong, Li	−71.264030	42.326259	
Charles River	MassDEP	10-D005–05	−71.264030	42.326259	
Charles River	MassDEP	Field Survey 6/26/2017 Wong, Li	−71.254393	42.325843	2007
Charles River	MassDEP	07-A017–06	−71.254393	42.325843	2007
Charles River	MassDEP	MassDEP/WPP 303d List 2012 extract			
Charles River	Individual	Joy Trahan-Liptak	−71.257339	42.353321	
Charles River	Individual	Joy Trahan-Liptak	−71.250210	42.360594	
Charles River	Individual	Joy Trahan-Liptak	−71.259812	42.350683	
Charles River	MassDEP	Field Survey 6/26/2017 Li, Wong	−71.513910	42.147718	2007
Charles River	MassDEP	07-A014–01	−71.513910	42.147718	2007
Chauncy Lake	MassDEP	MassDEP/WPP 303d List 2012 extract			
Cheshire Reservoir, Middle Basin	MassDEP	David Worden			
Cheshire Reservoir, Middle Basin	DCR	DCR Data from ACT,GeoSyntec EM-ACT W-A. Madden FEW			1999
Cheshire Reservoir, North Basin	MassDEP	David Worden			
Cheshire Reservoir, North Basin	DCR	David Worden			1999
Cheshire Reservoir, North Basin	Individual	Joy Trahan-Liptak	−73.173237	42.547261	
Cheshire Reservoir, North Basin	Individual	Joy Trahan-Liptak	−73.173237	42.547261	
Cheshire Reservoir, North Basin	Individual	Joy Trahan-Liptak	−73.173237	42.547261	

(Continued)

TABLE 8.1
Table 8.1a Eurasian Milfoil (Continued)

Waterbody	Agency	Report Source	Longitude	Latitude	First Year Reported
Cheshire Reservoir, South Basin	MassDEP	MassDEP/WPP 303d List 2012 extract			
Cheshire Reservoir, South Basin	DCR	DCR Data from ACT, GeoSyntec EM-ACT W-A. Madden FEW			1999
Chicopee River	MassDEP	Field Survey 06/20/2017 Wong, Li	−72.408085	42.178198	
Chicopee River	MassDEP	08-B012–02	−72.408085	42.178198	
Coes Reservoir	MassDEP	MassDEP/WPP 303d List 2012 extract			
Coes Reservoir	Individual	Joy Trahan-Liptak	−71.841568	42.253969	
Coes Reservoir	College of the Holy Cross	Robert Bertin	−71.841584	42.253967	
Concord River	MassDEP	MassDEP/WPP 303d List 2012 extract			
Concord River	MassDEP	MassDEP/WPP 303d List 2012 extract			
Congamond Lakes, Middle Basin	MassDEP	MassDEP/WPP 303d List 2012 extract			
Congamond Lakes, Middle Basin	DCR	DCR Data from Lakes and Ponds, 2005			2005
Congamond Lakes, North Basin	MassDEP	MassDEP/WPP 303d List 2012 extract			
Congamond Lakes, North Basin	DCR	DCR Data from Lakes and Ponds, 2005			2005
Congamond Lakes, South Basin	MassDEP	MassDEP/WPP 303d List 2012 extract			
Congamond Lakes, South Basin	DCR	DCR Data from Lakes and Ponds, 2005			2005
Cranberry Pond	MassDEP	MassDEP/WPP 303d List 2012 extract			
Dark Brook Reservoir	MassDEP	MassDEP/WPP 303d List 2012 extract			
Dark Brook Reservoir	MassDEP	MassDEP/WPP 303d List 2012 extract			
Dark Brook Reservoir	Individual	Joy Trahan-Liptak	−71.863653	42.193762	
Dark Brook Reservoir	Individual	Joy Trahan-Liptak	−71.863653	42.193762	
Devils Dishfull Pond	MassDEP	MassDEP/WPP 303d List 2012 extract			
Dorothy Pond	MassDEP	MassDEP/WPP 303d List 2012 extract			
Dudley Pond	MassDEP	MassDEP/WPP 303d List 2012 extract			

Eurasian Milfoil and Variable Milfoil

Waterbody	Agency	Report Source	Longitude	Latitude	First Year Reported
Ellis Pond	MassDEP	MassDEP/WPP 303d List 2012 extract			
Farm Pond	MassDEP	MassDEP/WPP 303d List 2012 extract			
Fisherville Pond	Individual	Joy Trahan-Liptak	−71.692178	42.184408	
Fisherville Pond	Individual	Joy Trahan-Liptak	−71.692178	42.184408	
Fisk Pond	DCR	DCR Data from Lakes and Ponds, 2008			2008
Flint Pond	MassDEP	MassDEP/WPP 303d List 2012 extract			
Flint Pond	MassDEP	MassDEP/WPP 303d List 2012 extract			
Flint Pond	College of the Holy Cross	Robert Bertin	−71.725087	42.241352	
Flint Pond	College of the Holy Cross	Robert Bertin	−71.725087	42.241352	
Flint Pond	College of the Holy Cross	Robert Bertin	−71.725087	42.241352	
Forest Lake	MassDEP	MassDEP/WPP 303d List 2012 extract			
Forge Pond	DCR	DCR Data from ACT, GeoSyntec			
Fort Meadow Reservoir	MassDEP	MassDEP/WPP 303d List 2012 extract			
Fort Meadow Reservoir	DCR	DCR Data from Lakes and Ponds, 2005	−71.547603	42.369941	2005
Framingham Reservoir #1	MassDEP	MassDEP/WPP 303d List 2012 extract			
Framingham Reservoir #3	MassDEP	MassDEP/WPP 303d List 2012 extract			
Goose Pond Brook	MassDEP	MassDEP/WPP 303d List 2012 extract	−73.226149	42.294173	
Greenwater Pond	MassDEP	EBT Environmental Consultants, Inc			
Greenwater Pond	Individual	Joy Trahan-Liptak	−73.149701	42.284945	
Hayden Pond	DCR	DCR Data from Lakes and Ponds, 2002			2002
Hills Pond	MassDEP	MassDEP/WPP 303d List 2012 extract			
Hocomonco Pond	DCR	DCR Data from Lakes and Ponds, 2005			
Horse Pond	MassDEP	MassDEP/WPP 303d List 2012 extract			
Housatonic River	MassDEP	Field Survey 06/16/2017 Wong, Li, Maldonado	−73.240011	42.284636	
Housatonic River	MassDEP	07-D017–03	−73.240011	42.284636	

(Continued)

TABLE 8.1
Table 8.1a Eurasian Milfoil (Continued)

Waterbody	Agency	Report Source	Longitude	Latitude	First Year Reported
Housatonic River	MassDEP	Field Survey 06/16/2017 Wong, Li, Maldonado	−73.354869	42.231769	
Housatonic River	MassDEP	07-D017–09	−73.354869	42.231769	
Hovey Pond	Individual	Joy Trahan-Liptak	−71.714879	42.234214	
Hubbard Brook	MassDEP	MassDEP/WPP 303d List 2012 extract			
Indian Lake	MassDEP	MassDEP/WPP 303d List 2012 extract			
Jamaica Pond	MassDEP	Field Survey 6/26/2017 Li, Wong	−71.119016	42.317541	
Jamaica Pond	MassDEP	09-A010–07	−71.119016	42.317541	
Knops Pond/Lost Lake	MassDEP	MassDEP/WPP 303d List 2012 extract			
Lake Averic	MassDEP	MassDEP/WPP 303d List 2012 extract			
Lake Buel	MassDEP	MassDEP/WPP 303d List 2012 extract			
Lake Cochituate	Individual	Joy Trahan-Liptak	−71.378621	42.319373	
Lake Cochituate	Individual	Joy Trahan-Liptak	−71.378621	42.319373	
Lake Cochituate	MassDEP	MassDEP/WPP 303d List 2012 extract			
Lake Cochituate	DCR	DCR Data from Lakes and Ponds, 2004			2004
Lake Cochituate	Individual	Joy Trahan-Liptak	−71.371426	42.305669	
Lake Cochituate	Individual	Joy Trahan-Liptak	−71.371426	42.305669	
Lake Cochituate	MassDEP	MassDEP/WPP 303d List 2012 extract			
Lake Cochituate	DCR	DCR Data from Lakes and Ponds, 2003			2003
Lake Cochituate	Individual	Joy Trahan-Liptak	−71.371904	42.300685	
Lake Cochituate	MassDEP	MassDEP/WPP 303d List 2012 extract			
Lake Cochituate	Individual	Joy Trahan-Liptak	−71.369349	42.288313	
Lake Cochituate	Individual	Joy Trahan-Liptak	−71.369349	42.288313	
Lake Cochituate	MassDEP	MassDEP/WPP 303d List 2012 extract			
Lake Cochituate	DCR	DCR Data from Lakes and Ponds, 2004			2004
Lake Garfield	MassDEP	MassDEP/WPP 303d List 2012 extract			
Lake Garfield	DCR	DCR Data from Lakes and Ponds, 2004	−73.197212	42.182427	2004

Waterbody	Agency	Report Source	Longitude	Latitude	First Year Reported
Lake Lorraine	MassDEP	Chicopee River Basin 1998 Water Quality Assessment Report 36-AC-2 47.0, April 2001			
Lake Pearl	MassDEP	MassDEP/WPP 303d List 2012 extract			
Lake Quinsigamond	MassDEP	MassDEP/WPP 303d List 2012 extract			
Lake Quinsigamond	College of the Holy Cross	Robert Bertin	−71.749052	42.256062	
Lake Rico	MassDEP	Taunton River Watershed Water Quality Assessment Report 62-AC-1 CN 94.0, December 2005			
Lake Rico	DCR	DCR Data from Lakes and Ponds, 2002			2002
Lake Ripple	College of the Holy Cross	Robert Bertin	−71.697077	42.213605	
Lake Shirley	MassDEP	MassDEP/WPP 303d List 2012 extract			
Lake Shirley	DCR	DCR Data from ACT, GeoSyntec-ACT			
Lake Waban	MassDEP	MassDEP/WPP 303d List 2012 extract			
Lake Whalom	MassDEP	MassDEP/WPP 303d List 2012 extract			
Laurel Lake	MassDEP	MassDEP/WPP 303d List 2012 extract			
Leesville Pond	Individual	Joy Trahan-Liptak	−71.826444	42.229001	
Leverett Pond	MassDEP	MassDEP/WPP 303d List 2012 extract			
Lily Pond, Middle	DCR	Jamie Carr	−71.769540	42.376670	
Little Alum Pond	DCR	DCR Data from Lakes and Ponds			
Long Pond	MassDEP	MassDEP/WPP 303d List 2012 extract			
Mansfield Pond	MassDEP	MassDEP/WPP 303d List 2012 extract			
Middle Pond	MassDEP	Taunton River Watershed Water Quality Assessment Report 62-AC-1 CN 94.0, December 2005			
Middle Pond	DCR	DCR Data from Lakes and Ponds, 2002			2002

(Continued)

TABLE 8.1

Table 8.1a Eurasian Milfoil (Continued)

Waterbody	Agency	Report Source	Longitude	Latitude	First Year Reported
Middle Pond	DCR	DCR Data from Lakes and Ponds, 2007			2007
Monponsett Pond	MassDEP	10-B003–04	−70.836781	42.001467	
Monponsett Pond	MassDEP	14-B002–02	−70.836781	42.001467	
Monponsett Pond	MassDEP	14-B004–05	−70.836781	42.001467	
Monponsett Pond	MassDEP	14-B006–05	−70.836781	42.001467	
Monponsett Pond	MassDEP	14-B008–05	−70.836781	42.001467	
Monponsett Pond	MassDEP	13-B005–06	−70.836781	42.001467	
Monponsett Pond	MassDEP	13-B006–05	−70.836781	42.001467	
Monponsett Pond	MassDEP	13-B008–05	−70.836781	42.001467	
Monponsett Pond	MassDEP	12-B002–04	−70.836781	42.001467	
Monponsett Pond	MassDEP	12-B004–04	−70.836781	42.001467	
Monponsett Pond	MassDEP	12-B006–05	−70.836781	42.001467	
Monponsett Pond	MassDEP	12-B008–05	−70.836781	42.001467	
Monponsett Pond	MassDEP	11-B006–05	−70.836781	42.001467	
Monponsett Pond	MassDEP	11-B008–02	−70.836781	42.001467	
Monponsett Pond	Individual	Joy Trahan-Liptak	−70.837849	42.005701	
Morses Pond	MassDEP	MassDEP/WPP 303d List 2012 extract			
Mystic River	MassDEP	Field Survey 6/26/2017 Li, Wong	−71.100564	42.411965	2009
Mystic River	MassDEP	09-A008–07	−71.100564	42.411965	2009
Newfield Pond	MassDEP	MassDEP/WPP 303d List 2012 extract			
Oldham Pond	MassDEP	South Shore Coastal Watersheds 2001 Water Quality Assessment Report 94-AC-2 CN 93.0, March 2006			
Onota Lake	MassDEP	MassDEP/WPP 303d List 2012 extract			
Onota Lake	DCR	DCR Data from Lakes and Ponds, 2008			2008
Onota Lake	MassDEP	05-G008–01	−73.283941	42.464926	
Onota Lake	Individual	Joy Trahan-Liptak	−73.281319	42.470479	
Orrs Pond	MassDEP	MassDEP/WPP 303d List 2012 extract			
Otis Reservoir	DCR	Data from ACT,GeoSyntec-ACT	−73.040921	42.151148	
Pequot Pond	MassDEP	MassDEP/WPP 303d List 2012 extract			
Plunkett Reservoir	MassDEP	MassDEP/WPP 303d List 2012 extract			

Eurasian Milfoil and Variable Milfoil

Waterbody	Agency	Report Source	Longitude	Latitude	First Year Reported
Ponkapoag Pond	MassDEP	MassDEP/WPP 303d List 2012 extract			
Pontoosac Lake	MassDEP	MassDEP/WPP 303d List 2012 extract			
Pontoosac Lake	DCR	DCR Data from Lakes and Ponds, 2008			2008
Pontoosac Lake	DCR	DCR Data from ACT, GeoSyntec-ACT			
Purgatory Cove	Individual	Joy Trahan-Liptak	−71.247771	42.358386	
Quaboag Pond	MassDEP	MassDEP/WPP 303d List 2012 extract			
Quaboag Pond	College of the Holy Cross	Robert Bertin	−72.068036	42.197472	
Quacumquasit Pond	MassDEP	MassDEP/WPP 303d List 2012 extract			
Quinsigamond River	Individual	Joy Trahan-Liptak	−71.701242	42.221306	
Quinsigamond River	MassDEP	MassDEP/WPP 303d List 2012 extract			
Reservoir Pond	MassDEP	09-B009–02	−71.126217	42.170467	
Rice City Pond	Individual	Joy Trahan-Liptak	−71.622465	42.100003	
Rice City Pond	Individual	Joy Trahan-Liptak	−71.622465	42.100003	
Richmond Pond	MassDEP	MassDEP/WPP 303d List 2012 extract			
Richmond Pond	Individual	Joy Trahan-Liptak	−73.324741	42.415098	
Richmond Pond	Individual	Joy Trahan-Liptak	−73.324741	42.415098	
Shaker Mill Pond	MassDEP	MassDEP/WPP 303d List 2012 extract			
Shaker Mill Pond	DCR	DCR Data from National Heritage 2005			2005
Shaker Mill Pond	Individual	Joy Trahan-Liptak	−73.369417	42.338953	
Shaw Pond	MassDEP	MassDEP/WPP 303d List 2012 extract			
Silver Lake	DCR	DCR Data from Lakes and Ponds, 2008			2008
Singletary Pond	MassDEP	MassDEP/WPP 303d List 2012 extract			
Sluice Pond	MassDEP	MassDEP/WPP 303d List 2012 extract			
Sluice Pond	DCR	DCR Data from Lakes and Ponds, 2005			2005
Spy Pond	MassDEP	MassDEP/WPP 303d List 2012 extract			
Stetson Pond	MassDEP	Taunton River Watershed Water Quality Assessment Report 62-AC-1 CN 94.0, December 2005			

(Continued)

TABLE 8.1
Table 8.1a Eurasian Milfoil (Continued)

Waterbody	Agency	Report Source	Longitude	Latitude	First Year Reported
Stevens Pond	MassDEP	MassDEP/WPP 303d List 2012 extract			
Stockbridge Bowl	MassDEP	MassDEP/WPP 303d List 2012 extract			
Sudbury Reservoir	College of the Holy Cross	Robert Bertin	−71.510778	42.321064	
Sudbury River	MassDEP	Field Survey 6/26/2017 Li, Wong	−71.397364	42.325435	2008
Sudbury River	MassDEP	08-M003–02	−71.397364	42.325435	2008
Sunset Lake	MassDEP	MassDEP/WPP 303d List 2012 extract			
Thousand Acre Pond	MassDEP	MassDEP/WPP 303d List 2012 extract			
Unionville Pond	DCR	Jamie Carr	−71.842015	42.359704	
Unionville Pond	DCR	Joy Trahan-Liptak	−71.842015	42.359704	
Unionville Pond	MassDEP	MassDEP/WPP 303d List 2012 extract			
Upper Goose Pond	MassDEP	MassDEP/WPP 303d List 2012 extract			
Wachusett Reservoir	DCR	David Worden	−71.787817	42.397107	
Wachusett Reservoir	DCR	David Worden	−71.788251	42.379206	
Wachusett Reservoir	DCR	David Worden	−71.789929	42.389998	
Wachusett Reservoir	DCR	David Worden	−71.787817	42.397107	
Wachusett Reservoir	DCR	David Worden	−71.774821	42.375014	
Wachusett Reservoir	DCR	Jamie Carr	−71.730707	42.380071	
Wachusett Reservoir	DCR	Jamie Carr	−71.789929	42.389998	
Wachusett Reservoir	DCR	Jamie Carr	−71.787817	42.397107	
Wachusett Reservoir	DCR	Jamie Carr	−71.788251	42.379206	
Wachusett Reservoir	DCR	Jamie Carr	−71.795345	42.384187	
Wachusett Reservoir	MassDEP	MassDEP/WPP 303d List 2012 extract			
Wachusett Reservoir	DCR	DCR Data from ACT, GeoSyntec-ACT			
Wachusett Reservoir	College of the Holy Cross	Robert Bertin	−71.787817	42.397107	

Eurasian Milfoil and Variable Milfoil

Waterbody	Agency	Report Source	Longitude	Latitude	First Year Reported
Wachusett Reservoir	DCR	Joy Trahan-Liptak	−71.787060	42.414454	
Webster Lake	MassDEP	MassDEP/WPP 303d List 2012 extract			
White Island Pond, East Basin	MassDEP	07-T003–02	−70.617531	41.809183	
Whiting Street Reservoir	MassDEP	MassDEP/WPP 303d List 2012 extract			
Willard Brook	MassDEP	MassDEP/WPP 303d List 2012 extract			
Windsor Pond	MassDEP	MassDEP/WPP 303d List 2012 extract			
Windsor Pond	DCR	DCR Data from Lakes and Ponds, 2002			2002
Winning Pond	MassDEP	MassDEP/WPP 303d List 2012 extract			
Woolshop Pond	MassDEP	09-G009–01	−71.749543	42.194774	
Yokum Pond	DCR	DCR Data from Lakes and Ponds, 2003			2003
Yokum Pond	DCR	DCR Data from Lakes and Ponds, 2005			2005

Table 8.1b Variable Milfoil

Waterbody	Agency	Report Source	Longitude	Latitude	First Year Reported
Aaron Reservoir	Individual	Joy Trahan-Liptak	−70.827339	42.206855	
Aaron Reservoir	Individual	Joy Trahan-Liptak	−70.827339	42.206855	
Aaron Reservoir	Individual	Joy Trahan-Liptak	−70.827339	42.206855	
Aldrich Pond	MassDEP	Blackstone River Basin 1998 Water Quality Assessment Report 51-AC-1 48.0, May 2011			
Aldrich Pond	MassDEP	Field Survey 6/26/2017 Wong, Li	−71.740259	42.163314	2009
Aldrich Pond	MassDEP	09-G008–06	−71.740259	42.163314	2009
Ames Long Pond	MassDEP	Taunton River Watershed Water Quality Assessment Report 62-AC-1 CN 94.0, December 2005			
Arcade Pond	MassDEP	Field Survey 6/26/2017 Wong, Li	−71.677520	42.112961	
Arcade Pond	MassDEP	09-G010–02	−71.677520	42.112961	
Arcadia Lake	MassDEP	Connecticut River Basin 2003 Water Quality Assessment Report 34-AC-2 CN 105.5, October 2008			
Ashland Reservoir	MassDEP	SuAsCo Watershed 2001 Water Quality Assessment Report 82-AC-1 CN 92.0, August 2005			

(Continued)

TABLE 8.1
Table 8.1b Variable Milfoil (Continued)

Waterbody	Agency	Report Source	Longitude	Latitude	First Year Reported
Ashland Reservoir	DCR	DCR Data from Lakes and Ponds Pioneer Infestation, 2008	−71.464892	42.240261	2008
Baddacook Pond	MassDEP	05-G001–01	−71.530464	42.618962	
Baddacook Pond	DCR	DCR Data from Lakes and Ponds, 2002	−71.530464	42.618962	
Bailey Road Pond	DCR	Joy Trahan-Liptak	−71.854850	42.343790	
Bare Hill Pond	MassDEP	Nashua River Watershed 2003 Water Quality Assessment Report 81-AC-4 CN107.5, August 2008			
Bare Hill Pond	College of the Holy Cross	Robert Bertin	−71.597616	42.491779	
Bartlett Pond	College of the Holy Cross	Robert Bertin	−71.617660	42.318598	
Beaver Lake	MassDEP	Chicopee River Basin 1998 Water Quality Assessment Report 36-AC-2 47.0, April 2001			
Beaver Pond	MassDEP	Charles River Watershed 2002–2006 Water Quality Assessment Report 72-AC-4 CN136.5, April 2008			
Beaver Pond	DCR	DCR Data from Lakes and Ponds, 2002			
Bennett Pond	Individual	Joy Trahan-Liptak	−72.451889	42.091374	
Billings Street/East Street Pond	MassDEP	Neponset River Watershed 2004 Water Quality Assessment Report 73-AC-1 CN170.4, February 2010			
Billington Sea	MassDEP	08-F003–05	−70.681001	41.934830	
Black Mountain Pond	MassDEP	South Shore Coastal Watersheds 2001 Water Quality Assessment Report 94-AC-2 CN 93.0, March 2006			
Blackstone River	MassDEP	Field Survey 6/26/2017 Li, Wong	−71.778069	42.202922	
Blackstone River	MassDEP	08-A032–07	−71.778069	42.202922	
Boons Pond	Individual	Joy Trahan-Liptak	−71.502252	42.396447	
Boons Pond	Individual	Joy Trahan-Liptak	−71.502252	42.396447	
Boons Pond	MassDEP	SuAsCo Watershed 2001 Water Quality Assessment Report 82-AC-1 CN 92.0, August 2005			
Bouchard Pond	MassDEP	French and Quinebaug River Watersheds 2004–2008 Water Quality Assessment Report 41/42-AC-2 178.5, November 2009			

Waterbody	Agency	Report Source	Longitude	Latitude	First Year Reported
Brierly Pond	MassDEP	Blackstone River Basin 1998 Water Quality Assessment Report 51-AC-1 48.0, May 2011			
Brigham Pond	DCR	Jamie Carr	−71.998532	42.472474	
Brooks Pond	MassDEP	Chicopee River Basin 1998 Water Quality Assessment Report 36-AC-2 47.0, April 2001			
Brooks Pond	College of the Holy Cross	Robert Bertin	−72.043108	42.302192	
Brooks Pond	College of the Holy Cross	Robert Bertin	−72.043108	42.302192	
Browning Pond	MassDEP	Chicopee River Basin 1998 Water Quality Assessment Report 36-AC-2 47.0, April 2001			
Browning Pond	DCR	DCR Data from Lakes and Ponds, 2007			
Buck Pond	MassDEP	Westfield River Watershed 2001 Water Quality Assessment Report 32-AC-1 CN 090.0, April 2005			
Buffum Pond	MassDEP	French and Quinebaug River Watersheds 2001 Water Quality Assessment Report 41/42-AC-1 51.0, March 2002			
Buffumville Lake	MassDEP	French and Quinebaug River Watersheds 2001 Water Quality Assessment Report 41/42-AC-1 51.0, March 2002			
Buffumville Lake	College of the Holy Cross	Robert Bertin	−71.911424	42.112068	
Burncoat Pond	College of the Holy Cross	Robert Bertin	−71.948645	42.240126	
Carver Pond	MassDEP	Taunton River Watershed Water Quality Assessment Report 62-AC-1 CN 94.0, December 2005			
Cedar Meadow Pond	MassDEP	French and Quinebaug River Watersheds 2001 Water Quality Assessment Report 41/42-AC-1 51.0, March 2002			
Cedar Pond	MassDEP	French and Quinebaug River Watersheds 2001 Water Quality Assessment Report 41/42-AC-1 51.0, March 2002			
Cedar Swamp Pond	MassDEP	Charles River Watershed 2002–2006 Water Quality Assessment Report 72-AC-4 CN136.5, April 2008			

(Continued)

TABLE 8.1
Table 8.1b Variable Milfoil (Continued)

Waterbody	Agency	Report Source	Longitude	Latitude	First Year Reported
Cedar Swamp Pond	Individual	Joy Trahan-Liptak	−71.513609	42.153435	
Cedar Swamp Pond	College of the Holy Cross	Robert Bertin	−71.513609	42.153435	
Chaffin Pond	DCR	Joy Trahan-Liptak	−71.839483	42.331244	
Charles River	MassDEP	Charles River Watershed 2002–2006 Water Quality Assessment Report 72-AC-4 CN136.5, April 2008			
Clark Pond	MassDEP	Neponset River Watershed 2004 Water Quality Assessment Report 73-AC-1 CN170.4, February 2010			
Clear Pond	DCR	DCR Data from Lakes and Ponds, 2005			2005
Cleveland Pond	DCR	DCR Data from Lakes and Ponds, 2008			1999
Coachlace Pond	DCR	Jamie Carr	−71.697104	42.413367	
Cocasset Lake	Individual	Joy Trahan-Liptak	−71.259580	42.058531	
Collins Pond	DCR	DCR Data from Lakes and Ponds, 2008			2008
Comins Pond	College of the Holy Cross	Robert Bertin	−72.195658	42.203643	
Cook Pond	College of the Holy Cross	Robert Bertin	−71.858373	42.285515	
Crane Brook Bog Pond	MassDEP	Buzzards Bay Watershed 2000 Water Quality Assessment Report 95-AC-2 085.0, November 2003			
Crocker Pond	DCR	DCR Data from Lakes and Ponds, 2007			2007
Curtis Pond	College of the Holy Cross	Robert Bertin	−71.838502	42.241484	
Dark Brook	MassDEP	Blackstone River Watershed 2003–2007 Water Quality Assessment Report 51-AC-3 CN 240.0, March 2010			
Dark Brook Reservoir	MassDEP	Blackstone River Basin 1998 Water Quality Assessment Report 51-AC-148.0, May 2011			
Dawson Pond	MassDEP	Nashua River Watershed 2003 Water Quality Assessment Report 81-AC-4 CN107.5, August 2008			
Dawson Pond	DCR	Joy Trahan-Liptak	−71.852208	42.335114	

Waterbody	Agency	Report Source	Longitude	Latitude	First Year Reported
Dean Pond	MassDEP	Chicopee River Watershed 2003 Water Quality Assessment Report 36-AC-3 CN 106.5, October 2008			
Dean Pond	DCR	DCR Data from Lakes and Ponds, 2003			2003
Demond Pond	College of the Holy Cross	Robert Bertin	−71.970411	42.352339	
Doane Pond	College of the Holy Cross	Robert Bertin	−72.072370	42.285721	
Eagle Lake	MassDEP	Nashua River Watershed 2003 Water Quality Assessment Report 81-AC-4 CN107.5, August 2008			
Eagle Lake	DCR	Joy Trahan-Liptak	−71.885094	42.356095	
Eagle Lake	College of the Holy Cross	Robert Bertin	−71.884555	42.356373	
East Brimfield Reservoir	MassDEP	French and Quinebaug River Watersheds 2001 Water Quality Assessment Report 41/42-AC-1 51.0, March 2002			
East Brimfield Reservoir	DCR	DCR: Lakes and Ponds, 2007			2007
East Brimfield Reservoir	Individual	Joy Trahan-Liptak	−72.134224	42.109406	
East Brookfield River	MassDEP	Field Survey 06/16/2017 Wong, Li, Maldonado	−72.049996	42.225710	
East Brookfield River	MassDEP	08-B032–05	−72.049996	42.225710	
East Brookfield River	MassDEP	08-B021–05	−72.049996	42.225710	
East Brookfield River	MassDEP	08-B013–05	−72.049996	42.225710	
East Brookfield River	MassDEP	08-B005–05	−72.049996	42.225710	
East Freetown Pond	MassDEP	Taunton River Watershed Water Quality Assessment Report 62-AC-1 CN 94.0, December 2005			
East Head Pond	DCR	DCR Data from Lakes and Ponds, humile 2008			2008
Eddy Pond	MassDEP	Blackstone River Basin 1998 Water Quality Assessment Report 51-AC-1 48.0, May 2011			
Eddy Pond	College of the Holy Cross	Robert Bertin	−71.844001	42.181076	

(Continued)

TABLE 8.1
Table 8.1b Variable Milfoil (Continued)

Waterbody	Agency	Report Source	Longitude	Latitude	First Year Reported
Ellis Pond	MassDEP	Millers River Watershed 2000 Water Quality Assessment Report 35-AC-1 CN089.0, March 2004			
Ellis Pond	College of the Holy Cross	Robert Bertin	−72.204192	42.577244	
Factory Pond	MassDEP	Charles River Watershed 2002–2006 Water Quality Assessment Report 72-AC-4 CN136.5, April 2008			
Falls Pond, South Basin	MassDEP	Ten Mile River Watershed 2002 Water Quality Assessment Report 52-AC-2 CN 137.5, June 2006			
Farrington Pond	MassDEP	Neponset River Watershed 2004 Water Quality Assessment Report 73-AC-1 CN170.4, February 2010			
Federal Pond	MassDEP	Buzzards Bay Watershed 2000 Water Quality Assessment Report 95-AC-2 085.0, November 2003			
Field Pond	DCR	DCR Data from Lakes and Ponds, 2007			2007
First Pond	DCR	DCR Data from Lakes and Ponds, 2006			2006
Fish Pond	MassDEP	Blackstone River Basin 1998 Water Quality Assessment Report 51-AC-1 48.0, May 2011			
Fisk Pond	MassDEP	SuAsCo Watershed 2001 Water Quality Assessment Report 82-AC-1 CN 92.0, August 2005			
Fisk Pond	DCR	DCR Data from Lakes and Ponds, 2008			2008
Flannagan Pond	MassDEP	Nashua River Watershed 2003 Water Quality Assessment Report 81-AC-4 CN107.5, August 2008			
Flint Pond	MassDEP	Blackstone River Basin 1998 Water Quality Assessment Report 51-AC-1 48.0, May 2011			
Flint Pond	Individual	Joy Trahan-Liptak	−71.725688	42.240948	
Flint Pond	College of the Holy Cross	Robert Bertin	−71.725087	42.241352	

Waterbody	Agency	Report Source	Longitude	Latitude	First Year Reported
Flint Pond	MassDEP	Merrimack River Basin 1999 Water Quality Assessment Report 84-AC-1 52.0, November 2001			
Flint Pond	DCR	DCR Data from Lakes and Ponds, 2008			2008
Fort Meadow Reservoir	DCR	DCR Data from Lakes and Ponds, 2005	−71.547603	42.369941	2005
Framingham Reservoir #1	MassDEP	SuAsCo Watershed 2001 Water Quality Assessment Report 82-AC-1 CN 92.0, August 2005			
French River	MassDEP	Field Survey 06/16/2017 Wong, Li, Maldonado	−71.885074	42.050945	
French River	MassDEP	10-I002–05	−71.885074	42.050945	
French River	MassDEP	09-P004–05	−71.885074	42.050945	
French River	MassDEP	08-N006–04	−71.885074	42.050945	
French River	MassDEP	08-N005–04	−71.885074	42.050945	
French River	MassDEP	08-N004–04	−71.885074	42.050945	
French River	MassDEP	08-N003–04	−71.885074	42.050945	
French River	MassDEP	07-M005–04	−71.885074	42.050945	
French River	MassDEP	07-M004–04	−71.885074	42.050945	
French River	MassDEP	07-M003–04	−71.885074	42.050945	
French River	MassDEP	07-M001–04	−71.885074	42.050945	
French River	MassDEP	06-J006–04	−71.885074	42.050945	
French River	MassDEP	06-J005–04	−71.885074	42.050945	
French River	MassDEP	06-J004–04	−71.885074	42.050945	
French River	MassDEP	06-J003–04	−71.885074	42.050945	
French River	MassDEP	05-M004–04	−71.885074	42.050945	
French River	MassDEP	05-M003–04	−71.885074	42.050945	
Frye Pond	DCR	DCR Data from Lakes and Ponds, 2008			
Fuller Street Pond	MassDEP	Taunton River Watershed Water Quality Assessment Report 62-AC-1 CN 94.0, December 2005			
Gaston Pond	College of the Holy Cross	Robert Bertin	−72.130135	42.455926	
Gaston Pond	College of the Holy Cross	Robert Bertin	−72.130135	42.455926	
Gavins Pond	MassDEP	Taunton River Watershed Water Quality Assessment Report 62-AC-1 CN 94.0, December 2005			
Gilboa Pond	College of the Holy Cross	Robert Bertin	−71.701442	42.081995	
Glen Echo Pond	MassDEP	Neponset River Watershed 2004 Water Quality Assessment Report 73-AC-1 CN170.4, February 2010			

(Continued)

TABLE 8.1
Table 8.1b Variable Milfoil (Continued)

Waterbody	Agency	Report Source	Longitude	Latitude	First Year Reported
Gore Pond	MassDEP	French and Quinebaug River Watersheds 2001 Water Quality Assessment Report 41/42-AC-1 51.0, March 2002			
Granite Reservoir	MassDEP	French and Quinebaug River Watersheds 2001 Water Quality Assessment Report 41/42-AC-1 51.0, March 2002			
Greenville Pond	College of the Holy Cross	Robert Bertin	−71.922721	42.205981	
Griswold Pond	MassDEP	North Shore Coastal Watersheds 2002 Water Quality Assessment Report 93-AC-2 CN 138.5, March 2007			
Grove Pond	MassDEP	Nashua River Watershed 2003 Water Quality Assessment Report 81-AC-4 CN107.5, August 2008			
Gushee Pond	MassDEP	Taunton River Watershed Water Quality Assessment Report 62-AC-1 CN 94.0, December 2005			
Hamilton Reservoir	MassDEP	French and Quinebaug River Watersheds 2001 Water Quality Assessment Report 41/42-AC-1 51.0, March 2002			
Hardwick Pond	MassDEP	Chicopee River Basin 1998 Water Quality Assessment Report 36-AC-2 47.0, April 2001			
Hardwick Pond	College of the Holy Cross	Robert Bertin	−72.238600	42.313254	
Hobart Pond	MassDEP	Taunton River Watershed Water Quality Assessment Report 62-AC-1 CN 94.0, December 2005			
Hoosicwhisick Pond	Individual	Joy Trahan-Liptak	−71.095558	42.207250	
Hoosicwhisick Pond	DCR	DCR Data from Lakes and Ponds, 2008			2007
Hopkinton Reservoir	MassDEP	SuAsCo Watershed 2001 Water Quality Assessment Report 82-AC-1 CN 92.0, August 2005			
Hopkinton Reservoir	DCR	DCR Data from Lakes and Ponds, 2007			2007
Hopkinton Reservoir	DCR	DCR Data from Lakes and Ponds, 2008			2007
Hopkinton Reservoir	MassDEP	Field Survey 6/26/2017 Li, Wong	−71.513377	42.256563	

Eurasian Milfoil and Variable Milfoil

Waterbody	Agency	Report Source	Longitude	Latitude	First Year Reported
Hopkinton Reservoir	MassDEP	05-G007–02	−71.513377	42.256563	
Horse Pond	MassDEP	Westfield River Watershed 2001 Water Quality Assessment Report 32-AC-1 CN 090.0, April 2005			
Hovey Pond	Individual	Joy Trahan-Liptak	−71.714879	42.234214	
Howe Pond	DCR	DCR Data from Lakes and Ponds, 2008	−71.999715	42.215269	
Howe Pond	College of the Holy Cross	Robert Bertin	−71.999715	42.215269	
Howe Reservoirs	MassDEP	Blackstone River Basin 1998 Water Quality Assessment Report 51-AC-1 48.0, May 2011			
Indian Brook	MassDEP	Field Survey 7/18/2017 Wong, Maldonado	−70.538045	41.887150	
Indian Brook	MassDEP	08-F009–03	−70.538045	41.887150	
Indian Brook	MassDEP	08-F006–01	−70.538045	41.887150	
Ironstone Reservoir	College of the Holy Cross	Robert Bertin	−71.610900	42.024298	
Jacobs Pond	MassDEP	South Shore Coastal Watersheds 2001 Water Quality Assessment Report 94-AC-2 CN 93.0, March 2006			
Jenks Reservoir	MassDEP	Blackstone River Basin 1998 Water Quality Assessment Report 51-AC-1 48.0, May 2011			
Jewells Pond	MassDEP	Neponset River Watershed 2004 Water Quality Assessment Report 73-AC-1 CN170.4, February 2010			
Kettle Brook	MassDEP	Blackstone River Watershed 2003–2007 Water Quality Assessment Report 51-AC-3 CN 240.0, March 2010			
Knops Pond/Lost Lake	MassDEP	Merrimack River Basin 1999 Water Quality Assessment Report 84-AC-1 52.0, November 2001			
Knops Pond/Lost Lake	DCR	DCR Data from Lakes and Ponds, 2002			2002
Lake Cochituate	Individual	Joy Trahan-Liptak	−71.371426	42.305669	
Lake Cochituate	MassDEP	SuAsCo Watershed 2001 Water Quality Assessment Report 82-AC-1 CN 92.0, August 2005			

(Continued)

TABLE 8.1
Table 8.1b Variable Milfoil (Continued)

Waterbody	Agency	Report Source	Longitude	Latitude	First Year Reported
Lake Cochituate	DCR	DCR Data from Lakes and Ponds, 2003			2003
Lake Cochituate	MassDEP	SuAsCo Watershed 2001 Water Quality Assessment Report 82-AC-1 CN 92.0, August 2005			
Lake Cochituate	Individual	Joy Trahan-Liptak	−71.369349	42.288313	
Lake Cochituate	MassDEP	SuAsCo Watershed 2001 Water Quality Assessment Report 82-AC-1 CN 92.0, August 2005			
Lake Cochituate	DCR	DCR Data from Lakes and Ponds, 2004			2004
Lake Holland	MassDEP	Connecticut River Basin 2003 Water Quality Assessment Report 34-AC-2 CN 105.5, October 2008			
Lake Mattawa	DCR	DCR Data from Lakes and Ponds, 2003			2003
Lake Monomonac	MassDEP	Millers River Watershed 2000 Water Quality Assessment Report 35-AC-1 CN089.0, March 2004			
Lake Pearl	MassDEP	Charles River Watershed 2002–2006 Water Quality Assessment Report 72-AC-4 CN136.5, April 2008			
Lake Quinsigamond	MassDEP	Blackstone River Basin 1998 Water Quality Assessment Report 51-AC-1 48.0, May 2011			
Lake Quinsigamond	College of the Holy Cross	Robert Bertin	−71.749052	42.256062	
Lake Quinsigamond	College of the Holy Cross	Robert Bertin	−71.749052	42.256062	
Lake Rico	DCR	DCR Data from Lakes and Ponds, 2002			2002
Lake Ripple	MassDEP	Blackstone River Basin 1998 Water Quality Assessment Report 51-AC-1 48.0, May 2011			
Lake Rohunta	DCR	DCR Data from Lakes and Ponds, Mattawa			
Lake Sabbatia	MassDEP	Taunton River Watershed Water Quality Assessment Report 62-AC-1 CN 94.0, December 2005			
Lake Samoset	MassDEP	Nashua River Watershed 2003 Water Quality Assessment Report 81-AC-4 CN107.5, August 2008			

Waterbody	Agency	Report Source	Longitude	Latitude	First Year Reported
Lake Shirley	MassDEP	Nashua River Watershed 2003 Water Quality Assessment Report 81-AC-4 CN107.5, August 2008			
Lake Shirley	DCR	DCR Data from ACT, GeoSyntec-ACT			
Lake Whalom	MassDEP	Nashua River Watershed 2003 Water Quality Assessment Report 81-AC-4 CN107.5, August 2008			
Lake Whalom	College of the Holy Cross	Robert Bertin	−71.740747	42.574132	
Lake Winthrop	MassDEP	Charles River Watershed 2002–2006 Water Quality Assessment Report 72-AC-4 CN136.5, April 2008			
Lancaster Millpond	DCR	Jamie Carr	−71.684545	42.407616	
Larner Pond	MassDEP	French and Quinebaug River Watersheds 2001 Water Quality Assessment Report 41/42-AC-1 51.0, March 2002			
Leesville Pond	Individual	Joy Trahan-Liptak	−71.826444	42.229001	
Leesville Pond	College of the Holy Cross	Robert Bertin	−71.827414	42.230332	
Leonards Pond	MassDEP	05-R003–02	−70.804664	41.750263	2005
Lily Pond	MassDEP	South Shore Coastal Watersheds 2001 Water Quality Assessment Report 94-AC-2 CN 93.0, March 2006			
Little Chauncy Pond	MassDEP	SuAsCo Watershed 2001 Water Quality Assessment Report 82-AC-1 CN 92.0, August 2005			
Little Chauncy Pond	College of the Holy Cross	Robert Bertin	−71.617285	42.306107	
Little River	Individual	Joy Trahan-Liptak	−71.883731	42.110570	
Long Island Pond	MassDEP	South Shore Coastal Watersheds 2001 Water Quality Assessment Report 94-AC-2 CN 93.0, March 2006			
Long Pond	MassDEP	Chicopee River Basin 1998 Water Quality Assessment Report 36-AC-2 47.0, April 2001			
Long Pond	DCR	DCR Data from Lakes and Ponds, 2003			2003
Long Pond	DCR	DCR Data from Lakes and Ponds, 2007			2003

(Continued)

TABLE 8.1
Table 8.1b Variable Milfoil (Continued)

Waterbody	Agency	Report Source	Longitude	Latitude	First Year Reported
Long Pond	DCR	DCR Data from Lakes and Ponds, 2008			2003
Long Pond	MassDEP	Taunton River Watershed Water Quality Assessment Report 62-AC-1 CN 94.0, December 2005			
Longwater Pond	MassDEP	Taunton River Watershed Water Quality Assessment Report 62-AC-1 CN 94.0, December 2005			
Lorings Bogs Pond	MassDEP	South Shore Coastal Watersheds 2001 Water Quality Assessment Report 94-AC-2 CN 93.0, March 2006			
Louisa Lake	College of the Holy Cross	Robert Bertin	−71.523061	42.158817	
Low Pond	MassDEP	French and Quinebaug River Watersheds 2001 Water Quality Assessment Report 41/42-AC-1 51.0, March 2002	−70.707816	41.876262	
Manchaug Pond	MassDEP	Blackstone River Basin 1998 Water Quality Assessment Report 51-AC-1 48.0, May 2011			
Mansfield Pond	College of the Holy Cross	Robert Bertin	−71.583462	42.019005	
Maple Spring Pond	DCR	Jamie Carr	−71.882155	42.376553	
Maple Spring Pond	DCR	Joy Trahan-Liptak	−71.882155	42.376553	
Marble Pond	MassDEP	Blackstone River Basin 1998 Water Quality Assessment Report 51-AC-1 48.0, May 2011			
Marble Pond	MassDEP	Field Survey 6/26/2017 Wong, Li	−71.742251	42.165436	
Marble Pond	MassDEP	09-G008–05	−71.742251	42.165436	
Massapoag Lake	MassDEP	Neponset River Watershed 2004 Water Quality Assessment Report 73-AC-1 CN170.4, February 2010			2016
Massapoag Lake	Individual	Joy Trahan-Liptak	−71.177528	42.103486	
Massapoag Lake	Individual	Joy Trahan-Liptak	−71.177528	42.103486	
Massapoag Pond	MassDEP	Merrimack River Basin 1999 Water Quality Assessment Report 84-AC-1 52.0, November 2001			
Merrill Pond No.4	College of the Holy Cross	Robert Bertin	−71.794120	42.137816	

Eurasian Milfoil and Variable Milfoil

Waterbody	Agency	Report Source	Longitude	Latitude	First Year Reported
Metacomet Lake	MassDEP	Connecticut River Basin 2003 Water Quality Assessment Report 34-AC-2 CN 105.5, October 2008			
Middle River	MassDEP	Field Survey 06/16/2017 Wong, Li, Maldonado	−71.825842	42.239095	
Middle River	MassDEP	11-D006–07	−71.825842	42.239095	
Mill Brook	MassDEP	French and Quinebaug River Watersheds 2001 Water Quality Assessment Report 41/42-AC-1 51.0, March 2002			
Mill Pond	MassDEP	Blackstone River Basin 1998 Water Quality Assessment Report 51-AC-1 48.0, May 2011			
Mill Pond	MassDEP	Buzzards Bay Watershed2000 Water Quality Assessment Report 95-AC-2 085.0, November 2003			
Mill River	MassDEP	Blackstone River Watershed 2003–2007 Water Quality Assessment Report 51-AC-3 CN 240.0, March 2010			
Mill River	MassDEP	Field Survey 6/26/2017 Wong, Li	−71.564216	42.166266	
Mill River	MassDEP	09-G010–06	−71.564216	42.166266	
Millers River	MassDEP	Field Survey 06/20/2017 Wong, Li	−72.341352	42.598155	
Millers River	MassDEP	05-H005–06	−72.341352	42.598155	2005
Miscoe Lake	MassDEP	Blackstone River Basin 1998 Water Quality Assessment Report 51-AC-1 48.0, May 2011			
Monoosnuc Brook	MassDEP	Field Survey 06/20/2017 Wong, Li	−71.737768	42.524956	
Monoosnuc Brook	MassDEP	08-G025–09	−71.737768	42.524956	
Monoosnuc Brook	MassDEP	08-G018–09	−71.737768	42.524956	
Monponsett Pond	MassDEP	14-B002–02	−70.836781	42.001467	
Monponsett Pond	MassDEP	14-B004–05	−70.836781	42.001467	
Monponsett Pond	MassDEP	14-B006–05	−70.836781	42.001467	
Monponsett Pond	MassDEP	14-B008–05	−70.836781	42.001467	
Monponsett Pond	MassDEP	13-B005–06	−70.836781	42.001467	
Monponsett Pond	MassDEP	13-B006–05	−70.836781	42.001467	
Monponsett Pond	MassDEP	13-B008–05	−70.836781	42.001467	
Monponsett Pond	MassDEP	12-B002–04	−70.836781	42.001467	
Monponsett Pond	MassDEP	12-B004–04	−70.836781	42.001467	
Monponsett Pond	MassDEP	11-B006–05	−70.836781	42.001467	

(Continued)

TABLE 8.1
Table 8.1b Variable Milfoil (Continued)

Waterbody	Agency	Report Source	Longitude	Latitude	First Year Reported
Monponsett Pond	MassDEP	11-B008–02	−70.836781	42.001467	
Monponsett Pond	Individual	Joy Trahan-Liptak	−70.837849	42.005701	
Moosehorn Pond	DCR	Jamie Carr	−71.968290	42.469370	
Moosehorn Pond	MassDEP	Chicopee River Basin 1998 Water Quality Assessment Report 36-AC-2 47.0, April 2001			
Moosehorn Pond	Individual	Joy Trahan-Liptak	−71.968290	42.469370	
Moosehorn Pond	College of the Holy Cross	Robert Bertin	−71.968290	42.469370	
Morse Pond	College of the Holy Cross	Robert Bertin	−72.013852	42.031608	
Morses Pond	MassDEP	Charles River Watershed 2002–2006 Water Quality Assessment Report 72-AC-4 CN136.5, April 2008			
Mossy Pond	DCR	Jamie Carr	−71.701034	42.417156	
Nabnasset Pond	MassDEP	Merrimack River Watershed 2004–2009 Water Quality Assessment Report 84-AC-2 CN179.5, January 2010			
Nashua River	MassDEP	Field Survey 6/26/2017 Wong, Li	−71.593150	42.626477	2008
Nashua River	MassDEP	10-K002–05	−71.593150	42.626477	2008
Nashua River	MassDEP	08-Q005–05	−71.593150	42.626477	2008
Nashua River	MassDEP	08-Q004–05	−71.593150	42.626477	2008
Nashua River	MassDEP	Field Survey 6/26/2017 Li, Wong	−71.679300	42.429974	
Nashua River	MassDEP	08-G032–02	−71.679300	42.429974	
Nashua River	MassDEP	08-G028–02	−71.679300	42.429974	
Nashua River	MassDEP	08-G020–02	−71.679300	42.429974	
Nashua River	MassDEP	08-G008–02	−71.679300	42.429974	
Neponset River	MassDEP	Field Survey 7/7/2017 Wong, Maldonado	−71.185944	42.171871	
Neponset River	MassDEP	09-B018–02	−71.185944	42.171871	
Neponset River	MassDEP	09-B016–02	−71.185944	42.171871	
Neponset River	MassDEP	09-B014–02	−71.185944	42.171871	
Neponset River	MassDEP	09-B005–02	−71.185944	42.171871	
New Bedford Reservoir	MassDEP	Buzzards Bay Watershed 2000 Water Quality Assessment Report 95-AC-2 085.0, November 2003			
Newton Pond	MassDEP	Blackstone River Basin 1998 Water Quality Assessment Report 51-AC-1 48.0, May 2011			

Waterbody	Agency	Report Source	Longitude	Latitude	First Year Reported
Nipmuck Lake	Individual	Joy Trahan-Liptak	−71.569912	42.096429	
Noannet Pond	MassDEP	Charles River Watershed 2002–2006 Water Quality Assessment Report 72-AC-4 CN136.5, April 2008			
Noquochoke Lake	MassDEP	Buzzards Bay Watershed2000 Water Quality Assessment Report 95-AC-2 085.0, November 2003			
Noquochoke Lake	MassDEP	Buzzards Bay Watershed2000 Water Quality Assessment Report 95-AC-2 085.0, November 2003	−71.043280		
Noquochoke Lake	MassDEP	Buzzards Bay Watershed2000 Water Quality Assessment Report 95-AC-2 085.0, November 2003	−71.523061		
North Pond	MassDEP	Blackstone River Basin 1998 Water Quality Assessment Report 51-AC-1 48.0, May 2011			
North Pond	DCR	DCR Data from Lakes and Ponds, 2008			2008
Norton Reservoir	MassDEP	Taunton River Watershed Water Quality Assessment Report 62-AC-1 CN 94.0, December 2005			
Noyes Pond	MassDEP	Farmington River Watershed 2001 Water Quality Assessment Report 31-AC-2 CN 091.0, January 2005			
Old Oaken Bucket Pond	MassDEP	South Shore Coastal Watersheds 2001 Water Quality Assessment Report 94-AC-2 CN 93.0, March 2006			
Packard Pond	MassDEP	French and Quinebaug River Watersheds 2001 Water Quality Assessment Report 41/42-AC-1 51.0, March 2002			
Paradise Pond	DCR	David Worden	−71.856392	42.504057	
Paradise Pond	MassDEP	Nashua River Watershed 2003 Water Quality Assessment Report 81-AC-4 CN107.5, August 2008			
Paradise Pond	DCR	DCR Data from Lakes and Ponds, 2003	−71.856392	42.504057	
Paradise Pond	DCR	DCR Data from Lakes and Ponds, 2007	−71.856392	42.504057	
Paradise Pond	College of the Holy Cross	Robert Bertin	−71.856392	42.504057	

(Continued)

TABLE 8.1
Table 8.1b Variable Milfoil (Continued)

Waterbody	Agency	Report Source	Longitude	Latitude	First Year Reported
Parker Mills Pond	MassDEP	Buzzards Bay Watershed 2000 Water Quality Assessment Report 95-AC-2 085.0, November 2003			
Partridge Pond	MassDEP	Nashua River Watershed 2003 Water Quality Assessment Report 81-AC-4 CN107.5, August 2008			
Partridgeville Pond	DCR	DCR Data from Lakes and Ponds			2007
Pequot Pond	MassDEP	Westfield River Watershed 2001 Water Quality Assessment Report 32-AC-1 CN 090.0, April 2005			
Pierpoint Meadow Pond	MassDEP	French and Quinebaug River Watersheds 2001 Water Quality Assessment Report 41/42-AC-1 51.0, March 2002			
Pierpoint Meadow Pond	DCR	DCR Data from Lakes and Ponds, 2003			2003
Pierpoint Meadow Pond	College of the Holy Cross	Robert Bertin	−71.915681	42.084317	
Pinewood Pond	MassDEP	Neponset River Watershed 2004 Water Quality Assessment Report 73-AC-1 CN170.4, February 2010			
Ponkapoag Pond	MassDEP	Neponset River Watershed 2004 Water Quality Assessment Report 73-AC-1 CN170.4, February 2010			
Pottapaug Pond	College of the Holy Cross	Robert Bertin	−72.226015	42.406072	
Pratt Pond	MassDEP	Blackstone River Basin 1998 Water Quality Assessment Report 51-AC-1 48.0, May 2011			
Pratt Pond	College of the Holy Cross	Robert Bertin	−71.598913	42.181814	
Quaboag Pond	MassDEP	Chicopee River Basin 1998 Water Quality Assessment Report 36-AC-2 47.0, April 2001			
Quaboag Pond	College of the Holy Cross	Robert Bertin	−72.068036	42.197472	
Quacumquasit Pond	MassDEP	Chicopee River Basin 1998 Water Quality Assessment Report 36-AC-2 47.0, April 2001			

Waterbody	Agency	Report Source	Longitude	Latitude	First Year Reported
Quinebaug River	MassDEP	12-H005–01	−72.118569	42.109562	
Quinebaug River	MassDEP	12-H003–01	−72.118569	42.109562	
Quinebaug River	MassDEP	09-P002–01	−72.118569	42.109562	
Quinebaug River	MassDEP	08-N003–01	−72.118569	42.109562	
Quinebaug River	MassDEP	07-M005–01	−72.118569	42.109562	
Quinebaug River	MassDEP	07-M003–01	−72.118569	42.109562	
Quinebaug River	MassDEP	05-M003–01	−72.118569	42.109562	
Quinsigamond River	MassDEP	Field Survey 6/26/2017 Wong, Li	−71.708092	42.230538	
Quinsigamond River	MassDEP	08-K003–02	−71.708092	42.230538	
Quinsigamond River	MassDEP	Blackstone River Watershed 2003–2007 Water Quality Assessment Report 51-AC-3 CN 240.0, March 2010			
Railroad Pond	MassDEP	French and Quinebaug River Watersheds 2001 Water Quality Assessment Report 41/42-AC-1 51.0, March 2002			
Reservoir	MassDEP	13-B006–06	−70.852628	42.029884	
Reservoir Pond	MassDEP	Neponset River Watershed 2004 Water Quality Assessment Report 73-AC-1 CN170.4, February 2010			
Riverlin Street Pond	MassDEP	Blackstone River Basin 1998 Water Quality Assessment Report 51-AC-1 48.0, May 2011			
Rivulet Pond	MassDEP	Blackstone River Basin 1998 Water Quality Assessment Report 51-AC-1 48.0, May 2011			
Rocky Pond	MassDEP	SuAsCo Watershed 2001 Water Quality Assessment Report 82-AC-1 CN 92.0, August 2005			
Rocky Pond	College of the Holy Cross	Robert Bertin	−71.688349	42.346174	
Salisbury Brook	MassDEP	Field Survey 7/7/2017 Wong, Maldonado	−71.014062	42.079367	
Salisbury Brook	MassDEP	06-B021–04	−71.014062	42.079367	
Salisbury Brook	MassDEP	06-B017–04	−71.014062	42.079367	
Sampson Pond	MassDEP	05-R002–01	−70.752977	41.852065	
Sargent Pond	MassDEP	French and Quinebaug River Watersheds 2001 Water Quality Assessment Report 41/42-AC-1 51.0, March 2002			
Sawmill Pond	MassDEP	Nashua River Watershed 2003 Water Quality Assessment Report 81-AC-4 CN107.5, August 2008			

(Continued)

TABLE 8.1
Table 8.1b Variable Milfoil (Continued)

Waterbody	Agency	Report Source	Longitude	Latitude	First Year Reported
Sawmill Pond	College of the Holy Cross	Robert Bertin	−71.846389	42.544612	
Sewall Pond	DCR	DCR Data from Lakes and Ponds, 2008			2008
Sherman Pond	MassDEP	French and Quinebaug River Watersheds 2001 Water Quality Assessment Report 41/42-AC-1 51.0, March 2002			
Shovelshop Pond	MassDEP	Taunton River Watershed Water Quality Assessment Report 62-AC-1 CN 94.0, December 2005			
Silver Lake	MassDEP	Blackstone River Watershed 2003–2007 Water Quality Assessment Report 51-AC-3 CN 240.0, March 2010			
Silver Lake	Individual	Joy Trahan-Liptak	−71.654971	42.193369	
Silver Lake	College of the Holy Cross	Robert Bertin	−71.654894	42.193409	
Singletary Brook	MassDEP	Blackstone River Watershed 2003–2007 Water Quality Assessment Report 51-AC-3 CN 240.0, March 2010			
Smelt Pond	MassDEP	South Shore Coastal Watersheds 2001 Water Quality Assessment Report 94-AC-2 CN 93.0, March 2006			
South Meadow Pond, East Basin	DCR	Jamie Carr	−71.705732	42.415348	
South Meadow Pond, West Basin	DCR	Jamie Carr	−71.713092	42.414889	
South River	MassDEP	Field Survey 7/7/2017 Wong, Maldonado	−70.717896	42.094494	
South River	MassDEP	06-C014–03	−70.717896	42.094494	
South River	MassDEP	06-C017–03	−70.717896	42.094494	
South River	MassDEP	06-C011–03	−70.717896	42.094494	
South River	MassDEP	06-C008–03	−70.717896	42.094494	
Spectacle Pond	Individual	Joy Trahan-Liptak	−71.516164	42.564009	
Spectacle Pond	MassDEP	Merrimack River Basin 1999 Water Quality Assessment Report 84-AC-1 52.0, November 2001			
Spring Pond	DCR	DCR Data from Lakes and Ponds, 2006			
Stetson Brook	MassDEP	Field Survey 7/7/2017 Wong, Maldonado	−70.836605	42.014395	2011

Waterbody	Agency	Report Source	Longitude	Latitude	First Year Reported
Stetson Brook	MassDEP	15-B007–04	−70.836605	42.014395	2011
Stetson Brook	MassDEP	14-B008–02	−70.836605	42.014395	2011
Stetson Brook	MassDEP	11-B006–03	−70.836605	42.014395	2011
Stoneville Pond	Individual	Joy Trahan-Liptak	−71.846513	42.218616	
Stuart Pond	DCR	David Worden	−71.828492	42.482750	
Stuart Pond	MassDEP	Nashua River Watershed 2003 Water Quality Assessment Report 81-AC-4 CN107.5, August 2008			
Stuart Pond	College of the Holy Cross	Robert Bertin	−71.828492	42.482750	
Stump Pond	DCR	Joy Trahan-Liptak	−71.889471	42.361136	
Stump Pond	MassDEP	Nashua River Watershed 2003 Water Quality Assessment Report 81-AC-4 CN107.5, August 2008			
Sudbury Reservoir	College of the Holy Cross	Robert Bertin	−71.510778	42.321064	
Sudden Pond	DCR	DCR Data from Lakes and Ponds, 2008	−71.063113	42.610012	2008
Swans Pond	MassDEP	Blackstone River Basin 1998 Water Quality Assessment Report 51-AC-148.0, May 2011			
Sweets Pond	MassDEP	Taunton River Watershed Water Quality Assessment Report 62-AC-1 CN 94.0, December 2005			
Swift River	Individual	Joy Trahan-Liptak	−72.333500	42.245300	
Swift River	MassDEP	Field Survey 06/20/2017 Wong, Li	−72.334760	42.243266	
Swift River	MassDEP	08-B015–05	−72.334760	42.243266	
Swift River	MassDEP	Field Survey 06/20/2017 Wong, Li	−72.346422	42.210707	
Swift River	MassDEP	08-B015–06	−72.346422	42.210707	
Sylvestri Pond	MassDEP	French and Quinebaug River Watersheds 2001 Water Quality Assessment Report 41/42-AC-1 51.0, March 2002			
Taft Pond	MassDEP	Blackstone River Watershed 2003–2007 Water Quality Assessment Report 51-AC-3 CN 240.0, March 2010			
The Quag	DCR	David Worden	−71.771138	42.416555	
The Quag	DCR	Jamie Carr	−71.771138	42.416555	
The Quag	DCR	Joy Trahan-Liptak	−71.771138	42.416555	
Thompsons Pond	DCR	DCR Data from Lakes and Ponds, 2008			2008

(Continued)

TABLE 8.1
Table 8.1b Variable Milfoil (Continued)

Waterbody	Agency	Report Source	Longitude	Latitude	First Year Reported
Tinker Hill Pond	MassDEP	Blackstone River Basin 1998 Water Quality Assessment Report 51-AC-1 48.0, May 2011			
Town Brook	MassDEP	Field Survey 7/18/2017 Wong, Maldonado	−70.663983	41.954362	
Town Brook	MassDEP	06-C015–04	−70.663983	41.954362	
Town Brook	MassDEP	06-C013–04	−70.663983	41.954362	
Town Brook	MassDEP	06-C010–04	−70.663983	41.954362	
Town Brook	MassDEP	06-C006–04	−70.663983	41.954362	
Town Brook	MassDEP	06-C001–04	−70.663983	41.954362	
Town River	MassDEP	Field Survey 7/7/2017 Wong, Maldonado	−70.953869	41.997462	
Town River	MassDEP	13-C034–03	−70.953869	41.997462	
Tremont Mill Pond	MassDEP	Buzzards Bay Watershed 2000 Water Quality Assessment Report 95-AC-2 085.0, November 2003			
Tuckers Pond	MassDEP	Blackstone River Basin 1998 Water Quality Assessment Report 51-AC-148.0, May 2011			
Turkey Hill Pond	MassDEP	Chicopee River Basin 1998 Water Quality Assessment Report 36-AC-2 47.0, April 2001			
Turkey Hill Pond	College of the Holy Cross	Robert Bertin	−71.947735	42.336725	
Turnpike Lake	MassDEP	Taunton River Watershed Water Quality Assessment Report 62-AC-1 CN 94.0, December 2005			
Turnpike Lake	DCR	DCR Data from Lakes and Ponds, 2004			2004
Uncas Pond	MassDEP	Charles River Watershed 2002–2006 Water Quality Assessment Report 72-AC-4 CN136.5, April 2008			
Uncas Pond	DCR	DCR Data from Lakes and Ponds, 2003			2003
Unionville Pond	DCR	Jamie Carr	−71.842015	42.359704	
Unionville Pond	DCR	Joy Trahan-Liptak	−71.842015	42.359704	
Unnamed Pond	DCR	Jamie Carr	−71.701377	42.411892	
Upper Chandler Pond	MassDEP	South Shore Coastal Watersheds 2001 Water Quality Assessment Report 94-AC-2 CN 93.0, March 2006			

Waterbody	Agency	Report Source	Longitude	Latitude	First Year Reported
Upper Crow Hill Pond	DCR	DCR Data from Lakes and Ponds, 2007			2007
Vandys Pond	MassDEP	Taunton River Watershed Water Quality Assessment Report 62-AC-1 CN 94.0, December 2005			
Wachusett Reservoir	DCR	David Worden	−71.795345	42.384187	
Wachusett Reservoir	DCR	David Worden	−71.787817	42.397107	
Wachusett Reservoir	DCR	Jamie Carr	−71.730707	42.380071	
Wachusett Reservoir	DCR	Jamie Carr	−71.789929	42.389998	
Wachusett Reservoir	DCR	Jamie Carr	−71.787817	42.397107	
Wachusett Reservoir	DCR	Jamie Carr	−71.788251	42.379206	
Wachusett Reservoir	DCR	Jamie Carr	−71.795345	42.384187	
Wachusett Reservoir	DCR	Jamie Carr	−71.795345	42.384187	
Wachusett Reservoir	MassDEP	Nashua River Watershed 2003 Water Quality Assessment Report 81-AC-4 CN107.5, August 2008			
Wachusett Reservoir	DCR	DCR Data from ACT, GeoSyntec-ACT			
Wachusett Reservoir	MassDEP	Richard McVoy	−71.730707	42.380071	
Wachusett Reservoir	MassDEP	Richard McVoy	−71.789929	42.389998	
Wachusett Reservoir	MassDEP	Richard McVoy	−71.795345	42.384187	
Wachusett Reservoir	MassDEP	Richard McVoy	−71.787817	42.397107	
Wachusett Reservoir	MassDEP	Richard McVoy	−71.788251	42.379206	
Wachusett Reservoir	College of the Holy Cross	Robert Bertin	−71.721795	42.385614	
Wachusett Reservoir	DCR	Joy Trahan-Liptak	−71.765499	42.357845	
Waite Pond	College of the Holy Cross	Robert Bertin	−71.891967	42.249054	
Walker Pond	MassDEP	French and Quinebaug River Watersheds 2001 Water Quality Assessment Report 41/42-AC-1 51.0, March 2002			

(Continued)

TABLE 8.1
Table 8.1b Variable Milfoil (Continued)

Waterbody	Agency	Report Source	Longitude	Latitude	First Year Reported
Walker Pond	College of the Holy Cross	Robert Bertin	−72.060053	42.139112	
Ware River	MassDEP	Field Survey 06/16/2017 Wong, Li, Maldonado	−72.159534	42.340072	
Ware River	MassDEP	14-C031–02	−72.159534	42.340072	
Ware River	MassDEP	14-C017–02	−72.159534	42.340072	
Ware River	MassDEP	14-C010–02	−72.159534	42.340072	
Ware River	MassDEP	Field Survey 06/16/2017 Wong, Li, Maldonado	−72.157140	42.343550	
Ware River	MassDEP	08-B031–09	−72.157140	42.343550	
Ware River	MassDEP	Field Survey 06/20/2017 Wong, Li	−72.285755	42.238726	
Ware River	MassDEP	08-L007–04	−72.285755	42.238726	2008
Ware River	MassDEP	08-L006–04	−72.285755	42.238726	2008
Ware River	MassDEP	08-L005–04	−72.285755	42.238726	2008
Ware River	MassDEP	08-L003–04	−72.285755	42.238726	2008
Ware River	MassDEP	08-L001–04	−72.285755	42.238726	2008
Ware River	MassDEP	07-K005–04	−72.285755	42.238726	2008
Ware River	MassDEP	07-K004–04	−72.285755	42.238726	2008
Ware River	MassDEP	06-H005–04	−72.285755	42.238726	2008
Ware River	MassDEP	06-H004–04	−72.285755	42.238726	2008
Ware River	MassDEP	Field Survey 06/20/2017 Wong, Li	−72.278995	42.235461	
Ware River	MassDEP	14-C031–04	−72.278995	42.235461	
Ware River	MassDEP	14-C010–04	−72.278995	42.235461	
Ware River	MassDEP	Field Survey 06/16/2017 Wong, Li, Maldonado	−72.114099	42.380363	
Ware River	MassDEP	08-B031–07	−72.114099	42.380363	
Watson Pond	DCR	DCR Data from Lakes and Ponds, 2003			2003
Watson Pond	DCR	DCR Data from Lakes and Ponds, 2008			
Waushakum Pond	MassDEP	SuAsCo Watershed 2001 Water Quality Assessment Report 82-AC-1 CN 92.0, August 2005			
Webster Lake	MassDEP	French and Quinebaug River Watersheds 2001 Water Quality Assessment Report 41/42-AC-1 51.0, March 2002			
Webster Lake	MassDEP	Field Survey 06/16/2017 Wong, Li, Maldonado	−71.848724	42.054350	
Webster Lake	MassDEP	05-G014–01	−71.848724	42.054350	
Webster Lake	College of the Holy Cross	Robert Bertin	−71.848244	42.038004	

Waterbody	Agency	Report Source	Longitude	Latitude	First Year Reported
Welsh Pond	MassDEP	Blackstone River Basin 1998 Water Quality Assessment Report 51-AC-1 48.0, May 2011			
West Meadow Pond	MassDEP	Taunton River Watershed Water Quality Assessment Report 62-AC-1 CN 94.0, December 2005			
West River	MassDEP	Blackstone River Watershed 2003–2007 Water Quality Assessment Report 51-AC-3 CN 240.0, March 2010			
West River	MassDEP	Field Survey 6/26/2017 Wong, Li	−71.601117	42.100361	2005
West River	MassDEP	05-K005–03	−71.601117	42.100361	2005
West Waushacum Pond	DCR	Joy Trahan-Liptak	−71.764500	42.414394	
West Waushacum Pond	DCR	DCR Data from Lakes and Ponds			
West Waushacum Pond	College of the Holy Cross	Robert Bertin	−71.763731	42.414597	
Westville Lake	College of the Holy Cross	Robert Bertin	−72.060517	42.076893	
White Pond	MassDEP	Nashua River Watershed 2003 Water Quality Assessment Report 81-AC-4 CN107.5, August 2008			
White Pond	DCR	DCR Data from Lakes and Ponds, 2003			2003
White Pond	College of the Holy Cross	Robert Bertin	−71.716035	42.513314	
Whitehall Pond	DCR	DCR Data from Lakes and Ponds, 2007			2007
Whitehall Pond	DCR	DCR Data from Lakes and Ponds, 2008			2008
Whitehall Reservoir	Individual	Joy Trahan-Liptak	−71.573594	42.230720	
Whitehall Reservoir	MassDEP	SuAsCo Watershed 2001 Water Quality Assessment Report 82-AC-1 CN 92.0 August 2005			
Whitehall Reservoir	DCR	DCR Data from Lakes and Ponds, 2008			2008
Whitins Pond	MassDEP	Email communication between David Wong and Therese Beaudoin on July 7, 2017	−71.694011	42.112406	
Whitins Pond	College of the Holy Cross	Robert Bertin	−71.689583	42.113764	
Whitman River	MassDEP	Field Survey 06/20/2017 Wong, Li	−71.866052	42.559799	
Whitman River	MassDEP	11-D022–05	−71.866052	42.559799	

(Continued)

TABLE 8.1
Table 8.1b Variable Milfoil (Continued)

Waterbody	Agency	Report Source	Longitude	Latitude	First Year Reported
Whitman River	MassDEP	11-D007–06	−71.866052	42.559799	
Williamsville Pond	DCR	DCR Data from Lakes and Ponds, 2007			2007
Winnecunnet Pond	DCR	DCR Data from Lakes and Ponds, 2003			2003
Winter Pond	MassDEP	Mystic River Watershed And Coastal Drainage Area 2004–2008 Water Quality Assessment Report 71-AC-2 CN170.2, March 2010			
Woodbury Pond	MassDEP	Blackstone River Basin 1998 Water Quality Assessment Report 51-AC-1 48.0, May 2011			
Woodbury Pond	MassDEP	Field Survey 6/26/2017 Wong, Li	−71.731255	42.164983	
Woodbury Pond	MassDEP	09-G008–07	−71.731255	42.164983	
Woods Pond	MassDEP	Neponset River Watershed 2004 Water Quality Assessment Report 73-AC-1 CN170.4, February 2010			
Wyman Pond	MassDEP	Nashua River Watershed 2003 Water Quality Assessment Report 81-AC-4 CN107.5, August 2008			

Table 8.1c Unidentified Milfoil

Waterbody	Agency	Report Source	Longitude	Latitude	First Reported Year
Assabet River	MassDEP	SuAsCo Watershed 2001 Water Quality Assessment Report 82-AC-1 CN 92.0, August 2005			
Baddacook Pond	MassDEP	05-G001–01	−71.530464	42.618962	
Charles River	MassDEP	Charles River Watershed 2002–2006 Water Quality Assessment Report 72-AC-4 CN136.5, April 2008			
Charles River	MassDEP	Charles River Watershed 2002–2006 Water Quality Assessment Report 72-AC-4 CN136.5, April 2008			

Eurasian Milfoil and Variable Milfoil

Waterbody	Agency	Report Source	Longitude	Latitude	First Reported Year
East Head Pond	DCR	DCR Data from Lakes and Ponds, humile 2008			2008
First Pond	MassDEP	North Shore Coastal Watersheds 2002 Water Quality Assessment Report 93-AC-2 CN 138.5, March 2007			
Fresh Meadow Pond	MassDEP	Buzzards Bay Watershed 2000 Water Quality Assessment Report 95-AC-2 085.0, November 2003			
Hockomock River	MassDEP	13-C022–01	−71.035453	41.988368	
Hockomock River	MassDEP	13-C034–01	−71.035453	41.988368	
Hockomock River	MassDEP	13-C040–01	−71.035453	41.988368	
Houghton Pond	MassDEP	Charles River Watershed 2002–2006 Water Quality Assessment Report 72-AC-4 CN136.5, April 2008			
Lake Gardner	DCR	DCR Data from Lakes and Ponds, 2007			2007
Leonards Pond	MassDEP	05-R003–02	−70.804664	41.750263	2005
Little Rocky Pond	DCR	DCR Data from Lakes and Ponds, 2008			2008
Lower Porter Pond	MassDEP	Taunton River Watershed Water Quality Assessment Report 62-AC-1 CN 94.0, December 2005			
Monponsett Pond	MassDEP	14-B002–02	−70.836781	42.001467	
Monponsett Pond	MassDEP	14-B004–05	−70.836781	42.001467	
Monponsett Pond	MassDEP	14-B006–05	−70.836781	42.001467	
Monponsett Pond	MassDEP	14-B008–05	−70.836781	42.001467	
Monponsett Pond	MassDEP	13-B006–05	−70.836781	42.001467	
Monponsett Pond	MassDEP	13-B008–05	−70.836781	42.001467	
Monponsett Pond	MassDEP	12-B002–04	−70.836781	42.001467	
Monponsett Pond	MassDEP	12-B004–04	−70.836781	42.001467	
Monponsett Pond	MassDEP	12-B006–05	−70.836781	42.001467	
Monponsett Pond	MassDEP	12-B008–05	−70.836781	42.001467	
Monponsett Pond	MassDEP	11-B006–05	−70.836781	42.001467	
Monponsett Pond	MassDEP	11-B008–02	−70.836781	42.001467	
Mumford River	MassDEP	Blackstone River Basin 1998 Water Quality Assessment Report 51-AC-1 48.0, May 2011			

(Continued)

TABLE 8.1
Table 8.1c Unidentified Milfoil (Continued)

Waterbody	Agency	Report Source	Longitude	Latitude	First Reported Year
Mumford River	MassDEP	11-D006–05	−71.737090	42.093107	
Mumford River	MassDEP	11-D015–05	−71.737090	42.093107	
Nine Mile Pond	DCR	DCR Data from Lakes and Ponds, 2003			2003
Onota Lake	MassDEP	05-G008–01	−73.283941	42.464926	
Pottapaug Pond	MassDEP	Chicopee River Basin 1998 Water Quality Assessment Report 36-AC-2 47.0, April 2001			
Priest Brook	MassDEP	Field Survey 06/20/2017 Wong, Li	−72.115037	42.682797	
Priest Brook	MassDEP	08-P004–04	−72.115037	42.682797	
Priest Brook	MassDEP	08-P003–04	−72.115037	42.682797	
Quabbin Reservoir	MassDEP	Chicopee River Basin 1998 Water Quality Assessment Report 36-AC-2 47.0, April 2001			
Reservoir Pond	MassDEP	09-B009–02	−71.126217	42.170467	
Robinsons Pond	DCR	DCR Data from Lakes and Ponds			
Sampson Pond	MassDEP	05-R002–01	−70.752977	41.852065	
Spring Pond	MassDEP	North Shore Coastal Watersheds 2002 Water Quality Assessment Report 93-AC-2 CN 138.5, March 2007			
Thirtyacre Pond	MassDEP	Taunton River Watershed Water Quality Assessment Report 62-AC-1 CN 94.0, December 2005			
Thompsons Pond	DCR	DCR Data from Lakes and Ponds, 2005			2005
Upper Leach Pond	DCR	DCR Data from Lakes and Ponds, 2008			2008
Upper Porter Pond	MassDEP	Taunton River Watershed Water Quality Assessment Report 62-AC-1 CN 94.0, December 2005			
Waldo Lake	MassDEP	Taunton River Watershed Water Quality Assessment Report 62-AC-1 CN 94.0, December 2005			

Waterbody	Agency	Report Source	Longitude	Latitude	First Reported Year
West River	MassDEP	Blackstone River Watershed 2003–2007 Water Quality Assessment Report 51-AC-3 CN 240.0, March 2010			
White Island Pond, East Basin	MassDEP	08-F008–02	−70.617531	41.809183	
White Island Pond, East Basin	MassDEP	14-B005–01	−70.617531	41.809183	
White Island Pond, West Basin	MassDEP	14-B003–02	−70.627556	41.809994	
White Island Pond, West Basin	MassDEP	14-B005–02	−70.627556	41.809994	
Winnecunnet Pond	MassDEP	Taunton River Watershed Water Quality Assessment Report 62-AC-1 CN 94.0, December 2005			

TABLE 8.2
Towns and Infested Waterbodies

Table 8.2a Eurasian Milfoil

Number	Waterbody	Town 1	Town 2
1	Ashmere Lake	Hinsdale	Peru
2	Assabet River	Stow	Hudson/Maynard
3	Assabet River Reservoir	Westborough	–
4	Bartlett Pond	Northborough	–
5	Bartons Cove	Gill	–
6	Beaver Lake	Ware	–
7	Benton Pond	Otis	–
8	Berkshire Pond	Lanesborough	–
9	Big Bearhole Pond	Taunton	–
10	Billington Sea	Plymouth	–
11	Buffumville Lake	Charlton	Oxford
12	Center Pond	Becket	–
13	Charles River	Dover	Needham/Wellesley/Natick
14	Chauncy Lake	Westborough	–
15	Cheshire Reservoir, Middle Basin	Cheshire	Lanesborough
16	Cheshire Reservoir, North Basin	Cheshire	–
17	Cheshire Reservoir, South Basin	Lanesborough	Cheshire
18	Chicopee River	Palmer	Wilbraham/Ludlow

(Continued)

TABLE 8.2
Table 8.2a Eurasian Milfoil (Continued)

Number	Waterbody	Town 1	Town 2
19	Coes Reservoir	Worcester	–
20	Concord River	Concord	Billerica/Carlisle/Bedford
21	Congamond Lakes, Middle Basin	Southwick	–
22	Congamond Lakes, North Basin	Southwick	–
23	Congamond Lakes, South Basin	Southwick	Suffield, CT
24	Cranberry Pond	Sunderland	–
25	Dark Brook Reservoir	Auburn	–
26	Devils Dishfull Pond	Peabody	–
27	Dorothy Pond	Millbury	–
28	Dudley Pond	Wayland	–
29	Ellis Pond	Athol	–
30	Farm Pond	Framingham	–
31	Fisherville Pond	Grafton	–
32	Fisk Pond	Natick	–
33	Flint Pond	Shrewsbury	–
34	Forest Lake	Palmer	–
35	Forge Pond	Westford	Littleton
36	Fort Meadow Reservoir	Marlborough	Hudson
37	Framingham Reservoir #1	Framingham	–
38	Framingham Reservoir #3	Framingham	–
39	Goose Pond Brook	Lee	Tyringham
40	Greenwater Pond	Becket	–
41	Hayden Pond	Otis	–
42	Hills Pond	Arlington	–
43	Hocomonco Pond	Westborough	–
44	Horse Pond	Westfield	–
45	Housatonic River	Stockbridge	Lenox/Lee/Great Barrington
46	Hovey Pond	Grafton	–
47	Hubbard Brook	Sheffield	Egremont/Great Barrington
48	Indian Lake	Worcester	–
49	Jamaica Pond	Boston	–
50	Knops Pond/Lost Lake	Groton	–
51	Lake Averic	Stockbridge	–
52	Lake Buel	Monterey	New Marlborough
53	Lake Cochituate	Wayland	Framingham/Natick
54	Lake Garfield	Monterey	–
55	Lake Lorraine	Springfield	–
56	Lake Pearl	Wrentham	–
57	Lake Quinsigamond	Shrewsbury	Worcester
58	Lake Rico	Taunton	–
59	Lake Ripple	Grafton	–
60	Lake Shirley	Lunenburg	Shirley

Eurasian Milfoil and Variable Milfoil

Number	Waterbody	Town 1	Town 2
61	Lake Waban	Wellesley	–
62	Lake Whalom	Lunenburg	Leominster
63	Laurel Lake	Lee	Lenox
64	Leesville Pond	Auburn	Worcester
65	Leverett Pond	Leverett	–
66	Lily Pond, Middle	West Boylston	–
67	Little Alum Pond	Brimfield	–
68	Long Pond	Great Barrington	–
69	Mansfield Pond	Great Barrington	–
70	Middle Pond	Taunton	–
71	Monponsett Pond	Halifax	–
72	Morses Pond	Wellesley	Natick
73	Mystic River	Medford	Arlington
74	Newfield Pond	Chelmsford	–
75	Oldham Pond	Pembroke	Hanson
76	Onota Lake	Pittsfield	–
77	Orrs Pond	Attleboro	–
78	Otis Reservoir	Otis	Tolland/Blanford
79	Pequot Pond	Westfield	Southampton
80	Plunkett Reservoir	Hinsdale	–
81	Ponkapoag Pond	Canton	Randolph
82	Pontoosac Lake	Lanesborough	Pittsfield
83	Purgatory Cove	Waltham	Newton
84	Quaboag Pond	Brookfield	East Brookfield
85	Quacumquasit Pond	Brookfield	East Brookfield/Sturbridge
86	Quinsigamond River	Grafton	–
87	Reservoir Pond	Canton	–
88	Rice City Pond	Uxbridge	Northbridge
89	Richmond Pond	Richmond	Pittsfield
90	Shaker Mill Pond	West Stockbridge	–
91	Shaw Pond	Becket	Otis
92	Silver Lake	Wilmington	–
93	Singletary Pond	Sutton	Millbury
94	Sluice Pond	Lynn	–
95	Spy Pond	Arlington	–
96	Stetson Pond	Pembroke	–
97	Stevens Pond	Monterey	–
98	Stockbridge Bowl	Stockbridge	–
99	Sudbury Reservoir	Southborough	Marlborough
100	Sudbury River	Wayland	Sudbury/Framingham
101	Sunset Lake	Braintree	–
102	Thousand Acre Pond	New Marlborough	–
103	Unionville Pond	Holden	–
104	Upper Goose Pond	Lee	Tryingham

(Continued)

TABLE 8.2
Table 8.2a Eurasian Milfoil (Continued)

Number	Waterbody	Town 1	Town 2
105	Wachusett Reservoir	Boylston	West Boylston/Clinton/Sterling
106	Webster Lake	Webster	–
107	White Island Pond, East Basin	Plymouth	Wareham
108	Whiting Street Reservoir	Holyoke	–
109	Willard Brook	Sheffield	–
110	Windsor Pond	Windsor	–
111	Winning Pond	Billerica	–
112	Woolshop Pond	Millbury	–
113	Yokum Pond	Becket	–

Table 8.2b Variable Milfoil

Number	Waterbody	Town 1	Town 2
1	Aaron Reservoir	Cohasset	Hingham
2	Aldrich Pond	Sutton	–
3	Ames Long Pond	Stoughton	Easton
4	Arcade Pond	Northbridge	–
5	Arcadia Lake	Belchertown	–
6	Ashland Reservoir	Ashland	–
7	Baddacook Pond	Groton	–
8	Bailey Road Pond	Holden	–
9	Bare Hill Pond	Harvard	–
10	Bartlett Pond	Northborough	–
11	Beaver Lake	Ware	–
12	Beaver Pond	Franklin	–
13	Bennett Pond	Wilbraham	–
14	Billings Street/East Street Pond	Sharon	–
15	Billington Sea	Plymouth	–
16	Black Mountain Pond	Marshfield	–
17	Blackstone River	Millbury	Worcester/Grafton/Sutton
18	Boons Pond	Stow	Hudson
19	Bouchard Pond	Leicester	–
20	Brierly Pond	Millbury	–
21	Brigham Pond	Hubbardston	–
22	Brooks Pond	North Brookfield	New Braintree/Oakham/Spencer
23	Browning Pond	Oakham	Spencer
24	Buck Pond	Westfield	–
25	Buffum Pond	Charlton	Oxford
26	Buffumville Lake	Charlton	Oxford
27	Burncoat Pond	Leicester	Spencer
28	Carver Pond	Bridgewater	–

Eurasian Milfoil and Variable Milfoil

Number	Waterbody	Town 1	Town 2
29	Cedar Meadow Pond	Leicester	–
30	Cedar Pond	Sturbridge	–
31	Cedar Swamp Pond	Milford	–
32	Chaffin Pond	Holden	–
33	Charles River	Dover	Needham/Wellesley/Natick
34	Clark Pond	Walpole	–
35	Clear Pond	Lakeville	–
36	Cleveland Pond	Abington	–
37	Coachlace Pond	Clinton	–
38	Cocasset Lake	Foxborough	–
39	Collins Pond	Andover	–
40	Comins Pond	Warren	–
41	Cook Pond	Worcester	–
42	Crane Brook Bog Pond	Carver	–
43	Crocker Pond	Westminster	–
44	Curtis Pond	Worcester	–
45	Dark Brook	Auburn	–
46	Dark Brook Reservoir	Auburn	–
47	Dawson Pond	Holden	–
48	Dean Pond	Brimfield	Monson
49	Demond Pond	Rutland	–
50	Doane Pond	North Brookfield	–
51	Eagle Lake	Holden	–
52	East Brimfield Reservoir	Sturbridge	Brimfield
53	East Brookfield River	East Brookfield	–
54	East Freetown Pond	Freetown	–
55	East Head Pond	Carver	Plymouth
56	Eddy Pond	Auburn	–
57	Ellis Pond	Athol	–
58	Factory Pond	Holliston	–
59	Falls Pond, South Basin	North Attleborough	–
60	Farrington Pond	Stoughton	–
61	Federal Pond	Carver	Plymouth
62	Field Pond	Andover	–
63	First Pond	Saugus	–
64	Fish Pond	Northbridge	–
65	Fisk Pond	Natick	–
66	Flannagan Pond	Ayer	–
67	Flint Pond	Grafton	Worcester/Shrewsbury
68	Fort Meadow Reservoir	Marlborough	Hudson
69	Framingham Reservoir #1	Framingham	–
70	French River	Dudley	Webster
71	Frye Pond	Andover	–

(Continued)

TABLE 8.2
Table 8.2b Variable Milfoil (Continued)

Number	Waterbody	Town 1	Town 2
72	Fuller Street Pond	Middleborough	Carver
73	Gaston Pond	Barre	–
74	Gavins Pond	Sharon	Foxborough
75	Gilboa Pond	Douglas	–
76	Glen Echo Pond	Canton	Stoughton
77	Gore Pond	Dudley	Charlton
78	Granite Reservoir	Charlton	–
79	Greenville Pond	Leicester	–
80	Griswold Pond	Saugus	–
81	Grove Pond	Ayer	–
82	Gushee Pond	Raynham	–
83	Hamilton Reservoir	Holland	–
84	Hardwick Pond	Hardwick	–
85	Hobart Pond	Whitman	–
86	Hoosicwhisick Pond	Milton	–
87	Hopkinton Reservoir	Hopkinton	Ashland
88	Horse Pond	Westfield	–
89	Hovey Pond	Grafton	–
90	Howe Pond	Spencer	–
91	Howe Reservoirs	Millbury	–
92	Indian Brook	Plymouth	–
93	Ironstone Reservoir	Uxbridge	–
94	Jacobs Pond	Norwell	–
95	Jenks Reservoir	Bellingham	–
96	Jewells Pond	Medfield	–
97	Kettle Brook	Leicester	Auburn/Worcester
98	Knops Pond/Lost Lake	Groton	–
99	Lake Cochituate	Natick	Wayland
100	Lake Holland	Belchertown	–
101	Lake Mattawa	Orange	–
102	Lake Monomonac	Winchendon	–
103	Lake Pearl	Wrentham	–
104	Lake Quinsigamond	Shrewsbury	Worcester
105	Lake Rico	Taunton	–
106	Lake Ripple	Grafton	–
107	Lake Rohunta	New Salem	–
108	Lake Sabbatia	Taunton	–
109	Lake Samoset	Leominster	–
110	Lake Shirley	Lunenburg	Shirley
111	Lake Whalom	Lunenburg	Leominster
112	Lake Winthrop	Holliston	–
113	Lancaster Millpond	Clinton	–

Eurasian Milfoil and Variable Milfoil

Number	Waterbody	Town 1	Town 2
114	Larner Pond	Dudley	–
115	Leesville Pond	Auburn	Worcester
116	Leonards Pond	Rochester	–
117	Lily Pond	Cohasset	–
118	Little Chauncy Pond	Northborough	–
119	Little River	Oxford	–
120	Long Island Pond	Plymouth	–
121	Long Pond	Rutland	–
122	Longwater Pond	Easton	–
123	Lorings Bogs Pond	Duxbury	–
124	Louisa Lake	Milford	–
125	Low Pond	Dudley	–
126	Manchaug Pond	Douglas	Sutton
127	Mansfield Pond	Millville	–
128	Maple Spring Pond	Holden	–
129	Marble Pond	Sutton	–
130	Massapoag Lake	Sharon	–
131	Massapoag Pond	Dunstable	Groton/Tyngsborough
132	Merrill Pond No.4	Sutton	–
133	Metacomet Lake	Belchertown	–
134	Middle River	Worcester	–
135	Mill Brook	Brimfield	–
136	Mill Pond	Upton	–
137	Mill River	Hopedale	Milford/Upton/Mendon
138	Millers River	Orange	Athol/Phillipston/Royalston/Wendell/Erving
139	Miscoe Lake	Wrentham	–
140	Monoosnuc Brook	Leominster	Fitchburg
141	Monponsett Pond	Halifax	–
142	Moosehorn Pond	Hubbardston	–
143	Morse Pond	Southbridge	–
144	Morses Pond	Wellesley	Natick
145	Mossy Pond	Clinton	–
146	Nabnasset Pond	Westford	–
147	Nashua River	Groton	Pepperell/Ayer
148	Neponset River	Walpole	Norwood/Foxborough/Canton/Sharon
149	New Bedford Reservoir	Acushnet	–
150	Newton Pond	Shrewsbury	Boylston
151	Nipmuck Lake	Mendon	–
152	Noannet Pond	Westwood	Dover
153	Noquochoke Lake	Dartmouth	–
154	North Pond	Hopkinton	Milford/Upton
155	Norton Reservoir	Norton	Mansfield
156	Noyes Pond	Tolland	–
157	Old Oaken Bucket Pond	Scituate	–

(Continued)

TABLE 8.2
Table 8.2b Variable Milfoil (Continued)

Number	Waterbody	Town 1	Town 2
158	Packard Pond	Dudley	–
159	Paradise Pond	Princeton	–
160	Parker Mills Pond	Wareham	–
161	Partridge Pond	Westminster	–
162	Partridgeville Pond	Templeton	–
163	Pequot Pond	Westfield	Southampton
164	Pierpoint Meadow Pond	Dudley	Charlton
165	Pinewood Pond	Stoughton	–
166	Ponkapoag Pond	Canton	Randolph
167	Pottapaug Pond	Petersham	Hardwick
168	Pratt Pond	Upton	–
169	Quaboag Pond	Brookfield	East Brookfield
170	Quacumquasit Pond	Brookfield	East Brookfield/Sturbridge
171	Quinebaug River	Sturbridge	Brimfield/Holland
172	Quinsigamond River	Grafton	–
173	Railroad Pond	Charlton	–
174	Reservoir	Hanson	–
175	Reservoir Pond	Canton	–
176	Riverlin Street Pond	Millbury	–
177	Rivulet Pond	Uxbridge	–
178	Rocky Pond	Boylston	–
179	Salisbury Brook	Brockton	–
180	Sampson Pond	Carver	–
181	Sargent Pond	Leicester	–
182	Sawmill Pond	Fitchburg	Westminster
183	Sewall Pond	Boylston	–
184	Sherman Pond	Brimfield	–
185	Shovelshop Pond	Easton	–
186	Silver Lake	Bellingham	–
187	Singletary Brook	Millbury	–
188	Smelt Pond	Kingston	–
189	South Meadow Pond, East Basin	Clinton	–
190	South Meadow Pond, West Basin	Clinton	Lancaster
191	South River	Marshfield	–
192	Spectacle Pond	Littleton	Ayer
193	Spring Pond	Saugus	–
194	Stetson Brook	Halifax	–
195	Stoneville Pond	Auburn	–
196	Stuart Pond	Sterling	–
197	Stump Pond	Holden	–
198	Sudbury Reservoir	Southborough	Marlborough
199	Sudden Pond	North Andover	–

Eurasian Milfoil and Variable Milfoil

Number	Waterbody	Town 1	Town 2
200	Swans Pond	Sutton	Northbridge
201	Sweets Pond	Mansfield	–
202	Swift River	Belchertown	Ware/Palmer
203	Sylvestri Pond	Dudley	–
204	Taft Pond	Upton	–
205	The Quag	Sterling	–
206	Thompsons Pond	Spencer	–
207	Tinker Hill Pond	Auburn	–
208	Town Brook	Plymouth	–
209	Town River	Bridgewater	–
210	Tremont Mill Pond	Wareham	–
211	Tuckers Pond	Sutton	–
212	Turkey Hill Pond	Rutland	Paxton
213	Turnpike Lake	Plainville	–
214	Uncas Pond	Franklin	–
215	Unionville Pond	Holden	–
216	Unnamed Pond	Clinton	–
217	Upper Chandler Pond	Pembroke	Duxbury
218	Upper Crow Hill Pond	Westminster	–
219	Vandys Pond	Foxborough	–
220	Wachusett Reservoir	Boylston	West Boylston/Clinton/Sterling
221	Waite Pond	Leicester	–
222	Walker Pond	Sturbridge	–
223	Ware River	New Braintree	Hardwick/Ware
224	Watson Pond	Taunton	–
225	Waushakum Pond	Framingham	Ashland
226	Webster Lake	Webster	–
227	Welsh Pond	Sutton	–
228	West Meadow Pond	West Bridgewater	–
229	West River	Upton	Grafton
230	West Waushacum Pond	Sterling	–
231	Westville Lake	Sturbridge	–
232	White Pond	Lancaster	Leominster
233	Whitehall Pond	Rutland	–
234	Whitehall Reservoir	Hopkinton	–
235	Whitins Pond	Northbridge	Sutton
236	Whitman River	Westminster	–
237	Williamsville Pond	Hubbardston	–
238	Winnecunnet Pond	Norton	–
239	Winter Pond	Winchester	–
240	Woodbury Pond	Sutton	–
241	Woods Pond	Stoughton	–
242	Wyman Pond	Westminster	–

(Continued)

Table 8.2c Unidentified Milfoil

Number	Waterbody	Town 1	Town 2
1	Assabet River	Stow	Hudson/Maynard
2	Baddacook Pond	Groton	–
3	Charles River	Medfield	Millis/Norfolk/Medway/Dover/Sherborn/Natick
4	East Head Pond	Carver	Plymouth
5	First Pond	Saugus	–
6	Fresh Meadow Pond	Plymouth	Carver
7	Hockomock River	West Bridgewater	Bridgewater
8	Houghton Pond	Holliston	–
9	Lake Gardner	Amesbury	–
10	Leonards Pond	Rochester	–
11	Little Rocky Pond	Plymouth	–
12	Lower Porter Pond	Brockton	–
13	Monponsett Pond	Halifax	–
14	Mumford River	Uxbridge	Northbridge/Sutton/Douglas
15	Nine Mile Pond	Wilbraham	–
16	Onota Lake	Pittsfield	–
17	Pottapaug Pond	Petersham	Hardwick
18	Priest Brook	Royalston	Winchendon
19	Quabbin Reservoir	Petersham	New Salem/Pelham/Ware/Hardwick/Shutesbury/Belchertown
20	Reservoir Pond	Canton	–
21	Robinsons Pond	Oxford	–
22	Sampson Pond	Carver	–
23	Spring Pond	Saugus	–
24	Thirtyacre Pond	Brockton	–
25	Thompsons Pond	Spencer	–
26	Upper Leach Pond	Sharon	–
27	Upper Porter Pond	Brockton	–
28	Waldo Lake	Avon	Brockton
29	West River	Upton	Northbridge/Uxbridge
30	White Island Pond, East Basin	Plymouth	Wareham
31	White Island Pond, West Basin	Plymouth	Wareham
32	Winnecunnet Pond	Norton	–

beaches) to control invasive species (MA DCR 2016).

Herbicide application is the main chemical method used to control dense beds of Eurasian milfoil. Herbicides contain active ingredients that prove toxic to target plants at recommended concentrations, making this method very effective. However, herbicides can also harm or kill non-target plants and organisms by using the inappropriate type or concentration (Mattson et al. 2004). Several herbicides have been tested or used to control Eurasian milfoil, such as diquat, 2,4-D, fluridone (Hall et al. 1984), bensulfuron-methyl (Getsinger et al. 1994), triclopyr (Madsen and Getsinger 2005), endothall (Netherland et al. 1991), etc. Recovery and

TABLE 8.3
Infested Watersheds

1	Blackstone
2	Boston Harbor: Mystic
3	Boston Harbor: Neponset
4	Boston Harbor: Weymouth and Weir
5	Buzzards Bay
6	Charles
7	Chicopee
8	Concord (SuAsCo)
9	Connecticut
10	Farmington
11	French
12	Housatonic
13	Hudson: Hoosic
14	Ipswich
15	Merrimack
16	Millers
17	Nashua
18	North Coastal
19	Quinebaug
20	South Coastal
21	Taunton
22	Ten Mile
23	Westfield

survival of severely injured Eurasian milfoil in auxin herbicide–treated areas in Gun Lake, Michigan, have been detected and it is therefore suggested that management plans should include field monitoring of efficacy and regrowth whenever possible to best inform adaptive management decision-making (Thum et al. 2017). A recent analysis of aquatic plant communities found significant declines in native plant species in response to lake-wide herbicide treatments in 173 lakes in Wisconsin. This analysis reveals that whole lake chemical treatment can reduce the size of milfoil populations but have non-target effects (Mikulyuk et al. 2020). Furthermore, it is important to try and remove dead biological matter after a chemical treatment, as the matter can cause issues with dissolved oxygen and eutrophication as they decay (Nichols 1975). At the same time, treatment early in the growing season will result in less biomass decomposing.

It is also debatable that if there is no management at all, biomass of invasives would continue to build year by year. So strategically disrupting that cycle with a targeted and timely herbicide treatment can help to limit biomass buildup down the road (Amy Smagula, personal communication).

Biological methods have the objective of achieving control of plants without introducing toxic chemicals or using machinery. For example, the American native weevil (*Euhrychiopsis lecontei*) has been used for Eurasian milfoil control in Massachusetts since 1995, with success being seen in test lake experiments (Mattson et al. 2004). Research has found that weevil larvae significantly reduced plant growth in experiments where Eurasian milfoil exhibited a faster growth rate (Creed and Sheldon 1994). Also, there are instances of Eurasian milfoil populations suffering from declines due to pathogens.

In addition, another example of biological control methods occurred from 1964 to 1967 in Chesapeake Bay as the abundance of Eurasian milfoil declined heavily. This decline was attributed to Northeast and Lake Venice disease (Bayley et al. 1968). While it may be hard to utilize these pathogens for targeted control and management purposes, it is possible populations of Eurasian milfoil will decline naturally when exposed to these diseases. Aquatic macrophyte moth (*Acentria ephemerella*) and the milfoil midge (*Cricotopus myriophylli*) are also known to limit the growth of milfoil growth.

Variable Milfoil

Like Eurasian milfoil, variable milfoil can be controlled by physical methods, chemical methods, and biological methods. Hand harvesting, drawdowns, and benthic barriers are several common physical ways to manage populations and impede the spread of variable milfoil. Hand harvesting is recommended for use in sparsely infested sites, while benthic barriers are one of the most effective choices in areas with dense populations of variable milfoil (Bailey and Calhoun 2008). Many herbicides have been confirmed to have the potential to control this invasive species and are often used alongside other control methods such as hand pulling. Effective herbicides known for variable milfoil control includes 2,4-D ester, carfentrazone-ethyl (Glomski and Netherland 2007, 2008a), triclopyr, fluridone, penoxsulam, and diquat (Glomski and Netherland 2008b). Variable milfoil shows a high tolerance to diquat from the research of Glomski and Netherland (2008b). In terms of the biological control, weevils are now marketed commercially as a milfoil removal tool, with a recommended stocking rate of 3,000 adults per acre (Mattson et al. 2004). However, it should be noted the effectiveness of milfoil weevils on variable milfoil and Eurasian milfoil may not be the same. Furthermore, weevil introduction may not work for all because every body of water has a different configuration of plants and bugs that make it very difficult to determine if weevils will damage watermilfoil plants. It is suggested that a feasibility pilot study should be conducted before a large-scale implementation to a waterbody.

In recent years, florpyrauxifen-benzyl (active ingredient of ProcellaCOR™) has emerged as a useful tool in target-specific variable milfoil (or Eurasian milfoil) control in the region. More information about chemical control on Eurasian milfoil and variable milfoil, as well as other 17 invasive species can be found in Appendix III. Any chemical used for aquatic invasive species control requires a WM04 Chemical Application License issued by the Massachusetts Department of Environmental Protection.

Additionally, efforts should be made to better educate the public to minimize the risk of spreading invasive aquatic plants between waterbodies. For example, in countries with a history of invasive species control and management, it is common practice to put up educational signage and warnings outside waterbodies with populations of invasive species (Nichols 1975). Boaters should be encouraged to take steps to remove any vegetation and mud from their watercraft, trailer, and recreational equipment to drain all compartments, including the bilge and motor, and allow for a period of drying between operation in different bodies of water. Boaters can also be warned about potential mats of milfoil sitting on the surface of the water that they want to operate in. These mats should be avoided by boats, as the engines can cause great fragmentation of the plant, which could then cause further spreading. It is also suggested to set up restricted use areas or quarantine areas to keep people out of zones of active growth, where fragmentation and spread are possible.

SUCCESS STORY

There are many successful examples of Eurasian milfoil control. A case study of Eurasian Milfoil Removal (Lyman and Eichler 2005) reports that milfoil sites have increased from 3 in 1985 to 127 in 1998 at Lake George, NY. By 2004, around a hundred of these sites have been managed successfully by a combination of physical management techniques, which includes hand pulling, suction/hand harvesting, and benthic barriers. Although there was an increase of two to three sites per year, it was a slow rate of invasive species expansion. This case study proved the physical treatment is an effective management method for Eurasian milfoil control. Another case study that occurred in Washington state, utilizing the herbicide triclopyr, found positive results in the treatment of a river and cove (Getsinger et al. 1997). Eurasian milfoil was reduced by 99% after just four weeks of treatment. Additionally, native populations of aquatic species were able to be restored and rejuvenated because of the reduction in the invasive milfoil, with species richness and plant diversity increasing a year after the treatments had been completed.

For variable milfoil, a field trial was performed by using the herbicide Renovate at Captains Pond, Salem, NH, during the summer of 2008, with promising results (Exotic Aquatic Species Program 2008). Renovate is a systemic aquatic herbicide, which targets both roots and shoots of the plant, effectively controlling the spread of variable milfoil.

CONCLUSION

Though there are many examples of invasive milfoil management, further management plans must be tailored to the regions where invasive outbreaks occur. Therefore, there must be a dissemination of information regarding invasive milfoil, to discuss the appearances and threat of Eurasian and variable milfoil in local waterbodies. With the use of monitoring tools such as ArcGIS, a collaborative effort can be used to track the spread of invasive milfoil and implement strategic and longer-lived management methods and regulations. Successful management of watermilfoil populations requires years of dedicated financial and human resources and frequent population surveys to evaluate the effectiveness of the management approach (Meg Modley, personal communication).

REFERENCES

Aiken, S.G. 1981. A conspectus of Myriophyllum (Haloragaceae) in North America. *Brittonia* 33(1): 57–69.

Aiken, S.G., P.R. Newroth, and I. Wile. 1979. The biology of Canadian weeds. 34. Myriophyllum spicatum L. *Canadian Journal of Plant Science* 59: 201–215.

Bailey, J.E., and A.J.K. Calhoun. 2008. Comparison of three physical management techniques for controlling variable-leaf milfoil in Maine lakes. *Journal of Aquatic Plant Management* 4(6): 163–167.

Bayley, S., H. Rabin, and C.H. Southwick. 1968. Recent decline in the distribution and abundance of Eurasian milfoil in Chesapeake Bay. *Chesapeake Science* 9(3): 173–181.

Cameron, D., and M. Wallhead. 2004. Bulletin #2530, Maine INVASIVE Plants: Variable-Leaf Milfoil, Myriophyllum Heterophyllum (Water MILFOIL family)—cooperative EXTENSION publications—University of Maine cooperative extension. https://extension.umaine.edu/publications/2530e/

Chase, R.F., and W.H. Wong. 2015. Standard Operating Procedure: Field Equipment Decontamination to Prevent the Spread of Invasive Aquatic Organisms. Massachusetts Department of Environmental Protection, Watershed Planning Program. CN 59.6.29 pp.

Creed, R.P. Jr., and S.P. Sheldon. 1994. The effect of two herbivorous insect larvae on Eurasian watermilfoil. *Journal of Aquatic Plant Management* 32: 21–26.

Crow, G.E., and C.B. Hellquist. 2000. Aquatic and Wetland Plants of Northeastern North America (vol. 1) Pteridophytes, Gymnosperms, and Angiosperms: Dicotyledons. The University of Wisconsin Press, Madison WI, USA, p. 480.

Dutartre, A., C. Chauvin, and J. Grange. 2006. Colonisation végétale du canal de Bourgogne à Dijon: bilan 2006, propositions de gestion. irstea. *Rapport Cemagref Bordeaux, France*; pp. 87.

Eichler, L.W., R.T. Bombard, and C.W. Boylen. 1994. *Final Report on the Lake George Eurasian Watermilfoil Survey for 1993.* Troy: Fresh Water Institute Technical Report, pp. 94–91, 53.

Eiswerth, M., G. Susan, B. Donaldson, and W. Johnson. 2000. Potential Environmental Impacts and Economic Damages of Eurasian Watermilfoil (Myriophyllum spicatum) in Western Nevada and Northeastern California. *Weed Technology*, 14(3): 511–518.

Exotic Aquatic Species Program. 2008. Report of the New Hampshire Exotic Aquatic Species Program. New Hampshire Department of Environmental Services, www.des.nh.gov/organization/commissioner/pip/publications/wd/documents/r wd-09-08.pdf (Accessed February 20, 2020).

Getsinger, K.D., G.O. Dick, R.M. Crouch, and L.S. Nelson. 1994. Mesocosm evaluation of bensulfuron methyl activity on Eurasian watermilfoil, vallisneria, and American pondweed. *Journal of Aquatic Plant Management* 32: 1–6.

Getsinger, K.D., E.G. Turner, J.D. Madsen, and M.D. Netherland. 1997. Restoring native vegetation in a Eurasian water-milfoil dominated plant community using the herbicide triclopyr. *Regulated Rivers: Research & Management: An International Journal Devoted to River Research and Management* 13(4): 357–375.

Glomski, L.M., and M.D. Netherland. 2007. Efficacy of diquat and carfentrazone-ethyl on variable-leaf milfoil. *Journal of Aquatic Plant Management* 45: 136–138.

Glomski, L.M., and M.D. Netherland. 2008a. Effect of water temperature on 2,4-D ester and carfentrazone-ethyl applications for control of variable-leaf milfoil. *Journal of Aquatic Plant Management* 46: 119–121.

Glomski, L.M., and M.D. Netherland. 2008b. Efficacy of fluridone, penoxsulam, and bispyribac-sodium on variable-leaf milfoil. *Journal of Aquatic Plant Management* 46(1): 193–196.

Hall, J.F., H.E. Westerdahl, and T.J. Stewart. 1984. Growth response of Myriophyllum spicatum and Hydrilla verticillata when exposed to continuous low concentrations of fluridone. US Army Engineers Waterways Experimental Station, Vicksburg, MS, USA. *Technical Report* A-84–1.

Howard, V. 2020. Myriophyllum heterophyllum Michx.: U.S. Geological Survey, Nonindigenous Aquatic Species Database, Gainesville, FL, https://nas.er.usgs.gov/queries/FactSheet.aspx?speciesID=236, Revision Date: 10/31/2008 (Accessed June 26, 2020).

Invasive Eurasian Watermilfoil: Cutting Back invasive species in Lake George. 2021. from www.lakegeorgeassociation.org/educate/science/lake-george-invasive-species/eurasian-milfoil/ (Accessed June 27, 2021).

Isabel, P. 2011. Variable Watermilfoil, Myriophyllum heterophyllum. https://sites.google.com/a/rsu5.org/invasive/maine-invasive-species/variable-watermilfoil-myriophyllum-heterophyllum (Accessed June 27, 2021).

ITIS (Integrated Taxonomic Information System). 2021. www.itis.gov (Accessed June 26, 2021).

Lyman, L., and L. Eichler. 2005. Successes and Limits of Hand Harvesting, Suction Harvesting, and Benthic Barriers in Lake George, NY. Presentation at the Northeast Aquatic Plant Management Society annual meeting, Saratoga Springs, NY.

MA DCR (Department of Conservation & Recreation, MA). 2016. A guide to aquatic plants in Massachusetts. Department of Conservation & Recreation, MA, http://lakemirimichi.org/Assets/Aquatic%20life/A%20Guide%20to%20Aquatic%20Plants_Booklet.PDF (Accessed February 19, 2020).

Madsen, J.D., and K.D. Getsinger. 2005. Selective control of invasive submersed aquatic plants. In: *Invasive Plants: Arming to Defend and Win, Southeast Exotic Pest Plant Council's Seventh Ann. Conf.*, Birmingham, AL, pp. 34–35.

MaineVLMP. 2009. Variable water-milfoil. maine volunteer lake monitoring program. www.mainevlmp.org/mciap/herbarium/VariableWatermilfoil.php (Accessed January 29, 2020).

MassDEP (Massachusetts Department of Environmental Protection) 2021. Final Massachusetts Integrated List of Waters for the Clean Water Act 2018/2020 Reporting Cycle. Division of Watershed Management, Watershed Planning Program. CN: 505.1. www.mass.gov/doc/final-massachusetts-integrated-list-of-waters-for-the-clean-water-act-20182020-reporting-cycle/download

Mattson, M.D., P.J.G. Barletta, A. Aiello, and K.J. Wagner. 2004. Eutrophication and aquatic plant management in Massachusetts: Final generic environmental impact report. *Commonwealth of Massachusetts, Executive Office of Environmental Affairs Commonwealth of Massachusetts* 1–514. pp. 4–11.

Mikulyuk, A., E. Kujawa, M.E. Nault, S. Van Egeren, K.I. Wagner, M. Barton, J. Hauxwell, and M.J. Vander Zanden. 2020. Is the cure worse than the disease? Comparing the ecological effects of an invasive aquatic plant and the herbicide treatments used to control it. *FACETS* 5: 353–366.

Netherland, M.D., W.R. Green, and K.D. Getsinger. 1991. Endothal concentration and exposure time relationships for the control of Eurasian watermilfoil and hydrilla. *Journal of Aquatic Plant Management* 29: 61–67.

New York Invasive Species (IS) Information. 2019. *Eurasian Watermilfoil*. New York: New York Invasive.

Nichols, S.A. 1975. Identification and management of Eurasian watermilfoil in Wisconsin. *Transactions of the Wisconsin Academy of Science, Arts, and Letters*, Vol. 63 pp. 116–128.

Olden, J.D., and M. Tamayo. 2014. Incentivizing the public to support invasive species. management: Eurasian Milfoil reduces lakefront property values. *PLoS One* 9: e110458. https://doi.org/10.1371/journal.pone.0110458

Pfingsten, I.A., L. Berent, C.C. Jacono, and M.M. Richerson. 2021. Myriophyllum spicatum L.: U.S. Geological Survey, Nonindigenous Aquatic Species Database, Gainesville, FL, https://nas.er.usgs.gov/queries/factsheet.aspx?SpeciesID=237 (Accessed December 4, 2020).

Rapid Response Plan for Eurasian Watermilfoil. n.d. Westford: ENSR. [RRP.doc]. www.mass.gov/doc/eurasian-milfoil/download

Robinson, M. 2002a. Variable Milfoil: An Invasive Aquatic Plant Myriophyllum Heterophyllum. MA DCR (Department of Conservation & Recreation, MA) (http://macolap.org/wp-content/uploads/2015/11/MA-DCR-Variable-Milfoil.pdf (Accessed January 29, 2020).

Robinson, M. 2002b. Eurasian Milfoil: An Invasive Aquatic *Myriophyllum spicatum*. MA DCR (Department of Conservation & Recreation, MA) www.mass.gov/files/documents/2017/09/06/eurasian-milfoil.pdf (Accessed January 29, 2020).

Scheers, K., L. Denys, J. Packet, and T. Adriaens. 2016. A second population of *Cabomba caroliniana* Gray (Cabombaceae) in Belgium with options for its eradication. *BioInvasions Records* 5(4):227–232.

Smith, C.S., and J.W. Barko. 1990. Ecology of Eurasian Watermilfoil [PDF]. *Journal of Aquatic Plant Management* 28: 55–64.

Smith, D.G. 1993. The Potential for Spread of the Exotic Zebra Mussel (Dreissena polymorpha) in Massachusetts. Report MS-Q-11. Department of Biology, University of Massachusetts Amherst, Massachusetts and Museum of Comparative Zoology, Harvard University, Cambridge, Massachusetts. From www.mass.gov/eea/docs/dcr/watersupply/lakepond/downloads/zebra-mussel-massdep-ms-q-11.pdf (Accessed June 27, 2018).

Thum, R.A., and J.T. Lennon. 2006. Is hybridization responsible for invasive growth of non-indigenous water-milfoils? *Biological Invasions* 8(5): 1061–1066.

Thum, R.A., S. Parks, J.N. Mcnair, P. Tyning, P. Hausler, L. Chadderton, A. Tucker, and A. Monfils. 2017. Survival and vegetative regrowth of Eurasian and hybrid watermilfoil following operational treatment with auxinic herbicides in Gun Lake, Michigan. *Journal of Aquatic Plant Management* 55: 103–107.

VT DEC (Vermont Department of Environmental Conservation). 2022. Aquatic invasive species control. https://dec.vermont.gov/watershed/lakes-ponds/aquatic-invasives/control (Accessed May 29, 2022).

9 Parrot-feather (*Myriophyllum aquaticum*)

ABSTRACT

Parrot-feather (*Myriophyllum aquaticum*) is an aquatic plant in the watermilfoil family native to South America. It is widely distributed across North America, Europe, Asia, and Africa as an invasive species. Outside of its native range, parrot-feather is regarded as a troublesome weed, due to its ability to grow quickly and clog or stagnate shallow waterways. This chapter describes the basic biology of parrot-feather and presents a listing of known sightings in the state of Massachusetts. Approaches to control this invasive species, such as mechanical removal, chemical treatment (i.e., herbicides), and potential biological agents, are also discussed.

INTRODUCTION

Taxonomic Hierarchy (ITIS 2021)

Kingdom	Plantae
Subkingdom	Viridiplantae
Infrakingdom	Streptophyta
Superdivision	Embryophyta
Division	Tracheophyta
Subdivision	Spermatophytina
Class	Magnoliopsida
Superorder	Saxifraganae
Order	Saxifragales
Family	Haloragaceae
Genus	*Myriophyllum* L.
Species	*Myriophyllum aquaticum* (Vell.) Verdc.

Parrot-feather (*Myriophyllum aquaticum*) is native to the Amazon River Basin in South America, but it has been introduced as an ornamental plant around the world (Wersal et al. 2021). Today, the plant is found on nearly every continent (Lastrucci et al. 2018). Parrot-feather is a type of watermilfoil, classified within the same genus as Eurasian watermilfoil and variable milfoil, two other invasive species. These three species of watermilfoil, including parrot-feather, are included on the Massachusetts Prohibited Plant List; therefore, it is illegal to import, sell, or trade parrot-feather within the state of Massachusetts (Commonwealth of Massachusetts 2021).

Considered an amphibious and highly adaptive plant species, parrot-feather is heterophyllous in its growth, meaning submerged sections of the plant grow to take on a different form and character to sections of the stem that emerge from the water (Wersal 2010; Wersal et al. 2021). The sections above water are solidly light green and dense with small feather-shaped leaves arranged in whorls of four to six around the stem (Smitha et al. 2007), while the submerged parts of the plant are much sparser, with relatively elongated green leaves around a reddish-brown stem (Figures 9.1 and 9.2). In response to a change in position or in water level, the stem is able to adjust and rapidly change; under experimental conditions, parts of the stem were observed to change from the emergent to the submersed form in a matter of days after a rise in water level (Wersal and Madsen 2011). The majority of the plant's biomass appears to be positioned above the water, but the stems can extend downward up to 2 m, where a rhizome is anchored to the sediment by thin roots (Cook 1985; Murphy 2007; Haberland 2014).

As a dioecious plant, parrot-feather has separate male and female flowers. The plant is capable of achieving pollination through wind and reproducing by seed, but sexual reproduction is thought to be a negligible means of reproduction outside of the plant's native range, since the vast majority of invasive specimens collected appear to be female plants, and flowers are rarely seen (Cook 1985; Murphy 2007). When present, flowers are small, white if female and yellow if male, and they grow along the stem between leaf-whorls (Murphy 2007). Parrot-feather reproduces on a local scale by cloning, with mature plants producing numerous offshoots and allocating resources to younger plants in order to maximize their survival (You

DOI: 10.1201/9781003201106-9

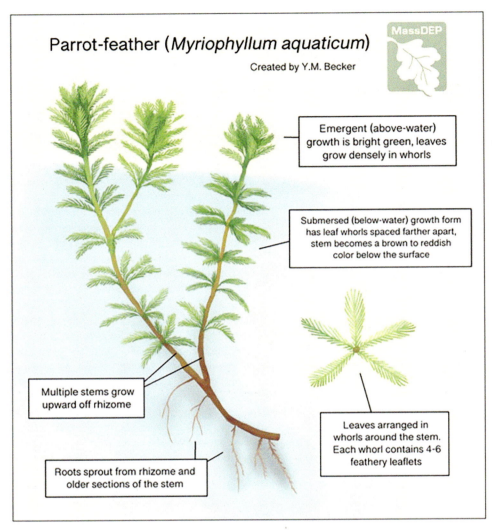

FIGURE 9.1 Illustration of parrot-feather. (Modified from Karwath (2005), Lurvey (2021), and UF IFAS (2021).)

et al. 2013). Since the plant lacks tubers or any other kind of root specialized for nutrient storage and dispersal, these functions are served by the stolons connecting offshoots to their parents (Wersal et al. 2021). Parrot-feather can also reproduce via stem fragmentation, when dislodged or senescent pieces of stem fall into the sediment, where they begin to grow roots and new stems (Figure 9.2).

Native and Invasive Range, Mechanisms of Spread

The earliest recorded specimen of *M. aquaticum* in the United States was collected from New Jersey in 1890, having been introduced to the area as a garden ornamental (Wersal 2010; Wersal et al. 2021). By the 1940s, *M. aquaticum* was well-established in the region of Southern New York, and populations could be found all the way on the west coast, in Washington state (Wersal et al. 2021). Today, this invasive species is established throughout the United States, especially along the coasts and in southern states east of Texas (USGS 2021).

After an initial introduction, parrot-feather is observed to secondarily spread to new habitats mainly by clonal growth and fragmentation (You et al. 2013; Murphy 2007). The species is

FIGURE 9.2 Photos of parrot-feather (King County NWCP 2018). Specimen of a rooted fragment held in hand with roots and young stems growing off fragment (*left*). Examples of dense wild parrot-feather growth (*right*, *top*, and *bottom*).

also capable of flowering and reproducing by seed, but this method of spread is thought to be less common outside of the plant's native range due to the rarity of male introduced specimens (Murphy 2007). Either stem fragments or seeds from an established parrot-feather stand are prone to being carried downstream to colonize new areas, where a population then grows and expands to capacity by producing clonal offshoots. Improperly cleaned boats and traveling waterfowl are also considered vectors for secondary spread, potentially enabling even broader dispersal of plant fragments to new waterways beyond the reach of simple downstream water movement (Murphy 2007; Kuehne et al. 2016).

Systems at the greatest risk of parrot-feather invasion are those which are shallow and prone to disturbance (Lastrucci et al. 2018). Regularly occurring mechanical disturbances facilitate stem fragmentation and create conditions that favor the dominance of *M. aquaticum* in shallow systems (Wersal and Madsen 2011). Since parrot-feather thrives in nutrient-rich environments, pollution and runoff are also risk factors for invasion (Xie et al. 2010; Wersal et al. 2021). Though populations will often fail to establish when faced with severe winters, parrot-feather is overall a hardy plant capable of withstanding moderate frost, short-term changes in water level, and even some degree of saltwater inundation (Wersal and Madsen 2011; Wersal et al. 2021).

Ecological and Human Impacts

M. aquaticum is known to be a competitive and fast-growing plant species, often dominating over native plant species as well as influencing the species composition in animal and bacterial communities (Kuehne et al. 2016; Sun et al. 2017; Lastrucci et al. 2018). Parrot-feather has been observed in several instances to compete with and displace native flora, forming dense monospecific stands (Stiers et al. 2011; Lastrucci et al. 2018). Due to the plant's inability to reproduce by seed in its introduced range, these stands are formed through clonal growth. Like other plant species which reproduce in this way, *M. aquaticum* stands are prone to low genetic diversity, which is considered a liability for the plant populations' health and long-term success (Lambertini et al. 2010). Though low genetic diversity does not reflect upon likelihood of invasion success (Roman and Darling 2007; Rollins et al. 2013), the replacement of genetically and taxonomically diverse plant populations with uniform clonal populations threatens the long-term resilience of an ecosystem (Hughes et al. 2008).

Parrot-feather invasion has also been observed to have effects on macroinvertebrate and fish species composition. Studies have found certain non-native fish and arthropod species living in higher density in areas dominated by *M. aquaticum* as compared to non-invaded areas (Lastrucci et al. 2018; Kuehne et al. 2016). Notably, there is a well-established correlation between the density of *M. aquaticum* and the presence of mosquitoes (Orr and Resh 1989; Lastrucci et al. 2018; Wersal et al. 2021 https://europepmc.org/article/med/2614408). Increased mosquito abundance is a human health risk, given the dangers of mosquito-borne illnesses (Wersal and Madsen 2007; Wersal et al. 2021). In Massachusetts, mosquitoes are known to seasonally carry and spread several diseases, including West Nile virus and eastern equine encephalitis (Cambridge Public Health Department n.d.).

The increased mosquito risk is brought about because of changes parrot-feather makes to the character of the habitats it invades. Parrot-feather grows into thick, dense mats, clogging already shallow waterways so that the flow of the water is reduced or even made stagnant (Hill 2003). The reduction in water movement, along with the protective cover provided by *M. aquaticum*'s emergent growth, creates perfect habitat for mosquitoes to breed and deposit their eggs, and for larvae to mature (Wersal et al. 2021). Blockages in waterways also negatively impact other species, preventing the movement of fish and inhibiting human recreational activities such as swimming and boating (Hill 2003; Lastrucci et al. 2018).

A 2016 study found that dense parrot-feather cover was associated with lower dissolved oxygen (DO) in the water column (Kuehne et al. 2016). In 1999, it was reported that irrigating tobacco with water drawn from sources infested by *M. aquaticum* lead to red discoloration of the harvested tobacco product, resulting in a less profitable harvest (Cilliers 1999), though the exact cause of the discolored crop was unclear. Parrot-feather is also thought to be capable of increasing evapotranspiration, with a higher rate of water loss where the water surface is covered by *M. aquaticum* (Cilliers 1999).

In spite of the risks posed by wild overabundant parrot-feather growth, a study on waste treatment in constructed wetlands found that when *M. aquaticum* is cultivated in water, it is highly efficient in reducing chemical oxygen demand (a measure of organic waste) and enriching communities of denitrifying bacteria (Sun et al. 2017). Though *M. aquaticum* was the only macrophyte included in this study, the authors suggest that impacts on bacterial communities may be specific to certain plant species (Sun et al. 2017). Both *M. aquaticum* and *M. spicatum*, another related milfoil species, have been found to contain allelopathic chemicals capable of inhibiting blue-green algae growth (Nakai et al. 2000; Cheng et al. 2008).

M. aquaticum has also been found to be highly efficient in removing phosphorus, tetracycline, heavy metals, and other pollutants from water, whether for purposes of assessing pollutant concentrations or for ecological restoration (Harguinteguy et al. 2013; Souza et al. 2013; Luo et al. 2017; Colzi et al. 2018; Guo et al. 2019). The plant may not even need to be implanted alive in order to provide these benefits: the dead biomass of *M. aquaticum* has been found useful in removing heavy metal contamination from water, most effectively removing zinc and cadmium specifically (Colzi et al. 2018). These findings point to a potential valuable purpose for the reuse of waste material collected after parrot-feather management efforts, though extreme caution should be taken not to introduce live plant material to high-risk waterways. Complete decomposition of *M. aquaticum* debris will also result in a complex variety of impacts to water quality, involving the re-release of nutrients (Luo et al. 2020).

Parrot-feather (*Myriophyllum aquaticum*)

TABLE 9.1

Sightings and Report Agencies of Infested Waterbodies

Waterbody	Watershed	Agency	Town	Year
Jones River	South Coastal	MassDEP	Kingston	2017
Jones River	South Coastal	MassDEP	Kingston	2006
Jones River	South Coastal	MassDEP	Kingston	2006
Jones River	South Coastal	MassDEP	Kingston	2006
Mill River	Charles	MassDEP	Norfolk	2015
Satucket River	Taunton	MassDEP	East Bridgewater	2017
Satucket River	Taunton	MassDEP	East B ridgewater	2006
Satucket River	Taunton	MassDEP	East Bridgewater	2006
Great Pond	Islands	USGS NAS Database	Tisbury	2020
Burchell's Pond	Islands	USGS NAS Database	Nantucket	2016
Big West Pond	Buzzards Bay	USGS NAS Database	Plymouth	2017

MONITORING AND SIGHTINGS

The data in this report were collected by Massachusetts Department of Environmental Protection (MassDEP) and US Geological Survey (USGS) (Table 9.1). The standard operating procedure was developed for all field surveys by MassDEP, including field sheet development, species identification, and quality control and assurance. MassDEP compiled data from all agencies. Data layers and maps of sites with parrot-feather were created using QGIS open-source software (OSGeo, Beaverton, Oregon) and ArcMap 10.1 (ESRI, Redlands, California).

Parrot-feather (*M. aquaticum*) was detected for the first time in Massachusetts in 2006, in the Jones River at Kingston. Since then, it has been confirmed that a total of six waterbodies in the state, including three rivers and three lakes, have been invaded by this species. These waters are within five watersheds: South Coastal, Charles River, Taunton River, Islands, and Buzzards Bay (Figure 9.3). Most of these waterbodies are in the southeastern region of the state. Monitoring and prevention are needed to better manage this invasive species and prevent its further spread to other waters in Massachusetts. A map depicting all known infested waterbodies and watersheds in the state is included in this report (Figure 9.3). Monitoring for parrot-feather in Massachusetts has so far been carried out by conventional visual assessment and identification. With recent advancements in molecular technologies, monitoring by analyzing environmental DNA (eDNA) is becoming an increasingly accessible and valuable tool for detecting invasive species on a broad scale. Specific identifiers and protocols for the detection of *M. aquaticum* have recently been developed, allowing for this species to be detected and identified through standard PCR-based methods (Shah et al. 2014).

MANAGING ACTIONS

Early detection and response measures need to be developed to monitor the establishment and spread of this invasive species. Like many invasive species, parrot-feather is most able to take hold and become invasive in bodies of water that are already at risk due to other factors—both anthropogenic disturbance and excess nutrients in a system due to pollution are conditions that benefit the proliferation of parrot-feather and eliminating these risk factors is an important step in preventing overabundant growth (Haberland 2014).

Another step to avoid parrot-feather invasion is the prevention of dispersal through human activities. Properly cleaning watercraft, swimming gear, and construction equipment before transporting items between waterbodies will prevent the accidental dispersal of plant fragments from infested systems. Care should be taken not to introduce exotic ornamental garden or aquarium plants to the wild, and the individual selection of native plants for outdoor home or commercial gardens should be encouraged and promoted.

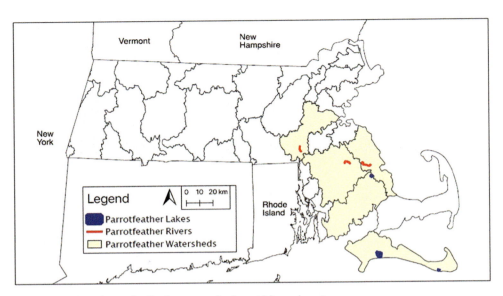

FIGURE 9.3 Infested waterbodies by parrot-feather at Massachusetts.

CHEMICAL CONTROL

Targeted application of chemical herbicides is a popular method of managing nuisance plants and several chemicals are legal to use in Massachusetts. Many different herbicides have been used with success, including glyphosate, endothall, diquat, 2,4-D, triclopyr, and imazapyr (Patten 2003; Hofstra et al. 2006; Souza et al. 2012). In recent years, florpyrauxifen-benzyl (active ingredient of ProcellaCOR™) is a relatively new herbicide for all milfoils, including parrot-feather. Success rates vary across different documented trials, and the effectiveness of a given herbicide application is likely to depend on characteristics of the site, the method of applying the herbicide, and the concentration and composition of the herbicide solution.

Though glyphosate is one of the most commonly used systemic herbicides, opinions vary on its effectiveness against parrot-feather. Glyphosate can be useful, but some advise against it due to its inability to prevent regrowth without multiple applications (Patten 2003; Hofstra et al. 2006; Wersal and Madsen 2007; Kuehne et al. 2018). On the other hand, a study conducted under greenhouse conditions found that certain additives to glyphosate can increase the herbicide's effectiveness on management of *M. aquaticum*. Mixing additives such as Aterbane® and Veget'oil® to the herbicide solution brought control effectiveness above 90% at certain dosages, and several additives caused reduction in regrowth (Cerveira et al. 2020).

Imazapyr is another chemical herbicide that is considered useful against parrot-feather. As imazapyr tends to break down after a short time when exposed to water and sunlight, it is typically used to control emergent vegetation (Tu et al. 2001). Field experiments comparing the efficacy of various herbicides have found imazapyr-based treatments more effective than those using 2,4-D as a main ingredient (Kuehne et al. 2018). Another experiment using imazapyr resulted in 100% parrot-feather mortality when applying high concentrations of the herbicide (Wersal and Madsen 2007). Imazamox may be useful too because it is the same class of chemicals but made for submergent vegetations, if applied at earlier growths of parrot-feather (Ken Wagner, personal communication).

Another set of experiments were carried out comparing the effects of endothall, triclopyr, dichlobenil, fluridone, clopyralid, and glyphosate on *M. aquaticum* (Hofstra et al. 2006). After initial treatments, clopyralid and fluridone were found to have a minimal impact on parrot-feather biomass and percent cover and were thus rejected. Triclopyr, dichlobenil, and endothall each significantly reduced the biomass of the experimental plants, with triclopyr standing out as the most efficacious, while also being less environmentally persistent than dichlobenil.[1] The second-year trials, conducted in the field, compared only triclopyr and glyphosate, finding triclopyr to provide "substantially" better control than glyphosate (Hofstra et al. 2006).

The relatively new herbicide, ProcellaCOR™, may have higher effectiveness on parrot-feather or other milfoil species without non-target damage. However, there is no data available to support its efficacy in parrot-feather control yet. Methods for application of this product in Massachusetts are restricted to in-water applications and foliar applications from a boat or ground equipment. It should be excluded from use in state-listed aquatic species habitats, unless otherwise authorized in writing on a case-by-case basis by the MA Division of Fisheries and Wildlife pursuant to MA Endangered Species Act (321 CMR 10.14 or 10.18).

Additionally, it is worth noting that, in spite of experimentally demonstrated effectiveness of many herbicides on parrot-feather, some agencies recommend against the use of chemical herbicides on the basis of low efficiency. The Invasive Species Council of Metro Vancouver (2019) lists chemical treatments as "not recommended" due to "poor absorption" and risks to wildlife. King County, WA's Noxious Weed Control Program best practice documentation, mentions that the texture of the stem and leaves demands chemical additives for effective herbicide delivery, and that herbicide applications may need to be repeated over several growing seasons, while altogether the documentation describes chemical management as "the most reasonable option for eradication of large parrotfeather infestations" (King County NWCP 2014). Altogether, there is ample experimental evidence to demonstrate the effectiveness of several chemical herbicides on parrot-feather.

Although herbicides can be very precise and efficient in eliminating target plant species, they may have significant impacts to other species and the environment if not used with care. Proper use is essential to best results in terms of target control and minimized non-target species influences. Therefore, it is critical to apply any herbicide product correctly, read and follow the directions on the product's label, and follow any state or federal laws applicable to herbicide treatments. More information about chemical control on parrot-feather and other 18 invasive species can be found in Appendix III. In the state of Massachusetts, it is required to obtain an aquatic nuisance species control license (BRP WM04 Form) from the Massachusetts Department of Environmental Protection before applying a chemical herbicide.

Physical Control

Harvesting plant matter, either by hand or by machine, is a simple and intuitive way to reduce the amount of invasive vegetation in a short period of time. However, like many other invasive plant species, parrot-feather is capable of reproducing by fragmentation. This growth strategy poses challenges to physical removal efforts, since mechanically cutting or damaging parrot-feather stems in any way could create loose stem fragments which inadvertently facilitate the spread of the invasive species. A Portugal study comparing mechanical and chemical control found that mechanical removal achieved immediate clearance followed by gradual regrowth back to initial density over the course of the next two years, while herbicide application using glyphosate was slow at first but provided better long-term control (Machado and Rocha 1998).

Another physical technique for removing invasive plants involves making adjustments to water level in an infested area by artificially enacting floods or drawdown. *M. aquaticum* is well-adapted to survive most short-term rises or falls in water level, but experimentation has shown that the species grows poorly under sustained deep flooding conditions (Wersal and Madsen 2011). When applicable, permanently or extensively raising water level could be a good way of mitigating invasive parrot-feather growth. Extended periods of drawdown can also be effective at controlling *M. aquaticum*, though the plants must be kept in dry soil for a long period of time in order to see positive results. A 2013 experiment found an insignificant decrease in parrot-feather survival after a 2-week drawdown, but in contrast survival was down to 18% after a 12-week drawdown (Wersal et al. 2013). The effects of drawdown and flooding on parrot-feather populations are regarded as unpredictable and ill-advised (Metro Vancouver 2019) because this technique is weather-dependent and becoming less reliable with climate change.

Shading and smothering through use of a gas-permeable benthic-barrier is another useful management strategy for aquatic invasive plants, including *M. aquaticum*. Parrot-feather has been found to thrive in partial shade (30–50% shaded) and suffer somewhat in full sunlight. When light is significantly reduced (in conditions of 70% shade), stem length increases while overall biomass decreases (Wersal 2010). Interestingly, when grown in 70% shade, the apical tips of *M. aquaticum* take on the submersed growth form, further indicating stress under insufficient light conditions. Shaded and full-sun conditions also directly impact water temperature, which could contribute to the plant's stress at extremes (Wersal 2010). In Richmond, Vancouver, trials were carried out to determine the effectiveness of shading and smothering on *M. aquaticum* in infested drainage ditches (Metro Vancouver 2019). Barriers were carefully applied to avoid leaving exposed seams that might be exploited by parrot-feather rhizomes.[2] Both the shading and benthic barrier trials were found effective in significantly reducing parrot-feather's biomass within the drainage ditches. However, while inexpensive on the small scale, these methods were acknowledged to be costly and impractical to apply in large open areas (Metro Vancouver 2019).

BIOLOGICAL CONTROL

Biological control of an invasive species entails the intentional release of an organism that is known to feed on the target species, in the hopes that the control agent will either completely eliminate the invader or simply reduce the invasive population so that it will not grow unchecked or dominate over native species. An ideal biological control agent is one that feeds on its target species sufficiently to suppress the target's growth and feeds exclusively or with strong preference on its target species, so that the control agent does not pose a risk to native or non-target species. Several organisms are known to feed on parrot-feather, including some insects and larger herbivores. While no parrot-feather-specific biocontrol agent has been approved for release in the United States, insect biocontrol programs have seen success in other parts of the world (Hill 2003). This section will discuss a range of species known to have potential for parrot-feather biocontrol, as well as the risks and benefits associated with each species.

Insect Control Agents

A bio-control program initiated in South Africa in the early 1990s saw the release of leaf-feeding beetles (*Lysathia* spp.) at 25 infested locations, resulting in a pattern of repeated defoliation and regrowth followed by an ultimate collapse of the parrot-feather population (Cilliers 1999; Hill 2003). While the project saw a degree of success, the control by the *Lysathia* sp. beetles was considered insufficient, and so research has been underway to determine the suitability of a South American weevil (*Listronotus marginicollis*) as another control species (Hill 2003; Oberholzer et al. 2007). *L. marginicollis* was experimentally determined to have host specificity with *M. aquaticum* and deemed safe to release in South Africa (Oberholzer et al. 2007). Additionally, the CABI Invasive Species Compendium recognizes *L. marginicollis* as a "natural enemy" of *M. aquaticum* (CABI 2019).

In 2020, a certain population of *Galerucella grisescens* beetle was found feeding on invasive *M. aquaticum* in Chiba Prefecture, Honshu, Japan (Okamoto et al. 2020). Though the natural host plant of these beetles is a different species, in the family Polygonaceae, reproductive beetles from the Chiba population were found to preferentially lay eggs on *M. aquaticum*, suggesting this species could be useful as biological control if further risk assessment and research to determine suitability are carried out. The authors of this study also note that this beetle population might be viewed not only as a tool for biological control, but perhaps as a hopeful example of a native species broadening its host plant range in order to adapt to the increased presence of an invasive species. If other insect species in Japan and worldwide are commonly able to adapt their feeding preferences in this way, as suggested by other examples of adaptation to non-native food sources or competitors (Carroll 2007; Berthon 2015; Golec et al. 2019), ecosystems around the world could have internal mechanisms for mitigating the threats posed

Fish and Mammal Control Agents

Grass carp (*Ctenopharyngodon idella*) are herbivorous fish native to Asia that are popularly stocked in a controlled manner as a way of reducing invasive vegetation (Reyes 2021). These fish tend to ravenously clear out all plant matter accessible to them, leaving their habitat barren of plants in a relatively short amount of time (Garner et al. 2013). Grass carp can therefore be a useful means of controlling nuisance vegetation or a troublesome force of ecological destruction. Observations on grass carp food preferences have found that the fish prefer to eat most other plant species over parrot-feather, suggesting that they would not be useful as a parrot-feather control agent (Pine and Anderson 1991; Madsen and Wersal n.d.; King County NWCP 2014). However, an in situ study found that grass carp will clear out all available parrot-feather vegetation despite the fact that parrot-feather is not a preferred food source (Garner et al. 2013).

Due to the intense pressure grass carp grazing inflicts on native and non-native vegetation, and the potential for the carp themselves to become established as an invasive species, grass carp should only be considered as a control agent after careful assessment of ecological risk. Upon implementation, a plan should be made for monitoring and regulating grass carp population in the long term, to ensure the success of the invasive species control as well as to prevent damage to local ecosystems. Grass carp are most appropriate as biological control in large, isolated man-made impoundments, with low diversity of native plant species (Reyes 2021). In Massachusetts, the introduction of grass carp is prohibited.

Rather than importing a non-native herbivore to graze on invasive species, one might also achieve management of invasive parrot-feather with the help of a native herbivore: the beaver. Field experiments by Parker et al. (2007) observed the effects of "beaver exclusion" on freshwater plant communities and found that removing beavers from certain plots lead to an extreme disparity in the abundance of the exotic *M. aquaticum*. Where beavers were permitted to graze and construct their nests, *M. aquaticum* biomass was reduced by 90%. This case serves as evidence that reintroducing and protecting native herbivores can act as a preventative measure against noxious plant growth and ecological invasion. In Massachusetts, the practitioners need to check with Division of Fisheries & Wildlife, local Conservation Commissions, or Department of Environmental Protection to get appropriate approvals for an introduction of a vertebrate due to beavers' damming and tree damage.

SUCCESS STORY

Over the course of 14 weeks from August to November 2006, Ryan Wersal and John D. Madsen, at Mississippi State University, performed outdoor mesocosm experiments to test the efficiencies of two systemic herbicides, imazapyr and imazamox, on parrot-feather (Wersal and Madsen 2007). For the first four weeks, parrot-feather was planted and grown in mesocosms (small-scale, simulated ecosystems). Each herbicide was applied to one of three mesocosms in either a low, medium, or high concentration, and the mesocosms were then monitored for ten weeks posttreatment. A non-ionic surfactant called Dyne-Amic® was added to each mixture to help the sprayed herbicide solution stick onto the surface of the plants. Between the two herbicides, imazapyr performed better, achieving 100% mortality of the parrot-feather after eight weeks, at both the medium and high concentrations (Wersal and Madsen 2007).

In 2018, a field study was carried out by Kuehne et al. at four sites along the Chehalis River in Washington State, assessing the efficiency of three chemical herbicide mixtures: imazapyr only, imazapyr mixed with the contact herbicide carfentrazone (known to be ineffective on parrot-feather when used alone), and 2,4-D mixed with carfentrazone (Kuehne et al. 2018). Six weeks after each treatment, the biomass of parrot-feather at the 2,4-D-solution-treated sites had only been reduced 23%, but at each of the sites where an imazapyr solution had been used, parrot-feather cover was reduced by 67–69%, a promising and significant reduction. The concentration of imazapyr used in this field study was at maximum strength, exceeding the highest concentration used in the 2007 Mississippi State study, and a surfactant was also added at twice the volume of that used in the mesocosm study (Kuehne et al. 2018). The incomplete control achieved during the field study is likely the result of variation in outdoor environmental conditions. The wild-grown parrot-feather may also have been tougher on account of being older and better-established than the 4-week-old crop in the mesocosm study. Regardless, a control rate of 67–69% is significant and speaks to the promise of imazapyr solutions as chemical control agents for parrot-feather infestations.

NOTES

1. Dichlobenil is not a permitted chemical in Massachusetts.
2. After benthic barriers were installed to cover parrot-feather in areas of Burchell Pond, Massachusetts, in 2017, the area covered by parrot-feather decreased significantly in 2018. Then, in 2018, benthic barriers reinstalled on areas previously not covered but in 2019, the area covered with parrot-feather increased substantially as the plants grew around the barriers seeking sunlight. After that, the herbicide ProcellaCOR was used to treat the plants and it worked well. After two applications there is hardly any parrot-feather left and the natural vegetation, as well as the animal species inhabiting the pond, does not seem to be impacted (personal communication, Rachel Freeman, dated July 5, 2022).

REFERENCES

Berthon, K. 2015. How do native species respond to invaders? Mechanistic and trait-based perspectives. *Biological Invasions* 17: 2199–2211.

CABI Invasive Species Compendium. 2019. *Listronotus marginicollis*. www.cabi.org/isc/datasheet/28361. (Accessed June 29, 2021).

Cambridge Public Health Department. n.d. Mosquito-borne diseases. www.cambridgepublichealth.org/services/environmental-health/mosquito-borne-diseases/. (Accessed June 29, 2021).

Carroll, S.P. 2007. Brave New World: The epistatic foundations of natives adapting to invaders. *Genetica* 129: 193–204.

Cerveira, W.R., A.F. Silva, J.H.C. Cervoni, C. Cruz, and R.A. Pitelli. 2020. The addition of adjuvants on glyphosate enhances the control of aquatic plant *Myriophyllum aquaticum* (Vell.). *Planta Daninha* 38.

Cheng, W., C. Xuexiu, D. Hongjuan, L. Difu, and L. Junyan. 2008. Allelopathic inhibitory effect of *Myriophyllum aquaticum* (Vell.) Verdc. on *Microcystis aeruginosa* and its physiological mechanism. *Acta Ecologica Sinica* 28(6): 2595–2603.

Cilliers, C.J. 1999. *Lysathia* n. sp. (Coleoptera: Chrysomelidae), a host-specific beetle for the control of the aquatic weed *Myriophyllum aquaticum* (Haloragaceae) in South Africa. *Hydrobiologia* 415: 271–276.

Colzi, I., L. Lastrucci, M. Rangoni, A. Coppi, and C. Gonnelli. 2018. Using *Myriophyllum aquaticum* (Vell.) Verdc. to remove heavy metals from contaminated water: Better dead or alive? *Journal of Environmental Management* 213(1): 320–328.

Commonwealth of Massachusetts. 2021. Massachusetts prohibited plant list. www.mass.gov/massachusetts-prohibited-plant-list. (Accessed June 25, 2021).

Cook, C.D.K. 1985. Worldwide distribution and taxonomy of *Myriophyllum* species. In: *1st International Symposium on Watermilfoil (Myriophyllum spicatum) and Related Haloragaceae Species*. Vancouver, B.C. Canada: Aquatic Plant Management Society.

Garner, A.B., T.J. Kwak, K.L. Manuel, and D.H. Barwick. 2013. High-density grass-carp stocking effects on a reservoir invasive plant and water quality. *Journal of Aquatic Plant Management* 51: 27–33.

Golec, J.R., J.J. Duan, K. Rim, J. Hough-Goldstein, and E.A. Aparicio. 2019. Laboratory adaptation of a native North American parasitoid to an exotic wood-boring beetle: Implications for biological control of invasive pests. *Journal of Pest Science* 92: 1179–1186.

Guo, X., Q. Mu, H. Zhong, P. Li, C. Zhang, D. Wei, and T. Zhao. 2019. Rapid removal of tetracycline by *Myriophyllum aquaticum*: Evaluation of the role and mechanisms of adsorption. *Environmental Pollution* 254: 113101.

Haberland, M. 2014. *Parrot Feather (Myriophyllum aquaticum): A Non-Native Aquatic Plant in New Jersey Waterways*. Hoboken, NJ: New Jersey Agricultural Experiment Station. Rutgers, The State University of New Jersey. https://njaes.rutgers.edu/fs1232/ (Accessed June 25, 2021).

Harguinteguy, C.A., R. Schreiber, and M.L. Pignata. 2013. *Myriophyllum aquaticum* as a biomonitor of water heavy metal input related to agricultural activities in the Xanaes River (Córdoba, Argentina). *Ecological Indicators* 27: 8–16.

Hill, M.P. 2003. The impact and control of alien aquatic vegetation in South African aquatic ecosystems. *African Journal of Aquatic Science* 28(1): 19–24.

Hofstra, D., P.D. Champion, and T.M. Dugdale. 2006. Herbicide trials for the control of parrotsfeather. *Journal of Aquatic Plant Management* 44: 13–18.

Hughes, A.R., B.D. Inouye, M.T.J. Johnson, N. Underwood, and M. Vellend. 2008. Ecological consequences of genetic diversity. *Ecology Letters* 11: 609–623.

ITIS (Integrated Taxonomic Information System). 2021. www.itis.gov/servlet/SingleRpt/SingleRpt?search_topic=TSN&search_value=503904#null (Accessed April 23, 2021).

Karwath, A. 2005. Parrotfeather (Myriophyllum aquaticum). https://en.wikipedia.org/wiki/Myriophyllum_aquaticum#/media/File:Myriophyllum_aquaticum_-_side_(aka).jpg. (Accessed June 30, 2021).

King County Noxious Weed Control Program (NWCP). 2014. Parrotfeather. *Best Management Practices*. https://your.kingcounty.gov/dnrp/library/water-and-land/weeds/BMPs/Parrotfeather-control.pdf. (Accessed June 29, 2021).

King County Noxious Weed Control Program (NWCP). 2018. Parrotfeather photos. https://kingcounty.gov/services/environment/animals-and-plants/noxious-weeds/weed-identification/parrot-feather.aspx. (Accessed June 30, 2021).

Kuehne, L.M., A.K. Adey, T.M. Brownlee, and J.D. Olden. 2018. Field-based comparison of herbicides for control of parrot-feather (*Myriophyllum aquaticum*). *Journal of Aquatic Plant Management* 56: 18–23.

Kuehne, L.M., J.D. Olden, and E.S. Rubenson. 2016. Multi-trophic impacts of an invasive aquatic plant. *Freshwater Biology* 61(11): 1846–1861.

Lambertini, C., T. Riis, B. Olesen, J.S. Clayton, B.K. Sorrell, and H. Brix. 2010. Genetic diversity in three invasive clonal aquatic species in New Zealand. *BMC Genetics* 11: 52.

Lastrucci, L., L. Lazzaro, L. Dell'Olmo, B. Foggi, and F. Cianferoni. 2018. Impacts of *Myriophyllum aquaticum* invasion in a Mediterranean wetland on plant and maco-arthropod communities. *Plant Biosystems* 152(3): 427–435.

Luo, P., F. Liu, X. Liu, X. Wu, R. Yao, L. Chen, X. Li, R. Xiao, and J. Wu. 2017. Phosphorus removal from lagoon-pretreated swine wastewater by pilot-scale surface flow constructed wetlands planted with *Myriophyllum aquaticum*. *Science of the Total Environment* 576: 490–497.

Luo, P., X. Tong, F. Liu, M. Huang, J. Xu, R. Xiao, and J. Wu. 2020. Nutrients release and greenhouse gas emission during decomposition of *Myriophyllum aquaticum* in a sediment water system. *Environmental Pollution* 260: 114015.

Lurvey. 2021. Parrots feather 1 qt. www.lurveys.com/products/lurvey-select-green-goods/pond-plants/AQPLMYRAQU1QT. (Accessed June 30, 2021).

Machado, C., and F. Rocha. 1998. Control of *Myriophyllum aquaticum* in drainage and irrigated channels of Mondego river valley, Portugal. In: *Management and Ecology of Aquatic Plants. Proceedings of the 10th EWRS International Symposium on Aquatic Weeds.* European Weed Research Society, pp. 373–375.

Madsen, J.D., and R.M. Wersal. n.d. Parrotfeather [*Myriophyllum aquaticum* (Vellozo) Verdecourt]. Mississippi State University, Geosystems Research Institute. www.gri.msstate.edu/research/invspec/factsheets/2P/Parrotfeather.pdf. (Accessed June 29, 2021).

Metro Vancouver. 2019. Best Management Practices for Parrot's Feather in the Metro Vancouver Region. www.metrovancouver.org/services/regional-planning/PlanningPublications/ParrotsFeatherBMP.pdf. (Accessed June 29, 2021).

Murphy, K. 2007. *Myriophyllum aquaticum* (parrot's feather). *CABI Invasive Species Compendium.* www.cabi.org/isc/datasheet/34939. (Accessed June 25, 2021).

Nakai, S., Y. Inoue, M. Hosomi, and A. Murakami. 2000. *Myriophyllum spicatum*-released allelopathic polyphenols inhibiting growth of blue-green algae *Microcystis aeruginosa*. *Water Research* 34(11): 3026–3032.

Oberholzer, I.G., D.L. Mafokoane, and M.P. Hill. 2007. The biology and laboratory host range of the Weevil *Listronotus marginicolis* (Hustache) (Coleoptera: Curculionidae), a Natural Enemy of the Invasive Aquatic Weed *Myriophyllum aquaticum* (Velloso) Verde (Haloragaceae) (Parrot's Feather). *Report to the Water Research Commission*, p. 22. www.wrc.org.za/wp-content/uploads/mdocs/KV180.pdf. (Accessed June 29, 2021).

Okamoto, U., S. Shirahama, S. Nasu, H. Miyauchi, and M. Tokuda. 2020. Host range expansion of a Polygonaceae-associated leaf beetle to an invasive aquatic plant *Myriophyllum aquaticum* (Haloragaceae). *Arthropod-Plant Interactions* 14: 491–497.

Orr, B.K., and V.H. Resh. 1989. Experimental test of the influence of aquatic macrophyte cover on the survival of *Anopheles* larvae. *Journal of the American Control Association* 5(4): 579–585.

Parker, J.D., C.C. Caudill, and M.E. Hay. 2007. Beaver herbivory on aquatic plants. *Oecologia* 151: 616–625.

Patten, K. 2003. Evaluating Imazapyr in Aquatic environments. *Agricultural and Environmental News* 205: 77.

Pine, R.T., and L.W.J. Anderson. 1991. Plant preferences of triploid grass carp. *Journal of Aquatic Plant Management* 29: 80–82.

Reyes, A. 2021. Using grass carp to control aquatic vegetation: Practices, uncertainties, and consequences. *Northeast Aquatic Research*, p. 20. https://nysfola.org/wp-content/uploads/Using-Grass-Carp-to-Control-Aquatic-Vegetation-NYSFOLA.pdf. (Accessed June 29, 2021).

Rollins, L.A., A.T. Moles, S. Lam, R. Buitenwerf, J.M. Buswell, C.R. Brandenburger, H. Flores-Moreno, K.B. Nielsen, E. Couchman, G.S. Brown, F.J. Thomson, F. Hemmings, R. Frankham, and W.B. Sherwin. 2013. High genetic diversity is not essential for successful introduction. *Ecology and Evolution* 3(13): 4501–4517.

Roman, J., and J.A. Darling. 2007. Paradox lost: genetic diversity and the success of aquatic invasions. *Trends in Ecology & Evolution* 22(9): 454–464.

Shah, M.A., M.A. Ali, F.M. Al-Hemaid, and Z.A. Reshi. 2014. Delimiting invasive *Myriophyllum aquaticum* in Kashmir Himalaya using a molecular phylogenetic approach. *Genetics and Molecular Research* 13(3): 7564–7570.

Smitha, P., P. Nazeem, T. James, M. Mohan, P.M. Sherif, R. Keshavachandran, P. Nazeem, D. Girija, P. John, and K. Peter. 2007. Micropropagation of the aquarium plant-parrot feather milfoil-*Myriophyllum aquaticum* (Velloso) Verdcourt. In: *Recent Trends in Horticultural Biotechnology.* New India Publishing Agency, pp. 333–336.

Souza, F.A., M. Dziedzic, S.A. Cubas, and L.T. Maranho. 2013. Restoration of polluted waters by phytoremediation using *Myriophyllum aquaticum* (Vell.) Verdc., Haloagaceae. *Journal of Environmental Management* 120: 5–9.

Souza, G.S.F., M.R.R. Pereira, H.S. Vitorino, C.F. Campos, and D. Martins. 2012. Influência da Chuva na Eficácia do Herbicida 2,4-D no Controle de *Myriophyllum Aquaticum*. *Planta Daninha* 30(2): 263–267.

Stiers, I., N. Crohain, G. Josens, and L. Triest. 2011. Impact of three aquatic invasive species on native plants and macroinvertebrates in temperate ponds. *Biological Invasions* 13: 2715–2726.

Sun, H., F. Liu, S. Xu, S. Wu, G. Zhuang, Y. Deng, J. Wu, and X. Zhuang. 2017. *Myriophyllum aquaticum* constructed wetland effectively removes nitrogen in swine wastewater. *Frontiers in Microbiology* 8: 1932.

Tu et al. 2001. Weed control methods handbook. *The Nature Conservancy.* www.invasive.org/gist/products/handbook/17.imazapyr.pdf. (Accessed June 29, 2021).

USGS. 2021. Myriophyllum aquaticum. *NAS—Nonindigenous Aquatic Species.* https://nas.er.usgs.gov/viewer/omap.aspx-?SpeciesID=235. (Accessed June 25, 2021).

Wersal, R.M. 2010. *The Conceptual Ecology and Management of Parrotfeather.* Mississippi: Mississippi State University, p. 216.

Wersal, R.M., E. Baker, J. Larson, K. Dettloff, A.J. Fusaro, D.D. Thayer, and I.A. Pfingsten. 2021. *Myriophyllum aquaticum (Vell.) Verdc. U.S. Geological Survey, Nonindigenous Aquatic Species Database,* Gainesville, FL. https://nas.er.usgs.gov/queries/FactSheet.aspx?speciesID=235. (Accessed June 25, 2021).

Wersal, R.M., and J.D. Madsen. 2007. Comparison of imazapyr and imazamox for control of parrotfeather (*Myriophyllum aquaticum* (Vell.) Verdc.). *Journal of Aquatic Plant Management* 45: 132–136.

Wersal, R.M., and J.D. Madsen. 2011. Comparative effects of water level variations on growth characteristics of *Myriophyllum aquaticum*. *Weed Research* 51(4): 386–393.

Wersal, R.M., J.D. Madsen, and P.D. Gerard. 2013. Survival of parrotfeather following simulated drawdown events. *Journal of Aquatic Plant Management* 51: 22–26.

Xie, D., D. Yu, L. Yu, and C. Liu. 2010. Asexual propagations of introduced exotic macrophytes *Elodea nuttallii*, *Myriophyllum aquaticum*, and *M. propinquum* are improved by nutrient-rich sediments in China. *Hydrobiologia* 655: 37–47.

You, W., D. Yu, C. Liu, D. Xie, and W. Xiong. 2013. Clonal integration facilitates invasiveness of the alien aquatic plant *Myriophyllum aquaticum* L. under heterogeneous water availability. *Hydrobiologia* 718: 27–39.

10 Carolina Fanwort (*Cabomba caroliniana*)

ABSTRACT

In Massachusetts, Carolina fanwort (*Cabomba caroliniana*) was first detected in 1930 in Hatfield. The sightings of invasive *C. caroliniana* species were analyzed based on historical data (1983–2017) collected mainly by the Massachusetts Department of Environmental Protection. By now fanwort has become highly invasive in Massachusetts. Currently, there are around 200 waterbodies within 20 watersheds infested by fanwort. This chapter provides a better understanding on the status of its spread in Massachusetts which will help the general public and water users to minimize the further dispersal of *C. caroliniana* in Massachusetts. In addition, this report also provides different methods that have been used or tested for control of *C. caroliniana* such as physical (e.g., drawdown and dredging), chemical (e.g., herbicides), and biological (e.g., weevil or grass carp) control tools.

INTRODUCTION

Taxonomy Hierarchy (ITIS 2021)

Kingdom	Plantae
Subkingdom	Viridiplantae
Infrakingdom	Streptophyta
Superdivision	Embryophyta
Division	Tracheophyta
Subdivision	Spermatophytina
Class	Magnoliopsida
Superorder	Nymphaeanae
Order	Nymphaeales
Family	Cabombaceae
Genus	*Cabomba* Aubl.
Species	*Cabomba caroliniana* A. Gray

BASIC BIOLOGY

Fanwort is a fully submerged aquatic plant that roots in the soft substrates in waterbodies, with stems that branch up to the surface of the water (Figure 10.1). Its fan-like leaves are found in pairs, with each pair of leaves opposite to the other. The underwater leaves are fan-shaped while the floating leaves that support the flowers are diamond-shaped, which are about 5 cm across, and secrete a mucous that coats the submerged portion of the plant (Larson et al. 2020). In late summer, *C. caroliniana* usually blooms with tiny flowers over oval floating leaves (Figure 10.2), while its stems are under the water surface and in thick mats in shallow waters of Massachusetts (MA DCR 2016). The flowers, which are usually less than 2 cm across, can range from a white to pale yellow color, and sometimes can exhibit small amounts of pink or purple coloration, as shown in Figure 10.2 (Larson et al. 2020). The stems will generally have white or reddish-brown hair. Mature plants can reach up to 10 m long and generally fall between 30 and 80 cm, or between 12 and 31 inches (Wilson et al. 2007). The plant produces a leathery, indehiscent fruit with a three-seeded follicle (MA DCR 2005). Fanwort can tolerate a wide range of temperatures, pH levels, water chemistry conditions, and nutrient conditions (MA DCR 2002). However, in waters with high levels of calcium, the growth of the plant can be restrained (MA DCR 2005). While fanwort grows in a wide variety of waters, it does best in acidic water with a pH around 6 (Tobias Bickel, personal communication). *C. caroliniana* usually can be found in slow-moving waterbodies (ponds, lakes, small rivers, etc.) with silty substrates, as well as in rivers and even turbid waterbodies (Larson et al. 2020). There are at least three confirmed phenotypes of fanwort (green, red, and aquarium), of which the invasive green phenotype is the most difficult to control with herbicides (Bultemeier et al. 2009). The phenotype color is related to the leaf coloration, not the flowers, and also that the phenotypes are aquarium cultivars, not the subspecies occurring in its natural environment. More information about the biology

DOI: 10.1201/9781003201106-10

FIGURE 10.1 Fanwort sample from Federal Pond (*left*) and underwater fanwort photo from Arcade Pond (*right*), MA. (Photo by Wai Hing Wong.)

FIGURE 10.2 Fanwort floating leaves and flower buds and flower. (Left photo by Lyn Gettys from https://plants.ifas.ufl.edu; right photo by Tobias O Bickel.)

and taxonomy of fanwort can be obtained from more references: Schneider et al. (1982), Ørgaard (1991), and Mackey and Swarbrick (1997).

NATIVE RANGE

C. caroliniana is a native plant to subtropic–temperate regions of the Americas, specifically to the countries of Brazil, Paraguay, Uruguay, and Argentina, and to the Southern and Eastern United States (Larson et al. 2020), where it lives in slow-flowing and stagnant freshwater (Scheers et al. 2016).

INVASIVE RANGE

C. caroliniana has invaded many regions in the world, such as several European countries, China, India, Japan, and the United States (Brundu 2015). Fanwort is considered as an invasive species in northern and western United Sates. In Australia, the weed has been declared as a Weed of National Significance due to severe economic and ecological impacts (CHAH 2011).

MECHANISMS/VECTORS OF SPREAD

C. caroliniana is highly adaptive and competitive, and can grow quickly and densely. It can easily spread through seeds and rhizome or stem fragmentation (MA DCR 2002; Scheers et al. 2016). Certain parts of the plant that become fragmented can survive free floating for six to eight weeks, allowing these fragments to easily spread to new waterbodies or repopulate areas in which treatments have been applied (Larson et al. 2020). Unintentional transport on boat trailers is one important way that *C. caroliniana* and other aquatic plants can spread by fragmentation (Rothlisberger et al. 2010; Bruckerhoff et al. 2015). While the plant is sensitive to drying out and generally requires a permanent source of at least shallow water to survive, its fragments can survive for at least 3 hours in a desiccated environment, making it highly resilient and improving its ability to spread (Bickel 2015; Larson et al. 2020).

ECOLOGICAL IMPACTS

As a nuisance species, *C. caroliniana* grows prolifically and forms dense canopy under and over the surface of the water (Figure 10.1). The dense growths of *C. caroliniana* can have a negative influence on the ecosystem. These impacts involve, but are not limited to, reducing biodiversity, displacing native macrophyte species, impeding water flow, and altering nutrient cycling and water quality (Sheldon 1994; Mackey and Swarbrick 1997; Hogsden et al. 2007). Large dense mats of *C. caroliniana* on the water surface can reduce the space that native species have to live because fanwort is highly competitive and creates monocultures that displace other macrophytes. This can affect the fish and other aquatic species that rely on the displaced species, potentially causing them to have to relocate or perish. Further, habitat becomes unsuitable for many native aquatic animals due to the anoxic environment created by the decay of *C. caroliniana* mainly from herbicides or by dense growth of fanwort which is more about the exclusion of light from deeper water, hence no photosynthesis, and that fanwort stands can interfere with water flow (i.e., create stagnant conditions and water doesn't exchange). According to the "Fanwort: An Invasive Aquatic Plant" report by the Department of Conservation and Recreation (2002), *C. caroliniana* mats can intercept the sunlight, excluding other submerged plants. The mats reduce the amount of light to varying degrees in all cases and the amount of light is one of the most important factors that determine aquatic plant distribution in lakes. Additionally, the growth of *C. caroliniana* can also alter the sediment chemistry.

ECONOMIC IMPACTS

Due to the infestation of *C. caroliniana*, different levels of socioeconomic impacts have arisen in many regions. For instance, fishing ability has decreased, tourism and recreational activities have declined, the value of real estate has been influenced, etc.

POSITIVE ASPECTS

Although *C. caroliniana* is an invasive species, there are some positive aspects associated with it. First, it can serve as the habitat for many fish, micro and macro invertebrates, and is a food source for waterfowl and wildlife (Mackey 1996). It should be noted that almost all submersed macrophytes can provide some ecosystem services as what fanwort can do; but it is still preferable to have a diverse macrophyte community than a monoculture. Second, *C. caroliniana* has been widely used in the aquarium industry around the world. However, this is also one of the reasons that fanwort has spread to many regions. The trade of fanwort is banned in Massachusetts.

MONITORING AND SIGHTING DATA

The invasive species data in each waterbody were collected by the Massachusetts Department of Environmental Protection (MassDEP), the Massachusetts Department of Conservation and Recreation (MA DCR), field surveys, Water Quality Assessment Reports, Diagnostic/Feasibility Reports, personal communications, application files, etc. The standard operating procedures, including sampling methodology, species identification, quality control and assurance, were implemented for all samples collected by MassDEP. Data from other agencies have been confirmed by experts. Sites with aquatic invasive species (AIS) were mapped as a data layer with ArcGIS® ArcMap 10.1 (ESRI, Redlands, California). Such a map will help make the general public aware of the presence of fanwort in Massachusetts, hopefully to assist minimizing unintentional transportation between different waterbodies.

Through the reports and surveys of *C. caroliniana*, different locations with fanwort have

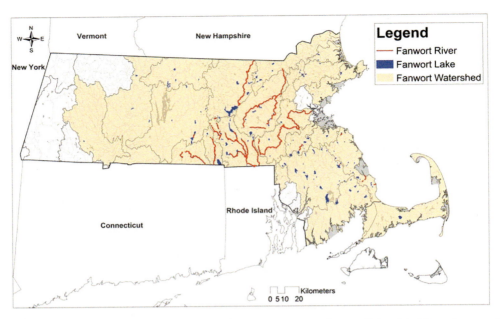

FIGURE 10.3 Distribution map depicting Carolina Fanwort (*Cabomba caroliniana*) in Massachusetts. (See Table 10.1 for site descriptions.)

been mapped using GIS (Figure 10.3). GIS is able to pinpoint the exact area that *C. caroliniana* has spread too, and this can help to inform future decision-making for these waterbodies, or regulations that involve efforts to limit the spread of this aquatic invasive species. *C. caroliniana* is a very aggressive invasive species, and therefore was able to spread in a short period of time throughout Massachusetts (Table 10.1). The first verified sighting by the Department of Environmental Protection in Massachusetts was in 1983 at Whitmans Pond. *C. caroliniana* was detected while completing a Report to Massachusetts Division of Water Pollution Control on Feasibility Study of Lake Restoration for Whitmans Pond. According to MA DCR (2002), Carolina fanwort was detected in Massachusetts as early as 1930 in Hatfield, MA. Currently, there are 196 waterbodies (Table 10.2) within the 23 watersheds in Massachusetts that are infested by *C. caroliniana* (Table 10.3). Among them, 173 are lakes and 23 are rivers. Most of the spread are recorded much later in the 1990s which is mainly due to the fact few monitoring on fanwort were conducted in earlier years.

MANAGEMENT OPTIONS

Currently, this species is banned from the trade in Massachusetts because it is in the prohibited plant list. More actions can be used to prevent the spread of *C. caroliniana*. For example, building a coalition to monitor for *C. caroliniana*, improving the monitoring and enforcement of the distribution and sale of *C. caroliniana*, educating aquarium owners and the industry to be aware of the hazards associated with the spread of invasive species, providing boat washing stations for high-traffic public lake access points, and developing a water recreation vehicle and trailer inspection program are all forms of effective social management (Maki and Galatowitsch 2004; Hussner et al. 2013; Verbrugge 2014; Bickel 2015; State of Michigan 2017).

There are many other different methods that have been tested for a range of fanwort management goals, from early detection and eradication to containment to prevent spread and subsequent maintenance or not doing anything once the infestation is too large or containment is not an option anymore. Effective management

Carolina Fanwort (*Cabomba caroliniana*)

TABLE 10.1
Fanwort Sightings in MA Waters as Shown in Figure 10.3

Waterbody	Agency	Report Source	Longitude	Latitude	First Year Reported
Whitmans Pond	MassDEP	Report to Massachusetts Division of Water Pollution Control on Feasibility Study of Lake Restoration for Whitmans Pond, Weymouth, MA			1983
Forge Pond	BEC	A Diagnostic/Feasibility Study for the Management of Lost Lake/Knopp's Pond Groton, Massachusetts, 1987			1987
Forge Pond	DCR	DCR Data from ACT, GeoSyntec			1987
North Pond	Metcalf & Eddy	Final Report to Town of Hopkinton on Diagnostic Feasibility Study of North Pond Hopkinton MA, 1987			1987
North Pond	DCR	DCR Data from Lakes and Ponds, 2008			1987
Knops Pond/Lost Lake	BEC	A Diagnostic/Feasibility Study for the Management of Lost Lake/Knopp's Pond Groton, Massachusetts, 1992			1992
Knops Pond/Lost Lake	DCR	DCR Data from Lakes and Ponds, 2002			1992
Arcade Pond	MassDEP	09-G010-02	−71.6775195	42.1129609	1994
Arcade Pond	Individual	Joy Trahan-Liptak	−71.67707	42.113303	1994
Arcade Pond	MassDEP	Synoptic lake survey field sheets 1994—Blackstone River Watershed Lakes, 1994			1994
Fish Pond	MassDEP	Synoptic lake survey field sheets 1994—Blackstone River Watershed Lakes, 1994			1994
Fish Pond	MassDEP	09-G010-01	−71.6879542	42.1209182	1994
Girard Pond	MassDEP	Synoptic lake survey field sheets 1994—Blackstone River Watershed Lakes, 1994			1994
Hayes Pond	MassDEP	Synoptic lake survey field sheets 1994—Blackstone River Watershed Lakes, 1994			1994
Kettle Brook	MassDEP	Synoptic lake survey field sheets 1994—Blackstone River Watershed Lakes, 1994			1994
Lake Quinsigamond	MassDEP	Synoptic lake survey field sheets 1994—Blackstone River Watershed Lakes, 1994			1994
Lake Quinsigamond	College of the Holy Cross	Robert Bertin	−71.749052	42.256062	1994
Lake Quinsigamond	College of the Holy Cross	Robert Bertin	−71.749052	42.256062	1994
Lake Quinsigamond	College of the Holy Cross	Robert Bertin	−71.749052	42.256062	1994
Leesville Pond	MassDEP	Synoptic lake survey field sheets 1994—Blackstone River Watershed Lakes, 1994			1994
Leesville Pond	College of the Holy Cross	Robert Bertin	−71.827414	42.230332	1994

(Continued)

TABLE 10.1 (Continued)

Waterbody	Agency	Report Source	Longitude	Latitude	First Year Reported
Leesville Pond	Individual	Joy Trahan-Liptak	−71.826444	42.229001	1994
Mill Pond	MassDEP	Synoptic lake survey field sheets 1994—Blackstone River Watershed Lakes, 1994			1994
Miscoe Lake	MassDEP	Synoptic lake survey field sheets 1994—Blackstone River Watershed Lakes, 1994			1994
Pondville Pond	MassDEP	Synoptic lake survey field sheets 1994—Blackstone River Watershed Lakes, 1994			1994
Pratt Pond	MassDEP	Synoptic lake survey field sheets 1994—Blackstone River Watershed Lakes, 1994			1994
Pratt Pond	College of the Holy Cross	Robert Bertin	−71.598913	42.181814	1994
Quinsigamond River	MassDEP	11-F004-02	−71.7080924	42.2305379	1994
Quinsigamond River	Individual	Joy Trahan-Liptak	−71.701242	42.221306	1994
Quinsigamond River	MassDEP	Synoptic lake survey field sheets 1994—Blackstone River Watershed Lakes, 1994			1994
Stevens Pond	MassDEP	Synoptic lake survey field sheets 1994—Blackstone River Watershed Lakes, 1994			1994
Unnamed Tributary	MassDEP	Synoptic lake survey field sheets 1998—Blackstone River Watershed Lakes, 1998			1994
West River	MassDEP	Synoptic lake survey field sheets 1994—Blackstone River Watershed Lakes, 1994			1994
West River	MassDEP	Synoptic lake survey field sheets 1994—Blackstone River Watershed Lakes, 1994			1994
Whitins Pond	MassDEP	Synoptic lake survey field sheets 1994—Blackstone River Watershed Lakes, 1994			1994
Whitins Pond	College of the Holy Cross	Robert Bertin	−71.689583	42.113764	1994
Whitins Pond	MassDEP	Email communication between David Wong and Therese Beaudoin on July 7, 2017	−71.688119	42.119622	1994
Woodbury Pond	MassDEP	Synoptic lake survey field sheets 1994—Blackstone River Watershed Lakes, 1994			1994
Woodbury Pond	MassDEP	09-G008-07	−71.7312552	42.164983	1994
Cook Pond	College of the Holy Cross	Robert Bertin	−71.858373	42.285515	1995
Cook Pond	College of the Holy Cross	Robert Bertin	−71.858373	42.285515	1995
Curtis Pond	College of the Holy Cross	Robert Bertin	−71.838502	42.241484	1995
Flint Pond	MassDEP	Synoptic lake survey field sheets 1998—Blackstone River Watershed Lakes, 1998			1995
Flint Pond	College of the Holy Cross	Robert Bertin	−71.725087	42.241352	1995
Flint Pond	College of the Holy Cross	Robert Bertin	−71.725087	42.241352	1995

Carolina Fanwort (*Cabomba caroliniana*)

Location	Affiliation	Contact	Source	Longitude	Latitude	Year
Flint Pond	College of the Holy Cross	Robert Bertin		−71.725087	42.241352	1995
Flint Pond	College of the Holy Cross	Robert Bertin		−71.725087	42.241352	1995
Flint Pond	Individual	Joy Trahan-Liptak		−71.725688	42.240948	1995
Flint Pond	MassDEP		Synoptic lake survey field sheets 1998—Blackstone River Watershed Lakes, 1998			1995
Massapoag Brook	MassDEP		The Neponset River Watershed 1994 Resource Assessment Report, 1995			1995
Lake Winthrop	MassDEP		Synoptic lake survey field sheets 1997—Charles River Watersheds lakes			1997
Morses Pond	MassDEP		Synoptic lake survey field sheets 1997—Charles River Watersheds lakes			1997
Arcadia Lake	MassDEP		Synoptic lake survey field sheets—Connecticut River Watershed Lakes			1998
Dark Brook	MassDEP		Synoptic lake survey field sheets 1998—Blackstone River Watershed Lakes, 1998			1998
Hardwick Pond	College of the Holy Cross	Robert Bertin		−72.2386	42.313254	1998
Hardwick Pond	MassDEP		Open lake survey files			1998
Ironstone Reservoir	MassDEP		Synoptic lake survey field sheets 1998—Blackstone River Watershed Lakes, 1998			1998
Ironstone Reservoir	College of the Holy Cross	Robert Bertin		−71.6109	42.024298	1998
Lake Holland	MassDEP		Synoptic lake survey field sheets—Connecticut River Watershed Lakes			1998
Lake Lashaway	Individual	Joy Trahan-Liptak		−72.045061	42.235541	1998
Lake Lashaway	MassDEP		Open lake survey files			1998
Lake Ripple	MassDEP		Synoptic lake survey field sheets 1998—Blackstone River Watershed Lakes, 1998			1998
Lake Ripple	College of the Holy Cross	Robert Bertin		−71.697077	42.213605	1998
Lake Ripple	College of the Holy Cross	Robert Bertin		−71.697077	42.213605	1998
Lake Ripple	MassDEP		09-G008-04	−71.6936628	42.2141715	1998
Lake Ripple	Individual	Joy Trahan-Liptak		−71.696072	42.213862	1998
Manchaug Pond	MassDEP		Synoptic lake survey field sheets 1998—Blackstone River Watershed Lakes, 1998			1998
Manchaug Pond	College of the Holy Cross	Robert Bertin		−71.775563	42.099183	1998
Metacomet Lake	MassDEP		Synoptic lake survey field sheets—Connecticut River Watershed Lakes			1998
Mill River	MassDEP		Synoptic lake survey field sheets 1998—Blackstone River Watershed Lakes, 1998			1998
Mill River	MassDEP		Synoptic lake survey field sheets 1998—Blackstone River Watershed Lakes, 1998			1998
Newton Pond	MassDEP		Synoptic lake survey field sheets 1998—Blackstone River Watershed Lakes, 1998			1998
Newton Pond	College of the Holy Cross	Robert Bertin		−71.747947	42.312773	1998
Quaboag Pond	College of the Holy Cross	Robert Bertin		−72.068036	42.197472	1998

(Continued)

TABLE 10.1 (Continued)

Waterbody	Agency	Report Source	Longitude	Latitude	First Year Reported
Quaboag Pond	MassDEP	Open lake survey files			1998
Quacumquasit Pond	MassDEP	Open lake survey files			1998
Tatnuck Brook	MassDEP	Synoptic lake survey field sheets 1998—Blackstone River Watershed Lakes, 1998			1998
Newfield Pond	MassDEP	DWM 1999 Lake TMDL field sheets			1999
Chebacco Lake	MassDEP	North Coastal Watershed 1997/1998 Water Quality Assessment Report, May 2000			2000
Griswold Pond	MassDEP	North Coastal Watershed 1997/1998 Water Quality Assessment Report, May 2000			2000
Lake Como	MassDEP	Ten Mile River Basin 1997 Water Quality Assessment Report, DWM CN 18.0.2000			2000
Lake Mascuppic	MassDEP	License applications for herbicide treatment: 1996 through 2000.2000			2000
Plain Street Pond	MassDEP	Ten Mile River Basin 1997 Water Quality Assessment Report, DWM CN 18.0.2000			2000
Spring Pond	MassDEP	North Coastal Watershed 1997/1998 Water Quality Assessment Report, May 2000			2000
Spring Pond	DCR	DCR Data from Lakes and Ponds, 2006			2000
Chaffin Pond	MassDEP	Nashua River Basin 1998 Water Quality Assessment Report CN046.0.2001			2001
Chaffin Pond	College of the Holy Cross	Robert Bertin	−71.840022	42.33112	2001
Chaffin Pond	DCR	Joy Trahan-Liptak	−71.839483	42.331244	2001
Dawson Pond	MassDEP	Nashua River Basin 1998 Water Quality Assessment Report CN046.0.2001			2001
Dawson Pond	DCR	Joy Trahan-Liptak	−71.852208	42.335114	2001
Flannagan Pond	MassDEP	Nashua River Basin 1998 Water Quality Assessment Report CN046.0.2001			2001
Grove Pond	MassDEP	Nashua River Basin 1998 Water Quality Assessment Report CN046.0.2001			2001
Lake Shirley	MassDEP	Nashua River Basin 1998 Water Quality Assessment Report CN046.0.2001			2001
Lake Shirley	DCR	DCR Data from ACT, GeoSyntec-ACT			2001
Pentucket Pond	MassDEP	Parker River Watershed Year 3 Assessment Report, June 2001			2001
Plow Shop Pond	MassDEP	Nashua River Basin 1998 Water Quality Assessment Report CN046.0.2001			2001

Location	Source	Reference	Longitude	Latitude	Year
Spectacle Pond	ESS	A Diagnostic/Feasibility Study of Spectacle Pond, Littleton/Ayer, Massachusetts, 2001			2001
Spectacle Pond	DCR	DCR Data from ACT, GeoSyntec-ACT			2001
Wachusett Reservoir	DCR	Water Quality Report: 2001 Wachusett Reservoir and Watershed			2001
Wachusett Reservoir	College of the Holy Cross	Robert Bertin	−71.787817	42.397107	2001
Wachusett Reservoir	DCR	David Worden	−71.787817	42.397107	2001
Wachusett Reservoir	DCR	David Worden	−71.789929	42.389998	2001
Wachusett Reservoir	DCR	David Worden	−71.788251	42.379206	2001
Wachusett Reservoir	DCR	David Worden	−71.774821	42.375014	2001
Wachusett Reservoir	DCR	Jamie Carr	−71.789929	42.389998	2001
Wachusett Reservoir	DCR	Jamie Carr	−71.787817	42.397107	2001
Wachusett Reservoir	DCR	Jamie Carr	−71.788251	42.379206	2001
Wachusett Reservoir	DCR	Jamie Carr	−71.795345	42.384187	2001
Wachusett Reservoir	DCR	DCR Data from ACT, GeoSyntec-ACT			2001
Baddacook Pond	MassDEP	05-G001-01	−71.530464	42.6189623	2002
Baddacook Pond	DCR	DCR Data from Lakes and Ponds, 2002	−71.530464	42.6189623	2002
Bearse Pond	Individual	Joy Trahan-Liptak	−70.333056	41.675875	2002
Bearse Pond	Individual	Joy Trahan-Liptak	−70.333056	41.675875	2002
Bearse Pond	MassDEP	Cape Cod Watershed Water Quality Assessment Report CN 50.0.			2002
Beaver Pond	DCR	Excel spreadsheet of non-native aquatic and wetland plants in Massachusetts lakes and ponds dated January 2005			2002
Beaver Pond	DCR	DCR Data from Lakes and Ponds, 2002			2002
Big Bearhole Pond	MassDEP	Appendix C—Table C1.1996 Taunton River Watershed Lake observations and trophic status estimates. (Taunton River Watershed 2001 Water Quality Assessment Report 62-AC-1 CN 94.0, December 2005)			2002
Big Bearhole Pond	DCR	DCR Data from Lakes and Ponds, 2002			2002
Big Bearhole Pond	DCR	DCR Data from Lakes and Ponds, 2007			2002
Big Bearhole Pond	DCR	DCR Data from Lakes and Ponds, 2008			2002
Bolivar Pond	MassDEP	Boston Harbor 1999 Water Quality Assessment Report CN049.0.2002			2002
Cedar Meadow Pond	MassDEP	French and Quinebaug River Watersheds 2001 Water Quality Assessment Report 41/42-AC-1 51.0, March 2002			2002

(Continued)

TABLE 10.1 (Continued)

Waterbody	Agency	Report Source	Longitude	Latitude	First Year Reported
Ellis Pond	MassDEP	Boston Harbor 1999 Water Quality Assessment Report CN049.0.2002			2002
Ellis Pond	DCR	DCR Data from Lakes and Ponds, 2005			2002
First Pond	MassDEP	Herbicide license applications for 2002			2002
First Pond	DCR	DCR Data from Lakes and Ponds, 2006			2002
Lake Rico	MassDEP	Appendix C—Table C1.1996 Taunton River Watershed Lake observations and trophic status estimates (Taunton River Watershed 2001 Water Quality Assessment Report 62-AC-1 CN 94.0 December 2005)			2002
Lake Rico	DCR	DCR Data from Lakes and Ponds, 2002			2002
Little Bearhole Pond	DCR	DCR Data from Lakes and Ponds, 2002			2002
Little Bearhole Pond	DCR	DCR Data from Lakes and Ponds, 2007			2002
Little Bearhole Pond	DCR	DCR Data from Lakes and Ponds, 2008			2002
Massapoag Lake	MassDEP	Boston Harbor 1999 Water Quality Assessment Report CN049.0.2002			2002
Massapoag Lake	Individual	Joy Trahan-Liptak	−71.177528	42.103486	2002
Massapoag Lake	Individual	Joy Trahan-Liptak	−71.177528	42.103486	2002
Moulton Pond	College of the Holy Cross	Robert Bertin	−71.954051	42.388392	2002
Neponset Reservoir	MassDEP	Boston Harbor 1999 Water Quality Assessment Report CN049.0.2002			2002
Reservoir Pond	MassDEP	Boston Harbor 1999 Water Quality Assessment Report CN049.0.2002			2002
Swains Pond	MassDEP	Herbicide license applications for 2002			2002
Town Pond	MassDEP	Boston Harbor 1999 Water Quality Assessment Report CN049.0.2002			2002
Turner Pond	MassDEP	Boston Harbor 1999 Water Quality Assessment Report CN049.0.2002			2002
Webster Lake	DCR	DCR Data from Lakes and Ponds, 2002			2002
Webster Lake	MassDEP	05-G014-01	−71.8487243	42.0543495	2002
Webster Lake	College of the Holy Cross	Robert Bertin	−71.848244	42.038004	2002
Webster Lake	College of the Holy Cross	Robert Bertin	−71.848244	42.038004	2002
Wequaquet Lake	Individual	Joy Trahan-Liptak	−70.35087	41.675829	2002

Carolina Fanwort (*Cabomba caroliniana*)

Location	Source	Reference	Longitude	Latitude	Year
Wequaquet Lake	Individual	Joy Trahan-Liptak	−70.35087	41.675829	2002
Wequaquet Lake	Individual	Joy Trahan-Liptak	−70.329647	41.670658	2002
Wequaquet Lake	Individual	Joy Trahan-Liptak	−70.35087	41.675829	2002
Wequaquet Lake	MassDEP	Cape Cod Watershed Water Quality Assessment Report CN 50.0			2002
Ballardvale Impoundment	MassDEP	Appendix D—Table D4.1995 Shawsheen River Watershed summer lake status (Shawsheen River Watershed 2000 Water Quality Assessment Report 83-AC-2 86.0, July 2003)			2003
Federal Pond	MassDEP	Buzzards Bay Watershed 2000 Water Quality Assessment Report 95-AC-2 085.0, November 2003			2003
Fosters Pond	MassDEP	Appendix D—Table D4.1995 Shawsheen River Watershed summer lake status. (Shawsheen River Watershed 2000 Water Quality Assessment Report 83-AC-2 86.0, July 2003)			2003
Fresh Meadow Pond	MassDEP	Buzzards Bay Watershed 2000 Water Quality Assessment Report 95-AC-2 085.0, November 2003			2003
Nashua River	Nashua River Watershed Association	2003 Water Quality Reports for the Nashua River and Tributaries			2003
Pomps Pond	MassDEP	Appendix D—Table D4.1995 Shawsheen River Watershed summer lake status (Shawsheen River Watershed 2000 Water Quality Assessment Report 83-AC-2 86.0, July 2003)			2003
Sampson Pond	MassDEP	05-R002–01	−70.7529767	41.8520645	2003
Sampson Pond	MassDEP	Buzzards Bay Watershed 2000 Water Quality Assessment Report 95-AC-2 085.0, November 2003			2003
Watson Pond	DCR	DCR Data from Lakes and Ponds, 2003			2003
Watson Pond	MassDEP	Appendix C—Table C1.1996 Taunton River Watershed Lake observations and trophic status estimates (Taunton River Watershed 2001 Water Quality Assessment Report 62-AC-1 CN 94.0, December 2005)			2003
Watson Pond	DCR	DCR Data from Lakes and Ponds, 2008			2003
White Island Pond, East Basin	MassDEP	07-T003–02	−70.6175309	41.8091834	2003
White Island Pond, East Basin	MassDEP	08-F008–02	−70.6175309	41.8091834	2003

(Continued)

TABLE 10.1 (Continued)

Waterbody	Agency	Report Source	Longitude	Latitude	First Year Reported
White Island Pond, East Basin	MassDEP	11-B007–01	−70.6175309	41.8091834	2003
White Island Pond, East Basin	MassDEP	14-B005–01	−70.6175309	41.8091834	2003
White Island Pond, East Basin	MassDEP	14-B007–01	−70.6175309	41.8091834	2003
White Island Pond, East Basin	MassDEP	Buzzards Bay Watershed2000 Water Quality Assessment Report 95-AC-2 085.0. November 2003			2003
White Island Pond, West Basin	MassDEP	11-B002–02	−70.6275557	41.8099941	2003
White Island Pond, West Basin	MassDEP	11-B005–02	−70.6275557	41.8099941	2003
White Island Pond, West Basin	MassDEP	11-B007–02	−70.6275557	41.8099941	2003
White Island Pond, West Basin	MassDEP	12-B003–02	−70.6275557	41.8099941	2003
White Island Pond, West Basin	MassDEP	13-B007–02	−70.6275557	41.8099941	2003
White Island Pond, West Basin	MassDEP	13-B009–03	−70.6275557	41.8099941	2003
White Island Pond, West Basin	MassDEP	14-B003–02	−70.6275557	41.8099941	2003
White Island Pond, West Basin	MassDEP	14-B005–02	−70.6275557	41.8099941	2003
White Island Pond, West Basin	MassDEP	14-B007–02	−70.6275557	41.8099941	2003
White Island Pond, West Basin	MassDEP	Buzzards Bay Watershed 2000 Water Quality Assessment Report 95-AC-2 085.0. November 2003			2003

Waterbody	Source	Reference	Longitude	Latitude	Year
Winnecunnet Pond	DCR	DCR Data from Lakes and Ponds, 2003			2003
Baldpate Pond	MassDEP	05-G004-02	−71.0014233	42.698862	2004
Baldpate Pond	MassDEP	Baseline Lake Survey 2003 Technical Memo. TM-S-16 DWM Control Number CN 205.0.2007			2004
Baldpate Pond	DCR	DCR Data from National Heritage 2004			2004
Baldpate Pond	DCR	DCR Data from Lakes and Ponds, 2004			2004
Bare Hill Pond	College of the Holy Cross	Robert Bertin	−71.597616	42.491779	2004
Edgewater Office Park Pond	MassDEP	Herbicide license applications for 2004			2004
Field Pond	DCR	DCR Data from Lakes and Ponds, 2007			2004
Field Pond	MassDEP	Appendix C—Table C1.1995 Ipswich River Watershed Lake observations and trophic status estimates. (Ipswich River Watershed 2000 Water Quality Assessment Report 92-AC-1 088.0, April 2004)			2004
Lake Ellis	MassDEP	Appendix B—Table B1. Millers River Watershed 1995 Lake Synoptic Survey Data and Trophic Status Estimates (Millers River Watershed 2000 Water Quality Assessment Report 35-AC-1 CN089.0, March 2004)			2004
Lake Ellis	College of the Holy Cross	Robert Bertin	−72.204192	42.577244	2004
Lake Rohunta	MassDEP	Millers River Watershed 2000 Water Quality Assessment Report 35-AC-1 CN089.0, March 2004			2004
Lake Rohunta	MassDEP	Appendix B—Table B1. Millers River Watershed 1995 Lake Synoptic Survey Data and Trophic Status Estimates (Millers River Watershed 2000 Water Quality Assessment Report 35-AC-1 CN089.0, March 2004)			2004
Lake Rohunta	MassDEP	Millers River Watershed 2000 Water Quality Assessment Report 35-AC-1 CN089.0, March 2004			2004
Lake Sabbatia	MassDEP	Appendix C—Table C1.1996 Taunton River Watershed Lake observations and trophic status estimates (Taunton River Watershed 2001 Water Quality Assessment Report 62-AC-1 CN 94.0, December 2005)			2004
Lake Warner	Massachusetts Water Watch Partnership, UMass Extension and the Town of Hadley	Lake Warner 2003 Volunteer Monitoring Program Report			2004

(Continued)

TABLE 10.1 (Continued)

Waterbody	Agency	Report Source	Longitude	Latitude	First Year Reported
Lowe Pond	MassDEP	Appendix C—Table C1.1995 Ipswich River Watershed Lake observations and trophic status estimates (Ipswich River Watershed 2000 Water Quality Assessment Report 92-AC-1 088.0, April 2004)			2004
Martins Pond	MassDEP	Appendix C—Table C1.1995 Ipswich River Watershed Lake observations and trophic status estimates (Ipswich River Watershed 2000 Water Quality Assessment Report 92-AC-1 088.0, April 2004)			2004
Parker Pond	MassDEP	Appendix B—Table B1. Millers River Watershed 1995 Lake Synoptic Survey Data and Trophic Status Estimates (Millers River Watershed 2000 Water Quality Assessment Report 35-AC-1 CN089.0, March 2004)			2004
South Athol Pond	MassDEP	Appendix B—Table B1. Millers River Watershed 1995 Lake Synoptic Survey Data and Trophic Status Estimates (Millers River Watershed 2000 Water Quality Assessment Report 35-AC-1 CN089.0, March 2004)			2004
Tully Lake	College of the Holy Cross	Robert Bertin	−72.215667	42.644638	2004
Tully Lake	College of the Holy Cross	Robert Bertin	−72.215667	42.644638	2004
Tully Lake	College of the Holy Cross	Robert Bertin	−72.215667	42.644638	2004
Turnpike Lake	MassDEP	Appendix C—Table C1.1996 Taunton River Watershed Lake observations and trophic status estimates (Taunton River Watershed 2001 Water Quality Assessment Report 62-AC-1 CN 94.0, December 2005)			2004
Turnpike Lake	DCR	DCR Data from Lakes and Ponds, 2004			2004
White Pond	MassDEP	Appendix B—Table B1. Millers River Watershed 1995 Lake Synoptic Survey Data and Trophic Status Estimates (Millers River Watershed 2000 Water Quality Assessment Report 35-AC-1 CN089.0, March 2004)			2004
Ames Long Pond	MassDEP	Appendix C—Table C1.1996 Taunton River Watershed Lake observations and trophic status estimates (Taunton River Watershed 2001 Water Quality Assessment Report 62-AC-1 CN 94.0, December 2005)			2005
Assabet River	MassDEP	SuAsCo Watershed 2001 Water Quality Assessment Report 82-AC-1 CN 92.0, August 2005			2005

Assabet River	Individual	Joy Trahan-Liptak	−71.5393	42.403	2005
Assabet River	MassDEP	SuAsCo Watershed 2001 Water Quality Assessment Report 82-AC-1 CN 92.0, August 2005			2005
Bartlett Pond	College of the Holy Cross	Robert Bertin	−71.61766	42.318598	2005
Bartlett Pond	MassDEP	SuAsCo Watershed 2001 Water Quality Assessment Report 82-AC-1 CN 92.0, August 2005			2005
Barton Cove	DCR	Excel spreadsheet of non-native aquatic and wetland plants in Massachusetts lakes and ponds dated January 2005			2005
Blair Pond	MassDEP	Appendix F—Table F1.1996 Westfield River Watershed Lake observations and trophic status estimates (Westfield River Watershed 2001 Water Quality Assessment Report 32-AC-1 CN 090.0, April 2005)			2005
Brockton Reservoir	MassDEP	Appendix C—Table C1.1996 Taunton River Watershed Lake observations and trophic status estimates (Taunton River Watershed 2001 Water Quality Assessment Report 62-AC-1 CN 94.0, December 2005)			2005
Cleveland Pond	DCR	DCR Data from Lakes and Ponds, 2008			2005
Cleveland Pond	MassDEP	Appendix C—Table C1.1996 Taunton River Watershed Lake observations and trophic status estimates (Taunton River Watershed 2001 Water Quality Assessment Report 62-AC-1 CN 94.0, December 2005)			2005
Cobbs Pond	DCR	Excel spreadsheet of non-native aquatic and wetland plants in Massachusetts lakes and ponds dated January 2005			2005
Concord River	MassDEP	SuAsCo Watershed 2001 Water Quality Assessment Report 82-AC-1 CN 92.0, August 2005			2005
Concord River	MassDEP	SuAsCo Watershed 2001 Water Quality Assessment Report 82-AC-1 CN 92.0, August 2005			2005
Cushing Pond	MassDEP	Appendix C—Table C1.1996 Taunton River Watershed Lake observations and trophic status estimates (Taunton River Watershed 2001 Water Quality Assessment Report 62-AC-1 CN 94.0, December 2005)			2005
Farm Pond	MassDEP	SuAsCo Watershed 2001 Water Quality Assessment Report 82-AC-1 CN 92.0, August 2005			2005
Fort Meadow Reservoir	DCR	DCR Data from Lakes and Ponds, 2005	−71.5476027	42.36994107	2005

(Continued)

TABLE 10.1 (Continued)

Waterbody	Agency	Report Source	Longitude	Latitude	First Year Reported
Gushee Pond	MassDEP	Appendix C—Table C1.1996 Taunton River Watershed Lake observations and trophic status estimates (Taunton River Watershed 2001 Water Quality Assessment Report 62-AC-1 CN 94.0, December 2005)			2005
Heard Pond	MassDEP	SuAsCo Watershed 2001 Water Quality Assessment Report 82-AC-1 CN 92.0, August 2005			2005
Island Grove Pond	MassDEP	Appendix C—Table C1.1996 Taunton River Watershed Lake observations and trophic status estimates (Taunton River Watershed 2001 Water Quality Assessment Report 62-AC-1 CN 94.0, December 2005)			2005
Johnson Pond	MassDEP	Appendix C—Table C1.1996 Taunton River Watershed Lake observations and trophic status estimates (Taunton River Watershed 2001 Water Quality Assessment Report 62-AC-1 CN 94.0, December 2005)			2005
Lake Boon	MassDEP	SuAsCo Watershed 2001 Water Quality Assessment Report 82-AC-1 CN 92.0, August 2005			2005
Lake Boon	Individual	Joy Trahan-Liptak	−71.502252	42.396447	2005
Lake Boon	Individual	Joy Trahan-Liptak	−71.502252	42.396447	2005
Lake Mirimichi	MassDEP	Appendix C—Table C1.1996 Taunton River Watershed Lake observations and trophic status estimates. (Taunton River Watershed 2001 Water Quality Assessment Report 62-AC-1 CN 94.0, December 2005)			2005
Lake Nippenicket	MassDEP	Appendix C—Table C1.1996 Taunton River Watershed Lake observations and trophic status estimates (Taunton River Watershed 2001 Water Quality Assessment Report 62-AC-1 CN 94.0, December 2005)			2005
Long Pond	MassDEP	Appendix C—Table C1.1996 Taunton River Watershed Lake observations and trophic status estimates (Taunton River Watershed 2001 Water Quality Assessment Report 62-AC-1 CN 94.0, December 2005)			2005
Long Pond	Individual	Joy Trahan-Liptak	−71.47025	42.530021	2005
Lower Porter Pond	MassDEP	Appendix C—Table C1.1996 Taunton River Watershed Lake observations and trophic status estimates (Taunton River Watershed 2001 Water Quality Assessment Report 62-AC-1 CN 94.0, December 2005)			2005

Waterbody	Source	Reference	Station	Longitude	Latitude	Year
Middle Pond	MassDEP	Appendix C—Table C1.1996 Taunton River Watershed Lake observations and trophic status estimates (Taunton River Watershed 2001 Water Quality Assessment Report 62-AC-1 CN 94.0, December 2005)				2005
Middle Pond	DCR	DCR Data from Lakes and Ponds, 2007				2005
Monponsett Pond, East Basin	MassDEP	Appendix C—Table C1.1996 Taunton River Watershed Lake observations and trophic status estimates (Taunton River Watershed 2001 Water Quality Assessment Report 62-AC-1 CN 94.0, December 2005)				2005
Monponsett Pond, East Basin	MassDEP		09-G006–05	−70.836781	42.0014672	2005
Monponsett Pond, East Basin	MassDEP		10-B005–03	−70.836781	42.0014672	2005
Monponsett Pond, East Basin	MassDEP		11-B006–05	−70.836781	42.0014672	2005
Monponsett Pond, East Basin	MassDEP		11-B008–02	−70.836781	42.0014672	2005
Monponsett Pond, East Basin	MassDEP		12-B002–04	−70.836781	42.0014672	2005
Monponsett Pond, East Basin	MassDEP		12-B004–04	−70.836781	42.0014672	2005
Monponsett Pond, East Basin	MassDEP		12-B006–05	−70.836781	42.0014672	2005
Monponsett Pond, East Basin	MassDEP		12-B008–05	−70.836781	42.0014672	2005
Monponsett Pond, East Basin	MassDEP		13-B005–06	−70.836781	42.0014672	2005
Monponsett Pond, East Basin	MassDEP		13-B006–05	−70.836781	42.0014672	2005
Monponsett Pond, East Basin	MassDEP		13-B008–05	−70.836781	42.0014672	2005
Monponsett Pond, East Basin	MassDEP		14-B004–05	−70.836781	42.0014672	2005
Monponsett Pond, East Basin	MassDEP		14-B006–05	−70.836781	42.0014672	2005

(Continued)

TABLE 10.1 (Continued)

Waterbody	Agency	Report Source	Longitude	Latitude	First Year Reported
Monponsett Pond, East Basin	MassDEP	14-B008–05	−70.836781	42.0014672	2005
Monponsett Pond, East Basin	Individual	Joy Trahan-Liptak	−70.837849	42.005701	2005
Monponsett Pond, West Basin	MassDEP	Appendix C—Table C1.1996 Taunton River Watershed Lake observations and trophic status estimates (Taunton River Watershed 2001 Water Quality Assessment Report 62-AC-1 CN 94.0, December 2005)			2005
Monponsett Pond, West Basin	MassDEP	09-G006–01	−70.8452535	42.0045958	2005
Monponsett Pond, West Basin	MassDEP	11-B006–01	−70.8452535	42.0045958	2005
Monponsett Pond, West Basin	MassDEP	12-B008–01	−70.8452535	42.0045958	2005
Monponsett Pond, West Basin	MassDEP	13-B005–02	−70.8452535	42.0045958	2005
Monponsett Pond, West Basin	MassDEP	13-B006–01	−70.8452535	42.0045958	2005
Monponsett Pond, West Basin	MassDEP	13-B008–01	−70.8452535	42.0045958	2005
Monponsett Pond, West Basin	MassDEP	Field Survey 7/7/2017 Wong, Maldonado	−70.845253	42.004596	2005
Mount Hope Mill Pond	MassDEP	Appendix C—Table C1.1996 Taunton River Watershed Lake observations and trophic status estimates (Taunton River Watershed 2001 Water Quality Assessment Report 62-AC-1 CN 94.0, December 2005)			2005
Muddy Pond	MassDEP	Appendix C—Table C1.1996 Taunton River Watershed Lake observations and trophic status estimates (Taunton River Watershed 2001 Water Quality Assessment Report 62-AC-1 CN 94.0, December 2005)			2005

Water Body	Source	Reference	Longitude	Latitude	Year
New Pond	MassDEP	Appendix C—Table C1.1996 Taunton River Watershed Lake observations and trophic status estimates (Taunton River Watershed 2001 Water Quality Assessment Report 62-AC-1 CN 94.0, December 2005)			2005
Norton Reservoir	MassDEP	Appendix C—Table C1.1996 Taunton River Watershed Lake observations and trophic status estimates (Taunton River Watershed 2001 Water Quality Assessment Report 62-AC-1 CN 94.0, December 2005)			2005
Richmond Pond	MassDEP	Appendix C—Table C1.1996 Taunton River Watershed Lake observations and trophic status estimates (Taunton River Watershed 2001 Water Quality Assessment Report 62-AC-1 CN 94.0, December 2005)			2005
Russell Pond	MassDEP	05-G010-02	−70.7470003	41.9778691	2005
Savery Pond	MassDEP	Appendix C—Table C1.1996 Taunton River Watershed Lake observations and trophic status estimates (Taunton River Watershed 2001 Water Quality Assessment Report 62-AC-1 CN 94.0, December 2005)			2005
Saxonville Pond	MassDEP	SuAsCo Watershed 2001 Water Quality Assessment Report 82-AC-1 CN 92.0, August 2005			2005
Snipatuit Pond	MassDEP	05-R007-02	−70.8620237	41.7809072	2005
Snipatuit Pond	DCR	DCR Data from Lakes and Ponds, 2007			2005
Thirtyacre Pond	MassDEP	Appendix C—Table C1.1996 Taunton River Watershed Lake observations and trophic status estimates (Taunton River Watershed 2001 Water Quality Assessment Report 62-AC-1 CN 94.0, December 2005)			2005
Upper Porter Pond	MassDEP	Appendix C—Table C1.1996 Taunton River Watershed Lake observations and trophic status estimates (Taunton River Watershed 2001 Water Quality Assessment Report 62-AC-1 CN 94.0, December 2005)			2005
Waldo Lake	MassDEP	Appendix C—Table C1.1996 Taunton River Watershed Lake observations and trophic status estimates (Taunton River Watershed 2001 Water Quality Assessment Report 62-AC-1 CN 94.0, December 2005)			2005
Whitehall Reservoir	MassDEP	SuAsCo Watershed 2001 Water Quality Assessment Report 82-AC-1 CN 92.0, August 2005			2005
Whitehall Reservoir	DCR	DCR Data from Lakes and Ponds, 2008			2005
Whitehall Reservoir	Individual	Joy Trahan-Liptak	−71.573594	42.23072	2005
Whittenton Impoundment	MassDEP	Appendix C—Table C1.1996 Taunton River Watershed Lake observations and trophic status estimates (Taunton River Watershed 2001 Water Quality Assessment Report 62-AC-1 CN 94.0, December 2005)			2005

(Continued)

TABLE 10.1 (Continued)

Waterbody	Agency	Report Source	Longitude	Latitude	First Year Reported
Winnecunnet Pond	MassDEP	Appendix C—Table C1.1996 Taunton River Watershed Lake observations and trophic status estimates (Taunton River Watershed 2001 Water Quality Assessment Report 62-AC-1 CN 94.0, December 2005)			2005
Woods Pond	MassDEP	Appendix C—Table C1.1996 Taunton River Watershed Lake observations and trophic status estimates (Taunton River Watershed 2001 Water Quality Assessment Report 62-AC-1 CN 94.0, December 2005)			2005
Aaron River	MassDEP	South Shore Coastal Watersheds 2001 Water Quality Assessment Report 94-AC-2 CN 93.0, March 2006			2006
Beaver Dam Pond	MassDEP	South Shore Coastal Watersheds 2001 Water Quality Assessment Report 94-AC-2 CN 93.0, March 2006			2006
Briggs Reservoir	MassDEP	South Shore Coastal Watersheds 2001 Water Quality Assessment Report 94-AC-2 CN 93.0, March 2006			2006
Briggs Reservoir	MassDEP	South Shore Coastal Watersheds 2001 Water Quality Assessment Report 94-AC-2 CN 93.0, March 2006			2006
Charles River	Charles River Watershed Association	Draft Upper Charles River Watershed Total Maximum Daily Load Project (Project Nos. 2001–03/104 and 2004–04/319) Volume I: Phase II Final Report and Phase III Data Report			2006
Charles River	Individual	Joy Trahan-Liptak	−71.264994	42.25732	2006
Charles River	Charles River Watershed Association	Draft Upper Charles River Watershed Total Maximum Daily Load Project (Project Nos. 2001–03/104 and 2004–04/319) Volume I: Phase II Final Report and Phase III Data Report			2006
Cooks Pond	MassDEP	South Shore Coastal Watersheds 2001 Water Quality Assessment Report 94-AC-2 CN 93.0, March 2006			2006
Eel River	MassDEP	South Shore Coastal Watersheds 2001 Water Quality Assessment Report 94-AC-2 CN 93.0, March 2006			2006
Forge Pond	MassDEP	South Shore Coastal Watersheds 2001 Water Quality Assessment Report 94-AC-2 CN 93.0, March 2006			2006

Carolina Fanwort (*Cabomba caroliniana*)

Herring Brook	MassDEP	South Shore Coastal Watersheds 2001 Water Quality Assessment Report 94-AC-2 CN 93.0, March 2006			2006
Island Creek Pond	MassDEP	South Shore Coastal Watersheds 2001 Water Quality Assessment Report 94-AC-2 CN 93.0, March 2006			2006
Island Pond	MassDEP	South Shore Coastal Watersheds 2001 Water Quality Assessment Report 94-AC-2 CN 93.0, March 2006			2006
Jacobs Pond	MassDEP	South Shore Coastal Watersheds 2001 Water Quality Assessment Report 94-AC-2 CN 93.0, March 2006			2006
Lily Pond	MassDEP	South Shore Coastal Watersheds 2001 Water Quality Assessment Report 94-AC-2 CN 93.0, March 2006			2006
Long Island Pond	MassDEP	South Shore Coastal Watersheds 2001 Water Quality Assessment Report 94-AC-2 CN 93.0, March 2006			2006
Lower Chandler Pond	MassDEP	South Shore Coastal Watersheds 2001 Water Quality Assessment Report 94-AC-2 CN 93.0, March 2006			2006
Old Oaken Bucket Pond	MassDEP	South Shore Coastal Watersheds 2001 Water Quality Assessment Report 94-AC-2 CN 93.0, March 2006			2006
Pembroke Street South Pond	MassDEP	South Shore Coastal Watersheds 2001 Water Quality Assessment Report 94-AC-2 CN 93.0, March 2006			2006
Reeds Millpond	MassDEP	South Shore Coastal Watersheds 2001 Water Quality Assessment Report 94-AC-2 CN 93.0, March 2006			2006
Silver Lake	College of the Holy Cross	Robert Bertin	−71.654894	42.193409	2006
Silver Lake	Individual	Joy Trahan-Liptak	−71.654971	42.193369	2006
Smelt Pond	MassDEP	South Shore Coastal Watersheds 2001 Water Quality Assessment Report 94-AC-2 CN 93.0, March 2006			2006
Torrey Pond	MassDEP	South Shore Coastal Watersheds 2001 Water Quality Assessment Report 94-AC-2 CN 93.0, March 2006			2006
Wampatuck Pond	MassDEP	South Shore Coastal Watersheds 2001 Water Quality Assessment Report 94-AC-2 CN 93.0, March 2006			2006
Wampatuck Pond	DCR	DCR Data from Lakes and Ponds, 2007	−70.8668332	42.06111681	2006
Wampatuck Pond	DCR	DCR Data from Lakes and Ponds, 2008	−70.8668332	42.06111681	2006
Wampatuck Pond	MassDEP	10-B002–05	−70.8657554	42.0647472	2006
Brooks Pond	College of the Holy Cross	Robert Bertin	−72.043108	42.302192	2007

(Continued)

TABLE 10.1 (Continued)

Waterbody	Agency	Report Source	Longitude	Latitude	First Year Reported
Brooks Pond	College of the Holy Cross	Robert Bertin	−72.043108	42.302192	2007
Harris Pond	College of the Holy Cross	Robert Bertin	−71.509471	42.020057	2007
Houghtons Pond	DCR	DCR Data from Lakes and Ponds, 2007			2007
Houghtons Pond	Individual	Joy Trahan-Liptak	−71.095558	42.20725	2007
Johns Pond	DCR	DCR Data from Lakes and Ponds, 2007			2007
Whitehall Pond	DCR	DCR Data from Lakes and Ponds, 2007			2007
Billington Sea	MassDEP	08-F007–05	−70.681001	41.9348301	2008
Billington Sea	MassDEP	08-F007–05	−70.681001	41.9348301	2008
Billington Sea	MassDEP	08-F005–01	−70.681001	41.9348301	2008
Billington Sea	MassDEP	08-F003–05	−70.681001	41.9348301	2008
Billington Sea	MassDEP	09-G007–06	−70.681001	41.9348301	2008
Billington Sea	MassDEP	09-G004–04	−70.681001	41.9348301	2008
Collins Pond	DCR	DCR Data from Lakes and Ponds, 2008			2008
East Brookfield River	MassDEP	Chicopee River Watershed 2003 Water Quality Assessment Report 36-AC-3 CN 106.5, October 2008			2008
East Head Pond	DCR	DCR Data from Lakes and Ponds, humile 2008			2008
Indian Brook	MassDEP	08-F009–03	−70.538045	41.8871496	2008
Indian Brook	MassDEP	Field Survey 7/18/2017 Wong, Maldonado	−70.538045	41.8871496	2008
Lackey Pond	College of the Holy Cross	Robert Bertin	−71.689012	42.096707	2008
Lackey Pond	Individual	Joy Trahan-Liptak	−71.689618	42.097854	2008
Ponkapoag Pond	DCR	DCR Data from Lakes and Ponds, 2008			2008
Ponkapoag Pond	MassDEP	09-B013–01	−71.0929681	42.1921829	2008
Sewall Pond	DCR	DCR Data from Lakes and Ponds, 2008			2008
Singletary Pond	College of the Holy Cross	Robert Bertin	−71.77917	42.159969	2008

Location	Source	Reference/Collector	Longitude	Latitude	Year
State Street Pond	DCR	Excel spreadsheet of non-native aquatic and wetland plants in Massachusetts lakes and ponds dated July 2008			2008
Stetson Pond	DCR	DCR Data from Lakes and Ponds, 2008			2008
Mumford River	MassDEP	09-G010-03	-71.6783156	42.1104152	2009
Mumford River	Individual	Joy Trahan-Liptak	-71.665758	42.109325	2009
Stoneville Pond	College of the Holy Cross	Robert Bertin	-71.846641	42.218518	2009
Stoneville Pond	Individual	Joy Trahan-Liptak	-71.846513	42.218616	2009
Reservoir (White Oak Reservoir)	MassDEP	10-B005-04	-70.8526283	42.0298844	2010
Reservoir (White Oak Reservoir)	MassDEP	12-B004-06	-70.8526283	42.0298844	2010
Reservoir (White Oak Reservoir)	MassDEP	12-B008-06	-70.8526283	42.0298844	2010
Reservoir (White Oak Reservoir)	MassDEP	13-B006-06	-70.8526283	42.0298844	2010
Unnamed Pond	DCR	Jamie Carr	-71.844452	42.445836	2011
Unnamed Pond	DCR	David Worden	-71.844452	42.445836	2011
Auguteback Pond	Individual	Joy Trahan-Liptak	-71.877796	42.117964	2013
French River	Individual	Joy Trahan-Liptak	-71.8832	42.1098	2013
Queen Lake	Individual	Joy Trahan-Liptak	-72.114214	42.53513	2013
Stetson Brook	MassDEP	13-B005-03	-70.8366053	42.0143947	2013
Stetson Brook	MassDEP	13-B006-02	-70.8366053	42.0143947	2013
Blackstone River	Individual	Joy Trahan-Liptak	-71.617101	42.092183	2015
Bryant Pond	DCR	Joy Trahan-Liptak	-71.85485	42.34379	2015
Caprons Pond	Individual	Joy Trahan-Liptak	-71.627869	42.07709	2015
Fisherville Pond	Individual	Joy Trahan-Liptak	-71.692178	42.184408	2015
Hovey Pond	Individual	Joy Trahan-Liptak	-71.714879	42.234214	2015
Sudbury River	Individual	Joy Trahan-Liptak	-71.356919	42.462852	2015
Quinebaug River	MassDEP	Field Survey 06/16/2017 Wong, Li, Maldonado	-72.1185692	42.1095615	2017

TABLE 10.2
Towns and Infested Waterbodies

Number	Waterbody	Town 1	Town 2
1	Aaron River	Cohasset	Hingham
2	Ames Long Pond	Stoughton	Easton
3	Arcade Pond	Northbridge	–
4	Arcadia Lake	Belchertown	–
5	Assabet River	Stow	Hudson/Maynard
6	Auguteback Pond	Oxford	–
7	Baddacook Pond	Groton	–
8	Baldpate Pond	Boxford	–
9	Ballardvale Impoundment	Andover	–
10	Bare Hill Pond	Harvard	–
11	Bartlett Pond	Northborough	–
12	Barton Cove	Gill	–
13	Bearse Pond	Barnstable	–
14	Beaver Dam Pond	Plymouth	–
15	Beaver Pond	Franklin	–
16	Big Bearhole Pond	Taunton	–
17	Billington Sea	Plymouth	–
18	Blackstone River	Uxbridge	Millville
19	Blair Pond	Blandford	–
20	Bolivar Pond	Canton	–
21	Briggs Reservoir	Plymouth	–
22	Brockton Reservoir	Avon	–
23	Brooks Pond	North Brookfield	New Braintree/Oakham/Spencer
24	Bryant Pond	Holden	–
25	Caprons Pond	Uxbridge	–
26	Cedar Meadow Pond	Leicester	–
27	Chaffin Pond	Holden	–
28	Charles River	Medfield	Millis/Norfolk/Medway/Dover/Sherborn/Natick
29	Chebacco Lake	Essex	Hamilton
30	Cleveland Pond	Abington	–
31	Cobbs Pond	Walpole	–
32	Collins Pond	Andover	–
33	Concord River	Concord	Billerica/Carlisle/Bedford
34	Cook Pond	Worcester	–
35	Cooks Pond	Plymouth	–
36	Curtis Pond	Worcester	–
37	Cushing Pond	Abington	–
38	Dark Brook	Auburn	–
39	Dawson Pond	Holden	–
40	East Brookfield River	East Brookfield	–
41	East Head Pond	Carver	Plymouth
42	Edgewater Office Park Pond	Wakefield	–

Carolina Fanwort (*Cabomba caroliniana*)

Number	Waterbody	Town 1	Town 2
43	Eel River	Plymouth	–
44	Ellis Pond	Norwood	–
45	Farm Pond	Framingham	–
46	Federal Pond	Carver	Plymouth
47	Field Pond	Andover	–
48	First Pond	Saugus	–
49	Fish Pond	Northbridge	–
50	Fisherville Pond	Grafton	–
51	Flannagan Pond	Ayer	–
52	Flint Pond	Shrewsbury	–
53	Forge Pond	Westford	Littleton
54	Fort Meadow Reservoir	Marlborough	Hudson
55	Fosters Pond	Andover	Wilmington
56	French River	Oxford	–
57	Fresh Meadow Pond	Plymouth	Carver
58	Girard Pond	Sutton	–
59	Griswold Pond	Saugus	–
60	Grove Pond	Ayer	–
61	Gushee Pond	Raynham	–
62	Hardwick Pond	Hardwick	–
63	Harris Pond	Blackstone	–
64	Hayes Pond	Grafton	–
65	Heard Pond	Wayland	–
66	Herring Brook	Cohasset	–
67	Houghtons Pond	Milton	–
68	Hovey Pond	Grafton	–
69	Indian Brook	Plymouth	–
70	Ironstone Reservoir	Uxbridge	–
71	Island Creek Pond	Duxbury	–
72	Island Grove Pond	Abington	–
73	Island Pond	Plymouth	–
74	Jacobs Pond	Norwell	–
75	Johns Pond	Carver	–
76	Johnson Pond	Taunton	–
77	Kettle Brook	Leicester	Auburn/Worcester
78	Knops Pond/Lost Lake	Groton	–
79	Lackey Pond	Uxbridge	Sutton
80	Lake Boon	Stow	Hudson
81	Lake Como	Attleboro	–
82	Lake Ellis	Athol	–
83	Lake Holland	Belchertown	–
84	Lake Lashaway	North Brookfield	East Brookfield
85	Lake Mascuppic	Tyngsborough	Dracut

(Continued)

TABLE 10.2
(Continued)

Number	Waterbody	Town 1	Town 2
86	Lake Mirimichi	Plainville	Foxborough
87	Lake Nippenicket	Bridgewater	Raynham
88	Lake Quinsigamond	Shrewsbury	Worcester
89	Lake Rico	Taunton	—
90	Lake Ripple	Grafton	—
91	Lake Rohunta	New Salem	Athol/Orange
92	Lake Sabbatia	Taunton	—
93	Lake Shirley	Lunenburg	Shirley
94	Lake Warner	Hadley	—
95	Lake Winthrop	Holliston	—
96	Leesville Pond	Auburn	Worcester
97	Lily Pond	Cohasset	—
98	Little Bearhole Pond	Taunton	—
99	Long Island Pond	Plymouth	—
100	Long Pond	Lakeville	Freetown
101	Long Pond	Littleton	—
102	Lowe Pond	Boxford	—
103	Lower Chandler Pond	Duxbury	Pembroke
104	Lower Porter Pond	Brockton	—
105	Manchaug Pond	Douglas	Sutton
106	Martins Pond	North Reading	—
107	Massapoag Brook	Sharon	Canton
108	Massapoag Lake	Sharon	—
109	Metacomet Lake	Belchertown	—
110	Middle Pond	Taunton	—
111	Mill Pond	Upton	—
112	Mill River	Hopedale	Milford/Upton/Mendon
113	Miscoe Lake	Wrentham	—
114	Monponsett Pond, East Basin	Halifax	—
115	Monponsett Pond, West Basin	Halifax	Hanson
116	Morses Pond	Wellesley	Natick
117	Moulton Pond	Rutland	—
118	Mount Hope Mill Pond	Taunton	Dighton
119	Muddy Pond	Carver	—
120	Mumford River	Uxbridge	Northbridge/Sutton/Douglas
121	Nashua River	Groton	Pepperell/Ayer
122	Neponset Reservoir	Foxborough	—
123	New Pond	Easton	—
124	Newfield Pond	Chelmsford	—
125	Newton Pond	Shrewsbury	Boylston

Carolina Fanwort (*Cabomba caroliniana*)

Number	Waterbody	Town 1	Town 2
126	North Pond	Hopkinton	Milford/Upton
127	Norton Reservoir	Norton	Mansfield
128	Old Oaken Bucket Pond	Scituate	–
129	Parker Pond	Gardner	–
130	Pembroke Street South Pond	Kingston	–
131	Pentucket Pond	Georgetown	–
132	Plain Street Pond	Mansfield	–
133	Plow Shop Pond	Ayer	–
134	Pomps Pond	Andover	–
135	Pondville Pond	Auburn	Millbury
136	Ponkapoag Pond	Canton	Randolph
137	Pratt Pond	Upton	–
138	Quaboag Pond	Brookfield	East Brookfield
139	Quacumquasit Pond	Brookfield	East Brookfield/Sturbridge
140	Queen Lake	Phillipston	–
141	Quinebaug River	Sturbridge	Brimfield/Holland
142	Quinsigamond River	Grafton	–
143	Reeds Millpond	Kingston	–
144	Reservoir (White Oak Reservoir)	Hanson	–
145	Reservoir Pond	Canton	–
146	Richmond Pond	Taunton	–
147	Russell Pond	Kingston	–
148	Sampson Pond	Carver	–
149	Savery Pond	Middleborough	–
150	Saxonville Pond	Framingham	–
151	Sewall Pond	Boylston	–
152	Silver Lake	Grafton	–
153	Singletary Pond	Sutton	Millbury
154	Smelt Pond	Kingston	–
155	Snipatuit Pond	Rochester	–
156	South Athol Pond	Athol	–
157	Spectacle Pond	Littleton	Ayer
158	Spring Pond	Saugus	–
159	State Street Pond	Newburyport	–
160	Stetson Brook	Halifax	–
161	Stetson Pond	Pembroke	–
162	Stevens Pond	Sutton	–
163	Stoneville Pond	Auburn	–
164	Sudbury River	Concord	Lincoln/Sudbury/Wayland
165	Swains Pond	Melrose	–
166	Tatnuck Brook	Worcester	Holden
167	Thirtyacre Pond	Brockton	–
168	Torrey Pond	Norwell	–

(Continued)

TABLE 10.2
(Continued)

Number	Waterbody	Town 1	Town 2
169	Town Pond	Stoughton	–
170	Tully Lake	Royalston	Athol
171	Turner Pond	Walpole	–
172	Turnpike Lake	Plainville	–
173	Unnamed Pond	Princeton	–
174	Unnamed Tributary	Worcester	–
175	Upper Porter Pond	Brockton	–
176	Wachusett Reservoir	Boylston	West Boylston/Clinton/Sterling
177	Waldo Lake	Avon	Brockton
178	Wampatuck Pond	Hanson	–
179	Watson Pond	Taunton	–
180	Webster Lake	Webster	–
181	Wequaquet Lake	Barnstable	–
182	West River	Upton	Grafton
183	White Island Pond, East Basin	Plymouth	Wareham
184	White Island Pond, West Basin	Plymouth	Wareham
185	White Pond	Athol	–
186	Whitehall Pond	Rutland	–
187	Whitehall Reservoir	Hopkinton	–
188	Whitins Pond	Northbridge	Sutton
189	Whitmans Pond	Weymouth	–
190	Whittenton Impoundment	Taunton	–
191	Winnecunnet Pond	Norton	–
192	Woodbury Pond	Sutton	–
193	Woods Pond	Middleborough	–

measures include drawdown, dredging, benthic barriers, introducing biological control agents such as weevil or grass carp, herbicides, and other control methods.

Drawdown is a lake management tool that tends to reduce the density of susceptible rooted plants, and could be helpful for the control of Carolina fanwort. As this method is a process of lowering the water level, it is more suitable for a waterbody with available structures that allow manipulation of the water level, as well as the acceptability of draining the water to all water users. Additionally, it can only achieve control when sediments are completely dry for an extended period of time or the sediments and plants are completed removed (Dutartre et al. 2006; Scheers et al. 2016). In order to reduce impacts to non-target plants and animals during the growing season, drawdown in Massachusetts is normally conducted in fall and winter (Mattson et al. 2004).

Dredging and benthic barriers both are effective physical methods to impede the expansion of *C. caroliniana*. Dredging is a sediment removal process that controls the rooted plant growth through light limitation during operations or substrate limitation. Dry dredging appears to result in the removal of more soft sediments and hydraulic dredging usually involves a suction type of dredge to produce slurry which is typically pumped (or barged in rare cases) to a nearby containment area on

TABLE 10.3
Infested Watersheds

Number	Infested Watersheds
1	Blackstone
2	Boston Harbor: Neponset
3	Boston Harbor: Weymouth and Weir
4	Buzzards Bay
5	Cape Cod
6	Charles
7	Chicopee
8	Concord (SuAsCo)
9	Connecticut
10	French
11	Ipswich
12	Merrimack
13	Millers
14	Nashua
15	North Coastal
16	Parker
17	Quinebaug
18	Shawsheen
19	South Coastal
20	Taunton
21	Ten Mile
22	Westfield

shore where the excess water can be separated from the solids by settling (Mattson et al. 2004). The dredging is very efficient if performed well in removing most plants, the regrowth is from missed bits and also if the material is not collected well and starts floating around, and this is an issue with all mechanical harvesting operations. Meanwhile, dredge causes high impacts to the ecosystem as the substrate is disturbed and it is costly and limited to suitable water depths. If the dredge volume is more than 100 cubic yards, a dredging permit is required from MassDEP (see more in the "Regulation and Permitting" section of Chapter 1). Benthic barriers are a control method usually with layers of geofabric or coconut fiber mesh material that is anchored above the weeds. The application of benthic barriers limits the plants growth by a cover of clay, silt, sand, gravel, or different types of mats (Caffrey et al. 2010). But there are some limitations to this method. For instance, it requires constant maintenance and it can harm other benthic organisms (Washington State Department of Ecology n.d.). Other potential methods of management include manual removal or suction harvesting, in which the plants are manually removed either by hand or through a suction apparatus. Harvesting is great for clearing larger areas, like swimming areas as a long-term maintenance option. Hand removal is usually either an emergency tool to control new invasions and used for clearing small areas (e.g., around boat ramps) or as a tool to remove remnants after other control methods. There are many examples of smaller ponds and waterbodies throughout Massachusetts that utilize mechanical harvesting to alleviate the stressors caused by *C. caroliniana* and other invasive species. These waterbodies, such as Wellesley Pond in Wellesley, MA, or Island Creek Pond in Duxbury, MA, generally perform annual mechanical harvests which allow for improved recreation (Mattson et al. 2004). These methods require high levels of manpower and efforts and are generally only successful when treating low to moderate densities of Carolina fanwort (MA DCR 2005). It also depends on the management goal, even if a whole lake is covered by fanwort, it might still be a viable option to use mechanical tools if the goal is simply to maintain public access or swimming areas. These mechanical methods also only result in a temporary solution, and not long-term eradication. Additionally, suction harvesting can result in elevated turbidity in treatments areas, which is often undesired.

Biological control involves the introduction of species such as the aquatic weevil (*Hydrotimetes natans*) or grass carp (*Ctynopharyngodon idella*). In general, biocontrol will always be a tool to reduce invasive plants to a certain level and it is a great tool for management. The weevil is a classical biocontrol tool with a specialist insect, the grass carp is a herbivorous fish that eats all aquatic vegetation. Both tools are used completely different and the limitations and risks are completely different as well. Aquatic weevil is a specialist feeder and it might aid with fanwort control. But aquatic weevils cannot achieve permanent removal and may have an influence on non-target plants (Louda et al. 2003). Grass carp have to be stocked at the appropriate rate otherwise they don't work. Grass carp will also consume all aquatic plants in a waterbody if stocked incorrectly, so they have to be removed once control is achieved so that macrophytes can reestablish. Grass carp are not approved in Massachusetts as a biological control agent (Mattson et al. 2004). Further, high densities of grass carp can change the sediment composition and limit the habit quality for other organisms (Pípalová 2006).

Many herbicides (e.g., endothall amine salt, fluridone, triclopyr, diquat, 2,4-D, and flumioxazin) have been tested for fanwort control (Nelson et al. 2002). Herbicides contain active and inert ingredients that are toxic to target plants. However, the use of inappropriate herbicides or applying the incorrect dose of herbicide can harm or kill non-target plants and organisms (Mattson et al. 2004). Hunt et al. (2015) found that endothall amine salt could be an effective tool for *C. caroliniana* control, even at low concentrations such as 0.5 mg ae/l. The Department of Conservation and Recreation also recommends the use of fluridone and triclopyr. The recommended doses for the control of fanwort is >10 ppb for fluridone and 0.75–2.5 ppm for triclopyr (MA DCR 2005). Flumioxazin is one

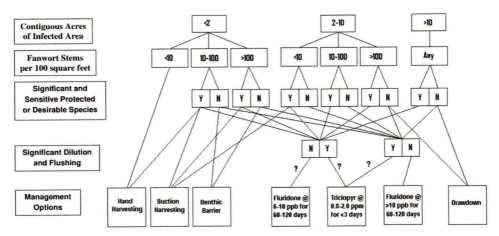

FIGURE 10.4 Decision tree for the control of Carolina fanwort (*Cabomba caroliniana*) (MA DCR, 2005). Hand harvesting and suction harvesting must include root system removal. Benthic barriers should remain in place for 30–60 days. Fluridone is effective at >10 ppb with >60 days exposure; lesser doses and exposure times may yield some control. Triclopyr was approved for use in MA in late 2004; experience is limited in MA. Drawdown use is dependent on many factors, including hydrology and use as a water supply. Moderate to dense growth over an extensive area (>10 acres) may not be appropriate for rapid response consideration.

of the best herbicides to control fanwort with a label rate of 200–400 ppb. More information about chemical control on fanwort and other 18 invasive species can be found in Appendix III. Any chemical used for aquatic invasive species control requires a WM04 Chemical Application License issued by the Massachusetts Department of Environmental Protection.

Other effective methods to suppress the growth of fanwort can also be used, for instance, increasing the shading by trees or shrubs to block the direct sunlight, developing a tall helophyte belt (e.g., Phragmites and Typha) along the shore to reduce the open water area, covering the area with a light-blocking synthetic foil or geo-textile, etc. (Scheers et al. 2016; Schooler 2008).

The MA Department of Conservation and Recreation provided a guideline on how to choose the best technique for *C. caroliniana* control based on different situations (Figure 10.4). This can be helpful when selecting the optimal control method.

SUCCESS STORY

In August 2004, Carolina fanwort was found growing throughout nearly half of Foster's Pond in Andover, MA (ACT 2011). An EPA/DEP registered aquatic herbicide, Sonar AS, which contains 42% fluridone and was chosen for the fanwort control (Mattson et al. 2004). During the control period in 2005, a maintenance herbicide treatment and monitoring program was initiated. This initial whole lake treatment consisted of three low-dose applications of Sonar AS, maintaining 10–20 ppb of the herbicide in the water for more than 60 days. This was followed by a partial lake treatment in 2007. The overall success of the fanwort control program was evaluated in surveys taken in 2008 and 2009. Although fanwort began to reemerge, it covered only 6.1% of Foster Pond, or roughly a ninth of the area it had previously dominated, and there were more native plants found in the pond in 2009 than in 2004. Spot treatments were applied in 2010 to areas where *C. caroliniana* remained and another whole lake treatment with Sonar was proposed for 2011. Therefore, this is a successful example of Carolina fanwort control.

REFERENCES

Aquatic Control Technology, Inc. 2011. Letter titled "Schedule and Program for Proposed 2011 Sonar and Reward Herbicide Treatment of Foster's Pond". *Aquatic Control Technology, INC.* www.fosterspond.org/ACT_2011_Treatment_Plan.pdf (Accessed February 19, 2020).

Bickel, T.O. 2015. A boat hitchhiker's guide to survival: *Cabomba caroliniana* desiccation resistance and survival ability. *Hydrobiologia* 746: 123–134.

Bruckerhoff, L., J. Havel, and S. Knight. 2015. Survival of invasive aquatic plants after air exposure and implications for dispersal by recreational boats. *Hydrobiologia* 746: 113–121.

Brundu, G. 2015. Plant invaders in European and Mediterranean inland waters: Profiles, distribution, and threats. *Hydrobiologia* 746: 61–79.

Bultemeier, B., M. Netherland, J. Ferrell, and W. Haller. 2009. Differential herbicide response among three phenotypes of *Cabomba caroliniana*. *Invasive Plant Science and Management* 2(4): 352–359.

Caffrey J.M., M. Millane, S. Evers, H. Moran, and M. Butler. 2010 A novel approach to aquatic weed control and habitat restoration using biodegradable jute matting. *Aquatic Invasions* 5: 123–129.

Council of Heads of Australasian Herbaria (CHAH). 2011. *Cabomba caroliniana*, https://profiles.ala.org.au/opus/weeds-australia/profile/Cabomba%20caroliniana (Accessed December 10, 2020).

Dutartre, A., C. Chauvin, and J. Grange. 2006. Colonisation végétale du canal de Bourgogne à Dijon: bilan 2006, propositions de gestion. In: *Rapport Cemagref Bordeaux*. Douai, France: Agence de l'Eau Artois-Picardie, p. 87.

Hogsden, K.L., E.P.S. Sager, T.C. Hutchinson. 2007. The impacts of the non-native macrophyte *Cabomba caroliniana* on littoral biota of Kasshabog Lake, Ontario. *Journal of Great Lakes Research* 33(2): 497–504.

Hunt, T.D., T.D. Dugdale, D. Clements, and M. Fridman. 2015. Concentration– exposure time relationships for controlling fanwort (*Cabomba caroliniana*) with endothall amine salt and carfentrazone. *Journal of Aquatic Plant Management* 53: 144–149.

Hussner, A., S. Nehring, and S. Hilt. 2013. From first reports to successful control: A plea for improved management of alien aquatic plant species in Germany. *Hydrobiologia* 737: 321–331.

ITIS (Integrated Taxonomic Information System). 2021. www.itis.gov/servlet/SingleRpt/SingleRpt?search_topic=TSN&search_value=18408#null (Accessed February 28, 2021).

Larson, J.L., L. Berent, and S. Iott. 2020. *Cabomba caroliniana* A. Gray: *U.S. Geological Survey, Nonindigenous Aquatic Species Database*. Gainesville, FL. https://nas.er.usgs.gov/queries/FactSheet.aspx?SpeciesID=231 (Accessed December 9, 2020).

Louda, S.M., R.W. Pemberton, M.T. Johnson, and P.A. Follett. 2003. Nontarget effects—The Achilles' heel of biological control? Retrospective analyses to reduce risk associated with biocontrol introductions. *Annual Reviews of Entomology* 48: 365–396.

MA DCR (Department of Conservation and Recreation). 2002. Fanwort: An invasive aquatic plant. www.mass.gov/files/documents/2016/08/ne/fanwort.pdf (Accessed February 19, 2020).

MA DCR (Department of Conservation and Recreation). 2005. Rapid Response Plan for Fanwort (*Cabomba caroliniana*) in Massachusetts. www.mass.gov/doc/fanwort-1/download (Accessed December 9, 2020).

MA DCR (Department of Conservation and Recreation). 2016. A Guide to aquatic plants in Massachusetts. http://lakemirimichi.org/Assets/Aquatic%20life/A%20Guide%20to%20Aquatic%20Plants_Booklet.PDF (Accessed February 19, 2020).

Mackey, A.P. 1996. *Cabomba (Cabomba spp.). Pest Status Review Series—Land Protection Branch*. Queensland: Queensland Government Department of Natural Resources and Mines.

Mackey, A.P., and J.T. Swarbrick. 1997. The biology of Australian weeds 32. *Cabomba caroliniana* Gray. *Plant Protection Quarterly* 12: 154–165.

Maki, K., and S. Galatowitsch. 2004. Movement of invasive aquatic plants into Minnesota (USA) through horticultural trade. *Biological Conservation* 118: 389–396.

Mattson, M.D., P.L. Godfrey, R.A. Barletta, and A. Aiello. 2004. *Eutrophication and Aquatic Plant Management in Massachusetts: Final Generic Environmental Impact Report*. Executive Office of Environmental Affairs, Commonwealth of Massachusetts, p. 514.

Nelson, L.S., A.B. Stewart, and K.D. Getsinger. 2002. Fluridone effects on fanwort and water marigold. *Journal of Aquatic Plant Management* 40: 58–63.

Ørgaard, M. 1991. The genus *Cabomba* (Cabombaceae)–A taxonomic study. *Nordic Journal of Botany* 11(2): 179–203.

Pípalová, I. 2006. A review of grass carp use for aquatic weed control and its impact on water bodies. *Journal of Aquatic Plant Management* 44: 1–12.

Rothlisberger, J.R., W.L. Chadderton, J. McNulty, and D.M. Lodge. 2010. Aquatic invasive species transport via trailered boats: what is being moved, who is moving it, and what can be done? *Fisheries* 35: 121–132.

Scheers, K., L. Denys, J. Packet, and T. Adriaens 2016. A second population of *Cabomba caroliniana* Gray (Cabombaceae) in Belgium with options for its eradication. *BioInvasions Records* 5(4): 227–232.

Schneider, E.L., and J.M. Jeter. 1982. Morphological studies of the Nymphaeaceae. XII. The floral biology of *Cabomba caroliniana*. *American Journal of Botany* 69(9): 1410–1419.

Schooler, S.S. 2008. Shade as a management tool for the invasive submerged macrophyte, *Cabomba caroliniana*. *Journal of Aquatic Plant Management* 46: 168–171.

Sheldon, S.P. 1994. Invasions and declines of submersed macrophytes in New England, with particular reference to Vermont lakes and herbivorous invertebrates in New England. *Lake and Reservoir Management* 10(1): 13–17.

State of Michigan. 2017. State of Michigan's Status and Strategy for Carolina Fanwort (*Cabomba caroliniana* A. Gray) Management. www.michigan.gov/documents/deq/wrd-ais-cabomba-caroliniana_499690_7.pdf.

Verbrugge, L.N.H. 2014. Going global: Perceiving, assessing and managing biological invasions. Thesis, Radboud University, Nijmegen, p. 171.

Washington State Department of Ecology. n.d. swollen bladderwort. *Wendy Scholl Invasion Ecology*. http://depts.washington.edu/oldenlab/wordpress/wp-content/uploads/2013/03/Ultricularia-inflata_Scholl_2007R.pdf (Accessed January 22, 2020).

Wilson, C.E., S.J. Darbyshire, and R. Jones. 2007. The biology of invasive alien plants in Canada. 7. *Cabomba caroliniana* A. Gray. *Canadian Journal of Plant Science* 87: 615–638.

11 European Naiad (*Najas minor*)

ABSTRACT

Najas minor is an invasive aquatic plant introduced to the United States from Europe. According to historical data collected mainly by Massachusetts Department of Environmental Protection, there are at least 20 waterbodies in Massachusetts infested by *N. minor*. Understanding the status of the infestation can help raise awareness among the general public and inform those who interact with water sources to help minimize its further spread. This report also describes different methods that have been used for controlling European naiad, including physical (e.g., harvesting and benthic barriers) and chemical treatments (e.g., herbicides).

INTRODUCTION

Taxonomy Hierarchy (ITIS 2021)

Kingdom	Plantae
Subkingdom	Viridiplantae
Infrakingdom	Streptophyta
Superdivision	Embryophyta
Division	Tracheophyta
Subdivision	Spermatophytina
Class	Magnoliopsida
Superorder	Lilianae
Order	Alismatales
Family	Hydrocharitaceae
Genus	*Najas*
Species	*Najas minor* All.

BASIC BIOLOGY

European naiad (*Najas minor*) is also called brittle naiad or brittle water-nymph. *N. minor* is a submersed rooted plant with an annual life cycle. At the height of its growth, *N. minor*'s stem can reach up to 120 cm in length and 1 mm in diameter, before it breaks apart into seeded fragments to reproduce. The leaves are usually stiff, pointed, and recurved, and have a length of 0.5–3.4 cm (Figure 11.1). Leaves are arranged in pairs oppositely at nodes on the stem but appear to grow in bushy whorls at the growing tip of the plant (MN DNR 2021a). There are spines along the leaf margin which are visible to the naked eye. Flowers of *N. minor* present carpellate in light green to purple, growing on the upper axils; purplish seeds are slightly recurved, which are usually 1.5–3.0 mm long and 0.5–0.7 mm wide (Meriläinen 1968; Haynes 1979). The species shares many subtle morphological characteristics with the other seven *Najas* species known to the United States, leading *N. minor* to frequently be misidentified as native naiads such as *N. marina* or *N. gracillima* at different stages of its growth. For this reason, the surest way to confirm the identity is using genetics (Les et al. 2015).

When young, *N. minor* and *N. gracillima* are indistinguishable by appearance, as they both have narrow leaves and truncate to auriculate sheathing leaf bases (Meriläinen 1968). Wentz and Stuckey (1971) also mention that *N. minor* does not have its stiff recurved leaves at the beginning of its growth, so young plants could be easily misidentified as *N. gracillima*. However, Jouko Meriläinen (1968) developed a method for differentiating these two plants based on several morphological characteristics. First, *N. minor* is dark green with a curvy leaf margin, while *N. gracillima* is light green with a straight leaf margin. Second, the length of the fruit is different in each plant: *N. minor*'s fruit is relatively long and *N. gracillima*'s fruit is relatively short. Third, the areolae of seed coat for *N. minor* is transversely elongate, but it is longitudinally elongate for *N. gracillima*. Another often confused species, *N. marina*, can be distinguished in that it has thicker stems and leaves than *N. minor*, and the leaves of *N. marina* are not strongly recurved (MN DNR 2021b). A guide to visually distinguishing *Najas* species of North America (at their adult stages before fragmentation) is included in this report (Figure 11.2).

DOI: 10.1201/9781003201106-11

FIGURE 11.1 Microscopic photos of European Naiad (*left*, 10×) and its stem (*right*, 50×). (Photos by Wai Hing Wong.)

NATIVE AND INVASIVE RANGE

Though relatively rare in its native range in Europe, western Asia, and northern Africa, *N. minor* has become invasive in North America, in some cases aggressively displacing native aquatic plants (Triest 1988; Les et al. 2015; Pfingsten et al. 2021). According to US Geological Survey (Pfingsten et al. 2021), *N. minor* was first found in 1932 at Lake Cardinal, Ashtabula, OH, by Freudenstein and Tadesse.

From the 1930s to the 1960s, the invasive range of *N. minor* expanded from Lake Ontario west to Illinois, and to the south as far as northern Florida (Meriläinen 1968). Currently, it is reported that the number of states populated by *N. minor* has increased to 37 (Pfingsten et al. 2021). The eastern and midwestern regions of the United States are the main areas infected by this species, but specimens of *N. minor* have been uncovered as far as California, which had been previously misidentified as *N. marina* when originally collected in 2003 (Les 2012).

MECHANISMS/VECTORS OF SPREAD

N. minor, as a sexual species, disperses primarily by seeds, and does so very efficiently and prolifically (Les et al. 2015). During the reproductive season, the stem of the plant breaks apart while the seeds remain attached to the leaf axils, so that the fragmented pieces can be easily carried by wind and water to disperse the seeds, which can overwinter in dry conditions (GISD 2021).

The plant itself is also said to tolerate a high-pollutant water environment, allowing *N. minor* to proliferate opportunistically when bodies of water are polluted or degraded. In the literature, *N. minor* and *N. marina* are described as preferring eutrophic, lentic, shallow, and turbid habitats, perhaps with more calcareous water (Baart et al. 2013; Les et al. 2015).

Les et al. (2015) theorize that *N. minor*'s initial introduction to the United States in Lake Cardinal occurred following residential development of the area surrounding the lake, when the plant was used in water gardening by private residents and unintentionally released into the lake. Aside from sporadic aquacultural introduction (i.e., through aquaria), *N. minor* may continue to spread along flyways of waterfowl, with seeds being dispersed by ducks and shore birds who eat them (Meriläinen 1968). As the plant reproduces by splitting into many small, easily transmittable seeded fragments, the seeds could also spread in connection with shipping activities, water and air movement, or by sticking to other live aquatic plants or vegetation that are being transported (Clausen 1936; Martin and Uhler 1939; Chase 1947; McIntyre and Barrett

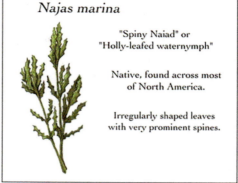
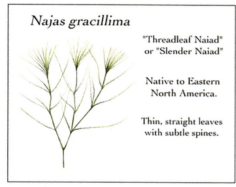
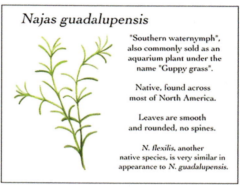

FIGURE 11.2 Guide to differentiating different North American native and introduced species in the genus *Najas* based on general visual characteristics. The plants are represented here in their adult form by one portion of a growing tip. (Illustrations and descriptions by Y.M. Becker. Photos of *N. minor* (GISD 2021; Native Plant Trust 2021; Lovel 2021; Mehrhoff n.d.; Skawinski n.d.; Na and Choi 2012), *N. marina*, (Topic n.d.; Wunderlin et al. 2021; USDA n.d.b), *N. gracillima*, (USDA n.d.a; Hilty 2019), and *N. guadalupensis* (Dressler 1996; Chayka and Dziuk n.d.) used as reference for illustrations.)

1985). Since *N. minor* can dissipate its seeds in many different ways, the spread of the species is difficult to control once it is established.

ECOLOGICAL IMPACTS

N. minor can thrive in the eutrophic waters, growing in decaying mud on the bottom. While the turbid, anoxic water conditions created by eutrophication harm many plants and animals, *N. minor* has an advantage under these conditions and can outcompete native species (Wentz and Stuckey 1971). According to Robinson (2004), *N. minor* mats can clog waterways, decrease the sediment level in the water, and intercept the sunlight, which leads to the exclusion of other submerged plants. When large mats of *N. minor* decay at the end of a growing season (because of the plant's annual growth habit), the organisms breaking down the plant matter deplete the water of oxygen, creating a eutrophic, anoxic environment that can cause fish and other aquatic animals to die in large numbers. These eutrophic conditions also allow future populations of *N. minor* to thrive, perpetuating the plant's life cycle and preventing other plants and animals from reestablishing.

N. minor, like other *Najas* species, has other impacts on aquatic systems. Research has found that *N. minor* and *N. marina* contain and exude allelopathic compounds with the ability to suppress algal growth, which might control algal blooms in eutrophic waterbodies (Wang et al. 2010). Additionally, *N. minor* is easily accessible to ducks, waterfowl, and shore birds as a food source since the plant prefers to grow in calm, shallow water (Clausen 1936; Martin and Uhler 1939). Martin and Uhler (1939) mentioned that *Najas* spp. ranked as the eighth most important food sources for wild ducks in the United States and Canada. However, transmission by migrating waterfowl is believed to be one of the ways *N. minor* spreads to new habitats, so consumption by ducks and other birds is also a potential risk factor for invasion (Meriläinen 1968).

Economic Impacts

Dense, bushy *N. minor* in the water may inhibit boating, swimming, and other recreational activities, resulting in economic loss. The spines on *Najas* plants have the potential to irritate skin, leading to an unpleasant swimming experience (Les 2012). With serious infestations, development could be hampered, the value of waterfront real estate could be influenced (Robinson 2004), and the water discharge capacity of channels could be reduced (Pfingsten et al. 2021).

Though rice is generally not a major agricultural product of Massachusetts, *Najas* spp. are often found in association with rice farming and are considered a weed of rice (Pinke et al. 2014). *N. minor* has the potential to cause economic loss if it is introduced as an agricultural pest in rice fields or among other crops that are grown in standing water.

MONITORING AND SIGHTINGS

The invasive species data detected in each waterbody were collected by the Massachusetts Department of Environmental Protection (MassDEP), the Department of Conservation and Recreation (DCR), the College of Holy Cross, as well as one individual, Joy Trahan-Liptak. The standard operating procedures, including sampling methodology, species identification, quality control and assurance, are implemented by samples collected by MassDEP. Data from other agencies are confirmed by experts. Sites with *N. minor* were mapped as a data layer with ArcGIS® ArcMap 10.1 (ESRI, Redlands, California). This tool can show how *N. minor* has spread, which can help to inform future decisions on use of these waterbodies or regulations to limit the spread of this aquatic invasive species.

Data from different sources are shown in Table 11.1. A map using ArcGIS has been created to show the spatial distribution of *N. minor* in Massachusetts waterbodies (Figure 11.3).

The first sighting of European Naiad (*Najas minor*) in Massachusetts was in the Lily Brook and Stockbridge Bowl in West Stockbridge, Berkshire County, in June 1974 (Hellquist 1977). It was generally thought that *Najas minor* traveled eastward and from there to waters adjacent to the Turnpike. For example, one of the early detections is in the upper basin of Dorothy Pond in Millbury, which functions as a stormwater basin for the Turnpike (Observed by Therese Beaudoin, personal communication). Currently, there are 20 waterbodies in Massachusetts (Table 11.2) with reported sightings of *N. minor* representing eight watersheds (Table 11.3 and Figure 11.3). So far, no invasive European naiad has been detected in Massachusetts rivers, not unexpected as this species prefers to grow in static waters (Clausen 1936; Martin and Uhler 1939). The infested waterbodies are lakes, ponds, and reservoirs mainly located in western, midwestern, and southern Massachusetts. Among the 20 infested bodies of water, 13 of them are reported by MassDEP. According to the data from MassDEP collected between 1994 and 2016, there are 2,050 waterbodies that have been investigated. Therefore, these 13 lakes/ponds represent 0.6% of the investigated waterbodies. Since the sampling is not randomly designed, the sighting ratio likely cannot accurately reflect the true presence of *N. minor* in Massachusetts.

MANAGING ACTIONS

The most efficient way to protect the environment from invasive species is integrated management, including education and prevention, early detection, control, ecosystem restoration, and environmental regulation and enforcement. Among these management options,

TABLE 11.1
Location and Report Source of Each Infested Waterbody in Massachusetts

Waterbody	Agency	Report Source	Longitude	Latitude	First Year Reported
Lake Buel	MassDEP	Housatonic River Watershed 2002 Water Quality Assessment Report 21-AC-4 CN141.5, September 2007			
Laurel Lake	MassDEP	Housatonic River Watershed 2002 Water Quality Assessment Report 21-AC-4 CN141.5, September 2007			2014
Onota Lake	MassDEP	Housatonic River Watershed 2002 Water Quality Assessment Report 21-AC-4 CN141.5, September 2007			
Onota Lake	Individual	Joy Trahan-Liptak	−73.2813	42.4705	
Plunkett Reservoir	MassDEP	Housatonic River Watershed 2002 Water Quality Assessment Report 21-AC-4 CN141.5, September 2007			
Pontoosac Lake	MassDEP	Housatonic River Watershed 2002 Water Quality Assessment Report 21-AC-4 CN141.5, September 2007			
Pontoosac Lake	DCR	DCR Data from Lakes and Ponds, 2008			2008
Pontoosac Lake	DCR	DCR Data from ACT, GeoSyntec-ACT			
Richmond Pond	MassDEP	Housatonic River Watershed 2002 Water Quality Assessment Report 21-AC-4 CN141.5, September 2007			
Leverett Pond	MassDEP	Connecticut River Basin 2003 Water Quality Assessment Report 34-AC-2 CN 105.5, October 2008			
Dark Brook Reservoir	MassDEP	Blackstone River Basin 1998 Water Quality Assessment Report 51-AC-1 48.0, May 2011			
Dorothy Pond	MassDEP	Blackstone River Basin 1998 Water Quality Assessment Report 51-AC-1 48.0, May 2011			
North Pond	DCR	DCR Data from Lakes and Ponds, 2008			2008
Tinker Hill Pond	MassDEP	Blackstone River Basin 1998 Water Quality Assessment Report 51-AC-1 48.0, May 2011			

(Continued)

TABLE 11.1
(Continued)

Waterbody	Agency	Report Source	Longitude	Latitude	First Year Reported
Flint Pond	College of the Holy Cross	Robert Bertin	−71.7251	42.2414	
Lake Shirley	DCR	DCR Data from ACT, GeoSyntec-ACT			
Flint Pond	MassDEP	Merrimack River Basin 1999 Water Quality Assessment Report 84-AC-1 52.0, November 2001			
Martins Pond	MassDEP	Ipswich River Watershed 2000 Water Quality Assessment Report 92-AC-1 088.0, April 2004			
White Island Pond, East Basin	MassDEP	14-B003–01	−70.6175	41.8092	
White Island Pond, East Basin	MassDEP	13-B007–01	−70.6175	41.8092	
White Island Pond, West Basin	MassDEP	12-B003–02	−70.6276	41.8100	
Chicoppee Reservoir	DCR	DCR Data from Lakes and Ponds, 2005	−72.5513	42.1707	2005
Chicoppee Reservoir	DCR	DCR Data from Lakes and Ponds, 2007	−72.5513	42.1707	2007
Lily Pond, Middle	DCR	Jamie Carr	−71.7695	42.3767	
Wachusett Reservoir, Muddy Pond	DCR	Jamie Carr	−71.7871	42.4145	
Lily Pond, West	DCR	Jamie Carr	−71.7720	42.3773	
Lily Pond, East	DCR	Jamie Carr	−71.7671	42.3759	
Lily Brook and Stockbridge Bowl, West Stockbridge	USGS	Hellquist, C.B. (via USGS)	−73.3109	42.3363	1974
The Quag	DCR	Joy Trahan-Liptak	−71.7711	42.4166	
West Waushacum Pond	DCR	Joy Trahan-Liptak	−71.7645	42.4144	

prevention is the most efficient and cost-effective approach in stopping or minimizing the spread of aquatic invasive species. Mapped locations of European naiad provide a spatial understanding of the status of this invasive species in Massachusetts lakes to increase public awareness of this invasive species. For waterbodies that haven't been invaded but may be at risk, proactive prevention should be researched and promoted.

In Massachusetts, waterbodies infested with European naiad will be included in the 303d list of impaired or threatened waters during water quality assessments, fulfilling the requirements of the Clean Water Act. For projects within infested watersheds subject to the jurisdiction of the 401 Water Quality Certification, conditions on invasive species prevention and decontamination are needed in the certificate. In addition, water quality monitoring gear and watercrafts in these infested

European Naiad (*Najas minor*)

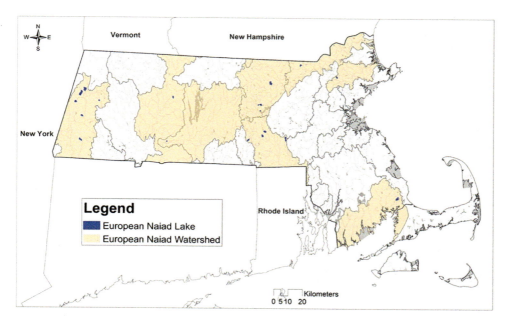

FIGURE 11.3 Distribution map depicting European Naiad (*Najas minor*) in Massachusetts.

TABLE 11.2
Towns and Infested Waterbodies

Number	Waterbody	Town_1	Town_2
1	Chicoppee Reservoir	Chicopee	–
2	Dark Brook Reservoir	Auburn	–
3	Dorothy Pond	Millbury	–
4	Flint Pond	Grafton	Worcester/Shrewsbury
5	Lake Buel	Monterey	New Marlborough
6	Lake Shirley	Lunenburg	Shirley
7	Laurel Lake	Lee	Lenox
8	Leverett Pond	Leverett	–
9	Lily Pond	West Boylston	–
10	Martins Pond	North Reading	–
11	North Pond	Hopkinton	Milford/Upton
12	Onota Lake	Pittsfield	–
13	Plunkett Reservoir	Hinsdale	–
14	Pontoosac Lake	Lanesborough	Pittsfield
15	Richmond Pond	Richmond	Pittsfield
16	The Quag	Sterling	–
17	Tinker Hill Pond	Auburn	–
18	Wachusett Reservoir, Muddy Pond	Sterling	–
19	West Waushacum Pond	Sterling	–
20	White Island Pond	Plymouth	Wareham

TABLE 11.3
Infested Watersheds

Number	Infested Watersheds
1	Blackstone
2	Buzzards Bay
3	Chicopee
4	Connecticut
5	Housatonic
6	Ipswich
7	Merrimack
8	Nashua

watersheds shall be decontaminated before being used in other watersheds to prevent the potential spread of invasive European naiad.

Several control methods for eradicating or reducing the abundance of *N. minor* in places where it is established are provided in this report. Known effective management measures include mechanical/physical control such as harvesting and benthic barriers, and chemical treatments (i.e., herbicides application). However, it is important to use these control methods carefully to avoid unintended consequences and choose a treatment for a specific site that will minimize any potential ecological harm.

When multiple invasive plants occupy the same habitat, a specific plan must be made to combat all invaders simultaneously, to avoid worsening the situation by sparing one or more invasive species from the competitive pressure of the other species (Richardson 2008). For example, if a pond contains three invasive plants in equal numbers, and measures are taken to eliminate only two of those species, the third species might thrive in the absence of its competitors and take over the entire pond, resulting in a less balanced system, and the original problem not being solved by the treatment.

All in all, control is only one small piece of an integrated management plan. It is essential to follow up any measures to eliminate nuisance species from an ecosystem with committed efforts to monitor, restore, and remediate the system. If a body of water is vulnerable to an *N. minor* invasion because ongoing pollution has caused the water to become eutrophic (containing excess nutrients), the site will remain vulnerable even if the invasive species is eliminated. Only by remediating pollution on the site and working to cultivate and reestablish native plant species in place of the ones removed will an infestation of *N. minor* be fully alleviated.

Chemical Control

Chemical control is one of the most popular management approaches for nuisance plants and several chemicals are legal to use in Massachusetts. Endothall, fluridone, and diquat are chemical herbicides that have been recognized as consistently effective against *N. minor* when used with the correct dose, proper formulation, and suitable conditions. Another active ingredient, 2,4-dichlorophenoxyacetic acid (abbreviated 2, 4-D), can also be used but its effectiveness varies as it can be influenced by dose and applying conditions (Mattson et al. 2004). More information about chemical control on *N. minor* and other 18 invasive species can be found in Appendix III.

Herbicides contain active ingredients that have specific biological toxicity to plants with acceptable risks to humans or other animals at the recommended dose. However, to avoid unintended effects, herbicides should be applied per the label and to achieve the concentration to be effective, they should be applied with care to limit exposure to non-target plants which might be indiscriminately damaged by the chemical (Mattson et al. 2004). It is also important to avoid overuse of herbicides because of the emerging possibility of herbicide resistance in aquatic plants (Richardson 2008). Before any chemical application, it is required to obtain an aquatic nuisance species control license (BRP WM04 Form) from Massachusetts Department of Environmental Protection.

PHYSICAL CONTROL

Harvesting of invasive plants can often achieve short-term success. Common harvesting techniques include mechanical harvesting and hand pulling (Mattson et al. 2004). Although this method is easily accessible and, in some cases, cheaper than alternatives, harvesting at the wrong time of the plant's life cycle can be counterproductive and disadvantageous for the removal of *N. minor* since the plant reproduces by breaking into many small seeded fragments (Meriläinen 1968; GISD 2021). Breaking the mature, fruiting plant or moving its pieces around could help the plant reproduce and spread rather than removing it (Robinson 2004). Mechanical removal by cutting or harvesting is therefore not recommended during the reproductive season of the plant (mid to late summer). Before the plant is mature, however, hand pulling is preferable to mechanical harvesting and mainly applicable when small-scale *N. minor* appears in the waterbody, or when *N. minor* is mixed with other aquatic plants.

Benthic barriers, large coverings placed on the bottom of waterbodies to smother benthic organisms, could be an effective physical control against *N. minor* by limiting the invasive population's access to light and oxygen. These barriers could consist of sheets of synthetic gas-impermeable material or layers of sediment such as clay, sand, or gravel deposited over the bottom. As *N. minor* grows submersed and rooted to the ground, if benthic barrier material is thick enough and low in nutrients, it could greatly reduce *N. minor* populations (Mattson et al. 2004). The cost of materials and labor in this technique can be high, and the barrier can often require additional maintenance (Robinson 2004). It is also suggested that, unless covering an entire population, barriers can be moved to cover other infested areas and eventually removed entirely from the waterbody (John McPheDran, personal communication). Benthic barriers also have the potential to harm non-invasive benthic plants and wildlife (Washington State Department of Ecology n.d.). However, in limited areas that are carefully chosen, such as swimming beaches or densely infested waterbodies, benthic barriers could be a good choice for managing *N. minor*.

BIOLOGICAL CONTROL

As mentioned in a previous section, ducks and other waterfowl are known to feed on *Najas* spp., but their feeding does not lead to reduced abundance of *Najas* spp., rather it helps in its propagation (Martin and Uhler 1939; Meriläinen 1968). Therefore, wild birds are unlikely to be valuable as biological control of *N. minor*.

Introduced populations of grass carp, often genetically modified to be sterile, have often been used to combat invasive aquatic plants, but their introduction can lead to elimination of non-target plant species and other ecological problems (Richardson 2008). The effectiveness of introduced fish or other herbivore species in reducing *N. minor* populations has not been specifically documented.

SUCCESS STORY

In 2016, an aquatic vegetation management survey was developed by SOLitude Lake Management (SLM) for protecting the Borough of Mount Lakes, in Morris, New Jersey. Five nuisance aquatic macrophytes were observed during the survey from June to August in a set of nine waterbodies collectively known as the Mountain Lakes (SLM 2016, 2017, 2018, 2019). *N. minor* was detected among these nuisance plants. As a part of the SLM (2016) plan for dealing with these aquatic invasions, specific herbicides and algaecides were applied at each of the lakes to treat different target plants. Alongside the application of herbicides and algaecides, a water quality monitoring program was conducted under the local regulations.

Naiad species, which includes *N. minor*, were found in Sunset Lake and Wildwood Lake. At these two lakes, a herbicide product called Reward® was used to target naiad species. The active ingredient of Reward® is diquat dibromide and the formulation is intended for use on aquatic plants.

At Wildwood Lake, Reward® was applied over about 8 acres of the lake in mid-July. At Sunset Lake, Reward® was applied later in the season (mid-August) over a smaller area of 4 acres. After the summer of 2016, the effects of the herbicide treatment on *Najas* spp. in Wildwood Lake were limited, and *Najas* spp. were detected growing at nuisance abundance in September and October of 2016. Therefore, SOLitude Lake Management was ready to apply a more aggressive method to control the growth of *Najas* species in their next plan. No specific information was given in this report regarding the abundance of *Najas* species at Sunset Lake within the year following the 2016 treatment, but for the following years through 2019, naiad populations were reported as sparse in Sunset Lake and additional naiad-targeted treatment was not deemed necessary. The 2019 season also saw renewed growth of native bass weed (*Potamogeton amplifolius*) in Sunset Lake, along with reduced algal growth, consistently high dissolved oxygen levels, and low nitrate and phosphate in the water, representing the overall success of the management program. Between 2007 and 2019, Sunset Lake was treated non-aggressively, only with algaecides and herbicides, since water quality in the lake was generally good compared to other lakes falling under the SLM plan throughout this time (SLM 2019).

At Wildwood Lake, *N. minor* continued to grow in years following the treatment, so two new herbicides, Tribune® and Schooner®, were used to control *Najas* species during 2017–2018. Tribune® is another formulation of diquat dibromide, and Schooner® has flumioxazin as the active ingredient. Flumioxazin is a herbicide registered for aquatic use in Massachusetts, but it is also regarded as moderately to acutely toxic to fish and aquatic invertebrates (MDAR/MassDEP 2013). Wildwood Lake was also treated with alum for general nutrient management. However, reduction of *N. minor* in Wildwood Lake was limited, and in 2019, *N. minor* returned in huge densities, taking up an estimated 70% of the lake basin (SLM 2019). Therefore, in 2019, lake management changed tack and a product called Aquastrike® (active ingredients: diquat dibromide and endothall) was used to target *N. minor* instead with two applications, one in July and one in August. According to the 2019 report, Aquastrike® "proved to be a great management tool for this lake for both naiad, and other submersed aquatic plants for localized management" (SLM 2019).

In this case, though *Najas* levels were eventually reduced from nuisance levels, the plants reappeared each year in spite of treatment, so repeated application of chemical herbicides may be necessary to achieve this reduction. The success found in this case through targeted chemical treatment was also in large part due to persistent and thorough monitoring of macrophyte coverage, phytoplankton, and water quality, which contributed in large part to the improved condition of these lake ecosystems. Chemical treatment alone would likely not have resulted in the same outcome in the Mountain Lakes without the strategic management plan surrounding it.

REFERENCES

Baart, I., S. Hohensinner, Z. Istvan, and T. Hein. 2013. Supporting analysis of floodplain restoration options by historical analysis. *Environmental Science & Policy* 34: 92–102.

Chase, S.S. 1947. Preliminary studies in the genus *Najas* in the United States. Ph.D. dissertation. Cornell University, Ithaca, NY, pp. 51–56.

Chayka, K., and M. Dziuk. n.d. Najas guadalupensis (Southern Waternymph). *Minnesota Wildflowers*. Via www.minnesotawildflowers.info/aquatic/southern-waternymph (Accessed March 23, 2021).

Clausen, R.T. 1936. Studies in the genus *Najas* in the northern United States. *Rhodora* 38: 333–345.

Dressler, K. 1996. University of Florida/IFAS/Center for Aquatic & Invasive Plants. https://plants.ifas.ufl.edu/plant-directory/najas-guadalupensis/. (Accessed March 23, 2021).

Global Invasive Species Database (GISD). 2021. Species profile: Najas minor. www.iucngisd.org/gisd/species.php?sc=1560 on 29–01–2021. (Accessed January 29, 2021).

Haynes, R. 1979. Revision of North and Central American *Najas* (Najadaceae). *Sida, Contributions to Botany* 8(1): 34–56.

Hellquist, C.B. 1977. Observations on some uncommon vascular aquatic plants in New England. *Rhodora* 79: 445–452.

Hilty, J. 2019. Thread-Leaf Naiad. Illinois Wildflowers. Via www.illinoiswildflowers.info/wetland/plants/th_naiad.html. (Accessed March 23, 2021).

ITIS (Integrated Taxonomic Information System). 2021. www.itis.gov/servlet/SingleRpt/SingleRpt?search_topic=TSN&search_value=39002#null (Accessed April 22, 2021).

Les, D.H. 2012. Noteworthy collection. *Madroño* 59(4): 230–233.

Les, D.H., E.L. Peredo, N.P. Tippery, L.K. Benoita, H. Razifarda, U.M. Kinga, H.R. Nab, H.K. Choib, L. Chenc, R.K. Shannona, and S.P. Sheldond. 2015. *Najas minor* (Hydrocharitaceae) in North America: A reappraisal. *Aquatic Botany* 126: 60–72.

Lovel, G. 2021. Brittle Naiad (water nymph). Finger Lakes PRISM. http://fingerlakesinvasives.org/invasive_species/brittle-naiad/. (Accessed March 23, 2021).

Martin, A.C., and F.M. Uhler. 1939. *Food of Game Ducks in the United States and Canada*. Washington, DC: United States Department of Agriculture.

Massachusetts Department of Agricultural Resources (MDAR) Pesticide Program and Massachusetts Department of Environmental Protection (MassDEP) Office of Research and Standards. 2013. Flumioxazin. www.mass.gov/doc/flumioxazin/download. (Accessed January 29, 2021).

Mattson, M.D., P.L. Godfrey, R.A. Barletta, and A. Aiello. 2004. Eutrophication and aquatic plant management in Massachusetts: Final generic environmental impact report. *Commonwealth of Massachusetts, Executive Office of Environmental Affairs Commonwealth of Massachusetts* 4: 29–80.

McIntyre, S., and S.C.H. Barrett. 1985. A comparison of weed communities of rice in Australia. *Proc. Ecol. Soc. Aust.* 14: 237–250.

Mehrhoff, L.J. n.d. USGS. Najas minor all. https://nas.er.usgs.gov/queries/FactSheet.aspx?SpeciesID=1118. (Accessed March 23, 2021).

Meriläinen, J. 1968. Najas minor all. In North America. *Rhodora* 70: 161–175.

Minnesota Department of Natural Resources (MN DNR). 2021a. Brittle Naiad (*Najas minor*), also called Brittle Waternymph. www.dnr.state.mn.us/invasives/aquaticplants/brittlenaiad/index.html. (Accessed January 28, 2021).

Minnesota Department of Natural Resources (MN DNR). 2021b. *Najas marina* L. www.dnr.state.mn.us/rsg/profile.html?action=elementDetail&selectedElement=PMNAJ01060. (Accessed January 28, 2021).

Na, H., and H. Choi. 2012. Numerical taxonomic study of Najas L. (Hydrocharitaceae) in Korea. *Korean Journal of Plant Taxonomy* 42(2): 126–140.

Native Plant Trust. 2021. Najas minor. Go Botany (3.4). https://gobotany.nativeplanttrust.org/species/najas/minor/. (Accessed March 23, 2021).

Pfingsten, I.A., L. Cao, and L. Berent. 2021. *Najas Minor All.: U.S. Geological Survey, Nonindigenous Aquatic Species Database.* Ann Arbor, MI and Gainesville, FL: NOAA Great Lakes Aquatic Nonindigenous Species Information System. https://nas.er.usgs.gov/queries/GreatLakes/FactSheet.aspx?SpeciesID=1118 (Accessed January 27, 2021).

Pinke, G., J. Csiky, A. Mesterházy, L. Tari, R.W. Pál, Z. Botta-Dukát, and B. Czúcz. 2014. The impact of management on weeds and aquatic plant communities in Hungarian rice crops. *European Weed Research Society* 54: 388–397.

Richardson, R.J. 2008. Aquatic plant management and the impact of emerging herbicide resistance issues. *Weed Technology* 22(1): 8–15.

Robinson, M. 2004. *European Naiad: An Invasive Aquatic Plant (Najas minor).* Cambridge, MA: Massachusetts Department of Conservation and Recreation; Office of Water Resources; Lakes and Ponds Program.

Skawinski, P. n.d. *Aquatic Invasive Species Quick Guide. Brittle Naiad (Najas minor All.).* Golden Sands Resource Conservation & Development Council, Inc. www.uwsp.edu/cnr-ap/UWEXLakes/Documents/programs/CLMN/AISfactsheets/04BrittleNaiad.pdf. (Accessed March 23, 2021).

SOLitude Lake Management (SLM). 2016. 2016 year-end report lakes management program borough of mountain lakes. https://mtnlakes.org/wp-content/uploads/2014/09/2016-Lakes-Year-End-Report.pdf. (Accessed January 29, 2021).

SOLitude Lake Management (SLM). 2017. 2017 year-end report lakes management program borough of mountain lakes. https://mtnlakes.org/wp-content/uploads/2014/09/Mtn-Lakes2017YEReport_BS.pdf. (Accessed January 29, 2021).

SOLitude Lake Management (SLM). 2018. 2018 year-end report lakes management program borough of mountain lakes. https://mtnlakes.org/wp-content/uploads/2014/09/2018-Lakes-Year-End-Report.pdf. (Accessed January 29, 2021).

SOLitude Lake Management (SLM). 2019. 2019 year-end report lakes management program borough of mountain lakes. https://mtnlakes.org/wp-content/uploads/2014/09/2019-Lakes-Year-End-Report.pdf. (Accessed January 29, 2021).

Topic, J. n.d. USGS. Najas marina L. https://nas.er.usgs.gov/queries/factsheet.aspx?SpeciesID=2674. (Accessed March 23, 2021).

Triest, L. 1988. A revision of the genus *Najas* L. (Najadaceae) in the old world. In: *Academie Royale des Sciences d'Outre-Mer.* Brussels.

U.S. Department of Agriculture (USDA). n.d.a. *Najas gracillima (A. Braun ex Engelm.) Magnus slender waternymph.* Natural Resources Conservation Service. https://plants.usda.gov/core/profile?symbol=NAGR. (Accessed March 23, 2021).

U.S. Department of Agriculture (USDA). n.d.b. *Najas marina L. spiny naiad.* Natural Resources Conservation Service. https://plants.usda.gov/core/profile?symbol=nama. (Accessed March 23, 2020).

Wang, H., H. Zhu, K. Zhang, L. Zhang, and Z. Wu. 2010. Chemical Composition in Aqueous Extracts of *Najas marine* and *Najas minor* and their Algae Inhibition Activity. Conference on Environmental Pollution and Public Health, CEPPH, pp. 806–809.

Washington State Department of Ecology. n.d. swollen bladderwort. *Wendy Scholl Invasion Ecology.* http://depts.washington.edu/oldenlab/wordpress/wp-content/uploads/2013/03/Ultricularia-inflata_Scholl_2007R.pdf. (Accessed March 23, 2020).

Wentz, W.A., and R.L. Stuckey. 1971. The changing distribution of the genus *Najas* (Najadaceae) in Ohio. *Ohio Journal of Science* 71: 292–302.

Wunderlin, R.P., B.F. Hansen, A.R. Franck, and F.B. Essig. 2021. Atlas of Florida Plants (http://florida.plantatlas.usf.edu/). [S. M. Landry and K. N. Campbell (application development), USF Water Institute.] Institute for Systematic Botany, University of South Florida, Tampa. https://florida.plantatlas.usf.edu/Plant.aspx?id=2087&display=photos. (Accessed March 23, 2021).

12 South American Waterweed (*Egeria densa*)

ABSTRACT

According to monitoring data, there are seven waterbodies in Massachusetts that are infested by South American waterweed (*Egeria densa*). This report serves to provide the general public with information about the status of South American waterweed in Massachusetts and help water users to minimize unintentional spread to new waterbodies. This report also provides biological and identification information about the plant, as well as descriptions of methods for control and management.

INTRODUCTION

Taxonomy Hierarchy (ITIS 2021)

Kingdom	Plantae
Subkingdom	Viridiplantae
Infrakingdom	Streptophyta
Superdivision	Embryophyta
Division	Tracheophyta
Subdivision	Spermatophytina
Class	Magnoliopsida
Superorder	Lilianae
Order	Alismatales
Family	Hydrocharitaceae
Genus	*Egeria* Planch.
Species	*Egeria densa* Planch.

South American waterweed or Brazilian waterweed (*Egeria densa*, hereafter referred to by its monotypic genus name, *Egeria*) is a submersed perennial monocot with a tendency for aggressive growth (Robinson 2002). It is a rooted macrophyte usually attached to the mud or sediment at the bottom of water, but it can also be found as a free-floating mat or in the surface water as fragments (Hoshovsky and Anderson 2001). *Egeria*'s stems are covered in small leaves arranged in whorls of four, or eight on a double node, making the whole stem resemble long, fuzzy cylinders, and the stems themselves can reach 1–3 m in length, though they are usually shorter (Cook and Urmi-König 1984; CABI 2019). They often grow until they reach the water surface and, after that, the plants start branching out. Leaves are bright green and longer than they are wide (about 1–3 cm long, Figure 12.1), with a lanceolate shape, smooth surface, and very fine serration on the leaf margins (Robinson 2002). *Egeria* is a dioecious plant, but only male plants have been observed outside of the plant's native range (CABI 2019). Bare floral peduncles, each containing a single flower, emerge from a node pathway down the stem and extend to the surface of the water. The flowers have three white, rounded petals with a yellow center which are the stamens (male reproductive organ) (Figure 12.2).

Egeria densa was previously named *Elodea densa* and classified within the genus *Elodea*. In spite of the species *E. densa* being transferred into the genus *Egeria*, it is still commonly referred to as an "elodea" in some circumstances, which, along with visual similarities, leads to confusion between *Egeria densa* and the currently canonized members of the *Elodea* genus. The singular member of another aquatic plant genus, *Hydrilla verticillata* (L.f.) Royle, is also visually similar to *Egeria* (Robinson 2002). To further complicate things, the genus *Elodea* was previously called *Anacharis*, a now defunct genus name, and all *Elodea*, *Egeria*, and *Hydrilla* species are prone to being marketed within the aquarium trade as "*Anacharis*." Other common names for *Egeria* include Brazilian waterweed, Brazilian Elodea, and dense waterweed (CABI 2019). Frequent reference is made in the aquatic macrophyte literature to a species named *Egeria najas*, but as of 2010, ITIS does not accept *E. najas* as a species (ITIS 2021). Specimens identified as *E. najas* can be keyed for identification as either *Egeria densa* or *Hydrilla verticillata*

FIGURE 12.1 South American waterweed (a) and its whorl of leaves (b) and single leaf (c). (Photos by Z. Jakubowska, M. Kiełbasa, and J. Nosek (see Krawczyk and Gabka 2019).)

on account of the formerly accepted waterweed *E. najas* sharing features with each of these accepted species (Catling and Mitrow 2001).

Several visual characteristics can be used to distinguish *Egeria* from *Hydrilla verticillata*, though both are considered invasive in the state of Massachusetts (Figure 12.2; see more about *Hydrilla* in Chapter 6). Generally, *Egeria densa* has four leaves per whorl, whereas *Elodea* spp. have three and *Hydrilla verticillata* five. Hydrilla has slightly shorter leaves, making the stem look thicker and more prominent than the stem of *Egeria* (Jacono et al. 2021); however, it may not be the reliable difference because, sometimes, leaf length will change depending on environment (density of stand, nutrient availability, light penetration, etc.) of the waterbody (Rosali Smith, personal communication). The flowers of *Hydrilla* are also much smaller than the flowers of *Egeria*, and they are light pink in color with darker pink streaks running through the center of the petals. *Hydrilla* also has tuber-like rhizomes which are absent in *Egeria* (Bossard et al. 2000).

South American Waterweed (*Egeria densa*)

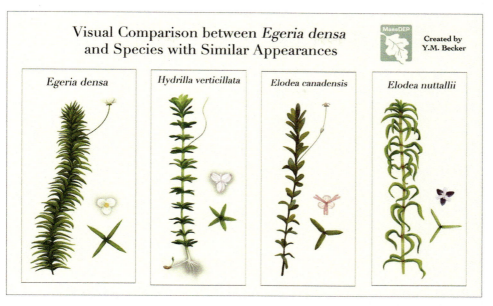

FIGURE 12.2 Guide to native and invasive waterweeds found in North America from the genera *Egeria*, *Hydrilla*, and *Elodea*. Illustrations and written descriptions of vegetated stems, flowers, and leaf whorl cross sections are provided to aid in visual identification. Simplified maps showing native and invasive ranges are also provided with each entry. Photo references used to ensure accuracy of illustrations of *Egeria densa* (Krawczyk and Gabka 2019; King County 2021), *Hydrilla verticillata* (Winterton n.d.; State of Michigan 2021; Houston Advanced Research Center 2021; Finger Lakes PRISM 2021), *Elodea canadensis* (Fischer 2008; Lukavský 2013; Lindman 1917), and *Elodea nuttalli* (Dixon 2019; Fischer 2011).

True *Elodea* spp. can be distinguished from *Egeria* by looking at the number and arrangement of leaves: while *Egeria*'s leaves are arranged in whorls of usually four leaves around each node on the stem, *Elodea* leaf whorls contain only three leaves. *Elodea* flowers are also pink, with thin, stringy petals, being very visually distinct from those of *Egeria*. Three species of *Elodea* are native to the continental United States. More information on differentiating *Egeria* from similar aquatic plants is provided in Figure 12.2 in a visual guide attached at the end of this chapter.

Native and Invasive Range

Egeria is native to Brazil and the surrounding region in South America including parts of Argentina and Peru. Introduced populations can now be found on all continents except Antarctica (Yarrow et al. 2009). The wide-scale naturalization of this weed is believed to be caused by the aquarium trade and possibly exacerbated by boating (Yarrow et al. 2009; Walsh et al. 2012; Rimac et al. 2018).

It is an invasive aquatic plant that has spread to 27 countries and 39 states in the United States (Bugbee et al. 2020). In the United States, *Egeria* was first found in 1893 at Mill Neck in Long Island, New York, according to a journal article by Weatherby (1932). From the early 1900s to present, most states in the United States have been found to contain populations of *Egeria*; the plant has not been found in some northern and midwestern states (Robinson 2002; MaineVLMP 2009).

Spread and Impacts

In its native habitat, *Egeria* commonly spreads by seed; the plants are pollinated mainly by flies traveling between male and female flowers, which grow on a long stalk and sit on the surface of the water. However, in North America,

Egeria is commonly seen to reproduce asexually by fragmentation and regrowth. Similarly, double nodes on stems can either be reproductive, bearing a flower, lateral branch, or root buds or it can be sterile (Yarrow *et al.* 2009).

Stem fragments from mature *Egeria* plants can easily form roots and develop into new dense mats of vegetation (Haynes 1988). *Egeria* is remarkably efficient at reproducing itself in this way and can rapidly establish dominance over an ecosystem, replacing other vegetation (Tanner et al. 1990). Because of the plant's ability to modify its habitat by controlling sediment suspension, nutrients, and algae growth, *Egeria* has been described as an "ecosystem engineer" (Yarrow et al. 2009). This term is commonly used to describe species that strongly modify their surroundings; for example, beavers are considered "ecosystem engineers" because they construct dams to modify the landscape. Corals can also be considered "ecosystem engineers" because of their ability to form coral reefs (Jones et al. 1994).

Rapid asexual reproduction allows *Egeria* to form large monocultural beds in the water, potentially depriving other plants of nutrients, space, and sunlight. *Egeria* also modifies its environment by slowing or preventing the flow of water, sometimes to an extent that is economically detrimental. Dense growth of *Egeria* could clog manmade plumbing, preventing water movement and potentially causing damage (Yarrow et al. 2009). *Egeria* infestation can also prevent larger fish from moving through waterways, especially posing a threat to the well-being of anadromous fish, which rely on passage through rivers and small tributaries to complete their life cycles (Johnson et al. 2006). In this way, the value of waterways for recreational fishing can be reduced. Boating, swimming, and other recreational activities could also be limited due to reduced water flow. Changes made by *Egeria* infestations might also reduce the aesthetic value of waterbodies or reduce the value of surrounding real estate (Robinson 2002).

Though dense, rapid growth of non-native *Egeria* can negatively impact large fish and outcompete native plants, *Egeria* could also have some ecosystem benefits. Small fish and zooplankton could take shelter in *Egeria*'s fronds, and wild waterfowl have been observed to use *Egeria* as a food source (Yarrow et al. 2009). *Egeria* also draws nutrients from the water column, limiting the growth of phytoplankton and potentially sequestering nutrients sufficiently to reverse the effects of eutrophication when established (Yarrow et al. 2009), though it is not clear that this nutrient sequestering ability is unique to *Egeria*, as related *Elodea* species have also been observed to sequester nitrogen. Mesocosm experiments by Vanderstukken et al. (2011) have directly demonstrated *Egeria*'s ability to suppress phytoplankton growth through nutrient competition, while another common aquatic macrophyte failed to produce an effect.

In spite of costs associated with removing unwanted *Egeria*, the plant has significant economic value, as well. While millions of dollars have been spent toward removing *Egeria* from the wild, a considerable amount of money is also spent by individuals looking to bring the plant into their own home fish tanks. A mere handful of *Egeria* (containing "at least four stems") commands a price of $3.99 through Walmart's website, plus $7.95 shipping (Walmart.com, 2021). Other scientific or aquarium-centered businesses sell *Egeria* stems at even higher prices, though sellers are not always clear about the precise species being sold (often using the names "*Anacharis*," "*Elodea*," "*Egeria*," and numerous other common names interchangeably, with photos of multiple different species attached to a listing). *Egeria* (along with other types of "*Anacharis*") is prized by aquarium keepers for its ecological services: while alive and photosynthesizing, *Egeria* effectively oxygenates water, improving the habitat for captive aquatic animals.

Egeria could also have potential value in industrial agriculture, either in aquaculture (because of its ability to take in nutrients and oxygenate water) or even as livestock feed. Research has found that sun-dried *Egeria* is a good source of nutrients to broiler chicks and human bred waterfowl; this fact combined with the known feasibility of growing *Egeria* quickly, at a low cost, and without taking up a large amount of space, makes *Egeria* appear to be a promising, potentially lucrative animal feed crop (Boyd and McGinty 1981; Maurice et al. 1984; Dillon et al. 1988).

South American Waterweed (*Egeria densa*)

MONITORING AND SIGHTINGS

The invasive species data detected in each waterbody were collected by the Massachusetts Department of Environmental Protection (MassDEP), the Department of Conservation and Recreation (DCR), the College of Holy Cross, as well as by Joy Trahan-Liptak as an individual before she joined DCR. The standard operating procedures, including sampling methodology, species identification, quality control and assurance, are implemented for samples collected by MassDEP. Data from other agencies are confirmed by experts. Sites with *Egeria* were mapped as a data layer with ArcGIS® ArcMap 10.1 (ESRI, Redlands, California). This tool is able to pinpoint the area that *Egeria* has spread, which can help to inform future decisions on processes that can happen in these waterbodies, or regulations and permitting that involve efforts to control or limit the spread of this aquatic invasive species.

Sightings of this species in Massachusetts are shown in (Table 12.1). A map using GIS has been created in order to show the visual distribution of *Egeria* in Massachusetts waterbodies (Figure 12.3). South American waterweed is only found in two lakes out of the 2,050 MassDEP-monitored waterbodies. Five sightings are reported by other agencies. Therefore, there are a total of seven lakes (Table 12.2) within six watersheds in Massachusetts that are infested by *Egeria* (Table 12.3). These infested waterbodies are mainly located in the central and eastern regions of the state. Invasive *Egeria* was first found in Massachusetts in 1939 in the pond at the Memorial Park, Plymouth, and a brook in Furnace Brook Parkway, Norfolk (USGS 2020).

MANAGING ACTIONS

The most efficient way to protect the environment from invasive species is integrated management, including education and prevention,

TABLE 12.1
Infested Waterbodies in Massachusetts

Waterbody	Agency	Report Source	Longitude	Latitude	First Year Reported
Clamshell Pond	DCR	Joy Trahan-Liptak	−71.678456	42.399324	
Clamshell Pond	College of the Holy Cross	Robert Bertin	−71.678197	42.399340	
Clamshell Pond	DCR	DCR Data from Lakes and Ponds, 2008			2008
Days Pond	MassDEP	North Shore Coastal Watersheds 2002 Water Quality Assessment Report 93-AC-2 CN 138.5, March 2007			
Hemenway Pond	DCR	DCR Data from ACT, GeoSyntec Barre Hellquist, 1971			1971
Lake Archer	MassDEP	Charles River Watershed 2002–2006 Water Quality Assessment Report 72-AC-4 CN136.5, April 2008			
Lake Archer	DCR	DCR Data from Lakes and Ponds, 2002	−71.338521	42.069854	2002
Lake Archer	DCR	DCR Data from Lakes and Ponds, 2003	−71.338521	42.069854	2003
Lake Cochituate	Individual	Joy Trahan-Liptak	−71.358646	42.284193	
Lake Rico	DCR	DCR Data from Lakes and Ponds, 2007			2007
Lake Rico	DCR	DCR Data from Lakes and Ponds, 2008			2008
North Pond	DCR	DCR Data from ACT, GeoSyntec, 2003			2003

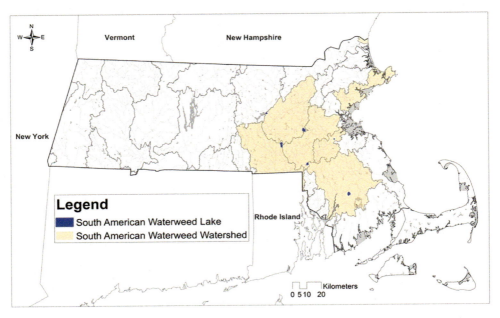

FIGURE 12.3 Distribution map depicting South American Waterweed (*Egeria densa*) in Massachusetts.

TABLE 12.2
Towns and Infested Waterbodies

Number	Waterbody	Town 1	Town 2	Town 3
1	Clamshell Pond	Clinton	–	–
2	Days Pond	Gloucester	–	–
3	Hemenway Pond	Milton	–	–
4	Lake Archer	Wrentham	–	–
5	Lake Cochituate	Framingham	Wayland	Natick
6	Lake Rico	Taunton	–	–
7	North Pond	Florida	–	–

early detection, control, ecosystem restoration, and environmental regulation and enforcement. Among these management options, prevention is the most efficient and cost-effective approach in stopping or minimizing the spread of aquatic invasive species. Mapping sightings of *Egeria* provides a spatial understanding of the status of this invasive species in Massachusetts' lakes to increase public awareness of this invasive species. For waterbodies that haven't been invaded but may be at risk, proactive prevention should be researched and promoted.

In Massachusetts, waterbodies infested with *Egeria* will be included in the 303d list of impaired or threatened waters during water quality assessments to fulfill the requirements of the Clean Water Act. For projects within infested watersheds subject to the jurisdiction of the 401 Water Quality Certification, conditions on invasive species prevention and decontamination must be provided to receive certification. In addition, water quality monitoring gear and watercrafts in these infested watersheds must be decontaminated before being used in other watershed to prevent the potential spread of invasive species.

To combat existing *Egeria* infestations, there are many different methods tested and found

TABLE 12.3
Infested Watersheds

1	Blackstone
2	Boston Harbor
3	Charles
4	North Coastal
5	SuAsCo
6	Taunton

applicable. Effective management measures include chemical, physical, and biological techniques. These techniques are described in the following sections.

CHEMICAL CONTROL

Chemical control is one of the most popular management approaches for nuisance plants and several chemicals are legal to use in Massachusetts. Fluridone, 2,4-dichlorophenoxyacetic acid (abbreviated 2, 4-D), and diquat are chemical herbicides that have been recognized as consistently effective against *Egeria* when used with the correct dose, proper formulation, and suitable conditions (Mattson et al. 2004).

Herbicides usually contain active ingredients that have specific biological toxicity to plants so that they are not dangerous to humans or other animals at the conventional dosage. However, to avoid unintended effects, herbicides should not be used in excess, and they should be applied with care to limit exposure to non-target plants, which might be indiscriminately damaged by the chemical (Mattson et al. 2004). It is also important to avoid overuse of herbicides because of the emerging possibility of herbicide resistance in aquatic plants (Richardson 2008).

Hanson et al. (2006) carried out a microcosm study to observe the effects of oxytetracycline on *Egeria*. The density of the plant was found to decrease in the presence of the chemical, but the decline in growth was attributed to reduced light availability caused by accumulating oxytetracycline by-products, and the research team determined that oxytetracycline does not pose any direct harm to *Egeria*.

More information about chemical control on *Egeria* and other 18 invasive species can be found in Appendix III. Prior to any chemical application to bodies of water, it is required to obtain an aquatic nuisance species control license (BRP WM04 Form) from Massachusetts Department of Environmental Protection.

PHYSICAL CONTROL

Mechanical harvesting, or physical removal, is one of the simplest methods of reducing an invasive plant population in a short period of time. Aquatic plants can be harvested by hand or by machine depending on site conditions (Mattson et al. 2004). Hand pulling is a suitable control method for sparse, emerging, or poorly established *Egeria* stands, especially if non-target plants requiring protection are present, while mechanical harvesting may be practicable where growth is denser, and problems are more severe. Although physical harvesting of *Egeria* is an easily accessible control method, there are some pronounced disadvantages. Since *Egeria* has the capability to regrow by fragments, this being its main reproductive strategy outside of its native range, physically removing *Egeria* stands may inadvertently create plant fragments which facilitate its spread (Curt et al. 2010). If *Egeria* fragments are left behind in the water after harvesting, or if mechanical equipment is not properly decontaminated before beginning work in another waterbody, new infestations could arise following removal efforts.

Benthic barriers, large coverings placed on the bottom of waterbodies to smother benthic organisms, could be an effective physical control against *Egeria*, limiting the whole invasive population's access to light and oxygen. These barriers could consist of sheets of synthetic gas-impermeable material, or layers of sediment such as clay, sand, or gravel deposited over the bottom. The cost of materials and labor in this technique can be high, and the barrier can often require additional maintenance (Robinson 2002). Benthic barriers also have the potential to harm non-invasive benthic plants and wildlife (Washington State Department of Ecology n.d.). However, in limited areas that are carefully chosen, such as swimming beaches or densely infested waterbodies, benthic barriers could be a good choice for managing aquatic nuisance plants.

Drawdown, or temporarily lowering the water level in a body of water, is potentially a very effective method of eliminating *Egeria* stands, as past experimentation has found that *Egeria* plants cannot survive more than an hour out of the water (Yarrow et al. 2009). Because this method involves removing a large portion of water from the site, it can be difficult to accomplish depending on the volume of water present. Drawdown can also be harmful to non-target aquatic species dependent on water for survival, so care should be taken to mitigate and prevent ecological damage. In order to reduce impacts to non-target plants and animals during the growing season, drawdowns in Massachusetts are normally conducted in fall and winter (Mattson et al. 2004).

Biological Control

The only well-known specialized herbivore of *Egeria* is the leaf-mining fly named *Hydrellia egeriae* Rodrigues-Júnior (Walsh et al. 2012). Risk assessments evaluated under quarantine conditions demonstrated that the fly could not discriminate between *E. densa* and *Elodea canadensis* and as a result, the host range of *H. egeriae* is too broad for use as a biological control agent of *E. densa* in the United States (Pratt et al. 2019). Another study has found that non-target aquatic macrophytes in South Africa cannot sustain multiple generations of a leaf-mining fly population, meaning the fly is not likely to reduce the abundance of any plant other than *Egeria* on a population scale. Based on this risk assessment study, permission has been obtained to release *H. egeriae* for *Egeria* control in South Africa (Smith et al. 2019).

A fungus from the genus *Fusarium* has also been found to have potential as biological control against *Egeria*, causing stem necrosis and foliar chlorosis (Nachtigal and Pitelli 1999; Neto et al. 2004). The use of fungi or pathogens as biological control against nuisance plants is precedented and laboratory experimentation of this method has appeared promising, but field applications have not yet been broadly successful in eliminating target plants (Hussner et al. 2017). Since several other fungi in the genus *Fusarium* are known to be destructive agricultural pathogens, causing a disease known as "Fusaric wilt," additional risk assessment is needed to determine whether the species previously evaluated is safe to release as a mycoherbicide (Singh et al. 2017).

Yarrow et al. (2009) reported observations of waterfowl using *Egeria* as a food source. Allowing ducks or other birds to graze may in fact be an effective means of controlling *Egeria*, demonstrated by the results of a case study in Spain (Curt et al. 2010). This case is discussed in greater detail in the "Success Story" section ahead.

SUCCESS STORIES

Chemical Control

Fence Rock Lake is a private 16.9 acre lake in Guilford, CT (CAES IAPP n.d.; Bugbee et al. 2020). In 2009, the Connecticut Agricultural Experiment Station (CAES) Invasive Aquatic Plant Program (IAPP) developed a survey at this lake, which resulted in documentation of the first appearance of the invasive species *Egeria*. Their vegetation surveys at Fence Rock Lake in the following years (2009–2013) showed that *Egeria* was rapidly expanding to cover large areas of the lake (CAES IAPP n.d.). In 2009, there is only a small amount of *Egeria* growing at the edge of the lake. However, during 2010–2012, *Egeria* spread from the western shoreline of the lake to the lake center, where it spanned to surrounding large areas. By 2013, almost the whole shoreline was covered by *Egeria*, and it was found in great quantities in the deeper water column. Abundances of native species were also decreased in these years (Figure 12.4).

In order to remove *Egeria* completely from Fence Rock Lake, CAES IAPP made a

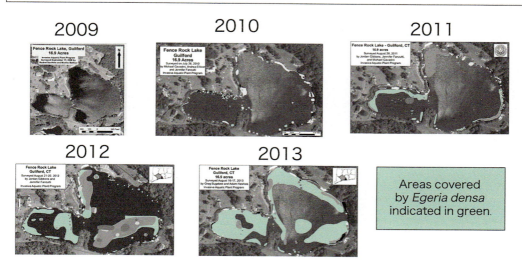

FIGURE 12.4 Maps produced from surveys by CASE IAPP at Fence Rock Lake during 2009–2013. (Modified to highlight areas covered by *Egeria densa* in each consecutive year.)

strategic plan (Bugbee et al. 2020). In 2014, they applied the herbicide diquat (Reward®) across 8.4 acres in the lake using a bottom injection technique. Generally, the effectiveness of herbicides can be seen after several repeated applications. Likewise, after two applications of diquat in Fence Rock Lake, *Egeria* was reportedly successfully controlled, with a survey and aquatic vegetation map from 2016 showing no *Egeria* anywhere in the lake (CAES IAPP n.d.). Not only were nuisance plants eliminated, but the treatment was applied precisely enough so that no native aquatic plants populations were affected. According to the records from the surveys of CAES IAPP, no *Egeria* appeared again at the Fence Rock Lake in the following two years after this chemical treatment (Bugbee et al. 2020). In the most recent survey at the lake, miniscule *Egeria* populations appear at only one point on the lake's shore.

DOMESTIC DUCKS AS BIOLOGICAL CONTROL

Years ago, *Egeria* was accidentally introduced into a small, family-run nursery reservoir in Galicia, northwest Spain (Curt et al. 2010). The introduction was suspected to have occurred when the nursery began intentionally cultivating water hyacinth *Pontederia crassipes* (formerly *Eichhornia crassipes*, see Chapter 15 of this book); fragments of *Egeria* were believed to have been mixed in with the roots of the *Pontederia* plants. About seven years after the initial introduction, the *Egeria* infestation had become serious, and management efforts began. Unsuccessful physical removal of *Egeria* was carried out for four years, a strategy which was described as "utterly ineffective; indeed, removal seemed to enhance the growth of the waterweed" (Curt et al. 2010). However, the tides changed when two domestic Peking white ducks were incidentally introduced to the property. The ducks were observed to feed on the nuisance plant, preferring the leaves and soft growing tips of the plant. Leafless, fragmented stems left behind by the ducks were unable to propagate and were observed to simply decay. Under specific conditions, even though stems may be leafless, nodes on the stems can still develop into new shoots, roots, etc.; often, damage to shoots stimulates branching of the plant (Mangan and Baars 2016). In the years following the introduction of the waterfowl, the dense infestation of *Egeria* was significantly reduced. Though the invasive plant was not entirely eliminated, its population remained under control as long as the ducks grazed (Curt et al. 2010).

REFERENCES

Bossard, C.C., J.M. Randall, and M.C. Hoshovsky. 2000. *Invasive Plants of California's Wildlands*. Berkeley, CA: University of California Press.

Boyd, C.E., and P.S. McGinty. 1981. Percentage digestible dry matter and crude protein in dried aquatic weeds. *Economic Botany* 35: 296–299.

Bugbee, G.J., C.S. Robb, and S.E. Stebbins. 2020. Efficacy of diquat treatments on Brazilian waterweed, effects on native macrophytes and water quality: A case study. *Journal of Aquatic Plant Management* 58: 83–91.

CABI. 2019. *Egeria densa* (leafy elodea). *Centre for Agriculture and Bioscience International (CABI)*. www.cabi.org/isc/datasheet/20491. (Accessed March 27, 2020).

Catling, P.M., and G. Mitrow. 2001. *Egeria najas* at the Canadian Border and its separation from the related aquatic weeds *Egeria densa* and *Hydrilla verticillata* (Hydrocharitaceae). *Botanical Electronic News 278*. www.ou.edu/cas/botany-micro/ben/ben278.html. (Accessed March 2, 2021).

Connecticut Agricultural Experiment Station, Invasive Aquatic Plant Program (CAES IAPP). n.d. Fence rock lake survey results. https://portal.ct.gov/-/media/CAES/Invasive-Aquatic-Plant-Program/Survey-Results/F/Fence-Rock-Lake/FenceRockLakepdf.pdf. (Accessed March 1, 2021).

Cook, C.D.K., and K. Urmi-König. 1984. A revision of the genus *Egeria* (Hydrocharitaceae). *Aquatic Botany* 19: 73–96.

Curt, M.D., G. Curt, P.L. Aguado, and J. Fernández. 2010. Proposal for the biological control of *Egeria densa* in small reservoirs: A Spanish case study. *Journal of Aquatic Plant Management* 48: 124–127.

Dillon, C.R., D.V. Maurice, and J.E. Jones. 1988. Chemical composition of *Egeria densa*. *Journal of Aquatic and Plant Management* 26: 44–45.

Dixon, C.J. 2019. *Elodea nuttalli*. MAKAQueS. www.makaques.com/gallery.php?sp=2508. (Accessed March 2, 2021).

Finger Lakes PRISM. 2021. Hydrilla. http://fingerlakesinvasives.org/invasive_species/hydrilla/. (Accessed March 2, 2021).

Fischer, C. 2008. Canadian Waterweed. https://en.wikipedia.org/wiki/Elodea_canadensis#/media/File:ElodeaCanadensis.jpg. (Accessed March 2, 2021).

Fischer, C. 2011. Parts of the western waterweed (*Elodea nuttalli*). https://en.wikipedia.org/wiki/Elodea_nuttallii#/media/File:ElodeaNuttallii2.jpg. (Accessed March 2, 2021).

Hanson, M.L., C.W. Knapp, and D.W. Graham. 2006. Field assessment of oxytetracycline exposure to the freshwater macrophytes *Egeria densa* Planch., and *Ceratophyllum demersum* L. *Environmental Pollution* 141: 434–442.

Haynes, R.R. 1988. Reproductive biology of selected aquatic plants. *Annals of the Missouri Botanical Garden* 75: 805–810.

Hoshovsky, M.C., and L. Anderson. 2001. *Egeria densa* Planchon. In C.C. Bossard, J.M. Randall, and M.C. Hoshovsky (eds.), *Invasive Plants of California's Wildlands* (1st edition). Santa Rosa, CA: Pickleweek Press.

Houston Advanced Research Center. 2021. Galveston Bay Field Guide. http://blog.microscopeworld.com/2016/07/hydrilla-verticillatea-leaf-under.html. (Accessed March 2, 2021).

Hussner, A., I. Stiers, M.J.J.M. Verhofstad, E.S. Bakker, B.M.C. Grutters, J. Haury, J.L.C.H. van Valkenburg, G. Brundu, J. Newman, J.S. Clayton, L.W.J. Anderson, and D. Hofstra. 2017. Management and control methods of invasive alien freshwater aquatic plants: A review. *Aquatic Botany* 136: 122–137.

Interagency Taxonomic Information System (ITIS). 2021. Egeria. www.itis.gov/servlet/SingleRpt/SingleRpt?search_topic=TSN&search_value=38972#null. (Accessed March 2, 2021).

Jacono, C.C., M.M. Richerson, H.V. Morgan, and I.A. Pfingsten. 2021. *Hydrilla verticillata* (L.f.) Royle: U.S. Geological Survey, Nonindigenous Aquatic Species Database. Gainesville, FL. https://nas.er.usgs.gov/queries/FactSheet.aspx?SpeciesID=6. (Accessed February 10, 2021).

Johnson, D., M. Carlock, and T. Artz. 2006. *Egeria densa* Control Program Second Addendum to 2001 Environmental Impact Report with Five-year Program Review and Future Operations Plan. California: The State of California Department of Boating and Waterways.

Jones, C.G., J.H. Lawton, and M. Shachak. 1994. Organisms as ecosystem engineers. *Oikos* 69(3): 373–386.

King County, WA. 2021. Egeria (Brazilian elodea) identification and control. www.kingcounty.gov/services/environment/animals-and-plants/noxious-weeds/weed-identification/brazilian-elodea.aspx. (Accessed March 2, 2021).

Krawczyk, R., and M. Gabka. 2019. Egeria densa (Hydrocharitaceae)—Nowy gatunek antropofita we florze Polski. *Fragmenta Floristica et Geobotanica Polonica* 26(1): 41–48.

Lindman, C.A.M. 1917. Elodea Canadensis. https://fr.wikipedia.org/wiki/%C3%89lod%C3%A9e#/media/Fichier:Elodea_canadensis_nf.jpg. (Accessed March 2, 2021).

Lukavský, J. 2013. Canadian Waterweed. www.biolib.cz/en/image/id223880/. (Accessed March 2, 2021).

MaineVLMP. 2009. Brazilian waterweed, Brazilian Elodea, *Anacharis*, *Egeria densa*. Maine Volunteer Lake Monitoring Program (MaineVLMP). www.mainevlmp.org/mciap/herbarium/VariableWatermilfoil.php. (Accessed March 27, 2020).

Mangan R., and J.R. Baars. 2016. Can leaf-mining flies generate damage with significant impact on the submerged weed *Lagarosiphon major*? *BioControl* 61: 803–813.

Mattson, M.D., P.J. Godfrey, R.A. Barletta, and A. Aiello. 2004. Eutrophication and aquatic plant management in Massachusetts: Final generic environmental impact report. *Commonwealth of Massachusetts, Executive Office of Environmental Affairs Commonwealth of Massachusetts* 4: 29–80pp.

Maurice, D.V., J.E. Jones, C.R. Dillon, and J.M. Weber. 1984. Chemical composition and nutritional value of Brazilian elodea (*Egeria densa*) for the chick. *Poultry Science* 63: 317–323.

Nachtigal, G.F., and R.E. Pitelli. 1999. Fusarium sp. as a potential biocontrol agent for Egeria densa and Egeria najas. In: *Program Abstracts, X International Symposium on Biological Control of Weeds*. Bozeman, MT: USDA-ARS and Montana State University, p. 68.

Neto, C.R.B., C.Q. Gorgati, and R.A. Pitelli. 2004. Effects of photoperiod and temperature in the development of disease caused *Fusarium graminearum* on *Egeria densa* and *E. najas*. *Fitopatologia Brasileira* 29(3): 252–258.

Pratt, P.D., J.C. Herr, R.I. Carruthers, and G.C. Walsh. 2019. Complete development on *Elodea canadensis* (Hydrocharitaceae) eliminates *Hydrellia egeriae* (Diptera, Ephydridae) as a candidate biological control agent of *Egeria densa* (Hydrocharitaceae) in the U.S.A. *Biocontrol Science and Technology* 29(4): 405–409.

Richardson, R.J. 2008. Aquatic plant management and the impact of emerging herbicide resistance issues. *Weed Technology* 22(1): 8–15.

Rimac, A., I. Stankovic, A. Alegro, S. Gottstein, N. Koletic, N. Vukovic, V. Segota, and A. Zizic-Nakic. 2018. The Brazilian elodea (*Egeria densa* Planch.) invasion reaches Southeast Europe. *BioInvasions Records* 7(4): 381–389.

Robinson, M. 2002. *South American Waterweed: An Exotic Invasive Plant (Egeria densa)*. Cambridge, MA: Massachusetts Department of Conservation and Recreation; Office of Water Resources; Lakes and Ponds Program.

Scheers, K., L. Denys, J. Packet, and T. Adriaens. 2016. A second population of *Cabomba caroliniana* Gray (Cabombaceae) in Belgium with options for its eradication. *BioInvasions Records* 5(4): 227–232.

Singh, V.K., H.B. Singh, and R.S. Upadhyay. 2017. Role of fusaric acid in the development of '*Fusarium* wilt' symptoms in tomato: Physiological, biochemical and proteomic perspectives. *Plant Physiology and Biochemistry* 118: 320–332.

Smith, R., R. Mangan, and J.A. Coetzee. 2019. Risk assessment to interpret the physiological host range of *Hydrellia egeriae*, a biocontrol agent for *Egeria densa*. *BioControl* 64: 447–456.

State of Michigan. 2021. Hydrilla. www.michigan.gov/invasives/0,5664,7-324-68002_74188-367843--00.html. (Accessed March 2, 2021).

Tanner, C., J. Clayton, and B. Coffey. 1990. Submerged-vegetation changes in lake Rotoria (Hamilton, New Zealand) related to herbicide treatment and invasion by *Egeria densa*. *New Zealand Journal of Marine and Freshwater Research* 24: 45–57.

U.S. Geological Survey (USGS). 2020. *Specimen observation data for Najas minor All., Nonindigenous Aquatic Species Database*. Gainesville, FL, https://nas.er.usgs.gov/queries/CollectionInfo.aspx?SpeciesID=1107. (Accessed March 26, 2020).

Vanderstukken, M., N. Mazzeo, W. Van Colen, S.A.J. Declerck, and K. Muylaert. 2011. Biological control of phytoplankton by the subtropical submerged macrophytes *Egeria densa* and *Potamogeton illinoensis*: A mesocosm study. *Freshwater Biology* 56(9): 1837–1849.

Walmart. 2021. 1 Anacharis Bunch—4+ Stems | *Egeria Densa*—Beginner Tropical Live Aquarium Plant. www.walmart.com/ip/1-Anacharis-Bunch-4-Stems-Egeria-Densa-Beginner-Tropical-Live-Aquarium-Plant/170556602. (Accessed March 2, 2021).

Walsh, G.C., Y.M. Dalto, F.M. Mattioli, R.I. Carruthers, and L.W. Anderson. 2012. Biology and ecology of Brazilian elodea (*Egeria densa*) and its specific herbivore *Hydrellia sp.*, in Argentina. *BioControl* 58: 133–147.

Washington State Department of Ecology. n.d. swollen bladderwort. *Wendy Scholl Invasion Ecology*. http://depts.washington.edu/oldenlab/wordpress/wp-content/uploads/2013/03/Ultricularia-inflata_Scholl_2007R.pdf. (Accessed March 30, 2020).

Weatherby, C.A. 1932. *Anacharis densa* on Long Island. *Rhodora* 34(403): 151–152.

Winterton, S. n.d. Aquarium and pond plants of the world, Edition 3, USDA APHIS PPQ, Bugwood.org. Via www.invasive.org/browse/detail.cfm?imgnum=5563004 (Accessed March 2, 2021).

Yarrow, M., V.H. Marin, M. Finlayson, A. Tironi, L.E. Delgado, and F. Fischer. 2009. The ecology of *Egeria densa* Planchon (Liliopsida: Alismatales): A wetland ecosystem engineer? *Revista Chilena de Historia Natural* 82: 299–313.

13 Swollen Bladderwort (*Utricularia inflata*)

ABSTRACT

In 1990, swollen bladderwort, otherwise known as *Utricularia inflata* (*U. inflata*), was first detected in the Federal Pond in Carver and Plymouth of southeast Massachusetts. Since then, there have been 15 sightings from central to eastern Massachusetts. The documented sightings and findings can provide the public with information regarding *U. inflata* infestations and the effects of infestations in Massachusetts to minimize future spread of this invasive species. This chapter describes the ecological and economic impacts of *U. inflata*. Control and treatment methods such as mechanical removal (e.g., benthic barriers and hands harvesting) and chemical treatment (e.g., herbicides application) are summarized in this chapter.

INTRODUCTION

Taxonomy Hierarchy (ITIS 2021)

Kingdom	Plantae
Subkingdom	Viridiplantae
Infrakingdom	Streptophyta
Superdivision	Embryophyta
Division	Tracheophyta
Subdivision	Spermatophytina
Class	Magnoliopsida
Superorder	Asteranae
Order	Lamiales
Family	Lentibulariaceae
Genus	*Utricularia*
Species	*Utricularia inflata* Walter

Swollen bladderwort is a rootless, carnivorous, free-floating, bushy, submerged plant which can be found just above the sediment (Figure 13.1). Some of its leaves float at the surface of the water. Even so, lateral submerged leaf-like branches fork into two unequal, bushy portions. The leaves are not actually leaves but stems that grow along the main stem (i.e., stolon) (Figure 13.2), which have numerous small bladders (Figure 13.3). In early spring, 3–15 yellow snap-dragon shaped flowers develop on emergent stalks. The stalks are supported by a floating pontoon comprised of four to ten leaves arranged like the spokes of a wheel (Figure 13.2). The pontoon leaves are 1.5 inches long and appear inflated.

Like other *Utricularia* species, swollen bladderwort lures its prey by secreting chemical attractants into its surroundings. They prey on a wide range of organism such as zooplankton (Robinson n.d.), insects (water fleas, worms, insect larvae), and some benthic animals such as arthropods and annelids. In addition, they can eat rotifers and protozoa from water soil (Clark n.d.).

Organisms are lured to the bladders with a sweet scent, and when trigger hairs on the bladder are brushed, a "trap door" opens, and a vacuum force pulls the prey inside to be digested. These traps are laterally inserted on the leaf segments (Figure 13.3). The dynamics of this plant for capturing small aquatic animals is quite similar to neuronal dynamics (Llorens et al. 2012). Glands pump water out of the trap, yielding a negative pressure difference between the plant and its surroundings. The trap door is set into a metastable state and opens quickly as extra pressure is generated by the displacement of a potential prey. As the door opens, the pressure difference sucks the animal into the trap (Figure 13.4). Bladderwort's ability to consume small organisms, in addition to absorbing nutrients directly from the water column, provides a competitive advantage over other species.

U. inflata can thrive due to its ability to reproduce. Swollen bladderwort reproduces by both vegetative methods and seed formation. Vegetatively, *U. inflata* reproduces by stem (stolon) fragmentation which can resprout and grow into new plants. Branches

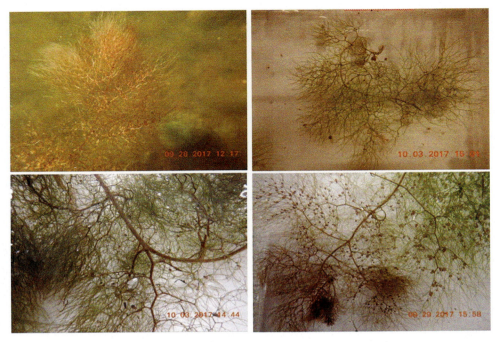

FIGURE 13.1 Swollen bladderwort (*Ultricularia Inflata*) at Indian Brook (*top left*) and samples collected from Monponsett Pond (*top right*), Ponkapog Pond (*bottom left*), and White Island Pond (*bottom right*). (Photos by Wai Hing Wong.)

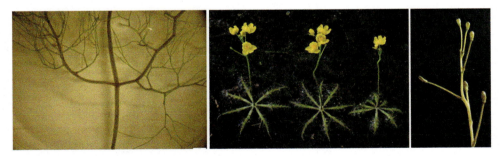

FIGURE 13.2 Picture of swollen bladderwort stem (*left*), flowers (middle), and sterile fruits (right). (Left microscopic photo by Wai Hing Wong; middle photo by Alan Cressler; right photo modified from Kadono et al. (2019).)

may emerge along the stem and form new individuals when they separate from the original plant (Urban and Dwyer 2016). Seeds can also be produced, resulting in regrowth from seeds remaining in lake or pond sediment. The average flower number is 10–11 (Reinert and Godfrey 1962). However, the morphology of flowers may be different in *U. inflata* depending on their location. For example, the apex of the spur is obtuse in *U. inflata* in Japan. On the other hand, the apex of the bracts in North American individuals is acute (Taylor 1989; Crow 2014) or subacute to obtuse (Reinert and Godfrey 1962). During the winter season, this species can be under ice and dormant in the frozen lakes of northern climates. Individuals grow under a wide range of water chemistry conditions and can be found in oligotrophic

Swollen Bladderwort (*Utricularia inflata*)

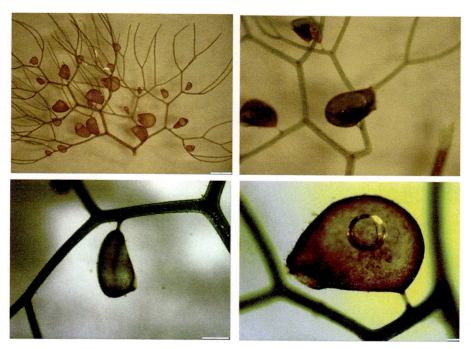

FIGURE 13.3 Microscopic photos of bladderworts of *U. inflata* (*top left:* 10×; *top right:* 25×; *bottom left:* 50×; *bottom right:* 60×. (Photos by Wai Hing Wong.)

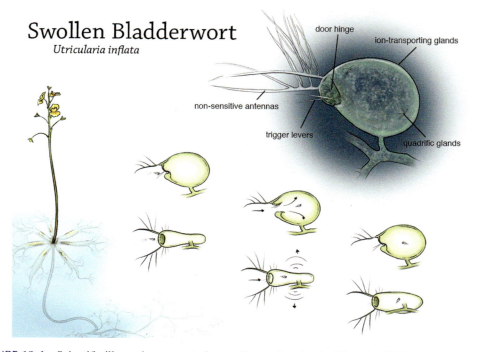

FIGURE 13.4 Scientific illustration on capturing small aquatic animals. (Photo by U-Bin Li.)

(low-nutrient), eutrophic (nutrient-rich), and acidic waters.

Swollen bladderwort prefers slow-moving waters, including lakes, ponds, and slow-moving rivers. In fact, swollen bladderwort is more susceptible to water movement and may spread downstream at a faster rate than common bladderwort (*Utricularia vulgaris*) and attached bladderwort species (Urban and Dwyer 2016). Despite its potential to grow well in shallow water, water movement can prevent the accumulation of *U. inflata* (Urban and Titus 2010).

In Massachusetts, there are other *Utricularia* species such as common bladderwort (*Utricularia vulgaris*) (Figure 13.5), Purple Bladderwort (*Utricularia pupurea*), Little floating bladderwort (*Utricularia radiata*), and Flatleaf Bladderwort (*Utricularia intermedia*). All bladderwort species are rootless and have carnivorous traps (Taylor 1989). Although these bladderwort plants are similar, they have their specific characteristics (MA DCR 2017) and some are as follows:

- Common bladderwort is the biggest bladderwort. Its bladders are large, and the tip of the plant has a tuft of branches with yellow flowers.
- Purple Bladderwort has clusters of branches with the bladders at the very tips of the branches with purple flowers.
- Little floating bladderwort's bladders only appear on underwater leaves. Underwater leaves' forks are more zigzag compared to the common bladderwort. This plan also has yellow flowers.
- Flatleaf Bladderwort has bladders on stems grown into the sediment.

FIGURE 13.5 Photos of common bladderwort (top panel, top right photo was taken under microscope 7×) and Purple Bladderwort (bottom panel). (Top panel photos by Wai Hing Wong; bottom panel photo by Michelle Kirby.)

NATIVE AND INVASIVE RANGE

Swollen bladderwort is native to southern and eastern North America, but it has been confirmed as an invasive species in Pennsylvania, Massachusetts, New York, New Jersey, Rhode Island, and the state of Washington (Urban and Dwyer 2016; Native Plant Trust 2021). This invasive species can dominate the waterbodies in a short time and displace other native species.

VECTORS OF SPREAD

Swollen bladderwort's northern spread is uncertain, but it is likely fragments were carried on boats, boat trailers, or waterfowl (Johnstone et al. 1985; Figuerola and Green 2002; but see Urban and Dwyer 2016). Once introduced, swollen bladderwort can grow by both sexual and asexual reproduction as described earlier. It may also spread by currents, boaters' activities, and waterfowls (Titus and Urban 2013). In addition, it has been documented that water movement and successful asexual reproduction have facilitated swollen bladderwort's downstream spread into Adirondack lakes connected by the Raquette River and the Middle Branch of the Moose River (Titus and Urban 2013).

In a greenhouse experiment comparing the vegetative propagation of swollen bladderwort and common bladderwort (*U. vulgaris*), it was found that swollen bladderwort and common bladderwort both produced potential propagules but exhibited differences in their asexual reproduction (Urban and Dwyer 2016). New common bladderwort branches grew significantly longer but swollen bladderwort fragments exhibited a greater number of new branches. Each new branch has the potential to develop into a new individual as the original stolon decays which may explain how swollen bladderwort is quickly establishing populations in newly colonized lakes (Urban and Dwyer 2016).

ECOLOGICAL IMPACTS

The existence of this harmful invasive species may cause multiple negative environmental impacts. For example, *U. inflata* may deplete nutrients from waterbodies, leading to the decline of native vegetation. Meanwhile, fish and other aquatic animals that rely on these vegetation could not survive. Furthermore, fish and other aquatic animals are also threatened by a low-oxygen environment created by large quantities of decaying swollen bladderwort.

Swollen bladderwort may negatively affect small aquatic animals, as it feeds on a wide range of organism. Therefore, its feeding habits may affect the populations of aquatic species and insects which can result in a decline in native wildlife populations.

Because of swollen bladderwort's strong ability to reproduce, it can cover the water surface creating dense mats. It can also form dense canopies underwater without reaching the water surface (top left panel of Figure 13.1). This phenomenon may increase light attenuation, causing a decline in biomass, even the death of isoetids (Urban et al. 2013). As a result, isoetids that work to oxidize and take up CO_2 from sediments, and therefore balance chemistry of the sediment and water, may be indirectly changed by swollen bladderwort. This may lead to a decline in the sediment's redox potential, more NH_4^+, and the release of mineral nutrients Fe into the water column, and accelerate the growth of algae and *U. inflata* (MA DCR 2007; Urban et al. 2009; Urban et al. 2013). This positive feedback loop, if continued, may further *U. inflata*'s impact on the environment.

ECONOMIC IMPACTS

Economically, massive swollen bladderwort can impede a series of human activities, such as fishing and water recreations, and could reduce the real estate values (MA DCR 2007). In addition, dense mats can limit the ability to navigate waters which interferes with recreational actives. Furthermore, the combination of low-water quality and denes mats can create conditions that may be dangerous for swimmers and recreational boaters (Scholl 2007).

POSITIVE EFFECTS

Although swollen bladderwort is an invasive species, there are a few positive effects of its expansion. A self-stabilizing ecosystem state could be formed in the water column by the proliferation of rootless swollen bladderwort. In addition, many types of wildlife such as turtles,

TABLE 13.1
Locations of Waters Infested by *Utricularia inflata* in Massachusetts

Site Number	Waterbody	First Year Reported	Longitude	Latitude	Report Agency	Report Source
1	Federal Pond	1992	−70.707816	41.876262	Sorrie 1992	Rhodora
2	First Pond	2006	−71.051194	42.475409	DCR	DCR Data from Lakes and Ponds, 2006
3	Long Pond	2008	−71.992134	42.356772	DCR	DCR 2008 (Data from National Heritage, DowCullina)
4	Noquochoke Lake	2008	−71.043280	41.647114	DCR	DCR 2008 (Data from National Heritage, DowCullina)
5	Lake Rico	2008	−70.996974	41.874723	DCR	DCR 2008 (Data from National Heritage, DowCullina)
6	Cooks Pond	2008	−70.665355	41.922381	DCR	DCR 2008 (Data from National Heritage, DowCullina)
7	Whitehall Reservoir	2008	−71.575363	42.229421	DCR	DCR 2008 (Data from National Heritage, DowCullina)
8	North Pond	2008	−71.555872	42.196528	DCR	DCR 2008 (Data from National Heritage, DowCullina)
9	Louisa Lake	2008	−71.523061	42.158817	DCR	DCR 2008 (Data from National Heritage, DowCullina)
10	Ponkapoag Pond	2017	−71.092968	42.192183	MassDEP	MassDEP Field Survey 10/2/17
11	White Island Pond	2017	−70.617531	41.809183	MassDEP	MassDEP Field Survey 9/28/17
12	Sampson Pond	2017	−70.752977	41.852064	MassDEP	MassDEP Field Survey 09/28/17
13	Monponsett Pond	2017	−70.845254	42.004596	MassDEP	MassDEP Field Survey 10/02/2017
14	Turner Pond	2017	−70.970963	41.683796	MassDEP	MassDEP Field Survey 9/28/17
15	Taunton River	2017	−70.942830	41.936230	MassDEP	MassDEP Field Survey 9/28/2017

salamanders, bullfrogs, and even potential prey use Bladderwort as their shelter (USDA n.d.). Further, swollen bladderwort could dominate an area, which may provide greater habitat for phytophilous littoral zone invertebrate, and thus enliven trophic interactions in the waterbodies (Urban et al. 2013).

MONITORING AND SIGHTINGS

The infested waterbody sightings were mainly collected by the Massachusetts Department of Environmental Protection (MassDEP) and Massachusetts Department of Conservation and Recreation (MA DCR) (Table 13.1). The standard

Swollen Bladderwort (*Utricularia inflata*)

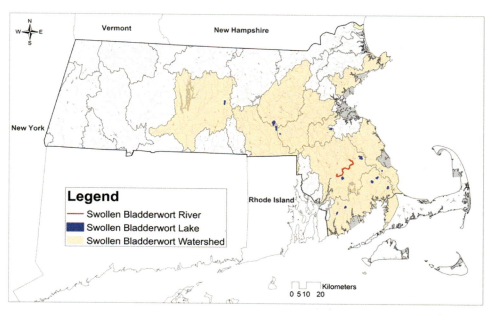

FIGURE 13.6 ArcGIS map depicting distribution of swollen bladderwort (*Ultricularia inflata*) in Massachusetts.

operating procedures, including sampling methodology, species identification, quality control and assurance, are implemented by samples collected by MassDEP. Sites with swollen bladderwort were mapped as a data layer with ArcGIS® ArcMap 10.1 (ESRI, Redlands, California). All locations infested by swollen bladderwort are shown in Figure 13.6. The ArcGIS map can pinpoint and confirm swollen bladderwort infestations which can help to inform future decisions on processes and activities that can happen in these bodies of water, or regulations that involve efforts to limit the spread of this aquatic invasive species.

Swollen bladderwort is a very aggressive invasive species. Although it was first detected in Federal Pond in Carver and Plymouth of southeast Massachusetts in 1990 (Sorrie 1992), multiple sightings have been documented since then. In total, it has been detected in 15 waterbodies (Figure 13.6 and Table 13.1). The first sighting documented by MassDEP staff was found in the Charles River in 2001. This can be reviewed in MassDEP's Charles River Watershed 2002–2006 Water Quality Assessment Report. These waterbodies are distributed in the following ten major watersheds: Chicopee, Concord (SuAsCo), Blackstone, Charles River, Taunton, Boston Harbor, South Coastal, Buzzards Bay, North Coastal, and Cape Cod (Table 13.2).

MANAGING ACTIONS

Common management tools for swollen bladderwort include mechanical removal and hand pulling/harvesting, drawdown, benthic barriers, and herbicides application.

Mechanical removal and hand pulling/harvesting may be effective, but these methods may aid in the spread of fragmented swollen bladderwort into new waterbodies if cautions are not taken.

Drawdowns can be used for aquatic plant control by lowering water levels to achieve drying and prompting the freezing of plants. To reduce impacts to non-target plants and animals during the growing season, drawdowns in Massachusetts are normally conducted in fall and winter (Mattson et al. 2004). But mild season or higher level of groundwater seepage may lead to rapid reestablishment of extensive seed beds. Further, lowering the water level may result in a temporary impact to the water quality (e.g., reducing the dissolved oxygen concentration and water clarity level), and a temporary loss of desirable plants, fish, or aquatic animals.

TABLE 13.2
Infested Watersheds and Waterbodies

Watershed	Waterbody
Blackstone	North Pond
Boston Harbor: Neponset	Ponkapoag Pond
Buzzards Bay	Federal Pond
	Noquochoke Lake
	Sampson Pond
	Turner Pond
	White Island Pond
Charles	Louisa Lake
Chicopee	Long Pond
Concord (SuAsCo)	Whitehall Reservoir
North Coastal	First Pond
South Coastal	Cooks Pond
Taunton	Lake Rico
	Monponsett Pond
	Taunton River

Drawdowns are usually useful in dammed waterways, while *U. inflata* is mostly found in quieter ponds. Therefore, it is not the first choice of managing swollen bladderwort.

Benthic barriers are another control method proposed by Massachusetts authorities, which could be applied in small areas such as swimming beaches to control this invasive species (MA DCR 2007). The application of benthic barriers limit plant growth by a cover of clay, silt, sand, or gravel. However, there are some limitations on this method. For instance, it requires constant maintenance, and it causes damage to benthic organisms (Washington State Department of Ecology 2020). Almost all covered plants will be harmed, and the habitat of fish will be influenced. MassDEP endorses the issuance of a Negative Determination of Applicability when these projects are conducted in accordance with the management techniques approved by DEP and described in the DCR Guidance, Standard Operating Procedures for Hand Pulling of Aquatic Vegetation and Benthic Barriers to Control Aquatic Vegetation dated May 15, 2003 (Langley et al. 2004).

Meanwhile, herbicides contain active ingredients that are toxic to target plants, but it may also harm or kill non-target plants and organisms by using inappropriate herbicides or applying high-rate usage (Mattson et al. 2004). In Massachusetts, the following chemicals/herbicides have been used for treating swollen bladderwort and other Bladderwort species: AquaPro, Aquathol K, Captain, Captain XTR, Clearcast, Clipper, Copper Sulfate, ProcellaCOR, Sonar Genesis, and Tribune. More information about chemical control on swollen bladderwort and other 18 invasive species can be found in Appendix III. Before chemicals are applied in Massachusetts waters, it is required to obtain an aquatic nuisance species control license (BRP WM04 Form) from Massachusetts Department of Environmental Protection.

There are no known biological methods for swollen bladderwort control. In La Center Bottoms Park, Washington, some animals such as mallards, wood ducks, muskrats, and turtles eat bladderworts (USDA n.d.). Introducing these animals probably may effectively manage bladderworts, but other native species might also be eaten or impacted and these animals could also spread bladderworts.

SUCCESS STORY

The application of herbicides may be effective in impeding the spread of swollen bladderwort. In 1996, Sonar (fluridone) treatment was tried in

Lake Limerick in Mason County, WA, and it has been shown to be successful on controlling the swollen bladderwort population for around two years (Washington State Department of Ecology 2020). But fluridone can also damage or even kill non-target plants by disrupting carotenoid synthesis (SERA, Inc. 2008). Inappropriate usage of herbicides could cause negative impacts on water quality and human health.

CONCLUSION

As described in this chapter, swollen bladderwort as an invasive species can have a negative impact not only on the ecosystem, but also on economic factors such as the recreational use of Massachusetts waterbodies. Therefore, it is of great importance to continue to raise awareness of the impacts of swollen bladderworts to decrease spread, increase precautionary steps, and implement treatment methods.

REFERENCES

Clark, A. n.d. Bladderwort-Adaptations, uses, habitats, eats (Common Plant). *LotusMagus*. https://lotusmagus.com/bladderwort/

Crow, G.E. 2014. Lentibulariaceae Richard. Flora of North America, Provisional publication. Flora of North America Association. October 27, 2014. http://floranorthamerica.org/files/Lentibulariaceae%20provisional. pdf. (Accessed January 31, 2021).

Figuerola, J., and A.J. Green. 2002. Dispersal of aquatic organisms by waterbirds: A review of past research and priorities for future studies. *Freshwater Biology* 47(3): 483–494.

ITIS (Integrated Taxonomic Information System). 2021. www.itis.gov/servlet/SingleRpt/SingleRpt?search_topic=TSN&search_value=34443#null (Accessed January 29, 2021).

Johnstone, I.M., B.T. Coffey, and C. Howard-Williams. 1985. The role of recreational boat traffic in Interlake dispersal of macrophytes—A New-Zealand case-study. *Journal of Environmental Management* 20(3): 263–279.

Kadono, Y., T. Noda, K. Tsubota, K. Shutoh, and T. Shiga. 2019. The Identity of an Alien Utricularia (Lentibulariaceae) Naturalized in Japan. *Acta Phytotaxonomica et Geobotanica* 70(2): 129–134.

Langley, L., L. Rhodes, and M. Stroman. 2004. *Guidance for Aquatic Plant Management in Lakes and Ponds as It Relates to the Wetlands Protection Act*. Cambridge, MA: Massachusetts Department of Environmental Protection, p. 30.

Llorens, C., M. Argentina, Y. Bouret, P. Marmottant, and O. Vincent. 2012. A dynamical model for the Utricularia trap. *Journal of the Royal Society Interface* 9: 3129–3139.

MA DCR (Massachusetts Department of Conservation & Recreation). 2007. *Swollen bladderwort: An Exotic Aquatic Plant*. Cambridge, MA: MA DCR, p. 3.

MA DCR (Massachusetts Department of Conservation & Recreation). 2017. *A Guide to Aquatic Plants in Massachusetts*. Cambridge, MA: MA DCR, p. 32.

Mattson, M.D., P.J. Godfrey, R.A. Barletta, and A. Aiello. 2004. *Eutrophication and Aquatic Plant Management in Massachusetts: Final Generic Environmental Impact Report*. Cambridge, MA: Commonwealth of Massachusetts, Executive Office of Environmental Affairs Commonwealth of Massachusetts, p. 514.

Native Plant Trust. 2021. Characteristics of Utricularia inflate. *Native Plant Trust*, https://gobotany.nativeplanttrust.org/species/utricularia/inflata/ (Accessed January 29, 2021).

Reinert, G.W., and R.K. Godfrey. 1962. Reappraisal of *Utricularia inflata* and *U. radiata* (Lentibulariaceae). *American Journal of Botany* 49: 213–220.

Robinson, M. n.d. *swollen bladderwort: An Exotic Aquatic Plant Utricularia inflata*. Cambridge, MA: DCR.

Scholl, W. 2007. *Invasion Ecology: swollen bladderwort*. Washington, DC: Washington State Department of Ecology.

SERA, Inc. 2008. *Fluridone Human Health and Ecological Risk Assessment Final Report*. Syracuse Environmental Research Associates, Inc. www.fs.fed.us/foresthealth/pesticide/pdfs/0521002a_Fluridone.pdf

Sorrie, B.A. 1992. *Utricularia inflata Walter* (Lentibulariaceae) in Massachusetts. *Rhodora* 94: 391–392.

Taylor, P. 1989. *The Genus Utricularia: A Taxonomic Monograph*. Kew Bulletin Additional Series XIV. London: HMSO, p. 724.

Titus, J.E., and R.A. Urban. 2013 Invasion in progress: *Utricularia inflata* in Adirondack submersed macrophyte communities. *Journal of the Torrey Botanical Society* 140: 506–516.

United Stated Department of Agriculture (USDA). n.d. Warning! carnivorous plant! Natural resources conservative service, USA, www.nrcs.usda.gov/Internet/FSE_DOCUMENTS/nrcs144p2_033271.pdf (Accessed January 23, 2020).

Urban, R.A., and M.E. Dwyer. 2016. Asexual reproduction and its potential influence on the distribution of an invasive macrophyte. *Northeastern Naturalist* 23: 408–419, https://doi.org/10.1656/045.023.0308

Urban, R.A., and J.E. Titus. 2010. Exposure provides refuge from a rootless invasive macrophyte. *Aquatic Botany* 92: 265–272.

Urban R.A., J.E. Titus, and H.H. Hansen. 2013. Positive feedback favors invasion by a submersed freshwater plant. *Oecologia* 172: 515–523, https://doi.org/10.1007/s00442-012-2496-4

Urban, R.A., J.E. Titus, and W.X. Zhu. 2009. Shading by an invasive macrophyte has cascading effects on sediment chemistry. *Biological Invasions* 11: 265.

Washington State Department of Ecology. 2020. Swollen bladderwort. *Wendy Scholl Invasion Ecology*, http://depts.washington.edu/oldenlab/wordpress/wp-content/uploads/2013/03/Ultricularia-inflata_Scholl_2007R.pdf. (Accessed January 22, 2020).

14 Water Chestnut (*Trapa natans*)

ABSTRACT

The earliest record of water chestnut (*Trapa natans*) was documented in Cambridge, MA, in 1877. Since then, sightings of water chestnut have increased to include 18 rivers and 96 lakes located within 17 of Massachusetts' 33 major watersheds. The purpose of this chapter is to present the location and spread of the invasive water chestnut and raise awareness of their ecologic and economic impacts. This process may aid in minimizing the unintentional transportation of water chestnuts between waterbodies. In addition, this chapter provides previous treatment methods that have been useful in controlling the abundance of water chestnut. These methods include physical management (e.g., mechanical harvesting, including pulling by hand, benthic barriers, and dredging), chemical treatments (e.g., fluridone and triclopyr), and biological agents (e.g., leaf beetle).

INTRODUCTION

Taxonomic Hierarchy (ITIS 2021)

Kingdom	Plantae
Subkingdom	Viridiplantae
Infrakingdom	Streptophyta
Superdivision	Embryophyta
Division	Tracheophyta
Subdivision	Spermatophytina
Class	Magnoliopsida
Superorder	Rosanae
Order	Myrtales
Family	Lythraceae
Genus	*Trapa* L.
Species	*Trapa natans* L.

BASIC BIOLOGY

As a floating annual macrophyte, water chestnut has alternate floating leaves with a shiny upper side and fine hairs on the underside (Mass. DCR 2015). Leaf blades are broadly rhomboid, triangular, or deltoid in shape, and can be up to 5 cm wide, with sharp, irregular, serrated margins. The petiole of each floating leaf is inflated like an air bladder to allow the formation of floating rosettes that can reach up to 30 cm in diameter (Crow and Hellquist 2000). Beneath the water surface, feathery, opposite submerged leaves attach to a stem 1–5 m long which connects to the rosettes. Submerged leaves are progressively replaced by fine, pinnately branched, leaf-like adventitious roots (Crow and Hellquist 2000; Mass. DCR 2015). Their slender roots also emerge at the lower stem, usually buried in the substrate, which anchors the plant in the water (Groth et al. 1996; Crow and Hellquist 2000). Flowers have been observed with four white petals emerging in axils of floating leaves from June to September (Hummel and Kiviat 2004; Chorak et al. 2019).

The fruit of water chestnut is a tetrahedral woody nut (or nutlet) with four sharp barbed spines (Crow and Hellquist 2000; Mass. DCR 2015). They are green and malleable when fresh, ultimately turning turn black and hard. Each is 2–4 cm wide and 6 g wet at maturity, and are produced from mid-July to September (Countryman 1978; Gleason and Cronqusit 1991). However, viable plants have been observed to come from nuts only ½ inch (1.27 cm) long (C. Boettner, personal communication). When the nuts mature, they fall off the plant and sink to the bottom of the waterbody (Naylor 2003). Nuts are then anchored by horns underneath the sediment of waterbodies throughout winter and start germination when the water temperature reaches above 8°C (Kurihara and Ikusima 1991), with an estimated germination rate of 86–87% (Kurihara and Ikusima 1991; Cozza et al. 1994). After germination, the remaining spent black casing of the nut may remain in the sediment for several decades or float to the surface. The parent plants decompose in late fall and winter.

After this, the sharp black spent seed casings can often be found along the shoreline of waterbodies, even in winter. Dormant seeds of water chestnut can survive up to 10–12 years, but the viability of seeds is quickly lost if seeds are dried out (Hummel and Kiviat 2004).

Each water chestnut seed can give rise to 10–15 rosettes, with each rosette producing up to 20 seeds (O'Neill 2006). Thus, each seed can, in turn, produce up to 300 seeds in the next generation that can then germinate within one of the following ten years. The density of the rosettes can reach up to 100 rosettes/m^2 when water chestnut is abundant (Pemberton 2002).

NATIVE RANGE

Water chestnut (*Trapa natans* L.), also known as European Water Chestnut, water caltrop, and bull nut, is native to temperate and tropical rivers, lakes, wetlands, and estuaries in Europe, Asia, and Africa (Hummel and Kiviat 2004; Chorak et al. 2019; Pfingsten et al. 2020). It tends to favor aquatic environments with abundant nutrients, a pH range between 6.7 and 8.2, moderate alkalinity (12–128 mg/l of calcium carbonate), and soft substrate (Pemberton 2002; Pfingsten et al. 2020). *Trapa natans* L. was introduced to North America in 1874 and cultivated in Asa Gray's botanical garden at Harvard University in Cambridge in 1877 (Countryman 1978; Naylor 2003). Due to a series of detrimental effects on ecosystem services caused by its aggressive growth, water chestnut is now considered a noxious weed in the northeastern United States (Figure 14.1) (Hummel and Kiviat 2004; Chorak et al. 2019).

INVASIVE RANGE

Seeds of water chestnuts can disperse to new sites by using its barbed spines to attach to moving objects, including animals, human clothing, nets, motorboat trailer carpets, life jackets, boats, and other vehicles. Plants can also spread by fragmentation, such as severed rosettes growing new roots and floating downstream. However, humans

FIGURE 14.1 Water chestnut. (Photo by Wai Hing Wong.)

also aid in the spread of water chestnuts through introduction to water gardens and aquarium releases (Mass. DCR 2002; Hummel and Kiviat 2004; Pfingsten et al. 2020). Water chestnut has been reported in states, including Connecticut, Delaware, Maryland, Massachusetts, New Hampshire, New Jersey, New York, Pennsylvania, Vermont, Virginia, and Washington, DC (Pemberton 2002; EDDMapS 2019).

ECOLOGICAL IMPACT

Water chestnut can have negative impacts on ecosystems when they dominate waterbodies. Though sharp fluctuations in water level and swift water flow can prohibit colonization, when conditions are favorable, water chestnuts can cover 100% of the water surface by generating a dense bed, sometimes stacked two to three layers (Pemberton 2002). As a result, these beds can intercept 95% of sunlight and suppress other submerged and floating aquatic plants (Pemberton 2002; Hummel and Kiviat 2004). Compared to native species, water chestnut provides less nutrients as a food source for wildlife once it dominates habitats (Feldman 2001; Wu and Wu 2007). Interestingly, Strayer et al. (2003) found densities of macroinvertebrates were lower in native *Vallisneria* beds than in *Trapa* beds in the Hudson River in New York. However, they speculated that macroinvertebrates in *Trapa* beds may not be available to fish due to low oxygen concentrations. A reduction of dissolved oxygen under water chestnut beds is consistently observed in both laboratories and field settings. Furthermore, these dense beds can reach to hundreds of hectares in size and can induce states of hypoxia or even anoxia (Caraco and Cole 2002). This phenomenon is detrimental to many aquatic invertebrates and fish (Hummel and Findlay 2006; Kornijów et al. 2010). Due to these conditions, water chestnut beds are often sites of low species richness, as few species can tolerate low-oxygen conditions found within them (Feldman 2001). However, a study by Kornijów et al. (2010), which took place in a 120-ha bed of water chestnut in the Hudson River, found high species richness, biodiversity, fish production, and invertebrate production, despite highly hypoxic conditions underneath the bed (Kornijów et al. 2010). A possible explanation that was put forth by Kornijów et al. (2010) stated that the species found inhabiting the bed possessed one or more behavioral or physiological mechanisms that allowed them to survive in hypoxic conditions. Even so, a survey of the fauna under the bed found that the species were not known to possess these traits. Therefore, more research is needed to determine the specific conditions under which water chestnut beds prove either beneficial or harmful to their aquatic environments.

ECONOMIC IMPACT

The infestation of water chestnut has considerable impacts on commercial and recreational water uses (Hummel and Kiviat 2004). In the Chesapeake Bay and other regions, dense water chestnut beds have blocked waterways and impeded activities, including boating and swimming (Pemberton 2002; Wu andWu 2007). Injuries to swimmers and beach visitors caused by the hard spines found on the outside of the nuts have also been reported (Countryman 1978; Giddy 2003). Furthermore, the control and removal of water chestnut can be costly. For example, over 14 million dollars was spent on Lake Champlain, Vermont, from 1982 to 2020 in controlling the spread of water chestnut with some success in the reduction of mechanical harvesting operations to the southern region, where mats continue to present challenges for the long-term ability to eradicate the species. Hand pulling and monitoring operations also continue throughout most of the initial locations where the species was found (K. Jensen, personal communication; Mass. DCR 2002). At the same time, other economic impacts occur due to lost recreational activities such as fishing and boating which cannot be ignored. To summarize, the main economic impacts associated with water chestnut are due to the cost of mechanical and chemical treatments, although these costs are often low if infestations are caught and treated in early stages of water chestnut establishment (Naylor 2003).

POSITIVE ASPECTS

Although recognized as an invasive species, water chestnut exhibits a few positive effects on ecosystems. Water chestnut is capable of phytoremediation by accumulating excess nitrogen and heavy metals in the water, which could present a solution for the treatment of municipal wastewater (Kumar and Chopra 2018). However, this function can only be performed effectively by harvesting the plants before decomposition.

Another potential wastewater treatment solution comes from using the husks of water chestnut plants to create an activated carbon solution that removes chromium compounds from water (Liu et al. 2010). This method entails using dried plant material and could work well with several physical management methods discussed later in this report. In addition, the presence of water chestnut beds also provides shelter and foraging grounds to juvenile fish, insects, and water birds (Hummel and Kiviat 2004). However, these positive effects are outweighed by the overall ecological, economic, and recreational damages caused by water chestnut.

MONITORING AND SIGHTINGS

Data for this project were collected by staff from MassDEP, the Massachusetts Department of Conservation and Recreation (DCR), the US Geological Survey (USGS), the US Fish and Wildlife Service, and other agencies through field visits and individual reports (Table 14.1). Sites with water chestnut were mapped as a data layer with ArcGIS® ArcMap 10.6 (ESRI, Redlands, California).

Since the early observation in Middlesex County, Massachusetts, in 1874, water chestnut has been reported at multiple waterbodies, including both rivers and lakes (Figure 14.2 and Table 14.1). More detailed information about the geographic coordinates of sites, the agencies that reported the sightings, and the specific report sources can be found in Table 14.1. Based on 395 records of water chestnut infestations, water chestnut was detected in 18 rivers and 96 lakes in Massachusetts, totaling 17 out of 33 DWM-WPP watersheds (modified by MassDEP from the MassGIS "Major Basins" layer). Infested watersheds were mainly distributed in the western, central, and northeastern regions of Massachusetts. Watersheds with multiple infested waterbodies or repeatedly reported waterbodies include Blackstone, Boston Harbor, Charles, Connecticut, Concord (SuAsCo), Housatonic, Mystic, and Nashua. As shown in Figure 14.2 and Tables 14.2 and 14.3, the risk of potential spread from these watersheds/waterbodies to others is quite high. Within the Connecticut River watershed, there are a few recent sightings that may not be included in this chapter.[1]

The distribution pattern of water chestnut in Massachusetts demonstrates the persistence of water chestnut infestations and its ability to spread to new locations. The presence of water chestnut in Sudbury River has been documented from 1879 to 2017 (OARS 2017) and continues to present, at total of 142 years. In terms of water salinity, although Vuorela and Aalto (1982) indicate that seeds fail to germinate when NaCl concentrations exceed 0.1%, water chestnut has been found in both freshwater and brackish water systems like the Mystic River Estuary, demonstrating the plants' highly adaptive nature.

MANAGEMENT ACTIONS

Water chestnut is listed as a prohibited plant and this species is banned from the trade in Massachusetts. The sightings as mapped in this chapter serve as an aid in creating awareness on the presence of water chestnut in Massachusetts, which may be helpful in minimizing unintentional transportation between different waterbodies and alerting local constituencies that management should be undertaken. Waterbodies infested with invasive species such as water chestnuts are reported in the biennial Massachusetts Water quality assessment and 303(d) list water quality. This integrated report is to fulfil the requirement of the federal Clean Water Act. In addition, projects that take place in infested waterbodies/watersheds are subject to the jurisdiction of 401 Water Quality Certifications with conditions to prevent potential spread of invasive species during the project. Furthermore, water quality monitoring gear and watercraft that operate in infested watersheds must be decontaminated before they are used in other watersheds to prevent the potential spread of invasive species such as the water chestnut.

In addition, water chestnut is an annual plant that begins to flower and form seeds in mid-July

Water Chestnut (*Trapa natans*)

TABLE 14.1
Latitude and Longitude for Each Waterbody with Water Chestnut (*Trapa natans*)

Waterbody	Agency	Report Source	N Latitude	W Longitude	First Year Reported
Ashfield Pond	USGS	USGS 6/23/2017 http://nas.er.usgs.gov/default.aspx	42.5313	−72.803	2007
Ashley Pond	USGS	USGS 6/27/2017 http://nas.er.usgs.gov/default.aspx	42.17	−72.6605	2013
Assabet River	MassDEP	SuAsCo Watershed 2001 Water Quality Assessment Report 82-AC-1 CN 92.0, August 2005	42.4	−71.51	2005
Bachelor Brook	USGS	USGS 6/30/2017 http://nas.er.usgs.gov/default.aspx	42.27	−72.595	2013
Bare Hill Pond	USGS	USGS 6/28/2017 http://nas.er.usgs.gov/default.aspx	42.4972	−71.5953	1999
Barrowsville Pond	USGS	USGS 6/30/2017 http://nas.er.usgs.gov/default.aspx	41.95269	−71.2054	2008
Bartlett Pond	College of the Holy Cross	Robert Bertin	42.318598	−71.61766	2009
Barton Cove	MassDEP	USGS 6/27/2017 http://nas.er.usgs.gov/default.aspx	42.6051	−72.5414	2009
Beaver Brook	MassDEP	Charles River Watershed 2002–2006 Water Quality Assessment Report 72-AC-4 CN136.5, April 2008			2008
Blacks Nook	MassDEP	Mystic River Watershed And Coastal Drainage Area 2004–2008 Water Quality Assessment Report 71-AC-2 CN170.2, March 2010			2010
Blackstone River	MassDEP	08-A035-05	42.098719	−71.622314	2008
Carding Mill Pond	MassDEP	SuAsCo Watershed 2001 Water Quality Assessment Report 82-AC-1 CN 92.0, August 2005			2001
Charles River	USGS	USGS 6/30/2017 http://nas.er.usgs.gov/default.aspx	42.360573	−71.181622	1994
Cheshire Reservoir, Middle Basin	DCR	DCR Data from ACT, GeoSyntec EM-ACT W-A. Madden FEW			
Cheshire Reservoir, North Basin	DCR	DCR Data from ACT, GeoSyntec EM-ACT W-A. Madden FEW			
Cheshire Reservoir, South Basin	DCR	DCR Data from ACT, GeoSyntec EM-ACT W-A. Madden FEW			
Chicopee Falls Impoundment	USGS	USGS 6/27/2017 http://nas.er.usgs.gov/default.aspx	42.1604	−72.5678	2007
Clamshell Pond	College of the Holy Cross	Robert Bertin	42.39934	−71.678197	2008
Clark Pond	MassDEP	Neponset River Watershed 2004 Water Quality Assessment Report 73-AC-1 CN170.4, February 2010			2010

(*Continued*)

TABLE 14.1 (Continued)

Waterbody	Agency	Report Source	N Latitude	W Longitude	First Year Reported
Clarks Pond	USGS	USGS 6/30/2017 http://nas.er.usgs.gov/default.aspx	42.86065	−70.92521	2007
Coes Pond	USGS	USGS 6/28/2017 http://nas.er.usgs.gov/default.aspx	42.250027	−71.834364	2001
Coes Reservoir	College of the Holy Cross	Robert Bertin	42.253967	−71.841584	1995
Concord River	USGS	USGS 6/28/2017 http://nas.er.usgs.gov/default.aspx	42.569644	−71.281614	1970
Connecticut River	USGS	USGS 6/27/2017 http://nas.er.usgs.gov/default.aspx	42.212592	−72.602312	2001
Cusky Pond	College of the Holy Cross	Robert Bertin	42.323429	−72.091626	2009
Danks Pond	USGS	USGS 6/30/2017 http://nas.er.usgs.gov/default.aspx	42.2873	−72.6416	2013
Ellis Pond	MassDEP	Neponset River Watershed 2004 Water Quality Assessment Report 73-AC-1 CN170.4, February 2010			2005
Exposition Grounds Pond	USGS	USGS 6/27/2017 http://nas.er.usgs.gov/default.aspx	42.0936	−72.6107	2013
Fisherville Pond	DCR	Joy Trahan-Liptak	42.184408	−71.692178	2015
Fisk Pond	USGS	USGS 6/28/2017 http://nas.er.usgs.gov/default.aspx	42.2819	−71.37107	2004
Flint Pond	USGS	USGS 6/28/2017 http://nas.er.usgs.gov/default.aspx	42.67278	−71.4327	2015
Forge Pond	USGS	USGS 6/28/2017 http://nas.er.usgs.gov/default.aspx	42.273	−72.468	2002
Franklin Reservoir Northeast	USGS	USGS 6/30/2017 http://nas.er.usgs.gov/default.aspx	42.09551	−71.38076	2003
Fresh Pond	USGS	USGS 6/30/2017 http://nas.er.usgs.gov/default.aspx	42.384263	−71.148942	1879
Great Meadows Pond #3	MassDEP	SuAsCo Watershed 2001 Water Quality Assessment Report 82-AC-1 CN 92.0, August 2005			2005
Great Pond	USGS	USGS 6/27/2017 http://nas.er.usgs.gov/default.aspx	42.3938	−72.6063	2013
Greenville Pond	College of the Holy Cross	Robert Bertin	42.205981	−71.922721	2007
Grist Mill Pond	MassDEP	SuAsCo Watershed 2001 Water Quality Assessment Report 82-AC-1 CN 92.0, August 2005			2005
Hardys Pond	MassDEP	Charles River Watershed 2002–2006 Water Quality Assessment Report 72-AC-4 CN136.5, April 2008			2008
Heard Pond	MassDEP	SuAsCo Watershed 2001 Water Quality Assessment Report 82-AC-1 CN 92.0, August 2005			2005

Water Chestnut (*Trapa natans*)

Heart Pond	MassDEP	Email communication between David Wong and Matthew Reardon on 7/12/2017	42.565626	−71.391319	2017
Hockanum Road Pond	USGS	USGS 6/27/2017 http://nas.er.usgs.gov/default.aspx	42.2986	−72.6149	2012
Housatonic River	MassDEP	Housatonic River Watershed 2002 Water Quality Assessment Report 21-AC-4 CN141.5 September 2007	42.394038	−73.240401	2002
Hubbard Brook	MassDEP	Housatonic River Watershed 2002 Water Quality Assessment Report 21-AC-4 CN141.5, September 2007			2007
Hulberts Pond	USGS	USGS 6/27/2017 http://nas.er.usgs.gov/default.aspx	42.2917	−72.644	2003
Ingraham Brook Pond	MassDEP	Connecticut River Basin 2003 Water Quality Assessment Report 34-AC-2 CN 105.5, October 2008			2008
Kingfisher Pond	USGS	USGS 6/28/2017 http://nas.er.usgs.gov/default.aspx	42.1084	−71.3212	2013
Lackey Pond	College of the Holy Cross	Robert Bertin	42.096707	−71.689012	2008
Lake Attitash	DCR	DCR Data from Lakes and Ponds, 2007			2007
Lake Bray	USGS	USGS 6/27/2017 http://nas.er.usgs.gov/default.aspx	42.2666	−72.6164	2013
Lake Cochituate	DCR	DCR Data from Lakes and Ponds, 2005			2005
Lake Quinsigamond	MassDEP	Email communication between David Wong and Barbara Kickham on June 23, 2017	42.296228	−71.754669	2017
Lake Ripple	College of the Holy Cross	Robert Bertin	42.213605	−71.697077	2008
Lake Warner	USGS	USGS 6/27/2017 http://nas.er.usgs.gov/default.aspx	42.3882	−72.5764	2002
Laurel Lake	USGS	USGS 6/23/2017 http://nas.er.usgs.gov/default.aspx	42.325555	−73.269367	2011
Linwood Pond	DCR	Joy Trahan-Liptak	42.101497	−71.651349	2016
Little Pond	USGS	USGS 6/30/2017 http://nas.er.usgs.gov/default.aspx	42.40001	−71.158834	2001
Log Pond Cove	USGS	USGS 6/27/2017 http://nas.er.usgs.gov/default.aspx	42.2148	−72.6117	2005
Long Pond	USGS	USGS 6/30/2017 http://nas.er.usgs.gov/default.aspx	42.598461	−71.251831	2016
Lower Mill Pond	MassDEP	USGS 6/27/2017 http://nas.er.usgs.gov/default.aspx	42.2737	−72.6573	2007
Lower Pond	USGS	USGS 6/27/2017 http://nas.er.usgs.gov/default.aspx	42.2546	−72.5723	2005
Lower Van Horn Park Pond	USGS	USGS 6/27/2017 http://nas.er.usgs.gov/default.aspx	42.1252	−72.5967	2004
Meadow Brook Pond	DCR	Joy Trahan-Liptak	42.078539	−71.592303	2009
Meadow Pond	MassDEP	SuAsCo Watershed 2001 Water Quality Assessment Report 82-AC-1 CN 92.0, August 2005			2005

(*Continued*)

TABLE 14.1 (Continued)

Waterbody	Agency	Report Source	N Latitude	W Longitude	First Year Reported
Mill River	MassDEP	Parker River Watershed And Coastal Drainage Area 2004–2008 Water Quality Assessment Report 91-AC-3 CN 173.0, March 2010			2010
Mumford River	DCR	Joy Trahan-Liptak	42.109325	−71.665758	2016
Mystic River	MassDEP	09-A012–05	42.417852	−71.118136	2009
Nashawannuck Pond	USGS	USGS 6/27/2017 http://nas.er.usgs.gov/default.aspx	42.2617	−72.6652	2007
Nashua River	MassDEP	08-G027–03	42.66415	−71.577006	2008
North Great Meadows	MassDEP	USGS 6/28/2017 http://nas.er.usgs.gov/default.aspx	42.479261	−71.32867	1983
North Great Meadows	MassDEP	SuAsCo Watershed 2001 Water Quality Assessment Report 82-AC-1 CN 92.0, August 2005			1983
Nutting Lake, East Basin	MassDEP	SuAsCo Watershed 2001 Water Quality Assessment Report 82-AC-1 CN 92.0, August 2005			2005
Onota Lake	USGS	USGS 6/23/2017 http://nas.er.usgs.gov/default.aspx	42.469691	−73.281212	2003
Oxbow	USGS	USGS 6/27/2017 http://nas.er.usgs.gov/default.aspx	42.2877	−72.6375	2004
Oxbow Cutoff	USGS	USGS 6/27/2017 http://nas.er.usgs.gov/default.aspx	42.295	−72.6218	2003
Pepperell Pond	USGS	USGS 6/28/2017 http://nas.er.usgs.gov/default.aspx	42.6547	−71.58197	2000
Pequot Pond	USGS	USGS 6/24/2017 http://nas.er.usgs.gov/default.aspx	42.1888	−72.6957	2007
Pontoosac Lake	USGS	USGS 6/23/2017 http://nas.er.usgs.gov/default.aspx	42.495897	−73.248425	2003
Purgatory Cove	DCR	Joy Trahan-Liptak	42.358386	−71.247771	2012
Rice City Pond	DCR	Joy Trahan-Liptak	42.100003	−71.622465	2011
River Meadow Brook	MassDEP	SuAsCo Watershed 2001 Water Quality Assessment Report 82-AC-1 CN 92.0, August 2005			2005
Riverdale Impoundment	DCR	Joy Trahan-Liptak	42.141777	−71.639295	2015
Rubber Thread Pond	USGS	USGS 6/27/2017 http://nas.er.usgs.gov/default.aspx	42.2647	−72.671	2013
Russell Cove	USGS	USGS 6/27/2017 http://nas.er.usgs.gov/default.aspx	42.2875	−72.604	2002
Russell Millpond	MassDEP	SuAsCo Watershed 2001 Water Quality Assessment Report 82-AC-1 CN 92.0, August 2005			2005

Water Chestnut (*Trapa natans*)

Location	Source	Reference	Latitude	Longitude	Year
Saxonville Pond	USGS	USGS 6/28/2017 http://nas.er.usgs.gov/default.aspx	42.31673	−71.41685	2015
Shaker Mill Pond	DCR	DCR Data from National Heritage, 2005			2005
Shirley Street Pond	MassDEP	Email from David Wong 6/28/2016	42.29933	−71.75352	2016
Silver Lake	DCR	Joy Trahan-Liptak	42.195614	−71.655275	2016
Spectacle Pond	DCR	DCR Data from ACT, GeoSyntec B. Hartzel, 2007			2007
Stearns Mill Pond	MassDEP	SuAsCo Watershed 2001 Water Quality Assessment Report 82-AC-1 CN 92.0, August 2005			2005
Stony Brook	MassDEP	Connecticut River Basin 2003 Water Quality Assessment Report 34-AC-2 CN 105.5, October 2008			2008
Sudbury Reservoir	College of the Holy Cross	Robert Bertin	42.321064	−71.510778	2006
Sudbury River	USGS	USGS 6/28/2017 http://nas.er.usgs.gov/default.aspx	42.46509	−71.35839	1879
Unnamed Pond	USGS	USGS 6/27/2017 http://nas.er.usgs.gov/default.aspx	42.2088	−72.6463	2013
Unnamed Pond	USGS	USGS 6/27/2017 http://nas.er.usgs.gov/default.aspx	42.2238	−72.6424	2006
Unnamed Pond	USGS	USGS 6/27/2017 http://nas.er.usgs.gov/default.aspx	42.2629	−72.6118	2013
Unnamed Pond	USGS	USGS 6/28/2017 http://nas.er.usgs.gov/default.aspx	42.2136	−72.5212	2013
Unnamed Pond	USGS	USGS 6/23/2017 http://nas.er.usgs.gov/default.aspx	42.18486	−72.7474	2016
Unnamed Pond	USGS	USGS 6/27/2017 http://nas.er.usgs.gov/default.aspx	42.2274	−72.6107	2003
Unnamed Pond	USGS	USGS 6/27/2017 http://nas.er.usgs.gov/default.aspx	42.2896	−72.6206	2002
Unnamed Pond	USGS	USGS 6/27/2017 http://nas.er.usgs.gov/default.aspx	42.3523	−72.6665	2013
Unnamed Pond	USGS	USGS 6/27/2017 http://nas.er.usgs.gov/default.aspx	42.2646	−72.6749	2013
Unnamed Pond	USGS	USGS 6/27/2017 http://nas.er.usgs.gov/default.aspx	42.2693	−72.5752	2013
Unnamed Pond	USGS	USGS 6/30/2017 http://nas.er.usgs.gov/default.aspx	42.2095	−72.6017	2003
Unnamed Pond	USGS	USGS 6/30/2017 http://nas.er.usgs.gov/default.aspx	42.2408	−72.5937	2002
Upper Pond	USGS	USGS 6/27/2017 http://nas.er.usgs.gov/default.aspx	42.258095	−72.567401	2001
Warners Pond	MassDEP	SuAsCo Watershed 2001 Water Quality Assessment Report 82-AC-1 CN 92.0, August 2005			2005
West River	MassDEP	09-G010–05	42.092409	−71.602293	2009
Wheeler Pond	DCR	DCR Data from Lakes and Ponds, 2006			2006
Whiting Street Reservoir	USGS	USGS 6/27/2017 http://nas.er.usgs.gov/default.aspx	42.2396	−72.638	2013

(Continued)

TABLE 14.1 (Continued)

Waterbody	Agency	Report Source	N Latitude	W Longitude	First Year Reported
Whitins Pond	MassDEP	Email communication between David Wong and Therese Beaudoin on July 7, 2017	42.119714	−71.688739	2017
Wilton Brook	MassDEP	Connecticut River Basin 2003 Water Quality Assessment Report 34-AC-2 CN 105.5, October 2008			2008
Woods Pond	DCR	DCR Data from MA Department of Fish and Game			

Water Chestnut (*Trapa natans*)

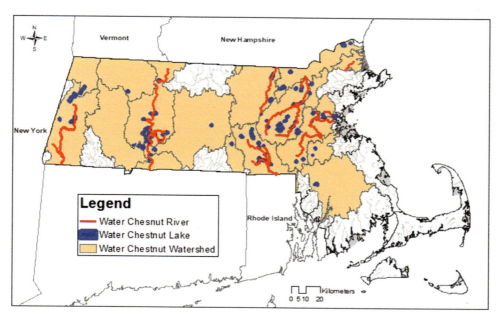

FIGURE 14.2 Distribution map depicting water chestnut (*Trapa natans*) in Massachusetts.

TABLE 14.2
Watersheds Infested with Water Chestnut

Blackstone River
Boston Harbor: Mystic River
Boston Harbor: Neponset River
Charles River
Chicopee River
Concord River (SuAsCo)
Connecticut River
Deerfield River
French River
Housatonic River
Hudson: Hoosic River
Merrimack River
Nashua River
Parker River
Shawsheen River
Taunton River
Westfield River

through fall with each seed producing 10–15 rosettes. Therefore, to manage it more effectively, physical removal or chemical treatments should be performed before seeds develop. This will reduce the number of seeds available for recolonization during the following growing season (Chorak et al. 2019). For best results, most management actions should begin before mid-July, regarding both the four-horned and two-horned variants of water chestnut (Rybicki

TABLE 14.3
Towns and Waterbodies

Town	Waterbody
Amesbury	Clarks Pond
	Lake Attitash
Ashfield	Ashfield Pond
Belmont	Little Pond
Berlin	Wheeler Pond
Billerica	Concord River
	Nutting Lake, East Basin
Boston	Charles River
	Mystic River
Cambridge	Blacks Nook
	Fresh Pond
Carlisle	Meadow Pond
Chelmsford	Heart Pond
	River Meadow Brook
	Russell Millpond
Cheshire	Cheshire Reservoir, Middle Basin
	Cheshire Reservoir, North Basin
Chicopee	Chicopee Falls Impoundment
Clinton	Clamshell Pond
Concord	Concord River
	Great Meadows Pond #3
	North Great Meadows
	Sudbury River
	Warners Pond
Deerfield	Connecticut River
Dover	Charles River
Easthampton	Lower Mill Pond
	Nashawannuck Pond
	Rubber Thread Pond
	Wilton Brook
Framingham	Saxonville Pond
Franklin	Franklin Reservoir Northeast
Gill	Barton Cove
Grafton	Fisherville Pond
	Lake Ripple
	Silver Lake
Granby	Forge Pond
	Ingraham Brook Pond
	Stony Brook
Groton	Nashua River
Hadley	Lake Warner
	Russell Cove

Water Chestnut (*Trapa natans*)

Town	Waterbody
Harvard	Bare Hill Pond
Hatfield	Great Pond
Holyoke	Ashley Pond
	Connecticut River
	Lake Bray
	Log Pond Cove
	Whiting Street Reservoir
Lanesborough	Cheshire Reservoir, South Basin
	Pontoosac Lake
Lee	Laurel Lake
Leicester	Greenville Pond
Lenox	Housatonic River
	Woods Pond
Littleton	Spectacle Pond
Maynard	Assabet River
Medfield	Charles River
Medford	Mystic River
Mendon	Meadow Brook Pond
Montague	Connecticut River
Natick	Fisk Pond
	Lake Cochituate
New Braintree	Cusky Pond
Newton	Charles River
Norfolk	Kingfisher Pond
Northampton	Danks Pond
	Hockanum Road Pond
	Hulberts Pond
	Oxbow
	Oxbow Cutoff
	Bartlett Pond
Northbridge	Blackstone River
	Linwood Pond
	Riverdale Impoundment
	Whitins Pond
Norton	Barrowsville Pond
Norwood	Ellis Pond
Pepperell	Nashua River
	Pepperell Pond
Pittsfield	Onota Lake
Rowley	Mill River
Sheffield	Hubbard Brook
Shirley	Nashua River
Shrewsbury	Lake Quinsigamond
	Shirley Street Pond

(Continued)

TABLE 14.3 (Continued)

Town	Waterbody
South Hadley	Bachelor Brook
	Connecticut River
	Lower Pond
	Upper Pond
Southborough	Sudbury Reservoir
Springfield	Lower Van Horn Park Pond
Stow	Assabet River
Sudbury	Carding Mill Pond
	Grist Mill Pond
	Stearns Mill Pond
Tewksbury	Long Pond
Tyngsborough	Flint Pond
Upton	West River
Uxbridge	Lackey Pond
	Mumford River
	Lackey Pond
	Rice City Pond
Walpole	Clark Pond
Waltham	Beaver Brook
	Hardys Pond
	Purgatory Cove
Wayland	Heard Pond
	Sudbury River
West Springfield	Exposition Grounds Pond
West Stockbridge	Shaker Mill Pond
Westfield	Pequot Pond
Westford	Forge Pond
Worcester	Coes Pond
	Coes Reservoir

2019) and followed up with checks for regrowth and new emergence until late August.

PHYSICAL CONTROL

Hand pulling and mechanical harvesting are commonly applied methods to remove invasive populations of water chestnut (Mass. DCR 2002). Hand pulling is highly selective and well-suited for shallow waterbodies and small-scale infestations or as follow-up once an infestation is reduced using other modes of management (Pearson 2021). Hand removal works especially well when plants are harvested "early and often" starting in early June, and repeated every few weeks to harvest plants when they are smaller and easier to handle (see the description of the Connecticut River watershed hand pulling protocols provided subsequently). A benefit of hand harvesting is that it is feasible to remove the entire plant, including the seed from which it grew. While the high cost of training and labor can be concerning, previous or ongoing control programs in the Potomac River, Lake Champlain, Connecticut River, and Chesapeake Bay utilize(d) less expensive volunteer programs. It is also useful to mention the utility of long handled rakes, as they may be useful in waterbodies where hand pulling may not be feasible and uproot plants (Rybicki 2019). Furthermore, in infested sites with dense and extensive water chestnut beds, mechanical harvesting may serve as an effective approach even though the cost and potential impacts on aquatic fauna may be higher (OARS 2017). Mechanical harvesting utilized by the Connecticut River Watershed Invasive Plant Control Initiative in Log Pond Cove, cost $80,000 in 1999 and $51,000 in 2000 (Massachusetts Aquatic Invasive Species Working Group 2002). Traditional mechanical harvesting entails cutting the plants about 18 inches below the water surface and collecting and disposing of the cut portion. Because plants can regrow and may have time to produce seeds, careful timing of this method, or implementing a second later cut is necessary. Timing can get undermined by low water levels (OARS 2017). However, when successful, mechanical harvesting can reduce a population to a level that can later be managed by hand pulling (OARS 2017).

Regardless of the methods employed, harvesting before the fruits are mature and potentially dropping during the harvesting activity, and harvesting the entire plant, stems, and roots will ensure a successful operation. Care must be taken to ensure the removal of harvested plant parts so that no damaged or fragmented pieces of the plant can continue to grow, fruit, and spread. Once harvested, all plant parts must be disposed of either by composting at an upland site or incinerated (Hummel and Kiviat 2004; Rybicki 2019). Even if a population is thought to be eliminated, due to the unpredictable nature of the long-lived seedbank (seeds that have dropped from previous years), annual monitoring must persist to prevent a resurgence (OARS 2017; Pearson 2021).

Chorak et al. (2019) found that there is a two-horn variety of water chestnut in the Potomac River, Virginia, and suggests that this morphologically similar species may exhibit a different pattern of development. Even though the two-horn water chestnut has not been reported in Massachusetts, it is recommended that an accurate identification of plants should be completed prior to any treatment.

Other physical control methods, including hydro raking, drawdown, dredging, and benthic barriers, can also be used for certain situations but have their own limitations (OARS 2017). For example, dredging can be effective at removing the nuts (or nutlets) from water chestnut that have fallen into the sediment at the bottom of waterbodies, as was the case at Hills Pond in Arlington, MA (Furgo East, Inc. 1996; Mattson et al. 2004). Additionally, since the barbed nuts of water chestnut can stick onto plumage or fur, fencing can be installed around the perimeter of infested waterbodies to keep mammals out and minimize spread (Rybicki 2019); however, waterfowl could still move seeds if they can fly in and out.

BIOLOGICAL CONTROL

Researchers have been looking for biological control agents for water chestnut. An efficient biological control agent should be host-specific to decimate or severely damage its target plant. It is suggested that the leaf beetle *Galerucella birmanica*, originally imported from China, can cause complete defoliation of whole populations of water chestnut and, therefore, is a promising biological control agent of *T. natans* (Ding et al. 2006a, b). *Galerucella birmanica* is only restricted to a quarantine facility (Bernd Blossey, personal communication) and has not been approved for release by the US Department of Agriculture (USDA) or by individual states as a Plant Protection and Quarantine (PPQ) 526 permit from the USDA. Such a permit is required to transport biological control agents across state lines and for release into the environment (OARS 2017). In addition, several other species of insects have potential as possible biological control agents, such as two species of *Nanophyes* weevil and an Italian species of weevil, *Bagous rufimanus* (Naylor 2003).

CHEMICAL CONTROL

Chemical treatment with herbicides is often coupled with physical removal of water chestnut to improve the efficiency of control. 2,4-Dicholorophenoxy acetic acid (2,4-D) and fluridone are currently recognized as being able to control water chestnut, with 2,4-D leading to consistent control and fluridone resulting in partial control of water chestnut according to the Eutrophication and Aquatic Plant Management in Massachusetts Final Generic Environmental Impact Report (Mattson et al. 2004). 2,4-D, a herbicide registered by the EPA for use in aquatic environments since 1959, was successfully used in the Mohawk River, the Hudson River, and Lake Champlain to control water chestnut (Countryman 1978). However, due to toxicity and concerns about migration into groundwater, the use of 2,4-D has been banned in Zone II wellhead protection areas (Aquatic Control Technology 2015). Common alternatives include triclopyr, imazapyr, glyphosate, and the imidazole-based herbicide Clearcast™ (Hummel and Kiviat 2004; OARS 2017). More information about chemical control on water chestnut and other 18 invasive species can be found in Appendix III. Any chemical used for aquatic invasive species control requires a WM04 Chemical Application License issued by the Massachusetts Department of Environmental Protection, as well as an Order of Conditions from the local town's Conservation Commission. Previous control programs that utilized chemical control often involve the monitoring of water quality and nutrient levels to assess the impacts on general water quality conditions from herbicide applications (Harman et al. 2012). Aquatic herbicides must be registered with the EPA (under the Federal Insecticide, Fungicide, and Rodenticide Act) and the Massachusetts Department of Agricultural Resources and approved for legal use in Massachusetts.

SUCCESS STORY

CONNECTICUT RIVER WATERSHED

Water chestnut has been a problem in the Connecticut River watershed since at least the early 1940s when an infestation was documented and management activities began at Lower Pond on Mt. Holyoke College campus in South Hadley (Sigler 2008). An especially dense and persistent infestation exists at Log Pond Cove, a 20-acre cove of the Connecticut River in Holyoke. There, several partnering agencies, including the US Fish and Wildlife Service (specifically, the Silvio O. Conte National Fish and Wildlife Refuge), the City of Holyoke, the Connecticut River Conservancy, and Holyoke Gas and Electric company have tried various modes of mechanical harvesting, chemical control, and integrated management (with augmentation from hand-pullers), with the population fluctuating through time. Control has remained out of reach. The species has spread to scores of other waterbodies, including other coves of the Connecticut River and shallow ponds within the watershed. A volunteer-based initiative was undertaken about 2000 under the leadership of the Silvio O. Conte National Fish and Wildlife Refuge and later taken over by the Connecticut River Conservancy in 2019. As of early 2022, water chestnut sporadically ranges within the watershed from mid-Vermont and New Hampshire, through Massachusetts and Connecticut, until salinity limits its viability north of Long Island Sound (see Figure 14.1).

The best long-term successes in the Massachusetts portion of the watershed have been through hand pulling efforts. Ideally, the goal is to catch new infestations and physically remove them before they ever have a chance to drop seeds. Unfortunately, most infestations are not detected until they have established a seedbank. Because a single water chestnut plant can produce around 100 seeds, successful management requires greater than 99% plant removal for the population to show any sign of decline.

The US Fish and Wildlife Service, the Connecticut River Conservancy, and other partnering organizations have been seeing very promising results on numerous ponds once they started an "Early and Often" approach to finding and removing as many plants as possible, primarily by hand. This has entailed pulling all visible plants four times during the growing season, starting in early June as soon as rosettes surface. In Massachusetts, this is around the first or second week of June and at that point, rosettes are only about 1–3 inches in diameter. Stewards follow up again two weeks later (late June), and then again two to three weeks after that (in July). A final pull (in mid-August) is conducted to catch any regrowth, late seed emergence, or missed plants and this prevents almost all seed drop. The idea is to be constantly vigilant for small, newly germinating plants and catching any regrowth (from previously snapped stems) long before any seeds can form.

Another benefit of pulling plants while small is the volume of plants handled is reduced. This minimizes the amount of storage area required in the boats, which, in turn, reduces the time required for paddling to offload sites. Depending on the size of the infestation, less people may be required as well (Larger infestations or infestations where water chestnut plants are hidden among other vegetation, can require many more people to find and remove all water chestnut).

Cozza et al. (1994) found that 86% of the water chestnut seedbank germinates the year after seed drop at their study site. Subsequently, 85% of the remaining seeds were able to germinate after a second winter. With this high germination rate the first two years, it should follow that if an intensive effort is put forth to find and remove all plants, it shouldn't take very long to exhaust the bulk of the seedbank and reduce the population significantly. Then it is a matter of catching seeds that will germinate in any one of the next eight to ten years of viability.

This high germination rate observed by Cozza et al. has indeed been observed in data collected on numerous sites in the Connecticut River watershed. One such site in Westfield, MA (Brickyard West), was discovered in September of 2014 after seed drop, extremely dense sections were observed. In 2015, the US Fish and Wildlife Service staff and youth crew, along with many volunteers, did a massive harvest using canoes, kayaks, and a john boat to remove water chestnut by hand in most of the 20 small man-made ponds (14 acres of water). Because of a late start and the large size of plants, they were unable to cover all the ponds that year. In 2016, they increased the effort and completed removal in all the ponds, which required 681 person-hours to hand-pull 18,383 pounds of water chestnut. This exhaustive effort likely prevented seed drop for that year. By the following year (2017), the total plant weight in the ponds had dropped (97.5%) to 454 pounds and then continued to drop by 100 pounds a year until 2021 when only 32 pounds were found within a total of 16 person-hours. The drop in labor since 2016 was 97.7%. Part of the reason for the substantial drop in weight of plants removed is that, starting in 2017, ponds were monitored early in the season and then regularly after that (four total visits per year), so all plants were found and pulled when they were still very small. Even late in the season plants were small because pulled material was typically either newly germinated plants or regrowth from snapped stems (C. Boettner and G. Boettner, personal communication).

Theoretically, an infestation could be extinguished after a total of 12 years, but practically speaking, it may be impossible to find those last hidden plants each year. It is hoped that, for the most part, the Brickyard West water chestnut population may now be kept in check, by just one or two people on the water for 4 hours, four times a year—quite a difference from the labor-intensive effort from just five years previous. Stewards at several other sites using this regimen are also experiencing similar drops in infestation size.

As of this writing in early 2022, there are many other ponds and coves in the Connecticut River watershed that have water chestnut populations. In general, it appears that the sites that are larger and more difficult to cover thoroughly in a growing season are those that have been harder to bring down to a more manageable level. Having a designated site coordinator in charge of planning and promoting harvesting events has proven essential. Challenges to thorough removal at various sites include lack of a site coordinator, garnering adequate human power (or the vessels needed) to effectively remove all plants before they drop seeds, the ability of plants to effectively escape notice in duckweed or other emergent or floating vegetation, and safe access issues due to heavy flow or water quality issues (e.g., cyanobacteria) during the prescribed time for effective plant removal. Each year partners meet to discuss successes and challenges. New reporting mechanisms are being implemented and tested by the Connecticut River Conservancy and the hope is that new infestations will be detected sooner, which will make them easier to bring under control.

CONCLUSION

Water chestnuts often negatively impact the well-being of waterbodies, as well as commercial and recreational water uses. Therefore, more mapping and collecting and publishing of data is needed to aid in implementing appropriate control methods in eradicating invasive water chestnuts. In doing so, it is important to continue to create public awareness of water chestnuts' impacts, as well as implement reporting mechanisms and multifaceted treatments methods such as physical, biological, and chemical controls. Raising awareness about the effectiveness of well-organized and well-timed persistent hand pulling efforts can involve individuals. Even so, more research concerning water chestnut is critical for future management plans.

NOTE

1 According to an email from Summer Stebbins, the Connecticut Agricultural Experiment Station, to David W.H. Wong, Massachusetts Department of Environmental Protection, dated June 21, 2022.

REFERENCES

Aquatic Control Technology. 2015. *2015 Baseline Assessment Sudbury River Survey Findings and Management Recommendations.* Sheridan, CO: Aquatic Control Technology.

Caraco, N.F., and J.J. Cole. 2002. Contrasting impacts of a native and alien macrophyte on dissolved oxygen in a large river. *Ecological Applications* 12: 1496–1509.

Chorak, G.M., L.L. Dodd, N. Rybicki, K. Ingram, M. Buyukyoruk, Y. Kadono, Y.Y. Chen, and R.A. Thum. 2019. Cryptic introduction of water chestnut (Trapa) in the northeastern United States. *Aquatic Botany*, 155: 32–37. doi: 10.1016/j.aquabot.2019.02.006

Countryman, W. 1978. *Nuisance aquatic plants in Lake Champlain: Lake Champlain Basin Study.* Burlington, VT: US Department of Commerce, National Technical Information Service PB-293 439.

Cozza, R., G. Galanti, M.B. Bitonti, and A.M. Innocenti. 1994. Effect of Storage at low Temperature on the Germination of the Waterchestnut (*Trapa natans* L.) Phyton (Horn Austria) 34(2): 315–320.

Crow, G., and C.B. Hellquist. 2000. *Aquatic and Wetland Plants of Northeastern North America.* Madison, WI: University of Wisconsin Press, pp. 206–209.

Ding, J., B. Blossey, Y. Du, and F. Zheng. 2006a. Impact of Galerucella birmanica (Coleoptera: Chrysomelidae) on growth and seed production of Trapa natans. *Biological Control* 37(3): 338–345, doi: 10.1016/j.biocontrol.2005.12.003

Ding, J., B. Blossey, Y. Du, and F. Zheng. 2006b. Galerucella birmanica (Coleoptera: Chrysomelidae), a promising potential biological control agent of water chestnut, Trapa natans. *Biological Control* 36(1): 80–90. doi: 10.1016/j.biocontrol.2005.08.001

EDDMapS (Early Detection & Distribution Mapping System). 2019. The University of Georgia—Center for invasive species and ecosystem health. www.eddmaps.org/ (Accessed December 19, 2019).

Feldman, R.S. 2001. Taxonomic and size structures of phytophilous macroinvertebrate communities in Vallisneria and Trapa beds of the Hudson River, New York. *Hydrobiologia* 452(1): 233–245, doi: 10.1023/A:1011903315998

Furgo East, Inc. 1996. *Summary Report on the Restoration of Hills Pond in Menotomy Rocks Park.* Arlington, MA; Northborough, MA: Furgo East.

Giddy, I.H. 2003. *The Hudson River Water Trail Guide.* Hudson: Hudson River Watertrail Association.

Gleason, H.A., and A. Cronquist. 1991. *Manual of Vascular Plants of Northeastern United States and Adjacent Canada* (2nd edition). Bronx, NY: New York Botanical Garden.

Groth, A., L. Lovett-Doust, and J. Lovett-Doust. 1996. Population Density and Module Demography in Trapa natans (Trapaceae), an Annual, Clonal Aquatic Macrophyte. *American Journal of Botany* 83, doi: 10.2307/2446095

Harman, W.N., H.A. Waterfield, and M.F. Albright. 2012. *DEC Invasive Species Eradication and Control Grant Final Report 1.* Cooperstown, NY: State University of New York at Oneonta Biological Field Station.

Hummel, M., and S. Findlay. 2006. Effects of water chestnut (Trapa natans) beds on water chemistry in the tidal freshwater Hudson River. *Hydrobiologia* 559(1): 169–181, doi: 10.1007/s10750-005-9201-0

Hummel, M., and E. Kiviat. 2004. Review of world literature on water chestnut with implications for management in North America. *Journal of Aquatic Plant Management* 42: 17–28.

ITIS (Integrated Taxonomic Information System). 2021. www.itis.gov/servlet/SingleRpt/SingleRpt?search_topic=TSN&search_value=27170#null (Accessed January 29, 2021).

Kornijów, R., D.L. Strayer, and N.F. Caraco. 2010. Macroinvertebrate communities of hypoxic habitats created by an invasive plant (*Trapa natans*) in the freshwater tidal Hudson River. *Fundamental and Applied Limnology/Archiv für Hydrobiologie*, 176(3): 199–207.

Kumar, V., and A.K. Chopra. 2018. Phytoremediation potential of water caltrop (*Trapa natans* L.) using municipal wastewater of the activated sludge process-based municipal wastewater treatment plant. *Environmental technology*, 39(1): 12–23.

Kurihara, M., and I. Ikusima. 1991. The ecology of the seed in Trapa natans var. Japonica in a eutrophic lake. *Vegetatio* 97(2): 117–124, doi: 10.1007/BF00035385

Lake Champlain Basin Atlas Water Chestnut. 2019. https://atlas.lcbp.org/issues-in-the-basin/aquatic-invasive-species/water-chestnut/ (Accessed December 15, 2019).

Liu, W., J. Zhang, C. Zhang, Y. Wang, and Y. Li. 2010. Adsorptive removal of Cr (VI) by Fe-modified activated carbon prepared from Trapa natans husk. *Chemical Engineering Journal*, 162(2): 677–684.

Mass. DCR. 2002. *Water Chestnut: An Invasive Aquatic Plant.* Cambridge, MA: Mass. DCR.

Mass. DCR. 2015. *A Guide to Aquatic Plants in Massachusetts.* Cambridge, MA: Mass. DCRL: Massachusetts Department of Conservation and Recreation, p. 19.

Massachusetts Aquatic Invasive Species Working Group. 2002. *Massachusetts Aquatic Invasive Species Management Plan.* Cambridge, MA: Massachusetts Aquatic Invasive Species Working Group.

Mattson, M.D., K.J. Wagner., R.A. Barletta, and A. Aiello. 2004. *Eutrophication and Aquatic Plant Management in Massachusetts: Final Generic Environmental Impact Report.* Cambridge, MA: Commonwealth of Massachusetts, Executive Office of Environmental Affairs Commonwealth of Massachusetts, p. 514.

Naylor, M. 2003. *Water Chestnut (Trapa natans) in the Chesapeake Bay Watershed: A Regional Management Plan.* Lanham, MD: Maryland Department of Natural Resources.

OARS. 2017. Water Chestnut Management Guidance & Five-year Management plan for the Sudbury, Assabet, and Concord River Waterseds. Concord, MA: OARS (Planning and Guidance for Water Chestnut Management in the SuAsCo Watershed).

O'Neill, C.R. 2006. *Water chestnut (Trapa natans) in the Northeast.* New York: New York Sea Grant, Invasive Species Factsheet Series 06–1, Brockport.

Pearson, S. 2021. A Persistent Seed Bank: The Case for Annual Water Chestnut Monitoring Once a Population is Presumed Eradicated. Northeast Aquatic Plant Management Society Annual Meeting. www.neapms.org/2021-virtual-conference-archive

Pemberton, R.W. 2002. *Water Chestnut. USDA Forest Service Publication FHTET-2002-04.* Morgantown, WV: USDA, p. 413.

Pfingsten, I.A., L. Cao, and L. Berent. 2020. *Trapa Natans L.: U.S. Geological Survey, Nonindigenous Aquatic Species Database.* Gainesville, FL. https://nas.er.usgs.gov/queries/factsheet.aspx?SpeciesID=263 (Accessed December 14, 2020).

Rybicki, N. 2019. *Recent Detection and Spread of a new type of Trapa, an Invasive Aquatic Plant, in the Potomac River Watershed.* Washington, DC: U.S. Geological Survey, emerita.

Sigler, M. 2008. Dams and dredging: An overview of Mount Holyoke College's lake history. *Mt. Holyoke College Institutional Digital Archive.* https://ida.mtholyoke.edu/handle/10166/4673

Strayer, D.L.C. Lutz, H.M. Malcom, K. Munger, and W.H. Shaw. 2003. Invertebrate Communities Associated with a Native (Vallisneria americana) and an alien (Trapa natans) macrophyte in a large river. *Freshwater Biology* 48: 1938–1949.

Vuorela, I., and M. Aalto. 1982. Palaeobotanical investigations at a Neolithic dwelling site in southern Finland, with special reference to Trapa natans. *Ann. Bot. Fenn.* 19: 81–92.

Wu, M., and J. Wu. 2007. In-vitro investigations on ultrasonic control of water Chestnut. *Journal Aquatic Plant Manage* 45: 76–83.

15 Water Hyacinth (*Eichhornia crassipes*)

ABSTRACT

Water hyacinth *Eichhornia crassipes* is an invasive free-floating aquatic plant in the United States. Currently, there are only two known infected waterbodies in Massachusetts, Lake Ellis in the Millers Watershed and Mansfield Pond in the Housatonic Watershed. Meanwhile, the spreading capability of *E. crassipes* could not be ignored due to its ecological and economic impacts. Since it is still in an early stage of invasion to Massachusetts waters, rapid response to eradication should be tried as a management strategy. Physical methods such as manual or mechanical harvesting, chemical control such as diquat and glyphosate, and biological control using agent such as weevil species (*Neochetina eichhorniae* and *Neochetina bruchi*) can treat water hyacinth separately or can be implemented complementary according to the status of infestation. The challenge to manage this species continues in many countries worldwide.

INTRODUCTION

Taxonomic Hierarchy (ITIS 2021)

Kingdom	Plantae
Subkingdom	Viridiplantae
Infrakingdom	Streptophyta
Superdivision	Embryophyta
Division	Tracheophyta
Subdivision	Spermatophytina
Class	Magnoliopsida
Superorder	Lilianae
Order	Commelinales
Family	Pontederiaceae
Genus	*Eichhornia* Kunth
Species	*Eichhornia crassipes* (Mart.) Solms

BIOLOGY

Water hyacinth (*Eichhornia crassipes*) is also called floating water hyacinth. *E. crassipes* is mainly a free-floating macrophyte which can be found on the water surface (Figure 15.1). They are also able to survive in wetlands by using their complex root structure to directly absorb nutrients from the soil (Yu et al. 2019). Recently, *Pontederia crassipes* is also used as the scientific name for this species. *E. crassipes* may grow up to 1 m, but it usually appears 0.5 m of the height; its leaves are very thick and waxy with a circular or elliptical size, appearing shiny green; the leaves width are around 10–20 cm, leaf vein are performing numerous and dense, and leaf stalks are inflated and spongy; roots occupy around half of the plant biomass, and the dark violet roots has a feathery appearance; lavender-colored flowers grows in set of 8–15 on each spike, and every flower generally consists of six petals with a yellow blue-lined center (Gopal 1987; Robinson 2003).

When *E. crassipes* is not in the blooming period, it has a similar look with a native plant, frog's-bit (*Limnobium spongia*). They are relatively difficult to distinguish since these two plants both can be found floating on the water surface with thick and rounded green leaves. In addition, frog's-bit can clump up on the surface forming dense mats in the water similar to water hyacinth. When in bloom, the flowers of *L. spongia* are white with three petals and three sepals, and *E. crassipes* flowers are lavender with around six petals (DWFS n.d.). Without the presence of flowers, identification becomes trickier. However, there are key distinctions between the two species found by examining the root stems. *E. crassipes* has dark and feathery roots and inflated spongy leaf stalks (Robinson 2003), while *L. spongia* has whitish roots and slender firm leaf stalks (UF/IFAS n.d.) (Figure 15.2).

FIGURE 15.1 Water hyacinth. (Modified from Patel (2012).)

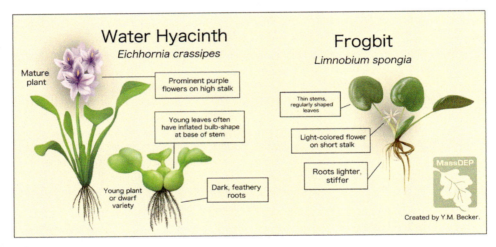

FIGURE 15.2 Water hyacinth comparison to native plant frog's-bit (*Limnobium spongia*). (Photo by Y.M. Becker.)

Native and Invasive Range

E. crassipes is native to the northern neotropics of South America. It can easily and rapidly establish itself in the various waterbodies, from small pond to reservoir. In addition, it can also be tolerant to extreme conditions of water level fluctuation, nutrient availability, pH, and toxic substances (Gopal 1987). However, cold weather and freezing temperatures prove challenging for this aquatic plant which may experience winter diebacks (Nesslage et al. 2016).

Currently, it is distributed through North America, South America, eastern Africa, Asia, and Australia, except Europe as a result of the climatic condition (GISD 2006). However, recent report is that this species has invaded in Italy in the first half of the 19th century (Brundu et al. 2013) and other European countries (Uremis et al. 2014; Coetzee et al. 2017). It is reported that *E. crassipes* was first spread from its native habitats to other countries during late 18th century and early 19th century, especially, it was introduced to the United States in the 1880s (Osei-Agyemang 2002).

Due to climate change, *E. crassipes* may be able to spread within and beyond its range as temperatures increase and winters become warmer. Although one study found that even with warming winters, *E. crassipes* populations didn't rebound significantly (Nesslage et al. 2016). Another study showed through two future greenhouse emission scenarios, temperature gradients in the northern hemisphere are too steep for significant geographical range expansion (Kriticos and Brunel 2016). At the same time, it is found in several studies that warming enhanced survival and regrowth of water hyacinth (You et al. 2013; Liu et al. 2016; Yu et al. 2019; Zhang et al. 2021).

Nevertheless, research suggests states plan accordingly and incorporate climate change–related actions and strategies into future management plans as warming creates conditions favorable to various species (Thomas et al. 2008).

Mechanisms/Vectors of Spread

In controlling *E. crassipes*, it may be useful to understand reproduction and dispersal mechanisms. *E. crassipes* can reproduce by both sexual and vegetative methods. Vegetative reproduction is the main cause for population increases (Barrett 1980) and the vegetative reproduction of *E. crassipes* occurs as short runner stems (stolons) break apart and float off. The new rosettes (daughter plants) grow from the floating stolon of the original plant (Barrett 1980; Robinson 2003). As plant fragments are easily transported by wind, waves, or boat movement, they can reproduce and infest additional areas, spreading the challenge for managers to continually control this aquatic plant species. Much of the spread may be contained by limiting human activity through infested areas such as avoiding boating activities and movement through infested waters.

Although the most common form of spread is vegetative reproduction, *E. crassipes* is capable of additional vectors of spread through seed and sexual reproduction (Barrett 1980; Pérez et al. 2011a, 2011b). Pollination of the *E. crassipes* is completed by bees between its flowers. In North America, the flowering season can last five to nine months, producing abundant amounts of inflorescences (Barrett 1980). Furthermore, seeds are produced in the mild season, and may be viable for decades (Robinson 2003). However, low light and low temperature can prevent seeds germination, as well as seedling reproduction.

Whether *E. crassipes* reproduces by vegetative method or sexual method, it has the potential to produce large amounts of individuals rapidly making for proper control important to reduce catastrophic impacts.

Ecological Impacts

E. crassipes is a very noxious aquatic invasive plant because it can thrive in a variety of waters. Once this plant species invades the waterbody and replaces the local vegetation, the natural ecosystems will be affected. According to multiple research (Robinson 2003; Villamagna and Murphy 2010; Koutika and Rainey 2015), the invasion of *E. crassipes* causes various threats and impacts to the ecosystem. Dense mats of *E. crassipes* inhibit the big fish migration, increase the sedimentation and evapotranspiration rates, degrade water quality, and intercept the sunlight which leads to the exclusion of other submerged plants. Massive and thick *E. crassipes* clog canals and waterways, providing a breeding environment for mosquitoes. Moreover, large amount of *E. crassipes* existing in the waterbodies compete with other native species and inhibit the light to the algae. This would cause fish or animals which rely on these native species to relocate or perish. Further, during the decomposition time of *E. crassipes*, fish or other aquatic animals may be harmed or even killed due to the anoxic environment. Therefore, in terms of the spread of *E. crassipes*, it significantly and negatively influences the ecosystem and biodiversity (Waltham et al. 2020). Several reports have revealed impacts or potential impacts from *E. crassipes*, such as the Great Lakes (North America) (Adebayo et al. 2011), Rift-Valley Lake (Ethiopia) (Mengistu et al. 2017), River Nile (Egypt) (Shanab et al. 2010), Lake Dianchi (China) (Wang et al. 2012), and different waters in China (Wang et al. 2012).

Economic Impacts

In addition to the impacts to the environment, the enormous impacts to human and society caused by *E. crassipes* should not be neglected. *E. crassipes* in the water may inhibit the boating and swimming recreational activities, resulting in economic loss. Other water activities such as fishing could also be reduced as plants overgrowth and less fish. Further, tourism development could be hampered, the value of surrounding real estate could be influenced (Robinson 2003), channels and waterways could be blocked, aesthetic value could be decreased, etc. The water use, irrigation, and electric power generation which are associated with agricultural, fishery, and other business would also be indirectly influenced by this nuisance plant (Koutika and Rainey 2015). Because of the thrive of *E. crassipes*, reduced water flow might lead to flooding and damage to canal banks (DWFS n.d.).

The benefits of management greatly outweigh the costs of control. Even after implementation of successful management practices, studies show the importance of long-term maintenance programs (Waltham et al. 2020). Many management decisions are made based on "least-cost control" options and tend to fail the consideration of long-term control effects. As mechanical shredding is a budget-friendly option (Greenfield et al. 2006), there are significant consequences of allowing widespread plant decomposition within an ecosystem. Although alternative treatments such as herbicides may be more expensive initially, over time they may become more cost-effective as the time of regrowth is slower and damaging effects may be minimized (Villamagna and Murphy 2010). Even though treatment may be costly, one study used evidence-based economic analysis which demonstrated that the ecosystem service benefits from water hyacinth management greatly exceed research and control costs. The study performed on a long-term treatment site in Louisiana estimated that peak plant cover would be 76% higher without substantial growth rate suppression (Wainger et al. 2018). The study also found the most cost-effective approach of combined biological and herbicide control programs 34:1 with costs-benefit of ecosystem services from management (Wainger et al. 2018).

Utilization of Water Hyacinth

In spite of *E. crassipes* having negative influences to the ecosystem and economy, special structure and biomass may let *E. crassipes* create many benefits. First, it can be used for animals and birds feed as well as organic fertilizers (GISD 2006). Second, prior research (Rommens et al. 2003) found that *E. crassipes* can be applied to absorb nutrients, such as nitrate, ammonium, and phosphate, for the evaluation of specific water system. This means it can also be applied to trap pollutants for water purification by plant harvesting (Greenfield et al. 2007); thus this benefit might limit the application in soil fertilizing. Third, *E. crassipes* can provide foraging places for Great Egret, Snowy Egret, Tri-colored Heron, Great Blue Heron, etc. large wading birds (Villamagna 2009). Finally, *E. crassipes* as a reusable energy can be used for producing bio-hydrogen and biomethane (Chuang et al. 2011). A recent review demonstrates that water hyacinth has gained attentions in biochar production, biomethane, biohydrogen, biogas, and utilization in case of wastewater treatment (Gaurav et al. 2020). In regions where permanent eradication proves difficult or impossible, research into finding alternatives for *E. crassipes* may prove more beneficial than focusing all efforts on control techniques (Güereña et al. 2015).

MONITORING AND SIGHTINGS

The invasive species data in this chapter were collected by the Massachusetts Department of Environmental Protection (MassDEP) and the Department of Conservation and Recreation (DCR). The standard operating procedures, including sampling methodology, species identification, quality control and assurance, are implemented by samples collected by MassDEP. Sites with *E. crassipes* were mapped as a data layer with ArcGIS® ArcMap 10.1 (ESRI, Redlands, California). This tool is able to pinpoint the area that *E. crassipes* has spread, which can help to inform future decisions on processes that can happen in these waterbodies, or regulations that involve efforts to limit the spread of this aquatic invasive species.

By using Geographic Information Systems (GIS), the presence of *E. crassipes* has been mapped in order to aid in future decisions that can be made on these waterbodies. From the collected data (Table 15.1), a map using GIS has been created in order to show the distribution of *E. crassipes* in Massachusetts waterbodies (Figure 15.3). Currently, there are two known waterbodies (Table 15.2) infested by *E. crassipes*, and two watersheds in Massachusetts are infested by *E. crassipes* (Table 15.3). These

Water Hyacinth (*Eichhornia crassipes*)

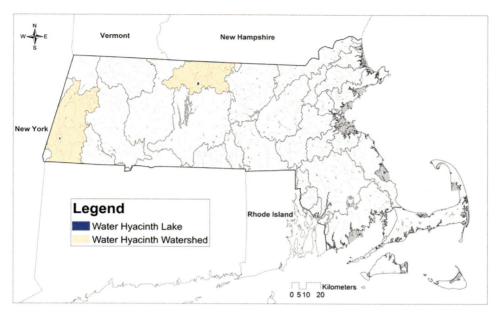

FIGURE 15.3 Distribution map depicting water hyacinth (*Eichhornia crassipes*) in Massachusetts.

TABLE 15.1
Infested Waterbodies in Massachusetts

Waterbody	Agency	Report Source
Lake Ellis	MassDEP	Millers River Watershed 2000 Water Quality Assessment Report 35-AC-1 CN089.0, March 2004
Mansfield Pond	DCR	DCR Data from Lake Association

TABLE 15.2
Towns and Infested Waterbodies

Number	Waterbody	Town 1
1	Lake Ellis	Athol
2	Mansfield Pond	Great Barrington

TABLE 15.3
Infested Watersheds

1	Millers
2	Housatonic

infested waterbodies are located in western and mid-northern Massachusetts.

Through the reports and surveys of *E. crassipes*, it is noted that *E. crassipes* is a very aggressive invasive species, and therefore has the ability to spread in a short period of time throughout Massachusetts. Although there is no massive *E. crassipes* spreading situation present in recent years in Massachusetts, the potential economic loss and ecological impact demonstrate that *E. crassipes* invading could not be neglected. A pointed and effective control method should be applied for infected waterbodies. For waterbodies haven't been invaded or under the risk to be invaded, the prevention methods should be conducted before the expansion of the invasive species.

MANAGEMENT

There are different methods tested for controlling the spread of *E. crassipes*. Effective management measures include physical, chemical, biological, and combined methods. The choice of these methods depends on the invasion range, the water condition, weather, management budget, regulation restrictions, etc.

PHYSICAL

Physical methods include harvesting (manual or mechanical) and in situ cutting (Villamagna and Murphy 2010). Mechanical harvesting is suitable for large-scale *E. crassipes* removal, especially the waterbody is invaded by massive and dense *E. crassipes*. Hand pulling is better than mechanical harvesting when small-scale *E. crassipes* appears in the waterbody, or when *E. crassipes* is mixed with other aquatic plants (Mattson et al. 2004). Although this easily accessible method could solve the problem, some disadvantages need to be noticed. Due to *E. crassipes*' ability to regrow by its fragments, harvesting can cause further spreading. When *E. crassipes* fragments drop in the water, it might be carried by animals or mechanical tools to other waterbodies (Robinson 2003). In situ cutting is another effective mechanical way. By applying this method, *E. crassipes* would die and decompose in the water (Greenfield et al. 2007). But it would release phosphorus, which might accelerate the eutrophication (Perna and Burrows 2005; Bicudo et al. 2007). Moreover, physical control might be time-consuming and expensive when large-scale *E. crassipes* needs to be removed. Transportation and disposal of large amount of *E. crassipes* may also bring health risk and environment problem owing to its pollution absorption capability (Villamagna and Murphy 2010).

CHEMICAL

Instead of the aforementioned methods, chemical control is also one of the most popular management approaches for undesirable plants control. Diquat, 2, 4-D, and glyphosate have been recognized effectively for controlling *E. crassipes* (Seagrave 1988; Mattson et al. 2004). Diquat and 2, 4-D can be used as consistent control method with correct dose, proper formulation, and suitable conditions (Mattson et al. 2004). Herbicides contain active ingredients that provide the toxicity to target plants but can also harm or kill non-target plants and organisms by using inappropriate herbicides or applying high-rate usage (Mattson et al. 2004). More information about chemical control on water hyacinth and other 18 invasive species can be found in Appendix III. Any chemical used for aquatic invasive species control requires a WM04 Chemical Application License issued by the Massachusetts Department of Environmental Protection.

Water quality conditions, specifically dissolved oxygen, should be minded in arial spray operations. Studies locations show that spraying using a helicopter to control invasive species does not dramatically effect water quality, DO, after mitigation (Tobias et al 2019). Any effects on dissolved oxygen and turbidity are able to recover to regional averages after treatment due to tidal hydrology. However, for wetland cases, this treatment method is appropriate when species cover is minor and restricted to wetland margins. In areas with higher plant cover, with ongoing spraying and low rainfall, hypoxia becomes of concern for coastal wetland function and productivity (Waltham and Fixler 2017). Here, the issue is the rate of consumption of oxygen for decomposition is greater than the amount of oxygen diffused in the water. The suggestion to avoid such cases is to avoid routine spraying and paying close attention to antecedent weather conditions before treatment (Waltham and Fixler 2017).

Additionally, studies show additional concern for plant decay in relation to breeding grounds for insects. Research found within herbicide-treated areas, there was an increase in mosquito larva as plant decay increased. This study suggests the need for integrated approach of invasive weed management with herbicides and larval mosquito control practice (Portilla and Lawler 2020).

Biological

Biological methods mainly involve the introduction of the insects and plant pathogen. Two weevil species (*Neochetina eichhorniae* and *Neochetina bruchi*) have been verified as an effective control method for *E. crassipes* (Robinson 2003; Sosa et al. 2007). These two species can reduce water hyacinth buoyancy so that plants could fall down and decompose (Wilson et al. 2007). However, successful control by these two species can only occur in some waters, other conditions (such as large mats of *E. crassipes* or shallow waters) might influence the control result (Julien 2001; Villamagna and Murphy 2010). Additionally, even with increased weevil densities in waters, not enough damage occurs during cooler seasons for year-round control resulting in the need for other control measures to be implemented in such regions (Hopper et al. 2017).

Another biological control agent, *Megamelus scutellaris* (Hemiptera: Delphacidae), a planthopper, may prove as an effective control method in warmer locations. *M. scutellaris* is native to the subtropical climate of South America and is more effective in warmer waters as peak densities are observed in warmer months (Hopper et al. 2017). Additionally, *M. scutellaris* perform better in shaded or regions of partial cover rather than open areas most likely due to the increased humidity created in such locations (Tipping et al. 2014). Similar to the two weevil species listed earlier, *M. scutellaris* is able to damage leaves to a significant amount (Hopper et al. 2017).

Furthermore, prior research found that some fungus, *Acremonium zonatum*, *Alternaria eichhorniae*, and *Cercospora piaropi*, can control *E. crassipes* with proper conditions (Shabana and Mohamed 2005; Dagno 2011). When pretreated with 3,4-methylenedioxy *trans*-cinnamic acid (MDCA), plants are more susceptible to *A. eichhorniae* as MDCA is a phenylpropanoid pathway inhibitor and weakens the plant's defense system (Shabana and Mohamed 2005). Although caution has been advised as *A. eichhorniae* has been tested to only target *E. crassipes*, effects of both agents on others plants have not been widely studied. But the performance of the application can vary with the change of water activity and temperature, so studies advise the need for understanding how the physical environment will affect the agent's survival (Dagno 2011).

The use of biological control methods coupled with winter diebacks has been found to be extremely effective in some areas (Nesslage et al. 2016). However, biological methods are typically implemented after large quantities of plants are removed by physical or chemical management (Adekoya et al. 1993).

SUCCESS STORY

More successful control locations include infestations found in tropical and subtropical areas as well as infestations from monocultures existing as free-floating mat that are able to sink as a whole when damaged (Driesche et al. 2002). Factors that may accelerate control include wave action, reduced growth due to biological control agents, and high nutrient levels that lead to higher plant quality and thus increased insect population growth (Hill and Olckers 2000). Limiting factors may include the removal of mats by herbicidal or mechanical means or disrupting agent populations, shallow water where damaged plants are unable to sink, ephemeral waterbodies, polluted waters, lower temperatures at high altitude or temperate sites, high nutrients at temperate sites, and smaller frequency releases as opposed to mass or serial releases (Driesche et al. 2002).

In South Africa, biological control methods have been successfully applied to against *E. crassipes* during 1974–1996 (Hill and Olcker

2000). Researchers have tried to release six species, which include five arthropods and one pathogen, for eradicating *E. crassipes*. But only two species were found to contribute the most in this *E. crassipes* control process. These two species are *Neochetina eichhorniae* and *Neochetina bruchi*. Hill and Olcker (2000) highlight that larger waterbodies are more proper for applying this biological method. This is because the greater wave action produced by wind can promote the mortality of plants.

In 1990, 80% area of New Year's Dam in South Africa was found covered by *E. crassipes*; therefore, 200 adult *N. eichhorniae* were released in the dam. In the next few years, the population size of *N. eichhorniae* gradually became larger. By 1994, it was found that in New Year' Dam there was only 10% area that was occupied by *E. crassipes*, which was successfully achieved by the application of biological management with *N. eichhorniae*. The remaining plants were seen in a very small size. But the short-term success did not inhibit the regrowth of *E. crassipes*. This time, other species (*Niphograpta albiguttalis*, *O. terebrantis*, and *E. catarinensis*) were used as a new biological method, but it did not help in *E. crassipes* control. In 1998, the same situation of large area coverage occurred again as increased precipitation accelerated the growth of *E. crassipes*. *N. eichhorniae* was used the second time at the dam, reducing the coverage to 10% in 2000. According to the research analysis, this success was summarized into three important reasons: (1) the dam system is oligotrophic, so less nutrient for *E. crassipes* growth; (2) the life cycle of *N. eichhorniae* was extended by seasonal weather; and (3) biological control was conducted without any pressure of *E. crassipes* removal.

For over a century, water hyacinth has been presented as a problematic invasive species to water systems in Louisiana. Primary treatment strategies up until the 1970s included mechanical removal and herbicide control. Since then, biological control agents have become more prominent. Four insect biological control agents have been introduced in Louisiana: *Neochetina eichhorniae* and *N. bruchi* from 1974 to 1977, *Niphograpta albiguttalis* from 1979 to 1981, and *Megamelus scutellaris* from 2010 to 2016, with the most successful being *N. eichhorniae*, or the mottled water hyacinth weevil, at establishing and dispersing throughout the state (Wainger et al. 2018). *Neochetina* spp. reduces water hyacinth vigor through larval and adult feeding which reduces production, fertility and spread, and increases susceptibility to herbicides. *Neochetina* spp. remains widespread in Louisiana despite lack of any new release since the late 1980s. Additionally, no other biological control agents have been released since 2017 with the primary management tool currently being herbicide treatments (Wainger et al. 2018).

Remaining Challenges

Some areas, despite best efforts to eradicate the invasion of *E. crassipes*, have not been successful. New research suggests control efforts move away from eradication and instead focus on utilization of the species. Through an integrated approach of removal and usage, one study poses a solution for Lake Victoria, where even after millions of dollars spent in control programs, water hyacinth remains a serious issue for the East African region (Guerena et al. 2015). While the study points to energy production being a viable usage for water hyacinth, it is also mentioned that current technologies hinder the effectiveness and efficiency as well as produce high operating costs for such a process to be achieved. However, theoretical capabilities of water hyacinth becoming a sustainable fuel supply are very high since an individual plant can produce daughter plants equivalent to 28,000 tons of fresh weight in a single year (Ruan et al. 2016). More research and efforts should be focused on novel uses of biomass in order to produce better management strategies of invaded regions.

REFERENCES

Adebayo, A.A., E. Briski, O. Kalaci, M. Hernandez, S. Ghabooli, B. Beric, F.T. Chan, A. Zhan, E. Fifield, T. Leadley, and H.J. MacIsaac. 2011. Water hyacinth (*Eichhornia crassipes*) and water lettuce (*Pistia stratiotes*) hit the Great Lakes: Playing with fire? *Aquatic Invasions* 6(1): 91–96.

Adekoya, B.B., G.N. Ugwuzor, K.B. Olurin, O.A. Sodeinde, and O.A. Ekpo 1993. A comparative assessment of the methods of control of water hyacinth infestation with regards to fish production. In: 10th Annual Conference of the Fisheries Society of Nigeria (FISON), 16–20 November 1992, Abeokuta, pp. 181–184.

Barrett, S.C.H. 1980. Sexual reproduction in Eichornia crassipes (water hyacinth) II. Seed production in natural populations. *Journal of Applied Ecology* 17: 113–124.

Bicudo, D.D., B.M. Fonseca, L.M. Bini, L.O. Crossetti, C.E.D. Bicudo, and T. Araujo-Jesus. 2007. Undesirable side-effects of water hyacinth control in a shallow tropical reservoir. *Freshwater Biology* 52: 1120–1133.

Brundu, G., M.M. Azzella, C. Blasi, L. Camarda, M. Iberite, and L. Celesti-Grapow. 2013. The silent invasion of *Eichhornia crassipes* (Mart.) Solms. in Italy. *Plant Biosystems-An International Journal Dealing with all Aspects of Plant Biology* 147(4): 1120–1127.

Chuang, Y.S., C.H. Lay, B. Sen, C.C. Chen, K. Gopalakrishnan, J.H. Wu, C.S. Lin, and C.Y. Lin. 2011. Biohydrogen and biomethane from water hyacinth (Eichhornia crassipes) fermentation: effects of substrate concentration and incubation temperature. *International Journal of Hydrogen Energy* 36: 14195–14203.

Coetzee, J.A., M.P. Hill, T. Ruiz-Téllez, U. Starfinger, and S. Brunel. 2017. Monographs on invasive plants in Europe N° 2: Eichhornia crassipes (Mart.) *Solms. Botany Letters* 164(4): 303–326.

Dagno, K., R. Lahlali, M. Diourté, and M.H. Jijakli. 2011. Effect of Temperature and Water Activity on Spore Germination and Mycelial Growth of Three Fungal Biocontrol Agents against Water Hyacinth (Eichhornia Crassipes). *Journal of Applied Microbiology* 110 (2): 521–28.

Department of Wildlife & Fisheries Sciences (DWFS) (n.d.) Frog's-Bit, Limnobium spongia. Department of Wildlife & Fisheries Sciences, Texas A&M AgriLife Extension Service https://agrilife.org/aquaplant/plant-identification/alphabetical-index/frogs-bit/ (Accessed March 30, 2020).

Driesche, F.V., B. Blossey, M. Hoodle, S. Lyon, and R. Reardon. 2002. Biological Control of Invasive Plants in the Eastern United States. United States Department of Agriculture Forest Service, Forest Health Technology Enterprise Team, Morgantown, West Virginia. 413 p.

Gaurav, G.K., T. Mehmood, L. Cheng, J.J. Klemeš, and D.K. Shrivastava. 2020. Water hyacinth as a biomass: A review. *Journal of Cleaner Production* 277: 122214.

Global Invasive Species Database (GISD). 2006. Species profile: Eichhornia crassipes. Downloaded from www.iucngisd.org/gisd/species.php?sc=70 (Accessed March 30, 2020).

Gopal, B. 1987. Water hyacinth. Elsevier Science Publishers, Amsterdam, 477 p.

Greenfield, B.K., M. Blankinship, and T.J. McNabb. 2006. Control costs, operation, and permitting issues for non-chemical plant control: Case studies in the San Francisco Bay-Delta Region, California. *Journal of Aquatic Plant Management* 44: 40–49.

Greenfield, B.K., G.S. Siemering, J.C. Andrews, M. Rajan, S.P. Andrews, and D.F. Spencer. 2007. Mechanical shredding of water hyacinth (Eichhornia crassipes): effects on water quality in the Sacramento-San Joaquin River Delta, California. *Estuaries and Coasts* 30: 627–640.

Güereña, D., H. Neufeldt, J. Berazneva, and S. Duby. 2015. Water hyacinth control in Lake Victoria: Transforming an ecological catastrophe into economic, social, and environmental benefits. *Sustainable Production and Consumption* 3: 59–69.

Hill, M.P., and T. Olckers. 2000. Biological control initiatives against water hyacinth in South Africa: constraining factors, success and new courses of action, M.H. Julien, T.D. Center, M.P. Hill (Eds.), Second IOBC Global Working Group on the Biological and Integrated Control of Water Hyacinth, ACIAR, Beijing, China pp. 33–38.

Hopper, J., P. Pratt, K. Mccue, M. Pitcairn, P. Moran, and J. Madsen. 2017. Spatial and temporal variation of biological control agents associated with Eichhornia crassipes in the Sacramento-San Joaquin River Delta, California. *Biological Control* 111: 13–22.

ITIS (Integrated Taxonomic Information System). 2021. *www.itis.gov/servlet/SingleRpt/SingleRpt#null* (Accessed February 2, 2021).

Julien, M. 2001. Biological control of water hyacinth with arthropods: a review to 2000. In: Julien, M., Hill, M., Center, T., Ding, J. (Eds.), *Proceedings of the Meeting of the Global Working Group for the Biological and Integrated Control of Water Hyacinth, Beijing, China*, 9–12 December. Australian Centre for International Agricultural Research, Canberra pp. 8–20.

Koutika, L.S., and H.J. Rainey. 2015. A review of the invasive, biological and beneficial characteristics of aquatic species *Eichhornia Crassipes* and *salvinia molesta*. *Applied Ecology and Environmental Research*. 13: 263–275.

Kriticos, D.J., and S. Brunel. 2016. Assessing and Managing the Current and Future Pest Risk from Water Hyacinth, (Eichhornia crassipes), an Invasive Aquatic Plant Threatening the Environment and Water Security. *PLoS One* 11(8): e0120054.

Liu, J., X. Chen, Y. Wang, X. Li, D. Yu, and C. Liu. 2016. Response differences of Eichhornia crassipes to shallow submergence and drawdown with an experimental warming in winter. *Aquatic Ecology* 50(2) 307–314.

Mattson, M.D., P.J. Godfrey, R.A. Barletta, A. Aiello, and K.J. Wagner 2004. *Eutrophication and Aquatic Plant Management in Massachusetts: Final Generic Environmental Impact Report*. Washington, DC: Commonwealth of Massachusetts, Executive Office of Environmental Affairs Commonwealth of Massachusetts, vol. 4, pp. 29–80.

Mengistu, B.B., D. Unbushe, and E. Abebe. 2017. Invasion of Water Hyacinth (*Eichhornia crassipes*) Is Associated with Decline in Macrophyte Biodiversity in an Ethiopian Rift-Valley Lake—Abaya. *Open Journal of Ecology* 7(13): 667–681.

Nesslage, G.M., L.A. Wainger, N.E. Harms, and A.F. Cofrancesco. 2016. Quantifying the population response of invasive water hyacinth, Eichhornia crassipes, to biological control and winter weather in Louisiana, USA. *Biological Invasions* 18(7): 2107–2115.

Osei-Agyemang, M. 2002. Introduced Species Summary Project, Water Hyacinth (Eichhorinia crassipies) www.columbia.edu/itc/cerc/danoff-burg/invasion_bio/inv_spp_summ/water%252520hyacinth.html (Accessed March 30, 2020).

Pérez, E.A., J.A. Coetzee, T.R. Tellez, and M.P. Hill. 2011a. A first report of water hyacinth (*Eichhornia crassipes*) soil seed banks in South Africa. *South African Journal of Botany* 77(3): 795–800.

Pérez, E.A., T.R. Téllez, and J.M. Sánchez Guzmán. 2011b. Influence of physico-chemical parameters of the aquatic medium on germination of *Eichhornia crassipes* seeds. *Plant Biology* 13(4): 643–648.

Perna, C., and D. Burrows 2005. Improved dissolved oxygen status following removal of exotic weed mats in important fish habitat lagoons of the tropical Burdekin River floodplain, Australia. *Marine Pollution Bulletin* 51: 138–148.

Portilla, M.A., and S.P. Lawler. 2020. Herbicide treatment alters the effects of water hyacinth on larval mosquito abundance. *Journal of Vector Ecology* 45(1): 69–81.

Robinson, M. 2003. *Potential Invader, Water Hyacinth: An Exotic Aquatic Plant*. Cambridge, MA: Massachusetts Department of Conservation and Recreation; Office of Water Resources; Lakes and Ponds Program, p. 3.

Rommens, W., J. Maes, N. Dekeza, P. Inghelbrecht, T. Nhiwatiwa, E. Holsters, F. Ollevier, B. Marshall, and L. Brendonck 2003. The impact of water hyacinth (*Eichhornia crassipes*) in a eutrophic subtropical impoundment (Lake Chivero, Zimbabwe). I. Water quality. *Archiv Fur Hydrobiologie* 158: 373–388.

Ruan, T., R. Zeng, X. Yin, S. Zhang, and Z. Yang. 2016. Water hyacinth (Eichhornia crassipes) biomass as a biofuel feedstock by enzymatic hydrolysis. *BioResources* 11(1): 2372–2380.

Seagrave, C. 1988. *Aquatic Weed Control.* Surrey: Fishing New Books.

Shabana, Y.M., and Z.A. Mohamed 2005. Integrated control of water hyacinth with a mycoherbicide and phenylpropanoid pathway inhibitor. *Biocontrol Science and Technology* 15: 659–669.

Shanab, S.M.M., E.A. Shalaby, D.A. Lightfoot, and H.A. El-Shemy. 2010. Allelopathic effects of water hyacinth [*Eichhornia crassipes*]. *PLoS One* 5(10): e13200.

Sosa, A.J., H.A. Cordo, and J. Sacco 2007. Preliminary evaluation of *Megamelus seutellaris* Berg (Hemiptera: Delphacidae), a candidate for biological control of water hyacinth. *Biological Control* 42: 129–138.

Thomas, R., A. Kane, and B.G. Bierwagen. 2008. *Effects of Climate Change on Aquatic Invasive Species and Implications for Management and Research.* Lincoln, NE: University of Nebraska—Lincoln.

Tipping, P.W., M.R. Martin, E.N. Pokorny, K.R. Nimmo, D.L. Fitzgerald, F.A. Dray, and T.D. Center. 2014. Current levels of suppression of waterhyacinth in Florida USA by classical biological control agents. *Biological Control* 71: 65–69.

Tobias, V.D., Conrad, J.L., Mahardja, B., and S. Khanna. 2019. Impacts of water hyacinth treatment on water quality in a tidal estuarine environment. *Biological Invasions* 21: 3479–3490.

UF/IFAS, Center for Aquatic and Invasive Plants. n.d. *Limnobium Spongia.* University of Florida, Institute of Food and Agricultural Sciences, Center for Aquatic and Invasive Plants http://plants.ifas.ufl.edu/plant-directory/limnobium-spongia/ (Accessed March 30, 2020).

Uremis, I., A. Uludag, Z.F. Arslan, and O. Abaci. 2014. A new record for the flora of Turkey: *E ichhornia crassipes* (Mart.) Solms (Pontederiaceae). *EPPO Bulletin* 44(1): 83–86.

Villamagna, A.M. 2009. The Ecological Effects of Water Hyacinth (*Eichhornia crassipes*) on Lake Chapala, Mexico. PhD Thesis. Virginia Polytechnic Institute and State University, Blacksburg, VA.

Villamagna, A.M., and B. Murphy. 2010. Ecological and socio-economic impacts of invasive water hyacinth (*Eichhornia crassipes*): A review. *Freshwater Biology* 55: 282–298.

Wainger, L.A., N.E. Harms, C. Magen, D. Liang, G.M. Nesslage, A.M. Mcmurray, and A.F. Cofrancesco. 2018. Evidence-based economic analysis demonstrates that ecosystem service benefits of water hyacinth management greatly exceed research and control costs. *PeerJ* 6: e4824.

Waltham, N.J., L. Coleman, C. Buelow, S. Fry, and D. Burrows. 2020. Restoring fish habitat values on a tropical agricultural floodplain: Learning from two decades of aquatic invasive plant maintenance efforts. *Ocean & Coastal Management* 198: 105355.

Waltham, N.J., and S. Fixler. 2017. Aerial herbicide spray to control invasive water hyacinth (*Eichhornia crassipes*): Water quality concerns fronting fish occupying a tropical floodplain wetland. *Tropical Conservation Science* 10: 1–10.

Wang, H., Q. Wang, P.A. Bowler, and W. Xiong. 2016. Invasive aquatic plants in China. *Aquatic Invasions* 11(1): 1–9.

Wang, Z., Z. Zhang, J. Zhang, Y. Zhang, H. Liu, and S. Yan. 2012. Large-scale utilization of water hyacinth for nutrient removal in Lake Dianchi in China: the effects on the water quality, macrozoobenthos and zooplankton. *Chemosphere* 89(10): 1255–1261.

Wilson, J.R., O. Ajuonu, T.D. Center, M.P. Hill, M.H. Julien, FF. Katagira, P. Neuenschwander, S.W. Njoka, J. Ogwang, R.H. Reeder, and T. Van. 2007. The decline of water hyacinth on Lake Victoria was due to biological control by Neochetina spp. *Aquatic Botany* 87: 90–93.

Wilson, J.R., N. Holst, and M. Rees. 2005. Determinants and patterns of population growth in water hyacinth. *Aquatic Botany* 81(1): 51–67.

You, W., D. Yu, D. Xie, and L. Yu. 2013. Overwintering survival and regrowth of the invasive plant Eichhornia crassipes are enhanced by experimental warming in winter. *Aquatic Biology* 19(1): 45–53.

Yu, H., X. Dong, D. Yu, C. Liu, and S. Fan. 2019. Effects of eutrophication and different water levels on overwintering of *Eichhornia crassipes* at the northern margin of its distribution in China. *Frontiers in Plant Science* 10: 1261.

Yu, H., N. Shen, D. Yu, and C. Liu, C. 2019. Clonal integration increases growth performance and expansion of *Eichhornia crassipes* in littoral zones: A simulation study. *Environmental and Experimental Botany* 159: 13–22.

Zhang, X., H. Yu, T. Lv, L. Yang, C. Liu, S. Fan, and D. Yu. 2021. Effects of different scenarios of temperature rise and biological control agents on interactions between two noxious invasive plants. *Diversity and Distributions* 27(12): 2300–2314.

16 European Waterclover (*Marsilea quadrifolia* L.)

ABSTRACT

European waterclover *Marsilea quadrifolia*, also called water shamrock, is an herbaceous perennial aquatic plant, which grows in slow-moving water environments. *M. quadrifolia* has been established in the northeastern United States for around 100 years. Prior research reported that *M. quadrifolia* spreads at a slow speed and poses a relatively weak threat to the environment (Benson et al. 2004). The distribution of known *M. quadrifolia* species was mapped based on historical data for Massachusetts. More comprehensive monitoring on *M. quadrifolia* has been developed for a better understanding on its distribution, so that further spread of *M. quadrifolia* can be minimized in Massachusetts, and the general public can be aware of the infestations of this species.

INTRODUCTION

Taxonomic Hierarchy (ITIS 2021)

Kingdom	Plantae
Subkingdom	Viridiplantae
Infrakingdom	Streptophyta
Superdivision	Embryophyta
Division	Tracheophyta
Subdivision	Polypodiophytina
Class	Polypodiopsida
Subclass	Polypodiidae
Order	Salviniales
Family	Marsileaceae
Genus	*Marsilea* L.
Species	*Marsilea quadrifolia* L.

BIOLOGY

European waterclover *Marsilea quadrifolia* is an amphibious heterosporous fern that can produce submerged and emergent leaves on the same plant (Kao and Lin 2010) (Figure 16.1). In the aquatic environment, it usually is found in ponds, rivers, streams, muddy shorelines, or roadside ditches (Benson et al. 2004). The species may grow in dense patches or interspersed among other vegetation and be found in shallow waters as well as survive some water-level fluctuation (Kiran et al. 2007). The roots of *M. quadrifolia* are fleshy and creeping; the thin green stems from rhizomes bear only one leaf with four leaflets resembling a four-leaf clover. The mature green clover-like leaves are usually glabrous and 1.5–4 cm in width (Benson et al. 2004; Cao and Berent 2020). Sporocarps form at approximately 1.2 cm above where the leaf branches from the rhizome and are spherical, approximately 4–5 mm long and either hairy or smooth (Holm et al. 1997). They contain both small, male microspores and larger, female megaspores. Additionally, *M. quadrifolia* is able to form dense mats and has the ability to adjust leaflet angle for sunlight optimization, both of which allow it to outcompete native species causing for local concern (Hackett et al. 2018).

M. quadrifolia may be distinguished from other plant species by its four-leaflet arrangement, aquatic habitat, and sporocarps found near the base of the leaves. However, sporocarps typically develop after the leaves and may not always be present, as they do not mature until the leaf has withered for the winter (Johnson 1986).

Additional detection methods may include the use of aerial imagery as well as identifying genetic markers in the aquatic system. Aerial imagery has been used by experts to distinguish emergent and floating aquatic vegetation (Husson et al. 2013). However, due to the size of *M. quadrifolia* in addition to its variable density, detection may be difficult without high spatial resolution. This method may also be limited in its ability to distinguish *M. quadrifolia* from other aquatic vegetation in mixed stands or along shores with tree canopies. In using genetic markers, any genetic material shed by organisms into the environment can be detected early via monitoring and has

FIGURE 16.1 European waterclover. (Photo by A.A. Reznicek (Reznicek et al. 2011).)

been demonstrated in various studies (Hackett et al. 2018). Using such methods has the potential to increase the efficacy of field detection and monitoring of *M. quadrifolia* during the growing season. Although little research has been conducted on identifying genetic material shed from this aquatic plant species, this sampling approach could reduce the need for labor-intensive field surveys until *M. quadrifolia* was already detected in the area (Scriver et al. 2015).

Marsilea quadrifolia might be considered as *Marsilea minuta* or *Marsilea mutica* by mistake because they all have glabrous, fleshy leaves. However, *Marsilea minuta* or *Marsilea mutica* prefer the warmer climate of the southeast, while *Marsilea quadrifolia* has not been identified in south regions (Cao and Berent 2020). In addition, *Marsilea mutica* has obvious characteristics that are different from *Marsilea quadrifolia* (Benson et al. 2004). The *Marsilea mutica* leaves have two colors, lighter in the center and darker toward the margins, and the sporocarps completely lack teeth. However, the *Marsilea quadrifolia* leaves are solid green and the sporocarps bear a tooth.

Native and Invasive Range

M. quadrifolia is native to tropical and warm temperate regions from areas of Eurasia to North and South America. The native range includes Caucasia, western Siberia, Afghanistan, southwest India, China, Japan, and Americas (Cao and Berent 2020). However, in some research,

M. quadrifolia was reported as a non-indigenous plant with a century of establishment history in the United States (Benson et al. 2004). While globally classified as a species of least concern, *M. quadrifolia* is labeled as a vulnerable and endangered species in Japan as well as 21 European countries (Strat 2012). In many European countries, such as Italy, Portugal, and Spain, *M. quadrifolia* has been assessed as Endangered or even Critically Endangered (Bruni et al. 2013). Other countries in southeast Asia and the Mediterranean consider *M. quadrifolia* a weed, particularly in rice fields (Holm et al. 1997). In North America, *M. quadrifolia* has been documented in at least 19 states as well as Ontario, Canada. In the United States, it is listed as a priority exotic species on the Michigan "Watch List" as an immediate and significant threat to natural resources (Hackett et al. 2018).

According to the USGS (2020) database, *M. quadrifolia* was first found at Lacey-Keosauqua State Park, Van Buren, Iowa, in 1821. It was first reported in Connecticut at Bantam Lake in 1860 with conflicting ideas of origin and threat; however, it was later found to have spread to parts of Massachusetts and other areas of New England by 1900 (Les and Mehrhoff 1999). Recently, it has been confirmed in 21 states of the United States (USGS 2020). Massachusetts is reported to have the most extensive infestations in the Charles, Concord, Sudbury, and Connecticut Rivers (Benson et al. 2004). The first time *M. quadrifolia* was detected in Massachusetts was at a Botanical Garden in Middlesex county in 1868 (USGS 2020).

Plant species are directly affected by regional rainfall and evaporation patterns as the physiological functions involved in seed dormancy and germination are interrupted through the processes of drying and soaking. Due to climate change, areas around the coasts and wetlands especially experience increased flooding events, changes in rainfall distribution patterns, in addition to more severe downpours, storms, and hurricanes (Kathiresan and Gualbert 2016). In the Cauvery River delta region in India, the average rainfall in recent decades has increased while the rate of evaporation has decreased in comparison to the prior decade (Kathiresan and Gualber 2016). A survey of this region found *M. quadrifolia* invading wetland rice fields, dominating over native weeds such as *Echinochloa* spp. (barnyard grass or cockspur grass) as well as others. This is believed to be due to the species' adaptation and ability to live in alternating flooded and higher soil moisture conditions, which have been prevalent in recent years in the region. These findings suggest, as warming temperatures and rainfall trends continue to increase, *M. quadrifolia*, as well as other amphibious plant species, may have a higher advantage over native species and continue to expand their invasive range (Kathiresan and Gualber 2016).

Furthermore, in the sexual reproduction process of *M. quadrifolia*, it was found that the optimal temperature for male spores was 77–86°F (25–30°C) (Hackett et al. 2018). As waterbodies warm, there may be more optimal conditions for *M. quadrifolia* to spread and reproduce effectively.

Mechanisms/Vectors of Spread

M. quadrifolia can reproduce by vegetative and sexual methods (Cao and Berent 2020). The vegetative method relies on its rhizome structure, which is its main reproductive approach. It can also persist throughout the winter seasons because of the underground rhizomes (Benson et al. 2004). During the growing season, *M. quadrifolia* plants are able to adjust the angle of the floating leaflets to optimize access to sunlight and the ability to photosynthesize (Kao and Lin 2010). *M. quadrifolia* can easily spread within connected waterbodies as the rhizome apex sheds and drift around, which allows for reproduction (Hackett et al. 2018). It is unknown what effect asexual reproduction has on long-distance dispersal as research has not concluded how long rhizome fragments can survive desiccation (Johnson 1986).

In addition, *M. quadrifolia* can also reproduce by male and female spore germination and cross-fertilization (Benson et al. 2004). The plant produces sporocarps, which are considered to be a modified leaf or leaflet. As sporocarps are disturbed or lightly abraded while immersed in water, they swell and burst to release spores which are germinated (Soni and Singh 2012). The sporocarp itself doesn't fully mature until the leaves have withered and it is believed light triggers sporocarp germination, which typically occurs after the leaves have matured (Johnson 1986). Furthermore, sporocarps have two external cell layers and internal gelatinous tissue which protect the spores from the environment and premature release in animal digestive tracts (Bloom 1955). The sporocarps can be easily dispersed by waterfowl or remain dormant in the soil for decades (Benson et al. 2004).

ECOLOGICAL IMPACTS

The plant is labeled as a noxious weed in India and becoming an increasing concern while also being considered a vulnerable species in Japan (Luo and Ikeda 2007). There are only few studies that have explored the ecological impacts of *M. quadrifolia*. As previously mentioned, in some European countries, it has been listed as an endangered species. *M. quadrifolia* is reported to have been previously managed in Massachusetts, and is considered as a problem species in at least some instances (Mattson et al. 2004; Wagner 2004). However, there is not enough scientific literature or research found evaluating any negative effects from *M. quadrifolia* on native species, food web, animals, water environment, etc. (SOM 2018).

There are conflicting reports whether *M. quadrifolia* spreads aggressively and how much of a threat it poses ecologically. In one study, *M. quadrifolia* was found to have only migrated 151 ft per year and a total of 1 mile downstream in 35 years (Henry and Myers 1983).

As for possible impacts, *M. quadrifolia* has the ability to adjust the angle of floating leaflets for sunlight optimization, which may allow it to outcompete neighboring species (Kao and Lin 2010). Additionally, *M. quadrifolia* creates dense monoculture of stands that can survive through winter seasons due to underground rhizomes (NOAA n.d.). This strategy proves beneficial in competition against native plants as well.

ECONOMIC IMPACTS

The economic impacts of *M. quadrifolia* have not been quantitatively studied (SOM 2018), but in some instances there might be some expenditure on control or management.

POSITIVE ASPECTS

Plenty of researchers have certified the medical values of *M. quadrifolia* (Longman 1997; Ripa et al. 2009; Khan and Manzoor 2010; Ashwini et al. 2012; Manjula and Mythili 2012; Mathangi and Prabahakaran 2012; Reddy et al. 2012; Soni and Singh 2012; Uma and Pravin 2013; Gopalakrishnan and Udayakumar 2014; Agarwal et al. 2018). *M. quadrifolia* is high in nutrient content, which can be used to reduce body heat and thirst. It can also be used to treat cough, bronchitis, diabetes, psychiatric diseases, eye diseases, diarrhea, and skin diseases. *M. quadrifolia* has been used in traditional treatments for hypnotic, leprosy, hemorrhoids, fever, insomnia, as a cough expectorant, etc. In addition, this plant was found posing potential antimicrobial activity.

For the environment, *M. quadrifolia* can promote nutrient mitigation from freshwater and contribute to wetland restoration.[1] In studies of sequestering of heavy metal by aquatic plants, *M. quadrifolia* showed the bioaccumulation of cadmium and chromium (SOM 2018).

MONITORING AND SIGHTINGS

The *M. quadrifolia* observation records in Massachusetts waterbodies were collected by the Massachusetts Department of Environmental Protection (MassDEP) and the Department of Conservation & Recreation (DCR). The standard operating procedures, including sampling methodology, species identification, quality control and assurance, were implemented during the sample collections. Sites with *M. quadrifolia* were mapped as a data layer with ArcGIS® ArcMap 10.1 (ESRI, Redlands, California). Mapping the *M. quadrifolia* distribution areas can help to inform future decisions and regulations for controlling the spread of this potentially invasive species.

Data was collected from MassDEP Water Quality Assessment Reports and DCR Lakes and Ponds Program Database (Table 16.1). An ArcGIS map was created to show the distribution of *M. quadrifolia* in Massachusetts (Figure 16.2), which can be used for the future decisions on nuisance plant control and prevention. Currently, there are 9 waterbodies (Table 16.2) within 6 watersheds (Table 16.3) that are infested by *M. quadrifolia* in Massachusetts. Among them, 6 are lakes/ponds and three are rivers (Tables 16.1 and 16.2).

TABLE 16.1
Waterbodies Infested by European Waterclover

Waterbody	Agency	Report Source	First Year Reported
Batemans Pond	MassDEP	SuAsCo Watershed 2001 Water Quality Assessment Report 82-AC-1 CN 92.0, August 2005	2005
Charles River	MassDEP	Charles River Watershed 2002–2006 Water Quality Assessment Report 72-AC-4 CN136.5, April 2008	2008
First Pond	DCR	DCR Data from Lakes and Ponds, 2006	2006
Lake Waban	MassDEP	Charles River Watershed 2002–2006 Water Quality Assessment Report 72-AC-4 CN136.5, April 2008	2008
Lake Waban	DCR	DCR Data from ACT, GeoSyntec-ACT	Not Available
Massapoag Brook	MassDEP	1994 Resource Assessment Report	1994
Prospect Lake	MassDEP	Housatonic River Watershed 2002 Water Quality Assessment Report 21-AC-4 CN141.5, September 2007	2007
Saxonville Pond	MassDEP	SuAsCo Watershed 2001 Water Quality Assessment Report 82-AC-1 CN 92.0, August 2005	2005
Stevens Pond	MassDEP	Ipswich River Watershed 2000 Water Quality Assessment Report 92-AC-1 088.0, April 2004	2004
Sudbury River	Individual	Joy Trahan-Liptak	2013

TABLE 16.2
Towns and Infested Waterbodies

Number	Waterbody	Town
1	Batemans Pond	Concord
2	Charles River	Dover, Newton
3	First Pond	Saugus
4	Lake Waban	Wellesley
5	Massapoag Brook	Sharon, Canton
6	Prospect Lake	Egremont
7	Saxonville Pond	Framingham
8	Stevens Pond	Boxford
9	Sudbury River	Concord, Lincoln, Sudbury, and Wayland

M. quadrifolia is a highly valuable plant for the ecosystem and human health. Currently, this species does not pose aggressive competition and fast spreading. According to the records from MassDEP, there is no significant *M. quadrifolia* distribution that has occurred in recent years in Massachusetts, but the potential economic loss and ecological impact cannot be underestimated. An effective control method should be applied for an infested waterbody. For a waterbody has not been invaded or is at risk to be invaded, prevention methods should be conducted before the expansion of this species.

MANAGING ACTIONS

There are various methods for controlling the spread of *M. quadrifolia*. The management measures range from preventative measures to physical and chemical management methods.

TABLE 16.3
Infested Watersheds

Number	Infested Watersheds
1	Housatonic River
2	Charles River
3	Concord (SuAsCo) River
4	Ipswich River
5	North Coastal Drainage
6	Boston Harbor (Neponset) Drainage

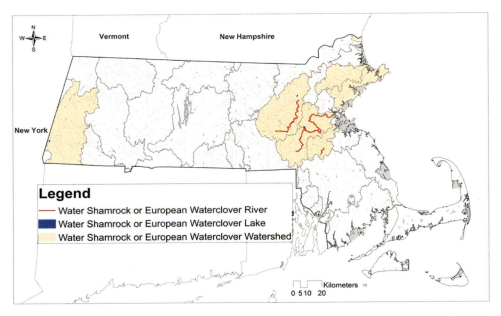

FIGURE 16.2 Distribution map depicting European waterclover (*M. quadrifolia*) in Massachusetts. (See Table 16.1 for site descriptions.)

Biological method of control for *M. quadrifolia* is currently unknown. The choice of management method(s) depends on the invasion range, water quality conditions, weather, management budget, regulatory restrictions, etc.

Preventative measures may assist in minimizing the spread and distribution of a particular invasive species. *M. quadrifolia* is considered a "Watch List species" in certain states. Sometimes species may be subject to restrictions or prohibition on the possession, introduction, importation, or selling of a species (Hackett et al. 2018). These are examples of ways to prevent the spread of an invasive species. In the case of *M. quadrifolia*, further methods include encouraging water garden and aquarium enthusiasts to use native or non-invasive species and educating user groups of the proper disposal of unwanted plants. The identification and monitoring of waterbodies at higher risk of invasion as well as actively managing known *M. quadrifolia* sites aid in preventative measures as well (Hackett et al. 2018).

Physical management methods include hand pulling, shading, dredging, and benthic barriers (SOM 2018). Hand pulling was found to be as effective as, or even more effective than chemical control methods, in rice field infestations of *M. quadrifolia* (Anwar et al. 2013; Popy et al. 2017). *M. quadrifolia* prefers semi-shade or no shade environment, which means physical shading by completely blocking sunlight can inhibit the plant's growth. Dredging is a sediment removal process that controls the rooted plant growth through light limitation (by adding depth to a waterbody) or substrate limitation (by removing or changing the substrate in which the plant would survive). Benthic barriers are a control method proposed by MassDEP, which could be applied in small areas such as swimming beaches to control this invasive species.

Instead of the above methods, chemical control via herbicide use is also one of the most popular management approaches for nuisance and/or invasive plant control. For the management of *M. quadrifolia*, two types of experiments have been conducted to understand the impacts of chemical treatments on this species. These include the effectiveness of herbicides at controlling *M. quadrifolia* as a rice field weed without damaging rice production and researching the effects of herbicide runoff on growth of *M. quadrifolia* as an endangered species in Eurasia (Bruni et al. 2013). These studies, although different from the intent of this document, may be useful for further investigation of effective methods in *M. quadrifolia* management. Diquat and glyphosate have been recognized as effective for controlling *M. quadrifolia*, but do not achieve complete control and may require higher doses or special environmental conditions (Mattson et al. 2004; Wagner 2004). The State of Michigan reported a summary table of effective herbicide active ingredients for *M. quadrifolia* control (Hackett et al. 2018). The effective active ingredients include Bensulfuron-methyl, Bensulfuron-methyl + pretilachlor, Cyhalofop-butyl, Imazamox + Glyphosate, Mustard crop residue, Pendimethalin, Penoxsulam, Pretilachlor, Profoxydim, and Simetryn. The corresponding herbicide products include Londax™, Londax™ Power, Clincher®, Clearcast® + AquaPro®, Drexel Aquapen®, Viper® India, Aura® (Table 16.4). However, many of the above treatments have not been studied extensively either in field research or their effectiveness on regrowth. In addition, many of the listed chemicals such as Bensulfuron-methyl, Bensulfuron-methyl + pretilachlor, Cyhalofop-butyl, and Pendimethalin are toxic to fish and other invertebrates. Others such as Penoxsulam, Profoxydim, and Imazamox + glyphosate have restrictive usage especially in aquatic environments. The State of Michigan warns that directions on pesticide labels should always be followed and the appropriate state departments be consulted for up-to-date regulations, restrictions, permitting, licensing, and application information (Hackett et al. 2018). Plant regrowth can usually occur after an initial treatment, therefore repeated applications of herbicides are typically needed. Please note that all the aforementioned management methods have other potential impacts to a waterbody that should be considered when choosing a management approach and may require regulatory approval before proceeding. More information about chemical control on this species and other 18 invasive species can be found in Appendix III. Any chemical used for aquatic invasive species control requires a WM04 Chemical Application License issued by the Massachusetts Department of Environmental Protection.

SUCCESS STORY

Wet direct-sown rice planting is a very popular method of crop establishment among Asian countries in recent years. However, direct-sown rice is more easily affected by *M. quadrifolia* growth when compared to the transplanting system (Saha and Rao 2010). This is because the *M. quadrifolia* has a more similar growth period with wet direct-sown rice, leading to a competitive relationship (Saha 2008). Plant competition may cause a reduction of rice when harvested, therefore an effective management for *M. quadrifolia* control is needed.

In the dry seasons of 2016 and 2017, chemical herbicides were applied in the wet direct-sown rice field for weed control at Cuttack, Odisha, India. Bensulfuron-methyl was applied alone as well as mixed with pretilachlor in the rice field to examine the efficacy. After a month of sowing, the major weed flora in the rice field included *Echinochloa colona* (i.e., jungle rice) (8.7%), *Cyperus difformis* (i.e., variable flat-sedge, smallflower umbrella-sedge, or rice sedge) (26.1%), *Fimbristylis miliacea* (i.e., grasslike fimbry) (14.5%), *Sphenochlea zeylanica* (i.e., gooseweed or wedgewort) (27.5%), and *Marsilea quadrifolia* (i.e., European waterclover) (23.2%). Unfortunately, the results showed that there was

TABLE 16.4
Effective Herbicides for European Waterclover Control

Herbicide	Approved for Use in MA	Pros	Cons
Bensulfuron-methyl (Londax™)	No	• Effective in laboratory (90%) when applied at 0.022 pounds ai per acre, seven days after EWC transplant • Less harm to non-target plant species (Selective herbicide)	• Has not been tested in field • Regrowth not examined • Permitted for aquatic use in only rice fields • Moderate toxicity to fish, algae • Resistance can be built • Application in water less than 70°F delays activity
Bensulfuron-methyl + pretilachlor (e.g., Londax™ Power)	No	• Effective in rice field (88.1–95.1%) when applied at 0.054 + 0.54 pounds ai per acre, three days after rice transplant • Slightly more efficient than hand weeding	• Regrowth not examined • Experimented in rice field • Moderate toxicity to fish, aquatic invertebrates, algae
Cyhalofop-butyl (e.g., Clincher®)	No	• Effective in laboratory (80%) when applied at 0.005 ppm, four days after EWC transplant	• Has not been tested in field • Regrowth not examined • Toxic to fish and macroinvertebrates • Permitted for aquatic use in only rice fields • May contaminate groundwater • May harm non-target plant species (broad-spectrum, contact herbicide)
Imazamox + glyphosate (e.g., Clearcast® + AquaPro®)	Yes	• Possibly effective in pond in Michigan (anecdotal)	• Regrowth not yet monitored • Restricted concentration when near potable water intakes • Prohibited for use in waterbodies <½ mile from a potable water intake • May harm non-target species (broad-spectrum, systemic herbicide)
Mustard crop residue	No	• Effective in rice field (83.98–91.73%) at 2.0 ton/ha	• Residue not thoroughly described • Low number of replicates • Non-target effects not measured

Herbicide	Selective	Effectiveness	Notes
Pendimethalin (e.g., Drexel Aquapen®)	Yes	• Effective in rice field (59.5–73.2%) when applied at 0.071–0.76 pounds ai per acre, two days after rice transplant • Less harm to non-target plant species (selective herbicide)	• Used as pre-emergent with a post-control treatment (e.g., penoxsolum, 2,4-D amine, hand pulling) • Regrowth not examined • Toxic to fish • Permitted for aquatic use in only rice fields • Does not control established weeds
Penoxsulam (e.g., CLEANTRAXX)	Yes	• Effective in rice field (71.3–75.2%) when applied at 0.0179–0.0201 pounds ai per acre, 3–12 days after rice transplant • Effective in laboratory (95%) when applied at 20 ppm • Less harm to non-target plant species (selective herbicide)	• Not effective in pond with glyphosate due to next season regrowth (anecdotal) • Performed at almost same effectiveness as hand pulling • Regrowth not examined • Posttreatment irrigation water restrictions
Pretilachlor	No	• Effective in rice field (88.1–95.1%) when applied at 0.071–0.54 pounds ai per acre, two days after rice transplant • Less harm to non-target plant species (selective herbicide)	• Used as pre-emergent with a post-control treatment (e.g., penoxsolum, 2,4-D amine, hand pulling) • Regrowth not examined • Moderate toxicity to fish, aquatic invertebrates, algae • Permitted for aquatic use in only rice fields
Profoxydim (e.g., Aura®)	No	• Effective in laboratory (82–95%) when applied at 0.02–0.2 ppm, four days after EWC transplant • More effective with Dash™ HC adjuvant • Less harm to non-target plant species (selective herbicide)	• Has not been tested in field • Regrowth not examined • Permitted for aquatic use in only rice fields
Simetryn	No	• Effective in laboratory (significantly different from controls) when applied at 0.0004–40 μmol/l, when inoculated for ten days • Less harm to non-target plant species (selective herbicide)	• Has not been tested in field • Measured fresh weight (not dry) • Regrowth not examined • High toxicity to beneficial algae • Moderate toxicity to fish, aquatic invertebrates

Source: Modified from and specific references in Hackett et al. (2018).

about 50% reduction on the grain yield of rice after herbicide treatment because of the weed competition existing. However, in terms of the efficacy on overall weed control, both Bensulfuron-methyl and Bensulfuron-methyl + pretilachlor performed well. The applications of Bensulfuron-methyl at 60 g/ha and Bensulfuron-methyl + pretilachlor at 50 + 450 g/ha each successfully reduced the total weed density (especially *M. quadrifolia* density) and dry matter production with approximately 90% control.

Furthermore, control measures may be learned through practices and studies performed in areas of conservation. Although the purpose of such studies would be to protect and rebound the *M. quadrifolia* population, it may be discovered what methods have led to its decline adding to information on effective control measurements. One study (Corli et al. 2021), aimed at species recovery in the Po Valley in Northern Italy within paddy fields, discussed the conditions in which *M. quadrifolia* would thrive. While water chemistry was found to have limited effects on the species due to its wide ecological range, it was found shady conditions provided by rice canopies created micro-habitats suitable for *M. quadrifolia* to grow. In this study, *M. quadrifolia* was found to have poor or no capacity to adjust pigment composition to light level, in addition to having lower chlorophyll fluorescence values, suggesting the species undergoes stress in full-light habitats. In management, avoiding opportunity for growth under shady regions and maintaining open spaces within an affected waterbody may contribute to control practices. Additionally, the study found *M. quadrifolia* survived better in organic rice fields (with no herbicide use) as well as at conventional farms with reduced herbicide use. The use of glyphosate during the early development phase of *M. quadrifolia* (mid-May) was found to have possible detrimental effects leading to the die-off of the species. These results show how data from conservation studies may be used in management practice techniques in areas where *M. quadrifolia* is of concern.

NOTE

1. Any invasive species should be inhibited for ecological restoration projects.

REFERENCES

Agarwal, S.K., S. Roy, P. Pramanick, P. Mitra, R. Gobato, and R. Mitra. 2018. Marsilea quadrifolia: A floral species with unique medicinal properties. *Parana Journal of Science and Education* 4(5): 15–20.

Anwar, B.M., A. Hussain, M.A. Ganai, and N.A. Teli. 2013. Efficacy of penoxsulam against weeds in transplanted rice (Oryza sativa L.) under temperate conditions of Kashmir. *Applied Biological Research* 15: 145–148.

Ashwini, G., P. Pranay, G. Thrinath, R.T. Karnaker, and P.V.S. Giri. 2012. Pharmacological evaluation of *Marsilea qudrifolia* plant extracts against Alzheimer's disease. *International Journal of Drug Development and Research* 4(2): 153–158.

Benson, A.J., C.C. Jacono, P.L. Fuller, E.R. McKercher, and M.M. Richerson. 2004. *Summary Report of Nonindigenous Aquatic Species in U.S. Fish and Wildlife Service Region 5*. Arlington, VA: U.S. Fish and Wildlife Service, p. 145.

Bloom, W.W., 1955. Comparative viability of sporocarps of Marsilea quadrifolia L. in relation to age. *Transactions of the Illinois State Academy of Science* 47: 72–76.

Bruni, I., R. Gentili, D.F. Mattia, P. Cortis, G. Rossi, and M. Labra. 2013. A multi-level analysis to evaluate the extinction risk of and conservation strategy for the aquatic fern *Marsilea quadrifolia* L. in Europe. *Aquatic Botany* 111: 35–42.

Cao, L., and L. Berent. 2020. *Marsilea quadrifolia L.: U.S. Geological Survey, Nonindigenous Aquatic Species Database*. Gainesville, FL and Ann Arbor, MI: NOAA Great Lakes Aquatic Nonindigenous Species Information System, https://nas.er.usgs.gov/queries/GreatLakes/FactSheet.aspx?SpeciesID=293 (Accessed May 5, 2020).

Corli, A., S. Orsenigo, R. Gerdol, S. Bocchi, A.P. Smolders, L. Brancaleoni, and G. Rossi. 2021. Coexistence of rice production and threatened plant species: Testing *Marsilea quadrifolia* L. in N-Italy. *Paddy and Water Environment* 19: 395–400.

Gopalakrishnan, K., and R. Udayakumar. 2014. Antimicrobial activity of *Marsilea quadrifolia* (L.) against some selected pathogenic microorganisms. *Microbiology Research Journal International* 4(9): 1046–1056.

Hackett, R.A., B.C. Cahill, and A.K. Monfils. 2018. *2018 Status and Strategy for European Water-clover (Marsilea quadrifolia L.) Management*. Lansing, MI: Michigan Department of Environmental Quality, p. 30.

Henry, R.D., and R.M. Myers. 1983. Spread of *Marsilea quadrifolia* in McDonough County, Illinois. *American Fern Journal* 73(1): 30.

Holm, L., J. Doll, E. Holm, J. Pancho, and J. Herberger. 1997. *World Weeds: Natural Histories and Distribution*. New York, USA: John Wiley and Sons, pp. 455–461.

Husson, E., O. Hagner, and F. Ecke. 2013. Unmanned aircraft systems help to map aquatic vegetation. *Appl Veg Sci* 17: 567–577.

ITIS (Integrated Taxonomic Information System). 2021. *www.itis.gov/servlet/SingleRpt/SingleRpt#null* (Accessed March 27, 2021).

Johnson, D.M. 1986. Systematics of the new world species of Marsilea (Marsileaceae). *Syst Bot Mon* 11: 1–87.

Kathiresan, R., and G. Gualbert. 2016. Impact of climate change on the invasive traits of weeds. *Weed Biology and Management*, 16(2): 59–66.

Kao, W.K., and B.L. Lin. 2010. Phototropic leaf movements and photosynthetic performance in an amphibious fern, *Marsilea quadrifolia. Journal of Plant Research* 123(5): 645–653.

Khan, M.A., and A.S. Manzoor. 2010. Studies on biomass changes and nutrient lock-up efficiency in a Kashmir Himalayan wetland ecosystem. *J Ecol Nat Environ* 2(8): 147–153.

Kiran, B.R., E.T. Puttaiah, S. Raghavendra, and M. Ravikumar. 2007. Ecological studies on aquatic macrophytic vegetation in Shivaji Tank, Karnataka, India. *Plant Archives* 7: 637–639.

Les, D.H., and L.J. Mehrhoff, 1999. Introduction of nonindigenous aquatic vascular plants in Southern New England: A historical perspective. *Biological Invasions* 1, 281–300.

Longman, O., 1997. Indian medicinal plants, vol. 4 (Orient Longman Pvt. Ltd., Chennai, India) pp. 5–9.

Luo, X.Y., and H. Ikeda. 2007. Effects of four rice herbicides on the growth of an aquatic fern, *Marsilea quadrifolia* L. *Weed Biology and Management*, 7(4): 237–241.

Manjula, R., and T. Mythili. 2012. Improved phytochemical production using biotic and abiotic elicitors in *Marsilea quadrifolia*. *International Journal of Current Science Research and Review* 98–101.

Mathangi, T., and P. Prabahakaran. 2012. Screening for antimicrobial activity of the leaf extracts of *Marsilea quadrifolia* against various bacterial pathogens. *Herbal Tech Industry* 11–12.

Mattson, M.D., P.J. Godfrey, R.A. Barletta, and A. Aiello. 2004. Eutrophication and Aquatic Plant Management in Massachusetts: Final Generic Environmental Impact Report. Cambridge, MA: Commonwealth of Massachusetts, Executive Office of Environmental Affairs Commonwealth of Massachusetts.

NOAA Great Lakes Environmental Research Laboratory. (n.d.). NOAA National Center for Research on Aquatic Invasive Species (NCRAIS). Retrieved from https://nas.er.usgs.gov/queries/GreatLakes/FactSheet.aspx?SpeciesID=293

Popy, F.S., A.M. Islam, A.K. Hasan, and M.P. Anwar. 2017. Integration of chemical and manual control methods for sustainable weed management in inbred and hybrid rice. *J Bangladesh Agric Univ* 15: 158.

Reddy, K.S., C.S. Reddy, and S. Ganapaty. 2012. Psychopharmacological studies of hydro alcoholic extract of whole plant of *Marsilea quadrifolia*. *Journal of Scientific Research* 4: 279–285.

Reznicek, A.A., E.G. Voss, and B.S. Walters. 2011. MICHIGAN FLORA ONLINE. University of Michigan. Web (Accessed March 28, 2021). http://michiganflora.net/species.aspx?id=1683.

Ripa, F.A., L. Nahar, M. Haque, and M. Islam. 2009. Antibacterial, cytotoxic and antioxidant activity of crude extract of *Marsilea quadrifolia*. *European Journal of Scientific Research* 3: 123–129.

Saha, S. 2008. Sustaining high rice productivity the IWM way. *Indian Farming* 58(3): 18–22.

Saha, S., and K.S. Rao. 2010. Evaluation of bensulfuron-methyl for weed control in wet direct-sown summer rice. *Oryza* 47(1): 38–41.

Scriver, M., A. Marinich, C. Wilson, and J. Freeland. 2015. Development of species-specific environmental DNA (eDNA) markers for invasive aquatic plants. *Aquatic Botany* 122: 27–31.

SOM (State of Michigan). 2018. *Status and Strategy for European Water-Clover (Marsilea quadrifolia L.) Management Scope*. Lansing, MI: State of Michigan, p. 30.

Soni, P., and L. Singh. 2012. *Marsilea quadrifolia* linn—A valuable culinary and remedial fern in Jaduguda, Jharkhand, India. *International Journal of Life Science & Pharma Research* 2(3): 99–104.

Strat, D. 2012. *Marsilea quadrifolia* L. in the protected wetlands from Romania. In: Proceedings of the International Conference on Water Resources and Wetlands, pp. 449–457.

Uma R., and B. Pravin. 2013. Invitro cytotoxic activity of *Marsilea quadrifolia* Linn of MCF-7 cells of human breast cancer. *International Research Journal of Medical Sciences* 1(1): 10–13.

U.S. Geological Survey (USGS). 2020. Specimen observation data for *Marsilea quadrifolia* L., Nonindigenous Aquatic Species Database, Gainesville, FL, https://nas.er.usgs.gov/queries/CollectionInfo.aspx?SpeciesID=293 (Accessed May 5, 2020).

Wagner K.J. 2004. *The Practical Guide to Lake Management in Massachusetts: A Companion to the Final Generic Environmental Impact Report on Eutrophication and Aquatic Plant Management in Massachusetts*. Boston, MA: Commonwealth of Massachusetts, Executive Office of Environmental Affairs Commonwealth of Massachusetts.

17 Yellow Floating Heart (*Nymphoides peltata*)

ABSTRACT

Yellow floating heart (*Nymphoides peltata*), also called water fringe, is an Eurasian invasive floating-leaved aquatic plant in Massachusetts. Currently, there are six reported sightings in Massachusetts including Scarboro Golf Course Pond in Boston and Lymans Pond in Dover, both within the Charles River Watershed. Since there are not many waterbodies in Massachusetts infested by this species, it is important to prevent the spread to other waterbodies and implement management strategies for the eradication of the *N. peltata*. Physical methods such as hand pulling and dredging and chemical control methods such as the application of glyphosate and diquat are suggested in this chapter.

INTRODUCTION

Taxonomy Hierarchy (ITIS 2021)

Kingdom	Plantae
Subkingdom	Viridiplantae
Infrakingdom	Streptophyta
Superdivision	Embryophyta
Division	Tracheophyta
Subdivision	Spermatophytina
Class	Magnoliopsida
Superorder	Asteranae
Order	Asterales
Family	Menyanthaceae
Genus	*Nymphoides* Hill
Species	*Nymphoides peltata* (S.G. Gmel.) Kuntze

BASIC BIOLOGY

Yellow floating heart (*Nymphoides peltata*), also called Water Fringe, Fringed Water Lily, or floating heart, is an aquatic floating-leaved perennial plant (Figure 17.1). It can grow long branching stolons (up to 2 m) that form new plants with a stem which resembles a rope arising from the roots (Pfingsten et al. 2021). Meanwhile, *N. peltata* has green leaves that appear circular or heart-shaped with a diameter of 3–15 cm (CABI 2019). These leaves grow alternately on the stem but appear oppositely at the flower stalks. *N. peltata* also has ripple margins, with the underside parts of the leaf appearing purple (Nault and Mikulyuk 2009). In addition, margin-fringed yellow flowers (top left panel, Figure 17.1) can be seen on the peduncles arising above the water surface. Each of these flowers has five petals, with a diameter around 3–5 cm (Robinson 2004). The seeds of *N. peltata* are very small (3–5 mm in length and 3 mm in width), with winged margins (Cook 1990; CABI 2019). The seed capsules are shown in the top right panel of Figure 17.1.

N. peltata could be mistakenly identified as the native Little floating heart (*Nymphoides cordata*) and native Yellow Water Lily (also called Yellow Pond Lily, *Nuphar variegata*) as they share some similarities (Figure 17.2). For example, *N. peltata*, *N. cordata*, and *N. variegata* have leaves that float on the water surface, with roots that grow on the water bottom, and flowers that float above their leaves. In addition, they all have dollar-sized, heart-shaped leaves. Even so, there are several distinguishing characteristics that set them apart, as the flowers of *N. cordata* are white without fringed margins, and the roots of *N. cordata* may be found in a bunch on the stem just below the surface (MA DCR 2016). Meanwhile, *N. variegata* has the largest leaves out of the other two species (*N. peltata* and *N. cordata*), which are 6–8 inch (Robinson 2004). Moreover, *N. variegata*'s flowers are cup-shaped, which is different from that of *N. peltata* (Figure 17.2).

NATIVE RANGE

N. peltata is native to Eastern Asia and the Mediterranean (Stuckey 1973). This hardy plant can establish itself in a wide range of

FIGURE 17.1 Yellow floating heart. (Photos by Lyn Gettys.)

waterbodies, but it prefers slow-moving waterbodies such as lakes, ponds, and streams (Robinson 2004). Meusel et al. (1978) reported in their research that *N. peltata* is the only *Nymphoides* species that appears in moderately cold temperature areas. For most circumstances, *N. peltata* is detected growing in neutral and alkaline waterbodies (Darbyshire and Francis 2008). Even so, they can sometimes be found in the acid waterbodies.

INVASIVE RANGE

Given its ability to inhabit a wide range of waterbodies, *N. peltata* has spread throughout many regions: Asia, Europe, North America, and Oceania (CABI 2019). In the United States, the earliest record of *N. peltata* invasion was recorded in Winchester, Massachusetts, in 1882 (Stuckey 1973; U.S. Fish and Wildlife Service 2018). There is also a report of *N. peltata* in New York City's Central Park in 1886.

FIGURE 17.2 Yellow water lily (*left*) and little floating heart (*right*). (Left photo by Les Mehrhoff from discoverlife.org, with permission from Dr. John Pickering; right photo by Alexey Zinovjev and Irina Kadis, with permission from salicicola.com)

Other first recordings include Missouri in 1893, Louisiana in 1899, and Pennsylvania in 1905. The earliest record of *N. peltata* in the Hudson River was in 1929 from New York, and its origin was speculated as being an escape from a water garden or pool (Stuckey 1973).

MECHANISMS/VECTORS OF SPREAD

N. peltata could have been introduced by "accident through flooding of ornamental ponds into surrounding natural waterways" (Stuckey 1973; Josefsson and Andersson 2001). Even so, *N. peltata* can reproduce by both vegetative and sexual methods which aids further spread (Robinson 2004). The reproduction by fragments can occur through the stolon, rhizomes, and leaves with part of a stem and part of the stolon. These fragments can then attach on vessels/boat moving from a waterbody to another waterbody, forming new *N. peltata* plant.

Sexual reproduction *N. peltata* also exists due to the production of seeds which are produced by either cross-pollination or self-pollination, but the former method can create more viable seeds than the latter (Ornduff 1966). Like fragments, seeds can also be attached to the boating vessels, causing possible dispersal. In addition, wildlife is another factor that can further the spread of seeds. For example, although seeds can be completely digested by animals, which decreases the possibility of seeds spreading, because of the special structure of the seed, seeds can easily attach to the fur or feather of birds or waterfowls (Cook 1990). Furthermore, prior research (Van Der Velde and Van Der Heijden 1981) mentioned some insects, such as bees (Apidae), hoverflies (Syrphidae), and shoreflies (Ephydridae) species, play an important role in the pollination among flowers, impacting the seeds production and the sexual reproduction of *N. peltata*.

ECOLOGICAL IMPACTS

N. peltata is a noxious aquatic invasive plant, which can thrive in a variety of waters. Once this plant species invades a waterbody, it may replace the local vegetation and as a result negatively impact the ecosystem. According to multiple research studies (Stuckey 1973; Robinson 2004), the invasion of *N. peltata* might severely impact ecosystems because dense mats of *N. peltata* can lead to an increase in sedimentation, degrade water quality, and intercept the sunlight which leads to the exclusion of other submerged plants. These massive, thick mats could clog drainage systems and waterways, reducing the water flow.

Furthermore, *N. peltata* can threaten food webs. For example, algae which serves as a food source for many species may be shaded out due to the abundance of *N. peltata* (Robinson 2004). Moreover, large amounts of *N. peltata* existing in the waterbodies could compete with other native species. This would cause fish or animals rely on these native species to relocate or perish. Furthermore, decomposing *N. peltata* may lower dissolved oxygen in the water, harming fish or other aquatic animals. Therefore, we can see that *N. peltata* may cause an enormous influence on the ecosystem and biodiversity.

Economic Impacts

N. peltata can have negative economic impacts. *N. peltata* in the water may negatively impact boating and swimming recreational activities, resulting in economic loss. Other water activities such as fishing could also be reduced as ecological habitats are threatened. Furthermore, tourism development could be hampered, the value of surrounding real estate could be influenced (Robinson 2004), channels and waterways could be blocked, and aesthetic value could be decreased. Control methods are expensive (Larson 2007) and time-consuming. For reference, control efforts in Sweden were estimated to cost SEK28,000 (US$4,500)/ha or SEK56,000 (US$9,000) annually (Gren et al. 2007).

POSITIVE ASPECTS

Although *N. peltata* has negative influences on the ecosystem and economy, there are a few benefits. The seeds of *N. peltata* provide food for animals, such as birds and waterfowls, and the plant can be used as a food for *Cataclysta lemnata* (L.) (a moth species) (Van Der Velde 1979). It can also be helpful in algal blooms control and be used to absorb heavy metal or organic pollutants from the wastewater (Wang et al. 2007; Wang et al. 2010). In addition, it is also found that *N. peltata* can be screened for constituents with antitumor activity (Du et al. 2015). However, invasive species are not allowed for any ecological restoration projects in Massachusetts.

MONITORING AND SIGHTINGS

The invasive species data in this chapter were provided in reports by the Massachusetts Department of Environmental Protection (MassDEP) and other agencies (Table 17.1). Sites with *N. peltata* were mapped as a data layer with ArcGIS® ArcMap 10.1 (ESRI, Redlands, California). This tool can pinpoint the area that *N. peltata* has spread to, which can help to inform future decisions on processes that can happen in these waterbodies, or regulations that involve efforts to limit the spread of this aquatic invasive species.

From the data collected from the Massachusetts Department of Environmental Protection (MassDEP) Water Quality Assessment Reports (Table 17.1), currently, there are two known waterbodies infested by *N. peltata*: Scarboro Golf Course Pond in Boston and Lymans Pond in Dover, MA. Both ponds are within the Charles River Watershed. According to other sources, it is also found in a small pond in the center of the complex of Rosewood Estates on routes 10/202 within the Westfield River Watershed, an ornamental koi pond adjacent to Burchell's Pond along 101 Miacomet Avenue at Nantucket (Table 17.1 and Figure 17.3). According to Stuckey (1973), this invasive species was first detected by C.E. Perkins in September 1882 in Winchester, Massachusetts. This is also the first sighting in the United States. However, the original record/sample was not able to be located. It is possible that the record of this specimen exists, but it has been out on loan for a very long time, or it may have been lost or destroyed.[1] At the same time, Harvard Herbarium have a sample of the little floating heart *N. cordata* (collected by C.E. Perkins, September, 1882) from Winter's Pond in Winchester, MA. So, it is not clear if this is the same specimen and was reidentified later, or if there might be other specimens collected by C.E. Perkins available elsewhere.[2] This invasive species was also reported in Hall's Pond within the Nashua River Watershed; however, no such pond is found in the area; therefore, it is identified as an unconfirmed sighting (Figure 17.3).

MANAGING ACTIONS

There are many different methods tested for controlling the spread of *N. peltata*. The management measures include physical methods, chemical methods, and biological methods. (*Note:* In choosing a particular method, it is important to determine the range or invasion, local water and weather conditions, budget, and restriction)

Physical Methods

Physical methods include mechanical harvesting, hand pulling, cutting, dredging, benthic

Yellow Floating Heart (*Nymphoides peltata*)   311

TABLE 17.1
Sightings of Yellow floating heart in Massachusetts

Waterbody	Watershed	Reporting Agency	Report Source	First Year Reported
Herbarium (not a waterbody)	Mystic River		Stuckey 1973	1882
Hall's Pond	Nashua		Invasive Plant Atlas of New England (IPANE) at the University of Connecticut online database. Reference ID: 2469430. www.eddmaps.org/ipane/	1983
Scarboro Golf Course Pond	Charles River	MassDEP 2008	Charles River Watershed 2002–2006 Water Quality Assessment Report 72-AC-4 CN136.5, April 2008	1997
Rosewood Estates on routes 10/202: small pond in center of the complex	Westfield River		Invasive Plant Atlas of New England (IPANE) at the University of Connecticut online database. Reference ID: 2469431. www.eddmaps.org/ipane/	1998
Lymans Pond	Charles River	MassDEP 2008	Charles River Watershed 2002–2006 Water Quality Assessment Report 72-AC-4 CN136.5, April 2008	2003
Ornamental Koi Pond adjacent to Burchell's Pond, 101 Miacomet Ave.	Islands		Kelly Omand, Nantucket Conservation Foundation. Ref. # 4742657 on www.eddmaps.org/distribution/	2016

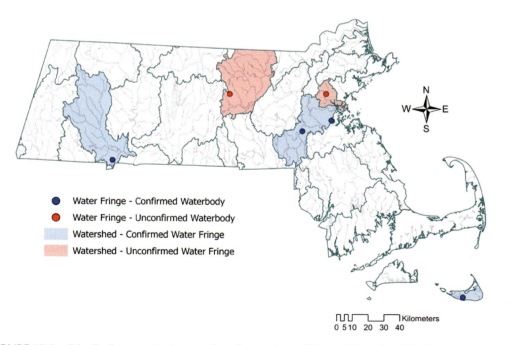

FIGURE 17.3 Distribution map depicting yellow floating heart (*Nymphoides peltata*) in Massachusetts.

barriers, and drawdowns (Robinson 2004; Darbyshire and Francis 2008; DiTomaso et al. 2013). Mechanical harvesting is suitable for large-scale *N. peltata* removal. On a smaller scale, hand pulling can be more efficient than mechanical harvesting, specifically when *N. peltata* is mixed with other aquatic plants (Mattson et al. 2004). However, any physical removal must be done with care to not generate plant fragments and spread the infestation. In addition, repeated cutting might be effective and a viable option (Darbyshire and Francis 2008).

Other physical methods such as dredging and drawdowns may be useful in controlling the spread of *N. peltata*. Dredging is described as a sediment removal process that controls the rooted plant growth through light limitation or substrate limitation. However, dredging sometimes leads to small amounts of regrowth due to fragments formed during the process. Meanwhile, benthic barriers are a control method proposed by Massachusetts authorities, which could be applied in small areas (such as swimming beaches) to control this invasive species. Drawdown is confirmed to successfully control the *N. peltata* when applying benthic barrier methods in the wintertime, but some plants can grow within the barriers margin (Darbyshire and Francis 2008). Although these methods may aid in controlling *N. peltata*, the drawbacks to these methods need to be considered when implemented in waterbodies. For example, physical methods could further spread *N. peltata*, as *N. peltata* can regrow through fragments, roots, and rhizomes (Darbyshire and Francis 2008).

CHEMICAL METHODS

Chemical control is a popular management approach for controlling invasive aquatic plants. Diquat, 2, 4-D, glyphosate, and dichlobenil have been recognized for effectively controlling *N. peltata* (Mattson et al.2004; Darbyshire and Francis 2008). Diquat can be used as consistent control method with correct dosage, proper formulation, and suitable conditions. Meanwhile, 2, 4-D can only achieve partial success (Mattson et al. 2004). Other chemicals such as glyphosate can be used from late spring to mid-late summer with a surfactant or spray (DiTomaso et al. 2013), and dichlobenil can be applied during spring, and reapplied in the following seasons (Darbyshire and Francis 2008). The relatively new aquatic herbicide ProcellaCOR™ (florpyrauxifen-benzyl) was able to reduce 90% of the total surface coverage of yellow floating heart in a 55-acre drinking water reservoir within 15 days after the treatment, and to less than 3.0 acres within 50 days after the treatment (Lamb et al. 2021) which demonstrates that ProcellaCOR™ has the potential to control yellow floating heart infestations with relatively short-term negative impacts on dissolved oxygen concentrations. More information about chemical control on yellow floating heart and other 18 invasive species can be found in Appendix III. Any chemical used for aquatic invasive species control requires a WM04 Chemical Application License issued by the Massachusetts Department of Environmental Protection.

BIOLOGICAL METHODS

In terms of the biological methods, there has yet to be a significant consensus on biological control methods for *N. peltata* (CEH 2004) as well as research on the results of implemented biological control methods in the United States. Therefore, below is a brief description of species that could be useful in controlling the abundance of *N. peltata*. Waterfowls sometimes feed on *N. peltata* (Steyermark 1963); Eurasian wigeons eat shoots of *N. peltata* (Gaevskaya 1969); Crayfish (*Cambaroides schrenckii*) eats leaves and stalks of *N. peltata* (Gaevskaya 1969); Eurasian coots eat seeds and leaves of *N. peltata*, and mallards also eat *N. peltata* seeds (Van Der Velde et al. 1982); Oligochaeta (earthworms) and Mollusca (clams) contribute in decomposing the *N. peltata* plants (Brock 1984; Xie et al. 2005). Although waterfowls or wigeons may provide some natural control in some areas, it is not suggested as a good idea as a tool of biological control because it might not control the yellow floating heart effectively and also might lead to the spread of *N. peltata* if its seeds are moved in feathers of waterfowls.

Harms and Nachtrieb (2019) as well as Stutz (2019) studied whether *N. peltata* is a suitable target for classical biological control in the United States. Harms concluded that *Nymphoides peltata* and *Nymphoides cristata* are appropriate targets for biological control in the United States. On the other hand, the Stutz study concluded that further surveys are necessary to find natural enemies of *N. peltata*. Before foreign insects are permitted by USDA APHIS for introduction as biological controls in the United States, they must undergo strict host-specificity testing and safety assessment. Therefore, it may take some time to begin implementing biological controls and recording significant results in the United States.

SUCCESS STORY

Lake Carl Blackwell is a mid-sized lake of 3,350 acres in Oklahoma in the United States, which is the only reservoir in Oklahoma known to be infested with *N. peltata* in recent years (Rigsby 2019). To eradicate this invasive species, OSU (Oklahoma State University) biologists created an aquatic plant management plan targeted to *N. peltata*. As a result, in July 2019, a new active and selective herbicide ProcellaCOR SC was applied at Lake Carl Blackwell. The special active ingredient of ProcellaCOR SC effectively achieved fast and long-term treatments. This herbicide is also an approved product by the EPA (US Environmental Protection Agency), designed as "partially nontoxic" to human and animals (SePRO n.d.).

During the application of ProcellaCOR SC, water samples were taken every day and water quality was tested weekly in 2019. The result showed that the concentration of the herbicide was lower than the detection level. At the end of the chemical treatment at Lake Carl Blackwell, there was only around 3 acres of the *N. peltata* found through satellite and drone images, and almost 96% of *N. peltata* was reduced by this treatment.

According to feedback from later observations, some regrowth occurred in the second growing season (Rigsby 2019). Some areas of regrowth were concentrated in narrow spaces where the boats could not easily access. For further control, OSU biologists are researching some alternative methods to test in the coming summer (July 2020).

CONCLUSION

N. peltata is currently in limited waters in Massachusetts. Given its ability to damage waterbodies and ecosystems, it is imperative to continue to gather information on the spatial range of *N. peltata* to limit the spread of the species to other neighboring waterbodies. For documented sightings, if infested area is manageable, it is recommended to eradicate this invasive species using one of the tools recommended in this document.

NOTES

1. According to an email from Matthew Pace, Assistant Curator of the Herbarium at New York Botanical Garden, to Davis Miller, MassDEP Intern, on September 23, 2021.
2. According to an email from Karen Merguerian, Northeastern University Library, to Davis Miller, MassDEP Intern, on September 17, 2021.

REFERENCES

Brock, T.C.M. 1984. Aspects of the decomposition of *Nymphoides peltata* (Gmel.) O. Kuntze (Menyanthaceae). *Aquat. Bot.* 19: 131–156.

CABI. 2019. Nymphoides peltata (yellow floating-heart). Centre for Agriculture and Bioscience International (CABI), www.cabi.org/isc/datasheet/107746#tosummaryOfInvasiveness (Accessed April 21, 2020).

CABI. 2017. *Nymphoides peltata (yellow floating-heart) [original text by A. Mikulyuk]. In Invasive Species Compendium*. Wallingford: CAB International. www.cabi.org/isc/datasheet/107746. (Accessed April, 2018).

Centre for Ecology and Hydrology (CEH). 2004. Information Sheet 6: Fringed Waterlily. Natural Environment Research Council, Centre for Aquatic Plant Management, p. 2.

Cook, C.D.K. 1990. Seed dispersal of Nymphoides peltata (S.G. Gmelin) O. Kuntze (Menyanthaceae). *Aquatic Botany* 37(4): 325–340.

Darbyshire, S.J., and A. Francis 2008. The Biology of Invasive Alien Plants in Canada. 10. Nymphoides peltata (S. G. Gmel.) Kuntze. *Canadian Journal of Plant Science* 88: 811–829.

DiTomaso, J.M., G.B. Kyser, S.R. Oneto, R.G. Wilson, S.B. Orloff, L.W. Anderson, S.D. Wright, J.A. Roncoroni, T.L. Miller, T.S. Prather, C. Ransom, K.G. Beck, C. Duncan, K.A. Wilson, and J.J. Mann. 2013. Weed Control in Natural Areas in the Western United States. Weed Research and Information Center, University of California, p. 544.

Du, Y., R. Wang, H. Zhang, and J. Liu. 2015. Antitumor constituents of the wetland plant *Nymphoides peltata*: A case study for the potential utilization of constructed wetland plant resources. *Natural Product Communications* https://doi.org/10.1177/1934578X1501000203.

Gaevskaya, N.S. 1969. The role of higher aquatic plants in the nutrition of the animals of fresh-water basins. National Lending Library for Science and Technology, Boston Spa, UK, p. 629.

Gren, I., L. Isacs, and M. Carlsson. 2007. Calculation of costs of alien invasive species in Sweden. Technical report. Uppsala, Sweden: Swedish University of Agricultural Sciences.

Harms, N.E., and J.G. Nachtrieb. 2019. Suitability of Introduced Nymphoides spp. (Nymphoides cristata, N. peltata) as Targets for Biological Control in the United States. https://apps.dtic.mil/sti/pdfs/AD1068632.pdf.

ITIS (Integrated Taxonomic Information System). 2021. www.itis.gov/servlet/SingleRpt/SingleRpt?search_topic=TSN&search_value=29998#null (Accessed April 22, 2021).

Josefsson, M., and B. Andersson. 2001. The environmental consequences of alien species in the Swedish Lakes Mälaren, Hjälmaren, Vänern and Vättern. A Journal of the human Environment 30(8): 514–521.

Lamb, B.T., A.A. McCrea, S.H. Stoodley, and A.R. Dzialowski. 2021. Monitoring and water quality impacts of an herbicide treatment on an aquatic invasive plant in a drinking water reservoir. *Journal of Environmental Management* 288: 112444.

Larson, D. 2007. Reproduction strategies in introduced *Nymphoides peltata* populations revealed by genetic markers. *Aquat. Bot* 86: 402–406.

MA DCR (Department of Conservation & Recreation). 2016. A Guide to Aquatic Plants in Massachusetts. 32 P.

MassDEP. 2008. Charles River Watershed 2002–2006 Water Quality Assessment Report. Report Number 72-AC-4/DWM Control Number CN136.5. Massachusetts Department of Environmental Protection, Division of Watershed Management, Worcester, Massachusetts. 210 P.

Mattson, M.D., P.L. Godfrey, R.A. Barletta, and A. Aiello. 2004. Eutrophication and Aquatic Plant Management in Massachusetts: Final Generic Environmental Impact Report. Commonwealth of Massachusetts, Executive Office of Environmental Affairs Commonwealth of Massachusetts 4: 29–80.

Meusel, H., E. Ja?ger, S. Rauschert, and E. Weinert. 1978. Vergleichende Chorologie der zentraleuropa?ischen. *Flora. Band.* 2. Verl. G. Fischer, Jena.

Nault, M.E., and A. Mikulyuk. 2009. Yellow floating heart (Nymphoides peltata): A Technical Review of Distribution, Ecology, Impacts, and Management. Wisconsin Department of Natural Resources Bureau of Science Services, PUB-SS-1051 2009. Madison, Wisconsin, USA.

Ornduff, R. 1996. The origin of dioecism from heterostyly in Nymphoides (Menyanthaceae). *Evolution* 20(3): 309–314.

Pfingsten, I.A., D.D. Thayer, L. Berent, and V. Howard. 2021. Nymphoides peltata (S.G. Gmel.) Kuntze: U.S. Geological Survey, Nonindigenous Aquatic Species Database, Gainesville, FL, https://nas.er.usgs.gov/queries/FactSheet.aspx?speciesID=243, Revision Date: 3/13/2018, Peer Review Date: 3/23/2016 (Accessed April 21, 2020).

Rigsby, S. 2019. Treatment of Yellow floating heart at Lake Carl Blackwell exceeds expectations. Oklahoma State University (OSU)https://news.okstate.edu/articles/communications/2019/treatment_of_yfh_exceeds_expectations_at_lcb.html (Accessed April 21, 2020).

Robinson, M. 2004. *Yellow floating heart: An Exotic Aquatic Plant, Nymphoides Peltata.* Cambridge, MA: Massachusetts Department of Conservation and Recreation; Office of Water Resources; Lakes and Ponds Program.

SePRO Corporation. n.d. ProcellaCOR®, Long-term control of milfoil, hydrilla, and more. www.sepro.com/aquatics/procellacor (Accessed April 21, 2020).

Steyermark, J.A. 1963. *Flora of Missouri.* Iowa: Iowa State University Press, p. 1725.

Stuckey, R.L. 1973. The introduction and distribution of Nymphoides peltata (Menyanthaceae) in North America. *Bartonia* 42: 14–23.

Stutz, S. 2019. *Identifying the origin of yellow floating heart, nymphoides peltata.* CABI.org. www.cabi.org/projects/identifying-the-origin-of-yellow-floating-heart-nymphoides-peltata/.

U.S. Fish and Wildlife Service. 2018. Yellow Floatingheart (*Nymphoides peltata*) Ecological Risk Screening Summary. www.fws.gov/fisheries/ans/erss/highrisk/ERSS-Nymphoides-peltata-FINAL.pdf.

Van Der Velde, G. 1979. Nymphoides peltata (Gmel.) O. Kuntze (Menyanthaceae) as a food plant for Cataclysta lemnata (L.) (Lepidoptera, pyralidae). *Aquatic Botany* 7: 301–304.

Van Der Velde, G., and L.A. Van Der Heijden. 1981. The floral biology and seed production of Nymphoides peltata (Gmel) O. Kuntze (Menyanthaceae). *Aquat. Bot* 10: 261–293.

Van Der Velde, G., L.A. Van Der Heijden, P.A.J. Van Grunsven, and P.M.M. Bexkens. 1982. Initial decomposition of Nymphoides peltata (Gmel.) O. Kuntze (Menyanthaceae), as studied by the leaf-marking method. *Hydrobiol. Bull.* 16: 51–60.

Wang, X., G. Shi, Q. Xu, and J. Hu. 2007. Exogenous polyamines enhance copper tolerance of Nymphoides peltatum. *Journal of Plant Physiology* 164: 1062–1070.

Wang, L., G. Wang, X.Y. Tang, and Z.Y. Chen. 2010. Inhibitory effect of Nymphoides peltatum on *Microcystis aerugnosa* and its mechanism. *Journal of Ecology and Rural Environment* 26: 257–263.

Xie, Z., T. Tang, K. Ma, R. Liu, X. Qu, J. Chen, and Q. Cai. 2005. The influence of environmental variables on macro- invertebrates in a macrophyte-dominated Chinese lake, with emphasis on the relationships between macrophyte heterogeneity and macroinvertebrate patterns. *J. Freshwater. Ecol.* 20: 503–512.

18 Common Reed Grass (*Phragmites australis*)

ABSTRACT

Common reed grass (*Phragmites australis*) locations recorded from 1994 to 2008 in Massachusetts lakes and rivers are summarized for a better overview of the status of this species in the state. As of 2008, there are 189 reported sites (representing 110 waterbodies) that contain common reed grass in Massachusetts. Brief description on the biology of common reed grass and its management are provided in this report. The mapped sightings will raise the general public's awareness of the presence of reed grass in Massachusetts, which may be helpful in minimizing unintentional spreading of invasive reed grass to other waterbodies. This report also describes different methods that have been used to control this invasive species, including physical (e.g., hand pulling, flooding, and mowing), chemical (e.g., glyphosate and imazapyr), and biological control (e.g., insects and livestock grazing). Depending on the site to be treated, optimal control of invasive common reed grass usually involves a combination of control methods.

INTRODUCTION

Taxonomic Hierarchy (ITIS 2021)

Kingdom	Plantae
Subkingdom	Tracheobionta
Superdivision	Spermatophyta
Division	Magnoliophyta
Class	Liliopsida
Subclass	Commelinidae
Order	Cyperales
Family	Poaceae-Gramineae
Genus	*Phragmites*
Species	*Phragmites australis* (Cav.) Trin. ex Steud.

The common reed, or common reed grass, *Phragmites australis*, is a perennial plant with a cosmopolitan distribution (Figure 18.1) (Packer et al. 2017). Typically seen by roadsides or in disturbed wetlands, *Phragmites australis* is a monocot in the Poaceae (Gramineae) family (Crow and Hellquist 2000). It is a wetland species that is able to tolerate its base and rhizome being submerged in water and conditions with high salinity. It is also capable of growing 2–4 m tall, prominently affecting the appearance of a landscape (Figure 18.2). The mature stalks of the plant have a distinctive brushy inflorescence, or panicle, on top containing seeds. The panicle, typically measuring between 15–38 cm long, is a deep purple when it first emerges, transitioning to a tan color as seeds mature (Del Tredici 2020). *Phragmites* plants have long, pointed dark green leaves that can grow to a length of 60 cm and a width of 5 cm. The leaves form sheaths around the stalks. *Phragmites* grows in large colonies, spreading rapidly via rhizomes as well as by seed (Kelly 1999). *Phragmites* also can produce up to 2,000 seeds annually (Figure 18.3), which can be carried by the wind or transported by wildlife to a new location (Avers et al. 2007). Seed germination is affected by flooding, salinity, and temperature. A depth of two inches or more of water and salinities above 20 parts per thousand (ppt) prevent germination, whereas salinities below 10 ppt do not affect germination (Tiner 1998). Germination usually increases with temperature (e.g., from 16–25°C), while sprouting time decreases with rising temperatures (e.g., from 25 to 10 days, respectively, for that temperature range). Optimal pH for common reed is circumneutral, from 5.5 to 7.5, with the most robust stands occurring in this range. However, it can tolerate acidic conditions as low as pH 3.6 and alkaline conditions up to pH 8.6 (Tiner 1998).

DOI: 10.1201/9781003201106-18

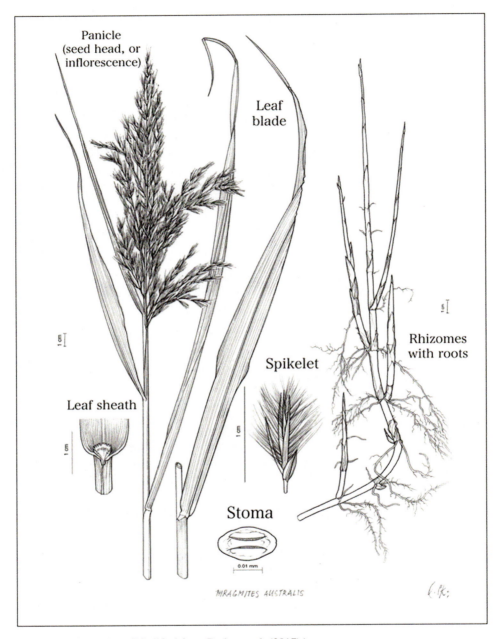

FIGURE 18.1 *Phragmites*. (Modified from Packer et al. (2017).)

The common reed grows under a wide range of environmental conditions, from salt to fresh marshes, to dry upland sites or shallow open water. This broad ecological amplitude has probably facilitated its nearly circumglobal occurrence. It grows in pristine wetlands as well as in altered wetlands, dredged material disposal sites (former wetlands), impoundment dikes, disturbed uplands, powerline rights-of-way, roadside ditches, railroad embankments, sandy soils, mine waste areas (refuse piles, acid spoil areas, and tipple areas), and in and around mine slurry impoundments. It can grow as a mat across shallow water and may be found in

Common Reed Grass (*Phragmites australis*)

FIGURE 18.2 *Phragmites australis* on the roadside of Massachusetts Turnpike (Interstate 90) (*left*) and along the shoreline of a pond nearby Interstate 90 (right). (Photos by W.H. Wong.)

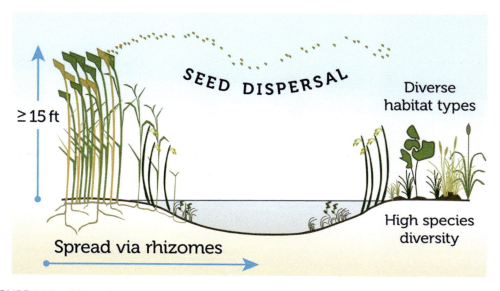

FIGURE 18.3 *Phragmites* spreads to new areas through seed and rhizome dispersal. (From Greatlakesphragmites.net.)

the shallows of lakes and ponds in water about 3 ft deep (Tiner 1998). Found throughout temperate regions of the world, common reed is quite likely the most widely distributed plant (Saltonstall and Meyerson 2016). Common reed quickly becomes the most dominate plant in areas where it occurs, forming a characteristic tall-grass monoculture throughout its global range.

Though it has been unclear in the past whether *P. australis* is a native or an invasive species in the United States, it is now understood that both native and invasive varieties can be found here. Both fossil and archaeological evidence have confirmed that native varieties of *Phragmites* have been present on the continent for thousands of years. The plant has long been important to Native American culture. Indigenous people have used reed grass for food, weaving, and medicine, and as components of tools, including pipes and musical instruments (Kiviat and Hamilton 2001; Tewksbury et al. 2002; Del Tredici 2020). In the early 19th century, the non-native variety, most likely European in origin, appeared in coastal ports in the eastern United States (US FWS n.d.). Prior to the 1900s, *Phragmites* was a relatively uncommon plant in North America. Since the 1960s, however, the plant has become extremely abundant, spreading aggressively and overwhelming wetland ecosystems. It is hypothesized that this rapid spread was a result of the introduction of a non-native variety (Saltonstall 2002). Historic and molecular evidence supports this theory. In 1877, a Eurasian strain of *Phragmites* was documented to have arrived in Philadelphia in ship's ballast, when a young common reed plant was found growing in a ballast dumping area. Burk (1877) wrote of the plant, "If this is not a distinct species, it is a very singular variety." This plant and others carried over in the same way are thought to have proliferated on the east coast and spread inland over time, competing with North American *Phragmites* varieties and other native wetland plants. The invasive behavior seen in the Eurasian *Phragmites* strain may have been exacerbated by increased development in and human disturbances to wetland habitats, including highway construction and pollution of various kinds (Jodoin et al. 2008).

Modern genetic analytical techniques have allowed for a better understanding of the introduction and spread of Eurasian *Phragmites*. A study by Saltonstall (2002) significantly supported the theory of an introduced aggressive *Phragmites* strain to explain the apparent sudden invasiveness of the plant in North America. By sequencing regions of the *Phragmites* genome with intraspecific variation from modern and herbarium-preserved plant samples, Saltonstall (2002) identified several native *Phragmites* haplotypes,[1] including 11 haplotypes A-H, S, Z, and AA, and haplotype I, found predominantly in the Gulf Coast, which have together been identified as a separate subspecies, *Phragmites australis* subsp. *americanus* (Saltonstall et al. 2004). The most prominent Eurasian haplotype was designated haplotype M. Preserved reed grass samples from earlier than 1910 show widespread abundance of native haplotypes and a limited range of haplotype M in North America. While modern-day analysis still shows the presence of native *P. australis americanus* in the United States, since 1960 haplotype M has expanded its range dramatically, to the point where it can be found across the country (Saltonstall 2002).

The Eurasian haplotype M has spread to an alarming extent, outcompeting native wetland species, including native *Phragmites australis* subsp. *Americanus*, and decreasing overall biodiversity (Tewksbury et al. 2002). It was originally reported that the three haplotypes of *Phragmites australis* subsp. *americanus* native to southern and central New England had been driven to extinction, including haplotype AA, which was unique to New England (Saltonstall 2002). While it is possible that some native strains, such as haplotype AA, have gone extinct due to competition from invasive common reed grass, native varieties can still be found in some areas of New England, lending hope to the survival of original North American varieties. For instance, populations of native *Phragmites australis* were discovered in Falmouth, Massachusetts, in 2004 and 2005 (Payne and Blossey 2007). In some locations, it is believed that there are native *Phgramites* such as those with red tint stems along the Carlisle section of the Concord River (Figure 18.4) but molecular analysis is still required for confirmation.

Native *Phragmites australis* subsp. *americanus* can be visually differentiated from invasive *P. australis* in several ways (Figure 18.5). The American subspecies is considered by some researchers to be sufficiently different from its Eurasian counterpart to justify its elevation to a fully separate species, under the name *Phragmites americanus*, a change which may be made official in the future (Haines 2010; Blossey et al. 2019). The stems of native *P. australis* are reddish, smooth, shiny, and flexible, compared to the tan, rough, dull, and rigid stems of invasive *P. australis*. Leaves of native *P. australis* are lighter yellow or green (Avers et al. 2007). The culms of native *P. australis* remain exposed during the winter, while invasive culms are not exposed. Finally, while invasive *P. australis* often

Common Reed Grass (*Phragmites australis*)

FIGURE 18.4 *Phragmites australis* along the Carlisle section of the Concord River that are about 21 ft tall. (Photo by Edward Reiner.)

occurs as a monoculture (stands with low genetic diversity resulting from a mainly clonal mode of growth), native *P. australis* rarely occurs as such (Saltonstall et al. 2004). Molecular analysis can be useful in distinguishing native and invasive strains as well as in tracking the spread of *Phragmites* between habitats. The invasive strain was unfortunately not differentiated from the native strain in the sightings included in this report.

Common reed has been reported in every county of Massachusetts. Drainage ditches found along the side of highways and major roads provide a suitable habitat for *Phragmites*. The plant is often found along roadsides. Increasing levels of road construction over the past hundred years may have created corridors facilitating the spread of *Phragmites*. Though roadside stands of *Phragmites* could be beneficial, potentially protecting roads from structural damage caused by ice and snow, abundant roadside *Phragmites* threatens to encroach on wetlands found near roads (Jodoin et al. 2008). The application of de-icing salts on roads goes hand in hand with *Phragmites*' intrusion as a threat to freshwater bog and fen habitats, as the increased salinity caused by road salt runoff harms many non-coastal wetland plant species while also creating conditions that are more favorable to salt-tolerant *Phragmites* (Richburg et al. 2001; Jodoin et al. 2008). In Jodoin et al.'s (2008) study, it was also found that *Phragmites* plants sampled on roadsides from Quebec were majorly composed of haplotype M, the invasive subspecies.

Phragmites seems to grow more abundantly in correlation with both warmer temperatures and higher levels of nutrients in agricultural runoff zones, especially if the density of surrounding competitive plant species is reduced by these factors (Minchinton and Bertness 2003; Jodoin et al. 2008; Legault et al. 2018). *Phragmites* can spread to new areas either in the form of seeds carried by wind or wildlife, with one individual capable of producing 2,000 seeds annually (Figures 18.1, 18.3, and 18.5), or vegetatively from rhizome fragments, which can be carried by water currents, animals, or on construction equipment (Tewksbury et al. 2002; Avers et al. 2007). Once established, reed grass is very difficult to remove or control. According to Martin and Blossey (2013), more than 4 billion dollars is spent annually by different municipal, state, federal, land trust, and private organizations to control common reed grass. Despite the high cost associated with eradication efforts, significant control has not been achieved with current conventional methods, which typically include chemical herbicides, mowing, burning, hand removal, and flooding.

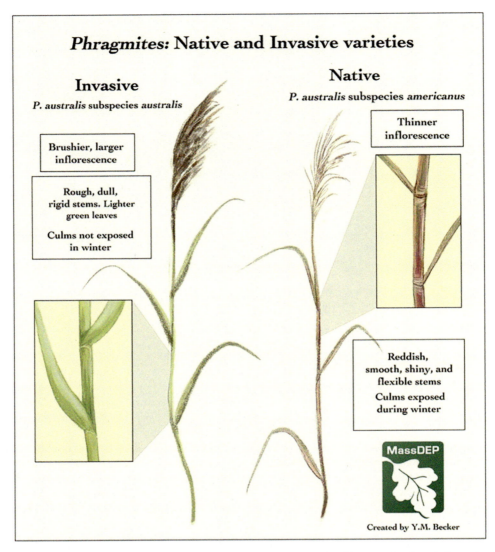

FIGURE 18.5 Differentiating native and invasive *Phragmites australis*. (Photos and written information from within this report and one external source (Tip of the Mitt Watershed Council n.d.) referenced.)

While introduced *Phragmites* is detrimental to many waterbodies, it has also been documented that these plants may be valuable for storm damage prevention and pollution attenuation (i.e., carbon storage and nutrient binding) (Bonham 1980; Gersberg et al. 1986; Gray and Biddlestone 1995; Weis et al. 2021). In the United States, *Phragmites australis* provides sustenance for certain native and introduced species of herbivores, but specialized herbivores of the plant are significantly less abundant in North America than they are in Europe. Effective long-term control of *Phragmites* invasion is required after *Phragmites* stands are removed, stable plant communities must be established in their place. Native wetlands species such as *Spartina alterniflora* (Medeiros et al. 2013) or freshwater bog species can maintain a competitive foothold against *Phragmites* while providing some of the same landscape and ecological benefits. Following efforts to remove *Phragmites*, it is also essential that salt and agricultural pollution are remediated to prevent its reemergence. In addition, it is documented that differences in native plant species abundance were attributed to invasive plant species-specific characteristics, and differences in species richness and composition were attributed to physical location (zonation) in the tidal Hudson River freshwater marshes (McGlynn 2008). "Invasive" status of a dominant plant species was less important in invasive plant–native plant interactions than species-specific characteristics and zonation.

MONITORING AND SIGHTINGS

The data in this report were collected by the Massachusetts Department of Environmental Protection (MassDEP) and the Massachusetts Department of Conservation and Recreation (MA DCR) during staff field visits. MassDEP compiled the data, which represent a portion of the 2,050 Massachusetts waterbodies surveyed by MassDEP from 1994 to 2008. Data layers and maps of sites with common reed grass were created using ArcGIS® ArcMap 10.1 (ESRI, Redlands, California).

Between 1994 and 2008, common reed grass has been reported in multiple waterbodies in Massachusetts, including both rivers and lakes (Figure 18.6 and Table 18.1). More detailed information about the latitude and longitude of specific sites and first reporting years can be found in Appendix A. Based on the MassDEP's records, common reed grass was detected in 82 of the 2,050 waterbodies assessed in Massachusetts. Within DCR's data, 26 additional waterbodies in Massachusetts are reported to contain common reed grass, for a total of 110 waterbodies in this report. For these 110 waterbodies, there are 189 reported sightings; 34 out of 110 waterbodies have been surveyed multiple times while the remaining waterbodies have been surveyed only once. Among these 110 waterbodies, 98 are lakes, 10 are rivers, and 2 are estuaries.

The map displays 110 waterbodies that contain common reed grass (Figure 18.6). It should be noted that this report excludes reed grass in wetlands and reed grass growing in other suitable conditions such as roadside habitats (Figure 18.2) created by road salt implementation (Jodoin et al. 2008). Thus, the sightings in this report underestimate the true presence of reed grass in Massachusetts. Future mapping needs to include information from wetlands, other areas, and other reports such as those reported in Falmouth, Massachusetts (Payne and Blossey 2007). Molecular data and information about the separate distribution of native and invasive haplotypes are also not included in this report, so some sightings may represent native reed grass.

MANAGING ACTIONS

The best results for controlling invasive *Phragmites* involve the use of multiple control methods together and depend on the site to be treated. Before applying treatments, the site must be evaluated to determine the level of the infestation and the density of the invasive *Phragmites* stands.

CHEMICAL CONTROL

Chemical control is one of the most frequently used methods to manage *Phragmites* (Marks 1994; Avers et al. 2007). Although herbicides can be very precise and efficient in eliminating target plant species, they can have detrimental effects on other species and on the environment if not used with care. Therefore, it is critical to apply any herbicide product correctly, read and follow the directions on the product's label, and follow any state or federal laws applicable to herbicide treatments.

Glyphosate is a general-use herbicide that works by targeting the shikimic acid pathway in plants. It does not typically travel through groundwater as it binds tightly to soil where it is broken down within a year of application. Pure glyphosate is not toxic to animals, but depending on the commercial mixture used, it may be combined with other ingredients that are toxic to humans or wildlife (Henderson et al. 2010). An aqueous form of glyphosate, made specifically to be used on plants growing in wetland resource areas water, is sold under the brand name Rodeo™ and has been found to be effective against *P. australis* (Marks 1994).

Another key chemical known to be useful in controlling *Phragmites* is imazapyr (Marks 1994; Avers et al. 2007). Recent studies have shown that imazapyr, either applied alone or in

TABLE 18.1
List of Town Names and Waterbodies that Contain *Phragmites australis*

Town	Waterbody	Town	Waterbody	Town	Waterbody
Ashland	Ashland Reservoir	Holland	Hamilton Reservoir	Pembroke	Furnace Pond
Barnstable	Hamblin Pond				Great Sandy Bottom Pond
Becket	Robin Hood Lake	Holliston	Bogastow Brook	Petersham	Quabbin Reservoir
	Long Bow Lake	Holyoke	Clear Pond		Town Barn Beaver Pond
	Silver Shield Pond	Hopedale	Mill River	Plainville	Wetherells Pond
Bellingham	Box Pond	Kingston	Foundry Pond	Plymouth	Billington Sea
	Jenks Reservoir		Tussock Brook		Ship Pond
	Silver Lake	Lakeville	Little Quittacas Pond		White Island Pond (East Basin)
Billerica	Richardson Pond North	Leicester	Southwick Pond		Five Mile Pond
Boston	Muddy River	Littleton	Fort Pond		Island Pond
Bourne	Flax Pond		Long Pond	Quincy	Blue Hills Reservoir
Brewster	Cliff Pond	Ludlow	Haviland Pond	Rochester	Turner Pond
	Little Cliff Pond	Lynn	Floating Bridge Pond	Rockport	Cape Pond
Brockton	Thirty Acre Pond	Marlborough	Fort Meadow Reservoir	Rutland	Long Pond
Canton	Forge Pond	Mashpee	Duxbury Bay		Moulton Pond
Charlton	Buffum Pond		Mashpee Pond		Muschopauge Pond
	Sibley Pond	Mattapoise	Tinkham Pond		Whitehall Pond
Chelmsford	Newfield Pond	Middleboro	Fuller Street Pond	Salem	Forest River
Cheshire	Cheshire Reservoir (Middle Basin)	Millbury	Hathaway Pond	Sandwich	Peters Pond
Chicopee	Chicoppee Reservoir	Milton	Gulliver Creek	Scituate	Musquashcut Pond
Clinton	Coachlace Pond	Monterey	Lake Garfield	Sheffield	Mansfield Pond
Cohasset	Aaron River Reservoir	Nantucket	Long Pond	Somerset	Somerset Reservoir
Danvers	Porters Pond	New Marlboro	York Lake	S.Hampton	Tighe Carmody Reservoir
	Crane River	New Salem	Lake Rohunta	Springfield	Bass Pond
	Seaplane Basin	N. Andover	Sudden Pond		Five Mile Pond
	Waters River	N. Attleboro	Sevenmile River	Sturbridge	Pistol Pond

Common Reed Grass (*Phragmites australis*)

Dighton	Broad Cove		Whiting Pond		Kings Pond
Douglas	Dudley Pond	N. Hampton	Roberts Meadow Reservoir		Segreganset River
	Wallum Lake	Otis	Benton Pond		Ponds
Dudley	Shepherd Pond		Creek Pond	Tewksbury	Round Pond
Fall River	Cook Pond		Otis Reservoir	Uxbridge	Lackey Pond
Gloucester	Mill Pond	Oxford	Hudson Pond		Rice City Pond
	Niles Pond	Paxton	Asnebumskit Pond	Wareham	Dicks Pond
Halifax	Monponsett Pond	Peabody	Cedar Pond		Parker Mills Pond
Hanover	Forge Pond		Crystal Pond	Warren	Snipatuit Pond
Hanson	Wampatuck Pond		Pierces Pond	Wrentham	Crocker Pond
Holden	Unionville Pond				Lake Archer

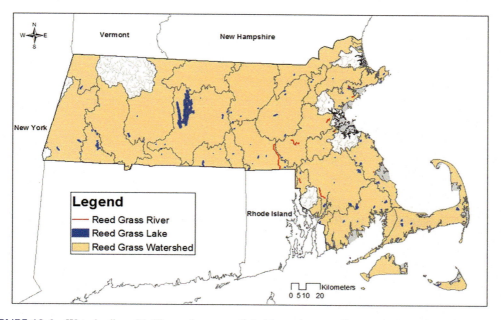

FIGURE 18.6 Waterbodies with *Phragmites australis* in Massachusetts. (See Table 18.1 for site descriptions.)

Note: This map underrepresents the full extent of *Phragmites* throughout of the states (see text for more information).

combination with glyphosate, achieves in more efficient control of *Phragmites* than glyphosate alone (Getsinger et al. 2007). However, while very effective at eliminating *Phragmites*, imazapyr persists in the environment for a longer period than glyphosate. When exposed to light in surface water, the chemical breaks down within days, but in soil it can persist for up to five months (Wisconsin DNR 2012). Stie monitoring after herbicide treatment has also indicated that heavier applications of imazapyr early in the growing season could be somewhat detrimental to recolonization by native plants (Mozdzer et al. 2008). Imazapyr can also move through soil and affect woody tree species in areas adjacent to the application. Therefore, applying an excessive amount of herbicide should be avoided.

The seasonal timing of herbicide application is an important factor in the treatment's success. Imazapyr is most effective on plants that are in stages of active growth, and should be applied to *Phragmites* after full leaf elongation in late spring and before plants have fully matured (Avers et al. 2007; Wisconsin DNR 2012). Glyphosate is more effective on mature plants once they have stopped growing and are in full bloom, i.e., in late summer (Avers et al. 2007). Therefore, for most effective chemical control, it is recommended to treat in early summer with imazapyr, in late summer with glyphosate, or in both seasons with each respective herbicide if necessary. Since imazapyr is more effective than glyphosate and requires fewer applications for complete removal, imazapyr application is generally recommended over glyphosate (Marks et al. 1994; Mozdzer et al. 2008).

Herbicides can be applied via a number of different methods. These include manually injecting stems, directly to a cut stem, spraying from a backpack, or aerial application in extreme cases. A practitioner on the Cape Cod developed a method of cutting *Phragmites* at about waist height, bundling the cut stems together, and wiping them with herbicide. Care should always be taken to avoid exposing nontarget plants to general-use herbicides to prevent environmental degradation. Common reed grass stems growing among or near desirable plants can be hand wiped (not something to do on acres of *Phragmites*). In this situation, applicator can wear an absorbent cotton glove over a rubber glove, then moistens the outer glove with herbicide, and each stem is then wiped from the bottom-up (Joan Deely, personal communication). Environmental monitoring is also needed for posttreatment assessment. It should also be noted that single-year applications of herbicide are never effective in fully eliminating *Phragmites*. A typical treatment cycle would be deployed over at least three growing seasons. Additionally, when herbicide regimens are not directly followed by replanting and cultivation of native plants, *Phragmites* often reemerges at the same site from remnant rhizomes or seeds (Hazelton et al. 2014). Therefore, chemical treatment plans should involve repetition of treatment for multiple years along with specific plans to simultaneously restore native flora. It is also found that native plant regeneration proceeds well in wetlands once the *Phragmites* has been removed and this is especially the case in salt marshes, where seed bank supplies are abundant, and ground moisture is continuous (Joan Deely, personal communication).

More information about chemical control on *Phragmites* and other 18 invasive species can be found in Appendix III. In the state of Massachusetts, an aquatic nuisance species control license (BRP WM04 Form) must be obtained from the Massachusetts Department of Environmental Protection before applying a chemical herbicide to *Phragmites* stands that are growing in or adjacent to open water.

Physical Control

Controlled burns and mechanical removal are often suggested as methods of control to be used in connection with herbicide treatment. It is not recommended to use prescribed fire treatments or mechanical removal (such as mowing or cutting vegetation either by hand or with machinery) without first applying herbicides, as physical destruction of aboveground plant matter promotes the growth of invasive *Phragmites* (Avers et al. 2007; Hazelton et al. 2014). Physical removal is recommended for eliminating dead plant material after herbicide treatment. When excess plant matter is removed from a site, it is also easier to apply follow-up herbicide spot treatments to remaining live *Phragmites*.

Fire treatments, if applicable and implemented safely, can be a cost-effective way to remove dead material and are of low risk to surrounding native plant life, as fires can promote general plant growth. However, *Phragmites* fires can be dangerous to humans and property, as dead or dry reed stalks are very flammable and can cause spot fires at unexpected locations (Marks et al. 1994), so burns should be planned carefully. The best timing for a controlled burn is during the driest part of the year. However, fires can spread as underground peat burns, which are difficult to control.

When physical removal is implemented without chemical treatment, mostly by cutting stems, higher rates of successful *Phragmites* eradication following physical removal have been reported when plastic is placed on top of the cut stems for the rest of the growing season (Hazelton et al. 2014). Flooding has also been found to be effective in preventing regrowth after manual removal. A study by Smith (2005) demonstrated that in flooded areas, manually cutting *Phragmites* stems below the water line prevents the plant from being able to transport oxygen efficiently. This method successfully prevented regrowth: 1.5 years after breaking the stems, reed grass was gone from all but one of the ponds in the trial (Smith 2005). Though techniques involving cutting and smothering stems are effective, they can be time-consuming and require many people to complete. Smothering can also have detrimental effects on soil biota, essentially sterilizing it and necessitating soil remediation efforts.

Deliberately increasing tidal flooding can also be a powerful method of *Phragmites* control, as it can raise salinity to a level that *Phragmites* cannot tolerate. This is especially useful in restoring salt marshes overtaken by *Phragmites*, since the native salt marsh grass *Spartina alterniflora* tolerates higher salinity than *Phragmites* (Medeiros et al. 2013). In the Buzzards Bay estuary, a culvert replacement intended to raise salinity by increasing tidal flow resulted in an ecological shift: where *Phragmites* initially made up 44% of the marsh vegetation, it made up 38% of the marsh five years after the culvert construction, and the portion of marsh covered by *Spartina* rose from 20% to 32% (US EPA 2007). A similar effort at the Trustees of Reservation Argilla road culvert replacement in Ipswich, Massachusetts, increased tidal flooding and saw the proportion of cover made up of *Phragmites* fall from 40% to 22% in a year, alongside the increased abundance of *Spartina alterniflora* (Buchsbaum et al. 2006). Flooding may additionally be effective if applied following herbicide and prescribed burning treatment, or together with other mechanical control methods.

One problem that is not easily solved by physical control is the extensive root system left behind after *Phragmites* stalks are removed (Figure 18.7). The roots can extend up to 2 m underground (Marks et al. 1994), making it very difficult to remove by pulling. Reed grass root systems or remnant aerial shoots can prevent the regrowth of other plant species because of the space they occupy in the soil. Furthermore, since *Phragmites* can propagate through its

FIGURE 18.7 The root and rhizome system of the common reed grass. (Photo by Robert E. Meadows.)

rhizome, the plant can produce new stalks even after all aboveground components of the plant have been removed. To effectively eradicate the plant, the roots must be completely starved or destroyed via flooding, smothering, or by repeated removal of stalks. The site must be well-monitored to watch for and quickly respond to new shoots emerging from the rhizome. In situations where complete removal on a very large scale is deemed necessary, and if sufficient time and funding are available, machine excavation might be considered (Hazelton et al. 2014). However, any such operation involving dredging on or adjacent to wetlands in the state of Massachusetts would require the landowners submit a 401 Water Quality Cert. application and receive clearance through the MassDEP.

BIOLOGICAL CONTROL

Many new avenues for biological control of introduced *Phragmites* have emerged in recent years. In 2002, Tewksbury et al. identified many organisms native to North America or to Europe (and introduced to North America) that feed either exclusively or in part on *Phragmites*,. Over the past two decades, through rigorous study and testing, the list was narrowed from nine to four, and then to two candidates for biological control. Finally, in 2018, Blossey et al. recommended the introduction of two stem-boring moths, *Archanara geminipuncta* and *Archanara neurica*, for the biological control of *Phragmites*, given the two species' extreme dietary specificity. Blossey et al. petitioned the USDA and equivalent regulatory agencies in Canada to approve the release of *A. geminipuncta* and *A. neurica* for this purpose. In April, 2019, the two species were officially "recommended for release" by the USDA (Blossey et al. 2019; USDA 2020).

These developments were met with some backlash that sparked debate in the scientific community (Kiviat et al. 2019; Blossey et al. 2019). There has been hesitation and concern surrounding the introduction of new non-native species as biological control, as unintended consequences may occur that are difficult to manage once introduction has been carried out (Tewksbury et al. 2002; Hazelton et al. 2014; Kiviat et al. 2019). Kiviat et al. (2019) expressed specific concern that *A. geminipuncta* and *A. neurica* will feed indiscriminately on the native *Phragmites australis americanus* along with the introduced strain, but Blossey et al. (2019) believe that this is not likely to occur, as accidentally introduced monophagous *Phragmites australis* herbivores in North America have not been observed to feed on native *P. australis americanus*. The effectiveness of these two promising moths has not yet been tested in the field, and neither *Archanara* species is yet commercially available, but the USDA has officially recommended *A. geminipuncta* and *A. neurica* for the biological control of introduced *Phragmites*. Though it has its risks, biological control is potentially cheaper and less labor-intensive than conventional methods of invasive plant control involving herbicides (Hazelton et al. 2014; Blossey et al. 2019).

Mammals have, at times, been employed as a form of biological control, thinning and removing *Phragmites* stands by grazing. Livestock have reportedly been grazed on *Phragmites* in its native Europe, but results have been mixed in the United States. Some field tests involving goats found that goats preferentially grazed on all plant matter except for *Phragmites* in an area (Hazelton et al. 2014). However, when goats are restricted to areas without alternative food sources, the goats can reduce *Phragmites* cover significantly (Hazelton et al. 2014; Silliman et al. 2014). Cows and horses may also readily consume this plant (Silliman et al. 2014). However, sites where grazing is implemented might suffer from expected problems such as trampling and compaction of soil (Hazelton et al. 2014). Phragmites may also be nutritionally insufficient to livestock as their only food source, and it is suggested other nutrients should also be made available to grazing animals such as goats (Sun et al. 2008).

Experience has shown that the most important and best proven ecological control of *Phragmites* is restoration of native plant assemblages. When *Phragmites* is removed from an area by any means, it is essential that the area is repopulated with native species to prevent another invasion and repair ecological damage caused by its aggressive growth. In estuarine habitats, *Phragmites* competes with the much shorter native salt-marsh grass *Spartina alterniflora* by shading it from the sunlight (Getsinger et al. 2007; Medeiros et al. 2013), but

S. alterniflora has the advantage of being able to withstand higher salinity than *Phragmites*. In salt marsh and tidal habitats, *Phragmites* may be effectively combated by increasing tidal flow to raise salinity while simultaneously supporting the regrowth of *S. alterniflora* in its place (Medeiros et al. 2013).

Restoration of native mammal habitat may also be a valuable method of ecological control. Small native mammals, though not typically considered for control of nuisance plants, may play an important role in limiting their expansion. Specifically in low-salinity marshes, small mammals were found to preferentially graze on *Phragmites*, not eliminating the reed grass but preventing its spread (Gedan et al. 2009). Muskrats, iconic inhabitants of New England's wetlands, have been observed to feed on *Phragmites* (Hazelton et al. 2014). Reintroduction of native mammals to degraded habitats, or restoration of habitats suitable to muskrats by installing muskrat platforms, could both prevent reed grass invasion and also be beneficial to wetland ecosystems. This method may be especially useful in freshwater wetlands, in areas of low salinity unfavorable to the reintroduction of *Spartina alterniflora*, or where intentional tidal flow increase is neither appropriate nor feasible.

GENERAL MANAGEMENT PLANS

The following general chemical and mechanical management plans were published by Avers et al. (2007) to be selected depending on characteristics of the site and the density of the *Phragmites* stand.

For large, dense stands at either a dry or wet site, the advised treatment is as follows:

1. Apply herbicide in early or late summer depending on what herbicides are being used (see the earlier section pertaining to chemical treatments for guidance) and wait at least three weeks to allow for plants to be exposed to the chemicals.
2. In the following year, conduct a prescribed fire in either late summer (mid-July through August) or winter (January to prior spring green-up) if a fire cannot be applied in the summer.
3. Assess the site the following growing season and spot-treat with herbicide as deemed necessary.

For large, dense stands in impoundments, the advised treatment is as follows:

1. Apply herbicide in late summer (late August and September) followed immediately by flooding to a minimum depth of 6 inches.
2. Dewater the site in late July of the following year.
3. Keep the site as dry as possible until mid-August and then treat with a prescribed fire.
4. Immediately following the burn, reflood the site to a minimum depth of 6 inches, maintaining this water level for at least a year.
5. Assess the site the following growing season and spot-treat with herbicide as deemed necessary.

For low-density stands at either a dry or wet site, the advised treatment is as follows:

1. Apply herbicide in early or late summer depending on what herbicides are being used (see the earlier section pertaining to chemical treatments for guidance) and wait at least two weeks to allow for plants to be exposed to the chemicals.
2. Mechanically treat the site either in late summer or fall prior to spring green-up. If the site is a wet site, wait until the ground is frozen. Use hand tools, weed whips, or small mowers on denser stands.
3. Assess the site the following growing season and spot-treat with herbicide as deemed necessary.

Using the methods already outlined, in combination with long-term monitoring and annual maintenance, invasive *Phragmites* can be controlled, and in some cases even eradicated from certain sites. An example of three different management plans over a three-year period can be found in Diagram 18.1. Due to the hardiness of the

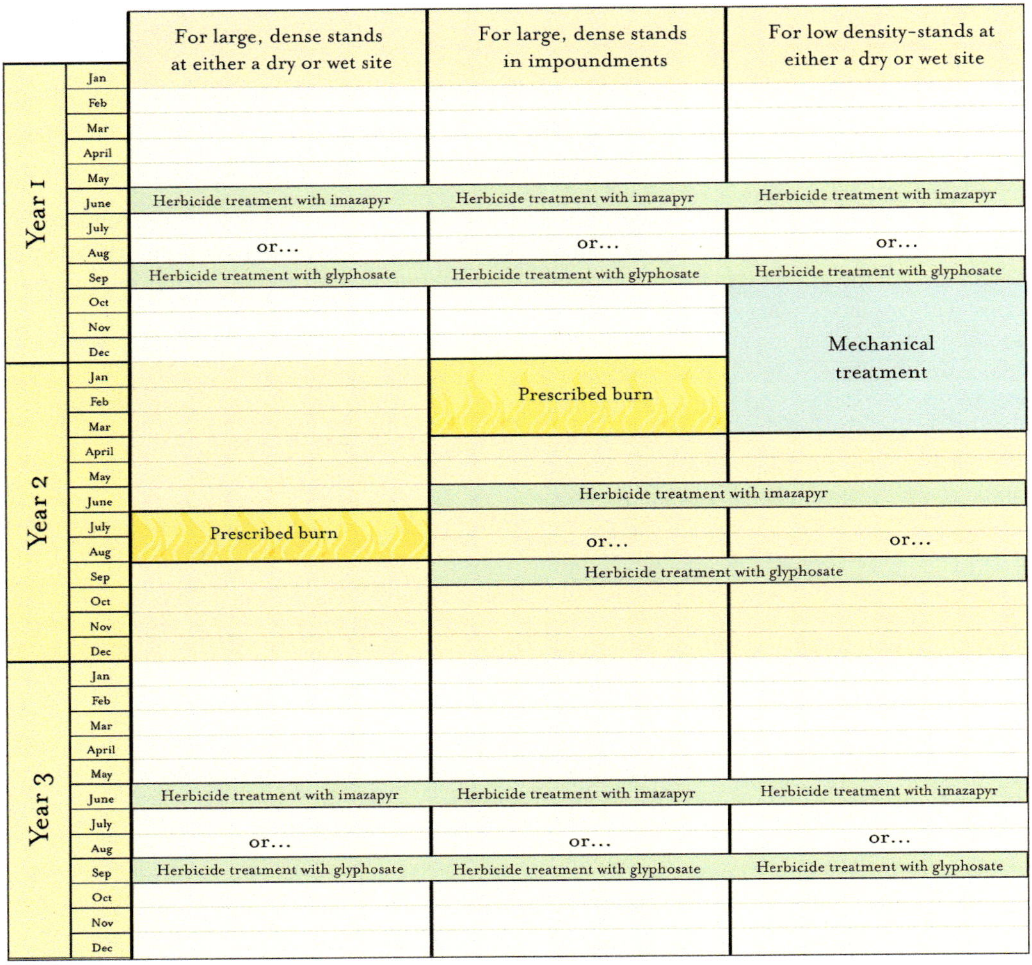

		For large, dense stands at either a dry or wet site	For large, dense stands in impoundments	For low density-stands at either a dry or wet site
Year 1	Jan			
	Feb			
	Mar			
	April			
	May			
	June	Herbicide treatment with imazapyr	Herbicide treatment with imazapyr	Herbicide treatment with imazapyr
	July	or…	or…	or…
	Aug			
	Sep	Herbicide treatment with glyphosate	Herbicide treatment with glyphosate	Herbicide treatment with glyphosate
	Oct			
	Nov			Mechanical treatment
	Dec			
Year 2	Jan		Prescribed burn	
	Feb			
	Mar			
	April			
	May			
	June		Herbicide treatment with imazapyr	Herbicide treatment with imazapyr
	July	Prescribed burn	or…	or…
	Aug			
	Sep		Herbicide treatment with glyphosate	Herbicide treatment with glyphosate
	Oct			
	Nov			
	Dec			
Year 3	Jan			
	Feb			
	Mar			
	April			
	May			
	June	Herbicide treatment with imazapyr	Herbicide treatment with imazapyr	Herbicide treatment with imazapyr
	July	or…	or…	or…
	Aug			
	Sep	Herbicide treatment with glyphosate	Herbicide treatment with glyphosate	Herbicide treatment with glyphosate
	Oct			
	Nov			
	Dec			

DIAGRAM 18.1 Three suggested management approaches over a three-year period. (Modified from Avers et al. (2007).)

species and its ability to spread, it is critical to commit to long-term management, repeated over multiple years, so that new patches and stands of *Phragmites* do not develop. This requires the cooperation of different agencies and organizations, as well as a specific restoration plan. An example of a successful chemical and mechanical management plan carried out with positive results is discussed in the "Success Story" section.

SUCCESS STORY

A study conducted in the Adirondack Park in upstate New York sought to manage invasive *Phragmites* using a glyphosate-based herbicide, with 346 populations receiving treatment over a seven-year period (Quirion et al. 2018). Prior to the beginning of treatment, 114 sites were monitored for three to six years to assess the annual increase in patch area and patch coverage in the absence of any control methods. Initial patches ranged from 0.36 to 4,314 m^2 with an initial site coverage ranging from 38% to 75%. For smaller patches of *Phragmites*, herbicide was applied by foliar spray, while large patches used a combination of foliar spray and stem injection (or cut and drip). A combination approach was also used in areas where the invasive species were found near native plants to reduce negative spillover effects that may occur when using a foliar spray application. Over the course of the study, a site-specific adaptive management approach was used; most sites required an additional treatment of herbicide following the first treatment. If resprouts were abundant in a patch, a foliar spray was applied; if resprouts were infrequent, isolated, or near native plants, stem injection was used. If no new growth was found, treatment at that site did not occur in that year. Any singular *Phragmites* plant found was removed manually.

A total of 243 sites were treated with foliar spray, with an average of 4.5 treatments per site. These smaller sites were generally treated intermittently, as sprouts would be present one year but absent the next. A total of 91 sites were treated with the combined application of foliar spray and stem injections. Eradication was determined to be achieved when a minimum of three consecutive years of *Phragmites* absence had been achieved. Following the seven-year study period, eradication had been achieved in 104 sites, with 88 of these sites receiving exclusively intermittent foliar spray. The probability of eradication decreased as the pretreatment patch size increased: the probability of eradicating smaller sites was 0.83, 0.26 for medium sites, and 0.02 for large sites.

Quirion et al. (2018) concluded that eradication of smaller sites was achievable, but with larger, well-established sites, eradication would be more difficult and require longer project periods and the extensive use of resources. They recommended responding rapidly and administering treatment to small and new patches of *Phragmites* in order to reduce its spread. They also noted a surprising lack of posttreatment evaluations, making it hard to determine what types of treatments are effective in different scenarios. They urged therefore that future projects aimed at the management of invasive species evaluate and publish their results, promoting accountability and aiding in decision-making for future projects. These takeaways, in conjunction with the goals of this project to map existing *Phragmites* locations in Massachusetts, can be used in the future to strategically pick which sites to administer treatment where it will be most effective. This method will also ensure that resources are not wasted by trying to treat patches where the probability of eradication are very slim. At existing sites, the methods laid out in the "Managing Actions" section can be used to treat existing sites, coupled with long-term monitoring.

NOTE

1 A haplotype is a set of DNA variations that are inherited together from a single parent.

REFERENCES

Avers, B., R. Fahlsing, E. Kafcas, J. Schafer, T. Collin, L. Esman, E. Finnell, A. Lounds, R. Terry, J. Hazelman, J. Hudgins, K. Getsinger, and D. Schuen. 2007. A Guide to the Control and Management of Invasive Phragmites. *Michigan Department of Environmental Quality, Lansing.*

Blossey, B., S.B. Endriss, R. Casagrande, P. Häfliger, H. Hinz, A. Dávalos, C. Brown-Lima, L. Tewksbury, and R.S. Bourchier. 2019. When misconceptions impede best practices: evidence supports biological control of invasive *Phragmites*. *Biological Invasions* 22: 873–883.

Bonham, A.J. 1980. Bank protection using emergent plants against boat wash in rivers and canals. Hydraulics Research Station #IT 206, UK, 28 pp.

Buchsbaum, R.N., J Catena, E. Hutchins, and M. James-Pirri. 2006. Changes in salt marsh vegetation, *Phragmites australis*, and nekton in response to increased tidal flushing in a New England salt marsh. *Wetlands* 26: 544–557.

Burk, I. 1877. List of Plants Recently Collected on Ships' Ballast in the Neighborhood of Philadelphia. *Proceedings of the Academy of Natural Sciences of Philadelphia* 29: 105–109.

Crow, G.E., and C.B. Hellquist. 2000. Aquatic and Wetland Plants of Northeastern North America: A Revised and Enlarged Edition of Norman C. Fassett's A Manual of Aquatic Plants (Volume Two) Angiosperms: Monocotyledons. University of Wisconsin Press, Madison WI, USA, p. 456.

Del Tredici, P. 2020. *Wild Urban Plants of the Northeast: A Field Guide*. Cornell University Press.

Gedan, K.M., C.M. Crain, and M.D. Bertness. 2009. Small-mammal herbivore control of secondary succession in New England tidal marshes. *Ecology* 90(2): 430–440.

Gersberg, R.M., B.V. Elkins, S.R. Lyon, and C.R. Goldman. 1986. Role of aquatic plants in wastewater treatment by artificial wetlands. *Water Research* 20(3): 363–368.

Getsinger, K.D., L.S. Nelson, L.M. Glomski, E. Kafcas, J. Schafer, S. Kogge, and M. Nurse. 2007. *Control of Phragmites in a Michigan Great Lakes Marsh*. U.S. Army Engineer Research and Development Center, Vicksburg, MS, p. 120.

Gray, K.R., and A.J. Biddlestone. 1995. Engineered reed-bed systems for wastewater treatment. *Trends in Biotechnology* 13(7): 248–252.

Haines, A. 2010. Botanical Notes 13: 5. *Stantec*. www.scribd.com/document/37804531/Botanical-Notes-13. (Accessed January 22, 2021).

Hazelton, E.L.G., T.J. Mozdzer, D. Burdick, K.M. Kettenring, and D. Whigham D. 2014. *Phragmites australis* management in the United States: 40 years of methods and outcomes. *Annals of Botany PLANTS* 6.

Henderson, A.M., J.A. Gervais, B. Luukinen, K. Buhl, D. Stone, A. Cross, and J. Jenkins. 2010. Glyphosate General Fact Sheet. *National Pesticide Information Center, Oregon State University Extension Services.* http://npic.orst.edu/factsheets/glyphogen.html. (Accessed January 20, 2021).

ITIS (Integrated Taxonomic Information System). 2021. www.itis.gov/servlet/SingleRpt/SingleRpt?search_topic=TSN&search_value=41072#null (Accessed April 9, 2021).

Jodoin, Y., C. Lavoie, P. Villeneuve, M. Theriault, J. Beaulieu, and F. Belzile. 2008. Highways as corridors and habitats for the invasive common reed *Phragmites australis* in Quebec, Canada. *Journal of Applied Ecology* 45 (2): 459–466.

Kelly, W. 1999. A Guide to Aquatic Plants in Massachusetts. New England Aquarium, Massachusetts Department of Environmental Management, Lakes and Ponds Program. Boston MA, USA, p. 32.

Kiviat, E., and E. Hamilton. 2001. *Phragmites* use by Native North Americans. *Aquatic Botany* 69(2–4): 341–357.

Kiviat, E., L.A. Meyerson, T.J. Mozdzer, W.J. Allen, A.H. Baldwin, G.P. Bhattarai, K. Brix, J.S. Caplan, K.M. Kettenring, C. Lambertini, J. Weis, D.F. Whigham, and J.T. Cronin. 2019. Evidence does not support the targeting of cryptic invaders at the subspecies level using classical biological control: the example of *Phragmites*. *Biological Invasions* 21: 2529–2541.

Legault, R., G.P. Zogg, and S.E. Travis. 2018. Competitive interactions between native *Spartina alterniflora* and non-native *Phragmites australis* depend on nutrient loading and temperature. *PLoS One* 13(2): e0192234.

Marks, M., B. Lapin, and J. Randall. 1994. *Phragmites australis* (*P. Communis*): Threats, management, and monitoring. *Natural Areas Journal* 14: 285–294.

Martin, L.J., and B. Blossey. 2013. The Runaway Weed: Costs and Failures of *Phragmites australis* Management in the USA. *Estuaries and Coasts* 36 (3): 626–32.

McGlynn, C.A. 2008. Native and invasive plant interactions in wetlands and the minimal role of invasiveness. *Biological Invasions* 11: 1929–1939.

Medeiros, D.L., D.S. White, and B.L. Howes. 2013. Replacement of *Phragmites australis* by *Spartina alterniflora*: The role of competition and salinity. *Wetlands* 33: 421–430.

Minchinton, T.E., and M.D. Bertness. 2003. Disturbance-mediated competition and the spread of *Phragmites australis* in a coastal marsh. *Ecological Applications* 13: 1400–1416.

Mozdzer, T.J., C.J. Hutto, P.A. Clarke, and D.P. Field. 2008. Efficacy of Imazapyr and Glyphosate in the Control of Non-Native *Phragmites australis*. *Restoration Ecology* 16(2): 221–224.

Packer, J.G., L.A. Meyerson, H. Skálová, P. Pyšek, and C. Kueffer. 2017. Biological Flora of the British Isles: *Phragmites australis*. *Journal of Ecology* 105(4): 1123–1162.

Payne, R.E., and B. Blossey. 2007. Presence and Abundance of Native and Introduced *Phragmites Australis* (Poaceae) in Falmouth, Massachusetts. *Rhodora* 109: 96–100.

Quirion, B., Z. Simek, A. Dávalos, and B. Blossey. 2018. Management of invasive *Phragmites australis* in the Adirondacks: a cautionary tale about prospects of eradication. *Biological Invasions* 20: 49–73.

Richburg, J.A., W.A. Patterson, and F. Lowenstein. 2001. Effects of Road Salt and *Phragmites australis* invasion on the vegetation of a western Massachusetts calcareous lake-basin fen. *Wetlands* 21(2): 247–255.

Saltonstall, K. 2002. Cryptic Invasion by a Non-native Genotype of the Common Reed, *Phragmites australis*, into North America. *Proceedings of the National Academy of Sciences of the United States of America* 99 (4): 2445–449.

Saltonstall, K., and L.A. Meyerson. 2016. *Phragmites australis*: from genes to ecosystems. *Biological Invasions* 18: 2415–2420.

Saltonstall, K., P.M. Peterson, and R.J. Soreng. 2004. Recognition of *Phragmites australis subsp.* americanus (Poaceae: Arundinoideae) in North America: Evidence from Morphological and Genetic Analysis. *SIDA, Contributions to Botany*, 683–692.

Silliman, B.R., T. Mozdzer, C. Angelini, J.E. Brundage, P. Esselink, J.P. Bakker, K.B. Gedan, J. van de Koppel, and A.H. Baldwin. 2014. Livestock as a potential biological control agent for an invasive wetland plant. *Peer J* 2: e567 10.7717/peerj.567.

Smith, S.M. 2005. Manual Control of *Phragmites australis* in Freshwater Ponds of Cape Cod National Seashore, Massachusetts, USA. *Journal of Aquatic Plant Management* 43: 50–53.

Sun, Z.W., D.W. Zhou, L.M.M. Ferreira, Q.Z. Zhong, and Y.J. Lou. 2008. Diet composition, herbage intake and digestibility in Inner Mongolian Cashmere goats grazing on native *Leymus chinensis* plant communities. *Livestock Science* 116 (1–3): 155–146.

Tewksbury, L., R. Casagrande, B. Blossey, P. Hälfliger, and M. Schwarzländer. 2002. Potential for biological control of *Phragmites australis* in North America. *Biological Control* 23(2): 191–212.

Tiner, R. 1998. Managing Common Reed (*Phragmites australis*) in Massachusetts. *U.S. Fish and Wildlife Service*. Boston, MA.

Tip of the Mitt Watershed Council. n.d. *Phragmites*. Photos via www.watershedcouncil.org/phragmites.html. (Accessed March 23, 2021).

US EPA (US Environmental Protection Agency). 2007. As Salt Water Returns to Winsegansett Marsh, So Does Natural Vegetation. www.epa.gov/sites/production/files/2015-11/documents/ma_winsegansett.pdf (Accessed March 15, 2017).

US FWS (US Fish and Wildlife Services). n.d. PHRAGMITES: Questions and Answers. www.fws.gov/gomcp/pdfs/phragmitesqa_factsheet.pdf (Accessed September 22, 2020).

USDA (US Department of Agriculture). 2020. Technical Advisory Group for Biological Control Agents of Weeds TAG Petitions—APHIS Actions. www.aphis.usda.gov/plant_health/permits/tag/downloads/TAGPetitionAction.pdf. (Accessed January 22, 2021).

Weis, J.S., E.B. Watson, B. Ravit, C. Harman, and M. Yepsen. 2021. The status and future of tidal marshes in New Jersey faced with sea level rise. *Anthropocene Coasts* 4: 168–192.

Wisconsin Department of Natural Resources (DNR). 2012. Imazapyr chemical fact sheet. https://dnr.wi.gov/lakes/plants/factsheets/ImazapyrFactsheet.pdf. (Accessed January 20, 2021).

APPENDIX A
Latitude and Longitude for Each Water body with *Phragmites australis*

Waterbody	Agency	Report Source	Longitude	Latitude	First Year Reported
Gulliver Creek	MassDEP	The Neponset River Watershed 1994 Resource Assessment Report	−71.05115043	42.27154821	1994
Long Pond	DCR	Complied Data from DEP Herbicide Files 98–05 (1995)	−70.17939013	41.27627396	1995
Broad Cove	MassDEP	Appendix C—DWM 1996 and 2001 Lake Survey Data in the Taunton River Watershed	−71.12887741	41.79206496	1996
Crocker Pond	MassDEP	Appendix C—DWM 1996 and 2001 Lake Survey Data in the Taunton River Watershed	−71.29478902	42.06769128	1996
Kings Pond	MassDEP	Appendix C—DWM 1996 and 2001 Lake Survey Data in the Taunton River Watershed	−71.05515697	41.93537918	1996
Little Quittacas Pond	MassDEP	Appendix C—DWM 1996 and 2001 Lake Survey Data in the Taunton River Watershed	−70.9161824	41.79260103	1996
Segreganset River	MassDEP	Appendix C—DWM 1996 and 2001 Lake Survey Data in the Taunton River Watershed	−71.1648734	41.85364572	1996
Somerset Reservoir	MassDEP	Appendix C—DWM 1996 and 2001 Lake Survey Data in the Taunton River Watershed	−71.13922277	41.78275579	1996
Thirty Acre Pond	MassDEP	Appendix C—DWM 1996 and 2001 Lake Survey Data in the Taunton River Watershed	−71.04550893	42.09554728	1996
Cape Pond	MassDEP	North Coastal Watershed 1997/1998 Water Quality Assessment Report	−70.630667	42.63992974	1997
Crane River	MassDEP	North Coastal Watershed 1997/1998 Water Quality Assessment Report	−70.93004499	42.55576425	1997
Floating Bridge Pond	MassDEP	North Coastal Watershed 1997/1998 Water Quality Assessment Report	−70.93984302	42.48535812	1997
Fuller Street Pond	MassDEP	Ten Mile River Basin 1997 Water Quality Assessment Report	−70.81318104	41.90716261	1997
Mill Pond	MassDEP	North Coastal Watershed 1997/1998 Water Quality Assessment Report	−70.67647849	42.63015993	1997
Mill River	MassDEP	Charles River Watershed 1997/1998 Water Quality Assessment Report			1997
Muddy River	MassDEP	Charles River Watershed 1997/1998 Water Quality Assessment Report 72-AC-3 16.0 February 2000	−71.10608544	42.34361819	1997
Niles Pond	MassDEP	North Coastal Watershed 1997/1998 Water Quality Assessment Report			1997
Porters Pond	MassDEP	North Coastal Watershed 1997/1998 Water Quality Assessment Report	−70.92704635	42.56318893	1997
Seaplane Basin	MassDEP	North Coastal Watershed 1997/1998 Water Quality Assessment Report	−71.01247661	42.43276228	1997
Sevenmile River	MassDEP	Ten Mile River Basin 1997 Water Quality Assessment Report	−71.34364142	41.94411787	1997
Waters River	MassDEP	North Coastal Watershed 1997/1998 Water Quality Assessment Report	−70.93863051	42.54647	1997
Wetherells Pond	MassDEP	Ten Mile River Basin 1997 Water Quality Assessment Report	−71.33702134	42.00018511	1997
Whiting Pond	MassDEP	Ten Mile River Basin 1997 Water Quality Assessment Report	−71.33522823	41.99363083	1997
Asnebumskit Pond	MassDEP	Appendix A—1998 DEP DWM Nashua River Basin QA/QC Report	−71.90908184	42.32300705	1998

(Continued)

APPENDIX A (Continued)

Waterbody	Agency	Report Source	Longitude	Latitude	First Year Reported
Box Pond	MassDEP	DEP WQAR (1998) NW	−71.49254045	42.09303602	1998
Coachlace Pond	MassDEP	Appendix A—1998 DEP DWM Nashua River Basin QA/QC Report	−71.69718294	42.413375	1998
Five Mile Pond	MassDEP	Chicopee River Basin 1998 Water Quality Assessment Report	−72.51066309	42.14168286	1998
Hathaway Pond	MassDEP	DEP WQAR (1998) NW	−71.75522937	42.17778252	1998
Haviland Pond	MassDEP	Chicopee River Basin 1998 Water Quality Assessment Report	−72.47399733	42.17244881	1998
Lackey Pond	MassDEP	Blackstone River Basin 1998 Water Quality Assessment Report	−71.6903591	42.09496427	1998
Moulton Pond	MassDEP	Chicopee River Basin 1998 Water Quality Assessment Report	−71.95411692	42.38905736	1998
Muschopauge Pond	MassDEP	Appendix A—1998 DEP DWM Nashua River Basin QA/QC Report	−71.92177215	42.38361307	1998
Quabbin Reservoir	MassDEP	Chicopee River Basin 1998 Water Quality Assessment Report 36-AC-2 47.0, April 2001	−72.30953364	42.39167411	1998
Roberts Meadow Reservoir	MassDEP	Connecticut River Basin 1998 Water Quality Assessment Report	−72.71269532	42.3511603	1998
Southwick Pond	MassDEP	DEP WQAR (1998) NW	−71.89129683	42.28423712	1998
Tighe Carmody Reservoir	MassDEP	Connecticut River Basin 1998 Water Quality Assessment Report	−72.7824297	42.22766881	1998
Town Barn Beaver Pond	MassDEP	Chicopee River Basin 1998 Water Quality Assessment Report	−72.1818303	42.47819577	1998
Unionville Pond	MassDEP	Appendix A—1998 DEP DWM Nashua River Basin QA/QC Report	−71.84205587	42.35973521	1998
Blue Hills Reservoir	MassDEP	Boston Harbor 1999 Water Quality Assessment Report	−71.05058786	42.22840255	1999
Dudley Pond	DCR	Compiled Data from DEP Herbicide Files 98–05 1999	−71.73810589	42.05104264	1999
Forge Pond	MassDEP	Boston Harbor 1999 Water Quality Assessment Report	−71.14075992	42.15619228	1999
Newfield Pond	MassDEP	Merrimack River Basin 1999 Water Quality Assessment Report	−71.3899233	42.63378436	1999
Bogastow Brook	MassDEP	Shawsheen River Watershed 2000 Water Quality Assessment Report	−71.39378189	42.1974852	2000
Cheshire Reservoir (Middle Basin)	MassDEP	Hudson River Basin 1997 Water Quality Assessment Report 11/12/13-AC-1 15.0, January 2000	−73.19187111	42.53145142	2000
Crystal Pond	MassDEP	Ipswich River Watershed 2000 Water Quality Assessment Report	−70.99999865	42.54906234	2000
Dicks Pond	MassDEP	Buzzards Bay Watershed 2000 Water Quality Assessment Report	−70.65766372	41.76031051	2000
Lake Rohunta	MassDEP	Millers River Watershed 2000 Water Quality Assessment Report 35-AC-1 CN089.0, March 2004	−72.27094837	42.53048841	2000
Pierces Pond	MassDEP	Ipswich River Watershed 2000 Water Quality Assessment Report	−70.996911	42.52940234	2000

Richardson Pond North	MassDEP	Shawsheen River Watershed 2000 Water Quality Assessment Report	−71.24628015	42.58771504	2000
Round Pond	MassDEP	Shawsheen River Watershed 2000 Water Quality Assessment Report	−71.23213478	42.602819	2000
Sudden Pond	MassDEP	Ipswich River Watershed 2000 Water Quality Assessment Report	−71.06311289	42.61001223	2000
Tinkham Pond	MassDEP	Buzzards Bay Watershed 2000 Water Quality Assessment Report	−70.85926672	41.68372684	2000
Benton Pond	MassDEP	Farmington River Watershed 2001 Biological Assessment	−73.04739091	42.1841285	2001
Buffum Pond	MassDEP	French and Quinebaug River Watershed 2001 Water Quality Assessment Report	−71.90231756	42.11611701	2001
Clear Pond	MassDEP	Westfield River Watershed 2001 Water Quality Assessment Report	−72.65945886	42.18564647	2001
Creek Pond	MassDEP	Farmington River Watershed 2001 Biological Assessment	−73.04844921	42.22894348	2001
Duxbury Bay	MassDEP	11-E008–01	−70.69884371	41.98662005	2001
Forge Pond	MassDEP	South Shore Coastal Watersheds 2001 Water Quality Assessment Report, South Coastal Watersheds DWM Year 2001 Water Quality Monitoring Data (PG. C2)	−70.88000386	42.10622436	2001
Fort Meadow Reservoir	MassDEP	Concord Watershed 2001 DWM Water Quality Monitoring Data	−71.54760267	42.36994107	2001
Foundry Pond	MassDEP	South Shore Coastal Watersheds 2001 Water Quality Assessment Report	−70.70910461	41.98428943	2001
Great Sandy Bottom Pond	MassDEP	South Shore Coastal Watersheds 2001 Water Quality Assessment Report, South Coastal Watersheds DWM Year 2001 Water Quality Monitoring Data (PG. C2)	−70.83153067	42.05287367	2001
Hudson Pond	MassDEP	French and Quinebaug River Watershed 2001 Water Quality Assessment Report	−71.83403839	42.14317709	2001
Long Bow Lake	MassDEP	Westfield River Watershed 2001 Water Quality Assessment Report	−73.09099528	42.25328255	2001
Mashpee Pond	MassDEP	05-G011–01	−70.4869729	41.66106655	2001
Monponsett Pond	MassDEP	09-G006–01	−70.8452535	42.0045958	2001
Musquashcut Pond	MassDEP	South Coastal Watersheds DWM Year 2001 Water Quality Monitoring Data (PG. C2)	−70.75814195	42.22765855	2001
Pistol Pond	MassDEP	French and Quinebaug River Watershed 2001 Water Quality Assessment Report	−72.06952873	42.11567299	2001
Robin Hood Lake	MassDEP	Westfield River Watershed DWM 2001 Water Quality Monitoring Data	−73.06232945	42.24891028	2001
Shepherd Pond	MassDEP	French and Quinebaug River Watershed 2001 Water Quality Assessment Report	−70.53373331	41.86995472	2001
Ship Pond	MassDEP	South Shore Coastal Watersheds 2001 Water Quality Assessment Report, South Coastal Watersheds DWM Year 2001 Water Quality Monitoring Data (PG. C2)	−72.00809455	42.14567651	2001
Sibley Pond	MassDEP	French and Quinebaug River Watershed 2001 Water Quality Assessment Report	−73.090534	42.24786439	2001
Silver Shield Pond	MassDEP	Farmington River Watershed 2001 Biological Assessment	−70.9709629	41.6837958	2001
Turner Pond	MassDEP	10-B004–01	−70.88759081	42.49586698	2002
Forest River	MassDEP	North Shore Coastal Watersheds 2002 Water Quality Assessment Report	−71.33852068	42.06985374	2002
Lake Archer	DCR	DCR Data from Lakes and Ponds, 2002			

(Continued)

APPENDIX A (Continued)

Waterbody	Agency	Report Source	Longitude	Latitude	First Year Reported
Snipatuit Pond	MassDEP	05-R010–02	−70.8620237	41.7809072	2002
Bass Pond	DCR	Complied Data from DEP Herbicide Files 98–05 2003	−72.5011394	42.10680081	2003
Fort Pond	DCR	Complied Data from DEP Herbicide Files 98–05 (2003)	−71.4659799	42.50759896	2003
Furnace Pond	MassDEP	Baseline Lake Survey 2003 Technical Memo	−70.82578292	42.05600568	2003
Island Pond	DCR	Complied Data from DEP Herbicide Files 98–05 (2003)	−70.64061553	41.90022056	2003
Jenks Reservoir	DCR	Complied Data from DEP Herbicide Files 98–05 (2003)	−71.4652706	42.03098393	2003
Lake Garfield	MassDEP	Baseline Lake Survey 2003 Technical Memo	−73.19721196	42.18242683	2003
Long Pond	DCR	DCR Data from Lakes and Ponds, 2003	−71.9921338	42.35677269	2003
Long Pond	DCR	Complied Data from DEP Herbicide Files 98–05 (2003)	−71.47077877	42.52992969	2003
Mill Pond	DCR	Complied Data from DEP Herbicide Files 98–05 (2003)	−73.36785604	42.20324203	2003
Parker Mills Pond	MassDEP	Buzzards Bay Watershed 2000 Water Quality Assessment Report 95-AC-2 085.0, November 2003	−70.71941257	41.77585128	2003
Wallum Lake	DCR	DCR Data from Lakes and Ponds, 2003	−71.76891342	42.01626694	2003
White Island Pond (East Basin)	MassDEP	Buzzards Bay Watershed2000 Water Quality Assessment Report 95-AC-2 085.0 November 2003			2003
Hamblin Pond	DCR	DCR Data from Lakes and Ponds, 2004	−70.40942032	41.66826289	2004
Hamilton Reservoir	DCR	Complied Data from DEP Herbicide Files 98–05 (2004)	−72.15477622	42.05095943	2004
Monponsett Pond	MassDEP	09-G005–04	−70.836781	42.0014672	2004
Peters Pond	DCR	DCR Data from Lakes and Ponds, 2004	−70.49118083	41.6888922	2004
Silver Lake	DCR	Complied Data from DEP Herbicide Files 98–05 VM (2004)	−71.46498695	42.06298288	2004
Billington Sea	MassDEP	08-F007–05	−70.68653428	41.93449681	2005
Chicoppee Reservoir	DCR	DCR Data from Lakes and Ponds, 2005	−72.55132737	42.17068898	2005
Cliff Pond	DCR	DCR Data from Lakes and Ponds, 2005	−70.02404774	41.75805904	2005
Little Cliff Pond	DCR	DCR Data from Lakes and Ponds, 2005	−70.01460736	41.75708527	2005
Tussock Brook	MassDEP	11-E014–05	−70.7221562	42.003955	2005

Common Reed Grass (*Phragmites australis*)

York Lake	DCR	DCR Data from Lakes and Ponds, 2005	−73.18290621	42.09800289	2005
Cedar Pond	MassDEP	North Shore Coastal Watersheds 2002 Water Quality Assessment Report 93-AC-2 CN 138.5, March 2007	−70.98205992	42.5183998	2007
Cook Pond	DCR	DCR Data from Lakes and Ponds, 2007	−71.17385703	41.67628843	2007
Flax Pond	DCR	DCR Data from Lakes and Ponds, 2007	−70.02643866	41.76683915	2007
Wampatuck Pond	DCR	DCR Data from Lakes and Ponds, 2007	−70.86683315	42.06111681	2007
Whitehall Pond	DCR	DCR Data from Lakes and Ponds, 2007	−71.99553739	42.37075916	2007
Aaron River Reservoir	DCR	DCR Data from Lakes and Ponds Pioneer Infestation, 2008	−70.82739822	42.20687841	2008
Ashland Reservoir	DCR	DCR Data from Lakes and Ponds, 2008	−71.46489203	42.2402613	2008
Five Mile Pond	DCR	DCR Data from Lakes and Ponds, 2008			2008
Otis Reservoir	DCR	Data from ACT, GeoSyntec EM-ACT	−73.04092109	42.15114776	NA
Rice City Pond	DCR	DCR Data from BWRA	−71.62321852	42.10152849	NA

19 Purple Loosestrife (*Lythrum salicaria*)

ABSTRACT

This study compiles information on 390 waterbodies in Massachusetts where purple loosestrife (*Lythrum salicaria*) has been documented in the surrounding riparian areas. These sightings are mapped to have a spatial understanding of the status of this species in the adjacent wetlands and/or riparian zones of Massachusetts' lakes and rivers. This enhances public awareness of the presence of purple loosestrife in Massachusetts which may be helpful in minimizing unintentional spreading of this species to other waterbodies. This chapter also provides different methods that have been used to control this invasive species which include physical (e.g., digging, hand pulling, and cutting), chemical treatments (e.g., triclopyr and rodeo), and biological control (e.g., beetles).

INTRODUCTION

Taxonomic Hierarchy

Kingdom	Plantae—plantes, Planta, Vegetal, plants
Subkingdom	Viridiplantae—green plants
Infrakingdom	Streptophyta—land plants
Superdivision	Embryophyta
Division	Tracheophyta—vascular plants, tracheophytes
Subdivision	Spermatophytina—spermatophytes, seed plants, phanérogames
Class	Magnoliopsida
Superorder	Rosanae
Order	Myrtales
Family	Lythraceae—loosestrife
Genus	*Lythrum* L.—loosestrife
Species	*Lythrum salicaria* L.—purple lythrum, rainbow weed, spiked loosestrife, purple loosestrife

BASIC BIOLOGY

Purple loosestrife *L. salicaria*, also called loosestrife, spiked loosestrife, salicaire, bouquet violet, and rainbow weed, is an invasive species in North America but a native species to Europe and Asia (Cao et al. 2020). Generally, it grows to 1–3 m tall (Figures 19.1 and 19.2). The root mass is fibrous with a canopy usually comprised of four to six stems. Root systems usually grow together as a bulk-sized block. If the thicker portion of the root becomes cut, it is capable of vegetatively reproducing another purple loosestrife plant (Cygan 2003). Each plant has on average 1–15 flowering stems, although a single plant can produce up to 50 stems (Figure 19.1) (Warne 2016). Matured stems are usually hard and woody, while young stems are soft, smooth, hairless, and green in color. Stems will have four to six sides and form a square shape. Purple loosestrife has surface aerenchyma cells that enable the species to live in standing water where there is little oxygen, which is typical of a wetland environment. Purple loosestrife tolerates slightly acidic soil (as low as pH 4) as well as soil that is low in nutrients (Shamsi and Whitehead 1974; Henderson 1987). Leaves are narrowly lanceolate with a cordate leaf base (Lesica 2012). The cordate, lanceolate leaf of purple loosestrife, is generally 13 cm long and 2 cm wide, and changes throughout the day in order to maximize light availability. The leaves grow on the stem in opposite directions or in a whorled arrangement from the bottom (Figure 19.1). Leaves of purple loosestrife have no stalk and instead attach directly to the stem of the plant (Warne 2016). Flowers of purple loosestrife are usually deep pink or purple, although there are on occasion lighter pink or white varieties (Figure 19.1) (Warne 2016). Each flower has five to seven petals and is arranged in a dense terminal spike cluster. The terminal

FIGURE 19.1 Purple loosestrife flower (*left*), stem (*top right*), and seed (*bottom right*). (Left photo by Owen Williams (Warne 2016); top right photo by Rob Routledge, from invadingspecies.com; bottom right, Photo by Donna MacKenzie (Warne 2016).)

spikes are usually 15–30 cm high. Three different floral morphs have been identified, known as tristyly, each with a different length and height. Purple loosestrife reproduces both sexually and asexually. The plant can generate 2.5–2.7 million seeds annually starting at the end of July and continuing until autumn, with a single stem being able to produce up to 1,000 seed pods (Figure 19.1). Senescence begins in winter and its stems will holdfast throughout the rest of year, sometimes standing for one or two years (Jacobs 2008). The very small, reddish to brown seeds average 1 mm in length and are found in rounded pods which range 3–6 mm in length. Seeds of purple loosestrife are buoyant, allowing them to be carried by water currents, and can attach to clothing (Regional Lythrum salicaria Working Group 2004). Seeds can also be carried by wetland animals. It takes eight to ten weeks with a temperature ranging from 15.5°C to 18.3°C (60–65°F) for the seeds to germinate (Cygan 2003). The preferred locations for purple

FIGURE 19.2 A plant community infested by purple loosestrife in the riparian zone of Otsego Lake, New York. (Photo by Wai Hing Wong.)

loosestrife to germinate are generally in sunny spots during late spring into early summer. In Minnesota, late-summer emerging purple loosestrife seedlings have survived overwinter (Katovich et al. 2003). After the 19th century, increased highway system speeds created strong wind currents which facilitated the transportation of dry *L. salicaria* seeds.

Considered a beautiful and vigorous plant, *L. salicaria* was used in the horticultural business in the 17th century (Thompson et al. 1987). In his 1814 book *Flora Americae Spetentrionalis*, Frederick T. Pursh recorded purple loosestrife in New England (Balogh 1986). *L. salicaria* survives across the northern hemisphere between the 39th parallel (Italy) and the 65th parallel (Norway) (Jacobs 2008). It is a very popular plant and can be found almost everywhere in the UK, the main islands of Japan, New Zealand, and eastern Africa. Besides its ornamental value, tonics made from the flowering branches, leaves, and roots are used medicinally to cure wounds, diarrhea, dysentery, sores, and ulcers (Thompson et al. 1987; Malecki et al. 1993). Beekeepers also profit from the abundant amount of nectar this plant produces which helped bee colonies survive through the winter (Pellet 1977; Malecki et al. 1991). In Europe and Asia, native insect species, like the beetle *Galerucella calmariensis*, feed on *L. salicaria* (Chandler et al. n.d.).

During the 19th century, *L. salicaria* seeds were unintentionally mixed with moist soil used as ballast to maintain the equilibrium of merchandise on cargo ships traveling from Europe to North America (Jacobs 2008). When the cargo arrived at North American shorelines, the seeds were given a chance to germinate. The plant was well-established in the New England area by the 1830s. The first herbarium specimen of purple loosestrife was collected in 1831 from Massachusetts (Lavoie 2009). Although purple loosestrife was accidentally introduced from the ballasts of ships, it was also introduced to North America intentionally because of its medicinal value (Lindgren and Clay 1993). It is possible that eradication of purple loosestrife could result in an economic loss for the honey industry (Thompson et al. 1987). However, if native plants are allowed to regain their habitat in local wetland systems, they could provide sustenance for bees, and the pollination provided by the bees in turn can help increase native plant populations. Purple loosestrife is also believed to have been introduced through imported livestock, fleece, for use in gardens, and as a beekeeping resource (Warne 2016).

ECOLOGICAL AND ECONOMIC IMPACTS

Regardless of the perception of horticultural, medicinal, or economic benefits, purple loosestrife is documented as a strong competitor in local ecosystems. Since there were no native insects that feed on its foliage, *L. salicaria* spread rapidly and became a pernicious weed to local wetlands in Quebec (Balogh 1986). After the first documented record in Neepawa, Manitoba, in 1896, more and more purple loosestrife appeared in local ecosystems. In the 1950s, huge amounts of purple loosestrife were documented near the Assiniboine River and the Red River in Winnipeg, Canada (Lindgren 1999). Purple loosestrife has been introduced throughout the Erie Canal as well as the St. Lawrence River (Cygan 2003). It became established around areas adjacent to the Great Lakes in both Canada and the United States from 1940 to 1985 (Stuckey 1980).

L. salicaria can be found throughout all of the United States with the exceptions of Florida and Hawaii (due to temperature). For now, the most serious infestation is located in the northeastern United States. The plant invades wetland ecosystems by displacing other native plants, leading to negative impacts to wetland habitats. While purple loosestrife prefers disturbed wetlands, it can also be found invading and colonizing both tidal and inland habitats such as riverbanks, natural wetlands (which are undisturbed), wet meadows, bogs, swamps, roadsides, and reservoirs (Regional Lythrum salicaria Working Group 2004). Animal populations, such as waterfowl, start to decline due to the loss of food resources displaced by purple loosestrife. Considered one of the most highly distributed species in North America, this perennial plant grows with strong vitality (Thomsen 2012). According to Jacobs (2008), purple loosestrife outcompeted over 20 wetland plant species under variable nutrient levels and seasonal flooding within a few years. It was observed by Mal et al. (1992) that an area with abundant *Typha angustifolia*, a common species of cattail, can be completely replaced by *L. salicaria* within four years. Species of waterfowl, such as the black tern, decreased in population due to habitat loss. For example, the disappearance of about 1,000 breeding pairs of black terns coincided with a large amount of purple loosestrife blooming in Montezuma National Wildlife Refuge, New York (Jacobs 2008). By occupying shallow water areas, fish species like northern pike cannot survive in areas where purple loosestrife is densely clustered. This can negatively affect other species that feed on fish who reside in shallow water, causing them to lose a source of food. Additionally, other species like reeds, sedges, rushes, cattails, muskrats, canvasback ducks, bog turtles, especially in Massachusetts and New York where the *L. salicaria* populations are high, are declining. The direct presence of purple loosestrife in a waterbody can lead to altered decomposition rates, nutrient cycling, and water chemistry (Warne 2016). The leaves of purple loosestrife decompose quicker than those of other aquatic plants and earlier in the season than endemic species, causing spikes in certain nutrients such as phosphorus. Therefore, the higher concentration of phosphorous in leaves of purple loosestrife can cause eutrophication in waterbodies and accelerate decomposition of plant material in the spring.

Invasive species have been attributed to a 42% decrease of endangered species in the United States (Stein and Flack 1997; Wilcove 1998). The losses caused by invasive species are too hard to calculate, let alone for one kind of notorious plant such as the purple loosestrife. A rough estimate of $45 million is spent annually to control *L. salicaria* and to repair forage losses up to 131,152 ha in the United States (Malecki et al. 1993; Blossey et al. 2001; Brown 2005) and annual costs of $2.6 million are lost indirectly due to the related degradation of agricultural activities (Malecki et al. 1991). Purple loosestrife can cause agricultural losses by reducing wetland pastures and hay meadows. Additionally, the plant is less desirable to livestock than native plants, and it can impede the flow of water in irrigation systems (Malecki et al. 1993). Invasions of purple loosestrife have also caused economic losses for wild rice and hay farmers, reducing the acreage of available pasture that can be used for growing crops (Thompson et al. 1987; Blossey and Schroeder 1992). In addition to economic costs associated with the agricultural industry, purple loosestrife can also affect municipalities by incurring costs due to decreased water flow and drainage (Mullin 1998). In studying the tidal Hudson River freshwater marsh system, McGlynn (2009) found that dominant plant species was less important in invasive plant–native plant interactions than species-specific characteristics and zonation.

MONITORING AND SIGHTINGS

The Massachusetts Department of Environmental Protection (MassDEP) is committed to protect, enhance, and restore the quality and value of the waters of the Commonwealth with guidance from the Federal Clean Water Act and works to secure the environmental, recreational, and public health benefits of clean water for the citizens of Massachusetts. This chapter summarizes monitoring result and sightings of purple loosestrife in Massachusetts' lake and river riparian areas. The data were compiled by MassDEP and Massachusetts Department of Conservation and Recreation (MA DCR) staff mostly in the summer field season (i.e., May to September). MassDEP compiled the data which represents a portion of the 2,290 Massachusetts waterbodies surveyed by MassDEP from 1994 to 2015. Data layers and maps of sites with purple loosestrife were created using ArcGIS® ArcMap 10.1 (ESRI, Redlands, California).

Purple loosestrife was found in many river and lake riparian areas in Massachusetts (Tables 19.1 and 19.2). Figure 19.3 depicts the distribution of purple loosestrife in Massachusetts which occurs mainly in the northern and eastern parts of the state. There are hitherto (as of April 12, 2017) 2,050 waterbodies that have been investigated and of these, 387 (18.8%) were found to have purple loosestrife during field visits. Of the 387 waterbodies (Figure 19.3), 58 are riverine (15.1%) and 329 are lakes (84.9%). Twenty-eight of the 33 major watersheds (84.8%) in Massachusetts contain *L. salicaria*. These numbers do not represent purple loosestrife in wetlands. Thus, the mapped sighting ratio (387 out of 2,050 waterbodies) likely underestimates the true presence of purple loosestrife in Massachusetts. Also, it is possible that early in the season, purple loosestrife could be hard to distinguish from native loosestrife, so there may be some discrepancies. Future mapping

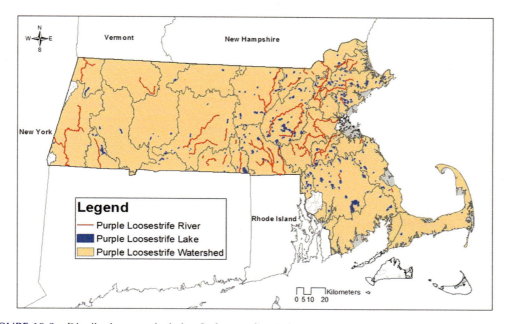

FIGURE 19.3 Distribution map depicting *Lythrum salicaria* in Massachusetts.

TABLE 19.1
List of Town Names and Waterbodies that Contain *Lythrum salicaria*

Town	Waterbody
Abington	Cleveland Pond
	Cushing Pond
	Island Grove Pond
	Cleveland Pond
	Cushing Pond
	Island Grove Pond
Andover	Bakers Meadow Pond
	Ballardvale Impoundment
	Brackett Pond
	Collins Pond
	Field Pond
	Fosters Pond
	Gravel Pit Pond
	Hussey Pond
	Pomps Pond
	Shawsheen River
	Unnamed Tributary
	Ballardvale Impoundment
	Gravel Pit Pond
	Pomps Pond
Ashburnham	Ward Pond
Ashland	Ashland Reservoir
Attleboro	Dodgeville Pond
	Farmers Pond
	Lake Como
	Luther Reservoir
	Manchester Pond Reservoir
	Mechanics Pond
	Orrs Pond
	Hebbronville Pond
Auburn	Dark Brook Reservoir (South Basin)
	Stoneville Pond
	Tinker Hill Pond
Avon	Brockton Reservoir
	Waldo Lake
Ayer	Flannagan Pond
	Grove Pond
	Plow Shop Pond
	Sandy Pond
Becket	Center Pond
	Shaw Pond
	Ward Pond
	Long Bow Lake
	Shaw Pond
Bedford	Fawn Lake
Bellingham	Spring Brook Silver Lake
Berlin	Gates Pond
	Wheeler Pond
Beverly	Wenham Lake

Purple Loosestrife (*Lythrum salicaria*)

Billerica	Content Brook
	Nutting Lake (East Basin)
	Pond Street Pond
	Richardson Pond North
	Winning Pond
Blackstone	Mill River
Bolton	West Pond
Boston	Sprague Pond
Boxford	Baldpate Pond
	Howes Pond
	Lowe Pond
	Lower Four Mile Pond
	Stevens Pond
	Baldpate Pond
	Spofford Pond
	Stiles Pond
	Towne Pond
Boylston	Sewall Pond
Brewster	Flax Pond
Bridgewater	Lake Nippenicket
Brimfield	Unnamed Tributary
Brockton	Ellis-Brett Pond
	Upper Porter Pond
Burlington	Butterfield Pond
	Sandy Brook
	Vine Brook
	Mill Pond
Canton	Glen Echo Pond
	Reservoir Pond
	Ponkapoag Pond
Carlisle	Fiske Street Pond
	Meadow Pond
Carver	Federal Pond
Charlton	Cady Brook
	Pikes Pond
	Sibley Pond
Chelmsford	Elm Street Pond
	Heart Pond
	Newfield Pond
	Russell Millpond
Cheshire	Cheshire Reservoir, Middle Basin
	Cheshire Reservoir, North Basin
Chester	Littleville Lake
Chicopee	Chicoppee Reservoir
Clinton	Clamshell Pond
	Coachlace Pond
	Lancaster Millpond
	South Meadow Pond (East Basin)
	South Meadow Pond (West Basin)
Cohasset	Aaron River Reservoir
	Lily Pond
Concord	Goose Pond
	Batemans Pond

(Continued)

TABLE 19.1
(Continued)

Town	Waterbody
	Great Meadow Pond #3
Danvers	Putnamville Reservoir
Deerfield	Deerfield River
Dighton	Muddy Cove Brook Pond
Douglas	Mumford River
Dover	Charles River
Dracut	Beaver Brook
	Richardson Brook
Dudley	Easterbrook Pond
	Larner Pond
	Sylvestri Pond
	Wallis Pond
	French River
Dunstable	Massapoag Pond
Duxbury	Lower Chandler Pond
Easton	Longwater Pond
	New Pond
	Shovelshop Pond
	Longwater Pond
	New Pond
	Shovelshop Pond
	Ward Pond
Egremont	Prospect Lake
Erving	Northfield Mountain Reservoir
Essex	Chebacco Lake
Fall River	Cook Pond
Fitchburg	Sawmill Pond
Foxborough	Beaumont Pond
	Bird Pond
	Carpenter Pond
	Cocasset Lake
	Neponset Reservoir
Framingham	Farm Pond
	Framingham Reservoir #1
	Framingham Reservoir #2
	Framingham Reservoir #3
	Saxonville Pond
	Waushakum Pond
	Learned Pond
Franklin	Beaver Pond
Gardner	Bents Pond
Georgetown	Penn Brook
	Parker River
Gloucester	Babson Reservoir
	Fernwood Lake
	Goose Cove Reservoir
	Haskell Pond
	Upper Banjo Pond
	Wallace Pond
Grafton	Blackstone River
	Flint Pond

Purple Loosestrife (*Lythrum salicaria*)

	Lake Ripple
	Quinsigamond River
Granby	Forge Pond
Great Barrington	Green River
Groton	Baddacook Pond
Groveland	Johnsons Pond
Halifax	Monponsett Pond
Hamilton	Beck Pond
	Gravelly Pond
	Round Pond
Hanover	Forge Pond
Hanson	Reservoir
	Riley Pond
	Wampatuck Pond
	Factory Pond
Harvard	Robbins Pond
Haverhill	Lake Saltonstall
Hingham	Weir River
Holden	Chaffin Pond
	Maple Spring Pond
	Quinapoxet Reservoir
	Dawson Pond
Holliston	Chicken Brook
Holyoke	Clear Pond
	Lake Bray
	Whiting Street Reservoir
	Wright Pond
Hopedale	Spindleville Pond
	Hopedale Pond
Hopkinton	North Pond
	Hopkinton Reservoir
	Whitehall Reservoir
Hudson	Assabet River
Ipswich	Hood Pond
Kingston	Foundry Pond
	Russell Pond
Lakeville	Assawompset Pond
	Long Pond
	Pocksha Pond
Lancaster	Nashua River
	North Nashua River
Lanesborough	Berkshire Pond
	Cheshire Reservoir, South Basin
Lawrence	Spicket River
Lee	Goose Pond Brook
	Housatonic River
Leicester	Moose Hill Reservoir
	Smiths Pond
	Town Meadow Brook
	Waite Pond
Lenox	Housatonic River

(Continued)

TABLE 19.1 (Continued)

Town	Waterbody
Leominster	Rockwell Pond
Lincoln	Farrar Pond
Littleton	Fort Pond
	Nagog Pond
	Spectacle Pond
Ludlow	Minechoag Pond
	Red Bridge Impoundment
Lunenburg	Lake Whalom
Lynn	Breeds Pond
	Flax Pond
	Floating Bridge Pond
	Walden Pond
Lynnfield	Hawkes Pond
	Pillings Pond
	Suntaug Lake
Mansfield	Sweets Pond
	Plain Street Pond
Marlborough	Fort Meadow Reservoir
	Hager Pond
	Milham Reservoir
Mashpee	Ashumet Pond
Medfield	Charles River
	Stop River
Mendon	Nipmuck Lake
Middleborough	Fuller Street Pond
Middleton	Creighton Pond
	Lower Boston Brook Pond
	Middleton Pond
	Unnamed Tributary
	Upper Boston Brook Pond
Millbury	Unnamed Tributary
Millis	Bogastow Brook
Millville	Blackstone River
Milton	Russell Pond
	Turners Pond
	Popes Pond
Monson	Chicopee Brook Pond
Natick	Fisk Pond
	Lake Cochituate
New Bedford	Sassaquin Pond
North Andover	Berry Pond
	Brook Street Pond
	Farnum Street Pond
	Salem Street Pond
	Stearns Pond
North Attleborough	Falls Pond (North Basin)

Purple Loosestrife (*Lythrum salicaria*)

	Falls Pond (South Basin)
	Whiting Pond
North Reading	Ipswich River
	Martins Pond
	Bradford Pond
	Eisenhaures Pond
	Swan Pond
Northborough	Assabet River
	Bartlett Pond
	Smith Pond
	Solomon Pond
Northbridge	Blackstone River
	Whitins Pond
	Linwood Pond
Norton	Chartley Pond
	Meadow Brook Pond
	Norton Reservoir
	Winnecunnet Pond
Norwell	Jacobs Pond
Norwood	Ellis Pond
	Hawes Brook
	Neponset River
Otis	Benton Pond
	Otis Reservoir
	Royal Pond
Oxford	Hudson Pond
	Texas Pond
Palmer	Palmer Reservoir
	Quaboag River
	Thompson Lake
	Forest Lake
Paxton	Asnebumskit Pond
Peabody	Browns Pond
	Crystal Pond
	Devils Dishfull Pond
	Elginwood Pond
	Pierces Pond
	Spring Pond
	Winona Pond
Pembroke	Furnace Pond
	Oldham Pond
Pepperell	Heald Pond
	Nashua River
	Pepperell Pond
Petersham	Connors Pond
Plainville	Lake Mirimichi
	Turnpike Lake
	Wetherells Pond
	Chestnut Street Pond
	Lake Mirimichi
Plymouth	Billington Sea
	Russell Millpond
	Ship Pond
	Unnamed Tributary

(Continued)

TABLE 19.1
(Continued)

Town	Waterbody
	White Island Pond (East Basin)
	White Island Pond (West Basin)
Rayham	Kings Pond
Rockland	Studleys Pond
Rockport	Cape Pond
	Rum Rock Lake
Rowley	Mill River
Rutland	Long Pond
	Muschopauge Pond
Sandisfield	West Branch Farmington River
Saugus	Birch Pond Reservoir
	First Pond
	Saugus River
	Spring Pond
	Griswold Pond
Scituate	Musquashcut Pond
	Old Oaken Bucket Pond
Sharon	Gavins Pond
	Massapoag Brook
	Upper Leach Pond
Sheffield	Konkapot River
Shrewsbury	Flint Pond
Somerset	Somerset Reservoir
South Hadley	Lower Pond
Southborough	Sudbury Reservoir
Southbridge	Morse Pond
Spencer	Sevenmile River
Springfield	Lake Lorraine
	Noonan Cove
	Fivemile Pond
	Lake Lookout
	Loon Pond
	Mona Lake
	Porter Lake
	Porter Lake West
	Watershops Pond
	Long Pond
	Mill Pond
Sterling	West Waushacum Pond
Stoughton	Ames Long Pond
	Farrington Pond
	Pinewood Pond
	Woods Pond
Sturbridge	Quinebaug River
Sudbury	Grist Mill Pond
	Stearns Mill Pond
Sutton	Aldrich Pond
	Blackstone River
	Marble Pond
	Singletary Pond
Taunton	Bear Hole Pond (little)
	Johnson Pond
	Lake Rico

Purple Loosestrife (*Lythrum salicaria*)

	Lake Sabbatia
	Middle Pond
	Prospect Hill Pond
	Watson Pond
	Whittenton Impoundment Middle Pond
Tewksbury	Ames Pond
	Long Pond
	Round Pond
	Shawsheen River
Tyngsborough	Althea Lake
	Flint Pond
Upton	West River
	Lake Wildwood
Uxbridge	Blackstone River
	Lackey Pond
Wakefield	Crystal Lake
	Lake Quannapowitt
Walpole	Cobbs Pond
	Ganawatte Farm Pond
	Neponset River
	Traphole Brook
	Willet Pond
Ware	Beaver Lake
	Ware River
Wareham	Glen Charlie Pond
Warren	Quaboag River
Wayland	Heard Pond
	Sudbury River
Webster	Webster Lake
Wellesley	Rosemary Brook
Wenham	Coy Pond
	Pleasant Pond
West Bridgewater	Hockomock River
	West Meadow Pond
Westborough	Assabet River
	Assabet River Reservoir
	Chauncy Lake
	Hocomonco Pond
Westford	Stony Brook
Westminster	Round Meadow Pond
Weston	Stony Brook
Whitman	Hobart Pond
Wilbraham	Nine Mile Pond
Williamstown	Green River
	Hoosic River
Wilmington	Lubber Pond East
	Lubber Pond West
	Lubbers Brook
	Maple Meadow Brook
Winchendon	Whitney Pond
Winchester	Winter Pond
Worcester	Coes Reservoir
	Patch Reservoir
	Salisbury Pond
Wrentham	Crocker Pond

TABLE 19.2
Geo-referenced Records of *Lythrum salicaria* in Massachusetts as Shown in Figure 19.3

Waterbody	Agency	Report Source	Longitude	Latitude	First Year Reported
Massapoag Brook	MassDEP	The Neponset River Watershed 1994 Resource Assessment Report	−71.1642662	42.1205358	1994
Neponset River	MassDEP	The Neponset River Watershed 1994 Resource Assessment Report	−71.2506977	42.1381175	1994
Neponset River	MassDEP	The Neponset River Watershed 1994 Resource Assessment Report	−71.2004073	42.1772345	1994
Hawes Brook	MassDEP	The Neponset River Watershed 1994 Resource Assessment Report	−71.2064474	42.1735363	1994
Traphole Brook	MassDEP	The Neponset River Watershed 1994 Resource Assessment Report	−71.2078652	42.1586282	1994
Ames Long Pond	MassDEP	Taunton River Watershed Water Quality Assessment Report 62-AC-1 CN 94.0, December 2005	−71.1187699	42.0875920	1996
Ames Long Pond	MassDEP	Appendix C—DWM 1996 and 2001 Lake Survey Data in the Taunton River Watershed	−71.1187699	42.0875920	1996
Brockton Reservoir	MassDEP	Appendix C—DWM 1996 and 2001 Lake Survey Data in the Taunton River Watershed	−71.0551783	42.1163914	1996
Brockton Reservoir	MassDEP	Taunton River Watershed Water Quality Assessment Report 62-AC-1 CN 94.0, December 2005	−71.0551783	42.1163914	1996
Cleveland Pond	MassDEP	Taunton River Watershed Water Quality Assessment Report 62-AC-1 CN 94.0, December 2005	−70.9828404	42.1199308	1996
Cleveland Pond	MassDEP	Appendix C—DWM 1996 and 2001 Lake Survey Data in the Taunton River Watershed	−70.9828404	42.1199308	1996
Crocker Pond	MassDEP	Taunton River Watershed Water Quality Assessment Report 62-AC-1 CN 94.0, December 2005	−71.2947890	42.0676913	1996
Crocker Pond	MassDEP	Appendix C—DWM 1996 and 2001 Lake Survey Data in the Taunton River Watershed	−71.2947890	42.0676913	1996
Cushing Pond	MassDEP	Taunton River Watershed Water Quality Assessment Report 62-AC-1 CN 94.0, December 2005	−70.9811913	42.1300566	1996
Cushing Pond	MassDEP	Appendix C—DWM 1996 and 2001 Lake Survey Data in the Taunton River Watershed	−70.9811913	42.1300566	1996
Gavins Pond	MassDEP	Taunton River Watershed Water Quality Assessment Report 62-AC-1 CN 94.0, December 2005	−71.2116854	42.0814356	1996
Gavins Pond	MassDEP	Appendix C—DWM 1996 and 2001 Lake Survey Data in the Taunton River Watershed	−71.2116854	42.0814356	1996
Hobart Pond	MassDEP	Taunton River Watershed Water Quality Assessment Report 62-AC-1 CN 94.0, December 2005	−70.9287075	42.0856020	1996
Hobart Pond	MassDEP	Appendix C—DWM 1996 and 2001 Lake Survey Data in the Taunton River Watershed	−70.9287075	42.0856020	1996
Island Grove Pond	MassDEP	Taunton River Watershed Water Quality Assessment Report 62-AC-1 CN 94.0, December 2005	−70.9399656	42.1110552	1996
Island Grove Pond	MassDEP	Appendix C—DWM 1996 and 2001 Lake Survey Data in the Taunton River Watershed	−70.9399656	42.1110552	1996
Johnson Pond	MassDEP	Taunton River Watershed Water Quality Assessment Report 62-AC-1 CN 94.0, December 2005	−71.0514379	41.9265631	1996
Johnson Pond	MassDEP	Appendix C—DWM 1996 and 2001 Lake Survey Data in the Taunton River Watershed	−71.0514379	41.9265631	1996
Long Pond	MassDEP	Appendix C—DWM 1996 and 2001 Lake Survey Data in the Taunton River Watershed	−70.9445534	41.8014573	1996
Longwater Pond	MassDEP	Taunton River Watershed Water Quality Assessment Report 62-AC-1 CN 94.0, December 2005	−71.0961075	42.0068526	1996

Purple Loosestrife (*Lythrum salicaria*)

Longwater Pond	MassDEP	Appendix C—DWM 1996 and 2001 Lake Survey Data in the Taunton River Watershed	Taunton River Watershed Water Quality Assessment Report 62-AC-1 CN 94.0, December 2005	−71.0961075	42.0068526	1996
Middle Pond	MassDEP	Taunton River Watershed Water Quality Assessment Report 62-AC-1 CN 94.0, December 2005	−70.9900826	41.8677608	1996
Middle Pond	MassDEP	Appendix C—DWM 1996 and 2001 Lake Survey Data in the Taunton River Watershed	−70.9900826	41.8677608	1996
Lake Mirimichi	MassDEP	Taunton River Watershed Water Quality Assessment Report 62-AC-1 CN 94.0, December 2005	−71.2917133	42.0272167	1996
Lake Mirimichi	MassDEP	Appendix C—DWM 1996 and 2001 Lake Survey Data in the Taunton River Watershed	−71.2917133	42.0272167	1996
New Pond	MassDEP	Taunton River Watershed Water Quality Assessment Report 62-AC-1 CN 94.0, December 2005	−71.1375423	42.0260035	1996
New Pond	MassDEP	Appendix C—DWM 1996 and 2001 Lake Survey Data in the Taunton River Watershed	−1.1375423	42.0260035	1996
Norton Reservoir	MassDEP	Taunton River Watershed Water Quality Assessment Report 62-AC-1 CN 94.0, December 2005	−71.2007819	41.9846846	1996
Norton Reservoir	MassDEP	Appendix C—DWM 1996 and 2001 Lake Survey Data in the Taunton River Watershed	−71.2007819	41.9846846	1996
Lake Rico	MassDEP	Taunton River Watershed Water Quality Assessment Report 62-AC-1 CN 94.0, December 2005	−70.9969743	41.8747225	1996
Lake Rico	MassDEP	Appendix C—DWM 1996 and 2001 Lake Survey Data in the Taunton River Watershed	−70.9969743	41.8747225	1996
Lake Sabbatia	MassDEP	Taunton River Watershed Water Quality Assessment Report 62-AC-1 CN 94.0, December 2005	−71.1081674	41.9445610	1996
Lake Sabbatia	MassDEP	Appendix C—DWM 1996 and 2001 Lake Survey Data in the Taunton River Watershed	−71.1081674	41.9445610	1996
Shovelshop Pond	MassDEP	Taunton River Watershed Water Quality Assessment Report 62-AC-1 CN 94.0, December 2005	−71.1009649	42.0691099	1996
Shovelshop Pond	MassDEP	Appendix C—DWM 1996 and 2001 Lake Survey Data in the Taunton River Watershed	−71.1009649	42.0691099	1996
Sweets Pond	MassDEP	Taunton River Watershed Water Quality Assessment Report 62-AC-1 CN 94.0, December 2005	−71.2566549	41.9916367	1996
Sweets Pond	MassDEP	Appendix C—DWM 1996 and 2001 Lake Survey Data in the Taunton River Watershed	−71.2566549	41.9916367	1996
Turnpike Lake	MassDEP	Taunton River Watershed Water Quality Assessment Report 62-AC-1 CN 94.0, December 2005	−71.3124012	42.0155418	1996
Turnpike Lake	MassDEP	Appendix C—DWM 1996 and 2001 Lake Survey Data in the Taunton River Watershed	−71.3124012	42.0155418	1996
Upper Porter Pond	MassDEP	Taunton River Watershed Water Quality Assessment Report 62-AC-1 CN 94.0, December 2005	−71.0442045	42.1032222	1996
Upper Porter Pond	MassDEP	Appendix C—DWM 1996 and 2001 Lake Survey Data in the Taunton River Watershed	−71.0442045	42.1032222	1996
Waldo Lake	MassDEP	Taunton River Watershed Water Quality Assessment Report 62-AC-1 CN 94.0, December 2005	−71.0482845	42.1094618	1996
Waldo Lake	MassDEP	Appendix C—DWM 1996 and 2001 Lake Survey Data in the Taunton River Watershed	−71.0482845	42.1094618	1996
Watson Pond	MassDEP	Taunton River Watershed Water Quality Assessment Report 62-AC-1 CN 94.0, December 2005	−71.1186846	41.9507941	1996
Watson Pond	MassDEP	Appendix C—DWM 1996 and 2001 Lake Survey Data in the Taunton River Watershed	−71.1186846	41.9507941	1996
West Meadow Pond	MassDEP	Taunton River Watershed Water Quality Assessment Report 62-AC-1 CN 94.0, December 2005	−71.0383792	42.0405202	1996
West Meadow Pond	MassDEP	Appendix C—DWM 1996 and 2001 Lake Survey Data in the Taunton River Watershed	−71.0383792	42.0405202	1996
Winnecunnet Pond	MassDEP	Taunton River Watershed Water Quality Assessment Report 62-AC-1 CN 94.0, December 2005	−71.1312668	41.9709330	1996
Winnecunnet Pond	MassDEP	Appendix C—DWM 1996 and 2001 Lake Survey Data in the Taunton River Watershed	−71.1312668	41.909330	1996

(Continued)

TABLE 19.2 (Continued)

Waterbody	Agency	Report Source	Longitude	Latitude	First Year Reported
Whittenton Impoundment	MassDEP	Taunton River Watershed Water Quality Assessment Report 62-AC-1 CN 94.0, December 2005	−71.1070860	41.9291042	1996
Whittenton Impoundment	MassDEP	Appendix C—DWM 1996 and 2001 Lake Survey Data in the Taunton River Watershed	−71.1070860	41.9291042	1996
Assawompset Pond	MassDEP	Appendix C—DWM 1996 and 2001 Lake Survey Data in the Taunton River Watershed	−70.9189452	41.8381170	1996
Beaumont Pond	MassDEP	Appendix C—DWM 1996 and 2001 Lake Survey Data in the Taunton River Watershed	−71.1989278	42.0522164	1996
Carpenter Pond	MassDEP	Appendix C—DWM 1996 and 2001 Lake Survey Data in the Taunton River Watershed	−71.2737942	42.0715149	1996
Chartley Pond	MassDEP	Appendix C—DWM 1996 and 2001 Lake Survey Data in the Taunton River Watershed	−71.2333304	41.9474469	1996
Cocasset Lake	MassDEP	Appendix C—DWM 1996 and 2001 Lake Survey Data in the Taunton River Watershed	−71.2597188	42.0588861	1996
Kings Pond	MassDEP	Appendix C—DWM 1996 and 2001 Lake Survey Data in the Taunton River Watershed	−71.0544926	41.9361331	1996
Meadow Brook Pond	MassDEP	Appendix C—DWM 1996 and 2001 Lake Survey Data in the Taunton River Watershed	−71.1641185	41.9375309	1996
Muddy Cove Brook Pond	MassDEP	Appendix C—DWM 1996 and 2001 Lake Survey Data in the Taunton River Watershed	−71.1312403	41.8142012	1996
Pocksha Pond	MassDEP	Appendix C—DWM 1996 and 2001 Lake Survey Data in the Taunton River Watershed	−70.8935724	41.8291440	1996
Prospect Hill Pond	MassDEP	Appendix C—DWM 1996 and 2001 Lake Survey Data in the Taunton River Watershed	−71.0931736	41.9343313	1996
Somerset Reservoir	MassDEP	Appendix C—DWM 1996 and 2001 Lake Survey Data in the Taunton River Watershed	−71.1384162	41.7824457	1996
Upper Leach Pond	MassDEP	Appendix C—DWM 1996 and 2001 Lake Survey Data in the Taunton River Watershed	−71.1513062	42.0702976	1996
Ward Pond	MassDEP	Appendix C—DWM 1996 and 2001 Lake Survey Data in the Taunton River Watershed	−71.1228875	42.0063244	1996
Ellis-Brett Pond	MassDEP	Appendix C—DWM 1996 and 2001 Lake Survey Data in the Taunton River Watershed	−71.0447806	42.0914975	1996
Mill River	MassDEP	Charles River Water Quality Assessment Report, 1997–2000	−71.5156703	42.0407739	1997
Charles River	MassDEP	Charles River Water Quality Assessment Report, 1997–2001	−71.3395731	42.1930188	1997
Berkshire Pond	MassDEP	Hudson River Basin 1997 Water Quality Assessment Report	−73.19612	42.504771	1997
Cheshire Reservoir, North Basin	MassDEP	Hudson River Basin 1997 Water Quality Assessment Report	−73.1739645	42.5473169	1997
Cheshire Reservoir, Middle Basin	MassDEP	Hudson River Basin 1997 Water Quality Assessment Report	−73.191871	42.531451	1997

Purple Loosestrife (*Lythrum salicaria*)

Cheshire Reservoir, South Basin	MassDEP	Hudson River Basin 1997 Water Quality Assessment Report	−73.1983974	42.5154111	1997
Lake Como	MassDEP	Ten Mile River Basin 1997 Water Quality Assessment Report	−71.3576397	41.9262715	1997
Falls Pond (South Basin)	MassDEP	Ten Mile River Basin 1997 Water Quality Assessment Report	−71.3242070	41.9602576	1997
Orrs Pond	MassDEP	Ten Mile River Basin 1997 Water Quality Assessment Report	−71.3326962	41.9286110	1997
Plain Street Pond	MassDEP	Ten Mile River Basin 1997 Water Quality Assessment Report	−71.2777427	42.0062287	1997
Fuller Street Pond	MassDEP	Ten Mile River Basin 1997 Water Quality Assessment Report	−70.8131810	41.9071626	1997
Chebacco Lake	MassDEP	North Coastal Watershed 1997/1998 Water Quality Assessment Report	−70.8111522	42.6119840	1997
Flax Pond	MassDEP	North Coastal Watershed 1997/1998 Water Quality Assessment Report	−70.9514364	42.4827035	1997
Griswold Pond	MassDEP	North Coastal Watershed 1997/1998 Water Quality Assessment Report	−71.0498670	42.4774936	1997
Lake Quannapowitt	MassDEP	North Coastal Watershed 1997/1998 Water Quality Assessment Report	−71.0785558	42.5149376	1997
Spring Pond	MassDEP	North Coastal Watershed 1997/1998 Water Quality Assessment Report	−71.0514912	42.4801724	1997
Lily Pond	MassDEP	North Coastal Watershed 1997/1998 Water Quality Assessment Report	−70.8159141	42.2246376	1997
Babson Reservoir	MassDEP	North Coastal Watershed 1997/1998 Water Quality Assessment Report	−70.6620453	42.6281521	1997
Beck Pond	MassDEP	North Coastal Watershed 1997/1998 Water Quality Assessment Report	−70.8228555	42.6040701	1997
Birch Pond Reservoir	MassDEP	North Coastal Watershed 1997/1998 Water Quality Assessment Report	−71.0014522	42.4786663	1997
Breeds Pond	MassDEP	North Coastal Watershed 1997/1998 Water Quality Assessment Report	−70.9786343	42.4797990	1997
Browns Pond	MassDEP	North Coastal Watershed 1997/1998 Water Quality Assessment Report	−70.9550201	42.4998821	1997
Cape Pond	MassDEP	North Coastal Watershed 1997/1998 Water Quality Assessment Report	−70.6308641	42.6404998	1997
Coy Pond	MassDEP	North Coastal Watershed 1997/1998 Water Quality Assessment Report	−70.8218642	42.5919722	1997
Falls Pond (North Basin)	MassDEP	Ten Mile River Basin 1997 Water Quality Assessment Report	−71.3233843	41.9689758	1997
Fernwood Lake	MassDEP	North Coastal Watershed 1997/1998 Water Quality Assessment Report	−70.6997665	42.6109725	1997
Floating Bridge Pond	MassDEP	North Coastal Watershed 1997/1998 Water Quality Assessment Report	−70.9398485	42.4855152	1997
Goose Cove Reservoir	MassDEP	North Coastal Watershed 1997/1998 Water Quality Assessment Report	−70.6639814	42.6439760	1997
Gravelly Pond	MassDEP	North Coastal Watershed 1997/1998 Water Quality Assessment Report	−70.8106273	42.5987887	1997

(*Continued*)

TABLE 19.2 (Continued)

Waterbody	Agency	Report Source	Longitude	Latitude	First Year Reported
Haskell Pond	MassDEP	North Coastal Watershed 1997/1998 Water Quality Assessment Report	−70.7384855	42.6113303	1997
Hawkes Pond	MassDEP	North Coastal Watershed 1997/1998 Water Quality Assessment Report	−71.0212112	42.5029144	1997
Pillings Pond	MassDEP	North Coastal Watershed 1997/1998 Water Quality Assessment Report	−71.0293596	42.5299953	1997
Rum Rock Lake	MassDEP	North Coastal Watershed 1997/1998 Water Quality Assessment Report	−70.6192624	42.6464618	1997
Saugus River	MassDEP	North Coastal Watershed 1997/1998 Water Quality Assessment Report	−70.9989210	42.4620059	1997
Upper Banjo Pond	MassDEP	North Coastal Watershed 1997/1998 Water Quality Assessment Report	−70.6943219	42.6122605	1997
Round Pond	MassDEP	North Coastal Watershed 1997/1998 Water Quality Assessment Report	−70.8179910	42.5983467	1997
Walden Pond	MassDEP	North Coastal Watershed 1997/1998 Water Quality Assessment Report	−71.0039981	42.4941163	1997
Wallace Pond	MassDEP	North Coastal Watershed 1997/1998 Water Quality Assessment Report	−70.7084723	42.6043935	1997
Whiting Pond	MassDEP	Ten Mile River Basin 1997 Water Quality Assessment Report	−71.3349764	41.9934412	1997
Rosemary Brook	MassDEP	Charles River Water Quality Assessment Report, 1997–2003	−71.2516891	42.3043036	1997
Stony Brook	MassDEP	Charles River Water Quality Assessment Report, 1997–2002	−71.2829360	42.3787810	1997
Crystal Lake	MassDEP	North Coastal Watershed 1997/1998 Water Quality Assessment Report	−71.0735447	42.4916140	1997
Dodgeville Pond	MassDEP	Ten Mile River Basin 1997 Water Quality Assessment Report	−71.2918061	41.9251093	1997
Farmers Pond	MassDEP	Ten Mile River Basin 1997 Water Quality Assessment Report	−71.3032357	41.9517620	1997
Hebbronville Pond	MassDEP	Ten Mile River Basin 1997 Water Quality Assessment Report	−71.3187011	41.9099740	1997
Luther Reservoir	MassDEP	Ten Mile River Basin 1997 Water Quality Assessment Report	−71.3388399	41.9383352	1997
Mechanics Pond	MassDEP	Ten Mile River Basin 1997 Water Quality Assessment Report	−71.2940074	41.9461536	1997
Wetherells Pond	MassDEP	Ten Mile River Basin 1997 Water Quality Assessment Report	−71.3375762	41.9999234	1997
Spring Pond	MassDEP	North Coastal Watershed 1997/1998 Water Quality Assessment Report	−70.9468041	42.4969367	1997
Chestnut Street Pond	MassDEP	Ten Mile River Basin 1997 Water Quality Assessment Report	−71.3597279	42.0216992	1997
Manchester Pond Reservoir	MassDEP	Ten Mile River Basin 1997 Water Quality Assessment Report	−71.3158334	41.9464202	1997
Prospect Lake	MassDEP	Chicopee River Basin 1998 Water Quality Assessment Report	−73.4522242	42.1949523	1998

Purple Loosestrife (*Lythrum salicaria*)

Lake Bray	MassDEP	Connecticut River Basin 1998 Water Quality Assessment Report	−72.6166715	42.2666603	1998
Forge Pond	MassDEP	Connecticut River Basin 1998 Water Quality Assessment Report	−72.4671967	42.2715846	1998
Porter Lake	MassDEP	Connecticut River Basin 1998 Water Quality Assessment Report	−72.5639194	42.0735051	1998
Whiting Street Reservoir	MassDEP	Connecticut River Basin 1998 Water Quality Assessment Report	−72.6377995	42.2389377	1998
Beaver Lake	MassDEP	Chicopee River Basin 1998 Water Quality Assessment Report 36-AC-2 47.0, April 2001	−72.3052244	42.2603274	1998
Fivemile Pond	MassDEP	Chicopee River Basin 1998 Water Quality Assessment Report	−72.5106631	42.1416829	1998
Forest Lake	MassDEP	Chicopee River Basin 1998 Water Quality Assessment Report	−72.3081122	42.2072563	1998
Long Pond	MassDEP	Chicopee River Basin 1998 Water Quality Assessment Report 36-AC-2 47.0, April 2001	−71.9921341	42.3567719	1998
Long Pond	MassDEP	Chicopee River Basin 1998 Water Quality Assessment Report	−71.9921341	42.3567719	1998
Coes Reservoir	MassDEP	Blackstone River Basin 1998 Water Quality Assessment Report	−71.8418253	42.2544586	1998
Dark Brook Reservoir (South Basin)	MassDEP	Blackstone River Basin 1998 Water Quality Assessment Report	−71.8658970	42.1882716	1998
Flint Pond	MassDEP	Blackstone River Basin 1998 Water Quality Assessment Report	−71.7360011	42.2495864	1998
Lake Ripple	MassDEP	09-G008–04	−71.6936628	42.2141715	1998
Lake Ripple	MassDEP	Blackstone River Basin 1998 Water Quality Assessment Report	−71.6963299	42.2134635	1998
Singletary Pond	MassDEP	Blackstone River Basin 1998 Water Quality Assessment Report	−71.7801300	42.1600274	1998
Tinker Hill Pond	MassDEP	Blackstone River Basin 1998 Water Quality Assessment Report	−71.8741419	42.1846460	1998
Whitins Pond	MassDEP	Blackstone River Basin 1998 Water Quality Assessment Report	−71.6901504	42.1140136	1998
Flint Pond	MassDEP	Blackstone River Basin 1998 Water Quality Assessment Report 51-AC-1 48.0, May 2011	−71.7306085	42.2415305	1998
Chaffin Pond	MassDEP	Appendix A—1998 DEP DWM Nashua River Basin QA/QC Report	−71.8391709	42.2309848	1998
Dawson Pond	MassDEP	Appendix A—1998 DEP DWM Nashua River Basin QA/QC Report	−71.8521791	42.3352095	1998
Flannagan Pond	MassDEP	Appendix A—1998 DEP DWM Nashua River Basin QA/QC Report	−71.5675232	42.5579469	1998
Grove Pond	MassDEP	Appendix A—1998 DEP DWM Nashua River Basin QA/QC Report	−71.5844890	42.5525657	1998
Plow Shop Pond	MassDEP	Appendix A—1998 DEP DWM Nashua River Basin QA/QC Report	−71.5923299	42.5558002	1998
Robbins Pond	MassDEP	Appendix A—1998 DEP DWM Nashua River Basin QA/QC Report	−71.6046534	42.5375850	1998
Sawmill Pond	MassDEP	Appendix A—1998 DEP DWM Nashua River Basin QA/QC Report	−71.8465410	42.5445173	1998
Lake Whalom	MassDEP	Appendix A—1998 DEP DWM Nashua River Basin QA/QC Report	−71.7404572	42.5739661	1998
Meadow Pond	MassDEP	Blackstone River Basin 1998 Water Quality Assessment Report	−71.3432969	42.5534691	1998

(*Continued*)

356 Invasive Animals and Plants in Massachusetts Lakes and Rivers

TABLE 19.2 (Continued)

Waterbody	Agency	Report Source	Longitude	Latitude	First Year Reported
Spectacle Pond	MassDEP	Chicopee River Basin 1998 Water Quality Assessment Report	−71.5168652	42.5633255	1998
Quaboag River	MassDEP	Chicopee River Basin 1998 Water Quality Assessment Report	−72.1796508	42.2233783	1998
Asnebumskit Pond	MassDEP	Appendix A—1998 DEP DWM Nashua River Basin QA/QC Report	−71.9090451	42.3231830	1998
Coachlace Pond	MassDEP	Appendix A—1998 DEP DWM Nashua River Basin QA/QC Report	−71.6974005	42.4131214	1998
East Waushacum Pond	MassDEP	Appendix A—1998 DEP DWM Nashua River Basin QA/QC Report	−71.7478236	42.4115697	1998
Heald Pond	MassDEP	Appendix A—1998 DEP DWM Nashua River Basin QA/QC Report	−71.6344636	42.6699219	1998
Lake Lookout	MassDEP	Connecticut River Basin 1998 Water Quality Assessment Report	−72.5382418	42.1147402	1998
Lancaster Millpond	MassDEP	Appendix A—1998 DEP DWM Nashua River Basin QA/QC Report	−71.6847860	42.4075777	1998
Loon Pond	MassDEP	Connecticut River Basin 1998 Water Quality Assessment Report	−72.4987251	42.1434933	1998
Maple Spring Pond	MassDEP	Appendix A—1998 DEP DWM Nashua River Basin QA/QC Report	−71.8818377	42.3766150	1998
Minechoag Pond	MassDEP	Chicopee River Basin 1998 Water Quality Assessment Report	−72.4587528	42.1633418	1998
Mona Lake	MassDEP	Chicopee River Basin 1998 Water Quality Assessment Report	−72.5206812	42.1426150	1998
Moose Hill Reservoir	MassDEP	Chicopee River Basin 1998 Water Quality Assessment Report	−71.9563492	42.2714098	1998
Muschopauge Pond	MassDEP	Appendix A—1998 DEP DWM Nashua River Basin QA/QC Report	−71.9213771	42.3838652	1998
Noonan Cove	MassDEP	Connecticut River Basin 1998 Water Quality Assessment Report	−72.5487494	42.1071250	1998
Northfield Mountain Reservoir	MassDEP	Connecticut River Basin 1998 Water Quality Assessment Report	−72.4405873	42.6134969	1998
Palmer Reservoir	MassDEP	Chicopee River Basin 1998 Water Quality Assessment Report	−72.3101546	42.1633650	1998
Porter Lake West	MassDEP	Connecticut River Basin 1998 Water Quality Assessment Report	−72.5711189	42.0736919	1998
Quinapoxet Reservoir	MassDEP	Appendix A—1998 DEP DWM Nashua River Basin QA/QC Report	−71.8832363	42.3962827	1998
Round Meadow Pond	MassDEP	Appendix A—1998 DEP DWM Nashua River Basin QA/QC Report	−71.8941192	42.5451980	1998
Sandy Pond	MassDEP	Appendix A—1998 DEP DWM Nashua River Basin QA/QC Report	−71.5556476	42.5618947	1998

Purple Loosestrife (*Lythrum salicaria*)

Location	Source	Report	Longitude	Latitude	Year
South Meadow Pond (East Basin)	MassDEP	Appendix A—1998 DEP DWM Nashua River Basin QA/QC Report	−71.7060627	42.4148445	1998
South Meadow Pond (West Basin)	MassDEP	Appendix A—1998 DEP DWM Nashua River Basin QA/QC Report	−71.7127434	42.4148406	1998
Thompson Lake	MassDEP	Chicopee River Basin 1998 Water Quality Assessment Report	−72.2990214	42.1749037	1998
Waite Pond	MassDEP	Blackstone River Basin 1998 Water Quality Assessment Report	−71.8911113	42.2491804	1998
Watershops Pond	MassDEP	Connecticut River Basin 1998 Water Quality Assessment Report	−72.5439428	42.1057506	1998
Long Pond	MassDEP	Chicopee River Basin 1998 Water Quality Assessment Report	−72.5081176	42.1542203	1998
Mill Pond	MassDEP	Connecticut River Basin 1998 Water Quality Assessment Report	−72.4951695	42.1117920	1998
Chicopee Brook Pond	MassDEP	Chicopee River Basin 1998 Water Quality Assessment Report	−72.3095784	42.1198885	1998
Connors Pond	MassDEP	Chicopee River Basin 1998 Water Quality Assessment Report	−72.1616303	42.4642839	1998
Hopedale Pond	MassDEP	Blackstone River Basin 1998 Water Quality Assessment Report	−71.5536066	42.1397139	1998
Lackey Pond	MassDEP	Blackstone River Basin 1998 Water Quality Assessment Report	−71.6921029	42.0931662	1998
Linwood Pond	MassDEP	Blackstone River Basin 1998 Water Quality Assessment Report	−71.6520998	42.1010953	1998
Lower Pond	MassDEP	Connecticut River Basin 1998 Water Quality Assessment Report	−72.5722162	42.2545682	1998
Patch Reservoir	MassDEP	Blackstone River Basin 1998 Water Quality Assessment Report	−71.8513623	42.2700807	1998
Red Bridge Impoundment	MassDEP	Chicopee River Basin 1998 Water Quality Assessment Report	−72.4020896	42.1802859	1998
Smiths Pond	MassDEP	Blackstone River Basin 1998 Water Quality Assessment Report	−71.8693452	42.2413182	1998
Stoneville Pond	MassDEP	Blackstone River Basin 1998 Water Quality Assessment Report	−71.8468045	42.2187351	1998
Rockwell Pond	MassDEP	Appendix A—1998 DEP DWM Nashua River Basin QA/QC Report	−71.7684382	42.5271890	1998
Salisbury Pond	MassDEP	Blackstone River Basin 1998 Water Quality Assessment Report Appendix B	−71.8058591	42.2771991	1998
Lake Wildwood	MassDEP	Blackstone River Basin 1998 Water Quality Assessment Report	−71.6412087	42.1763307	1998
Mill River	MassDEP	Parker River Watershed Water Quality Assessment Report Appendix C	−70.8990290	42.7396810	1999
Winter Pond	MassDEP	Boston Harbor 1999 Water Quality Assessment Report	−71.1530817	42.4563023	1999
Russell Pond	MassDEP	Boston Harbor 1999 Water Quality Assessment Report	−71.0734873	42.2362559	1999
Cobbs Pond	MassDEP	Boston Harbor 1999 Water Quality Assessment Report	−71.2445201	42.1595441	1999
Ellis Pond	MassDEP	Boston Harbor 1999 Water Quality Assessment Report	−71.2229887	42.1821424	1999
Neponset Reservoir	MassDEP	Boston Harbor 1999 Water Quality Assessment Report	−71.2445409	42.0846820	1999

(Continued)

TABLE 19.2 (Continued)

Waterbody	Agency	Report Source	Longitude	Latitude	First Year Reported
Pinewood Pond	MassDEP	Boston Harbor 1999 Water Quality Assessment Report	−71.1395441	42.1298261	1999
Farrington Pond	MassDEP	Boston Harbor 1999 Water Quality Assessment Report	−71.1155279	42.1101472	1999
Ponkapoag Pond	MassDEP	Boston Harbor 1999 Water Quality Assessment Report	−71.0951069	42.1923267	1999
Reservoir Pond	MassDEP	Boston Harbor 1999 Water Quality Assessment Report	−71.1231824	42.1688080	1999
Woods Pond	MassDEP	Boston Harbor 1999 Water Quality Assessment Report	−71.1127164	42.1167650	1999
Flint Pond	MassDEP	Merrimack River Basin 1999 Water Quality Assessment Report	−71.4318174	42.6729165	1999
Newfield Pond	MassDEP	Merrimack River Basin 1999 Water Quality Assessment Report	−71.3899233	42.6337843	1999
Massapoag Pond	MassDEP	Merrimack River Basin 1999 Water Quality Assessment Report	−71.4965387	42.6485085	1999
Ganawatte Farm Pond	MassDEP	Boston Harbor 1999 Water Quality Assessment Report	−71.2417500	42.1064274	1999
Memorial Pond	MassDEP	Boston Harbor 1999 Water Quality Assessment Report	−71.2474683	42.1454564	1999
Parker River	MassDEP	Parker River Watershed Water Quality Assessment Report Appendix C	−71.0122130	42.7302460	1999
Willet Pond	MassDEP	Boston Harbor 1999 Water Quality Assessment Report	−71.2372682	42.1793243	1999
Bird Pond	MassDEP	Boston Harbor 1999 Water Quality Assessment Report	−71.2231683	42.1613874	1999
Popes Pond	MassDEP	Boston Harbor 1999 Water Quality Assessment Report	−71.0955672	42.2487895	1999
Sprague Pond	MassDEP	Boston Harbor 1999 Water Quality Assessment Report	−71.1369968	42.2335018	1999
Beaver Brook	MassDEP	Merrimack River Basin 1999 Water Quality Assessment Report Appendix C	−71.3231210	42.6624310	1999
Spicket River	MassDEP	Merrimack River Basin 1999 Water Quality Assessment Report	−71.1836624	42.7191350	1999
Weir River	MassDEP	Boston Harbor 1999 Water Quality Assessment Report	−70.8677397	42.2372405	1999
Turners Pond	MassDEP	Boston Harbor 1999 Water Quality Assessment Report	−71.0773782	42.2608348	1999
Penn Brook	MassDEP	Parker River Watershed Water Quality Assessment Report Appendix C	−70.9871310	42.7297300	1999
Penn Brook	MassDEP	10-D020–04	−70.9841492	42.7187277	1999
Stony Brook	MassDEP	Merrimack River Basin 1999 Water Quality Assessment Report	−71.4096830	42.6102380	1999
Silver Lake	MassDEP	Ipswich River Watershed 2000 Water Quality Assessment Report	−71.4645777	42.0632423	2000
Fosters Pond	MassDEP	Shawsheen River Watershed 2000 Water Quality Assessment Report 83-AC-2 86.0, July 2003	−71.1369818	42.6067165	2000

Gravel Pit Pond	MassDEP	Shawsheen River Watershed 2000 Water Quality Assessment Report 83-AC-2 86.0, July 2003	−71.1604601	42.6722056	2000
Gravel Pit Pond	MassDEP	Shawsheen River Watershed 2000 Water Quality Assessment Report	−71.1604601	42.6722056	2000
Ballardvale Impoundment	MassDEP	Shawsheen River Watershed 2000 Water Quality Assessment Report 83-AC-2 86.0, July 2003	−71.1580528	42.6197553	2000
Ballardvale Impoundment	MassDEP	Shawsheen River Watershed 2000 Water Quality Assessment Report	−71.1580528	42.6197553	2000
Pomps Pond	MassDEP	Shawsheen River Watershed 2000 Water Quality Assessment Report 83-AC-2 86.0, July 2003	−71.1513484	42.6352457	2000
Pomps Pond	MassDEP	Shawsheen River Watershed 2000 Water Quality Assessment Report	−71.1513484	42.6352457	2000
Devils Dishfull Pond	MassDEP	Ipswich River Watershed 2000 Water Quality Assessment Report	−71.0068499	42.5406443	2000
Field Pond	MassDEP	Ipswich River Watershed 2000 Water Quality Assessment Report 92-AC-1 088.0, April 2004	−71.1087937	42.6083542	2000
Lower Boston Brook Pond	MassDEP	Ipswich River Watershed 2000 Water Quality Assessment Report 92-AC-1 088.0, April 2004	−71.0083967	42.6174828	2000
Lower Four Mile Pond	MassDEP	Ipswich River Watershed 2000 Water Quality Assessment Report 92-AC-1 088.0, April 2004	−71.0032797	42.6803774	2000
Lowe Pond	MassDEP	Ipswich River Watershed 2000 Water Quality Assessment Report 92-AC-1 088.0, April 2004	−70.9858738	42.6759112	2000
Lubber Pond East	MassDEP	Ipswich River Watershed 2000 Water Quality Assessment Report 92-AC-1 088.0, April 2004	−71.1974308	42.5562190	2000
Lubber Pond West	MassDEP	Ipswich River Watershed 2000 Water Quality Assessment Report 92-AC-1 088.0, April 2004	−71.2031072	42.5553548	2000
Martins Pond	MassDEP	Ipswich River Watershed 2000 Water Quality Assessment Report 92-AC-1 088.0, April 2004	−71.1252953	42.5955576	2000
Stevens Pond	MassDEP	Ipswich River Watershed 2000 Water Quality Assessment Report 92-AC-1 088.0, April 2004	−70.9973757	42.6836135	2000
Federal Pond	MassDEP	Buzzards Bay Watershed 2000 Water Quality Assessment Report 95-AC-2 085.0, November 2003	−70.7078164	41.8762623	2000
White Island Pond (East Basin)	MassDEP	07-T003−02	−70.6175309	41.8091834	2000
White Island Pond (East Basin)	MassDEP	07-T004−01	−70.6175309	41.8091834	2000
White Island Pond (East Basin)	MassDEP	08-F008−02	−70.6175309	41.8091834	2000
White Island Pond (East Basin)	MassDEP	11-B007−01	−70.6175309	41.8091834	2000

(Continued)

TABLE 19.2 (Continued)

Waterbody	Agency	Report Source	Longitude	Latitude	First Year Reported
White Island Pond (East Basin)	MassDEP	14-B007–01	−70.6175309	41.8091834	2000
White Island Pond (East Basin)	MassDEP	Buzzards Bay Watershed 2000 Water Quality Assessment Report 95-AC-2 085.0, November 2003	−70.6178754	41.8117381	2000
White Island Pond (East Basin)	MassDEP	Buzzards Bay Watershed 2000 Water Quality Assessment Report	−70.6178754	41.8117381	2000
White Island Pond (West Basin)	MassDEP	08-F008–01	−70.6275557	41.8099941	2000
White Island Pond (West Basin)	MassDEP	12-B003–02	−70.6275557	41.8099941	2000
White Island Pond (West Basin)	MassDEP	13-B007–02	−70.6275557	41.8099941	2000
White Island Pond (West Basin)	MassDEP	13-B009–03	−70.6275557	41.8099941	2000
White Island Pond (West Basin)	MassDEP	14-B005–02	−70.6275557	41.8099941	2000
White Island Pond (West Basin)	MassDEP	Buzzards Bay Watershed 2000 Water Quality Assessment Report 95-AC-2 085.0, November 2003	−70.6277405	41.8062552	2000
White Island Pond (West Basin)	MassDEP	Buzzards Bay Watershed 2000 Water Quality Assessment Report	−70.6277405	41.8062552	2000
Ames Pond	MassDEP	Shawsheen River Watershed 2000 Water Quality Assessment Report	−71.2253468	42.6382918	2000
Bakers Meadow Pond	MassDEP	Shawsheen River Watershed 2000 Water Quality Assessment Report	−71.1602603	42.6507736	2000
Bents Pond	MassDEP	Millers River Watershed 2000 Water Quality Assessment Report	−71.9846729	42.5580259	2000
Brackett Pond	MassDEP	Ipswich River Watershed 2000 Water Quality Assessment Report	−71.1095852	42.6134520	2000
Bradford Pond	MassDEP	Ipswich River Watershed 2000 Water Quality Assessment Report	−71.0789855	42.5999909	2000
Collins Pond	MassDEP	Ipswich River Watershed 2000 Water Quality Assessment Report	−71.1090134	42.6115557	2000

Purple Loosestrife (*Lythrum salicaria*)

Creighton Pond	MassDEP	Ipswich River Watershed 2000 Water Quality Assessment Report	−71.0442255	42.6269243	2000
Crystal Pond	MassDEP	Ipswich River Watershed 2000 Water Quality Assessment Report	−70.9999708	42.5491935	2000
Eisenhaures Pond	MassDEP	Ipswich River Watershed 2000 Water Quality Assessment Report	−71.0896937	42.5860316	2000
Elginwood Pond	MassDEP	Ipswich River Watershed 2000 Water Quality Assessment Report	−71.0032608	42.5477493	2000
Farnum Street Pond	MassDEP	Ipswich River Watershed 2000 Water Quality Assessment Report	−71.0833779	42.6549048	2000
Fawn Lake	MassDEP	Shawsheen River Watershed 2000 Water Quality Assessment Report	−71.2734103	42.5137746	2000
Glen Charlie Pond	MassDEP	Buzzards Bay Watershed 2000 Water Quality Assessment Report	−70.6462652	41.7920967	2000
Hood Pond	MassDEP	Ipswich River Watershed 2000 Water Quality Assessment Report	−70.9548440	42.6699159	2000
Hussey Pond	MassDEP	Shawsheen River Watershed 2000 Water Quality Assessment Report	−71.1523517	42.6727427	2000
Middleton Pond	MassDEP	Ipswich River Watershed 2000 Water Quality Assessment Report	−71.0280532	42.5917317	2000
Pierces Pond	MassDEP	Ipswich River Watershed 2000 Water Quality Assessment Report	−70.9969165	42.5293390	2000
Pleasant Pond	MassDEP	Ipswich River Watershed 2000 Water Quality Assessment Report	−70.8952933	42.6140959	2000
Pond Street Pond	MassDEP	Shawsheen River Watershed 2000 Water Quality Assessment Report	−71.2556560	42.5869750	2000
Putnamville Reservoir	MassDEP	Ipswich River Watershed 2000 Water Quality Assessment Report	−70.9468334	42.6008152	2000
Richardson Pond North	MassDEP	Shawsheen River Watershed 2000 Water Quality Assessment Report	−71.2457842	42.5879255	2000
Round Pond	MassDEP	Shawsheen River Watershed 2000 Water Quality Assessment Report	−71.2319936	42.6029166	2000
Salem Street Pond	MassDEP	Ipswich River Watershed 2000 Water Quality Assessment Report	−71.0455120	42.6366929	2000
Spofford Pond	MassDEP	Ipswich River Watershed 2000 Water Quality Assessment Report	−71.0207771	42.6959440	2000
Stearns Pond	MassDEP	Ipswich River Watershed 2000 Water Quality Assessment Report	−71.0694217	42.6173500	2000
Stiles Pond	MassDEP	Ipswich River Watershed 2000 Water Quality Assessment Report	−71.0366642	42.6889085	2000
Suntaug Lake	MassDEP	Ipswich River Watershed 2000 Water Quality Assessment Report	−71.0048430	42.5217843	2000
Swan Pond	MassDEP	Ipswich River Watershed 2000 Water Quality Assessment Report	−71.0504704	42.5915270	2000
Towne Pond	MassDEP	Ipswich River Watershed 2000 Water Quality Assessment Report	−71.0287626	42.6546551	2000
Wenham Lake	MassDEP	Ipswich River Watershed 2000 Water Quality Assessment Report	−70.8907252	42.5904622	2000
Whitney Pond	MassDEP	Baseline Lake Survey 2003 Technical Memo	−72.0412151	42.6830822	2000
Whitney Pond	MassDEP	Millers River Watershed 2000 Water Quality Assessment Report	−72.0347660	42.6814818	2000
Winona Pond	MassDEP	Ipswich River Watershed 2000 Water Quality Assessment Report	−71.0099919	42.5344892	2000

(Continued)

TABLE 19.2 (Continued)

Waterbody	Agency	Report Source	Longitude	Latitude	First Year Reported
Butterfield Pond	MassDEP	Shawsheen River Watershed 2000 Water Quality Assessment Report	−71.2106699	42.4697954	2000
Howes Pond	MassDEP	Ipswich River Watershed 2000 Water Quality Assessment Report	−71.0021204	42.6545333	2000
Long Pond	MassDEP	Shawsheen River Watershed 2000 Water Quality Assessment Report	−71.2518748	42.5978382	2000
Mill Pond	MassDEP	Ipswich River Watershed 2000 Water Quality Assessment Report	−71.1737213	42.5129751	2000
Upper Boston Brook Pond	MassDEP	Ipswich River Watershed 2000 Water Quality Assessment Report	−71.0184112	42.6199362	2000
Bogastow Brook	MassDEP	Shawsheen River Watershed 2000 Water Quality Assessment Report	−71.3920350	42.1861990	2000
Brook Street Pond	MassDEP	Ipswich River Watershed 2000 Water Quality Assessment Report	−71.0877541	42.6491289	2000
Shaw Pond	MassDEP	06-E012–01	−73.1227752	42.252142	2001
Shaw Pond	MassDEP	Farmington River Watershed 2001 Biological Assessment	−73.1239117	42.2544760	2001
Sylvestri Pond	MassDEP	French and Quinebaug River Watershed 2001 Water Quality Assessment Report	−71.9847640	42.0673699	2001
Larner Pond	MassDEP	French and Quinebaug River Watershed 2001 Water Quality Assessment Report	−71.9060326	42.0597896	2001
Lake Nippenicket	MassDEP	Taunton River Watershed 2001 Water Quality Assessment Report Appendix C	−71.0416911	41.9696598	2001
Ashland Reservoir	MassDEP	Concord Watershed 2001 DWM Water Quality Monitoring Data	−71.4648923	42.2402611	2001
Assabet River Reservoir	MassDEP	Concord Watershed 2001 DWM Water Quality Monitoring Data	−71.6459850	42.2636753	2001
Bartlett Pond	MassDEP	Concord Watershed 2001 DWM Water Quality Monitoring Data	−71.6183754	42.3179137	2001
Batemans Pond	MassDEP	Concord Watershed 2001 DWM Water Quality Monitoring Data	−71.3664673	42.4939747	2001
Chauncy Lake	MassDEP	Concord Watershed 2001 DWM Water Quality Monitoring Data	−71.6123353	42.2943741	2001
Fisk Pond	MassDEP	Concord Watershed 2001 DWM Water Quality Monitoring Data	−71.3683511	42.2819821	2001
Fort Meadow Reservoir	MassDEP	Concord Watershed 2001 DWM Water Quality Monitoring Data	−71.5481107	42.3686485	2001
Framingham Reservoir #1	MassDEP	Concord Watershed 2001 DWM Water Quality Monitoring Data	−71.4493238	42.2896421	2001
Framingham Reservoir #3	MassDEP	Concord Watershed 2001 DWM Water Quality Monitoring Data	−71.4695991	42.3001460	2001

Purple Loosestrife (*Lythrum salicaria*)

Great Meadow Pond #3	MassDEP	Concord Watershed 2001 DWM Water Quality Monitoring Data	−71.3349052	42.4756991	2001
Grist Mill Pond	MassDEP	Concord Watershed 2001 DWM Water Quality Monitoring Data	−71.4791471	42.3554728	2001
Hager Pond	MassDEP	Concord Watershed 2001 DWM Water Quality Monitoring Data	−71.4877578	42.3490361	2001
Heard Pond	MassDEP	Concord Watershed 2001 DWM Water Quality Monitoring Data	−71.3835387	42.3526192	2001
Hopkinton Reservoir	MassDEP	Concord Watershed 2001 DWM Water Quality Monitoring Data	−71.5210262	42.2547944	2001
Nutting Lake (East Basin)	MassDEP	Concord Watershed 2001 DWM Water Quality Monitoring Data	−71.2650031	42.5372640	2001
Russell Millpond	MassDEP	Concord Watershed 2001 DWM Water Quality Monitoring Data	−71.3329065	42.5703497	2001
Saxonville Pond	MassDEP	Concord Watershed 2001 DWM Water Quality Monitoring Data	−71.4136220	42.3201977	2001
Stearns Mill Pond	MassDEP	Concord Watershed 2001 DWM Water Quality Monitoring Data	−71.4530771	42.3858152	2001
Waushakum Pond	MassDEP	05-G006–02	−71.4233861	42.2641737	2001
Waushakum Pond	MassDEP	Concord Watershed 2001 DWM Water Quality Monitoring Data	−71.4262402	42.2639502	2001
Whitehall Reservoir	MassDEP	Concord Watershed 2001 DWM Water Quality Monitoring Data	−71.5753633	42.2294215	2001
Winning Pond	MassDEP	Concord Watershed 2001 DWM Water Quality Monitoring Data	−71.3013147	42.5514593	2001
Lake Cochituate	MassDEP	Concord Watershed 2001 DWM Water Quality Monitoring Data	−71.3670553	42.2894878	2001
Forge Pond	MassDEP	South Shore Coastal Watersheds 2001 Water Quality Assessment Report 94-AC-2 CN 93.0, March 2006	−70.8800038	42.1062243	2001
Jacobs Pond	MassDEP	South Shore Coastal Watersheds 2001 Water Quality Assessment Report 94-AC-2 CN 93.0, March 2006	−70.8492691	42.1619900	2001
Lower Chandler Pond	MassDEP	South Shore Coastal Watersheds 2001 Water Quality Assessment Report 94-AC-2 CN 93.0, March 2006	−70.7624539	42.0312782	2001
Old Oaken Bucket Pond	MassDEP	South Shore Coastal Watersheds 2001 Water Quality Assessment Report 94-AC-2 CN 93.0, March 2006	−70.7501611	42.1791203	2001
Old Oaken Bucket Pond	MassDEP	South Coastal Watersheds DWM YEAR 2001 Water Quality Monitoring Data (PG. C2)	−70.7501611	42.1791203	2001
Oldham Pond	MassDEP	South Shore Coastal Watersheds 2001 Water Quality Assessment Report 94-AC-2 CN 93.0, March 2006	−70.8364494	42.0664190	2001

(Continued)

TABLE 19.2 (Continued)

Waterbody	Agency	Report Source	Longitude	Latitude	First Year Reported
Oldham Pond	MassDEP	South Shore Coastal Watersheds 2001 Water Quality Assessment Report, South Coastal Watersheds DWM Year 2001 Water Quality Monitoring Data (PG. C2)	−70.8364494	42.0664190	2001
French River	MassDEP	French and Quinebaug River Watershed 2001 Water Quality Assessment Report	−71.8841820	42.0246995	2001
Quinebaug River	MassDEP	French and Quinebaug River Watershed 2001 Water Quality Assessment Report	−72.1185692	42.1095615	2001
Russell Pond	MassDEP	South Shore Coastal Watersheds 2001 Water Quality Assessment Report, South Coastal Watersheds DWM Year 2001 Water Quality Monitoring Data (PG. C2)	−70.7470003	41.9778691	2001
Gates Pond	MassDEP	Concord Watershed 2001 DWM Water Quality Monitoring Data	−71.6108718	42.3782027	2001
Clear Pond	MassDEP	Westfield River Watershed DWM 2001 Water Quality Monitoring Data	−72.6595532	42.1855163	2001
Easterbrook Pond	MassDEP	French and Quinebaug River Watershed 2001 Water Quality Assessment Report	−71.9249238	42.0537809	2001
Easterbrook Pond	MassDEP	French and Quinebaug River Watershed 2004 Benthic Macroinvertebrate Bioassessment	−71.9249240	42.0537810	2001
Elm Street Pond	MassDEP	Concord Watershed 2001 DWM Water Quality Monitoring Data	−71.3736433	42.5605568	2001
Farrar Pond	MassDEP	Concord Watershed 2001 DWM Water Quality Monitoring Data	−71.3542989	42.4141745	2001
Fiske Street Pond	MassDEP	Concord Watershed 2001 DWM Water Quality Monitoring Data	−71.3754055	42.5534551	2001
Fort Pond	MassDEP	Concord Watershed 2001 DWM Water Quality Monitoring Data	−71.4663567	42.5071911	2001
Foundry Pond	MassDEP	South Shore Coastal Watersheds 2001 Water Quality Assessment Report, South Coastal Watersheds DWM Year 2001 Water Quality Monitoring Data (PG. C2)	−70.7091488	41.9842148	2001
Framingham Reservoir #2	MassDEP	Concord Watershed 2001 DWM Water Quality Monitoring Data	−71.4439073	42.2744049	2001
Furnace Pond	MassDEP	South Shore Coastal Watersheds 2001 Water Quality Assessment Report, South Coastal Watersheds DWM Year 2001 Water Quality Monitoring Data (PG. C2)	−70.8255009	42.0557280	2001
Furnace Pond	MassDEP	Baseline Lake Survey 2003 Technical Memo	−70.8255009	42.0557280	2001
Heart Pond	MassDEP	Concord Watershed 2001 DWM Water Quality Monitoring Data	−71.3877340	42.5657450	2001
Hocomonco Pond	MassDEP	Concord Watershed 2001 DWM Water Quality Monitoring Data	−71.6497506	42.2724040	2001
Hudson Pond	MassDEP	French and Quinebaug River Watershed 2001 Water Quality Assessment Report	−71.8343498	42.1433074	2001
Learned Pond	MassDEP	Concord Watershed 2001 DWM Water Quality Monitoring Data	−71.4188407	42.2873503	2001
Littleville Lake	MassDEP	Westfield River Watershed 2001 Water Quality Assessment Report	−72.8866628	42.2789380	2001

Long Bow Lake	MassDEP	Westfield River Watershed DWM 2001 Water Quality Monitoring Data	−73.0914248	42.2529731	2001
Milham Reservoir	MassDEP	Concord Watershed 2001 DWM Water Quality Monitoring Data	−71.6092840	42.3422667	2001
Morse Pond	MassDEP	French and Quinebaug River Watershed 2001 Water Quality Assessment Report	−72.0144229	42.0319671	2001
Musquashcut Pond	MassDEP	South Coastal Watersheds DWM Year 2001 Water Quality Monitoring Data (PG. C2)	−70.7583101	42.2275200	2001
Nagog Pond	MassDEP	Concord Watershed 2001 DWM Water Quality Monitoring Data	−71.4412077	42.5151087	2001
Pikes Pond	MassDEP	French and Quinebaug River Watershed 2001 Water Quality Assessment Report	−71.9404468	42.1617335	2001
Royal Pond	MassDEP	Farmington River Watershed 2001 Biological Assessment	−73.1609142	42.1804095	2001
Russell Millpond	MassDEP	South Shore Coastal Watersheds 2001 Water Quality Assessment Report, South Coastal Watersheds DWM Year 2001 Water Quality Monitoring Data (PG. C2)	−70.6335513	41.9169630	2001
Ship Pond	MassDEP	South Shore Coastal Watersheds 2001 Water Quality Assessment Report, South Coastal Watersheds DWM Year 2001 Water Quality Monitoring Data (PG. C2)	−70.5337638	41.8697059	2001
Sibley Pond	MassDEP	French and Quinebaug River Watershed 2001 Water Quality Assessment Report	−72.0107046	42.1515962	2001
Smith Pond	MassDEP	Concord Watershed 2001 DWM Water Quality Monitoring Data	−71.6603615	42.2898519	2001
Studleys Pond	MassDEP	South Shore Coastal Watersheds 2001 Water Quality Assessment Report	−70.9209521	42.1195205	2001
Sudbury Reservoir	MassDEP	Concord Watershed 2001 DWM Water Quality Monitoring Data	−71.5058924	42.3172382	2001
Ward Pond	MassDEP	Farmington River Watershed 2001 Biological Assessment	−73.1012513	42.2492359	2001
Wright Pond	MassDEP	Westfield River Watershed 2001 Water Quality Assessment Report	−72.6586467	42.1812338	2001
Factory Pond	MassDEP	South Shore Coastal Watersheds 2001 Water Quality Assessment Report, South Coastal Watersheds DWM Year 2001 Water Quality Monitoring Data (PG. C2)	−70.8748442	42.0899688	2001
Town Meadow Brook	MassDEP	French and Quinebaug River Watershed 2001 Water Quality Assessment Report	−71.9200884	42.2220138	2001
West Branch Farmington River	MassDEP	Farmington River Watershed 2001 Biological Assessment	−73.0737135	42.1526264	2001
Texas Pond	MassDEP	French and Quinebaug River Watershed 2001 Water Quality Assessment Report	−71.8928149	42.1717096	2001
Wallis Pond	MassDEP	French and Quinebaug River Watershed 2001 Water Quality Assessment Report	−71.9070449	42.0660729	2001
Housatonic River	MassDEP	Housatonic River Watershed 2002 Water Quality Assessment Report Appendix C	−73.2404010	42.3940380	2002
Green River	MassDEP	Housatonic River Watershed 2002 Water Quality Assessment Report Appendix C	−73.3781260	42.1785560	2002
Charles River	MassDEP	Charles River Watershed 2002 Biological Assessment	−71.2724073	42.2621874	2002
Goose Pond Brook	MassDEP	Housatonic River Watershed 2002 Water Quality Assessment Report Appendix C	−73.2271930	42.2943020	2002
Shaw Pond	DCR	DCR(2008) Data from Lakes and Ponds, 2002	−73.1239117	42.2544760	2002

(Continued)

TABLE 19.2 (Continued)

Waterbody	Agency	Report Source	Longitude	Latitude	First Year Reported
Beaver Pond	DCR	DCR(2008) Data from Lakes and Ponds, 2002	−71.4175437	42.0799485	2002
Baddacook Pond	DCR	DCR(2008) Data from Lakes and Ponds, 2002	−71.5304640	42.6189623	2002
Chicken Brook	MassDEP	Charles River Watershed 2002 Biological Assessment	−71.4422633	42.1785228	2002
Green River	MassDEP	Appendix D—Hudson Watershed 2002 Biological Assessment	−73.2312640	42.6764870	2002
Hoosic River	MassDEP	Appendix D—Hudson Watershed 2002 Biological Assessment	−73.2092170	42.7293160	2002
Stop River	MassDEP	Charles River Watershed 2002 Biological Assessment	−71.3059926	42.1539616	2002
Housatonic River	MassDEP	Housatonic River Watershed 2002 Water Quality Assessment Report Appendix C	−73.2408830	42.2833520	2002
Nipmuck Lake	DCR	DCR(2008) Data from Lakes and Ponds, 2002	−71.5699120	42.0964290	2002
Bear Hole Pond (little)	DCR	DCR(2008) Data from Lakes and Ponds, 2002	−70.9934554	41.8688229	2002
Bear Hole Pond (little)	DCR	DCR(2008) Data from Lakes and Ponds, 2007	−70.9934554	41.8688229	2002
Bear Hole Pond (little)	DCR	DCR(2008) Data from Lakes and Ponds, 2008	−70.9934554	41.8688229	2002
Konkapot River	MassDEP	Housatonic River Watershed 2002 Water Quality Assessment Report Appendix C	−73.311830	42.047410	2002
Center Pond	DCR	DCR(2008) Data from Lakes and Ponds, 2003	−73.0687461	42.2967178	2003
Long Pond	DCR	DCR(2008) Data from Lakes and Ponds, 2003	−71.9921341	42.3567719	2003
Long Pond	DCR	DCR(2008) Data from Lakes and Ponds, 2008	−71.9921341	42.3567719	2003
Watson Pond	DCR	DCR(2008) Data from Lakes and Ponds, 2003	−71.1186846	41.9507941	2003
Watson Pond	DCR	DCR(2008) Data from Lakes and Ponds, 2008	−71.1186846	41.9507941	2003
Winnecunnet Pond	DCR	DCR(2008) Data from Lakes and Ponds, 2003	−71.1312668	41.9709330	2003
Farm Pond	MassDEP	Baseline Lake Survey 2003 Technical Memo	−71.4267259	42.2815529	2003
Baldpate Pond	MassDEP	05-G004-02	−71.0014233	42.6988862	2003
Baldpate Pond	MassDEP	Baseline Lake Survey 2003 Technical Memo	−71.0023711	42.6982584	2003
Quaboag River	MassDEP	07-K004-05	−72.2635427	42.1814299	2003
Quaboag River	MassDEP	08-L006-05	−72.2635427	42.1814299	2003

Purple Loosestrife (*Lythrum salicaria*) 367

Quaboag River	MassDEP	11-G004-05	−72.2635427	42.1814299	2003
Quaboag River	MassDEP	Baseline Lake Survey 2003 Technical Memo	−72.2630590	42.1686640	2003
Mumford River	MassDEP	Blackstone River Watershed 2003 Biological Assessment	−71.7293980	42.0832710	2003
Prospect Hill Pond	DCR	DCR(2008) Data from Lakes and Ponds, 2003	−71.0931736	41.9343313	2003
Spindleville Pond	MassDEP	Blackstone River Watershed 2003 Biological Assessment	−71.5312797	42.1161304	2003
Blackstone River	MassDEP	Blackstone River Watershed 2003 Biological Assessment	−71.5456216	42.0171721	2003
Pepperell Pond	MassDEP	Baseline Lake Survey 2003 Technical Memo	−71.5839579	42.6448131	2003
Nine Mile Pond	DCR	DCR (2008) Data from Lakes and Ponds, 2003	−72.4344914	42.1490848	2003
Turnpike Lake	DCR	DCR (2008) Data from Lakes and Ponds, 2004	−71.3124012	42.0155418	2004
Hood Pond	DCR	DCR(2008) Data from Lakes and Ponds, 2004	−70.9548440	42.6699159	2004
Richardson Brook	MassDEP	Merrimack River Watershed 2004 Benthic Macroinvertebrate Assessment	−71.2734717	42.6676737	2004
Unnamed Tributary	MassDEP	French and Quinebaug River Watershed 2004 Benthic Macroinvertebrate Bioassessment	−72.1988670	42.1223380	2004
Lake Saltonstall	DCR	DCR (2008) Data from Lakes and Ponds, 2004	−71.0658718	42.7827085	2004
Flax Pond	MassDEP	05-G012−01	−70.0260112	41.7659812	2005
Lake Lorraine	MassDEP	05-G013−02	−72.5129923	42.1450906	2005
Webster Lake	MassDEP	05-G014−01	−71.8487243	42.0543495	2005
Oldham Pond	DCR	DCR(2008) Data from Lakes and Ponds, 2005	−70.8364494	42.0664190	2005
Blackstone River	MassDEP	05-K004−04	−71.6520398	42.1538730	2005
Blackstone River	MassDEP	08-A028−03	−71.6800238	42.1748750	2005
Blackstone River	MassDEP	08-A035−05	−71.6223140	42.0987190	2005
Ashumet Pond	MassDEP	05-G011−02	−70.5318225	41.6347157	2005
Baddacook Pond	MassDEP	05-G001−01	−71.5304640	42.6189623	2005
Sudbury River	MassDEP	05-J003−02	−71.3973643	42.3254347	2005
Sudbury River	MassDEP	05-J004−02	−71.3973643	42.3254347	2005
Sudbury River	MassDEP	05-J005−02	−71.3973643	42.3254347	2005
Sudbury River	MassDEP	06-F003−02	−71.3973643	42.3254347	2005
Sudbury River	MassDEP	06-F004−02	−71.3973643	42.3254347	2005
Sudbury River	MassDEP	07-L003−02	−71.3973643	42.3254347	2005
Furnace Pond	DCR	DCR (2008) Data from Lakes and Ponds, 2005	−70.8255009	42.0557280	2005

(Continued)

TABLE 19.2 (Continued)

Waterbody	Agency	Report Source	Longitude	Latitude	First Year Reported
Hocomonco Pond	DCR	DCR (2008) Data from Lakes and Ponds, 2005	−71.6497506	42.2724040	2005
Chicoppee Reservoir	DCR	DCR (2008) Data from Lakes and Ponds, 2005	−72.5512770	42.1708408	2005
Chicoppee Reservoir	DCR	DCR (2008) Data from Lakes and Ponds, 2007	−72.5512770	42.1708408	2005
Goose Pond	DCR	DCR (2008) Data from Lakes and Ponds, 2005	−71.3312044	42.430841	2005
Johnsons Pond	DCR	DCR (2008) Data from Lakes and Ponds, 2005	−71.0535516	42.7316414	2005
Deerfield River	MassDEP	05-F013-01	−72.6266247	42.5228109	2005
Shawsheen River	MassDEP	05-I006-13	−71.1508026	42.6474461	2005
Shawsheen River	MassDEP	05-I003-08	−71.2151746	42.5681537	2005
Shawsheen River	MassDEP	05-I004-08	−71.2151746	42.5681537	2005
Shawsheen River	MassDEP	05-I003-10	−71.2151746	42.5681537	2005
Shawsheen River	MassDEP	05-I004-10	−71.2151746	42.5681537	2005
Shawsheen River	MassDEP	05-I004-11	−71.1930607	42.5996629	2005
Unnamed Tributary	MassDEP	05-Q003-10	−71.0109215	42.5930941	2005
Unnamed Tributary	MassDEP	05-Q004-07	−71.0109215	42.5930941	2005
Unnamed Tributary	MassDEP	05-Q005-07	−71.0109215	42.5930941	2005
Ipswich River	MassDEP	05-Q004-03	−71.1106017	42.5611646	2005
Lubbers Brook	MassDEP	05-Q004-02	−71.1466976	42.5588828	2005
Maple Meadow Brook	MassDEP	05-Q004-01	−71.1500663	42.5519109	2005
Spring Brook	MassDEP	05-I003-03	−71.2578761	42.4948081	2005
Spring Brook	MassDEP	05-I004-03	−71.2578761	42.4948081	2005
Spring Brook	MassDEP	05-I006-03	−71.2578761	42.4948081	2005
Vine Brook	MassDEP	05-I004-04	−71.2242658	42.4964526	2005

North Nashua River	MassDEP	05-O004-01	−71.7219246	42.4951686	2005
Content Brook	MassDEP	05-I004-09	−71.2182168	42.5796709	2005
Content Brook	MassDEP	05-I006-09	−71.2182168	42.5796709	2005
Sandy Brook	MassDEP	05-I004-05	−71.2125419	42.4974268	2005
Unnamed Tributary	MassDEP	05-I004-12	−71.1994003	42.6288780	2005
West River	MassDEP	11-F004-04	−71.601117	42.1003609	2006
West River	MassDEP	06-G004-03	−71.601117	42.1003609	2006
West River	MassDEP	11-F004-04	−71.601117	42.1003609	2006
Glen Echo Pond	DCR	DCR (2008) Data from Lakes and Ponds, 2006	−71.0887317	42.1521704	2006
First Pond	DCR	DCR(2008) Data from Lakes and Ponds, 2006	−71.0511939	42.4754089	2006
Blackstone River	MassDEP	06-G004-02	−71.5682244	42.0219477	2006
Blackstone River	MassDEP	07-J005-02	−71.5705414	42.0227186	2006
Wheeler Pond	DCR	DCR (2008) Data from Lakes and Ponds, 2006	−71.6304343	42.3572406	2006
Solomon Pond	DCR	DCR (2008) Data from Lakes and Ponds, 2006	−71.6260766	42.3397019	2006
West Pond	DCR	DCR (2008) Data from Lakes and Ponds, 2006	−71.5807312	42.4276008	2006
Unnamed Tributary	MassDEP	06-C001-03	−70.6135325	41.9260270	2006
Unnamed Tributary	MassDEP	06-C006-03	−70.6135325	41.9260270	2006
Assabet River	MassDEP	06-A008-03	−71.6284508	42.3048530	2006
Assabet River	MassDEP	06-A015-03	−71.6284508	42.3048530	2006
Assabet River	MassDEP	06-F003-01	−71.6284508	42.3048530	2006
Assabet River	MassDEP	06-F004-01	−71.6284508	42.3048530	2006
Assabet River	MassDEP	07-L004-01	−71.6284508	42.3048530	2006
Assabet River	MassDEP	07-L005-01	−71.6284508	42.3048530	2006
Assabet River	MassDEP	08-M003-01	−71.6284508	42.3048530	2006
Assabet River	MassDEP	08-M004-01	−71.6284508	42.3048530	2006
Assabet River	MassDEP	09-N004-01	−71.6284508	42.3048530	2006
Assabet River	MassDEP	06-A015-01	−71.6322420	42.2740602	2006
Assabet River	MassDEP	06-A008-08	−71.5861363	42.3803093	2006
Wampatuck Pond	DCR	DCR (2008) Data from Lakes and Ponds, 2007	−70.8668332	42.0611168	2007

(Continued)

TABLE 19.2 (Continued)

Waterbody	Agency	Report Source	Longitude	Latitude	First Year Reported
Wampatuck Pond	DCR	DCR (2008) Data from Lakes and Ponds, 2008	−70.8668332	42.0611168	2007
Cook Pond	DCR	DCR(2008) Data from Lakes and Ponds, 2007	−71.1748547	41.6752804	2007
Ward Pond	DCR	DCR (2008) Data from Lakes and Ponds, 2007	−71.8813490	42.6814691	2007
Cady Brook	MassDEP	07-M003–02	−72.0087044	42.1194732	2007
Quinsigamond River	MassDEP	09-L004–02	−71.7080924	42.2305379	2008
Quinsigamond River	MassDEP	08-K006–02	−71.7080924	42.2305379	2008
North Pond	DCR	DCR (2008) Data from Lakes and Ponds, 2008	−71.5558719	42.1965281	2008
Fisk Pond	DCR	DCR (2008) Data from Lakes and Ponds, 2008	−71.3683511	42.2819821	2008
Field Pond	DCR	DCR (2008) Data from Lakes and Ponds, 2008	−71.1087937	42.6083542	2008
Nashua River	MassDEP	08-Q005–04	−71.5677653	42.6696867	2008
Blackstone River	MassDEP	08-A028–02	−71.6881594	42.1795812	2008
Blackstone River	MassDEP	08-A028–01	−71.7306827	42.181217	2008
Ware River	MassDEP	08-L005–04	−72.2857550	42.2387258	2008
Billington Sea	MassDEP	08-F007–05	−70.6810010	41.9348301	2008
Collins Pond	DCR	DCR (2008) Data from Lakes and Ponds, 2008	−71.1090134	42.6115557	2008
Stearns Pond	DCR	DCR (2008) Data from Lakes and Ponds, 2008	−71.0694217	42.6173500	2008
Upper Leach Pond	DCR	DCR (2008) Data from Lakes and Ponds, 2008	−71.1513062	42.0702976	2008
Aaron River Reservoir	DCR	DCR (2008) Data from Lakes and Ponds Pioneer Infestation, 2008	−70.8270316	42.2076141	2008
Clamshell Pond	DCR	DCR (2008) Data from Lakes and Ponds, 2008	−71.6781971	42.3993398	2008
Althea Lake	DCR	DCR (2008) Data from Lakes and Ponds Pioneer Infestation, 2008	−71.3807537	42.6679916	2008
Berry Pond	DCR	DCR (2008) Data from Lakes and Ponds, 2008	−71.0868735	42.6200740	2008
Sewall Pond	DCR	DCR (2008) Data from Lakes and Ponds, 2008	−71.7461921	42.3230767	2008

Sevenmile River	MassDEP	08-L006-01	−72.0049161	42.2647794	2008
Nashua River	MassDEP	08-Q006-02	−71.6719879	42.4447381	2008
Unnamed Tributary	MassDEP	08-A032-06	−71.7877508	42.2054101	2008
Aldrich Pond	MassDEP	09-G008-06	−71.7402591	42.1633137	2009
Marble Pond	MassDEP	09-G008-05	−71.7422507	42.1654355	2009
Monponsett Pond	MassDEP	09-G006-01	−70.8452535	42.0045958	2009
Monponsett Pond	MassDEP	12-B004-01	−70.8452535	42.0045958	2009
Monponsett Pond	MassDEP	13-B008-01	−70.8452535	42.0045958	2009
Monponsett Pond	MassDEP	14-B006-01	−70.8452535	42.0045958	2009
Monponsett Pond	MassDEP	14-B008-01	−70.8452535	42.0045958	2009
Monponsett Pond	MassDEP	09-G005-04	−70.836781	42.0014672	2009
Monponsett Pond	MassDEP	09-G006-05	−70.836781	42.0014672	2009
Monponsett Pond	MassDEP	12-B002-04	−70.836781	42.0014672	2009
Monponsett Pond	MassDEP	12-B004-04	−70.836781	42.0014672	2009
Monponsett Pond	MassDEP	12-B006-05	−70.836781	42.0014672	2009
Monponsett Pond	MassDEP	12-B008-05	−70.836781	42.0014672	2009
Monponsett Pond	MassDEP	13-B006-05	−70.836781	42.0014672	2009
Monponsett Pond	MassDEP	13-B008-05	−70.836781	42.0014672	2009
Monponsett Pond	MassDEP	14-B004-05	−70.836781	42.0014672	2009
Monponsett Pond	MassDEP	14-B006-05	−70.836781	42.0014672	2009
Monponsett Pond	MassDEP	14-B008-05	−70.836781	42.0014672	2009
Monponsett Pond	MassDEP	15-B009-05	−70.836781	42.0014672	2009
Riley Pond	MassDEP	09-G010-04	−71.6704740	42.1044164	2009
Reservoir	MassDEP	10-B005-04	−70.8526283	42.0298844	2010
Reservoir	MassDEP	12-B004-06	−70.8526283	42.0298844	2010
Reservoir	MassDEP	13-B006-06	−70.8526283	42.0298844	2010
Saugus River	MassDEP	10-D020-01	−71.0364004	42.5095513	2010
Hockomock River	MassDEP	13-C040-01	−71.0354529	41.988368	2013
Benton Pond	DCR	DCR (2008) Data from Lakes and Ponds	−73.0473909	42.1841285	N/A

(Continued)

TABLE 19.2 (Continued)

Waterbody	Agency	Report Source	Longitude	Latitude	First Year Reported
Sassaquin Pond	MassDEP	Matfield River Watershed	−70.9487998	41.7347795	N/A
Otis Reservoir	DCR	DCR (2008) Data from ACT, GeoSyntec-ACT	−73.0383897	42.1507965	N/A
West Waushacum Pond	DCR	DCR (2008) Data from Lakes and Ponds	−71.7644996	42.4143945	N/A

MANAGING ACTIONS

The most efficient way to protect the environment from invasive species is integrated management, including education and prevention, early detection, control, ecosystem restoration, and environmental regulation and enforcement. Among these management options, prevention has been proved to be the most efficient and cost-effective approach in stopping or minimizing the spread of aquatic invasive species. Mapping sightings of purple loosestrife provides a spatial understanding of the status of this invasive species in Massachusetts' lake and river riparian areas. This can increase the public's awareness of this invasive species and ultimately help to minimize the human-mediated spread to other waterbodies. This type of proactive method should be promoted.

In the meantime, for areas with purple loosestrife, reactive actions should also be taken. Developing a long-term control plan is key, especially when time and resources are scarce (Warne 2016). When a new population of purple loosestrife is identified, landowners and managers should focus first on preventing immediate spread by targeting isolated plants or small mats which are susceptible to physical control methods. Critically important areas should receive priority, such as areas that are habitat for endangered or threated species. Follow-up monitoring is another crucial step to ensure that purple loosestrife populations that have been managed or are in the process of being managed do not reemerge.

CHEMICAL TECHNIQUES

Using herbicides from mid-summer to early fall to control purple loosestrife is possible. Herbicides can be ideal for treating smaller populations and require repeat treatments in order to get long-term results. Spraying the solution in mist form is not acceptable since mist can drift away and influence other vegetation. Similarly, rainy days should be avoided as the extra water could carry the solution further than intended (Minnesota Department of Natural Resources 2017). Triclopyr-formulated solutions (2, 4-D, Rodeo and Pondmaster) for wetland areas are needed at 0.5% by volume in spray solution and 50 gallons spray solution is suggested as standard requirement (Jacobs 2008). When using backpack spraying, the solution can be adjusted to 1–1.5%. Multi-year herbicide treatment is needed to eradicate purple loosestrife (Jacobs 2008). Herbicides such as 2, 4-D for *L. salicaria* might be considered as a control method, but it may lead to chemical pollution of the local soil and ecosystem. Other chemicals such as glyphosate and imazapyr are also used for chemical treatment. More information about chemical control on purple loosestrife and other 18 invasive species can be found in Appendix III. Regardless of the herbicide chosen for a purple loosestrife management project, the directions on the label should be followed. Before chemical application, it is required to obtain an aquatic nuisance species control license (BRP WM04 Form) from Massachusetts Department of Environmental Protection.

MECHANICAL OR PHYSICAL TECHNIQUES

When treating small areas, or areas that have plants less than 2 years old (i.e., root system is not well-developed), digging, hand pulling, cutting, and mowing are the most effective albeit time-consuming eradication methods (Jacobs 2008; Warne 2016). Digging, hand pulling, and cutting is best performed throughout the summer before the plant begins to seed. When plotting the soil around purple loosestrife, it is better to minimize the disturbance to the soil system. After removing the plant stem above ground, roots need to be removed and put into bags to prevent resprouting; the spreading of seeds potentially in the soil needs to be prevented too. Grazing and tilling are not recommended because it would be considered more likely to spread the seeds. Notwithstanding the aerenchyma cells can tolerate low-oxygen conditions, flooding can still be an effective method to control it and will eliminate almost all of purple loosestrife within an area, but sometimes it might also eliminate other desirable species (Jacobs 2008). However, flooding at levels less than 30 cm will not kill seedlings and can actually allow mature purple loosestrife to thrive.

BIOLOGICAL TECHNIQUES

There are several biological treatments for controlling the spread of purple loosestrife. In 1992, the Manitoba Purple Loosestrife Project was set up as an introduction to use biological management methods to control purple loosestrife. This project used *Neogalerucella* spp. and resulted in a reduction in purple loosestrife populations in targeted areas (Warne 2016). Currently, there are four kinds of tested beetles that feed on purple loosestrife. *Galerucella calmariensis* and *Galerucella pusilla* are two beetles that feed on the leaves of purple loosestrife (Figure 19.4) and eat the terminal bud area; also, the larvae feed on the bottom side of leaves. Massachusetts Association of Wetland Managers and its partners did a study to raise *Galerucella* sp. beetles for release in wetlands and only ten beetles were released at two spots along the Concord River in 2004 (Edward Rainer, personal communication). Ten years later, there is hardly any purple loosestrife along the Concord River in Billerica; however, loosestrife did come back from seed even the beetles are still eating the new plants (Figure 19.4). In Massachusetts, the leaf-eating *Galerucella* sp. is also used for purple loosestrife control in other areas such as along the Sudbury River (Flint 2014). Fifteen years ago, Massachusetts Office of Coastal Zone Management (MA CZM) Wetlands Restoration Program published a Guidance Document for the Purple Loosestrife Biocontrol briefly reviewing the use of biocontrol measures in Massachusetts to control purple loosestrife and providing information to people who may be interested in participating in the Project (MA CZM 2007). However, since 2010, new beetle release is not supported by MA Division of Ecological Restoration anymore. *Hylobius transversovittatus* is a weevil that feeds on the leaf from the edge toward the center while the larval form mines into the root of the plant depleting energy reserves. *Nanophyes marmoratus*, another beetle, forages on the seeds of purple loosestrife (Malecki et al. 1993; Blossey and Schroeder 1995; Hight et al. 1995). Two other species of beetle *Nanophyes brevis* and *Bayeriola salicariae* also eat seed capsules. Field testing of these two species has yet to be conducted and further

FIGURE 19.4 Purple loosestrife leaves eaten by *Galerucella* beetles along Concord River, Massachusetts. (Photos by Edward Rainer.)

research for these two subjects is required to prevent them from becoming the next new invasive species (Blossey 2002). More information about biological control on purple loosestrife is provided in the "Success Story" section.

There is no silver bullet to completely control purple loosestrife. For example, removing the plant during its pre-pollinating period would be considered an effective way of control, but it is costly and cannot be applied to a large area due to the requirement of manpower. Another option such as using flooding to extinguish the infested area is an undifferentiated method that may break the balance of local ecosystem. Therefore, integrated management practices are recommended in aquatic invasive species control and management (Wong and Gerstenberger 2015). Figure 19.5 provides an outline for choosing the best management techniques given the size of the area and the percent of the land that contains purple loosestrife. Following any management actions, restoration efforts should be conducted utilizing native plant species. Another example is that biocontrol has provided suppression of purple loosestrife at many sites in North America, it is not effective at or applicable to every infestation location (Blossey et al. 2015); so, the authors proposed that integrated purple loosestrife management is needed to control this invasive species with physical, cultural, and chemical control tools.

It is critical to not compost any plant material that may be live still as this can lead to the growth of new plants. Discarding plant waste in areas of critical importance should also be avoided. The ideal method of disposal for purple loosestrife is by burning. Composting of plant material can be conducted when brought to an upland waste management facility where the composting temperatures can reach high enough to ensure the death of any remaining live plant material. If the above methods of disposal cannot be achieved, another option is to seal the plant material into bags which are left in direct sunlight for at least three weeks.

SUCCESS STORY

The use of exotic biological control agents as a method of managing invasive pests is not widely accepted. Concerns exists about the safety of such treatment methods due to spillover effects on non-target species, as well as a lack of previous successful cases of introductions and a lack of monitoring of the impacts of biological controls on both target and non-target species (Malecki et al. 1993). However, it is proposed that biological control can be cost-effective, long-lasting, self-sustaining, and non-polluting given proper research and testing of the proposed control species (Malecki et al. 1993; Blossey et al. 1994). One initial study

Percent of Area Covered with Purple Loosestrife	Size of Area to be Managed			
	Isolated Plants	Small infestation <0.5 hectare / 1 acre	Medium <0.5 – 2 hectares / 1 - 4 acres	Large >2 hectares / > 4 acres
1-10%	• Mechanical • Chemical	• Mechanical • Chemical	• Biological	• Biological
10-25%	• Mechanical • Chemical	• Mechanical • Chemical	• Biological	• Biological
25-50%	• Mechanical • Chemical • Biological	• Mechanical • Chemical • Biological	• Biological	• Biological
>50%	• Biological	• Biological	• Biological	• Biological

FIGURE 19.5 Suggested control methods for purple loosestrife based on the size of the control area and the percentage of the area infested with purple loosestrife. (From Warne 2016.)

conducted jointly by the USDA Agricultural Research Service and the US Fish and Wildlife Service sought to find natural predators of *L. salicaria* by examining 120 species of insects native to habitats associated with that of purple loosestrife. Fourteen species were found to be host-specific, and three were further chosen as being the most promising control agents due to their substantial effect on the growth of *L. salicaria*: *Galerucella calmariensis*, *Galerucella pusilla*, and *Hylobius transversovittatus*. Fifty plants of similar taxonomy to purple loosestrife were also tested to determine selectivity of the proposed control agent. Only two species native to North America were identified: swamp loosestrife and winged loosestrife, both of the family Lythraceae (*Decodon verticillatus* and *Lythrum alatum*, respectively). However, it was observed that when given a choice between the North American plants and *L. salicaria*, the latter was predominantly chosen. Additionally, a separate study conducted by Blossey et al. (1994) tested the selectivity of *G. calmariensis* and *G. pusilla* on 48 non-target species; normal adult and larval feeding only occurred on the target plant with slight to moderate feeding occurring on several other species of *Lythrum*; normal oviposition only occurred on the target plant with moderate oviposition occurring only on winged loosestrife. In 1992, the three biological control species identified were approved for release into the United States (Malecki et al. 1993).

In 1994, populations of *G. calmariensis* and *G. pusilla* were released throughout central New York in four different release sizes (20, 60, 180, and 540) at 36 different sites (Grevstad 1999). Over the next three years, monitoring was conducted at each site to determine the remaining numbers of each species. Prior to the introductions, the size and density of each *L. salicaria* strand was measured to determine the effectiveness of the introduced control agents at managing purple loosestrife. Ten years later, Grevstad returned to examine the long-term effects of the introduction. He found that *G. pusilla* was present at 22 of the 36 original sites, and *G. calmariensis* was present at 10 sites (Grevstad 2006). Sites that had beetles during the final year of monitoring in 1997 were more likely to have beetles ten years after introduction, especially in the case of *G. pusilla*. Sites with higher release sizes were also found to have higher population persistence than those with lower release sizes. In terms of their effectiveness as a control agent for purple loosestrife, stems were found to be on average shorter after ten years; however, overall plant density and size did not change. Grevstad (2006) suggested several factors may have led to the low overall impact on the target species. First, he proposed that ten years may not have been a long enough time to see beneficial impacts. Second, the initial densities of the introduced control agents may not have been high enough. And third, seasonal variations in beetle abundances may have allowed purple loosestrife to rebound on a year-to-year basis. He proposed, therefore, that large-scale benefits could be achieved by releasing more biological control agents into more locations, ideally with release sizes of at least 500 individuals.

Herbicides are also a potential solution to combat the spread of *L. salicaria*. One study looked at the effectiveness of 14 herbicides administered at four sites over a ten-year period (Knezevic et al. 2018). Overall, purple loosestrife was significantly impacted by herbicides across all locations. However, the age of the *L. salicaria* strand had an effect on the number of treatments required for adequate control to be achieved. Strands that were 3 years old required on average two to three years of sequential treatment. Strands that were 5 years old required two to five years of sequential treatment. Strands that were 10 years old required three to nine years of sequential treatment. Additionally, certain older strands showed regrowth after treatment had ceased due to no new growth being observed. Because of this, it is advised older strands of *L. salicaria* be observed for several years after a final treatment to ensure that growth has been ceased. While this study showed that herbicides can be an effective control method, non-target grassy and broad-leaf plant species were negatively affected by treatment alongside *L. salicaria*.

Both studies which examined the long-term effects of the two different control methods (biological and chemical) showed promising results, but also came with several negative side effects. The best management technique then would integrate both management methods, coupled with active mapping of purple loosestrife locations statewide and long-term site monitoring. New or young strands that are identified can be treated with herbicides, which were shown to be most effective on younger *L. salicaria*. In areas that have larger or older strands of purple loosestrife, biological control methods can be applied, as they are long-lasting without the need for yearly reapplications.

REFERENCES

Balogh, G. 1986. Ecology, Distribution and Control of Purple Loosestrife (*Lythrum salicaria*) in Northwest Ohio. Thesis for Master of Science, Ohio State University, p. 107.

Blossey, B. 2002. Purple Loosestrife. In: Van Driesche R, Blossey B, Hoddle M, Lyon S, Reardon R (eds), Biological control of invasive plants in the Eastern United States. USDA Forest Service Publication FHTET-2002-04, Morgantown, West Virginia, p. 413.

Blossey, B., C.B. Randall, and M. Schwarzländer. 2015. *Biology and Biological Control of Purple Loosestrife* (2nd ed.). U.S. Department of Agriculture and U.S. Forest Service. 107 p.

Blossey, B., D. Schroeder. 1992. Biocontrol of *Lythrum salicaria* in the United States. Final Report. Cornell University, United States Fish and Wildlife Service, Washington State Dept. of Agriculture, and Washington State Dept. of Wildlife.

Blossey, B., D. Schroeder. 1995. Host specificity of three potential biological weed control agents attacking flowers and seeds of *Lythrum salicaria* (Purple Loosestrife). *Biological Control* 5: 47–53.

Blossey, B., D. Schroeder, S. Hight, and R. Malecki. 1994. Host specificity and environmental impact of two leaf beetles (*Galerucella calmariensis* and *G. pusilla*) for biological control of purple loosestrife (*Lythrum salicaria*). *Weed Science* 42: 134–140.

Blossey, B., L.C. Skinner, J. Taylor 2001. Impact and management of purple loosestrife (*Lythrum salicaria*) in North America. *Biodiversity and Conservation* 10: 1787–1807.

Brown, M.J. 2005. Purple loosestrife—*Lythrum salicaria* L. In: C.L. Duncan and J.K. Clark (eds). *Invasive Plants of Range and Wildlands and Their Environmental, Economic, and Societal Impacts*. Lawrence, KS: Weed Science Society of America, pp. 128–146.

Cao, L., J. Larson, R. Sturtevant. 2020. *Lythrum salicaria L.: U.S. Geological Survey, Nonindigenous Aquatic Species Database*. Gainesville, FL: U.S. Geological Survey.

Chandler, M.A., L.C. Skinner, L.C. Van Riper. n.d. *Biological Control of Invasive Plants in Minnesota*. Minnesota: Minnesota Department of Agriculture & Minnesota Department of Natural Resources. http://files.dnr.state.mn.us/natural_resources/invasives/biocontrolofplants.pdf (Accessed April 20, 2017).

Cygan, D. 2003. *Biological Control of Purple Loosestrife*. New Hampshire: New Hampshire Department of Agriculture, Markets & food, Plant Industry Division and New Hampshire Department of Transportation, Bureau of Environment.

Flint, S. 2014. *Loosestrife-eating Beetles Come to Local Backyard*. London: OARS For the Assabet Sudbury and Concord Rivers Newsletter. p. 1 and 6.

Grevstad, F. 2006. Ten-year impacts of the biological control agents *Galerucella pusilla* and *G. calmariensis* (Coleoptera: Chrysomelidae) on purple loosestrife (*Lythrum salicaria*) in Central New York State. *Biological Control* 39: 1–8.

Grevstad, F. 1999. Experimental invasions using biological control introductions: The influence of release size on the chance of population establishment. *Biological Invasions* 1: 313–323.

Henderson, R. 1987. Status and control of purple loosestrife in Wisconsin. *WDNR-Research Management Findings No. 4*, p. 4.

Hight, S.D., B. Blossey, J. Laing, and R. DeClerck-Floate. 1995 Establishment of insect biological control agents from Europe against *Lythrum salicaria* in North America. *Environmental Entomology* 44: 965–977.

Jacobs, J. 2008. Ecology and Management of Purple Loosestrife (*Lythrum salicaria* L.). *Invasive Species Technical Note No. MT-21*. United States Department of Agriculture, Natural Resources Conservation Service. www.nrcs.usda.gov/wps/portal/nrcs/detail/mt/home/?cid=nrcs144p2_056795 (Accessed April 10, 2017).

Katovich, E.J.S., R.L. Becker, and J.L. Byron. 2003. Winter survival of late emerging purple loosestrife (*Lythrum salicaria*) seedlings. *Weed Science* 51(4): 565–568.

Knezevic, S., O.A. Osipitan, M. Oliveira, and J. Scott. 2018. *Lythrum salicaria* (Purple Loosestrife) control with herbicides: Multiyear applications. *Invasive Plant Science and Management* 11: 143–154.

Lavoie, C. 2009. Should we care about purple loosestrife? The history of an invasive plant in North America. *Biological Invasions* 12(7): 1967–1999.

Lesica, P., M.T. Lavin, and P.F. Stickney. 2012. *Manual of Montana Vascular Plants*. Fort Worth, TX: BRIT Press. 771 p.

Lindgren, C.J. 1999. Performance of a biological control agent, *Galerucella calmariensis* L. (Coleoptera: Chrysomelidae) on purple loosestrife *Lythrum salicaria* L. in Southern Manitoba (1993–1998). *Proceedings of the X International Symposium on Biological Control of Weeds*, Stonewall, MB, pp. 367–382.

Lindgren, C.J., R.T. Clay. 1993. Fertility of 'morden pink' *Lythrum virgatum* L. transplanted into wild stands of *L. salicaria* L. in Manitoba. *Horticultural Science* 28(9): 954.

MA CZM (Massachusetts Office of Coastal Zone Management). 2007. *Guidance Document for the Purple Loosestrife Biocontrol Project*. Cambridge, MA: MA CZM, p. 34.

Mal, T.K., J. Lovett-Doust, L. Lovett-Doust, and G.A. Mulligan. 1992. The biology of Canadian weeds 100. *Lythrum salicaria*. *Canadian Journal of Plant Science* 72: 13051330.

Malecki, R.A., S. Hight, L. Kok, D. Schroeder, and J. Coulson. 1991. Information for the preparation of an environmental assessment. Host plant specificity testing of *Hylobius transversovittatus, Galerucella calmarienses* and *G. pusilla* for use in the biological control of *Lythrum salicaria* L. in North America. New York Cooperative Fish and Wildlife Research Unit, Department of Natural Resources, Fernow Hall, Cornell University, Ithaca, NY, p. 79.

Malecki, R.A., B. Blossey, S.D. Hight, D. Schroeder, L.T. Kok, and J.R. Coulson. 1993. Biological control of purple loosestrife; a case for using insects as control agents, after rigorous screening, and for integrating release strategies with research. *Biological Science* 43: 680–686.

McGlynn, C.A. 2008. Native and invasive plant interactions in wetlands and the minimal role of invasiveness. *Biological Invasions* 11: 1929–1939.

Minnesota Department of Natural Resources. 2017. Controlling purple loosestrife with herbicides. www.dnr.state.mn.us/invasives/aquaticplants/purpleloosestrife/control_herbicides.html (Accessed April 10, 2017).

Mullin, B.H. 1998. The biology and management of purple loosestrife (*Lythrum salicaria*). *Weed Technology* 12: 397–401.

Pellet, M. 1977. Purple loosestrife spreads down river. *The American Bee Journal*. 117: 214–215.

Regional *Lythrum salicaria* Working Group. 2004. *Purple Loosestrife (Lythrum salicaria) in the Chesapeake Bay Watershed: A Regional Management Plan*, p. 36.

Shamsi, S.R.A., F.H. Whitehead. 1974. Comparative eco-physiology of *Epilobium hirsutum* L., and *Lythrum salicaria* L. I. General biology, distribution and germination. *Journal of Ecology* 62: 279–290.

Stein, B.A., S.R. Flack 1997. *Species report card: The State of U.S. plants and animals*. Arlington, VA: The Nature Conservancy, p. 26.

Stuckey, R.L. 1980. Distributional history of *Lythrum salicaria* (purple loosestrife) in North America. *Bartonia* 47: 3–20.

Thomsen, A. 2012. Perennial self-sowers. *Fine Gardening* 143: 32–37.

Thompson, D.Q., R.L. Stuckey, and E.B. Thompson. 1987. *Spread, impact and control of purple loosestrife (Lythrum salicaria) in North American wetlands. United States Fish and Wildlife Service, Fish and Wildlife Research No. 2*. Washington, DC: United States Department of Interior, p. 55.

Warne, A. 2016. *Purple Loosestrife (Lythrum salicaria) Best Management Practices in Ontario*. Peterborough, ON: Ontario Invasive Plant Council, p. 40.

Wilcove, D.S., D. Rothstein, J. Bulow, A.L. Phillips, and E. Losos. 1998. Quantifying threats to imperiled species in the United States. *Bioscience* 48: 607–615.

Wong, W.H., S.L. Gerstenberger (eds). 2015. *Biology and Management of Invasive Quagga and Zebra Mussels in the Western United States*. Boca Raton, FL: CRC Press, p. 566.

Appendix I

MassDEP Equipment Decontamination Protocol[1]

Massachusetts Department of Environmental Protection Division of Watershed Management

STANDARD OPERATING PROCEDURE

Field Equipment Decontamination to Prevent the Spread of Invasive Aquatic Organisms

CN 59.6
August, 2015

1.0 SCOPE AND APPLICATION

The following SOP has been developed under the assumption that Massachusetts' waterways are threatened by the spread of non-indigenous species. This SOP provides guidance to DWM field staff on the prevention and minimization of the spread of invasive aquatic organisms from one waterbody to another. It covers field and lab decontamination procedures for any equipment and gear used in streams, rivers, lakes, ponds, and impoundments throughout Massachusetts whenever any invasives have been observed or are reasonably suspected to be present and spread to non-contaminated areas by monitoring activity. A complete list of confirmed and suspected aquatic invasive species sightings by WPP and other agencies in Massachusetts can be found from the WPP Toolbox named Mass AIS Waterbody List. If a survey is going to be conducted in any of the listed waterbodies, the decontamination procedures will be implemented.

This SOP applies to controlling the spread of invasive organisms only. For additional guidance regarding equipment decontamination procedures to prevent and minimize cross contamination of samples, see CN 59.0.

2.0 SUMMARY

By following simple checking and cleaning steps, the inadvertent spread of invasive organisms (e.g., Eurasian milfoil, Didymosphenia geminata or Didymo, zebra mussel, asian clam, others) from infected to non-infected waterbodies by the actions of DWM field staff can be avoided or minimized. Special procedures are required because infestation can occur from very small amounts of invasive material (in some cases, microscopic), which can remain viable long after being removed from the water.

3.0 SAFETY AND LOGISTICAL CONSIDERATIONS

Care should be taken at all times during decontamination activities. Although these procedures do not involve the use of hazardous chemicals, gloves and safety glasses are recommended when using washing solutions. Clean tap water should be available at all times in case of splashes on skin or into eyes. For cleaning at DWM-Worcester, a shower/eyewash station is available, if necessary.

Employ a mitigation-hierarchy approach in implementing this SOP by practicing stepwise decision-making. First, seek to avoid contact with invasives such as Didymo and thus the need to decontaminate equipment. If avoidance is not possible, minimize contact with invasives and recognize where/when decontamination is required.

Avoidance of the need to decontaminate equipment in the field is preferred. This can be achieved, for example, by using equipment only once at known or potentially contaminated sites, then bringing all equipment back to the lab for cleaning prior to reuse. It is recognized, however, that this is not always possible for DWM field activities.

Because application of these procedures requires additional time for preparation, use in the field, and post-survey cleanup, adequate planning is required to ensure implementation. Specifically, plan to sample known/suspected invasive sites toward the end of the survey, if possible.

4.0 DECONTAMINATION EQUIPMENT AND MATERIALS

The equipment and materials needed to ensure adequate decontamination (DECON) for invasives vary depending on the type of contaminate and the location of decontamination activity. Soaking baths are generally more effective to render organisms non-viable. Spray washing is more useful for physical rinsing of organisms.

In general, the materials that may be needed for decontamination are as follows:

Field DECON "Kit": EACH CREW/VEHICLE

- Cleaning solution bath (cooler): Solution varies (see Appendix B for options; e.g., 5% hand-dishwashing soap solution); in tub with secure lid; minimum non-displaced solution depth of 6 inches; include energy dissipation to avoid excessive splashing, if possible
- Cleaning solution spray: In pressure sprayer#1
- Decon tubes: Containing cleaning solution for unattended deployment tubes and attended multiprobe sondes
- Spare cleaning solution (preferably non-P-containing, non-anti-microbial)
- Rinse water spray (tap water): In pressure sprayer#2 (use tap water spray if P-detergent or bleach is the cleaning solution)
- Clean rags and paper towels
- Trash bags
- PPE (gloves, safety glasses)
- Wristwatch
- Dedicated plastic sample container (for specimens)
- Bleach (1 gallon in reserve if needed)
- Portable eye wash (w/tap water)
- Quarters ($) for manual, pressure-spray car wash

Lab Decontamination

- Hot water (>60°C or >140°F)
- Cleaning solution: Varies (e.g., 5% hand-dishwashing soap solution)
- Tap water rinse
- Brushes, clean rags, and paper towels
- Trash container
- Bleach
- Portable pressure hose (boat/trailer washing), if available
- PPE (gloves, safety glasses)

5.0 GENERAL PROCEDURES

Checking and cleaning equipment (e.g., removing plant fragments) prior to moving to another waterbody is a recognized best management practice that should normally be employed whenever and wherever appropriate and practicable, regardless of whether invasives are suspected or confirmed to be present or not. This is especially true for macroscopic plant fragments and visible organisms. The DECON procedures outlined in this SOP represent additional measures to be used when necessary.

Step 1: Determine Presence/Absence Potential for Invasives

In the office and the field, perform background review and pre-survey field reconnaissance adequate to determine the likelihood of invasive organisms being present at each area to be visited. Agencies, watershed groups, etc. can assist in this determination. Based on the results, plan accordingly.

In the field upon arrival at each site, CHECK for the visual presence of invasive organisms in the area to be sampled. If invasives are found or reasonably suspected to be present and spread to non-contaminated areas by sampling activity (see the Mass AIS Waterbody List in the WPP Toolbox), all activities involving contact with water must employ "DECON" procedures as contained in this SOP. If invasives are encountered but were not expected, do not perform the activity without the proper decontamination equipment or restrict the sampling equipment to a single waterway, and then clean/dry later at the office/lab.

Appendix I

> **Example DECON approach involving "Didymo":** As of January 2008, the only watershed in Massachusetts where Didymo has been found (albeit only out of state in upstream NH and VT tributaries) is the Connecticut River watershed. Therefore, the proposed Year-2 monitoring approach by DWM in 2008 will be to:
>
> - Employ DECON procedures at all DWM stations visited in the Connecticut River watershed *and* watch for actual Didymo outbreaks in this watershed as much as possible.
> - Watch for actual Didymo outbreaks as much as possible in other Year-2 watersheds. If observed in a watershed (in Massachusetts or upstream in other states), employ DECON procedures at all DWM stations visited in that watershed.

Any potential new invasive species observed in any site, whether it is a new site or a site has been infested by other invasive species, needs to be confirmed before it is reported to other agencies. A standard reporting protocol on invasive species sightings are described below (please also refer to Appendix K about field sampling protocol and verification for suspected invasives).

> **New Invasive Species Sightings Verification and Reporting Guidance:** WPP field survey crew will take an extra sample of the suspicious invasive species. If possible, a photo should also be taken to record the habitat of the suspicious invasive species. If the suspicious species is an animal, the sample needs to be preserved with 50% ETOH in a container. For a plant, the sample should be collected as a whole or a segment; if plants have fruits and/or flowers, the plants need to be collected as a whole. Keep the plant sample in a bag or bucket of water at all times: don't leave them out of the water in the sun because they will wither quickly and become useless as specimens. The extra sample will be brought back to the lab and examined by at least one additional WPP biologist for verification. If the sample is not confirmed within WPP, external research experts will be consulted until the sample is finally confirmed. Upon the final confirmation, the sighting will be added to the list of Mass AIS Waterbody List in the WPP Toolbox. This new invasive sighting will be reported to other agencies and shared with the general public. If the sample is not identified as an invasive species, the waterbody will not be added to the Mass AIS Waterbody list. Contact David Wong for AIS confirmation along with Richard Chase and Art Johnson for AIS reporting. Preserve specimens for further analysis if it is needed. Destroy specimens prior to disposal as trash.

Step 2: Assemble Field DECON "Kit"

At the office, prepare the field DECON kit and include it with survey equipment inside each DWM vehicle. The field DECON kit should be available at all times in case it is needed. The cleaning solution can also be made in the field as needed.

Step 3: Employ Check–Clean–Dry Procedures (and DECON as Necessary)

If You Are Visiting Waterways Known or Reasonably Suspected of Containing Invasives, You Must Use Check, Clean, Dry Procedures. If Cleaning or Drying in the Field Is Not Practical, Restrict Equipment to a Single Waterway, and Then Clean/Dry Later at the Office/Lab

In general, do not wear felt soled boots/kickers or boots with porous surfaces for monitoring activity, especially where Didymo is known or suspected to be present. If it must be done for some reason, restrict felt soles (and other "porous" equipment) to a single waterway, and then thoroughly clean/dry later at the office/lab. For traction (in lieu of felt-soles), use attachable, washable cleats. If cleats are used, do not drive vehicles with them on, and make sure to decontaminate Velcro straps.

Ensure that all washwater drains to isolated ground or to the sanitary sewer system. Keep washwater away from storm drains to prevent the spread of invasives (in case decontamination is not 100% effective).

> **CHECK:** Before you arrive at and leave a river or lake site, thoroughly inspect all equipment for plant/algal fragments and debris, *and*
> **CLEAN:** Remove all plant fragments and organic debris and dispose as trash. Clean equipment using the most practical treatment for your situation (which will not adversely affect your gear). See Appendices E–J for specific DECON cleaning procedures, *and/or*
> **DRY:** Drying will kill many invasive organisms, but must be complete. Slightly moist organisms may survive for months. To ensure effective drying, the item must be completely dry to the touch, inside and out, then left dry for at least another 48 hours before use.

STEP 4: POST-SURVEY CLEANUP

Perform post-survey cleanup to ensure proper disposal of all spent cleaning solutions and to ensure clean equipment for the next users.

6.0 TRAINING

All field staff using field equipment shall be trained in this SOP. Trained staff may also train designated interns in the procedures. Training shall consist of instruction on office and field procedures, including field identification of invasives and decontamination steps. Each trainee will conduct a cleaning procedure under supervision of the trainer. Training in lab microscopy for microscopic invasives (e.g., Didymo and zebra mussel veligers) is also planned.

7.0 QUALITY CONTROL

Random interviews and audits can be performed by DWM QA staff and others to ensure compliance with this SOP.

For surveys involving sample collection, application of these decontamination procedures must not impact sample integrity.

8.0 MAINTENANCE

Survey planning, preparation, and execution with regard to decontamination procedures is the responsibility of the monitoring coordinators and survey crew leads. If problems arise with decontamination equipment or procedures, see DWM's QA Analyst.

9.0 CORRECTIVE ACTIONS

Known failures to follow this SOP will be documented and corrective actions (e.g., communication with applicable staff) taken. Adjustments to this SOP will be made as needed based on hands-on experience, improvements in procedures, or the nature and extent of invasives.

10.0 POLLUTION PREVENTION AND WASTE MINIMIZATION

- When possible, use prescribed tap water spray and drying procedures as an alternative to chemical use.
- Use the prescribed amounts of cleaning reagents (not more than necessary). Use non-P-containing detergent only.
- Ensure proper disposal of waste materials throughout the decontamination procedure.
- Return spent washwater solutions used in the field to the office/lab for disposal down the sanitary sewer drain.

NOTES

1 Modified from Chase and Wong (2015).

REFERENCES

Kilroy, C. 2005. Tests to determine the effectiveness of methods for decontaminating materials that have been in contact with *Didymosphenia geminata*; Prepared for Biosecurity New Zealand; NIWA Client Report: CHC2005-005, NIWA Project: MAF05501 National Institute of Water and Atmospheric Research Ltd; www.niwa.co.nz. 36 p.

Mass DCR and Mass DFG August 2009. Massachusetts Interim Zebra Mussel Action Plan. www.mass.gov/eea/docs/dcr/watersupply/lakepond/downloads/zebra-mussel-interim-action-plan.pdf. (Accessed August 5, 2015).

Scholl. C. 2006. Aquatic invasive species: A guide for proactive and reactive management. Report to Wisconsin Department of Natural Resources. http://dnr.wi.gov/aid/documents/ais/aisguide06.pdf. (Accessed on August 4, 2015).

Spaulding, S., and L. Elwell. 2007. *Increase in Nuisance Blooms and Geographic Expansion of the Freshwater Diatom Didymosphenia geminata: Recommendations for Response*. Denver, CO: US EPA Region & Livingston MT: Federation of Fly Fishers, p. 33.

Special Session on *Didymosphenia geminata*, Western Division American Fisheries Society Meeting, May 15–16, 2006, Bozeman, Montana. post-meeting update.

Warrington P. 1994. Collecting and preserving aquatic plants. Environmental Protection Department, Ministry of Environment, Lands and Parks. Government of British Columbia. www.env.gov.bc.ca/wat/wq/plants/plantcollect.pdf. (Accessed August 4, 2015).

Zook, B., and S. Phillips. 2015. Recommended uniform minimum protocols and standards for watercraft interception programs for dreissenid mussels in the Western United States. In: W.H. Wong and S.L. Gerstenberger (eds). *Biology and Management of Invasive Quagga and Zebra Mussels in the Western United States*, pp. 175–204.

NOTE #1 CLEANING SOLUTIONS AND/OR ACTIONS TO PREVENT THE SPREAD OF INVASIVE AQUATIC ORGANISMS

Invasives of Concern	Disinfectant	Concentration	Contact Time	Reference
Dreissenid mussels (zebra and quagga mussels)	Vinegar	100%	20 minutes ^	1,2,3,4, 5
	Chlorine/bleach	1 oz per gallon water	1 hour	
	Power wash with hot wash	>45°C	20 seconds	
	Steam/scalding hot wash	60°C	10 seconds	
	Freeze	<0 °C	4–24 hours	
	Salt bath	Saturated	30 minutes ^	
	Ethanol	50%	10 minutes	
	Lysol	As sold	10 minutes	
	Drying	Dry to the touch	One week if kept dry; up to four weeks if subject to cool, wet weather	
Didymo (*Didymosphenia geminata*)	Dishwashing detergent[B] (non-absorbent)	5% (two large cups or 500 ml with water added to make 10 l)	>1 minute (soak or spray)	6
	Salt	5% v/v (e.g., 1 l dry salt in 19 l hot tap water)	>1 minute (soak or spray)	
	Bleach (non-absorbent)	2% (one small cup or 200 ml with water added to make 10 l)	>1 minute (soak or spray)	
	Hot water (non-absorbent)	Very hot water *kept above* 60°C (140°F; hotter than most tap water)	>1 minute (soak)	
		hot water *kept above* 45°C (uncomfortable to touch)	>20 minutes (soak)	
	Hot water (absorbent material)	hot water kept above 45°C	>60 minutes (soak)	
	Hot water plus detergent (absorbent material)	hot water kept above 45°C and containing 5% dishwashing detergent	>30 minutes (soak)	
	Freezing	<0 °C	12 hours	
	Drying	Dry to the touch	>2 days after dry	

(Continued)

NOTE #1 CLEANING SOLUTIONS AND/OR ACTIONS TO PREVENT THE SPREAD OF INVASIVE AQUATIC ORGANISMS
(Continued)

Invasives of Concern	Disinfectant	Concentration	Contact Time	Reference
	Other (TBD)	TBD	TBD	TBD
Other microscale invasives	BPJ similar to that for Didymo or mussels			
Aquatic macrophytes (following check–clean procedures)	Drying	Dry to the touch	>2 days after dry	
	Power wash with hot wash	≥60°C	2 minutes	7

A It is intended for zebra mussel veligers, not adults.
B If necessary, use unscented detergent to avoid nausea from prolonged breathing of perfumed air.

(1) DiVittorio, J., Grodowitz, M., Snow, J., Manross, T. (2012) Inspection and Cleaning Manual for Equipment and Vehicles to Prevent the Spread of Invasive Species. US Department of the Interior, Bureau of Reclamation, Technical Memorandum No. 86-68220-07-05.
(2) Massachusetts Department of Conservation and Recreation. 2010. Prevent the Spread of Zebra Mussels. Massachusetts DCR Lakes and Ponds Program. www.mass.gov/eea/docs/dcr/watersupply/lakepond/downloads/zebmussbro10.pdf. (Accessed on August 4, 2015).
(3) Comeau, S. Ianniello, R.S., Wong, W.H., Gerstenberger, S.L. 2015. Boat Decontamination with Hot Water Spray: Field Validation. In: Biology and Management of Invasive Quagga and Zebra Mussels in the Western United States (Eds Wong, W.H., Gerstenberger, S. L.). Pages 161–173.
(4) Wong, W.H., personal observation.
(5) Waller, D. L., Fisher, S.W., Dabrowska H. 1996. Prevention of Zebra Mussel Infestation and Dispersal during Aquaculture Operations. The Progressive Fish-Culturist. 58:77–84.
(6) New Zealand Ministry for Primary Industries. Didymo: *Didymosphenia geminate*. www.biosecurity.govt.nz/cleaning. (Accessed on August 4, 2015).
(7) Blumer, D.L., Newman, R.M., Gleason, F.K. 2009. Can Hot Water Be Used to Kill Eurasian Watermilfoil? *Journal of Aquatic Plant Management*. 47: 122–127.

NOTE #2 FIELD DECONTAMINATION EQUIPMENT CHECKLIST FOR MULTIPROBE DEPLOYMENT SURVEYS

- QuickGuide protocol for decon
- Non-porous (NP) waders *only*
- 6″-Diameter decon soaking tube (1) filled ¾ with decon solution 3″-diameter decon soaking tub with cable notch (1) filled ¾ with 5% decon solution
- Decon soaking can/cooler (1) filled 1/3–1/2 with 5% v/v decon solution (for misc. items)
- Decon sprayer (1 minimum; 2 each crew if possible) filled with 5% decon solution
- Extra decon ingredients
- Large bags for used/contaminated equipment
- Watch/timer
- Bungee cords sufficient to tie down decon tubes
- 2nd set of "new" bungee cords (if needed)
- 2nd set of "new" concrete blocks (if needed)
- 2nd set of "new" deploy tubes (if available/needed)

NOTE #3 GENERAL INSPECTION AND CLEANING PROTOCOL FOR DWM BOATING EQUIPMENT

Prior to departure from the DWM office/lab, thoroughly inspect and *check* all watercraft, motors, and trailers for the presence of plant/animal remnants and organic debris. Remove all plant fragments, algal clumps, and other organisms and dispose of as trash. If necessary, *clean*, rinse, and drain (as appropriate) boat motor, trailer, anchors, chains, bilge water, fish tanks, fishing gear, and other equipment using portable spray unit or tap water hose or, if a designated wash area is available,[1] use it to rinse all surfaces of boats and equipment. If available, use motor flusher or "muff" device with water hookup to rinse out engine cooling system for 2–3 minutes. If not available, run cold motor out of water for 3–5 seconds *max* to remove most of the water.

When removing boats/trailer from the water, repeat the procedure of checking/cleaning (at the lake just sampled or at a separate washing station prior to entering another waterbody): Check, clean, rinse with salt water, and drain surface areas of a boat, motor, trailer, anchors, chains, bilge water, fish tanks, fishing gear, and other equipment using portable spray unit or tap water hose. If a designated wash area is available, make sure that all water enters the sanitary sewer system. In general, avoid going from one lake (X) to another waterbody (Y) where the same boating equipment must be used *and* where invasives are known or reasonably suspected to be present and spread by sampling activity to non-contaminated areas. If this cannot be avoided and after extensive checking and cleaning, DECON by cleaning and rinsing all equipment and surfaces that came in contact with the water using a portable spray unit (containing either tap water or an appropriate non-phosphorus, non-antibacterial solution[2]), *or*, preferably if available, a designated hot water pressure wash area or manual hot water pressure-spray car wash facility. Drain bilge water on land away from storm drains. To remove cooling water remaining in the motor when exiting the lake, you can pull motor out of water while running and then turn off gas feed or turn motor off after 3–5 seconds. When reaching Lake Y, check for plant fragments again prior to launch.

Note: Avoid contaminating waterways with residual cleaning solution by using P-free, non-antimicrobial detergent. Although most liquid detergents for handwashing dishes are now phosphorus-free, detergents for automatic dishwashers typically can have a high phosphorus content, as tripolyphosphate is a preferred water-softening agent. Use of soap without anti-bacterial chemicals (e.g., triclosan, triclocarban) also avoids potential pollution with these persistent biocides.

[1]As of August 2015, DWM does NOT have a designated pressure washing area at the DWM-Worcester location. Use a nearby pressure-spray wash facility and request reimbursement for $ spent.

[2]Ensure that cleaning solution used is appropriate for the invasive(s) of concern. Readily available cleaners include bleach, salt, and hand-dishwashing detergents. 5% solution (v/v) = 1 part cleaner to 20 parts water. For a 3 gallon spray unit (w/max fill line of 2 ¼ gallons), add about 1 pint of liquid dishwashing detergent or bleach and fill to max line).

NOTE #4 DECON PROTOCOL FOR FIELD CLEANING SAMPLING EQUIPMENT AND GEAR

Examples of DWM sampling gear that come into contact with ambient water and require checking and cleaning include, but are not limited to, boots and waders, felt-soled kickers, nets, gloves, ropes/tapes, bottle baskets, sediment samplers, Van Dorn samplers, integrated tube samplers, attended multi-probe sondes, deployed multi-probe sonde tubes, anchor/cable/lock assemblies for deployed multi-probe sonde tubes, Secchi disk, velocimeters, boats, motors, and trailers.

The following procedures apply to checking and cleaning equipment used for all types of DWM surveys in which more than one location is visited on the same day using the same equipment *and* where invasives are known to be present or suspected to be spread by sampling activity to non-contaminated areas[1]:

1. **Check** for and manually remove plant/animal remnants and organic debris from all equipment prior to and following sampling at each site. Dispose as trash at the site.
2. **Clean** gloves, boots, and equipment by immersing in a tub(s) containing an appropriate non-phosphorus, non-antibacterial solution.[2] Keep immersed for

the recommended time to kill the invasive of concern. When done, remove the items and rinse with tap water (optional). Cover the tub with the lid for reuse at the next site.

Soak solution.

3. For equipment that cannot be soaked in the tub, clean by spraying with an appropriate non-phosphorus, non-antibacterial solution for the recommended time using a portable spray device (away from waterbody). Make sure to cover all surfaces thoroughly. Rinse with second sprayer containing tap water (optional).

Soak solution.   Tap water rinse (optional).

4. **Dry** items to suppress invasives. Where cleaning at the lab is appropriate, these same standards apply, but also include drying (to ensure effective drying, the item must be *completely dry* to the touch, inside and out, then left dry for at least another 2–30 days, depending on the invasive of concern) (see Appendix C).
5. Although strongly discouraged, if you wear felt soled boots/kickers where Didymo and/or other microscopic invasives are known or suspected to be present, restrict equipment to a single waterway, and then clean/dry later at the office/lab.
6. Dispose of all used tub washwater back at the lab down the sink.
7. The cleaning solution can be made up at the lab prior to departure or in the field as needed.
8. For attended and deployed multi-probe sondes (and tubes), employ the following special procedures:

   (a) In general, pre-design the deployment surveys to avoid the need to redeploy multi-probe sondes from one location to another. This will avoid the need for field decontamination, but they will still require decontamination washing at the office/lab. It is recognized that this is not always possible.

   (b) For lab or field washing, scrub and rinse or soak entire apparatuses (sondes, deployment tubes, cables, L-brackets, locks, bungee cords, and anchor blocks) with appropriate P-free non-antibacterial solution for the recommended contact time. Do not use bleach on sonde units. For bungee cords (and other porous surfaces), soak for 30 minutes in hot water kept above 45°C containing 5% dishwashing detergent or other applicable solution (at the lab).

   (c) If *unattended* deployment tubes must be moved from one location to another, use field decontamination kit at the retrieval site to clean/rinse the entire deployment apparatus using P-free, non-antibacterial solution, followed by tap water rinse, *and* use lab-cleaned bungee cords only.

   (d) For *attended* multi-probe sondes used at multiple sites on the same survey run, clean/rinse sondes and coiled cable after each use with P-free non-antibacterial cleaning solution for the recommended contact time. Do not use bleach on sonde units. Do not clean the datalogger or its comm. ports.

[1] DECON procedures are also required whenever work is performed outside Massachusetts where Didymo is known or suspected to be present.

[2] Ensure that cleaning solution used is appropriate for the invasive(s) of concern. Readily available cleaners include bleach, vinegar, hand-dishwashing detergents, and salt.

NOTE #5 USE OF DECON SPRAYERS

Setup: To be performed by lead monitoring coordinator

1. Sprayers have been preset to produce a flat spray (no adjustment needed).
2. Fill sprayer unit(s) to max fill line with decon solution. Do not exceed max fill line.
3. Pressurize unit(s) and test pressure relief valve and spray (to make it ready for use). Approximately 10–20 pump cycles should be sufficient. Do not exceed max pressure limits.
4. Lock pump top and load sprayer(s) on cart or in vehicle. Protect sprayer wand(s) from damage by securing it inside the vehicle.
5. In case additional decon solution is needed in the field and to avoid having to make it up in the field, a second decon sprayer per crew should be set up and provided.
6. For maintenance issues, see operator's manual,.
7. For inflation precautions, see below.

Using the Sprayer: By Survey Staff

1. To save time, one person can be spraying boots, gloves, and equipment while the other performs other decontamination tasks.
2. If needed, unlock pump and add more pressure to get a better spray.
3. Rinse all "contaminated" items sufficiently for the solution to have the required contact time (not 1 minute of constant spraying), but be aware of how much spray solution is being used at each site (especially if you don't have a spare sprayer).
4. If solution runs out, use spare sprayer or make up new solution.
5. If you need to open pressurized tank, pull on relief valve first to release pressure before opening.
6. For other precautions, see below.

WARNING
AIR COMPRESSOR
INFLATION PROCEDURE

An air compressor can be used to pressurize Solo sprayers equipped with a built-in inflation valve. Compressors pressurize sprayers much more rapidly than hand pumping; for this reason extra caution must be exercised when using compressed air. **Sprayers must be functioning properly, unmodified and have all component parts.** The following procedures must be followed. Failure to do so could result in serious injury to the operator or others.

1) Before **each** use of a compressor with the sprayer be certain that:
   a) The umbrella valve (or valve cone on older models) is present, installed and functioning properly. The valve is located on the bottom of the cylinder (see owner's manual, page 2, "Pump Maintenance" item #7).
   b) The pump assembly is screwed snug to the sprayer tank.
   c) The pressure relief valve is functioning properly. Check by pulling up on the valve until the red stem shows. The valve stem should move freely and spring back to its original position when released. The O-ring and the valve stem must be greased (see page 2, "Maintenance" in the owner's manual).

If any of the above items or other components is malfunctioning, STOP!, do not use an air compressor to pressurize. Repairs must be made prior to use.

2) Additional Precautions:
   a) Fill the sprayer with liquid formula.
   b) Do not stand over the sprayer handle while pressurizing with an air compressor.
   c) Do not stand over the sprayer while releasing the handle from the locked position. Compressed air can cause the pump handle to pop upward if the valve cone or umbrella valve is worn, damaged or if the pressure relief valve is not functioning (see item 1c above).

3) When pressurizing, place pump handle in the unlocked position, resting on top of the pump assembly. Begin pressurizing slowly. If the pump handle rises...**STOP!, DISCONTINUE PRESSURIZING.** Pull up on the pressure release valve and hold until all the pressure is released; then remove the pump, check and replace the umbrella valve (or valve cone). Compressed air can cause the pump handle to pop upward if the valve cone or umbrella valve is worn, damaged or not installed completely. Do not pressurize until the worn or damaged part has been replaced, installed properly and the handle does not rise during pressurization. Should you have questions, please call Solo (800) 296-7656.

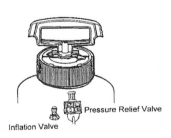

Figure 1 – Handle in the unlocked, resting position.

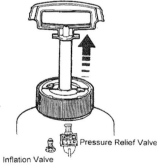

Figure 2 – Handle rising during pressurization; indicating a potentially unsafe condition.

Appendix II

A Guide for Using Hand Pulling and Benthic Barriers to Control Aquatic Invasive Species Pioneer Populations (Modified from MA DCR 2007)

CONTROL OF SUBMERGED AQUATIC INVASIVE PLANT SPECIES

HAND PULLING

Summary: This inexpensive techniques favored for controlling small pioneer infestations or where a large pool of volunteer labor is available. Although this technique is very species-specific and causes minimal damage to non-target species or other biota, many submerged non-native species spread by fragmentation, so extreme caution must be exercised when hand pulling to prevent additional spread. Although hand pulling is an inexpensive management technique, the use of SCUBA divers may increase the cost, and post-monitoring is essential.

Safety Considerations: It is essential to carry out this technique with a partner, rather than alone, and to take into consideration weather conditions, such as extreme heat or approaching storms. Life jackets are strongly recommended, and always follow the boating/water rules and regulations. If SCUBA divers are required, the divers will follow the safety guidelines outline by PADI, SCUBA, or the certifying company.

Materials: Plant bags and nets; spotter boat (if needed); scuba divers (if needed); plant guide, note pad, and markers (permanent ink); life vests; water, sunscreen, polarized glasses, hat with a brim.

Procedure:

1. If plants are in deep water, arrange for a spotter boat and two volunteers: one to drive and one to net any fragments that may float up. If the plants are confined to shallow waters, waders and view scopes (or mask/snorkel) may suffice.
2. Have someone on shore keep notes on the amount of plants removed, the time spent on removal, names of participants, etc. If using volunteer help, it is important to have them sign in and out so that they are accounted for.
3. Begin at the furthest boundary of the defined area and line up the participants along the boundary. Work toward the shore with the volunteers maintaining the line formation. Participants should go no more than chest deep, depending on the slope of the shore and type of bottom.
4. Remove target plants from the base, removing the entire root while disturbing the sediment as little as possible. Place the removed plants carefully in a collecting bag, and take care not to fragment the plants or leave any fragments in the water. The spotter boat should remain nearby, downwind/current, and have a volunteer with a net collect any fragments and place them in a storage bag. The boat operator needs to be very cautious of the volunteers in the water.
5. Repeat steps 3 and 4 until all the target plants have been removed. Depending

on the number of volunteers, type of sediment, depth of water, and other factors, expect this project to take a few days since the removal of the plants can create turbidity and make visibility very difficult.

6. Once the removal is complete, dispose of the contents of the storage bags far from the water so that they cannot cause a reinfestation.
7. Record the final details of the procedure and include date, time, site, town, volunteers involved, size of area pulled, approximate volume of plants removed, how they were disposed of, and other relevant notes.
8. To ensure effectiveness of treatment, monitor the site monthly during the growing season for reappearance of the non-native species. Remove any surviving plants.

BENTHIC BARRIERS

Summary: The installation of benthic barriers can be used to control the growth of aquatic submerged and floating-leaved plants. Benthic barriers are most suitable for small areas such as around docks and swim beaches. This technique can be repeated over a long period of time if the mats are maintained and cleaned.

Safety Considerations: The barrier needs to be securely anchored to the lake bottom or gases from decaying plants can build up beneath the barrier, causing it to rise off the bottom where it may create a hazard for boaters and swimmers. Caution must be used in selecting anchors so that they do not pose a hazard for swimmers, and will not roll as gases build up. Installation should be done on a day with appropriate weather conditions (calm and with no predicted storms). Use the buddy system when performing routine maintenance or inspection of the barrier.

Apparatus/materials: Anchors (sand bags, rocks, concrete blocks, flat weight discs); durable material (resistant to decay, limits light, and is less likely to float); area markers (anchored buoys/floating milk jugs) and rope; life vests; sunscreen, hat with brim, polarized glasses, water (optional); note pad and pen.

Procedure:

1. If possible, select a date in early spring for installation.
2. Purchase project materials, including benthic barriers, area markers, and weights. Note that there are many companies that both sell and install the benthic barriers.
3. If the barrier is not being professionally installed, identify an adequate number of volunteers who will install the barrier. Notify boaters, swimmers, and homeowners.
4. Define the area of barrier installation and mark area very clearly with visible, durable markers or buoys. Fishing lures and anchors can tear the fabric, so it is very important to forewarn boaters and fishermen of the barriers presence.
5. Record the details of the procedure and include date, time, site, town, number of volunteers (or name professional company involved), size of area covered, and other relevant notes.
6. One of the easier ways to install, maintain, and move a benthic barrier is to create a frame of marine plywood or rebar and PVC pipes for the barrier. Slits in the benthic material will allow gases to escape and sand bags can be used to secure the frame. Another option is to roll the material outward over the treatment area, anchoring as you proceed. Weights should then be placed along the edges, corners, and in the center of the barrier to anchor it down. Select weights that will not roll (such as cinder blocks).
7. Monitor the site monthly during the growing season to ensure that the mat remains well-anchored and free of sediments, and to assess effectiveness of treatment. Also monitor the area on a routine basis to check for reappearance of invasive species. Keep accurate records of the monitoring visits.

Appendix II

CONTROL OF FLOATING AQUATIC INVASIVE SPECIES

HAND PULLING

Summary: This inexpensive technique is favored for small- to medium-sized infestations or where a large pool of volunteer labors is available. Since the floating-leaved plants do not spread by fragmentation, this technique is very species-specific with minimal risk of additional spread. Although hand pulling is an inexpensive management technique, post-monitoring for regrowth and new plants is essential because many plants drop seeds that remain viable for years.

Safety Considerations: It is essential to carry out this technique with a partner and to take into consideration weather conditions. Life jackets are recommended and always follow the boating regulations.

Materials: Laundry baskets/leaf tip bags (or other containers to transport plants); kayak/canoe; pontoon boat (optional); plant guide, note pad, and pens; life vests; water, sunscreen, polarized lasses, hat with a brim; waders, mask/snorkel, view scope (optional); 100 pounds limit hanging scale (optional).

Procedure:

1. *Timing:* Mid-June is the best time to pull floating-leaved plants since they are visible at the water's surface, are still small, and have not produced seeds. Water chestnut must be pulled prior to August, before the nuts have formed. If hand pulling after August is inevitable, then take care to pull plants very carefully and to turn them upside down during retrieval to prevent the seeds from dropping into the water.

2. *Boats:* Kayaks and canoes are ideal vessels for hand pulling floating leaved species. Kayaks are easier to transport to remote locations, and are more maneuverable, especially in shallow water and dense plant growth. Since kayaks only require one person to paddle, their use maximizes the use of available volunteers. Canoes have the advantage of being able to carry a greater quantity of pulled plants, but generally require two volunteers to paddle and steer. Pontoon boats increase the efficiency of the hand pulling project in several ways. They can carry all the supplies, volunteers, and kayaks/canoes to the location and then once unloaded, can be used to store and transport the plants (e.g., an average pontoon boat can carry around 1,000 pounds of water chestnut plants). Kayakers and canoes can save time and energy by trading full laundry baskets for empty ones at the pontoon boat, instead of traveling to and from shore each time.

3. If plants are confined to shallow waters near shore, then volunteers with waders may suffice.

4. Plastic laundry baskets are ideal collection containers because they are inexpensive, lightweight, can be secured to the kayak with bungee cords, and drain excess water. Two handled plastic tubs also work well in canoes. For hand pulling projects near shore, leaf tip bags will suffice.

5. Prior to beginning a hand pulling event, give volunteers a brief history of the species, its impacts, and emphasize species identification.

6. Keep a list of the names of participants and have volunteers sign in and out so that they can be accounted. Remove target plants from the base, removing the entire root and stem. Place the removed plants carefully in the collecting basket/bag.

7. Once the basket is full, return to shore (or a stationary pontoon boat) and turn in the basket to be weighed (or plants counted). Assign a volunteer to keep notes on the weight or number of plants removed. This data is helpful for tracking population decreases year to year as a result of the hand pulling effort. If uniform bags or baskets are used, ten loads can be averaged to determine the approximate weight and plant count per load. This will eliminate the need

to weigh or count plants for every load collected. Plants should be disposed of on dry land, far above the high water mark. Some towns or local companies may be willing to haul away and compost or incinerate the removed plants.

8. Record the final details, including date, weather, beginning and end time, site, town, number of volunteers, size of area pulled, number (or weight) of plants removed, how they were disposed of, and other relevant notes.
9. Return to the site in one month and hand pull any new growth. Continue to monitor the site monthly (if possible) during the growing season.

CONTROL OF EMERGENT INVASIVE SPECIES

HAND PULLING

Summary: This inexpensive, labor-intensive technique is suitable for small pioneer infestations but is not feasible on a large scale. Although this technique is very species-specific and creates minimal damage to non-target species or other biota, it does require a long-term commitment. Both purple loosestrife and *Phragmites* have deep underground root systems and can regrow if any sections remain in the soil. Seeds already present in the soil rapidly germinate when the site has been disturbed, and therefore, continual monitoring and removal are necessary. These species need to be pulled prior to the formation of seeds; otherwise, the disturbance that occurs during hand pulling will only aid in their dispersal. Also, covering the area with black plastic or other light barrier may thwart new growth, and/or mowing the dry areas prevents returning plants from storing nutrients or developing seeds/flowers. Additional success may be achieved by planting native species in the disturbed area.

Safety Considerations: It is essential to carry out this technique with a partner or group and to take into consideration weather conditions, such as extreme heat or approaching storms. Dress appropriately by wearing long sleeves, long pants, and gloves. While working, volunteers should keep a 10-ft distance from each other to avoid accidental injury from rakes and other tools.

Materials: Shovels, rakes, trowels, clippers; plant guide, note pad, and permanent markers; water, sunscreen, polarized glasses, hat with a brim; long sleeve shirts, pants, and gloves; waders (optional).

Procedure:

1. If plants are in deep water, a boat can be used; if they are confined to shallow water and the shoreline, chest waders are ideal.
2. Have a volunteer keep notes on the amount of plants removed, the time spent on removal, names of participants, etc. It is important to have volunteers sign in and out so that they can remain accounted.
3. Timing for the removal of emergent plants is species-specific; however, it is best to hand-pull the plants in the spring when they are smaller, less established, and have not produced seeds. Although it is easier to identify purple loosestrife when it is in bloom, the plants need to be removed before they have formed seeds (usually mid-July). Pulling plants when they are in seed will only aid in distributing the 1–2 million seeds per plant. However, if the plants must be pulled after they have bloomed, place a plastic bag carefully over the flowering portion of the plant and secure it around the stem. This will minimize seed dispersal.
4. Begin on shore and slowly work outward into the stand.
5. Remove target plants and try to extract the entire root. Place the removed plants carefully in a collecting bag, and take care not to fragment the plants or leave any fragments in the water.
6. Proper disposal of the removed plants is very important. Do not compost *Phragmites* or purple loosestrife. The plants should be incinerated or burned. If this is not feasible, the plants should remain in plastic bags and allowed to rot.

Appendix III

Literature Research of Chemical Control Methods on 19 Invasive Species

Invasive Species	Chemicals*	Effective Minimal Concentration	Notes	References
Asian clam *Corbicula fluminea*	Ammonium nitrate	59.3 mg/l	Under hypoxic conditions, clam mortality rate began to steadily rise at 50 mg/l with effectiveness plateauing at around 200 mg/l. Under normoxic conditions. mortality rate did not begin to show signs of increase until around 125 mg/l. At 200 mg/l, normoxic testing began to show similar mortality levels to that of 75 mg/l under hypoxic conditions	Rosa et al. 2015; Rehman et al. 2021
	Potassium chloride	45 mg/l	Seemed to be most effective at increasing clam mortality rate from around 100 mg/l to 250 mg/l under hypoxic conditions. Under normoxic conditions, clam mortality rate saw a significant increase at around 150 mg/l to 900 mg/l with the highest mortality rate resulting from around 450 mg/l	Rosa et al. 2015; Densmore et al. 2018
	Niclosamide	0.08 mg/l	Required a significantly smaller concentration than other chemical agents to begin showing effectiveness at increasing Asian Clam mortality rates. Under hypoxic conditions, clam mortality rate increased to 10% with a 0.1 mg/l concentration of niclosamide, with effectiveness slowing at around 0.5 mg/l and 90% Asian clam mortality. Under normoxic conditions, niclosamide concentrations of around 0.2 mg/l began to slightly increase clam mortality. Clam mortality then reached about 90% at 1.2 mg/l under normoxic conditions and then began to plateau	Rosa et al. 2015
	Dimethoate	18 mg/l	Dimethoate concentration usage under hypoxic conditions began to increase clam mortality at around 45 mg/l. Effectiveness under hypoxic conditions then reached its maximum at around 100 mg/l and was near 100% clam mortality rate. Under normoxic conditions, clam mortality rate began to increase around 150 mg/l and reached its peak around 400 mg/l	Rosa et al. 2015; Van Scoy et al. 2016
	polyDADMAC	12.3 mg/l	Under hypoxic conditions, polyDADMAC effectiveness began to increase at approximately 10 mg/l, with mortality rate peaking at around 500 mg/l. Under normoxic conditions, polyDADMAC also began to increase at 10 mg/l and peaked at around 1200 mg/l. However, the clam mortality rate % difference between hypoxic and normoxic curves only varied slightly, with hypoxic conditions being more effective. Both hypoxic and normoxic curves also began to increase exponentially early on, but slowed quite quickly at around 200 mg/l	Rosa et al. 2015; Santos Ltd. 2021

Appendix III

Chlorpyrifos	0.05 mg/l	Exposure to substance between 0.5 ppm and 1 ppm, caused a significant reduction in cholinesterase activity and a reduced capacity to burrow into the substrate. All measured concentrations were within 25% of the nominal concentrations with all initial concentrations, and all but two of the final concentrations, falling above the nominal target concentration. Freshwater bivalves often occur in close association with agricultural landscapes and this, along with their near continuous contact with waterborne contaminants during feeding, makes the potential for exposure to agricultural chemicals quite high	Cooper and Bidwell 2006; Rosa et al. 2015
Zebra mussel *Dreissena polymorpha*	Potassium chloride (potash)	100 mg/l	During the winter of 2006, KCl was used at a concentration of approximately 100 mg/l (ppm) to successfully eradicate zebra mussels from a 12-acre abandoned rock quarry in Virginia without harming other aquatic fauna. Whereas KCl is not an US Environmental Protection Agency (EPA) approved pesticide and requires special permitting for use, it is generally considered a reasonably safe alternative to other molluscicides because of its low potential to impact non-target species (Densmore Et al. 2018). The acute lethal concentrations of the KCL on juvenile salmonoid populations are not expected to be of concern. Concentrations used to eradicate the zebra mussel populations (around 100 mg/l) are not nearly high enough to be of great concern as the salmonoid populations survived for 96 hours in a controlled environment with up to 800 mg/l of KCl exposure. However, as previously stated, long-term effects on the species were not accounted for and the buildup of the chemical agent in aquatic ecosystems was not fully examined. The warmer summer months required a smaller concentration of the chemical agent to reach the 48 h LC50 value. In June and July, the concentration used was just over 150 mg/l, while in the autumn and winter the concentrations required to reach the 48 h LC50 shot up to 500 mg/l by January. By using the mussels' filtering behavior to concentrate BioBullets, the absolute quantity of active ingredient added to the water can be reduced substantially. Another study was performed on the Colorado River but used KCl levels that far exceeded those of previous studies and would be deemed to a high concentration for the survival of other non-target species according to most of the other papers found	Fisher et al. 1991; Aldridge et al. 2006; Costa et al. 2008; Davis et al. 2018; Moffitt et al. 2016; Densmore et al. 2018

(Continued)

Invasive Species	Chemicals*	Effective Minimal Concentration	Notes	References
	polyDADMAC	6.25 mg/l	Chemical was tested with seasonal variability to find most effective concentration and time frame for usage. The warmer summer months required a smaller concentration of the chemical agent to reach the 48 h LC50 value. The concentration in use remained quite consistent at around 10–20 mg/l between June and October, with concentration requirements to reach 48 h LC50 reaching near 100 mg/l by November	Costa et al. 2008; Rosa et al. 2015
	Bayluscide WP 70 (active ingredient is the niclosamide ethanolamine salt) (Bayer 73) (Clonitralid)	0.006 mg/l	Chemical was tested with seasonal variability to find most effective concentration and time frame for usage. The warmer summer months required a smaller concentration of the chemical agent to reach the 48 h LC50 value. From June to August, the concentration hovered around 0.07 mg/l used, and more than doubled to 0.15 mg/l between August and September	Dawson 2003; Costa et al. 2008
	Sodium chloride	5,000 mg/l	Adult mussels required a 4× longer exposure period to exhibit complete mortality when exposed to NaCl at 30,000 mg/l (24 h) compared to KCl (6 h). At 10,000 mg/l, NaCl took 8× longer (96 h) than KCl (12 h) to cause 100% mortality of adult mussels. Sodium chloride is less effective at causing mortality than KCl within the exposure periods tested	Davis et al. 2015b; Davis et al. 2018
	Distilled white vinegar	25%	All concentrations (25, 50, 75, and 100%) caused complete mortality within 4 hours. The use of such an acid solution may be problematic in certain applications where the materials that need to be disinfected could be harmed by the chemical treatment. It could be assumed that the time needed to kill veligers is shorter than needed to kill adults	Claudi et al. 2012; Davis et al. 2015a
Chinese mystery snail *Cipangopaludina chinensis*	Rotenone	25 mg/l	The use of chemicals such as rotenone has a limited effect on *B. chinensis* due to the impenetrability of the shell, large shell size, and operculum	Haak et al. 2014; Dalu et al. 2015
	Copper sulfate	1.25 mg/l	Within one month of treatment, more than 27,000 dead snails were removed from two ponds	Freeman 2010; Boone et al. 2012; Haak et al. 2014

Species	Chemical	Concentration	Description	References
Northern snakehead *Channa argus*	Rotenone	0.025 ppm	It has been found that a rotenone concentration of 0.075 mg/l is strong enough to kill all northern snakehead in an enclosed area after 24 hours, but it also includes the most devastating damage. The commercial products are most commonly applied at a concentration 1.0–2.0 ppm which equates to 0.025–0.100 ppm of actual rotenone; however, treatment rates can range from 0.5 to 10.0 ppm	Lazur et al. 2011; Turner et al. 2007; Abdel-Fattah 2011; Stinson 2018
	Deltamethrin	0.061 µg/l (asked Jonathan on 8/27/22)	Environmentally relevant concentrations (0.121, 0.242, 0.485, and 0.970 µg/l) inhibited the biochemicals, antioxidants, and immune responses and disease resistance of snakehead fish. Deltamethrin exposure induced tissues damage, oxidative damage, and immunotoxicity in fish. The LC50 at 96 hours was determined to be 1.94 µg/l	(Kong et al. 2021; Shrivastava et al. 2011
Hydrilla *Hydrilla verticillata*	Diquat dibromide	0.25 ppm	Herbicide-treated hydrilla plants were severely necrotic indicating mortality 14 and 21 days after application (but not different from each). Greater than 95% control was observed against all floating species tested when either formulation was applied at 4.7 or 7.0 l/ha. The performance of diquat on *Eichhornia crassipes* (water hyacinth) and some other species can be enhanced if copper is also applied together. Copper is the most common active ingredient in algaecides	EPA 1995; Langeland et al. 2002; Mattson et al. 2004
	Endothall	1.0 mg ae/l	Hydrilla required higher concentrations and longer exposure times than did milfoil to achieve acceptable levels of control. Although root biomass was greatly reduced by some of these treatments (especially at concentrations of 4.0 and 5.0 mg/l), the presence of apparently healthy regrowth suggested that complete recovery could occur. It is also found that endothall killed coontail, lagarosiphon, and hydrilla and some species of *Myriophyllum* and *Potamogeton* but not *Egeria* or species of *Chara* or *Nitella*. Potassium endothall is used extensively in Florida	Netherland et al. 1991; Hofstra and Clayton 2001; Mattson et al. 2004; Poovey and Getsinger 2010; Wisconsin DNR 2012; Giamotti et al. 2014; Ortiz et al. 2019
	Triclopyr	0.25 mg/l	Triclopyr produced epinastic shoots in all species, except the charophytes; however, these growth effects along with some loss of turgor and color change in stems were temporary	Hofstra and Clayton 2001

(Continued)

Invasive Species	Chemicals*	Effective Minimal Concentration	Notes	References
	Dichlobenil	0.5 mg/l	All plants treated with dichlobenil exhibited some loss of vigor when compared to untreated control plants, and some species had more pronounced shoot loss, browning of stems, and stem fragmentation; however, all symptoms were transient with plant recovery in 35–50 days after treatment. The onset of symptoms was related to dichlobenil concentration rather than exposure time, with all susceptible species exhibiting symptoms irrespective of exposure time, but for some species only at the higher concentration	Hofstra and Clayton 2001
	Bispyribac-sodium	Not available	Bispyribac was registered by the EPA for aquatic uses in 2011 and is sold under the trade name Tradewind. Bispyribac is a systemic herbicide that blocks an enzyme necessary for growth and development specific to plants. As the herbicide accumulates in plant tissue, the plant dies over a period of weeks to months. Tradewind herbicide may be applied to slow-moving or quiescent bodies of water where there is minimum or no outflow; it is not applicable in flowing systems. There is no post-application restriction against use of treated water for drinking or recreational purposes (e.g., swimming, fishing)	Giannotti et al. 2014
	Copper complexes	3 ppm	Copper is a fast-acting, broad-spectrum, contact herbicide that kills a wide range of aquatic plants and algae. Although copper is a micronutrient required by living plants and animals in small amounts, too much copper kills plants by interfering with plant enzymes, enzyme co-factors, and plant metabolism in general. Copper has long been used in natural and industrial waters for algae control, often applied directly to water as copper sulfate crystals. Chelated copper (i.e., copper ion combined with an organic molecule) is typically used for aquatic plant management as it remains active in the water column longer than copper sulfate. Copper is toxic to fish, and because copper is an element, it will accumulate in the sediments regardless of its bioavailability. Drinking water considerations are not typically the limiting factor for copper application. National Primary Drinking Water Regulations include an action level for copper at 1.3 mg/l, but copper applied to lakes and reservoirs tends to quickly bind with sediment and organic matter, settling out of the water column. Copper can be highly toxic to mollusks and fish at relatively low doses (approximately 1–5 ppm), thus some states (e.g., Florida and New York) restrict its use to prevent impacts to fisheries. Copper alone may only provide fair control of hydrilla at application rates of approximately 3 ppm. Copper can be added at lower rates in combination with other herbicides (e.g., diquat or endothall) for better control of hydrilla	Giannotti et al. 2014

Penoxsulam	Not available	Penoxsulam is currently sold under the trade name of Galleon. It is a systemic herbicide that is applied to plant foliage to control floating or immersed plants, or to the water column for submersed plant control. Penoxsulam works by inhibiting the plant enzyme acetolactate synthase, similar to imazamox. Treatment must maintain herbicide concentrations at sufficient levels for 90–120 days for optimum performance. Penoxsulam is broken down in water both microbially and through photolysis, and its half-life in water is approximately 25 days. Because of the long contact time, penoxsulam is not generally applied in areas of high water exchange. Penoxsulam needs a surfactant for foliar and exposed sediment applications to increase efficacy by binding the herbicide to the plant. There are no restrictions on consumption of treated water for potable use or by livestock, pets, or other animals. The label for penoxsulam-containing herbicides includes a number of restrictions on irrigation usage after treatment	Wright et al. 2018
Topramezone	30 ppb	Topramezone is currently sold under the trade name Oasis. It is a systemic herbicide that is applied to the water column for submersed plant control, directly to foliage of floating and emergent vegetation or to dewatered sites. Topramezone is the first herbicide belonging to new chemical class called pyrazolones. In sensitive plant species, topramezone inhibits the enzyme 4-hydroxyphenylpyruvate dioxygenase, leading to a disruption of the synthesis and function of chloroplasts. Consequently, chlorophyll is destroyed by oxidation resulting in bleaching of the growing shoot tissue (white or pink coloration) and subsequent death of the aboveground portion of the pant. Generally, topramezone is applied at 30–50 ppb and maintained at or near the initial concentration for a minimum of 60 days. Applications are made to actively growing plants early in the growing season before mature plants can build tubers. Topramezone is absorbed into the plant tissue and symptoms generally first appear in seven to ten days. Water with concentrations higher than 45 ppb are restricted for potable uses. There are no restrictions on consumption of treated water by livestock, pets, or other animals up to the maximum concentration of 50 ppb. There are no restrictions on use of treated water for recreational purposes, including swimming and fishing up to the maximum concentration of 50 ppb	Giannotti et al. 2014

(Continued)

Invasive Species	Chemicals*	Effective Minimal Concentration	Notes	References
	Flumioxazin	Not available	Flumioxazin is sold under the trade name Clipper, Schooner, Redeagle, or Flumigard. It is a contact herbicide that causes chlorosis (yellowing) and necrosis (browning) of exposed plant tissue. It moves within treated leaves, but does not translocate to other areas of the plant. Plants exposed to flumioxazin die because of the disruption of cell membranes. Once inside the plant cell, flumioxazin inhibits a key enzyme, protoporphyrinogen oxidase. Plant necrosis and death is rapid, taking a few days, up to two weeks. In general, at least four hours of contact time is required for good control. The primary breakdown pathway of flumioxazin in water is by hydrolysis, and it is highly dependent on water pH. Under high pH values (>9), flumioxazin half-life in water is 15–20 minutes. Under more neutral pH values (7–8), half-life in water is approximately 24 hours. Flumioxazin controls a wide variety of submersed and floating aquatic weeds and can be tank-mixed with other contact or systemic herbicides. There is no post-application restriction against use of treated water for drinking or recreational purposes (e.g., swimming, fishing). Treated water is restricted for use for irrigation for up to five days	Giannotti et al. 2014
	Imazamox	50 ppb	Imazamox was registered for aquatic use in 2007. Imazamox is a systemic herbicide that works by inhibiting the plant enzyme acetolactate synthase (ALS), which regulates the production of amino acids in plants. When ALS is inhibited, plants die. Animals do not produce these enzymes, so imazamox has low toxicity to animals. Enzyme inhibiting herbicides act very slowly. Imazamox is broken down in the water by photolysis and microbial degradation. Its half-life in water is 7–14 days. Imazamox is absorbed rapidly into plant tissues, and growth of susceptible plants is inhibited within a few hours after application, dying in approximately one to two weeks. In Florida, aquatic plant management programs include submersed applications for hydrilla control. At concentrations of 50–150 ppb, imazamox acts as a growth regulator for hydrilla, persisting for up to several months. At concentrations of 150–250 ppb, imazamox acts with herbicidal activity, killing hydrilla in a few weeks after application. Imazamox application rates are restricted to less than 50 ppb within ¼ mile of potable drinking water intakes, and irrigation is restricted at rates above 50 ppb	Giannotti et al. 2014

	Fluridone	0.05 ppb	Low concentrations of fluridone (0.05 and 0.5 ppb) caused transient increases in the number of both subterranean and axillary turions by mature hydrilla, but higher concentrations (5 and 50 ppb) inhibited development of these tissues. Growth (shoot dry weight) of young plants treated with low concentrations of fluridone (0.05 and 0.5 ppb) was not affected. The 5.0 ppb-fluridone treatment did not affect the growth of young plants until after six weeks of exposure. The 50 ppb fluridone treatment prevented any significant change in young plant shoot dry weight over the 12-week study. There was no significant change in shoot dry weight of mature plants regardless of the treatment	Netherland et al. 1993b; Netherland and Getsinger 1995; Mattson et al. 2004
Curly-leaf pondweed *Potamogeton crispus*	Diquat	1 mg ai/l	Turion numbers and curly-leaf pondweed injury were observed. Although herbicide effects were more pronounced with the 21°C than the 16°C diquat treatments, plants showed signs of appreciable recovery by 6 week after treatment (WAT). Treatments conducted when water temperatures at 23°C were most effective in sustaining plant injury. All diquat treatments at the end of the study were effective in reducing shoot and root biomass. Endothall and diquat treatments in the early spring have resulted in effective biomass reduction and the inhibition of turion production	Poovey et al. 2002; Mattson Et al. 2004; Wisconsin DNR 2012; Barr and Ditomaso 2014
	2,4-D	10 µg/l	Low rates of endothall combined with 2,4-D or triclopyr can provide selective control of two invasive exotic species, Eurasian watermilfoil and curly-leaf pondweed, if applied in early spring when most native species are dormant	Poovey et al. 2002; Mattson et al. 2004; Belgers et al. 2007; Skogerboe and Netherland 2008)
	Endothall	1 mg ai/l	All endothall applications reduced shoot and root biomass; however, early and mid-spring treatments provided better control than late spring treatments. Both the 16°C and 21°C treatments reduced shoot biomass by 90% compared to the 23°C treatment, which reduced shoot biomass by 60%. Endothall and diquat treatments in the early spring have resulted in effective biomass reduction and the inhibition of turion production. Endothall effectively controlled Eurasian watermilfoil and curly-leaf pondweed at all of the application rates, and no significant regrowth was observed at 8 week after treatment (WAT)	Poovey et al. 2002; Skogerboe and Getsinger 2002; Mattson et al. 2004; Wisconsin DNR 2012); Barr and Ditomaso 2014

(Continued)

Invasive Species	Chemicals*	Effective Minimal Concentration	Notes	References
Eurasian watermilfoil, *Myriophyllum spicatum*	Fluridone	1 mg ai/l	During the first and second years after treatment, it is assumed that fluridone was no longer having a direct effect on the vegetation because concentration of the herbicide reached a low level of 2.3 ppb at 91 days after treatment (DAT) on August 29, 2002 (Figure 1)	Poovey et al. 2002; Mattson et al. 2004; Valley et al. 2006; Wisconsin DNR 2012
	Diquat	Not available	Eurasian watermilfoil was highly susceptible to diquat, with 85–100% biomass reductions for all diquat treatments. The dark exposure period did not increase diquat efficacy on Eurasian watermilfoil as all diquat treatments were similar. Reductions in Eurasian watermilfoil biomass of 97% to 100% was achieved using similar diquat concentrations at half-lives of 2.5 and 4.5 hours	Mattson et al. 2004; Wersal et al. 2010
	2,4-D	2 ppm ae (acid equivalent)	A plastic curtain suspended across the outlet of each treatment cove kept 94–98% of the herbicide from drifting into open water. Both control methods eliminated Eurasian watermilfoil from treatment sites within four to six weeks. The bottom fabrics eliminated all species of rooted, submerged aquatic plants. The 2,4-D treatments initially reduced the mean standing crop of coontail (*Ceratophyllum demersum* L.), elodea (*Elodea canadensis* Michaux), variable-leaf watermilfoil (*Myriophyllum heterophyllum* Michaux), and wild celery (*Vallisneria americana* Michaux) by 14–85%. These native plants, however, recovered about 80–120% of their standing crops within 10–12 weeks after herbicide treatments	Mattson et al. 2004; Hesel et al 1996; Thum et al. 2017
	Endothall	0.5 mg ae/l	Severe Eurasian watermilfoil injury (>85% biomass reduction) occurred when exposed to 0.5 mg ae/l for 48 hours, 1.0 mg ae/l for 36 hours, 3.0 mg ae/l for 18 hours, and 5.0 mg ae/l for 12 hours. Milfoil control increased with increasing endothall concentrations and/or exposure times. All treatments resulted in a significant reduction of shoot and root biomass levels compared to the untreated reference aquaria at four weeks posttreatment, except 1 mg/l for 2 hours	Netherland et al. 1991; Mattson et al. 2004
	Fluridone	10 µg/l	Fluridone concentrations ranging 10–100 µg/l were used on Eurasian watermilfoil treatment and reduction in root biomass ranged from 53% at 10 µg/l to 79% at 20 µg/l while shoot biomass saw a reduction of 68% at 10 µg/l and 84% at 90 µg/l	Hall et al. 1984; Netherland et al. 1993a; Mattson et al. 2004

Appendix III

	Carfentrazone-ethyl	0.1 mg ai/l	It is reported that carfentrazone-ethyl resulted in complete control (100% biomass reduction of this species; conversely, carfentrazone-ethyl was not efficacious against Eurasian watermilfoil because biomass reductions were only 25% and 37% for the 0.20 mg ai/l with light and dark treatments	Gray et al. 2007; Wersal et al. 2010; Wisconsin DNR 2012
	Triclopyr	1.00 mg/l	This chemical can be applied in either river or lake systems. The proposed potable water tolerance level is 0.5 mg/l	Getsinger et al. 1997; Thum et al. 2017
	Bensulfuron methyl	25 µg/l	Eurasian milfoil biomass averaged 50% less than that of untreated references approximately after six weeks of exposure to all treatments. By 12 weeks, the biomass was reduced to 96–98% compared to untreated plots for all chemical application rates	Getsinger et al. 1994
Variable milfoil *Myriophyllum heterophyllum*	Diquat	Not available	Contained infestation in the short term by reducing footprint and density of patch, but it did not eradicate the variable milfoil	Mattson et al. 2004; Carrol County 2008
	2,4-D	500 µg ai/l	"In greenhouse studies, 2,4-D ester at 500 and 1500 µg ai L^{-1} exposed for 3, 8, and 24 hours provided 98 to 100% control of variable-leaf milfoil (). Bugbee et al. (2003) also reported that 227 kg ha-1 2,4-D ester as Navigate controlled nearly all the variable-leaf milfoil in treated field sites" (Glomski and Netherland 2008)	Mattson et al. 2004; Netherland and Glomski 2007; Skogerboe and Netherland 2008; Glomski and Netherland 2008a
	4-Amino-3-chloro-6-(4-chloro-2-fluoro-3-methoxyphenyl)-5-fluoro-pyridine-2-benzyl ester (SX-1552 or XDE-848 BE; proposed ISO common name in review)	0.3 µg/l	Variable watermilfoil is one of the most sensitive species evaluated. Symptomology occurred within one week after treatment (WAT)	Richardson et al. 2016
	Endothall	0.5 mg ae/l	Variable milfoil can be partially controlled by endothall	Mattson et al. 2004
	Fluridone	8 ppb	Variable milfoil also tends to be quite susceptible to fluridone and the ALS inhibitors at rates in the range of 8–20 ppb. Studies suggest the phenology of variable milfoil will require that these treatments be applied early in the season prior to or just as the plants start to come out of winter dormancy	Mattson et al. 2004; Netherland 2007; Glomski and Netherland 2008b; Wisconsin DNR 2012

(Continued)

Invasive Species	Chemicals*	Effective Minimal Concentration	Notes	References
Parrot-feather *Myriophyllum aquaticum*	Carfentrazone-ethyl	100 µg ai/l	Carfentrazone at 100 µg ai/l for 6–30 hours was reported to provide 61–81% control of variable-leaf milfoil. Doubling the rate of carfentrazone did not improve efficacy. While there is no published literature regarding field applications of carfentrazone to control variable-leaf milfoil, recent field trials in North Carolina have demonstrated good control	Glomski and Netherland 2008a; Wisconsin DNR 2012
	Diquat	0.19 mg ai/l	In all treatments, diquat at each concentration and application time significantly reduced biomass of parrot-feather by 52–82% across diquat concentrations. Allowing for a dark exposure after herbicide application did not result in increased efficacy of diquat on parrot-feather at the concentrations tested. Although parrot-feather biomass was reduced with respect to untreated plants, regrowth was evident, and plants would have recovered given sufficient time. Plant recovery was occurring through regrowth via root crowns and the formation of new shoots from the nodes of surviving plants	EPA 1995; Langeland et al. 2002; Mattson et al. 2004; Hofstra et al. 2006; Wersal et al. 2010
	Endothall	2.5 mg ae/l	Endothall at 5.0 mg ae L21 and fluridone at 0.02 mg ai/l (0.02 ppmv) did reduce parrot-feather biomass; however, reductions were only 30% and 26% of untreated reference plants, respectively, at 6 WAT. Endothall was promising in reducing parrots-feather cover and biomass in the first year contained trial. It is also reported that reduction of parrot-feather biomass was not impressive (i.e., only 30% or 26% of untreated plants)	Hofstra et al. 2006; Wersal and Madsen 2010
	2,4-D	2.0 mg ae/l	It is one of the most effective herbicides for parrot-feather control. The foliar application of 2,4-D resulted in 85% control of parrot-feather at six week after treatment (WAT)	Wersal and Madsen 2010
	Imazamox	281 g ai/ha	At four week after treatment (WAT), imazamox at 561 and 281 g ai/ha controlled 63.3% and 78.3% of parrot-feather, respectively. However, by 6 WAT regrowth of plant tissue in the imazamox treatments was observed and control decreased to 63.3% and 56.7% for the 561 and 281 g ai/ha rates, respectively	Wersal and Madsen 2007

Imazapyr	584 g ai/ha	Imazapyr provided excellent control of parrot-feather. At four weeks after treatment (WAT), imazapyr at 1,123 and 584 g ai/l rates reduced 73.6% and 80.0%, respectively. Additionally, *M. aquaticum* treated with imazapyr at 1,123 and 584 g ai/ha was controlled 90.0% six WAT with an increase to 100.0% for both treatments by eight WAT. It was observed that beyond five WAT, *M. aquaticum* control with any imazamox rate was significantly less than all imazapyr treatments except imazapyr at 281 g ai/ha	Patten 2003; Wersal and Madsen 2007
Fluridone	0.01 mg ai/l	Fluridone applications were not efficacious on parrot-feather from one to six weeks after treatment (WAT). The fluridone-treated plants had symptomatic development of pink and chlorotic shoots within the first two WAT, although this did not appear to impact on percent cover and did not result in reduced biomass	Hofstra et al. 2006; Wersal and Madsen 2010
Glyphosate	1.5 l/ha	The best effectiveness of control of the glyphosate alone was 85% at the dose of 7.5 l/ha, increasing to 100% when associated with Aterbane® and Veget'oil®. The control reached 100% for all glyphosate doses associated with Dash®. Moreover, glyphosate at the dose of 7.5 l/ha associated with Assist® provided a 98% control, while glyphosate doses of 3.5, 5.5, and 7.5 l/ha associated with Agral® provided a 100% control. Glyphosate at doses of 5.5 and 7.5 l/ha associated with Dash® and Agral® was more effective in reducing the regrowth and dry biomass (100%). Thus, glyphosate + Dash® and Agral® promoted the highest control (above 95%), the lowest regrowth, and the highest reduction in the dry biomass of *M. aquaticum*	Cerveira et al. 2020
Dichlobenil	6.75 kg ai/ha	Dichlobenil (granular form of Prefix®-D) was scattered onto tanks at a rate of either 6.75 or 20.25 kg ai/ha. It was promising in reducing parrot-feather cover and biomass in the first year contained trial. Dichlobenil was seen as less likely to be an acceptable choice of product for parrots-feather control compared with triclopyr, due to the longer persistence of dichlobenil	Hofstra et al. 2006

(Continued)

Invasive Species	Chemicals*	Effective Minimal Concentration	Notes	References
	Clopyralid	1.5 kg ai/ha	Plants treated with clopyralid showed some initial loss of vigor, with reduced cover (and shoot number) for approximately eight weeks after treatment (WAT). By 17 WAT, the percent plant cover in the clopyralid tubs was within 20% of that observed in the control tubs, but the biomass did not differ significantly from control plants. Clopyralid was selected in this study because it provides selective control of a range of dicot species with little damage to monocots. The advantage of this for a drain-weed herbicide is that ditch bank grasses will not be damaged and continue to provide or maintain bank stability in the absence of other vegetation	Hofstra et al. 2006
	Triclopyr	2.0 kg ai/ha	Results indicate that triclopyr is effective at controlling parrot-feather under contained experimental conditions, reducing biomass to zero (or near), with little or no plant recovery in contrast to the results for glyphosate. Under field conditions, triclopyr has successfully reduced the cover and presence of parrot-feather. All triclopyr treatments had significantly lower percent cover than glyphosate tubs from 15 week after treatment (WAT). This trend continued for the duration of the study. Therefore, triclopyr provided substantially better control of parrot-feather than glyphosate	Hofstra et al. 2006
	Carfentrazone-ethyl	0.10 mg ai/l	Carfentrazone-ethyl has shown variable control of parrot-feather where ratings ranged from 29% to 70%. The use of carfentrazone-ethyl was also effective at reducing parrot-feather at both concentrations and application times. A 64% and 65% reduction in parrot-feather biomass was obtained when carfentrazone-ethyl was applied at 0.20 mg ai/l during a dark and light exposure period, respectively. In another study, similar biomass reductions of parrot-feather (63%) using carfentrazone-ethyl at 0.20 mg ai/l	Gray et al. 2007; Wersal et al. 2010
Fanwort *Cabomba caroliniana*	Fluridone	5 g/l	Treatments included static exposures of 0, 5, 7.5, 10, 15, 20, and 30 g fluridone per liter. For fanwort, phytoene levels increased 82% and β-carotene decreased 88% when exposed to 5 g fluridone per liter for 14 days. Effects on these two pigments persisted through 84 days after treatment (DAT) for fanwort. Leaf chlorophyll decreased with increasing fluridone concentration in fanwort, whereas in water marigold, decreased chlorophyll was observed in plants treated with rates of 7.5 g/l and higher. Despite these observed differences in pigment response, all fluridone treatments significantly reduced shoot dry weight biomass	Nelson et al. 2002

Appendix III

	Herbicide	Concentration	Notes	References
	Carfentrazone-ethyl	100 ug ai/l	At 2 mg ai/l, there was a 60–90% biomass reduction in mesocosms with likely eradication of a field site. Another study involving carfentrazone indicates that control of fanwort was not as effective as endothall amine salt was, but its performance may have been inhibited by the heavy shading employed to reduce algal growth in the study	Hunt et al. 2015; Hofstra et al. 2021
	Endothall	1 mg ai/l	Endothall (dipotassium salt) reduced fanwort biomass; however, with viable plant material remained, it indicates the potential for rapid regrowth after treatment, and a high degree of uncertainty of outcome where the herbicides are to be used for the management of field populations. Symptoms within three to seven days were less effective than endothall amine	Mattson et al. 2004; Willey 2012; (); Hunt et al. 2015; Hofstra et al. 2021
	Flumioxazin	0.1 mg ai/l	Flumioxazin reduced fanwort biomass; however, with viable plant material remained, it indicates the potential for rapid regrowth after treatment, and a high degree of uncertainty of outcome where the herbicides are to be used for the management of field populations	Hofstra et al. 2021
	Endothall amine salt	0.5 mg ae/l	It could be an effective tool for fanwort control, even at low concentration (0.5 mg ae/l) provided contact times can be maintained for at least 50 hours. Field verification is now required to confirm the findings of this research	Hunt et al. 2015
	Triclopyr	0.5 mg ai/l	Triclopyr reduced fanwort biomass; however, with viable plant material remained, it indicates the potential for rapid regrowth after treatment, and a high degree of uncertainty of outcome where the herbicides are to be used for the management of field populations	Hofstra et al. 2021
European naiad *Najas minor*	Diquat	Not available	In July of 2010, 3.5 acres of the pond was sprayed with the herbicide diquat to eradicate the newly discovered European spiny naiad without more information on this project	Mattson et al. 2004; Desmerais 2016
	2,4-D	Not available	Limited 2,4-D treatment information in the Final Generic Environmental Report	Mattson et al. 2004
	Endothall	Not available	Limited information on endothall treatment on European naiad in the Final Generic Environmental Report	Mattson Et al. 2004
	Imazamox	Not available	It is a systemic herbicide, so contact exposure time for submersed vegetation such as the European naiad may be lengthy	Richardson 2008

(Continued)

Invasive Species	Chemicals*	Effective Minimal Concentration	Notes	References
	Fluridone	Not available	Spiny naiad (*Najas marina* L.) is a native species susceptible to fluridone that was originally present in low abundances but its abundance decreased significantly following treatment and was undetected in transect surveys for at least three years	Mattson et al. 2004; Wagner et al. 2007
South American waterweed *Egeria densa*	Diquat	1.8 kg ai/ha	Control of this invasive waterweed and effects on native species of diquat (bottom injection) were assessed by the point intercept method. One year after treatment, the waterweed was absent from all points except one. After another diquat treatment, no invasive waterweed was found. The native plant community was resilient with an increase in species richness from 11 pretreatment to 18 two-year posttreatment	Mattson et al. 2004; Bugbee et al. 2020
	Oxytetracycline	5 µg/l + 20 µg/l oxytetracycline amended with nitrogen and phosphorus	In a microcosm study, increased susceptibility to oxytetracycline exposure was noted in some paired plantings (e.g., *E. densa* root development), relative to individual plants in these treatments; however, no clear explanation for this response is available	Hanson et al. 2006
	Fluridone	Not available	It can be used between March 1 and November 30). Fluridone is a slow-acting, selective, systemic herbicide used to control submersed aquatic weeds. It has an average half-life of 20 days in pond water and three months in pond hydrosol for fluridone formulations. Fluridone is applied at rates of 5–30 ppb depending on plant susceptibility. Because of the slow-acting nature of fluridone, 8–16 weeks of exposure is necessary. This usually requires monitoring and additional applications to maintain the prescribed dose	Mattson et al. 2004; Caudill et al. 2021
Swollen bladderwort *Utricularia inflata*	Diquat	Not available	Diquat is listed as "E" for "Excellent Control" for bladderwort	Miller and Lewis 1980
	Endothall	Not available	Endothall is listed as "G" for "Good Control" for bladderwort	Miller and Lewis 1980
	Fluridone	Not available	Fluridone as a 480 g/l aqueous suspension (4 pounds/gal AS) or 2.5% granule at rates 0.1–1.0 ppm ai total water treatment were applied over the water surface, directly under the water surface, or as a layered treatment to the bottom of the body of water provided control of many submersed and emersed aquatic plant species	Parka and Arnold 1979

Appendix III

Species	Herbicide	Dose	Notes	References
Water chestnut *Trapa natans*	2,4-D	0.5 mg ai/l	All application rates of 2,4-D significantly controlled water chestnut by 60–65% compared to the untreated reference. The Oswego County Soil and Water Conservation District turned to chemical control in 2005 when mechanical control methods were slowly losing effectiveness at fighting invasive water chestnut and 2,4-D is one of the two chemicals on large patches with erratic at best result	Mattson et al. 2004; Poovey and Getsinger et al. 2007; OARS 2017
	Fluridone	Not available	Partial control for water chestnut but control can sometimes be achieved with a higher dose or other conditions	Mattson et al. 2004; Mustafa et al. 2016
	Triclopyr	0.5 mg ai/l	Control of water chestnut with triclopyr significantly increased from 33% for plants treated with 0.5 mg ai/l to 66% for plants treated with 2.0 mg ai/l. Application rates of 2,4-D and triclopyr significantly reduced water chestnut shoot growth; Technology LLC claims to have success with the 2,4-D and not the triclopyr, when removing the water chestnut. Although triclopyr may not be as effective as 2,4-D, it can be used in public waters where 2,4-D use is not allowed or may be allowed with special conditions	Poovey and Getsinger 2007; Jacobs 2008; Mustafa et al. 2016; OARS 2017
	Imazapyr	Not available	It is one of the nine herbicides approved for control of water chestnut in Massachusetts	OARS 2017
	Imazamox	Not available	Since it is approved for control of water chestnut, imazamox has been used with initial good results	OARS 2017
	Glyphosate	7 l ha/l at 53.8% ai	Its application may have a significant impact on the surviving plants' ability to produce viable fruit. The seeds may either be non-viable or of smaller mass and lack vigor	Rector et al. 2015; OARS 2017
Water hyacinth *Eichornia crassipes*	Diquat	0.25 ppm	To protect aquatic organisms, EPA is requiring labeling that limits application of diquat dibromide to one-third or one-half of the dense weed areas in a waterbody, and prohibits subsequent applications for two weeks. Diquat dibromide's primary route of environmental dissipation is strong adsorption to soil particles. Diquat does not hydrolyze or photodegrade and is resistant to microbial degradation under aerobic and anaerobic conditions. When used as an aquatic herbicide, diquat dibromide is removed from the water column by adsorption to soil sediments, aquatic vegetation, and organic matter. Adsorbed diquat dibromide is persistent and immobile, and is not expected to be a groundwater contaminant. It can be used with copper, which also enhances the performance of diquat on *Eichhornia crassipes* (water hyacinth) and some other species	EPA 1995; Langeland et al. 2002; Mattson et al. 2004

(Continued)

Invasive Species	Chemicals*	Effective Minimal Concentration	Notes	References
	2,4-D	1.5 kg ai/ha	Maintenance of infestations at the "lowest feasible level" is generally accomplished by repeated applications of herbicides, most often 2,4-D. 1999). 2,4-D is sold in liquid or granular forms as sodium and potassium salts, as ammonia or amine salts, and as an ester. Doses of 50–150 pounds per acre are usual for submersed weeds. Herbicide 2,4-D application for plant suppression is excellent	Center Et al. 1999; Mattson et al. 2004; Fawad et al. 2015
	Glyphosate	2.0 kg ai/ha	A study showed that the spraying of the glyphosate freshwater mixture using a helicopter to control invasive aquatic plants does not dramatically reduce water quality conditions. It also found that the spraying did not fully repair the DO levels of the wetlands that were put into hypoxic conditions by the water hyacinth	Jacobs 2008; Fawad et al. 2015; Waltham and Fixler 2017
European water clover, *Marsilea quadrifolia*	Diquat	Not available	It is regarded as capable of only partial control for pepperwort. Control can sometimes be achieved, but may require a higher dose or specific natural conditions that are difficult to control	Mattson et al. 2004
	Glyphosate	10 mg/l	Glyphosate is regarded as capable of only partial control. Control can sometimes be achieved, but may require a higher dose of other conditions	Mattson et al. 2004
	Aryloxyphenoxypropionate (Clincher)	0.5 mg/l	Approximately 60–70% survival rate at the lowest of diluted concentrations. The toxicological tests showed that *M. quadrifolia* is sensitive to a wide range of herbicides that have different mechanisms of action, such as the interruption of fatty acid	Bruni et al. 2013
	Sulfonamide + triazolopyrimidine (Viper)	20 ml/l	Approximately 80% survival rate at the lowest of diluted concentrations. The inhibition of enzymes involved in amino acid biosynthesis (Viper)	Bruni et al. 2013
	Cyclohexanone (Aura)	10 mg/l	Under 50% survival rate at the lowest of diluted concentrations	Bruni et al. 2013
	Penoxsulam	Not available	Penoxsulam is the only herbicide tested for its effectiveness in controlling this invasive species that is approved for aquatic use in Michigan. It was shown to be effective in the laboratory. This may contribute to the reduced weed density detected in rice fields	Hackett et al. 2018
Yellow floating heart *Nymphoides peltata*	Diquat	Not available	Limited scholarly literature information on direct usage of diquat on yellow floating heart but it is listed as one of the herbicides capable of consistent control over the species	Mattson et al. 2004

Appendix III

2,4-D	Not available	Regulation of the use of herbicides in or near water is stringent in Canada and there are no reports of use to control *N. peltata*. Countryman reported that "some success" was achieved in Lake Champlain, VT, using "various formulations" of 2,4-D	Mattson et al. 2004; Darbyshire and Francis 2008
Glyphosate	Not available	To completely eradicate the plant, all rhizome fragments in the sediment must be removed or killed with a herbicide like glyphosate. In some trials, the application to floating leaves between July and September resulted in about 40–50% control (for one season), but in others regrowth occurred before the end of the season	Darbyshire and Francis 2008; Warren 2009; Willey 2012
Dichlobenil	Not available	In the UK, dichlobenil has been effective in small localized areas within a larger waterbody, although in Canada conditions under which this agent can be used are currently limited. In the UK, it was recommended that no more than 20% of a waterbody be treated at any one time and this herbicide was not recommended for use in water flowing at more than 90 m/hour	EPA 1995; Darbyshire and Francis 2008
Florpyrauxifen-benzyl**	3 (PDU)/ac-f	55-acre infestation of YFH at a rate of 3 Prescription Dose Units (PDU)/ac-f. Total surface coverage of yellow floating heart in the reservoir was reduced by more than 90% within 15 days after the treatment, and to less than 3 acres within 50 days after the treatment. No blooming flowers were observed after treatment and the surface coverage was close to 0% within 17 days after treatment in the cove. The effect of the herbicide treatment also appeared to carry over into the following growing season as the total surface coverage of yellow floating heart in the reservoir was less than 8 acres one year after the treatment in July 2020	Lamb et al. 2021
Endothall	Not available	A recent study on herbicide efficacy on *N. cristata* in south Florida showed endothall (dipotassium salt) was most effective, giving 98–100% control at 1.5–2.5 ppm. The longer term impacts of these treatments were not reported	Willey 2012

(Continued)

Invasive Species	Chemicals*	Effective Minimal Concentration	Notes	References
Common reed grass *Phragmites australis*	Glyphosate	25% strength rodeo (dosage not specified) + 1 l glyphosate + 2 l of water	Glyphosate and imazapyr are two broad-spectrum herbicides commercially available and known to control *Phragmites*. These herbicides are best applied in late summer/early fall after the plant has flowered either as a cut stump treatment or as a foliar spray. Together, glyphosate and imazapyr were found to be the only herbicides that resulted in greater than 90% biomass reduction of *Phragmites australis* in controlled mesocosm studies. However, it must be noted that these chemicals are non-selective and will impact native plants if they come in contact with the herbicides. Glyphosate should be applied after plants are in full bloom in late summer. Glyphosate is not as effective as imazapyr; however, it costs less and has good results with follow-up treatment or where water level management is available	Startford 1995; Avers et al. 2007; Hazelton et al. 2014
	Imazapyr	25% strength arsenal (dosage not specified)	Imazapyr should be applied to actively growing green foliage after full leaf elongation. If stand has substantial amount of old stem tissue, allow new growth to reach approximately 5 ft tall before treatment. In a long-term study, it was shown that imazapyr was 15% more successful than glyphosate in removing *Phragmites australis* as measured by the number of live stems, mean height, and percent cover remaining. No significant differences were observed between either herbicide treatments in regard to plant recolonization over the two-year time course	Startford 1995; Avers et al. 2007; Mozdzer et al. 2008
	Imazamox	280 g ai/ha	Compared to glyphosate and imazapyr, imazamox provided the lowest level of control	Knezevic et al. 2013
	Fluazifop-butyl	1 l fluazifop-butyl + 2 l of water	Increasing rates of glyphosate and fluazifop-butyl volumes of application increase the efficiency of the herbicides in the control of common reed. Rope-Wick method would better control compared with application of herbicide with sprayer. The cost of management of common reed has been reduced and glyphosate gave a good control on common reed compared to fluazifop-butyl	Al-Wagaa et al. 2019

Appendix III

Purple loosestrife *Lythrum salicaria*	Triclopyr	50 gallons spray solution per acre at 0.5 % solution (two quarts per 100 gallon solution)	Triclopyr formulated for use in wetlands applied as a foliar broadcast application at six to eight quarts per acre is most effective when purple loosestrife is in the bud to mid-bloom stage. This is when plants are actively growing, the toxic chemical is moved into roots, and when roots reserves needed to regenerate from defoliation are at their lowest level. The second optimum timing is in September when starches in the roots are being converted to sucrose important for cold tolerance and surviving freezing temperatures over winter. Annual application may be needed to target plants regrowing from root stocks and the seed bank. This herbicide is more selective and will not harm monocot species such as cattails	Jacobs 2008
	Glyphosate	2 quarts per acre as a 1% spray solution	Glyphosate herbicides are very effective for killing purple loosestrife. Glyphosate should be applied to actively growing plants and best results can be expected when it is applied during bloom. If applied at late bloom, plants may still produce seeds which can be clipped and bagged to prevent spread. One study found glyphosate most effective when applied in mid-August (late-bloom). Selective spot treatment can be used to avoid injuring neighboring non-target plants that can fill in the areas opened by removing the purple loose strife	Jacobs 2008
	2,4-D	1 quarter per acre	Broadcast applications of 2,4-D at one to two quarts per acre or a 0.5–1% solution applied to the bud or early bloom stage will kill top growth. Repeated applications will be needed to target plants regenerating from roots. An aquatic surfactant can be used to improve effectiveness	Jacobs 2008
	Imazapyr	1 pint per acre	A non-ionic surfactant with an aquatic label is needed for imazapyr to be effective	Jacobs 2008

Source: * Not all chemicals in this table are permitted in Massachusetts. More information about many chemicals' modes of actions, as well as their advantages and disadvantages, can be found in Table 1.6.

** Florpyrauxifen-benzyl (i.e., ProcellaCOR) is a relatively new chemical that has been used widely in selective control of milfoils and other aquatic invasive plants such as hydrilla, water hyacinth, and parrot-feather. However, there is very limited scholarly research.

REFERENCES

Abdel-Fattah, S. 2011. Aquatic Invasive Species Early Detection and Rapid Response- Assessment of Chemical Response Tools. International Joint Commission, Great Lakes Regional Office. 104 pp.

Aldridge, D.C., P. Elliott, and G.D. Moggridge. 2006. Microencapsulated BioBullets for the control of biofouling zebra mussels. *Environmental Science & Technology* 40: 975–979.

Al-Wagaa, A.H., I.A.H. Al-Obadui, H.A.K. Alfarttoosi, and O.A. AL-Gburi. 2019. Evaluating the performance of rope-wick herbicide applicator to control common reed. *IOP Conference Series: Earth and Environmental Science* 388: 012003.

Avers, B., R. Fahlsing, E. Kafcas, J. Schafer, T. Collin, L. Esman, E. Finnell, A. Lounds, R. Terry, J. Hazelman, J. Hudgins, K. Getsinger, and D. Schuen. 2007. A Guide to the Control and Management of Invasive Phragmites. Michigan Department of Environmental Quality, Lansing.

Barr, T.C.III., and J.M. Ditomaso. 2014. Curly leaf pondweed (*Potamogeton crispus*) turion control with acetic acid and benthic barriers. *Journal of Aquatic Plant Management* 52: 31–38.

Belgers, J.D.M., R.J. Van Lieverloo, L.J.T. Van Der Pas, and P.J. Van Der Brink. 2007. Effects of the herbicide 2,4-D on the growth of nine aquatic macrophytes. *Aquatic Botany* 86: 260–268.

Boone, C., C. Bond, K. Buhl, and D. Stone. 2012. Copper Sulfate. Oregon, USA: National Pesticide Information Center, Oregon State University. http://npic.orst.edu/factsheets/cuso4gen.html. (Accessed March 21, 2017).

Bruni, I., R. Gentili, F. De Mattia, P. Cortis, G. Rossi, and M. Labra. 2013. A multi-level analysis to evaluate the extinction risk of and conservation strategy for the aquatic fern *Marsilea quadrifolia* L. in Europe. *Aquatic Botany* 111: 35–42.

Bugbee, G.J., C.S. Robb, and S.E. Stebbins. 2020. Efficacy of diquat treatments on Brazilian waterweed, effects on native macrophytes and water quality: A case study. *Journal of Aquatic Plant Management* 58: 83–91.

Caudill, J., J.D. Madsen, and W. Pratt. 2021. Operational aquatic weed management in the California Sacramento–San Joaquin River Delta. *Journal of Aquatic Plant Management* 59: 112–122.

Center, T., F. Dray, Jr., G. Jubinsky, and M.J. Grodowitz. 1999. Biological Control of Water Hyacinth Under Conditions of Maintenance Management: Can Herbicides and Insects Be Integrated? *Environmental Management* 23: 241–256.

Cerveira, W.R., A.F. Silva, J.H.C. Cervoni, C. Cruz, and R.A. Pitelli. 2020. The addition of adjuvants on glyphosate enhances the control of aquatic plant *Myriophyllum aquaticum* (Vell.). *Planta Daninha* 38. DOI:10.1590/s0100-83582020380100090.

Claudi, R., A. Graves, A.C. Taraborelli, R.J. Prescott, and S. Mastitsky. 2012. Impact of pH on survival and settlement of dreissenid mussels. *Aquatic Invasions* 7: 21–28.

Cooper, N.L., and J.R. Bidwell. 2006. Cholinesterase inhibition and impacts on behavior of the Asian clam, *Corbicula fluminea*, after exposure to an organophosphate insecticide. *Aquatic Toxicology* 76: 258–267.

Costa, R., D.C. Aldridge, and G.D. Moggridge. 2008. Seasonal variation of zebra mussel susceptibility to molluscicidal agents. *Journal of Applied Ecology* 45: 1712–1721.

Dalu, T., R.J. Wasserman, M. Jordaan, W.P. Froneman, and O.L.F. Weyl. 2015. An assessment of the effect of rotenone on selected non-target aquatic fauna. *PLoS One* 10(11): e0142140.

Darbyshire, S.J., and A. Francis 2008. The biology of invasive alien plants in Canada. 10. *Nymphoides peltata* (S. G. Gmel.) Kuntze. *Canadian Journal of Plant Science* 88: 811–829.

Davis, E.A., W.H. Wong, and W.N. Harman. 2015a. Distilled white vinegar (5% acetic acid) as a potential decontamination method for adult zebra mussels. *Management of Biological Invasions* 6(4): 423–428.

Davis, E.A., W.H. Wong, and W.N. Harman. 2015b. Comparison of three sodium chloride chemical treatments for adult zebra mussel decontamination. *Journal of Shellfish Research* 34(3): 1029–1036.

Davis, E.A., W.H. Wong, and W.N. Harman. 2018. Toxicity of potassium chloride compared to sodium chloride for zebra mussel decontamination. *Journal of Aquatic Animal Health* 30: 3–12.

Dawson, V.K. 2003. Environmental fate and effects of the lampricide Bayluscide: A review, *Journal of Great Lakes Research* 29(Supplement 1): 475–492.

Densmore, C.L., L.R. Iwanowicz, A.P. Henderson, V.S. Blazer, B.M. Reed-Grimmett, and L.R. Sanders. 2018. An Evaluation of the Toxicity of Potassium Chloride, Active Compound in the Molluscicide Potash, on Salmonid Fish and Their Forage Base. *USGS Science for a Changing World* 1–46.

EPA R.E.D. 1995. *Diquat Dibromide*. The United States Environmental Protection Agency. https://archive.epa.gov/pesticides/reregistration/web/pdf/0288fact.pdf.

Fawad, M., H. Khan, B. Gul, M.A. Khan, and K.B. Marwat. 2015. Comparative effect of herbicidal and non-chemical control methods against water hyacinth. *Pakistan Journal of Weed Science Research* 21(4).

Fisher, S.W., P. Stromberg, K.A. Bruner, and L.D. Boulet. 1991. Molluscicidal activity of potassium to the zebra mussel, *Dreissena polymorpha*: Toxicity and mode of action. *Aquatic Toxicology* 20(4): 219–234.

Freeman M. 2010. Invasive snails pose threat if not eradicated. www.mailtribune.com/apps/pbcs.dll/article?AID=/20101030/NEWS/10300304. (Accessed March 21, 2017).

Getsinger, K.D., G.O. Dick, R.M. Crouch, and L.S. Nelson. 1994. Mesocosm evaluation of bensulfuron methyl activity on Eurasian watermilfoil, vallisneria, and American pondweed. *Journal of Aquatic Plant Management* 32: 1–6.

Getsinger, K.D., L.S. Nelson, L.M. Glomski, E. Kafcas, J. Schafer, S. Kogge, and M. Nurse. 2007. *Control of Phragmites in a Michigan Great Lakes Marsh*. Vicksburg, MS: U.S. Army Engineer Research and Development Center, p. 120.

Getsinger, K.D., E.G. Turner, J.D. Madsen, and M.D. Netherland. 1997. Restoring native vegetation in a Eurasian water-milfoil dominated plant community using the herbicide triclopyr. *Regulated Rivers: Research & Management: An International Journal Devoted to River Research and Management* 13(4): 357–375.

Giannotti, A.L., T.J. Egan, M.D. Netherland, M.L. Williams, and A.K. Knecht. 2014. Hydrilla Shows Increased Tolerance to Fluridone And Endothall In the Winter Park Chain of Lakes: Considerations for Resistance Management and Treatment Options. https://conference.ifas.ufl.edu/aw14/Presentations/Grand/Thursday/Session%209A/0850%20Giannotti.pdf

Glomski, L.M., and M.D. Netherland. 2008a. Effect of water temperature on 2, 4-D ester and carfentrazone-ethyl applications for control of variable-leaf milfoil. *Journal of Aquatic Plant Management* 46: 119–121.

Glomski, L.M., and M.D. Netherland. 2008b. Efficacy of fluridone, penoxsulam, and bispyribac-sodium on variable-leaf milfoil. *Journal of Aquatic Plant Management* 46(1): 193–196.

Gray, C.J., J.D. Madsen, R.M. Wersal, and K.D. Getsinger. 2007. Eurasian watermilfoil and parrotfeather control using carfentrazone-ethylethyl. *Journal of Aquatic Plant Management* 45: 43–46.

Haak, D.M., B.J. Stephen, R.A. Kill, N.A. Smeenk, and C.R. Allen. 2014. Toxicity of copper sulfate and rotenone to Chinese mystery snail (*Bellamya chinensis*). *Management of Biological Invasions* 5: 371–375.

Hackett, R.A., B.C. Cahill, and A.K. Monfils. 2018. *2018 Status and Strategy for European Water-clover (Marsilea quadrifolia L.) Management*. Lansing, MI: Michigan Department of Environmental Quality, p. 30.

Appendix III

Hall, J.F., H.E. Westerdahl, and T.J. Stewart. 1984. Growth response of *Myriophyllum spicatum* and *Hydrilla verticillata* when exposed to continuous low concentrations of fluridone. US Army Engineers Waterways Experimental Station, Vicksburg, MS, USA. Technical Report A-84-1.

Hanson, M.L., C.W. Knapp, and D.W. Graham. 2006. Field assessment of oxytetracycline exposure to the freshwater macrophytes *Egeria densa* Planch. and *Ceratophyllum demersum* L. *Environmental Pollution* 141: 434–442.

Hazelton, E.L.G., T.J. Mozdzer, D. Burdick, K.M. Kettenring, and D. Whigham D. 2014. Phragmites australis management in the United States: 40 years of methods and outcomes. *Annals of Botany Plants* 6.

Hesel, D.R., D.T. Gerber, and S. Engel. 1996. Comparing spring treatments of 2,4-D with bottom fabrics to control a new infestation of Eurasian watermilfoil. *Journal of Aquatic Plant Management* 34: 68–71.

Hofstra, D., P.D. Champion, and T.M. Dugdale. 2006. Herbicide trials for the control of parrotsfeather. *Journal of Aquatic Plant Management* 44: 13–18.

Hofstra, D.E., D. Clements, D.M. Rendle, and P.D. Champion. 2021. Response of fanwort (*Cabomba caroliniana*) to selected aquatic herbicides in New Zealand. *Journal of Aquatic Plant Management* 59(1): 35–39.

Hofstra, D.E., and J.S. Clayton. 2001. Evaluation of selected herbicides for the control of exotic submerged weeds in New Zealand: I The use of endothall, triclopyr and dichlobenil. *Journal of Aquatic Plant Management* 39: 20–24.

Hunt, T.D., T.D. Dugdale, D. Clements, and M. Fridman. 2015. Concentration–exposure time relationships for controlling fanwort (*Cabomba caroliniana*) with endothall amine salt and carfentrazone. *Journal of Aquatic Plant Management* 53: 144–149.

Jacobs, J. 2008. Ecology and Management of Purple Loosestrife (*Lythrum salicaria* L.). Invasive Species Technical Note No. MT-21. United States Department of Agriculture, Natural Resources Conservation Service. www.nrcs.usda.gov/wps/portal/nrcs/detail/mt/home/?cid=nrcs144p2_056795

Knezevic, S.Z., R.E. Rapp, A. Datta, and S. Irmak. 2013. Common reed (*Phragmites australis*) control is influenced by the timing of herbicide application. *International Journal of Pest Management* 59(3): 224–228.

Kong, Y., M. Li, X. Shan, G.n. Wang, and G. Han. 2021. Effects of deltamethrin subacute exposure in snakehead fish, Channa argus: Biochemicals, antioxidants and immune responses. *Ecotoxicology and Environmental Safety* 209: 111821.

Lamb, B, T.A.A. McCrea, S.H. Stoodley, and A.R. Dzialowski. 2021. Monitoring and water quality impacts of an herbicide treatment on an aquatic invasive plant in a drinking water reservoir. *Journal of Environmental Management* 288: 112444.

Langeland, K.A., O.N. Hill, T.J. Koshnick, and W.T. Haller. 2002. Evaluation of a New Formulation of Reward Landscape and Aquatic Herbicide for Control of Duckweed, Waterhyacinth, Waterlettuce, and Hydrilla. *Journal of Aquatic Plant Management* 40: 51–53.

Lazur, A., S. Early, and J.M. Jacobs. 2011. Acute toxicity of 5% rotenone to northern snakeheads. *North American Journal of Fisheries Management* 26(3): 628–630.

Mattson, M.D., P.J. Godfrey, R.A. Barletta, and A. Aiello. 2004. Eutrophication and aquatic plant management in Massachusetts. Final Generic Environmental Report. Edited by Kenneth J. Wagner. Department of Environmental Protection and Department of Conservation and Recreation, EOEA Commonwealth of Massachusetts.

Miller, J. F, and G.W. Lewis. 1980. Duckweeds water hyacinth coontail bladderwort emersed aquatic weeds. In: *Identification and Control of Weeds in Southern Ponds*. The University of Georgia Cooperative Extension Service, College of Agriculture, p. 26.

Moffitt, C.M., K.A. Stockton-Fiti, and R. Claudi. 2016. Toxicity of potassium chloride to veliger and byssal stage dreissenid mussels related to water quality. *Management of Biological Invasions* 7(3): 257–268.

Mozdzer, T.J., C.J. Hutto, P.A. Clarke, and D.P. Field. 2008. Efficacy of imazapyr and glyphosate in the control of non-native phragmites australis. *Restoration Ecology* 16(2): 221–224.

Mustafa, J., R. Smolenski, and R. Sullivan. 2016. The Future of Coes Reservoir: An Investigation of Removal Methods for Water Chestnuts. IQP-DR2-WS15. Worcester Polytechnic Institute, p. 121.

Nelson, L.S., A.B. Stewart, and K.D. Getsinger. 2002. Fluridone effects on fanwort and water marigold. *Journal of Aquatic Plant Management* 40: 58–63.

Netherland, M.D. 2007. Evaluation of registered and EUP herbicides for control of variable milfoil. In *Proceedings of the Sixty-First Annual Meeting—Northeastern Weed Science Society*, p. 123.

Netherland, M.D., and K.D. Getsinger. 1995. Laboratory evaluation of threshold fluridone concentrations under static conditions for controlling hydrilla and Eurasian watermilfoil. *Journal of Aquatic Plant Management* 33: 33–36.

Netherland, M.D., K.D. Getsinger, and E.G. Turner. 1993a. Fluridone concentration and exposure time requirements for control of Eurasian watermilfoil and hydrilla. *Journal of Aquatic Plant Management* 31: 189–189.

Netherland, M.D., and L.M. Glomski. 2007. Evaluation of Aquatic Herbicides for Selective Control of Variable Milfoil (*Myriophyllum heterophyllum* Michx). Final Report to the New Hampshire Dept. of Environ. Services, p. 96.

Netherland, M.D., W.R. Green, and K.D. Getsinger. 1991. Endothall concentration and exposure time relationships for the control of Eurasian watermilfoil and hydrilla. *Journal of Aquatic Plant Management* 29: 61–67.

Netherland, M.D., W.R. Green, and K.D. Getsinger. 1993b. Effects of fluridone on hydrilla growth and reproduction. *Journal of Aquatic Plant Management* 29: 189–194.

OARS. 2017. *Water chestnut management guidance & five-year management plan for the Sudbury, Assabet, and Concord River watersheds*. Concord, MA: OARS "Planning and Guidance for Water Chestnut Management in the SuAsCo Watershed".

Ortiz, M.F., S.J. Nissen, and C.J. Gray. 2019. Endothall behavior in *Myriophyllum spicatum* and *Hydrilla verticillate*. *Pest Management Science* 75(11): 2942–2947.

Parka, S., and W. Arnold. 1979. Fluridone, a new herbicide for aquatic plant management. *Journal of Aquatic Plant Management* 17: 27–30.

Patten, K. 2003. Evaluating Imazapyr in Aquatic environments. *Agricultural and Environmental News* 205.7 pp.

Poovey, A.G., and K.D. Getsinger. 2007. Subsurface applications of triclopyr and 2,4-D amine for control of water chestnut (*Trapa natans* L.). *Journal of Aquatic Plant Management* 45: 63–66.

Poovey, A.G., and K.D. Getsinger. 2010. Comparative response of monoecious and dioecious hydrilla to endothall. *Journal of Aquatic Plant Management* 48: 15–20.

Poovey, A.G., J.G. Skogerboe, and C.S. Owens. 2002. Spring treatments of diquat and endothall for curlyleaf pondweed control. *Journal of Aquatic Plant Management* 40: 63–67.

Rector, P.R., P.J. Nitzsche, and S.S. Mangiafico. 2015. Temperature and herbicide impacts on germination of water chestnut seeds. *Journal of Aquatic Plant Management* 53: 105–112.

Richardson, R.J. 2008. Aquatic plant management and the impact of emerging herbicide resistance issues. *Weed Technology* 22(1): 8–15.

Richardson, R.J., E.J. Haug, and M.D. Netherland. 2016. Response of seven aquatic plants to a new arylpicolinate herbicide. *Journal of Aquatic Plant Management* 54: 26–31.

Rosa, I., R. Garrido, A. Ré, J. Gomes, J. Peirera, F. Gonçalves, and R. Costa. 2015. Sensitivity of the invasive bivalve *Corbicula fluminea* to candidate control chemicals: The role of dissolved oxygen conditions. *Science of the Total Environment* 536: 825–830.

Santos Ltd. 2021. (rep.). *Qualitative Tier 2 Assessment* (PolyDAD-MAC). EHS Support.

Shrivastava, B., A. Shrivastava, A. Kumar, J.L. Bhatt, S.P. Bajpai, S.S. Parihar, and V. Bhatnaga. 2011. Impact of deltamethrin on environment, use as an insecticide and its bacterial degradation—A preliminary study. *International Journal of Environmental Sciences* 1(5): 977–985.

Skogerboe, J.G., and K.D. Getsinger. 2002. Endothall species selectivity evaluation: Northern latitude aquatic plant community. *Journal of Aquatic Plant Management* 40: 1–5.

Skogerboe, J.G., and M.D. Netherland. 2008. Draft Report Following April 2008 Aquatic Herbicide Treatments of Three Bays on Lake Minnetonka. October. Report to the Minnesota Department of Natural Resources.

Stinson, H. 2018. The Northern Snakehead, Channa Argus, as an Invasive Species. *Eukaryon*, Lake Forest College News.

Thum, R.A., S. Parks, J.N. Mcnair, P. Tyning, P. Hausler, L. Chadderton, A. Tucker, and A. Monfils. 2017. Survival and vegetative regrowth of Eurasian and hybrid watermilfoil following operational treatment with auxinic herbicides in Gun Lake, Michigan. *Journal of Aquatic Plant Management* 55: 103–107.

Turner, L., S. Jacobson, and L. Shoemaker. 2007. Risk Assessment for Piscicidal Formulations of Rotenone. Compliance Services International, p. 104.

Valley, R.D., W. Crowell, C.H. Welling, and N. Proulx. 2006. Effects of a low-dose fluridone treatment on submersed aquatic vegetation in a eutrophic Minnesota lake dominated by Eurasian watermilfoil and coontail. *Journal of Aquatic Plant Management* 44(1): 19–25.

Van Scoy, A, A. Pennell, X. Zhang. 2016. Environmental fate and toxicology of dimethoate. *Reviews of Environmental Contamination and Toxicology* 237: 53–70.

Wagner, K.I., J. Hauxwell, P.W. Rasmussen, F. Koshere, P. Toshner, K. Aron, D.R. Helsel, S. Toshner, S. Provost, M. Gansberg, J. Masterson, and S. Warwick. 2007. Whole-lake herbicide treatments for Eurasian watermilfoil in four Wisconsin lakes: effects on vegetation and water clarity. *Lake and Reservoir Management* 23(1): 83–94.

Waltham, N.J., and S. Fixler. 2017. Aerial herbicide spray to control invasive water hyacinth (*Eichhornia crassipes*): Water quality concerns fronting fish occupying a tropical floodplain wetland. *Tropical Conservation Science* 10: 1–10.

Warren, D. 2009. Invasive Species Management Plan for Oswego Lake. Planning & Building Services, City of Oswego, OR. 17 pp.

Wersal, R.M., and J.D. Madsen. 2007. Comparison of imazapyr and imazamox for control of parrotfeather (*Myriophyllum aquaticum* (Vell.) Verdc.). *Journal of Aquatic Plant Management* 45: 132–136.

Wersal, R.M., and J.D. Madsen. 2010. Comparison of subsurface and foliar herbicide applications for control of parrotfeather (*Myriophyllum aquaticum*). *Invasive Plant Science and Management* 3: 262–267.

Wersal, R.M., J.D. Madsen, J.H. Massey, W. Robles, and J.C. Cheshier. 2010. Comparison of Daytime and Night-time Applications of Diquat and Carfentrazoneethyl for Control of Parrotfeather and Eurasian Watermilfoil. *Journal of Aquatic Plant Management* 48: 56–58.

Willey, L.N. 2012. Biology and control of the invasive aquatic plant crested floating heart (*Nymphoides cristata*) (Thesis, University of Florida).

Wisconsin Department of Natural Resources (DNR). 2012a. *Endothall Chemical Fact Sheet*. Madison, WI. https://dnr.wi.gov/lakes/plants/factsheets/FluridoneFactsheet.pdf

Wisconsin Department of Natural Resources (DNR). 2012b. *Fluridone Chemical Fact Sheet*. Madison, WI. https://dnr.wi.gov/lakes/plants/factsheets/FluridoneFactsheet.pdf

Wright, B., H. Landis, and T. Nelson. 2018. Chemical Management of Hydrilla for Drinking Water Utilities. Project #4747, Water Research Foundation, Denver, Colorado, p. 120.

Appendix IV

Laws and Statutes Pertaining to Aquatic Invasive/Nuisance Species in the New England States and New York

This document serves as an overview of the major laws/statutes pertaining to aquatic species, wetlands, and invasive species, within the six New England States and New York. The laws are cited in the following tables by title, chapter, and section. The section titles are shown, as well as a summary and/or the full or abbreviated version of the section referenced.

CONNECTICUT

INVASIVE SPECIES

Title/Chapter/Section	Section Title	Summary	Penalty
Title 15. Ch. 268 § 15–180	Transporting vessel or trailer without inspecting for and properly removing and disposing of vegetation and aquatic invasive species. Penalty	• No person shall transport a vessel, as defined in section 15–127, or any trailer used to transport such vessel, in the state without first inspecting such vessel for the presence of vegetation and aquatic invasive species, as determined by the commissioner, and properly removing and disposing of any such vegetation and aquatic invasive species that are visible and identifiable without optical magnification from such vessel or trailer	Any person who violates the provisions of this section shall be fined a maximum $100 for each violation
Title 22a. Ch. 446i § 22a–381a	Duties and recommendations of the Invasive Plants Council	• To developed programs to educate the public on the issues of invasive plants; make recommendations, to control the spread of invasive plants and to make information available, publish updates	
Title 22a. Ch. 446i § 22a–381c	Prohibition on purchase of invasive or potentially invasive plants by state agencies	• No state agency, department or institution shall purchase any plant listed as invasive or potentially invasive	
Title 22a. Ch. 446i § 22a–381d	Prohibited actions on certain invasive plants. Exceptions. Municipal ordinances prohibited. Penalty	• List of 67 invasive species as well as 19 other invasive plants that no person shall import, move, sell, purchase, transplant, cultivate or distribute	Any person who violates the provision of this section will be find a maximum of $100 per plant

WETLANDS

Title/Chapter/ Section	Section	Summary	Penalty
Title 22a. Ch. 446i § 22a–381d	Prohibited actions re certain invasive plants. Exceptions. Municipal ordinances prohibited. Penalty	• No person shall import, move, sell, purchase, transplant, cultivate or distribute any of the following invasive plants: Curly leaved Pondweed (*Potamogeton crispus*); (2) fanwort (*Cabomba caroliniana*); (3) eurasian watermilfoil (*Myriophyllum spicatum*); (4) variable watermilfoil (*Myriophyllum heterophyllum*); (5) water chestnut (*Trapa natans*); (6) egeria (*Egeria densa*); (7) hydrilla (*Hydrilla verticillata*); (8) common barberry (*Berberis vulgaris*); (9) autumn olive (*Elaeagnus umbellata*) etc.	Any person who violates the provisions of this section shall be fined a maximum of $100 per plant

RELEVANT ACTS

Act	Summary	Year
Public Act 10–20: To authorize conservation officers to enforce certain prohibitions concerning invasive plants	• Any conservation officer, special conservation officer or patrolman may, within the boundaries of the state, may examine the contents of any boat, ship, automobile or other vehicle, box, locker, basket, creel, crate, game bag or game coat or other package in which he has probable cause to believe that any fish, crustacean, bird, or quadruped is being kept, in violation of any said statutory provisions or any regulation • Note: Section 1. Section 26–6 of the general statutes is repealed, and the following is substituted in lieu thereof (*Effective October 1, 2010*)	2010
Public Act 12–167: An act requiring the inspection of vessels and vessel trailers for aquatic invasive species	• Section 1. Section 15–180 of the general statutes is repealed, and the following is substituted in lieu thereof (Effective July 1, 2012) • No person shall transport a vessel, as defined in section 15–127, or any trailer used to transport such vessel, in the state without first inspecting such vessel for the presence of vegetation and aquatic invasive species, as determined by the commissioner, and properly removing and disposing of any such vegetation and aquatic invasive species that are visible and identifiable without optical magnification from such vessel or trailer	2012
Public Act No. 21–12 An act concerning aquatic invasive species effects on lakes and related funding, certain group fishing events and eliminating the season limitation for the taking or trout	• Section 1. Section 22a-339h of the general statutes is repealed and the following is substituted in lieu thereof (Effective October 1, 2021): • Section 2. Not later than October 1, 2021, the Commissioner of Energy and Environmental Protection shall submit a report, in accordance with section 11–4a of the general statutes having cognizance of matters relating to the environment on the amount of revenue collected from the Aquatic Invasive Species fees authorized pursuant to section 14–21bb of the general statutes and the number, value and purpose of any grants to municipalities and not-for-profit organizations awarded from the Connecticut Lakes, Rivers and Ponds Preservation account in accordance with section 14–21aa of the general statutes	2021

MAINE

Many of Maine's revised statutes have been repealed. As a result, as of August 2021, this section represents a summary of available information; some of the relevant laws that have been repealed as of the access date, August 5, 2021 are also noted.

Appendix IV

INVASIVE SPECIES

Title/Chapter/Section	Section Title	Summary	Penalty
Title 38. Ch. 3 § 410-N	Aquatic Nuisance Species Control	• Defines terms such as Aquatic Plant, and Invasive Aquatic Plant • Department shall prepare educational materials that inform the public about problems associated with invasive aquatic plants, how to identify invasive aquatic plants, why it is important to prevent the transportation of aquatic plants and the prohibitions relating to aquatic plants contained in section 419-C • The department shall investigate and document the occurrence of invasive aquatic plants in state waters and may undertake activities to control invasive aquatic plant populations	
Title 38. Ch. 3 § 419-C	Prevention of the spread of invasive aquatic plants	No person may: • Transport any aquatic plant or parts of any aquatic plant on the outside of a vehicle, boat, personal watercraft, boat trailer or other equipment on a public road • Possess, import, cultivate, transport, or distribute any invasive aquatic plant or parts of any invasive aquatic plant in a manner that could cause the plant to get into any state water • Sell or offer for sale in this State any invasive aquatic plant • Failure to remove any aquatic plant or parts of any aquatic plant, from the outside of a vehicle, boat, personal watercraft, boat trailer or other equipment on a public road	A person who violates this section commits a civil violation for which a forfeiture not to exceed $500 may be adjudged for the first violation and a forfeiture not to exceed $2,500 may be adjudged for a subsequent violation
Title 38. Ch 20-A § 1862	Program to prevent infestation of and to control invasive aquatic plants	• Program: The commissioner and commissioner of Inland Fisheries and Wildlife jointly shall implement to inspect watercraft, watercraft trailers and outboard motors at or near the border of the State and at boat launching sites for the presence of invasive aquatic plants and to provide educational materials to the public and to watercraft owners regarding invasive aquatic plants • The program will establish inspection stations at boat launching sites • The program will provide informational material	
Title 38. Ch 20-B §1872	Action plan to protect State's inland waters	• The task force shall also recommend to the department an action plan to protect the State's inland waters from invasive aquatic plants and nuisance species. This includes the identification of inland waters known to be infested, vulnerability assessment, lake monitoring program, response program, training, and public information material	
Title 38. Ch. 3 § 423	Discharge of waste from watercraft	• Discharge from watercraft prohibited. A person, firm, corporation, or other legal entity may not discharge, spill, or permit to be discharged sewage, septic fluids, garbage, or other pollutants from watercraft: Into inland waters of the State; On the ice of inland waters and on the banks of inland waters of the State	Penalty. Notwithstanding section 349, subsection 2, a person who is charged with a civil violation of this section is subject to a civil penalty, payable to the State, of not less than $500 and not more than $10,000 for each day of that violation

WETLANDS

Title/Chapter/Section	Section Title	Summary
Title 5. Ch. 357 § 6401	Water Resources Planning Committee	• Established in the department of agriculture, Conservation and Forestry who will plan for sustainable use of water resources focused on water withdrawal activities, watersheds at risk climate change, and review state of policy with regards to conserving water resources, effects of surface water quality improvements on water withdraws opportunities
Title 12. Ch. 200 § 401	Maine's rivers	• Rivers and streams are a natural resource, As the state has 32,000 miles of rivers and streams • Importance's of increasing the value and use of river and streams • Implementing policies that recognizes the importance of rivers and streams
Title 12. Part 5. Ch. 421 Wetlands		Repealed
Title 38. Ch. 3 § 401-L	Lake Assessment and Protection Program. Established	• Established within the department to monitor and protect the health and integrity of the State's Lakes
Title 38. Ch. 3 § 410-M	Lake Assessment and Protection	• The Lake Assessment and Protection Program (LAPP) will provide education and technical assistance relating to lake function and values, watershed planning and management to implement applicable laws and rule • The LAPP will conduct resource monitoring and research and promote the natural resources protections laws/protection of lakes laws

RELEVANT ACTS

Title/Chapter/Section	Section Title	Summary	Year
Title 38. Ch. 3 § 480. Natural Resource Protection Act	A finding; purpose; short title	• The State's rivers and streams, great ponds, fragile mountain areas, freshwater wetlands, significant wildlife habitat, coastal wetlands and coastal sand dunes systems are resources of state significance • The Legislature further finds and declares that there is a need to facilitate research, develop management programs and establish sound environmental standards that will prevent the degradation of and encourage the enhancement of these resources • The Legislature further finds and declares that the cumulative effect of frequent minor alterations and occasional major alterations of these resources poses a substantial threat to the environment and economy of the State and its quality of life	1987

Appendix IV

MASSACHUSETTS

Invasive Species

Title/Chapter/ Section	Section Title	Summary	Penalty
Title 2. Ch. 21 § 37B	Aquatic Nuisance Control Program (ANCP)	• The Department of Environmental Management will establish and maintain the ANCP and work with the department of fish and game to promulgate rules and regulation to suppress, eradicate/control Aquatic nuisances. Study and promote methods of suppressing/controlling/reducing the spread of aquatic nuisances • The ANCP shall receive and respond to complaints, work with municipalities, local interest organizations and agencies to develop log-range program to control aquatic nuisances • (f) Except as otherwise authorized by the department, no person shall knowingly or intentionally place, or cause to be placed, an aquatic nuisance in or upon inland waters. Mass. Ch. 21 §37B • (g) Except as otherwise authorized by the department, no person shall place in or upon inland waters any vessel that has an aquatic nuisance attached to the vessel unless it has been cleaned/decontaminated or treated to kill/remove the Aquatic nuisance in accordance with the department's regulations	• (h) Whoever: (1) violates subsection (f); (2) knowingly and willfully resists or obstructs the department/authorized employees/agents from suppressing or eradicating aquatic nuisances shall be subject to a civil assessment of not more than $5,000 for each violation; each day that such violation occurs or continues shall be deemed a separate violation • (3) Violate subsection (g) or knowingly violates any rule, regulation, order, or quarantine issued by the commissioner pursuant to this section shall be subject to the fines and sanctions set forth in section 5D of chapter 90B (Mass. Ch. 21 §37B)
Title 26. Ch. 111 § 5E	Application of chemicals to control aquatic nuisances; licenses; rules and regulations; violations; penalties; applicability of section	• No one may use chemicals in a waterbody to control aquatic nuisances without obtaining a license from DEP. After a public hearing, DEP may establish rules for licenses and the application of chemicals to control aquatic nuisances	• The regulations may include penalties not exceeding $500 per offense. Any unlicensed person who applies chemicals to a waterbody to control aquatic nuisances shall be fined a minimum of $25 and a maximum of $500
Title 19. Ch. 128 § 20A	Spread or growth of plants of water chestnuts (*Trapa natans*)	• Spread or growth of plants of water chestnuts (*Trapa natans*): no one many knowingly transplant, transport, plant, or traffic in water chestnuts or its seed or nuts or cause the water chestnuts' growth or spread	• Violations: Anyone who knowingly transplants, transports, plants, or traffics in water chestnut, or its seeds or nuts, or causes the water chestnuts' growth or spread, shall be fined a minimum of $10 and a maximum of $100 (Mass. Gen. Laws Ch. 128, § 29)

Title/Chapter/Section	Section Title	Summary	Penalty
Title 19. Ch. 131 § 40	Removal, fill, dredging or altering of land bordering waters	• No person shall remove, fill, dredge or alter any bank, riverfront area, freshwater wetland, coastal wetland, beach, dune, flat, marsh, meadow or swamp bordering on the ocean or on any estuary, creek, river, stream, pond, or lake, or any land under said waters or any land subject to tidal action, coastal storm flowage, or flooding, other than while maintaining, repairing, or replacing	• Whoever violates any provision of this section, (a) shall be punished by a fine of not more than twenty-five thousand dollars or by imprisonment for not more than two years, or both such fine and imprisonment; or (b), shall be subject to a civil penalty not to exceed twenty-five thousand dollars for each violation
Title 19. Ch 132 § 11	Suppression of moths, caterpillars, worms, and beetles and any invasive plant or animal species rules and regulation contracts: studies for control of public nuisances: annual recommendations	• The chief superintended, with the approval of the commissioner makes rules and regulation that governs all operation in cities, towns, or person for the purpose of suppressing moths, caterpillars, worms and beetles and any invasive plant or animal species • The chief superintended may make contracts on behalf of the commonwealth. Study and promote improved methods of suppression such as public nuisances • The chief superintended may conduct investigation, gather, and distributed information concerning public nuisances	

FISH AND MAMMALS AND OTHER

Title/Chapter/Section	Section Title	Summary	Penalty
Title 19. Ch. 131 § 26	Importation of fish, birds, mammals, reptiles, or amphibians; shipments; tags; violations; seizure and disposition	• Any animal that is lawfully taken/lawfully propagated without the commonwealth may be purchased by any dealer licensed under section 23. the Export and the sale must be lawful in the state, province/country in which the animal was taken from. All shipments need to bear the name of the consignee, consignor or to the carton, package, box/crate. A mark of identification is required by state/province/country. • The dealer purchasing/dealing any bird/mammal before offering the same for sale, required a number tag as discussed in section 25. Any tags required hereunder for fish shall be furnished by the director at cost	• Any fish, bird, mammal, reptile, or amphibian possessed, shipped, transported, or delivered in violation of this section or of any rule or regulation made under the authority thereof may be seized and shall be disposed of by the director of law enforcement for the best interest of the commonwealth.
Title 19. Ch. 131 § 19	License to put fish or spawn into inland waters; permit to import live fish or viable eggs, certification, inspection for disease, and disposition	• No one may put fish or spawn thereof into inland waters without a license issued under Ch. 131 section 23, or with the director's written approval • No one may bring, or cause to be brought into Massachusetts any live fish or viable fish eggs without a permit issued by the director	• Anyone who violates Ch. 131, § 19 shall be fined a minimum of $100 or a maximum of $500, or be imprisoned for a maximum of six months, or both fined and imprisoned (Mass. Gen. Laws Ch. 131, § 90)

Appendix IV

WETLANDS

Title/Chapter/Section	Section Title	Summary	Penalty
Title 19. Ch. 131 § 40	Removal fill dredging or altering of land boarding waters	No person shall remove, fill, dredge or alter any bank, riverfront area, freshwater wetland, coastal wetland, beach, dunce, flat, march, meadow or swam, bordering on the ocean or on any estuary, creek, river, stream pond, lake, or any land under said waters or any land subject to tidal action, coastal storm flowage, or flooding	

RELEVANT ACTS

Title/Chapter/Section	Summary	Penalty	Year
Title 19. Ch. 131 § 40. The Wetland Protection Act	• This act sets forth a public review and decision-making process by which activities affecting areas subject to protection under M.G.L. c. 131 section 40 are to be regulated to protect and control: public and private water supply, ground water supply, fisheries and wildlife habitat, control flooding, and prevent storm damage, pollution and land containing shellfish	• Penalties can be found for Ch. 131 in Section 90	2017

NEW HAMPSHIRE STATUTES

INVASIVE SPECIES

Title/Chapter/Section	Section Title	Summary	Penalty
Title 50. Ch. 487 § 43	Aquatic invasive species decal	• No person shall operate a powerboat registered in another state on New Hampshire public waters without displaying a New Hampshire aquatic invasive species decal from the department of environmental services	Any person who violates this section shall be guilty of a violation punishable by a fine of $50 for a first offense, $100 for a second offense, and $250 for any subsequent offense
Title 50. Ch. 487 § 16-a	Exotic aquatic weed prohibition	• No exotic aquatic weeds shall be offered for sale, distributed, sold, imported, purchased, propagated, transported, or introduced in the state. The commissioner may exempt any exotic aquatic weed from any of the prohibitions of this section consistent with the purpose of this subdivision	It shall be unlawful to offer for sale, distribute, sell, import, purchase, propagate, negligently transport, or introduce exotic aquatic weeds into New Hampshire waterbodies. Notwithstanding RSA 487:7, any person engaging in such an activity shall be guilty of a violation (RSA 487: 16-b)
Title 50. Ch. 487 § 16-c	Transport of aquatic plants or exotic aquatic weeds on outside of boats, vehicles, and equipment	• No person shall negligently transport any aquatic plants or plant parts, or exotic aquatic weed or weed parts to or from any New Hampshire waters on the outside of a vehicle, boat, ski craft as defined in RSA 270:73, trailer, or other equipment	Any person who violates RSA 487:16-c through 487:16-e shall be guilty of a violation punishable by a fine of $50 for a first offense, $100 for a second offense, and $250 for any subsequent offense (RSA 487: 16-f)

Title/Chapter/Section	Section Title	Summary	Penalty
Title 50. Ch. 487 § 16-d	Draining of water conveyances	• When leaving waters of the state, a person shall drain their boat and other water-related equipment that holds water, including live wells and bilges • Devices used to control the draining of water from ballast tanks, bilges, and live wells shall be removed or opened while transporting boats and other water-related equipment • Commercial enterprises shall drain all water-related equipment holding water and live wells and bilges prior to transporting the equipment to another waterbody	Any person who violates RSA 487:16-c through 487:16-e shall be guilty of a violation punishable by a fine of $50 for a first offense, $100 for a second offense, and $250 for any subsequent offense (RSA 487: 16-f)
Title 50. Ch 487 § 29	Milfoil and Other Exotic Aquatic Plants Prevention; Grant Fund Report and Budget	• The department of environmental services shall submit an annual report shall include, but not be limited to, a description of prevention and research projects funded by the milfoil and other exotic aquatic plants prevention program and the extent of aid to municipalities or subdivisions of the state, non-profit corporations, and research institutions	
Title 50. Ch 487 § 30	Exotic Aquatic Weeds and Species Committee	• It is a committee to study exotic aquatic weeds and exotic aquatic species of wildlife in the state of NH • The committee will also aid the department of environmental services in the control and eradication milfoil	

FISH AND MAMMALS AND OTHER

Title/Chapter/Section	Section Title	Summary	Penalty
Title 18. Ch. 207 § 22-c	Wildlife damage control program; Administration	• The general wildlife damage mitigation program will shall address conflicts between wildlife and human populations by disseminating educational and technical information and providing assistance	
Title 18. Ch. 207 § 14	Import, possession, or release of wildlife	• No person shall import, possess, sell, exhibit, or release any live marine species or wildlife, or the eggs or progeny thereof, without first obtaining a permit from the executive director except as permitted under title XVIII	Any person who violates this section or any rule adopted under this section shall be guilty of a violation and guilty of an additional violation for each marine species or wildlife possessed contrary to the provisions of this section

Appendix IV

WETLANDS

Title/Chapter/Section	Section Title	Summary
Title 50. Ch. 483 § 1	Statement of policy	• New Hampshire rivers are valued ecologic, economic, public health and safety, and social assets for the benefit of present and future generations • The state shall encourage and assist in the development of river corridor management plans and regulate the quantity and quality of instream flow along certain protected rivers or segments of rivers to conserve and protect outstanding characteristics including recreational, fisheries, wildlife, environmental, hydropower, cultural, historical, archaeological, scientific, ecological, aesthetic, community significance, agricultural, and public water supply so that these valued characteristics shall endure as part of the river uses to be enjoyed by New Hampshire people • If conflicts arise in the attempt to protect all valued characteristics within a river or stream, priority shall be given to those characteristics that are necessary to meet state water quality standards
Title 50. Ch. 483 § 3	Program established: Intent	• It is the intent of the legislature that the New Hampshire lakes management and protection program shall complement and reinforce existing state and federal water quality laws • The scenic beauty and recreational potential of lakes shall be maintained or enhanced, that wildlife habitat shall be protected, that opportunity for public enjoyment of lake uses be ensured, and that littoral interests shall be respected
Title 50.485 § 1	Declaration of purpose	• The purpose of this chapter is to protect water supplies, to prevent pollution in the surface and groundwaters of the state and to prevent nuisances and potential health hazards. In exercising all powers conferred upon the department of environmental services under this chapter, the department shall be governed solely by criteria relevant to the declaration of purpose set forth in this section

RELEVANT ACTS

Chapter and Section	Section Title	Summary	Year
Title 50 Ch. 482 § 1. Fill and Dredge in wetlands or Wetland Act	Finding public's purpose	• This act protects and preserves its submerged lands under tidal and fresh waters and its wetlands (both saltwater and freshwater), from despoliation and unregulated alteration as it will adversely affect the value of such areas as sources of nutrients for finfish, crustacea, shellfish and wildlife of significant value, will damage or destroy habitats and reproduction areas for plants, fish and wildlife of importance, will eliminate, depreciate, or obstruct the commerce, recreation and aesthetic enjoyment of the public, will be detrimental to adequate groundwater levels, will adversely affect stream channels and their ability to handle the runoff of waters, will disturb and reduce the natural ability of wetlands to absorb flood waters and silt, thus increasing general flood damage and the silting of open water channels, and will otherwise adversely affect the interest of the general public	1990

NEW YORK

INVASIVE SPECIES

Chapter/Article/Section	Section Title	Summary
Ch. 37. Article 3 § 33-C	Regulating disposal of sewage; littering of waterways	Regulating disposal of sewage; littering of waterways: • No person, whether engaged in commerce or otherwise, shall place, throw, deposit, or discharge, or cause to be placed, thrown, deposited, or discharged into the waters of this state, from any watercraft, marina or mooring, any sewage, or other liquid or solid materials which render the water unsightly, noxious, or otherwise unwholesome to be detrimental to the public health or welfare or to the enjoyment of the water for recreational purposes
Ch. 37. Article 3 § 35-D	Aquatic invasive species signs at public boat launches	• The department of environmental conservation shall design and establish universal signage which may be posted at any access point to the navigable waters of the state relating to the threat and mitigation of aquatic invasive species • Commencing within one year of the effective date of this section, owners of each public boat launch shall conspicuously post the universal sign of not less than eighteen inches by twenty-four inches
Title 6, Ch. 5, Subchapter C., Part 575.1	Purpose, scope, and applicability	• Establish procedures to identify and classify invasive species and to establish a permit system to restrict the sale, purchase, possession, propagation, introduction, importation, and transport of invasive species in New York
Title 6, Ch. 5, Subchapter C., Part 575.4	Regulated Invasive Species	• No person shall knowingly introduce into a free-living state or introduce by a means that one knew or should have known would lead to the introduction into a free-living state any regulated invasive species, although such species shall be legal to possess, sell, buy, propagate, and transport
Title 6, Ch. 5, Subchapter C., Part 575.9	Invasive Species Permits	• A person may possess, with the intent to sell, import, purchase, transport or introduce, a prohibited invasive species if the person has been issued a permit by the department for research, education, or other approved activity, under this Part • A person may only introduce a regulated invasive species into a free-living state if the person is issued a permit under this section expressly authorizing such introduction. Written application are required, noted criteria must be met
Title 6, Ch. 5, Subchapter C., Part 575.10	Penalties	• Any person who violates this Part or any license or permit or order issued by the department, or Department of Agriculture and Markets, pursuant to section 9–1709 of the Environmental Conservation Law or pursuant to the provisions of this Part shall be liable for all penalties and other remedies provided for in the Environmental Conservation Law including section 71–0703(9). With respect to Eurasian boars, any person who violates this Part shall also be liable for all penalties provided for in the Environmental Conservation Law, including section 71–0925. Such penalties and remedies may be in addition to any other penalty or remedy available under any other law, including but not limited to, permit revocation

Appendix IV

Fish and Mammal and Other

Chapter/Article/Title/Section	Section Title	Summary
Ch. 43-B. Article 11 Title 14 § 1703	Importation, possession, and sale of fish without license of permit; prohibitions	• No person shall possess or transport into the state any fish except eels caught in that part of Missisquoi Bay in Lake Champlain lying in the Province of Quebec or in the Richelieu River

Wetlands

Chapter/Article/Title/Section	Section Title	Summary
Ch. 43-B. Article 15. Title 1 § 0105	Declaration of policy	It is public policy of the state of New York that: • The regulation and control of the water resources of the state of New York be exercised only pursuant to the laws of this state • The waters of the state be conserved and developed for all public beneficial uses
Ch. 43-B. Article 17. Title 5 § 0501	General prohibition against pollution	• It shall be unlawful for any person, directly or indirectly, to throw, drain, run, or otherwise discharge into such water's organic or inorganic matter that shall cause or contribute to a condition in contravention of the standards adopted by the department pursuant to section 17–0301
Ch. 43-B. Article 24 Title 1 § 0103	Declaration of policy	• It is declared to be the public policy of the state to preserve, protect and conserve freshwater wetlands and the benefits derived therefrom, to prevent the despoliation and destruction of freshwater wetlands, and to regulate use and development of such wetlands to secure the natural benefits of freshwater wetlands, consistent with the general welfare and beneficial economic, social, and agricultural development of the state
Ch. 43-B. Article 24. Title 7 § 0701	Permits	• Activities subject to regulation shall include any form of draining, dredging, excavation, removal of soil, mud, sand, shells, gravel, or other aggregate from any freshwater wetland, either directly or indirectly; and any form of dumping, filling, or depositing of any soil, stones, sand, gravel, mud, rubbish or fill of any kind, either directly or indirectly, erecting any structures, roads, the driving of pilings, or placing of any other obstructions whether changing flow of the water; any form of pollution and any other activity which substantially impairs any of the several functions served by freshwater wetlands

Relevant Bills

Information	Title	Summary
Senate Bill S6858 (2011–2012 Legislative Session)	Requires Publication of Laws Relating to the Control of Invasive Species	*Purpose:* • "The purpose of this bill is to provide sportspersons with information on legislation intended to reduce the effects of invasive species and to prevent further invasions." *Summary of specific provisions:* • "This bill would require the Department of Environmental Conservation (DEC) to include in their existing publications information on legislation affecting the eradication, suppression, reduction, or management of invasive species."
Assembly Bill A7692 (2019–2020 Legislative Session)	Extends provisions relating to the Department of Environmental Conservation's Management of Aquatic Invasive Species, Spread Prevention and Penalties	• Extends provisions relating to the Department of Environmental Conservation's Management of Aquatic Invasive Species, Spread Prevention and Penalties
Senate Bill S7010C (2012–2022 Legislative Session	Authorizes the establishment of aquatic invasive species inspection stations in Adirondack Park to inspect motorized watercraft for the presence of organisms or organic material that may harbor invasive species	• Authorizes self-issuing certification; directs education and outreach; makes permanent certain provisions of law relating to aquatic invasive species spread prevention • To make permanent the requirement that boaters take reasonable precautions to clean, drain and dry their watercraft before launching in New York State Waters, and to grant the Department of Environmental Conservation with the authority to conduct inspections and decontaminations of watercraft for the prevention of invasive species within the Adirondack Park or a 10-mile radius of its boundary

RHODE ISLAND

Invasive Species

Title/Chapter/Section	Section Title	Summary	Penalty
Title 20. Ch. 1 § 26	Freshwater invasive aquatic plants—prohibition on importation and possession	• No person shall import, transport, disperse, distribute, introduce, sell, purchase, or possess in the state any species of non-native (exotic) freshwater invasive aquatic plants, as defined by the director. The director shall promulgate rules and regulations governing the prohibition and its applicability	Violations of this section shall be punishable by a fine of not more than five hundred dollars ($500)

Appendix IV

Title/Chapter/Section	Section Title	Summary	Penalty
Title 20. Ch. 1 § 27	Exotic invasive freshwater fish and invertebrate species—prohibition on liberation into freshwaters	• No person shall release or liberate, by design or accident, any species of non-native (exotic) fish or invertebrate, as defined by the director, into the freshwater lakes, ponds, rivers, streams, or wetlands of the state. The director shall promulgate rules and regulations governing the prohibition and its applicability	Violations of this section shall be punishable by a fine of not more than five hundred dollars ($500)
Title 20. Ch. 1 § 1–28	Regulation of exotic baitfish—prohibition on importation, sale, and transport of exotic baitfish species	• No person shall import, transport, culture, or sell exotic species of baitfish, as specified by the director, in Rhode Island. The director shall promulgate rules and regulations governing the prohibition and its applicability. The regulations shall include a list of approved native baitfish and a list of prohibited non-native or exotic species	Violations of this section shall be punishable by a fine of not more than five hundred dollars ($500)

Fish and Mammals and Other

Title/Chapter/Section	Section Title	Summary	Penalty
Title 20. Ch. 18 § 1.	Acquisition or control of land for protecting wildlife	• The director may acquire by gift, lease, purchase, or easement, land within the state for the purpose of protecting, conserving, cultivating, or propagating any species of wildlife, plant, or animal	

Wetlands

Title and Chapter	Section	Summary	Penalty
Title 46. Ch. 12 § 37	Waste from seagoing vessels	• Pertains to the owners and/or agents of any seagoing vessel entering the waters or waterways of this state which intends to transfer or discharge any type of waste or bilge at a certified shore facility or terminal pursuant to the Resource and Conservation Recovery Act (RCRA), 42 U.S.C. § 6901 et seq.	The first file a performance bond or other evidence of financial responsibility with the director in the amount of a minimum of $50,000 payable to the state of Rhode Island and Providence Plantations. If vessel causes damage to the environment, the bond shall be forfeited to the extent of the costs incurred by the state to rectify and clean up the damages. To the extent of any fine levied for violations of water pollution abatement laws. Any seagoing vessel transferring any type of waste or bilge without coverage shall be fined minimum of $5,000

Title and Chapter	Section	Summary	Penalty
Title 46. Ch. 15 § 46–15–10	Sec. 10. Public nuisances— abatement	• Any person, municipality, municipal water department or agency, special water district, or private water company, committing a violation shall be liable for the costs of abatement of any pollution and any public nuisance caused by the violation. The superior court is hereby given jurisdiction over actions to recover the costs of the abatement • Any activity or condition declared by this chapter to be a nuisance, or which is otherwise in violation of this chapter, shall be abatable in the manner provided by law or equity for the abatement of public nuisances. In addition, the water resources board may proceed in equity to abate nuisances or to restrain or prevent any violation of this chapter	
Title 46. Ch. 17.1 § 1–1	Transporting of waste and dredge materials over state waterways prohibited	• Except as permitted under § 46–23–18.1 or otherwise, no person, either as principal, agent, or servant, shall transport or cause to be transported, dump, or cause to be dumped within the territorial waters of the state, any waste or dredge material	Every person who shall violate any provision of this section shall, upon conviction, be fined not more than one thousand dollars ($1,000) or be imprisoned not more than one year, or both, for each offense
Title 46. Ch. 17.3 § 1	Legislative findings	• Non-indigenous aquatic species introduced into waters of the United States from ballast water have caused tremendous environmental and ecological damage, displacing native species, degrading water quality, and interfering with commerce, including the zebra mussel brought into the Great Lakes and the upper Susquehanna River • Ballast water practices of commercial shipping vessels may cause irreversible damage to waters of the state; and protective measures against the introduction of non-indigenous aquatic species from ballast water are necessary to minimize exposure of the waters of the state to unwanted contamination and damage caused by these species	Sec 11. Penalties and remedies. Any person who willfully or negligently violates any provision of this chapter, or any rule or regulation or other order promulgated by the water resources board, or any condition of any permit issued pursuant to the chapter, is guilty of a misdemeanor and, upon conviction, shall be subject to a fine of not more than five hundred ($500) dollars for each separate offense or to imprisonment for a period of not more than one year, or both (RI. Gen. Laws. Ch. 17.3 § 11)

Appendix IV

Relevant Acts

Act	Section Title	Summary	Year
Title 46. Ch. 23 § 2–3. The Comprehensive Watershed and Marine Monitoring Act of 2004	Purpose	• The purpose of this chapter is to establish a comprehensive watershed and marine monitoring system that provides consistent and useful data to resource managers, decision-makers and the public concerning the health of the marine environment of the state. The Rhode Island environmental monitoring collaborative is hereby established with the purposes of organizing, coordinating, maintaining, and supporting the watershed and marine monitoring system of the state	2004
Title 20 Chapter 20 § 3.2–2 and 3.2.3. Rhode Island Freedom to Fish and Marine Conservation Act	Findings Freedom to Fish	• The rights and interests of people to engage in commercial and recreational fishing in Rhode Island's marine waters need to be recognized and protected. Various management measures, including the closure of marine waters or portions thereof to fishing, can be utilized to manage marine animals, and resources, but such measures must be developed to specific conservation or restoration needs and be based on scientific information; and emanate from an open management and regulatory process, incorporating full input from all affected stakeholders, conducted pursuant to the general laws of the state of Rhode Island • Closer of recreational or commercial fishing will on occur if it is deemed necessary to protect, manage or restore marine fish, shellfish, crustaceans, and associated marine habitats or other marine resources, protect public health or safety, or address some other public purpose	2003
Title 20. Ch. 20–1 § 24. Wildlife Damage Act	General provisions	• For purposes of this section, "wildlife population" includes, but is not limited to deer, indigenous Canadian geese, mute swans, cormorants, wild turkeys, crows, coyotes, and furbearers • The department of environmental management shall establish a program of financial assistance to farmers, when state or federal funds become available, for the purpose of establishing preventive practices to protect damage to crops by wildlife. The director of the department is authorized and empowered to establish rules and regulations to enforce the provisions of this section	2002

VERMONT

Invasive Species

Title/Chapter	Section	Summary	Penalty
Title 6. Ch. 083 § 981	Adoption of compact	Party states: • An annual loss of approximately 137 billion dollars from the depredation of pest is certain to continue/increase • Varying climatic, geographic, and economic factors may be affected differently by pest, and may pose serious damages to all states • The migratory character of pest infestation makes it necessary for states adjacent to and distant from one another to complement each other's activities when faced with conditions of infestation and reinfestation • Pest can cause damage to crop and products. in the interest to all states established an operation of an Insurance Fund	

Title/Chapter	Section	Summary	Penalty
Title 6. Ch. 084 § 1033	Detection and abundance surveys; eradication and suppression	• The Secretary may conduct detection and abundance surveys for plant pests of an injurious nature that may be present in the State to determine the necessity for establishing control practices • When the Secretary determines that a new injurious plant pest exists within the State or that an established pest requires control and the nature of the pest dictates immediate action, he or she may proceed with a plan of eradication or suppression	
Title 10. Ch. 050 § 1453	Aquatic Nuisance Control Program	They shall: • Receive/respond to aquatic nuisance complaints • Work with municipalities, local interest organizations, private individuals, and agencies of the state to develop long-range programs regarding aquatic nuisance controls • Work with federal, state, and local governments to obtain funding for aquatic nuisance control programs. • Implement an aquatic species rapid response program • Administer a grant-in-aid program under section 1458 of this title • place a sign that states that the water is infected with an aquatic nuisance and that the sign is easily visible from a ramp used to launch vessels at any fish and wildlife access area on a body of water infected with an aquatic nuisance • Provide the Commissioner of Fish and Wildlife and the Commissioner of Motor Vehicles with written educational information about aquatic nuisances	Regarding the signage: in violation of section 1454 of this title may be subject to a penalty of up to $1,000.00 pursuant to 23 V.S.A. § 3317
Title 10. Ch. 050 § 1454	Transport of aquatic plants and aquatic nuisance species	• A person shall not transport an aquatic plant, aquatic plant part, or aquatic nuisance species to or from any Vermont water • The inspection of vessels entering or leaving water • No-cost boat wash; aquatic nuisance species inspection station is open for vessels • Requires for the draining of vessel when leaving the state and profit to transport away from the area where the vessel left the water (including equipment used, live wells, ballast tanks, bilge areas	Violations. Pursuant to 4 V.S.A. § 1102, a violation of this section may be brought in the Judicial Bureau by any law enforcement officer, as that term is defined in 23 V.S.A. § 3302(2), or, pursuant to section 8007 or 8008 of this title, a violation of this section may be brought in the Environmental Division of the Superior Court
Title 10. Ch. 050 § 1457	Entrance upon lands to prevent the introduction and spread of new aquatic species	In taking steps to prevent the introduction/spread of new aquatic species/invasive the Secretary may, after first obtaining the permission of the landowner or lessee, enter upon lands for the following purposes: • To survey for, inspect, or investigate conditions relating to new aquatic species that may become invasive. • To collect information to issue coverage under rapid response general permits under section 1456 of this title • To conduct or use control techniques that are available under or authorized by a rapid response general permit issued under section 1456 of this title • To determine whether the rules of the agency adopted or issued under this chapter are being complied with	

Appendix IV

Fish, Mammals, and Others

Title/Chapter/Section	Section Title	Summary	Penalty
Title 10. Ch. 111 § 4601	Taking fish; possession	• A person shall not take fish, except in accordance with this part and regulations of the Board, or possess a fish taken in violation of this part or regulations of the Board (Added 1961, No. 119, § 1, eff. May 9, 1961)	
Title 10. Ch. 001 § 18	Governing the importation and possession of wild animals, excluding fish	• It is the purpose of this regulation to carry out the mandate of the Vermont General Assembly to control through a permit program the importation and possession • It is the purpose of this statute and its regulations to protect the health, safety, and welfare of animals, both wild and domestic, to prevent damage to agriculture and livestock, and to protect the health, safety, and welfare of human inhabitants of the State of Vermont	Any wild animal that is taken, imported, or possessed in violation of this regulation, or is kept in violation of any permit issued may be confiscated and disposed of in accordance with 10 V.S.A. § 4513. Permit violations and violations of Part 4 of Title 10 may result in the revocation of the permit

Wetlands

Title/Chapter/Section	Section Title	Summary	Penalty
Title 10. Ch. 049 § 1421	Policy	• It is declared to be in the public interest to make studies, establish policies, make plans, make rules, encourage, and promote buffers adjacent to lakes, ponds, reservoirs, rivers, and streams of the State, • The purposes of the rules shall be to further the maintenance of safe and healthful conditions; prevent and control water pollution; protect spawning grounds, fish, and aquatic life; control building sites, placement of structures, and land uses; reduce fluvial erosion hazards; reduce property loss and damage; preserve shore cover, natural beauty, and natural stability; and provide for multiple use of the waters in a manner to provide for the best interests of the citizens of the State	Any person who violates a rule adopted under this chapter shall be subject to the civil penalty provision of 23 V.S.A. § 3317(b) (10 V.S.A. § 1426)

Index

Note: Page numbers in *italics* indicate figures; page numbers in **bold** indicate tables.

A

Acremonium zonatum, 291
Adirondack Park (New York), common reed grass (*Phragmites australis*), 328–329
Aetokthonos hydrillicola, 97
air compressor inflation procedure, 388
Alternaria eichhorniae, 291
aluminum, treating aquatic invasive species, **25**
Amazon River Basin, parrot-feather, 189
American native weevil (*Euhrychiopsis lecontei*), 185
Anacharis, 245
Angiostrongylus cantonensis, 73
apple snails, 69
Aquastrike®, European naiad, 242
aquatic invasive plant species
  benthic barriers, 390
  biological control options, **26**, 27
  hand pulling for control of emergent, 392
  hand pulling for floating, 391–392
  hand pulling for submerged, 389–390
aquatic macrophyte moth (*Acentria ephemerella*), 186
aquatic macrophytes (*Ceratophyllum demersum*), 41
aquatic weevil (*Hydrotimetes natans*), 230
Aral Sea, zebra mussel, 53
ArcGIS®, 236, 249, 263, 270, 288, 298
Archanara geminipuncta, 326
Archanara neurica, 326
Asian clam (*Corbicula fluminea*), 1
  benthic barrier control of, 47–48
  biological treatment, 47
  Charles River, 7
  chemical treatment of, 46
  clams attaching to drifting plant materials, *36*
  distribution of, *41*, 45
  dry ice study, 48
  ecological impacts, 36–37
  economic impacts, 37
  literature research of chemical control methods, **394–395**
  live clams and dead empty shells, *43*, **44**
  location of each waterbody, **38–40**
  managing actions, 45–47
  Massachusetts waterbodies infected by, **5**
  monitoring and sightings of, 37, 41–45
  physical treatment, 46–47
  sightings in MA waterbodies, **2**
  size of, from unnamed tributary to Porter Lake, **44**
  source of report, **38–40**
  success stories of, 47–48
  taxonomic hierarchy, 35
  unnamed tributary to Porter Lake, *43*
  watersheds and waterbodies infested by, **42**
Aspidogaster conchiola, 73
Assawompset Pond, 3

Aythya ferina, 60
Aythya fuligula, 60

B

banded mystery snails (*Viviparus georgianus*), Chinese mystery snails, 70
Barbus spp., 37
barcoding, 13
Bartlett Pond, invasive species in, **5**
bass weed (*Potamogeton amplifolius*), 242
Bayeriola salicariae, 374
Bellamya genus, snails, 69
Bellamya chinensis, *see* Chinese mystery snail (*Bellamya chinensis*)
benthic barriers
  aquatic invasive plant control, 16, **17**
  control of submerged aquatic invasive species, 390
Billington Sea, invasive species in, **5**
Billmeyer Quarry, zebra mussels, 62–63
BioInvasions Records (journal), 13
biological control
  aquatic invasive species, **26**, 27
  Asian clam (Corbicula fluminea), 47
  Carolina fanwort (*Cabomba caroliniana*), 230
  Chinese mystery snail (*Bellamya chinensis*), 79
  common reed grass (*Phragmites australis*), 326–327
  Eurasian milfoil (*Myriophyllum spicatum*), 185–186
  European naiad (*Najas minor*), 241
  hydrilla (*Hydrilla verticillata*), 102
  northern snakehead (*Channa argus*), 91
  parrot-feather (*Myriophyllum aquaticum*), 196
  purple loosestrife (*Lythrum salicaria*), 374–375, *375*
  South American waterweed (*Egeria densa*), 252
  variable milfoil (*Myriophyllum heterophyllum*), 185–186
  water chestnut (*Trapa natans*), 281
  water hyacinth (*Eichhornia crassipes*), 290
  yellow floating heart (*Nymphoides peltata*), 312–313
  zebra mussel (*Dreissena polymorpha*), 59–60
biological control options, aquatic invasive species, **26**
biological invasions, 7, 10
bivalve (*Limnoperna fortunei*), 97
Black Sea, zebra mussel, 53
black snail, 69
Blackstone River
  Asian clam, **39**, 41
  invasive species in, **5**
Blackstone River watershed, 4, 41
Boat Decontamination Program, Quabbin Reservoir, **11**
boaters, brochure by MA DCR, *9*
boats, invasive species as hitchhikers on, 6
Boreal Marstonia snail (*Marstonia lustrica*), 58
bowfin (*Amia calva*), 85, *86*

435

Brazilian waterweed, 245, *see also* South American waterweed (*Egeria densa*)
Brazillian waterweed (*Egeria densa*), 98
Bucephalus polymorphus, 60
bullseye snakehead (*Channa marulius*), *84*, 85, 89
burbot (*Lota lota*), 85, *86*
Burchell Pond (MA), parrot-feather, 198
Buzzards Bay, parrot-feather (*Myriophyllum aquaticum*), 193, **193**

C

Cabomba caroliniana, *see* Carolina fanwort (*Cabomba caroliniana*)
Caenogastropoda clade, 69
Campeloma sp., 70, *71*
Cape Cod Water Quality Assessment, 99
Captains Pond (NH), Eurasian milfoil, 187
carfentrazone, treating aquatic invasive species, 24
Carolina fanwort (*Cabomba caroliniana*), 2
　biological control, 230
　biology of, 201–202
　chemical treatment, 230–231, *230*
　decision tree for control of, *230*
　distribution map of, *204*
　ecological impacts, 203
　economic impacts, 203
　Federal Pond sample, *202*
　floating leaves and flower buds/flower, *202*
　infested watersheds, **229**
　invasive range, 202
　literature research of chemical control methods, **406–407**
　management options, 204, 228–231
　Massachusetts waterbodies infected by, **5**
　mechanisms/vectors of spread, 202–203
　monitoring and sighting data, 203–204
　native range, 202
　physical control, 228–29
　positive aspects, 203
　sightings in MA waterbodies, **2, 205–223**
　success story, 231
　taxonomic hierarchy, 201
　towns and infested waterbodies, **224–228**
　underwater photo, *202*
carp (*Cyprinidae*), 60
Caspian Sea, zebra mussel, 53
Catlin Creek, northern snakehead, 92
Cauvery River (India), European waterclover (*Marsilea quadrifolia* L.), 297
Cayuga Lake (New York), hydrilla, 104
CD3 Waterless Cleaning Systems, 10
Cercospora piaropi, 291
Channa argus, *see* northern snakehead (*Channa argus*)
Charles River, 3
　Asian clam, 7, 37, **38**, 41
　invasive species in, **5**
　parrot-feather (*Myriophyllum aquaticum*), 193, **193**
　swollen bladderwort (*Utricularia inflata*), 263
Charles River Watershed
　Chinese mystery snail, 73
　yellow floating heart (*Nymphoides peltata*), 310, **311**
Chehalis River (Washington), parrot-feather (*Myriophyllum aquaticum*), 197

Chemical Application License (WM 04), 29, 186, 282, 290, 301
chemical treatment
　aquatic invasive plant treatment, 16, **22–25**, 27
　Asian clam (*Corbicula fluminea*), 46
　Carolina fanwort (*Cabomba caroliniana*), 230–231, *230*
　Chinese mystery snail (*Bellamya chinensis*), 74, 76–78
　common reed grass (*Phragmites australis*), 321, 323–324
　curly-leaf pondweed (*Potamogeton crispus*), 130
　Eurasian milfoil (*Myriophyllum spicatum*), 138, 184–185
　European naiad (*Najas minor*), 240–241
　European waterclover (*Marsilea quadrifolia* L.), 300–301, **302–303**
　hydrilla (*Hydrilla verticillata*), 102–103
　literature research on invasive species, **394–413**
　northern snakehead (*Channa argus*), 90
　parrot-feather (*Myriophyllum aquaticum*), 194–195
　purple loosestrife (*Lythrum salicaria*), 373, *375*
　South American waterweed (*Egeria densa*), 251, 252–253
　swollen bladderwort (*Utricularia inflata*), 264
　variable milfoil (*Myriophyllum heterophyllum*), 186
　water chestnut (*Trapa natans*), 281–282
　water hyacinth (*Eichhornia crassipes*), 290–291
　yellow floating heart (*Nymphoides peltata*), 312
　zebra mussel (*Dreissena polymorpha*), 62
Chesapeake Bay
　Eurasian milfoil, 186
　water chestnut (*Trapa natans*), 269, 280
Chicopee River Basin, **3**, 4
Chinese mystery snail (*Bellamya chinensis*), 1
　adult and juvenile, *70*
　banded mystery snails (*Viviparus georgianus*) and, 70
　biological control, 79
　Campeloma species and, 70
　chemical control, 74, 76–78
　distribution map, *74*
　ecological control, 79
　ecological impacts, 72–73
　human impacts on, 73
　infested watersheds, **78**
　location of, 72
　managing actions, 74, 76–78
　Massachusetts waterbodies infected by, **5**
　monitoring and sightings, 73–74, **75–76**
　native and invasive range, mechanisms of spread, 72
　physical control, 78–79
　sightings and report sources of infested waterbodies, **75–76**
　sightings in MA waterbodies, **2**
　success story, 79–81
　taxonomic hierarchy, 69
　towns and infested waterbodies, **77**
　visual guide for differentiating, from similar species, *71*
Chinese mystery snail (*Cipangopaludina chinensis*), literature research of chemical control methods, **396**
Chinese soft-shelled marsh turtle (*Pelodiscus sinensis*), 1
Chinese vivipara, 69
Christmas Lake (Minnesota), zebra mussels, 60
Cipangopaludina chinensis, 69, **396**

Index

Clean Water Act (CWA), 28, 37, 88, 101, 238, 250, 270, 341
climate change, **420**
    Asian clam (Corbicula fluminea), 45
    European waterclover (*Marsilea quadrifolia*), 297
    freshwater invasive species, 7
    parrot-feather (*Myriophyllum aquaticum*), 196
    spread of invasive species, 12
    water hyacinth (*Eichhornia crassipes*), 286
College of the Holy Cross, 109, 112
Columbia River, Asian clam, 35, 37
common bladderwort (*Utricularia vulgaris*), 260, *260*, 261
common pochard (*Aythya ferina*), 60
common reed grass (*Phragmites australis*), 2
    biological control, 326–327
    biology, 315–321
    chemical control, 321, 323–324
    general management plans, 327–328
    haplotypes, 318
    illustration, *316*
    literature research of chemical control methods, **412**
    location of waterbodies with, **331–335**
    management approaches, *328*
    managing actions, 321, 323–327
    Massachusetts waterbodies infected by, **5**
    monitoring and sightings, 321
    native and invasive varieties, 317–321, *320*
    photographs of, *317, 319*
    physical control, 324–326
    root and rhizome system of, *325*
    seed and rhizome dispersal, *317*
    sightings in MA waterbodies, **2**
    success story, 328–329
    taxonomic hierarchy, 315
    towns and infested waterbodies, **322–323**
Concord River Basin, **3**, 4
Connecticut, laws and statutes pertaining to aquatic invasive/nuisance species, **417–418**
Connecticut Agricultural Experiment Station (CAES) Invasive Aquatic Plant Program (IAPP), 252–253
Connecticut River
    hydrilla, 95, 96, *97*, 98, **99**, **100**
    water chestnut (*Trapa natans*), 282–283
    zebra mussels, 52
Connecticut River Basin, 2, **3**
Connecticut River Watershed, water chestnut (*Trapa natans*), 282–283
Connecticut River Watershed Invasive Plant Control Initiative, Log Pond Cove, 280–281
Conservation Commission, 28
control and containment, invasive species, 15–16
copper, treating aquatic invasive species, **25**
Corbicula fluminea, *see* Asian clam (*Corbicula fluminea*)
crayfish *Procambarus clarkia*, 47
Crystal Lake (Connecticut), curly-leaf pondweed (*Potamogeton crispus*), 108
curly-leaf pondweed (*Potamogeton crispus*), 2, 43
    chemical methods, 130
    Crystal Lake (CT), *108*
    distribution map of, in Massachusetts, *130*
    ecological impact, 109
    economic impact, 109
    as invasive species, 107–109
    latitude and longitude of each waterbody, **113–129**
    literature research of chemical control methods, **401–402**
    management, 112, 130–131
    Massachusetts waterbodies infected by, **5**
    mechanical and physical methods, 112, 130
    Minnesota lakes, 131
    monitoring and sightings, 109, 112
    photograph, *108*
    positive aspects, 109
    prevention methods, 130–131
    sightings in MA waterbodies, **2**
    success story, 131–132
    taxonomy hierarchy, 107
    town names and waterbodies containing, **110–112**
cyanobacterium (*Aetokthonos hydrillicola*), 97
Cyperus difformis, 301
Cyprinus carpio, 37

D

diquat, treating aquatic invasive species, **22**
domestic ducks, South American waterweed (*Egeria densa*), 253–254
Dorothy Pond, European naiad (*Najas minor*), 236
dredging
    aquatic invasive plant control, 16, **18–19**
    Water Quality Certification (WQC), 28–29
Dreissena polymorpha, *see* zebra mussel (*Dreissena polymorpha*)
ducks, domestic, South American waterweed (*Egeria densa*), 253–254
dyes and surface covers, aquatic invasive plant control, 16, **19**

E

early detection and rapid response (EDRR)
    decision-making process, *13*
    invasive species, 12
EarthTec QZ®, zebra mussels and, 62–63
eastern mosquitofish (*Gambusia holbrooki*), 91
Echinochloa spp., 297
eel (Anguilliformes), 60
Egeria densa, *see* South American waterweed (*Egeria densa*)
Eichhornia crassipes, *see* water hyacinth (*Eichhornia crassipes*)
Eichinochloa colona, 301
Eichornia spp., 46
Elodea genus, *Egeria densa* and, 245, 246, *247*
Endothall, treating aquatic invasive species, **23**
environmental DNA (eDNA), 10, 14
    Chinese mystery snail, 74
    northern snakehead, 89, 92
    surveillance, 15
Equipment Decontamination Protocol (MassDEP), 379–382
    air compressor inflation procedure, 388
    cleaning solutions preventing invasive aquatic organisms, 383–384
    DWM boating equipment, 384–385
    equipment checklist for multiprobe deployment surveys, 384
    field cleaning sampling equipment and gear, 385–387

general procedures, 380–382
sprayer use, 387
eradication, functional, 16
Erie Canal, purple loosestrife (*Lythrum salicaria*), 340
Erie Canal Corridor (ECC), northern snakehead, 92
Eurasian milfoil (*Myriophyllum spicatum*),
see also milfoil(s); variable milfoil
(*Myriophyllum heterophyllum*)
  biological control, 185–186
  biology of, 133–135
  chemical treatment, 185
  distribution map, *137*, *138*
  ecological impacts, 136
  economic impacts, 136
  herbicide application, 184–185
  invasive range, 135
  latitude and longitude of waterbody, **140–149**
  leaves of, *134*
  management, 138–139, 184–186
  monitoring and sightings, 136–138
  native range, 135
  parrot-feather (*M. aquaticum*) and, 192
  physical treatment, 138–139, 185
  schematic depiction of, *134*
  stems of, *135*
  taxonomic hierarchy, 133
  towns and infested waterbodies, **175–178**
Eurasian watermilfoil (*Myriophyllum spicatum*), 2, 103
  literature research of chemical control methods, **402–403**
  Massachusetts waterbodies infected by, **5**
  sightings in MA waterbodies, **2**
  stems of, *135*
European naiad (*Najas minor*), 2
  biological control, 241
  biology, 233
  chemical control, 240–241
  distribution map of, *239*
  ecological impacts, 235–236
  economic impacts, 236
  guide to differentiating *Najas* genus, *235*
  infested waterbodies, **237–238**
  infested watersheds, **240**
  literature research of chemical control methods, **407–408**
  managing actions, 236, 238, 240
  Massachusetts waterbodies infected by, **5**
  mechanisms/vectors of spread, 234–235
  microscopic photos of, *234*
  monitoring and sightings, 236
  native and invasive range, 234
  physical control, 241
  sightings in MA waterbodies, **2**
  success story, 241–242
  taxonomic hierarchy, 233
  towns and infested waterbodies, **239**
European roach or common roach (*Rutilus rutilus*), 59
European waterclover (*Marsilea quadrifolia* L.), 2
  biology, 295–296
  chemical control, 301
  distribution map, *300*
  ecological impacts, 298
  economic impacts, 298
  herbicides for, **302–303**
  infested watersheds, **300**
  literature research of chemical control methods, **410**
  managing actions, 299–301
  Massachusetts waterbodies infected by, **5**
  mechanisms/vectors of spread, 297–278
  monitoring and sightings, 298–299
  native and invasive range, 296–297
  photograph, *296*
  physical control, 300–301
  positive aspects, 298
  sightings in MA waterbodies, **2**
  success story, 301, 304
  taxonomic hierarchy, 295
  towns and infested waterbodies, **299**
  waterbodies, **299**
Eutropication and Aquatic Plant Management, 16
Exotic Aquatic Mollusk Collections in the Illinois Natural History Survey, 73

F

Fall Creek (New York), hydrilla, 104
fanwort, *see* Carolina fanwort (*Cabomba caroliniana*)
Federal Pond, swollen bladderwort (*Utricularia inflata*), 263
Fence Rock Lake (CT), South American waterweed (*Egeria densa*), 252–253
Fimbristylis miliacea, 301
First International Snakehead Symposium (2018), 88
fish and mammal control agents, parrot-feather (*Myriophyllum aquaticum*), 197
flatleaf bladderwort (*Utricularia intermedia*), 260
Flint Pond, invasive species in, **5**
Flora Americae Spetentrionalis (Pursh), 339
florpyrauxifen-benzyl, treating aquatic invasive species, **24**
flumioxazin, treating aquatic invasive species, **24**
fluridone, treating aquatic invasive species, **22**
Fort Meadow Reservoir, invasive species in, **5**
Foster's Pond (MA), Carolina fanwort (*Cabomba caroliniana*), 231
freshwater ecosystems, ecological and economic damage, 7–8
freshwater invasive species
  climate change on, 7
  spread of, 6–7
freshwater jellyfish (*Craspedacusta sowerbii*), 1
frog's-bit (*Limnobium spongia*), water hyacinth (*Eichhornia crassipes*) and, 285, *286*
functional eradication, 16
Fusarium, South American waterweed (*Egeria densa*), 252

G

Galerucella sp., 374
Galerucella calmariensis beetle, 374, 376
  purple loosestrife (*Lythrum salicaria*) and, 339
Galerucella grisescens beetle, 196
Galerucella pusilla, 374, 376
Geographic Information Systems (GIS), 98, 136
giant snakehead (*Channa maculata*), *84*, 85
glyphosate
  parrot-feather (*Myriophyllum aquaticum*), 194
  treating aquatic invasive species, **22**
grass carp (Ctenopharyngodon idella), 230

Carolina fanwort (*Cabomba caroliniana*), 228, 230
parrot-feather (*Myriophyllum aquaticum*), 197
great blue heron (*Ardea herodias*), 91
Great Lakes
    northern snakehead, 92
    zebra mussel, 53, 57, 60
Green River, zebra mussel, 15
Gun Lake (Michigan), Eurasian milfoil, 185

H

hand pulling
    control of emergent invasive species, 392
    control of floating aquatic invasive species, 391–392
    control of submerged aquatic invasive species, 389–390
Harvard Herbarium, little floating heart, 310
harvesting, aquatic invasive plant control, 16, **19–20**
Herbarium, yellow floating heart, 310, **311**
Hills Pond (MA), water chestnut (*Trapa natans*), 281
Hoosic River Basin, zebra mussels, 52, 59
Housatonic River, zebra mussel, 15
Housatonic River Basin, zebra mussels, 52, 59
Housatonic River Watershed, **3**, 8, 41
Hudson River
    water chestnut (*Trapa natans*), 281
    zebra mussel, 53, 54
hydrilla (*Hydrilla verticillata*), 1
    biological control, 102
    biotypes, 95
    Cayuga Lake (New York), 104
    chemical treatment, 102–103
    description of, 95
    distribution of, *99*
    ecological effects, 96–97
    economic impacts, 97–98
    Fall Creek (New York), 104
    informational sign for preventing spread of, *101*
    literature research of chemical control methods, **397–401**
    management, 101–103
    monitoring and sightings, 98–99, **100–101**
    native and invasive range, 98
    photograph of, *96*
    physical control, 103
    Pickerel Pond (Maine), 104
    sightings in MA waterbodies, **2**
    success story, 104
    taxonomic hierarchy, 95
    tubers and turions, 97
    vectors of spread, 98, **99**
    waterbodies with invasive, **100–101**
Hydrilla verticillate, *Egeria densa* and, 245, 246
Hylobius transversovittatus, 374, 376

I

imaging flowcytometry, 14
imazamox, treating aquatic invasive species, **24**
imazapyr
    parrot-feather (*Myriophyllum aquaticum*), 194
    treating aquatic invasive species, **23**
Indian Brook, swollen bladderwort (*Utricularia inflata*), 258
Indian leaf-mining fly (*Hydrellia pakistanae*), 102

infested watersheds
    Carolina fanwort (*Cabomba caroliniana*), **229**
    Chinese mystery snail (*Bellamya chinensis*), **78**
    European naiad (*Najas minor*), **240**
    European waterclover (*Marsilea quadrifolia* L.), **300**
    milfoils, **18**
    South American waterweed (*Egeria densa*), **251**
    swollen bladderwort (*Utricularia inflata*), **264**
    water chestnut (*Trapa natans*), **277**
    water hyacinth (*Eichhornia crassipes*), **289**
    yellow floating heart (*Nymphoides peltata*), **311**
insect control agents, parrot-feather (*Myriophyllum aquaticum*), 196–197
Integrated Lists of Waters, MassDEP's biennial, 2
International Union for Conservation of Nature (IUCN), 8
invasion curve, *12*
invasive species, *see also* state laws and statutes on invasive species
    climate change on freshwater, 7
    control and containment, 15–16
    definition, 1
    early detection and monitoring, 13–15
    early detection and rapid response (EDRR), 12
    freshwater, in MA and US population size, *5*
    invasion curve, *12*
    literature research on chemical control methods, **394–413**
    MA lakes and rivers, 1–6
    management, 8
    permitting, 28–29
    physical removal and management options, **17–21**
    prevention, 10–12
    public education and awareness, 9–10
    regulation, 27–28
    spread of freshwater, 6–7
    weakness and strength of data, 30
Invasive Species Council of Metro Vancouver, parrot-feather (*Myriophyllum aquaticum*), 195
Island Creek Pond (MA), Carolina fanwort (*Cabomba caroliniana*), 229
Islands, parrot-feather (*Myriophyllum aquaticum*), 193, **193**

J

Jackson County Sports Park (OR), Chinese mystery snails, 79
Jones River, parrot-feather (*Myriophyllum aquaticum*), 193, **193**
Jordanelle Reservoir, Utah, 15

K

King County (WA), Noxious Weed Control Program, 195

L

Lacey Act (2002), 87
Lacey-Keosauqua State Park (Iowa), European waterclover (*Marsilea quadrifolia* L.), 297
Lake Bomoseen, Asian clam, 41
Lake Cardinal (OH), European naiad, 234
Lake Carl Blackwell (Oklahoma), yellow floating heart (*Nymphoides peltata*), 313

Lake Champlain (VT), water chestnut (*Trapa natans*), 269, 280, 281
Lake Cochituate, invasive species in, **5**
Lake Erie, zebra mussel, *52*, 52–54
Lake George (New York)
    Eurasian milfoil, 186
    hydrilla, 98
Lake Limerick (WA), swollen bladderwort (*Utricularia inflata*), 265
Lake Mead, 6
    invasive quagga mussel, 42
    quagga mussel, 41–42
Lake Moultrie, hydrilla, 98
Lake Quinsigamond, invasive species in, **5**
Lake Rico, invasive species in, **5**
Lake St. Clair, zebra mussel, 53
Lake Tahoe, Asian clams, 46, 47
Laurel Lake, zebra mussels, 6, 10, 57–59
Laurel Lee, 6
laws and statutes, *see* state laws and statutes on invasive species
leaf beetle (*Galerucella birmanica*), 281
leaf-feeding beetles (*Lysathia* spp.), 196
Lepomis gibbosus, 37
Lily Brook and Stockbridge Bowl, European naiad (*Najas minor*), 236
Limnobium spongia (frog's-bit), 285, *286*
    little floating bladderwort (*Utricularia radiata*), 260
little floating heart (*Nymphoides cordata*), 307, *309*
Long Pond, hydrilla, 99, **100**
loosestrife, *see* purple loosestrife (*Lythrum salicaria*)
low-watermilfoil (*Myriophyllum humile*), 133, *134*, *see also* milfoil(s)
Luciobarbus spp., 37
Luciobarbus bocagei, 47
Lymnaea stagnalis, 72
    Lythrum salicaria, *see* purple loosestrife (*Lythrum salicaria*)

M

MacQuilliam Pond (Maryland), northern snakehead success, 91–92
Madsen, John D., 197
Maine, laws and statutes pertaining to aquatic invasive/nuisance species, **418–420**
Manitoba (Canada), purple loosestrife (*Lythrum salicaria*), 340
Manitoba Purple Loosestrife Project, 374
maps, *see* Massachusetts maps (distribution)
Marsilea quadrifolia L., *see* European waterclover (*Marsilea quadrifolia* L.)
Maryland's Department of Natural Resources (MDNR), 91
Massachusetts
    lakes/ponds infested by invasive species, *4*
    laws and statutes pertaining to aquatic invasive/nuisance species, **421–423**
    number of infested waterbodies/watershed for invasive species, *4*
    rivers/streams infested by invasive species, *4*
    watershed codes and names, **3**
    zebra mussel monitoring, 57–59
Massachusetts Department of Agricultural Resources (MA DAR)
    Pesticide Bureau, 28
    Pesticide Program, 29
Massachusetts Department of Conservation and Recreation (MA DCR), 8, *9*, 27
    curly-leaf pondweed (*Potamogeton crispus*), 109
    Lakes and Ponds Program, 15
Massachusetts Department of Environmental Protection (MassDEP), 8, 10, 28, 37, 62, 73
    boat cleaning, *11*
    equipment cleaning, *11*
    equipment decontamination protocol, 379–382
Massachusetts Department of Fish and Game (DFG), 27, 29, 58
Massachusetts Division of Fisheries and Wildlife, northern snakehead, 90
Massachusetts Endangered Species Act (MESA), 28, 90
Massachusetts Environmental Policy Act (MEPA), 29
Massachusetts Generic Environmental Impact Report (GEIR), 16
Massachusetts maps (distribution)
    Asian clam (*Corbicula fluminea*), 41
    Carolina fanwort (*Cabomba caroliniana*), 204
    Chinese mystery snail (*Bellamya chinensis*), *74*
    common reed grass (*Phragmites australis*), *323*
    curly-leaf pondweed (*Potamogeton crispus*), *130*
    Eurasian milfoil (*Myriophyllum spicatum*), 137, 138
    European naiad (*Najas minor*), *239*
    European waterclover (*Marsilea quadrifolia* L.), *300*
    hydrilla (*Hydrilla verticillata*), 99
    lakes/ponds and rivers/streams infested by invasive species, *4*
    parrot-feather (*Myriophyllum aquaticum*), 194
    purple loosestrife (*Lythrum salicaria*), *341*
    South American waterweed (*Egeria densa*), *250*
    swollen bladderwort (*Utricularia inflata*), *263*
    unidentified milfoil, 137, *139*
    variable milfoil (*Myriophyllum heterophyllum*), 137, 138
    water chestnut (*Trapa natans*), *277*
    water hyacinth (*Eichhornia crassipes*), 289
    yellow floating heart (*Nymphoides peltata*), *311*
    zebra mussel (*Dreissena polymorpha*), 58
Massachusetts Office of Coastal Zone Management (MA CZM), 374
Massachusetts Prohibited Plant List, 189
Massachusetts Water Resource Authority (MWRA), 8
Massachusetts Wetlands Protection Act, 16, 28
Massapoag Pond, northern snakehead, 89
mechanical removal, aquatic invasive plant control, 16, **19–20**
Megamelus scutellaris, 291, 292
Meriläinen, Jouko, 233
Merrimack River, Asian clam, 41
MESA, *see* Massachusetts Endangered Species Act (MESA)
MESA-associated permits, 29
metsulfuron, treating aquatic invasive species, **24**
Meuse River, Asian clam, 37
Michigan, European waterclover (*Marsilea quadrifolia* L.), 301
milfoil(s), 187, *see also* Eurasian milfoil (*Myriophyllum spicatum*); low-watermilfoil (*Myriophyllum humile*); parrot-feather (*Myriophyllum aquaticum*); variable milfoil (*Myriophyllum heterophyllum*)

Index

distribution map of unidentified, *137, 139*
infested watersheds, **18**
latitude and longitude of each waterbody for unidentified, **172–175**
management, 187
Myriophyllum farwellii, 133
milfoil midge (Cricotopus myriophylli), 186
Mill Neck (NY), *Egeria densa*, 247
Mill River, invasive species, **5**
Minnesota, curly-leaf pondweed in lakes, 131
Mississippi State University, 197
Mohawk River, water chestnut (*Trapa natans*), 281
Monponsett Pond
　invasive species, **5**
　swollen bladderwort (*Utricularia inflata*), 258
Montezuma National Wildlife Refuge (NY), purple loosestrife (*Lythrum salicaria*), 340
Mountain Lakes, European naiad (*Najas minor*), 241, 242
Muddy River, Chinese mystery snail, 72, 73
Myriophyllum aquaticum, see parrot-feather (*Myriophyllum aquaticum*)
Myriophyllum farwellii, 133
Myriophyllum heterophyllum, see variable milfoil (*Myriophyllum heterophyllum*)
Myriophyllum humile, see low-watermilfoil (*Myriophyllum humile*)
　Myriophyllum spicatum, *see* Eurasian milfoil (*Myriophyllum spicatum*)
mystery snails, 69

N

Najas gracillima, 233, 235
Najas guadalupensis, 235
Najas marina, 233, 234, 235, 236
Najas minor, 235, *see also* European naiad (Najas minor)
Nanophyes brevis, 374
Nanophyes marmoratus, 374
Nashua watershed, **3**, 4
National Heritage and Endangered Species Program (NHESP), 29
National Sea Grant Law Center, 27
Neochetina bruchi, 292
Neochetina eichhorniae, 292
Neogalerucella spp., 374
New Hampshire, laws and statutes pertaining to aquatic invasive/nuisance species, **423–425**
Newton Pond, northern snakehead, 89
New York
　Department of Environmental Conservation Board Stewardship Inspection program, **99**
　laws and statutes pertaining to aquatic invasive/nuisance species, **426–428**
New York State Department of Environmental Conservation (NYSDEC), 92
Northeast Aquatic Nuisance Species (NEANS), hydrilla, 98, 101, 104
northern snakehead (*Channa argus*), 1
　appearance of, 83–85
　biological control, 91
　chemical control, 90
　distribution map of, *87*
　ecological control, 91
　ecological impacts, 88

human risks and benefits, 88–89
infested waterbodies, towns, and watersheds, **89**
invasive, in North America, *84*
invasive, in United States, *86*
life history of, 87–88
literature research of chemical control methods, **397**
MacQuilliam Pond (Maryland), 91–92
managing actions, 90–91
monitoring and sightings, 89, **89**
native and invasive range, mechanisms of spread, 85, 87–88
physical control, 90–91
Ridgebury Lake (New York), 92–93
sightings in MA waterbodies, **2**, **89**
success stories, 91–93
taxonomic hierarchy, 83
North Pond, invasive species in, **5**
Noxious Weed Control Program, King County, WA, 195
　Nymphoides peltata, see yellow floating heart (*Nymphoides peltata*)

O

Onota Lake, Asian clam, 41
operations and maintenance (O&M), 8
Orconectes rusticus, 72
Order of Conditions (OOC), 28
Oregon Department of Fish and Wildlife (ODFW), Chinese mystery snails, 79
osprey (Pandion haliaetus), 91

P

parrot-feather (*Myriophyllum aquaticum*), 2, 189–190
　biological control, 196
　chemical control, 194–195
　ecological and human impacts, 191–192
　fish and mammal control agents, 197
　illustration of, *190*
　infested waterbodies, **193**
　insect control agents, 196–197
　literature research of chemical control methods, **404–406**
　managing actions, 193–197
　map of infested waterbodies by, *194*
　mechanisms of spread, 190–191
　monitoring and sightings, 193
　native and invasive range, 190–191
　photos of, *191*
　physical control, 195–196
　sightings in MA waterbodies, **2**
　success story, 197–198
　taxonomic hierarchy, 189
pea clam (*Pisidium* spp.), 48
permitting
　Egeria, 249
　401 Water Quality Certification (Dredge), 28–29
　MESA-associated permits, 29
　Order of Conditions, 28
　regulation and, 27–29
　WM 04 Chemical Application License, 29
Phragmites americanus, 318
Phragmites australis, *see* common reed grass (Phragmites australis)

Physa gyrina, 72
physical control
    Asian clam (*Corbicula fluminea*), 46–47
    Carolina fanwort (*Cabomba caroliniana*), 228–230
    Chinese mystery snail (*Bellamya chinensis*), 78–79
    common reed grass (*Phragmites australis*), 324–326
    curly-leaf pondweed (*Potamogeton crispus*), 112, 130
    Eurasian milfoil (*Myriophyllum spicatum*), 138–139, 184
    European naiad (*Najas minor*), 241
    European waterclover (*Marsilea quadrifolia* L.), 300–301
    hydrilla (Hydrilla verticillata), 103
    northern snakehead (*Channa argus*), 90–91
    parrot-feather (*Myriophyllum aquaticum*), 195–196
    purple loosestrife (*Lythrum salicaria*), 373, *375*
    South American waterweed (*Egeria densa*), 251–252
    swollen bladderwort (*Utricularia inflata*), 263–264
    variable milfoil (*Myriophyllum heterophyllum*), 186
    water chestnut (*Trapa natans*), 280–281
    water hyacinth (*Eichhornia crassipes*), 290
    yellow floating heart (*Nymphoides peltata*), 310, 312
    zebra mussel (*Dreissena polymorpha*), 61–62
physical removal
    benthic barriers, 16, **17**
    control of aquatic invasive plants, **17–21**
    dredging, 16, **18–19**
    dyes and surface covers, 16, **19**
    mechanical removal (harvesting), 16, **19–20**
    water level control, 16, **20–21**
Pickerel Pond (Maine), hydrilla, 104
Polygonaceaeae, 196
polymerase chain reaction (PCR), 14
Pomacea genus, snails, 69, *71*
Ponkapog Pond, swollen bladderwort (*Utricularia inflata*), *258*
Pontederia crassipes, 285, see also water hyacinth (Eichhornia crassipes)
Pontederia crassipes (formerly Eichhornia crassipes), 253
Porter Lake, 42
    Asian clams, 42–44, *43*
    density of live Asian clams, **44**
    dry weight of dead/broken shells of Asian clams, **44**
    size of Asian clams, **44**
Potamogeton crispus, see curly-leaf pondweed (*Potamogeton crispus*) Page Number?
Potomac River (VA)
    northern snakehead, 87, 88, 90
    water chestnut (*Trapa natans*), 280, 281
Practical Guide to Aquatic Plant Management, Massachusetts, 16
prevention, invasive species, 10–12
ProcellaCOR™, parrot-feather (*Myriophyllum aquaticum*), 194, 195, 198
Pseudomonas fluorescens, 60
public education and awareness, invasive species, 8
purple bladderwort (*Utricularia pupurea*), 260, *260*
purple loosestrife (*Lythrum salicaria*), 2, 42
    biological control, 374–375, *375*
    biology, 337–340
    chemical treatment, 373, *375*
    control methods, *375*
    distribution map, *341*
    ecological impacts, 340–341
    economic impacts, 340–341
    Galerucella beetles eating, *374*
    geo-referenced records of, **350–372**
    hand pulling, 392
    literature research of chemical control methods, **413**
    managing actions, 373–375
    Massachusetts waterbodies infected by, **5**
    monitoring and sightings, 341, 373
    photographs, *338, 339*
    physical control, 373, *375*
    sightings in MA waterbodies, **2**
    success story, 375–377
    taxonomic hierarchy, 337
    towns and infested waterbodies, **342–349**
Pursh, Frederick T., 339

Q

Quabbin Reservoir, 3, 10
    Boat Decontamination Program, **11**
quagga mussels (*Dreissena rostriformis bugensis*), 42, 53, 60, 63
quantitative polymerase chain reaction (qPCR), 14
Quinsigamond Lake, Asian clam, 41

R

rapid response, 15, see also early detection and rapid response (EDRR)
rat lungworm (Angiostrongylus cantonensis), 73
redear sunfish (*Lepomis microlophus*), 60
regulation, 27–28, see also state laws and statutes on invasive species
    Connecticut, **417–418**
    Maine, **418–420**
    Massachusetts, **421–423**
    New Hampshire, **423–425**
    New York, **426–428**
    permitting and, 28–29
    Rhode Island, **428–431**
    Vermont, **431–433**
Reward®, European naiad, 241–242
Rhine River, Asian clam, 35
Rhode Island, laws and statutes pertaining to aquatic invasive/nuisance species, **428–431**
Ridgebury Lake (New York), northern snakehead success, 92–93
River Barrow, Asian clams, 48
Rockcastle River, Asian clam, 36

S

sacred lotus (*Nelumbo nucifera*), 1
St. Lawrence River, purple loosestrife (*Lythrum salicaria*), 340
Schooner®, European naiad, 242
sheepshead (*Archosargus*), 60
snakeheads, 83, *84*, see also northern snakehead (*Channa argus*)
sodium percarbonate + hydrogen peroxide, treating aquatic invasive species, **25**
Solitude Lake Management (SLM), vegetation management survey, 241

Index

South Africa, water hyacinth (*Eichhornia crassipes*), 291–292
South American waterweed (*Egeria densa*), 2, 98
   biological control, 252, 253–254
   biology of, 245–247
   chemical control, 251, 252–253
   distribution map, *250*
   domestic ducks as biological control, 253–254
   Fence Rock Lake, 252–253
   guide to native and invasive waterweeds, *247*
   infested waterbodies, **249**
   infested watersheds, **251**
   literature research of chemical control methods, **408**
   managing actions, 249–251
   maps from CAES IAPP, 252–253
   Massachusetts waterbodies, **5**
   monitoring and sightings, 249
   native and invasive range, 247
   photographs of, *246*
   physical control, 251–252
   sightings in MA waterbodies, **2**
   spread and impacts, 247–248
   success stories, 252–254
   taxonomic hierarchy, 245
   towns and infested waterbodies, **250**
South American weevil (*Listronotus marginicollis*), 196
South Coastal watershed, parrot-feather (*Myriophyllum aquaticum*), 193, **193**
Spartina alterniflora, 320, 325, 326, 327
Sphenochlea zeylanica, 301
spiny waterflea (*Bythotrephes longimanus*), 1
spread
   Asian clam (Corbicula fluminea), 36
   Carolina fanwort (*Cabomba caroliniana*), 202–203
   Chinese mystery snail (*Bellamya chinensis*), 72
   common reed grass (*Phragmites australis*), 315, *317*, 318–320
   curly-leaf pondweed (*Potamogeton crispus*), 107–109, 130–131
   Eurasian milfoil (*Myriophyllum spicatum*), 136–137
   European naiad (*Najas minor*), 234–235
   European waterclover (*Marsilea quadrifolia*), 297–298
   freshwater invasive species, 6–7
   hydrilla (Hydrilla verticillata), 98, **99**
   informational sign for preventing, of hydrilla, *101*
   northern snakehead (*Channa argus*), 85, 87–88
   parrot-feather (*Myriophyllum aquaticum*), 190–191
   purple loosestrife (*Lythrum salicaria*), 340, 373–374, 376
   South American waterweed (*Egeria densa*), 247–248
   swollen bladderwort (*Utricularia inflata*), 261
   variable milfoil (*Myriophyllum heterophyllum*), 186
   water chestnut (*Trapa natans*), 268–270
   water hyacinth (*Eichhornia crassipes*), 287
   yellow floating heart (*Nymphoides peltata*), 309
   zebra mussel (*Dreissena polymorpha*), 53–54, *58*
state laws and statutes on invasive species
   Connecticut, **417–418**
   Maine, **418–420**
   Massachusetts, **421–423**
   New Hampshire, **423–425**
   New York, **426–428**
   Rhode Island, **428–431**
   Vermont, **431–433**

Sudbury River (MA)
   invasive species in, **5**
   water chestnut (*Trapa natans*), 270
Sunset Lake, European naiad (*Najas minor*), 241, 242
Sweetwater Reservoir (California), quagga mussel study design, *61*
swollen bladderwort (*Utricularia inflata*), 2
   biology of, 257–258, 260
   chemical treatments, 264
   distribution map, *263*
   ecological impacts, 261
   economic impacts, 261
   literature research of chemical control methods, **408**
   locations of waters infested by, **262**
   managing actions, 263–264
   Massachusetts waterbodies infected by, **5**
   microscopic photos of, *259*
   monitoring and sightings, 262–263
   native and invasive range, 261
   photographs of, *258*
   physical controls, 263–264
   pictures of stem, flowers and sterile fruits, *258*
   positive effects, 261–262
   scientific illustration on capturing small aquatic animals, *259*
   sightings in MA waterbodies, **2**
   success story, 264–265
   taxonomic hierarchy, 257
   vectors of spread, 261

T

Taunton River, parrot-feather (*Myriophyllum aquaticum*), 193, **193**
Taunton River Basin, **3**, 4
taxonomic hierarchy
   Asian clam (Corbicula fluminea), 35
   Carolina fanwort (*Cabomba caroliniana*), 201
   Chinese mystery snail (*Bellamya chinensis*), 69
   common reed grass (*Phragmites australis*), 315
   curly-leaf pondweed (*Potamogeton crispus*), 107
   Eurasian milfoil (*Myriophyllum spicatum*), 133
   European naiad (*Najas minor*), 233
   European waterclover (*Marsilea quadrifolia* L.), 295
   hydrilla (Hydrilla verticillata), 95
   northern snakehead (*Channa argus*), 83
   parrot-feather (*Myriophyllum aquaticum*), 189
   purple loosestrife (*Lythrum salicaria*), 337
   South American waterweed (*Egeria densa*), 245
   swollen bladderwort (*Utricularia inflata*), 257
   variable milfoil (Myriophyllum heterophyllum), 133
   water chestnut (*Trapa natans*), 267
   water hyacinth (*Eichhornia crassipes*), 285
   zebra mussel (Dreissena polymorpha), 51
towns and infested waterbodies
   Carolina fanwort (*Cabomba caroliniana*), **224–228**
   Chinese mystery snails, **77**
   common reed grass (*Phragmites australis*), **322–323**
   curly-leaf pondweed (*Potamogeton crispus*), **110–112**
   Eurasian milfoil, **175–178**
   European naiad (*Najas minor*), **239**
   European waterclover (*Marsilea quaderifolia* L.), **299**
   northern snakehead, **89**
   purple loosestrife (*Lythrum salicaria*), **342–349**

South American waterweed (*Egeria densa*), 250
  unidentified milfoil, **184**
  variable milfoil, **178–183**
  water chestnut (*Trapa natans*), **278–280**
  water hyacinth (*Eichhornia crassipes*), **289**
  zebra mussels, **60**
Trapa natans, *see* water chestnut (Trapa natans)
trapdoor snail, 69
Tribune®, European naiad, 242
Triclopyr, treating aquatic invasive species, **23**
triploid grass carp (*Ctenopharyngodon idella* Val.), 102
tufted duck (*Aythya fuligula*), 60
2,4-D, treating aquatic invasive species, **23**
Typha angustifolia Cattail, purple loosestrife (*Lythrum salicaria*), 340

U

US Army Corps of Engineers, hydrilla, 97
US Bureau of Reclamation, 8
US Department of Agriculture (USDA), 281
US Department of Agriculture, Animal Plant Health Inspection Service (USDA-APHIS), 29
US Geological Survey (USGS), 37, 57, 73, 109, 234, 270
Utricularia inflata, *see* swollen bladderwort (*Utricularia inflata*)

V

Vallisneria, 269
variable milfoil (*Myriophyllum heterophyllum*), 2, *see also* Eurasian milfoil (*Myriophyllum spicatum*); milfoil(s)
  biological control, 186
  biology of, 133–135
  chemical treatment, 186
  distribution map, *137, 138*
  ecological impacts, 136
  economic impacts, 136
  florpyrauxifen-benzyl (ProcellaCOR™), 186
  invasive range, 135
  latitude and longitude of waterbody, **149–172**
  leaves of, *134*
  literature research of chemical control methods, **403–404**
  management, 186
  Massachusetts waterbodies infected by, **5**
  monitoring and sightings, 136–138
  native range, 135
  physical treatment, 186
  schematic depiction of, *134*
  sightings in MA waterbodies, **2**
  stems of, *135*
  taxonomic hierarchy, 133
  towns and infested waterbodies, **178–183**
Vermont, laws and statutes pertaining to aquatic invasive/nuisance species, **431–433**
Viviparidae, Chinese mystery snails, 69, 70
Viviparus georgianus, 70, *71*
Viviparus malleatus, 69

W

Wachusett Reservoir, 3
Washington state, Eurasian milfoil, 187

waterbodies, *see also* towns and infested waterbodies
  Asian clams, **42**
  Carolina fanwort (*Cabomba caroliniana*), **205–233**
  Chinese mystery snail, **75–76**, 77
  common reed grass (*Phragmites australis*), **322–323**, *323*, **331–335**
  curly-leaf pondweed (*Potamogeton crispus*), **110–112**, **113–129**
  Eurasian milfoil, **140–149**
  European naiad (*Najas minor*), **237–238**
  European waterclover (*Marsilea quaderifolia* L.), **299**
  hydrilla, **100–101**
  invasive species infecting, **5**
  northern snakehead, **89**
  purple loosestrife (*Lythrum salicaria*), **350–372**
  South American waterweed (*Egeria densa*), 249
  swollen bladderwort (*Utricularia inflata*), **262**, **264**
  unidentified milfoil, **172–175**
  variable milfoil, **149–172**
  water chestnut (*Trapa natans*), **271–276**
  water hyacinth (*Eichhornia crassipes*), **289**
  yellow floating heart (*Nymphoides peltata*), **311**
  zebra mussels, **60**
water chestnut (*Trapa natans*), 2, 282–283
  biological control, 281
  biology, 267–268
  chemical control, 281–282
  distribution map, *277*
  ecological impact, 269
  economic impact, 269
  infested watersheds, **277**
  invasive range, 268–269
  literature research of chemical control methods, **409**
  location of waterbodies, **271–276**
  management actions, 270, 277, 280
  Massachusetts waterbodies infected by, **5**
  monitoring and sightings, 270
  native range, 268
  photograph, *268*
  physical control, 280–281
  positive aspects, 269–270
  sightings in MA waterbodies, **2**
  taxonomic hierarchy, 267
  towns and waterbodies, **278–280**
watercraft inspection and decontamination (WID), 8
Watercraft Inspection Stations, Quabbin Reservoir, 10
water hyacinth (*Eichhornia crassipes*), 2
  biological control, 291
  biology, 285
  chemical control, 290–291
  distribution map, *289*
  ecological impacts, 287
  economic impacts, 287–288
  frog's-bit (*Limnobium spongia*) and, 285, *286*
  infested waterbodies, **289**
  infested watersheds, **289**
  literature research of chemical control methods, **409–410**
  management, 290–291
  mechanisms/vectors of spread, 287
  monitoring and sightings, 288, 290
  native and invasive range, 286–287
  photograph, *286*
  physical control, 290

Index

remaining challenges, 292
sightings in MA waterbodies, **2**
success story, 291–292
taxonomic hierarchy, 285
towns and infested waterbodies, **289**
utilization of, 288
water hyacinth Pontederia crassipes (formerly Eichhornia crassipes), 253
water level control, aquatic invasive plant control, 16, **20–21**
Water Quality Certification, 28–29, 99, 238, 250, 270
watersheds
   Asian clams, **42**
   Carolina fanwort (*Cabomba caroliniana*), **229**
   Chinese mystery snails, **78**
   codes and names, **3**
   northern snakehead, **89**
Webster Lake, invasive species in, **5**
weevil (*Bagous affinis*), 102
weevil (Bagous rufimanus), 281
weevil (Neochetina bruchi), 291
weevil (Neochetina eichhorniae), 291
Wellesley Pond (MA), Carolina fanwort (*Cabomba caroliniana*), 229
Wersal, Ryan, 197
Wetlands Protection Act, 29
Wetlands Protection Act Regulations, 28
White Island Pond
   invasive species, **5**
   swollen bladderwort (*Utricularia inflata*), 258
White River (Arkansas), northern snakehead, 90
Wildwood Lake, European naiad (*Najas minor*), 241, 242
Wisconsin, lake-wide herbicide treatments, 185
WM 04 Chemical Application License, 29, 241

Y

yellow floating heart (*Nymphoides peltata*), 2
   biological methods, 312–313
   biology, 307
   chemical methods, 312
   distribution map, *311*
   ecological impacts, 309–310
   economic impacts, 310
   invasive range, 308–309
   literature research of chemical control methods, **410–411**
   managing actions, 310, 312–313
   mechanisms/vectors of spread, 309
   monitoring and sightings, 310, **311**
   native range, 307–308
   photographs, *308, 309*
   physical methods, 310, 312
   positive aspects, 310
   sightings in MA waterbodies, **2**
   success story, 313
   taxonomic hierarchy, 307
yellow pond lily (*Nuphar variegata*), 307, *309*

Z

zebra mussel (*Dreissena polymorpha*), 1, 48
   adult, and bed in Lake Erie, *52*
   biological control, 60
   chemical treatment of, 62
   dead zebra mussel density in drawdown zone, *59*
   distribution map depicting, *58*
   EarthTec QZ®, 62–63
   economic impact of, 55, 57
   filtration rate of, **56–57**
   Great Lakes beaches, 57
   Hudson River, 54
   invasion pathway of, 53–55
   Lake Erie and, 52–54
   life cycle of, 52–53
   literature research of chemical control methods, **395–396**
   managing actions, 59–62
   monitoring and sightings, 57–59
   physical treatment of, 61–62
   potential ecological impacts on aquatic ecosystem, 55, *55*
   quagga mussel and, 14
   risk categories of invasions by water quality parameters, **53**
   sightings in MA waterbodies, **2**
   success story, 62–63
   taxonomic hierarchy, 51
   towns and waterbodies containing, **60**

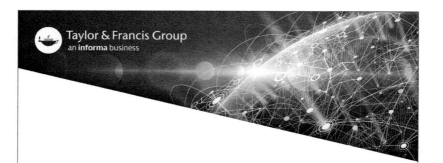